D0700154

Blackwell Handbook of Perception

Blackwell Handbook of Perception

Edited by

E. Bruce Goldstein

Consulting editors:

Glyn Humphreys

Margaret Shiffrar

William Yost

First published 2001

2 4 6 8 10 9 7 5 3 1

Blackwell Publishers Inc.
350 Main Street
Malden, Massachusetts 02148
USA

Blackwell Publishers Ltd
108 Cowley Road
Oxford OX4 1JF
UK

Library of Congress Cataloging-in-Publication Data has been applied for.

Blackwell handbook of perception / edited by E. Bruce Goldstein ; consulting editors,
William Yost, Margaret Schiffrar, Glyn Humphreys.
p. cm. — (Handbooks in experimental psychology series)
Includes bibliographical references and index.
ISBN 0-631-20683-3 (alk. paper)
1. Perception. 2. Senses and sensation. I. Title: Handbook of perception. II. Goldstein,
E. Bruce, 1941– III. Series.

BF311 .B537 2001
152.1—dc21

00-063050

British Library Cataloguing in Publication Data

A CIP catalogue record for this book is available from the British Library.

Typeset in 10½ on 12½ pt Adobe Garamond
by Ace Filmsetting Ltd, Frome, Somerset
Printed in Great Britain by T.J. International, Padstow, Cornwall

This book is printed on acid-free paper.

The editor and publishers gratefully acknowledge permission to reproduce copyright material. All such material is acknowledged where it appears in the text. The publishers apologize for any errors or omissions in the copyright acknowledgements and would be grateful to be notified of any corrections that should be incorporated in the next edition or reprint of this book.

Contents

Preface

This handbook surveys the field of perception, including vision, hearing, taste, olfaction, and cutaneous sensibility. Covering a field as vast as perception in one volume is a challenge, because it involves selection – first, of the chapters to be included in the Table of Contents, and then, of the material to be included within each of these chapters. In creating the Table of Contents, my goal was to include a chapter on each of the basic perceptual qualities plus a few chapters on topics that cut across senses, such as coding, development, sense interactions, and modularity.

In selecting material to include within each chapter, the authors were faced with the challenge of summarizing their area in about 30 pages. In reality, short of creating a telegraphic list of key findings and concepts, it is not possible to satisfactorily cover any of the areas in this handbook in one short chapter. But creating an introduction that crystallizes the basic ideas of an area and provides the orientation necessary for further reading is possible. This is what the distinguished group of authors who have written chapters for this handbook have strived for. Their goal has been to write introductions to their areas that will be useful to researchers and teachers who are familiar with the field, but who want succinct, state-of-the-art overviews of areas outside their specialty.

To increase breadth of coverage, two features are included at the end of each chapter. "Suggested Readings" points the reader to general references that offer detailed treatments of the chapter's topic. "Additional Topics" provides references to important topics which, because of space limitations, could not be included in the chapter.

My personal experience in editing this handbook has confirmed the principle that to truly understand something you must do it. Receiving advice from someone else about how to raise children, do empirical research, write a college textbook, or edit a handbook provides knowledge that may seem reasonable when it is received, but which can be most fully appreciated only in hindsight, after one has been through the experience. Such was the case for my first-time experience of editing a handbook.

Before beginning this project, I received advice from others who had edited multiauthor texts. They regaled me with stories related mainly to the difficulties involved in receiving all of a book's chapters in an acceptable form, on a reasonable time schedule. Having been forewarned, I felt I would avoid the problems they had experienced. However, I am now in a position to report that my experience mirrors the experiences of my predecessors, and that I now feel qualified to dispense my own advice to any first-time editor who wishes to listen.

Luckily, I am also able to report that I found the overall process of creating this book to be extremely rewarding. The main rewards came from my dealings with the authors who graciously agreed to contribute to this volume, and who diligently wrote their chapters and responded to my suggestions. In many cases I had to ask authors to cut sections or to rewrite parts of their chapters to make the material more accessible for our intended audience. I thank these authors for their patience and willingness to respond to my feedback.

I also thank the people at Blackwell who conceived of this project, and who have supported me from our initial conversations that shaped the book, to the process of production, which is occurring as I write this preface. I especially thank Alison Mudditt, who convinced me to undertake this project, and Alison Dunnett, who took it over near the beginning and who has supported me throughout the creation of this handbook. I also thank all of the other people at Blackwell, with whom, through the magic of e-mail, I have had many helpful and pleasant interactions.

Bruce Goldstein
Pittsburgh, PA, April, 2000

Contributors

Israel Abramov
Department of Psychology
Brooklyn College of CUNY
Brooklyn, NY 11221
Jgordon@gc.cuny.edu

Ilene L. Bernstein
Department of Psychology
Box 351525
University of Washington
Seattle, WA 98195
ileneb@u.washington.edu

Eileen E. Birch
Retina Foundation of the Southwest
9900 North Central Expressway
Dallas, TX 75231
gwiazdaj@ne-optometry.edu

Marvin M. Chun
Department of Psychology and Vanderbilt Vision Research Center
Vanderbilt University
531 Wilson Hall
Nashville, TN 37240
marvin.chun@vanderbilt.edu

Miranda Cleary
Department of Psychology
Indiana University
Bloomington, IN 47405
micleary@indiana.edu

Beverly J. Cowart
Monell Chemical Senses Center
3500 Market Street
Philadelphia, PA 19104-3308
cowart@monell.org

W. Jay Dowling
Program in Cognitive Science
University of Texas at Dallas
Richardson, TX 75083-0688
jdowling@utdallas.edu

Laura J. Frishman
College of Optometry
University of Houston
4901 Calhoun Rd.
Houston, TX 77204-5872
lfrishman@uh.edu

E. Bruce Goldstein
Department of Psychology
University of Pittsburgh
Pittsburgh, PA 15260
bruceg+@pitt.edu

Melvyn A. Goodale
Department of Psychology
University of Western Ontario
London, Ontario N6A 5C2
Canada
keith@julian.uwo.ca

James Gordon
Psychology Department
Hunter College
695 Park Avenue
New York, NY 10021
Jgordon@gc.cuny.edu

Jane Gwiazda
The New England College of Optometry
424 Beacon Street
Boston, MA 02115
gwiazdaj@ne-optometry.edu

G. Keith Humphrey
Department of Psychology
University of Western Ontario
London, Ontario
Canada N6A 5C2
keith@julian.uwo.ca

Glyn W. Humphreys
School of Psychology
University of Birmingham
Edgbaston
Birmingham B15 2TT
UK
g.w.humphreys@bham.ac.uk

Harry T. Lawless
Department of Food Science
Cornell University
Stocking Hall
Ithaca, NY 14853
htl1@cornell.edu

Michael W. Levine
Department of Psychology M/C 285
University of Illinois
1007 W. Harrison St.
Chicago, Illinois 60607
mikel@uic.edu

Brian C. J. Moore
Department of Experimental Psychology
University of Cambridge
Downing Street
Cambridge CB2 3EB
UK
bcjm@cus.cam.ac.uk

Ken Nakayama
Department of Psychology
Harvard University
33 Kirkland Street
Cambridge, MA 02138-2044
ken@wjh.harvard.edu

Mary A. Peterson
Department of Psychology
University of Arizona
Tucson, AZ 85721
mapeters@u.arizona.edu

David B. Pisoni
Department of Psychology
Indiana University
Bloomington, IN 47405
micleary@indiana.edu

Nancy E. Rawson
Monell Chemical Senses Center
3500 Market Street
Philadelphia, PA 19104-3308
rawson@monell.org

M. Jane Riddoch
School of Psychology
University of Birmingham
Edgbaston
Birmingham B15 2TT
g.w.humphreys@bham.ac.uk

H. A. Sedgwick
SUNY College of Optometry
100 E 24th Street
New York, NY 10010
hsedgwick@sunyopt.edu

Maggie Shiffrar	Department of Psychology Rutgers University Newark, NJ 07102 mag@psychology.rutgers.edu
Terrence R. Stanford	Department of Neurobiology and Anatomy Bowman Grey School of Medicine Winston-Salem, NC 27157 nstein@wfubmc.edu
Barry E. Stein	Department of Neurobiology and Anatomy Bowman Grey School of Medicine Winston-Salem, NC 27157 nstein@wfubmc.edu
Mark T. Wallace	Department of Neurobiology and Anatomy Bowman Grey School of Medicine Winston-Salem, NC 27157 nstein@wfubmc.edu
Janet M. Weisenberger	Office of the Dean Ohio State University 1010 Derby Hall 154 North Oval Mall Columbus, OH 43210-1341 jan+@osu.edu
Lynne A. Werner	Department of Speech and Hearing Sciences 1417 NE 42nd St Seattle, WA 9815 lawerner@u.washington.edu
Jeremy M. Wolfe	Center for Ophthalmic Research 221 Longwood Avenue Boston, MA 02115 marvin.chun@vanderbilt.edu
William A. Yost	Parmly Hearing Institute Loyola University 6525 N. Sheridan Rd. Chicago, IL 60626 wyost@wpo.it.luc.edu

Chapter One

Cross-Talk Between Psychophysics and Physiology in the Study of Perception[1]

E. Bruce Goldstein

> All perception is neural activity.
>
> Casagrande & Norton, 1991, p. 42

> You can observe a lot by watching.
>
> Yogi Berra

The illusion that perception is a simple process follows from the ease with which we perceive. The reality, however, is that perception is the outcome of an extraordinary process that is accomplished by mechanisms which, in their exquisite complexity, work so well that the outcome – our awareness of the environment and our ability to navigate through it – occurs effortlessly under most conditions.

This *Handbook* is a record of the progress we have made towards uncovering the complexities of perception. This progress has been achieved by research that has approached the study of perception psychophysically (studying the relationship between the stimulus and perception) and physiologically (studying the relationship between physiological events and perception). The purpose of this chapter is to show that the psychophysical and physiological approaches not only make their individual contributions to understanding perception, but also that they often function in collaboration with one another. The message of this chapter is that this collaboration, or "cross-talk," has been and will continue to be a crucial component of perceptual research.

Psychophysical, Physiological and Linking Relationships in Perceptual Research

The basic relationships of perceptual research are diagramed in Figure 1.1. The three relationships are (a) relationship ϕ, between stimuli and the physiological response; (b) relationship ψ, between stimuli and the perceptual response; and (c) relationship L, between the physiological response and the perceptual response.

Relationship ϕ, the physiological relationship, is the dominant method for studying the physiological workings of perceptual mechanisms. Emblematic of this approach is classic research such as Hubel and Wiesel's (1959, 1962) specification of the response and organization of neurons in the cat and monkey visual system; Kiang's (1965) measurement of frequency tuning curves in the cochlear nucleus of the cat; and Mountcastle and Powell's (1959) research on the relationship between tactile stimulation and the response of neurons in the monkey's somatosensory cortex.

Relationship ψ is studied by what are usually called the psychophysical methods. These methods include the classic Fechnerian methods used to determine thresholds (Fechner, 1860), and Stevens' (1961) magnitude estimation techniques for scaling above-threshold experience. For the purposes of this chapter, we will also include as psychophysics any technique that measures the relationship between stimuli and response, including phenomenological observations (cf. Katz, 1935) and measures such as identification, recognition, and reaction time.

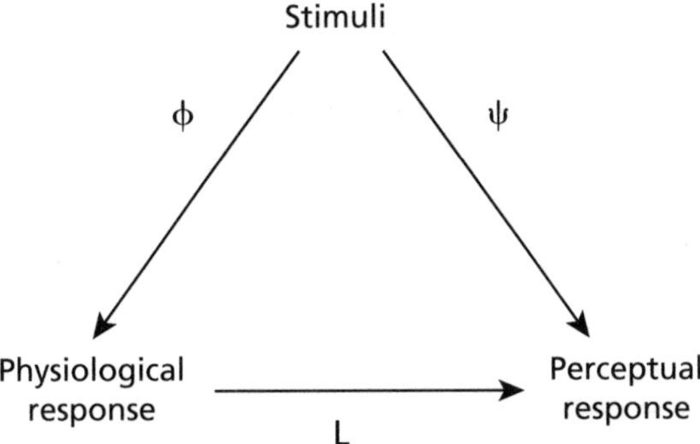

Figure 1.1. The basic relationships of perceptual research. See text for details.

Relationship L is the linking relationship between physiology and perception. Determining this relationship is often the ultimate goal for those concerned with determining the physiological basis of perception, but it is the most problematic to measure. The core problem is that it is difficult to measure both physiological responding and perceptual response in the same subject (although, as we will see, not impossible). Because of the difficulty in simultaneously measuring physiological and perceptual responding, relationship L has often been inferred from independent measurements of relationships ψ and ϕ, often with relationship ψ determined in humans, and relationship ϕ in animals. When relationship L is determined by inference from relationships ψ and ϕ, it is called a linking hypothesis (see Teller, 1984, who considers in some detail the factors involved in making this inference; also see Teller & Pugh, 1983).

One goal of this chapter is to show how these three relationships are interrelated. This may seem like a modest goal, because these relationships must, of necessity, be related, as they are all components of the same system. However, our interest extends beyond simply identifying relationships, to considering the *processes* by which these relationships have been discovered. Approached from this perspective, it becomes clear that the discovery of one relationship has often been dependent on or facilitated by knowledge gained from another of the relationships, with the physiological and psychophysical approaches being engaged in "cross-talk," which directs, informs, and enhances the creation of knowledge on both sides of the methodological divide. We begin by considering how psychophysics provides the foundation for physiological research on perception, and will then consider examples of how cross-talk between psychophysics and physiology has helped determine (a) the mechanisms, and (b) the locus of operation of these mechanisms.

Before beginning the discussion, a few caveats are in order. The highlighting of instances of cross-talk between psychophysics and physiology does not mean that the psychophysical and physiological approaches cannot be profitably pursued independently of one another. There is a vast physiological literature that is concerned primarily with determining basic physiological mechanisms of sensory systems (although even these experiments are often motivated by a desire to link physiological functioning and perceptual outcomes). Conversely, some psychologists have taken a purely psychophysical approach, with the idea being to explain perception by focusing solely on psychophysically defined relationships (cf. Gibson, 1950, 1979; Sedgwick, Chapter 5 for visual examples; Yost, Chapter 14 and Dowling, Chapter 15 for auditory examples)[2]. This "pure psychophysics" approach is reminiscent of Skinner's (1953) behaviorism, which is based on determination of stimulus-response contingencies, without any reference to what is happening inside the "black box."

Psychophysics as Guiding Physiological Research

One of the primary outcomes of psychophysical research is determination of the stimulus parameters that are relevant for perception. Knowing that there is a relationship between wavelength and hue, frequency and pitch, binocular disparity and depth perception, and the temporal relationship between two flashing lights and the movement that is perceived between them, not only defines the phenomena of perception, but focuses attention on the stimulus information that is relevant to perception.

Consider, for example, the discovery that binocular disparity can provide sufficient information for depth perception (Julesz, 1964; Wheatstone, 1838). This finding not only formed the basis of psychophysical research on binocular depth perception, but guided physiological research as well. Imagine what the search for the neural signal for depth perception would have been like had disparity been unknown. Physiologists might still have discovered neurons that respond best to objects located at different distances, but to understand the nature of the stimulus information driving these neurons, the role that binocular disparity plays in depth perception would eventually have had to be discovered as well. Luckily, the psychophysicists had made this discovery long before the physiologists recorded from neurons that respond to binocular disparity in the striate cortex (Barlow, Blakemore, & Pettigrew, 1967).

In addition to identifying relevant stimulus parameters, psychophysics has often determined ψ relationships that have provided "system specifications" for physiology to explain. The classic example of this "system specification" is Hecht, Shlaer, and Pirenne's (1942) conclusion, based on psychophysical measurements, that the absolute threshold for rod vision is about 7 quanta, and that these quanta are absorbed by 7 visual pigment molecules, each located in a different receptor. From this conclusion it follows that isomerization of a single visual pigment molecule is adequate to excite a receptor.

This conclusion that isomerizing only one visual pigment molecule can excite a receptor threw down the gauntlet to researchers who were searching for the molecular mechanism of visual transduction, by requiring that this mechanism explain how isomerization of only one out of the 100 million molecules in a receptor (cf. Wandell, 1995) can cause such a large effect. Researchers realized that the answer probably involved some type of amplification mechanism (Wald, 1968; Wald, Brown, & Gibbons, 1963) but it wasn't until over 40 years after Hecht et al.'s psychophysical observation that the "enzyme cascade" responsible for this amplification was described (Baylor, 1992; Ranganathan, Harris, & Zuker, 1991; Stryer, 1986).

What is notable about the role of psychophysics in the Hecht et al. example is that a psychophysical result led to a physiological prediction at the molecular level. Not all psychophysical research has achieved specification at that level, but there are numerous examples of situations in which psychophysical data have helped guide further physiological research. Consider, for example, the ψ finding in the auditory system that listeners can detect frequency differences of just a few Hz (depending on the frequency range being tested). However, Bekesy's (1942, 1960) determination of the ϕ relationship between frequency and basilar membrane vibration indicated tuning too broad to explain this frequency selectivity, especially at low frequencies. This mismatch between the ϕ and ψ relationships motivated a search for a physiological mechanism that would discriminate between nearby frequencies. Eventually, more accurate measurement of basilar membrane vibration using Mossbauer techniques in living animals revealed that the tuning of basilar membrane vibration was much sharper than indicated by Bekesy's original measurements (Johnstone & Boyle, 1967; Johnstone, Patuzzi, & Yates, 1986). (See Moore, Chapter 12, p. 389.)

Specifying Physiological Mechanisms

The two examples above describe situations in which psychophysical results motivated further physiological research. In both cases, the psychophysical results furnished physiological researchers with specific goals: identification of the molecular amplification mechanism in the visual example, and identification of physiological responses that can signal small frequency differences in the auditory example. But psychophysical results can go beyond simply posing questions for physiologists to answer. They can suggest theories regarding physiological mechanisms. The rationale behind this inference of physiological mechanisms from psychophysics is illustrated in Figure 1.2.

Figure 1.2a shows a mechanical device consisting of two rods protruding from a black box. The rod at A represents the *stimulus* in a psychophysical relationship, and the rod at B represents the *response*. Our goal is to determine what is happening inside the black box, by determining the relationship between the stimulus at A and the response at B. In our first "psychophysical" experiment, we move the rod at A to the right and observe a corresponding rightward movement at B. Based on this stimulus-response relationship, we can venture a guess as to what is happening inside the black box. One possibility is that the rods at A and B are connected, or are part of the same rod (Figure 1.2b). To check the validity of this hypothesis we do another experiment, pulling rod A to the left. When we do this, rod B remains motionless, a result that invalidates our original hypothesis, and leads to a new one, shown in Figure 1.2c. To determine whether this is the correct hypothesis, we can do further psychophysical experiments, or we can move to the physiological approach and look inside the black box. What we see may confirm our psychophysically based hypothesis, may partially confirm it (the physiology and psychophysics match, but not exactly), or may disconfirm it altogether. All of these outcomes have occurred in perceptual research. We now consider color vision, which provides an example of a situation in which psychophysical results led to predictions of physiological mechanisms long before physiological measurements were available.

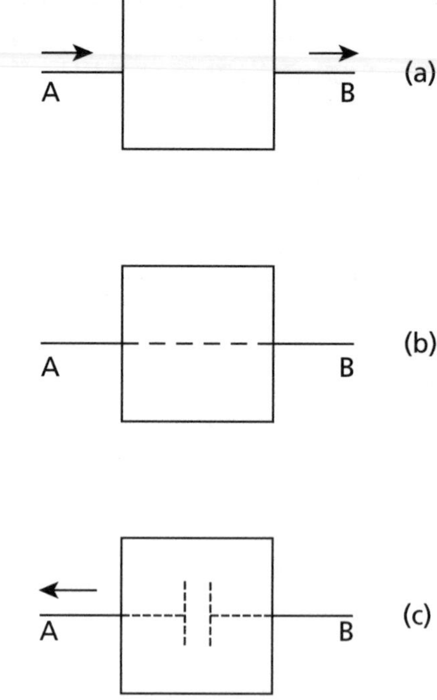

Figure 1.2. Mechanical analogue illustrating the process of inferring mechanisms within the black box, based on relationships observed between stimulus at A and response at B. (a) Moving the rod to the right at A causes rightward movement at B. (b) Hypothesized internal mechanism: The rod is continuous from A to B. (c) Moving the rod to the left at A causes no response at B, so a new mechanism, shown by the dashed line, replaces the old hypothesis.

Theories of Color Vision

Color vision provides the classic example of psychophysics predicting physiology, because color vision research and theorizing stretches from the 19th century, when psychophysics stood alone because the necessary physiological technology was unavailable, to the present, when psychophysical and physiological research often occur side by side. Adding to the interest in color vision is the proposal of two competing theories, the trichromatic (Helmholtz, 1852; Young, 1802) and opponent-process (Hering, 1878, 1964) theories of color vision. Trichromatic theory has its roots in the following assertion, by Young (1802):

> Now as it is almost impossible to conceive each sensitive point of the retina to contain an infinite number of particles . . . . it becomes necessary to suppose the number limited; for instance to the three principal colours, red, yellow, and blue . . . . each sensitive filament of the nerve may consist of three portions, one for each principal colour.

This statement is derived mainly from psychophysics but assumes some physiology. On the physiological side is the mention of the retina, which was known to be the light-sensitive surface upon which images were formed and vision began. On the psychophysical side are color-matching experiments, which indicate that people with normal color vision can match any wavelength by mixing a minimum of three other wavelengths. This psychophysical fact was the evidence behind the idea of "three principal colours."

Another important psychophysical fact that followed from the color-matching experiments was the phenomenon of metamerism. When subjects match one wavelength by mixing the correct proportions of two other wavelengths, they have created two fields that are physically different, but perceptually identical. The fact that physically different stimuli can lead to the same perception implies that the physiology underlying these perceptual responses may be identical (see Teller, 1984), a property which is a key feature of trichromatic theory's assertions (a) that the basis of color vision is the pattern of firing of three mechanisms, and (b) that two physically different wavelength distributions can result in the same patterns of firing.

In the years following the proposal of trichromatic theory, various functions were proposed for the three mechanisms (e.g., Stiles, 1953), but accurate specification of these mechanisms had to await physiological measurement of cone absorption spectra (Bowmaker & Darntall, 1980; Brown & Wald, 1964). Thus, the general form of the physiology (three mechanisms) was correctly predicted by psychophysics, but it was necessary to look into the black box to determine the details (pigment absorption spectra).

Opponent-process theory, as described by Hering, postulated that color vision was the result of three opposing processes, red-green, blue-yellow, and black-white, with white, yellow, and red causing a chemical reaction that results in the buildup of a chemical and black, blue, and green causing a reaction that results in a breakdown of the chemical. These physiological predictions were based on phenomenological observations, such as the fact that it is difficult to imagine a bluish-yellow or a reddish-green.

Years after Hering's proposal, modern physiological research revealed opponent S-potentials in the fish retina (Svaetichin, 1956) and opponent single unit responding in the monkey lateral geniculate nucleus (DeValois, 1965; DeValois, Jacobs, & Jones, 1963), thus confirming Hering's predicted opponency and replacing his proposed chemical reactions with neural excitation and inhibition. Around the same time that these opponent physiological mechanisms were being revealed, Jameson and Hurvich (1955; also Hurvich & Jameson, 1957) were using a quantitatively precise psychophysical cancellation procedure to specify the strengths of the opponent mechanisms. Cross-talk, if it existed, between physiology and psychophysics is not obvious from journal citations (e.g., the Hurvich and Jameson papers were not liberally cited in physiological papers of the time), although Hurvich and Jameson's papers are now considered classics.

Whatever the nature of the interaction between opponent psychophysics and color vision physiology, the physiological research was necessary not only to confirm Hering's prediction of opponency, but to gain the theory's acceptance by color vision researchers. A contest pitting Helmholtz's prestige and the quantitative nature of color-matching data against an unlikely physiological mechanism derived from Hering's phenomenological observations translated into color vision research of the 1950s being a largely trichromatic world. As late as the 1960s, Hering's theory was mentioned only briefly or not at all in the discussions of color vision in prominent texts, even after publication of the Hurvich and

Jameson papers (Brindley, 1960; LeGrand, 1957; Pirenne, 1967; but see Graham, 1959 for an early acknowledgement of the Hurvich and Jameson work). Eventually, opponent physiology, with DeValois' single-unit work being especially important, gained acceptance for opponent theory, and the "contest" was over, with trichromatic responding being recognized as the outcome of receptor physiology, and opponent responding as the outcome of subsequent neural wiring.

The story of color vision does not, however, end with the physiological confirmation of trichromatic and opponent-process theories, because what the physiologists saw inside the black box matched the psychophysics on a general level only. There is not a one-to-one match, for example, between many of the electrophysiologically determined opponent functions and Hurvich and Jameson's psychophysically determined functions. Also psychophysical experiments in which parameters such as spot size and illumination are varied have revealed complexities that demand further physiological investigation (Hood & Finkelstein, 1983), and we are far from understanding the physiology of color vision at the cortical level (Lennie, 2000; Chapter 4, this volume).

In summary, color vision provides an instructive story of continuing cross-talk between psychophysics and physiology. Early psychophysics led to the proposal of physiological theories, later physiological research confirmed the general outlines of these theories, and then further psychophysical research raised new questions to be answered by additional physiological research. This is similar in some respects to the example, described above, of auditory frequency discrimination, in which the absence of a match between physiologically and psychophysically determined capacities led to further physiological research.

Lateral Interactions in the Retina

Another example of psychophysics predicting physiology is provided by Mach bands, the illusory light and dark bands seen at the borders of contours. Ernst Mach (1865) carried out a mathematical analysis of these bands, and concluded that the bands "can only be explained on the basis of a reciprocal action of neighboring areas of the retina" (Ratliff, 1965, p. 98). Mach further described this reciprocal interaction in terms of excitatory and inhibitory influences. Although Mach's conclusions were correct, they were largely ignored, because the necessary physiological techniques were not available for confirmation (Ratliff, 1965). This situation, which is reminiscent of the fate of Hering's opponent-process theory, was finally rectified almost 100 years later by electrophysiological demonstrations of lateral inhibition in the Limulus (Barlow, 1953; Hartline, 1949; Hartline, Wagner, & Ratliff, 1956; Ratliff & Hartline, 1959). Again, physiology resurrected a psychophysically based physiological theory. However, as was the case for color vision, numerous discrepancies between the psychophysics and physiology remained to be worked out (Ratliff, 1965).

Mechanisms of Pitch Perception

The auditory system provides a number of examples of cross-talk between psychophysics and physiology. We note the following three psychophysical findings, which have had physiological repercussions: (a) the ability to "hear out" components of a chord; (b) periodicity pitch, the constancy of pitch perception when a complex tone's fundamental frequency is removed (periodicity pitch); and (c) the effects of auditory masking (see Moore, Chapters 12 and 13).

Hearing Out Components of a Chord

In the early 19th century, Ohm proposed his acoustic law, which stated that the ear analyzes a complex tone into its components (Bekesy, 1960). Ohm's acoustic law, plus observations by Helmholtz and others that when a number of tones are combined to create a chord, it is possible for trained listeners to "hear out" the individual notes that make up the chord (see Plomp & Mimpen, 1968), indicated that pitch perception operates in an analytic fashion. This contrasts with vision, which operates in a synthetic fashion, so when two colors are mixed (say red and green) to create a third (yellow), the components of the mixture are not perceived.

The phenomenologically observed analytic nature of pitch perception was the basis of Helmholtz's (1865) resonance-place theory of pitch, which stated that a particular frequency was signaled by the vibration of individual fibers, arranged along the basilar membrane in a tonotopic fashion, like the strings inside a piano. This conception provided a system in which components of a complex tone stimulate different receptors and are processed in separate channels, thus enabling listeners to hear out the components of a chord.

Helmholtz's proposal provides an example of a psychophysically inspired physiological theory, but this time (in contrast with his proposal of trichromatic theory), the proposed physiology was wrong. After almost a century of dominating auditory theory, the resonance-place theory fell victim to Bekesy's (1942, 1943) observation that the basilar membrane vibrates in a traveling wave. Licklider's (1959) commentary that "Almost overnight, the problem that everyone had been theorizing about, was empirically solved" (p. 44) acknowledges the power of looking inside the Black Box. This observation of the actual physiology kept the place concept, but replaced resonating fibers with a wave traveling down the membrane. As noted above, Bekesy's measurement of the basilar membrane's vibration did not, however, put the problem of frequency discrimination to rest. More accurate specification of the basilar membrane vibration was needed to explain the precision of psychophysically measured frequency discrimination.

Periodicity Pitch

The psychophysical observation of excellent frequency discrimination was eventually explained physiologically. However, another psychophysical observation, that the pitch of a complex tone remains constant, even when its fundamental frequency is eliminated (Fletcher, 1929), has posed more difficult problems. This effect, which is called *periodicity pitch* or *the effect of the missing fundamental*, has had a large influence on auditory research and theorizing. Periodicity pitch is difficult for a strict place theory to explain, it provides evidence favoring a temporal approach to frequency coding, and it has caused some theorists to focus more centrally in the auditory system in their search for an explanation for auditory pitch coding (Meddis & Hewitt, 1991; Srulovicz & Goldstein, 1983).

The Effect of Masking

The auditory masking experiments of Fletcher (1938) and others provided psychophysical evidence for the localization of frequencies along the basilar membrane, and led to the concept of the critical band – channels that independently analyze a narrow band of frequencies. The cochlea's analysis of frequency occurs, according to this psychophysically based idea, through the action of filters tuned to small frequency ranges. (Also see Schafer, Gales, Shewmaker, and Thompson (1950), who explicitly equated the critical band with tuned filters.) These tuned filters were subsequently demonstrated physiologically by single unit recordings of frequency tuning curves from neurons in the cat's auditory nerve (Galambos & Davis, 1943) and cochlear nucleus (Kiang, 1965). (Also see Zwicker, 1974, who demonstrated a correspondence between Kiang's neural tuning curves and psychophysical tuning curves, determined using a different masking procedure.)

It could be argued that perhaps the electrophysiologists might have discovered the neural tuning curves on their own, without any prior knowledge of psychophysics. If, however, history had turned out that way, it would still have been necessary for the psychophysicists to give perceptual reality to the physiologists' neural filters. In fact, discovery of the neural filters for visual features provides an example of such a sequence of discovery, with the physiological discovery of visual feature detectors just preceding the psychophysical measurement of these detectors.

Detectors for Orientation, Size and Spatial Frequency

In the previous examples, psychophysical observations predated the relevant physiology by many years. In these situations, it is appropriate to call the relationship between psychophysics and physiology a predictive relationship. However, sometimes parallel developments in psychophysics and physiology have coexisted closely in time, a situation which might be called a synergistic relationship. This appears to be the case for research on neurons in the visual system that respond selectively to stimuli with specific orientations, directions of motion, or sizes. (Note that in the literature size has been discussed mainly in terms of spatial frequency, where small sizes correspond to high spatial frequencies, large sizes to low spatial frequencies.) We will focus on orientation and spatial frequency.

One of the earliest references to such neurons was Hubel and Wiesel's (1959) pioneering paper describing receptive fields of neurons in the cat striate cortex. In that paper they state that "the particular arrangements within receptive fields of excitatory and inhibitory regions seem to determine the form, size and orientation of the most effective stimuli . . ." (p. 588). Thus began a series of papers describing the properties of receptive fields of single neurons in the cat cortex (Hubel & Wiesel, 1962, 1965, 1968). These papers, plus others such as Lettvin, Maturana, McCulloch, and Pitts' (1959) cleverly titled paper, "What the frog's eye tells the frog's brain," led to the concept of specialized neural detectors in the visual system (see Frishman, Chapter 3; Levine, Chapter 2).

Campbell and Kulikowski (1966), in one of the first papers to look for psychophysical evidence of feature detectors, began their paper with a reference to Hubel and Wiesel, followed by a question: "Hubel and Wiesel (1959, 1962) have shown that many of the cells in the visual cortex of the cat respond only to lines with a certain orientation . . . Is it possible to demonstrate in man psychophysically a similar orientational selectivity?" (pp. 437–438). Campbell and Kulikowski's affirmative answer to their question was followed by a flurry of experiments demonstrating the existence of orientation, size, and spatial frequency channels in humans (Blakemore & Campbell, 1969; Blakemore & Sutton, 1969; Campbell & Kulikowski, 1966; Campbell & Robson, 1968; Gilinski, 1968; Pantle & Sekuler, 1968). The primary psychophysical procedure in most of these experiments was selective adaptation, in which the effect of an adapting exposure to a particular orientation, size, or spatial frequency on subsequent sensitivity to that feature was determined. The resulting decrease in sensitivity, which usually occurred across a narrow band of orientations or frequencies, was taken as an indication of the tuning of the relevant detector.

The synergy between psychophysics and physiology is symbolized in a number of ways. In summarizing the results of an electrophysiological study of the response of neurons in the cat striate cortex to spatial frequency, Campbell, Cooper, and Enroth-Cugell (1969) state that "these neurophysiological results support psychophysical evidence for the existence in the visual system of channels, each selectively sensitive to a narrow band of spatial frequencies." So Hubel and Wiesel's physiological results inspired the search for psychophysical channels, and now, just a decade later, new physiological results are supporting the psychophysical evidence!

To make the marriage between psychophysics and physiology complete, another paper from Campbell's laboratory is titled "On the existence of neurons in the human visual system selectively sensitive to the orientation and size of retinal images" (Blakemore & Campbell, 1969), even though the research reported in the paper is psychophysical, not neural. Similarly, in Thomas' (1970) paper titled "Model of the function of receptive fields in human vision," he describes a number of psychophysical procedures that can be used to study "the receptive fields of various detector systems," and provides a model of receptive field functioning, based solely on psychophysical results. A more recent example of a paper with a physiological title that reports psychophysical research is Yang and Blake's (1994) paper "Broad tuning for spatial frequency of neural mechanisms underlying visual perception of coherent motion." Thus, from the seed planted by electrophysiological research on feature detectors in the late 1950s and early 1960s grew a vast literature of interlocking physiological and psychophysical research. (See Graham, 1989, for an impressive compendium of psychophysical research on pattern analyzers.)

Object Recognition and the Binding Problem

We have seen how physiological research on feature detectors in animals inspired psychophysical research which established the existence of these detectors in humans. Physiological feature detectors have also inspired other psychophysically based research and theories. For example, a number of theories of object recognition have taken the lead from physiological feature detectors to propose basic perceptual units called "primitives" (Biederman, 1987; Julesz, 1984; Peterson, Chapter 6; Treisman & Gelade, 1980). One way to think about these primitives is that they are perceptual manifestations of neural feature detectors.

However, these primitives are not necessarily isomorphic with the neural detectors, as noted by Nakayama and Joseph's (1998) statement that

> Although Treisman and Gelade's and Julesz's theories were inspired by neurophysiological findings, they maintained a certain distance from these results, preferring to define the characteristics of these units a priori or to let them be characterized by the search experiments themselves. (p. 280)

Thus, while these psychophysically based theories of object recognition may have been inspired by physiological feature detectors, the detectors, as defined by the results of psychophysical search experiments, do not necessarily represent a one-to-one mapping of psychophysics onto physiology. This is not surprising, given the complexity of object recognition. This complexity is highlighted by one of the more challenging problems in object recognition – the binding problem.

The binding problem has been defined both perceptually and physiologically. From a perceptual perspective the binding problem asks how we generate a unitary perceptual experience of an object that combines object qualities such as color, shape, location, and orientation (Roskies, 1999; Treisman, 1999). Psychophysical experiments done in conjunction with Treisman's feature integration theory of object recognition have provided evidence for "illusory conjunctions" – misperceptions that are created when features are incorrectly combined during a brief period of preattentive processing (Treisman, 1986; Wolfe & Cave, 1999). These illusory conjunctions, which represent a case of incorrect feature binding, provide a psychophysical entree to the study of stimulus parameters that may be relevant to the binding process.

On the physiological side, the binding problem is represented by the fact that information about various visual features is processed in different areas (or modules, see Nakayama, Chapter 23) in the cortex. A large literature hypothesizing mechanisms such as temporal synchronization of neural firing represents current attempts to determine the physiological mechanism responsible for the unification of this spatially separated feature information (Gray, 1999; Singer, 1999). The relationship between psychophysical and physiological approaches to the binding problem is, like the relationship between psychophysically and physiologically defined feature detectors, not necessarily one-to-one, but it is not unreasonable to expect a coming together of these two perspectives as our knowledge of both the psychophysical and physiological aspects of object recognition increases.

Locating Physiological Mechanisms

Our discussion has been focused on how the collaboration between psychophysical and physiological research has helped determine physiological mechanisms. However, as Blake (1995) points out, it is possible to use what he calls "psychoanatomical strategies" to determine the location or relative ordering of these mechanisms. The examples below speak to how psychophysics and physiology have provided information both about the ordering of processing and the sites of physiological mechanisms.

The Locus of Orientation Perception

An example of how psychophysical measurements, combined with a knowledge of anatomy, can locate the site of a perceptual effect is provided by the tilt aftereffect, which occurs after a person is adapted to a grating with a particular orientation. When the vertical grating on the right of Figure 1.3 is viewed just after adaptation to the tilted grating on the left, the vertical grating appears to be tilted slightly to the right. The psychophysical evidence that one of the sites of this effect is beyond the lateral geniculate nucleus is that it transfers interocularly, so the effect occurs when the adapting grating is viewed with the left eye and the test grating is viewed with the right eye. This transfer indicates that binocular neurons in the cortex are involved, because the signals from the left and right eyes do not meet until they reach the striate cortex (Banks, Aslin, & Letson, 1975) (see Maffei, Fiorentini, & Bisti (1973) for interocular transfer measured in single neurons).

Early vs. Late Selective Attention

The event related potential (ERP), an electrophysiological response recorded using scalp electrodes, has been used to provide evidence relevant to a long-standing controversy in the field of attention: Does the selection that occurs when attention is focused on one stimulus occur early in processing or late in processing? Chun and Wolfe (Chapter 9, p. 291) refer to Hillyard, Hink, Schwent, and Picton's (1973) research, which showed that when subjects attend to information presented to one ear, ERP components that occur within 100 msec are enhanced for the attended stimuli. Similar results also occur for visual stimuli (see Mangun, Hillyard, & Luck, 1993), indicating that attentional modulation occurs very early in visual processing. Chun and Wolfe present similar arguments, based

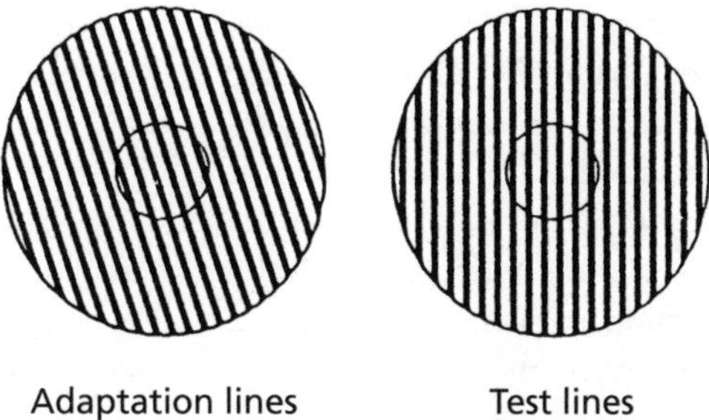

Figure 1.3. Stimuli for achieving the tilt aftereffect. Cover the test pattern on the right, and stare at the pattern on the left for about 60 seconds, moving your eyes around the circle in the middle. Then cover the left-hand pattern, and transfer your gaze to the test lines on the right. If you see the test lines as tilted to the right, you are experiencing the tilt aftereffect. To achieve interocular transfer, repeat this procedure viewing the left grating with the left eye, and the right with the right eye. This effect is usually weaker than the one that occurs when the adaptation and test lines are viewed with the same eye.

on the presence of specific components of the ERP, that words that are "blinked" during a Rapid Serial Visual Presentation (RSVP) procedure are semantically processed, even though they are not consciously perceived (Shapiro & Luck, 1999).

Linking Structures with Function

Linking structures with their functions has long been a goal of sensory neurophysiology. This has been accomplished in a number of ways, all of which necessarily involve correlating physiological and perceptual responses.

Perceptual Effects of Lesioning and Brain Damage

One of the major discoveries of the 1990s has been the identification of two processing streams in the visual cortex, the ventral stream from the striate cortex to the temporal lobe, and the dorsal stream from the striate cortex to the parietal lobe. The determination of the functions served by these streams has been achieved by assessing the behavioral effects of brain damage caused by (a) lesioning in animals and (b) accidental brain damage in humans.

The technique of lesioning a specific brain area, followed by assessment of the resulting behavioral deficits, is a time-honored way of localizing the functions of specific areas. This technique involves measuring the ψ relationship of Figure 1.1 with and without a specific structure present. Using this technique in monkeys, Ungerleider and Mishkin (1982) concluded that the ventral stream was responsible for providing information relevant to "what" an object is, and the dorsal stream provides information about "where" it is. These experiments are significant not only because they were the first to identify the functions of the dorsal and ventral streams, but also because they established an anatomical schema for future researchers.

Milner and Goodale (1995; also see Goodale & Humphrey, Chapter 10), came to a different conclusion, by assessing the behavior of brain-damaged human subjects (also see Humphreys & Riddoch, Chapter 7). They argue that the ventral stream is best characterized as being responsible for "perception" (roughly equivalent to "what"), whereas the dorsal stream is best characterized as being responsible for "action" – the sensory-motor coordination of movement with relation to an object. The main import of both the Ungerleider and Mishkin and the Milner and Goodale research for our purposes is that the conclusions from both lesion and neuropsychological studies involve a collaborative effort between physiology and psychophysics, with a physiological manipulation leading to a psychophysically measured outcome.

Comparing Animal Electrophysiology and Human Psychophysics

The most common way of determining the function of a particular structure is by measuring ϕ relationships, with the goal being to identify a neuron's preferred stimulus (cf. Hubel & Wiesel, 1959). Although these experiments typically have not included measurement of the ψ relationship, stimuli are used which have known perceptual effects. Thus, oriented or moving lines, and lights with different wavelength distributions, are used because they are known to be perceived as oriented, moving, or colored by humans.

The ψ relationship in these studies is often not determined because of the difficulty of training animals to make psychophysical judgments (but this has been done, see Stebbins (1971) and more recent examples described below), so the relationship between physiology and perception is usually a qualitative one. A further disadvantage of this method is that it requires generalizing from animals to humans, something electrophysiologists have never been shy about doing (see Adrian (1928) for some of the earliest examples of this, involving the eel) but which should be done with a sensitivity to interspecies differences. If comparisons between human psychophysics and animal physiology are to be made, it is clearly preferable that human psychophysics be compared to monkey physiology. A recent paper by Kapadia, Ito, Gilbert, and Westheimer (1995) which determines parallels between human contrast sensitivity and the response of monkey V1 neurons provides a good example of this approach.

Despite the disadvantages of only measuring neural responding in animals, localizing function by determining what stimuli neurons prefer has yielded a wealth of data, including identification of neurons in the monkey's IT cortex that respond selectively to complex objects (Tanaka, 1993) and faces (Rolls & Tovee, 1995), cells in area V4 that respond to color (Felleman & Van Essen, 1991), and cells in area MT that respond predominantly to the direction of movement (Felleman & Van Essen, 1987). These results provide suggestions, but not proof, of the functions of neurons in a particular brain area. For example, Gordon and Abramov (Chapter 4) discuss problems with assuming area V4 is the locus for color perception, even though it contains many neurons that respond selectively to specific wavelengths. More certain conclusions can be derived from experiments in which the ϕ and ψ relationships are determined in the same animal, as described in the next section.

Correlating Electrophysiology and Psychophysics in the Same Animal

Recent research from a number of laboratories has begun combining simultaneous measurement of electrophysiological and behavioral responding in the same animal. Newsome (see Movshon & Newsome, 1992; Newsome & Pare, 1988; Newsome, Britten, & Movshon, 1989; Newsome, Shadlen, Zohary, Britten, & Movshon, 1995) measured the firing of MT neurons as the monkey makes a discrimination of the direction of movement of "dynamic random dot" stimuli that vary in correlation between 0 percent (all dots moving randomly) to 100 percent (all dots moving in the same direction). The result, plots of "neurometric" and "psychometric" functions (proportion correct vs. correlation) for both neurons and behavior, revealed a close connection between the neural responding and perception. Newsome has also shown that electrical stimulation of MT neurons during behavior increases the monkey's ability to discriminate the direction of movement (see Shiffrar, Chapter 8, p. 242).

Leopold and Logothetis (1996) also achieved simultaneous measurement of behavior and electrical responding in monkeys. The stimulus, a vertical grating presented to one eye and a horizontal grating presented to the other, is designed to create binocular rivalry, so the monkey's perception flips from one perception to the other. The monkey indicates, by a key press, which stimulus it is seeing, while electrical activity is simultaneously recorded from neurons in area V4 of extrastriate cortex. The link between perception and physiology is established by changes in firing that are time-locked to changes in the monkey's perception of the gratings (also see Logothetis & Schall, 1989). Note that in this experiment the physical stimulus remains constant, but perceptual changes occur that are associated with changes in neural firing. We now describe a similar procedure, which has recently been applied to humans using cortical imaging techniques to measure the physiological response.

Correlating Cortical Imaging and Perception in Humans

Moore and Engel (1999) devised a procedure in which perceptual changes elicited to a constant stimulus are correlated with neural activity in the lateral occipital region (LO) of cortex. They first measured the fMRI response of an area in LO that had previously been shown to respond well to three-dimensional stimuli. They measure the fMRI response to a high-contrast stimulus, which is initially perceived as a two-dimensional black and white pattern (Figure 1.4a) and then presented a gray-scale image of the same object (Figure 1.4b). This gray-scale image biases the subject to see the high-contrast stimulus as a three-dimensional volumetric object, and when the fMRI response to the high-contrast stimulus (Figure 1.4c) is remeasured, the response in LO increases, even though the stimulus pattern has not changed. This result is particularly interesting because it demonstrates a link between electrical responding and *interpretation* of a stimulus.

It is fitting to end this chapter with this experiment, because this collaboration between psychophysics and physiology reflects recent increases in interest in (a) cognitive contributions to perception (cf. Ballesteros, 1994; Rock, 1983), and (b) the role of inferential processes built into our nervous system, which provide heuristics that help us decode ambiguous information in the environment (cf. Goldstein, 1998; Ramachandran, 1990; Shepard, 1984). As with the other research discussed in this chapter, the operation of these aspects of perception will eventually be elucidated through cross-talk between psychophysical and physiological research.

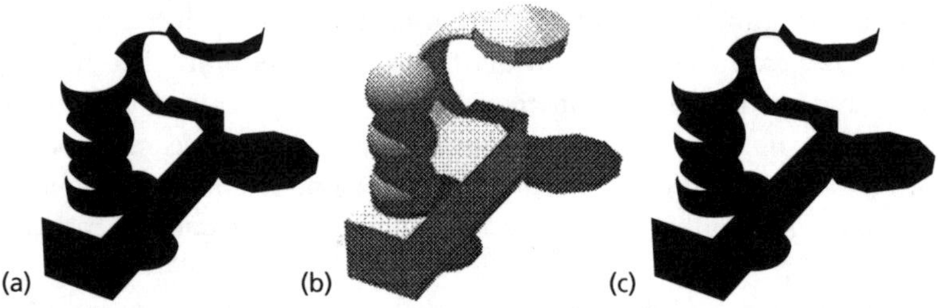

Figure 1.4. Stimuli used by Morre and Engel (1999). (a) High contrast object, which is initially perceived as two-dimensional. (b) Gray-scale image of the same object. (c) Same object as (a), which appears three-dimensional after viewing (b).

Conclusion

The various examples above make a case for the idea that a full understanding of perception demands using both psychophysical and physiological approaches and that the issue is not simply one of measurement at different levels of analysis, but of a true cross-fertilization between the information derived from one level and the information derived from the other level.

This type of cross-talk between behavior and physiology has been noted by Schacter (1986) as applied to research on memory. Schacter distinguishes three kinds of relations between cognitive psychology and neuroscience:

1. Collateral relations, in which an issue pursued in one field can't be mapped onto the other field. Schacter cites the issues of whether memory occurs presynaptically or postsynaptically as having little to say about the mnemonic facilities that interest many cognitive psychologists.
2. Complementary relations, in which description of a phenomenon in one discipline can supplement description of similar phenomena in the other discipline. Localization of function, in which the mental mechanisms hypothesized by memory researchers can sometimes be mapped onto neuroanatomical structures, is an example of such a complementary relation.
3. Convergent relations, in which cognitive psychologists and neuroscientists "coordinate their agenda to bring to bear the various conceptual and experimental tools of their respective disciplines to analyze it." When this happens, according to Schacter, findings at the cognitive level may help neuroscientists understand phenomena at the physiological level, and vice versa.

Schacter concludes that convergent relations are difficult to achieve for much of memory research (or at least they were in 1986. Recent human event related potential and neuroimaging research, such as that of Fernandez et al. (1999) and Smith and Jonides (1999), have brought the achievement of convergent relationships in cognition closer to reality). It is clear, however, that in the field of perception, convergent relations are common, and, in fact, that this convergence has evolved to the point that many perceptual researchers do not consider the psychophysical and physiological approaches to be coming from different disciplines. Instead, they see psychophysics and physiology as simply two different ways of understanding the three relationships of Figure 1.1, with special emphasis on determining linking relationships between physiology and perception. The various chapters in this Handbook illustrate how research in perception has progressed along both psychophysical and physiological lines, with the relation between them being at least complementary, and often convergent.

Notes

1. I thank Norma Graham, Donald Hood, Donald McBurney, Davida Teller, and William Yost for their comments on an early draft of the manuscript.
2. References to "Chapters," such as occurs here, refer to Chapters in this Handbook.

Suggested Readings

Brindley, G. S. (1960). *Physiology of the retina and the visual pathway*. London: Edward Arnold.
Teller, D. Y. (1984). Linking propositions. *Vision Research, 24*, 1233–1246.
Teller, D. Y. (1990). The domain of visual science. In L. Spillman and J. S. Werner (Eds.), *Visual perception: The neurophysiological foundations*. San Diego, CA: Academic Press.

Additional Topics

Basic Taste Qualities

The psychophysically derived idea of basic taste qualities has been supported by physiological research demonstrating different molecular transduction mechanisms for each of the basic qualities (Kinnamon, 1988; McBurney, 1988; Schiffman & Erickson, 1993).

Experiential Effects on Physiology and Perception

There is a large literature showing that changes in an organism's experience both during early development and in adulthood can cause parallel physiological and perceptual changes (Blake & Hirsch, 1975; Merzenich, Recanzone, Jenkins, Allard, & Nudo, 1988; Rauschecker, 1995; Wiesel, 1982).

Developmental Effects

Corresponding changes in psychophysical sensory functioning and physiological functioning occur during development, beginning in early infancy (Gwiazda & Birch, Chapter 20 (for vision); Werner & Bernstein, Chapter 21 (for auditory, somatosensory, and chemical)).

References

Adrian, E. D. (1928). *The basis of sensation*. London: Christophers.
Ballesteros, S. (1994). *Cognitive approaches to human perception*. Hillsdale, NJ: Erlbaum.
Banks, M. S., Aslin, R. N., & Letson, R. D. (1975). Sensitive period for the development of human binocular vision. *Science, 190*, 675–677.
Barlow, H. B., Blakemore, C., & Pettigrew, J. D. (1967). The neural mechanism of binocular depth discrimination. *Journal of Physiology, 193*, 327–342.
Baylor, D. (1992). Transduction in retinal photoreceptor cells. In P. Corey & S. D. Roper (Eds.), *Sensory transduction* (pp. 151–174). New York: The Rockefeller University Press.
Bekesy, G. von (1943). Über die Resonanzkurve und die Abklingzeit der verschiedenen Stellen der Schneckentrennwand. *Akust. Z., 8*, 66–76. (On the resonance curve and the decay period at various points on the cochlear partition. *Journal of the Acoustical Society of America, 21*, 245–254, 1949.)
Bekesy, G. von (1960). *Experiments in hearing*. New York: McGraw-Hill.

Bekesy, G. von. (1942). Über die Schwingungen der Schneckentrennwand beim Präparat und Ohrenmodell. *Akust. Z.*, *7*, 173–186. (The vibration of the cochlear partition in anatomical preparations and in models of the inner ear. *Journal of the Acoustical Society of America, 21*, 233–245, 1949.)

Biederman, I. (1987). Recognition-by-components: A theory of human image understanding. *Psychological Review, 94*,115–147.

Blake, R. (1995). Psychoanatomical strategies of studying human visual perception. In T. Papathomas (Ed.), *Early vision and beyond* (pp. 17–25). Cambridge, MA: MIT Press.

Blake, R., & Hirsch, H. V. B. (1975). Deficits in binocular depth perception in cats after alternating monocular deprivation. *Science, 190*, 1114–1116.

Blakemore, C. B., & Sutton, P. (1969). Size adaptation: A new aftereffect. *Science, 166*, 245–247.

Blakemore, C., & Campbell, F. (1969). On the existence of neurons in the human visual system selectively responsive to the orientation and size of retinal images. *Journal of Physiology, 203*, 237–260.

Bowmaker, J. K., & Dartnall, H. J. A. (1980). Visual pigments of rods and cones in a human retina. *Journal of Physiology, 298*, 501–511.

Brindley, G. S. (1960). *Physiology of the retina and the visual pathway*. London: Edward Arnold.

Brown, P. K., & Wald, G. (1964). Visual pigments in single rods and cones of the human retina. *Science, 144*, 45–52.

Campbell, F. W., & Kulikowski, J. J. (1966). Orientational selectivity of the human visual system. *Journal of Physiology, 187*, 437–445.

Campbell, F. W., & Robson, J. G. (1968). Application of Fourier analysis to the visibility of gratings. *Journal of Physiology, 197*, 551–566.

Campbell, F. W., Cooper, G. F., & Enroth-Cugell, C. (1969). The spatial selectivity of the visual cells of the cat. *Journal of Physiology, 203*, 223–235.

Casagrande, V. A., & Norton, T. T. (1991). Lateral geniculate nucleus: A review of its physiology and function. In J. R. Coonley-Dillon & A. G. Leventhal (Eds.), *Vision and visual dysfunction: The neural basis of visual function* (Volume 4, pp. 41–84). London: Macmillan.

DeValois, R. L. (1965). Analysis and coding of color vision in the primate visual system. *Cold Spring Harbor Symposia on Quantitative Biology, 30*, 567–579.

DeValois, R. L., Jacobs, G. G., & Jones, A. E. (1963). Responses of single cells in primate red-green color vision system. *Optik, 20*, 87–98.

Fechner, G. (1860). *Elements of psychophysics* (H. E. Adler, Trans.). New York: Holt, Rinehart and Winston.

Felleman, D. J., & Van Essen, D. C. (1991). Distributed hierarchical processing in the primate cerebral cortex. *Cerebral Cortex, 1*, 1–47.

Fernandez, G., Effern, A., Grunwald, T., Pezer, N., Lehnertz, K., Dumpelmann, M., Van Roost, D., & Elger, C. E. (1999). Real-time tracking of memory formation in the human rhinal cortex and hippocampus. *Science, 285*, 1582–1585.

Fletcher, H. (1929). *Speech and hearing*. New York: Van Nostrand.

Fletcher, H. (1938). The mechanism of hearing as revealed through an experiment on the masking effect of thermal noise. *Proceedings of the National Academy of Sciences, 24*, 265–274.

Galambos, R., & Davis, H. (1943). The response of single auditory-nerve fibers to acoustic stimulation. *Journal of Neurophysiology, 7*, 287–304.

Gibson, J. J. (1950). *The perception of the visual world*. Boston: Houghton Mifflin.

Gibson, J. J. (1979). *The ecological approach to visual perception*. Boston: Houghton Mifflin.

Gilinski, A. S. (1968). Orientation-specific effects of patterns of adapting light on visual acuity. *Journal of the Optical Society of America, 58*, 13–18.

Goldstein, E. B. (1998). When does visual processing become cognitive? *Contemporary Psychology, 43*, 127–129.

Graham, C. H. (1959). Color theory. In S. Koch (Ed.), *Psychology: A study of a science. Volume 1* (pp. 145–285). New York: McGraw-Hill.

Graham, N. (1989). *Visual pattern analyzers*. New York: Oxford University Press.

Gray, C. M. (1999). The temporal correlation hypothesis of visual feature integration: Still alive and well. *Neuron, 24,* 31–47.

Hartline, H. K. (1949). Inhibition of activity of visual receptors by illuminating nearby retinal elements in the *Limulus* eye. *Federation Proceedings, 8,* 69.

Hartline, H. K., Wagner, H. G., & Ratliff, F. (1956). Inhibition in the eye of *Limulus. Journal of General Physiology, 39,* 651–673.

Hecht, S., Shlaer, S., & Pirenne, M. H. (1942). Energy, quanta, and vision. *Journal of General Physiology, 25,* 819–840.

Helmholtz, H. L. F. von (1865). *Die Lehre von den Tonempfindungen als physiologische Grundlage für die Theorie der Musik,* (2nd ed.). Braunschweig: Viewig & Sohn. (*On the sensations of tone.* New York: Dover, 1954. Reprint of the 2nd English edition, 1885.)

Helmholtz, H. von (1852). On the theory of compound colors. *Philosophical Magazine, 4,* 519–534.

Hering, E. (1878). *Zur Lehre vom Lichtsinn.* Vienna: Gerold.

Hering, E. (1964). *Outlines of a theory of the light sense* (L. M. Hurvich & D. Jameson, Trans.). Cambridge: Harvard University Press.

Hillyard, S. A., Hink, R. F., Schwent, V. L., & Picton, T. W. (1973). Electrical signs of selective attention in the human brain. *Science,* 177–180.

Hood, D. C., & Finkelstein, M. A. (1983). A case for the revision of textbook models of color vision: The detection and appearance of small brief lights. In J. D. Mollon & L.T. Sharpe (Eds.), *Color vision: Physiology and psychophysics* (pp. 385–398). New York: Academic Press.

Hubel, D. H., & Wiesel, T. N. (1959). Receptive fields of single neurons in the cat's striate cortex. *Journal of Physiology, 148,* 574–591.

Hubel, D. H., & Wiesel, T. N. (1962). Receptive fields, binocular interaction and functional architecture in the cat's visual cortex. *Journal of Physiology, 160,* 106–154.

Hubel, D. H., & Wiesel, T. N. (1965). Receptive fields and functional architecture in two nonstriate visual areas (18 & 19) of the cat. *Journal of Neurophysiology, 28,* 229–289.

Hurvich, L. M., & Jameson, D. (1957). An opponent-process theory of color vision. *Psychological Review, 64,* 384–404.

Jameson, D., & Hurvich. L. M. (1955). Some quantitative aspects of an opponent-colors theory: I. Chromatic responses and spectral saturation. *Journal of the Optical Society of America, 45,* 546–552.

Johnstone, B. M., & Boyle, A. J. F. (1967). Basilar membrane vibrations examined with the Mossbauer technique. *Science, 158,* 390–391.

Johnstone, B. M., Patuzzi, R., & Yates, G. K. (1986). Basilar membrane measurements and the traveling wave. *Hearing Research, 22,* 147–153.

Julesz, B. (1964). Binocular depth perception without familiarity cues. *Science, 145,* 356–362.

Julesz, B. (1984). A brief outline of the texton theory of human vision. *Trends in Neuroscience, 7,* 41–45.

Kapadia, M. K., Ito, M., Gilbert, C. D., & Westheimer, G. (1995). Improvement in visual sensitivity by changes in local context: Parallel studies in human observers and in V1 of alert monkeys. *Neuron, 15,* 843–856.

Katz, D. (1935). *The world of colour.* London: Kegan Paul, Trench, Trubner.

Kiang, N. (1965). *Discharge patterns of single fibers in the cat's auditory nerve.* Cambridge, MA: MIT Press.

Kinnamon, S. C. (1988). Taste transduction: A diversity of mechanisms. *Trends in Neurosciences, 11,* 491–496.

LeGrand, Y. (1957). *Light, color and vision.* London: Chapman & Hall.

Lennie, P. (2000). Color vision. In E. R. Kandel, J. H. Schwartz, & T. M. Jessell (Eds.), Principles of neural science, 4th edn. (pp. 572–589). New York: McGraw-Hill.

Leopold, D. A., & Logothetis, N. K. (1996). Activity changes in early visual cortex reflect monkeys' percepts during binocular rivalry. *Nature, 379,* 549–553.

Lettvin, J. Y., Maturana, H. R., McCulloch, W. S., & Pitts, W. H. (1959). What the frog's eye tells

the frog's brain. *Proceedings of the Institute of Radio Engineers, 47,* 1940–1951.
Licklider, J. C. R. (1959). Three auditory theories. In S. Koch (Ed.), *Psychology: A study of a science. Volume 1* (pp. 41–144). New York: McGraw-Hill.
Logothetis, N. K., & Schall, J. D. (1989). Neuronal correlates of subjective visual perception. *Science, 245,* 761–763.
Mach, E. (1959). *The analysis of sensations.* New York: Dover. (Original work published 1914.)
Maffei, L., Fiorentini, A., & Bisti, S. (1973). Neural correlate of perceptual adaptation to gratings. *Science, 182,* 1036–1038.
Mangun, G. R., Hillyard, S. A., & Luck, S. J. (1993). Electrocortical substrates of visual selective attention. In D. Meyer and S. Kornblum (Eds.), *Attention and performance XIV* (pp. 219–243). Cambridge, MA: MIT Press.
McBurney, D. H. (1969). Effects of adaptation on human taste function. In C. Pfaffmann (Ed.), *Olfaction and taste* (pp. 407–419). New York: Rockefeller University Press.
Meddis, R., & Hewitt, M. J. (1991). Virtual pitch and phase sensitivity of a computer model of the auditory periphery: I. Pitch identification. *Journal of the Acoustical Society of America, 89,* 2866–2882.
Merzenich, M. M., Recanzone, G., Jenkins, W. M., Allard, T. T., & Nudo, R. J. (1988). Cortical representational plasticity. In P. Rakic & W. Singer (Eds.), *Neurobiology of neocortex* (pp. 42–67). Berlin: Wiley.
Milner, A. D., & Goodale, M. A. (1995). *The visual brain in action.* New York: Oxford University Press.
Moore, C., & Engel, S. A. (1999). Neural response to 2D and 3D objects measured with fMRI. *Investigative Ophthalmology and Visual Science, 40,* S351.
Mountcastle, V. B., & Powell, T. P. S. (1959). Neural mechanisms subserving cutaneous sensibility, with special reference to the role of afferent inhibition in sensory perception and discrimination. *Bulletin of the Johns Hopkins Hospital 105,* 201–232.
Movshon, J. A., & Newsome, W. T. (1992). Neural foundations of visual motion perception. *Current Directions in Psychological Science, 1,* 35–39.
Nakayama, K., & Joseph, J. S. (1998). Attention, pattern recognition, and pop-out in visual search. In R. Parasuramon (Ed.), *The attentive brain* (pp. 279–298). Cambridge, MA: MIT Press.
Newsome, W. T., & Pare, E. B. (1988). A selective impairment of motion perception following lesions of the middle temporal visual area (MT). *Journal of Neuroscience, 8,* 2201–2211.
Newsome, W. T., Britten, K. H., & Movshon, J. A. (1989). Neuronal correlates of a perceptual decision. *Nature, 341,* 52–54.
Newsome, W. T., Shadlen, M. N., Zohary, E., Britten, K. H., & Movshon, J. A. (1995). Visual motion: Linking neuronal activity to psychophysical performance. In M. S. Gazzaniga (Ed.), *The cognitive neurosciences* (pp. 401–414). Cambridge, MA: MIT Press.
Pantle, A., & Sekuler, R. (1968). Size-detecting mechanisms in human vision. *Science, 162,* 1146–1148.
Pirenne, M. H. (1967). *Vision and the eye* (2nd ed.). London: Chapman and Hall.
Plomp, R., & Mimpen, A. M. (1968). The ear as a frequency analyzer. II. *Journal of the Acoustical Society of America, 43,* 764–767.
Ramachandran, V. S. (1990). Visual perception in people and machines. In R. Blake & T. Troscianko (Eds.), *AI and the eye* (pp. 21–77). New York: Wiley.
Ranganathan, R., Harris, W. A., & Zuker, C. S. (1991). The molecular genetics of invertebrate phototransduction. *Trends in Neurosciences, 14,* 486–493.
Ratliff, F. (1965). *Mach bands: Quantitative studies on neural networks in the retina.* New York: Holden-Day.
Ratliff, F., & Hartline, H. K. (1959). The response of *Limulus* optic nerve fibers to patterns of illumination on the receptor mosaic. *Journal of General Physiology, 42,* 1241–1255.
Rauschecker, J. P. (1995). Compensatory plasticity and sensory substitution in the cerebral cortex. *Trends in Neurosciences, 18,* 36–43.
Rock, I. (1983). *The logic of perception.* Cambridge, MA: MIT Press.

Rolls, E. T., & Tovee, M. J. (1995). Sparseness of the neuronal representation of stimuli in the primate temporal visual cortex. *Journal of Neurophysiology, 73*, 713–726.
Roskies, A. L. (1999). The binding problem. *Neuron, 24*, 7–8.
Schacter, D. L. (1986). A psychological view of the neurobiology of memory. In J. E. LeDouxs & W. Hirst (Eds.), *Mind and brain* (pp. 265–269). Cambridge: Cambridge University Press.
Schafer, T. H., Gales, R. S., Shewmaker,C. A., & Thompson, P. O. (1950). The frequency selectivity of the ear as determined by masking experiments. *Journal of the Acoustical Society of America, 49*, 1218–1231.
Schiffman, S. S., & Erickson, R. P. (1993). Psychophysics: Insights into transduction mechanisms and neural coding. In S. A. Simon & S. D. Roper (Eds.), *Mechanisms of taste transduction* (pp. 395–424). Boca Raton, FL: CRC Press.
Shapiro, K. L., & Luck, S. J. (1999). The attentional blink: A front-end mechanism for fleeting memories. In V. Coltheart (Ed.), *Fleeting memories: Cognition of brief visual stimuli*. Cambridge, MA: MIT Press.
Shepard, R. N. (1984). Ecological constraints on internal representation: Resonant kinematics of perceiving, imagining, thinking, and dreaming. *Psychological Review, 91*, 417–447.
Singer, W. (1999). Neuronal synchrony: A versatile code for the definition of relations? *Neuron, 24*, 49–65.
Skinner, B.F. (1953). *Science and human behavior*. New York: Macmillan.
Smith, E. E., & Jonides, J. (1999). Storage and executive processes in the frontal lobes. *Science, 283*, 1657–1661.
Srulovicz, P., & Goldstein, J. L. (1983). A central spectrum model: A synthesis of auditory-nerve timing and place cues in monaural communication of frequency spectrum. *Journal of the Acoustical Society of America, 34*, 371–380.
Stebbins, W. C. (Ed.) (1971). *Animal psychophysics*. New York: Appleton-Century Crofts.
Stevens, S. S. (1961). To honor Fechner and repeal his law. *Science, 133*, 80–86.
Stiles, W. S. (1953). Further studies of visual mechanisms by the two-color threshold method. Coloquio sobre problemas opticos de la vision. Madrid: *Union Internationale de Physique Pure et Appliquée, 1*, 65.
Stryer, L. (1986). Cyclic GMP cascade of vision. *Annual Review of Neuroscience, 9*, 87–119.
Svaetichin, G. (1956). Spectral response curves from single cones. *Acta Physiologica Scandinavica Supplementum, 134*, 17–46.
Tanaka, K. (1993). Neuronal mechanisms of object recognition. *Science, 262*, 684–688.
Teller, D. Y. (1984). Linking propositions. *Vision Research, 24*, 1233–1246.
Teller, D. Y., & Pugh, E. N., Jr. (1983). Linking propositions in color vision. In J. D. Mollon & T. Sharpe (Eds.), *Colour vision: Physiology and psychophysics* (pp. 11–21). New York: Academic Press.
Thomas, J. P. (1970). Model of the function of receptive fields in human vision. *Psychological Review, 77*, 121–134.
Treisman, A. (1986). Features and objects in visual processing. *Scientific American, 255*, 114–125.
Treisman, A. (1999). Solutions to the binding problem: Progress through controversy and convergence. *Neuron, 24*, 105–110.
Treisman, A., & Gelade, G. (1980). A feature-integration theory of attention. *Cognitive Psychology, 12*, 97–136.
Ungerleider, L. G., & Mishkin, M. (1982). Two cortical visual systems. In D. J. Ingle, M. A. Goodale, & R. J. Mansfield (Eds.), *Analysis of visual behavior* (pp. 549–580). Cambridge: MIT Press.
Wald, G. (1968). The molecular basis of visual excitation. *Science, 162*, 230–239.
Wald, G., Brown, P., & Gibbons, I. (1963). The problem of visual excitation. *Journal of the Optical Society of America, 53*, 20–35.
Wandell, B. A. (1995). *Foundations of vision*. Sunderland, MA: Sinauer Associates.
Wheatstone, C. (1838). On some remarkable, and hitherto unobserved phenomena of binocular vision. Part I. *Transactions of the Royal Society of London*, 371–394.

Wiesel, T. N. (1982). Postnatal development of the visual cortex and the influence of the environment. *Nature, 299,* 583–591.
Wolfe, J. M., & Cave, K. R. (1999). The psychophysical evidence for a binding problem in human vision. *Neuron, 24,* 11–17.
Yang, Y., & Blake, R. (1994). Broad tuning for spatial frequency of neural mechanisms underlying visual perception of coherent motion. *Nature, 371,* 793–796.
Young, T. (1802). On the theory of light and colours. *Transactions of the Royal Society of London, 92,* 12–48.
Zwicker, E. (1974). On the psychoacoustic equivalent of turning curves. In E. Zwicker & E. Terhardt (Eds.), *Facts and models in hearing* (pp. 132–141). Berlin: Springer-Verlag.

Chapter Two

Principles of Neural Processing

Michael W. Levine

A major purpose of our sensory systems is perception, which means organizing a comprehensible internal representation of the external world. The processing depends upon the information embodied in energy gathered by the sense organs. This chapter introduces the basic concepts essential for understanding how energy in the environment becomes information in the nervous system, and the basic principles of how the nervous system processes that information. What is intended is enough background to facilitate understanding of the chapters that follow.

Components of Sensory Systems

Receptors and Transduction

Specialized receptor cells in each of the sense organs convert the energy gathered from the environment into neural energy, a process called transduction. Small currents in a receptor cell result in changes of polarization of the cell membrane (see below). In the visual system, the receptors are the rods and the cones. Each rod or cone contains molecules of pigment that absorb light; when light is absorbed, its energy changes the conformation of the pigment molecule, initiating a chain of chemical reactions that ultimately close channels through which sodium ions enter the cell (Yau, 1994). In the auditory system, the receptors are the hair cells. Motion induced by sound waves bends cilia on the hair cells, opening ionic channels through which depolarizing current enters the cell (Hudspeth, 1985). Similarly, receptors in the other sensory systems change their polarization in response to energy from the environment.

Glia and Neurons

The receptors transduce energy, but this volume is about how the information it embodies is processed. The processing is done by the central nervous system, a large portion of which is devoted to sensation and perception. There are two important aspects of this processing: how the components of the nervous system operate, and the ways in which information may be represented in the nervous system.

The nervous system comprises two cell types: glia and neurons. Glia have generally been considered supporting elements of the nervous system. Support includes providing physical structure, housekeeping, providing nutrition, and guiding the development and regeneration of neurons. Glia may also participate in the processing of information. For example, the radial glia of the retina (Müller cells) help maintain potassium concentrations, which may influence the neural elements (Newman & Zahs, 1998).

Neurons, however, are considered the principal players in the nervous system. Each neuron must be able to receive information, integrate information (both in time and from various other neurons), and transmit information (often over some distance, always to other cells). How this is accomplished will be outlined in the next sections.

Most neurons receive information from a number of other neurons, having an extensively branched set of dendrites upon which other cells can make contacts. Dendrites are generally a receiving structure, although many are also capable of transmitting messages to other cells, and information can be received by other parts of a neuron. Integration is a result of the combined currents from all synapses anywhere on the neuron converging on the cell body, or soma.

There are two aspects to the transmission of information: transmission over a distance, and communication with other cells. Some neurons convey information over a considerable distance to link different parts of the nervous system. Sensory cells must transmit information to the brain; cells in the thalamus send information to the cortex and cells in one cortical region in the brain send information to other cortical regions and to subcortical structures; cells in the central nervous system pass the command signals to muscles and glands. Sensory cells are called afferents, cells carrying information from the brain are called efferents.

Transmission is along a thin process called the axon. For transmission over long distances, the active properties of axons avoid losses as the message travels. Neurons that process information within a small brain region for use within that region may not have an axon, or at least not an axon that relies on active processes. These "local" cells are called interneurons.

The second aspect is that information must be transmitted to other neurons. There are several means of transmitting information. The best studied is direct neuron-to-neuron transmission at a synapse. The common synapse is chemical: the presynaptic neuron releases a chemical messenger, or transmitter; the transmitter binds to specific molecules on the postsynaptic neuron. Other synapses form a direct electrical connection between cells. These are electrical synapses, which occur at physical contacts known as gap junctions.

The Structure of Neurons

A membrane surrounds every neuron, isolating its inside from the external environment and controlling what comes in or gets out. The membrane separates two water compartments: intracellular and extracellular. The fluids in these compartments differ in composition, and in that difference lies the key to the operation of the neuron.

The cell membrane is "doped" with protein molecules. Some of these act as pores or channels through the membrane, allowing ions to flow from one compartment to another. Channels may be specific for a particular ionic species, or may act like a general breach through which any ion may flow. Still other molecules use the cell's energy stores to pump ions or molecules against their natural gradients and maintain the concentrations within the cell that provide a ready energy supply.

Operation of Neurons

Basic Definitions and Properties

The operation of neurons is best understood in terms of electrical phenomena. There are three fundamental quantities in electricity: current, potential, and impedance. Current, which is the flow of charged particles down a gradient of potential energy, is measured in amperes (or amps, abbreviated A). Potential is the energy gradient that causes electrical current to flow. Potential, also known as electromotive force (EMF, or voltage), is measured in volts (V) relative to an arbitrary point; usually the body as a whole is taken as the reference.

The final quantity, impedance, refers to opposition to the flow of current. Impedance is a general term that includes the ability to accumulate charge (capacitance, measured in farads, F), and thus imparts temporal properties. The memoryless portion is called resistance, measured in ohms (Ω). Since changes in resistance are usually effected by opening channels through the membrane, it is common to consider the inverse of resistance, called conductance.

Electrical current flows when there is a potential energy to act as a driving force and a conductive pathway through which it can flow. The greater the potential, the greater the flow; the greater the resistance, the smaller the flow. These relationships are captured by Ohm's law:

$$i = \frac{V}{R} \qquad [1]$$

where V is voltage, i is current, and R is resistance. In terms of the conductance, g:

$$i = V \cdot g \qquad [2]$$

In electrical devices, the current is carried by electrons; in the nervous system the charged particles are ions. Ions are atoms that obtained charge by gaining or losing one or more electrons. Atoms that lose electrons form positively charged ions that are attracted to the negative pole (cathode) of a battery, and so are called cations. The lost electrons are captured by another atom, creating ions with a net negative charge. Negatively charged particles are attracted to the positive pole (anode), and so are called anions.

Potentials Across the Membrane

Equilibrium and Steady-State Potentials

Neurons are bathed in filtered blood: water, sodium chloride (a mix of the sodium cation Na^{+} and the chlorine anion chloride, Cl^{-}), and traces of other cations like calcium (Ca^{+2}), potassium (K^+), and magnesium (Mg^{+2}), plus some negative radicals. Cytoplasm is also salt water, but its principal salt is potassium chloride.

The differential concentrations of specific ions inside and outside the neuron, especially Na^+ and K^+, lead to a potential across the membrane. Consider K^+, which is relatively free to cross the membrane. The higher internal concentration leads to diffusion of potassium from the cell. But each K^+ that exits carries with it a positive charge, leaving behind an unescorted anion making the inside negative. Separation of charges creates an electrical potential, a voltage across the membrane. Negative voltage attracts the positively charged K^+, drawing it back into the cell. When the electrical attraction equals the force of diffusion, there is no net flow of K^+ across the membrane; equilibrium is achieved. The potential at which this occurs, which is the voltage that would be established across the membrane in the absence of any other ionic flows, is called the Nernst equilibrium potential, given by:

$$V_{K^+} = -\frac{RT}{F}\ln\left(\frac{[\mathrm{K}^+]_{\mathrm{in}}}{[\mathrm{K}^+]_{\mathrm{out}}}\right) \qquad [3]$$

where the voltage is inside the cell (outside is defined as 0); T is the absolute temperature (degrees Kelvin), R and F are universal constants; ln is the natural logarithm, and square brackets indicate concentration (e.g.: $[K^+]_{in}$ is the concentration of K^+ inside the cell).

A similar analysis applies to sodium. Sodium is more concentrated outside the cell, so the ratio is less than one, making the logarithm negative and the potential positive. Obviously, the inside cannot at one time be both negative and positive, so both of these species cannot simultaneously be at equilibrium.

When a species is not at equilibrium, there is a net flow across the membrane. The rate at which specific ions cross (the current) depends on the difference from their equilibrium potential times the ability of that species to cross the membrane, as given in equation 2. Positive current is usually defined as a flow of positive charges into the cell; a flow of positive charges out of the cell, or a flow of negative ions into the cell, is a negative current. The membrane settles to a steady-state condition in which the total current is zero; this is the resting potential of the neuron.

Graded Potentials

Tapping the battery is accomplished by changing the ability of one or more ion species to cross the membrane. Opening channels that allow a flow of K^+ out of the cell (increasing K^+ conductance) brings the membrane potential nearer the Nernst potential for K^+. That is, the membrane becomes even more polarized than normally, a condition referred to as hyperpolarization. Similarly, allowing Na^+ to enter the cell more readily brings the potential nearer the Na^+ Nernst potential. Such a change, which reduces (or even reverses) the polarization of the membrane, is referred to as depolarization. Because the amount of current (and hence potential change) depends on the conductance change, these potentials are graded in size.

Opening channels results in a current through the membrane at that point. Because currents must always complete a circuit, an equal but opposite current crosses the membrane elsewhere. How far the current spreads depends on the relative resistance in the route it must travel inside the cytoplasm versus the resistance of the membrane. Resistance decreases with the area through which current passes, so the spread is larger for larger diameter processes. Opening channels reduces membrane resistance and thereby confines the spread. As current crosses the membrane, it changes the potential according to equation 1; the result is that potential declines with distance from the point at which current was injected. The passive spread of current is called electrotonic conduction.

The Nerve Impulse

The nervous system uses a regenerative process to carry signals over a greater distance than electrotonic conduction can reasonably support. Information is encoded in a stream of nerve impulses, also called action potentials or spikes.

The biophysics of the impulse were established in a series of papers from the Physiological Laboratory at Cambridge University (Hodgkin & Huxley, 1952a–d; Hodgkin, Huxley, & Katz, 1952). These researchers measured the current crossing a membrane as a function of voltage and time. By altering ionic concentrations of the bathing solution they were able to identify the currents due to each ionic species. They found that depolarization of the axon caused a transient inward spurt of Na^+, followed by a slower but sustainable outward flow of K^+. They correctly hypothesized that this could be explained if the membrane contains a large number of Na^+-specific and K^+-specific channels, each guarded by gates that block the flow of ions.

When the membrane is depolarized slightly, a sequence of events summarized in Figure 2.1 is initiated. Figure 2.1a shows the membrane at resting potential. A depolarizing current raises membrane potential; if the depolarization is sufficient to open the m-gates guarding the sodium channels, a level of depolarization called the threshold, sodium channels open (Figure 2.1b). Na^+ enters the cell, further depolarizing it and opening more m-gates. Were it not for h-gates, the membrane would switch to a new potential near the sodium equilibrium and stay there. But h-gates respond to the depolarization by closing (Figure 2.1c), blocking the sodium channels. With closed sodium channels, the membrane returns to its normal resting potential. Another factor also comes into play: The slower n-gates respond to the previous depolarization, opening the potassium channels (Figure 2.1d). The outward potassium current pulls the membrane potential toward potassium equilibrium potential, hyperpolarizing it. This closes the m-gates, then reopens the h-gates, and finally closes the n-gates.

Two features of the impulse deserve comment. First, since the depolarization phase is driven by inward sodium currents and not the original depolarizing current, the size and shape of the impulse is essentially independent of the original stimulus. This is comparable to lighting a fire; the resulting blaze is independent of the size of match used to ignite it. Like a fire, the impulse takes its energy from the medium in which it travels (the axon), and not from its initiator.

Second, the action of h-gates in extinguishing the inward sodium current also precludes restarting the process until the h-gates have reopened. Reopening the m-gates by a second pulse of current immediately after an impulse can have no effect because the h-gates still block the sodium channels (Figure 2.1c). This is the absolute refractory period, the time after an impulse when another cannot be initiated. There is also a relative refractory period

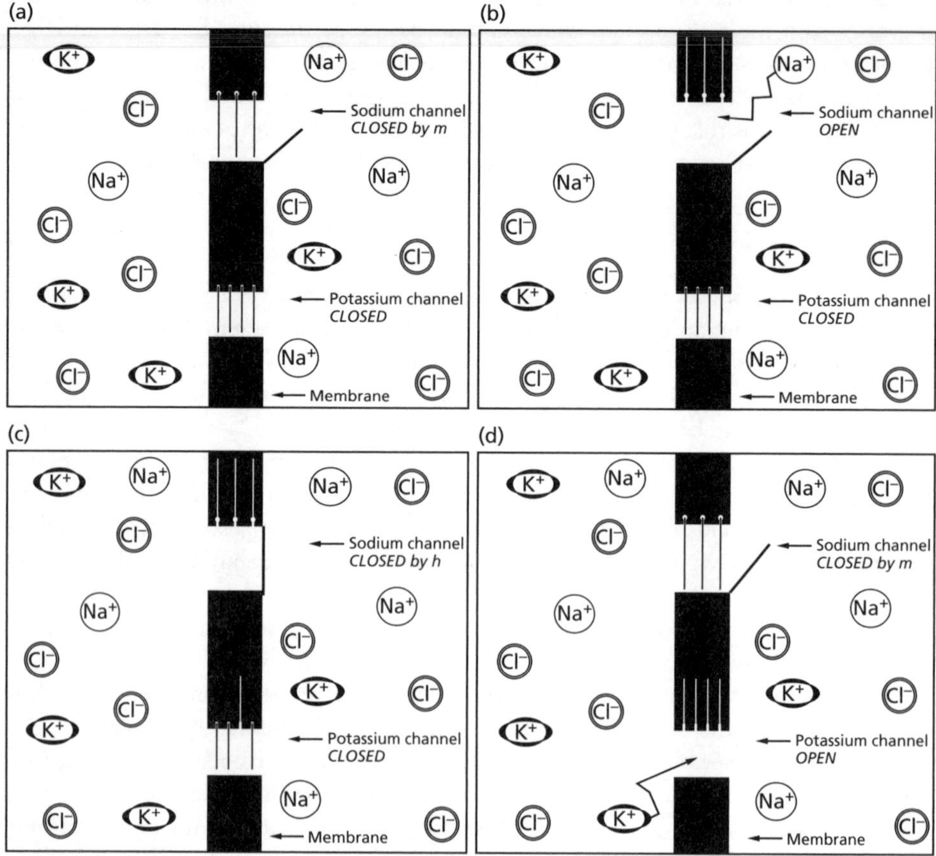

Figure 2.1. Sequence of channel openings and closings during an impulse. One representative sodium and one potassium channel are shown traversing the section of membrane. The sodium channel is guarded by three m-gates, which open rapidly in response to depolarization, and one h-gate, which closes upon depolarization but opens at resting potential. The potassium channel is guarded by four n-gates, which open slowly upon depolarization. On the left of the membrane is the cytoplasm inside of the cell with a high concentration of K^+ ions; on the right is the ECF outside the cell with a higher Na^+ concentration. Cl^- ions are on both sides. (a) Resting state. Both channels are blocked, so the only ionic currents are those that cross through the membrane itself. Potential is about −70 mV inside the cell. (b) Upon threshold depolarization, the m-gates open, allowing positive Na^+ to enter the cell, further depolarizing it (to about +10 mV). (c) Depolarization causes the slightly slower acting h-gate to shut, stopping the influx of Na^+; resting potential is restored. This is the absolute refractory period. (d) The previous depolarization finally has its effect on the n-gates, opening the potassium channel. Positive K^+ leaves the cell more readily, further polarizing it (to about −80 mV); this is the relative refractory period. The m-gates and h-gate return to their resting state. The hyperpolarization "gradually" allows the n-gates to close, returning the membrane to the resting state shown in (a). The entire cycle takes about 0.001 second.

that lasts somewhat longer; during this period, the cell is hyperpolarized by the open potassium channels; considerably more current would be required to overcome the decreased membrane resistance and the larger difference between membrane potential and threshold potential (Figure 2.1d).

Since the impulse is all-or-none, it cannot convey information about the amount of depolarization that initiated it. That information is encoded by the frequency of firing impulses. A weak depolarizing current takes a long time to reach threshold, especially during the relative refractory period of a preceding impulse. A stronger depolarizing current can quickly overcome the relatively refractory period, firing impulses in a rapid volley. This idea will recur later in this chapter.

Synapses and Synaptic Potentials

Chemical Synapses

At a chemical synapse, depolarization of the presynaptic neuron initiates the release of a chemical transmitter. Transmitter diffuses across a short synaptic gap, and binds to receptor sites on the membrane of the postsynaptic cell. The union of transmitter and receptor opens channels that allow ions to cross the membrane, changing the potential across it.

Transmitter is generally stored in small bubble-like containers (vesicles) within the presynaptic process. When the presynaptic process depolarizes, calcium channels in the membrane open. Calcium enters the cell, enabling the vesicles to move to the membrane (Katz & Miledi, 1967). At some synapses, the vesicle fuses with the plasma membrane, like a bubble at the top of a glass of soda; at others, it docks and a pore opens to the outside (Matthews, 1996). In either case, the contents of the vesicle are released (del Castillo & Katz, 1954; Fatt & Katz, 1952).

At some synapses, the release is calcium-independent. The transmitter may be in the cytoplasm, with no vesicles present. An active transporting mechanism extrudes transmitter when the cell depolarizes (Ayoub & Lam, 1984; Schwartz, 1986).

The result of transmitter binding to receptor sites is to open an ion channel. (Less commonly, the transmitter may act to close an ion channel; Toyoda, 1973.) In ionotropic systems, the receptor molecule or complex of molecules itself embodies an ion channel that opens when transmitter is bound. Metabotropic synapses work by means of an intermediary molecule called a second messenger. Typically, the binding moiety combines with a molecule of transmitter to become an active enzyme that initiates a chain of reactions to ultimately operate the ion channels.

The end result, regardless of the process, is a change in polarization of the postsynaptic cell. The potential of the postsynaptic cell approaches the equilibrium potential of the ion whose conductance increases when the channel opens; this change may be either a depolarization or a hyperpolarization.

Depolarization causes increased release of transmitter by the postsynaptic cell to neurons postsynaptic to it. If the postsynaptic cell fires impulses, a depolarizing postsynaptic response increases the probability that one will be initiated. Depolarization is therefore generally considered to be excitatory, and a depolarizing postsynaptic potential is referred to as an excitatory postsynaptic potential (EPSP). Conversely, hyperpolarization reduces the chances of releasing transmitter or initiating an impulse, and is thus inhibitory; a hyperpolarizing postsynaptic potential is referred to as an inhibitory postsynaptic potential (IPSP). However, because the effect of a stimulus may be either depolarization or hyperpolarization, it is often less confusing to refer to synapses as sign-conserving if the polarization of the postsynaptic cell mimics that of the presynaptic cell, and sign-inverting if the polarities are mirror imaged.

Not all inhibition is associated with an IPSP. A signal can be diminished by shunting; that is, by opening channels such that electrotonic spread is less efficient. In effect, the excitatory current is divided by the inhibitory influence. Thus, an inhibitory input can be slightly depolarizing, but the combination is less than the response to the excitatory signal alone.

When a train of impulses arrives at a presynaptic terminal, each represents a large depolarization that results in the release of many vesicles. The effect of each impulse lasts for a short time, so when the next arrives its influence is added to the surviving influence of the previous. The more rapidly the impulses arrive, the larger the surviving effect of each, and thus the greater the resulting mean polarization. In this way, rate is converted to a graded level, just as a graded potential was originally encoded as a firing rate. The synapse thus acts as decoder for the signal encoded by the frequency of firing of impulses.

The effect of transmitter on the postsynaptic cell is long lasting compared to an impulse, but it must not last too long, or synapses will saturate. In general, the transmitter-receptor binding is not very stable, and breaks apart. If the transmitter remains in the synapse, it may bind again and continue to have an effect. But transmitter is removed, partly by diffusion, and partly because of an active reuptake process in the presynaptic cell. In some cases, an enzyme on the postsynaptic membrane destroys the transmitter molecules so they cannot continue their effect; the reuptake is then of the inactivated transmitter. In many transmitter systems, receptors on the presynaptic membrane respond to the transmitter to regulate the amount of transmitter released.

Chemical Transmitters

Virtually all of the many chemical transmitters that have been identified in the nervous system have been found in sensory systems. Transmitters range from small gaseous molecules like nitric oxide to large proteins like the enkephalins. They are grouped into chemically related families: cholinergic (acetylcholine [ACh]); catecholaminergic (such as norepinephrine [NE] and dopamine [DA]); indoleaminergic (serotonin [5-hydroxytryptamine or 5-HT]); bioaminergic (gamma amino butyric acid [GABA]); amino acids (glutamate, aspartate, taurine, etc.); opioids; and peptides (neuropeptide Y [NPY]). For each of these, there are several to many different varieties of postsynaptic receptor. Receptors may differ in which ions pass through their channel, their speed of operation, and what other chemicals may affect them.

Pharmacological agents affecting a synapse may work in various ways. An agent that binds to a receptor and activates the same process as the natural transmitter is called a mimetic. Other chemically similar substances may bind to the receptor but not activate the ion channel. This precludes activation by the natural transmitter; such substances are competitive blockers. Other blockers allow the transmitter to bind, but interfere with the operation of the ion channel. Other agents may facilitate the opening of the channel, such that they alone have no effect but the natural transmitter has greater or lesser effect when the agent is present.

There are a number of other loci at which agents may exert an influence on a synapse. Antiesterases block the action of an enzyme that removes transmitter, allowing the effect to be prolonged, and thus enhanced. Reuptake inhibitors slow removal from the gap, again prolonging and enhancing the effect. Agents similar to the precursors for the transmitter may clog the synthesis machinery, depleting the supply of transmitter. An agent may have a very specific effect (a "clean" drug), or a broader effect with varying degrees of effectiveness for different receptors. Agents that enhance or mimic the natural transmitter are called agonists; those that oppose its effect are called antagonists.

Electrical Synapses

While much attention has been given to chemical synapses, connections are also made at gap junctions, or electrical synapses. In simple form, electrical synapses provide direct communication between the two cells. The connection can often be demonstrated by the spread of a small dye molecule, neurobiotin, which crosses gap junctions when it is injected into a neuron. Cells that make electrical contacts may link into a wide network, or syncytium. Thus, electrotonic spread can extend beyond a single cell.

There are several obvious advantages of chemical synapses over electrical, justifying the added delay (and energetic requirements) of chemical transmission. First, as noted above, the chemical synapse decodes the frequency code of impulses. Second, it allows a greater range of transmission strengths. By increasing the number of contacts between two cells, the polarization in the postsynaptic cell may be amplified to a level greater than that in the presynaptic cell. Third, the sign change of an IPSP would not occur in an electrical synapse. Finally, the chemical synapse is unidirectional; activity in the postsynaptic cell is not communicated to the presynaptic cell. As it turns out, however, some electrical synapses are at least partially rectifying; that is, spread from one cell to the other is more effective than spread from the other back to the first one.

Modulation of Synaptic Strength

There is still another wrinkle on the cell-to-cell connection so far outlined, one that is essential to neural network modeling: The effectiveness of synaptic connections can be altered. Experience, sometimes requiring concurrent activation of the synapse and postsynaptic cell, can modify the strength of a synapse. The NMDA type of glutamate receptor (and a few others) changes synaptic effectiveness as a function of the use of the synapse (Bear, 1996; Huang, Colino, Selig, & Malenka, 1992; Ohtsu, Kimura, & Tsumoto, 1995).

In addition, other chemicals present in the ECF can have temporary effects on the synapse. This process is neuromodulation. One form of modulation is by hormones, which are transported to the nucleus to effect changes in the cell. Other modulators are chemicals that also may act as transmitters. Either the agent leaks from nearby synapses, is released (perhaps by a different mechanism) at the same synapse, or is released into the general vicinity by other neurons. Neuromodulators generally reach binding sites separate from the transmitter binding sites on the receptors. The modulator alone has no effect, but when present, it affects the ability of the normal transmitter to open the ion channel. This is reminiscent of pharmacological agents alluded to above. For example, the $GABA_A$ receptor (and $GABA_C$) receptor can be modulated by a metabotropic action of glutamate (Euler & Wässle, 1998); it also has a locus for alcohol, another for pentobarbital, and still another for benzodiazepines. These drugs work by altering the ability of GABA to open a chloride channel. One suspects that some endogenous substances normally bind to these sites to modulate the GABA receptors. The natural neuromodulator is unknown, but pharmacologists capitalize on their binding sites.

Neural Coding

Frequency Coding

Cells that produce impulses must use a code to represent different messages. The simplest coding scheme, which follows from the Hodgkin/Huxley model, suggests that a steady depolarizing current is converted into a steady stream of impulses. The rate of firing impulses is proportional to the current (Shapley, 1971). The code is therefore the firing rate, or frequency. Figure 2.2 indicates ways in which firing rate may be represented.

Many models of neural firing predict a current to rate relationship. Most of these models are simplifications of the Hodgkin/Huxley model, modified so that the variability of firing can be represented mathematically (e.g., Gerstein & Mandelbrot, 1964; Stein, 1965). A popular simplification is the integrate-and-fire model; in this model, current charges the membrane until a threshold level is obtained, at which point an impulse is produced and the membrane resets. The reset is usually, but not necessarily, to resting level (Bugmann, Christodoulou, & Taylor, 1997). The integrator is often made "leaky"; that is, the charge decays toward the resting level so that an input current that ceases is soon forgotten (Knight, 1972). The leaky integrate-and-fire can conveniently be studied with Monte Carlo simulations (Levine, 1991, 1997).

Variability of Firing

The conversion from stimulus to signal is not a noise-free process, and there is considerable variability in the firing of impulses. If the neural code is actually a frequency code, the variability is unwanted noise superimposed upon the signal (but see the "additional topic" about stochastic resonance). In experiments, this purported noise is typically removed by averaging the responses to several repetitions of the same stimulus (see Figure 2.2b). An average reveals the underlying rate, which may be obscured in each single noise-ridden realization. The assumption is that the variability, being uncorrelated with the stimuli, has an expected value of zero in the average. Of course, the nervous system does not have

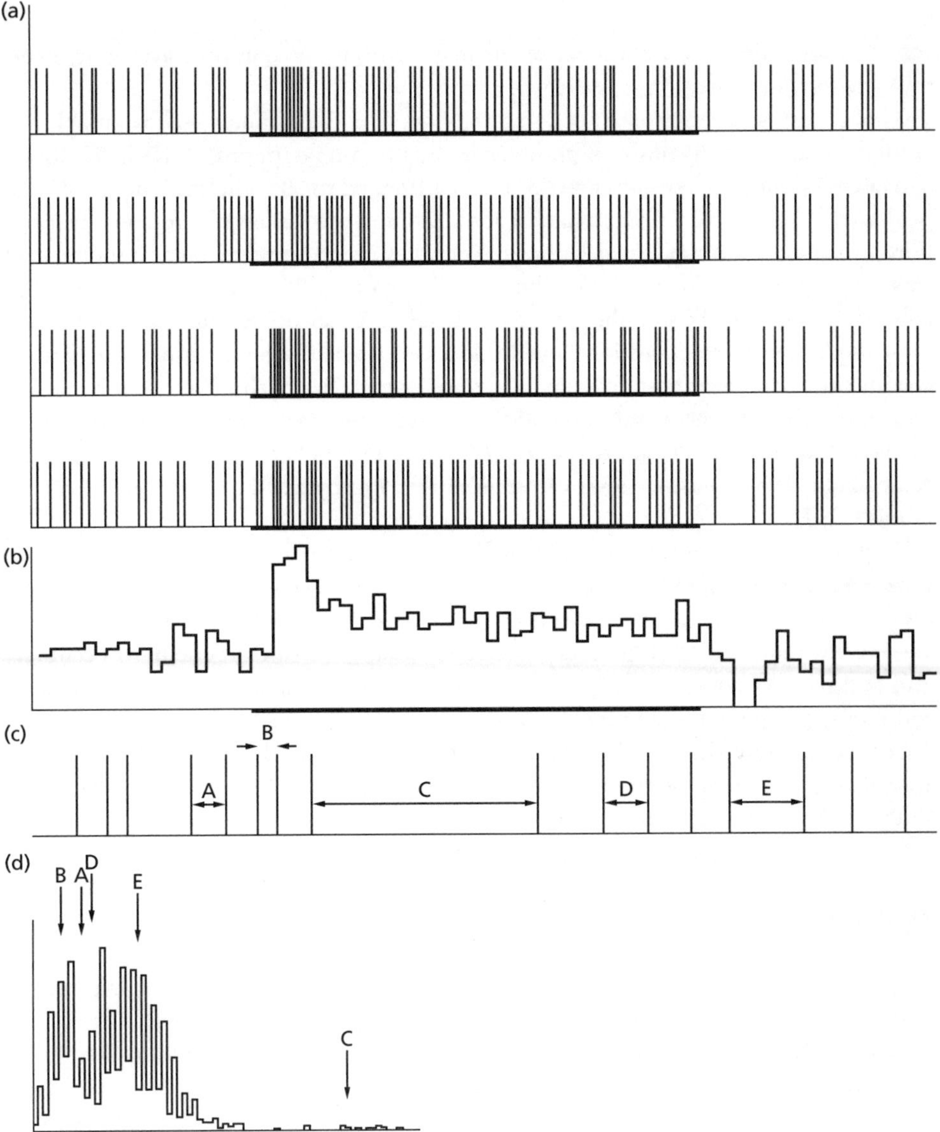

Figure 2.2. Analyses of impulse trains. (a) Four exemplars of firing in response to a 1 sec stimulus presentation (1 mm diameter spot projected on the center of the receptive field of a ganglion cell in the retina of a goldfish). Potential is plotted versus time; impulses are represented by vertical lines. A stimulus was present during the time marked by the thickened time axis. (b) Peristimulus time histogram (PSTH) derived from 11 such responses to the identical stimulus. The time axis is divided into 25 msec bins; the ordinate is the rate (number of impulses divided by total time) in each bin. (c) A half-second portion of a long record of firing in the absence of any changing stimulation. As in (a), impulses are shown versus time. Five representative intervals, labeled A through E, are indicated. (d) Interspike interval distribution derived from the record of which C is a portion. The abscissa is the time between successive intervals, in 2 ms bins; the ordinate is the number of intervals of each length found in the record. The bins containing the five intervals marked in C are indicated.

access to multiple repeated stimuli, but it may perform an equivalent averaging across multiple redundant neurons (see below).

The sources of variability are not completely known. The stimulus itself is variable; for example, visual stimuli consist of photons released by a random process (Poisson noise). Synapses also produce Poisson noise in the quantized release of vesicles (Ashmore & Copenhagen, 1983; del Castillo & Katz, 1954). Complicated interspike interval distributions can result from random deletions of impulses in a relatively regular impulse train (Bishop, Levick, & Williams, 1964; Funke & Wörgötter, 1997; Ten Hoopen, 1966), or failure to respond at the stimulus rate (Rose, Brugge, Anderson, & Hind, 1968). Finally, the complicated interconnections and feedback loops of the highly nonlinear nervous system present a nonlinear dynamical system, which may exhibit chaotic behavior. Unmeasurable differences lead to very different outcomes, making the system appear unpredictable and random (Canavier, Clark, & Byrne, 1990; Diez Martinez, Pérez, Budelli, & Segundo, 1988; Jensen, 1987; Ornstein, 1989; Przybyszewski, Lankheet, & van de Grind, 1993).

A related aspect of the variability of neural responses is the variability of the firing rate in response to a stimulus. In the retina, the variance of the firing rate generally increases when the mean rate is increased by presenting a more effective or stronger stimulus (Levine, Cleland, & Zimmerman, 1992). The overall variability increases as one moves centrally into the brain (Wilson, Bullier, & Norton, 1988), while the relationship between variance and mean rate grows more linear, at least among the cells most likely to be involved in pattern recognition (Levine, Cleland, Mukherjee, & Kaplan, 1996). In cortex, the variance of rate is directly proportional to the mean rate (Snowden, Treue, & Andersen, 1992; Tolhurst, Movshon, & Dean, 1983).

Temporal Coding

The preceding discussion of variability invoked the pejorative term "noise", conveying the implicit assumption that variability is disruptive. It is common in psychophysics to consider variability as noise, and, for example, to consider threshold as that level of stimulus sufficient to rise reliably above the noise level.

On the other hand, the orderly rise of variability with mean response, especially in central processing, suggests that variability may play a useful role in the process of perception. A neural network faced with an array of inputs that do not exactly fit the canonical form of any particular stimulus category must solve the statistical problem of determining what is the most likely possible input. To do so, it must search a "solution space" for the best-fit answer (Amit, 1989). Perhaps noise provides the necessary "jiggle" to prevent the system from settling on a second-best solution to the problem in determining what stimulus is actually present (Levine et al., 1996).

Another indication that the variability may be beneficial is that it is not independent in neighboring units. Neighboring ganglion cells in the retina show cross-correlation between their discharges (Levine, 1997; Mastronarde, 1983; Meister, Lagnado, & Baylor, 1995). The cause may be accidental, but its effect may be important; the coincident arrival of impulses converging on a postsynaptic cell can be conducive to temporal integration (Fetz,

1997). Note, however, that high correlation between neurons eliminates any advantage of averaging their responses to reduce variability.

Coincidences such as those suggested in the preceding paragraph may hold a key to a puzzle in perception called the binding problem. A natural scene produces activity in many cells in various areas of the cortex; how do the spatially separated parts of the same visual object become associated into a unit distinct from all the other objects in the scene? Simple proximity cannot be responsible, for parts of other objects are often closer than other portions of any given object; often, they may partially occlude a section of an object that is nevertheless seen as a whole. One theory of how the cortex collates the disparate parts of an object within a scene is that neurons representing its various features fire in temporally synchronous patterns (Eckhorn & Obermueller, 1993; Eckhorn et al., 1988; Engel, König, Kreiter, Schillen, & Singer,1992; Funke & Wörgötter, 1997; Gray & Singer, 1989; Singer & Gray, 1995). Synchrony is then the common bond relating all the cells responding to the same object. There are indications from motor cortex that synchronization may increase independently of mean rates as part of the cognitive process (Riehle, Grün, Diesmann, & Aertsen, 1997). Recent work has shown that when attention shifts (due to interocular rivalry), only cells responding to the stimulus being perceived continue to oscillate in synchrony (Fries, Roelfsema, Engel, König, & Singer, 1997; Logothetis, 1998).

Another possible explanation for the irregular distribution of impulses within a response is that temporal patterning could encode information. Richmond and Optican (1987) examined the responses of cortical cells to a set of stimuli from which any other possible stimulus of the same type could be constructed. They performed an analysis that identifies a set of firing patterns, called the principal components, that can be summed to reproduce any of the observed response waveforms. These components form a basis for a multidimensional response space, just as the stimuli formed the basis for a multidimensional stimulus space. The identity of the input stimulus eliciting each response could be better inferred from the values of the largest few of these components than from the mean firing rate (which is captured by the first component). It is unclear whether the nervous system actually makes use of information in this form.

Information Theory

If many cells participate in conveying a message, how many cells are required? What is the contribution of each neuron? Information theory provides a way to approach these questions and many others.

Consider the information capacity of a single axon. The informational content of any message depends on the probability of that message being produced in response to a particular stimulus, weighted by the probability of that message and the probability of that stimulus. But the maximum theoretical capacity of the axon is limited by the number of distinguishable signals it can support. The information capacity, I_{cap}, is expressed in bits (binary digits):

$$I_{cap} = \log^2(Nr) \qquad [4]$$

where *Nr* is the number of possible (equiprobable) messages, and the logarithm is base 2. Thus if there are 8 distinguishable messages the axon can convey, its maximum capacity is 3 bits; if there are 16 messages, it can transmit 4 bits, and so forth.

Single Cells

Evaluation of the number of distinguishable messages, and hence the information capacity, is not straightforward. One might think that because firing rate is a continuous variable, an infinite number of messages are possible. The key word is "distinguishable": One could not hope to discriminate a difference of one impulse per second when the variance is larger than 100 (impulses/second)^2. A reasonable estimate of the number of discriminable firing rates in a one-second sample is about 8 to 16, or a capacity of slightly under 4 bits (Rolls & Tovee, 1995b). Warland, Reinagel, and Meister (1997) found that ganglion cells have a theoretical capacity nearer 14 bits, but actually use only about 3 bits. Three to four bits seems a reasonable estimate for the capacity of a single neuron.

This estimate assumes information is conveyed only by the mean firing rate. As noted above, this is not the only possible code for information conveyed by an impulse train. One could easily distinguish among steady firing in which every interimpulse interval was exactly 100 ms, variable firing in which the mean interval was 100 ms, or firing in which 195 ms intervals alternated with 5 ms intervals, although all have the identical rate (10 impulses/sec). More complex patterning can be revealed by principal component analyses (Richmond & Optican, 1987). However, mean firing rate apparently does account for most of the information conveyed by neurons, with the additional components providing only a small contribution (Rolls & Tovee, 1995b).

Populations: Multiplexing and Redundancy

No neuron stands as the sole member of a pathway; other neurons convey information about many of the same stimuli. The information capacity of the channel depends on the combined action of many neurons.

If the responses of each neuron were independent of those of every other, the information capacity of the group would be the sum of the capacities of each of its members. That is, the total number of possible messages would be the product of the number of messages each could convey. This is the theoretical upper limit on the total information capacity. But the neurons in an ensemble are not independent; they respond to many of the same stimuli, and there may be cross-correlations among their impulse trains. Insofar as two neurons are not independent, the information carried by the pair is less than the sum of their separate capacities. In other words, some of the information is redundant.

One form redundancy could take is for two or more neurons to convey identical information. At this extreme, the information content of the group of cells is identical to that of any of its members. No capacity is gained by adding neurons to the group, but neither is any capacity lost in the event that some cells are damaged as long as at least one survives.

More commonly, some information is shared across cells. Suppose a class of neurons has a 4-bit capacity. One such cell could convey 4 bits. Add a second cell that shares 1 bit with the first; it adds 3 bits, giving 7 total. A third cell sharing 1 bit with each of the others would add only 2 bits; a fourth would add only one more. As the ensemble grows, the total information approaches an asymptote (Warland et al., 1997), while the deficit caused by the loss of any cell becomes minimal. This compromise between economy of neurons (no redundancy, high risk) and maximum safety (total redundancy, reducing risk by adding "stand-by" neurons) seems to be the actual situation in the nervous system. In at least two visual cortical areas, redundancy of about 20% seems to be the norm (Gawne, Kjaer, Hertz, & Richmond, 1996).

Redundancy limits the information capacity of groups of neurons, but the restriction may not be as severe as the above analysis indicates. Once again, it is important to recognize that there can be encoding schemes richer than simple firing rate. Meister (1996) has shown how a pair of retinal ganglion cells could in principle "multiplex" information about a third receptive field. The firing rates of each cell indicate the stimulation within each receptive field (with the redundancy that these fields are partially overlapped on the retina); the rate of impulses that are produced simultaneously by the two cells (coincidences) signals the activation of a "hidden" field at the intersection of the two.

Neural Computation

Convergence, Divergence, Summation, and Inhibition

Despite what is known of neuromodulation, electrical synapses, and autoregulation, we tend to think of the nervous system as a collection of neurons with discrete one-way connections. Within this framework, information diverges from one neuron to many (Figure 2.3a), and converges from many neurons onto one (Figure 2.3b). A neuron receiving inputs from many other neurons must integrate that information.

The simplest form of integration of multiple inputs is summation (bottom of Figure 2.3b). The currents from each activated synapse spread by electrotonic conduction; the net current in the soma is the sum of these currents, each weighted by its attenuation during its spread. Currents due to IPSPs subtract from those due to EPSPs. (As noted above, some inputs may act to divide the currents due to others.) The total current determines membrane potential, according to equation 1, thereby affecting the rate of firing impulses or altering the release of transmitter.

Inhibition as a Tuning Mechanism

Inhibition is a necessary counterbalance to excitation. If neurons could only excite each other, there would be runaway overexcitation (when a major inhibitory system is disabled, as by a drug like strychnine, convulsions result). Rapid, potent excitation requires an inhibitory system to counterbalance it and rapidly quench it.

In sensory systems, inhibition also serves to shape the specificity of neurons. For example, the responses of each retinal neuron depend on stimulation (light) in a limited region of the retina known as its receptive field. The responses depend on a difference between the illumination in a small central region compared with that in a larger surrounding

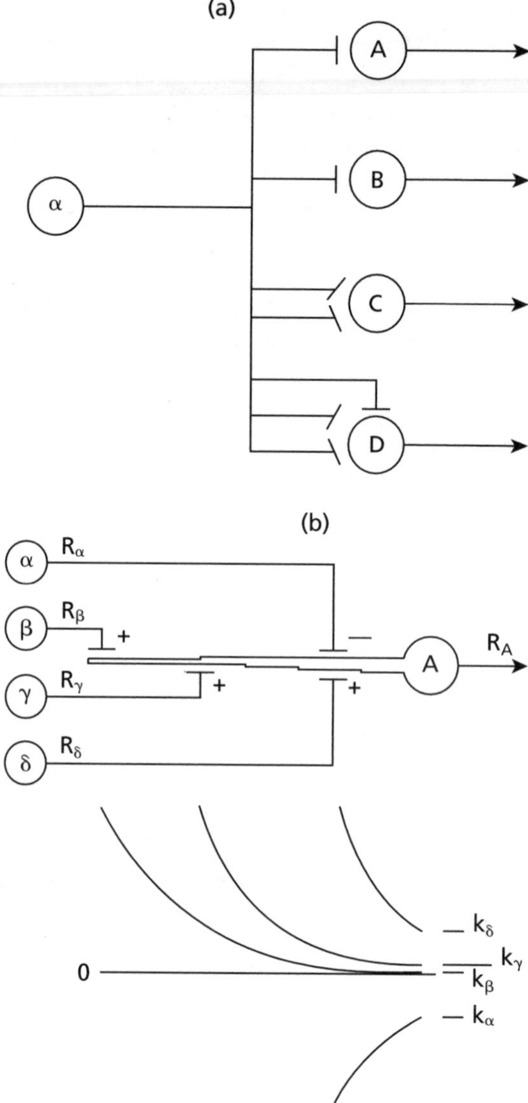

Figure 2.3. Divergence, convergence, and computation in neurons. (a) Divergence: neuron α provides inputs to neurons A, B, C, and D. Note that because of the number of synapses (and their locations), the effect on different neurons is different; in this case, α has more effect upon C and D than upon A and B. (b) Convergence: neuron A receives inputs from neurons α, β, γ, and δ. The effectiveness of each is determined by how much of the current engendered by its activation actually reaches the summation point (the soma). The electrotonic conduction of current along the dendritic tree (shown as a single dendrite for illustrative purposes) is represented by the curves below the dendrite (the synapse from δ is inhibitory, so its curve is shown inverted). The proportion of the original current at the cell body is indicated by the values k_j at the right. Thus, the net current at the cell body of A is the sum of each k times the relevant synaptic current, and its response is a function, f, of the current, I_A:

$$R_A = f(I_A) = f(I_\alpha k_\alpha + I_\beta k_\beta + I_\gamma k_\gamma + I_\delta k_\delta) = f(\textstyle\sum I_i k_i)$$

region. This general property was first described in invertebrates (Hartline, 1949; Hartline & Ratliff, 1957) and called lateral inhibition. It is a property of all retinas studied (Kuffler, 1953; Rodieck, 1979). In vertebrate ganglion cells, it is manifested as antagonism between concentric center and surround regions of the receptive field (see Chapter 3). Light in the center of an ON-center ganglion cell field excites it, but light in the surround inhibits it. (Because the reverse is true in the complementary OFF-center cells, it is preferable to refer to lateral antagonism, rather than "inhibition"). Thus, the inhibitory interaction of responses from a circumscribed region compared to those from a broader surrounding region makes the ganglion cells sensitive to contrast rather than absolute levels of illumination. Firing therefore represents "brighter here" (or "darker here"), rather than an absolute level of illumination. A white object is white because it is lighter than surrounding objects, not because its luminance exceeds some predetermined level.

A cell that responds to a wide range of stimuli cannot indicate which stimulus is present. An inhibitory interaction among cells with broad but somewhat different sensitivities leads to responses based on the differences of these sensitivities, and this can be sharply selective. There are numerous examples of inhibitory interactions sharpening the tuning of neurons. The orientation selectivity of cortical neurons depends in part on antagonistic regions that flank the elongated receptive field center (Hubel & Wiesel, 1962, 1965). A simple elongated region would show an orientation preference because a bar aligned with it would be more effective than one at an angle to it (Figure 2.4a–c). But the antagonistic flanks are stimulated when the bar is at an angle (Figures 2.4b and 2.4c), counteracting the response from the center and thereby rendering the cell considerably more selective. Orientation selectivity is further sharpened by inhibition from cells with similar preferred orientations, as illustrated schematically in Figures 2.4d and 2.4e (Allison & Bonds, 1994; Bonds, 1989; Crook, Kisvárdy, & Eysel, 1998; Hata, Tsumoto, Sato, Hagihara, & Tamura, 1988).

Another example may be found in color vision. The three cone types are each sensitive to a wide spectral range (see Chapter 4). Subsequent layers of cells difference the outputs, creating opponent cells with far more restricted spectral ranges of excitation (Calkins, Tsukamoto, & Sterling, 1998; Dacey, 1996; De Monasterio, Gouras, & Tolhurst, 1975; DeValois, 1965).

Inhibition can also tune the sensitivity to temporal patterning. If excitation and inhibition arrive simultaneously, the inhibition can negate the excitation; if they arrive asynchronously, the excitation is unaffected. This mechanism underlies direction selectivity for moving visual stimuli. A stimulus at any point in the receptive field triggers an excitatory signal, but also initiates an inhibitory signal that arrives at a position to one side with some delay. If the stimulus is moving in the same direction as the inhibitory signals, its excitatory effect at the next position is cancelled by the inhibition. Moving in the opposite direction, it precedes the inhibition and the excitation prevails (Barlow, Hill, & Levick, 1964; Livingstone, 1998).

Hierarchies and Feedback

There is a tendency to think of the visual system as a hierarchy: The eyes tell the thalamus, which tells primary cortex, which tells extrastriate cortex, which tells whatever is the seat of

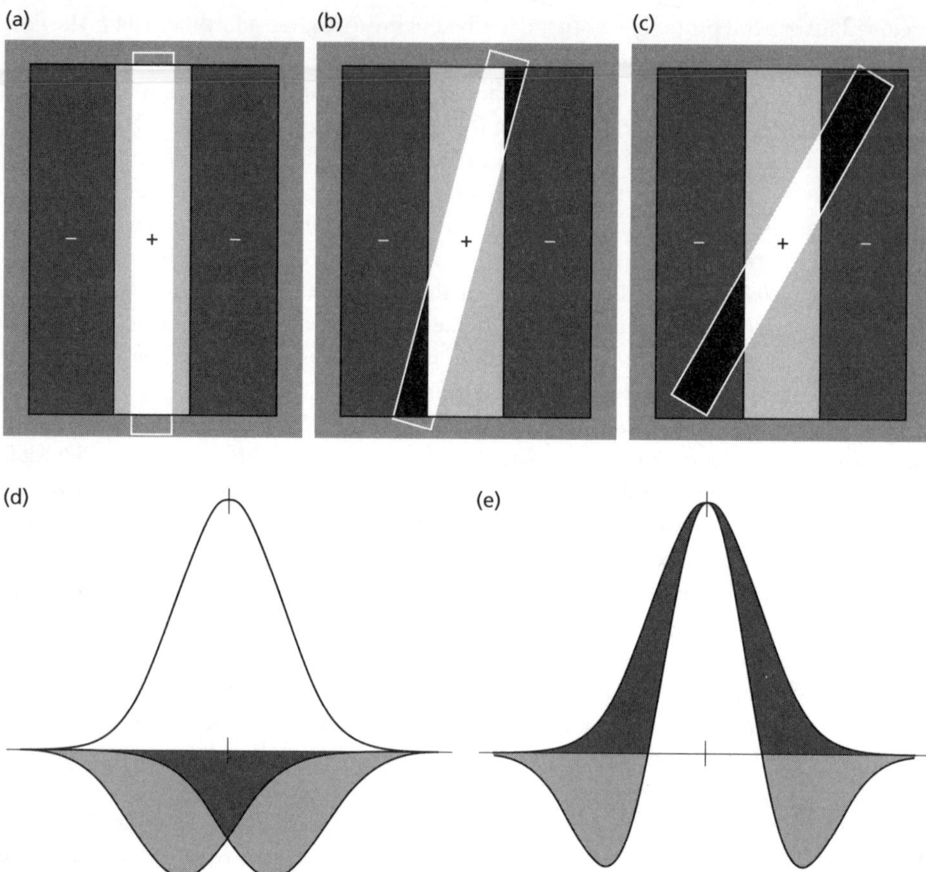

Figure 2.4. Sharpening of tuning properties by inhibition. (a–c) Orientation selectivity of a simple cortical cell. The receptive field consists of a vertically oriented excitatory area (marked "+" and lightly shaded) flanked by two inhibitory areas (marked "−" and shaded dark gray). The stimulus, a rectangular bar of light outlined in white, is shown white where it falls on the excitatory area and black in inhibitory areas; elsewhere, it is the same medium gray as the rest of the area outside the traditional field. (a) The bar of light is aligned with the excitatory region, resulting in a large excitation. (b) At 15° to vertical, the bar not only covers less of the excitatory region, but also encroaches on the inhibitory area. The black areas nearly equal the white, so the net response would be very small. (c) At 30° to vertical, the inhibition exceeds the excitation; because these cells have very low maintained discharges, there would be essentially no response. (d–e) Inhibitory interactions among neurons with somewhat different preferred stimuli sharpen the tuning of each. The relative responses are represented by curves that are centered upon the optimal stimulus. The x-axis could represent orientation (so the top curve might represent the receptive field of the cell shown in (a)–(c), while the inhibiting cells would have preferred orientations several degrees to clockwise or anticlockwise); it could represent preferred position in the visual field, preferred velocity of motion, preferred sound frequency in the cochlear nucleus, preferred odorant sensitivity along some dimension among glomeruli in the olfactory bulb, or any number of other possible stimulus dimensions. (d) The "natural" range of the cell in question is shown by the upright curve with tic marks at the optimum stimulus value. Curves for the inhibiting neurons are shown shaded and inverted to represent their

perception. The properties of cells at higher levels tend to be more generalized, with receptive fields less localized in space. For example, cells in visual area 4 have larger receptive fields and are responsive to relatively complex stimuli compared to cells in earlier visual areas (Kobatake & Tanaka, 1994). A monotonic increase in receptive field size (at the same eccentricity) as one ascends the visual hierarchy has been traced by Gross and his colleagues (Gross, Rodman, Gochin, & Colombo, 1993). Complexity, including insensitivity to the position of a complex stimulus, may be observed in the next higher area, inferotemporal cortex (Tovee, Tolls, & Azzopardi, 1994); cells in this area are sensitive even to the presence of multiple objects in their receptive fields (Rolls & Tovee, 1995a; Sato, 1989), and can respond to their preferred object even when it is partially occluded (Kovács, Vogels, & Orban, 1995). This tendency toward perceptually relevant encoding at higher levels reinforces the hierarchical view of the organization of visual processing.

While there is generalization toward more perceptually relevant responses at higher levels, the supposedly higher-ups also send information "down" to the more primary areas, creating a vast, interconnected web. Response properties of lower-order cells are affected by the responses of higher-order cells. For example, cooling the primary visual cortex (which temporarily disables it) weakens the surrounds of LGN cell receptive fields (McClurkin & Marrocco, 1984), and even affects retinal ganglion cell discharges (Molotchnikoff & Tremblay, 1983).

Feedback also applies at local levels. The inner layers of the retina send messages to the outer layers via interplexiform cells (see Chapter 3); the layers of cortex project to each other. Even at single synapses, the postsynaptic cell may synapse upon the presynaptic cell, as at the dyads of the retina, and autoreceptors control the release of transmitter. Some feedback is synaptic, but some may be neuromodulatory.

A difficulty that feedback presents is that it can mask the functions of the components of a feedback loop. Each neuron responds not only to the ascending influences from lower-level cells, but to the results of its own and its neighbors' responses. For example, a cell that receives inhibition from the cells it excites would reduce its response even in the continued presence of an excitatory input from lower-order cells. (The bipolar cell to amacrine cell and back to bipolar cell circuit at the dyads in the retina is an example of such a loop.) The response is transient, but not because of the properties of that particular cell. It would be hard to understand this operation without considering that it is within a closed loop.

←

negative effect. (e) The sum of the curves in (d) is compared to the "natural" curve (reproduced from (d)). Since the inhibiting curves are negative, this represents the central curve minus the inhibiting cell responses. The resultant curve is amplified to match the peak of the "natural" curve. The negative lightly shaded regions would result in no response if there is minimal maintained discharge. The difference is shaded dark gray; notice how much narrower is the range of the difference curve compared to the "natural" function without inhibition.

Single Cells and Populations

Neurons and Perception

The rationale for examining the operation of neurons and the codes by which they convey information is the assumption that, at some level, neurons are responsible for perception. This has been expressed formally by Horace Barlow (1972, 1995) as the "neuron doctrine." His thesis is that neurons are the fundamental unit of perceptual systems, the atoms of which all perceptual computations and experiences are composed.

While individual neurons are certainly the most obvious anatomical components of the brain, it is not assured that the functional units are coincident with the physical units. As Barlow acknowledges, cohorts of neurons may be the significant units for perception. At the other extreme, different parts of a single neuron may serve computationally different functions; for example, the properties of complex cortical cells may be explained by the nonlinear combination of independent computations on each dendritic branch (Mel, Ruderman, & Archie, 1998; Spitzer & Hochstein, 1985).

Evidence for single neurons that are linked directly to perceptual experience can be found by comparing the sensitivities of sensory cells to the psychophysical sensitivity of the behaving organism. Many studies have found changes in the discharge of single neurons that were statistically about as reliable as the animal's detection abilities. For example, the sensitivity of individual neurons in visual area MT (a movement-sensitive area) was found to have thresholds very similar to the psychophysical thresholds for moving patterns, measured from the same animals on the same trials as the physiological recordings (Britten, Shadlen, Newsome, & Movshon, 1992). Moreover, modifications of the stimulus had corresponding effects upon the psychophysical thresholds and physiological responses of cells in the related nearby area MST, further implicating individual neuronal responses in detection (Celebrini & Newsome, 1994; for further discussion, see Parker & Newsome, 1998).

The stimuli in experiments of this type were those to which the cell being recorded was most sensitive, but other cells would have presumably been sensitive to other stimuli that the animal could detect and the recorded cell could not (Barlow & Tripathy, 1997). Threshold performance would therefore be the lower envelope of the thresholds of the various cells. If single cells can perform at that level, there would be no need no invoke averaging the signals of multiple cells.

Although single cells may sometimes be able to provide an adequate signal for detection, it seems unlikely that a single cell would be the sole messenger bearing some critical news. Neurons are too fragile for such specificity, so some redundancy must be built in. Even when single cells have the requisite properties, it is assumed that a small pool of neurons bears the information (Britten et al., 1992; Britten, Newsome, Shadlen, Celebrini, & Movshon, 1996). One possibility is that a single trigger event could be obtained by averaging the outputs of these cells, which would be a way to reduce the variability inherent in the firing of individual cells. Alternatively, the next neuron (or neurons) could respond to whichever cell is most active, a "winner take all" mode of operation (Salzman & Newsome, 1994). Of course, this argument applies to the psychophysical detection of a stimulus, which is not the same problem as the perception of objects and scenes.

A somewhat different question is whether the activity of a particular neuron (or collection thereof) might represent a particular perception. Such representational cells have a long history in sensory physiology, ranging from "bug detectors" in the frog's retina (Lettvin, Maturana, McCullough, & Pitts, 1959), to detectors specific to "handlike dark stimuli" in inferotemporal cortex (Gross, Rocha-Miranda, & Bender, 1972), to the "line" and "edge" detectors of primary visual cortex (Hubel & Wiesel, 1962, 1965, 1977). Individual cells are often differentially responsive to different stimuli, and cells tuned to particular aspects of the stimulus have become known as feature detectors. A generalization of this idea may be seen in the concept of parallel processing pathways, suggesting that particular aspects of a scene are processed by different groups of cells in what are often anatomically distinct areas of the brain.

The logical extension of the detector concept is the fabled "grandmother" cells (attributed to Jerome Lettvin by Barlow, 1995), or the "yellow Volkswagen detectors" of Harris (1980). The point of the extrapolations was that one would not expect cells with such flexibility and responsibility. Could one really have cells that depended on the conjunction of yellowness, a particular chassis, and all the attributes of an automobile, such that those attributes could nevertheless be associated with other objects, such as red Subarus, blue Volkswagens, and bananas? If all such cells were lost, what would one perceive if shown a yellow, bug-shaped automobile?

Nevertheless, cells have been found in "higher" cortical areas that do have remarkably versatile but specific response properties (Logothetis, 1998). One area that has received considerable attention is the inferotemporal region, which lies on the lateral and lower banks of the temporal lobes at the sides of the brain. Some cells in inferotemporal cortex respond best to a particular complex shape, even disregarding the angle from which it is viewed (Booth & Rolls, 1998); in some cases, cells respond only to a specific constellation of attributes such as color, shape, and texture (Kobatake & Tanaka, 1994; Komatsu & Ideura, 1993; Tanaka, Saito, Fukada, & Moriya, 1991). It is noteworthy that cells in inferotemporal cortex are found in columns or modules organized according to the complex visual features they encode (Fujita, 1993; Fujita, Tanaka, Ito, & Cheng, 1992; Ghose & Ts'o, 1997).

In the inferotemporal area, and slightly higher in the temporal lobe in the superior temporal sulcus, are cells that respond preferentially to faces (Bruce, Desimone, & Gross, 1981; Perrett, Hietenan, Oram, & Benson, 1992). Some of these cells can be specific for the identity of the individual whose face is shown or for the emotion being portrayed by the face (Hasselmo, Rolls, & Baylis, 1989). Some cells generalize across all views of the face, while others prefer certain views or lighting schema (Hietanen, Perrett, Oram, Benson, & Dittrich, 1992). Each face-sensitive cell responds to a limited subset of specific stimuli (Young & Yamane, 1992).

Coding by cells with highly specific properties is referred to as sparse coding. The firing of any given cell indicates the presence of the specific stimulus it encodes. Only a small fraction of the available cells would be active at a given time, because only a small subset of all possible stimuli can be present in a given image. Conversely, a given cell would be quiescent much of the time; how often is a yellow Volkswagen part of the scene?

An alternative to sparse coding is coarse coding, in which the stimulus attributes signaled by a given cell are much more general. It is the conjunction of such firings that denotes specific stimuli (Gross, 1992). As an illustration, the three cone types that subserve color vision are quite broad in their spectral sensitivities. The long-wavelength sensitive cone responds to some extent to light of any wavelength in the visible spectrum (and can hardly be called a "red" cone, although that is often its colloquial denotation). Other colors, such as yellow, are the result of the balance of activation of the long-wavelength and middle-wavelength sensitive cones; in fact, it is their activation in the locally colored region compared with activation of all the cones in the general vicinity that determines the yellowness of a stimulus.

In coarse coding, a stimulus is represented by a pattern of responses across a relatively large group of cells. Each cell participates in the encoding of many patterns, so the firing of a given neuron cannot be taken as an indicator that some particular stimulus is present. As a result, neurons act as part of a greater network, and it is the activity of this network that matters.

Perceptual Coding

Different cells within the same structure have different properties: They may receive stimuli from different positions in the visual field, they may be located differently on the basilar membrane, they may be receptive to different molecules. In other words, there is rarely complete redundancy among neurons; the information conveyed by an ensemble of cells increases with the size of the ensemble (Rolls, Treves, Robertson, Georges-François, & Panzeri, 1998). This implies sparse coding; however, there is some redundancy, indicating coarse coding by feature detectors.

A problem with the feature detector idea, and perhaps with parallel pathways as well, is the assumption that some "higher" center must be making sense of the information segregated in particular cell types or pathways. The question of how perception is achieved is simply displaced from the area under study to some ill-defined "higher" center.

The intense interconnections of cortical areas makes the idea of a "higher" area hard to defend (Barlow, 1997). Although the way these interconnections lead to perception is not well understood, the brain is an interconnected network; perception, and consciousness itself, is an "emergent property" of this complex network of networks (Edelman, 1987). Our ultimate understanding of the sensory systems will have to be in terms of neurons functioning within multiple plastic closed loops, and not as fixed encoders in a deterministic machine.

Suggested Readings

Barlow, H. B. (1995). The neuron doctrine in perception. In M. S. Gazzaniga (Ed.), *The cognitive neurosciences* (pp. 415–435). Cambridge, MA: MIT Press.

Logothetis, N. (1998). Object vision and visual awareness. *Current Opinion in Neurobiology, 8*, 536–544.

Matthews, G. G. (1998). *Cellular physiology of nerve and muscle* (3rd ed., Chapters 1 through 8, pp. 3–169). Oxford: Blackwell Science.

Parker, A. J., & Newsome, W. T. (1998). Sense and the single neuron: Probing the physiology of perception. *Annual Review of Neuroscience, 21*, 227–277.
Perrett, D. I., & Oram, M. W. (1998). Visual recognition based on temporal cortex cells: Viewer centered processing of pattern configuration. *Zeitschrift für Naturforschung, 53c*, 518–541.

Additional Topics

Dopaminergic Modulation of Electrical Synapses

Like other synapses, the strength of connection of electrical synapses can be modulated. In the retina, this modulation is by the transmitter dopamine (DA), and occurs at junctions between amacrine cells of the rod pathway (Hampson, Vaney, & Weiler, 1992), and between horizontal cells (Dong & McReynolds, 1991; McMahon, Knapp, & Dowling, 1989). At the horizontal cells, dopamine, released by interplexiform cells (Dowling, 1979; Savy et al., 1995; Takahashi, 1988), acts at the D_1 receptor subtype to decrease the gap junction coupling (Harsanyi & Mangel, 1992; see also the review by Witkovsky & Dearry, 1991).

Temporal Frequency Analyses of Impulse Trains

When stimuli are repeated in time, averaging techniques can extract small responses from noisy signals. A popular technique is *Fourier analysis*. Fourier analysis extracts the amplitudes and phases of the sinusoidal waves (of various frequencies) that best describe the response. The impulse train is treated as a series of delta functions, each of infinitesimal duration but unit area. These are multiplied by a cosine function of the stimulus frequency, and by a sine function of the same frequency.

For a more complete description of a nonlinear system, a stimulus that is a sum of several frequencies is often used. Considerable information about nonlinearities may be derived from responses to frequencies not actually in the stimulus but represented by sums and differences of the input frequencies (e.g., Chubb & Sperling, 1988; Shapley & Victor, 1978; Solomon & Sperling, 1994, 1995). These frequencies are extracted by a method that is a multidimensional generalization of Fourier analysis, called *Wiener kernal analysis* after the mathematician Norbert Wiener. These analyses are beyond the scope of this book.

Stochastic Resonance

In stochastic resonance, variability boosts a signal to detectable levels that it would not attain in the absence of "noise" (Barlow, Birge, Kaplan, & Tallent, 1993; Bulsara & Gammaitoni, 1996). Noise can improve the ability of a population of cells to replicate a stimulus (Knight, 1972). Similarly, noise can linearize a distorted signal. This method was used by Spekreijse (1969; Spekreijse & Oosting, 1970) to examine responses of goldfish ganglion cells.

References

Allison, J. D., & Bonds, A. B. (1994). Inactivation of the infragranular striate cortex broadens orientation tuning of supragranular visual neurons in the cat. *Experimental Brain Research, 101*, 415–426.
Amit, D. J. (1989). *Modeling brain function*. Cambridge: Cambridge University Press.
Ashmore, J. F., & Copenhagen, D. R. (1983). An analysis of transmission from cones to hyperpolarizing bipolar cells in the retina of the turtle. *Journal of Physiology, 340*, 569–597.
Ayoub, G. S., & Lam, D. M.-K. (1984). The release of γ-aminobutyric acid from horizontal cells of

the goldfish (*Carassius auratus*) retina. *Journal of Physiology, 355,* 191–214.
Barlow, H. B. (1972). Single units and sensation: A neuron doctrine for perceptual psychology? *Perception, 1,* 371–394.
Barlow, H. B. (1995). The neuron doctrine in perception. In M. S. Gazzaniga (Ed.), *The cognitive Neurosciences* (pp. 415–435). Cambridge, MA: MIT Press.
Barlow, H. B. (1997). The knowledge used in vision and where it comes from. *Philosophical Transactions of the Royal Society of London, series B, 352,* 1141–1147.
Barlow, R. B., Birge, R. R., Kaplan, E., & Tallent, J. R. (1993). On the molecular origin of photoreceptor noise. *Nature, 366,* 64–66.
Barlow, H. B., Hill, R. M., & Levick, W. R. (1964). Retinal ganglion cells responding selectively to direction and speed of image motion in the rabbit. *Journal of Physiology, 173,* 377–407.
Barlow, H. B., & Tripathy, S. P. (1997). Correspondence noise and signal pooling in the detection of coherent visual motion. *Journal of Neuroscience, 17,* 7954–7966.
Bear, M. F. (1996). Progress in understanding NMDA-receptor-dependent synaptic plasticity in the visual cortex. *Journal of Physiology (Paris), 90,* 223–227.
Bishop, P. O., Levick, W. R., & Williams, W. O. (1964). Statistical analysis of the dark discharge of lateral geniculate neurones. *Journal of Physiology, 170,* 598–612.
Bonds, A. B. (1989). Role of inhibition in the specification of orientation selectivity of cells in the cat striate cortex. *Visual Neuroscience, 2,* 41–55.
Booth, M. C. A., & Rolls, E. T. (1998). View-invariant representations of familiar objects by neurons in the inferior temporal visual cortex. *Cerebral Cortex, 8,* 510–525.
Britten, K. H., Newsome, W. T., Shadlen, M. N., Celebrini, S., & Movshon, J. A. (1996). A relationship between behavioral choice and the visual responses of neurons in macaque MT. *Visual Neuroscience, 13,* 87–100.
Britten, K. H., Shadlen, M. N., Newsome, W. T., & Movshon, J. A. (1992). The analysis of visual motion: A comparison of neuronal and psychophysical performance. *Journal of Neuroscience, 12,* 4745–4765.
Bruce, C. J., Desimone, R., & Gross, C. G. (1981). Visual properties of neurons in a polysensory area in superior temporal sulcus of the macaque. *Journal of Neurophysiology, 46,* 369–384.
Bugmann, G., Christodoulou, C., & Taylor, J. G. (1997). Role of temporal integration and fluctuation detection in the highly irregular firing of a leaky integrator neuron model with partial reset. *Neural Computation, 9,* 985–1000.
Bulsara, A. R., & Gammaitoni, L. (1996). Tuning in to noise. *Physics Today, March, 1996,* 39–45.
Calkins, D. J., Tsukamoto, Y., & Sterling, P. (1998). Microcircuitry and mosaic of a blue-yellow ganglion cell in the primate retina. *Journal of Neuroscience, 18,* 3373–3385.
Canavier, C. C., Clark, J. W., & Byrne, J. H. (1990). Routes to chaos in a model of a bursting neuron. *Biophysical Journal, 57,* 1245–1251.
Celebrini, S., & Newsome, W. T. (1994). Neuronal and psychophysical sensitivity to motion signals in extrastriate area MST of the macaque monkey. *Journal of Neuroscience, 14,* 4109–4127.
Chubb, C., & Sperling, G. (1988). Drift-balanced random stimuli: A general basis for studying non-Fourier motion perception. *Journal of the Optical Society of America, A, 5,* 1986–2007.
Crook, J. M., Kisvárday, Z. F., & Eysel, U. T. (1998). Evidence for a contribution of lateral inhibition to orientation tuning and direction selectivity in cat visual cortex: Reversible inactivation of functionally characterized sites combined with neuroanatomical tracing techniques. *European Journal of Neuroscience, 10,* 2056–2075.
Dacey, D. M. (1996). Circuitry for color coding in the primate retina. *Proceedings of the National Academy of Science (USA), 93,* 582–588.
del Castillo, J., & Katz, B. (1954). Quantal components of the end-plate potential. *Journal of Physiology, 124,* 560–573.
De Monasterio, F. M., Gouras, P., & Tolhurst, D. J. (1975). Trichromatic color opponence in ganglion cells of the rhesus monkey retina. *Journal of Physiology, 251,* 197–216.
De Valois, R. L. (1965). Analysis and coding of color vision in the primate visual system. *Cold Spring Harbor Symposia on Quantitative Biology, 30,* 567–579.
Diez Martinez, O., Pérez, P., Budelli, R., & Segundo, J. P. (1988). Phase locking, intermittency,

and bifurcations in a periodically driven pacemaker neuron: Poincaré maps and biological implications. *Biological Cybernetics, 60*, 49–58.

Dong, C.-J., & McReynolds, J. S. (1991). The relationship between light, dopamine release and horizontal cell coupling in the mudpuppy retina. *Journal of Physiology, 440*, 291–309.

Dowling, J. E. (1979). A new retinal neurone – the interplexiform cell. *Trends in Neurosciences, 2*, 189–191.

Eckhorn, R., Bauer, R., Jordan, W., Brosch, M., Kruse, W., Munk, M., & Reitboeck, H. J. (1988). Coherent oscillations: A mechanism of feature linking in the visual cortex? *Biological Cybernetics, 60*, 121–130.

Eckhorn, R., & Obermueller, A. (1993). Single neurons are differently involved in stimulus-specific oscillations in cat visual cortex. *Experimental Brain Research, 95*, 177–182.

Edelman, G. M. (1987). *Neural Darwinism.* New York: Basic Books.

Engel, A. K., König, P., Kreiter, A. K., Schillen, T. B., & Singer, W. (1992). Temporal coding in the visual cortex: New vistas on integration in the nervous system. *Trends in Neurosciences, 15*, 218–226.

Euler, T., & Wässle, H. (1998). Different contributions of $GABA_A$ and $GABA_C$ receptors to rod and cone bipolar cells in a rat retinal slice preparation. *Journal of Neurophysiology, 79*, 1384–1395.

Fatt, P., & Katz, B. (1952). Spontaneous subthreshold activity at motor nerve endings. *Journal of Physiology, 117*, 109–128.

Fetz, E. E. (1997). Temporal coding in neural populations? *Science, 278*, 1901–1902.

Fries, P., Roelfsema, P. R., Engel, A. K., König, P., & Singer, W. (1997). Synchronization of oscillatory responses in visual cortex correlates with perception in interocular rivalry. *Proceedings of the National Academy of Sciences, 94*, 12699–12704.

Fujita, I. (1993). Columns in the inferotemporal cortex: Machinery for visual representation of objects. *Biomedical Research, 14, supplement 4*, 21–27.

Fujita, I., Tanaka, K., Ito, M., & Cheng, K. (1992). Columns for visual features of objects in monkey inferotemporal cortex. *Nature, 360*, 343–346.

Funke, K. & Wörgötter, F. (1997). On the significance of temporally structured activity in the dorsal lateral geniculate nucleus (LGN). *Progress in Neurobiology, 53*, 67–119.

Gawne, T. J., Kjaer, T. W., Hertz, J. A., & Richmond, B. J. (1996). Adjacent visual cortical complex cells share about 20% of their stimulus-related information. *Cerebral Cortex, 6*, 482–489.

Gerstein, G. L., & Mandelbrot, B. (1964). Random walk models for the spike activity of a single neuron. *Biophysical Journal, 4*, 41–68.

Ghose, G. M., & Ts'o, D. Y. (1997). Form processing modules in primate area V4. *Journal of Neurophysiology, 77*, 2191–2196.

Gray, C. M., & Singer, W. (1989). Stimulus-specific neuronal oscillations in orientation columns of cat visual cortex. *Proceedings of the National Academy of Science, 86*, 1698–1702.

Gross, C. G. (1992). Representation of visual stimuli in inferior temporal cortex. *Philosophical Transactions of the Royal Society of London, series B, 335*, 3–10.

Gross, C. G., Rocha-Miranda, C. E., & Bender, D. B. (1972). Visual properties of neurons in inferotemporal cortex of the macaque. *Journal of Neurophysiology, 35*, 96–111.

Gross, C. G., Rodman, H. R., Gochin, P. M., & Colombo, M. W. (1993). Inferior temporal cortex as a pattern recognition device. In E. Baum (Ed.), *Computational learning and cognition, Proceedings of the 3rd NEC Research Symposium, Siam.*

Hampson, E. C. G. M., Vaney, D. I., & Weiler, R. (1992). Dopaminergic modulation of gap junction permeability between amacrine cells in mammalian retina. *Journal of Neuroscience, 12*, 4911–4922.

Harris, C. S. (1980). Insight or out of sight? Two examples of perceptual plasticity in the human adult. In C. S. Harris (Ed.), *Visual coding and adaptability* (pp. 95–149). Hillsdale, NJ: Lawrence Erlbaum.

Harsanyi, K., & Mangel, S. C. (1992). Activation of a D_2 receptor increases electrical coupling between retinal horizontal cells by inhibiting dopamine release. *Proceedings of the National Academy of Science, 89*, 9220–9224.

Hartline, H. K. (1949). Inhibition of activity of visual receptors by illuminating nearby retinal areas

in the *Limulus* eye. *Federation Proceedings, 8,* 69.
Hartline, H. K. & Ratliff, F. (1957). Inhibitory interaction of receptor units in the eye of *Limulus. Journal of General Physiology, 40,* 357–376.
Hasselmo, M. E., Rolls, E. T., & Baylis, G. C. (1989). The role of expression and identity in the face-selective responses of neurons in the temporal visual cortex of the monkey. *Behavioural Brain Research, 32,* 203–218.
Hata, Y., Tsumoto, T., Sato, H., Hagihara, K., & Tamura, H. (1988). Inhibition contributes to orientation selectivity in visual cortex of cat. *Nature, 336,* 815–817.
Hietanen, J. K., Perrett, D. I., Oram, M. W., Benson, P. J., & Dittrich, W. H. (1992). The effects of lighting conditions on responses of cells selective for face views in the macaque temporal cortex. *Experimental Brain Research, 89,* 157–171.
Hodgkin, A. L., & Huxley, A. F. (1952a). Currents carried by sodium and potassium ions through the membrane of the giant axon of *Loligo. Journal of Physiology, 116,* 449–472.
Hodgkin, A. L., & Huxley, A. F. (1952b). The components of membrane conductance in the giant axon of *Loligo. Journal of Physiology, 116,* 473–496.
Hodgkin, A. L., & Huxley, A. F. (1952c). The dual effect of membrane potential on sodium conductance in the giant axon of *Loligo. Journal of Physiology, 116,* 497–506.
Hodgkin, A. L., & Huxley, A. F. (1952d). A quantitative description of membrane current and its application to conduction and excitation in nerve. *Journal of Physiology, 117,* 500–544.
Hodgkin, A. L., Huxley, A. F., & Katz, B. (1952). Measurement of the current-voltage relations in the membrane of the giant axon of *Loligo. Journal of Physiology, 116,* 424–448.
Huang, Y.-Y., Colino, A., Selig, D. K., & Malenka, R. C. (1992). The influence of prior synaptic activity on the induction of long-term potentiation. *Science, 255,* 730–733.
Hubel, D. H., & Wiesel, T. N. (1962). Receptive fields, binocular interaction and functional architecture in the cat's visual cortex. *Journal of Physiology, 160,* 106–154.
Hubel, D. H., & Wiesel, T. N. (1965). Receptive fields and functional architecture in two nonstriate visual areas (18 and 19) of the cat. *Journal of Neurophysiology, 28,* 229–289.
Hubel, D. H., & Wiesel, T. N. (1977). Functional architecture of macaque monkey visual cortex. *Proceedings of the Royal Society of London, Series B, 198,* 1–59.
Hudspeth, A. J. (1985). The cellular basis of hearing: The biophysics of hair cells. *Science, 230,* 745–752.
Jensen, R. V. (1987). Classical chaos. *American Scientist, 75,* 168–181.
Katz, B., & Miledi, R. (1967). The timing of calcium action during neuromuscular transmission. *Journal of Physiology, 189,* 535–544.
Knight, B. W. (1972). Dynamics of encoding in a population of neurons. *Journal of General Physiology, 59,* 734–766.
Kobatake, E., & Tanaka, K. (1994). Neuronal selectivities to complex object features in the ventral visual pathway of the macaque cerebral cortex. *Journal of Neurophysiology, 71,* 856–867.
Komatsu, H., & Ideura, Y. (1993). Relationships between color, shape, and pattern selectivities of neurons in the inferior temporal cortex of the monkey. *Journal of Neurophysiology, 70,* 677–694.
Kovács, G., Vogels, R., & Orban, G. A. (1995). Selectivity of macaque inferior temporal neurons for partially occluded shapes. *Journal of Neuroscience, 15,* 1984–1997.
Kuffler, S. W. (1953). Discharge patterns and functional organization of mammalian retina. *Journal of Neurophysiology, 16,* 37–68.
Lettvin, J. Y., Maturana, H. R., McCulloch, W. S., & Pitts, W. H. (1959). What the frog's eye tells the frog's brain. *Proceedings of the Institute of Radio Engineers, 47,* 1940–1951.
Levine, M. W. (1991). The distribution of the intervals between neural impulses in the maintained discharges of retinal ganglion cells. *Biological Cybernetics, 65,* 459–467.
Levine, M. W. (1997). An analysis of the cross-correlation between ganglion cells in the retina of goldfish. *Visual Neuroscience, 14,* 731–739.
Levine, M. W., Cleland, B. G., Mukherjee, P., & Kaplan, E. (1996). Tailoring of variability in the lateral geniculate nucleus of the cat. *Biological Cybernetics, 75,* 219–227.
Levine, M. W., Cleland, B. G., & Zimmerman, R. P. (1992). Variability of responses of cat retinal ganglion cells. *Visual Neuroscience, 8,* 277–279.

Livingstone, M. S. (1998). Mechanisms of direction selectivity in macaque V1. *Neuron, 20*, 509–526.

Logothetis, N. (1998). Object vision and visual awareness. *Current Opinion in Neurobiology, 8*, 536–544.

Mastronarde, D. N. (1983). Correlated firing of cat retinal ganglion cells. I. Spontaneously active inputs to X- and Y- cells. *Journal of Neurophysiology, 49*, 303–324.

Matthews, G. (1996). Neurotransmitter release. *Annual Review of Neuroscience, 19*, 219–233.

McClurkin, J. W. & Marrocco, R. T. (1984). Visual cortical input alters spatial tuning in monkey lateral geniculate nucleus cells. *Journal of Physiology, 348*, 135–152.

McMahon, D. G., Knapp, A. G., & Dowling, J. E. (1989). Horizontal cell gap junctions: Single-channel conductance and modulation by dopamine. *Proceedings of the National Academy of Science, 86*, 7639–7643.

Meister, M. (1996). Multineuronal codes in retinal signaling. *Proceedings of the National Academy of Sciences, 93*, 609–614.

Meister, M., Lagnado, L., & Baylor, D. A. (1995). Concerted signaling by retinal ganglion cells. *Science, 270*, 1207–1210.

Mel, B. W., Ruderman, D. L., & Archie, K. A. (1998). Translation-invariant orientation tuning in visual "complex" cells could derive from intradendritic computations. *Journal of Neuroscience, 18*, 4325–4334.

Molotchnikoff, S. & Tremblay, F. (1983). Influence of the visual cortex on responses of retinal ganglion cells in the rat. *Journal of Neuroscience Research, 10*, 397–409.

Newman, E. A. & Zahs, K. R. (1998). Modulation of neuronal activity by glial cells in the retina. *Journal of Neuroscience, 18*, 4022–4028.

Ohtsu, Y., Kimura, F., & Tsumoto, T. (1995). Hebbian induction of LTP in visual cortex: Perforated patch-clamp study in cultured neurons. *Journal of Neurophysiology, 74*, 2437–2444.

Ornstein, D. S. (1989). Ergodic theory, randomness, and "chaos". *Science, 243*, 182–187.

Parker, A. J. & Newsome, W. T. (1998). Sense and the single neuron: Probing the physiology of perception. *Annual Review of Neuroscience, 21*, 227–277.

Perrett, D. I., Hietenan, J. K., Oram, M. W., & Benson, P. J. (1992). Organization and functions of cells responsive to faces in the temporal cortex. *Philosophical Transactions of the Royal Society of London, series B, 335*, 23–30.

Przybyszewski, A. W., Lankheet, M. J. M., & van de Grind, W. A. (1993). Irregularities in spike trains of cat retinal ganglion cells. In: W. Ditto, L. Pecora, M. Schlesinger, M. Spano, & S. Vohra (Eds.), *Proceedings of the 2nd Experimental Chaos Conference* (pp. 218–225). London: World Scientific Publishing.

Richmond, B. J. & Optican, L. M. (1987). Temporal encoding of two-dimensional patterns by single units in primate inferior temporal cortex. II. Quantification of response waveform. *Journal of Neurophysiology, 57*, 147–161.

Riehle, A., Grün, S., Diesmann, M., & Aertsen, A. (1997). Spike synchronization and rate modulation differentially involved in motor cortical function. *Science, 278*, 1950–1953.

Rodieck, R. W. (1979). Visual pathways. *Annual Review of Neuroscience, 2*, 193–225.

Rolls, E. T., & Tovee, M. J. (1995a). The responses of single neurons in the temporal visual cortical areas of the macaque when more than one stimulus is present in the receptive field. *Experimental Brain Research, 103*, 409–420.

Rolls, E. T. & Tovee, M. J. (1995b). Sparseness of the neural representation of stimuli in the primate temporal visual cortex. *Journal of Neurophysiology, 73*, 713–726.

Rolls, E. T., Treves, A., Robertson, R. G., Georges-François, P., & Panzeri, S. (1998). Information about spatial view in an ensemble of primate hippocampal cells. *Journal of Neurophysiology, 79*, 1797–1813.

Rose, J. E., Brugge, J. F., Anderson, D. J., & Hind, J. E. (1968). Patterns of activity in single auditory nerve fibers of the squirrel monkey. In A. V. S. DeReuck & J. Knight (Eds.), *Hearing mechanisms in vertebrates* (pp. 144–157). London: Churchill.

Salzman, C. D., & Newsome, W. T. (1994). Neural mechanisms for forming a perceptual decision. *Science, 264*, 231–237.

Sato, T. (1989). Interactions of visual stimuli in the receptive fields of inferior temporal neurons in awake macaques. *Experimental Brain Research, 77,* 23–30.

Savy, C., Moussafi, F., Durand, J., Yelnik, J., Simon, A., & Nguyen-Legros, J. (1995). Distribution and spatial geometry of dopamine interplexiform cells in the retina. II. External arborizations in the adult rat and monkey. *Journal of Comparative Neurology, 355,* 392–404.

Schwartz, E. A. (1986). Synaptic transmission in amphibian retinae during conditions unfavorable for calcium entry into presynaptic terminals. *Journal of Physiology, 376,* 411–428.

Shapley, R. M. (1971). Fluctuations of the impulse rate in *Limulus* eccentric cells. *Journal of General Physiology, 57,* 539–555.

Shapley, R. M., & Victor, J. D. (1978). The effect of contrast on the transfer properties of cat retinal ganglion cells. *Journal of Physiology, 285,* 275–298.

Singer, W., & Gray, C. M. (1995). Visual feature integration and the temporal correlation hypothesis. *Annual Review of Neuroscience, 18,* 555–586.

Snowden, R. J., Treue, S., & Andersen, R. A. (1992). The response of neurons in areas V1 and MT of the alert rhesus monkey to moving random dot patterns. *Experimental Brain Research, 88,* 389–400.

Solomon, J. A., & Sperling, G. (1994). Full-wave and half-wave rectification in second-order motion perception. *Vision Research, 34,* 2239–2257.

Solomon, J. A., & Sperling, G. (1995). 1st- and 2nd-order motion and texture resolution in central and peripheral vision. *Vision Research, 35,* 59–64.

Spekreijse, H. (1969). Rectification in the goldfish retina: Analysis by sinusoidal and auxiliary stimulation. *Vision Research, 9,* 1461–1472.

Spekreijse, H., & Oosting, H. (1970). Linearizing: A method for analysing and synthesizing nonlinear systems. *Kybernetik, 7,* 22–31.

Spitzer, H., & Hochstein, S. (1985). A complex-cell receptive-field model. *Journal of Neurophysiology, 53,* 1266–1286.

Stein, R. B. (1965). A theoretical analysis of neuronal variability. *Biophysical Journal, 5,* 173–194.

Takahashi, E. S. (1988). Dopaminergic neurons in the cat retina. *American Journal of Optometry & Physiological Optics, 65,* 331–336.

Tanaka, K., Saito, H.-A., Fukada, Y., & Moriya, M. (1991). Coding visual images of objects in the inferotemporal cortex of the macaque monkey. *Journal of Neurophysiology, 66,* 170–189.

Ten Hoopen, M. (1966). Multimodal interval distributions. *Kybernetik, 3,* 17–24.

Tolhurst, D. J., Movshon, J. A., & Dean, A. F. (1983). The statistical reliability of signals in single neurons in cat and monkey visual cortex. *Vision Research, 23,* 775–785 .

Tovee, M. J., Rolls, E. T., & Azzopardi, P. (1994). Translation invariance in the responses to faces of single neurons in the temporal visual cortival areas of the alert macaque. *Journal of Neurophysiology, 72,* 1049–1060.

Toyoda, J.-I. (1973). Membrane resistance changes underlying the bipolar cell response in the carp retina. *Vision Research, 13,* 283–294.

Warland, D. K., Reinagel, P., & Meister, M. (1997). Decoding visual information from a population of retinal ganglion cells. *Journal of Neurophysiology, 78,* 2336–2350.

Wilson, J. R., Bullier, J., & Norton, T. T. (1988). Signal-to-noise comparisons for X and Y cells in the retina and lateral geniculate nucleus of the cat. *Experimental Brain Research, 70,* 399–405.

Witkovsy, P., & Dearry, A. (1991). Functional roles of dopamine in the vertebrate retina. In N. N. Osborne & G. J. Chader (Eds.), *Progress in retinal research* (Vol. 11, pp. 247–292). Oxford: Pergamon Press.

Yau, K.-W. (1994). Phototransduction mechanism in retinal rods and cones: The Friedenwald Lecture. *Investigative Ophthalmology and Visual Science, 35,* 9–32.

Young, M. P., & Yamane, S. (1992). Sparse population coding of faces in the inferotemporal cortex. *Science, 256,* 1327–1331.

Chapter Three

Basic Visual Processes

Laura J. Frishman

Visual perception is a very complicated and evolved function, the basis of which has interested scholars of disciplines as disparate as philosophy and molecular biology. This chapter on basic visual processing will begin to address the problem of how we see by identifying the structures, cells, and pathways of the visual system, and by describing the specific functions that are performed by these elements. The focus will be upon the lower-level processes that occur early in the visual pathways where information about the visual scene is coded and then transmitted to higher levels. This early processing determines the fidelity of the coded information and sets limits for the sensitivity and acuity of our visual perceptions. An understanding of the higher-level processes that underlie object recognition, color, and motion perception will be left to subsequent chapters.

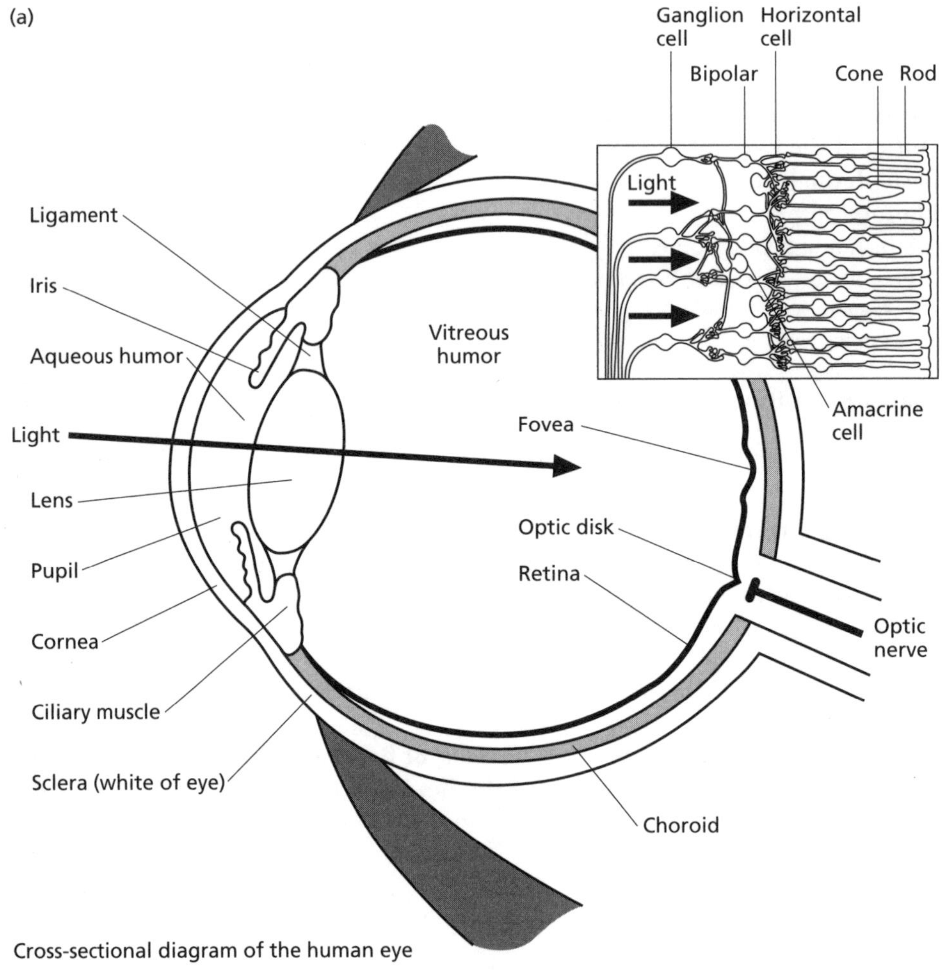

Cross-sectional diagram of the human eye

This chapter first will present an overview of the structures of the visual system as a whole. Then most of the chapter will focus on describing the structures and functions of the eye and the retina where the stage is set for what happens downstream. Later portions of the chapter will return to the visual cortex, and then consider briefly the difficult issue of how the various functional attributes of the visual neurons described in the chapter are bound together to produce coherent perceptions.

Overview of the Visual Pathways

What are the first steps in seeing? As illustrated in Figure 3.1a, light emanating from a source, or reflected from a scene or object, enters the eye, and passes through optics, the

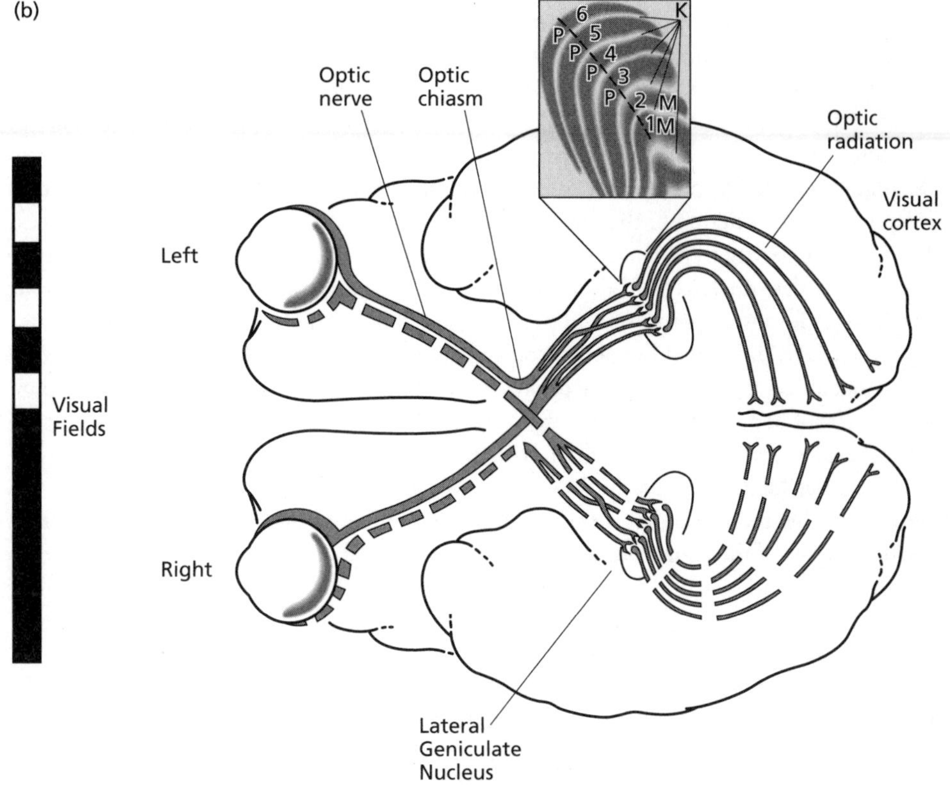

Figure 3.1. The primate eye and visual pathways. (a) A cross-section of the eye and the vertical organization of the retina (modified from Tovée, 1996; reprinted with permission of Cambridge University Press). (b) The visual pathway to the primary visual cortex. Signals travel from the retina via the optic nerve to the lateral geniculate nucleus (LGN) via the optic radiations to the primary visual cortex. The LGN slice is from Hendry and Calkins, 1998.

pupil, and humors to the back of the eye where it is imaged on the retina. The optics and the humors are essentially transparent, a feature that minimizes distortions and light losses in the ocular media. In primates such as humans, and Old World monkeys (macaques) whose visual capabilities are similar to those of humans, light in the range of about 400 to 700 nanometers (nm) is absorbed by visual pigment molecules and transduced to electrical neural signals by the photoreceptor cells of the retina. These signals are then transmitted through the retinal circuitry, out of the eye in the optic nerve, and eventually to brain areas where neural representations of images become perceptions.

A schematic of the primate visual pathways from the retina to the visual cortex appears in Figure 3.1b. Visual signals leave the eye via the axons of the retinal ganglion cells. These cells provide the last stage of processing in the retina. Their axons cross the retina in the nerve fiber layer and converge at the optic disc to form the optic nerve that exits the eye. Because there are no photoreceptors in the optic disc, that region, about 1.5 mm across, is blind. As the optic nerve enters the cranium, fibers from the nasal portions of each retina cross to the opposite side of the brain in the optic chiasm. In addition, a few fibers project to the suprachiasmatic nucleus that is involved in circadian rhythms (Rodieck, Brening, & Watanabe, 1993; Rodieck, 1998). Past the chiasm, the fibers form the optic tracts that carry information in each brain hemisphere about the opposite hemifield of vision (see Figure 3.1b). A small percent (<10%) of the fibers project to the prectectum and superior colliculus of the midbrain, and the pregeniculate. The pretectum is involved in control of the pupil (see below), the superior colliculus is important for directing the eyes to points of interest, and the function of the pregeniculate is unknown (Rodieck et al., 1993; Rodieck, 1998). The majority (~90%) of the axons in each optic tract in primates terminate in the lateral geniculate nucleus (LGN) of the thalamus. The pathways through the LGN are the critical ones for visual perception in primates, and will be the focus of this chapter.

In the LGN, the retinal signals are transmitted to the LGN cells, which are arranged in layers that are segregated according to the eye of origin, as well as according to the morphological type of neuron. Axons from large parasol ganglion cells of the retina, named for the umbrella-like appearance of their dendritic trees, synapse on the large cells that form the two magnocellular layers of the LGN, and axons of small "midget" cells of the retina synapse on the small cells that form the four parvocellular layers of the LGN. Inputs from the nasal retina of the contralateral eye, which had crossed in the chiasm, synapse with cells in layers 1, 4, and 6, while inputs from the temporal retina of the ipsilateral eye contact cells in layers 2, 3, and 5 (see inset to Figure 3.1b).

Each LGN layer contains an orderly, retinotopic map of the contralateral hemifield of vision, and the maps in the six layers are aligned. Signals from LGN cells travel to the primary visual cortex (V1) via their axons in the optic radiations. V1, which is Brodmann's cortical area 17, also is known as the striate cortex, due to the distinctive dense accumulation of incoming radiation fibers to layer 4. V1 in each hemisphere, like its LGN afferents, contains a retinotopic map of the contralatereral hemifield. Within the map, the central area of the visual field is magnified so that it receives a disproportionately large representation.

V1 is just the first of more than 30 cortical areas in the primate brain that process visual information (Van Essen, Anderson, & Felleman, 1992). Some of these cortical regions are shown in the brain diagram of Figure 3.2a. Much recent work in humans and macaques has probed the functions and interconnections of the striate (V1) and extrastriate visual areas. A broad generalization that has emerged from these studies is that visual information is processed in two streams: a "dorsal" or "parietal" stream, and a "ventral" or "temporal" stream.

As illustrated in Figure 3.2, the dorsal stream is dominated by inputs from the magnocellular layer of the LGN, and projects from V1 to V2 to V3 to MT to MST, as well as directly from V1 to MT. The ventral stream, which has inputs from the parvocellular

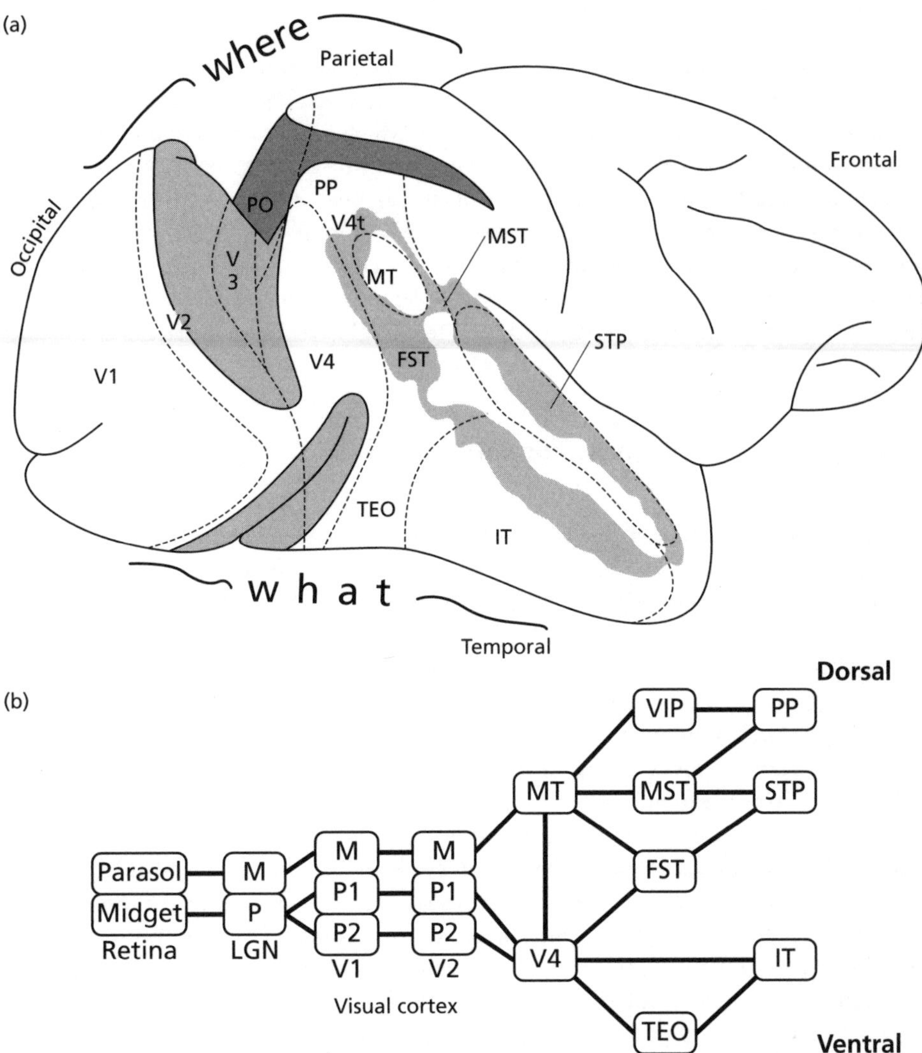

Figure 3.2. Dorsal and ventral visual pathways. (a) The dorsal and ventral pathways in the visual cortex (redrawn from Albright, 1993, with permission from Elsevier Science). (b) The visual pathway to the primary visual cortex. The LGN slice is reprinted from Hendry & Calkins, 1998, with permission from Elsevier Science.

(but also magnocellular) layers of the LGN, projects from V1 to V2 to V3 to V4 to IT and TEO (Merigan & Maunsell, 1993; Ungerleider & Mishkin, 1982). Based on results of brain lesion studies in macaques, Ungerleider and Mishkin (1982; Mishkin, Ungerleider, & Macko, 1983) suggested that the dorsal stream is concerned with location in space and motion, and it therefore has been described as the " where" stream. In contrast, the ventral stream was thought to be concerned with object identification, form and color, and has been called the "what" stream.

Other investigators, studying deficits resulting from parietal damage in human patients, have suggested that a more appropriate name for the "where" stream is the "how" stream (Goodale, Milner, Jacobsen, & Carey, 1991; Goodale & Milner, 1992). Despite these controversies, a valuable contribution of the dorsal/ventral distinction is that it has provided an organizing theoretical framework for ongoing investigations. Evaluation of its appropriateness is beyond the scope of this chapter, which focuses on basic, or lower, visual processes (but see Chapter 10 for more consideration of these streams). However, this chapter will consider the peripheral origins of the putative streams. As described in later sections, the initial separation of the parallel pathways that project from retina to the magnocellular and parvocellular layers of the LGN occurs at the first synapse in the retina between the photoreceptor cells and the second-order retinal cells, the bipolar cells. Processing at subsequent stages of the visual pathways further differentiates the streams.

Optics of the Eye and Image Formation

The light that enters the eye passes through a succession of transparent structures that refract (bend) the light and, in an optically normal or "emmetropic" eye, focus the image, inverted, on the retina. As shown in Figure 3.1a, light passes first through the cornea and the aqueous humor, and then reaches the crystalline lens in the anterior segment of the eye via the pupil aperture in the pigmented iris. The smooth muscles of the iris can adjust the size of the pupil, thereby altering the amount of light that enters the eye. The refraction and focusing of light on the retina is due to the optical power of the cornea and the crystalline lens. This optical power can be quantified in diopters, where one diopter is equivalent to the reciprocal of the focal length, in meters, of the lens. For viewing distant objects, the distance between the middle of the cornea and the crystalline lens is about 0.017 meters, which means that optical power of the human eye is about 60 diopters (Wandell, 1995). Considered another way, for an eye whose focus is fixed at infinity, a one-diopter lens will focus an image that is one meter from the eye on the retina. The cornea normally has a power of about 43 diopters, which is about two-thirds of the total power of the optics. More refraction occurs in the cornea than in the crystalline lens because the change in index of refractive as light waves propagate through air, and then through the cornea, is greater than the change between the aqueous humor that fills the anterior chamber and the crystalline lens.

Although both the cornea and the crystalline lens refract the light that enters the eye, the corneal power is fixed, whereas the lens power can be adjusted through changes in its curvature. This adjustment, called accommodation, may be as great as 12–16 diopters in a person under 20 years of age. Accommodation allows objects at a range of different distances from the retina to be brought into sharp focus. Due to an age-related loss of accommodation called "presbyopia," accommodative amplitude declines gradually over time. In persons over 55 years of age accommodation generally will be restricted to a range of less than one diopter. This age-related change is due mainly to a reduction in the elasticity of the lens and the capsule that holds the lens. However, the changes in extra-lenticular factors in presbyopia such as configurational changes in the muscles controlling accommodation, and changes in the position of zonular fibers that hold the lens in position, remain an active area of investigation (Glasser & Campbell, 1999).

As noted above, the pupil regulates the amount of light that enters the eye. The size of its aperture is adjusted by a pupillary light reflex. The reflex is controlled by retinal illumination which is signaled by retinal ganglion cells (Rodieck et al., 1993; Rodieck, 1998) that project to the pretectum in the midbrain. The midbrain, in turn, sends signals via the ciliary ganglion to neurons that innervate the iris sphincter muscles, causing the pupil to dilate when illumination is low and constrict when illumination is high. The aperture area, which controls the amount of light that can enter the eye, changes maximally by about 10 fold. The pupil size affects image quality as well. A constricted pupil improves the focus of the image on the retina by increasing the depth of field. A small pupil aperture also reduces the effects of aberrations in the cornea and lens that differentially affect focus as the wavelength of the incoming light varies. However, a small aperture also increases diffraction, which distorts the image. When all factors are considered, a pupil diameter of 2–3 mm provides the best image quality (see Charmin, 1991; and Wandel, 1995 for reviews).

The final retinal image is subject not only to diffraction and chromatic aberrations, but also to other factors (for example, pigmentation and blood vessels) that reduce the number of photons reaching the photoreceptors. Media losses are such that only about 70% of the light measured at the cornea reaches the photoreceptors. Of that light, less than 50% is transduced by the photoreceptors to visual signals.

It is possible to specify the effect of the preretinal optics on the image quality at the retina by measuring the modulation transfer function (MTF) of the optics. The MTF of the eye's optics has been measured, using both optical and psychophysical approaches and applying linear systems theory. Linear systems theory provides analytical tools for assessing transformations that systems make between inputs and outputs, and in the case of the eye, predicting the image quality at the retina after light has passed through the optics. The MTF of a lens (or of the visual system as a whole) can be measured using a pattern of alternating light and dark bars, called a grating. The length of the spatial period of the luminance modulation formed by one dark and one light bar is varied to create a range of spatial frequencies. For the eye, the spatial frequencies are quantified in cycles per degree (c/deg) of visual angle. A degree is equal to one centimeter viewed at distance of 57.3 cm, which corresponds roughly to 300 microns on the human retina.

When using such stimuli, the amplitude of the luminance modulation between the dark and light bars, which is the grating contrast, can be varied using sinusoidal waveforms. For a linear system, according to Fourier's theory, sinusoidal waveforms are the fundamental building blocks for other waveforms. Other waveforms (such as square waves, etc.) can be synthesized by adding harmonic frequencies (scaled to the appropriate amplitudes) that are multiples of the fundamental frequency. Conversely, complicated waveforms can be analyzed, using Fourier analysis, into their fundamental sinusoid component, and the harmonics of the fundamental that are present. For a linear system (in this case, the preretinal optics), if the luminance modulation is sinusoidal, then the image will retain the sinusoidal luminance pattern, but the contrast will be reduced as the optical resolution limit is reached. Thus, for lenses, the MTF can be determined by measuring the transfer of contrast at each spatial frequency.

For the human eye Campbell and Green (1965) assessed the MTF of the preretinal optics by measuring the MTF of the entire human visual system psychophysically using sinusoidal gratings generated on a CRT, and comparing results with measurements when the optics were bypassed by using interference fringes. In both cases, the contrast necessary for subjects to report resolving gratings of different spatial frequencies, that is, the contrast thresholds, were measured. From these data they derived the MTF of the preretinal optics. They found (for <3 mm pupils) that the transfer of contrast was reduced by a factor of 2 when spatial frequency was increased from low spatial frequencies (<1 c/deg) to about 12 c/deg, and that there was essentially no transfer of contrast for spatial frequencies above about 50 c/deg. These values for the MTF are close to those derived from optical measurements of the line spread function (the blur produced by the image of a very fine line on the retina) by Campbell and Gubisch (1966). They also are close to those made more recently by Williams, Brainard, McMahon, and Navarro (1994) who implemented various improvements to reduce errors in the measurements.

Importantly, the spatial resolution limit for the preretinal optics is well matched to that established for the cone photoreceptor mosaic (Curcio, Sloan, Kalina, & Hendrickson, 1990; see the later section on spatial resolution). The resolution is also well matched to the psychophysically determined spatial MTF of the whole visual system, called the spatial contrast sensitivity function (CSF), which includes optical and neural factors. A CSF for a human observer reproduced from the classic study by Campbell and Robson (1968) is shown in Figure 3.3. The function shows that contrast sensitivity (the reciprocal of contrast threshold) is highest for spatial frequencies between about 3 and 6 c/deg, and gratings of frequencies up to about 50 c/deg can be resolved.

Basic Retinal Circuitry

The main functions of the retina are to receive and to transmit information about the visual scene to the brain. In considering the contributions of the various retinal elements to these functions, it is useful to review the cells and signal pathways of the primate retina. The primate retina is a thin neural tissue with three different cell layers, three fiber layers, and two blood supplies. The basic cell types forming these layers are illustrated in the inset to Figure 3.1a. The photoreceptors are the most distally located cells of the neural retina. They are of critical importance because they convert light energy to neural signals. Their cell bodies form the outer nuclear layer (ONL). Light passes through the other essentially transparent layers of the neural retina to reach the photoreceptors' elongated, light-sensitive, receptor outer segments. The outer segments are in apposition to the apical processes of the cells of the retinal pigment epithelium (RPE), a monolayer of cells forming the

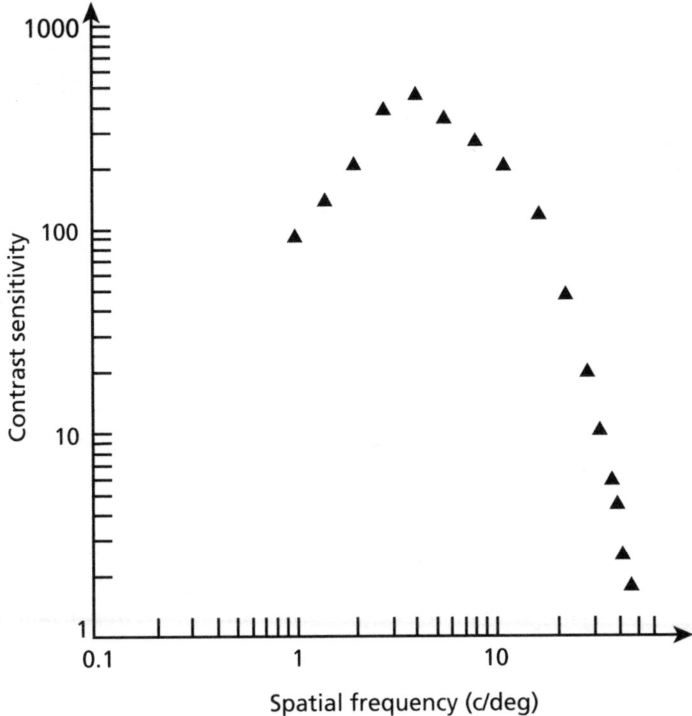

Figure 3.3. The human spatial contrast sensitivity function. The psychophysically determined contrast sensitivity of the human visual system. Spatially sinusoidal grating stimuli were generated on a CRT, and contrast was turned on and off at 0.5 Hz. (From Campbell & Robson, 1968.)

selective blood-retina barrier for the photoreceptor's private blood supply from the choriocapillaris vessels of the choroid (see Feeney-Burns & Katz, 1998 for a review). The blood supply provides oxygen for photoreceptors' high metabolic demands, as well as other nutrients, including the vitamin A that forms the light-sensitive chromophore of their visual pigment molecules. The central retinal artery that enters the eye via the optic nerve and disc supplies the other retinal cells.

The photoreceptor axon terminals contact dendrites of bipolar cells and horizontal cells in the outer plexiform layer (OPL). The bipolar cells are crucial retinal interneurons that transmit signals from the outer retina to the amacrine and ganglion cells (and less common interplexiform cells) in the inner (or proximal) retina, making contact with those cells in the inner plexiform layer (IPL). There are various types of bipolar cells, providing the substrate for parallel visual streams. For example, some bipolar cells provide input to the high-resolution parvocellular stream that preserves specific information such as type of photoreceptor input, and other bipolar cells pool photoreceptor inputs for the lower-resolution, higher-gain magnocellular stream. There also are bipolar cells that distinguish whether the light has increased or decreased in the region of the visual field over which stimuli affect the activity of the cell, which is called its receptive field.

Cell bodies of bipolar and horizontal cells, as well as cell bodies of amacrine, interplexiform, and retinal glial cells called Müller cells, are in the inner nuclear layer (INL). Retinal ganglion and displaced amacrine cells form the ganglion cell layer, with axons of various ganglion cell classes carrying the retinal output signals in parallel streams to the LGN. Because the signals must travel a long distance, approximately 8 cm to the LGN in adult humans, the ganglion cells produce action potentials rather than local potentials. All other retinal neurons, except amacrine cells, signal via local potentials. The differences between local and action potentials are described in Chapter 2.

Horizontal and amacrine cells of the INL participate in lateral interactions in the retina, and interplexiform cells form a feedback from inner to outer retina. Lateral interactions between horizontal cells integrate photoreceptor signals over large areas. Inhibitory lateral interactions via feedback from horizontal cells to photoreceptors, or amacrine cells to bipolar cells, or other amacrine cells are important for forming inhibitory surround regions of receptive fields that serve to accentuate effects of changes in illumination, and for adjusting the gain of retinal circuits. Lateral interactions also may synchronize ganglion cell activity over long distances (Neuenschwander, Costelo-Branco, & Singer, 1999). The Müller cells of the INL do not transfer visual signals, but they are important for maintaining the ionic microenvironment, clearing neurotransmitters from the extracellular space, providing trophic factors, and perhaps in modulating neuronal activity (Newman, 2000; Newman & Zahs, 1998).

Photoreceptors

Photoreceptors are the cells in the retina that initiate vision. They have light-sensitive pigments in their outer segment membranes that convert light to neural signals. This section will first examine the structure and distribution of these important cells, and then describe the process of phototransduction, the nature of the resulting signals, and some of their functional consequences.

Structure and Distribution

As illustrated in Figure 3.1a, and in the retinal circuit diagrams of Figure 3.4, there are two major classes of photoreceptor cells: rods and cones. In human retinas, as in other diurnal mammals, there are many more rods than cones. Humans have 100–125 million rods, and 5–6.4 million cones. Thus, in humans, cones comprise only about 5% of the photoreceptors. As suggested by their names, rods and cones can be distinguished morphologically by the rod-like and conical shapes of their outer segments and, except in the central retina, cones are larger in diameter and less densely distributed than rods. The outer segments of both photoreceptor types have adaptations that increase the surface area available for photon capture. In rods the outer segments consist of a stack of membranous discs surrounded by the plasma membrane, and in cones there are numerous infoldings of the outer segment plasma membrane. A basic functional distinction between rods and cones is that rods

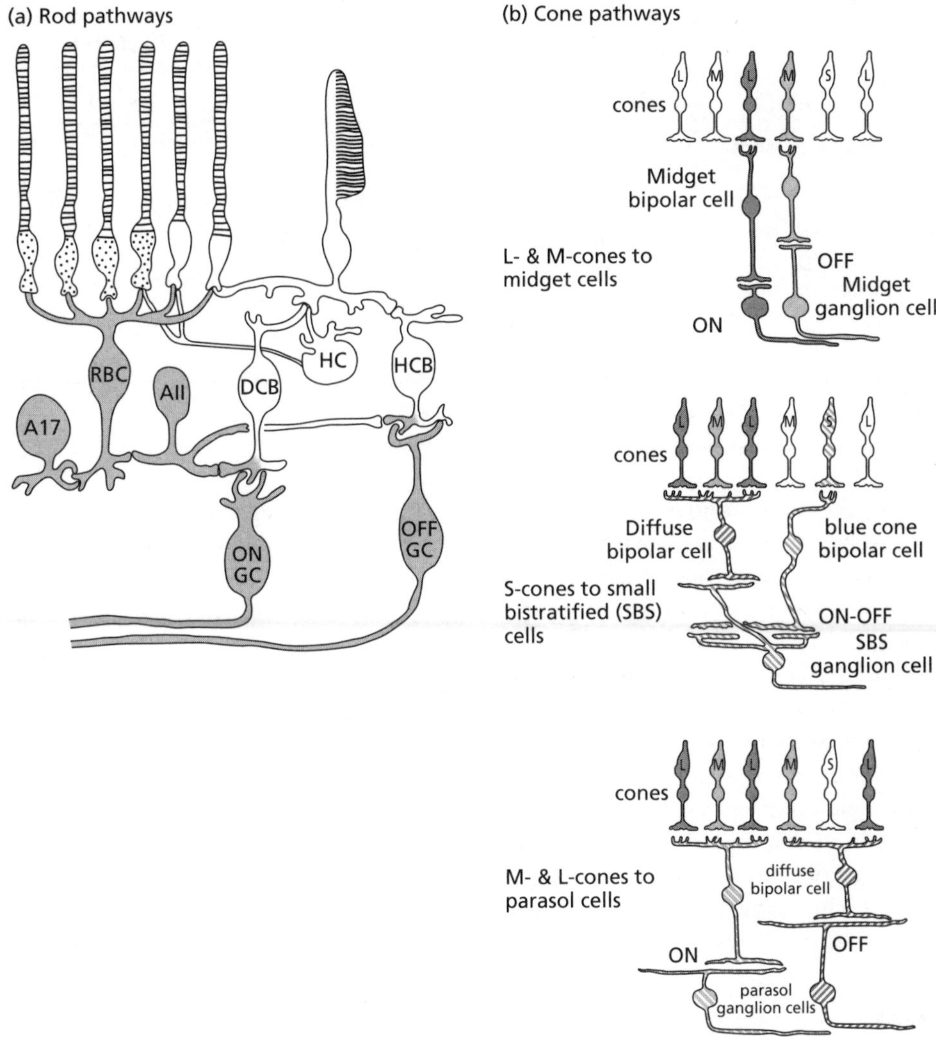

Figure 3.4. Rod and cone circuits through the macaque retina. (a) The rod pathway: The rod pathway carrying rod signals via the rod bipolar cells (RBC) to AII amacrine cells to On (depolarizing – DCB) cone bipolar cells via a gap junction, and to Off (hyperpolarizing – HCB) cone bipolar cells via a chemical synapse. The bipolar cells transmit the rod signals to On- and Off-center retinal ganglion cells. (b) The cone pathways. Top: The midget pathways carry signals of L- and M-cones via the midget bipolar cells to midget ganglion cells. Middle: The S-cone pathway carries S-cone signals via the blue bipolar cells to the small bistratified ganglion cells, and M- + L-cone signals via the diffuse bipolar cells. Bottom: The diffuse bipolar cells carry L- and M-cone signals to parasol cells. (Modified from Martin, 1998.)

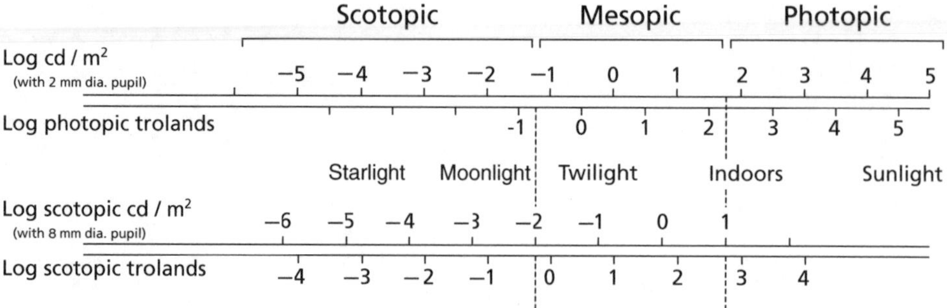

Figure 3.5. Scotopic, mesopic and photopic ranges for the macaque retina. (R. G. Smith, personal communication).

mediate the most sensitive vision at low light levels, called scotopic conditions, whereas cones subserve vision at higher light levels called photopic conditions. Under photopic conditions, we enjoy high resolution and color vision. Figure 3.5 shows the ranges of illumination for scotopic and photopic conditions, and a range where rods and cones both function, which is called the mesopic range.

Rods and cones tile the retina in a distinctive arrangement called the photoreceptor mosaic. The cone mosaic and its relation to subsequent circuitry is critical for determining the chromaticity of color vision and the limits of acuity. Humans, Old World monkeys, and some New World monkeys have trichromatic color vision, and primates have a central foveal region that has very high spatial resolution due to the small size and high density of the cones in that region (Figure 3.6b) and to the private channel wiring for individual cones, described in more detail in a later section.

The trichromatic color vision of humans and macaque monkeys (cf. Chapter 4) has its origins in three classes of cones that can be identified by the visual pigments in their outer

⟶

Figure 3.6. Photoreceptors of the primate retina. (a) The spectral sensitivity of the rods, the S-, M- and L-cones. (modified from Dartnall, Bowmaker, & Mollen, 1983, with permission of the Royal Society). (b) Top: The cone mosaic in the fovea of a human retina (nasal retina, 1 deg of eccentricity), measured using adaptive optics and densitometry (Roorda & Williams, 1999; reprinted by permission from *Nature*, Macmillan Magazines Ltd.). Bottom: The peripheral photoreceptor mosaic. L- and M-cones are not distinguished in this mosaic derived from histological analysis. Rods fill in the spaces between cones (Scale bar = 10 microns). (From Curcio et al., 1990; reprinted by permission of Wiley-Liss Inc., a subsidiary of John Wiley & Sons Inc.) (c) The dark current and transduction cascade in the rod photoreceptor. The dark current is maintained by the inward current in the outer segment of the cations: Na^+, Ca^+, and Mg^+ (Yau, 1994), and the outward leak from the inner segment of K^+ ions. The Na^+-K^+ ATPase maintains concentration gradient of cations. The countertransporter contributes to changes in intracellular $[Ca^+]$ that adjust sensitivity in the photoreceptor. (d) Interruption of the photoreceptor dark current in response to a range of light intensities. Recordings with suction electrodes from outer segments of rods and cones of macaque retina. Bottom: plots of flash response vs. log photon density for the A rod and cone (from Walraven et al., 1990; copyright © 1990 by Academic Press, reproduced by permission of the publisher. All rights of reproduction in any form reserved).

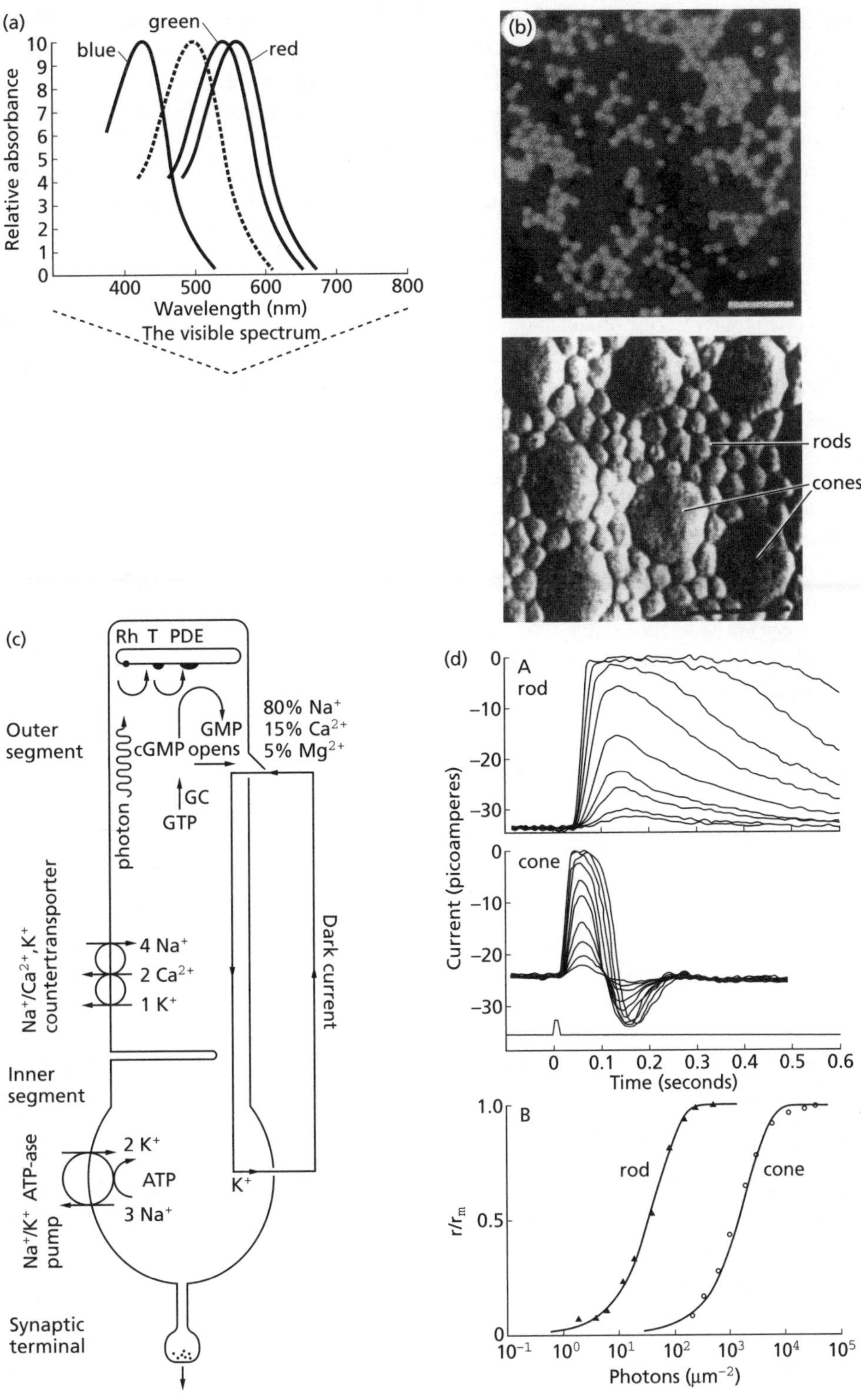
(a)
green
blue
red
Relative absorbance
10
9
8
7
6
5
4
3
2
1
0
400
500
600
700
800
Wavelength (nm)
The visible spectrum
(b)
rods
cones
(c)
Rh T PDE
Outer segment
photon
cGMP
GMP
opens
GC
GTP
80% Na⁺
15% Ca²⁺
5% Mg²⁺
Na⁺/Ca²⁺,K⁺ countertransporter
4 Na⁺
2 Ca²⁺
1 K⁺
Dark current
Inner segment
Na⁺/K⁺ ATP-ase pump
2 K⁺
ATP
3 Na⁺
K⁺
Synaptic terminal
(d)
A
rod
cone
Current (picoamperes)
0
−10
−20
−30
0
0.1
0.2
0.3
0.4
0.5
0.6
Time (seconds)
B
1.0
0.5
0
r/r_m
rod
cone
10⁻¹
10⁰
10¹
10²
10³
10⁴
10⁵
Photons (μm⁻²)

segments. As shown in Figure 3.6a, spectral sensitivities in humans of the short (S, or blue), the medium (M, or green), and the long (L, or red) wavelength cones peak around 420, 530, and 565 nm respectively. The rod pigment, rhodopsin, peaks at 499 nm. The figure also shows that the spectral tuning curves are sufficiently broad that there is substantial overlap in their ranges, particularly for L- and M-cones.

Photoreceptor spectral sensitivities have been determined using several different approaches, including direct measures of pigment density and electrophysiological studies. The human measurements using these approaches coincide well with inferences made from psychophysical studies, and are only slightly different from values for various types of macaques (Jacobs, 1996; Tovée, 1994, 1996). Many other diurnal mammals have only two cone pigments, one of which peaks at a short wavelength, the other at a longer wavelength. The separation of L- and M-cones in primates can be viewed as a special evolutionary alteration in the longer wavelength pigment (see Tovée, 1996 for a review).

The spectral selectivity of the visual pigments is determined by membrane-spanning proteins called opsins that tune the chromophore, 11-*cis* retinaldehyde, to which they are bound. These opsins constitute most of the protein in the outer segment disc membranes. In humans, the genes that code the L- and M-cone opsins are on the same leg of the X-chromosome. The amino acid sequences of the two opsins are 96% identical (Nathans, Thomas, & Hogness, 1986). In contrast, the gene that codes the S-cone opsin is on chromosome 7, and the gene for rod pigment rhodopsin is on 3. In both cases, their amino acid sequences are only about 40% identical to each other and to the M-cone sequence. X-linked color deficiencies such that either medium or long wavelength cones are not present in normal amounts are more common in males than females.

Phototransduction and Receptor Signaling

Conversion of Photons to Membrane Potentials

Light absorbed by the pigments in the photoreceptor outer segments is transduced into neural signals. Absorption of a photon by rhodopsin or a cone pigment leads to isomerization of the pigment's chromophore, 11-*cis* (vitamin A) to all-*trans* retinaldehyde. In classic psychophysical experiments, Hecht, Shlaer, and Pirenne (1942) concluded that only one visual pigment molecule must be isomerized in order to activate a rod photoreceptor, and that activating 7 to 10 receptors at once is sufficient for us to detect the light. Physiologists and biochemists have actively researched the mechanisms that allow the isomerization of a single pigment molecule to create a physiological effect large enough to activate the rod receptor.

An important discovery in the search for the basis of transduction was the observation by Hagins, Penn, and Yoshikami (1970) of a continuous current of positively charged ions, mainly sodium (Na^+), into the rod photoreceptor outer segment in the dark, creating an inward cation current that they called the dark current (see Figure 3.6c). This finding indicated that the photoreceptor was active in the dark. We now know that depolarization of the photoreceptor by the dark current leads to continuous release of neurotransmitter (glutamate) from the cell's axon terminal in the dark. In contrast, as reported by Hagins et al., illumination of the photoreceptor interrupts the dark current, and this hyperpolarizes the cell, reducing transmitter release, which means that reduced transmitter release signals the presence of light.

Biochemical and physiological studies have since shown that the photoreceptor dark current is interrupted in the presence of light via an enzyme cascade that decreases the concentration of cGMP, the substance that keeps the cation channels open in the dark (see Baylor, 1996 for a review). In this cascade, as illustrated in Figure 3.6c, the absorption of a photon by rhodopsin leads to isomerization of the pigment. This activates the pigment (indicated by Rh), leading to catalytic activation of many molecules of the GTP-binding protein (G-protein) transducin. Transducin, in turn, activates another protein, cGMP-PDE which hydrolyzes cGMP to 5'-GMP. Because cGMP is required to hold cation channels open, this destruction of cGMP causes the channels to shut.

An important characteristic of the phototransduction cascade is amplification. The isomerization of one pigment molecule leads to the hydrolysis of one hundred thousand molecules of cGMP, which closes hundreds of cation channels and blocks the flow of about a million Na^+ ions. The process of visual transduction is similar in rods and cones, but rods produce electrical signals that are larger and slower than those in cones (see Figure 3.6d). In both types of photoreceptor, excitation of the visual pigment by an absorbed photon leads, via an amplifying biochemical cascade, to closure of cation channels in the outer segments.

As important as the activation of the visual pigment is the termination of its catalytic activity so that the photoreceptor will not continue to signal the presence of light. In rods this involves the binding of rhodopsin kinase to rhodopsin, leading to its phosphorylation, as well as the binding to rhodopsin of a protein called arrestin (Baylor, 1996).

Interruption of the Dark Current

Electrophysiological recordings from individual photoreceptor outer segments of the interruption of the dark current by light stimuli have provided valuable data on the kinetics, sensitivity, and gain of the rod and cone photoreceptors. Figure 3.6d shows recordings from macaque rod and cone outer segments in response to brief flashes from darkness of increasing intensity (reviewed Walraven, Enroth-Cugell, Hood, MacLeod, & Schnapf, 1990; also see Baylor, Nunn, & Schnapf, 1984; Schnapf, Nunn, Meister, & Baylor, 1990). The smallest response shown for the rod recordings is the single photon response. Thus, just as predicted by Hecht and co-workers (1942), a single photon can activate a rod photoreceptor.

The kinetics of the rod response are much slower than those of the cone response. As shown in Figure 3.6d, the rod single photon response rises to a peak in 150–200 msec, and then recovers slowly to baseline. As light intensity is increased, the response amplitude increases in proportion to intensity and then saturates. When the response is saturated, higher intensities simply prolong the duration over which the current is interrupted. In contrast, cone responses (Figure 3.6d) peak earlier, terminate sooner, and hardly increase in duration as stimulus intensity is increased. Due to the brevity of their responses, cones can modulate their activity in response to high temporal frequency flicker (>30 Hz). In contrast, the slow recovery of rods to baseline limits their temporal resolution. This difference in the kinetics of the rods and cones forms the foundation for well-known differences in temporal frequency response and temporal resolution (critical fusion frequency) of scotopic and photopic vision (see Hart, 1992 for a review). The temporal properties of the visual system are further refined by postreceptoral neurons in the retina and central visual pathways.

The gain of individual rod responses is much higher than that of cones. This difference can be appreciated in the roughly 70-fold difference in their sensitivities, illustrated by the horizontal separation between their (interrupted) current versus log photon density in Figure 3.6d. Whereas rods signal single photon absorptions with roughly a pico (10^{-12}) amp reduction in current (about one-fifth of their operating range), cones' single photon responses are extremely small and cone signals relevant for vision occur only for stimulus strengths that deliver many photons. Furthermore, there is inherent noise in all stimuli, and both rods and cones are noisy due to spontaneous isomerizations and other internal noise (reviewed by Baylor, 1996). For rods, single photon signals are sufficiently large that they can be passed to more proximal neurons despite the noise, whereas for cones this is not the case. The differences in overall sensitivity of the two receptor systems determined psychophysically relies not only upon the factors described here for individual photoreceptors, but also upon the postreceptoral neural circuitry to be described in the later sections on spatial resolution of the rod and cone pathways.

The Output Signal of the Retina

Although recordings of the interruption of the dark current have improved our understanding of rod and cone photoreceptor function, they reflect only the outer segment function. The output signal of individual photoreceptors can be measured with voltage recordings of the inner segment membrane potential. Recent recordings from macaque photoreceptor inner segments by Schneeweis and Schnapf (1995, 1999) show that their hyperpolarizations in response to light increments are similar in sensitivity and timecourse to the outer segment current responses previously recorded by Schnapf and co-workers (Baylor et al., 1984; Schnapf et al., 1990), although the voltage responses to saturating stimulus strengths show larger initial transients. Rods signal a single photon with about a milli (10^{-3}) volt reduction in membrane, again about 5% of their operating range. Interestingly, recordings from M- and L-cones revealed the presence of rod signals in the cones. Rod signals spread through gap junctions between rod spherules and cone pedicles (Figure 3.4a) (Raviola & Gilula, 1973; Schneeweis & Schnapf, 1995, 1999). This finding is an important one for considerations of the extent of rod-cone interactions in visual pathways, and light adaptation of rod signals (see section on adaptation).

Spatial Resolution

Photopic

Visual resolution is highest, and hence acuity is best, when images fall on the fovea. The foveal region of the human retina is about five degrees in diameter and it is populated predominantly by L- and M-cones. Only L- and M-cones (no rods, no S-cones, no postreceptoral retinal neurons, no blood vessels) are present at the center of the fovea in a region of about 1.4 degrees in diameter called the foveola. S-cones are present outside the foveola, but they are sparsely distributed, representing only about 7 % of the cone population (reviewed by Hagstrom, Neitz, & Neitz, 1998). The high acuity of the foveola is a consequence of the high packing density (averaging about 160,000/mm^2) of cones in that small region (Curcio et al., 1990). During early postnatal development, the cone outer segments elongate and their thin processes migrate into the foveal region, pushing the other cell layers aside to form the foveal pit where only photoreceptors and Müller cells are present. Resolution in the fovea is further improved by the directional selectivity of the cone outer segments, which causes light to be most effective when traveling almost parallel to the visual axis rather than from other angles (McIlwain, 1996). This property of the cones is called the Stiles-Crawford effect for the scientists that first described it.

The neurally determined upper limit of visual acuity can be calculated from the foveal cone spacing because there are dedicated pathways for signals from individual foveal cones to visual cortex. This limit is about 60 cycles per degree, or about ½ min of arc, a value close, on the one hand, to the limit for the MTF of the preretinal optics, and on the other hand to the upper limit of spatial resolution measured psychophysically (Williams, 1986).

Psychophysical studies using short wavelength stimuli show that S-cone resolution is relatively low, about 9 min of arc (Williams et al., 1981). This is close to the value predicted from morphological studies of S-cone spacing, which is 5–7 per degree of visual angle in the central retina (Curcio et al., 1991 using an antibody to S-cone opsin; de Monasterio, McCrane, Newlander, & Schein, 1985, using dye infusion). It should be noted, however, that for isoluminant stimuli for which the luminance is equated for stimuli that differ in wavelength, S-cone system resolution in central retina has been reported to be as high as 10 c/deg (see Calkins & Sterling, 1999 for review).

Although the spacing of the L- and M-cones has been measured, it has not been easy to determine which are M and which L, or their relative ratios. This is because the L- and M-cones are very similar structurally and genetically. However, these cones now have been distinguished by Roorda and William (1999) using adaptive optics that correct for retinal blur, in combination with retinal densitometry. Figure 3.6b shows the resulting distribution of L-, M- and S-cones determined for the central retina of one human subject. For this subject, the L-cones outnumber the M-cones, a finding corroborated in a study by Hagstrom and co-workers (1998) that sampled the messenger RNAs of L- and M-cones to determine their ratios as a function of retinal eccentricity. The average ratio of L to M in the central retina was 3:2 (23 eyes). This ratio increased with eccentricity, and in peripheral retina past 40 degrees it was 3:1 on average, but variability was high.

Spatial resolution is determined not only by the photoreceptor mosaic, but also by the presence of bipolar and retinal ganglion cells in sufficient numbers to provide private transmission lines for individual M- and L-cones. Labeled lines for the signals transmitted from individual receptors through the retina and on to the LGN ensure that the high resolution provided by the photoreceptor mosaic is preserved. Labeled lines for single cones, or several cones tuned to the same wavelength, also allow spectral information to be preserved.

The circuits associated with L-, M-, and S-cones are shown in Figure 3.4b; S-cones travel in a dedicated S-cone pathway (Figure 3.4b, middle). Figure 3.4b (top) shows the circuits that carry single L- or M-cone signals. Midget bipolar cells contact individual cones and relay the cone signals to midget retinal ganglion cells. As shown in Figure 3.1b, these cells in turn send their signals to the parvocellular layers of the LGN. A study of human midget ganglion cells indicates that for eccentricities up to 2 mm (7–9 deg) from the central fovea, midget ganglion cells receive input from single cones (Dacey, 1993). At greater retinal eccentricities, there is some convergence of cones onto midget ganglion cells. The size of the individual cones and the distance between them also increase with eccentricity. Consistent with increasing convergence and inter-cone spacing, densities of cone bipolar (Martin & Grünert, 1992) and retinal ganglion cells (Curcio & Allen, 1990) decrease with distance from the fovea. These factors all contribute to the decline in spatial resolution with increasing eccentricity that is well documented in psychophysical studies (Wertheim, 1891; Thibos, Cheney, & Walsh, 1987; Anderson, Mullen, & Hess, 1991).

Scotopic

In contrast to foveal cone vision, the highest scotopic resolution measured in humans is only about 6 c/deg (Lennie & Fairchild, 1994). The resolution is low despite the fact that rods are thinner and more densely packed than cones in all but the central regions of the retina (Figure 3.6b). Maximum rod density (~150,000/mm^2), which approaches that of foveal cones, occurs in an elliptical region 2–5 mm from the foveola, with density highest in the superior retina (Curcio et al., 1990). The resolution of rod vision is low because of the enormous amount of convergence associated with rods, with retinal ganglion cells pooling signals from more than 1,000 rods.

Although the high density of the rods does not provide high scotopic acuity, the density and pooling of rod signals are responsible for the high absolute sensitivity of rod vision. The high density provides a rich substrate for capturing photons at the very lowest light levels, conditions under which very few photons enter the eye. Pooling at later stages in the pathway then provides spatial summation of rod signals. For a brief full field flash, the absolute threshold is about 1–3 photons per deg^2 (Frishman, Reddy, & Robson, 1996). As noted in an earlier section, Hecht and co-workers (1942) found that humans can detect light when as few as 7–10 rods are activated in a small region of retina where rod density is high (see Chapter 1). The dedicated rod pathway, depicted in Figure 3.4a, carries discrete rod signals to inner retina where signaling of single photon events can be detected in the spiking activity of retinal ganglion cells (Barlow, Levick, & Yoon, 1971). In addition to high density and convergence, the high absolute sensitivity of rod vision also benefits from the high gain of the transduction process (see Baylor, 1996 for a review).

Adaptation

As indicated in Figure 3.5, our visual system can operate over more than 10 log units of retinal illuminations. This range of illuminations includes scotopic conditions where only starlight is present to photopic conditions in bright sunlight. Over much of this range, due to light adaptation, but we have fairly constant relative sensitivity to light increments and decrements regardless of the steady level of illumination. This combination of reduced absolute sensitivity and relatively constant contrast sensitivity has been the subject of many psychophysical and physiological investigations. Adaptation of rod-mediated vision has been studied more thoroughly than cone vision-mediated vision and the sites of the underlying mechanisms have been better localized.

As the background illumination is increased, the human psychophysical threshold increases, following a slope of between 0.5 and 1.0 on logarithmic coordinates (see Sharpe et al., 1993 for a review). Figure 3.7a illustrates results from the classic study of Aguilar and Stiles (1954) of light adaptation of the human rod system. A slope of 1.0 (Weber's Law) means that the increase in incremental threshold is proportional to the increase in background illumination. Stated another way, contrast sensitivity remains constant because the increment in light necessary to reach the contrast threshold is a constant proportion of the background illumination. A comparison of psychophysical results with microelectrode recordings from retinal ganglion cells in cats indicates that most of the light adaptation of rod signals reported by human subjects can be observed in the individual ganglion cells (reviewed by Shapley & Enroth-Cugell, 1984; Frishman & Robson, 1999). This finding also has been confirmed in studies of humans for whom psychophysical sensitivity and noninvasive electrical recordings of retinal sensitivity (electroretinograms) were compared in the same subjects for the same stimulus conditions (Frishman et al., 1996). The electroretinogram (ERG), a potential change in response to light that can be recorded at the cornea, provides access, in noninvasive recordings, to signals from most retinal cells, including retinal ganglion cells (see Robson & Frishman, 1999 for a review). Thus the major components of adaptation occurs in the retina before the rod signals travel to the brain for further processing.

Although most light adaptation of rod signals is retinal, a substantial portion of the adaptation occurs after the photoreceptors. The reduction in rod sensitivity predicted from human rod outer segments current recordings is illustrated in Figure 3.7a. It shows that over at least a 1,000-fold range of scotopic background illuminations that are too weak to appreciably reduce the absolute sensitivity of the rod photoreceptor response, the rod-driven threshold is reduced (reviewed by Walraven et al., 1990).

Although photoreceptor responses show little desensitization through the scotopic range, single cell and ERG studies show that they do desensitize in the mesopic range (see Frishman & Robson, 1999 for a review). This desensitization is less than would be predicted if the desensitization were completely the result of rod hyperpolarization in response to the background illumination causing compression of the response. A small intracellular adjustment improves sensitivity in the presence of background illuminations that nearly saturate their responses. This improvement in sensitivity does not restore the entire operating range, as it does for ganglion cells (see below). The functional significance of this adaptation is unclear, for it occurs at the end of the mesopic range where cone vision dominates. Experiments on single rods (and cones) in several laboratories have shown that calcium, via intracellular feedback pathways that increase cGMP, reopening cation channels, is responsible for this adjustment of sensitivity in photoreceptors (see Koutalos & Yau, 1996 for a review).

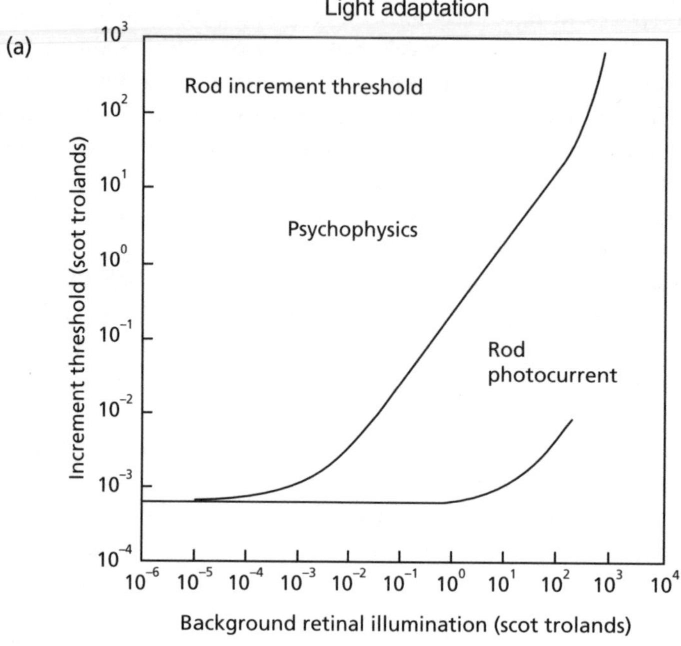

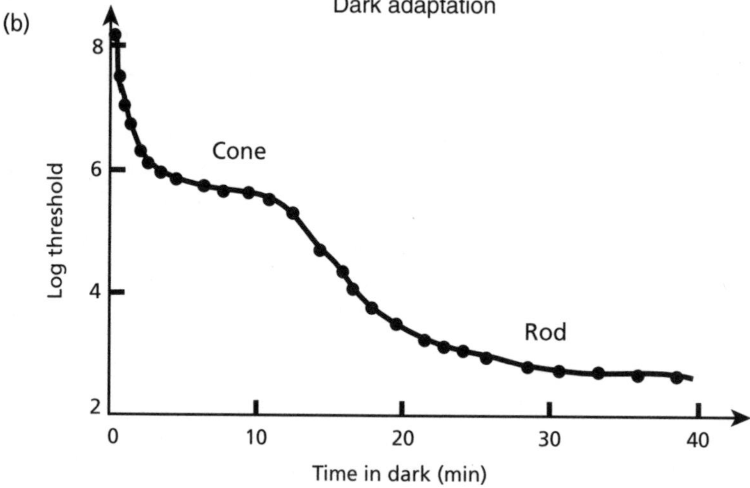

Figure 3.7. Adaptation. (a) Increment sensitivity and inverse sensitivity curves. The curve on the left is the average result of the classical psychophysical study of four human subjects by Aguilar and Stiles (1954). The curve on the right is a fit of Weber's Law to current recordings from isolated rod outer segments of humans (Kraft, Schneeweis, & Schnapf, 1991). (b) Psychophysical threshold intensity for a large violet flash of light as a function of time in the dark after exposure to a bleaching light. (From Hecht, Haig, & Chase, 1937.)

Rod-driven bipolar cells, as judged by ERG recordings, desensitize at intensities that are 10 to 100 times lower than affecting photoreceptor responses (Xu, Frishman, & Robson, 1998), but are at least 100 times higher than those affecting psychophysical and ganglion cell responses. Again, as observed for photoreceptors, there is an adjustment of sensitivity of the bipolar cells, perhaps due to intracellular mechanisms like those in photoreceptors, but the entire operating range is not restored.

In contrast to photoreceptors and bipolar cells, retinal ganglion cells, as noted above, are desensitized by the very weak backgrounds that desensitize psychophysical responses. Ganglion cells are unique in that they demonstrate automatic gain control when increases in background illumination occur. This means that their entire operating range from threshold to saturation shifts so that sensitivity is reduced in proportion to background illumination (Weber's Law), but contrast sensitivity and Rmax are preserved (Sakmann & Creutzfeld, 1969; Frishman et al., 1996). This shifting of the operating range forms the basis for the visual system's ability to maintain high contrast sensitivity over a large range of retinal illuminations.

Saturation of rod responses occurs when only 1% of the rod's visual pigment is isomerized. However, very intense lights will totally bleach the rod and cone photoreceptor pigments, changing of virtually all 11-*cis* retinaldehyde to the all-*trans* form that detaches from the disc opsin. The process of dark adaptation that occurs following pigment bleaches has been well studied. Restoration of 11-*cis* retinaldehyde occurs in the RPE, and then it is shuttled back to rejoin the photoreceptors. As shown in Figure 3.7b, following a complete bleach, it takes more than 40 minutes to reestablish full (absolute) rod psychophysical threshold (rod branch of curve). Restoration of full sensitivity occurs much more rapidly in cones, within about 10 minutes following complete bleaches (see the cone branch of the curve in Figure 3.7b) because cone pigment regenerates faster than rod pigment. The prolonged rod recovery involves recovery from residual activation of rhodopsin created by interim photoproducts of the bleaching of the pigment (Leibrock, Reuter, & Lamb, 1998). Recovery times for both rods and cones become briefer as smaller proportions of the pigment are bleached, but rods always take longer than cones to recover.

Response saturation with increased light levels occurs postreceptorally as well as in the photoreceptors. For example, the rod bipolar cells of the dedicated rod pathway (Figure 3.4a) saturate at background illuminations well below those for which the rods themselves saturate (Robson & Frishman, 1995). However, rod signals continue to traverse the retina at mean higher illumination levels by invading cones and entering cone pathways (reviewed by Sharpe & Stockman, 1999).

Light adaptation of cone signals has been studied more extensively in psychophysical than in physiological investigations. Studies of macaque retinal ganglion cells (Purpura, Tranchina, Kaplan, & Shapley, 1990) indicate that, as for rod signals, adaptation of cone signals is retinal, but the retinal loci for the adaptation have not been as well localized as for rod signals. However, adaptation may occur earlier in the retinal circuitry. Although adaptation at low and moderate photopic levels has not been detected in macaque photoreceptor voltage responses (Schneeweis & Schnapf, 1999), both psychophysical studies in humans (see Hood, 1998 for a review) and physiological recordings from macaque horizontal cells (Lee, Dacey, Smith, & Pokorny, 1999) suggest that there may be substantial adaptation of cone signals in the synapses between cones and horizontal, or bipolar, cells that they contact.

Processing Streams

As described in the overview to the visual pathways, the dorsal and ventral pathways of the extrastriate cortex represent, at least to some extent, extensions of the magno- and parvocellular streams that are established earlier in the visual pathways. In this section we will consider how these streams originate in the retina, and we will trace their progress through the retina and the LGN.

Bipolar Cells: Origin of the Parvocellular, Magnocellular and Koniocellular Streams and the On and Off Pathways

The major classes of bipolar cells of the macaque retina are illustrated in Figure 3.8a (Boycott & Wässle, 1999). There is only one type of rod bipolar cell (RB). RB cells contact only rods, about 40 rods per RB cell (Kolb, Linberg, & Fisher, 1992), and they relay rod signals via amacrine cells (AII) to cone bipolar cells that pass the signals to ganglion cells (Figure 3.4a).

In contrast to the rod bipolar cells, there are several types of cone bipolar cell, and these cells play a central role in setting up the parallel visual streams. For example, foveal midget cone bipolar cells (IMB and FMB) relay single L- or M-cone signals to midget ganglion cells. These cells are critical in maintaining the fidelity of single cone information in foveal regions.

There are two types of midget bipolar cells. The IMB cells depolarize at light onset, producing On responses, whereas the FMB cells depolarize at light offset, producing Off responses. On bipolar cells terminate in the inner half of the IPL, in the On-sublaminae; Off bipolar cells terminate in the outer half, in the Off-sublaminae. The On and Off cone bipolar cells, in turn, determine the response polarity of the retinal ganglion cells that synapse with them in the IPL (Figure 3.4b, top). A functional advantage of having both On and Off responses is that the dynamic range is extended, with signaling of both light increments and decrements from a mean level of illumination. The On and Off pathways remain parallel to the first stage of processing in visual cortex.

The diffuse cone bipolar cells (DB1–6), like the midget cone bipolars, receive input from L- and M-cones. However, each diffuse cell receives inputs from several L- and M-

⟶

Figure 3.8. Parallel processing streams. (a) The bipolar cells of the primate retina. The figure includes diffuse bipolar cells (DB 1–6), Flat (F) and invaginating (I) midget bipolar cells (MB), short wavelength (Blue) cone bipolar cells (BB) and rod bipolar cells (RB) that terminate in the inner plexiform layer (IPL). The dendrites of the bipolar cells contact cones in the outer plexiform layer (OPL), and they pass signals to the ganglion cell dendrites in the outer (Off) and inner (On) sublaminae of the IPL (Boycott & Wässle, 1999, with acknowledgment to the Association of Research in Vision and Ophthalmology, the copyright holder). (b) Retinal ganglion cells in the primate retina. Plot of dendritic field sizes of midget, parasol, and small bistratified cells. (Modified from Rodieck, 1998.) (c) Contrast response functions of midget (8) and parasol cells (28) of the macaque retina under photopic conditions to gratings of optimal spatial frequency drifted at 4 Hz (Kaplan & Shapley, 1986).

(a) Bipolar cells

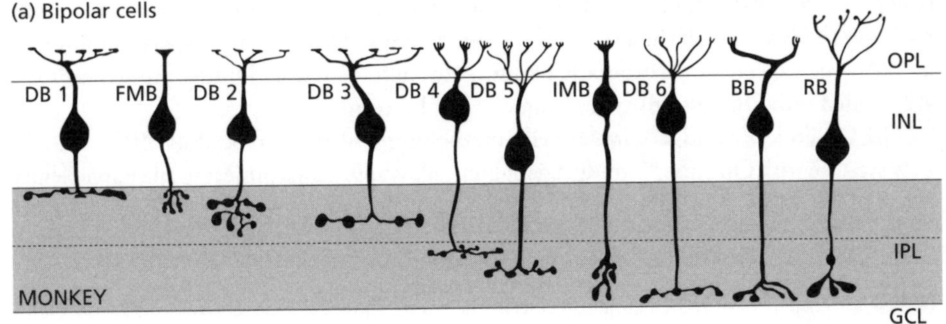

(b) Retinal ganglion cells

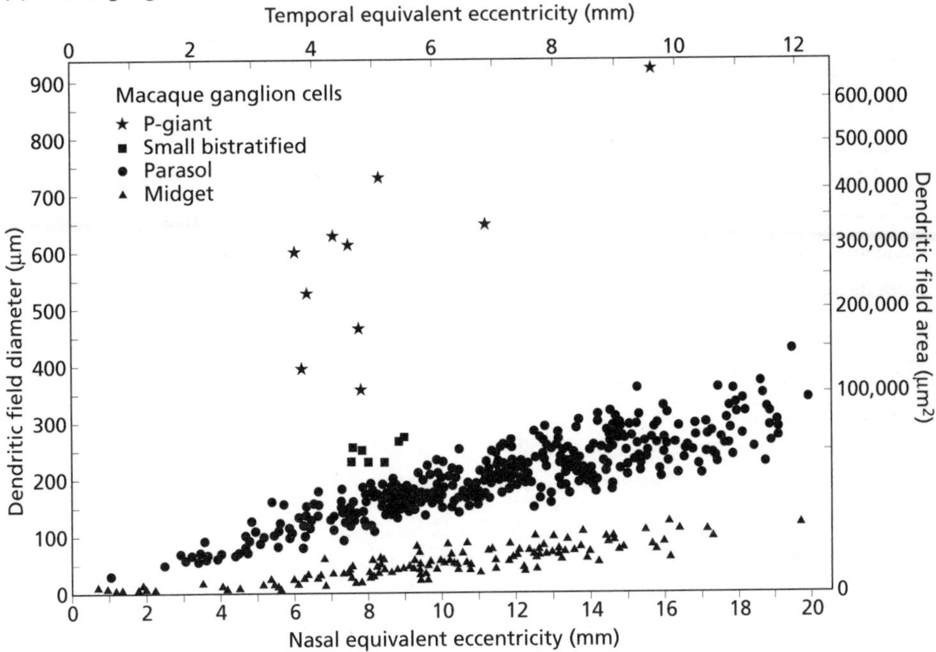

(c) Contrast gain

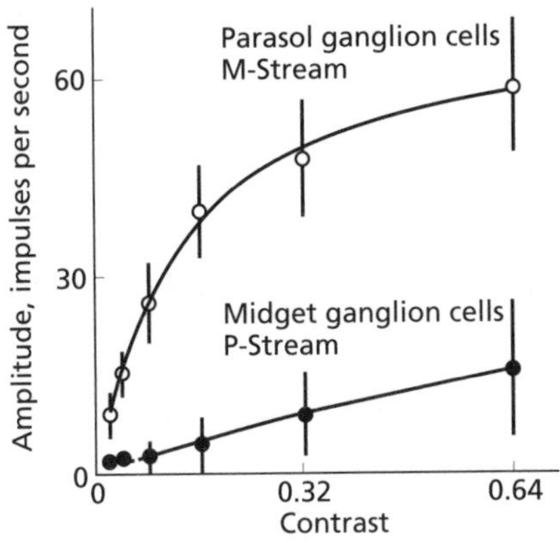

cones (Figure 3.4b, bottom). This means that single cone information is lost, and the cells' receptive fields are larger than those of the midget cells. The pooling of spectral inputs (L- and M-cones) creates an achromatic pathway through the retina. Diffuse bipolar cells also are divided into On and Off types (Figure 3.4b, bottom).

The On and Off midget bipolar cells are the origin of the parvocellular (P-) stream as they synapse with On and Off midget ganglion cells whose axons project to the parvocellular layers of the LGN. Similarly, the diffuse bipolar cells synapse with parasol ganglion cells

Table 3.1 Properties of retinal ganglion cells in the parvocellular, magnocellular, and koniocellular streams

Processing streams	*Parvocellular*	*Magnocellular*	*Koniocellular*
Morphology			
Retinal ganglion cell class	Midget	Parasol	Small bistratified
% of ganglion cell population	70%	10%	10%
Cell body (soma) area	Small	Large	Small
Dendritic field area	Small	Large	Large
Axon diameter	Thin	Thick	Very thin
Response properties			
Axonal conduction velocity	Slow	Fast	Very slow
Receptive field configuration	Center/Surround (Surround > Center)	Center/Surround (Surround > Center)	Center/Surround (Surround > Center)
Spatial resolution	High	Low	Low
Temporal resolution	Low	High	Low
Contrast gain	Low	High	Low
Spectral selectivity	Yes (L vs M wavelengths)	No (Broadband)	S vs LM wavelengths
Linearity of spatial summation	Linear	75% Linear 25% Nonlinear	?
Circuitry			
Bipolar cell input	Midget	Diffuse	Short wavelength (Blue) Bipolar
LGN layers	Parvocellular (P) layers (2–6)	Magnocellular (M) layers (1–2)	Intercalated koniocellular (K) layers between P layers
Projections to primary visual cortex (V1	V1 layer 4Cb, 6 (upper half)	V1 layer 4Ca, 6 (lower half)	V1 layers 2/3 (blobs)

whose axons project to the magnocellular (M-) stream. Both P- and M-streams also carry signals from rods that invade the cones in the OPL, and the cone bipolar cells in the IPL (Figure 3.4a). The rod signals are more prominent in the achromatic magnocellular stream.

Signals from S-cones travel to the inner retina via short wavelength (BB) cone bipolar cells (BB). BB cells synapse on a third class of retinal ganglion cells called small bistratified cells (Figure 3.4b, middle). These small bistratified cells project to koniocellular cells in the intercalated regions between the parvocellular layers of the LGN, forming a parallel koniocellular or K-stream. There probably are only On-type S-cone bipolar cells (Dacey, 1996; Martin, 1998).

Retinal Ganglion Cells: Receptive Field Characteristics of Parvocellular, Magnocellular, and Koniocellular Streams

The parallel parvo-, magno-, and koniocellular streams each have morphologically identified ganglion cells: midget, parasol, and small bistratified respectively. The morphological and physiological characteristics of the ganglion cells of the different streams are described in this section, and summarized in Table 3.1.

Since Kuffler's (1953) classic study of cat retinal ganglion cell receptive fields, it has been known that ganglion cells have receptive field centers of one polarity (On or Off) and antagonistic surrounds of the opposite polarity. The centers and surrounds in cat and macaque ganglion cells are generally overlapping, with a spatially dome-like (Gaussian) distribution of their sensitivity (see Kaplan, 1989 for a review). The polarity of the center response is determined by the cell's contacts in the IPL with bipolar cells. Surrounds originate from feedback in the OPL (Packer, Diller, Lee, & Dacey, 1999). Additional lateral interactions in the IPL from amacrine cells add to surrounds, especially of parasol cells. For a minority of these cells the lateral interactions produce nonlinear behavior such as that described for cat Y-cells (Enroth-Cugell & Robson, 1966; also see Sterling, 1998 for a review).

In contrast to the parasol and midget cells, the small bistratified ganglion cells, as their name implies, ramify in both sublaminae of the IPL (see Figure 3.4b, middle). This produces color-opponent receptive fields with short wavelength-sensitive On-centers and medium-long Off-surrounds. At least some of the midget ganglion cells also have color-opponent receptive fields. However, the degree to which midget ganglion cells show spectrally opponent centers and surrounds is controversial. The existence of still another class of color-opponent ganglion cells, that project, like the K-stream, to the intercalated layers in the parvocellular portion of the LGN, recently has been suggested (Calkins & Sterling, 1999).

Cells of the three functional streams completely tile the retina, thereby covering the entire visual field, and presumably contributing to vision over the whole area. For the midget and parasol cells, the retina is covered twice: once by On- center cells, and once by Off-center cells. Midget cells are most numerous, representing about 70% of the ganglion cells, and perhaps as high as 95% in the cone-dense fovea where there are 3–4 ganglion cells per photoreceptor. However, this relationship changes in the periphery, where pooling over many photoreceptors occurs, and receptive fields are large. Overall, there are about 5 times as many cones and 100 times as many rods as retinal ganglion cells. Parasol cells represent only about 10% of the ganglion cell population, and small bistratified cells perhaps another 10%.

Midget ganglion cell fields show higher spatial resolution than parasol or small bistratified cells at the same retinal eccentricity (Croner & Kaplan, 1995). High spatial resolution is correlated with small receptive field size. The size of a ganglion cell receptive field center also is well predicted by the size of its dendritic field (Dacey, 1993), and plots of dendritic field size vs. eccentricity (Figure 3.8b) best illustrate the differences among the classes. At each eccentricity, the parasol and small bistratified dendritic fields are larger than those of the midgets, and the midget and parasol cell field sizes do not overlap.

The parasol cells have larger cell bodies and thicker axons than the midget and small bistratified retinal ganglion cells. The diameter of the axon determines conduction velocity, so parasol cell axons conduct signals faster than the other cells. These differences in conduction velocity can lead to differences in visual latency with latencies being shortest in the M-pathway would be appropriate for a system signaling movement and change, rather than focussing on detail. However, the visual latency of P-pathway may be shortened at cortical levels where large numbers of P-cell inputs are pooled, increasing the size of the signal at early times after the stimulus (Maunsell et al., 1999).

Although the midget ganglion cells have higher spatial resolution than parasol cells, their small number of cone inputs limits their sensitivity to contrast. This can be quantified as contrast gain, defined as the response amplitude per unit contrast (the slope) of the linear portion of the contrast response function. Figure 3.8c shows average contrast response functions for samples of macaque midget and parasol cells (Kaplan & Shapley, 1986). Whereas the midget cell responses were small and increased linearly with contrast over the entire contrast range, the parasol cell responses were large and saturated at fairly low contrasts. The contrast gain for parasol cells is 6–8 times greater for midget cells at every retinal eccentricity, and over a range of mesopic and photopic background levels (Croner & Kaplan, 1995; Kaplan, Lee, & Shapley, 1990). At scotopic levels the contrast gain of the midget cells is extremely low (Lee, Smith, Pokorny, & Kremers, 1997).

In addition to their higher contrast gain, the parasol cells have higher temporal resolution and produce more transient response than the midget or small bistratified cells, whose responses are more sustained to standing contrast.

In summary, as shown in Table 3.1, the midget cells that form the P-pathway have high spatial resolution and, along with the K-pathway, color sensitivity, and sustained responses compatible with form vision such as occurs in the ventral stream. In contrast, parasol cells form an achromatic path to the LGN that has lower spatial resolution, but higher contrast gain and temporal resolution; characteristics more compatible with signaling movement and rapid changes, such as occurs in the dorsal stream.

Lateral Geniculate Cells: Laminar Segregation of the Parallel Streams

The various classes (midget, parasol, and small bistratified) and functional types (On or Off) of retinal ganglion cells project in parallel to and through the LGN. Response characteristics of LGN cells closely resemble those of their retinal inputs, so the response characteristics of the parallel streams listed in Table 3.1 also are applicable for the LGN cells. Each LGN cell receives excitatory input from very few, and predominantly from one, ganglion cell that confers its properties upon the cell. P-, M-, and K-layer LGN cells are designated by P-cells, M-cells, and K-cells respectively. Retinal ganglion cells that project to LGN P- and M- layers often are called P- and M-cells as well. P-cells, especially those representing foveal vision, may increase in number in the LGN relative to retina, but this issue is controversial (Azzopardi, Kirstie, & Cowey, 1999). Such an increase might contribute to the over-representation of central vision in V1, and may serve to boost the overall contrast gain of the P-pathway (see next section on contrast sensitivity).

In addition to relaying signals to cortex, the LGN also contains circuitry for processing the signal. Retinal inputs to the macaque LGN represent only about 30% of the afferents to the LGN. About 40% of the inputs arrive via local inhibitory interneurons and the thalamic reticular nucleus (Wilson, 1993). Also, there is massive excitatory (positive) feedback from cortical area V1, and direct input from the brainstem. A major function of this LGN circuitry is to modulate the transfer ratio of signals from retina to cortex. Low arousal states, signaled by the brain stem inputs, leads to low transfer ratios. High arousal states improve the ratios, although they are still less than one (Kaplan, Mukherjee, & Shapley, 1993). The LGN circuitry also provides temporal filtering at high and low frequencies that makes the bandpass of LGN frequency responses narrower than those of the retinal inputs. In cats, whose LGN circuitry is similar to that of macaques, this filtering is pronounced during low arousal states (Kaplan et al., 1993). The function of the positive feedback from individual cortical cells in V1 to their LGN inputs may be to synchronize the activity of the inputs (Sillitto, Jones, Gerstein, & West, 1996).

Because of its laminar structure and its retinotopic organization, the LGN provides an opportunity for selective lesioning of either the M- or P-pathway input to the visual cortex in a specific location in the visual field. When this was done in macaques trained to perform visual psychophysical tasks, the effect on visual performance of removing either pathway could be assessed. The results of the selective lesion studies support the generalizations from the previous section, and are summarized in Table 3.1 regarding the spectral selectivity and the spatial and temporal resolution of the two streams. When P-layers (including the intercalated regions) are destroyed, the macaque's color discrimination and pattern detection, particularly at high spatial frequencies, deteriorates (Merigan, Byrne, & Maunsell, 1991; Merigan, Katz, & Maunsell, 1991; Schiller, Logothetis, & Charles, 1990). In contrast, magnocellular lesions reduce the animal's sensitivity to low spatial frequency stimuli modulated at high temporal frequencies.

Contrast Sensitivity

Throughout this chapter, results of contrast sensitivity measurements have been used to describe the visual spatial and temporal resolution, measured either psychophysically or in physiological experiments. A general question to be addressed here is whether the visual system analyzes scenes into its frequency components. We will examine the case for spatial vision.

Figure 3.3 shows the human contrast sensitivity function from the classic study of Campbell and Robson (1968). The question of whether the visual system has channels, or filters, for different spatial frequencies, and the width of those filters, was addressed psychophysically by exposing subjects to particular spatial frequencies and observing the effect on the spatial contrast sensitivity function. These experiments supported the existence of channels (Blakemore & Campbell, 1969; Campbell & Robson, 1968).

Physiological studies in visual cortex also have supported the hypothesis that there are spatial frequency channels. As noted in the next section, spatial tuning of individual neurons is narrower in primary visual cortex than in the LGN, providing a possible substrate for channels or filters (Campbell, Cooper, & Enroth-Cugell, 1969; see DeValois and DeValois, 1990 for a review). It is also possible, by incorporating filters of physiologically plausible dimensions, six in the case of Wilson and Regan (1984), to construct a model of the psychophysically determined contrast sensitivity function of the entire system (see Graham, 1989 for a review).

Stepping back from the visual cortex to its LGN inputs, can we say anything about the contribution of the M- and P-pathways to the contrast sensitivity function of the entire system? Most importantly, which pathway determines the spatial resolution; which pathway determines the sensitivity? The logical choice for the resolution is the P-pathway due to its high spatial resolution. A problem with this choice is that the human peak contrast sensitivity is quite high, whereas the responsiveness of individual P-stream cells is very low. Although responsiveness of individual M-stream cells is much higher, and it is tempting to match it to the psychophysical findings, it is important to take the relative numbers of cells in the two streams into account. There are many more P- than M-stream cells, and the manner in which signals are pooled in visual cortex could increase the overall gain of the P-pathway sufficiently to predict the high sensitivity of the psychophysical function.

Primary Visual Cortical Cells: An Overview of Processing in V1

The parallel projections of P-, M- and K-streams are maintained through the LGN and into V1. As summarized in Figure 3.2b, these streams remain at least partially segregated at higher stages of processing. P- and M-cells synapse predominantly on cortical cells in layer 4 of the V1, whereas K-cells terminate in layers 2 and 3. More specifically, P-cells synapse in layers 4Cβ, 4A (and the deepest cortical layer, 6), whereas M-cells synapse in layers 4Cα and weakly to layer 6. K-cells project to regions in layers 2/3 called "blobs." This designation is due to blob-like concentrations in layers 2/3 of V1 of the mitochondrial enzyme, cytochrome oxidase (CO), demonstrated using a histological stain for CO. In V2, the stain forms thick and thin stripes. The cells in the blobs project to thin stripe regions in V2, and then to V4, perhaps forming a special color-sensitive pathway.

Receptive field characteristics of V1 cells differ in several respects from the characteristics of their LGN inputs. A prominent emergent property is elongation of receptive fields, with the preferred stimulus being a bar oriented along the long axis of the field, rather than a spot filling the receptive field center. This property is common for V1 cells, although at least some cells receiving direct LGN input retain non-oriented center-surround properties.

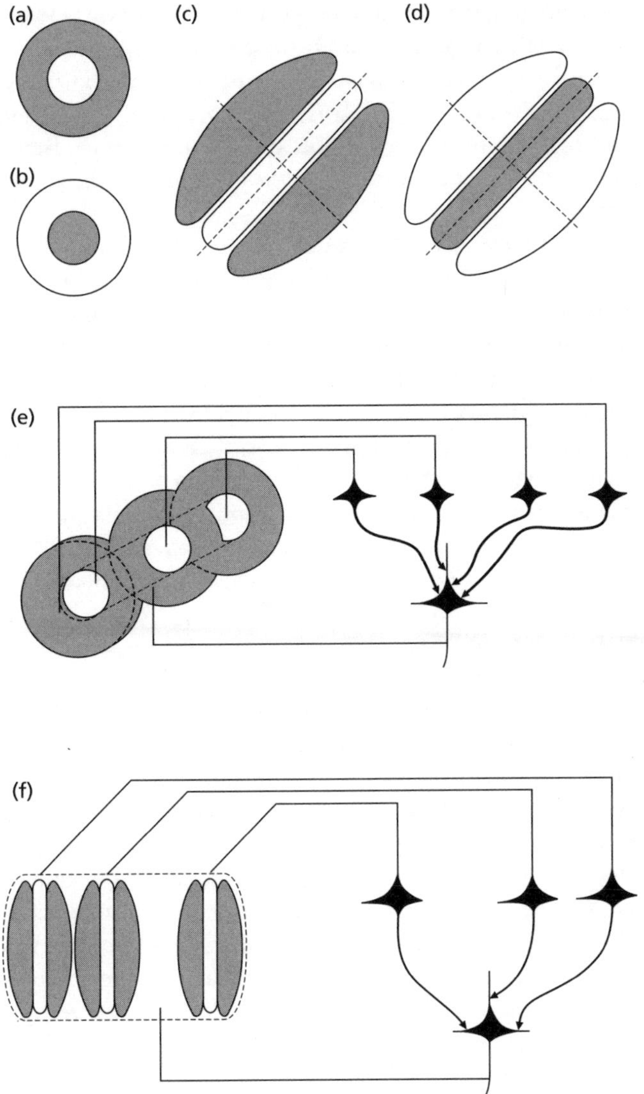

Figure 3.9. Hubel and Wiesel's (1962) model of hierarchical organization of the visual cortex for simple and complex cells. (a) and (b) On-center and Off-center LGN cell receptive fields respectively. (c) and (d) Simple cell receptive fields. (e) Convergence of LGN cells onto a V1 simple cell. (f) Convergence of simple cells onto a complex cell.

In classic studies in cats, Hubel and Wiesel (1962) proposed that cortical processing is hierarchical. In their model, visual cortical cells progress from those having simple receptive fields to those having complex, and then hypercomplex, receptive fields. The progression from simple to complex receptive fields is generally accepted today, but hypercomplex receptive fields are no longer believed to be a single category (see below). The simple cell receptive fields are composed of rows of On-center and Off-center LGN inputs (Figure 3.9e). Simple receptive fields can be mapped into discrete On and Off regions arranged in abutting excitatory and inhibitory bands (Figure 3.9c & d). Spatial summation within each band is linear, as are the interactions between flanking bands. Responses to gratings show a spatial phase-dependence predicted by the placement of the gratings relative to the On and Off regions.

In the next stage of hierarchical processing, simple cells feed into complex cells (Figure 3.9f). Complex cell receptive fields cannot be mapped into discrete On and Off regions, and no longer show linear spatial summation. Responses occur at light onset and light offset, and for grating stimuli, are phase-independent. A common feature of simple and complex cells is their preference for stimulus bars of a particular orientation, a property called orientation selectivity. Because complex cell responses are not tightly tied to the specific stimulus location or polarity (light or dark), they can signal the presence of an appropriately oriented bar anywhere in the receptive field. This higher-order function of signaling a particular stimulus attribute (orientation in this case) regardless of location is more fully developed in extrastriate visual areas, and may form the basis for perceptual constancy (Reid, 1999). Receptive field characteristics of simple and complex cells in macaque V1 are similar to those described by Hubel and Wiesel in cats (Hubel & Wiesel, 1977).

As noted above, Hubel and Wiesel (1962) described a further step in hierarchical processing that produced hypercomplex cells. These cells, in addition to showing orientation selectivity, also preferred a particular optimal length for a bar stimulus. Extending the bar beyond the optimal length inhibited the cells' responses. This characteristic is called end-stopping. Because end-stopping emerges in both simple and complex cells, the current view is that hypercomplex cells do not represent a separate higher-level class (see Reid, 1999 for a review).

Cortical cells show spatial and temporal frequency tuning. The tuning is more selective, and hence contrast sensitivity functions are narrower than in their LGN P- and M-cell inputs, indicating a role for cortical circuits in refining the tuning (DeValois & DeValois, 1990) of the possible physiological substrate for spatial frequency channels.

Another emergent property of cortical cells is the directional selectivity that many cells in cats, but only about 20% of the complex cells in V1 in macaque (Tovée, 1996), show for bars moving orthogonal to the long axis of their receptive fields. Movement in the preferred direction elicits strong responses whereas movement in the opposite, null, direction evokes little or no response. This property, as well as orientation selectivity, is due, at least in part, to the spatial and temporal arrangement of the cortical cell inputs. However, further refinements due to cortical circuits also can be demonstrated (reviewed by Reid & Alonso, 1996).

Preference for a particular direction of movement, and tuning for a particular velocity, are characteristics of motion-sensitive cells. In a true motion detector, the preferred velocity would be independent of the spatial and temporal tuning of the cell. However, most cells in V1 show velocity preferences for grating stimuli that can be predicted from the cells' spatial and temporal frequency responses using the simple relation: velocity equals temporal frequency divided by spatial frequency. True motion detectors exist in areas such as MT of the dorsal pathway that receive input from the cortical extension of the M-stream.

A final property of visual neurons that emerges in V1 to be described in this chapter is the binocular interaction that occurs in these cells. Input from the two eyes alternates spatially in layer 4 and, although responses of layer 4 cells are driven only by one eye, the cells in other cortical layers to which they project are binocular. Binocular cells can be divided into classes that are dominated by one eye, the other eye, or equally influenced by the two eyes. This property is called ocular dominance (Hubel & Wiesel, 1962). The fact that visual processing becomes binocular only after visual signals reach striate cortex can be utilized in analyzing the locus of perceptual effects that show intraocular transfer (see Chapter 1).

In addition to charting the properties of cortical cells, in their classic work Hubel and Wiesel (1962) observed that the visual cortex is organized into functional units called columns. Hierarchical and parallel processing occurs in the columns of V1 as the cells receiving LGN inputs project to other layers of the cortex before projecting to other cortical areas (see Callaway, 1998 for a review). The columns in visual cortex first were identified in microelectrode recordings. In penetrations perpendicular to the cortical layers, the preferred orientation, the ocular dominance, and perhaps spatial frequency tuning (De Valois & DeValois, 1990) are similar for all of the cells encountered. The properties varied smoothly and continuously across the cortex when tangential penetrations were made. For each point in the visual field, in a short distance over the cortex (a "module" of about 0.5 mm) the entire range of orientation preferences and ocular dominance was represented. Hubel and Wiesel (1977) called these modules "hypercolumns."

Anatomical studies of the functional architecture of visual cortex, using metabolic markers to identify regions activated by particular stimuli, have verified the existence of the cortical columns. For example, the alternation of inputs from the eyes to layer 4 has been visualized. In vivo optical imaging studies have further clarified the topography of the orientation columns (Bartfield & Grinvald, 1992; Blasdel & Salma, 1986; Grinvald, Lieke, Frostig, Gilbert, & Wiesel, 1988). However, the columns are not organized as predicted by the physiological studies. They have occasional discontinuities, and single points around which all of the orientation preferences are arranged that have been called pinwheels. Imaging studies will continue to yield new information, not only about columns and local processing modules, but also about higher-level processing in cortex.

Single Neurons, Parallel Streams and the Binding Problem

This chapter on basic visual processes has explored the functional architecture of the visual pathways from retina to primary visual cortex, and has examined receptive field characteristics of neurons at each stage of processing. The emphasis has been upon the relation between response properties of individual neurons and lower order perceptual processes. As summarized in the overview, a common view of higher order processing beyond primary visual cortex is that processing is modular, with parallel streams to cortical areas involved in signaling specific attributes of the stimulus. A central issue that remains, which has been referred to as the "binding problem" (see Chapter 1), is how information from the various different visual areas is integrated to provide coherent representations of visual objects and scenes.

Basic Data

In humans there are about 5–6.4 * 10^6 cones, and 1 * 10^8 to 1.25 * 10^8 rods
Cones make up about 5% of the photoreceptor population. (Rodieck: *The first steps in seeing*, 1998)
Maximum density of cones in central fovea – 161,000 per mm^2 (Curcio et al., 1987)
Maximum density of rods in the elliptical high density ring 2–5 deg. eccentricity ≥ 150,000 per mm^2 (Curcio et al., 1990; Østerberg, 1935)
Spectral sensitivities of the short (S, or blue), the medium (M, or green), and the long (L, or red) wavelength cones in humans peak around 420, 530, and 565 nm respectively
The rod pigment, rhodopsin, peaks around 499 nm (Tovée, 1996)
Spacing of foveal cones – 0.5 min of arc (Curcio et al., 1987)
Spatial resolution at fovea – 0.5 min of arc (Williams, 1986)
Isoluminant resolution for L- and M-cone vision: 20–27 c/deg (from Calkins & Sterling review, 1999)
Resolution of rod vision – 6 min (Lennie & Fairchild, 1994)
Resolution of blue cones: 9 min of arc determined psychophysically (Williams et al., 1981) and anatomically (Curcio et al., 1991)
Detection of an isoluminant grating: 10 c/deg by S-cone system (reviewed by Calkins and Sterling, 1999)
Foveola rod free, blue cone free, avascular region – 0.7 deg. in radius (Kolb, 1991)
Number of retinal ganglion cells: 0.7 to 1.5 million. Their highest density: 32–38 * 103 /mm^2 (Curcio & Allen, 1990)
Absolute dark adapted sensitivity – 1–3 photons per deg^2 (Frishman et al., 1996); 7–10 rods photons at the photoreceptors (Hecht, Shlaer, & Pirenne, 1942)
Rod absolute sensitivity = isomerizations in 7–10 rods (Hecht et al., 1942) (Wandel (1995): 1–5 rods). Hecht et al.: 1 photon in about every 85 min.
Cones: absolute sensitivity = <50 isomerizations per cone (Hood & Finkelstein, 1986; Schnapf et al., 1990) (Wandel (1995) says 10–15 for detection)
Number of visual cortical areas – more than 30 (Van Essen et al., 1992)

Suggested Readings

Barlow, H. B. (1972). Single units and sensation: A neuron doctrine for perceptual psychology? *Perception, 1*, 371–394. [This classic paper addresses the important issue of the relation between neuronal responses and perception.]

Baylor, D. (1996). How photons start vision. *Proceedings of the National Academy of Science USA, 93*, 582–588. [This is a very good review of rod photoreceptor function.]

Boycott, B. B., & Wässle, H. (1999). Parallel processing in the mammalian retina. *Investigative Ophthalmology & Visual Science, 40*, 1313–1327. [This review provides a current view of the role of bipolar cells in setting up parallel streams in the primate retina.]

Charmin, W. N. (1991). Optics of the human eye. In *Visual optics and instrumentation* (pp. 1–26). Boca Raton: CRC Press. [(This chapter provides a good overview of the optics of the human eye.]

Hood, D. C. (1998). Lower-level processing and models of light adaptation. *Annual Review of Psychology, 49*, 503–535. [This review provides a current view of data and models pertaining to photopic adaptation in humans.]

Kolb, H., Fernandez, E., & Nelson, R. Web Vision, the organization of the vertebrate retina. http:/

insight.med.utah.edu/Webvision. [This Web site provides a many illustrations of the retina, and explanatory text.]

Parker, A.J., & Newsome, W. T. (1998). Sense and the single neuron: Probing the physiology of perception. *Annual Review of Neuroscience, 21*, 227–277. [This reviews recent attempts in awake, behaving primates to relate physiology and perception.]

Reid, R. C. (1999). Vision. In M.J. Zigmond, F.E. Bloom, S.C. Landis, J.L. Roberts, & L.R. Squire (Eds.), *Fundamental Neuroscience* (Ch. 28, pp. 821–851). New York: Academic Press. [This is an up-to-date review of the visual pathways, their anatomy and physiology.]

Rodieck, R. W. (1998). *The first steps in seeing.* Sunderland, MA: Sinauer Associates. [This book provides a very thorough description of the primate retina, its anatomy and function.]

Wandell, B. (1995). *Foundations of vision.* Sunderland, MA: Sinauer Associates. [This book is a good source for reviewing the contributions of photoreceptors to vision, and quantitative approaches to the analysis of visual function.]

Additional Topics

Retinal Neurotransmitters

The functional properties of retinal neurons are determined to a large extent by the neurotransmitters and neuromodulators present in the retina, and the selective distribution of specific neurotransmitter receptor types on retinal neurons. Over the past decade there have been enormous advances in our knowledge of retinal neuropharmacology. See Brandstätter, Koulen, and Wässle (1998), Koulen (1999), Massey and Maguire (1995), and Wässle, Koulen, Brandstätter, Fletcher, and Becker (1998).

Cortical Development and Critical Periods

Development of the visual cortex has been studied extensively. From these studies we have learned a great deal about which characteristics of cortical neurons are present from birth, which develop, and which are plastic and can be altered during an early critical period in development. See Blakemore, Vital-Durand, and Garey (1981), Burkhalter, Bernardo, and Charles (1993), Daw (1994), Chino, Smith, Hatta, and Cheng (1997), and Knudsen (1999).

Plasticity in Adult Cortex

Although the classic view is that plasticity in the functional anatomy of the visual system can occur only during a critical period early in development, new evidence indicates that alterations can occur even in adults. See Chino (1995), Das and Gilbert (1995), Sur (1999), and Gilbert, Das, Kapidia, and Westheimer (1996).

Neural Mechanisms of Binocular Vision and Stereopsis

This chapter focused mainly on monocular visual capacities, and we can see very well with just one eye. However, binocular vision is very important for our very accurate depth perception, called stereopsis. The mechanisms for stereopsis are considered in papers by Freeman (1998), Horton and Hocking (1990), Livingstone and Tsao (1999), and Poggio, Gonzales, and Krause (1998).

References

Aguilar, M., & Stiles, W. S. (1954). Saturation of the rod mechanism at high levels of stimulation. *Optica Acta*, 1, 59–65.

Albright, T. D. (1993). Cortical processing of visual motion. In F. A. Miles & J. Wallman (Eds.), *Vision motion and its role in the stabilization of gaze* (pp. 177–201). Amsterdam: Elsevier Science Publishers.

Anderson, S. J., Mullen, K. T., & Hess, R. F. (1991). Human peripheral spatial resolution for achromatic and chromatic stimuli: Limits imposed by optical and retinal factors. *Journal of Physiology, 442*, 47–64.

Azzopardi, P., Kirstie, E. J., & Cowey, A. (1999). Uneven mapping of magnocellular and parvocellular projections from the lateral geniculate nucleus to the striate cortex in the macaque monkey. *Vision Research, 39*, 2179–2189.

Banks, M. S., Sekuler, A. B., & Anderson, S. J. (1991). Peripheral spatial vision: Limits imposed by optics, photoreceptors, and receptor pooling. *Journal of the Optical Society of America A*, 1775–1787.

Barlow, H. B., Levick, W. R., & Yoon, M.(1971). Responses to single quanta of light in retinal ganglion cells of the cat. *Vision Research, 11, Supplement 3*, 87–102.

Bartfeld, E., & Grinvald, A. (1992). Relationships between orientation-preference pinwheels, cytochrome oxidase blobs, and ocular-dominance columns in primate striate cortex. *Proceedings of the National Academy of Science, USA, 89*, 11905–11909.

Baylor, D. (1996). How photons start vision. *Proceedings of the National Academy of Science USA, 93*, 582–588.

Baylor, D. A. , Nunn, B. J., & Schnapf, J. L. (1984). The photocurrent, noise and spectral sensitivity of rods of the monkey *Macaca Fascicularis*. *Journal of Physiology, 357*, 575–607.

Bennet, A. G., & Rabbetts, R. B. (1989). The eye's optical system. *Clinical visual optics* (2nd ed.). London: Butterworth-Heinemann Ltd.

Blakemore, C., & Campbell, F. (1969). On the existence of neurons in the human visual system selectively responsive to the orientation and size of retinal images. *Journal of Physiology, 203*, 237–260.

Blakemore, C., Vital-Durand, F., & Garey, L. (1981). Recovery from monocular deprivation in the monkey. I. Recovery of physiological effects in the visual cortex. *Proceedings of the Royal Society London [Biology], 213*, 399–423.

Blasdel, G. G., & Salma, G. (1986). Voltage sensitive dyes reveal a modular organization in the monkey striate cortex. *Nature, 321*, 579–585.

Boycott, B. B., & Wässle, H. (1999). Parallel processing in the mammalian retina. *Investigative Ophthalmology & Visual Science, 40*, 1313–1327.

Brandstätter, H., Koulen., P., & Wässle, H. (1998). Diversity of glutamate receptors in the mammalian retina. *Vision Research, 38*, 1385–1398.

Burkhalter, A. Bernardo, K. I., & Charles, V. (1993). Development of local circuits in human visual cortex. *Journal of Neuroscience, 13*, 1916–1931.

Calkins, D. J., & Sterling, P. (1999). Evidence that circuits for spatial and color vision segregate at the first retinal synapse. *Neuron, 24*, 313–321.

Callaway, E. M. (1998). Local circuits in primary visual cortex of the macaque monkey. *Annual Review of Neuroscience, 12*, 47–74.

Campbell, F. W., Cooper, G.F., & Enroth-Cugell, C. (1969). The spatial selectivity of the visual cells of the cat. *Journal of Physiology, 203*, 223–235.

Campbell, F. W., & Green, D. G. (1965). Optical and retinal factors affecting visual resolution. *Journal of Physiology, 181*, 576–593.

Campbell, F. W., & Gubisch, R. W. (1966). Optical quality of the human eye. *Journal of Physiology, 186*, 558–578.

Campbell, F. W., & Robson J. G. (1968). Application of Fourier analysis to the visibility of gratings. *Journal of Physiology, 197*, 551–566.

Charmin, W. N. (1991). Optics of the human eye. In *Visual optics and instrumentation* (pp. 1–26). Boca Raton: CRC Press.

Chino, Y. M. (1995). Adult plasticity in the visual system. *Canadian Journal of Physiological Pharmacology, 73*, 1323–38.

Chino, Y. M., Smith, E. L. 3rd., Hatta, S., & Cheng, H. (1997). Postnatal development of binocular disparity sensitivity in neurons of the primate visual cortex. *Journal of Neuroscience, 17*, 296–307.

Croner L. J., & Kaplan E. (1995). Receptive fields of P and M ganglion cells across the primate retina. *Vision Research, 35*, 7–24.

Curcio, C. A., & Allen, K. A. (1990). Topography of retinal ganglion cells in human retina. *Journal of Comparative Neurology, 300*, 5–25.

Curcio, C. A., Allen, K. A., Sloan, K. R., Lerea, C. L., Hurley, J. B., Klock, I. B., & Milam, A. H. (1991). Distribution and morphology of human cone photoreceptors stained with anti-blue opsin. *Journal of Comparative Neurology, 312*, 610–624.

Curcio, C. A., Sloan, K. R., Kalina, R. E., & Hendrickson, A. E. (1990). Human photoreceptor topography. *Journal of Comparative Neurology, 292*, 497–523.

Curcio, C. A., Sloan, K. R., Packer, O., Hendrickson, A. E., & Kalina, R. E. (1987). Distribution of cones in human and monkey retina: Individual variability and radial asymmetry. *Science, 236*, 579–582.

Dacey, D. M. (1993). The mosaic of midget ganglion cells in the human retina. *Journal of Neuroscience, 13*, 5334–5355.

Dacey, D. M. (1996). Circuitry for color coding in the primate retina. *Proceedings of the National Academy of Science, USA, 93*, 582–588.

Dartnall, H. J. A., Bowmaker, J. K., & Mollen, J. D. (1983). Human visual pigments, microspectrophotometric results from the eyes of seven persons. *Proceedings of the Royal Society London B, 220*, 114–130.

Das, A., & Gilbert, C. D. (1995). Long-range horizontal connections and their role in cortical reorganization revealed by optical recording of cat primary visual cortex. *Nature, 375*, 780–784.

Daw, N. W. (1994). Mechanisms of plasticity in the visual cortex. *Investigative Ophthalmology & Visual Science, 35*, 1133–1138.

De Monasterio, F., McCrane, E. P., Newlander, J. K., & Schein, S. (1985). Density profile of blue-sensitive cones along the horizontal meridian of macaque retina. *Investigative Ophthalmology & Visual Science, 26*, 289–302.

DeValois, R. L., & DeValois, K. K. (1990). *Spatial vision*. New York: Oxford University Press.

Engel, A. K., Konig, P., Kreiter, A. K., Schillen, T. B., & Singer, W. (1992). Temporal coding in the visual cortex: New vistas on integration in the nervous system. *Trends in Neuroscience, 15*, 218–226.

Engel, A. K., Roelfsema, F. P., Brecht, M., & Singer, W. (1997). Role of the temporal domain for response selection and perceptual binding. *Cerebral Cortex, 7*, 571–582.

Engel, A. K., Fries, P., Konig, P., Brecht, M., & Singer, W. (1999). Temporal binding, binocular rivalry, and consciousness. *Conscious Cognition, 8*, 128–151.

Enroth-Cugell, C., & Robson, J. G. (1966). The contrast sensitivity of retinal ganglion cells of the cat. *Journal of Physiology, 187*, 517–552.

Feeney-Burns, M., & Katz, M. (1998). Retina pigment epithelium. In W. Tamsan & E. A. Jaeger (Eds), *Duane's foundations of clinical ophthalmology* (Ch. 21). Philadelphia, PA: Lippincott Williams & Wilkin.

Freeman, R. D. (1998). Binocular vision: The neural integration of depth and motion. *Current Biology, 8*, R761–764.

Frishman, L. J., Reddy, M. G., & Robson, J. G. (1996). Effects of background light on the human ERG dark-adapted ERG and psychophysical threshold. *Journal of the Optical Society of America A, 13*, 601–612.

Frishman, L. J., & Robson, J. G. (1999). Inner retinal signal processing: Adaptation to environmental light. In Archer et al. (Eds.), *Adaptive mechanisms in the ecology of vision* (pp. 383–412). London: Chapman & Hall.

Gilbert, C. D., Das, A., Kapidia, M., & Westheimer, G. (1996). Spatial integration and cortical dynamics. *Proceedings of the National Academy of Science USA, 93*, 615–622.

Glasser, A., & Campbell, M. C. (1999). Biometric, optical and physical changes in the isolated human crystalline lens with age in relation to presbyopia. *Vision Research, 39*, 1991–2015.

Goodale, M. A., & Milner, A. D. (1992). Separate visual pathways for perception and action. *Trends in Neuroscience, 15*, 20–25.

Goodale, M. A., Milner, A. D., Jacobsen, L. S., & Carey, D. P. (1991). A neurological distinction between perceiving objects and grasping them. *Nature, 349*, 154–156.

Graham, N. (1989). *Visual pattern analyzers*. New York: Oxford University Press.

Grinvald, A., Lieke, E., Frostig, R. D., Gilbert, C. D., & Wiesel, T. N. (1988). Functional architecture of cortex revealed by optical imaging of intrinsic signals. *Nature, 324*, 361–364.

Hagins, W. A., Penn, R. D., & Yoshikami, S. (1970). Dark current and photocurrent in retinal rods. *Biophysical Journal, 10*, 380–409.

Hagstrom, S. A., Neitz, J., & Neitz, M. (1998). Variations in cone populations for red-green color vision examined by analysis of mRNA. *Neuroport, 9*, 1963–1967.

Hart, W. M. (1992). The temporal responsiveness of vision. In W. H. Hart (Ed.), *Adlers physiology of the eye* (9th ed., pp. 548–576). Mosby Year Book, Inc.

Hecht, S., Haig, C., & Chase, A.M. (1937). The influence of light adaptation on subsequent dark adaptation of the eye. *Journal of General Physiology, 20*, 831–850.

Hecht, S., Shlaer, S., & Pirenne, M. H. (1942). Energy, quanta, and vision. *Journal of Physiology, 25*, 819–840.

Hendry, S. H. C., & Calkins, D. J. (1998). Neuronal chemistry and functional organization of the primate visual system. *Trends in Neuroscience, 21*, 345–349.

Hood, D. C. (1998). Lower-level processing and models of light adaptation. *Annual Review of Psychology, 49*, 503–535.

Hood, D. C., & Finkelstein, M. A. (1987). Sensitivity to light. In K. R. Boeff, L. Kaufman, & J. P. Thomas (Eds.), *Handbook of perception and human performance: Vol. 1. Sensory processes and perception* (pp. 5:1–66). New York: John Wiley & Sons.

Horton, J. C., & Hocking, D. R. (1990). Arrangement of ocular dominance columns in human visual cortex. *Archives of Ophthalmology, 108*, 1025–1031.

Hubel, D. H., & Wiesel, T. N. (1962). Receptive fields, binocular interaction, and functional architecture in the cat's visual cortex. *Journal of Physiology, 160*, 106–154.

Hubel, D. H., & Wiesel, T. N. (1977). Functional architecture of macaque visual cortex (Ferrier Lecture). *Proceedings of the Royal Society London B, 198*, 1–59.

Jacobs, G. H. (1996). Primate photopigments and primate color vision. *Proceedings of the National Academy of Science USA, 93*, 577–581.

Kaplan, E. (1989). The receptive field structure of retinal ganglion cells in cat and monkey. In A. Leventhal (Ed.), *Vision and visual dysfunction: Vol. 5. The electrophysiology of vision* (pp. 10–40). London: Macmillan Press.

Kaplan, E., Lee, B. B., & Shapley, R. M. (1990). New views of primate retinal function. In N. N. Osborne & G. J. Chader (Eds.), *Progress in retinal research* (Vol. 9, pp. 273–336). Oxford, UK: Pergamon.

Kaplan, E., Mukherjee, P., & Shapley, R. (1993). Information filtering in the lateral geniculate nucleus. In R. Shapley & Dm-K. Lam (Eds.), *Proceedings of the Retinal Research Foundation Symposium* (pp. 183–200).

Kaplan, E., & Shapley, R. M. (1986). The primate retina contains two types of ganglion cells, with high and low contrast sensitivity. *Proceedings of the National Academy of Science USA*, 2755–2757.

Knudsen, E. I. (1999). Early experience and critical periods. In M. J. Zigmond, F. E. Bloom, S. C. Landis, J. L. Roberts, & L. R. Squire (Eds.), *Fundamental neuroscience* (Ch. 32, pp. 637–654). San Diego, CA: Academic Press.

Kolb, H. (1991). The neural organization of the human retina. In J. Heckenlively & G. B. Arden (Eds.), *Principles and practice of clinical electrophysiology of vision* (pp. 25–52). Mosby Year Book Publishers, Inc.,

Kolb, H. (1994). The architecture of functional neural circuits in the vertebrate retina. The Proctor lecture. *Investigative Ophthalmology & Visual Science, 35*, 2385–2404.

Kolb, H., Linberg, K. A., & Fisher, S.K. (1992). Neurons of the human retina: A Golgi study. *Journal of Comparative Neurology, 318*, 147–187.

Koulen, P. (1999). Clustering of neurotransmitter receptors in the mammalian retina. *Journal of Membrane Biology, 171*, 97–105.

Koutalos, Y., & Yau, K-W. (1996). Regulation of sensitivity in vertebrate rod photoreceptors by calcium. *Trends in Neuroscience, 19*, 73–81.

Kraft, T. W., Schneeweis, D. M., & Schnapf, J. S. (1991). Visual transduction in human rod photoreceptors. *Journal of Physiology, 464*, 747–765.

Kuffler, S. W. (1953). Discharge patterns and functional organization of mammalian retina. *Journal of Neurophysiology, 16*, 37–68.

Lee, B. L., Smith, V. C., Pokorny, J., & Kremers, J. (1997). Rod inputs to macaque ganglion cells. *Vision Research, 37*, 2813–2828.

Lee, B., Dacey, D. M., Smith, V. C., & Pokorny, J. (1999). Horizontal cells reveal cone type-specific adaptation in primate retina. *Proceedings of the National Academy of Science USA, 96*, 14611–14616.

Leibrock, C. S., Reuter, T., & Lamb, T. D. (1998). Molecular basis of dark adaptation in rod photoreceptors. *Eye, 12*, 511–520.

Lennie, P., & Fairchild, M. D. (1994). Ganglion cell pathways for rod vision. *Vision Research, 34*, 477–482.

Levick, W. R., & Zack, J. L. (1970). Responses of cat retinal ganglion cells to brief flashes of light. *Journal of Physiology, 206*, 677–700.

Levine, M. W., & Sheffner, J. M. (1991). *Sensation and perception* (2nd ed.). Belmont, CA: Brooks/Cole Publishing Company.

Livingstone, M. S., & Tsao, D. Y. (1999). Receptive fields of disparity-selective neurons in macaque striate cortex. *Nature Neuroscience, 2*, 825–832.

Martin, P. R. (1998). Colour processing in the primate retina: Recent progress. *Journal of Physiology, 513*, 631–638.

Martin, P., & Grünert, U. (1992). Spatial density and immunoreactivity of bipolar cells in the macaque monkey retina. *Journal of Comparative Neurology, 322*, 269–287.

Massey, S. C., & Maguire, G. (1995). The role of glutamate in retinal circuitry. In H. Wheal & A. Thomson (Eds.), *Excitatory amino acids and synaptic transmission* (Ch. 15, pp. 201–221). New York: Academic Press.

Maunsell, J. H. R., & Newsome, W. T. (1987). Visual processing in monkey extrastriate cortex. *Annual Review of Neuroscience, 10*, 363–401.

Maunsell, J. H., Ghose, G. M., Assad, J. A., McAdams, C. J., Boudreau, C.E., & Noerager, B.D. (1999). Visual response latencies of magnocellular and parvocellular LGN neurons in macaque monkeys. *Visual Neuroscience, 16*, 1–14.

McIlwain, J. T. (1996). *An introduction to the biology of vision.* New York: Cambridge University Press.

Meister, M. (1996). Multineuronal codes in retinal signaling. *Proceedings of the National Academy of Science USA*, 609–614.

Merigan, W. H., Byrne, C. E., & Maunsell, J. H. R. (1991). Does primate motion detection depend on the magnocellular pathway? *Journal of Neuroscience, 11*, 3422–3429.

Merigan, W. H., Katz, L. M., & Maunsell, J. H. R. (1991). Effects of parvocellular lesions on the acuity and contrast sensitivity of macaque monkeys. *Journal of Neuroscience, 11*, 994–1001.

Merigan, W., & Maunsell, J. (1993). How parallel are the primate visual pathways? *Annual Review of Neuroscience, 16*, 369–402.

Mishkin, M., Ungerleider, L. G., & Macko, K. A. (1983). Object vision and spatial vision: Two cortical pathways. *Trends in Neuroscience, 6*, 414–417.

Nathans, J., Thomas, D., & Hogness, D. S. (1986). Molecular genetics of color vision: The genes encoding blue, green and red pigments. *Science, 232*, 193–202.

Neuenschwander, S., Costelo-Branco, M., & Singer, W. (1999). Synchronous oscillations in the cat retina. *Vision Research, 39*, 2485–2497.

Newman, E.A. (2000). Müller cells and the retinal pigment epithelium. In D. M. Albert & F. A. Jakobiec (Eds.), *The principles and practice of ophthalmology. Retina and vitreous* (2nd ed., Ch.

118, pp. 1763–1785). Philadelphia, PA: W. B. Saunders.
Newman, E. A., & Zahs, K. R. (1998). Modulation of neuronal activity by glial cells in the retina. *Journal of Neuroscience, 18*, 4022–4028.
Nicholls, J. G. (1992). In J. G. Nicholls, A. R. Martin, & B. G. Wallace (Eds.), *From neuron to brain* (3rd ed.). Sunderland, MA: Sinauer Associates.
Østerberg, G. (1935). Topography of the layer of rods and cones in the human retina. *Acta Ophthalmologica, 6*, 1–103.
Packer, O. S., Diller, L., Lee, B. B., & Dacey, D. M. (1999). Diffuse cone bipolar cells in macaque retina are spatially opponent. *Investigative Ophthalmology & Visual Science, 40*, S790.
Poggio, G. F., Gonzales, F., & Krause, F. (1998). Stereoscopic mechanisms in monkey visual cortex: Binocular correlation and disparity selectivity. *Journal of Neuroscience, 8*, 4531–4550.
Purpura, K., Tranchina, D., Kaplan, E., & Shapley, R. M. (1990). Light adaptation in primate retina: Analysis of changes in gain and dynamics of monkey retinal ganglion cells. *Visual Neuroscience, 4*, 75–83.
Raviola, E., & Gilula N.B. (1973). Gap junctions between photoreceptor cells in the vertebrate retina. *Proceedings of the National Academy of Science USA, 70*, 1677–1681.
Reid, R. C. (1999). Vision. In M. J. Zigmond, F. E. Bloom, S. C. Landis, J. L. Roberts, & L.R. Squire (Eds.), *Fundamental neuroscience* (Ch. 28, pp. 821–851). San Diego, CA: Academic Press.
Reid, R. C., & Alonso, J.-M. (1996). The processing and encoding of information in visual cortex. *Current Opinion in Biology, 6*, 475–480.
Robson, J. G. (1966). Spatial and temporal contrast sensitivity functions of the visual system. *Journal of the Optical Society of America, 56*, 1141–1142.
Robson, J. G., & Frishman, L. J. (1995). Response linearity and dynamics of the cat retina: The bipolar cell component of the dark-adapted ERG. *Visual Neuroscience, 12*, 837–850.
Robson, J. G., & Frishman, L. J. (1998). Dissecting the dark-adapted electroretinogram. *Documenta Ophthalmologica, 95*, 187–215.
Rodieck, R. W. (1998). *The first steps in seeing*. Sunderland, MA: Sinauer Associates.
Rodieck, R. W., Brening, R. K., & Watanabe, M. (1993). The origin of parallel visual pathways. In R. Shapley, & Dm-K. Lam (Eds.), *Proceedings of the Retinal Research Foundation Symposium* (pp. 117–144).
Roorda, A., & Williams, D. R. (1999). The arrangement of the three cone classes in the living human eye. *Nature, 397*, 520–522.
Sakman, B., & Creutzfeldt, O. D. (1969). Scotopic and mesopic light adaptation in the cat's retina. *Pflügers Archiv, 313*, 168–185.
Schiller, P. H., Logothetis, N. K., & Charles, E. R. (1990). Functions of the colour-opponent and broad-band channels of the visual system. *Nature, 343*, 68–70.
Schnapf, J. L., Nunn, B. J., Meister, M., & Baylor, D. A (1990). Visual transaction in cones of the monkey, Macaca Fascicularis. *Journal of Physiology, 427*, 618–713.
Schneeweis, D. M., & Schnapf, J. L. (1995). Photovoltage of rods and cones in the macaque retina. *Science, 268*, 1053–1056.
Schneeweis, D. M., & Schnapf, J. L. (1999). The photovoltage of macaque cone photoreceptors: Adaptation, noise, and kinetics. *Journal of Neuroscience, 19*, 1203–1216.
Shapley, R. M., & Enroth-Cugell, C. (1984). Visual adaptation and retinal gain controls. *Progress in Retinal Research, 3*, 263–346.
Sharpe, L. T., Stockman, A., Fach, C. C., & Markstahler, U. (1993). Temporal and spatial summation in the human rod visual system. *Journal of Physiology, 461*, 325–348.
Sharpe, L. T., & Stockman, A. (1999). Rod pathways: The importance of seeing nothing. *Trends in Neuroscience, 22*, 497–504.
Sherman, S. M., & Koch, C. (1998). Thalamus. In G. Shepherd (Ed.), *Synaptic organization of the brain* (Ch. 8, pp. 289–328). Oxford: Oxford University Press.
Sillito, A. M., Jones, H. E., Gertstein, G. L., & West, D. C. (1996). Feature-linked synchronization of thalamic relay cell firing induced by feedback from the visual cortex. *Nature, 369*, 479–482.
Singer, W., & Gray, C. M. (1995). Visual feature integration and the temporal correlation hypoth-

esis. *Annual Review of Neuroscience, 18*, 555–586.

Sterling, P. (1998). Retina. In G. Shepherd (Ed.), *Synaptic organization of the brain* (Ch. 6, pp. 205–254). Oxford: Oxford University Press.

Sur, M. (1999). Rewiring cortex the role of patterned activity in development and plasticity of neocortical circuits. *Journal of Neurobiology, 41*, 33–43.

Thibos, L. N., Cheney, F. E., & Walsh, D. J. (1987). Retinal limits to the detection and resolution of gratings. *Journal of the Optical Society of America, 67*, 696–698.

Tovée, M. J. (1994). The molecular genetics and evolution of primate colour vision. *Trends in Neuroscience, 17*, 30–37.

Tovée, M. J. (1996). *An introduction to the visual system*. Cambridge, UK: Cambridge University Press.

Ungerleider, L. G., & Mishkin, M. (1982). Two cortical visual systems. In D. J. Ingle, R. J. W. Mansfield, & M. S. Goodale (Eds.), *The analysis of visual behavior* (pp. 549–586). Cambridge, MA: MIT Press.

Usrey, W. M., & Reid, R. C. (1999). Synchronous activity in the visual system. *Annual Review of Physiology, 61*, 435–456.

Van Essen, D. C., Anderson, C. H., & Felleman, D. J. (1992). Information processing in the primate visual system: An integrated systems perspective. *Science, 255*, 419–423.

Walraven, J., Enroth-Cugell, C., Hood, D. C., MacLeod, D. I. A., & Schnapf, J. L. (1990). The control of visual sensitivity: Receptoral and postreceptoral processes. In L. Spillman & J. Werner (Eds.), *Vision perception: The neurophysiological foundations* (pp. 53–101). New York: Academic Press.

Wandell, B. (1995). *Foundations of vision*. Sunderland, MA: Sinauer Associates Inc.

Wässle, H., Koulen, P., Brandstätter, J. H., Fletcher, E. L., & Becker, C.-M. (1998). Glycine and GABA receptors in the mammalian retina. *Vision Research, 38*, 1411–1430.

Wertheim, T. (1981). Peripheral visual acuity. Reprint (I. L. Dunsky, Trans.). *American Journal of Optometry and Phyisological Optics, 57*, 915–924, 1980.

Williams, D. R. (1986). Seeing through the photoreceptor mosaic. *Trends in Neurosience, 9*, 193–197.

Williams, D. R., Brainard, D. H., McMahon, M. J., & Navarro, R. (1994). Double-pass and interferometric measures of optical quality of the eye. *Journal of the Optical Society of America A, 11*, 3123–3135.

Williams, D., MacLeod, D. I. A., & Hayhoe, M. (1981). Punctate sensitivity of the blue sensitive mechanisms. *Vision Research, 21*, 1357–1375.

Wilson, H. R., & Regan, D. (1984). Spatial-frequency adaptation and grating discrimination: Predictions of a line-element model. *Journal of the Optical Society of America A, 1*, 1091–1096.

Wilson, J. R. (1993). Circuitry of the dorsal lateral geniculate nucleus in the cat and monkey. *Acta Anatomica, 147*, 1–13.

Xu, L., Frishman, L. J., & Robson, J. G. (1998). Effects of light adaptation on the sensitivity and kinetics of the rod P2 component of the cat ERG. *Investigative Ophthalmology & Visual Science Supplement, 39*, S976.

Yau, K.-W. (1994). Phototransduction mechanisms in retinal rods and cones. The Friedenwald Lecture. *Investigative Ophthalmology & Visual Science, 35*, 9–32.

Chapter Four

Color Vision[1]

James Gordon and Israel Abramov

Introduction

Contrary to popular misconceptions, some form of color vision is probably the rule rather than the exception, at least among mammals (Jacobs, 1991, 1998; Neumeyer, 1991). But what exactly is "color vision"?

Color vision is the ability to discriminate among different wavelengths of light regardless of their relative intensities: Two lights of sufficiently different wavelengths will always appear different in some fashion – the experience of color is indeed associated with wavelength. But, this does not mean that if the wavelength is known, the resulting sensation must always be known. Color sensation derives entirely from processing by the nervous system: "For the rays to speak properly are not coloured. In them there is nothing else than a certain power and disposition to stir up a sensation of this or that Colour" (Newton, 1704). In this chapter, we will concentrate on how lights stir up different sensations of color.

The absence of invariant correspondence between wavelength and color is exemplified by additive color mixing: A mixture of two wavelengths can be exactly equivalent visually to a third wavelength. Such visual equivalences of physically different stimuli are termed "metamers." For example, when a light of a wavelength that looks blue is added to one that looks yellow, the result appears white; or, a mixture of red-appearing and green-appearing wavelengths can be made indistinguishable from a completely different wavelength that appears yellow. Another, and more familiar way of mixing colors is subtractive color mixing, when two paints are mixed to produce a third color. In this case each of the pigments subtracts or absorbs some wavelengths from the illumination falling on it and reflects the rest; the color of the mixture is determined by the wavelengths subtracted by neither pigment. Thus, when yellow and blue paint are mixed the only wavelengths reflected are those that usually appear green. But always, color sensation depends on the wavelengths entering the eye and how they stir up the nervous sysem.

Minimum Requirements for Color Vision

The retinal light receptors are the rods and cones. Rods subserve vision under dim, scotopic, illumination, whereas cones require more intense, photopic, illumination. We will confine ourselves to cones. The fovea has only cones and has excellent color vision. Are all

(a)

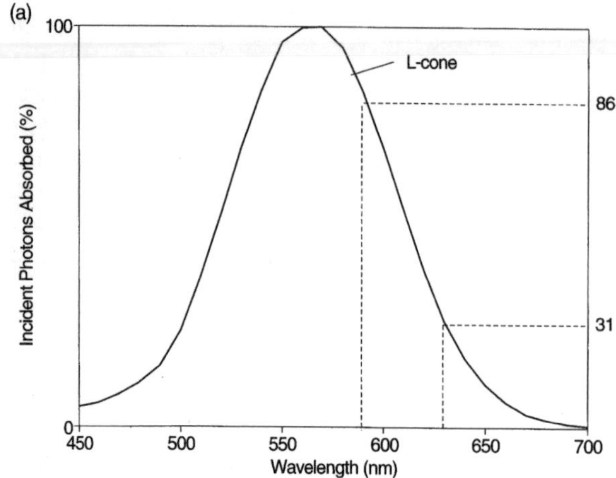

Stimulus		Photone absorbed by cones	
Wavelength (nm)	Photons	L	M
590	1,000	860	
630	1,000	310	
590	1,000	860	
630	2,774	860	

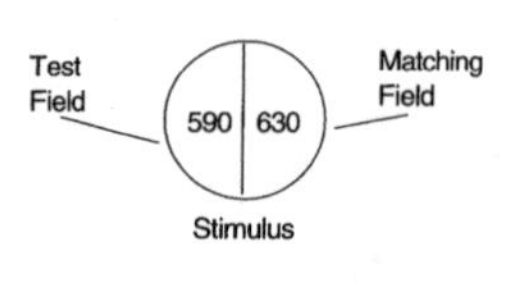

(b)

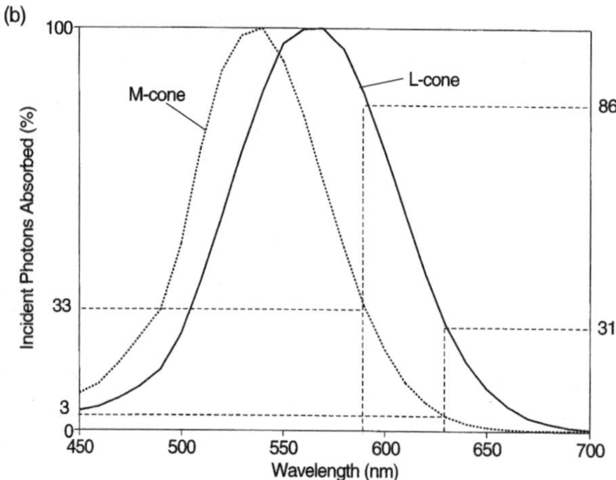

Stimulus		Photone absorbed by cones	
Wavelength (nm)	Photons	L	M
590	1,000	860	330
630	2,774	860	83
590	2,606	2,241	860
630	28,667	8,867	860

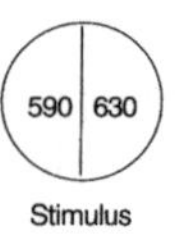

(c)

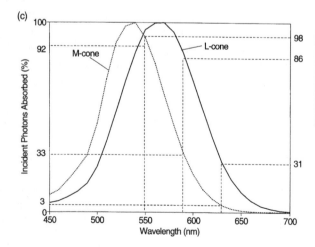

100
98
92
M-cone
L-cone
86
33
31
3
0
450
500
550
600
650
700
Wavelength (nm)
Incident Photons Absorbed (%)

Stimulus		Photone absorbed by cones	
Wavelength (nm)	Photons	L	M
590	1,000	860	330
550	299	293	275
+	+	+	+
630	1,830	567	55
		860	330

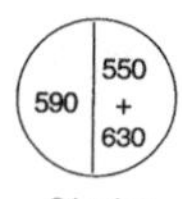

cones the same? All receptors transduce light through their photopigments, but different receptors have different photopigments, which determine the receptors' spectral sensitivities. When a photopigment molecule absorbs a photon its chemical structure is changed (bleached); the resultant chemical cascade leads to a neural response by the receptor. (See Bowmaker, 1991; Goldsmith, 1991; Piantanida, 1991; Rodieck, 1998.)

Figure 4.1a illustrates the consequences if all cones contain the same photopigment. In this example, a subject views a bipartite field with a test wavelength of 590 nm on the left and a different wavelength, 630 nm, on the right, whose intensity will be adjusted to try to match the appearance of the test light. The table indicates the numbers of incident photons of each wavelength that are absorbed (these numbers are not intended to be realistic but to illustrate the argument). When the two fields are equal in intensity, the cones stimulated by the 590 nm test field absorb more photons and respond more strongly. But if intensity of the 630 nm matching field is increased to compensate for the difference in ability of the pigment to absorb that wavelength, the cones on each side absorb the same numbers of photons. The two sides are now indistinguishable because of a basic property of a photoreceptor: univariance. Any visible photon absorbed by a photopigment molecule causes the same change in the structure of the molecule. Thus any information about the wavelength of the photon is lost once it has been absorbed. An observer with only these cones would not be able to distinguish the two fields other than by differences in their relative intensities; the observer would not have color vision and would be termed a monochromat – this is in principle what happens when only rods subserve vision (dim lights viewed peripherally).

Minimally, two spectrally distinct cone types are needed for color vision. As illustrated in Figure 4.1b, in which we have added a second cone, there is no intensity for the matching field that results in the same response to the two wavelengths for both cone types simultaneously. Two spectrally different receptors resolve the spectral ambiguity that exists for just one receptor type. If the absorptions from the two sides are equal for one of the cone types, they will not be equal for the other. However, if a third wavelength (550 nm) is added to the matching side, the relative intensities of each of the additively mixed wavelengths can be adjusted so that each cone type absorbs the same total number of photons from matching and test fields and the two fields become indistinguishable. The two matching wavelengths are called "primaries"; the only restriction on choice of primary wavelengths is that they be independent – it should not be possible to match the appearance of one primary with the other. When only two cone types exist, *any* test light can be matched with two primaries; an individual with only two cone types is termed a dichromat.

←

Figure 4.1. Absorption of photons by cone photopigments and additive color mixing. Bipartite stimulus field with test wavelength of 590 nm; observer adjusts intensity of matching field to try to make the two half fields appear identical. Tables show numbers of photons incident on the cones and numbers actually absorbed. (a) All observer's cones contain the same photopigment; intensity of matching field can be adjusted so that cone absorptions (and therefore responses) are exactly the same from both field sides. (b) Observer has two types of cones, equally distributed across the entire stimulus field; with a single matching wavelength; absorptions can be equalized for one or other cone type but not simultaneously for both. (c) Same as (b), except that matching field is an additive mixture of two wavelengths; by separately adjusting the intensities of the matching wavelengths it is possible to equate simultaneously absorptions by both cone types.

Extending these arguments, individuals with three cone types require three primaries and are trichromats. When we describe the neuronal processing of cone responses that leads to color sensation, we will show why a third cone type is necessary to resolve spectral ambiguities that still remain if the retina contains only two cone types. While all cone pigments are sensitive to a broad spectral range, one is more sensitive to short wavelengths (S-cone), another to middle wavelengths (M-cone), and the third to long wavelengths (L-cone). (Spectra in Figure 4.1 are those for L- and M-cones.) As we shall see later, many humans have more than three cone types and trichromacy must be imposed by the nervous system which somehow melds cone responses into three fundamental channels (Jacobs, 1993). For the moment we will simplify by continuing to speak of three cone types.

Chromaticity and Luminance

Chromaticity

The existence of metamers shows that the spectra of stimuli may not be enough to specify their appearance. We need to describe stimuli in a way that takes note of how spectrally different stimuli might elicit identical sensations.

Color-normal humans are trichromats and need only three primaries to match exactly any test light (Boynton, 1996). Typically, three widely separated wavelengths are chosen as primaries and mixed to match the appearance of all other visible wavelengths. Because each investigator is free to choose the three primaries, the empirical functions need not resemble each other, but each data set presumably reflects the operation of the same three spectral filters in the visual system. Despite a century's collection of precise three-primary color matches, it has been difficult to deduce a unique trio of spectral functions to describe the visual system's fundamental filters. Indeed, if these fundamental filters are linear operators, there is an infinite number of filter trios that satisfy the data. In response to this problem, in 1931 the CIE (Commission Internationale de l'Eclairage, the body that codifies photometric and colorimetric standards) settled on a specific set of spectral weighting coefficients. These are denoted $\bar{x}$, $\bar{y}$, $\bar{z}$ (Figure 4.2a) and can be used to weight the spectral energies of any stimulus (e.g., Figure 4.2b).

A stimulus can then be specified in terms of its metameric equivalent; that is, the relative amounts of activation of the three fundamentals needed to produce the same appearance as the given stimulus (see inset equation; also, Additional Topics). The calculated equivalent stimulus can be plotted in a two-dimensional color space (Figure 4.2c). The horseshoe-shaped curve is the locus of all single wavelengths and is the outer boundary of all realizable light stimuli; stimuli that plot inside the diagram appear more washed out, or desaturated, and tend towards white. The weighting functions in Figure 4.2a can be linearly remapped onto other trios of coefficients; while the resulting color spaces will look different, they will still embody exactly the same matching data – the CIE has subsequently specified several such variants.

More recent forms of chromaticity diagrams are based on currently acceptable estimates of the spectra of the visual system's three fundamental filters, which may correspond to three cone types (see next section). Such color spaces have all the same general properties as

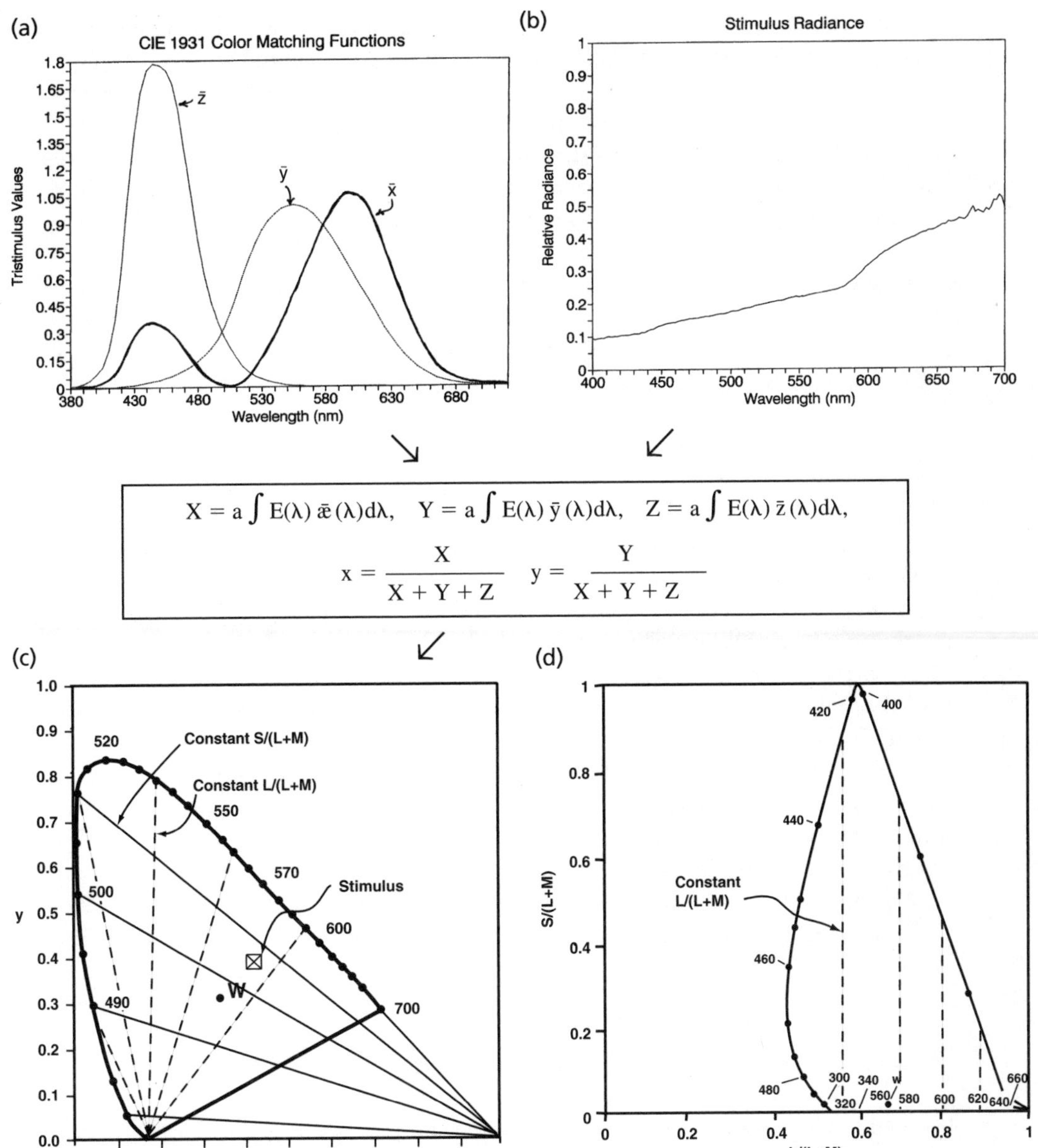

Figure 4.2. Chromaticity. Trichromatic observers can exactly match any stimulus with an additive mixture of three primary lights. (a) Spectral distributions of the three "primaries" adopted by the CIE in 1931. (b) Spectral distribution of light from a stimulus; the functions in (a) are used to weight the spectrum of the stimulus – see upper equations in box. (c) CIE 1931 chromaticity diagram; lower equations in box show normalization of weighted stimulus spectrum so that it can be located in the two-dimensional diagram; horseshoe-shaped curve is the locus of all single wavelengths and is the outer boundary of physically realizable stimuli; W, center of diagram, denotes equal-energy white; see text, P and M Pathways, for explanation of the radiating lines. (d) Chromaticity diagram using spectral sensitivities of L-, M-, and S-cones as the "primaries."

does the CIE space in Figure 4.2c, with the advantage that they would relate directly to physiological processes; an example is shown in Figure 4.2d (MacLeod & Boynton, 1979).

The above chromaticity diagrams, including those based on cone spectra, are systems for describing in standard terms how different lights, including reflections by real objects, stimulate the visual system. If two stimuli with different spectra nonetheless plot to the same location on a chromaticity diagram after their spectra are appropriately weighted, then those stimuli are metamers and exert the same effect on vision – they are visually indistinguishable. By itself, this tells us little about their actual appearance: If a light is surrounded by a different light its appearance may change, though its specification on the chromaticity diagram remains exactly as it was. For example, a gray field surrounded by green will appear tinged with red, but the spectrum of the gray has not physically changed – its position on the chromaticity diagram is unchanged.

Luminance

Metamers, as described above, are indistinguishable. This, however, ignores the "intensive" dimension – for chromaticity calculations, everything is normalized so that absolute intensities of the primaries are factored out (see equations, Figure 4.2). But one side of the matched bipartite field can be made to appear more or less "intense" or "luminous" simply by adjusting its overall intensity, for example, by placing a dark filter over one side. For visual purposes, stimulus intensity is measured in units of luminance, which are derived from the findings that we are not equally sensitive to all parts of the spectrum. Two wavelengths that appear different (e.g., one looks red and the other green) can be made equally luminous or visible by adjusting their relative intensities. By adjusting the intensities of a series of wavelengths, viewed in the fovea, so that each is just visible, we can specify a spectral sensitivity function for the visual system as a whole. For the cone-based photopic system this was defined by the CIE as V_λ, which, incidentally, is identical with the weighting function in the standard chromaticity diagram (Figure 4.2). Note that this spectral sensitivity curve is an average across observers and is specific to one particular set of viewing conditions – in practice, relative luminosity will vary across individuals and conditions.

Spectra of the Visual System's Three Fundamentals

It would be illuminating were it possible to base a chromaticity diagram on actual spectral properties of the visual system's initial filters, the cones, as was attempted for the diagram in Figure 4.2d. What are the measured cone spectra?

Psychophysical Estimates

Psychophysical measures of these spectra usually depend either on the fact that the visual system adapts (sensitivity reduces as ambient light intensity increases), or that some individuals, the so-called genetically color-blind, may lack a cone type.

Adaptation studies use background lights of wavelengths that might affect one spectral channel more than the others; that channel would be differentially desensitized, thus facilitating measurement of the spectrum of the remaining channel(s). There are many variants of this approach (Stiles, 1978; Pugh & Kirk, 1986; Stockman, MacLeod, & Johnson, 1993; Hood, 1998). Ultimately, intense chromatic adaptation bleaches one cone's photopigment to the point that a three-cone trichromatic subject is reduced to a dichromat or even a monochromat, allowing direct measurement of the remaining cones' spectra (e.g., Brindley, 1960). We will consider later the problem of channels that behave as if they were single cone types when in fact their responses are amalgams of several cone types.

An alternative psychophysical approach is to use individuals who, because of genetic defects, lack one or more of the three cone types. Since the foveas of normal individuals have relatively few S-cones, the foveas of those who lack either L- or M-cones (protanopes and deuteranopes, respectively) are assumed to be populated largely by a single cone type whose spectral sensitivity can be measured readily (Figure 4.3a).

Photopigment Absorption Spectra

Spectral sensitivity of a photoreceptor is determined by the ability of its photopigment to absorb photons of different wavelengths. Unlike rhodopsin, the rod photopigment, cone photopigments cannot be readily extracted to form a solution whose spectral absorption can be measured. They are usually measured *in situ* using isolated cones (microspectrophotometry; e.g., MacNichol, 1986) or by measuring, in the intact eye, light not absorbed by any pigments – that is, by measuring the light reflected back out of the eye (e.g., Rushton, 1972). A problem is that whereas the wavelengths to which the cone is most sensitive are well specified by these techniques, wavelengths away from the peak of the absorption function are severely noise-limited. Moreover, non-photopigment structures in the measuring beam may influence the measurements. For example, the spectra of isolated cones are not the same as their *effective* spectra in the intact eye. Usually, stimulus intensity is measured at the cornea, but ocular structures absorb some light before it reaches the receptors. Much of this pre-retinal absorption (Figure 4.3b) is in the lens and cornea; additionally, central retina, including the fovea (macula), is overlain by a pigment that also filters out short wavelengths.

Spectrophotometric methods, despite their difficulties, showed the existence of three distinct populations of cones in Old World primates, such as humans and macaque monkeys (Bowmaker, 1991).

Electrophysiology

Recently, spectra have been obtained from measurements of the electrical responses of single primate cones: Spectra are derived directly by measuring, at each wavelength, stimulus intensity required to elicit a criterion response. Thus, the cone itself is being used as a very sensitive, univariant photon counter. Unlike spectrophotometry, noise associated with recording does not vary with wavelength and spectra can be extended over a wide range. The clearest data, from macaques, show that each cone contains one of three photopigments (Baylor, Nunn, & Schnapf, 1987), whose peaks, at approximately 430, 530 and 560 nm, agree well with spectrophotometry. (See Figure 4.3a for similar data from humans.) Although all such spectra appear progressively broader on a linear wavelength axis, all have

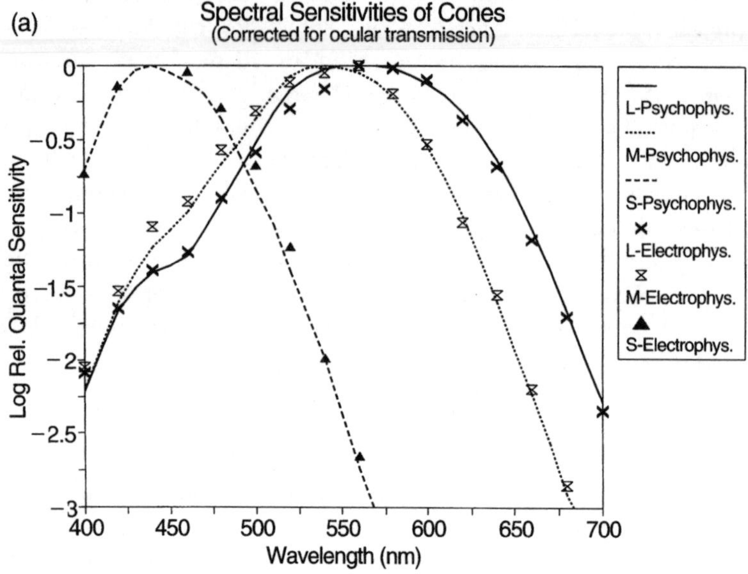

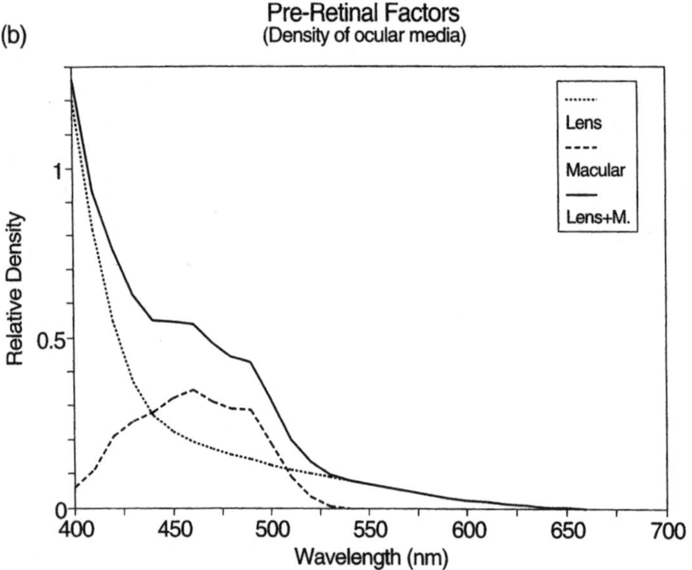

Figure 4.3. Spectral properties of the eye. (a) Spectral sensitivities of L-, M-, and S-cones measured psychophysically (lines; Smith and Pokorny, 1975) and electrophysiologically (symbols; Schnapf et al., 1987). (b) Light absorption by pre-retinal structures (lens and macular pigment); in (a), the "Lens+M" curve was used to adjust the single cone spectra for comparison with psychophysical data. (c) Responses of a spectrally opponent ganglion cell that combines opposed inputs from L- and

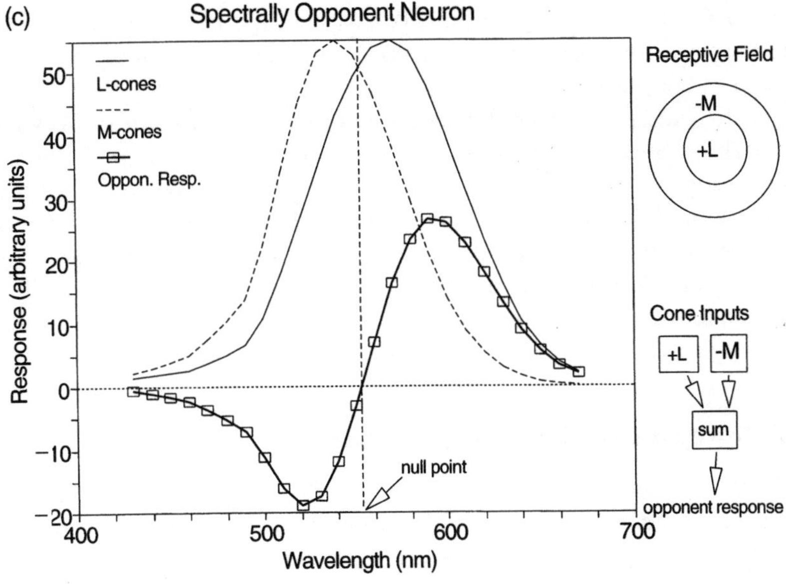

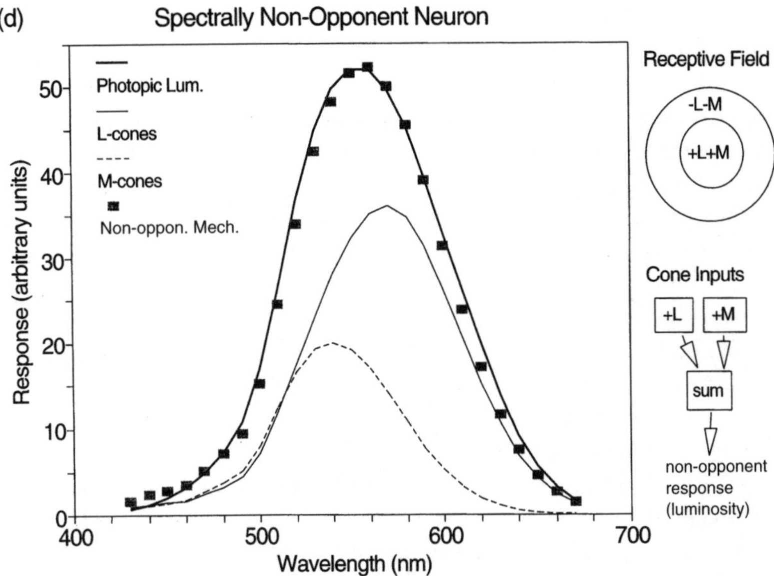

M-cones; simplified schematic of combination (bottom right) and spatial organization of receptive field (upper right). (d) Responses of spectrally non-opponent ganglion cell (symbols) combining, with same sign, inputs from L- and M-cones; heavy line represents CIE photopic luminosity function; simplified schematic of combination (bottom right) and spatial organization of receptive field (upper right).

exactly the same shape when plotted in a coordinate space that directly relates to the quantal nature of light absorption (Mansfield, 1985; MacNichol, 1986); this observation of a common shape is useful because a cone's spectrum is fully specified when its peak wavelength is known (Dartnall, 1953).

To compare cone spectra from different techniques, all must be treated comparably. Figure 4.3a shows human psychophysical spectra (Smith & Pokorny, 1975), for which stimulus intensity was measured at the cornea; of necessity they include the effects of pre-retinal absorption. To compare these curves with the superimposed points from isolated cones (Schnapf, Kraft, & Baylor, 1987), the cone spectra were corrected for pre-retinal absorption (Figure 4.3b). The nice fit between the two sets of data is at least partly due to this correction for pre-retinal factors.

Spectral Processing by the Nervous System

Different cone spectra, by themselves, are not enough for color vision. Here we will consider the other essentials: What are the necessary operations, and what criteria must be met before we assert that given neurons perform these operations? We then outline known physiology and how it might be related to the needed operations.

Gedanken or Hypothetical Physiology

At least two cone types are needed for any color vision (Figure 4.1). Equally essential are neurons that compare the outputs of these cones and report that they were not equally stimulated by different wavelengths; such neurons are spectrally opponent. A hypothetical spectrally opponent neuron (Figure 4.3c) would be excited by its associated L-cones and inhibited by its M-cones. This neuron reports the sum of these inputs: For longer wavelengths the net sum is positive and for shorter it is negative. Also, there is a wavelength at which the opposed inputs equal each other (null point) and no overt response is elicited. While this neuron signals something about wavelength, its responses are still ambiguous: It fails to respond either when there is no light, or when a light's wavelength is the same as its null point, or when combinations of wavelengths and intensities produce canceling excitatory and inhibitory responses.

A spectrally opponent neuron divides the spectrum into two zones on either side of a spectral neutral point. Wavelengths on one side of the neutral point elicit excitation, possibly perceived as one particular hue; wavelengths on the other side elicit inhibition, perceived as a second hue. But the neuron's spectral responses are still partially confounded with responses to changes in intensity. Responses to any two excitatory wavelengths can be equated simply by adjusting their relative intensities. Many of these ambiguities can be resolved by having another type of neuron, a spectrally non-opponent neuron (Figure 4.3d), that combines the same cone inputs but with the same sign; such a neuron is inherently color-blind, for the same reasons that a single cone is color-blind. Individuals with only these two neuronal types would be termed dichromats, whose color vision would still have major ambiguities: All wavelengths on one side of a neutral point would appear very similar. Further, responses of the opponent neuron can be nullified either by presenting light at the wavelength of the null point or some canceling combination of wavelengths, such as in "white" light. A trichromat's third cone allows for different spectrally opponent neurons with different null points; thus, no spectral region appears colorless.

We have considered only the spectral response properties of neurons. However, each neuron also has a receptive field, the area of retina whose cones provide the inputs to the neuron. These receptive fields may be spatially antagonistic; the insets to Figures 4.3c and 4.3d show how the different cone types might be divided across the receptive fields.

Before discussing possible models of these neurons we will describe propositions to link physiological and psychological domains and outline what is known from real physiology. The aim is to assess how well the physiology, as we know it now, accounts for color vision.

Psycho-Physiological Linking Propositions

"We experience red when neuron A is excited" is not the same as "we experience red *only* when neuron A is excited." We avoid using color terminology unless we explicitly mean a link with sensation. An L-cone is not a red-cone; trivially, it responds to some degree to all wavelengths, and the wavelength at its spectral peak (560 nm) usually appears yellowish-green. Similarly, a spectrally opponent neuron is wavelength-selective, but is "color-coded" only if one asserts that its responses directly determine sensation of some color.

Our psycho-physiological linking proposition is that for any particular category of sensation (e.g., red) there is a neural mechanism whose response properties match those of the related psychophysical functions; when, and only when, that mechanism responds do we experience that sensation (Brindley, 1960; Teller, 1984). We will use the term *mechanism* only in this restricted sense. However, a sensation need not be determined entirely by responses of a single neuron – the mechanism might be delineated by the joint activities of a group of neurons none of which, by itself, fulfills all the requirements.

Human color vision is trichromatic, and three dimensions are necessary and sufficient to specify appearance of any light. But the dimensions need not be the primaries of chromaticity diagrams. Additive color-matching experiments specify only that color vision can be described along three dimensions. The dimensions could equally well be the three sensory dimensions of hue, saturation, and brightness, which together comprise color. Hue is described by words such as red or purple. Saturation is the "concentration" of hue; white has no hue (zero saturation), while a pastel is a weakly saturated hue – pink is a weakly saturated red. Brightness is the apparent intensity of a light – as physical intensity of a light increases, brightness increases, though not necessarily in proportion.

Rather than attempting a complete, abstract hierarchy of propositions, we will describe what is currently known about spectral properties of neurons and then apply particular examples of propositions to show why given neurons might or might not be color mechanisms. Our central principle is that *all* relevant attributes of color sensation must be included in the responses of any putative color mechanism.

Wet Physiology

We concentrate on the macaque monkey, an Old World primate that has been extensively studied and has cone pigments, anatomical organization, and psychophysical color discriminations very similar to those of humans (Jacobs, 1991, 1998).

Retina and Thalamus

In the fovea and near periphery, each cone provides an input to two midget bipolar cells, ON and OFF types, which are the inputs to spectrally opponent ganglion cells (Wässle & Boycott, 1991; Dacey, 1996); additionally, each cone feeds into diffuse bipolars, which are the inputs to spectrally non-opponent ganglion cells. Axons of several classes of ganglion cells exit the retina to synapse in the visual system's thalamic relay center, the lateral geniculate nucleus (LGN), whose neurons, in turn, project to primary visual cortex ("striate" cortex, or V1). Responses of LGN and retinal ganglion cells are effectively the same, since each LGN cell is driven primarily by one ganglion cell (Kaplan & Shapley, 1984). Three-quarters of a macaque's ganglion cells are spectrally opponent and terminate in the parvocellular layers of the LGN (P-cells). Most of the remaining ganglion cells are spectrally non-opponent and terminate in the magnocellular layers of the LGN (M-cells) – warning: An M-*cell* is either a ganglion cell or its LGN target, while an M-*cone* is a particular type of receptor. Both pathways are divided between ON and OFF varieties, which refers to the spatial organization of their receptive fields; mostly, these are circular, with centers whose responses are antagonized by responses from a larger surround; for example, an ON-cell is excited by light falling on the center of its field (Kaplan, Lee, & Shapley, 1990).

Most spectrally opponent P-cells are associated only with L- and M-cones, by far the most numerous cone types. For the fovea and near periphery, the center of each cell's receptive field is driven by a single cone (Wässle & Boycott 1991; Dacey, 1996); whichever cone drives the center, the best evidence is that the other is the exclusive input to the surround (Reid & Shapley, 1992; Lee, Kremers, & Yeh, 1998); therefore, these cells must all be spectrally opponent and are usually also spatially opponent (Figure 4.3c). Input to the centers of M-cell receptive fields is a combination, with same sign, of L- and M-cone responses, and the same types, with changed sign, constitute the surrounds of the fields (Figure 4.3d). Thus, M-cells are spatially opponent but spectrally non-opponent (Lee, Pokorny, Smith, Martin, & Valberg, 1990).

Figure 4.4 summarizes the cone inputs to known cell types – six spectrally opponent and two non-opponent. When stimuli are large enough to cover entire receptive fields, neurons no longer respond to variations in spatial patterning but continue to respond to spectral variations. For such stimuli, LGN P-cells have been divided into four classes (bottom of Figure 4.4); both LM cell types have similar spectral null points, and can be thought of as a single spectral system; S/LM types also have null points similar to each other, but at shorter wavelengths (De Valois, Abramov, & Jacobs, 1966; Derrington, Krauskopf, & Lennie, 1984). These two spectral classes of P-cells, with widely separated null points, are the minimum needed to disambiguate information available from only one spectrally opponent system (Gedanken Physiology, above) – comparing responses of one spectrally

Ganglion Cells – Receptive Fields

	Spectrally Opponent (P)			Spectrally Non-opponent (M)
ON	[+L]−M	[+M]−L	[+ S]−(+L+M)*	[+L+M]−(+L+M)
OFF	[−L] + M	[−M]+L	[−S]+(+ L+M)*	[−L−M]+(+L+M)

P-Ganglion Cells – Spectral Types

LM Cells	S/LM Cells
+L−M	+S−(+L+M)
+M−L	−S+(+L+M)

Notes:

[ ] denotes cone input to center of receptive field.

* due to chromatic aberration, centers and surrounds of these fields may be spatially co-extensive (Calkins et al., 1998).

Figure 4.4. Cone inputs to spatially opponent and non-opponent cells.

opponent system to those of the other yields continuous information about changes in wavelength.

P and M Pathways

P- and M-cells project to cortical area V1 and are the inputs to parallel pathways, thought to continue through the visual system, that subserve separate visual functions. Beyond V1 there are multiple secondary representations of the visual world (V2, V3, and so on), each thought to emphasize a different aspect of visual information. Anatomically, one stream goes dorsally from V1 to parietal centers, while the other courses ventrally to the temporal lobe. The major sources are said to be M-cells for the dorsal stream and P-cells for the ventral stream. But this greatly oversimplifies the anatomy. Most realistic wiring diagrams include massive interactions between P and M pathways beyond V1 (Van Essen, Anderson, & Felleman, 1992).

Dorsal and ventral streams had been said to subserve "where" and "what" functions (Ungerleider & Mishkin, 1982); recently it has been argued that their functions are more properly described as "how" and "what" (Milner & Goodale, 1995). At a basic sensory level, the P-pathway is said to deal mainly with form and color, while the M-pathway subserves motion, stereoscopic depth, and luminance (Hubel & Livingstone, 1987; Merigan & Maunsell, 1993).

How can we separate P- and M-contributions to specific sensory functions? Stimuli can be configured to modulate only the responses of one cell type. For example, because the spectral sensitivity of an M-cell matches the psychophysical luminosity function V_λ (Lee et al., 1990), alternating between wavelengths equated for luminance will produce no *change* in that cell's responses; however, the same equi-luminant stimuli will produce vigorous changes in responses of P-cells.

More generally, one can use a technique (originally devised for psychophysical experiments; Krauskopf, Williams, & Heeley, 1982) that allows choice of sets of stimuli that modulate responses of only M-cells or only a single class of P-cell. For example, stimuli that lie on one of the lines marked "constant L/(L+M)" in Figure 4.2c will elicit different responses from S-cones while keeping the difference between L- and M-cones fixed; this means that only the responses of P-cells with S-cone inputs (see Figure 4.4) will be modulated (Derrington et al., 1984). Each of the two sets of radiating lines in Figure 4.2c represents stimuli that modulate a single class of P-cell; they represent two "cardinal axes" or directions in color space.

Findings from the above methods have been confirmed by physically lesioning either the P- or M-layers (Schiller, Logothetis, & Charles, 1990; Merigan & Maunsell, 1993). When M-layers are lesioned, there are no losses of visual acuity or chromatic contrast sensitivity and losses are confined mostly to luminance-varying stimuli that change rapidly and are relatively large. Lesions in P-layers, on the other hand, reduce sensitivity to relatively small stimuli slowly varying in luminance; most importantly, much of color vision is lost. But this oversimplifies the findings (Cavanagh, 1991) – each of these neurons simultaneously carries information relevant to many functions.

Are There Neurons That Are Hue Mechanisms?

None of the neurons we have described qualifies as a sensory mechanism. P-cells are not hue mechanisms, despite their sometimes being called color-coded or labeled with terms such as +R−G, implying that they encode redness when excited and greenness when inhibited (De Valois et al., 1966; Derrington et al., 1984; Hubel & Livingstone, 1987). Although our strictures apply to all P- and M-cells, we will use as an illustration only the "+R−G" cells (more appropriately labeled +L−M):

1. They respond to achromatic white and therefore cannot uniquely signal redness.
2. The wavelength at which their spectral response functions cross from excitation to inhibition should correspond to a lack of R and G, which would define the wavelength of a uniquely yellow (Y) hue – the +Y−B cells are strongly excited by this same wavelength. However, null points of these RG neurons are not wavelengths that we see as Y – they appear chartreuse (greenish-yellow).
3. *Sensory* null points remain remarkably stable across conditions, but the *neuronal* null points are easily shifted by changing stimulus conditions (Marrocco & De Valois, 1977).

4. None of the response functions of +R−G cells cross back to excitation at short wavelengths, and yet short wavelengths elicit a sensation that includes some R (violet).
5. Modulation along one of the cardinal axes (Figure 4.2c) affects only one type of P-cell, but, psychophysically, shifts the appearance of all chromatic stimuli, regardless of whether they are on or off that axis (Webster & Mollon, 1991).

Usually, spectrally non-opponent M-cells are said to underlie the sensation of luminosity, largely because their spectral sensitivities match the standard photopic luminosity function (Lee et al., 1990). This is not the same as a brightness function. The standard luminosity function is measured by flicker photometry, and corresponds to $\bar{y}$ in Figure 4.2a. Spectral sensitivity functions, however, change markedly with measurement technique (Lee, 1991). The function obtained by adjusting non-flickering stimuli to appear equally bright is not the same as the function from M-cells – it includes marked inputs from spectrally opponent P-cells (Sperling, 1992).

Thus, while spectrally opponent P-cells are not themselves hue mechanisms, they do transmit some information about stimulus wavelength and must provide inputs to the sensory/perceptual hue mechanisms at later stages of the visual system; this, of course, requires disambiguation in order to strip from their responses those components that do not directly determine hue.

Where Do Hue Mechanisms Reside?

Hue mechanisms must derive from cortical recombinations of spectrally opponent responses of P-cells. Many cortical neurons, in areas V1 and V2, are spectrally opponent (Thorell, De Valois, & Albrecht, 1984; Dow & Vautin, 1987; Hubel & Livingstone, 1987; Lennie, Krauskopf, & Sclar, 1990), and some are even double opponent (e.g., +L−M center and +M−L surround), which has been said to be needed for color contrast (Gouras,1991a). However, none shows the disambiguation needed to separate hue from other attributes of a stimulus that are also derived from responses of P-cells – for example, most of these cortical cells still respond to achromatic patterns.

An area often touted as the color center is V4, a designation that applies strictly to the macaque monkey and whose human homologue is still being debated (Zeki, 1990; Plant, 1991). Many V4 neurons respond to narrow spectral ranges and, when stimulated with complex colored patterns, seem to exhibit color constancy (Zeki 1983; Schein & Desimone, 1990). But V4 cells by themselves cannot be the hue mechanisms – most respond well to achromatic stimuli, so their color responses are still ambiguous (Schein & Desimone, 1990). Furthermore, lesions of V4 disrupt many forms of learned visual discriminations, not just color (Schiller & Lee, 1991).

Looking for a color center assumes that visual sensations can be subdivided into separate processes and that color sensations can be dissociated from other sensory/perceptual dimensions (Davidoff, 1991). Evidence for an area dedicated to color processing comes from studies of achromatopsia, a loss of color vision associated with damage to some area of the central nervous system. It is not a loss of color knowledge – affected individuals can correctly state that leaves are green, or the sky is blue, but they cannot correctly identify the color of any object currently being viewed (Mollon, 1989; Zeki, 1990; Davidoff, 1991;

Plant, 1991). From brain-imaging studies (MRI and PET scans) candidate areas for hue or color centers are the temporal lobe's lingual and fusiform gyri, bordering V1 (Howard et al., 1998).

Severe achromatopsia may not be the same as complete loss of color vision, or inability to *discriminate* spectrally different stimuli regardless of intensity. Some individuals with achromatopsia can still discriminate spectrally different stimuli without being able to identify their hues (Victor, Maiese, Shapley, Sidtis, & Gazzaniga, 1989). This raises a problem. As we will show in the next section, sensory descriptions of color appearance can be used to derive traditional wavelength discrimination functions, implying that discrimination is based on *identifiable* differences in appearance.

Color Appearance

Our aim is to link physiology and sensation. One approach, "bottom-up," is to examine responses of neurons at successive levels of the visual system to find where the requisite linkage exists. As yet, we have not identified any physiological units whose responses directly determine sensations. An alternative is to use color sensations to constrain analyses of neuronal responses and guide creation of models. Such a use of phenomenology to infer physiology is the basis of Ewald Hering's (1920) seminal derivation of opponent processes underlying color vision. Following this "top-down" approach, we start by evaluating the techniques used to define color appearance.

Additive color mixing, used to generate chromaticity diagrams (Figure 4.2), cannot be used to describe color appearance: The position of a stimulus in such a color space is determined exclusively by its spectrum (see Figure 4.2 equations). However, the color *appearance* of a given stimulus (red, or pink, etc.) can change if viewing conditions change – for example, introducing a colored surround or changing adaptation state.

Many standardized systems have been devised to describe appearance along dimensions of perceived color space, such as hue, saturation, and brightness (Derefeldt, 1991). Most systems are realized as a set of colored chips varying in discrete steps along the perceptual axes, but there is little agreement on how to segment the hue dimension. We have found it very useful to ask subjects to describe their color sensations using a standard set of color words. But first, we must examine the justification for using linguistic terms as sensory measures.

Color Appearance and Color Terms

Contrary to the prevailing tradition of cultural relativism of all linguistic terms (Sapir-Whorf hypothesis), there is good evidence that denotations of common color words are universal and not culture-specific (Berlin & Kay 1969; Kay & McDaniel 1978; Kay, Berlin, & Merrifield, 1991; Hardin & Maffi, 1997). Across some 100 languages, 11 basic color terms have been identified, with the English equivalents of: white, black, red (R), yellow (Y), green (G), blue (B), brown, purple, pink, orange, and gray. These terms appear to have evolved in a particular sequence because a fixed set of rules seems to specify which terms are present in any language with less than the full set. Languages with only two basic terms have white and black, and those with three have white, black, and R; beyond this there are some variations in the sequence of inclusion of terms, although Y, G, and B precede any others.

Basic color terms have been said to reflect universal properties of the human nervous system and are linked explicitly to spectrally opponent physiological mechanisms (Ratliff, 1976). Similarity of the denotations of the basic color terms across languages is central to the universalist thesis. Although the range of colors to which a term applies varies with the number of basic terms in a language, within that range there is a privileged location, the "focus." Across languages with equivalent terms, foci fall on the same tight regions of color space. (Note: It is impossible to separate laundry correctly unless a culture has all 11 basic terms; Shirriff, 1991.)

Is there a set of basic color terms that is both necessary and sufficient to describe color sensations? Several lines of evidence converge on the fundamental nature of R, Y, G, B; though no one line is conclusive, together they are convincing. Studies range from multidimensional scaling (Gordon & Abramov, 1988; Shepard & Cooper, 1992) to experiments in which individual terms are omitted in order to test whether the remaining ones are still sufficient to describe sensation completely. R, Y, G, and B are necessary and sufficient – orange, violet, purple, brown are not necessary (Sternheim & Boynton, 1966; Fuld et al., 1983; Quinn, Rosano, & Wooten, 1988).

Is there a necessary pair of perceptual axes for hue space? Stemming from Hering's (1920) original work, the accepted bipolar hue axes are spectrally opponent RG and YB (Hurvich & Jameson, 1955). These axes are certainly sufficient – two completely different psychophysical techniques based on these axes yield very similar functions. In one technique (see below), observers use these hue terms to scale their color sensations. In the other, hue cancellation, one hue can be used to cancel its spectrally opponent counterpart. For example, any stimulus eliciting some sensation of G can be added to one eliciting R in order to cancel the R; the intensity of the added canceler measures the sensation that was canceled (Hurvich, 1981). Spectral functions of RG and YB mechanisms obtained from either method are approximately the same (Werner & Wooten, 1979). But, there is no obvious *a priori* justification for these precise axes – they might be chartreuse-violet and teal-cherry. Introspectively, we find it virtually impossible to think of canceling or scaling all hues in these terms and ultimately this is the principal justification for using RG and YB.

Hue and Saturation Scaling

Using the four unique hue sensations of R, Y, G, B, subjects can directly scale the magnitudes of their sensations (Jameson & Hurvich, 1959). In our method (Gordon & Abramov, 1988; Gordon, Abramov, & Chan, 1994), observers state percentages of their sensations using any combination of the four unique terms for a total of 100%; they also describe apparent saturation (percentage of their entire sensation, chromatic and achromatic, that was chromatic; Figures 4.5a, 4.5b). These four hue terms do not denote separate perceptual

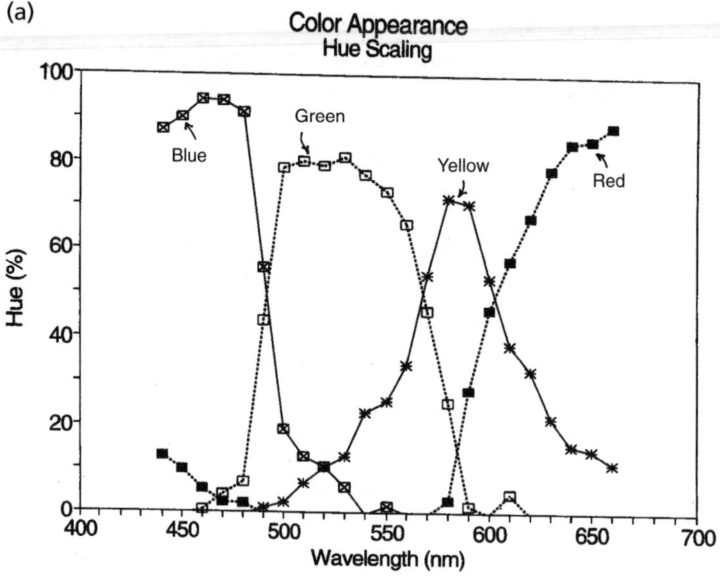

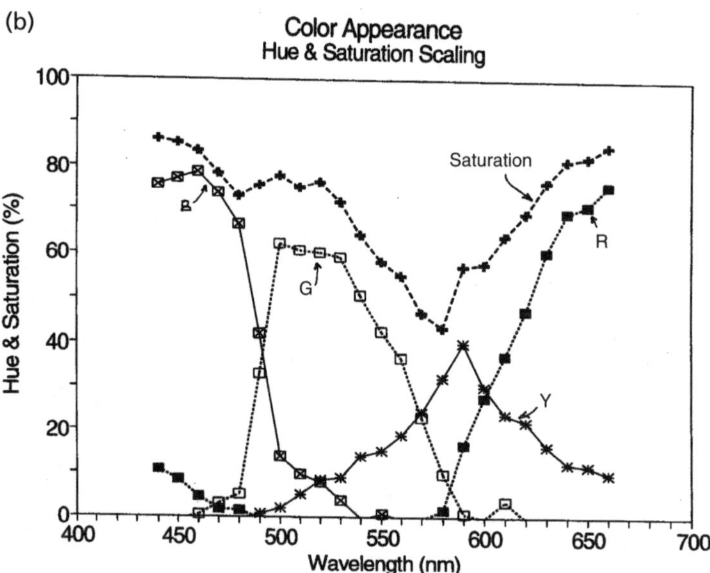

Figure 4.5. Color appearance of monochromatic lights equated for luminance. (a) Percentages of sensations of red, yellow, green, and blue elicited by each wavelength; mean data from a representative observer. (b) Upper curve shows percent saturation of each wavelength; hue curves are the same as those in (a) rescaled by percent saturation at each wavelength. (c) Uniform Appearance Diagram; smoothed, two-dimensional representation of the rescaled hue curves in (b). (d) Wavelength discrimination (symbols) from adjustment of wavelength to produce just noticeable differences; relative spacings of stimuli on UAD (c) used to derive the heavy curve.

(c)

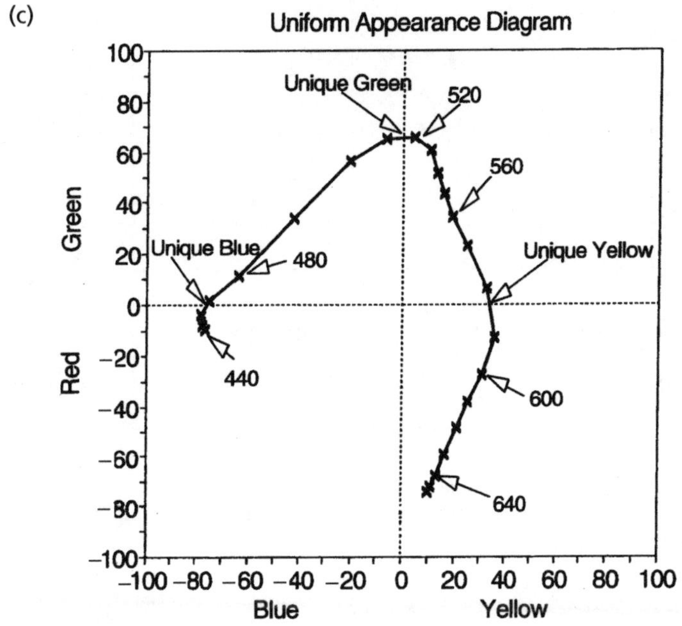
Uniform Appearance Diagram
Unique Green
520
560
Unique Blue
480
Unique Yellow
440
600
640
Green
Red
Blue
Yellow
100
80
60
40
20
0
−20
−40
−60
−80
−100
−100 −80 −60 −40 −20 0 20 40 60 80 100

(d)

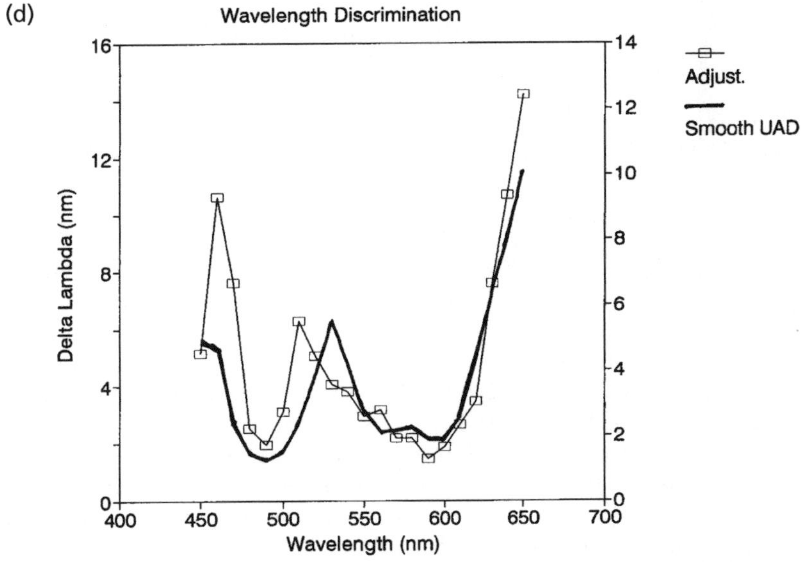
Wavelength Discrimination
Adjust.
Smooth UAD
Delta Lambda (nm)
Wavelength (nm)
16
12
8
4
0
14
12
10
8
6
4
2
0
400 450 500 550 600 650 700

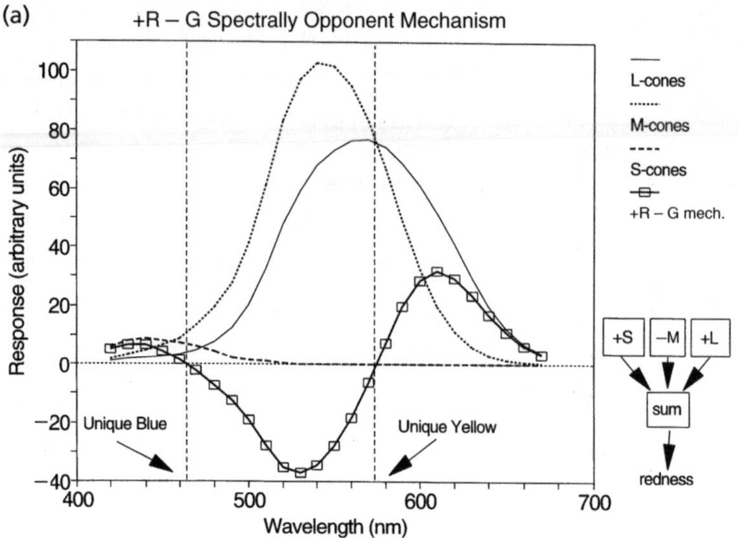

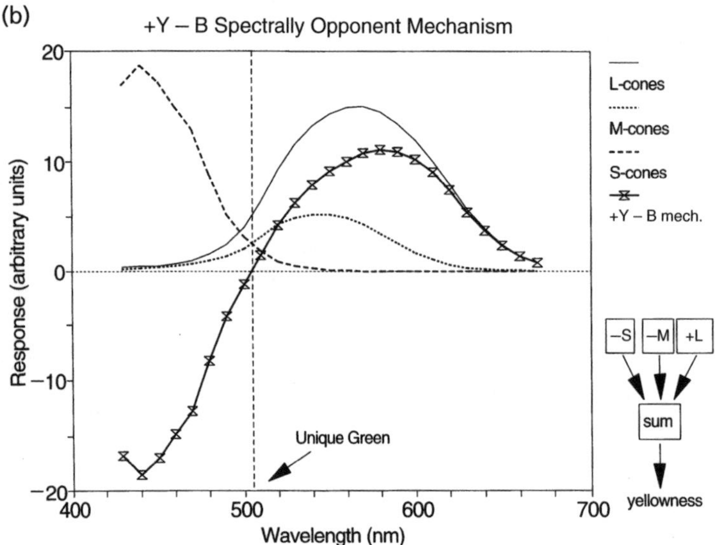

Figure 4.6. Hue mechanisms and color appearance. (a) +R−G spectrally opponent mechanism derived from weighted combination of responses of L-, M-, and S-cones – see schematic (lower right); changing signs yields a +G−R mechanism; zero R or G responses are the spectral loci of unique blue and unique yellow, as indicated. (b) +Y−B spectrally opponent mechanism derived from weighted combination of responses of L-, M-, and S-cones – see schematic (lower right); changing signs yields a +B−Y mechanism; zero Y or B responses is the spectral locus of unique green, as indicated. (c) Plausible combination of P-cell receptive fields to yield a +R−G hue mechanism; similar combinations, but with different signs, yield the other hue mechanisms. (d) Hue functions derived from responses of RG and YB hue mechanisms; at any wavelength, the percentage for any given hue is the ratio of that mechanism's response to the total responses of all hue mechanisms; curves derived from response functions in (a) and (b). (e) Saturation, from responses of hue and luminosity mechanisms; derived from ratio of responses of summed hue mechanisms (a, b) to sum of hue mechanisms plus spectrally non-opponent luminosity mechanisms (Figure 4.3d).

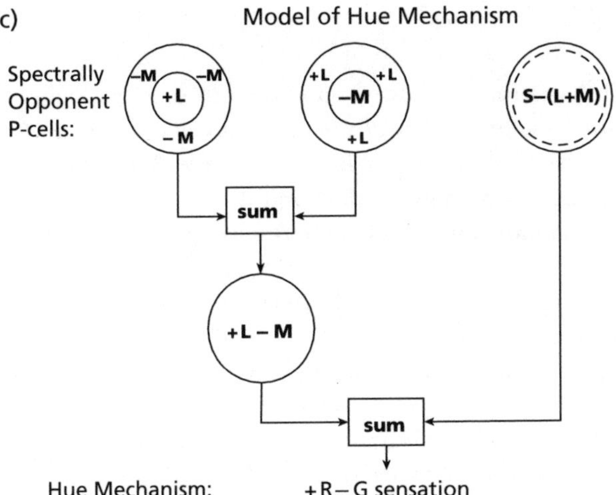
(c)
Model of Hue Mechanism
Spectrally Opponent P-cells:
–M
–M
+L
– M
+L
+L
–M
+L
S–(L+M)
sum
+L – M
sum

Hue Mechanism:

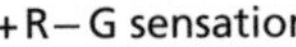
+R– G sensation

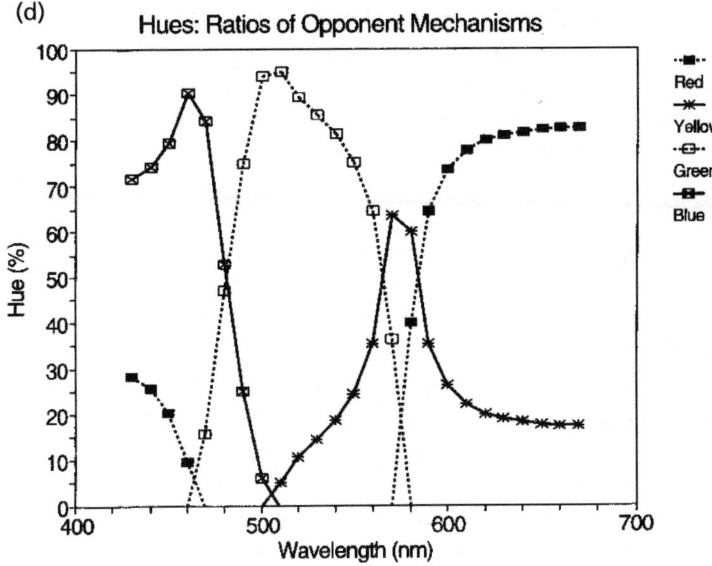
(d)
Hues: Ratios of Opponent Mechanisms
Hue (%)
Wavelength (nm)
Red
Yellow
Green
Blue

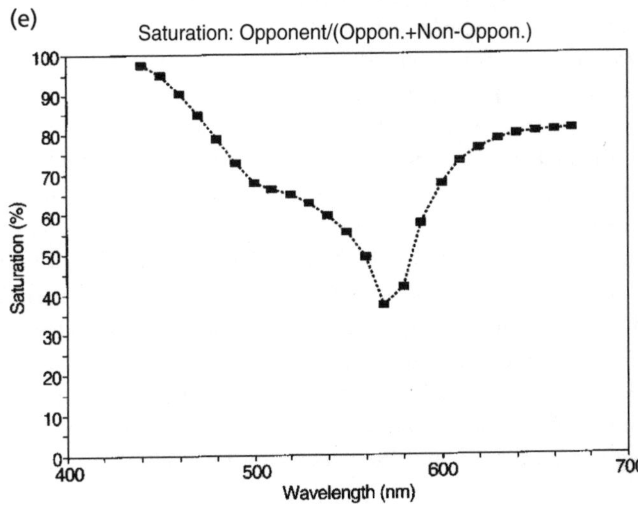
(e)
Saturation: Opponent/(Oppon.+Non-Oppon.)
Saturation (%)
Wavelength (nm)

categories in the sense that sensation must belong only to one or another – sensation shades continuously from one to another of the adjacent categories (Kay & McDaniel, 1978). However, there is very little overlap of R with G or Y with B. Thus, R and G form a mutually exclusive pairing of sensations, as do Y and B.

To combine hue and saturation, hue values can be rescaled by their associated saturations so that the sum of the hue values for each stimulus equals the saturation (Figure 4.5b). These hue values can be replotted on a two-dimensional uniform appearance diagram (UAD) whose orthogonal and bipolar axes are Y-B and G-R (Figure 4.5c); location of each stimulus defines its hue, and distance from the origin represents saturation. This perceptual mapping of stimuli is "uniform" because distances between stimuli are directly proportional to discriminability steps; to illustrate, we show in Figure 4.5d that a subject's wavelength discrimination function, obtained traditionally by adjusting wavelength to produce a just-noticeable difference, is closely comparable to the function derived from the relative distances between adjacent stimuli as plotted on the UAD in Figure 4.5c (Abramov, Gordon, & Chan, 1990; Chan, Abramov, & Gordon, 1991).

Other color-spaces, closely related to ours, include: hue-brightness-saturation (HBS) space, derived from hue cancellation (Hurvich & Jameson, 1956), and the Natural Color System, based on hue and saturation scaling (Hård & Sivik, 1981).

Possible Wiring Diagrams of Hue Mechanisms

We asserted earlier that no known neurons qualify as hue mechanisms. Clearly, though, outputs of the LGN's P- and M-neurons must somehow be combined to form hue mechanisms. How? We start by specifying cone combinations needed to produce response functions of the two necessary spectrally opponent mechanisms. We then suggest how responses of real LGN neurons might be combined cortically to yield such functions.

Figures 4.6a, 4.6b depict the cone combinations needed for the +R−G and +Y−B spectrally opponent hue mechanisms that are the minimum needed for hue sensations (Abramov & Gordon, 1994). The cone functions were weighted to meet two major constraints: that the mechanisms' null points, corresponding to wavelengths eliciting unique hue sensations, be in the correct regions of the spectrum, and that these mechanisms not respond to achromatic ("white") stimuli, else they would violate the requirement that when a hue mechanism responds, we experience that specific hue. The stimuli that elicit unique hue and achromatic sensations are known from psychophysical studies. Wavelengths of unique hues can be estimated from UADs (Figure 4.5c); these loci have also been obtained from adjustment and constant-stimuli studies (Ayama, Nakatsue, & Kaiser, 1987; Schefrin & Werner, 1990). The best estimates of achromatic stimuli cluster near equal-energy white lights (Hurvich & Jameson, 1951; Walraven & Werner, 1991; Sternheim & Drum, 1993).

When a +R−G mechanism is excited, we experience R and when inhibited, we experience G. Such a mechanism (Figure 4.6a) has +L−M+S cone inputs (spectra from human psychophysics; Figure 4.3a). Consider first the locus of unique-Y, the null point of the +R−G mechanism (i.e., a sensation of unique-Y cannot include any R or G); only the other hue mechanism (+Y−B) can respond to this wavelength. Only L- and M-cones absorb this wavelength (Figure 4.3a) and their responses must be so weighted that their inputs to the mechanism cancel each other (Figure 4.6a). These weighted L- and M-cone inputs are sufficient to divide middle and long wavelengths into R and G on either side of unique-Y. But this combination by itself cannot provide for the reappearance of R at short wavelengths (violet). S-cones must be included to provide this signal. To determine the range of short wavelengths eliciting a sensation with some R, the weighting of S-cone inputs must be sufficient to create a second null point at a short wavelength corresponding to unique-B (Figure 4.6a). This combination of cone inputs also satisfies our second constraint, that a hue mechanism not respond to an achromatic stimulus – in Figure 4.6a, summed excitatory responses equal summed inhibitory responses.

Weightings of cone inputs to the +R−G mechanism are well constrained. Figure 4.6b shows a plausible model for the +Y−B mechanism, which is less well constrained. In this case, inputs are +L−M−S and the null point corresponds to unique-G; because all three cones absorb at this wavelength, many sets of cone weightings could be used. For the version shown, unique-G is appropriately located and there is no response to equal-energy white.

The cone weightings depicted in Figures 4.6a, 4.6b are specific to those mechanisms; they cannot also be estimates of the relative numbers of cones in the retina because the weights are not the same for the two hue mechanisms we have just described. We also emphasize that the different cones cannot be specific color receptors: S-cones contribute to both B and R, M-cones contribute to both B and G, and L-cones contribute to both R and Y (Drum, 1989; Shevell, 1992).

By showing only two hue mechanisms, we have implied that excitation and inhibition signal separate, opposed hue sensations; for example, when the +R−G mechanism (Figure 4.6a) is excited, we experience R and when inhibited we experience G. Cortical neurons, however, have very low background, or spontaneous, activity and can only be driven effectively by stimuli that elicit excitation (Movshon, Thompson, & Tolhurst, 1978; Spitzer & Hochstein, 1988). A more complete model is that R is seen when the +R−G mechanism is excited, but to see G we need excitation from a +G−R mechanism. Inhibition serves to limit the spectral ranges of the excitatory responses. Having four separate hue mechanisms (two RG and two YB) permits each to have different properties along other stimulus dimensions, such as size (Abramov, Gordon, & Chan, 1991; see below). But, a mechanism such as +R−G must still have precisely the same weighted cone inputs, except for sign changes, as its inverse, +G−R; otherwise, sensations of R and G would not be mutually exclusive.

The LGN cells, whose responses must be summed to produce RG and YB mechanisms, carry both spatial and chromatic information. Their responses must be processed cortically to extract the chromatic component (Mullen & Kingdom, 1991; Valberg & Seim, 1991; De Valois & De Valois, 1993). Among other things, any processing must eliminate spatial opponency in receptive fields. Also, each hue mechanism (Figures 4.6a, 4.6b) must receive inputs from all three cone types, but most LGN cells have inputs only from M- and L-cones.

Figure 4.6c shows how a spatially homogeneous +R–G hue mechanism might be assembled from a subset of LGN P-cells. The center component of each neuron's receptive field is chromatically homogeneous, driven by only one cone type. Neurons with either L- or M-cone centers have surrounds driven exclusively by the other cone type, while those with S-cone centers have mixed surrounds with little spatial opponency (Wet Physiology, above). In the notation of Figure 4.4, summing responses of [+L]−M and [−M]+L cells produces spectral opponency [+L−M] without spatial opponency. When this is additionally combined with responses of [+S]−(+L−M) cells, the result is a +R−G mechanism (Figure 4.6a). Note that these combinations are weighted and could be distributed over many neuronal stages. Similar assemblies can be made to derive other hue mechanisms. The sort of combination described in Figure 4.6c effectively disambiguates responses of LGN cells: Hue mechanisms are no longer spatially opponent, do not respond to achromatic stimuli, and divide the spectrum at appropriately placed null points.

However, responses of our hypothetical hue mechanisms (Figures 4.6a, 4.6b) are not, by themselves, the same as hue sensations: The sensation elicited by any spectral light depends on the relative degrees of excitation across all the mechanisms. For example, the R sensation at any wavelength is the ratio of +R responses to the sum of +R, +Y, +G, and +B responses at that wavelength. These ratios, derived directly from Figures 4.6a, 4.6b, are shown in Figure 4.6d, and are strikingly similar to real psychophysical functions, as in Figure 4.5a.

The sensory quality of saturation involves yet another level of comparison across neuronal assemblies. Saturation is the amount of chromatic response, regardless of specific hue, relative to the weighted sum of the responses of chromatic and achromatic mechanisms. When stimuli are adjusted to produce equal photopic responses, M-cells (which are achromatic, or spectrally non-opponent) respond equally to all of them and their contribution to saturation is constant. A saturation function can be derived by summing the responses of the hue mechanisms to an equal luminosity spectrum and dividing by that sum plus a constant for the contribution of M-cells (Figure 4.6e). Again, the derived curve is strikingly similar to a real psychophysical curve (Figure 4.5b).

Critique of the Standard Model: Here Be Dragons

The model we have presented is the framework currently accepted by most students of color appearance, even though it is acknowledged to be deficient in many details. Here, we delineate the problems we find the most puzzling.

Do We Have Three Cone Types?

The above models assume that color vision is based on three spectrally distinct cone types. Is this tenable, and, if not, what are the perceptual consequences?

Genetics of Cone Photopigments

The explosion of information about cone photopigment genetics can only be treated briefly here. The consensus is that the earliest forms of color vision compared signals from an S-cone and a single L/M-cone, and this is still the case for most mammals, which are dichromats

(Jacobs, 1998). Trichromacy evolved much later from a divergence of the gene coding the opsin of the ancestral L/M into separate, but closely related L- and M-genes. In humans, the S-cone gene is on chromosome 7. M- and L-genes are on the X-chromosome, as is abundantly clear from sex-linked inheritance of the major forms of dichromacy (Nathans, Thomas, & Hogness, 1986). And it is these L- and M-genes that form the first dragon. The story for Old World primates has been greatly complicated by discovery of more than the canonical two gene loci on this chromosome (Nathans et al., 1986; Dulai, Bowmaker, Mollon, & Hunt, 1994); many humans actively express more than two pigments in the L/ M range (Neitz & Neitz, 1998). (Note that a fundamentally different pattern evolved in New World primates; Jacobs, 1998.)

Variations among human L- and M-genes are such that L-cones have a wider range of spectral peaks (Neitz & Neitz, 1998). We can divide L-cones into short (L_S) and long (L_L) subvarieties, which are expressed roughly equally across the male population; although most individuals express predominantly one form, a substantial fraction of males actively express more than one L-cone gene. Even more possibilities exist for females, who have two X-chromosomes. Adding the possibilities of M-gene variations, we conclude that a substantial number of humans (possibly more than 50%) possess more than the canonical number of three cone types. This is supported by direct recording of the spectra of single human cones (Kraft, Neitz, & Neitz, 1998).

Trichromacy and Photopigment Polymorphism

A century of research confirms that the overwhelming majority of humans are exactly trichromatic – three primaries are necessary and sufficient to match any light. Thus, trichromacy must be imposed by neural processing of cone responses. For example, responses of L_S and L_L cones could be combined early in the retina to form a single composite channel whose spectral sensitivity would be the sum of the individual cone sensitivities and could fulfill all the requirements of univariance – it might be termed a pseudo-pigment (Sirovich & Abramov, 1977). However, at least for fovea and near periphery, this cannot be the case: P-ganglion cells have single cone centers, which could be either L_S or L_L, but not both, and this organization carries through the LGN. The inescapable conclusion is that the neural locus of trichromacy is in the cortex, the first place at which there is summation across arrays of P-cells.

Are there any perceptual consequences of cone polymorphism? The example of additive color mixing in Figure 4.1 (the Rayleigh anomaloscope match) is for wavelengths sufficiently long that the S-cones no longer contribute and so depends exclusively on M- and L-cones. Any population variations in these "cones," real pigments or pseudo-pigments, should lead to variations in the precise amounts of the two primaries needed to match the Y appearance of the test field. Such variations have been reported, with multi-modal frequency distributions corresponding to the expected expression frequencies of the different pigments (Neitz & Jacobs, 1990). But the range of these multi-modal distributions is small. The consequences of cone polymorphism seem subtle at best and the evolutionary benefits to humans are unclear.

Is Color Vision Stable?

A monochrome, black-and-white view of the world is mostly acceptable. Computational models of object perception often concentrate on intensity boundaries in the image, because they are likely linked to real discontinuities in the world (e.g., Marr, 1982). But color certainly adds something and may be vital to parsing a visual image into its component objects – differentiating ripe fruit from a leafy background replete with shadows (Mollon, 1989, 1991), or deciding when an intensity boundary is not a real edge but merely a shadow lying across the object (e.g., Cavanagh, 1991). Indeed, we may be more sensitive to chromatic than luminance differences (Chaparro, Stromeyer, Huang, Kronauer, & Eskew, 1993).

For useful color vision in the real world it is probably more important to have several clearly discriminable and stable color categories – a red, ripe apple should appear reddish under most illuminations, from dawn to midday, against most backgrounds, and at most distances. The sensory boundaries between hue categories are set by the unique hue sensations and their associated stimuli. In our simple linear models (Figures 4.6a, 4.6b), spectral loci of the unique hues are necessarily invariant. However, the models do not include changes with intensity, light adaptation, or spatio-temporal variation. We now consider some of these variables.

Size, Eccentricity, and Perceptive Fields

When stimuli are degraded, color vision suffers. If stimuli are too small, normal color vision reduces to one of the standard forms of dichromacy, tritanopia (Willmer & Wright, 1945), presumably because the sparse S-cones are being undersampled; similar effects are noted when stimuli are too dim or too brief (Weitzman & Kinney, 1969). Also, there is a long history of plotting color zones across the visual field and showing how various hues drop out away from the fovea (e.g., Ferree & Rand, 1919; Johnson, 1986). These changes with retinal eccentricity probably reflect the increasing sizes of receptive fields; to maintain tiled coverage of the visual field, the smaller sizes of central receptive fields require more ganglion cells, and these are associated with the magnified cortical representation of the central visual field (M-scaling: Rovamu & Virsu, 1979).

We have used hue and saturation scaling to estimate the size-scales for color across the retina (Abramov et al., 1991; Abramov, Gordon, & Chan, 1992). At each eccentricity, as size was increased, saturations of each of the hues increased to an asymptote, as if the stimuli were filling each hue mechanism's *perceptive* field. Even at 40° eccentricities hue and saturation functions are almost fovea-like, provided stimuli are locally sufficiently large. Others have made similar observations for wavelength discrimination and photopic spectral sensitivity (Wooten & Wald, 1973; Stabell & Stabell, 1982; Van Esch, Koldenhoff, Van Doorn, & Koenderink, 1984). Interestingly, the retinal size-scales of the hue mechanisms are not the same: Everywhere, estimated sizes of G and Y perceptive fields are large, whereas those for R and B are quite small (Abramov et al., 1991, 1992). This is additional evidence for four separate hue mechanisms. The increases in sizes of these perceptive fields with eccentricity is more than would be expected from M-scaling at the level of V1, which underscores our view that the hue mechanisms probed by sensory scaling reside at cortical levels beyond V1.

In the fovea, a 0.25° stimulus is sufficient for all hue channels and well exceeds the size of the B perceptive field. But, this area covers only a very small number of S-cones compared with L- and M-cones. In the average human fovea, there is a zone as large as 0.3° that is totally devoid of S-cones, and even within the central 1° we compute that there may be as few as 60 S-cones compared with at least 8,000 L- and M-cones (Curcio, Sloan, Kalina, & Hendrickson, 1990; Curcio et al., 1991). Contributions of S-cones to chromatic pathways must be massively amplified. Any loss of S-cones, due to disease or light-induced damage, will have a much larger impact on color vision than similar losses of the other, more numerous, cone types (Abramov & Hainline, 1991).

For sufficiently large stimuli, the spectral loci of the unique hues are quite stable across the retina (Abramov et al., 1991, 1992; Nerger, Volbrecht, Ayde, & Imhoff, 1998). This requires stability of weighted cone inputs to hue mechanisms, and suggests stability of the ratios of L/M/S-cones across the retina. Unfortunately, genetic analyses suggest otherwise – L/M ratios vary across the retina, with the periphery heavily dominated by L-cones (Hagstrom, Neitz, & Neitz, 1998). If these genetic data hold up, we are left with the unappealing conclusion that the weights assigned to the contributions of cones to hue mechanisms must change systematically across the retina in order to preserve hue boundaries.

Intensity, Adaptation, and Color Constancy

As required by our models (Figures 4.6a, 4.6b), it is possible that cones are linear over large intensity ranges (Schnapf, Nunn, Meister, & Baylor, 1990; Hood & Birch, 1993). This raises problems for later stages whose neurons fire action potentials and thus have a limited dynamic range. For good discrimination, at least these later stages must be nonlinear and must adapt by shifting their response ranges to match ambient light levels (Hood, 1998).

Colors of real objects remain remarkably constant from dawn to dusk, despite large changes in intensity and in spectral composition of illumination (Jameson & Hurvich, 1989). This implies existence of a process for "discounting the illuminant": If illumination is reddish, sensitivity of a red-sensitive mechanism must be selectively reduced so that, for example, a white object continues to look white (Brainard & Wandell, 1992). Such constancy cannot be perfect, however, else we would not distinguish candlelight from sunlight. These adaptations could occur at all stages of the visual system, including cognitive ones: Something lit by different illuminants maintains a constant appearance when instructions emphasize its object properties rather than its abstract color (Arend, Reeves, Schirillo, & Goldstein, 1991). (See Additional Topics.)

Hues change with intensity – the Bezold-Brücke hue shift (Boynton & Gordon, 1965) – indicating that the intensity-response functions of R, G, Y, and B mechanisms cannot be the same (Hurvich, 1981) – at least some might be nonlinear (Valberg & Seim, 1991). For example, at higher intensities longer wavelengths appear more Y, either because R has a compressive function so that as intensity increases, R tends towards a ceiling while Y continues to grow, or the Y mechanism has a steeper response-vs.-intensity function.

However, even large intensity variations have little effect on spectral loci of the unique hues, the hue category boundaries (Hurvich & Jameson, 1955; Boynton & Gordon, 1965; Ayama et al., 1987); similarly, achromatic white is intensity-invariant over an impressively large range (Walraven & Werner, 1991). It is difficult to postulate adaptational processes to stabilize spectral loci of unique hues, while still producing a Bezold-Brücke hue shift for intermediate hues.

Tuning the Unique Hues and White

The major sensory color categories are typified by stimuli corresponding to the unique hues and to white, which are sensations that depend on precise ratios of cone inputs to their respective mechanisms. There is little variation across individuals and across viewing conditions; spectral loci of unique hues and spectra of the best achromatic stimuli are tightly clustered (Schefrin & Werner, 1990; Walraven & Werner, 1991; Werner & Schefrin, 1993). While this consistency may be ecologically useful, it is not obvious how it arises.

The primary constraint must be imposed by the numbers of the different cones available in the retinal mosaic. The ranges of L/M cone ratios for central retina vary considerably: psychophysics, about 1.5 to 7 (Cicerone & Nerger, 1989; Wesner, Pokorny, Shevell, & Smith, 1991), electrophysiology, 0.7 to 9 (Jacobs & Neitz, 1993), genetic analyses, 0.8 to 3 (Hagstrom et al., 1998), and *in vivo* imaging of the receptor mosaic, 1.2 to 3.8 (Roorda & Williams, 1999). The problem is compounded when we consider the entire retina: L/M ratios vary across the retina (Hagstrom et al., 1998), as does the proportion of S-cones (Curcio et al., 1991).

Given so much variation in the receptors, the stability of the spectral loci of the unique hues must rest on compensatory changes in the weights with which the different cones feed into the hue mechanisms. What controls this?

The "gray world" hypothesis, which postulates that the average chromaticity of real-world scenes is equivalent to that of an achromatic stimulus, provides a possible tuning mechanism (Buchsbaum, 1980; Dannemiller, 1993). A truly gray world would provide an external standard for one of the unique sensory qualities and could be used to tune outputs of hue mechanisms so that they failed to respond to a real achromatic target; the weights of the cone inputs needed for this would also specify the spectral null points of the hue mechanisms. Such tuning could occur once and for all or could be a continuous dynamic process; evidence favors the latter, because changes in spectrum of the illuminant rarely produce gross changes in color appearance of objects. However, this adaptive process is never perfect even though the degree of retuning seems to be greater with real-world scenes (Brainard, 1998). The problem is that this reweighting of cone inputs must vary greatly across individuals and across the retina, because the ratios of the cones vary greatly and yet the spectral loci of the unique hues show very little variation.

Closing Comments

Color vision evolved to allow organisms to identify important objects in their environments. But color cannot come at the expense of spatial resolution. Minimal color vision has two spectrally distinct receptor types whose outputs are compared in spectrally opponent channels; provided that the centers of their receptive fields are small enough, spatial resolution can still be maintained along with some spectral information. However, this dichromatic form of color vision splits the spectrum into two categories; continuous discrimination across the spectrum requires the addition of at least one more receptor type.

Although humans have evolved several loci for cone pigments on their X-chromosomes, they seem to reduce the system to the minimum consonant with continuous color discrimination across the spectrum: three spectral parameters. By contrast, some non-mammalian species developed color vision that is more than trichromatic; many fish, insects, reptiles, and birds are at least tetrachromatic (Neumeyer, 1991). Presumably this improves color discrimination and may extend the range of the visible spectrum, but the selection pressures for this are not obvious. Perhaps because of less stringent environmental pressures, humans have a relatively high prevalence of color abnormalities, especially among males, abnormalities that have never been found in macaques (Jacobs, 1991).

Accepting that our color vision evolved for detecting real things, it becomes important to place objects into one or other of a limited set of categories, categories that remain acceptably stable across viewing conditions. And this is precisely what is needed for behaviors linked to food gathering, recognition of con-specifics, especially when sexually receptive, and warning displays.

Note

1. Preparation of this chapter was supported in part by the following grants: National Park Service/NCPTT (MT-2210–8–NC-2); NYState/Higher Education Advanced Technology; NSF (IBN-9319683); NEI/NIH (1472); PSC-BHE/CUNY Research Awards Program (669255, 669259).

Suggested Readings

Kaiser, P. K., & Boynton, R. M. (1996). *Human color vision* (2nd ed.). Washington, DC: Optical Society of America.

Rodieck, R. W. (1998). *The first steps in seeing.* Sunderland, MA: Sinauer.

Cronly-Dillon, J. R. (Gen. Ed.) (1991). *Vision and visual dysfunction: Vol. 6.* Gouras, P. (Ed.), *The perception of colour.* Boca Raton, FL: CRC.

Cronly-Dillon, J. R. (Gen. Ed.) (1991). *Vision and visual dysfunction: Vol. 7.* Foster, D. H. (Ed.), *Inherited and acquired colour vision deficiencies.* Boca Raton, FL: CRC.

Additional Topics

Specifying Color Stimuli

Accurate specification of stimuli used to study color vision must include spectral and intensive domains. They can be measured either in strict physical terms (e.g., spectral distribution and radiance), or they can be measured in terms of their effectiveness for eliciting visual sensations (e.g., chromaticity and luminance). For detailed descriptions of the quantitative manipulations, see

Kaiser and Boynton (1996); Wyszecki and Stiles (1982).

Color Constancy

Objects in the real world maintain their color appearance across a wide range of illuminants. However, changing the illuminant must change objects' reflectance spectra. How does the visual system "discount the illuminant" to allow for this color constancy? See Pokorny, Shevell, and Smith (1991); Wandell (1995).

Historical Background

There is a very long history of studies of color vision. Unfortunately this richness means that we often end by rediscovering the wheel. See the following for starting points into this wide field: Gouras (1991b); Wright (1991); Graham (1965); Mollon (1997).

References

Abramov, I., & Gordon, J. (1994). Color appearance: On seeing red – or yellow, or green, or blue. *Annual Review of Psychology, 45*, 451–485.

Abramov, I., Gordon, J., & Chan, H. (1990). Using hue scaling to specify color appearance. *Proceedings of the Society of Photo Optical Instrumentation Engineers, 1250*, 40–51.

Abramov, I., Gordon, J., & Chan, H. (1991). Color appearance in the peripheral retina: Effects of stimulus size. *Journal of the Optical Society of America, A8*, 404–414.

Abramov, I., Gordon, J., & Chan, H. (1992). Color appearance across the retina: Effects of a white surround. *Journal of the Optical Society of America, A9*, 195–202.

Abramov, I., & Hainline, L. (1991). Light and the developing visual system. In J. Cronly-Dillon (Gen. Ed.), *Vision and visual dysfunction: Vol. 16*. J. Marshall (Ed.), *The susceptible visual apparatus* (pp. 104–133). Boca Raton, FL: CRC Press.

Arend, L. E., Jr., Reeves, A., Schirillo, J., & Goldstein, R. (1991). Simultaneous color constancy: Papers with diverse Munsell values. *Journal of the Optical Society of America, A8*, 661–672.

Ayama, M., Nakatsue, T., & Kaiser, P. K. (1987). Constant hue loci of unique and binary balanced hues at 10, 100, and 1000 Td. *Journal of the Optical Society of America, A4*, 1136–1144.

Baylor, D. A., Nunn, B. J., & Schnapf, J. L. (1987). Spectral sensitivity of cones of the monkey, *Macaca fascicularis. Journal of Physiology, 390*, 145–160.

Berlin, B., & Kay, P. (1969). *Basic color terms: Their universality and evolution.* Berkeley, CA: University of California Press.

Bowmaker, J. K. (1991). Visual pigments, oil droplets and photoreceptors. In J. R. Cronly-Dillon (Gen. Ed.), *Vision and visual dysfunction: Vol. 6*. Gouras, P. (Ed.), *The perception of colour* (pp. 108–127). Boca Raton, FL: CRC Press.

Boynton, R. M. (1996). History and current status of a physiologically based system of photometry and colorimetry. *Journal of the Optical Society of America, A13*,1609–1621.

Boynton, R. M., & Gordon, J. (1965). Bezold–Brücke hue shift measured by color-naming technique. *Journal of the Optical Society of America, 55*, 78–86.

Brainard, D. H. (1998). Color constancy in the nearly natural image. 2. Achromatic loci. *Journal of the Optical Society of America, A15*, 307–325.

Brainard, D. H., & Wandell, B. A. (1992). Asymmetric color matching: How color appearance depends on the illuminant. *Journal of the Optical Society of America, A9*, 1433–1448.

Brindley, G. S. (1960). *Physiology of the retina and the visual pathway.* London: Edward Arnold.

Buchsbaum, G. (1980). A spatial processor model for object colour perception. *Journal of the Franklin Institute, 310*, 1–26.

Calkins, D. J., Tsukamoto, Y., & Sterling, P. (1998). Microcircuitry and mosaic of a blue-yellow ganglion cell in the primate retina. *Journal of Neuroscience, 18*, 3373–3385.

Cavanagh, P. (1991). Vision at equiluminance. In J. R. Cronly-Dillon (Gen. Ed.), *Vision and visual dysfunction: Vol. 5*. J. J. Kulikowski, V. Walsh, & I. J. Murray (Eds.), *Limits of vision* (pp. 234–250). Boca Raton, FL: CRC Press.

Chan, H., Abramov, I., & Gordon, J. (1991). Large and small color differences: Predicting them from hue scaling. *Proceedings of the Society of Photo Optical Instrumentation Engineers, 1453*, 381–389.

Chaparro, A., Stromeyer, C. F., III, Huang, E. P., Kronauer, R. E., & Eskew, R. T., Jr. (1993). Colour is what the eye sees best. *Nature, 361*, 348–350.

Cicerone, C. M., & Nerger, J. L. (1989). The relative numbers of long-wavelength-sensitive to middle-wavelength-sensitive cones in the human fovea centralis. *Vision Research, 29*, 115–128.

Curcio, C. A., Allen, K. A., Sloan, K R., Lerea, C. L., Hurley, J. B., Klock, I. B., & Milam, A. H. (1991). Distribution and morphology of human cone photoreceptors stained with anti-blue opsin. *Journal of Comparative Neurology, 312*, 610–624.

Curcio, C. A., Sloan, K. R., Kalina, R. E., & Hendrickson, A. E. (1990). Human photoreceptor topography. *Journal of Comparative Neurology, 292*, 497–523.

Dacey, D. M. (1996). Circuitry for color coding in the primate retina. *Proceedings of the National Academy of Sciences, 93*, 582–588.

Dannemiller, J. L. (1993). Rank orderings of photoreceptor photon catches from natural objects are nearly illuminant-invariant. *Vision Research, 33*,131–40.

Dartnall, H. J. A. (1953). The interpretation of spectral sensitivity curves. *British Medical Bulletin, 9*, 24–30.

Davidoff, J. (1991). *Cognition through color.* Cambridge, MA: Bradford Book/MIT.

Derefeldt, G. (1991). Colour appearance systems. In J. R. Cronly-Dillon (Gen. Ed.), *Vision and visual dysfunction: Vol. 6*. P. Gouras (Ed.), *The perception of colour* (pp. 62–89). Boca Raton, FL: CRC Press.

Derrington, A. M., Krauskopf, J., & Lennie, P. (1984) Chromatic mechanisms in lateral geniculate nucleus of macaque. *Journal of Physiology, 357*, 241–265.

De Valois, R. L., Abramov, I., & Jacobs, G. H. (1966). Analysis of response patterns of LGN cells. *Journal of the Optical Society of America, 56*, 966–977.

De Valois, R. L., & De Valois, K. K. (1993). A multi-stage color model. *Vision Research, 33*, 1053–1065.

Dow, B. M., & Vautin, R. G. (1987). Horizontal segregation of color information in the middle layers of foveal striate cortex. *Journal of Neurophysiology, 57*, 712–739.

Drum, B. (1989). Hue signals from short- and middle-wavelength-sensitive cones. *Journal of the Optical Society of America, A6*, 153–157.

Dulai, K. S., Bowmaker, J. K., Mollon, J. D., & Hunt, D. M. (1994). Sequence divergence, polymorphism and evolution of the middle-wave and long-wave visual pigment genes of great apes and Old World monkeys. *Vision Research, 34*, 2483–2491.

Ferree, C. E., & Rand, G. (1919). Chromatic thresholds of sensation from center to periphery of the retina and their bearing on color theory. *Psychological Review, 26*, 16–41.

Fuld, K., Werner, J. S., & Wooten, B. R. (1983). The possible elemental nature of brown. *Vision Research, 23*, 631–637.

Goldsmith, T. H. (1991). The evolution of visual pigments and colour vision. In J. R. Cronly-Dillon (Gen. Ed.), *Vision and visual dysfunction: Vol. 6*. P. Gouras (Ed.), *The perception of colour* (pp. 62–89). Boca Raton, FL: CRC Press.

Gordon, J., & Abramov, I. (1988). Scaling procedures for specifying color appearance. *Color Research & Application, 13*, 146–152.

Gordon, J., Abramov, I., & Chan, H. (1994). Describing color appearance: Hue and saturation scaling. *Perception & Psychophysics, 56*, 27–41.

Gouras, P. (1991a). Cortical mechanisms of colour vision. In J. R. Cronly-Dillon (Gen. Ed.), *Vision and visual dysfunction: Vol. 6.* P. Gouras (Ed.), *The perception of colour* (pp. 179–197). Boca Raton, FL: CRC Press.

Gouras, P. (1991b). History of colour vision. In J. R. Cronly-Dillon (Gen. Ed.), *Vision and visual dysfunction: Vol. 6.* P. Gouras (Ed.), *The perception of colour* (pp. 1–9). Boca Raton, FL: CRC Press.

Graham, C. H. (Ed.) (1965). *Vision and visual perception.* New York: Wiley.

Graham, N., & Hood, D. C. (1992). Modeling the dynamics of light adaptation: The merging of two traditions. *Vision Research, 32,* 1373–1393.

Hagstrom, S. A., Neitz, J., & Neitz, M. (1998). Variations in cone populations for red–green color vision examined by analysis of mRNA. *NeuroReport, 9,* 1963–1967.

Hård, A., & Sivik, L. (1981). NCS – Natural Color System: A Swedish standard for color notation. *Color Research & Application, 6,* 129–138.

Hardin, C. L., & Maffi, L. (Eds.) (1997). *Color categories in thought and language.* Cambridge: Cambridge University Press.

Hering, E. (1920). *Grundzüge der Lehre vom Lichtsinn.* Berlin: Springer-Verlag. (*Outlines of a theory of the light sense* (L. M. Hurvich & D. Jameson, Trans.). Cambridge, MA: Harvard University Press, 1964.)

Hood, D. C. (1998). Lower-level visual processing and models of light adaptation. *Annual Review of Psychology, 49,* 503–535.

Hood, D. C., & Birch, D. G. (1993). Human cone receptor activity: The leading edge of the a-wave and models of receptor activity. *Visual Neuroscience, 10,* 857–871.

Howard, R. J., ffytche, D. H., Barnes, J., McKeefry, D., Ha, Y., Woodruff, P. W., Bullmore, E. T., Simmons, A., Williams, S. C., David, A. S., & Brammer, M. (1998). The functional anatomy of imagining and perceiving colour. *NeuroReport, 9,* 1019–1023.

Hubel, D. H., & Livingstone, M. S. (1987). Segregation of form, color, and stereopsis in primate area 18. *Journal of Neuroscience, 7,* 3378–3415.

Hurvich, L. M. (1981). *Color vision.* Sunderland, MA: Sinauer Associates.

Hurvich, L. M., & Jameson, D. (1951). A psychophysical study of white. I. Neutral adaptation. *Journal of the Optical Society of America, 41,* 521–527.

Hurvich, L. M., & Jameson, D. (1955). Some quantitative aspects of an opponent-colors theory. II. Brightness, saturation, and hue in normal and dichromatic vision. *Journal of the Optical Society of America, 45,* 602–616.

Hurvich, L. M., & Jameson, D. (1956). Some quantitative aspects of an opponent-colors theory. IV. A psychological color specification system. *Journal of the Optical Society of America, 46,* 416–421.

Jacobs, G. H. (1991). Variations in colour vision in non-human primates. In J. R. Cronly-Dillon (Gen. Ed.), *Vision and visual dysfunction: Vol. 7.* D. H. Foster (Ed.), *Inherited and acquired colour vision deficiencies* (pp. 199–214). Boca Raton, FL: CRC Press.

Jacobs, G. H. (1993). The distribution and nature of colour vision among the mammals. *Biological Reviews, 68,* 413–71.

Jacobs, G. H. (1998). Photopigments and seeing – lessons from natural experiments: The Proctor Lecture. *Investigative Ophthalmology and Visual Science, 39,* 2205–2216.

Jacobs, G. H., & Neitz, J. (1993). Electrophysiological estimates of individual variation in the L/M cone ratio. In B. Drum (Ed.), *Colour vision deficiencies XI (Documenta Ophthalmologica Proceedings Series, 56)* (pp. 107–112). Dordrecht, Netherlands: Kluwer.

Jameson, D., & Hurvich, L. M. (1959). Perceived color and its dependence on focal surrounding, and preceding stimulus variables. *Journal of the Optical Society of America, 49,* 890–898.

Jameson, D., & Hurvich, L. M. (1989). Essay concerning color constancy. *Annual Review of Psychology, 40,* 1–22.

Johnson, M. A. (1986). Color vision in the peripheral retina. *American Journal of Optometry and Physiological Optics, 63,* 97–103.

Kaiser, P. K., & Boynton, R. M. (1996) *Human color vision* (2nd ed.). Washington, DC: Optical Society of America.

Kaplan, E., & Shapley, R. (1984). The origin of the S (slow) potential in the mammalian lateral geniculate nucleus. *Experimental Brain Research, 55,* 111–116.

Kaplan, E., Lee, B. B., & Shapley, R. M. (1990). New views of primate retinal function. In N. N.

Osborne & G. J. Chader (Eds.), *Progress in retinal research* (Vol. 9, pp. 273–336). New York: Pergamon Press.

Kay, P., & McDaniel, C. K. (1978). The linguistic significance of the meanings of basic color terms. *Language, 54*, 610–645.

Kay, P., Berlin, B., & Merrifield, W. (1991). Biocultural implications of systems of color naming. *Journal of Linguistic Anthropology, 1*, 12–25.

Kraft, T. W., Neitz, J., & Neitz, M. (1998). Spectra of human L cones. *Vision Research, 38*, 3663–3670.

Krauskopf, J., Williams, D. R., & Heeley, D. W. (1982). Cardinal directions of color space. *Vision Research, 22*, 1123–1131.

Lee, B. B. (1991). Spectral sensitivity in primate vision. In J. R. Cronly-Dillon (Gen. Ed.), *Vision and visual dysfunction: Vol. 5*. J. J. Kulikowski, V. Walsh, & I. J. Murray (Eds.), *Limits of vision* (pp. 191–201). Boca Raton, FL: CRC Press.

Lee, B. B., Kremers, J., & Yeh, T. (1998). Receptive fields of primate retinal ganglion cells studied with a novel technique. *Visual Neuroscience, 15*, 161–175.

Lee, B. B., Pokorny, J., Smith, V. C., Martin, P. R., & Valberg, A. (1990). Luminance and chromatic modulation sensitivity of macaque ganglion cells and human observers. *Journal of the Optical Society of America, A7*, 2223–2236.

Lennie, P., Krauskopf, J., & Sclar, G. (1990). Chromatic mechanisms in striate cortex of macaque. *Journal of Neuroscience, 10*, 649–669.

MacLeod, D. I. A., & Boynton, R. M. (1979). Chromaticity diagram showing cone excitation by stimuli of equal luminance. *Journal of the Optical Society of America, 69*, 1183–1186.

MacNichol, E. F., Jr. (1986). A unifying presentation of photopigment spectra. *Vision Research, 26*, 1543–1556.

Mansfield, R. J. W. (1985). Primate photopigments and cone mechanisms. In A. Fein & J. S. Levine (Eds.), *The visual system* (pp. 89–106). New York: Liss.

Marr, D. (1982). *Vision.* New York: W.H. Freeman.

Marrocco, R. T., & De Valois, R. L. (1977). Locus of spectral neutral point in monkey opponent cells depends on stimulus luminance relative to background. *Brain Research, 119*, 465–470.

Merigan, W. H., & Maunsell, J. H. R. (1993). How parallel are the primate visual pathways? *Annual Review of Neuroscience, 16*, 369–402.

Milner, A. D., & Goodale, M. A. (1995). *The visual brain in action.* New York: Oxford University Press.

Mollon, J. D. (1989). "Tho' she kneel'd in that place where they grew . . . " The uses and origins of primate colour vision. *Journal of Experimental Biology, 146*, 21–38.

Mollon, J. D. (1991). Uses and evolutionary origins of primate colour vision. In J. R. Cronly-Dillon (Gen. Ed.), *Vision and visual dysfunction: Vol. 2*. J. R. Cronly-Dillon & R. L. Gregory (Eds.), *Evolution of the eye and visual system* (pp. 306–319). Boca Raton, FL: CRC Press.

Mollon, J. D. (1997). ' . . . aus dreyerley Arten von Membranen oder Molekülen': George Palmer's legacy. In C. R. Cavonius (Ed.), *Colour vision deficiencies XIII (Documenta Ophthalmologica Proceedings Series, 59)* (pp. 3–20). Dordrecht, Netherlands: Kluwer.

Movshon, J. A., Thompson, I. D., & Tolhurst, D. J. (1978). Spatial summation in the receptive fields of simple cells in the cat's striate cortex. *Journal of Physiology, 283*, 53–77.

Mullen, K. T., & Kingdom, F. A. A. (1991). The perception of colour. In J. R. Cronly-Dillon (Gen. Ed.), *Vision and visual dysfunction: Vol. 6*. P. Gouras (Ed.), *The perception of colour* (pp. 198–217). Boca Raton, FL: CRC Press.

Nathans, J., Thomas, D., & Hogness, D. S. (1986). Molecular genetics of human color vision: The genes encoding blue, green and red pigments. *Science, 232*, 193–202.

Neitz, J., & Jacobs, G. H. (1990). Polymorphism in normal human color vision and its mechanism. *Vision Research, 30*, 621–636.

Neitz, M., & Neitz, J. (1998). Molecular genetics and the biological basis of color vision. In W. G. K. Backhaus, R. Kliegl, & J. S. Werner (Eds.), *Color vision: Perspectives from different disciplines* (pp. 101–119). Berlin: Walter de Gruyter.

Nerger, J. L., Volbrecht, V. J., Ayde, C. J., & Imhoff, S. M. (1998). Effect of the S-cone mosaic and rods on red/green equilibria. *Journal of the Optical Society of America, 15A*, 2816–2826.

Neumeyer, C. (1991). Evolution of colour vision. In J. R. Cronly-Dillon (Gen. Ed.), *Vision and visual dysfunction: Vol. 2*. J. R. Cronly-Dillon & R. L.Gregory (Eds.), *Evolution of the eye and visual system* (pp. 284–305). Boca Raton, FL: CRC Press.

Newton, I. (1704). *Opticks: Or a treatise of the reflexions, refractions, inflexions and colours of light*. London: Sam. Smith and Benj. Walford.

Piantanida, T. P. (1991). Molecular biology of colour vision. In J. R. Cronly-Dillon (Gen. Ed.), *Vision and visual dysfunction: Vol. 6*. P. Gouras (Ed.), *The perception of colour* (pp. 90–107). Boca Raton, FL: CRC Press.

Plant, G. T. (1991). Disorders of colour vision in diseases of the nervous system. In J. R. Cronly-Dillon (Gen. Ed.), *Vision and visual dysfunction: Vol. 7*. D. H. Foster (Ed.), *Inherited and acquired colour vision deficiencies* (pp. 173–198). Boca Raton, FL: CRC Press.

Pokorny, J., Shevell, S. K., & Smith, V. C. (1991). Colour appearance and colour constancy. In J. R. Cronly-Dillon (Gen. Ed.), *Vision and visual dysfunction: Vol. 6*. P. Gouras (Ed.), *The perception of colour* (pp. 43–61). Boca Raton, FL: CRC Press.

Pugh, E. N. J., & Kirk, D. B. (1986). The π mechanisms of W S Stiles: An historical review. *Perception, 15*, 705–728.

Quinn, P. C., Rosano, J. L., & Wooten, B. R. (1988). Evidence that brown is not an elemental color. *Perception & Psychophysics, 43*, 156–164.

Ratliff, F. (1976). On the psychophysiological bases of universal color terms. *Proceedings of the American Philosophical Society, 120*, 311–330.

Reid, R. C., & Shapley, R. M. (1992). Spatial structure of cone inputs to receptive fields in primate lateral geniculate nucleus. *Nature, 356*, 716–718.

Rodieck, R. W. (1998). *The first steps in seeing*. Sunderland, MA: Sinauer.

Roorda, A., & Williams, D. A. (1999). The arrangement of the three cone classes in the living human eye. *Nature, 397*, 520–522.

Rovamu, J., & Virsu, V. (1979). An estimation and application of the human cortical magnification factor. *Experimental Brain Research, 37*, 495–510.

Rushton, W. A. H. (1972). Visual pigments in man. In H. J. A. Dartnall (Ed.), *Photochemistry of vision, Vol. VII/1, Handbook of sensory physiology* (pp. 364–394). Berlin: Springer-Verlag.

Schefrin, B. E., & Werner, J. S. (1990). Loci of spectral unique hues throughout the life span. *Journal of the Optical Society of America, A7*, 305–311.

Schein, S. J., & Desimone, R. (1990). Spectral properties of V4 neurons in the macaque. *Journal of Neuroscience, 10*, 3369–3389.

Schiller, P. H., & Lee, K. (1991). The role of the primate extrastriate area V4 in vision. *Science, 251*, 1251–1253.

Schiller, P. H., Logothetis, M. K., & Charles, E. R. (1990). Role of the color-opponent and broad-band channels in vision. *Visual Neuroscience, 5*, 321–346.

Schnapf, J. L., Kraft, T. W., & Baylor, D. A. (1987). Spectral sensitivity of human cone photoreceptors. *Nature, 325*, 439–441.

Schnapf, J. L., Nunn, B. J., Meister, M., & Baylor, D. A. (1990). Visual transduction in cones of the monkey *Macaca fascicularis*. *Journal of Physiology, 427*, 681–713.

Shepard, R. N., & Cooper, L. A. (1992). Representation of colors in the blind, color-blind, and normally sighted. *Psychological Science, 3*, 97–104.

Shevell, S. K. (1992). Redness from short-wavelength-sensitive cones does not induce greenness. *Vision Research, 32*, 1551–1556.

Shirriff, K. (1991). Laundry and the origin of basic color terms. *Journal of Irreproducible Results, 36*, 10.

Sirovich, L., & Abramov, I. (1977). Photopigments and pseudopigments. *Vision Research, 17*, 5–16.

Smith, V. C., & Pokorny, J. (1975). Spectral sensitivity of the foveal cone photopigments between 400 and 500 nm. *Vision Research, 15*, 161–171.

Sperling, H. G. (1992). Spatial discrimination of heterochromatic stimuli: A review and a new experimental approach. In B. Drum (Ed.), *Colour vision deficiencies XI* (pp. 35–50). Dordrecht, Netherlands: Kluwer.

Spitzer, H., & Hochstein, S. (1988). Complex-cell receptive field models. *Progress in Neurobiology, 31*, 285–309.

Stabell, U. & Stabell, B. (1982). Color vision in the peripheral retina under photopic conditions. *Vision Research, 22*, 839–844.

Sternheim, C. E., & Boynton, R. M. (1966). Uniqueness of perceived hues investigated with a continuous judgmental technique. *Journal of Experimental Psychology, 72*, 770–776.

Sternheim, C. E., & Drum, B. (1993). Achromatic and chromatic sensation as a function of color temperature and retinal illuminance. *Journal of the Optical Society of America, A10*, 838–843.

Stiles, W. S. (1978). *Mechanisms of colour vision.* London: Academic Press.

Stockman, A., MacLeod, D. I. A., & Johnson, N. E. (1993). Spectral sensitivities of the human cones. *Journal of the Optical Society of America, A10*, 2491–2521.

Teller, D. Y. (1984). Linking propositions. *Vision Research, 24*, 1233–1246.

Thorell, L. G., De Valois, R. L., & Albrecht, D. G. (1984). Spatial mapping of monkey V1 cells with pure color and luminance stimuli. *Vision Research, 24*, 751–769.

Ungerleider, L. G., & Mishkin, M. (1982). Two cortical visual systems. In D. J. Ingle, M. A. Goodale, & R. J. Mansfield (Eds.), *Analysis of visual behavior* (pp. 549–580). Cambridge, MA: MIT Press.

Valberg, A., & Seim, T. (1991). On the physiological basis of higher colour metrics. In A. Valberg & B. B. Lee (Eds.), *From pigments to perception* (pp. 425–436). New York: Plenum.

Van Esch, J. A., Koldenhoff, E. E., Van Doorn, A. J., & Koenderink, J. J. (1984). Spectral sensitivity and wavelength discrimination of the human peripheral visual field. *Journal of the Optical Society of America, A1*, 443–450.

Van Essen, D. C., Anderson, C. H., & Felleman, D. J. (1992). Information processing in the primate visual system: An integrated systems perspective. *Science, 255*, 419–423.

Victor, J. D., Maiese, K., Shapley, R., Sidtis, J., & Gazzaniga, M. S. (1989). Acquired central dyschromatopsia: Analysis of a case with preservation of color discrimination. *Clinical Vision Science, 4*, 183–196.

Walraven, J., & Werner, J. S. (1991). The invariance of unique white; a possible implication for normalizing cone action spectra. *Vision Research, 31*, 2185–2193.

Wandell, B. A. (1995). *Foundations of vision.* Sunderland, MA: Sinauer.

Wässle, H., & Boycott, B. B. (1991). Functional architecture of the mammalian retina. *Physiological Reviews, 71*, 447–480.

Webster, M. A., & Mollon, J. D. (1991). Changes in colour appearance following post-receptoral adaptation. *Nature, 349*, 235–238.

Weitzman, D. O., & Kinney, J. A. S. (1969). Effect of stimulus size, duration, and retinal location upon the appearance of color. *Journal of the Optical Society of America, 59*, 640–643.

Werner, J. S., & Schefrin, B. E. (1993). Loci of achromatic points throughout the life span. *Journal of the Optical Society of America, A10*, 1509–1516.

Werner, J. S., & Wooten, B. R. (1979). Opponent chromatic mechanisms: Relation to photopigments and hue naming. *Journal of the Optical Society of America, 69*, 422–434.

Wesner, M. F., Pokorny, J., Shevell, S. K., & Smith, V. C. (1991). Foveal cone detection statistics in color-normals and dichromats. *Vision Research, 31*, 1021–1037.

Willmer, E. N., & Wright, W. D. (1945). Colour sensitivity of the fovea centralis. *Nature, 156*, 119–121.

Wooten, B. R., & Wald, G. (1973). Color-vision mechanisms in the peripheral retinas of normal and dichromatic observers. *Journal of General Physiology, 61*, 125–145.

Wright, W. D. (1991). The measurement of colour. In J. R. Cronly-Dillon (Gen. Ed.), *Vision and visual dysfunction: Vol. 6.* P. Gouras (Ed.), *The perception of colour* (pp. 10–21). Boca Raton, FL: CRC Press.

Wyszecki, G., & Stiles, W. S. (1982). *Color science: Concepts and methods, quantitative data and formulae* (2nd ed.). New York: Wiley.

Zeki, S. (1983). Colour coding in the cerebral cortex: The reaction of cells in monkey visual cortex to wavelengths and colours. *Neuroscience, 9*, 741–765.

Zeki, S. (1990). A century of cerebral achromatopsia. *Brain, 113*, 1721–1777.

Chapter Five

Visual Space Perception

H. A. Sedgwick

Introduction

What Is Space Perception?

Almost all animals rely on vision to help them interact with their environments. Finding their way around, looking for food, seeking shelter, avoiding predators, and many other activities require the perception of various features of the *spatial layout* of visible environmental surfaces, such as their sizes, distances, shapes, and orientations. This aspect of perceptual activity is referred to as *visual space perception.*

Perceiving a given feature of spatial layout, such as the size of an object, may be useful in a wide range of activities, so this perception has most commonly been thought of as occurring somewhat independently of the particular activity of the moment. Thus a rock in a field may be thought of as having a particular perceived size that is more or less independent of whether one is going to sit on it or jump over it. This is the premise of most psychophysical research on space perception, which examines the perception of size, for example, using specialized psychophysical tasks, such as adjusting a comparison object to match the perceived size of a standard object, but assumes that its results are more generally informative about perceived size in real-world activities such as sitting or jumping.

This view – that there is something we can call "space perception" that exists independently of the particular activities of the animal – can be questioned. It may be a more accurate description of an animal's perception to say that it doesn't perceive the rock's size per se but instead perceives simply that "I can sit on this rock" or that "I can jump over this rock"; what is perceived, according to this alternate view, is the behavior that the environment affords, called an *affordance* (Gibson, 1977; Gibson, 1979, p. 18; Greeno, 1994), rather than the physical characteristics of the environment (Warren, 1995, p. 264). It is possible to combine these two views and hypothesize that at least some "higher" animals, such as the primates, perceive both the underlying spatial layout of their environment and the affordances of this layout. This combined view will be adopted in this chapter because it invites us to consider the widest range of information about space perception and also because neither of the alternative views has yet developed a compelling argument for its exclusive validity.

Even if an animal's perception of spatial layout is to some degree independent of the animal's current activity, it seems reasonable that the features of spatial layout that the animal perceives are those that are potentially relevant for its behavior. That is, the animal's perception is *adapted* to be helpful in its interactions with its environment (Gibson, 1966, p. 154). This adaptation may have occurred through evolution, through maturation, through learning, or through short-term or momentary adjustments; which of these processes predominates and how they occur are fascinating questions that are beyond the scope of this chapter. What is important for us is that an animal's space perception cannot be understood independently of the behaviors and environments to which it is adapted. We shall see in the course of this chapter that this applies to the space perception of humans as well as other animals, even though the versatility of our species can make it seem as though our potential behaviors and environments are unlimited.

What Is the Problem of Visual Space Perception?

The problem of visual space perception is how an observer, human or otherwise, can perceive a three-dimensional spatial layout of environmental surfaces using only the light that is reflected from these surfaces to the eyes of the observer. A solution is possible because this reflected light, called the *optic array* (Gibson, 1961), has been structured by its interaction with the environment. Different environments produce different optic arrays, so that the particular structure of each optic array reaching the observer is in some ways specific to the environment that produced it. This makes it possible within some limitations to work backward from the structure in the optic array to recover the structure of the environment – a process called *inverse projection*. When such inverse projection is possible, the optic array is said to carry *visual information* that specifies the environment (Gibson, 1966, p. 186).

For inverse projection to be possible there must be, for a particular optic array, only one spatial layout that could have produced it. If every conceivable spatial layout is considered, then there are generally infinitely many distinct layouts that could have given rise to any particular optic array. If, however, only spatial layouts that conform to the natural environment of the observer are considered, then a unique solution may be possible. In asserting that certain visual information is specified by some structure in the optic array, we need to identify the *ecological constraints* that ensure the validity of this information (Cantril, 1960, p. 41; Marr, 1982, p. 104; Sedgwick, 1983, p. 427). This chapter will describe some of these ecological constraints, but they will not be detailed in every instance.

There is disagreement over how the human visual system makes use of the information in the optic array. Some theorists suggest that the visual system is, or becomes, finely attuned to at least some of this information (Gibson, 1979; Marr, 1982; Runeson, 1995; Runeson & Vedeler, 1993). Other theorists argue that, rather than using the precise information that is available, perception relies on fairly crude approximations, called *heuristics*, that are close enough to be useful but lack the complexity required to determine the actual inverse projections (Caudek & Proffitt, 1993; Gilden & Proffitt, 1994; Ramachandran & Anstis, 1986). The term "*cues*" is sometimes used instead of "information" to suggest that the optical structures responded to by the perceptual system are rather fragmentary, incomplete, and in need of considerable internal elaboration (Gregory, 1997, p. 5; Woodworth, 1938, p. 651). Much research continues to be directed toward determining precisely which information, heuristics, or cues are actually used in perception.

The sections that follow introduce the major sources of visual information for space perception and consider how each of them is utilized. How multiple sources of information are combined is then considered. The final section addresses the neurophysiology of space perception.

Optic Array Information

We begin our discussion of visual information by considering the optic array of a stationary observer.

The Textured Ground

Humans have evolved as terrestrial organisms, living mostly on the surface of the earth, and getting around by walking on two legs. The simplest human spatial layout, then, could be said to consist of a person standing on a *ground plane* that extends away toward the horizon. If we consider the optic array arising from this layout, we can see that there is already visual information in this situation. Locations on the ground that are increasingly far from the observer are optically projected to increasingly high angular elevations in the optic array. A simple trigonometric relation links the distance along the ground ("d") to the angular elevation in the optic array ("A") and to the height of the observer's eye above the ground ("h"): d = h*tan A (Figure 5.1a). By making use of this angular *height in the visual field*, an observer could accurately perceive distances along the ground (Epstein, 1966; Gibson, 1950a, p. 72; Wallach & O'Leary, 1982).

Notice that the height of the observer's eye enters into this relationship. This means that for a given angular elevation in the optic array the specified distance increases with the height of the observer. We could say that in this relationship distance is *scaled* by eye height or that *eye height* is a natural unit of measurement, based on the observer's own body.

The surface of the ground or floor usually has some *texture*, such as grass, pebbles, or shag carpet. This provides a *texture scale* that also could be used in perceiving distance (Gibson, 1950a). The angular separation between two objects resting on the ground will vary with the position of the observer, but the amount of texture, or number of texture elements, separating the two objects will not change (Figure 5.1d). Thus, texture scale provides information for the distance between any two objects (called "*exocentric distance*"), and also between the observer and an object (called "*egocentric distance*"). For this texture scale information to be valid, the texture elements must have a statistically uniform distribution across the surface; this is an example of an ecological constraint.

Estimates of egocentric distance increase linearly out to quite large distances (reviewed in Gillam, 1995; Sedgwick, 1986; Wiest & Bell, 1985). This can be ascertained either psychophysically, for example by obtaining verbal estimates, or behaviorally, by specifying a location and then asking observers to close their eyes and walk to it. Interestingly, the behavioral method tends to produce more accurate results than the psychophysical method, which may lend some support to the hypothesis, discussed above, that perception is better attuned to affordances than to the reportable physical characteristics of the environment (Fukusima, Loomis, & Da Silva, 1997; Loomis, Da Silva, Fujita, & Fukusima, 1992; Philbeck, Loomis, & Beall, 1997; Thomson, 1983).

Researchers have measured exocentric distance perception by scattering a number of objects on the ground and asking observers either to estimate the distances between all possible pairs of objects or to make a map of the objects' positions. The spatial relations in

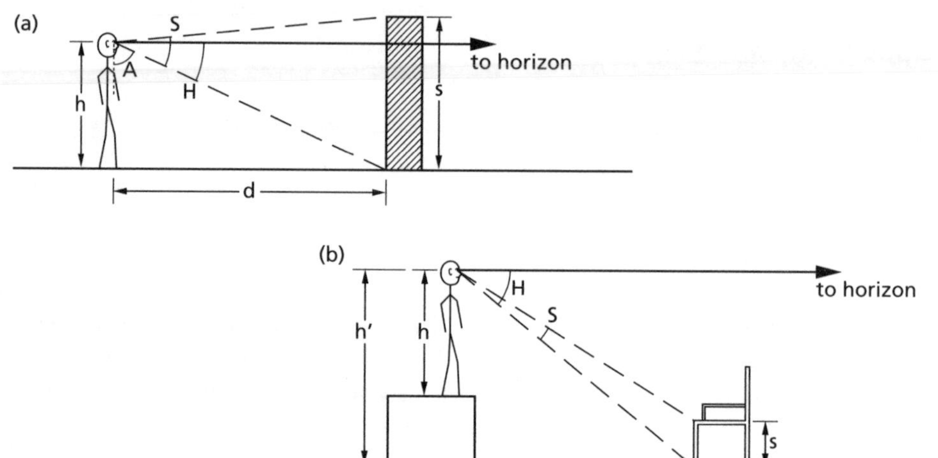
(a)
S
A
H
h
to horizon
s
d
(b)
H
S
h'
h
to horizon
s

(c)

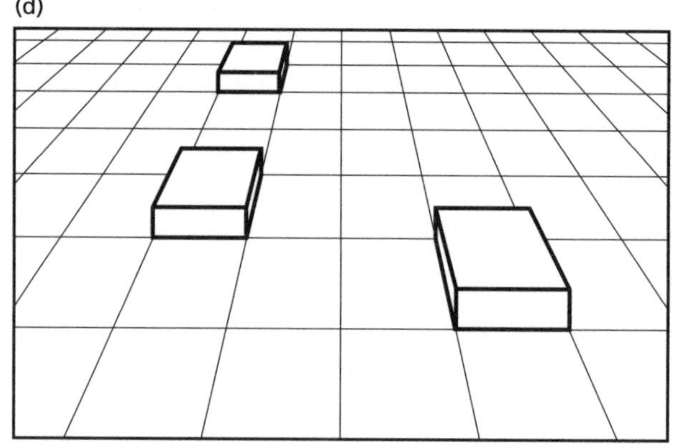
(d)

such perceptual maps are quite accurate except that perceived distance along a radial line from the observer tends to be compressed (by 15 to 50%) relative to distance in the frontal plane of the observer (Levin & Haber, 1993; Toye, 1986; Wagner, 1985).

Other information, discussed below, sometimes makes it possible to perceive small distances even in the absence of a ground plane, but the distances of objects at larger distances are difficult to perceive accurately if they cannot be located relative to the ground or some equivalent plane, such as the floor of a room. The distance of an unfamiliar object in the sky, for example, may be quite unclear; it could be a large object at a great distance or a much smaller object that is also much closer. Recent research has demonstrated the importance of a continuous ground surface to distance perception. For example, if there is a gap in the ground between the observer and the object whose distance is being judged then distance perception is less accurate (Sinai, Ooi, & He, 1998).

The size of an object resting on the ground is specified by its relation to the scale of the ground texture, discussed above, and is also specified by its relation to the horizon. Because the horizon is very far away, the line of sight to the horizon is almost parallel to the ground, so it intersects the object at a height above the ground equal to the eye height of the observer. Thus the height ("s") of the entire object, relative to the eye height ("h") of the observer, is approximately equal to the optic array angle ("S") subtended by the object, relative to the optic array angle ("H") subtended by the portion of the object below the horizon: $s/h = S/H$ (Figure 5.1a). This relationship is referred to as the *horizon-ratio relation* (Sedgwick, 1973, 1983). If the horizon is not visible, its position in the optic array may still be specified either by other optic array information, such as linear perspective, or by vestibular information, discussed below.

The horizon-ratio relation enters into a variety of affordances, such as whether a doorway is wide enough to pass through or whether a platform is low enough to step up on. These affordances are all naturally scaled by eye height to the particular body size of the observer. Research has found that observers are quite accurate in using this information either in planning or performing their actions (Jiang & Mark, 1994; Warren, 1984; Warren & Whang, 1987).

If an observer is relying on the horizon-ratio relation and if the observer's own eye height is misperceived (for example, if the observer is standing on a box, as in Figure 5.1b), then the sizes of objects and their affordances may also be misperceived (Mark, 1987; Wraga, forthcoming). If several objects are visible, however, then their *relative sizes* are still correctly specified because the error cancels out (Sedgwick, 1983; Figure 5.1c). Recent research suggests that size perception based on this information is most accurate when the object height is similar to the observer's eye height (Bertamini, Yang, & Proffitt, 1998).

←

Figure 5.1. The textured ground. (a) Distance is specified by height in the field and size is specified by the horizon ratio. (b) If eye height is underestimated then the perceived size of the chair may be too small to afford sitting. (c) The relative heights of the trees (twice eye height) and bushes (half eye height) are specified by the horizon ratio even if eye height is unknown. (d) The relative sizes and separations of the blocks are specified by the texture scale of the ground.

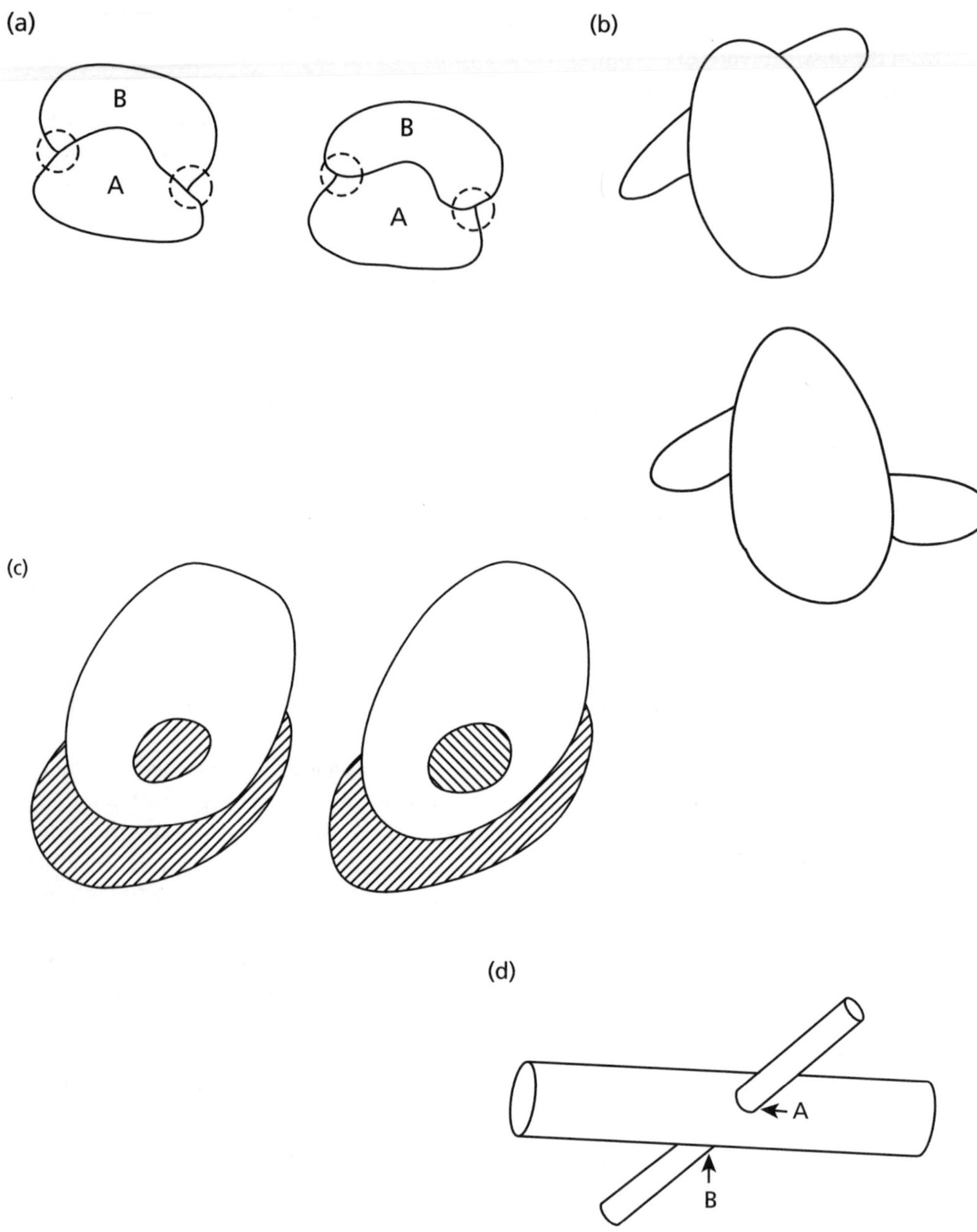

Figure 5.2. Occlusion. (a) T-junctions determine which blob is seen in front. (b) The perception of partial occlusion is stronger when the small blobs' contours can be perceptually related to each other (through colinearity in this example). (c) Matching areas of texture produce a stronger perception of one surface continuing under another. (d) The perception of one volume penetrating and being partially occluded occurs without T-junctions at A.

Occlusion

A typical environment is cluttered with objects. Various forms of visual information are available that help to specify the spatial relations between these objects. From a given point of observation only some surfaces are visible; others are hidden either by other objects or because they are facing away from the observer. When one surface only partially hides another, this *partial occlusion* provides information about the relative distance of the surfaces from the observer. The surface that is partially occluded is necessarily farther away. Partial occlusion specifies little more than the *order of depth*; it provides no information about the size of the depth interval that separates two objects, although the occluded object at least must be farther away by an amount equal to the thickness of the occluding object.

To see that a surface is partially occluded, it is logically necessary to see that there is more to the surface than is visible. How is it possible to see the existence of the part of a surface that is not visible? With some objects or forms, familiarity may play a role; it more likely that a chair continues under a table than that it is chopped off abruptly just as it reaches the table's edge. But partial occlusion is readily perceived with unfamiliar forms and objects. One powerful indicator of occlusion lies in the way that the contours of two objects meet. If one surface passes behind another then the projected contours of the occluded surface usually terminate abruptly when they meet the contours of the occluding surface (Helmholtz, 1962/1925; Ratoosh, 1949). This meeting, or junction, of projected contours in the optic array is called a *T-junction* because of its resemblance to the letter "T"; the terminated, occluded contour is the stem of the T and the continuing, occluding contour is the crossbar of the T (Guzman, 1969). When T-junctions are embedded in appropriate global configurations, then occlusion tends to be seen (Shipley & Kellman, 1990; Figure 5.2a). Other contour characteristics, such as abrupt changes in curvature (Tse & Albert, 1998; Figure 2d) and the perceived continuation of the occluded contour (Boselie & Wouterlood, 1992; Kellman & Shipley, 1991; Wouterlood & Boselie, 1992; Figure 5.2b) also contribute to the perception of occlusion. Although the role of contours in the perception of occlusion has been most extensively investigated, recent work has shown that specific characteristics of surfaces (Yin, Kellman, & Shipley, 1997; Figure 5.2c) and of three-dimensional volumes (Tse, 1999; Figure 2d) can also contribute to the perception of occlusion.

Context

When one surface is in contact with, or in the neighborhood of, other surfaces, the surrounding surfaces provide a *context* for it. The size, shape, and location of the surface may then be perceived relative to this context (Sedgwick, 1986). To take a very simple example, a line surrounded by a small rectangle will tend to be perceived as longer than a line of equal length surrounded by a larger rectangle because the first line is longer relative to its context (Rock & Ebenholtz, 1959). Context is a complex subject that has not been extensively investigated but that may play a considerable role in the perception of spatial layout in complex environments (Figure 5.3d). The information for size provided by texture scale and by the horizon-ratio relation, both discussed above, may be thought of as particular examples of contextual influences.

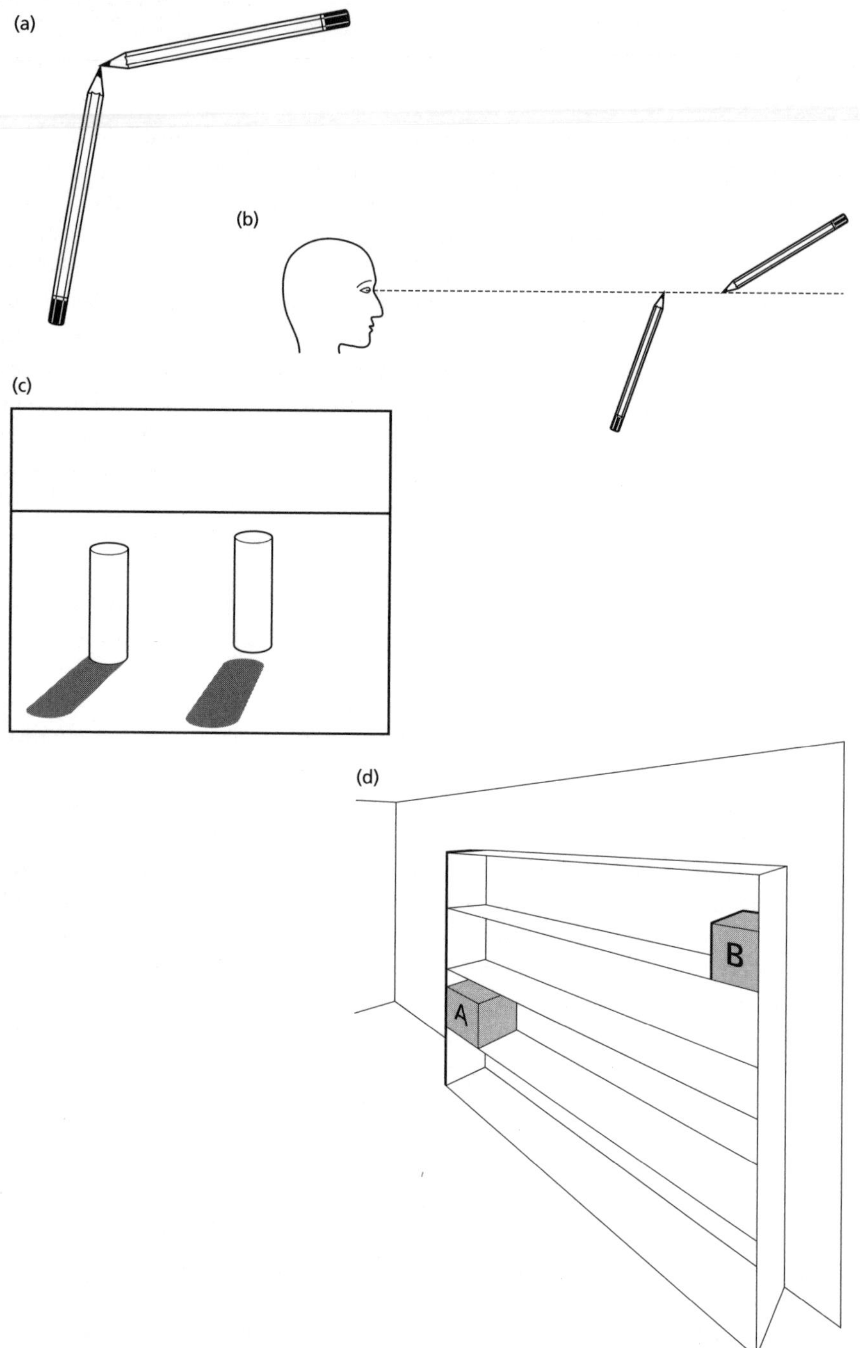

Figure 5.3. Optical contact and context. (a) Optical contact produces the perception that the pencils are touching. (b) A side view shows that the pencils are not physically touching; the optical contact is accidental. (c) Cast shadows can specify whether or not two objects are touching. (d) The context of the bookshelf specifies that A is larger and farther away than B even though A's projection is smaller and lower in the field than B's.

Some forms of contextual information depend critically on whether and how one surface contacts another. For example, the texture scale of a background surface only correctly specifies the relative sizes of two smaller surfaces along whatever edges of those surfaces are in contact with the background (Gibson, 1950a, p.181; Gillam, 1981; Figure 5.1d). If one visible edge of a surface is in *physical contact* with another surface, then the optical projection of that edge necessarily is superimposed on the optical projection of the surface, a configuration referred to as *optical contact* (Gibson, 1950a, p. 178). Optical contact, on the other hand, need not imply physical contact, because it can also arise when one surface is suspended in space between the observer and the other surface. Nevertheless, in the absence of information to the contrary there is a strong tendency for optical contact to give rise to the perception of physical contact (Gibson, 1950a, p. 180).

Cast shadows are one form of visual information that can either confirm or disconfirm physical contact (Madison & Kersten, 1999). For example, if an object is suspended slightly above the ground there will be a visible gap between the bottom of the object and the corresponding end of its shadow on the ground. In this case, the cast shadow not only shows that the object is not in contact with the ground but also helps to establish the spatial relation between the floating object and the ground (Rock, Wheeler, Shallo, & Rotunda, 1982; Ujjike & Saida, 1998; Yonas, Goldsmith, & Hallstrom, 1978; Figure 5.3c). For example, it has been shown that the perceived path of motion of a suspended or flying object can be strongly influenced by the path of the shadow it is perceived to cast on the ground (Kersten, Knill, Mamassian, & Bulthoff, 1996; Kersten, Mamassian, & Knill, 1997).

In some instances it is possible but highly unlikely that optical contact would be present without physical contact. For example, if two projected contours meet at a point, it is possible that they are actually the projections of edges whose endpoints are separated in space but are arranged so that they lie along the same line of sight (Figure 5.3a). This is highly unlikely because if the point of observation were displaced even slightly then there would be a visible gap between the endpoints (Figure 5.3b). Thus of all possible points of observation only a tiny fraction would produce optical contact; the rest would not. The assumption that a slight change in viewpoint will not produce a qualitative change in the optic array has been called the *general position assumption* (Huffman, 1971, p. 298) and has wide application in understanding how perception operates (Nakayama & Shimojo, 1992; Rock, 1983, p. 143). Violating the general position assumption by forcing the observer to maintain an atypical viewpoint is a common way of fooling the eye and creating a variety of visual illusions (e.g., Gregory, 1970, pp. 50–60; Ittleson, 1968, pp. 17–21). The general position assumption is another example of an ecological constraint.

Most environments contain a rich and complex set of contact relations. Some objects rest directly on the ground, but many rest on, or are attached to, other objects. Except for floating or flying objects, each object is eventually linked to the ground, and hence to other objects, by a set of *nested contact relations* (Sedgwick, 1989). Some of the information specifying these relations has been analyzed in detail (Sedgwick, 1987b, 1989), but there has been little research on how perception utilizes such information. Recent initial results suggest that observers can accurately perceive spatial relations mediated by such contact relations, although their perception may become more variable as the relations become more extended (Meng & Sedgwick, 1998, 1999).

The idea that the spatial layout of the environment can be conceptualized as a *continuous layout of surfaces* whose spatial relations with each other are mediated by their relations with the ground plane has been called the *ground theory of space perception* (Gibson, 1950a, p. 6). This way of thinking about space perception was clearly articulated by Alhazen about 1000 years ago (Alhazen, 1989/d.1039, p. 152), but appears not to have entered into modern thinking about perception until it was independently rediscovered by Gibson.

Linear Perspective

As things of constant size get farther away, the visual angles that they subtend in the optic array decrease. Depending on the particular structure of the environment, this relation between size, distance, and visual angle gives rise to a variety of optic array structures that can be informative about spatial layout.

In the absence of any information about distance, objects tend to appear to be at the same distance, an effect that is known as the *equidistance tendency* (Gogel, 1969b). If, however, two objects differ in angular size, then there is a strong perceptual effect of *relative angular size* on perceived distance (Burnham, 1983; Gogel, 1969a; Hochberg & McAlister, 1955; Newman, 1972). The object with the larger angular size tends to be perceived as physically larger as well as closer (Epstein & Landauer, 1969; Higashiyama, 1979).

When a textured surface is slanted away from the observer, the projected angular size of the surface's texture features will decrease steadily with increasing distance. This produces an optic array structure called a *gradient of texture size* in the direction of surface slant; the angular separation of texture features also decreases, producing a *gradient of texture density* (Gibson, 1950a; Purdy, 1960; Sedgwick, 1983). The more slanted the surface, the steeper the texture gradient; thus texture gradients provide information about the amount and direction of surface slant. Research has shown that texture gradients do influence perceived slant. Direction of slant is perceived quite accurately (Stevens, 1983), but typically the amount of slant that is perceived is considerably less than the slant that is optically specified by the texture gradient (reviewed in Blake, Bulthoff, & Sheinberg, 1993; Buckley, Frisby, & Blake, 1996; Knill, 1998a; Knill, 1998b; Sedgwick, 1986; Stevens, 1981; Stevens, 1984; Turner, Gerstein, & Bajcsy, 1991).

If a slanted surface has parallel contours, such as the top and bottom of an open door, then the angular separation of the projected contours will decrease with increasing distance, causing the projections of the contours to converge. This convergence is called *linear perspective.* If these converging projected contours are extended they will eventually meet at a point, called the *vanishing point,* which would be the projection of the parallel contours if they could be extended to infinity, where the angular projection of their separation would decrease to zero. All contours that are parallel to each other have the same vanishing point. Thus each vanishing point in the optic array is uniquely specific to an orientation in space; the vanishing point determined by the converging projections of parallel contours provides unequivocal information about their three-dimensional orientation (Hay, 1974; Sedgwick, 1983). Linear perspective produces a reasonably accurate perception of slant if the surface subtends a sufficiently wide visual angle (reviewed in Sedgwick, 1986). Even if a slanted surface has no visible edges or contours, linear perspective is still implicit in the angular size and density of its texture features (Sedgwick, 1983). Although such textural perspective also produces a perception of slant, it is much more effective if the pattern of texture features is regular, and thus contains implicit contours, than if the texture elements have an irregular, random distribution on the surface (Gibson, 1950b; Kraft & Winnick, 1967; Turner et al., 1991).

Compression

If a surface is slanted away from the observer, its projection is compressed in the direction of the slant. Thus, for example, the projection of a slanted circular surface is approximately elliptical. The *aspect ratio* is the ratio of the short axis to the long axis of a projected form; if the form's unprojected dimensions are equal, as they are with a circle, the aspect ratio is a measure of the *projective compression* and is directly related to the amount of slant. The perceived slant of a projected form seen in isolation is at least weakly related to its aspect ratio, so that a projected ellipse will tend to be seen both as more circular and as slanted (Clark, Smith, & Rabe, 1955).

If the slanted surface is textured, then its texture will also be compressed. Although natural textures are varied and complex, one simple model of surface texture is circular texture elements scattered over the surface. These circular texture elements are then each compressed into an approximate ellipse. An extended slanted surface, such as a ramp, has a slant relative to the ground, called its *geographical slant*, that can be expressed as a single angle for the entire surface (e.g., 30°). The compression of the surface texture depends, however, on the local slant of the surface relative to the line of sight of the observer, called its *optical slant*, and this slant changes with distance along the surface (Gibson & Cornsweet, 1952). If we consider the ground plane, for example, as the line of sight sweeps from the feet of the observer to the horizon, the angle it makes with the ground changes gradually from perpendicular to parallel. The projection of circular texture elements changes from circular to progressively narrower ellipses, finally being compressed into a single line at the horizon. This gradual change in the compression of the projected texture is called a *gradient of texture compression* (Purdy, 1960; Sedgwick, 1983). The rate of change of texture compression, that is, the steepness of the texture gradient, is directly related to the slant of the surface and thus provides visual information that could potentially be used in the perception of surface slant. This information is more robust than the aspect ratios of individual texture elements because it does not depend on their underlying unprojected shapes. For example, if the texture elements are themselves elliptical then their individual aspect ratios will not be reliably related to their slant, but the gradient of texture compression will correctly specify the surface slant. It appears that both the aspect ratios of the texture elements and the gradient of texture compression have some influence on perceived slant (Knill, 1998a; Rosenholtz & Malik, 1997). Texture compression has more effect on perceived surface curvature than on the perceived slant of a flat surface (Cumming, Johnston, & Parker, 1993; Cutting & Millard, 1984; Goodenough & Gillam, 1997).

Shading

How much light a surface reflects in the direction of the observer depends not only on the intrinsic reflectance of the surface but also on the angle at which the illumination strikes the surface. A surface receives and reflects less light from glancing illumination and receives and reflects only indirect light if it is facing away from the source. The amount of light reflected from a curved surface changes gradually as the orientation of the surface changes, thus creating a *gradient of shading* along the surface. Gradients of shading contribute to the perception of surface curvature (De Haan, Erens, & Noest, 1995; Horn & Brooks, 1989; Kleffner & Ramachandran, 1992; Koenderink, van Doorn, Christou, & Lappin, 1996; Mingolla & Todd, 1986; Ramachandran, 1988; Todd & Mingolla, 1983). As with gradients of texture, however, they are most effective when they produce or are accompanied by visible contours (Christou, Koenderink, & van Doorn, 1996; Christou & Koenderink, 1997; Erens, Kappers, & Koenderink, 1993; Mamassian & Kersten, 1996; Todd & Reichel, 1989).

The information described so far is available in the optic array at a single, stationary point of observation. It is thus information that can be captured by taking a photograph or, to some extent, by making a careful drawing or painting from that point of observation. For this reason it is sometimes referred to as *pictorial information* (Gibson, 1971; Hochberg, 1962; Sedgwick, 1980).

Motion Transformations

Animals are usually mobile. Their movements serve many purposes, including gathering information about their environment. The transformations of the optic array produced by an animal's movements generate a variety of forms of useful information about the spatial layout of the environment.

Varying Structures and Invariant Structures in the Optic Array

An animal's movements bring distant surfaces nearer and bring hidden surfaces into sight, thus allowing it to explore the layout of its environment according to its needs and interests. Although the usefulness of such exploratory movements for space perception has been clearly stated (Gibson, 1966, p. 206), they have been little studied. New impetus for research in this area may come from the recent development in mathematics and computer science of formal techniques, called *aspect graphs*, for studying the visibility of objects and scenes from different points of observation (Plantinga & Dyer, 1990; Van Effelterre, 1994).

As the animal moves, many but not all of the informative optic array structures discussed so far are gradually *transformed.* Height in the visual field, relative angular sizes of objects at different distance, perspective convergence and compression, texture gradients,

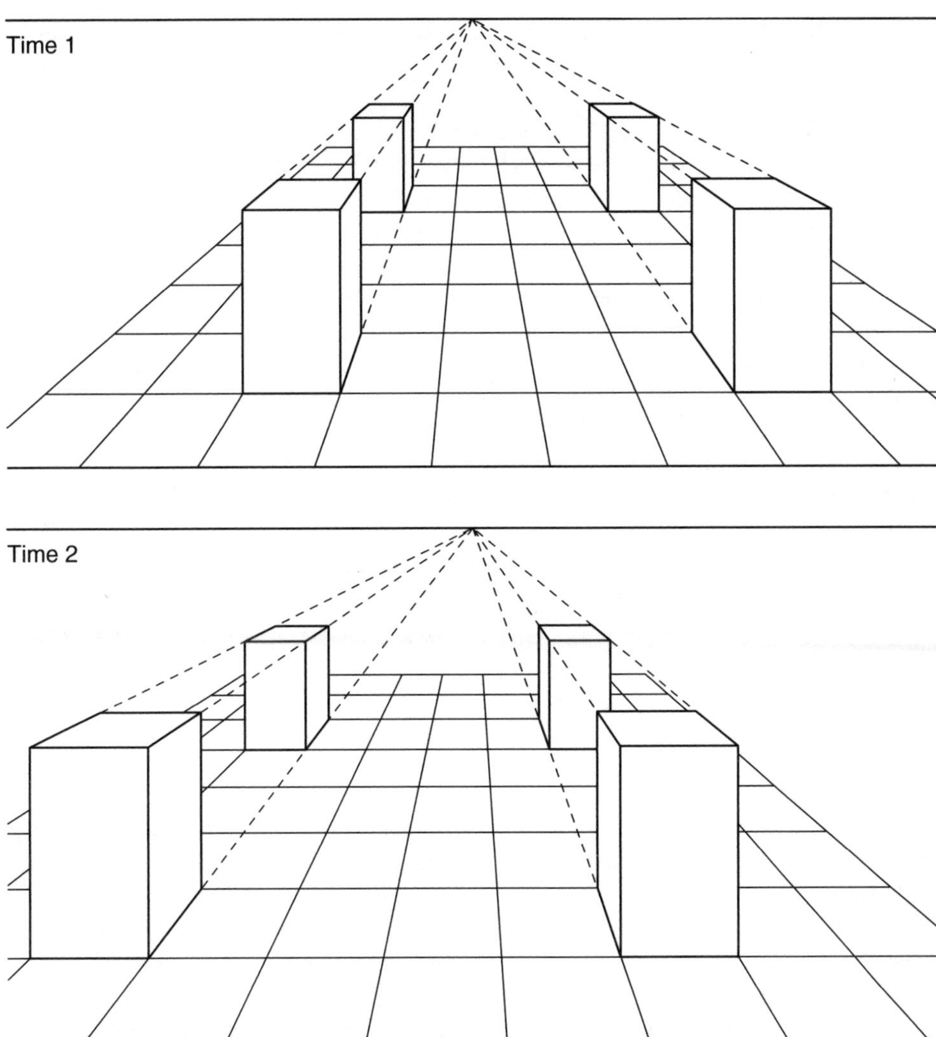

Figure 5.4. Motion transformation and invariance. Between Time 1 (top frame) and Time 2 (bottom frame), the observer moves forward and to the right. Optic array transformations include projective sizes and shapes, relative directions, and dynamic occlusion and disocclusion. Invariant optic array structures include points of contact with the ground, texture scale specification of relative sizes and separations, relative horizon-ratios, and directions of the vanishing points.

occlusion relations, and some optical contact relations all typically change, and these changes can themselves be informative (Figure 5.4).

For example, if the observer's movements cause a partially occluded textured surface to be gradually revealed, or disoccluded, then new texture elements will become visible at the occlusion boundary (Gibson, 1966, p. 203). This accretion of texture elements occurs only on the side of the boundary belonging to the surface that is hidden. If the observer moves in the other direction then texture elements of the surface being hidden will be deleted at the boundary. Research has shown that this progressive *accretion and deletion of texture* carries effective information both about the existence of a boundary between two surfaces (Andersen & Cortese, 1989; Anderson & Sinha, 1997; Bruno & Bertamini, 1990; Shipley & Kellman, 1994) and about which surface is in front and which is behind (Granrud et al., 1984; Kaplan, 1969; Ono, Rogers, Ohmi, & Ono, 1988; but also see Craton & Yonas, 1988, 1990).

On the other hand, some optical structures are unaffected by movements of the observer. Consider texture scale, for example; the projected number of texture elements separating two objects does not change as the observer moves. Similarly, relative horizon-ratios, the relative directions of vanishing points, and the angular size of an object relative to its local context remain unchanged, or *invariant*, with movements of the observer (Figure 5.4). Such invariance during movement can itself be informative. As the observer moves, for example, the vanishing point of an edge, and hence its orientation in space, is revealed as the unchanging point of intersection of the edge's successive optic array projections (Hay, 1974; Sedgwick, 1983).

If two surfaces are in physical contact with each other, then when the observer moves, their optical contact will remain invariant. If the surfaces are not in physical contact, however, then their optical contact will usually change. Thus whether or not their optical contact remains invariant specifies whether or not the surfaces are in physical contact.

Optical Flow

When the observer moves in a straight line, this translatory motion produces a change in the angular direction of most locations in the environment (Figure 5.5a). This complex, continuous, overall transformation of the optic array is called an *optical flow field.* The location toward which the observer is moving is called the *focus of expansion* because it maintains a fixed position in the optic array while the surrounding locations gradually move, in angular terms, away from it (Gibson, 1950a, p. 128; Figure 5.5b). Thinking of the optic array as a globe having the observer's direction of motion as its axis, the optical flow follows imaginary lines of longitude, flowing outward from the center of expansion at the pole, flowing past the observer on all sides, and flowing together again at the location away from which the observer is moving (Gibson, 1950a, p. 123; Gibson, Olum, & Rosenblatt, 1955).

The overall structure of the optical flow field, and the direction of the center of expansion in particular, provide information specifying the direction of movement, or *heading*, of the observer (Gibson, 1950a, p. 123). Much research has been done showing that observers are able to use this information with considerable accuracy, although exactly which aspects of this complex information are most useful remains a matter of debate and investigation (reviewed in Warren, 1995). If the observer moves in a curved path, as happens for example in driving on a curving road, the optical flow field becomes more complex, but judgments of heading remain quite accurate (Turano & Wang, 1994; Warren, Mestre, Blackwell, & Morris, 1991). The visual perception of self-motion has been termed *visual kinesthesis* (Gibson, 1950a, p. 124).

When the observer's eyes rotate, possibly in conjunction with a rotation of the head or

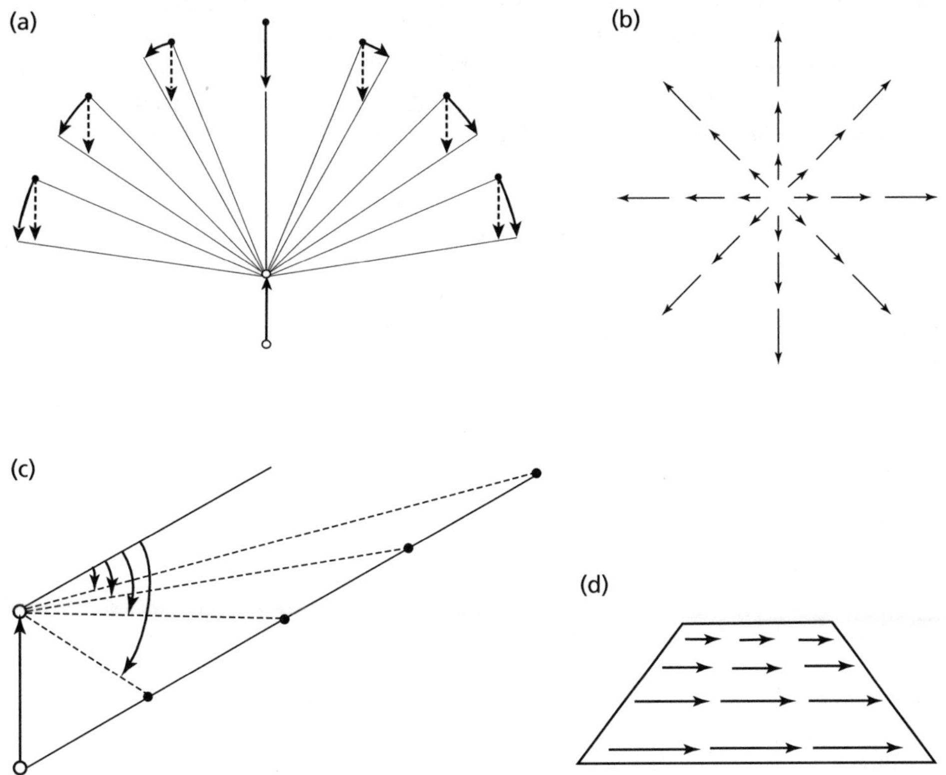

Figure 5.5. Optic flow fields. (a) The amount of flow produced by translatory movement (seen from above) varies with direction. (b) The center of expansion in the optic array is the point toward which the observer is moving. (c) The amount of flow produced by translatory movement (seen from above) also varies with distance. (d) Movement relative to a slanted surface produces an optic array gradient of motion parallax.

body, the angular directions of the entire optic array change relative to the eye and retina. Considered from a retinal point of view, a *rotational flow field* is added to whatever optical transformations are being produced by translatory movements of the observer (Gibson, 1950a, p. 126). Research shows that observers continue to be able to perceive their heading with considerable accuracy in this situation; it seems that they are able to separate the translational flow from the rotational retinal flow, perhaps in part by taking into account the rotation of the eye in its orbit (Banks, Ehrlich, Backus, & Crowell, 1996; Warren, 1995).

A location's change in angular direction as the observer moves is also a function of its distance from the observer. The farther away a location is, the smaller is the angular change produced by a given translation of the observer (Figure 5.5c). Locations that are effectively infinitely far, such as locations on the horizon, do not change their angular direction at all (Helmholtz, 1962/1925, p. 295). The amount of angular motion of a single location, as a function of its distance, is called its *absolute motion parallax*. The difference in angular motion between two locations that is produced by their different distances from the observer is called their *relative motion parallax*. There is little evidence that human observers are able to make much use of absolute motion parallax in the perception of distance (Gogel & Tietz, 1973; Philbeck & Loomis, 1997), but relative motion parallax produces the clear perception that one location is farther away than the other (Bruno & Cutting, 1988; Eriksson, 1974; Ono et al., 1988; reviewed in Sedgwick, 1986, p. 21–43).

When an extended surface slants away from the observer, the distances of locations along the direction of slant change gradually, producing a *gradient of motion parallax*, which is also called *motion perspective* (Gibson, 1950a, p. 124; Figure 5.5d). Such a gradient has been shown to produce a vivid and accurate perception of the slant of the surface (Braunstein, 1968; Flock, 1964; Gibson, Gibson, Smith, & Flock, 1959). The gradient of motion parallax produced by a more complexly shaped three-dimensional surface, such as a surface corrugated in depth, produces a compelling perception of its three-dimensional shape (Rogers & Graham, 1979; reviewed in Todd, 1995). The motion parallax itself is not noticed; that is, although the surface's projection is deforming, the surface itself is perceived to be rigid and motionless.

Illusions of Self-Motion and Orientation

In principle, all motion is relative. Thus when we speak of the observer moving through the environment we might equally well speak of the environment as moving past a stationary observer. Perception, however, usually does not reflect this ambiguity. Thus rather than being uncertain about whether the observer or the environment is moving, the observer's perception is unambiguously of self-motion. The environment is perceived as the *stable framework* or background against which movement occurs.

If the observer is surrounded by a local environment, such as the cabin of a ship or a room in an experimental laboratory, that is moving relative to the larger terrestrial environment, then the observer will tend to see the visible local environment as stationary and to perceive self-motion in relation to that local environment (Helmholtz, 1962/1925, p. 266). This tendency leads to a variety of effects. On a ship or airplane that is cruising at a steady speed, the observer's perception is of being stationary because the observer is not moving relative to the local environment. In a laboratory it is possible to suspend the observer in an experimental room in such a way that the room is moving but the observer is held stationary (relative to the larger terrestrial environment). Then if the room moves back and forth, the observer perceives an illusory translatory motion of the self in the opposite direction (Lishman & Lee, 1973), which is called *linear vection* (Figure 5.6a); if the room rotates around the vertical axis, the observer perceives an opposite illusory rotation of the self, which is called *circular vection* (Brandt, Dichgans, & Koenig, 1973; Warren, 1995, p. 297; Figure 5.6b).

These vection effects can also be produced by *simulated motion* of the environment, as occurs sometimes in movies, video games, flight simulators, and *virtual reality* displays. In these situations, as in some local environments such as buses and trains, the observer is often able to see some portion of the larger stationary environment as well as seeing the

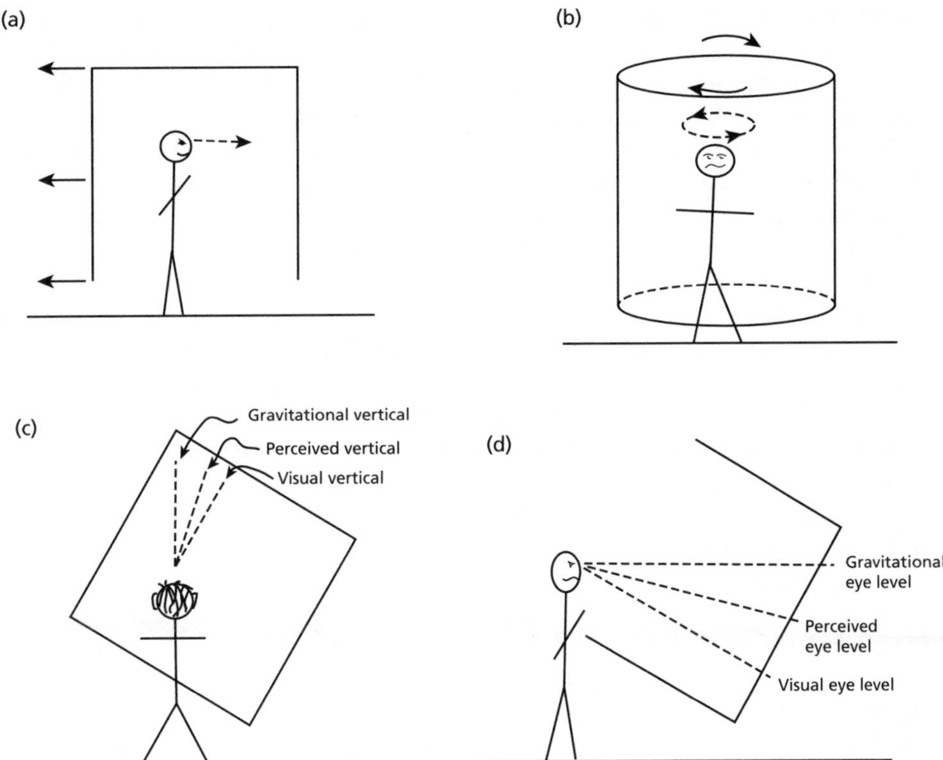

Figure 5.6. Illusions of self-motion and orientation. (a) Linear vection: movement of the room toward the observer produces the perception that the observer is moving forward. (b) Circular vection: Rotation of the room relative to the observer produces the perception that the observer is rotating. (c) Rod and frame effect: A tilted visual framework produces a partial tilt in the perceived gravitational vertical. (d) Eye level: A pitched visual framework produces a partial shift in perceived eye level.

relative motion or simulated motion of the local environment. These situations can produce instability in the perception of self-motion, with the perceptual choice of a reference frame being affected by a number of factors, such as which environment takes up the largest portion of the visual field or which environment is perceived as being farther away (Brandt, Dichgans, & Koenig, 1973; Brandt, Wist, & Dichgans, 1975; Howard & Heckmann, 1989; Ohmi, Howard, & Landolt, 1987).

It must be noted here, although the topic is beyond the scope of this chapter, that the observer's vestibular system is another source of information about self-motion. In vection situations, vestibular information often conflicts with the visual information provided by optical flow fields. The vestibular system is sensitive to acceleration rather than to constant linear motion, so such conflicts occur most with starting or stopping, speeding up or slowing down, or changing direction. Conflicts between vestibular and visual information can produce instability in the perception of self-motion, although in many situations perception tends to be more consistent with visual information (Howard, 1982, p. 388). These conflicts also are thought to be a major factor in producing motion sickness, although individuals vary widely in their susceptibility to this effect (Yardley, 1992).

The vestibular system is sensitive to the accelerational force of gravity and so provides the observer with information about the direction of the gravitational vertical. If the local environment rotates around a horizontal axis, this creates a conflict between visual and vestibular information. If the rotation of the local framework is from side to side, it is said to be rolling, and a stationary observer perceives a rolling self-motion, called *roll vection,* in the opposite direction. If the rotation of the local framework is from front to back, then the room is said to be pitching and the resulting illusion of self-motion for a stationary observer is called *pitch vection.* With both roll vection and pitch vection the conflict between visual information and the vestibular information specifying the gravitational vertical tends to reduce the amount of vection that is perceived (Dichgans, Held, Young, & Brandt, 1972; Held, Dichgans, & Bauer, 1975; Previc & Donnelly, 1993; Previc, Kenyon, Boer, & Johnson, 1993; Reason, Mayes, & Dewhurst, 1982; Young, Mendoza, Groleau, & Wojcik, 1996; Young, Oman, & Dichgans, 1975).

When a room rolls or pitches, the vertical or horizontal orientations that are visually specified by this local framework roll or pitch along with it. Even if the room is frozen in a stationary position at some roll or pitch angle to the terrestrial environment, an observer looking into the room will misperceive the orientation of the vertical or horizontal. If a local framework containing an adjustable rod is rolled to the side, an observer asked to set the rod to the true vertical will set it at some angle between the true gravitational vertical, which is specified vestibularly, and the visually specified vertical. This misperception of the true vertical is sometimes called the *rod and frame effect* (Asch & Witkin, 1948; Figure 5.6c). The strength of this effect varies considerably across individuals and also depends upon how visually compelling the local framework is (Howard, 1982, p. 419; Matin & Li, 1992). A similar effect is obtained if the observer looks into a room that is pitched forward or backward and attempts to set a marker to indicate true eye level. Here again the *perceived eye level,* or horizontal, is somewhere midway between the true eye level specified vestibularly and the eye level specified by the visual framework (Cohen, Ebenholtz, & Linder, 1995; Matin & Fox, 1989; Stoper & Cohen, 1986, 1989; Figure 5.6d).

Structure From Motion

Another kind of relative motion occurs when a visible object moves in the environment. The local optical transformations produced by the object's motion are necessarily the same as if the observer were making a corresponding movement relative to a stationary object. But because the observer is actually stationary relative to the environment, these local optical transformations occur within the context of an unchanging optic array and so specify that the object rather than the observer is moving. A local optical expansion pattern is thus perceived as a surface coming toward the observer (this perceptual effect is called *looming*) (Braunstein, 1966; Kilpatrick & Ittleson, 1951; Schiff, 1965). A local gradient of motion parallax is perceived as a slanted surface translating past the observer (Braunstein, 1968; Flock, 1964). And a surface undergoing an appropriate continuous perspective and compressive transformation is perceived as rotating (Gibson & Gibson, 1957).

These local optical transformations simultaneously specify both the motion of the object and its three-dimensional shape. Thus as an object rotates, the progressive occlusion and disocclusion of its component surfaces, their transforming patterns of shading, their gradients of motion parallax, and their perspective and compressive transformations all specify the three-dimensional shapes of these surfaces and their orientations relative to each other. Even the transforming silhouette of the rotating object contributes to the perception of its three-dimensional structure (Norman & Todd, 1994). The perceptual effect of these transformations is called *structure-from-motion* (Ullman, 1979).

A special case of structure from motion is created if all forms of depth information that would be present in a stationary object, such as perspective, shading, and occlusion, are artificially eliminated from the display of a rotating object. The continuous transformation of the projected lengths and orientations of its contours is generally sufficient in itself to produce a compelling perception of a three-dimensional object rotating in depth. The perception of a rotating three-dimensional shape that is produced purely from motion is called the *kinetic depth effect* (Wallach & O'Connell, 1953). The geometrical information on which the kinetic depth effect and structure from motion are based and the perceptual conditions under which they arise have been studied extensively (reviewed in Braunstein, 1976; Lappin, 1995; Todd, 1995; Ullman, 1979).

Stereopsis

Most animals have two eyes and thus see the world simultaneously from two slightly different points of view. For many animals the two eyes mostly view different parts of the world and may function fairly independently of each other perceptually (Howard & Rogers, 1995, pp. 645–657). For some animals, however, such as cats and primates, there is considerable overlap between the visual fields of the two eyes, creating a *binocular visual field.* Although the differences between the two views of the binocular visual field are quite small, they carry potentially useful visual information about the spatial layout of the environment. The perceptual use of this information is called *stereopsis.* Stereopsis can be investigated by presenting separate images of the same scene to the left and right eyes; such displays are called *stereograms.*

Horizontal Binocular Disparity

Any difference between the two eyes' views of something is referred to as *binocular disparity.* There is an underlying similarity between the disparities produced by binocular vision and the transformations produced by the observer's movements, discussed above. With motion each eye successively occupies different locations, whereas with binocular vision the two eyes simultaneously occupy different locations. Thus all of those optic array structures that are transformed by motion also give rise to binocular disparities; conversely, those optic array structures that remain invariant when the observer moves do not produce binocular disparity.

There are also, however, substantial differences between motion transformations and binocular disparities. Movements of the observer are continuous, are often large, and occur in any direction, whereas the two eyes have a small, fixed separation that always has the same orientation relative to the observer's head. These differences have substantial implications for the relative usefulness of the visual information carried by the various forms of binocular disparity in comparison with the analogous motion transformations.

When the head is held upright, the two eyes have a fixed horizontal separation. Until recently, most research on stereopsis has concentrated on the resulting *horizontal binocular disparities*. The *absolute horizontal disparity* of a single location depends upon the reference system that is used to measure it. Measured relative to the optic arrays of the two eyes, absolute horizontal disparity is, like absolute motion parallax, inversely related to distance (Figure 5.7a). There is no disparity between locations at the horizon, and disparity increases steadily for locations increasingly close to the observer.

Commonly, however, absolute horizontal disparity has been measured relative to the retinas of the two eyes, and so depends upon eye position. If we imagine the two retinas, centered on the foveae, as being superimposed on each other, then retinal locations that lie one on top of the other are called *corresponding retinal points.* Any location that is accurately fixated by the two eyes will be imaged on the centers of the two foveae and will have zero retinal disparity. Any other locations that are imaged on corresponding retinal points will also have zero retinal disparity. The set of all locations in space that have zero retinal disparity, for a given posture of the eyes, is called the *horopter*. In the horizontal plane, the *geometrical horopter* is a circle (called the *Vieth-Mueller circle*) that passes through the fixation point and the optical centers of the two eyes. Locations closer to the observer than the horopter are imaged on non-corresponding points and are referred to as having *crossed retinal disparity*; locations farther from the observer than the horopter are also imaged on non-corresponding points and are referred to as having *uncrossed retinal disparity*. Both crossed and uncrossed absolute horizontal retinal disparities increase with distance from the horopter (Figure 5.7b). The complexities of the horopter have been investigated in great detail (Howard & Rogers, 1995, pp. 31–68; Ogle, 1950).

Relative horizontal disparity refers to the difference in horizontal disparity between two locations. In taking the difference between the disparities of two locations, the effect of the choice of reference system is subtracted out; thus relative horizontal disparities do not depend upon eye position and are the same whether measured relative to the optic array or relative to the retinas (Figures 5.7c and 5.7d). Human stereopsis is exquisitely sensitive to relative disparities, but is not very sensitive to absolute retinal disparity. One recent study estimated that human perception is roughly one hundred times more sensitive to relative horizontal disparity than to absolute horizontal disparity (Ledgeway & Rogers, 1997).

For locations that are fairly close to the straight ahead, the relative horizontal disparity "η" of two locations depends upon the distance "D" of the nearer location from the observer, on the depth interval "d" from the nearer to the farther location, and on the separation "I" between the two eyes: η (in radians) $\approx d*I/(D*(D + d))$(Ittleson, 1960, p. 116).

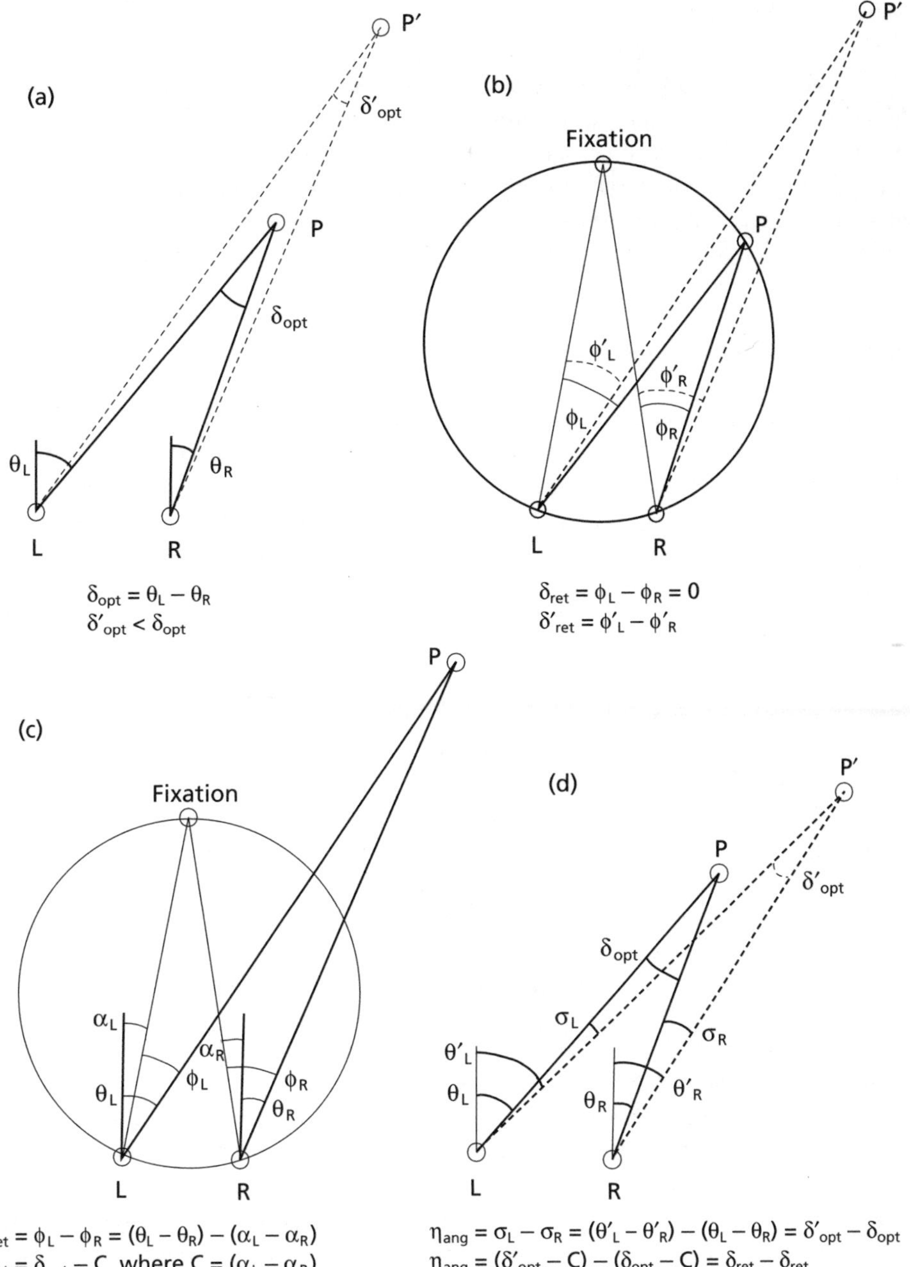

Figure 5.7. Binocular disparity. (a) In optic array coordinates, the absolute disparity δ_{opt} of the point P equals the difference in direction $\theta_L - \theta_R$ from the two points of observation L and R. As distance increases (to P′), disparity decreases (to δ'_{opt}). (b) In retinal coordinates, absolute horizontal disparity δ_{ret} is the difference in direction $\phi_L - \phi_R$ relative to the fixation point. For points (P) on the horopter, disparity is zero; disparity (δ'_{ret}) increases with distance of the point (P′) from the horopter. (c) For a given fixation, absolute retinal disparity (δ_{ret}) equals absolute optic array disparity (δ_{opt}) minus the angular convergence (C) of the eyes (note that α_R is a negative angle in this figure). (d) Relative angular disparity η_{ang} is the same for optic array and retinal coordinates (convergence is a constant that subtracts out).

If d is quite small relative to D, then this relation can be approximated by $\eta \approx d^*I/D^2$. Under these conditions, for a fixed I and D, the relative disparity η is directly related to the depth interval d. The sensitivity of stereopsis can be determined by measuring the minimum depth interval that can be reliably perceived. Under optimum conditions, the stereoscopic threshold for relative horizontal disparity is as little as a few seconds of visual angle (Schor & Badcock, 1985; Westheimer & McKee, 1978).

Stereoscopic Depth Constancy

We can rewrite the expression relating depth and disparity as $d \approx \eta^*D^2/I$. The rewritten expression emphasizes that the depth interval between two locations depends not only on their relative horizontal disparity but also on their distance from the observer and on the separation between the observer's eyes. The interocular separation I is a fixed property of the observer that, as with eye height, may be thought of as a natural unit of measurement based on the body. For a given disparity, however, the corresponding depth interval varies as a function of the square of its distance from the observer. This dependence on distance has two implications. The first is that the minimum depth interval that can be perceived based on relative horizontal disparity will increase dramatically with distance; for example, if the distance increases by a factor of 10, the minimum depth interval increases by a factor of 100. Thus stereopsis is much more sensitive at close distances.

The second implication of the dependence of stereoscopic depth on distance is that relative horizontal disparity by itself is not a sufficient basis for the stereoscopic perception of spatial layout. To perceive depth correctly using this relationship, the disparity would have to be adjusted, or *scaled*, according to distance. The perceptual result of scaling stereoscopically perceived depth according to distance is called *depth constancy* (Wallach & Zuckerman, 1963). Stereoscopically perceived depth intervals tend to be fairly constant as their distance from the observer increases (Collett, Schwarz, & Sobel, 1991; Glennerster, Rogers, & Bradshaw, 1996; reviewed in Ono & Comerford, 1977; Tittle, Todd, Perotti, & Norman, 1995). If distance is misperceived, then the depth scaling will accordingly be inappropriate (Foley, 1985).

What information for distance is used to scale disparity? One possibility is that the information discussed above in the sections on pictorial information and on motion transformations is used. A second possibility is that oculomotor information is used (see Additional Topics, below). A third possibility is that other stereoscopic information is used; one such kind of stereoscopic information arises from the vertical component of binocular disparities.

Any location that is above or below the horizontal plane through the eyes will have some angular elevation (positive or negative) in the optic array. If the location is in the median plane of the observer then its angular elevation will be the same in the two arrays. If the location is not in the median plane, however, then it will be at different distances from the two eyes and so will have different elevations in the two arrays (Figure 5.8a). This *vertical disparity* has been shown to provide information for distance that can be used to scale horizontal disparities (Gillam, Chambers, & Lawergren, 1988a; Gillam & Lawergren, 1983). This information is most effective when the observer has a wide field of view, which can thus take in locations having large angular deviations from the median plane (Rogers & Bradshaw, 1993). The relative influence of oculomotor information increases as the field of view decreases (Bradshaw, Glennerster, & Rogers, 1996).

Stereoscopic Slant Perception

A surface that is slanted in depth projects a gradient of binocular disparities. The nature of this gradient differs according to whether the slant is in the horizontal or vertical direction. For a horizontally slanted surface, the horizontal disparities are horizontally compressed in one array relative to the other (Gillam, 1995; Figure 5.8b), whereas in a vertically slanted surface the horizontal disparities increase along the vertical direction of slant, so that forms in one array are sheared relative to the other (Gillam, 1995; Figure 5.8c). This difference in the underlying optical structure produces a difference in perception. Vertical slants are seen easily, quickly, and accurately. Horizontal slants, however, are difficult to see, are often seen only after a latency of many seconds, and are often strongly underestimated (Gillam, Chambers, & Russo, 1988b; Rogers & Graham, 1983). Such a difference in perception, which depends on direction, is called an *anisotropy.* The anisotropy of stereoscopic slant perception suggests that stereopsis is more sensitive to the information carried by *shear* than to the information carried by *compression* (Gillam, 1995).

The difficulty in seeing the horizontal slant of a surface disappears if an unslanted surface is located just above or below it (Gillam, Flagg, & Finlay, 1984). Along the optical boundary between these two surfaces there is a gradient of disparity discontinuities, with these discontinuities increasing as the depth in terval between the slanted and frontal surfaces increases. This observation has led to the suggestion that there are two modes of stereopsis: a *surface mode,* which integrates local disparities across the extent of a surface, and a *boundary mode,* which responds to disparity discontinuities at the edges of a surface (Gillam, 1995; Gillam et al., 1984; Gillam & Blackburn, 1998).

Array Disparity and Occlusion

Stereopsis has traditionally been understood as arising from disparities between pairs of points in the images reaching the two eyes. When one surface partially occludes another, however, there are often some locations on the occluded surface that are visible to one eye but are not visible to the other. The projections of these locations are *unpaired points* and so cannot be said to have any local binocular disparity. They may be said, however, to be part of the overall *array disparity,* that is, the complete set of differences between the optic arrays at the two binocular points of observation. Such array disparities, involving unpaired points arising from occlusion, carry useful information about spatial layout and have recently been shown to give rise to compelling perceptions of depth (Anderson, 1994; Gillam & Borsting, 1988; Gillam & Nakayama, 1999; Nakayama & Shimojo, 1990; for a particularly striking example see Gillam, Blackburn, & Nakayama, 1999, illustrated in Figure 5.8d).

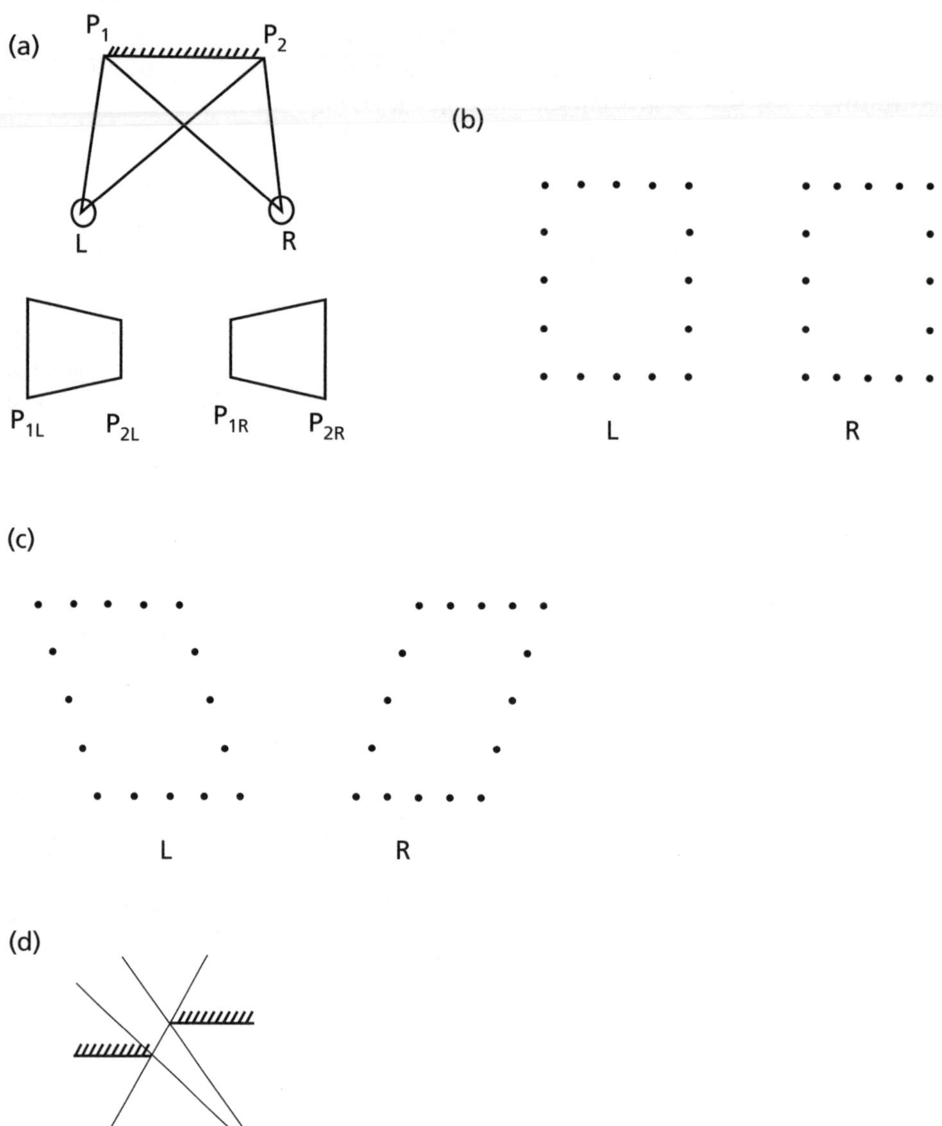

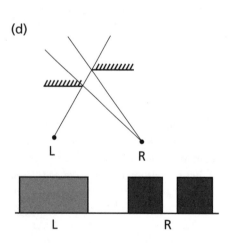

Figure 5.8. Stereoscopic configurations. (a) Vertical disparity is illustrated by a frontal square whose left side is closer to the left eye and whose right side is closer to the right eye. (b) With slant around a vertical axis, one eye's image is compressed relative to the other image. (c) With slant around a horizontal axis, one eye's image is sheared relative to the other image. (d) A stereogram with no local disparity but with a vertical gap in one image is seen as two surfaces arranged in depth so that only one eye sees the background between them.

Multiple Sources of Information

In a typical environment, multiple sources of visual information for spatial layout are simultaneously available to perception. These sources of information are partially redundant, often specifying the same or closely related characteristics of the environment, and they are deeply and complexly interrelated. How perception responds to multiple sources of information has been a question of considerable interest in recent years.

The Modularity Hypothesis

One widely influential hypothesis, suggested by the methodology of computer programming, is that the complex process of space perception is made more manageable and robust by a *modular* organization (Marr, 1982, p. 102). In this view spatial layout is specified by a number of distinct sources of visual information, such as binocular disparity, texture gradients, and shading, each of which is processed more or less independently by a separate module within the visual system. Each module generates its own representation of spatial layout, expressed in terms such as distance from the observer, and then these multiple representations are combined in some fashion to obtain the perception of the scene. One way of combining representations would be to take a *weighted average*, with the weights being based on considerations such as the relative reliability and accuracy of each source of information (Landy, Maloney, Johnston, & Young, 1995).

The hypothesis of modularity within visual space perception can be seen as one example of a broader hypothesis of modularity within the cerebral cortex and the cognitive functions that it supports, including vision. This broader hypothesis derives from the well-documented observation of *distributed processing* over multiple distinct cortical areas (Mountcastle, 1997; Zeki & Bartels, 1998; Zeki, 1978). Recent work, however, has challenged this concept of modularity as oversimplifying the fluid, dynamic, reciprocal interactions at many levels that characterize cortical functioning (Burr, 1999; Goldberg, 1995; Ishai, Ungerleider, Martin, Schouten, & Haxby, 1999; Lee, Mumford, Romero, & Lamme, 1998; Plaut, 1995; Pollen, 1999; Swindale, 1990, 1998). In any case, the specific hypothesis of the modular processing of different forms of information for spatial layout must be evaluated in its own right.

Using computer-generated images, it is possible to create displays having two sources of visual information that differ in the shape or distance of the surface that they specify. It is often possible to successfully model the resulting perception as arising from the weighted average of the two sources of information (reviewed in Landy et al., 1995). Although such results are consistent with the modular hypothesis they are weak evidence for it because such linear combinations could just as readily occur within a single integrated system. Perhaps the greatest weakness of the modular hypothesis is that it is based on the examination of highly simplified situations. It is far from clear how the complexly related sources of visual information for spatial layout existing in a typical environment could be divided up into separate modules.

Non-Modular Systems

A non-modular system would be one in which all of the various sources of visual information were processed together. Compared to a modular system, the dynamic flow of processing in such a system might be more complex and difficult to follow, but the underlying structure, treating all sources of information by a uniform set of rules, might be simpler. For example, one might simply have learned (or have evolved) to *associate* certain complexes of optic array structures with certain environmental structures (Berkeley, 1910/1709, pp. 16–17; Brunswik, 1955).

Recently there has been considerable interest in the use of *Bayesian* statistical methods to model the behavior of the perceptual system (Knill & Richards, 1996). Given a particular optic array, Bayesian methods make it possible in theory to calculate the probability, called the *posterior probability,* of each of the possible scenes that might give rise to that array, and so to choose, or perceive, the most likely one. To perform this calculation, however, it is necessary to know in advance the *conditional probability* that each of these scenes might have given rise to this array and also to know the *prior probability* of occurrence of each of these scenes.

In principle Bayesian methods are better suited than modular models to describing the dramatic alterations in the perception of spatial layout that can be produced by complex dependencies among sources of information. Bayesian theory, on the other hand, is so broad in its formulation that it gives us little *a priori* understanding of how particular forms of information are combined. It has been suggested that a modified form of Bayesian statistics that ignores (or equalizes) the prior probabilities of different scenes might be a better model of visual space perception, which sometimes appears to mechanistically follow certain rules without regard either for the likelihood of the resulting perception or for the prior knowledge the observer may have concerning the scene (Nakayama & Shimojo, 1992).

The conditional probabilities of Bayesian statistics are conceptually related to the environmental constraints discussed earlier. These constraints, however, being based on geometry, optics, and the persisting physical qualities of the environment, are often *determinant,* or non-probabilistic. Another non-modular way of modeling the combination of multiple sources of information is as the interaction of a large number of *conditional inference rules,* such as form the basis of *expert systems* (Sedgwick, 1987a, b). Although the world can certainly be conceptualized in probabilistic terms (including probabilities close to one or zero), the degree to which perception depends upon statistical operations remains an open question.

Effective and Ineffective Information

However the various sources of visual information are organized and combined by the perceptual system, it is apparent that sources of information differ widely in their perceptual effectiveness. Some of these differences are situational; thus each source of information is most effective over a particular range of distances, with stereopsis, for example, being most effective at near distances, whereas occlusion is equally effective at all distances (Cutting & Vishton, 1995). Other differences may depend upon the particular sensitivities of the perceptual system. Several examples have been mentioned above in which perception is more sensitive to shear and to perspective, which involve differences in orientation, than to compression (Gillam, 1995). Likewise, information carried by contours, junctions of contours, and discontinuities at contours appears to be highly salient, whereas information that must be statistically inferred from, or integrated across, distributions of elements, is often less effective perceptually (reviewed in Sedgwick, 1986, p. 21–34). Information present within a local context, such as local size ratios, tends to outweigh more globally distributed information, which would establish relationships between widely separated local contextual frameworks (Hochberg, 1968; Rock & Ebenholtz, 1959). The careful differentiation and delineation of the characteristics of effective and ineffective information has so far received little systematic attention. This may, however, prove to be a useful approach to uncovering some structure within the processes of visual space perception. If so, it could provide an alternative to current efforts that take the various sources of information as the organizational principles of space perception.

Neurophysiology of Space Perception

The functional capabilities of the visual system are densely interwoven, so that one structure may serve many functions, and those involved in the perception of spatial layout may not be easily separable from those that process other information about the animal's environment. Thus, for example, neurons that respond selectively to contour orientation are certainly essential for the perception of spatial layout but are presumably also involved in other functions, such as object recognition.

Some electrophysiological studies recording the activity of single neurons in primates have set out to search for, and have found, *receptive field properties* that appear to be specifically adapted for space perception. The activity of some neurons in *Visual Area 1 (V1)* and *Visual Area 4 (V4)* is modulated by the distance of the object being viewed, even when its image size on the retina is held constant; this modulation may contribute to size constancy (Dobbins, Jeo, Fiser, & Allman, 1998; Trotter, Celebrini, Stricanne, Thorpe, & Imbert, 1992, 1996). Neurons have been found in several cortical visual areas that are selective for some particular range of absolute binocular disparities; such selectivity is presumed to contribute to the process of stereopsis (DeAngelis, Ohzawa, & Freeman, 1991, 1995; Fischer & Poggio, 1979; Gonzalez & Perez, 1998; Hubel & Wiesel, 1970; Poggio & Fischer, 1977; Poggio, Motter, Squatrito, & Trotter, 1985). Many neurons in the *Medial-Temporal (MT)* cortical area are selective for disparity and for motion and may help to integrate these two sources of information in the perception of three-dimensional structure (Bradley & Andersen, 1998; Bradley, Chang, & Andersen, 1998; Bradley, Qian, & Andersen, 1995; DeAngelis, Cumming, & Newsome, 1998; DeAngelis & Newsome, 1999). Some neurons in the *Medial Superior Temporal (MST)* cortical area are selective for patterns of radial optical flow and so may be involved in the perception of self-motion and heading (Duffy & Wurtz, 1991; Graziano, Andersen, & Snowden, 1994; Lagae, Maes, Raiguel, Xiao, &

Orban, 1994). It thus appears that many cortical areas are involved in, and have specific adaptations for, visual space perception, although each of these areas probably serves other functions as well.

Single-cell evidence such as the above gives only a fragmentary view of visual functioning. A more coherent view of higher-order neural processes such as space perception probably requires a better understanding of how large aggregates of neurons function together. For example, there is as yet no accepted explanation of the neural processes that underlie the perception of an extended surface.

There is much promise in the recent development of sophisticated non-invasive techniques for imaging the brain in action, such as *positron emision tomography (PET)* and *functional magnetic resonance imaging (fMRI)*. Although these techniques do not have the spatial or temporal resolution of single-neuron recording, they can be used with humans and can provide information about which areas of the brain are most involved in particular activities such as stereopsis (Nagahama et al., 1996), the perception of shape from shading (Humphrey et al., 1997), and the perception of self-motion (de Jong, Shipp, Skidmore, Frackowiak, & Zeki, 1994). For example, early evidence now suggests that the *parahippocampal* area, buried within the temporal lobe of each hemisphere, is selectively involved in the perception of complex spatial layouts (Epstein & Kanwisher, 1998).

Neurophysiological research has received a significant source of guidance from psychophysical and theoretical studies of space perception and has produced important findings that are consistent with these studies. Neurophysiology has not yet reached the point, however, of being able to help answer functional questions about the processes of space perception. New techniques and a deeper understanding of how the brain functions may be necessary before neurophysiology is ready to make such a contribution.

Suggested Readings

Much of the research on visual space perception over the past 50 years has been stimulated by the ideas of James J. Gibson, which are well summarized in three of his publications:

Gibson, J. J. (1950). The perception of visual surfaces. *American Journal of Psychology, 63*, 367–384.
Gibson, J. J. (1966). *The senses considered as perceptual systems.* Boston: Houghton Mifflin.
Gibson, J. J. (1979). *The ecological approach to visual perception.* Boston: Houghton Mifflin.

A clear and highly influential exposition of the computational approach, which in some ways is closely related to Gibson's approach, is given in David Marr's book:

Marr, D. (1982). *Vision.* San Francisco: Freeman.

More detailed reviews of many of the topics covered here are given in the chapters included in the section on "space and motion perception," edited by Sedgwick, in:

Boff, K., Kaufman, L., & Thomas, J. (Eds.) (1986). *Handbook of perception and human performance* (Vol. 1). New York: Wiley.

Two useful collections of chapters reviewing various aspects of visual space perception have been assembled by Epstein and his colleagues:

Epstein, W. (Ed.) (1977). *Stability and constancy in visual perception: Mechanisms and processes.* New York: Wiley.
Epstein, W., & Rogers, S. J. (Eds.) (1995). *Perception of space and motion.* San Diego: Academic Press.

Also, a collection of chapters reviewing the constancies has recently been published:
Walsh, V., & Kulikowski, J. (Eds.) (1998). *Perceptual constancy: Why things look as they do.* Cambridge, UK: Cambridge University Press.

A detailed and comprehensive review of binocular vision is provided by:
Howard, I. P., & Rogers, B. J. (1995). *Binocular vision and stereopsis.* Oxford: Oxford University Press.

Additional Topics

The Representation of Spatial Layout

Does one representation of spatial layout best describe what we see? Or are multiple representations required? Researchers have suggested *viewer-centered* (Marr, 1982), *object-centered* (Marr, 1982), or *environment-centered* representations (Sedgwick, 1983; Sedgwick & Levy, 1985); also, a variety of geometries for describing space perception have been discussed, including *Euclidean, affine, ordinal, differential,* and *perspective* geometries, among others (Koenderink, 1984, 1990; Lappin, 1995; Pizlo, 1994; Todd, Chen, & Norman, 1998; Todd & Reichel, 1989).

Direct and Indirect Perception

An ongoing theoretical debate concerns whether or not visual perception consists of forming one or more internal *representations* of the environment. Those supporting *direct perception* argue that perception does not need to be mediated by such representations (Brooks, 1991; Gibson, 1979; Katz, 1983; Michaels & Carello, 1981; O'Regan, 1992); those supporting *indirect perception* argue that it does (Marr, 1982; Rock, 1997; Ullman, 1980).

Visual-Spatial Behaviors

The question of how visual information for spatial layout is used in a wide range of complex, meaningful activities has been receiving increased attention (Oudejans, Michaels, Bakker, & Davids, 1999; Rushton & Wann, 1999; Warren, 1995). Also see Chapter 10 in this Handbook.

Spatial Displays

Increasingly sophisticated technologies are being used to create the perception of virtual three-dimensional environments, displayed via static images, stereograms, moving pictures, and interactive virtual reality systems. The perceptual basis for the efficacy and limitations of such displays is the subject of growing research interest (Ellis, 1991; Hochberg, 1986; Rogers, 1995). Also see Chapter 11 in this Handbook.

Oculomotor Information

At near distances, up to one or two meters, the oculomotor adjustments of *convergence* and *accommodation* influence the perception of size and, more weakly, distance (Fisher & Ciuffreda, 1988; Gillam, 1995; Howard & Rogers, 1995, pp. 427–435). Also, the resting state of convergence is correlated with the tendency, in the absence of any information for distance, to see an object's distance as being about one to two meters (the *specific distance tendency*) (Owens & Leibowitz, 1976).

References

Alhazen, I. (1989/d.1039). Book of optics. In A. I. Sabra (Ed.), *The optics of Ibn Al-Haytham.* London: Warburg Institute, University of London.

Andersen, G. J., & Cortese, J. M. (1989). 2–D contour perception resulting from kinetic occlusion. *Perception & Psychophysics, 46*, 49–55.

Anderson, B. L. (1994). The role of partial occlusion in stereopsis. *Nature, 367*, 365–368.

Anderson, B. L., & Sinha, P. (1997). Reciprocal interactions between occlusion and motion computations. *Proceedings of the National Academy of Science, USA, 94*, 3477–3480.

Asch, S. E., & Witkin, H. A. (1948). Studies in space orientation: II. Perception of the upright with displaced visual fields and with body tilted. *Journal of Experimental Psychology, 38*, 455–477.

Banks, M. S., Ehrlich, S. M., Backus, B. T., & Crowell, J. A. (1996). Estimating heading during real and simulated eye movements. *Vision Research, 36*, 431–443.

Berkeley, G. (1910/1709). *A new theory of vision and other writings.* New York: Dutton.

Bertamini, M., Yang, T. L., & Proffitt, D. R. (1998). Relative size perception at a distance is best at eye level. *Perception & Psychophysics, 60*, 673–682.

Blake, A., Bulthoff, H. H., & Sheinberg, D. (1993). Shape from texture: Ideal observers and human psychophysics. *Vision Research, 33*, 1723–1737.

Boselie, F., & Wouterlood, D. (1992). A critical discussion of Kellman and Shipley's (1991) theory of occlusion phenomena. *Psychological Research, 54*, 278–285.

Bradley, D. C., & Andersen, R. A. (1998). Center-surround antagonism based on disparity in primate area MT. *Journal of Neuroscience, 18*, 7552–7565.

Bradley, D. C., Chang, G. C., & Andersen, R. A. (1998). Encoding of three-dimensional structure-from-motion by primate area MT neurons. *Nature, 392*, 714–717.

Bradley, D. C., Qian, N., & Andersen, R. A. (1995). Integration of motion and stereopsis in middle temporal cortical area of macaques. *Nature, 373*, 609–611.

Bradshaw, M. F., Glennerster, A., & Rogers, B. J. (1996). The effect of display size on disparity scaling from differential perspective and vergence cues. *Vision Research, 36*, 1255–1264.

Brandt, T., Dichgans, J., & Koenig, E. (1973). Differential effects of central versus peripheral vision on egocentric and exocentric motion perception. *Experimental Brain Research, 16*, 476–491.

Brandt, T., Wist, E. R., & Dichgans, J. (1975). Foreground and background in dynamic spatial orientation. *Perception & Psychophysics, 17*, 497–503.

Braunstein, M. L. (1966). Sensitivity of the observer to transformations of the visual field. *Journal of Experimental Psychology, 72*, 683–689.

Braunstein, M. L. (1968). Motion and texture as sources of slant information. *Journal of Experimental Psychology, 78*, 247–253.

Braunstein, M. L. (1976). *Depth perception through motion.* New York: Academic Press.

Brooks, R. (1991). Intelligence without representation. *Artificial Intelligence, 47*, 139–159.

Bruno, N., & Bertamini, M. (1990). Identifying contours from occlusion events. *Perception & Psychophysics, 48*, 331–342.

Bruno, N., & Cutting, J. E. (1988). Minimodularity and the perception of layout. *Journal of Experimental Psychology: General, 117*, 161–170.

Brunswik, E. (1955). Representative design and probabilistic theory in a functional psychology. *Psychological Reviews, 62*, 193–217.

Buckley, D., Frisby, J. P., & Blake, A. (1996). Does the human visual system implement an ideal observer theory of slant from texture? *Vision Research, 36*, 1163–1176.

Burnham, D. K. (1983). Apparent relative size in the judgment of apparent distance. *Perception, 12*, 683–700.

Burr, D. (1999). Vision: Modular analysis – or not? *Current Biology, 9*, R90–92.

Cantril, H. (Ed.) (1960). *The morning notes of Adelbert Ames, Jr.* New Brunswick: Rutgers University Press.

Caudek, C., & Proffitt, D. R. (1993). Depth perception in motion parallax and stereokinesis. *Jour-*

nal of Experimental Psychology: Human Perception and Performance, 19, 32–47.
Christou, C., Koenderink, J. J., & van Doorn, A. J. (1996). Surface gradients, contours and the perception of surface attitude in images of complex scenes. *Perception, 25*, 701–713.
Christou, C. G., & Koenderink, J. J. (1997). Light source dependence in shape from shading. *Vision Research, 37*, 1441–1449.
Clark, W. C., Smith, A. H., & Rabe, A. (1955). Retinal gradient of outline as a stimulus for slant. *Canadian Journal of Psychology, 9*, 247–253.
Cohen, M. M., Ebenholtz, S. M., & Linder, B. J. (1995). Effects of optical pitch on oculomotor control and the perception of target elevation. *Perception & Psychophysics, 57*, 433–440.
Collett, T. S., Schwarz, U., & Sobel, E. C. (1991). The interaction of oculomotor cues and stimulus size in stereoscopic death constancy. *Perception, 20*, 733–754.
Craton, L. G., & Yonas, A. (1988). Infants' sensitivity to boundary flow information for depth at an edge. *Child Development, 59*, 1522–1529.
Craton, L. G., & Yonas, A. (1990). Kinetic occlusion: Further studies of the boundary-flow cue. *Perception & Psychophysics, 47*, 169–179.
Cumming, B. G., Johnston, E. B., & Parker, A. J. (1993). Effects of different texture cues on curved surfaces viewed stereoscopically. *Vision Research, 33*, 827–838.
Cutting, J. E., & Millard, R. T. (1984). Three gradients and the perception of flat and curved surfaces. *Journal of Experimental Psychology: General, 113*, 198–216.
Cutting, J. E., & Vishton, P. M. (1995). Perceiving layout and knowing distances: The integration, relative potency, and contextual use of different information about depth. In W. Epstein & S. Rogers (Eds.), *Perception of space and motion*. New York: Academic Press.
DeAngelis, G. C., Cumming, B. G., & Newsome, W. T. (1998). Cortical area MT and the perception of stereoscopic depth. *Nature, 394*, 677–680.
DeAngelis, G. C., & Newsome, W. T. (1999). Organization of disparity-selective neurons in macaque area MT. *Journal of Neuroscience, 19*, 1398–1415.
DeAngelis, G. C., Ohzawa, I., & Freeman, R. D. (1991). Depth is encoded in the visual cortex by a specialized receptive field structure. *Nature, 352*, 156–159.
DeAngelis, G. C., Ohzawa, I., & Freeman, R. D. (1995). Neuronal mechanisms underlying stereopsis: How do simple cells in the visual cortex encode binocular disparity? *Perception, 24*, 3–31.
De Haan, E., Erens, R. G., & Noest, A. J. (1995). Shape from shaded random surfaces. *Vision Research, 35*, 2985–3001.
De Jong, B. M., Shipp, S., Skidmore, B., Frackowiak, R. S., & Zeki, S. (1994). The cerebral activity related to the visual perception of forward motion in depth. *Brain, 117*, 1039–1054.
Dichgans, J., Held, R., Young, L. R., & Brandt, T. (1972). Moving visual scenes influence the apparent direction of gravity. *Science, 178*, 1217–1219.
Dobbins, A. C., Jeo, R. M., Fiser, J., & Allman, J. M. (1998). Distance modulation of neural activity in the visual cortex. *Science, 281*, 552–555.
Duffy, C. J., & Wurtz, R. H. (1991). Sensitivity of MST neurons to optic flow stimuli. I. A continuum of response selectivity to large-field stimuli. *Journal of Neurophysiology, 65*, 1329–1345.
Ellis, S. R. (Ed.) (1991). *Pictorial communication in virtual and real environments*. London: Taylor and Francis.
Epstein, R., & Kanwisher, N. (1998). A cortical representation of the local visual environment. *Nature, 392*, 598–601.
Epstein, W. (1966). Perceived depth as a function of relative height under three background conditions. *Journal of Experimental Psychology, 72*, 335–338.
Epstein, W. (Ed.) (1977). *Stability and constancy in visual perception: Mechanisms and processes*. New York: Wiley.
Epstein, W., & Landauer, A. A. (1969). Size and distance judgments under reduced conditions of viewing. *Perception & Psychophysics, 6*, 269–272.
Epstein, W., & Rogers, S. J. (Eds.) (1995). *Perception of space and motion*. San Diego: Academic Press.
Erens, R. G., Kappers, A. M., & Koenderink, J. J. (1993). Perception of local shape from shading.

Perception & Psychophysics, 54, 145–156.
Eriksson, E. S. (1974). Movement parallax during locomotion. *Perception & Psychophysics, 16*, 197–200.
Fischer, B., & Poggio, G. F. (1979). Depth sensitivity of binocular cortical neurons of behaving monkeys. *Proceedings of the Royal Society of London, B: Biological Science, 204*, 409–414.
Fisher, S. K., & Ciuffreda, K. J. (1988). Accommodation and apparent distance. *Perception, 17*, 609–621.
Flock, H. R. (1964). Some conditions sufficient for accurate monocular perceptions of moving surface slants. *Journal of Experimental Psychology, 67*, 560–572.
Foley, J. M. (1985). Binocular distance perception: Egocentric distance tasks. *Journal of Experimental Psychology: Human Perception and Performance, 11*, 133–149.
Fukusima, S. S., Loomis, J. M., & Da Silva, J. A. (1997). Visual perception of egocentric distance as assessed by triangulation. *Journal of Experimental Psychology: Human Perception and Performance, 23*, 86–100.
Gibson, E. J., Gibson, J. J., Smith, O. W., & Flock, H. R. (1959). Motion parallax as a determinant of perceived depth. *Journal of Experimental Psychology, 58*, 40–51.
Gibson, J. J. (1950a). *The perception of the visual world.* Boston: Houghton Mifflin.
Gibson, J. J. (1950b). The perception of visual surfaces. *American Journal of Psychology, 63*, 367–384.
Gibson, J. J. (1961). Ecological optics. *Vision Research, 1*, 253–262.
Gibson, J. J. (1966). *The senses considered as perceptual systems.* Boston: Houghton Mifflin.
Gibson, J. J. (1971). The information available in pictures. *Leonardo, 4*, 27–35.
Gibson, J. J. (1977). The theory of affordances. In R. Shaw & J. Bransford (Eds.), *Perceiving, acting, and knowing: Toward an ecological psychology* (pp. 67–82). Hillsdale, NJ: Erlbaum.
Gibson, J. J. (1979). *The ecological approach to visual perception.* Boston: Houghton Mifflin.
Gibson, J. J., & Cornsweet, J. (1952). The perceived slant of visual surfaces – optical and geographical. *Journal of Experimental Psychology, 44*, 11–15.
Gibson, J. J., & Gibson, E. J. (1957). Continuous perspective transformations and the perception of rigid motion. *Journal of Experimental Psychology, 54*, 129–138.
Gibson, J. J., Olum, P., & Rosenblatt, F. (1955). Parallax and perspective during aircraft landings. *American Journal of Psychology, 68*, 372–385.
Gilden, D. L., & Proffitt, D. R. (1994). Heuristic judgment of mass ratio in two-body collisions. *Perception & Psychophysics, 56*, 708–720.
Gillam, B. (1981). False perspectives. *Perception, 10*, 313–318.
Gillam, B. (1995). The perception of spatial layout from static optical information. In W. Epstein & S. Rogers (Eds.), *Perception of space and motion.* New York: Academic Press.
Gillam, B., Blackburn, S., & Nakayama, K. (1999). Stereopsis based on monocular gaps: Metrical encoding of depth and slant without matching contours. *Vision Research, 39*, 493–502.
Gillam, B., & Borsting, E. (1988). The role of monocular regions in stereoscopic displays. *Perception, 17*, 603–608.
Gillam, B., Chambers, D., & Lawergren, B. (1988a). The role of vertical disparity in the scaling of stereoscopic depth perception: An empirical and theoretical study. *Perception & Psychophysics, 44*, 473–483.
Gillam, B., Chambers, D., & Russo, T. (1988b). Postfusional latency in stereoscopic slant perception and the primitives of stereopsis. *Journal of Experimental Psychology: Human Perception and Performance, 14*, 163–175.
Gillam, B., Flagg, T., & Finlay, D. (1984). Evidence for disparity change as the primary stimulus for stereoscopic processing. *Perception & Psychophysics, 36*, 559–564.
Gillam, B., & Lawergren, B. (1983). The induced effect, vertical disparity, and stereoscopic theory. *Perception & Psychophysics, 34*, 121–130.
Gillam, B., & Nakayama, K. (1999). Quantitative depth for a phantom surface can be based on cyclopean occlusion cues alone. *Vision Research, 39*, 109–112.
Gillam, B. J., & Blackburn, S. G. (1998). Surface separation decreases stereoscopic slant but a

monocular aperture increases it. *Perception, 27*, 1267–1286.

Glennerster, A., Rogers, B. J., & Bradshaw, M. F. (1996). Stereoscopic depth constancy depends on the subject's task. *Vision Research, 36*, 3441–3456.

Gogel, W. C. (1969a). The absolute and relative size cues to distance. *American Journal of Psychology, 82*, 228–234.

Gogel, W. C. (1969b). Equidistance effects in visual fields. *American Journal of Psychology, 82*, 342–349.

Gogel, W. C., & Tietz, J. D. (1973). Absolute motion parallax and the specific distance tendency. *Perception & Psychophysics, 13*.

Goldberg, E. (1995). Rise and fall of modular orthodoxy. *Journal of Clinical Experimental Neuropsychology, 17*, 193–208.

Gonzalez, F., & Perez, R. (1998). Neural mechanisms underlying stereoscopic vision. *Progress in Neurobiology, 55*, 191–224.

Goodenough, B., & Gillam, B. (1997). Gradients as visual primitives. *Journal of Experimental Psychology: Human Perception and Performance, 23*, 370–387.

Granrud, C. E., Yonas, A., Smith, I. M., Arterberry, M. E., Glicksman, M. L., & Sorknes, A. C. (1984). Infants' sensitivity to accretion and deletion of texture as information for depth at an edge. *Child Development, 55*, 1630–1636.

Graziano, M. S., Andersen, R. A., & Snowden, R. J. (1994). Tuning of MST neurons to spiral motions. *Journal of Neuroscience, 14*, 54–67.

Greeno, J. G. (1994). Gibson's affordances. *Psychological Reviews, 101*, 336–342.

Gregory, R. (1997). *Eye and brain: The psychology of seeing*. (5th ed.). Princeton, New Jersey: Princeton University Press.

Gregory, R. L. (1970). *The intelligent eye*. New York: McGraw-Hill.

Guzman, A. (1969). Decomposition of a visual field into three-dimensional bodies. In A. Grasselli (Ed.), *Automatic Interpretation and Classification of Images* (pp. 243–276). New York: Academic Press

Hay, J. C. (1974). The ghost image: A tool for the analysis of the visual stimulus. In R. B. MacLeod & H. L. Pick, Jr. (Eds.), *Perception: Essays in honor of James J. Gibson*. Ithaca, NY: Cornell University Press.

Held, R., Dichgans, J., & Bauer, J. (1975). Characteristics of moving visual scenes influencing spatial orientation. *Vision Research, 15*, 357–365.

Helmholtz, H. v. (1962/1925). *Treatise on physiological optics* (J. P. C. Southall, Trans.). New York: Dover.

Higashiyama, A. (1979). The perception of size and distance under monocular observation. *Perception & Psychophysics, 26*, 230–234.

Hochberg, J. (1962). The psychophysics of pictorial perception. *Audio-Visual Communication Review, 10*, 22–54.

Hochberg, J. (1968). In the mind's eye. In R. N. Haber (Ed.), *Contemporary theory and research in visual perception*. New York: Holt, Rinehart and Winston.

Hochberg, J. (1986). Representation of motion and space in video and cinematic displays. In K. R. Boff, L. Kaufman, & J. P. Thomas (Eds.), *Handbook of perception and human performance* (Vol. 1). New York: John Wiley and Sons.

Hochberg, J. E., & McAlister, E. (1955). Relative size vs. familiar size in the perception of represented depth. *American Journal of Psychology, 68*, 294–296.

Horn, B. K. P., & Brooks, M. J. (Eds.) (1989). *Shape from shading*. Cambridge, MA: MIT Press.

Howard, I. P. (1982). *Human visual orientation*. New York: Wiley.

Howard, I. P., & Heckmann, T. (1989). Circular vection as a function of the relative sizes, distances, and positions of two competing visual displays. *Perception, 18*, 657–665.

Howard, I. P., & Rogers, B. J. (1995). *Binocular vision and stereopsis*. Oxford: Oxford University Press.

Hubel, D. H., & Wiesel, T. N. (1970). Stereoscopic vision in macaque monkey. Cells sensitive to binocular depth in area 18 of the macaque monkey cortex. *Nature, 225*, 41–42.

Huffman, D. A. (1971). Impossible objects as nonsense sentences. In B. Meltzer & D. Michie (Eds.), *Machine intelligence, 6*. Edinburgh: Edinburgh University Press.

Humphrey, G. K., Goodale, M. A., Bowen, C. V., Gati, J. S., Vilis, T., Rutt, B. K., & Menon, R. S. (1997). Differences in perceived shape from shading correlate with activity in early visual areas. *Current Biolology, 7*, 144–147.

Ishai, A., Ungerleider, L. G., Martin, A., Schouten, J. L., & Haxby, J. V. (1999). Distributed representation of objects in the human ventral visual pathway. *Proceedings of the National Academy of Science, USA, 96*, 9379–9384.

Ittleson, W. H. (1960). *Visual space perception*. New York: Springer.

Ittleson, W. H. (1968). *The Ames demonstrations in perception*. New York: Hafner Publishing Company.

Jiang, Y., & Mark, L. S. (1994). The effect of gap depth on the perception of whether a gap is crossable. *Perception & Psychophysics, 56*, 691–700.

Kaplan, G. A. (1969). Kinetic disruption of optical texture: The perception of depth at an edge. *Perception & Psychophysics, 6*, 193–198.

Katz, S. (1983). R L Gregory and others: The wrong picture of the picture theory of perception. *Perception, 12*, 269–279.

Kellman, P. J., & Shipley, T. F. (1991). A theory of visual interpolation in object perception. *Cognitive Psychology, 23*, 141–221.

Kersten, D., Knill, D. C., Mamassian, P., & Bulthoff, I. (1996). Illusory motion from shadows. *Nature, 379*, 31.

Kersten, D., Mamassian, P., & Knill, D. C. (1997). Moving cast shadows induce apparent motion in depth. *Perception, 26*, 171–192.

Kilpatrick, F. P., & Ittleson, W. H. (1951). Three demonstrations involving the perception of movement. *Journal of Experimental Psychology, 42*, 394–402.

Kleffner, D. A., & Ramachandran, V. S. (1992). On the perception of shape from shading. *Perception & Psychophysics, 52*, 18–36.

Knill, D. C. (1998a). Discrimination of planar surface slant from texture: Human and ideal observers compared. *Vision Research, 38*, 1683–1711.

Knill, D. C. (1998b). Surface orientation from texture: Ideal observers, generic observers and the information content of texture cues. *Vision Research, 38*, 1655–1682.

Knill, D. C., & Richards, W. (Eds.) (1996). *Perception as Bayesian inference*. Cambridge: Cambridge University Press.

Koenderink, J. J. (1984). What does the occluding contour tell us about solid shape? *Perception, 13*, 321–330.

Koenderink, J. J. (1990). The brain a geometry engine. *Psychological Research, 52*, 122–127.

Koenderink, J. J., van Doorn, A. J., Christou, C., & Lappin, I. S. (1996). Perturbation study of shading in pictures. *Perception, 25*, 1009–1026.

Kraft, A. L., & Winnick, W. A. (1967). The effect of pattern and texture gradient on slant and shape judgments. *Perception & Psychophysics, 2*, 141–147.

Lagae, L., Maes, H., Raiguel, S., Xiao, D. K., & Orban, G. A. (1994). Responses of macaque STS neurons to optic flow components: A comparison of areas MT and MST. *J Neurophysiol, 71*, 1597–1626.

Landy, M. S., Maloney, L. T., Johnston, E. B., & Young, M. (1995). Measurement and modeling of depth cue combination: In defense of weak fusion. *Vision Research, 35*, 389–412.

Lappin, J. S. (1995). Visible information about structure from motion. In W. Epstein & S. Rogers (Eds.), *Perception of space and motion* (pp. 165–199). New York: Academic Press.

Ledgeway, T., & Rogers, B. J. (1997). Measuring the visual system's sensitivity to absolute disparity using open-loop vergence. *Investigative Ophthalmology and Visual Science, 38*, S903.

Lee, T. S., Mumford, D., Romero, R., & Lamme, V. A. (1998). The role of the primary visual cortex in higher level vision. *Vision Research, 38*, 2429–2454.

Levin, C. A., & Haber, R. N. (1993). Visual angle as a determinant of perceived interobject distance. *Perception & Psychophysics, 54*, 250–259.

Lishman, J. R., & Lee, D. N. (1973). The autonomy of visual kinesthesis. *Perception, 2*, 287–294.
Loomis, J. M., Da Silva, J. A., Fujita, N., & Fukusima, S. S. (1992). Visual space perception and visually directed action. *Journal of Experimental Psychology: Human Perception and Performance, 18*, 906–921.
Madison, C. J., & Kersten, D. J. (1999). Use of interreflection and shadow for surface contact. *Investigative Ophthalmology and Visual Science, 40*, S748.
Mamassian, P., & Kersten, D. (1996). Illumination, shading and the perception of local orientation. *Vision Research, 36*, 2351–2367.
Mark, L. S. (1987). Eyeheight-scaled information about affordances: A study of sitting and stair climbing. *Journal of Experimental Psychology: Human Perception and Performance, 13*, 361–370.
Marr, D. (1982). *Vision*. San Francisco: Freeman.
Matin, L., & Fox, C. R. (1989). Visually perceived eye level and perceived elevation of objects: Linearly additive influences from visual field pitch and from gravity. *Vision Research, 29*, 315–324.
Matin, L., & Li, W. (1992). Mislocalizations of visual elevation and visual vertical induced by visual pitch: The great circle model. *Annals of the New York Academy of Science, 656*, 242–265.
Meng, J., & Sedgwick, H. A. (1998). Perception of relative distance through nested contact relations with the ground plane. *Investigative Ophthalmology & Visual Science, 39*, S626.
Meng, J., & Sedgwick, H. A. (1999). Spatial parameters of distance perception mediated by nested contact relations with the ground plane. *Investigative Ophthalmology and Visual Science, 40*, S415.
Michaels, C. F., & Carello, C. (1981). *Direct perception*. Englewood Cliffs, NJ: Prentice-Hall.
Mingolla, E., & Todd, J. T. (1986). Perception of solid shape from shading. *Biology and Cybernetics, 53*, 137–151.
Mountcastle, V. B. (1997). The columnar organization of the neocortex. *Brain, 120*, 701–722.
Nagahama, Y., Takayama, Y., Fukuyama, H., Yamauchi, H., Matsuzaki, S., Magata, Y., Shibasaki, H., & Kimura, J. (1996). Functional anatomy on perception of position and motion in depth. *Neuroreport, 7*, 1717–1721.
Nakayama, K., & Shimojo, S. (1990). da Vinci stereopsis: Depth and subjective occluding contours from unpaired image points. *Vision Research, 30*, 1811–1825.
Nakayama, K., & Shimojo, S. (1992). Experiencing and perceiving visual surfaces. *Science, 257*, 1357–1363.
Newman, C. V. (1972). Familiar and relative size cues and surface texture as determinants of relative distance judgments. *Journal of Experimental Psychology, 96*, 37–42.
Norman, J. F., & Todd, J. T. (1994). Perception of rigid motion in depth from the optical deformations of shadows and occlusion boundaries. *Journal of Experimental Psychology: Human Perception and Performance, 20*, 343–356.
Ogle, K. N. (1950). *Researches in binocular vision*. New York: Hafner.
Ohmi, M., Howard, I. P., & Landolt, J. P. (1987). Circular vection as a function of foreground-background relationships. *Perception, 16*, 17–22.
Ono, H., & Comerford, J. (1977). Stereoscopic depth constancy. In W. Epstein (Ed.), *Stability and constancy in visual perception* (pp. 91–128). New York: John Wiley & Sons.
Ono, H., Rogers, B. J., Ohmi, M., & Ono, M. E. (1988). Dynamic occlusion and motion parallax in depth perception. *Perception, 17*, 255–266.
O'Regan, J. K. (1992). Solving the "real" mysteries of visual perception: The world as an outside memory. *Canadian Journal of Psychology, 46*, 461–488.
Oudejans, R. R., Michaels, C. F., Bakker, F. C., & Davids, K. (1999). Shedding some light on catching in the dark: Perceptual mechanisms for catching fly balls. *Journal of Experimental Psychology: Human Perception and Performance, 25*, 531–542.
Owens, D. A., & Leibowitz, H. W. (1976). Oculomotor adjustments in darkness and the specific distance tendency. *Perception & Psychophysics, 20*, 2–9.
Philbeck, J. W., & Loomis, J. M. (1997). Comparison of two indicators of perceived egocentric distance under full-cue and reduced-cue conditions. *Journal of Experimental Psychology: Human Perception and Performance, 23*, 72–85.

Philbeck, J. W., Loomis, J. M., & Beall, A. C. (1997). Visually perceived location is an invariant in the control of action. *Perception & Psychophysics, 59*, 601–612.

Pizlo, Z. (1994). A theory of shape constancy based on perspective invariants. *Vision Research, 34*, 1637–1658.

Plantinga, H., & Dyer, C. (1990). Visibility, occlusion, and the aspect graph. *International Journal of Computer Vision, 5*, 137–169.

Plaut, D. C. (1995). Double dissociation without modularity: Evidence from connectionist neuropsychology. *Journal of Clinical and Experimental Neuropsychology, 17*, 291–321.

Poggio, G. F., & Fischer, B. (1977). Binocular interaction and depth sensitivity in striate and prestriate cortex of behaving rhesus monkey. *Journal of Neurophysiology, 40*, 1392–1405.

Poggio, G. F., Motter, B. C., Squatrito, S., & Trotter, Y. (1985). Responses of neurons in visual cortex (V1 and V2) of the alert macaque to dynamic random-dot stereograms. *Vision Research, 25*, 397–406.

Pollen, D. A. (1999). On the neural correlates of visual perception. *Cerebral Cortex, 9*, 4–19.

Previc, F. H., & Donnelly, M. (1993). The effects of visual depth and eccentricity on manual bias, induced motion, and vection. *Perception, 22*, 929–945.

Previc, F. H., Kenyon, R. V., Boer, E. R., & Johnson, B. H. (1993). The effects of background visual roll stimulation on postural and manual control and self-motion perception. *Perception & Psychophysics, 54*, 93–107.

Purdy, W. C. (1960). *The hypothesis of psychophysical correspondence in space perception* (General Electric Technical Information Series No. R60ELC56). Ithaca, NY: General Electric Advanced Electronics Center.

Ramachandran, V. S. (1988). Perception of shape from shading. *Nature, 331*, 163–166.

Ramachandran, V. S., & Anstis, S. M. (1986). The perception of apparent motion. *Scientific American, 254*, 102–109.

Ratoosh, P. (1949). On interposition as a cue for the perception of distance. *Proceedings of the National Academy of Science, 35*, 257–259.

Reason, J. T., Mayes, A. R., & Dewhurst, D. (1982). Evidence for a boundary effect in roll vection. *Perception & Psychophysics, 31*, 139–144.

Rock, I. (1983). *The logic of perception*. Cambridge, MA: The MIT Press.

Rock, I. (1997). *Indirect perception*. Cambridge, MA: The MIT Press.

Rock, I., & Ebenholtz, S. (1959). The relational determination of perceived size. *Psychological Reviews, 66*, 387–401.

Rock, I., Wheeler, D., Shallo, J., & Rotunda, J. (1982). The construction of a plane from pictorial information. *Perception, 11*, 463–475.

Rogers, B., & Graham, M. (1979). Motion parallax as an independent cue for depth perception. *Perception, 8*, 125–134.

Rogers, B. J., & Bradshaw, M. F. (1993). Vertical disparities, differential perspective and binocular stereopsis. *Nature, 361*, 253–255.

Rogers, B. J., & Graham, M. E. (1983). Anisotropies in the perception of three-dimensional surfaces. *Science, 221*, 1409–1411.

Rogers, S. (1995). Perceiving pictorial space. In W. Epstein & S. Rogers (Eds.), *Perception of space and motion*. New York: Academic Press.

Rosenholtz, R., & Malik, J. (1997). Surface orientation from texture: Isotropy or homogeneity (or both)? *Vision Research, 37*, 2283–2293.

Runeson, S. (1995). Support for the cue-heuristic model is based on suboptimal observer performance: Response to Gilden and Proffitt (1994). *Perception & Psychophysics, 57*, 1262–1273.

Runeson, S., & Vedeler, D. (1993). The indispensability of precollision kinematics in the visual perception of relative mass. *Perception & Psychophysics, 53*, 617–632.

Rushton, S. K., & Wann, J. P. (1999). Weighted combination of size and disparity: A computational model for timing a ball catch. *National Neuroscience, 2*, 186–190.

Schiff, W. (1965). Perception of impending collision: A study of visually directed avoidant behavior. *Psychological Monographs, 79*, (Whole No. 604).

Schor, C. M., & Badcock, D. R. (1985). A comparison of stereo and vernier acuity within spatial channels as a function of distance from fixation. *Vision Research, 25*, 1113–1119.

Sedgwick, H. A. (1973). The visible horizon: A potential source of visual information for the perception of size and distance (Doctoral Dissertation, Cornell University, 1973). *Dissertation Abstracts International, 34*, 1301B–1302B. (University Microfilms No. 73–22,530).

Sedgwick, H. A. (1980). The geometry of spatial layout in pictorial representation. In M. A. Hagan (Ed.), *The perception of pictures* (Vol. 1, pp. 33–90). New York: Academic Press.

Sedgwick, H. A. (1983). Environment-centered representation of spatial layout: Available visual information from texture and perspective. In J. Beck, B. Hope, & A. Rosenfeld (Eds.), *Human and machine vision* (pp. 425–458). New York: Academic Press.

Sedgwick, H. A. (1986). Space perception. In K. Boff, L. Kaufman, & J. Thomas (Eds.), *Handbook of perception and human performance* (Vol. 1). New York: Wiley.

Sedgwick, H. A. (1987a). Layout2: A production system modeling visual perspective information. *Proceedings of the IEEE First International Conference on Computer Vision*. London, England, June 8–11, 1987.

Sedgwick, H. A. (1987b). *A production system modeling high-level visual perspective information for spatial layout* (Technical Report No. 298). New York University Department of Computer Science.

Sedgwick, H. A. (1989). Combining multiple forms of visual information to specify contact relations in spatial layout. In Paul S. Schenker (Ed.), *Sensor fusion II: Human and machine strategies*. SPIE Proceedings, *1198*, 447–458.

Sedgwick, H. A. & Levy, S.(1985). Environment-centered and viewer-centered perception of surface orientation. *Computer Vision, Graphics, and Image Processing, 31*, 248–260.

Shipley, T. F., & Kellman, P. J. (1990). The role of discontinuities in the perception of subjective figures. *Perception & Psychophysics, 48*, 259–270.

Shipley, T. F., & Kellman, P. J. (1994). Spatiotemporal boundary formation: Boundary, form, and motion perception from transformations of surface elements. *Journal of Experimental Psychology: General, 123*, 3–20.

Sinai, M. J., Ooi, T. L., & He, Z. J. (1998). Terrain influences the accurate judgement of distance. *Nature, 395*, 497–500.

Stevens, K. A. (1981). The information content of texture gradients. *Biology and Cybernetics, 42*, 95–105.

Stevens, K. A. (1983). Surface tilt (the direction of slant): A neglected psychophysical variable. *Perception & Psychophysics, 33*, 241–250.

Stevens, K. A. (1984). On gradients and texture "gradients." *Journal of Experimental Psychology: General, 113*, 217–224.

Stoper, A. E., & Cohen, M. M. (1986). Judgments of eye level in light and in darkness. *Perception & Psychophysics, 40*, 311–316.

Stoper, A. E., & Cohen, M. M. (1989). Effect of structured visual environments on apparent eye level. *Perception & Psychophysics, 46*, 469–475.

Swindale, N. V. (1990). Is the cerebral cortex modular? *Trends in Neuroscience, 13*, 487–492.

Swindale, N. V. (1998). Cortical organization: Modules, polymaps and mosaics. *Current Biology, 8*, R270–3.

Thomson, J. A. (1983). Is continuous visual monitoring necessary in visually guided locomotion? *Journal of Experimental Psychology: Human Perception and Performance, 9*, 427–443.

Tittle, J. S., Todd, J. T., Perotti, V. J., & Norman, J. F. (1995). Systematic distortion of perceived three-dimensional structure from motion and binocular stereopsis. *Journal of Experimental Psychology: Human Perception and Performance, 21*, 663–678.

Todd, J. T. (1995). The visual perception of three-dimensional structure from motion. In W. Epstein & S. Rogers (Eds.), *Perception of space and motion* (pp. 201–226). New York: Academic Press.

Todd, J. T., Chen, L., & Norman, J. F. (1998). On the relative salience of Euclidean, affine, and topological structure for 3–D form discrimination. *Perception, 27*, 273–282.

Todd, J. T., & Mingolla, E. (1983). Perception of surface curvature and direction of illumination

from patterns of shading. *Journal of Experimental Psychology: Human Perception and Performance, 9*, 583–595.
Todd, J. T., & Reichel, F. D. (1989). Ordinal structure in the visual perception and cognition of smoothly curved surfaces. *Psychological Review, 96*, 643–657.
Toye, R. C. (1986). The effect of viewing position on the perceived layout of space. *Perception & Psychophysics, 40*, 85–92.
Trotter, Y., Celebrini, S., Stricanne, B., Thorpe, S., & Imbert, M. (1992). Modulation of neural stereoscopic processing in primate area V1 by the viewing distance. *Science, 257*, 1279–1281.
Trotter, Y., Celebrini, S., Stricanne, B., Thorpe, S., & Imbert, M. (1996). Neural processing of stereopsis as a function of viewing distance in primate visual cortical area V1. *Journal of Neurophysiology, 76*, 2872–2885.
Tse, P. U. (1999). Volume completion. *Cognitive Psychology, 39*, 37–68.
Tse, P. U., & Albert, M. K. (1998). Amodal completion in the absence of image tangent discontinuities. *Perception, 27*, 455–464.
Turano, K., & Wang, X. (1994). Visual discrimination between a curved and straight path of self motion: Effects of forward speed. *Vision Research, 34*, 107–114.
Turner, M. R., Gerstein, G. L., & Bajcsy, R. (1991). Underestimation of visual texture slant by human observers: A model. *Biology and Cybernetics, 65*, 215–226.
Ujjike, H., & Saida, S. (1998). Similarity and interaction of shadow and disparity cues of depth. *Perception, 27, supplement*, 116b.
Ullman, S. (1979). The interpretation of structure from motion. *Proceedings of the Royal Society of London, B: Biological Science, 203*, 405–426.
Ullman, S. (1980). Against direct perception. *The Behavioral and Brain Sciences, 3*, 373–415.
Van Effelterre, T. (1994). Aspect graphs for visual recognition of three-dimensional objects. *Perception, 23*, 563–582.
Wagner, M. (1985). The metric of visual space. *Perception & Psychophysics, 38*, 483–495.
Wallach, H., & O'Connell, D. N. (1953). The kinetic depth effect. *Journal of Experimental Psychology, 45*, 205–217.
Wallach, H., & O'Leary, A. (1982). Slope of regard as a distance cue. *Perception & Psychophysics, 31*, 145–148.
Wallach, H., & Zuckerman, C. (1963). The constancy of stereoscopic depth. *American Journal of Psychology, 76*, 404–412.
Warren, W. H., Jr. (1984). Perceiving affordances: Visual guidance of stair climbing. *Journal of Experimental Psychology: Human Perception and Performance, 10*, 683–703.
Warren, W. H., Jr. (1995). Self-motion: Visual perception and visual control. In W. Epstein & S. Rogers (Eds.), *Perception of space and motion* (pp. 263–325). New York: Academic Press.
Warren, W. H., Jr., Mestre, D. R., Blackwell, A. W., & Morris, M. W. (1991). Perception of circular heading from optical flow. *Journal of Experimental Psychology: Human Perception and Performance, 17*, 28–43.
Warren, W. H., Jr., & Whang, S. (1987). Visual guidance of walking through apertures: Body-scaled information for affordances. *Journal of Experimental Psychology: Human Perception and Performance, 13*, 371–83.
Westheimer, G., & McKee, S. P. (1978). Steroscopic acuity for moving retinal images. *Journal of the Ophthalmic Society of America, 68*, 450–455.
Wiest, W. M., & Bell, B. (1985). Stevens's exponent for psychophysical scaling of perceived, remembered, and inferred distance. *Psychological Bulletin, 98*, 457–470.
Woodworth, R. S. (1938). *Experimental psychology*. New York: Henry Holt.
Wouterlood, D., & Boselie, F. (1992). A good-continuation model of some occlusion phenomena. *Psychological Research, 54*, 267–277.
Wraga, M. (forthcoming). Using eye height in different postures to scale the heights of objects. *Journal of Experimental Psychology: Human Perception and Performance.*
Yardley, L. (1992). Motion sickness and perception: A reappraisal of the sensory conflict approach. *British Journal of Psychology, 83*, 449–471.

Yin, C., Kellman, P. J., & Shipley, T. F. (1997). Surface completion complements boundary interpolation in the visual integration of partly occluded objects. *Perception, 26*, 1459–1479.

Yonas, A., Goldsmith, L. T., & Hallstrom, J. L. (1978). Development of sensitivity to information provided by cast shadows in pictures. *Perception, 7*, 333–341.

Young, L. R., Mendoza, J. C., Groleau, N., & Wojcik, P. W. (1996). Tactile influences on astronaut visual spatial orientation: Human neurovestibular studies on SLS-2. *Journal of Applied Physiology, 81*, 44–49.

Young, L. R., Oman, C. M., & Dichgans, J. M. (1975). Influence of head orientation on visually induced pitch and roll sensation. *Aviation and Space Environment Medicine, 46*, 264–268.

Zeki, S., & Bartels, A. (1998). The autonomy of the visual systems and the modularity of conscious vision. *Philosophical Transactions of the Royal Society of London, B: Biological Science, 353*, 1911–1914.

Zeki, S. M. (1978). Functional specialisation in the visual cortex of the rhesus monkey. *Nature, 274*, 423–428.

6

Object Perception

Mary A. Peterson

What Is Object Perception?

Visual perception in general, and the visual perception of objects in particular, seems so immediate and effortless that it is difficult to comprehend its complexity. Consider, for example, the non-trivial question of what constitutes an object. Both philosophers and psychologists have occupied themselves with trying to find the necessary and sufficient properties of objects (Hirsch, 1982; Wiggins, 1980). Based on infant research, Elizabeth Spelke and her colleagues have defined objects as solid entities that (a) exhibit spatio-temporal continuity, (b) cohere within their boundaries when they move, and (c) move only when contacted by another object (Spelke, 1990; Spelke, Guthiel, & Van de Walle, 1995). On Spelke's definition, animals and immaterial entities are excluded from the object category, and well they should be, at least for common usage of the term "object." Bloom (1996) correctly excludes other entities, including puddles, shadows, holes, illusory objects, and parts of objects (e.g., fingers and cup handles). Ittelson (1996) excludes pictures of objects because they are two-dimensional (2-D) rather than three-dimensional (3-D), as real objects are.

Distinctions between those entities that count as real objects and those that do not are critical if one is concerned with classifying those entities we *judge or know* to be real objects. However, most investigators of visual perception use the term "object perception" both more broadly and more narrowly than it is used by the authors discussed above. The term *object perception* is used more broadly by perception psychologists because it encompasses processes that

- integrate within and segregate between elements in the visual input;
- assign shape and 3-D structure to some of those elements;
- permit recognition of previously-seen shaped entities; and
- determine the manner in which attention is focused on the shaped entities.

Hence, investigators of visual perception typically use the term *object perception* to apply to both animate and inanimate objects, to pictured (2-D) as well as real (3-D) objects, and even to illusory objects.

This chapter will cover research and theory on both shape and object perception. The first section of this chapter will cover the processes involved in segmenting the visual field into contours and grouped regions; the second section will cover shape assignment. Object recognition theories will be summarized in the third section, and different visual architectures that specify the relationships among segmentation, shape assignment and recognition will be presented in the fourth section. Finally, the relationship between attention and object perception will be covered in the fifth section.

Before continuing, I should note the ways in which vision scientists use the term *object perception* more narrowly than it is used by philosophers and theorists concerned with defining what constitutes an object. The critical difference is that many of the conceptual or judgmental processes necessary to distinguish real objects from other entities are not included in the term *object perception,* as typically used by perception psychologists. Although visual perception is affected by some types of knowledge embodied in previous experience, it seems immune to influences from other types of knowledge (e.g., Peterson, Harvey, & Weidenbacher, 1991; Peterson, Nadel, Bloom, & Garrett, 1996). Consider, for example, the classic demonstration shown in Figure 6.1a (Hochberg, 1978). Figure 6.1b shows that the number 4 is embedded in Figure 6.1a. However, this familiar shape is not perceived unless the viewer is informed that the display contains the number 4, and unless time sufficient for careful inspection is provided. Göttschaldt (1926) created displays like Figure 6.1a to demonstrate that familiar shape does not affect segmentation, a position that has subsequently been shown to be incorrect (Peterson, 1994a). What Göttschaldt's (1926) demonstrations actually show is that objects cannot be perceived effortlessly unless the critical features defining those objects can be readily extracted from the display. The line terminator features of the number 4 are obscured by the continuous contour in Figure 6.1a (Hochberg, 1971; M. G. Moore, 1930; Woodworth, 1938). On subsequent encounters with Figure 6.1a, the initial percept of a closed loop might be supplemented quickly by knowledge of past experience, which might initiate a search for the number 4. However, the search processes employed under such conditions are secondary to the initial, or primary, perception.

Research designed to distinguish between primary versus secondary perceptual processes and between object knowledge based upon those different processes would certainly be worthwhile, and might be useful in bridging the terminological gaps between philosophers and psychologists, and between investigators of infant and adult perception. It might even allow bridges between the study of object perception and object categorization. Because object perception research is mostly concerned with initial perception, however, the distinction between primary and secondary perceptual processes will not be considered further in this chapter.

Segmentation

This section will summarize research and theory concerning processes by which the visual field is segmented, or differentiated, into contours, regions, and groups. We start with contour segregation because it is fundamental for object perception. Grouping processes and region-detecting processes are considered next.

Contour Perception

The General Case

Objects are bounded by contours. Although the boundaries of physical objects are continuous, the contours extracted by visual processes are likely to be discontinuous, or fragmented. Therefore, as part of the process of segregating contours from other elements, some process must integrate the contour segments (Grossberg & Mingolla, 1985; Ullman, 1990). Ullman proposed that contour segregation occurs more readily for more "salient" contours. According to Ullman, contour salience increases as the orientation similarity between neighboring contour segments increases.

Ullman's salience computation implemented the Gestalt psychologists' proposal that the visual system has an inherent tendency to group segments into contours along paths entailing the smallest change in curvature. This tendency, called "good continuation," operates to group both segments of fragmented contours, as in Figure 6.1c, and segments of continuous contours where they intersect other contours, as in Figure 6.1d. The Gestalt view was that, by virtue of integration by good continuation, fragmented contours (termed "virtual contours" by Kanizsa, 1987) were as real as real contours. (For recent behavioral evidence consistent with this hypothesis, see Rensink & Enns, 1995; Han, Humphreys, & Chen, 1999a).

The Gestalt psychologists supposed that good continuation operates very early in the course of perceptual organization. After Hubel and Wiesel (1968) showed that cells in the first layer of visual cortex (V1) were differentially sensitive to stimulus bars of different orientations, it was thought that V1 might be the neural substrate for contour integration and segregation mechanisms. Recent psychophysical, computational, and neurophysiological work has elucidated contour integration mechanisms, and has confirmed a role for V1 cells. (For an excellent brief history, see Westheimer, 1999.)

Field, Hayes, and Hess (1993) used Gabor patches as both contour elements and background elements (see Figure 6.1e), and examined the conditions under which the contour could be segregated from the background. Field et al. found that, as long as the elements' principal axes were misaligned by less than 60°, observers could accurately segregate contours from backgrounds even when (a) the elements differed in phase, and (b) the inter-element distance was up to seven times the element width. (See also Beck, Rosenfeld, & Ivry, 1990.) These effects at a distance demonstrated by Field et al. (1993) were inconsistent with the classic understanding of the receptive field properties of V1 cells. However, Kapadia, Ito, Gilbert, and Westheimer (1995) later showed that V1 cell responses to a stimulus bar were enhanced substantially when a bar with the same orientation was located nearby, yet outside their receptive field. Strikingly, the patterning of the effects demonstrated in V1 cells was very similar to the pattern obtained in psychophysical studies (e.g., Field et al., 1993; Kapadia et al., 1995). The degree to which V1 cell activity was enhanced by nearby bars decreased as the principal axes of the bars became increasingly misaligned, and as the distance between the two bars increased. Together, these psychophysical and physiological results support the hypothesis that V1 cells do indeed play a role in contour integration and segregation.

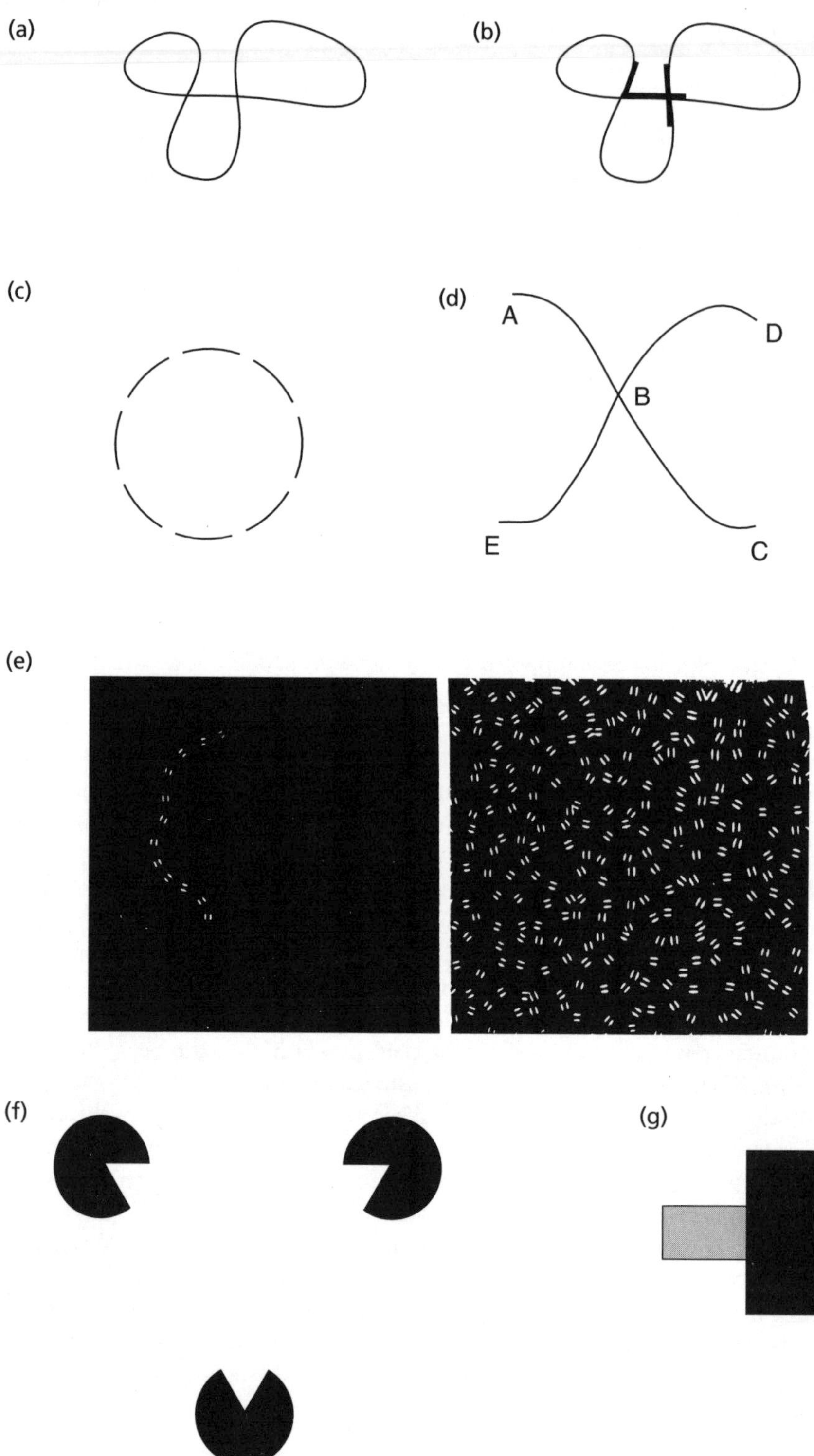
(a)
(b)
(c)
(d)
A
D
B
E
C
(e)
(f)
(g)

Modal and Amodal Contour Completion

So far, the discussion has focused on real and fragmented, or "virtual" contours. In contrast, *modal* completion occurs where no explicit contour is present, yet an illusory, or subjective, contour is perceived. An example is shown in Figure 6.1f, which appears to be a white triangle resting on three black circles. The bounding contour of the white triangle is a modal contour, in that it can be perceived. Yet it is a subjective contour because, despite appearances, there are simply no white contours in the display. The black pacmen shapes with two straight edges serve as the inducing elements for the subjective contour. When the subjective triangle is seen in Figure 6.1f, the black shapes appear to be circles completed behind the subjective triangle, due to *amodal* completion (see below).

Both physiological and behavioral evidence suggest that subjective contours are generated by early visual processes. Physiological investigations have identified cells in V1 and V2 that respond to both real and subjective contours shortly after stimulus onset (Grosof, Shapley, & Hawken, 1993; Peterhans & von der Heydt, 1989; von der Heydt & Peterhans, 1989). Behavioral evidence indicates that the time required to find subjective contour targets does not increase as the number of locations to be searched increases. Such results suggest that subjective contours are generated in parallel across the visual field; focal attention is unnecessary (Davis & Driver, 1994; Gurnsey, Humphrey, & Kapitan, 1992). In addition, psychophysical investigations demonstrate that, similar to real and virtual contours, modal contours are perceived between contrast reversed elements (Prazdny, 1983). Thus, although the perceived outcomes are very different, there are clear similarities in the early processes that produce real and subjective contours.

The only straight contours present in Figure 6.1f are those of the three black inducing elements. Nevertheless, the straight edges are not perceived as belonging to the black shapes. Rather, the black shapes are completed as circles lying behind the subjective triangle. This is a case of *amodal* contour completion. Amodal contour completion occurs when two lines (or edges) are perceived to connect behind occluding surfaces. This implicit contour completion is considered amodal because a connecting edge is not seen – in contrast to modal completion, where contours that are not present in the physical display are nonetheless perceived. (For review, see Kanizsa, 1987.) Psychophysical investigations indicate that amodal contours (and the amodal surfaces bounded by those contours) are completed sufficiently early in processing that observers cannot ignore them even when doing so would improve their performance on experimental tasks (He & Nakayama, 1992, 1994).

←

Figure 6.1. (a & b) The number 4, visible in the drawing in (b), is hidden in the drawing in (a). (a) is reprinted from *Perception*, 2/e by Hochberg, J., © 1964. Reprinted by permission of Prentice-Hall, Inc., Upper Saddle Riber, NJ. (c) Fragmented contours grouped by good continuation. (d) Intersecting contours grouped by good continuation into continuous segments ABC and EBD. (e) The left and right fields show a sample target and comparison display used by Field et al. (1993), reproduced with permission from Elsevier Science. (f) A subjective contour triangle. (g) A gray rectangle occluded by a black rectangle. According to Kellman and Shipley's (1991) relatability rule, the edges of the gray rectangle do not complete amodally.

Kellman and Shipley (1991) articulated a relatability rule that predicts when amodal completion will occur. The relatability rule states that amodal contour completion will occur only when smoothly curving extensions of interrupted contours meet at an angle less than 90°. Hence, the black inducing elements complete amodally as circles in Figure 6.1f, because the smoothly curving extensions of the outer contours of the inducing elements meet each other. The edges of the gray shape in Figure 6.1g would not complete amodally, however, because the smoothly curving extensions of the inducing element do not meet. The relatability rule captures local constraints on contour connectivity.

I end this section by raising the possibility that both modal and amodal completions are generated by the same processes that integrate real and virtual lines; hence, neither may be special cases after all. Consistent with this possibility, Kellman, Yin, and Shipley (1998) showed that those amodal contours that satisfy the relatability rule have some of the same properties as modal contours. Dresp and Bonnet (1993) showed that the properties of real and modal contours overlap. Moreover, real and subjective contours function similarly as substrates for certain higher-level processes (Peterson & Gibson, 1994b).

Looking Beyond V1 to Explain Contour Segregation, Integration, and Completion

A number of investigators, including Kanizsa (1987), Rock (1987), and Wallach and Slaughter (1988), showed that familiarity affects modal completion. C. Moore and Cavanagh (1998) demonstrated familiarity effects on virtual contour completion. Furthermore, Hochberg and Peterson (1993) and Zemel, Behrmann, Mozer, and Bavelier (under review) demonstrated that familiar shapes are more likely than unfamiliar shapes to be completed amodally. And, Sekuler (1994) showed that in addition to local processes, more global processes, such as the symmetry of the completed figure, play a role in early amodal completion processes. These results suggest that one must look beyond V1 to gain a full understanding of contour integration and segregation processes.

Grouping

Grouping Factors

In addition to good continuation, the Gestalt psychologists identified a number of factors that increase the likelihood that a set of entities will be grouped together and segregated from other entities. For instance, elements that are *similar* are likely to be grouped together. *Similarity* can be determined over any number of dimensions, such as shape, color, or size. An example of grouping by similarity can be seen in Figure 6.2a. In addition, elements that are *close to* one another are likely to group together. The display in Figure 6.2b is likely to be grouped into columns because of the factor of *proximity.* Proximity appears to be determined by the perceived distance separating the elements rather than by the physical distance, when the two differ (Rock & Brosgole, 1964). As well, elements that *move together* are likely to be grouped together. If the elements in columns 1, 3, and 5 of Figure 6.2c were to move upward while the elements in columns 2 and 4 remained stationary, the moving elements would group together by virtue of sharing a *common fate* and would segregate from the stationary elements. Although common fate was traditionally defined for moving versus stationary elements, or for elements moving in opposite directions, Leonards, Singer, and Fahle (1996) recently found that temporal modulation of brightness operates to segregate the visual field as well.

Level at Which Grouping Operates

Evidence obtained from a variety of sources suggests that grouping processes are early visual processes, as the Gestalt psychologists proposed. Supporting evidence was obtained in a task in which observers are asked to categorize a target letter appearing at fixation as one of two letters. The target letter is surrounded by a number of distractor letters lying on its right and left sides (B. A. Eriksen & C. W. Eriksen, 1974). Distractors located at a given distance from the target are more likely to interfere with the target response when they group with the target (by virtue of similarity or common fate) than when they do not

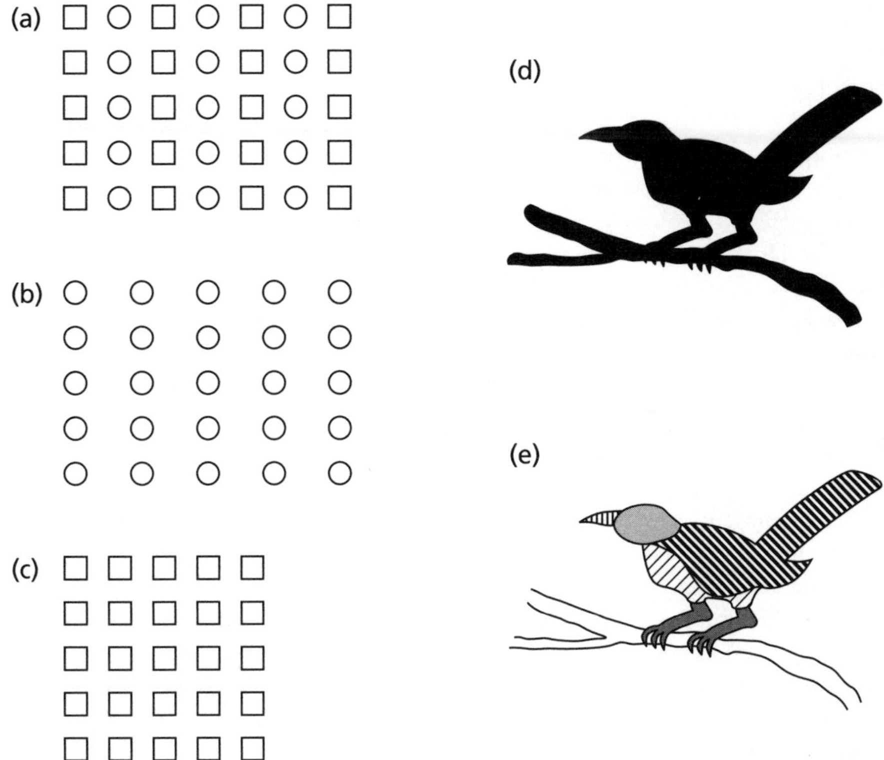

Figure 6.2. (a) An example of grouping by similarity. (b) An example of grouping by proximity. (c) Grouping by common fate would occur if the elements in columns 1, 3, and 5 were to move upward while the elements in columns 2 and 4 remained stationary. (d) According to Palmer and Rock (1994), this display would first be perceived as a unified connected region and later segregated into two objects, a bird and a branch. (e) Because of the different textures in this display, it would be treated as up to eight regions at the entry level. Later processes would integrate across the uniform connected regions to yield two objects, a bird and a branch.

group with the target (Baylis & Driver, 1992; Driver & Baylis, 1989; Fox, 1998; Harms & Bundeson, 1983; Humphreys, 1981; Kramer & Jacobson, 1991). These results can be taken as evidence that the Gestalt grouping laws are early automatic processes that are not overridden by task-dependent attentional allocation. It remains difficult to pinpoint how early or late the relevant grouping is accomplished, especially because physiological investigations have not shed light on where the grouping factors operate (but see Tononi, Sporns, & Edelman, 1991). Nevertheless, these behavioral results suggest that attention spreads across the entities defined by grouping factors, even when task performance would be improved by focusing attention on the target.

The grouping factors do not all follow the same time course, however. For example, Ben-Av and Sagi (1995) found that proximity grouping is perceived faster than similarity grouping and dominates performance under brief exposure conditions; whereas similarity grouping is perceived somewhat later in time and dominates performance under long exposure conditions (see also Han et al., 1999a; Han, Humphreys, & Chen, 1999b). Thus, the grouping factors should not be considered a homogeneous set.

Region Formation

Integration and segregation processes are required for regions of homogeneous stimulation as well as for contours and groups of elements (Koffka, 1935). The detection of closed contours might be involved in integrating and segregating homogeneous regions from the outside-in. Homogeneous regions can also be formed from the inside-out by a "region-growing" type of integration processes, analogous to contour integration processes, whereby neighboring image locations are linked by virtue of sharing the same property (e.g., Mumford, Kosslyn, Hillger, & Herrnstein, 1987).

Uniform Connectedness

Recently, Palmer and Rock (1994) outlined a theory of perceptual organization in which regions of homogeneous or uniform visual properties ("uniform connected regions," UCRs) serve as "entry level units" – that is, as the units forming the substrate for other segregation and integration processes. Palmer and Rock (1994) proposed that once UCRs have been isolated in the visual array, subsequent processes can operate either to create divisions within UCRs, as in Figure 6.2d, where a homogeneous black region is seen as two objects – a bird and a branch; or to integrate across UCRs, as in Figure 6.2e, where the regions of different luminance and texture are integrated into a single object – a bird. According to Palmer and Rock, the principle of "uniform connectedness" (UC) has the privileged position of defining the fundamental units for later segregation and grouping processes.

A Privileged Cue?

Uniform connectedness is surely one of the early integration/segmentation factors employed by the visual system; but the claim that it is the fundamental factor is controversial. Two issues of continued relevance to object perception underlie the debate. A first issue is whether the fundamental units for object perception are global, bounded regions, or whether they are smaller units (see Boselie, 1994; Boselie & Leeuwenberg, 1986; Hochberg, 1968, 1980; Kimchi, 1998; Peterson & Hochberg, 1983, 1989). A second issue is whether any one factor constitutes the fundamental, or dominant, segmentation factor, or whether UC and the Gestalt grouping and configural factors constitute a subset of a larger set of factors that cooperate to organize the visual field (Peterson, 1994b, 1999).

Consistent with Peterson's view that UC operates as one cue among many, Han et al. (1999) found that grouping by a cue known to operate quickly – proximity – was accomplished as fast as grouping by UC and was not enhanced when combined with UC. However, they found that grouping by a cue known to operate more slowly – similarity – was accomplished more slowly than grouping by UC and was enhanced when combined with UC. Furthermore, developmental research suggests that UC is not a dominant factor in infants' organization of the visual world (Spelke, 1988). However, consistent with Palmer and Rock's view that UC defines the entry level elements for perception, Watson and Kramer (1999) found that, in adults, other things being equal, attention may select regions defined by UC, even when the selection of larger units would speed task performance (Watson & Kramer, 1999). Additional research is required to determine whether UC has the privileged position of defining the first fundamental units for perceptual organization or whether it is simply one of many cues, each of which has different strengths and time courses.

Shape Assignment

The integration and segregation of contours, groups, and regions is not sufficient for shape perception because not all regions in the visual field are perceived to have shape; some are perceived as shapeless backgrounds. Contours can be described as shared by two regions, one lying on each side. Whenever two regions share a contour, two perceptual outcomes are possible. One outcome is that the contour is assigned to one region only; whereas the adjacent region is left contour-less. In this case, the region to which the contour is assigned is the "figure"; the adjacent region is the "ground." By virtue of contour ownership, the figure appears to have a definite shape, whereas the adjacent ground does not, at least near the contour it shares with the figure. When this outcome, termed *figure-ground segregation,* is perceived the shared contour is seen as an occluding contour, in that it appears to occlude parts of the ground (i.e., the ground appears to continue behind the figure). An example is shown in Figure 6.3a.

A second outcome that can be perceived when two adjacent regions share a contour is that the shared contour can be assigned to both regions rather than to just one region (Kennedy, 1973, 1974). When this outcome, called *figure-figure segregation,* is perceived, the shared contour signifies the meeting of two surfaces or objects, both of which appear to be shaped by the contour. The two surfaces can appear to lie on the same depth plane, as in a tile pattern (Figure 6.3b), or to slant in depth, as in the two surfaces of a cube that meet at a common edge (Figure 6.3c). Examples such as Figures 6.3b & 6.3c demonstrate that one-sided contour assignment is not "obligatory," as some have claimed (Baylis & Driver, 1995).

In some situations, such as the one depicted in Figure 6.3c, figure-figure segregation is

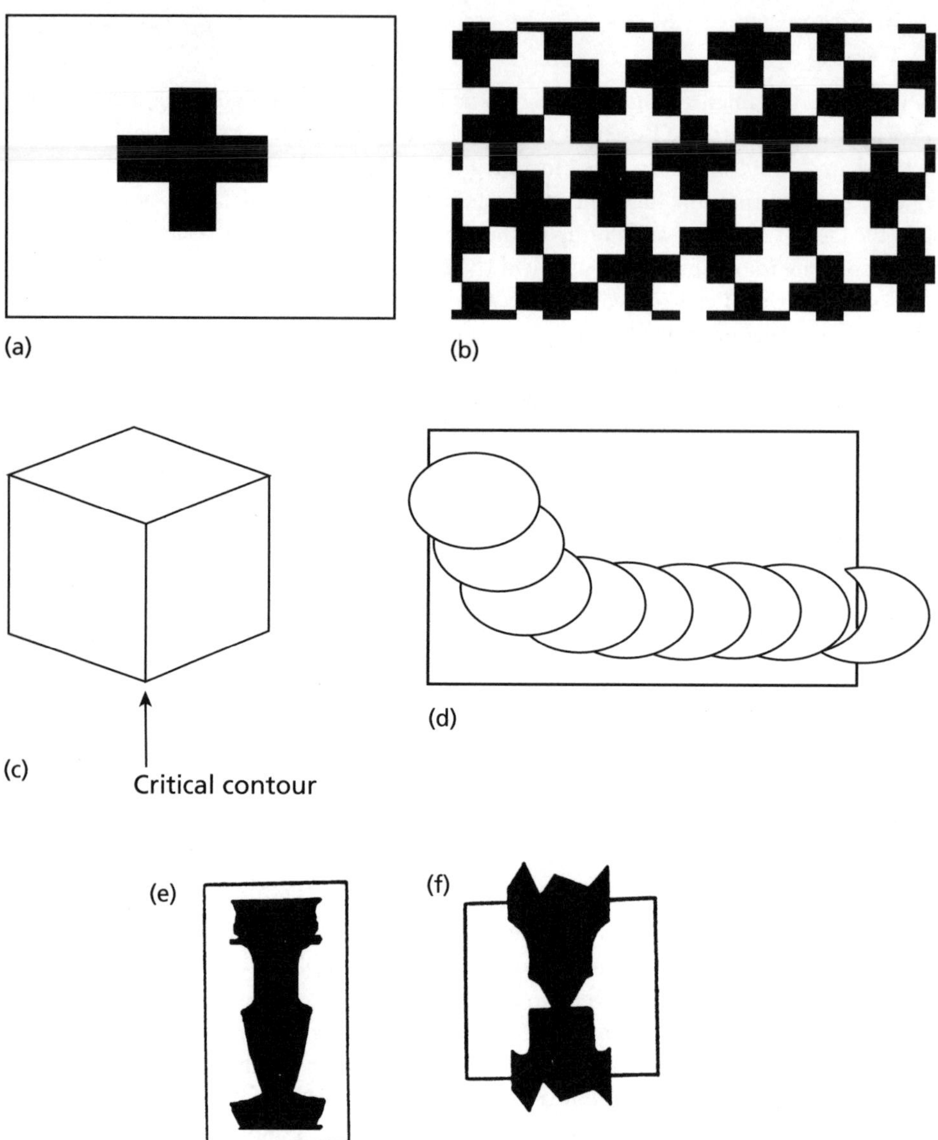

Figure 6.3. (a) An example of figure-ground organization in which the contour shared by the black and white regions bounded by the rectangle is assigned to the black region. The black region is seen as the shaped figure (a cross), whereas the white region appears to be a shapeless ground, continuing behind the cross. (b) A tile pattern in which the contours shared by the black and white regions are assigned to both regions. Both regions appear to be shaped and to lie on the same depth plane. (c) The critical contour signifies the meeting of two faces of a cube. (d) Eight ovals and one crescent. The contours in this display are assigned to one side only. All regions, except the outer two, appear to be figures along one portion of their bounding contour and grounds along another portion of their bounding contours. (From Hochberg (1980), copyright © 1980 by Academic Press, reproduced by permission of the publisher.) (e, f) Displays used by Peterson et al. (1991). The white high-denotative surrounds are more likely to be seen as figures when the displays are upright rather than inverted. (Reprinted with permission from the American Psychological Association.)

clearly the preferred organization. That may be because the Y- and arrow junctions in the figure are themselves early cues to 3-D structure (Enns & Rensink, 1991; Hummel & Biederman, 1992). In other situations, such as the one depicted in Figure 6.3a, however, figure-ground segregation seems to be preferred. The likelihood of seeing figure-figure versus figure-ground segregation can be attributed to the cross-region balance of (a) configural factors identified by the Gestalt psychologists and others, (b) contour recognition processes, and (c) monocular and binocular depth cues. These factors are discussed next.

Gestalt Configural Factors

The Gestalt psychologists elucidated a number of factors that affect the likelihood that a region will be attributed figural status while its adjacent region will be attributed ground status; these factors are called the Gestalt configural factors. Regions that are (a) smaller in area than their surrounds, (b) symmetric (especially around a vertical axis), (c) convex, and/or (d) enclosed are likely to be seen as figures; whereas their adjacent regions are likely to be seen as grounds. Demonstrations devised by Gestalt psychologists in the first half of the twentieth century supported these claims (for reviews, see Hochberg, 1971; Pomerantz & Kubovy, 1986).

Recent research replicated and extended the demonstrations of the Gestalt psychologists. For instance, Kanizsa & Gerbino (1976) tested the importance of global convexity and found that it is a stronger cue to figural status than symmetry. The importance of closure as a Gestalt configural cue was recently confirmed by Kovács & Julesz (1994) who used a detection task rather than the phenomenological reports favored by the Gestalt psychologists. Kovács and Julesz (1994) obtained lower detection thresholds for targets presented near the center of a region bounded by a closed curve than for targets presented at an equivalent distance from the contour outside the bounded region. Given that closed regions tend to be seen as figures, these results replicate and extend research conducted by Wong and Weisstein (1983) who reported that detection of high spatial frequency targets is superior when targets fall on the figure rather than the ground. Similarly, using a contour-matching paradigm as an indirect measure of perceived organization, to avoid some of the demand character of phenomenological report, Driver, Baylis and Rafal (1992) recently confirmed the importance of smallness of relative area as a segregation cue.

Modern research has revealed new factors that can be added to the list of configural cues. Brown and Weisstein (1988) showed that when different spatial frequency patterns cover two adjacent regions, the region covered with the higher spatial frequency is likely to be seen as the figure. O'Shea, Blackburn and Ono (1994) showed that the region that contrasts more with the background is likely to be seen as the figure. And, Hoffman and Singh (1997) showed that regions with distinctive parts (defined as large area, convex excursions into adjacent regions) are more likely to be seen as figures than grounds.

Does "Configural" Imply "Global"?

Although configural cues are often considered global, holistic cues, recent research indicates that configural factors can be computed locally. For instance, Hoffman and Singh's

(1997) part distinctiveness is measured locally. Further, Stevens and Brooks (1988) showed that convexity can operate locally. In addition, Han et al. (1999b) and Kimchi (1994) have shown that configural factors are not necessarily mediated by global, object-wide mechanisms. These findings are important because they are consistent with the evidence indicating that figural status need not be assigned to an entire bounded region. A region can be figure along one portion of its contour and ground along another portion (Hochberg, 1980, 1998; Hoffman & Singh, 1997; Peterson & Hector, 1996), as illustrated in Figure 6.3d.

Level at Which Configural Cues Operate

Recent research confirms the Gestalt claim that configural factors are computed early in processing. Peterson and Gibson (1994a) showed that symmetry can determine figure assignment in masked exposures as short as 28 ms (but not in 14-ms masked exposures). An approach used recently to partition perception into early and late-acting processes has been to test brain-damaged individuals who distribute attention preferentially toward the side of space or the side of an object contralateral to the brain damage (contralesional spaces or contralesional sides of objects; Heilman & Van Den, 1980; Kinsbourne, 1970; see Chapter 7 for more details.) Processing that occurs in unattended contralesional space can be considered "preattentive" – that is, can be considered to occur before the intentional allocation of attention. Driver et al. (1992) showed that the configural cue of smallness of relative area operates effectively to determine figure-ground segregation in contralesional space. Similarly, Driver et al. (1992) found that the configural cue of symmetry affected figure-ground segregation normally in a patient who was unable to consciously attend to the contralesional sides of the figures he saw, and hence, unable to judge accurately whether or not the figures he perceived were symmetric.

None of the factors described above determined which of two adjacent regions will appear to be shaped (i.e., will be seen as the figure) 100% of the time, especially when other competing configural cues are present. Furthermore, the likelihood of assigning shape to one region or the other is affected by contour recognition cues and depth cues, as well as by configural cues. The perceived segregation depends upon the balance of cues across regions competing for figural status (Peterson, 1994a, 1999).

Quick Access to Memories of Object Structure

It was traditionally assumed that access to memories of objects occurs only after grouping and segregation processes have produced the figures or objects in the visual array (e.g., Köhler, 1929; Neisser, 1967; Biederman, 1987). Contrary to this assumption, Peterson and her colleagues found evidence that object memories activated by contours can serve as one more shape-assignment cue. Their results were obtained using stimuli like those shown in Figures 6.3e and 6.3f in which adjacent regions sharing a contour differed in the degree to which they resembled known objects. One, "high denotative," region was a good depiction of an upright known object when it was seen as figure (e.g., the white regions in Figures 6.3e and 6.3f), whereas the other, "low denotative," region was not (i.e., the black regions in Figures 6.3e and 6.3f). (The denotivity of each region was determined by between-subjects agreement in a pre-test in which observers listed all the known objects each region resembled when it was seen as figure.) Other relevant cues, such as configural cues and the monocular and binocular depth cues, were sometimes present in these displays, and when they were present, these cues favored the interpretation that the low-denotative region was the shaped figure (e.g., Peterson, Harvey & Weidenbacher, 1991; Peterson & Gibson, 1993, 1994a).

Peterson et al. (1991) compared the likelihood that the high-denotative region was seen as the shaped figure when the displays were upright (as shown in Figures 6.3e and 6.3f) versus inverted (i.e., as seen when you turn the book upside down). Such rotation in the picture plane does not change the configural or depth cues present in the displays shown in Figures 6.3e and 6.3f. However, rotation in the picture plane does slow down access to object memories (Jolicoeur, 1985, 1988; Tarr & Pinker, 1989). Peterson et al. (1991) reasoned that the delay induced by inversion in the picture plane might be sufficient to remove, or to reduce, any influence from object memories that normally affects the segregation outcome. Therefore, Peterson and her colleagues argued that any increased tendency to see high-denotative regions as figures in upright compared to inverted displays would constitute evidence that object memories, activated early in the course of perceptual processing, can affect the segregation outcome. Consistent with this prediction, Peterson et al. (1991; Gibson & Peterson, 1994; Peterson & Gibson, 1994a, 1994b) found that high-denotative regions were more likely to be seen as figures when the displays were upright than inverted. They attributed these effects to a set of quick recognition processes operating simultaneously on both sides of the contour shared by two adjacent regions.

The objects portrayed by inverted high-denotative regions are not necessarily unrecognizable; they can be recognized once they are seen as figure. Nevertheless, influences from object memories on shape assignment are diminished or absent for inverted displays. This finding indicates that only those object memories that are accessed quickly affect shape assignment; object memories accessed later in time (as when misoriented displays are used) do not influence shape assignment. Consistent with this conclusion, neither priming nor knowledge of what the inverted high-denotative region portrays alters the orientation effects (Gibson & Peterson, 1994; Peterson et al., 1991). Effects of object memories on shape assignment are evident only when a match between the stimulus and a memory representation coding the structure of the object can be made quickly. Additional evidence implicating access to memories of object structure is that no effects of object memories on shape assignment are observed when the parts of the known object portrayed by the high-denotative region are retained, but their spatial interrelationships are rearranged, or scrambled. Furthermore, effects of object memories on shape assignment have been found only when the contours that serve as the substrate for access to object memories are detected early in processing. For example, luminance contours and subjective contours support contour recognition effects, whereas binocular disparity contours, available later in processing, do not (Peterson & Gibson, 1993, 1994b).

Neuropsychological investigations are consistent with the proposal that the processes subserving quick access to object memories should be considered early visual processes. For instance, a visual agnosic individual whose object identification was severely impaired nevertheless showed normal influences from contour recognition processes on figure-ground responses (Peterson, de Gelder, Rapcsak, Gerhardstein, & Bachoud-Lévi, 2000). These results indicate that contour recognition processes operate outside of conscious awareness, and are a subset of the processes required for conscious object recognition/identification.

In addition, Peterson, Gerhardstein, Mennemeier, and Rapcsak (1998) tested individuals with unilateral brain damage whose attention was biased away from the contralesional contours of the regions of the experimental displays. Nevertheless, contour recognition processes seemed to operate normally on the unattended contralesional contours, suggesting that contour recognition processes proceed without the benefit of focused attention.

Physiological evidence is consistent with the claim that shape assignment is accomplished early in visual processing. Zipser, Lamme, and Schiller (1996) measured a response in V2 cells 80–100 ms after stimulus onset that was evident when near, shaped, figures, but not grounds, fell on the cells' receptive fields. If this differential activation indeed indicates that shape assignment or figure-ground segregation has been accomplished, these data confirm the view that those processes occur early in visual processing. Because the inferior temporal cortex, located downstream from V2, and important for object recognition, can be activated 60 ms after stimulus onset, however, these data are also consistent with the proposal that object memories can affect figure-ground segregation.

Just as for the other segregation-relevant cues, the likelihood that the region providing a good fit to object memories will be seen as figure depends on the balance of other cues. In other words, the cue originating in quick access to object memories does not always dominate the configural and depth cues (Peterson & Gibson, 1993, 1994a). Indeed, just as none of the other configural cues or depth cues is a necessary component of the segregation process, neither is a good fit to an object memory. Therefore, segregation can proceed without substantial contributions from object memories for novel objects, as it can proceed without contributions from the configural cue of symmetry for asymmetric objects (or without convexity for concave objects). However, when known objects are present, the segregation process can benefit from prior experience, as it can benefit from convexity when convex objects are present.

Depth Cues

Many depth cues, including binocular disparity (stereo), contour, motion parallax, texture, and shading, affect the likelihood that shape will be assigned to the region lying on one or the other side of a contour. Some of these cues, such as shape from shading, are determined early in processing (Braun, 1993; Ramachandran, 1988; Sun & Perona, 1997), whereas others, such as shape-from-stereo, may unfold over a longer time course (Julesz, 1971; Sun & Perona, 1997).

Cue combination studies address the question of whether these cues to 3-D shape interact early in processing or whether they are computed independently until each pathway produces an estimate of depth. Some evidence indicates that the 3-D cues combine linearly to determine shape, a finding that is consistent with the latter possibility. But departures from linear combination have also been obtained, and these departures are consistent with the possibility that the cues to 3-D shape interact early in processing (Bülthoff, 1991; Parker, Cumming, Johnston, & Hurlburt, 1995). Neuropsychological case studies of patients who are impaired at seeing shape from shading, but relatively intact at seeing shape from edge cues (and vice versa) provide evidence consistent with the hypothesis of separate pathways (Battelli, Casco, & Sartori, 1997; Humphrey, Symona, Herbert, & Goodale,

1996), but do not necessarily speak to the independence of those pathways.

Investigations of how depth cues interact with configural cues and activated object memories are, unfortunately, rare. Hence, it is not possible at this point in time to draw any conclusions about how these different cues to shape are combined. In conducting research to address this question, it will be important to bear in mind a consideration recently raised by Tittle, Norman, Perotti, and Phillips (1997) that different depth cues may be important for different properties of 3-D structure. For instance, Tittle et al. (1997) showed that binocular disparity is relatively more important for the perception of scale-independent aspects of shape (e.g., whether a shape is spherical versus cylindrical) than for scale-dependent aspects of shape (e.g., magnitude of surface curvature).

As for the configural cues, none of the depth cues is 100% predictive of perceived depth, especially when other, contradictory depth cues are present. Instead, it seems that perceived depth corresponds to the depth signaled by the ensemble of cues in any particular scene (Landy, Maloney, & Young, 1990), although different depth cues may have different strengths (Cutting & Vishton, 1995), as different configural cues do.

A review the object perception processes must address the question of what object memories are like, and how object recognition occurs. Accordingly, a brief review of theories of object recognition is given next.

Theories of Object Recognition

An adequate theory of object recognition must account for

- the accuracy of object recognition over changes in object size, location, and orientation (and it would be preferable if this account did not posit a different memory record for each view of every object ever seen);
- the means by which the spatial relationships between the parts or features of an object are represented; and
- the attributes of both basic-level and subordinate-level recognition (e.g., recognition of a finch as both a bird and as a specific kind of bird).

Current competing object recognition theories differ in their approach to each of these attributes (see Biederman, 1987, 1995; Tarr, 1995; Tarr & Bülthoff, 1998).

Recognition by Components Theory

According to the Recognition by Components (RBC) theory, proposed by Biederman (1985, 1987), objects are parsed into parts at concave portions of their bounding contours, and the parts are represented in memory by a set of abstract 3-D components, called "geons." Before RBC was proposed, other theorists had stressed the importance for recognition of both concave regions of the bounding contour of objects (e.g., Hoffman & Richards, 1985; Marr, 1982; Marr & Nishihara, 1978) and 3-D representational components (i.e., cylinders, Binford,

1981; Marr, 1982; Marr & Nishihara, 1978). Biederman expanded the set of components from cylinders to generalized cones (i.e., cross-sections swept out in depth along an axis). Further, Biederman (1995) showed that a finite set of 3-D geons (N = 24) can be defined by combining a small set of binary or trinary contrasts that can easily be extracted from two-dimensional images. Thus, in RBC, a representation of an object's 3-D structure was derived from contrasts extracted from a single 2-D view. The contrasts specify the shape of the cross-section of a geon, the shape of the axis of the geon, and changes in the size of the cross-section as it is swept along the axis. (Contrasts include the following: for edges, whether they are straight or curved, parallel or non-parallel, converging or diverging; and for cross-sections, whether they shrink, expand, or remain constant in size as they move along the geon axis.) Sample geons and some objects constructed from them are shown in Figure 6.4a.

The contrasts from which the geons are constructed are viewpoint invariant properties or "non-accidental properties," in that they are unlikely to occur in the image as an accident of viewing position (Lowe, 1985, 1987; Witkin & Tenenbaum, 1983). For instance, under most viewing conditions, except for accidental views, curved lines do not look straight, nor do converging lines appear parallel. Biederman and his colleagues (Biederman, 1987, 1995; Biederman & Gerhardstein, 1993, 1995) argued that geon extraction is viewpoint invariant because the contrasts that specify the geons are viewpoint invariant. The prediction that object recognition should be viewpoint invariant followed, provided that the same geons (and geon relations, see below) could be extracted from the image in different views. Thus, according to RBC theory, only a small number of views of each object need to be represented in memory.

RBC specified that the spatial relations between the geons comprising an object are specified in terms of categorical relationships such as "top-of," below, or "next-to," rather than in metric terms (Biederman, 1987; Hummel & Biederman, 1992). It is known that object recognition fails when the parts are rearranged (Cave & Kosslyn, 1993; Peterson et al., 1991). Nevertheless, prior to RBC, little consideration had been given to the question of how the spatial relationships between the parts of an object are coded.

Evidence: Pro and Con

As all good theories should be, RBC makes testable predictions and consequently, is falsifiable. After the publication of Biedermans' (1987) article, research and theorizing on object recognition flourished, and continues to flourish today. Research investigated questions such as whether or not (a) bounding contours and concave cusps are as important as claimed by RBC, (b) object recognition is viewpoint invariant, (c) RBC can account for both subordinate and basic level recognition, and (d) RBC's proposals concerning the coding of spatial relationships. The fact that many objects can be recognized from their bounding contour alone indicates that bounding contours are highly important for object

→

Figure 6.4. (a) Sample geons and objects constructed from them. Reprinted from Biederman (1995), with permission of MIT Press. (b) Paperclip objects (top row) and spheroid objects (bottom row) used in tests of Multiple Views Theory (reprinted from Logothetis et al. (1994), with permission from Elsevier Science). (c) Examples of the shapes that activated cells at various levels in the ventral processing stream.

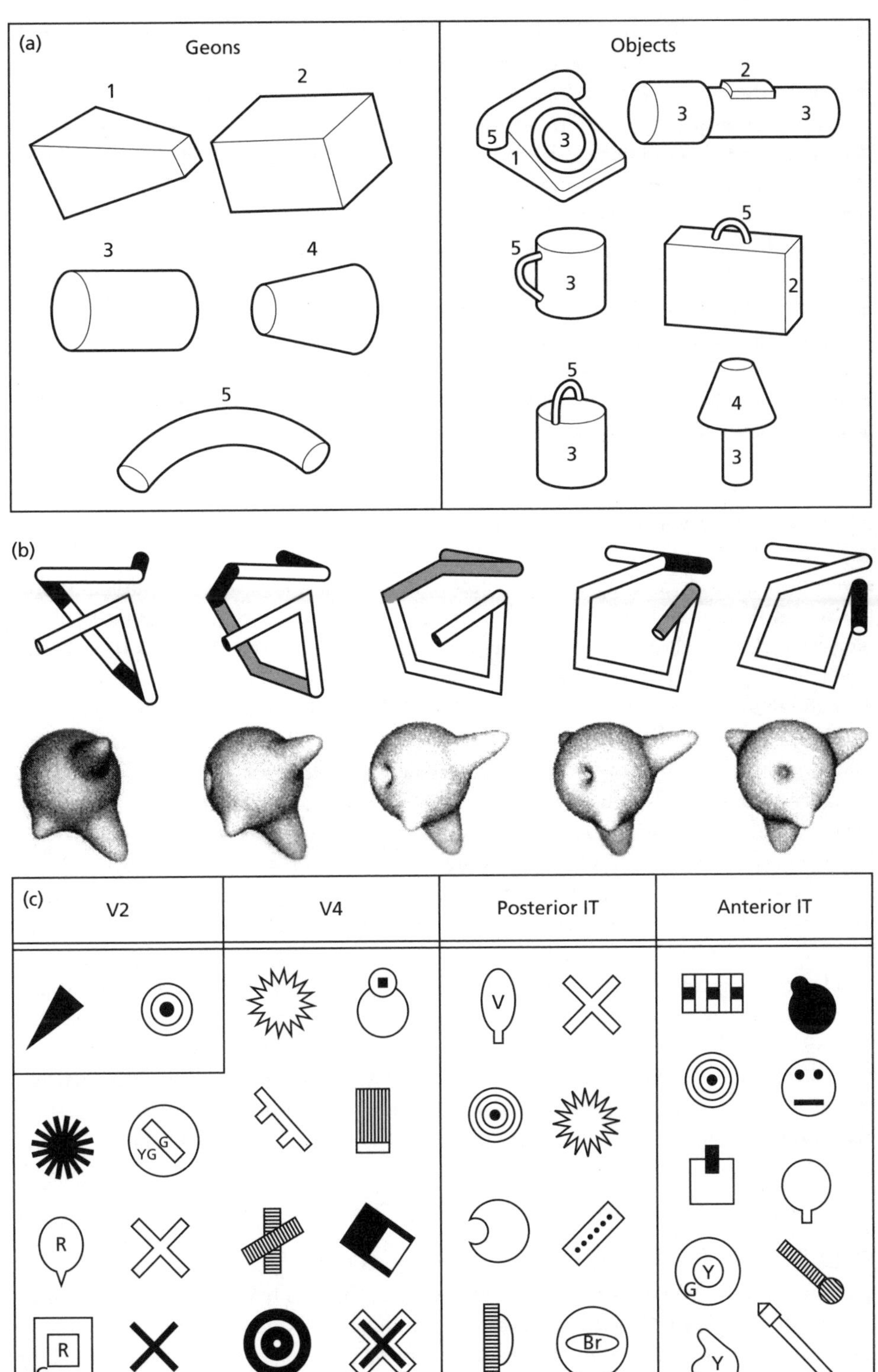

(a)
Geons
1
2
3
4
5
Objects
5
1
3
2
3
3
5
3
5
2
5
3
4
3
(b)
(c)
V2
V4
Posterior IT
Anterior IT
YG
G
R
R
G
V
Br
Y
G
Y

recognition, as specified by RBC (Hayward, 1998; Peterson, 1994a), although bounding contours are clearly not the whole story (Riddoch & Humphreys, 1987). Consistent with part-based theories such as RBC, evidence suggests that the concave portions of bounding contours are more important than other contour segments (Baylis & Driver, 1994; Biederman, 1987; Hoffman & Singh, 1997; Hoffman & Richards, 1985; Braunstein, Hoffman, & Saidpour, 1989). Furthermore, recent research by Saiki and Hummel (1998) indicates that the spatial relationships between parts of objects are represented differently than spatial relationships between different objects. Although this last finding does not directly support RBC, it does suggest that a complete theory of object recognition must account for the coding of spatial relationships between object parts.

Overall, the research suggests that certain elements of RBC theory must be retained, but other elements should probably be abandoned. In particular, evidence that neither geon extraction nor object recognition is viewpoint invariant (Brown, Weisstein & May, 1992; Tarr & Pinker, 1989) led to the formulation of a competing theory, discussed next.

Multiple Views: Evidence and Theory

Psychophysical evidence suggests that object recognition is not viewpoint invariant as proposed by RBC (e.g., Bülthoff & Edelman, 1993; Tarr & Pinker, 1989). Furthermore, physiological evidence indicates that cells may code for individual views of objects (Logothetis, Pauls, & Poggio, 1995) and faces (Perrett et al., 1985). Accordingly, Bülthoff, Edelman, Tarr and their colleagues (Bülthoff & Edelman, 1993; Edelman & Weinshall, 1991; Tarr, 1995; Tarr & Bülthoff, 1995) adopted a different theoretical approach to object recognition, proposing that multiple two-dimensional views of objects are represented rather than just a few 3-D views. According to Multiple Views Theory, object recognition is view-dependent (rather then view-independent) in that objects seen in new views must undergo some time-consuming process before they are matched to stored views and recognized.

In addition, Tarr and Bülthoff (1995) argue that the geon-based representations of RBC theory fail to account for either basic or subordinate level recognition (see also Kurbat, 1994). They criticize the RBC geons for their coarseness, arguing that geon-based representations could not distinguish between members of different basic level categories such as a horse and a cow, and could not represent the differences between two horses, two cows, or two dogs. Yet humans can easily make these sorts of distinctions. In contrast to RBC, exemplar representations, such as those in Multiple Views Theory, can readily represent the differences between objects by representing their different salient features. Similarities between objects can be made explicit through multidimensional feature interpolation (Poggio & Edelman, 1990).

Criticisms of Multiple Views Theory

Multiple Views Theory has not yet specified the exact form of the representation used for common objects. Much of the research supporting RBC has been conducted with open "paperclip" or spheroid objects such as those in Figure 6.4b, where all of the parts were identical save for length, and the bends in the paperclips were the salient features used for recognition. But such objects may not be representative of the objects humans recognize.

Another criticism is that the object representations in Multiple Views Theory are too much like two-dimensional templates. It is well known that template-like representations leave perception susceptible to disruption by slight changes in any object features (Neisser, 1967), regardless of whether they lie on, or internal to, the object's bounding contour. Yet human perception is notoriously robust to such changes. It was just this robustness of object perception that led early theorists to propose that object memories were view-independent, size-independent, location-independent, etc. (i.e., in Marr's (1982) terminology, they were "object-centered" representations). It is feared that Multiple Views Theory might require an unreasonably large number of representations for each object. Moreover, it is not clear how different views of objects are determined to be the same object, rather than similar but different objects. Another criticism is that in Multiple Views Theory there is no provision, save for that implied in template matching, for representing the spatial relations between parts of objects. This is a drawback, given the importance of the spatial relations between features, and the behavioral distinctions between the spatial relations between objects per se, and between parts of objects (see above).

These criticisms point to research that must be done to elaborate Multiple Views Theory. Current attempts to resolve these problems include (a) using the bounding contour of the object to integrate different views, and (b) exploring the feasibility of categorical coding for spatial relations between features (for a summary of recent research see Tarr and Bülthoff, 1998). Recall that both bounding contours and categorically coded spatial relations play important roles in RBC. It may turn out that a complete theory of object recognition must incorporate principles of both RBC and Multiple Views Theory (Suzuki, Peterson, Moscovitch, & Behrmann, under review; Tarr & Bülthoff, 1998). There also remains the possibility that, in addition to orientation-dependent representations (such as those identified by Logothetis et al., 1995), there exist object-centered representations (i.e., representations that permit orientation-independent object recognition) (Corballis, 1988; Solms, Turnbull, Kaplan-Solms, & Miller, P., 1998; Turnbull & Mccarthy, 1996).

Open Issues

In addition to the issues discussed at the end of the preceding section, two other issues must be considered in order to understand object recognition. The first concerns the role of local features in object memories. For the most part, theorists assume that object recognition is a global or holistic process. However, both behavioral and computational evidence (Mozer, Zemel, Behrmann, & Williams, 1992; Peterson & Hector, 1996; Ullman, 1998) suggests that object recognition can be mediated by local cues. Those local cues that are necessary and sufficient for object recognition have yet to be determined. Furthermore, mounting evidence suggests that the local components of representation are affected by experience (Lin & Murphy, 1997; Mozer et al., 1992; Schyns, Goldstone, & Thilbaut, 1998; Zemel et al., under review). Future research exploring the nature of the local cues mediating object recognition, the degree to which they are learned, and the interactions between local and global cues will be important for object recognition theory.

The second open issue concerns the nature of the representational primitives. In both Multiple Views Theory and RBC Theory, there is a clear resemblance between the object and the representational components. Indeed, it is easier to think about the components of object representations as being similar to the nameable or visible parts of objects than it is to think about them as abstractions bearing little or no resemblance to the consciously perceived object parts. However, alternative conceptions exist. One possibility is that objects are represented by their Fourier components (e.g., Graham, 1989, 1992). Another possibility is that objects are represented by complex shape components such as those suggested by research by Tanaka (1993; Kobatake & Tanaka, 1994) (see Figure 6.4c). Tanaka and his colleagues discovered that cells in monkey temporal cortex are selective for complex shape components, many of which bear little resemblance to either whole objects or parts of objects. Furthermore, these investigators uncovered a columnar organization in the temporal cortex, where cells within a column share a similar selectivity. Many questions about these components await further investigation: Can ensembles of these components be used to represent the entire set of objects the monkeys can recognize? Is the selectivity changed by experience? Are some components best described as coding global features and others as coding local features? The answers to these questions will constrain future theories of object recognition.

Models of the Relationship Between Segmentation, Shape Assignment, and Object Recognition

In order to understand how object perception proceeds, it is important to understand how the component processes of integration and segmentation, shape assignment, and object recognition are ordered. Which precede the others? Which serve as substrates for others? In what follows, I first discuss traditional hierarchical models. Next, I summarize a parallel model my colleagues and I have proposed. Finally, I point out the open questions that must be addressed to adjudicate between these models.

Hierarchical Models

The Gestalt psychologists proposed that segmentation, shape assignment and recognition were ordered serially and hierarchically, with grouping and segmentation completed first and forming the substrate for shape assignment, and shaped regions in turn providing the substrate for, and necessarily being determined prior to, access to object memories. (For some evidence consistent with the proposal that segmentation is completed before shape assignment see Sekuler & Palmer, 1992; for contradictory evidence see Bruno, Bertamini, & Domini, 1997; Peterson et al., 1991; Kellman et al., 1998.)

An influential model of vision proposed by David Marr (1982) was also serial and hierarchical. Unlike the Gestalt psychologists, Marr concentrated on the traditional depth cues at the expense of the configural cues, arguing that the sphere of influence of the latter was restricted to 2-D displays, which represent only a small subset of the conditions under which the visual system operates. (The current isolationism between those who study the perception of shape based upon configural cues versus depth cues can be traced to Marr's position.)

According to Marr, visual input proceeds through a number of stages, illustrated in

Figure 6.5a. The first stage of processing is the primal sketch, in which edges are made explicit. The second stage entails the construction of the 2½-D sketch, in which surfaces and viewer-relative orientations emerge. The third stage is the construction of the 3-D model, and as a final step, the 3-D model is matched to 3-D object models stored in memory. In Marr's theory, there is a clear sequence from edge extraction through 3-D shape assignment before object memories are accessed. (Marr's theory was proposed before either the RBC Theory or the Multiple Views Theory of object recognition. Indeed, the RBC Theory owes much to Marr and Nishihara's (1978) work.)

More recent interactive hierarchical models of the relationship among segmentation, shape assignment, and object recognition allow feedback from higher levels to influence processing at lower levels. However, these models maintain a hierarchical structure in that lower-level processes must at least be initiated before higher-level processes are initiated, as illustrated in Figure 6.5b (McClelland, 1979, 1985; McCelland & Rumelhart, 1986; Rumelhart & McClelland, 1982, 1986; Vecera & O'Reilly, 1998).

In hierarchical views of perceptual organization, configural and depth cues are considered lower-level, or bottom-up, cues – cues that do not require access to higher-level memory representations, and shape assignment based upon these cues is considered a lower-level process than object recognition. Consequently, according to these accounts, object memories cannot be accessed before shape assignment and perception is at least partially accomplished. On the basis of the evidence that contour recognition processes influence shape assignment, my colleagues and I proposed a parallel model, discussed next.

A Parallel Model

Recall that investigations with figure-ground displays indicated that object memories accessed quickly in the course of processing affect the shape assignment. The cues arising from these activated object memories did not dominate the other configural cues or depth cues; nor did the configural and depth cues constrain access to object memories. Rather, activated object memories seem to serve as one more cue among the many cues that contribute to the likelihood that a region will be seen as a shaped figure rather than a shapeless ground. Critically, object memories affected shape assignment only when they were accessed quickly. Influence from object memories could be removed either by inverting the stimuli (and thereby delaying the access to object memories), or by using contours detected later rather than earlier in processing (e.g., random-dot stereo edges versus luminance edges).

On the basis of this evidence, my colleagues and I proposed that, as soon as contours are segmented in the visual input, quick access to object memories via contours is initiated. The model is a parallel model because object memories are accessed via contour-based mechanisms at the same time that other processes assess the Gestalt configural cues and the depth cues, and all of these processes interact to affect shape assignment (see Figure 6.5c). We do not suppose that time course of all of these processes is the same. We suppose only that shape assignment based upon configural cues and/or depth cues does not precede access to object memories, either partially or wholly, as would be assumed on hierarchical models (Peterson, 1994a, 1999; Peterson & Gibson, 1994a, 1994b).

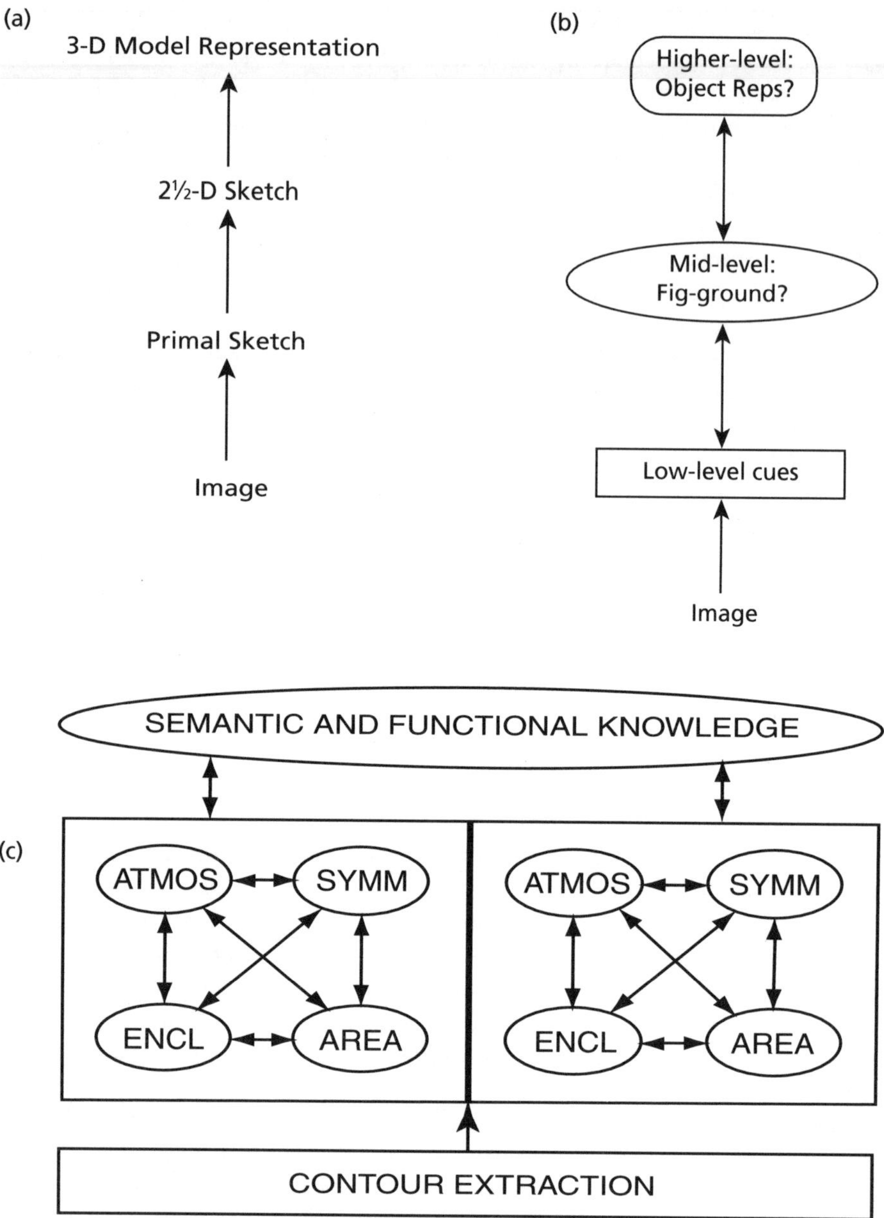

Figure 6.5. (a) A sketch of Marr's serial hierarchical theory. (b) An interactive hierarchy. (c) The parallel interactive model proposed by Peterson et al. (2000). A selection of shape processes are shown operating on both sides of a contour extracted early in processing, including ATMOS (Access to Memories of Object Structure), SYMM (Symmetry), ENCL (Enclosure), and AREA. Facilitatory connections exist between shape processes operating on the same side of the contour (indicated by double-headed arrows). Inhibitory connections exist between shape processes operating on opposite sides of the contour (indicated by T-endings). Feed-forward and feedback connections to and from Semantic and Functional Knowledge are also indicated by double-headed arrows. (Originally published in Peterson et al. (2000, Figure 9); reprinted with permission from Pergamon Press.)

A Continuing Debate

Hierarchical interactive models have been adapted to account for the evidence indicating that shape assignment is affected by access to object memories (e.g., Vecera & O'Reilly, 1998, 2000). In Vecera and O'Reilly's (2000) model, lower-level processes do not constrain the operation of higher-level recognition processes and effects of recognition processes on the processing at lower levels are evident at the earliest time slices. It will be difficult to distinguish this version of an interactive hierarchical model from a parallel model (e.g., Peterson, 1999; Peterson et al., 2000).

Many theorists prefer hierarchical models (serial or interactive) to parallel models because they believe that hierarchical models are better able than parallel models to account for the perception of novel or unrecognized objects (e.g., Marr, 1982; Warrington, 1982). However, this belief is based on the incorrect assumptions that (a) in parallel accounts, inputs from higher-level object memories are necessary for shape assignment and perception, and (b) high-level influences must dominate low-level factors. Neither of these assumptions is necessary and neither is held in the parallel models proposed by Peterson (1999; Peterson et al., 2000; also see above).

A hierarchical model implicitly underlies the notion of object files proposed by Kahneman and Treisman (1984) to account for perceived object continuity over changes in perceived identity, shape, color, or location. They proposed that temporary representations of objects are created at an intermediate hierarchical level, before object identity is established. These "object files" mediate object continuity over changes in object features such as location, color, and shape, provided that the changes are not too extreme. Priming experiments support the existence of object files (e.g., Kahneman, Treisman, & Gibbs, 1992; Treisman, Kahneman, & Burkell, 1983), but experimental evidence suggests that object files may code some aspects of object identity as well (Gordon & Irwin, 1996; Henderson & Anes, 1994). Thus, object files must be understood within a hierarchical model only if one assumes that spatio-temporal continuity is less likely to be maintained over changes in object identity than over changes in other object features. Although this prediction might be generated by a serial hierarchical model, it is not necessary on a parallel account.

Another reason underlying a preference for both serial and interactive hierarchical approaches to perceptual organization is that brain structures are thought to be arranged hierarchically. For instance, occipital cortex is initially activated via cortical connections earlier in time than temporal and parietal cortices, which in turn, are initially activated before frontal cortex. (Indeed, Vecera and O'Reilly (2000) argue that their hierarchical interactive model of figure-ground assignment is an architectural model rather than a processing model.) It is tempting to associate functional stages such as those proposed by Marr (1982) with these sequentially activated brain regions. However, it must be remembered that there are massive feedback connections between brain regions as well as feed-forward connections (Felleman & Van Essen, 1991; Zeki, 1993). These feedback connections from brain regions activated later in time via cortical connections can alter the activity in brain regions activated earlier in time. When these feedback connections are taken into consideration, it becomes very difficult to pinpoint the stage at which various aspects of perceptual organization are accomplished (Braddick, 1992; Peterson, 1999).

Consider the V2 cells that respond differentially to figures than to grounds (Zipser et al., 1996). This "figure" response in V2 occurs after some cells in temporal cortex have responded, so feedback may be involved (Zipser et al., 1996). This is not to say that activity did not occur in V2 prior to the measured "figure" response. But it is simply not clear whether or not the prior activity should be taken as constituting emergent figure-ground segregation, as might be predicted on any interactive hierarchical view. Alternatively, the prior activity represents some other perceptual function, such as border detection or grouping (see Zipser et al., 1996), neither of which can properly be said to produce emergent figure-ground segregation, as discussed previously.

At this time, we simply cannot distinguish between an interactive hierarchical account and a parallel account of how object (or contour) recognition processes interact with other early visual processes. Attempts to elucidate what aspects of object memories (i.e., structure, function, semantics) are accessed at various processing stages will be critical in resolving this debate. (For research relevant to this issue see Gordon & Irwin, 1996; Henderson & Anes, 1994; Kahneman & Treisman, 1984; Kahneman, Treisman, & Gibbs, 1992; Peterson et al., 1991; Peterson et al., 1996; Treisman, 1988; Treisman, Kahneman, & Burkell, 1983.)

Attention and Object Perception

In this section, we consider research concerning the relationship between object perception and attention. We begin by considering whether attention makes something an object. Imagine attending to entities in order to count them, for example. Wolfe and Bennett (1997) define an object as ". . . a numerable thing as distinct from a collection of numerable things and as distinct from unenumerable 'stuff'." We can certainly count objects, but we can also count other things, like the spaces between the words on this line of text, for example. Enumerability does not make something an object. Similarly, one can attend to spaces as well as to objects, but attending does not necessarily make a space an object (Rubin, 1915/1958; Peterson & Gerhardstein, under review; Peterson, Gerhardstein, Mennemeier, & Rapcsak, 1998; Peterson & Gibson, 1994b). Thus, neither attention nor enumerability is sufficient for object perception. The related question of whether attention, or intention, on the viewer's part is necessary for object perception is currently being explored, as a consequence of pioneering work by Mack and Rock (1998). This topic is covered next. Then, in the following section, we consider the evidence indicating that there exists an object-based form of attention that is distinct from spatial attention.

Is Attention Necessary for Object Perception?

Inattentional Blindness

Mack and Rock (1998; Mack, Tang, Tuma, Kahn, & Rock, 1992; Rock, Linnett, Grant, & Mack, 1992) found that a large percentage of observers were effectively blind to the unexpected onset of an object when they were performing a difficult discrimination task. The discrimination task entailed judging which of the two arms of a cross was longer, when the difference between the arms was quite small. The cross was exposed briefly (e.g., 200 ms) and followed by a masking stimulus. On the third trial on which observers performed this task, a simple geometric object was presented in one of the four quadrants sketched by the cross at the same time that the cross was presented. When questioned shortly after this critical trial, many observers reported that they had not seen anything unusual. Some observers did report that something unusual had happened on the critical trial, but they were unable to report the simple geometric shape of the object that had been shown (e.g., a square or a triangle). Mack and Rock called this phenomenon "inattentional blindness." They argued that if the observer's attention or intention is not directed to perceiving an object, then object perception does not occur. Note that inattentional blindness is necessarily inferred from performance on a memory task rather than from performance on an online perception task. (Presumably, if observers knew they would have to occasionally detect objects, their perceptual intentions would change to accommodate this object detection task.)

The phenomenon of inattentional blindness raises the possibility that one may need attention (or intention) to perceive objects consciously. This in turn raises a question about terminology: Should the term "perception" (and the term "object perception" in particular) be reserved only for conditions in which observers can report being consciously aware of what they perceived? I argue that it should not. Research summarized in this chapter indicates that many of the component processes involved in object perception can be computed outside the observer's attentional focus, outside of awareness. Other evidence comes from work by C. M. Moore and Egeth (1997), who adapted the Mack and Rock paradigm and presented convincing evidence that grouping occurs without intention or attention. Regardless of whether or not the term "object perception" is ultimately reserved for conscious object perception, the important question of how attention or intention contributes to *conscious* object perception remains.

Stimulus Selection

A related debate in the search literature concerns whether or not it is possible for a stimulus to draw attention automatically if an observer is not intending to search for that stimulus in the first place. Pop-out effects have often been taken as evidence that unusual stimulus features or abrupt stimulus onsets can attract attention (e.g., Treisman, 1988; Yantis, 1993, 1996). "Pop-out" occurs when a single target stimulus differing on some basic feature from other "distractor" stimuli is detected quickly, and target detection latency does not increase as the number of distractors increases (e.g., the time to detect a red dot amongst green dots does not increase appreciably as the number of green dots increases). The quick detection responses were originally attributed to "stimulus selection" – the automatic allocation of attention to the distinct stimulus feature in the display. But Mack, Rock, and others pointed out that, in experiments demonstrating pop-out effects, observers are typically given advance information about the identity of their target feature or stimulus. Therefore, pop-out effects cannot serve as evidence that targets automatically attract attention in virtue of being different from the other display items. In experiments in which attention and task set were carefully controlled, Folk, Remington, and Johnston (1992) and Gibson and Kelsey (1998) failed to find evidence for stimulus selection, consistent with the view that task set determines what observers perceive. These results are consistent with the hypothesis that attention/intention is necessary for conscious perception, although it must be remembered that no "consciousness standard" exists; surely no single task currently in the experimentalist's repertoire provides a universally accepted standard.

Binding

Attention may be required to bind together the various properties of an object, such as its color, form, and movement (Treisman, 1988; Treisman & Gelade, 1980) as well. Treisman and her colleagues argued that, without attention, such features can be combined incorrectly, and illusory conjunctions can occur (e.g., illusory conjunctions of color and form, or form and motion). Prinzmetal (1981, 1995) showed that, when grouped displays are not attended, illusory conjunctions are more likely to occur within grouped entities than across grouped entities. (Note that Prinzmetal's results, like Moore and Egeth's, suggest that grouping itself can occur without attention.) Wolfe and Bennet (1997) recently demonstrated that attention is necessary to conjoin the features of an object, at least for conscious report. These authors argue that, prior to the allocation of attention, objects are nothing more than loose collections of basic features organized on the basis of spatio-temporal properties (i.e., Kahneman & Treisman's object files). However, it is important to remember that inaccessibility to conscious report does not necessarily imply that perceptual organization has not occurred. There is some evidence that binding has occurred, even when it cannot be measured via conscious reports (Robertson, 1998; Wojciulik & Kanwisher, 1998).

Experiments such as these indicate that attention must be considered if we are to understand object perception, but so must the relationship between perception and conscious report. I turn next to consider the evidence indicating that a specialized form of object-based attention exists.

Object-Based Attention

It has long been known that attention can be allocated to locations in space that are different from the location where the eyes are directed (Posner, 1980). More recently, it has been shown that attention can be allocated to objects independent of the spaces they occupy (e.g., Duncan, 1984; Driver & Halligan, 1991; Gibson & Egeth, 1994; Treisman, Kahneman & Burkell, 1983). Evidence that attention can be "object-based" and not just "space-based" takes various forms. One form of evidence for "object-based" attention, is that it takes longer to move attention a given distance between two objects than the same distance within an object (Egly, Driver, & Rafal, 1994; Egly, Rafal, Driver, & Starrveveld, 1994). Another manifestation of object-based attention is that observers require less time to report about two features of a single object than about two features of different objects. This second effect is obtained even when the two objects overlap each other and occupy essentially the same location (Duncan, 1984; Goldsmith, 1998), and even when portions of the single object are occluded by another object (Behrmann, Zemel, & Mozer, 1998). A third demonstration of object-based attention entails moving objects. When a cued object moves to a new location, attention moves with the object, rather than (or in addition to) staying in the cued location (Kahneman, Treisman, & Gibbs, 1992; Tipper, Brehaut, & Driver, 1990; Tipper, Driver, & Weaver, 1991). Thus, attention seems (a) to spread more readily within an attended object than between two objects, (b) to encompass the perceptible features of an attended object, and (c) to move with an object.

In summary, the study of object perception and the study of attention are currently intertwined. Objects may not be perceived consciously unless they are encompassed by the observer's intentions. Once objects are perceived consciously, they form a unique substrate for the spread of attention that is distinct from a purely spatial substrate. Questions regarding the relationship between space and objects have been raised throughout this chapter, and will continue to be raised in the future. Questions regarding the relationship between conscious perception and action are important as well (see Chapters 7 and 10) for elaboration of these points.

Suggested Readings

Parasuraman, R. (Ed.) (1998). *The attentive brain.* Cambridge, MA: MIT Press.

Hochberg, J. (Ed.) (1998). *Perception and cognition at century's end.* NY: Academic Press.

Inui, T., & McClelland, J. L. (Eds.) (1996). *Attention and performance, XVI: Information integration in perception and communication.* Cambridge, MA: MIT Press.

Tarr, M. J, & Bülthoff, H. (Eds.) (1999). *Object recognition in man, monkey, and machine.* Cambridge, MA: MIT Press. (Printed from a special issue of *Cognition* (1998), 67 (1–2).)

Additional Topics

Colour and Surface Detail

To what extent do color and surface detail influence object recognition? (Biederman & Ju, 1988; Price & Humphreys, 1989; J. W. Tanaka & Presnell, 1999)

Are Holes Objects?

For discussions of holes, see Cassati & Varzi (1995); Bloom (1996); Bloom & Giralt (in press); Hochberg, 1998.

Tactile and Auditory Object Perception

What general principles cut across different modalities in which object perception occurs (e.g., what principles are shared by visual, tactile, and auditory object perception and what specific principles are employed in each modality)? For work on auditory object perception see Darwin and Hakin (1999). For work on tactile object perception see Klatzsky and Lederman (1995, 1999).

References

Battelli, L., Casco, C., & Sartori, G. (1997). Dissociation between contour-based and texture-based shape perception: A single case study. *Visual Cognition, 4*, 275–310.

Baylis, G. C., & Driver, J. (1992). Visual parsing and response competition: The effect of grouping factors. *Perception & Psychophysics, 51*, 141–162.

Baylis, G. C., & Driver, J. (1993). Visual attention and objects: Evidence for the hierarchical encoding of location hypothesis. *Journal of Experimental Psychology: Human Perception & Performance, 19*, 451–470.

Baylis, G. C., & Driver, J. (1994). Parallel computation of symmetry, but not repetition in single visual objects. *Visual Cognition, 1*, 377–400.

Baylis, G. C., & Driver, J. (1995). Obligatory edge-assignment in vision: The role of figure- and part-segmentation in symmetry detection. *Journal of Experimental Psychology: Human Perception & Performance, 21*, 1323–1342.

Beck, J., Rosenfeld, A., & Ivry, R. (1990). Line segregation. *Spatial Vision, 4*, 75–101.

Behrmann, M., Zemel, R. S., & Mozer, M. C. (1998). Object-based attention and occlusion: Evidence from normal participants. *Journal of Experimental Psychology: Human Perception & Performance, 24*, 1011–1036.

Ben-Av, M. B., & Sagi, D. (1995). Perceptual grouping by similarity and proximity: Experimental results can be predicted by intensity autocorrelations. *Vision Research, 35*, 853–866.

Biederman, I. (1985). Human image understanding: Recent research and a theory. *Computer Vision, Graphics, and Image Processing, 32*, 29–73.

Biederman, I. (1987). Recognition by components: A theory of human image understanding. *Psychological Review, 94*, 115–147.

Biederman, I. (1995). Visual object recognition. In S. F. Kosslyn & D. N. Oshershon (Eds.), *An invitation to cognitive science* (2nd ed., pp. 121–165). Cambridge, MA: The MIT Press.

Biederman, I., & Gerhardstein, P.C. (1993). Recognizing depth-rotated objects: Evidence and conditions for three-dimensional viewpoint invariance. *Journal of Experimental Psychology: Human Perception & Performance, 19*, 1162–1182.

Biederman, I., & Gerhardstein, P.C. (1995). Viewpoint-dependent mechanisms in visual object recognition: A reply to Tarr and Bülthoff (1995). *Journal of Experimental Psychology: Human Perception & Performance, 21,* 1506–1514.

Biederman, I., & Ju, G. (1988). Surface versus edge-based determinants of visual recognition. *Cognitive Psychology, 20*, 38–64.

Binford, T. O. (1981). Inferring surfaces from images. *Artificial Intelligence, 17*, 205–244.

Bloom, P. (1996). Possible individuals in language and cognition. *Current Directions in Psychological Science, 5*, 90–94.

Bloom, P., & Girault, N. (in press). *Psychological Science.*

Boselie, F. (1994). Local and global factors in visual occlusion. *Perception, 23*, 517–528.

Boselie, F., & Leeuwenberg, E. (1986). A test of the minimum principle requires a perceptual coding system. *Perception, 15*, 331–354.

Braddick, O. (1992). Motion may be seen but not used. *Current Biology, 2*, 597–599.

Braun, J. (1993). Shape-from-shading is independent of visual attention and may be a 'texton.' *Spatial Vision, 7*, 311–322.

Braunstein, M. L, Hoffman, D. D., & Saidpour, A. (1989). Parts of visual objects: An experimental test of the minima rule. *Perception, 18*, 817–826.

Brown, J. M., & Weisstein, N. (1988). A spatial frequency effect on perceived depth. *Perception & Psychophysics, 44*, 157–166.

Brown, J. M., Weisstein, N., & May, J. G. (1992). Visual search for simple volumetric shapes. *Perception & Psychophysics, 51*, 40–48.

Bruno, N., Bertamini, M., & Domini, F. (1997). Amodal completion of partly occluded surfaces: Is there a mosaic stage? *Journal of Experimental Psychology: Human Perception & Performance, 23*, 1412–1426.

Bülthoff, H. H. (1991). Shape from X: Psychophysics and computation. In M. S. Landy & J. A. Movshon (Eds.), *Computational models of visual processing.* Cambridge, MA: The MIT Press.

Bülthoff, H. H., & Edelman, S. (1993). Evaluating object recognition theories by computer psychophysics. In T. A. Poggio & D. A. Glaser (Eds.), *Exploring brain functions: Models in neuroscience* (pp. 139–164). NY: Wiley.

Cassati, R., & Varzi, A. C. (1995). *Holes and other superficialities*. Cambridge, MA: MIT Press.

Cave, C. B., & Kosslyn, S. M. (1993). The role of parts and spatial relations in object identification. *Perception*, 22, 229–248.

Corballis, M. C. (1988). Recognition of disoriented shapes. *Psychological Review*, *95*, 115–123.

Cutting, J. E., & Vishton, P. M. (1995). Perceiving layout and knowing distances: The integration, relative potency, and contextual use of different information about depth. In W. Epstein & S. Rogers (Eds.), *Perception of space and motion* (pp. 71–118). San Diego: Academic Press.

Darwin, C. J., & Hukin, R. W. (1999). Auditory objects of attention: The role of interaural time differences. *Journal of Experimental Psychology: Human Perception & Performance, 25*, 617–629.

Davis, G., & Driver, J. (1994). Parallel detection of Kanizsa subjective figures in the human visual system. *Nature, 371*, 791–793.

Dresp, B., & Bonnet, C. (1993). Psychophysical measures of illusory form perception: Further evidence for local mechanisms. *Vision Research, 33*, 759–766.

Driver, J., & Baylis, G. C. (1989). Movement and visual attention: The spotlight metaphor breaks down. *Journal of Experimental Psychology: Human Perception & Performance, 15*, 448–456.

Driver, J., Baylis, G. C., & Rafal, R. D. (1992). Preserved figure-ground segregation and symmetry perception in visual neglect. *Nature* (London), *360*, 73–75.

Driver, J., & Halligan, P. W. (1991). Can visual neglect operate in object-centered coordinates? An affirmative single case study. *Cognitive Neuropsychology, 8*, 475–496.

Duncan, J. (1984). Selective attention and the organization of visual information. *Journal of Experimental Psychology: General, 119*, 501–517.

Edelman, S., & Weinshall, D. (1991). A self-organizing multiple view representation of 3D objects. *Biological Cybernetics, 64*, 209–219.

Egly, R., Driver, J., & Rafal, R. D. (1994). Shifting visual attention between objects and locations: Evidence from normal and parietal lesion subjects. *Journal of Experimental Psychology: General, 123*, 161–177.

Egly, R., Rafal, R., Driver, J., & Starrveveld, Y. (1994). Covert orienting in the split brain reveals hemispheric specialization for object-based attention. *Psychological Science, 5*, 380–383.

Enns, J. T., & Rensink, R. A. (1991). Preattentive recovery of three-dimensional orientation from line drawings. *Psychological Review, 98*, 335–351.

Eriksen, B. A., &. Eriksen, C. W. (1974). Effects of noise letters upon the identification of a target letter in a nonsearch task. *Perception & Psychophysics, 16*, 143–149.

Felleman, D. J., & Van Essen, D. C. (1991). Distributed hierarchical processing in primate visual cortex. *Cerebral Cortex, 1*, 1–47.

Field, D. J., Hayes, A., & Hess, R. F. (1993). Contour integration by the human visual system: Evidence for a local "association field." *Vision Research, 33*, 175–193.

Folk, C.L., Remington, R.W., & Johnston, J. C. (1992). Involuntary covert orienting is contingent on attentional control settings. *Journal of Experimental Psychology: Human Perception & Performance, 18*, 1030–1044.

Fox, E. (1998). Perceptual grouping and visual selective attention. *Perception & Psychophysics, 60*, 1004–1021.

Gibson, B. S., & Egeth, H. (1994). Inhibition and disinhibition of return: Evidence from temporal order judgments. *Perception & Psychophysics, 56*, 669–680.

Gibson, B. S., & Kelsey, E. M. (1998). Stimulus-driven attentional capture is contingent on attentional set for displaywide visual features. *Journal of Experimental Psychology: Human Perception & Performance, 24*, 699–706.

Gibson, B. S., & Peterson, M. A. (1994). Does orientation-independent object recognition precede orientation-dependent recognition? Evidence from a cueing paradigm. *Journal of Experimental Psychology: Human Perception & Performance, 20*, 299–316.

Goldsmith, M. (1998). What's in a location? Comparing object-based and space-based models of feature integration in visual search. *Journal of Experimental Psychology: General, 27*, 189–219.

Gordon, R. D., & Irwin, D. E. (1996). What's in an object file? Evidence from priming studies. *Perception & Psychophysics, 58*, 1260–1277.

Göttschaldt, K. (1926/1938). Gestalt factors and repetition (continued). In W. D. Ellis (Ed.), *A sourcebook of Gestalt psychology*. London: Kegan Paul, Trech, Tubner, and Co., Ltd.
Graham, N. V. S. (1989). *Visual pattern analyzers*. New York: Oxford University Press.
Graham, N. V. S. (1992). Breaking the visual stimulus into parts. *Current Directions in Psychological Science, 1*, 55–60.
Grosof, D. H., Shapley, R. M., & Hawken, M. J. (1993). Macaque V1 neurons can signal illusory contours. *Nature, 365*, 550–552.
Grossberg, S., & Mingolla, E. (1985). Neural dynamics of perceptual grouping: Textures, boundaries and emergent segmentations. *Perception & Psychophysics, 38*, 141–171.
Gurnsey, R., Humphrey, G. K., & Kapitan, P. (1992). Parallel discrimination of subjective contours defined by offset gratings. *Perception & Psychophysics, 52*, 263–276.
Han, S., Humphreys, G., & Chen L. (1999a). Uniform connectedness and classical Gestalt principles of perceptual grouping. *Perception & Psychophysics, 61*, 661–674.
Han, S., Humphreys, G. W., & Chen L. (1999b). Parallel and competitive processes in hierarchical analysis: Perceptual grouping and encoding of closure. *Journal of Experimental Psychology: Human Perception & Performance, 25*, 1411–1432.
Harms, L., & Bundeson, C. (1983). Color segregation and selective attention in a nonsearch task. *Perception & Psychophysics, 33*, 11–19.
Hayward, W. G. (1998). Effects of outline shape in object recognition. *Journal of Experimental Psychology: Human Perception & Performance, 24*, 427–440.
He, Z. J., & Nakayama, K. (1992). Surfaces versus features in visual search. *Nature, 359*, 231–233.
He, Z. J., & Nakayama, K. (1994). Perceiving textures: Beyond filtering. *Vision Research, 34*, 151–162.
Heilman, K. M., & Van Den, A. (1980). Right hemisphere dominance for attention: The mechanism underlying hemispheric asymmetries of inattention (neglect). *Neurology, 30*, 327–330.
Henderson, J. M., & Anes, M. D. (1994). Roles of object-file review and type priming in visual identification within and across eye fixations. *Journal of Experimental Psychology: Human Perception & Performance, 20*, 826–839.
Hirsch, E. (1982). *The concept of identity*. New York: Oxford University Press.
Hochberg, J. (1968). In the mind's eye. In R. N. Haber (Ed.), *Contemporary theory and research in visual perception* (pp. 309–331). New York: Holt, Rinehart, & Winston.
Hochberg, J. (1971). Perception I: Color and shape. In J. W. Kling & L. A. Riggs (Eds.), *Woodworth and Schlossberg's experimental psychology*, (3rd ed., pp. 395–474). New York: Hold, Rinehart, & Winston.
Hochberg, J. (1978). *Perception* (2nd ed.). Englewood Cliffs, NJ: Prentice Hall, Inc.
Hochberg, J. (1980). Pictorial functions and perceptual structures. In M. A. Hagen (Ed.), *The perception of pictures* (Vol. 2, pp. 47–93). New York: Academic Press.
Hochberg, J. (1998). Gestalt theory and its legacy. In J. Hochberg (Ed.), *Perception and cognition at century's end* (pp. 253–306). New York: Academic Press.
Hochberg, J., and Peterson, M. A. (1993). Mental representations of occluded objects: Sequential disclosure and intentional construal. *Giornale Italiano di Psicologia, 20*, 805–820. (Monograph edition published in English in honor of Gaetano Kanizsa.)
Hoffman, D. D., & Richards, W. A. (1985). Parts of recognition. In S. Pinker (Ed.), *Visual cognition*. Cambridge, MA: MIT Press.
Hoffman, D. D., & Singh, M. (1997). Saliende of visual parts. *Cognition, 63*, 29–78.
Hubel, D. H., & Wiesel, T. N. (1968). Receptive fields and functional architecture of monkey striate cortex. *Journal of Physiology (London), 166*, 106–154.
Hummel, J., & Biederman, I. (1992). Dynamic binding in a neural network for shape recognition. *Psychological Review, 99*, 480–517.
Humphrey, G. K., Symons, L. A., Herbert, A. M., & Goodale, M. A. (1996). A neurological dissociation between shape from shading and shape from edges. *Behavioral Brain Research, 76*, 117–125.
Humphreys, G. W. (1981). Flexibility of attention between stimulus dimensions. *Perception &*

Psychophysics, 30, 291–302.
Ittelson, W. (1996). Visual perception of markings. *Psychonomic Bulletin & Review, 3,* 171–187.
Jolicoeur, P. (1985). The time to name disoriented objects. *Memory & Cognition, 13,* 289–303.
Jolicoeur, P. (1988). Mental rotation and the identification of disoriented objects. *Canadian Journal of Psychology, 42,* 461–478.
Julesz, B. (1971). *Foundations of Cyclopean perception.* Chicago: University of Chicago Press.
Julesz, B. (1981). Textons, the elements of texture perception, and their interactions. *Nature (London), 290,* 91–97.
Kahneman, D., & Treisman, A. (1984). Changing views of attention and automaticity. In R. Parasuraman (Ed.), *Varieties of attention* (pp. 29–61). New York: Academic Press.
Kahneman, D., Treisman, A., & Gibbs, B. J. (1992). The reviewing of object files: Object specific integration of information. *Cognitive Psychology, 24,* 175–215.
Kanizsa, G. (1987). Quasi-perceptual margins in homogeneously stimulated fields. In S. Petry & G. Meyer (Eds.), *The perception of illusory contours* (W. Gerbino, Trans.) (pp. 40–49). New York: Springer-Verlag.
Kanizsa, G., & Gerbino, W. (1976). Convexity and symmetry in figure-ground organization. In M. Henle (Ed.), *Vision and artifact.* New York: Springer Publishing Co.
Kapadia, M. K., Ito, M., Gilbert, C. D., & Westheimer, G. (1995). Improvement in visual sensitivity by changes in local context: Parallel studies in human observers and in V1 of alert monkeys. *Neuron, 15,* 843–856.
Kellman, P. J., & Shipley, T. F. (1991). A theory of visual interpolation in object perception. *Cognitive Psychology, 23,* 141–221.
Kellman, P. J., Yin, C., & Shipley, T.F. (1998). A common mechanism for illusory and occluded object completion. *Journal of Experimental Psychology: Human Perception & Performance, 24,* 859–869.
Kennedy, J. M. (1973). Misunderstandings of figure and ground. *Scandinavian Journal of Psychology, 14,* 207–209.
Kennedy, J. M. (1974). *A psychology of picture perception.* San Francisco: Jossey-Bass Publishers.
Kimchi, R. (1994). The role of wholistic/configural properties versus global properties in visual form perception. *Perception, 23,* 489–504.
Kimchi, R. (1998). Uniform connectedness and grouping in the perceptual organization of hierarchical patterns. *Journal of Experimental Psychology: Human Perception & Performance.*
Kinsbourne, M., (1970). The cerebral basis of lateral asymmetries in attention. *Acta Psychologica, 33,* 193–201.
Klatzky, R. L., & Lederman, S. J. (1995). Identifying objects from a haptic glance. *Perception & Pychophysics, 57,* 1111–1123.
Klatzky, R. L., & Lederman, S. J. (1999). The haptic glance: A route to rapid object identification and manipulation. In D. Gopher & A. Koriat (Eds.), *Attention and performance XVII. Cognitive regulation of performance: Integration of theory and application.* Mahwah, NJ: Erlbaum.
Kobatake, E., & Tanaka, K. (1994). Neuronal selectivities to complex object features in the ventral visual pathway of the macaque cerebral cortex. *Journal of Neurophysiology, 71,* 856–867.
Koffka, K. (1935) *Principles of Gestalt psychology.* New York: Harcourt, Brace, & World, Inc.
Köhler, W. (1929/1947) *Gestalt psychology.* New York: New American Library.
Kovács, I., & Julesz, B. (1994). Perceptual sensitivity maps within globally defined visual shapes. *Nature, 370,* 25 August, 644–646.
Kramer, A. F., & Jacobson, A. (1991). Perceptual organization and focused attention: The role of objects and proximity in visual processing. *Perception & Psychophysics, 50,* 267–284.
Kurbat, M. (1994). Structural description theories: Is RBC/JIM a general purpose theory of human entry-level object recognition? *Perception, 23,* 1339–1368.
Landy, M. S., Maloney, L. T, & Young, M. J. (1990). Psychophysical estimation of the human depth combination rule. Sensor Fusion III: 3-D perception and recognition. *SPIE, 1383,* 247–254.
Leonards, U., Singer, W., & Fahle, M. (1996). The influence of temporal phase differences on

texture segmentation. *Vision Research, 36*, 2689–2697.
Lin, E. L., & Murphy, G. L. (1997). Effects of background knowledge on object categorization and part detection. *Journal of Experimental Psychology: Human Perception & Performance, 23*, 1153–1169.
Logothetis, N. K., Pauls, J., Bueltoff, H. H., & Poggio, T. (1994). Viewpoint dependent object recognition in monkeys. *Current Biology, 4*, 401–414.
Logothetis, N. K., Pauls, J., & Poggio, T. (1995). Shape representation in the inferior temporal cortex of monkeys. *Current Biology, 5*, 552–563.
Lowe, D. (1985). *Perceptual organization and visual recognition.* Boston: Kluwer.
Lowe, D. (1987). Three-dimensional object recognition from single two-dimensional images. *Artificial intelligence, 31*, 355–395.
Mack, A., & Rock, I. (1998). *Inattentional blindness.* Cambridge, MA: MIT Press.
Mack, A., Tang, B., Tuma, R., Kahn, S., & Rock, I. (1992). Perceptual organization and attention. *Cognitive Psychology, 24*, 475–501.
Marr, D. (1982). *Vision.* San Francisco: W. H. Freeman.
Marr, D., & Nishihara, H. K. (1978). Representation and recognition of the spatial organization of three-dimensional shapes. *Proceedings of the Royal Society of London, B, 200*, 269–291.
McClelland, J. L. (1979). On the time relations of mental processes: An examination of systems of processes in cascade. *Psychological Review, 86*, 287–330.
McClelland, J. L. (1985). Putting knowledge in its place: A scheme for programming parallel processing structures on the fly. *Cognitive Science, 9*, 113–146.
McClelland, J. L., & Rumelhart, D. E. (1986). *Parallel distributed processing: Explorations in the microstructure of cognition* (Vol. 2). Cambridge, MA: The MIT Press.
Moore, C., & Cavanagh, P. (1998). Recovery of 3D volume from 2–tone images of novel objects. *Cognition, 67*, 45–71.
Moore, C. M., & Egeth, H. (1997). Perception without attention: Evidence of grouping under conditions of inattention. *Journal of Experimental Psychology: Human Perception & Performance, 23*, 339–352.
Moore, M. G. (1930). Gestalt vs. experience. *American Journal of Psychology, 42*, 543–455.
Mozer, M. C., Zemel, R. S., Behrmann, M., & Williams, C. K. (1992). Learning to segment images using dynamic feature binding. *Neural Computation, 4*, 650–665.
Mumford, D., Kosslyn, S. M., Hillger, L. A., & Herrnstein, R. J. (1987). Discriminating figure from ground: The role of edge detection and region-growing. *Proceedings of the National Academy of Sciences, 84*, 7354–7358.
Neisser, U. (1967). *Cognitive psychology.* New York: Appleton, Century, Crofts.
O'Shea, R. P., Blackburn, S. G., & Ono, H. (1994). Contrast as a depth cue. *Vision Research, 34*, 1595–1604.
Palmer, S., & Rock, I. (1994a). Rethinking perceptual organization: The role of uniform connectedness. *Psychonomic Bulletin & Review, 1*, 29–55.
Parker, A. J., Cumming, B. G., Johnston, E. B., & Hurlbert, A. C. (1995). Multiple cues for three-dimensional shape. In M. S. Gazzaniga (Ed.), *The cognitive neurosciences* (pp. 351–364). Cambridge, MA: The MIT Press.
Perrett, D., Smith, P., Potter, D., Mistlin, A., Head, A., Milner, A., & Jeeves, M. (1985). Visual cells in the temporal cortex sensitive to face view and gaze direction. *Proceedings of the Royal Society, London*, [Biol], *223*, 293–317.
Peterhans, E., & von der Heydt, R. (1989). Mechanisms of contour perception in monkey visual cortex. II. Contours bridging gaps. *Journal of Neuroscience, 9*, 1749–1763.
Peterson, M. A. (1994a). Shape recognition can and does occur before figure-ground organization. *Current Directions in Psychological Science, 3*, 105–111.
Peterson, M. A. (1994b). The proper placement of uniform connectedness. *Psychonomic Bulletin and Review, 1*, 509–514.
Peterson, M. A. (1999). What's in a stage name? *Journal of Experimental Psychology: Human Perception & Performance, 25*, 276–286.

Peterson, M. A., de Gelder, B., Rapcsak, S. Z., Gerhardstein, P. C., & Bachoud-Lévi, A.-C. (2000). Object memory effects on figure assignment: Conscious object recognition is not necessary or sufficient. *Vision Research, 40,* 1549–1567.
Peterson, M. A., & Gerhardstein, P. C. (under review). Effects of region-centered attention and object memory on figure assignment.
Peterson, M. A., Gerhardstein, P., Mennemeier, M., & Rapcsak, S. V. (1998). Object-centered attentional biases and object recognition contributions to scene segmentation in right hemisphere- and left hemisphere-damaged patients. *Psychobiology, 26,* 557–570.
Peterson, M. A., & Gibson, B. S. (1993). Shape recognition contributions to figure-ground organization in three-dimensional displays. *Cognitive Psychology, 25,* 383–429.
Peterson, M. A., & Gibson, B. S. (1994a). Must shape recognition follow figure-ground organization? An assumption in peril. *Psychological Science, 5,* 253–259.
Peterson, M. A., & Gibson, B. S. (1994b). Object recognition contributions to figure-ground organization: Operations on outlines and subjective contours. *Perception & Psychophysics, 56,* 551–564.
Peterson, M. A., Harvey, E. H., & Weidenbacher, H. L. (1991). Shape recognition inputs to figure-ground organization: Which route counts? *Journal of Experimental Psychology: Human Perception & Performance, 17,* 1075–1089.
Peterson, M. A., & Hector, J. E. (1996, November). *Evidence for the piecemeal nature of pre-depth object recognition processes.* Paper presented at the Annual Meeting of the Psychonomic Society, Chicago, IL.
Peterson, M. A., & Hochberg, J. (1983). Opposed-set measurement procedure: A quantitative analysis of the role of local cues and intention in form perception. *Journal of Experimental Psychology: Human Perception & Performance, 9,* 183–193.
Peterson, M. A., & Hochberg, J. (1989). Necessary considerations for a theory of form perception: A theoretical and empirical reply to Boselie and Leeuwenberg. *Perception, 18,* 105–119.
Peterson, M. A., Nadel, L., Bloom, P., & Garrett, M. F. (1996). Space and language. In P. Bloom, M. A. Peterson, L. Nadel, & M. F. Garrett (Eds.), *Language and space* (pp. 553–577). Cambridge, MA: MIT Press.
Poggio, T., & Edelman, S. (1990). A network that learns to recognize three-dimensional objects. *Nature, 343,* 263–266.
Pomerantz, J. R., & Kubovy, M. (1986). Theoretical approaches to perceptual organization: Simplicity and likelihood principles. In K. R. Boff, L. Kaufman, & J. P. Thomas (Eds.), *Handbook of perception and performance, volume II: Cognitive processes and performance* (pp. 36:1–46). New York: John Wiley & Sons.
Posner, M. I. (1980). Orienting of attention. *Quarterly Journal of Experimental Psychology, 32,* 23–25.
Prazdny, K. (1983). Illusory contours are not caused by simultaneous brightness contrast. *Perception & Psychophysics, 34,* 403–404.
Price, C. J., & Humphreys, G. W. (1989). The effects of surface detail on object categorization and naming. *Quarterly Journal of Experimental Psychology, 41A,* 797–828.
Prinzmetal, W. (1981). Principles of feature integration in visual perception. *Perception & Psychophysics, 30,* 330–340.
Prinzmetal, W. (1995). Visual feature integration in a world of objects. *Current Directions in Psychological Science, 4,* 90–94.
Ramachandran, V. S. (1988). Perception of shape from shading. *Nature* (London), *331,* 163–166.
Rensink, R., & Enns, J. T. (1995). Preemption effects in visual search: Evidence for low-level grouping. *Psychological Review, 102,* 101–130.
Riddoch, M. J., & Humphreys, G. W. (1987). A case of integrative visual agnosia. *Brain, 110,* 1431–1462.
Robertson, L. C. (1998). Visuospatial attention and cognitive function: Their role in object perception. In R. Parasuraman (Ed.), *The attentive brain.* Cambridge, MA: MIT Press.
Rock, I. (1987). A problem-solving approach to illusory contours. In S. Petry & G. Meyer (Eds.),

The perception of illusory contours (pp. 462–70). New York: Springer-Verlag.
Rock, I., & Brosgole, L. (1964). Grouping based on phenomenal proximity. *Journal of Experimental Psychology, 67*, 531–538.
Rock, I., Linnett, C. M., Grant, P., & Mack, A. (1992). Perception without attention: Results of a new method. *Cognitive Psychology, 24*, 502–534.
Rubin, E. (1958). Figure and ground. In D. Beardslee & M. Wertheimer (Ed. and Trans.), *Readings in perception* (pp. 35–101). Princeton, NJ: Van Nostrand. (Original work published 1915.)
Rumelhart, D. E., & McClelland, J. L. (1982). An interactive activation model of context effects in letter perception: Part 2. The contextual enhancement effect and some tests of and extensions of the model. *Psychological Review, 89*, 60–94.
Rumelhart, D. E., & McClelland, J. L. (1986). *Parallel distributed processing: Explorations in the microstructure of cognition* (Vol. 1). Cambridge, MA: The MIT Press.
Saiki, J., & Hummel, J. (1998). Connectedness and the integration of parts with relations in shape perception. *Journal of Experimental Psychology: Human Perception & Performance, 24*, 227–251.
Schyns, P., Goldstone, R. L., & Thilbaut, J-P. (1998). The development of features in object concepts. *Behavioral & Brain Sciences, 21*, 1–54.
Sekuler, A. B. (1994). Local and global minima in visual completion: Effects of symmetry and orientation. *Perception, 23*, 529–545.
Sekuler, A. B., & Palmer, S. E. (1992). Perception of partly occluded objects: A microgenetic analysis. *Journal of Experimental Psychology: General, 121*, 95–111.
Solms, M., Turnbull, O. H., Kaplan-Solms, K., & Miller, P. (1998). Rotated drawing: The range of performance and anatomical correlates in a series of 16 patients. *Brain & Cognition, 38*, 358–368.
Spelke, E. S. (1988). Where perceiving ends and thinking begins: The apprehension of objects in infancy. In A. Yonas (Ed.), *Perceptual development in infancy: The Minnesota symposium on child psychology* (Vol. 20, pp. 197–234). Hillsdale. NJ: Lawrence Erlbaum Associates.
Spelke, E. S. (1990). Principles of object perception. *Cognitive Science, 14*, 29–56.
Spelke, E. S., Gutheil, G., & Van de Walle, G. (1995). The development of object perception. In S. M. Kosslyn & D. N. Osherson (Eds), *Visual cognition: An invitation to cognitive science* (Vol. 2, 2nd ed.). Cambridge, MA: MIT Press.
Stevens, K. A., & Brooks, A. (1988). The concave cusp as determiner of figure-ground. *Perception, 17*, 35–42.
Sun, J., & Perona, P. (1997). Shading and stereo in early perception of shape and reflectance. *Perception, 26*, 519–529.
Suzuki, S., Peterson, M. A., Moscovitch, M., & Berhmann, M. (under review). Identification of one-part and two-part volumetric objects: Selective deficits in coding spatial arrangement of part in visual object agnosia.
Tanaka, J. W., & Presnell, L. M. (1999). Color diagnosticity in object recognition. *Perception & Psychophysics, 61*, 1140–1153.
Tanaka, K. (1993). Neuronal mechanisms of object recognition. *Science, 262*, 685–688.
Tarr, M. J. (1995). Rotating objects to recognize them: A case study on the role of viewpoint dependency in the recognition of three-dimensional objects. *Psychonomic Bulletin & Review, 2*, 55–82.
Tarr, M. J., & Bülthoff, H. H. (1998). Image-based recognition in man, monkey, and machine. *Cognition, 67*, 1–20.
Tarr, M. J., & Bülthoff, H. H. (1995). Is human object recognition better described by geon structural descriptions or by multiple views? Comment on Biederman and Gerhardstein (1993). *Journal of Experimental Psychology: Human Perception & Performance, 21*, 1494–1505.
Tarr, M. J., & Pinker, S. (1989). Mental rotation and orientation-dependence in shape recognition. *Cognitive Psychology, 21*, 233–282.
Tipper, S. P., Brehaut, J., & Driver, J. (1990). Selection of moving and static objects for the control of spatially-directed attention. *Journal of Experimental Psychology: Human Perception & Performance, 16*, 492–504.
Tipper, S. P., Driver, J., & Weaver, B. (1991). Object-centered inhibition of return of visual atten-

tion. *Quarterly Journal of Experimental Psychology, 43A,* 289–298.

Tittle, J. S., Norman, J. F., Perotti, V. J., & Phillips, F. (1997). The perception of scale-dependent and scale-independent surface structure from binocular disparity, texture, and shading. *Perception, 26,* 147–166.

Tononi, G., Sporns, O., & Edelman, G. M. (1991). Modeling perceptual grouping and figure-ground segregation by means of active reentrant connections. *Proceedings of the National Academy of Sciences, 88,* 129–133.

Treisman, A., & Gelade, G. (1980). A feature-integration theory of attention. *Cognitive Psychology, 12,* 97–136.

Treisman, A. (1988). Features and objects: The fourteenth Bartlett memorial lecture. *Quarterly Journal of Experimental Psychology, 40A,* 201–237.

Treisman, A., Kahneman, D., & Burkell, J. (1983) Perceptual objects and the costs of filtering. *Perception & Psychophysics, 33,* 527–532.

Turnbull, O. H., & McCarthy, R. A. (1996). When is a view unusual? A single case study of orientation-dependent visual agnosia. *Brain Research Bulletin, 40,* 497–503.

Ullman, S. (1990). Three-dimensional object recognition. *Cold Spring Harbor Symposium on Quantitative Biology, 50,* 1243–1258.

Vecera, S. P., & O'Reilly, R. C. (1998). Figure-ground organization and object recognition processes: An interactive account. *Journal of Experimental Psychology: Human Perception & Performance, 24,* 441–462.

Vecera, S. P., & O'Reilly, R. C. (2000). A reply to Peterson. *Journal of Experimental Psychology: Human Perception & Performance.*

von der Heydt, R., & Peterhans, E. (1989). Mechanisms of contour perception in monkey visual cortex. I. Lines of pattern discontinuity. *Journal of Neuroscience, 9,* 1731–1748.

Wallach, H., & Slaughter, V. (1988). The role of memory in perceiving subjective contours. *Perception & Psychophysics, 43,* 101–106.

Warrington, E. K. (1982). Neuoropsychological studies of object recognition. *Philosophical Transactions of the Royal Society of London, B, 298,* 15–33.

Watson, S. E., & Kramer, A. F. (1999). Object-based visual selective attention and perceptual organization. *Perception & Psychophysics, 61,* 31–49.

Westheimer, G. (1999). Gestalt theory reconfigured: Max Wertheimer's anticipation of recent developments in visual neuroscience. *Perception, 18,* 5–15.

Wiggins, D. (1980). *Sameness and substance.* Oxford, UK: Basil Blackwell.

Witkin, A. P., & Tenenbaum, J. M. (1983). On the role of structure in vision. In J. Beck, B. Hope, & A. Rosenfeld (Eds.), *Human and machine vision.* NY: Academic Press.

Wojciulik, E., & Kanwisher, N. (1998). Implicit but not explicit feature binding in a Balint's patient. *Visual Cognition, 5,* 157–181.

Wolfe, J. M., & Bennett, S. C. (1997). Preattentive object files: Shapeless bundles of basic features. *Vision Research, 37,* 25–43.

Wong, E., & Weisstein, N. (1983). Sharp targets are detected better against a figure, and blurred targets are detected better against a background. *Journal of Experimental Psychology: Human Perception & Performance, 9,* 194–202.

Woodworth, E. G. (1938). *Experimental psychology.* New York: Henry Holt & Company.

Yantis, S. (1993). Stimulus-driven attentional capture. *Current Directions in Psychological Science, 2,* 156–171.

Yantis, S. (1996). Attentional capture in vision. In A. F. Kramer, M. G. H. Coles, & G.D. Logan (Eds.), *Converging operations in the study of visual selective attention* (pp. 45–76). Washington, DC: American Psychological Association.

Zeki, S. (1993). *A vision of the brain.* Oxford: Blackwell.

Zemel, R. S., Behrmann, M., Mozer, M. C., & Bavelier, D. (under review). Experience-dependent perceptual grouping and object-based attention.

Zipser, K., Lamme, V. A. F., & Schiller, P. H. (1996). Contextual modulation in primary visual cortex. *The Journal of Neuroscience, 16,* 7376–7389.

Chapter Seven

The Neuropsychology of Visual Object and Space Perception[1]

Glyn W. Humphreys and M. Jane Riddoch

Introduction

One of the difficulties in explaining vision to a member of the general public is that, normally, processes such as object and space perception operate with a kind of "seamless" efficiency. We are able to recognize objects and faces, read words, reach and avoid stimuli without paying undue care to each task. There hardly seems to be much that requires explanation. However, this efficiency of normal visual processing can break down following selective damage to the brain. People can fail to recognize objects and faces, even though they can remember what such things should look like and even though they can draw the stimuli placed in front of them. People can fail to react to or show appreciation of the whole of a stimulus, acting as if parts of the object or the world are missing. People can suddenly find that printed words no longer make sense to them. Neuropsychological disorders of object and space perception lead to problems in many of the everyday tasks that vision normally does so rapidly and with little apparent effort. The study of such disorders, then, can provide important insights into how the affected processes might operate. The disorders can tell us whether object and face recognition depend on the same or on distinctive processes, they address whether perceptual processing can be distinguished from perceptual memory, they can tell us something about the kinds of representation that mediate object and space perception. In this chapter we will review evidence on disorders of object and space perception, discussing the implications of the disorders for understanding how visual perception normally operates. Studies of patients with impaired visual processing tell us both about the functional nature of the normal perceptual system, and also about its anatomical underpinnings.

Visual Recognition

Visual Agnosias

Apperceptive and Associative Agnosia

The term visual agnosia was introduced to the literature by the German neurologist Lissauer in 1890. Lissauer used the term to describe patients with acquired deficits of visual object recognition which were not contingent on poor sensory processing. Agnosic patients can show good sensory processing of elementary image properties such as luminance and color, yet fail to make sense of their percepts. The term applies to patients with recognition and not just naming disorders, because such patients are typically unable to gesture how to use objects and they are unable to provide detailed semantic information about the objects they are confronted with (e.g., they cannot describe their use or where they might be found etc.). Lissauer made a major distinction between two general forms of agnosia, which continues to be influential to the present day. He separated "apperceptive agnosia" from "associative agnosia." By "apperceptive agnosia," he meant patients who seemed unable to achieve a stable visual perception of stimuli, despite intact sensation. By "associative agnosia," Lissauer meant patients who failed to recognize objects because their deficit was in associating their percepts to their stored knowledge. Clinically, the distinction has typically been made by asking patients to copy the objects they fail to recognize. On Lissauer's definition, associative but not apperceptive agnosics should be able to copy objects despite their recognition impairment.

Lissauer's work indicated that different forms of visual recognition deficit can be distinguished; however, the dichotomy between apperceptive and associative agnosia has proved to be too simple, and more recent accounts have indicated that a more subtle range of deficits can occur within what might broadly be termed the perceptual/apperceptive or memorial/associative agnosias. We will illustrate this in relation to a patient we have studied in detail, HJA (Riddoch & Humphreys, 1987a; Riddoch, Humphreys, Gannon, Blott, & Jones, 1999).

Distinguishing Different Perceptual Deficits

HJA was the European agent in charge of handling exports for a North American firm. However, aged 61 he suffered a stroke due to occlusion of the posterior cerebral artery, with the result that regions of inferior cortex transversing between the occipital and temporal lobes were damaged, on both sides of the brain. Coming to in a hospital ward, HJA found that he was no longer able to recognize many of the objects placed in front of him; he failed to recognize his own face in the mirror or even that of his wife when she visited him – though he could recognize her immediately from her voice. He also found it difficult to read words, particularly if they were presented in unfamiliar print or if they were handwritten. HJA's brain damage had in fact resulted in a number of neuropsychological problems – agnosia for objects, prosopagnosia (impaired face recognition) and alexia (impaired visual recognition of words) (Humphreys & Riddoch, 1987a). The world he faced after the stroke appeared strange, fragmented and incoherent. We asked: Do HJA's problems in object recognition conform to the apperceptive-associative agnosic distinction introduced by Lissauer, and what is the nature of the process that has been impaired by the stroke?

Deficits in Shape Coding

Let us begin by considering the problem of object recognition. There are numerous ways in which visual processing could be disturbed so as to impair object recognition. For example, there might be a deficit in the ability to encode some of the basic features of shapes, so that the shapes cannot be identified. Patients with deficits in shape coding have been described by Benson and Greenberg (1969; see also Efron, 1968), Campion and Latto (1985) and Milner and colleagues (Milner et al., 1991). In each of these cases the patient suffered carbon monoxide poisoning, which tends to produce multiple, small disseminated lesions in the cerebral cortex; these lesions may limit the linking together of activity in cells coding basic properties of shape, such as edge orientation and spatial frequency, preventing recognition from taking place. Such patients are not blind, because they can demonstrate light and also color perception, and indeed they may be able to act appropriately when reaching and grasping objects, a point we return to later (and see also Goodale & Humphrey, this volume). However, the patients are poor at drawing objects placed in front of them and they fail standard tests of shape perception such as the Efron shape discrimination task. This task requires a patient to discriminate squares from rectangles, matched for area and brightness, and is used as a clinical assessment of shape perception (see Figure 7.1a).

HJA, on the other hand, was able to produce generally accurate copies of objects, though this sometimes took him a long time (see Figure 7.1b for an example of HJA's copying) (Riddoch & Humphreys, 1987a). He was also able to perform the Efron shape discrimination task at a normal level (Humphreys, Riddoch, Quinlam, Donnelly, & Price, 1992). Thus he appeared to "see" objects, even though he failed to recognize them. He also succeeded at other tests that have been used to diagnose high-level problems in visual perception. Figure 7.1c shows two example shapes from a test of "unusual view" matching. In such a test, a patient may be given two drawings or photographs of a common object on each trial, with one depicting the object in a canonical viewing position while in the other the object is depicted at an unusual angle. The task does not require the object to be recognized, only a decision as to whether the same object is shown in the two views (see Warrington & James, 1986; Warrington & Taylor, 1973, 1978). This ability, to match objects across different views, can be selectively disturbed after damage to the right parietal lobe (Warrington & Taylor, 1978, 1973). HJA, on the other hand, could perform unusual view matches providing salient features of objects were available in each view (Humphreys & Riddoch, 1984). HJA was not only able to extract visual features to enable him to copy objects from a given viewpoint, he could also translate those features to enable him to judge how they would appear from a different viewing angle.

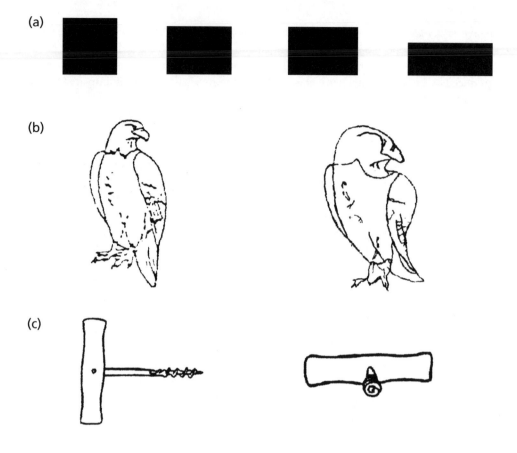

(a)

(b)

(c)

(d) Define a nail:

First this is a pin-shaped, sharp-pointed, thin cone of metal, with one end expanded and flattened to form a head-piece, to provide the striking point for a hammer to drive the nail into timber.

Second, nails are the hard, sharp-edged ends of human fingers and toes.

(e)

Figure 7.1. (a) Example stimuli from the Efron shape matching task. (b) Example of a copy of an eagle by the agnosic patient HJA; the copy is on the right. (c) Example of two stimuli that should be matched together in an unusual view matching task. (d) Example of a verbal definition of an object by HJA. (e) Example of a pair of overlapping figures.

Impaired Stored Knowledge?

Another reason why object recognition might break down is that the patient has lost stored knowledge about objects (see below for a fuller discussion of such problems). Without stored knowledge, recognition could not take place. However, our tests with HJA also went counter to this suggestion. HJA was able to give precise verbal definitions of objects when given their names, often providing details of the appearance of the stimuli (see Figure 7.1d). He could also draw objects from memory. These results suggest that HJA's visual memories were reasonably intact (Riddoch & Humphreys, 1987a). Why then was he unable to link the basic visual features he seemed to perceive to his stored memories, in order for recognition to occur?

Impairments In Integrating Shape Features

To understand HJA's problem, we need to realize that fragmentary visual features, taken in isolation, do not provide satisfactory input to recognition processes. Features need to be coded in relation to one another, and the features belonging to one object need to be segmented from those belonging to other objects, when several objects are present in a scene. Perception needs to be organized, as has been pointed out from the Gestalt psychologists onward. HJA was poor at perceptual organization. For example, his errors in naming revealed that he often segmented objects incorrectly into parts, as if the parts belonged to different objects (e.g., he described a paintbrush as two objects lying close to one another). This difficulty was most apparent when he was asked to name line drawings, where the internal details provide segmentation cues between the parts. HJA was particularly poor at naming line drawings, and he was even worse with line drawings than he was with silhouettes. In contrast, normal observers find line drawings easier to identify than silhouettes, presumably because they find the extra detail in line drawings useful (Riddoch & Humphreys, 1987a; Lawson & Humphreys, 1999). HJA was also impaired when given sets of overlapping line drawings to identify (see Figure 7.1e). With such overlapping figures, there needs to be appropriate grouping of features belonging to each object and segmentation of these features from the other objects present. These tests indicate a deficit in visual grouping and in segmenting objects in complex scenes.

A more precise analysis of the nature of this grouping deficit was revealed by HJA's performance on visual search tasks that depend on grouping between relatively complex image features. In such tasks, participants are asked to detect a target amongst varying numbers of distractor stimuli, and the efficiency of search is measured in terms of the effects of the number of distractors on performance. Efficient search can be conducted across all the distractors in parallel, so that they have little effect on search times or accuracy. Humphreys et al. (1992) used tasks in which complex feature targets (e.g., an inverted T) had to be detected amongst distractors containing the same features but in different arrangements (e.g., upright Ts). Such search tasks can be performed efficiently if the distractors are homogeneous and so can be segmented into a group separate from the target. When the distractors are heterogeneous (e.g., Ts at different angles), disrupting grouping, search is normally more difficult and affected by the number of distractors (see also Duncan & Humphreys, 1989; Humphreys, Quinlan & Riddoch, 1989). In the difficult search task, with heterogeneous distractors, HJA performed at the same level as normal observers. In this task normal observers seem to search serially, treating each cluster of features as a separate item. HJA was able to do this. However, relative to the controls, HJA was impaired with homogeneous distractors, and his error rate with such displays increased even when compared with the condition with heterogeneous distractors. This suggests that there was a specific problem in grouping the feature clusters in a spatially parallel manner. Interestingly it seemed that HJA's perceptual system continued to attempt to group the feature clusters, leading to more errors with homogeneous displays than with heterogeneous displays, when grouping was minimized.

The analysis of the deficit in HJA shows how the simple distinction between apperceptive and associative agnosia needs to be refined. Superficially HJA might be characterized as an associative agnosic, because he can copy objects and because he can perform some perceptual tests. More detailed testing, though, reveals subtle problems in perceptual organization. HJA is impaired at integrating the features of shapes, and at segmenting them apart from other shapes. This problem in feature integration occurs at a level above the encoding of basic shape features, which is reasonably intact. It is HJA's ability to code the basic features of shapes that allowed him to match simple shapes and even to copy more complex ones provided he treated each part of a display separately; however, it would be incorrect to assume from this that he could "see" normally. Instead the data indicate that his ability to code and interrelate parts broke down as the complexity of the displays increased and as a function of the number of segmentation cues present. This is a form of "intermediate" level deficit, separable from deficits in low-level feature coding and higher-level matching to memory (for recognition to occur).

Integrating Local and Global Forms

One other point to note concerning HJA is that his deficit in grouping visual features was dissociated from his ability to perceive the global shape of objects. We have already noted that he was better able to recognize silhouettes of objects than line drawings, though silhouettes only convey outline shape information (Riddoch & Humphreys, 1987a). Other tests required him to match fragmented line drawings of objects using either the overall global shape of the items or information gained from grouping the local line fragments (e.g., when the fragments were collinear; Boucart & Humphreys, 1992). HJA performed normally at global shape matching but he was unable to improve his performance when the local line segments could group; normal observers improve their performance when information for grouping is available.

HJA's coding and integration of local and global forms was examined in further detail using the Navon task (1977). Compound global letters were presented made up from small, local letters, and HJA was asked to identify either the global or the local forms (see Figure 7.2a). The letters at the local and global levels were either the same or they required opposite responses. Normal subjects show faster responses to global than to local letters, and the identity of the global letter interferes with responses to the local letter. HJA, like the controls, showed fast responses to "global" letters made out of local letters. However, in addition to this there were slow responses to local letters and there was no interference from global letters onto local letters when the stimuli had conflicting identities (Humphreys,

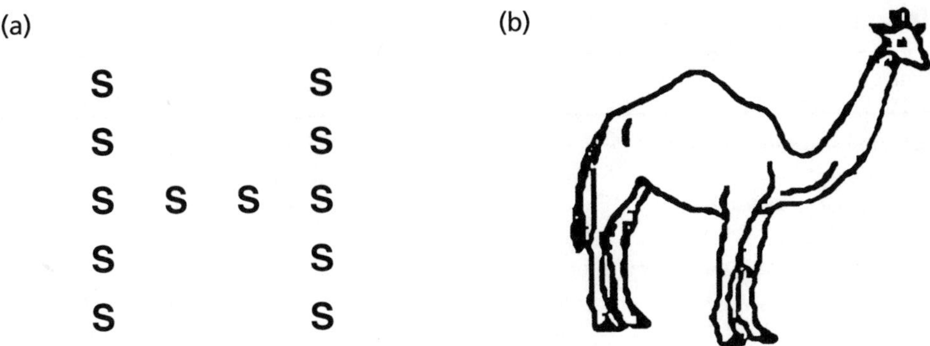

Figure 7.2. (a) Compound letters of the type introduced by Navon (1977). (b) Example nonobject from an object decision test (after Riddoch & Humphreys, 1987b).

Riddoch & Quinlan, 1985). Subsequently, Lamb, Robertson, and Knight (1990) have reported a similar pattern of results (with no interference from global onto local identities) in patients with damage to the superior temporal gyrus (at the top of the temporal lobe). Lamb et al. proposed that this brain area was concerned with integrating information derived in parallel from local and more global representations of shape, and this process may itself be influenced by perceptual integration in which local properties of stimuli are linked together. It is this last process that seems to be disrupted in HJA. The superior temporal gyrus connects with the inferior occipito-temporal region damaged in HJA via area MT (Kaas, 1989), and so lesions to the superior temporal gyrus (to link local and global representations) may disconnect this region from more inferior cortical regions concerned with local perceptual integration (which are damaged bilaterally in HJA's case).

Other Cases of Impaired Perceptual Grouping

A summary of the main results with HJA are given in Table 7.1. We must ask, how typical is HJA's case relative to other patients with perceptual forms of agnosia? Similar deficits have now been documented in several cases (e.g., Butter & Trobe, 1994), and aspects of HJA's piecemeal attempts to identify objects serially from their parts is a characteristic of patients of this type (Behrmann, Moscovitch, & Winocur, 1994; Goldstein & Gelb, 1918; Grossman, Galetta, & d'Esposito, 1997; Sirigu, Duhamel, & Poncet, 1991; Wapner, Judd, & Gardner, 1978). However, in other patients the problems in perception can be coupled with deficits in long-term knowledge about objects (DeRenzi & Lucchelli, 1993; Grailet, Seron, Bruyer, Coyette, & Frederix, 1990). HJA presents us with a clearer case in which the damage to perceptual processing nevertheless left stored memories for objects intact. The distinction between impaired perception and relatively intact stored knowledge is important, because it indicates that perceptual processes can be encapsulated from memorial processes to at least some degree (see Pylyshyn, 1999).

Table 7.1 Summary of the perceptual tests performed by the agnosic patient HJA

Test	*Performance*	*Reference*
(a) Efron shape discrimination	Good	Humphreys et al. (1992)
(b) Copying	Good	Riddoch & Humphreys (1987a)
(c) Unusual view matching	Good when distinctive features are available	Humphreys & Riddoch (1984)
(d)Identifying overlapping forms	Impaired	Riddoch & Humphreys (1987a)
(e) Identifying fragmented forms	Impaired	Boucart & Humphreys (1992)
(f) Identifying silhouettes	Relatively good	Riddoch & Humphreys (1987a); Lawson & Humphreys (1999)
(g) Search for form conjunctions	Impaired with homogeneous displays	Humphreys et al. (1992)
(h) Identifying compound letters	Global advantage but no global interference	Humphreys et al. (1985)

Coding Feature Conjunctions

A somewhat different approach to the argument that agnosia can reflect a high-level perceptual impairment comes from the work of Arguin, Bub and Dudek (1996; see also Dixon, Bub, & Arguin, 1997). They used computer generated shapes based on differences in elongation, tapering and bending along their main axes (e.g., a banana can be described as having positive values on the elongation and bending dimensions, but a zero value on tapering). In one task four shapes were presented simultaneously, one in each quadrant of the screen, and these were followed by a target. The task was to point to the location where the target had appeared. They tested a patient with impaired recognition following infection by herpes simplex encephalitis. When the items presented were different along a single dimension (e.g., elongation), performance was reasonably good; in contrast, the patient's performance was impaired when items varied along two dimensions simultaneously (e.g., tapering as well as elongation). Arguin et al. propose that patients may fail to represent more than one visual dimension at a time, and this reduces their sensitivity to features that co-vary across dimensions. Interestingly this problem was exacerbated when the patient had to learn to label the shapes using the names of semantically close items (e.g., fruits). A failure to represent the visual dimensions of objects appropriately may lead to particular difficulties in discriminating within sets of objects that are also semantically close as well as perceptually close (see Forde & Humphreys, 1999, for a review of recognition deficits affecting selective categories of object).

Distinguishing Different Memorial Deficits

Patients such as HJA show that the syndrome of apperceptive agnosia can be fractionated, so that different forms of perceptual deficit can be distinguished (e.g., coding basic attributes of shape, grouping local shape attributes, integrating local and global properties of objects, etc.). We can similarly distinguish between different forms of memorial deficit in associative agnosia. In all of the following patients, tests of perceptual processing were relatively intact, nevertheless object recognition remained impaired. In some cases, poor recognition seems to be related to a loss of stored knowledge about the visual properties of objects. For example, when shown drawings of real objects and nonobjects constructed from the parts of real objects, some patients are deficient in distinguishing which are real and which constructed (in so-called "object decision tests"; see DeRenzi & Lucchelli, 1993; Riddoch & Humphreys, 1987b; see Figure 7.2b for an example nonobject). Note that this task requires only that objects be registered as familiar; patients do not need to name the stimuli or even to be able to retrieve functional or contextual knowledge about how to use the object or where it may be found. A deficit on this task, when coupled with good performance on tests of visual perception (see above), may be taken to reflect impaired visual knowledge.

Some patients, however, may perform even difficult object decision tasks at normal levels while concurrently showing impaired access to functional and contextual information about objects (see Hillis & Caramazza, 1995; Riddoch & Humphreys, 1987b; Sheridan & Humphreys, 1993; Stewart, Parkin & Hunkin, 1992). JB, the patient studied by Riddoch and Humphreys (1987b), performed at a control level on object decision tasks, often remarking the objects looked familiar to him. On the other hand, when given three objects visually and asked to choose which two were related and would be used together (e.g., hammer, nail, screw), JB was impaired. This was not due to his having poor semantic knowledge per se: When given the names of the objects and asked to choose which two were related, he unerringly chose the more related stimuli. JB was also poor at naming visually presented objects but could nevertheless give names to verbal definitions. Thus in this case semantic knowledge was relatively intact when accessed verbally, but there was an impairment in accessing that knowledge from vision. The problem in visual recognition occurred after access to knowledge about the familiar form of the objects had been achieved (measured by means of the object decision task). This indicates that we can distinguish between different forms of stored knowledge about objects: Stored perceptual knowledge is dissociable from functional and contextual knowledge (see also Cooper, Schacter, Ballesteros, & Moore, 1992; Schacter & Cooper, 1993; Schacter, Cooper, & Delaney, 1990, for converging evidence from studies of priming with normal observers). The data also indicate that contrasting forms of memorial deficit exist. In some patients there is loss of stored perceptual knowledge; in other patients this knowledge is intact but they cannot access further forms of knowledge to enable full recognition to take place.

Prosopagnosia

HJA had problems not only with objects but also with faces. He had the clinical symptoms of prosopagnosia, failing to recognize any faces, no matter how familiar (including those of his wife or close family). Such disorders of face recognition have long been associated with object agnosia and may simply reflect the fact that faces as a class are perceptually highly similar – so a disorder in visual coding or in perceptual organization that is sufficient to disrupt object recognition should also affect face recognition (see Damasio, Damasio, & Van Hoesen, 1982). On the other hand, it may be that there are particular procedures specialized respectively for the processing of faces and objects, each of which can be affected selectively by neural damage. In the latter case, patients who lose just the procedures specialized for faces will be prosopagnosic but not agnosic. The converse is that patients who lose procedures used in object but not face recognition will be agnosic but not prosopagnosic. In other cases, though (HJA being one), either both procedures are affected or the damage influences some earlier stage of processing prior to specialization.

Evidence for specialized face processing procedures can be drawn from the normal literature. For example, studies with normal observers show that face recognition is highly sensitive to (a) parts being presented within the configuration of the face (parts are easier to link to an individual if shown within a face than if shown in isolation, Tanaka & Farah, 1993; parts are also difficult to extract from the context of a face when parts of different faces are intermixed; Young, Hellawell, & Hay, 1987); (b) inversion (Farah, Wilson, Drain, & Tanaka, 1998; Yin, 1969); (c) masking by whole as opposed to part stimuli (Farah et al., 1998); (d) metric variation in the parts; (e) changes in contrast polarity and luminance direction; and (f) rotation in depth (see Biederman & Kalocsai, 1997, for a review of the last results). Though effects of these variables can be found on object recognition, they are very often not of the same order of magnitude (though see Diamond & Carey, 1986; Gauthier & Tarr, 1997; Gauthier, Williams, Tarr, & Tanaka, 1998, for counter-examples). This has led authors to argue that the processes specialized for face recognition involve coding wholistic, non-decomposed visual representations, different from the kinds of parts-based representations used for object recognition (see Biederman & Kalocsai, 1997; Farah, 1990). Such wholistic representations may be particularly vulnerable to changes in the configural context, to inversion, metric variations, and so forth. Does the neuropsychological evidence fit with this argument for specialist face processing?

Prosopagnosia Without Agnosia

Most patients in the literature, like HJA, have a deficit that affects objects as well as faces. Some exceptions have been reported, however. For example, DeRenzi (1986) documented a prosopagnosic patient who could identify individual exemplars of common objects. This finding is important because it suggests that the problem in face recognition was not simply because faces, relative to objects, require the identification of specific exemplars within their class (who it is, rather than it simply being a person). However, because the tests required discrimination between the patient's own and other objects of the same type, it is possible that performance was relatively good because the stimuli were highly familiar and examined under forced-choice conditions. Sergent and Signoret (1992) found a similar improvement in performance when prosopagnosics had to make forced-choice discriminations between highly familiar faces. Nevertheless, one of their prosopagnosic patients remained very good at discriminating between makes and even years of cars, demonstrating a retained ability to differentiate items in a fixed, visually similar set.

Recognition of Nonhuman Faces

Other investigators have noted that prosopagnosic patients can maintain an ability to discriminate between the faces of animals other than humans. Bruyer et al. (1983) discussed a prosopagnosic farmer who was able to tell individual cows apart but not members of his family. A similar pattern of deficit, but this time showing retained recognition of individual sheep, was examined formally by McNeil and Warrington (1993). Their patient, a hill farmer, was better than many controls at discriminating between individual sheep but was profoundly impaired with faces. Assal, Favre, and Anderes (1984) discussed an opposite impairment, of a prosopagnosic patient whose problem with faces recovered to some degree but who reported that he was still unable to identify his individual cows.

These contrasting deficits are consistent with face and object recognition being dependent to some degree on different processes, which can be selectively impaired or spared in patients, but the studies do not pin-point the precise impairments involved. To do this, experiments are needed to assess which processes, specific to words or to faces, are vulnerable to neuronal damage. One study along these lines was reported by Perrett et al. (1988), who used a task in which a patient was required to state whether a stimulus was a face or not (the non-faces being created by scrambling the parts of the faces, but keeping the stimuli symmetrical). Normal observers were faster with faces than with non-faces, presumably because decisions to faces can be based on wholistic visual information. In contrast the prosopagnosic was faster with non-faces. Faster decisions to faces suggest that the task was performed by checking individual features; faces would then be slow because all of their features must be checked before a response can be made. The result fits with the proposal that prosopagnosic patients are deficient in responding to wholistic visual information, though it is also true that the same pattern would occur if the patient was unable to code and group the features of faces in a spatially parallel fashion – a process that subserves object recognition (see the discussion of patient HJA above).

Agnosia Without Prosopagnosia

There are also some patients who, despite being severely agnosic, do not suffer even a transitory problem with faces. The patient documented by Moscovitch, Winocur, and Behrmann (1997; see also Behrmann et al., 1994), for example, showed relatively good face recognition while being very poor at recognizing both objects and words. Face recognition was affected, however, when the face was cut into separate portions. This suggests that face recognition was highly dependent on the whole configuration being present, and that recognition via separate regions of faces was not possible. This patient's object recognition was also sensitive to visual manipulations (e.g., using overlapping figures), consistent with there being an underlying perceptual deficit. The authors argued that the deficit involved coding objects with multiple parts, while wholistic representations could still be derived. Other cases of agnosia for objects without prosopagnosia have been reported by Humphreys and Rumiati (1998) and by Rumiati, Humphreys, Riddoch, and Bateman (1994), though in these cases a memorial deficit for objects might be suspected. Both patients performed well at perceptual matching tasks but were impaired at tasks such as object decision, in which objects had to be compared to memory.

Memorial Deficits for Faces

Like disorders of object recognition, impairments of face recognition are not necessarily due to a perceptual deficit; some seem to reflect problems in accessing stored memories for faces. McNeil and Warrington (1991) contrasted three patients on a range of tests assessing both perceptual processing of faces and a test of face-name learning. The patient with the worst performance on the perceptual tests showed some evidence of accessing stored face memories, since he showed better learning of correct than incorrect pairings between faces and names (see below for further discussion of similar results suggesting "covert" recognition of stimuli, in some patients). In contrast the patient with the best performance on the perceptual tests did not demonstrate improved learning of correct compared with incorrect pairings. McNeil and Warrington proposed that, in the last case, there was impaired access to stored face memories. Interestingly, poor access to stored memory could not be attributed to a perceptual deficit, because patients with worse perceptual problems still seemed able to access stored memories. McNeil and Warrington argued instead that there was damage to the face memories themselves.

Functional Brain Imaging of Object and Face Processing

Other evidence that faces and objects depend on functionally separate processes comes from study of the lesion sites affected in different patients. Though both agnosia and prosopagnosia are found after lesions to ventral parts of the visual system, leading from the occipital to the temporal cortex, the precise localization differs. Prosopagnosia may be found after unilateral right hemisphere damage (DeRenzi, 1986). Perceptual forms of agnosia may require bilateral damage (Humphreys & Riddoch, 1987b), and memorial forms can be found after unilateral left hemisphere damage (e.g., Riddoch & Humphreys, 1987b).

The argument for anatomical localization is supported also by data on functional brain imaging in normal observers. In an early PET study, Sergent, Ohta, and MacDonald (1992) directly contrasted face and object classification tasks. In one task they had to judge whether faces were of politicians or actors; in the other they judged whether objects were living or non-living. Sergent and Signoret (1992) found more selective left hemisphere activation for objects relative to faces, and more selective right hemisphere activation for faces relative to objects, when they subtracted activity in each task from the other. Object classification was associated with enhanced activity in the lateral tempero-occipital region and the middle temporal gyrus of the left hemisphere; face classification was associated with enhanced activation of the right fusiform gyrus, the right hippocampal gyrus and the anterior temporal lobes bilaterally. The involvement of the right fusiform gyrus has been confirmed in other studies of face processing using PET (Haxby et al., 1993), fMRI (Puce, Allison, Asgari, Gore, & McCarthy, 1995), and visual evoked responses (Allison, McCarthy, Nobre, Puce, & Belger, 1994).

Studies of object processing, in contrast, reveal bilateral activity in the middle occipital gyrus and the inferior temporal sulcus when subjects view objects or structurally plausible non-objects compared with noise or meaningless shape baselines (Kanwisher, Woods, Iacoboni, & Mazziotta, 1997; Martin, Wiggs, Ungerleider, & Haxby, 1996; Price, Moore, Humphreys, Frackowiak, & Friston, 1996a; Schacter et al.,1995). Early object processing,

Table 7.2 Summary of findings of example functional brain imaging of faces, words and objects

Stimulus	*Region activated relative to baseline*	*Reference*
Objects		
Living things	bilateral inferior occipito-temporal	Damasio et al. (1996); Martin et al. (1997); Moore & Price (1999); Perani et al. (1995)
Non-living things	middle temporal & inferior frontal(left)	Damasio et al. (1996); Martin et al. (1996); Moore & Price (1999); Perani et al. (1995)
Faces		
	fusiform gyrus & anterior temporal lobe (right)	Damasio et al. (1996); Haxby et al. (1993); Puce et al. (1994); Sergent et al. (1992)
Words		
	medial extra-striate & inferior occipito-temporal (left)	Howard et al. (1992); Petersen et al. (1990); Price et al. (1996); Puce et al. (1995)

sensitive to structural properties of objects, appears to be bilaterally represented. In identification tasks, though, there is differentiation between the neural areas selectively activated by different objects: enhanced medial extra-striate and inferior temporal activation for the identification of living things but enhanced activation of the medial temporal and the lateral inferior frontal cortex for the identification of non-living things, especially in the left hemisphere (with the precise areas involved depending on the details of the particular study; Damasio, Grabowski, Tranel, Hichwa, & Damasio, 1996; Martin et al., 1996; Moore & Price, 1999; Perani et al., 1995). These results are summarized in Table 7.2.

From these studies we may conclude that there is some degree of specialization within the neural networks subserving object and face processing, though the evidence as yet does not specify which processes are neurally distinct, for which stimuli (e.g., whether differences reflect contrasts in access to stored perceptual or semantic memories)(though see Vandenberghe, Price, Wise, Josephs, and Frackowiak (1996) for some evidence distinguishing structural from semantic properties of objects). Behavioral evidence, from normal and neuropsychological observers, indicates that at least some differences arise in perceptual processing, and concern the dependence on wholistic, configural processes.

Alexia

The third class of visual stimulus that HJA found difficult to recognize was words, particularly when the words appeared in an unusual format or when they were handwritten. His reading in fact depended on the serial identification of letters in words, so that the time to name individual words increased monotonically as a function of the number of letters present (Humphreys, 1998). This pattern of performance, with there being abnormally strong effects of word length on reading time, is the hallmark of alexia or letter-by-letter reading (see Howard, 1991; Patterson & Kay, 1982; Warrington & Shallice, 1980).

Several accounts of alexia have been offered, including a deficit in visually encoding the letters in words simultaneously (Farah & Wallace, 1991), a deficit in accessing abstract information about letter identities (Arguin & Bub, 1993; Kay & Hanley, 1991), a deficit in stored word representations (Warrington & Shallice, 1980), and an impairment to a left hemisphere visual recognition system along with slowed transmission of information across the corpus callosum (e.g., Coslett & Saffran, 1993). Certainly there are some grounds for arguing that the deficits can differ across different patients. For example, some patients show a retained ability to read some words rapidly or under short exposure conditions, whereas others do not (see Howard, 1991; Price & Humphreys, 1992). In these last patients, there are grounds for arguing for some form of perceptual deficit. Also some patients can be abnormally affected by degrading the visual information present in words (Farah & Wallace, 1991), suggesting a visual locus for their deficit. Some patients show qualitatively similar patterns of performance with pictures as well as words (Friedman & Alexander, 1984), as would be expected if these stimuli depend to some degree on common visual descriptions which were jointly affected by the damage. On the other hand, there are alexic patients who remain able to identify single letters across briefly presented letter strings, showing few signs of a visual processing limitation (Arguin & Bub, 1994; Warrington & Shallice, 1980). For the latter patients the deficit may be better explained in terms of a loss of stored memories for words, or to impoverished activation of these memories based on letter identity codes.

Parallel Processing in Skilled Word Recognition

Studies of word recognition in normal, skilled readers suggest that it can operate by means of parallel activation of the letter identities present. For example, recognition is little affected by the number of letters present (at least for words containing up to six letters; see Frederiksen & Kroll, 1976). Also effects of altering the familiarity of the whole shape, by CaSe MiXiNg, are no greater on words than on pronounceable nonwords (Adams, 1979; McClelland, 1976), though it should be noted that both are affected. If words are recognized wholistically, we might expect effects of CaSe MiXiNg to be larger on words than on pronounceable nonwords. On the other hand, this may not be the only means by which words are recognized. If letter identities alone are important it is difficult to understand why spacing the letters in MiXeD CaSe words (M i X e D C a S e) improves their reading, an effect reported by Mayall, Humphreys, and Olson (1997); after all, the same letter identities are present in both spaced and unspaced formats. The improvement with spacing also does not seem due to reductions in lateral masking between the letters, which could generate better letter coding. A beneficial effect of spacing would arise, however, if letters were grouped and these supra-letter groups used in recognition alongside individual letter identities. Normally this is useful for reading. However, with CaSe MiXiNg incorrect letter groups can be formed between letters having the same case (MXN, for example, in the word MiXiNg), and this disrupts recognition. The grouping process is weakened by spacing and so the detrimental effects of CaSe MiXiNg are then reduced. Supra-letter groups may be extracted from words and pronounceable nonwords alike, leading to both being affected to an equal degree by CaSe MiXiNg (Adams, 1979; McClelland, 1976).

Neuropsychological Evidence on Supra-Letter Reading: Attentional Dyslexia

This view, that supra-letter information as well as individual letter identities are used in word recognition, is useful for explaining other patterns of neuropsychological data. The term attentional dyslexia is used to describe patients whose ability to read single words is relatively good but who are impaired at identifying the individual letters present, even when asked to identify them serially (Shallice & Warrington, 1977). Such patients can also show very marked effects of CaSe MiXiNg, showing abnormal sensitivity to changes in the familiar form of words. They may also retain an ability to identify abbreviations (BBC, IBM), but only if the letters are shown in their familiar case; the same items are not identified when the opposite case is used (bbc, ibm), though letter identities are then the same (Hall, Humphreys, & Cooper, in press; see also Howard, 1987). Such patients seem to rely on visually familiar letter groups and have poor access to individual letter identities. Unlike alexic patients who read letter-by-letter, the reading of such patients cannot even be supported by serial coding of letters, because this process also seems impaired.

Functional Imaging of Word Recognition

Functional imaging studies of reading implicate areas in the posterior left hemisphere in visual word recognition. Petersen, Fox, Snyder, and Raichle (1990), for example, reported that, relative to a baseline involving fixation only, there was enhanced activity in the medial extrastriate cortex of the left hemisphere when people viewed words but not when they viewed meaningless symbols. They suggested that this area was linked to the perceptual memory system for written words. Other PET studies have found increased activation in the left lateral, posterior temporal lobe for words compared with meaningless symbol patterns (Howard et al., 1992; Price, Wise, & Frackowiak, 1996b), though an fMRI study by Puce et al. (1995) found more posterior activation, in the left occipitotemporal and the left inferior occipital sulcus, for letter strings when compared to faces and random textures. Evoked potential studies, using epileptic patients with implanted electrodes, have also linked to letter strings a specific component of the visual evoked response (the N200) originating from the medial extrastriate cortex (Allison et al., 1994; Nobre, Allison, & McCarthy, 1994). Though the precise anatomical locus has varied across the studies, the research does suggest lateralization of visual processes specialized for letter strings and words (see Table 7.2). Interestingly, the electrodes that record an N200 response to letter strings do not do so to faces, and vice versa, supporting the argument for some degree of functional separation between the processing of words and faces (Allison et al., 1994). Whether the differences lie in localization of the memory stores for words and faces, or in the forms of visual information that are important, remains to be assessed.

Faces, Objects and Words

The data indicate that the recognition of faces, objects, and words differs in terms of the kinds of visual information processing involved. Face recognition in particular is sensitive to wholistic visual codes, word recognition to parallel coding of letter identities (though with some support from supra-letter groups) and object recognition dependent on grouping of parts. These different forms of information are either processed, or access memory systems, in specialized areas of cortex and are vulnerable to different brain lesions.

Farah (1990) argued further that there were particular relations between agnosia, prosopagnosia, and alexia that are informative about the nature of the visual information used to recognize the different classes of stimulus. In a review of historical cases, she noted that there were cases of "pure" alexia and "pure" prosopagnosia (i.e., without concomitant deficits with other classes of stimulus), and cases of mixed deficits where patients had agnosia and alexia, agnosia and prosopagnosia, and also all three deficits (as in patient HJA, with whom we began; Humphreys & Riddoch, 1987a). However, there were no convincing cases with "pure" agnosia (i.e., without problems in reading or face recognition) and no cases with a "mixed" impairment including alexia and prosopagnosia without agnosia. From this she concluded that there were two underlying visual processes that could be affected and lead to recognition deficits in patients: one concerned with processing wholistic visual representations (needed for face recognition), and one concerned with processing multiple parts in parallel (e.g., the letters in words). These two processes would each contribute to object recognition, to different degrees, depending on the properties of the object. Lesions to the process dealing with wholistic representations would disrupt face recognition and possibly also object recognition (if the lesions are more severe). Lesions to processes dealing with multiple parts would disrupt word recognition and again object recognition to some degree (for those objects dependent on these processes, with joint impairments found with more severe damage). However it should not be possible to generate a "pure" agnosia, because there is not a unique process used for object recognition. Similarly it should not be possible to damage both face and word recognition without there also being some disruption to object recognition, which will depend on the same processes.

Farah's proposal presents a useful way to summarize the deficit across many of the patients in the literature; however, it may not provide a complete account of recognition deficits. We have already noted cases of "pure" agnosia, affecting objects but not words. Some of these patients remain good at word as well as face recognition, contrary to Farah's account. Rumiati, Humphreys, and colleagues (Humphreys & Rumiati, 1998; Rumiati et al., 1994) reported patients who seemed to have good face and word recognition (reading words at a normal rate), but impaired object recognition. Both patients suffered degenerative impairments and had some problems in retrieving semantic information about objects even from words, but the problems were more serious with visually presented objects. Both were impaired at object decision tasks and one primarily made visual errors when naming objects. This pattern of impairment is consistent with the patients having damage to stored visual memories for objects, and both performed well on a range of perceptual tests (including unusual view matching).

A second pattern of deficit that goes against a simple two-process account has also been documented recently by Buxbaum, Glosser, and Coslett (1999) and by DeRenzi and Di Pellegrino (1998). These investigators have reported patients with alexia and prosopagnosia (impaired reading and face recognition) but without agnosia (having relatively preserved object recognition). The data suggest that memory representations for faces, objects, and words can differ, so that there can be selective degeneration of visual memories for objects rather than for words or faces (and perhaps also vice versa). The results also emphasize that not all recognition deficits are perceptual in nature, and that some reflect memorial rather than perceptual impairments – as we have pointed out when reviewing each syndrome. It may be the case that the dichotomy between wholistic and parts-based descriptions accounts for many of the perceptual differences between face, object, and word recognition, but memorial differences also need to be taken into account. In addition, the dichotomy in its simplest terms makes no distinction between parts-based descriptions that are coded independently for individual parts (e.g., the letters in words) and those that are grouped to form a larger perceptual unit (e.g., supra-letter codes in words). We suggest that a full account of face, object, and word processing will need to accommodate effects of grouped features in recognition.

Space Perception

So far we have considered how neuropsychological deficits of visual recognition affect different classes of stimulus. Brain lesions can also affect the ability of patients to make perceptual judgements to the spatial properties of objects. Perhaps the clearest example of this is in the syndrome of unilateral neglect, where patients may fail to respond to stimuli presented on the side of space contralateral to their lesion (e.g., to stimuli on the left side following a right hemisphere lesion). However, other disorders of space perception can also arise; for example, in the syndrome of simultanagnosia patients seem to be very poor at having sense of the spatial layout of their visual environment, and may only report on the presence of a single object at a time. We now consider what these disorders tell us about the nature of spatial perception. The uses of spatial information for action are taken up in Chapter 10 of this volume.

Unilateral Neglect

A patient with unilateral neglect may fail to eat the food on one side of their plate, they may fail to read words on one side of the page, or the letters on one side of a word. This disorder is classically associated with damage to the right parietal lobe (particularly the tempero-parietal region), though it can also be found after damage to several other sites, including the right frontal lobe (Husain & Kennard, 1996). It is as if the patient is unaware of a stimulus presented to the affected side. However, it is not the case that neglect results simply from a visual field deficit; patients with a field deficit do not necessarily show neglect (such patients can scan to the affected side and show awareness of stimuli presented there), and patients with neglect do not necessarily have a field cut (Halligan, Marshall, & Wade, 1990). Also neglect can be demonstrated on tests using imagery in which no visual stimulus is presented to the patient (Bisiach & Luzzatti, 1978).

Most clinical tests of neglect require both that a stimulus be perceived and that an action be directed towards it (e.g., line cancellation and line bisection being two examples). On such tests it is difficult to distinguish effects on space perception from those affecting action to a particular part of space (or an action to an object in that part of space). Nevertheless deficits even on purely perceptual tests can be established. Patients can judge that bisections to the unaffected side are at the true centre of a line (Harvey, Milner, & Roberts, 1995), they can judge that objects on the affected side are smaller (Milner & Harvey, 1995), they can fail to detect targets in search (Humphreys & Heinke, 1998; Riddoch & Humphreys, 1987c), they can fail to identify objects whose critical features fall on the affected side (Seron, Coyette, & Bruyer, 1989), they fail to perceive half of a chimeric face on the affected side (Walker, Findlay, Young, & Lincoln, 1996), they fail to identify letters at the affected ends of words (Ellis, Flude, & Young, 1987), and so forth. Such results indicate that, in addition to any problem in action, there is also a deficit in perceiving the spatial properties of objects.

Neglect Within and Between Objects

One way to fractionate the deficits within the neglect syndrome is to define the nature of the spatial information that seems to be affected. Of particular relevance to accounts of how the spatial properties of objects are coded for object recognition are cases where visual elements are neglected according to their position within an object. There are now several examples of this. For instance, in reading, right hemisphere lesioned patients can fail to report the left letters in words even when the words are briefly presented in their right visual field (Young, Newcombe, & Ellis, 1991), suggesting that the positions of the letters in a word can be more important than their position on the retina. Whether patients neglect a gap in an equilateral triangle is influenced by how the triangle aligns with other contextual shapes, with the shapes affecting which axis is taken as the main axis in the triangle (Driver, Baylis, Goodrich, & Rafal, 1994; see Figure 7.3a). Patients can show neglect of the left parts of objects even when the objects are rotated in the plane so that these parts now fall in the right field (but still fall to the left of the main axis of the shapes; Driver & Halligan, 1991).

Interestingly, these effects seem closely linked to stimuli being represented as parts within objects. Young, Hellawell, and Welch (1992), for instance, studied a patient with neglect of the left half of chimeric faces. Neglect of this left half-face was reduced if the right half-face was shifted slightly more to the right, so that the two halves did not cohere into a single object but appeared instead as separate objects. The same point is apparent in our own case study of a patient, JR, with bilateral brain lesions who demonstrated neglect on either the left or the right of space depending on how stimuli were represented for the task

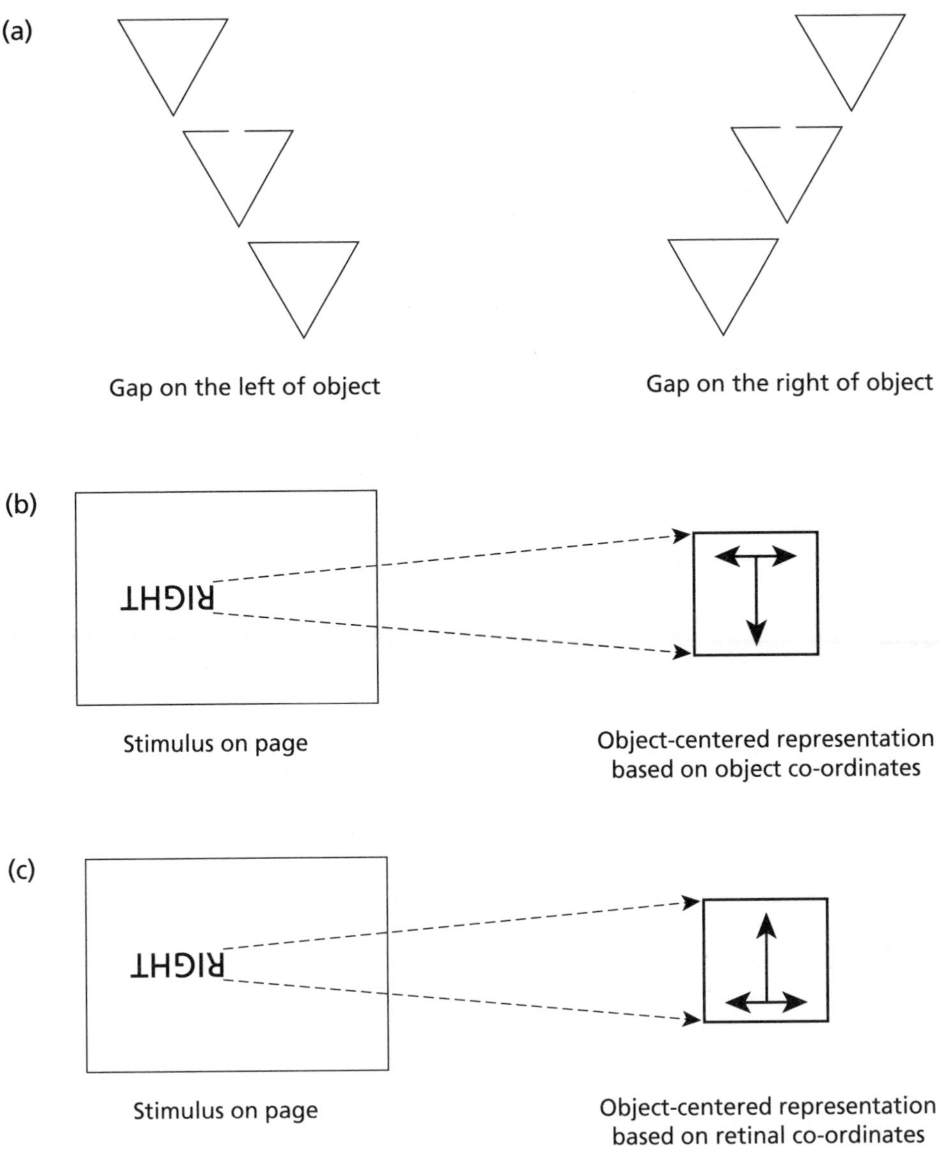

Figure 7.3. (a) Stimuli of the type used by Driver et al. (1994). The task was to detect a gap in the central equilateral triangle. This gap is in the same retinal position in the configuration on the left and the one on the right. However, relative to the contextual shapes present, the gap falls on the left of the axis in the central shape in the left-side configuration. Relative to the contextual shapes the gap falls on the right of the axis in the right-side configuration. Neglect is more pronounced in the left-side configuration. (b) Example of a "true" object-centered representation. Irrespective of the position of the object on the page, a representation is generated with its origin at the center of the word and with the co-ordinate system oriented according to the features that normally fall at the top of the word. (c) Example of a representation centered on the word but with its co-ordinate system retaining top, left, and right positions determined by retinal locations.

(Humphreys & Riddoch, 1994a, 1995). Most dramatically, when asked to read aloud letter strings and words JR neglected the left-side letters (e.g., reading "ditch" as "bitch"). However, when asked to treat each letter as a separate object, reading each aloud in sequence, he made right-side errors; he now reported the left-side letters he had formerly neglected and neglected the right-side letters he had formerly reported ("ditch" → "d, i, t, c")! The two forms of neglect manifested by JR likely reflect his bilateral lesions, which may affect two different forms of spatial representation: a representation in which elements are coded with respect to the object they are part of (a "within-object" representation), and a representation in which stimuli are coded as independent objects (a "between-object" representation). Neglect may occur following spatially selective damage to either form of representation.

Co-ordinate Systems in Neglect

The nature of these different forms of representation, for instance the kinds of co-ordinate system they are coded within, remains to be specified. For example, some patients show strong effects of the position of stimuli with regards to the body midline (Karnath, Schenkel, & Fischler, 1991; Riddoch & Humphreys, 1983), and it is possible that between-object codes represent the positions of stimuli with respect to the body. There may also be some further differentiation between representations for objects close to the body (in "peri-personal space") and those for objects far from the body (in "extra-personal space")(see Halligan & Marshall, 1991; Cowey, Small, & Ellis, 1994; for evidence with human patients; Rizzolatti, Gentilucci, & Matelli, 1985, for data from the monkey).

Concerning neglect of the parts within-objects, it is not clear whether the form of representation affected is truly "object-centered" or whether it is a more a hybrid representation in which "left" and "right" features are assigned with respect to their positions on the retina (or in head or even body-space) relative to the main axis of an object (Figures 7.3b and 7.3c; see Heinke & Humphreys, 1998, for one example). A test of this is to invert the object. In a true object-centered representation, features would still be coded as being on the left side of the inverted objects even when they fall on the right of the retina. In the example given in Figure 7.3b, the letter "R" remains on the left of the inverted word. However, if the left and right positions of features are coded in terms of their positions on the retina relative to the main axis, then the original left features would fall on the right side of this representation when the object is inverted (Figure 7.3c). In at least some instances, patients showing within-object neglect remain unable to recover features on the affected side with respect to the retina, even when objects are inverted (e.g., Young et al., 1992). On the other hand, cases have also been reported in which the side neglected changes with respect to the retina; a patient who shows neglect of the features on the left of the retina when a stimulus is first presented may show neglect of those same features even when they fall on the right (and now reports the features on the right of the object but the left of the retina). One example is a patient reported by Caramazza and Hillis (1990) who showed this behavior in reading tasks (always neglecting the endings of words, even when the stimuli were mirror reversed so the ends fell on the left rather than the right of the retina). Behrmann and Tipper (1994, 1999; Tipper & Behrmann, 1996) used a rather different procedure but to a quite similar effect. Patients with right hemisphere lesions and left neglect had to detect a target presented on the left or right side of an object which rotated slowly through 180 degrees. The usual slowed detection of left-side targets shifted to slowed detection of right-side targets as the object rotated so that the original left-part appeared on the right side. This reversal only occurred when a bar connected the two parts, so that the parts grouped to form a single object. In this case, neglect seemed tied to the original coding of the part within a frame of reference based on the object, which is maintained as the object is rotated in the field. Other workers, though, have suggested that patients who show such shifts in neglect do so because they mentally rotate a stimulus back to its standard or starting position, where the parts maintain their positions with respect to the observer (Buxbaum, Coslett, Montgomery, & Farah, 1996). Future work must adjudicate whether neglect occurs within a true object-centered coordinate system or whether this is simulated because patients adopt a mental rotation strategy.

Visual Attention in Neglect

Although we have discussed the perceptual deficit in neglect in terms of impairments to particular forms of spatial representation, other aspects of the syndrome have led to it being interpreted in terms of a deficit in visual attention. For instance, patients with neglect may find it difficult to refrain from attending to stimuli on their unimpaired side, as if these stimuli capture attention (Ladavas, Petronio, & Umilta, 1990), and they have abnormal problems in reorienting attention from the unimpaired to the impaired side (Posner, Walker, Friedrich, & Rafal, 1984). Nevertheless performance can be improved when patients are cued to attend to the affected side (Posner et al., 1984; Riddoch & Humphreys, 1983). Heilman and colleagues (e.g., Heilman, Bowers, Valenstein, & Watson, 1987) and Kinsbourne (1987) have both argued that neglect is caused by a spatial imbalance in the systems that orient attention to each side of space. Each hemisphere acts to direct attention to the opposite side of space, with the right hemisphere also having the capability of directing attention to the same side (the right)(see Corbetta, Miezen, Shulman, & Petersen, 1995). Damage to the right hemisphere results in strong orienting to the right, directed by the left hemisphere. Left hemisphere damage, however, produces a less severe imbalance in attention because the right hemisphere is able to direct attention rightwards as well as leftwards. These accounts thus accommodate both strong effects of attentional orienting found in neglect and the relative prevalence of the disorder, which is more frequent after right hemisphere lesions (see Heilman et al., 1987).

Of course we should not think that the representational and attentional accounts of neglect are contradictory. Indeed, current models suggest that accounts need to be integrated for a full explanation to be provided. In one recent view, object recognition depends on computing different forms of representation of stimuli, moving from representations that are viewpoint-specific to those that are viewpoint-independent (see Marr, 1982, for one example). Mapping from one representation to another, though, may need to be competitive so that it operates optimally for one stimulus at a time. Lesioning such a system can lead to biases in computing certain representations and also to biases in the "attentional" competition to favor stimuli in one part of "space" (defined in terms of the representation affected) (see Heinke & Humphreys, 1998, for a explicit simulation along these lines). A fronto-parietal network may be important for achieving the mappings for viewpoint-independent recognition to take place, and in regulating the competition between objects that enable mappings to be achieved. Lesions to the network may disturb both particular forms of spatial coding and the attentional competition involved. This network may overlap with, but be separable from, networks in more dorsal brain regions concerned with using visual information for action (Goodale & Humphrey, this volume).

Simultanagnosia

Another deficit in spatial perception is simultanagnosia, associated in this case with bilateral damage to the parietal lobe (see Balint, 1909). Patients with simultanagnosia, as the term implies, seem only to perceive a single object at a time. Clinically such patients may be able to recognize single objects relatively well but they can have problems in interpreting complex scenes in which several objects have to be interrelated. They also need abnormally protracted times between stimuli in order to report the presence of multiple items.

The stimuli that can be reported by such patients are influenced by grouping and not simply by the spatial locations they occupy. Luria (1959) described an example in which such a patient could identify a "star of David" symbol derived from two equilateral triangles. However, when each triangle was depicted in a different color, the patient only reported seeing a single triangle. Here the cue to segment the shapes apart, based on the color difference, dominated perception, even though the shapes fell in the spatial area as before. Similar results have been reported more formally by Humphreys and Riddoch (1993). They reported two patients who were impaired at identifying whether circles of different colors were present in the field. The patients remained poor at the task when lines connected circles of the same color, but they improved dramatically when the lines joined circles of different color (though the circles were spaced the same distances apart in each condition)(see Figure 7.4). Humphreys et al. (1994) also examined the factors that determined which stimulus such a patient might report, when two were presented simultaneously. Contrasting stimuli that varied in their strength of grouping, they found that the patient tended to report the stimulus whose elements grouped most strongly while being unaware of the stimulus that grouped less strongly (see also Ward & Goodrich, 1996, for similar findings following unilateral damage).

In such patients the grouping processes important for object recognition (which are impaired in some agnosics) may operate in a relatively normal fashion. However, the patients seem poor at assimilating the presence of, and spatial interrelationships between, separate objects. This contrast can be demonstrated by comparing identification and counting responses in these patients. Identification requires that the parts of objects be grouped. Counting requires that they are treated as separate objects. Humphreys (1998) showed that simultanagnosic patients could identify objects efficiently while being quite unable to count the separate parts (see also Friedman-Hill, Robertson, & Treisman, 1995). Humphreys argued that simultanagnosics are deficient at assimilating, in parallel, information about a small number of separate objects (around three to four) – a process normally subserved by the parietal cortex. This description of a small number of objects is important in helping us achieve a coherent spatial representation of the visual environment, and it may also play a role in focusing attention on objects of interest. Due to damage to this representation, simultanagnosics are severely impaired in scene perception.

Different Forms of Simultanagnosia?

Kinsbourne and Warrington (1962) noted that patients with unilateral left ventral lesions also manifested some of the symptoms of simultanagnosia – in particular they needed very extended inter-stimulus intervals in order to be able to report multiple items. However, in other respects the problems experienced by such patients seem different from those found in simultanagnosics with bilateral parietal lesions (see also Farah, 1990). For example, the patients with unilateral ventral lesions show few signs of difficulty in negotiating the environment, unlike the parietal patients. Ventral patients also have no difficulty in counting small numbers of visual stimuli in parallel ("subitizing"; see Humphreys, 1998; Kinsbourne & Warrington, 1962), though are slow at identifying the same items. We suggest that patients with posterior ventral lesions show slowed identification of individual objects, which leads to the deficit in identifying multiple items simultaneously. In contrast, unlike the patients with parietal lesions, there is no deficit in assimilating a number of separate objects in parallel.

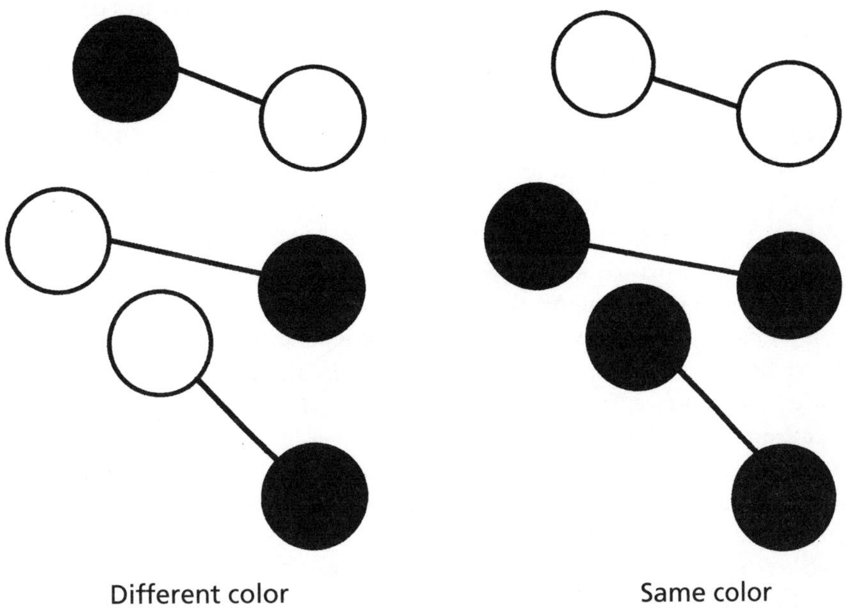

Figure 7.4. Example stimuli used by Humphreys and Riddoch (1993). In the same color condition, circles having the same color are linked by a line. In the different color condition circles having different colors are linked by a line. Simultanagnosic patients were better able to discriminate the presence of two colors in the same color condition, even though the colors were separated by the same distance in each case.

Covert Processing

Standard clinical tests of object and space perception typically probe visual processing in an explicit manner, with patients being required to respond directly to the process involved – tests of semantic access depend on judgments of semantic relatedness between items, tests of reading require words to be named, tests of neglect may require judgments about the spatial extent of objects. Patients are assigned to clinical categories (agnosia, prosopagnosia, alexia, etc.) based on their impairment on such tests relative to the normal population. However, in almost all the syndromes we have reviewed, patients have been reported as showing "covert" processing of stimuli, with the patients often being unaware that processing has taken place. We have in fact already discussed one such effect, evidenced when simultanagnosic patients show effects of grouping on the items they can report (Humphreys & Riddoch, 1993; Luria, 1959). For grouping to influence report, the elements that group (or do not group, depending on their properties) must be coded prior to the patient being aware that the stimulus is present. Such patients, unlike normal subjects, may be unable to detect stimuli that do not group (see Humphreys et al., 1994 for one example). Even more dramatic examples of covert processing in neuropsychological patients can be found in the syndrome of unilateral neglect. Marshall and Halligan (1988), for example, reported the case of a patient unable to report any differences between two houses, one of which had fire coming from a left-side (neglected) window. However, when asked to choose which house would be better to live in, the patient consistently chose the house without the fire! Neglect patients have also been shown to be sensitive to semantic priming from words they cannot detect (McGlinchey-Berroth, Milberg, Verfaellie, Alexander, & Kilduff, 1993; McGlinchey-Berroth et al., 1996), and, like patients with simultanagnosia, patients are influenced by grouping between items that would otherwise be neglected (Grabowecky, Robertson, & Treisman, 1993; Kartsounis & Warrington, 1989). Alexic patients may be surprisingly accurate when shown words for brief exposures and asked to guess at their meaning, though the patients may deny seeing the words under these conditions (Coslett & Saffran, 1993). Prosopagnosic patients can show semantic interference from faces on responses to the names of people, as well as better learning of correct over incorrect face-name pairings (for faces the patients fail to identify; de Haan, Young, & Newcombe, 1987).

In each of these examples, the information is used covertly in recognition or perceptual judgment tasks, rather than being used for other sets of tasks that might draw on different neural regions (e.g., as when visual information is used for action rather than recognition; see Goodale & Humphrey, this volume). Hence the effects cannot be attributed to a set of processes that simply operate in parallel to those affected in the patients. It may be, rather, that information is sometimes represented below a threshold level and this can be raised above threshold level by priming or by forcing patients to guess (see Burton, Young, Bruce, Johnston, & Ellis, 1991, for one simulation). It may also be that the explicit and the more covert tests differ in sensitivity, or that information that is processed normally by patients can be used to help recover otherwise degraded representations (an example here might be grouping between elements in the intact and impaired fields, in neglect; see Farah, Monheit,

& Wallace, 1991). It should also be noted that by no means all patients show evidence of covert processing (see Price & Humphreys, 1992, for evidence on alexia; see de Haan, Young, & Newcombe, 1991, for evidence on agnosia and prosopagnosia). The work of McNeil and Warrington (1991), which we have discussed as evidence for memorial forms of prosopagnosia, also indicates that what is important is where the deficits arise within a processing system.[2] They found covert face recognition in a patient with poor perception, whereas a patient with better perceptual processing showed no covert effect. Presumably the patient with poor perception and covert recognition maintained sufficient perceptual abilities for some access to stored knowledge to occur. The patient with better perception but no covert recognition may have lost stored memories for faces. An important question for future research will be to elucidate whether a lack of covert processing is indicative of impaired stored memories for stimuli.

Summary

In this chapter we have reviewed data on the neuropsychology of object and space perception. For both object and spatial processing, a number of different types of disorder can be established. In each instance, the disorder can be related to impaired perceptual or memorial processes underlying normal object and space perception, and the deficits illustrate something of the complexity of the processes that normally lead to our "seamless perceptions" of the world. Studies of such disorders not only guide our understanding of normal perception, but, via investigations of covert processing, they provide insights into the mechanisms that generate conscious awareness of perceptual processes. Both object recognition and space perception are contingent on a number of component processes that can be isolated following selective brain lesions.

Notes

1. This work was supported by program and cooperative grants from the MRC to both authors, and from a grant from the Humboldt Foundation to the first author.
2. Speculatively, we might suppose that covert recognition might not be shown in cases where there is loss of stored representations, but this remains to be tested.

Suggested Readings

Farah, M. J. (1990). *Visual agnosia.* Cambridge, MA: MIT Press. [A short book providing a historical review of cases of agnosia along with a discussion of the relations between agnosia, prosopagnosia, alexia, and simultanagnosia]

Humphreys, G. W., & Riddoch, M. J. (1987). *To see but not to see: A case study of visual agnosia.* London: Lawrence Erlbaum Associates. [A short book detailing the nature of the investigation into the agnosic patient, HJA, plus also a description of his experience]

Robertson, I., & Marshall, J.C. (Ed.) (1993). *Unilateral neglect: Clinical and experimental studies.* Hove: Lawrence Erlbaum Associates. [An edited book containing recent accounts of visual neglect]

Additional Topics

Rehabilitation and Recovery

One of the most practical questions in neuropsychology is whether patients can recover cognitive functions following brain damage. Therapy can be aimed either at reconstituting damaged processes, or at bypassing the processes by means of compensatory strategies. These strategies can, in turn, be guided by theories of the normal cognitive system. Examples of studies aimed at rehabilitating neuropsychological patients are provided in Humphreys and Riddoch (1994b).

Vision and Action

Despite having severe problems in recognizing objects by sight, many agnosics may interact appropriately with objects – they are able to reach accurately and they can avoid objects in the environment. Patients with deficits in space perception, such as unilateral neglect, can also manifest problems to different degrees if contrasting actions are used. For example, patients may show neglect when asked to point to the center of a bar but not when asked to grasp the bar to pick it up (see Edwards & Humphreys, 1999; Robertson, Nico, & Hood, 1997). This suggests that action can influence perception, with perhaps different perceptual descriptions being used for contrasting actions. The relations between the uses of vision for recognition and for action are taken up in Chapter 10, this volume, and they are discussed more fully in Milner and Goodale (1995).

References

Adams, M. J. (1979). Models of word recognition. *Cognitive Psychology, 11*, 133–176.

Allison, T., McCarthy, G., Nobre, K., Puce, A., & Belger, A. (1994). Human extrastriate visual cortex and the perception of faces, words, numbers and colours. *Cerebral Cortex, 5*, 544–554.

Arguin, M., & Bub, D. (1993). Single character processing in a case of pure alexia. *Neuropsychologia, 31*, 435–458.

Arguin, M., & Bub, D. (1994). Functional mechanisms in our alexia: Evidence from letter processing. In M. J. Farah & G. Ratcliff (Eds.), *The neuropsychology of high-level vision.* Hillsdale, NJ: Lawrence Erlbaum Assoc..

Arguin, M., Bub, D., & Dudek, G. (1996). Shape integration for visual object recognition and its implication in category-specific visual agnosia. *Visual Cognition, 3*, 221–275.

Assal, G., Favre, C., & Anderes, J. (1984). Nonrecognition of familiar animals by a farmer. Zooagnosia or prosopagnosia for animals. *Revue Neurologie, 25*, 51–81.

Balint, R. (1909). Seelenlahmung des "Schauens", optische Ataxie, räumliche Störung der Aufmerksamkeit. *Monatschrift für Psychiatrie und Neurologie, 25*, 51–81.

Behrmann, M., Moscovitch, M., & Winocur, G. (1994). Intact imagery and impaired visual perception in a patient with visual agnosia. *Journal of Experimental Psychology: Human Perception and Performance, 20*, 1068–1087.

Behrmann, M., & Tipper, S. P. (1994). Object-based visual attention: Evidence from unilateral neglect. In C. Umilta & M. Moscovitch (Eds.), *Attention and performance XV.* Cambridge, MA: MIT Press.

Behrmann, M., & Tipper, S. P. (1999). Attention across multiple reference frames: Evidence from visual neglect. *Journal of Experimental Psychology: Human Perception and Performance, 25*, 83–

101.
Benson, D. F., & Greenberg, J. P. (1969). Visual form agnosia. A specific deficit in visual discrimination. *Archives of Neurology, 20*, 82–89.
Biederman, I., & Kalocsai, P. (1997). Neurocomputational bases of object and face recognition. *Philosophical Transactions of the Royal Society, B352*, 1203–1220.
Bisiach, E., & Luzzatti, C. (1978). Unilateral neglect of representational space. *Cortex, 14*, 129–133.
Boucart, M., & Humphreys, G. W. (1992). The computation of perceptual structure from collinearity and closure: Normality and pathology. *Neuropsychologia, 30*, 527–546.
Bruyer, R., Laterre, C., Seron, X., Feyereison, P., Strypstein, E., Pierrard, E. et al. (1983). A case of prosopagnosia with some preserved covert remembrance of familiar faces. *Brain and Cognition, 2*, 257–284.
Burton, A. M., Young, A. W., Bruce, V., Johnston, R., & Ellis, A. W. (1991). Understanding covert recognition. *Cognition, 39*, 129–166.
Butter, C. M., & Trobe, J. D. (1994). Integrative agnosia following progressive multifocal leukoencephalopathy. *Cortex, 30*, 145–158.
Buxbaum, L. J., Coslett, H. B., Montgomery, M. W., & Farah, M. J. (1996). Mental rotation may underlie apparent object-based neglect. *Neuropsychologia, 14*, 113–126.
Buxbaum, L. J., Grosser, G., & Coslett, H. B. (1999). Impaired face and word recognition without object agnosia. *Neuropsychologia, 37*, 41–50.
Campion, J., & Latto, R. (1985). Apperceptive agnosia due to carbon monoxide poisoning. An interpretation based on critical band masking from disseminated lesions. *Behavioral Brain Research, 15*, 227–240.
Caramazza, A., & Hillis, A. E. (1990). Levels of representation, co-ordinate frames and unilateral neglect. *Cognitive Neuropsychology, 7*, 391–445.
Cooper, L. A., Schacter, D., Ballasteros, S., & Moore, C. (1992). Priming and recognition of transformed three dimensional objects: Effects of size and refraction. *Journal of Experimental Psychology: Learning, Memory and Cognition, 18*, 43–57.
Corbetta, M., Shulman, G. I., Miezen, F. M., & Petersen, S. E. (1995). Superior parietal cortex activation during attentional shifts and visual feature conjunctions. *Science, 270*, 802–805.
Coslett, H. B., & Saffran, E. (1993). Reading in pure alexia. *Brain, 116*, 21–37.
Cowey, A., Small, M., & Ellis, S. (1994). Left visuo-spatial neglect can be worse in far than in near space. *Neuropsychologia, 32*, 1059–1066.
Damasio, A. R., Damasio, H., & Van Hoesen, G. W. (1982). Prosopagnosia: Anatomic basis and behavioral mechanisms. *Neurology, 32*, 331–341.
Damasio, H., Grabowski, T. J., Tranel, D., Hichwa, R. D., & Damasio, A. R. (1996). A neural basis for lexical retrieval. *Nature, 380*, 499–505.
de Haan, E. H. F., Young, A. W., & Newcombe, F. (1987). Face recognition without awareness. *Cognitive Neuropsychology, 4*, 385–415.
de Haan, E. H. F., Young, A. W., & Newcombe, F. (1991). Covert and overt recognition in prosopagnosia. *Brain, 114*, 2575–2591.
DeRenzi, E. (1986). Current issues in prosopagnosia. In H. D. Ellis, M. A. Jeeves, F. Newcombe & A. W. Young (Eds.), *Aspects of face processing*. Dordrecht: Martinus Nijhoff.
DeRenzi, E., & Di Pellegrino, G. (1998). Prosopagnosia and alexia without object agnosia. *Cortex, 34*, 41–50.
DeRenzi, E. & Lucchelli, F. (1993). The fuzzy boundaries of apperceptive agnosia. *Cortex, 29*, 187–215.
Diamond, S., & Carey, S. (1986). Why faces are and are not special: An effect of expertise. *Journal of Experimental Psychology: General, 115*, 107–117.
Dixon, M., Bub, D. N., & Arguin, M. (1997). The interaction of object form and object meaning in the identification performance of a patient with category-specific visual agnosia. *Cognitive Neuropsychology, 14*, 1085–1130.
Driver, J., Baylis, G. C., Goodrich, S. J., & Rafal, R. D. (1994). Axis–based neglect of visual shapes.

Neuropsychologia, 32, 1358–1365.

Driver, J., & Halligan, P. W. (1991). Can visual neglect operate in object-centred co-ordinates? An affirmative case study. *Cognitive Neuropsychology, 8,* 475–496.

Duncan, J., & Humphreys, G. W. (1989). Visual search and visual similarity. *Psychological Review, 96,* 433–458.

Edwards, M. G., & Humphreys, G. W. (1999). Pointing and grasping in unilateral visual neglect: Effects of on-line visual feedback in grasping. *Neuropsychologia, 37,* 959–973.

Efron, R. (1968). What is perception? *Boston Studies in the Philosophy of Science, 4,* 137–173.

Ellis, A. W., Flude, B. M., & Young, A. W. (1987). "Neglect dyslexia" and the early visual processing of letters in words and nonwords. *Cognitive Neuropsychology, 4,* 439–464.

Farah, M. J. (1990). *Visual agnosia.* Cambridge, MA: MIT Press.

Farah, M. J., & Wallace, M. A. (1991). Pure alexia as a visual impairment: A reconsideration. *Cognitive Neuropsychology, 8,* 313–334.

Farah, M. J., Monheit, M. A., & Wallace, M. A. (1991). Unconscious perception of "extinguished" visual stimuli: Reassessing the evidence. *Neuropsychologia, 29,* 949–958.

Farah, M. J., Wilson, K. D., Drain, M., & Tanaka, J. N. (1998). What is "special" about face perception? *Psychological Review, 105,* 482–494.

Forde, E. M. E., & Humphreys, G. W. (1999). Category-specific recognition impairments: A review of important case studies and influential theories. *Aphasiology, 13,* 169–193.

Frederiksen, J. R. & Kroll, J. F. (1976). Spelling and sound: Approaches to the internal lexicon. *Journal of Experimental Psychology: Human Perception and Performance, 2,* 361–379.

Friedman-Hill, S. R., Robertson, L. C., & Treisman, A. (1995). Parietal contributions to visual feature binding: Evidence from a patient with bilateral lesions. *Science, 269,* 853–855.

Friedman, R. B. & Alexander, M. P. (1984). Pictures, images and pure alexia. *Cognitive Neuropsychology, 1,* 9–23.

Gauthier, I., & Tarr, M. J. (1997). Orientation priming of novel shapes in the context of viewpoint-dependent recognition. *Perception, 26,* 51–73.

Gauthier, I., Williams, P., Tarr, M. J., & Tanaka, J. (1998). Training "greeble" experts: A framework for studying expert object recognition processes. *Vision Research, 38,* 2401–2428.

Goldstein, K., & Gelb, A. (1918). Psychologische Analysen hirnpathologischer Fälle auf Grund von Untersuchungen Hirnverletzter. *Zeitschrift für die gesamte Neurologie und Psychiatrie, 41,* 1–142.

Grabowecky, M., Robertson, L. C., & Treisman, A. (1993). Preattentive processes guide visual search: Evidence from patients with unilateral visual neglect. *Journal of Cognitive Neuroscience, 5,* 288–302.

Grailet, J. M., Seron, X., Bruyer, R., Coyette, F., & Frederix, M. (1990). Case report of visual integrative agnosia. *Cognitive Neuropsychology, 7,* 275–309.

Grossman, M., Galetta, S., & D'Esposito, M. (1997). Object recognition difficulty in visual apperceptive agnosia. *Brain and Cognition, 33,* 306–342.

Hall, D., Humphreys, G. W., & Cooper, A. (in press). Neuropsychological evidence for case-specific reading: Multi-letter units in visual word recognition. *Quarterly Journal of Experimental Psychology.*

Halligan, P. W., & Marshall, J. C. (1991). Left neglect for near but not for far space in man. *Nature, 350,* 498–500.

Halligan, P. W., Marshall, J. C., & Wade, D. T. (1990). Do visual field deficits exacerbate visuospatial neglect? *Journal of Neurology, Neurosurgery and Psychiatry, 53,* 487–491.

Harvey, M., Milner, A. D., & Roberts, R. C. (1995). An investigation of hemispatial neglect using the landmark task. *Brain and Cognition, 27,* 59–78.

Haxby, J. V., Grady, C. L., Horowitz, B., Salerno, J., Ungerleider, L. G., Mishkin, M. et al. (1993). Dissociation of object and spatial visual pathways in human extrastriate cortex. In B. Gulyas, D. Ottoson, & P. E. Roland (Eds.), *Functional organisation of the human visual cortex.* Oxford: Pergamon Press.

Heilman, K. M., Bowers, D., Valenstein, E., & Watson, R. T. (1987). Hemispace and hemispatial neglect. In M. Jeannerod (Ed.), *Neurophysiological and neuropsychological aspects of spatial neglect.*

Amsterdam: Elsevier Science.

Hillis, A. E., & Caramazza, A. (1995). Cognitive and neural mechanisms underlying visual and semantic processing: Implications from "optical aphasia". *Journal of Cognitive Neuroscience, 7,* 457–478.

Howard, D. (1987). Reading without letters? In M. Coltheart, G. Sartori, & R. Job (Eds.), *The cognitive neuropsychology of language*. London: Lawrence Erlbaum Assoc.

Howard, D. (1991). Letter-by-letter readers: Evidence for parallel processing. In D. Besner & G. W. Humphreys (Eds.), *Basic processing in reading: Visual word recognition*. Hillsdale, NJ: Lawrence Erlbaum Associates.

Howard, D., Patterson, K. E., Wise, R., Douglas-Brown, W., Friston, K., Weiller, C. et al. (1992). The cortical localisation of the lexicons. *Brain, 115,* 1769–1782.

Humphreys, G. W. (1998). The neural representation of objects in space: A dual coding account. *Philosophical Transactions of the Royal Society, 353,* 1341–1352.

Humphreys, G. W., & Heinke, D. (1998). Spatial representation and selection in the brain: Neuropsychological and computational constraints. *Visual Cognition, 5,* 9–47.

Humphreys, G. W., Quinlan, P. T., & Riddoch, M. J. (1989). Grouping effects in visual search: Effects with single- and combined-feature targets. *Journal of Experimental Psychology: General, 118,* 258–279.

Humphreys, G. W., & Riddoch, M. J. (1984). Routes to object constancy: Implications from neurological impairments of object constancy. *Quarterly Journal of Experimental Psychology, 36A,* 385–415.

Humphreys, G. W., & Riddoch, M. J. (1987a). *To see but not to see: A case study of visual agnosia.* London: Lawrence Erlbaum Associates.

Humphreys, G. W., & Riddoch, M. J. (1987b). The fractionation of visual agnosia. In G. W. Humphreys & M. J. Riddoch (Eds.), *Visual object processing: A cognitive neuropsychological approach.* London: Lawrence Erlbaum Associates.

Humphreys, G. W., & Riddoch, M. J. (1993). Interactions between object and space vision revealed through neuropsychology. In D. E. Meyer & S. Kornblum (Eds.), *Attention and performance XIV* (pp. 143–162). Cambridge, MA: MIT Press.

Humphreys, G. W., & Riddoch, M. J. (1994a). Attention to within-object and between-object spatial representations: Multiple sites for visual selection. *Cognitive Neuropsychology, 11,* 207–242.

Humphreys, G. W., & Riddoch, M. J. (Eds.) (1994b). *Cognitive neuropsychology and cognitive rehabilitation.* London: Lawrence Erlbaum Associates.

Humphreys, G. W., & Riddoch, M. J. (1995). Separate coding of space within and between perceptual objects: Evidence from unilateral visual neglect. *Cognitive Neuropsychology, 12,* 283–312.

Humphreys, G. W., Riddoch, M. J., & Quinlan, P. T. (1985). Interactive processes in perceptual organisation: Evidence from visual agnosia. In M. I. Posner & O. S. M. Marin (Eds.), *Attention and performance XI.* Hillsdale, NJ: Lawrence Erlbaum Associates.

Humphreys, G. W., Riddoch, M. J., Quinlan, P. T., Donnelly, N., & Price, C. J. (1992). Parallel pattern processing and visual agnosia. *Canadian Journal of Psychology, 46,* 377–416.

Humphreys, G. W., Romani, C., Olson, A., Riddoch, M. J., & Duncan, J. (1994). Non-spatial extinction following lesions of the parietal lobe in humans. *Nature, 372,* 357–359.

Humphreys, G. W., & Rumiati, R. I. (1998). Agnosia without prosopagnosia or alexia: Evidence for stored visual memories specific to objects. *Cognitive Neuropsychology, 15,* 243–277.

Husain, M., & Kennard, C. (1996). Visual neglect associated with frontal lobe infarction. *Journal of Neurology, 243,* 652–657.

Kaas, J. H. (1989). Changing concepts of visual cortex organisation in primates. In J. W. Brown (Ed.), *Neuropsychology of visual perception.* Hillsdale, NJ: Lawrence Erlbaum Associates.

Kanwisher, N., Woods, R. P., Iacoboni, M., & Mazziotta, J. C. (1997). A locus in human extrastriate cortex for visual shape analysis. *Journal of Cognitive Neuroscience, 9,* 133–142.

Karnath, H.-O., Schenkel, P., & Fischer, B. (1991). Trunk orientation as the determining factor of the "contralesional" deficit in the neglect syndrome and as the physical anchor of the internal

representation of body orientation in space. *Brain, 114*, 1997–2014.
Kartsounis, L. D., & Warrington, E. K. (1989). Unilateral visual neglect overcome by cues implicit in stimulus arrays. *Journal of Neurology, Neurosurgery and Psychiatry, 52*, 1253–1259.
Kay, J., & Hanley, R. (1991). Simultaneous form perception and serial letter recognition in a case of letter-by-letter reading. *Cognitive Neuropsychology, 8*, 249–273.
Kinsbourne, M. (1987). Mechanisms of unilateral neglect. In M. Jeannerod (Ed.), *Neurophysiological and neuropsychological aspects of spatial neglect.* Amsterdam: North-Holland.
Kinsbourne, M., & Warrington, E. K. (1962). A disorder of simultaneous form perception. *Brain, 85*, 461–486.
Ladavas, E., Petronio, A., & Umilta, C. (1990). The deployment of visual attention in the intact field of hemineglect patients. *Cortex, 26*, 307–317.
Lamb, M. R., Robertson, L. C., & Knight, R. T. (1990). Component mechanisms underlying the processing of hierarchically organised patterns – inferences from patients with unilateral cortical lesions. *Journal of Experimental Psychology: Learning, Memory and Cognition, 16*, 471–483.
Lawson, R., & Humphreys, G. W. (1999). The effects of view in depth on the identification of line drawings and silhouettes of familiar objects: Normality and pathology. *Visual Cognition, 6*, 165–196.
Lissauer, H. (1890). Ein Fall von Seelenblindheit nebst einem Beitrag zur Theorie derselben. *Archiv für Psychiatrie und Nervenkrankheiten, 21*, 222–270.
Luria, A. R. (1959). Disorders of "simultaneous perception" in a case of bilateral occipito-parietal brain injury. *Brain, 82*, 437–449.
Marr, D. (1982). *Vision.* San Francisco: W.H. Freeman.
Marshall, J. C., & Halligan, P. W. (1988). Blindsight and insight in visuo-spatial neglect. *Nature, 336*, 766–767.
Martin, A., Wiggs, C. L., Ungerleider, L. G., & Haxby, J. V. (1996). Neural correlates of category–specific knowledge. *Nature, 379*, 649–652.
Mayall, K. A., Humphreys, G. W., & Olson, A. (1997). Disruption to letter or word processing? The origins of case-mixing effects. *Journal of Experimental Psychology: Learning, Memory and Cognition, 23*, 1275–1286.
McClelland, J. L. (1976). Preliminary letter recognition in the perception of words and nonwords. *Journal of Experimental Psychology: Human Perception and Performance, 2*, 80–91.
McGlinchey-Berroth, R., Milberg, W. P., Verfaellie, M., Alexander, M., & Kilduff, P. (1993). Semantic processing in the neglected visual field: Evidence from a lexical decision task. *Cognitive Neuropsychology, 10*, 79–108.
McGlinchey-Berroth, R., Milberg, W. P., Verfaellie, M., Grande, L., D'Esposito, M., & Alexander, M. (1996). Semantic processing and orthographic specificity in hemispatial neglect. *Journal of Cognitive Neuroscience, 8*, 291–304.
McNeil, J. E., & Warrington, E. K. (1991). Prosopagnosia: A real classification. *Quarterly Journal of Experimental Psychology, 43A*, 267–287.
McNeil, J. E., & Warrington, E. K. (1993). Prosopagnosia: A face specific disorder. *Quarterly Journal of Experimental Psychology, 46A*, 1–10.
Milner, A. D., & Goodale, M. (1995). *The visual brain in action.* London: Academic Press.
Milner, A. D., & Harvey, M. (1995). Distortion of size perception in visuospatial neglect. *Current Biology, 5*, 85–89.
Milner, A. D., Perrett, D. I., Johnston, R. S., Benson, P. J., Jordan, T. R. et al. (1991). Perception and action in "visual form agnosia". *Brain, 114*, 405–428.
Moore, C., & Price, C. J. (1999). A functional neuroimaging study of the variables that generate category-specific object processing differences. *Brain, 122*, 943–962.
Moscovitch, M., Winocur, G., & Behrmann, M. (1997). What is special about face recognition? Nineteen experiments on a person with visual agnosia and dyslexia but normal face recognition. *Journal of Cognitive Neuroscience, 5*, 555–604.
Navon, D. (1977). Forest before trees: The precedence of global features in visual perception. *Cognitive Psychology, 9*, 353–383.

Nobre, A. C., Allison, T., & McCarthy, G. (1994). Word recognition in the human inferior temporal lobe. *Nature, 372,* 260–263.
Patterson, K. E., & Kay, J. (1982). Letter-by-letter reading: Psychological characteristics of a neurological syndrome. *Quarterly Journal of Experimental Psychology, 34A,* 411–441.
Perani, C. A., Cappa, S. F., Bettinardi, V., Bressi, S., Gorno-Tempini, M. et al. (1995). Different neural systems for the recognition of animals and man-made tools. *NeuroReport, 6,* 1637–1641.
Perrett, D. I., Mistlin, A. J., Chitty. A. J., Harries, M. H., Newcombe, F., & De Haan, E. (1988). Neuronal mechanisms of face perception and their pathology. In C. Kennard & F. Clifford-Rose (Eds.), *Physiological aspects of clinical neuro-ophthalmology.* London: Chapman & Hall.
Petersen, S. E., Fox, P. T., Snyder, A., & Raichle, M. E. (1990). Activation of extrastriate and frontal cortical areas by visual words and word-like stimuli. *Science, 249,* 1041–1044.
Posner, M. I., Walker, J. A., Friedrich, F., & Rafal, R. D. (1984). Effects of parietal injury on covert orienting of attention. *Journal of Neuroscience, 4,* 1863–1874.
Price, C. J., & Humphreys, G. W. (1992). Letter-by-letter reading? Functional deficits and compensatory strategies. *Cognitive Neuropsychology, 9,* 427–457.
Price, C. J., Moore, C., Humphreys, G. W., Frackowiak, R. S. J., & Friston, K. J. (1996a). The neural regions sustaining object recognition and naming. *Proceedings of the Royal Society, B263,* 1501–1507.
Price, C. J., Wise, R., & Frackowiak, R. S. J. (1996b). Demonstrating the implicit processing of visually presented words and pseudowords. *Cerebral Cortex, 6,* 62–70.
Puce, A., Allison, T., Asgari, M., Gore, J. C., & McCarthy, G. (1995). Differential sensitivity of human visual cortex to faces, letter strings and textures: A functional magnetic imaging study. *Journal of Neuroscience, 16,* 5205–5215.
Pylyshyn, Z. (1999). Is vision continuous with cognition? The case for cognitive impenetrability of visual perception. *Behavioral and Brain Sciences, 22,* 341–423.
Riddoch, M. J., & Humphreys, G. W. (1983). The effect of cueing on unilateral neglect. *Neuropsychologia, 21,* 589–599.
Riddoch, M. J., & Humphreys, G. W. (1987a). A case of integrative agnosia. *Brain, 110,* 1431–1462.
Riddoch, M. J., & Humphreys, G. W. (1987b). Visual object processing in optic aphasia: A case of semantic access agnosia. *Cognitive Neuropsychology, 4,* 131–185.
Riddoch, M. J., & Humphreys, G. W. (1987c). Perceptual aand action systems in unilateral neglect. In M. Jeannerod (Ed.), *Neurophysiological and neuropsychological aspects of spatial neglect.* Amsterdam: North-Holland.
Riddoch, M. J., Humphreys, G. W., Gannon, T., Blott, W., & Jones, V. (1999). Memories are made of this: The effects of time on stored visual knowledge in a case of visual agnosia. *Brain, 122,* 537–559.
Rizzolatti, G., Gentilucci, M., & Matelli, M. (1985). Selective spatial attention: One centre, one circuit or many circuits? In M. I. Posner & O. S. M. Marin (Eds.), *Attention and performance XI.* Hillsdale, NJ: Lawrence Erlbaum Associates.
Robertson, I. H., Nico, D., & Hood, B. M. (1997). Believing what you feel: Using proprioceptive feedback to reduce unilateral neglect. *Neuropsychology, 11,* 53–58.
Rumiati, R. I., Humphreys, G. W., Riddoch, M. J., & Bateman, A. (1994). Visual object agnosia without prosopagnosia or alexia: Evidence for hierarchical theories of object recognition. *Visual Cognition, 1,* 181–225.
Schacter, D. L., & Cooper, L. A. (1993). Implicit and explicit memory for novel visual objects: Structure and function. *Journal of Experimental Psychology: Learning, Memory and Cognition, 19,* 995–1009.
Schacter, D. L., Cooper, L. A., & Delaney, S. M. (1990). Implicit memory for unfamiliar objects depends on access to structural descriptions. *Journal of Experimental Psychology: General, 119,* 5–24.
Schacter, D. L., Reimann, E., Uecker, A., Polster, M. R., Yun, L. S., & Cooper, L. A. (1995). Brain

regions associated with retrieval of structurally coherent visual information. *Nature, 376*, 587–590.

Sergent, J., Ohta, S., & MacDonald, B. (1992). Functional neuroanatomy of face and object processing. *Brain, 115*, 15–36.

Sergent, J., & Signoret, J.-L. (1992). Varieties of functional deficits in prosopagnosia. *Cerebral Cortex, 2*, 375–388.

Seron, X., Coyette, F., & Bruyer, R. (1989). Ipsilateral influences on contralateral processing in neglect processing. *Cognitive Psychology, 6*, 475–498.

Shallice, T., & Warrington, E. K. (1977). The possible role of selective attention in acquired dyslexia. *Neuropsychologia, 15*, 31–41.

Sheridan, J., & Humphreys, G. W. (1993). A verbal-semantic category-specific recognition impairment. *Cognitive Neuropsychology, 10*, 143–184.

Sirigu, A., Duhamel, J.-R., & Poncet, M. (1991). The role of sensorimotor experience in object recognition. *Brain, 114*, 2555–2573.

Stewart, F., Parkin, A. J., & Hunkin, H. N. (1992). Naming impairments following recovery from herpes simplex encephalitis. *Quarterly Journal of Experimental Psychology, 44A*, 261–284.

Tanaka, J., & Farah, M. J. (1993). Parts and wholes in face recognition. *Quarterly Journal of Experimental Psychology, 46A*, 225–245.

Tipper, S. P., & Behrmann, M. (1996). Object-centered not scene-based visual neglect. *Journal of Experimental Psychology: Human Perception and Performance, 22*, 1261–1278.

Vandenberghe, R., Price, C. J., Wise, R., Josephs, O., & Frackowiak, R. S. J. (1996). Semantic system(s) for words or pictures. *Nature, 383*, 254–256.

Walker, R., Findlay, J. M., Young, A. W., & Lincoln, N. (1996). Saccadic eye movements in object-based neglect. *Cognitive Neuropsychology, 13*, 569–615.

Wapner, W., Judd, T., & Gardner, H. (1978). Visual agnosia in an artist. *Cortex, 14*, 343–364.

Ward, R., & Goodrich, S. J. (1996). Differences between objects and nonobjects in visual extinction: A competition for visual attention. *Psychological Science, 7*, 177–180.

Warrington, E. K., & James, M. (1986). Visual object recognition in patients with right hemisphere lesions: Axes or features? *Perception, 15*, 355–356.

Warrington, E. K., & Shallice, T. (1980). Word-form dyslexia. Brain, *103*, 99–112.

Warrington, E. K., & Taylor, A. (1973). The contribution of the right parietal lobe to object recognition. *Cortex, 9*, 152–164.

Warrington, E. K., & Taylor, A. (1978). Two categorical stages of object recognition. *Perception, 9*, 152–164.

Yin, R. K. (1969). Looking at upside-down faces. *Journal of Experimental Psychology, 81*, 141–145.

Young, A. W., Hellawell, D. J., & Hay, D. C. (1987). Configural information in face perception. *Perception, 16*, 747–759.

Young, A. W., Hellawell, D. J., & Welch, J. (1992). Neglect and visual recognition. Brain, *112*, 51–71.

Young, A. W., Newcombe, F., & Ellis, A. W. (1991). Different impairments contribute to neglect dyslexia. *Cognitive Neuropsychology, 8*, 177–192.

Chapter Eight

Movement and Event Perception

Maggie Shiffrar

Introduction

Imagine that you are a pedestrian standing on the corner of a busy intersection. Before you can safely cross the street, you must interpret the motion of the nearby buses, cars, trucks, bicycles, and other pedestrians. Failure to do so in an accurate and timely fashion could have catastrophic consequences. This situation demonstrates that our daily survival depends upon our ability to perceive motion. Indeed, the survival of all animals depends upon their interpretations of the movements of their young, their prey, their predators, and themselves.

What is visual motion? In its most basic sense, visual motion consists of a perceived change in optical information over space and time. Different changes in optical information are usually associated with different types of motion (Gibson, 1979). For example, as you walk through your environment, changes are produced within your entire field of view. This type of change, known as optic flow, helps you to determine where you are headed as you walk. A different type of change occurs when you stare at a fixed point in a field and, for example, observe a hopping rabbit. In this example, changes only occur in those subregions of your field of view that are affected by the rabbit. Such spatially limited change is related to the perception of object motion. The goal of this chapter is to provide a concise overview into both of these types of motion; that is, how we use movement to understand objects and to navigate within our environment.

Through out this chapter, emphasis will be given to the constructive or inferential nature of motion perception. Photoreceptors in the retina only respond to changes in light intensity. The visual system must use these intensity changes to infer motion. The following examples illustrate just how complex these inferences can be. Firstly, imagine that you are standing in the middle of a field and you move your eyes to scan the horizon. As a result of your eye movements, an image of the field moves across the back of your eyes. Yet, the field appears stationary. Thus, movement of a retinal image does not, in and of itself, result in the perception of movement. Secondly, imagine that you are seated in a very dark room and the only thing that you can see is a single point of light. Even though the point of light remains perfectly stationary, after a few moments, the light will appear to move erratically (Koffka, 1935). The first example demonstrates that we can perceive no motion even though motion signals reach our eyes. The second example, known as the autokinetic effect, demonstrates that we can also perceive movement when none physically exists. The relative nature of motion perception produces yet another complexity. For example, moving clouds can cause the moon to appear to move rapidly (Duncker, 1929/1937). This phenomenon, known as induced motion, illustrates that the perception of an object's movement also depends upon the motion of its surround. Thus, motion perception is complex and cannot simply result from a change in position over time (Nakayama & Tyler, 1981).

How does the visual system construct motion percepts? We will systematically address this question by first examining the neural structures underlying our perception of movement. We will then discuss how the structure of the visual system creates certain ambiguities in the measurement of visual motion information and how the visual system overcomes these ambiguities. This will be followed by a discussion of the types of information that the visual system considers in its calculation of object and self motion. Finally, we will review recent evidence suggesting that sensory systems other than the visual system also contribute to the perception of visual movement

The Neural Basis of Motion Perception

Over the past 10 years, one of the hottest debates among vision researchers has been whether motion perception depends on a special information processing pathway (e.g., Livingstone & Hubel, 1988; Merigan & Maunsell, 1993; Zeki, 1993). Although the exact nature of motion processing pathways remains to be understood, researchers have determined that certain cortical areas are particularly responsive to motion. One intriguing example comes from a patient exhibiting "motion blindness." As a result of a stroke, L.H. suffered bilateral lesions to the medial temporal area (or area MT) of her visual cortex (Shipp et al., 1994). Although L.H.'s visual acuity and color vision are normal, she fails nearly all tests involving movement (Zihl, von Cramon, & Mai, 1983). L.H. reports that she can not even cross a street because, "When I'm looking at the car first, it seems far away. But then, when I want to cross the road, suddenly the car is very near" (Zihl et al., 1983). Thus, damage to particular cortical areas can have devastating repercussions for motion perception. The following section contains an overview of the basic neural substrate underlying motion perception.

Subcortical Mechanisms

The process of visual motion perception begins when retinal photoreceptors respond to photons of light energy. These responses are passed on to other neurons in the retina that modify the information. Eventually these visual signals exit the retina at the blind spot via a bundle of ganglion cell axons known as the optic nerve. For mammals, about 10% of the axons in the optic nerve project to the superior colliculus in the retinotectal pathway. Activity in the superior colliculus is associated with the planning of eye movements, among other things (Wurtz, Goldberg, & Robinson, 1982).

The remaining 90% of the axons leaving the retina project to the dorsal portion of the two lateral geniculate nuclei (LGN) of the thalamus thereby creating the first segment of the geniculostriate pathway (Silveira & Perry, 1991). The primate LGN has six layers. The outer four layers are known as the parvocellular layers and the two inner layers are called the magnocellular layers. Neurons in the magnocellular and parvocellular layers exhibit some important differences in their responsiveness to visual displays (for a thorough review, see Chapter 3 of this volume, Livingstone & Hubel, 1988 and Merigan & Maunsell, 1993). Although the vast majority of cells in the parvocellular layers are wavelength or color sensitive (Derrington & Lennie, 1984), cells in the magnocellular layer are much more sensitive to luminance than to wavelength (Shapley, Kaplan, & Soodak, 1981). Secondly, magnocellular neurons are also much more responsive to transient or moving stimuli whereas parvocellular neurons are more responsive to steady state displays. Furthermore, neurons in these magnocellular and parvocellular pathways project to different cortical areas. These and other differences have led some researchers to suggest that neurons in the magnocellular pathway are selectively responsive to movement information (Livingstone & Hubel, 1988). Subsequent analyses suggest that the magnocellular pathway may actually be dedicated to the analysis of middle and high velocity stimuli (Merigan & Maunsell, 1993) and/or edge-based motion information (Shapley, 1995). Researchers now believe that motion perception depends on the activity of both the magnocellular and parvocellular pathways (Merigan & Maunsell, 1993; Shapley, 1995; Shiffrar & Lorenceau, 1996).

Primary Visual Cortex

The output of the LGN is sent to the primary visual cortex (also known as the striate cortex or area V1). Our understanding of the neural coding of motion information in this large, six-layered structure is grounded in the research of David Hubel and Tornsten Wiesel. These researchers were the first to demonstrate that a subset of the neurons in area V1 exhibits directional selectivity; that is, they respond vigorously to motion in a particular direction (Hubel & Wiesel, 1968). By shining a bar of light within the receptive fields of individual neurons, these researchers identified cells that responded maximally when a bar moved in a particular direction and were less responsive or completely unresponsive when the bar moved in the opposite direction. Neurons exhibiting directional selectivity are most frequently found in layers 4 and 6; that is, those layers receiving input from the magnocellular layers of the LGN (Hawken, Parker, & Lund, 1988). An important quality of these neurons is that they are both direction and orientation selective. The implications of this property will be discussed in the section concerning the aperture problem.

Area MT

Directionally selective V1 neurons project directly to the medial temporal (MT) area (Movshon & Newsome, 1996). Whereas only a quarter of the neurons in area V1 exhibit directional selectivity (Hawken et al., 1988), nearly all of the neurons in area MT are directionally selective (Dubner & Zeki, 1971; Maunsell & Newsome, 1987). Indeed, evidence from a number of different techniques suggests that area MT plays a fundamentally important role in motion perception (Maunsell & Newsome, 1987). When this area is lesioned, motion perception, but not static visual perception, is severely disrupted (Siegel & Andersen, 1988). Furthermore, large lesions of area MT and neighboring area MST permanently disrupt both pursuit and saccadic eye movements (Yamasaki & Wurtz, 1991).

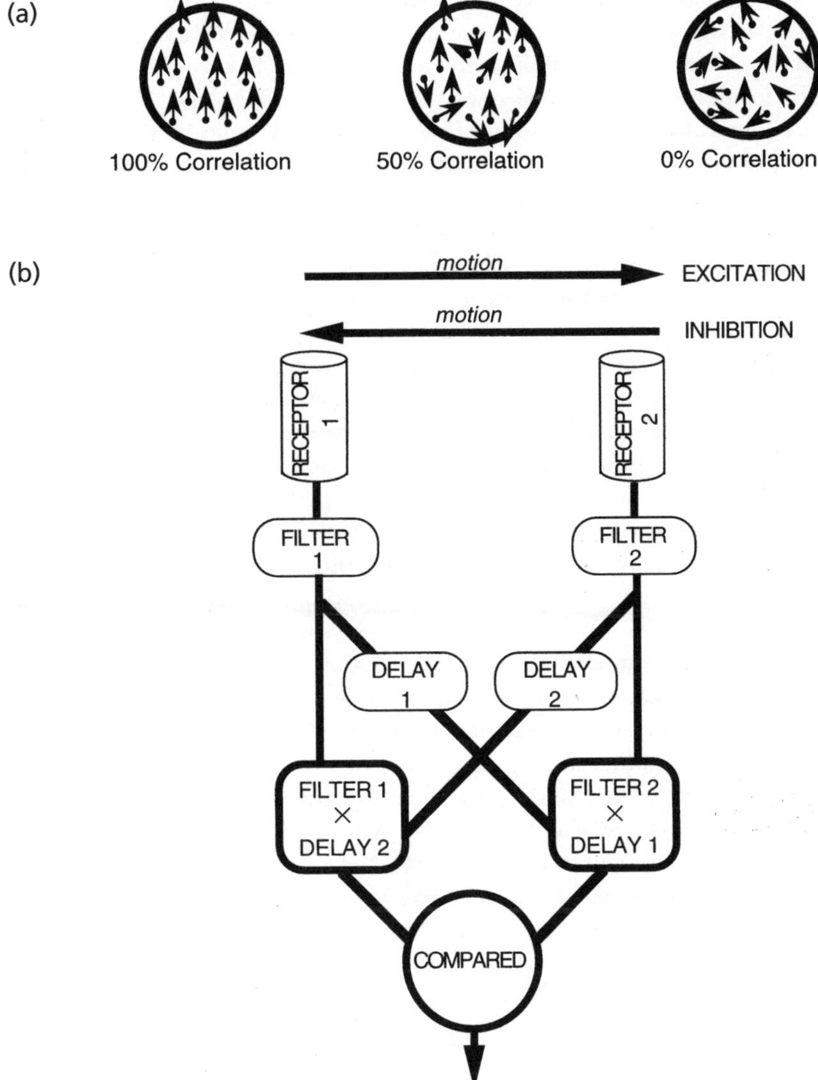

Figure 8.1. (a) Random dot kinematograms. When the dot motion is 100% correlated, all of the dots appear to move as a coherent cloud. When none of the dots are correlated, the dots appear to flicker. (b) A Reichardt detector for direction of translation. This circuit can discriminate between leftward and rightward motion. In this model, a filtered version of each receptor's output is multiplied by a temporally delayed version of the other receptor's response. The results are then compared. Rightward motion produces a positive value at comparison while leftward motion produces a negative value. For example, if a point of light moves rightward, receptor 2 will respond after receptor 1. If this temporal lag is similar to the value of delay 2, then the multiplication of the filtered output of receptor 1 × delay 2 will be large (relative to filter 2 × delay 1) and produce a positive value at the comparison stage. This positive value indicates rightward motion.

Recent neurophysiological techniques have been used to directly evaluate the relationship between the activity of individual MT neurons and motion perception. These studies have involved the use of random dot kinematograms. Such displays consist of a cloud of dots in which each dot is briefly flashed at a random position within the display area, as illustrated in Figure 8.1a. The correlation of the dot positions from frame to frame is varied. When the correlation is zero, a dot can appear anywhere in the subsequent frame of the display. At this correlation level, there is no net direction of motion and observers perceive only random flicker. The cloud of dots can be given a net motion by correlating some of the dot positions across frames. When the displacements of 100% of the dots are correlated, the dot cloud appears to move as a coherent whole. If half of the dots are correlated, then observers perceive a subset of dots translating together within a cloud of randomly flickering dots. Usually, an observer is asked to indicate whether the net direction of dot motion is in one of two directions, say up or down. When the motion of only 5% of the dots is correlated, direction discrimination performance is usually near chance (50% correct). When approximately 20% or more of the dots are displaced together, the discrimination becomes simple and performance is nearly perfect.

To understand the relationship between single cell activity in area MT and perceptual judgments of visual motion, researchers have presented the above kinematograms within the receptive fields of individual MT neurons of a behaving monkey (Britten, Shadlen, Newsome, & Movshon, 1992; Newsome, Britten, & Movshon, 1989). While the animal performs the direction discrimination task, the activity of the MT neuron is recorded. These researchers found that, on average, the response of a single MT neuron discriminates motion direction about as well as the animal does. Similarity between behavioral and neural sensitivity on this motion task supports the view that area MT is specialized for motion perception. Newsome and his colleagues found additional support for this hypothesis when they directly manipulated neural activity in area MT (Salzman, Britten, & Newsome, 1990; Salzman, Murasugi, Britten, & Newsome, 1992). A random dot kinematogram of variable coherence was projected within the receptive field of an MT neuron of a monkey who performed the same direction discrimination task. During half of the trials, the neuron was electrically stimulated. The microstimulation was directly associated with a change in the monkey's performance such that the electrical activation appeared to strengthen the motion signal in the direction of the neuron's best direction selectivity. For example, a monkey might be 20% more likely to report the perception of upward dot movement when a neuron selective for upward movement was stimulated.

Obviously, microelectrodes can not be used to study the activity of neurons in the human visual system. Therefore, researchers interested in the neural basis of human motion perception use brain imaging techniques such as positron emission tomography (PET) and functional magnetic resonance imaging (fMRI) to indirectly measure neuronal activity. Neuroimaging studies have confirmed that humans have a cortical area that is roughly equivalent to the monkey area MT. In one influential study, subjects observed a pattern of randomly distributed black and white squares. Cerebral blood flow, an indirect measure of neuronal activity, was measured with PET imaging while subjects viewed the squares as stationary and then again when the squares moved. Increased activity was found in an area now known as human area MT, that is, at the junction of the occipital and temporal lobes, during the perception of the moving display (Zeki et al., 1991). Furthermore, magnetically stimulating area MT in human subjects alters their perception of visual motion (Beckers & Zeki, 1995; Walsh et al., 1998).

Recall that under some conditions, such as those used to generate the autokinetic effect, stationary objects can appear to move. Thus, the perception of visual motion does not require the presence of physical movement. Within this context, it is particularly interesting to consider the finding that neural activity has been measured in human area MT during the perception of physically stationary objects (Tootell et al., 1995; Zeki et al., 1993). For example, in a PET study, subjects viewed line drawings of objects and were asked to identify the color or the action normally associated with each object. Area MT was activated when subjects verbally reported each object's action even though the object was completely stationary (Martin, Haxby, Lalonde, Wiggs, & Ungerleider, 1995). Importantly, human area MT was not activated during the identification of object color. These results suggest that area MT may play a critical role in our memory of object motion (Martin et al., 1995). Furthermore, these and other results (Treue & Maunsell, 1996; O'Craven, Rosen, Kwong, Treisman, & Savoy, 1997) indicate that area MT activity can be strongly modulated by attentional processes.

Areas MST and STP

The superior temporal sulcus of the primate brain contains several areas that are involved in the perception of visual motion. Area MT, which is one such area, sends much of its output to other areas that are located along this sulcus; namely areas MST (medial superior temporal) and STP (superior temporal polysensory). Whereas directionally selective V1 and MT neurons are most responsive to translational motion, neurons in these other areas respond to more complex types of motion. For example, MST neurons are selectively responsive to expanding, contracting, and rotating stimuli (Graziano, Andersen, & Snowden, 1994; Tanaka, Fukada, & Saito, 1989). Visual selectivity to expansion suggests that area MST may be involved in the perception of optic flow during locomotion (see Perception of Self Motion section). Furthermore, lesions in area MST produce deficits in certain eye movements (Dursteller & Wurtz, 1988). This combination of findings suggests that area MST may be important for the integration of optic flow and eye movement information. More specifically, neurons in the dorsal sub-division of area MST may help the visual system account for an observer's eye movements as that observer moves through the environment (Bradley, Maxwell, Andersen, Banks, & Shenoy, 1996).

Single cell recordings in the anterior region of area STP indicate that some of the neurons in this area are most responsive to the movement of humans and other primates (Perrett, Harries, Mistlin, & Chitty, 1990). For example, an STPa neuron might respond selectively to the visual depiction of a forearm extending outward from the elbow but not to a rotating bar that replicates the forearm's motion (Perrett et al., 1990). Moreover, although these STPa neurons respond vigorously to displays depicting whole body movements, they remain unresponsive to partial displays (Oram & Perrett, 1994). In the human, neuroimaging and case studies have also suggested the existence of specialized processing centers dedicated to the visual analysis of human movement (Bonda, Petrides, Ostry, & Evans, 1996; Vaina, Lemay, Bienfang, Choi & Nakayama, 1990).

Motion Measurement

The previous section provided an overview of many of the brain regions involved in the perception of visual motion. When the response properties and relative locations of these regions are considered together, one finds that neuronal receptive fields are relatively small in early visual areas and that receptive field size increases in subsequent processing areas. This situation creates some fundamental ambiguities in the measurement of object motion (see Zeki, 1993 for review). For example, motion measurements made by neurons with large receptive fields may be less accurate because they can not signal the precise location of a stimulus. On the other hand, neurons with small receptive fields can only respond to small changes, and as a result, can not be used to measure the motion of entire objects. Obviously, the visual interpretation of object motion is a tricky business. In the current section, we will address three aspects of motion measurement that have been extensively studied because they are central to the construction of motion percepts.

Early Motion Measurements

How does the visual system compute the speed and direction of a moving object? One aspect of this computation is clear. Visual motion must be determined from an integration of information across different retinal locations because neither direction nor speed can be determined from the changes that occur at a single location. Motion can be measured across pairs of locations because the movement of a stimulus produces changes that are correlated across neighboring retinal regions. Reichardt (1969) and his colleagues took advantage of this fact to construct a now classic correlational model of motion measurement. To compare changes across two locations on the retina, the response of the receptor at one location is multiplied with a temporally delayed version of the response of the other receptor as shown in Figure 8.1b. The difference between the two resulting values indicates the direction of image motion.

Variations on this cross-correlation method serve as the foundation for many computational models of motion measurement (e.g., Adelson & Bergen, 1985; van Santen & Sperling, 1984; Watson & Ahumada, 1985). Interestingly, the motion measurements provided by Reichardt detectors are ambiguous. For example, the speed calculated by Reichardt detectors is significantly influenced by the luminance contrast of a moving display. That is, the relative brightness of an object can change its apparent speed. Consistent with this computational ambiguity, the perception of visual speed by human observers is also contrast dependent (Stone & Thompson, 1992; Castet, Lorenceau, Shiffrar, & Bonnet, 1993). Thus, correlational models, of which the Reichardt detector is a classic example, do provide a good account of the measurement of visual motion by neurons exhibiting direction selectivity.

Motion Integration Over Space: The Aperture Problem

Once the speed and direction of a retinal image have been calculated for each pair of points in an image, a second stage of analysis is needed. This second stage serves two important purposes. Firstly, neurons in the early stages of the visual system can only respond to changes within very small regions of an observer's field of view. Therefore, in order to interpret the motion of a real object, motion information must be combined across much larger regions of retinal space. Secondly, early calculations of image motion are limited by something known as the aperture problem. This problem refers to the fact that directionally sensitive neurons with small receptive fields will sometimes give the same response to very different motions. As illustrated in Figure 8.2 (a and b), this problem can arise whenever the motion of long lines or edges must be estimated from the activity of a neuron having a small receptive field. More specifically, the motion of any line can be decomposed into the portion that is parallel to the line and the portion that is perpendicular to the line. Because a neuron can not track or "see" the ends of the line if those ends fall outside of its receptive field, the neuron can not measure any of the motion that is parallel to the line's orientation. As a result, many different motions will appear to be identical when viewed within a window or small receptive field. Because all known visual systems have neurons with receptive fields that are limited in size, this measurement ambiguity has been extensively studied (e.g., Hildreth, 1984; Wallach, 1935).

How can an observer construct an interpretation of object motion from such ambiguous measurements? Although the interpretation of a single translating line is ambiguous, the possible interpretations of its motion are limited to a large family of motions. All of the members of this family differ only in the component of translation that is parallel to the line's orientation (that is, along the length of the line). Members of two hypothetical families are illustrated by the groups of three arrows in Figure 8.2c. Notice that the arrows all line up along a dashed line. This dashed line, known as the constraint line, depicts the entire family of motions that is consistent with the motion measured from a single translating line or grating.

The visual system can solve the aperture problem by combining together the individually ambiguous motion information from two differently oriented lines. If two differently oriented lines are rigidly connected to each other, then their corresponding constraint lines will intersect at a single point. This point, known as the intersection of constraints or IOC, defines the only possible motion interpretation that is shared by both translating lines. Thus, if the visual system is correct in assuming that two lines are rigidly connected to each other, then the motion of an object defined by the lines can be uniquely interpreted.

Experimental support for this approach comes from studies examining the visual perception of and neural response to spatially overlapping edges and gratings. In behavioral experiments, Adelson and Movshon (1982) asked subjects to report whether superimposed sinusoidal gratings (represented by the lines on the right-hand side of Figure 8.2c) appeared to move as a coherent whole. When the luminance contrast and the spatial frequency of the two gratings were similar, subjects perceived a single translating plaid pattern. The perceived direction of translation was the same as the IOC solution for the two gratings, as shown in Figure 8.2c. On the other hand, when the two gratings differed

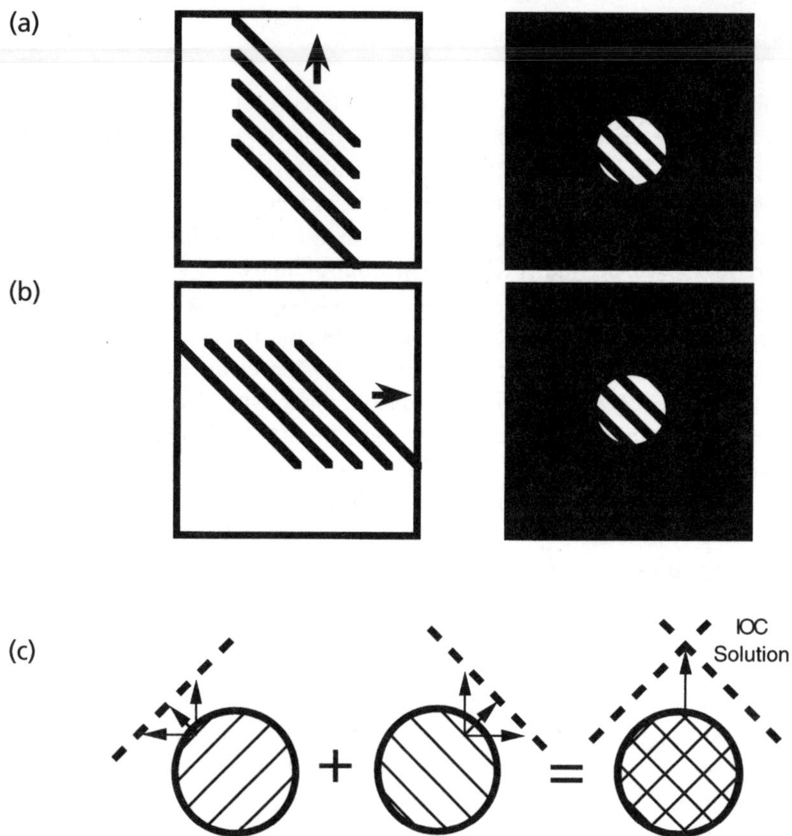

Figure 8.2. (a) On the left, a diagonal line translates upward. Each line segment shows the position of the translating line at a different time. On the right, the vertically translating line is viewed through a small window or aperture. Such apertures can be used to represent the receptive field of a neuron. (b) On the left, a diagonal line translates rightward. Again, each line segment illustrates the position of the translating line at a different time. On the right, the rightwardly translating line is viewed through an aperture. Notice that the upward and rightward motions appear to be identical when they are viewed through an aperture that hides the end points of the lines. This so-called aperture problem refers to the fact that the motion of a translating line or grating is ambiguous. This ambiguity arises from the fact that the component of translation parallel to a line's orientation can not be measured unless the real ends of the lines are visible. (c) The intersection of constraints solution to the aperture problem. Because of the aperture problem, the true motion of a line or grating viewed within an aperture could be any one of an infinitely large family of different motion interpretations defined by its constraint line (shown here as a dashed line). The visual system can overcome this ambiguity by considering the motion measurements from two or more differently oriented lines. That is, while the measured motion of a single translating line is consistent with infinitely many interpretations, measurements of differently oriented lines can be combined to uniquely interpret the line motion. This unique solution is defined by the point of intersection of two different constraint lines and is known as the intersection of constraints or IOC solution.

significantly in their spatial frequency or contrast, subjects reported the perception of two independently translating gratings. These results suggest that when overlapping stimuli are structurally similar, the visual system assumes that they belong to the same object, and as a result, their component motions are combined according to the IOC solution (Adelson & Movshon, 1982).

Other researchers have argued that the visual system performs a vector average of the individually ambiguous motion signals (Mingolla, Todd, & Norman, 1992; Wilson, Ferrera, & Yo, 1992). Finally, a third approach to the integration of motion information across space emphasizes the role of image discontinuities (Alais, Wenderoth, & Burke, 1997; Bowns, 1996; Rubin & Hochstein, 1993; Shiffrar, Lichtey, & Heptulla-Chatterjee, 1997; Shiffrar & Lorenceau, 1996; Shiffrar & Pavel, 1991; Wallach, 1976). As described in this next section, this class of theories argues that the visual system determines object motion by tracking the discontinuities in an object's image, such as its corners and line endings. Researchers do not yet agree on what type of motion analysis is actually conducted. It is even possible that the visual system performs competing motion analyses in parallel so that object motion can always be computed even when environmental conditions change the information available in a retinal image (e.g., a foggy evening versus a sunny day).

Neurophysiological evidence suggests that at least some MT neurons may perform an IOC analysis. In collecting this evidence, Movshon and his colleagues began by determining how the responses of MT neurons were tuned to the direction of translating sinusoidal gratings (Movshon et al., 1985). These researchers then examined how these responses to one-dimensional gratings could be used to predict responsiveness to two-dimensional plaid patterns formed by superimposing two one-dimensional gratings (Figure 8.2). One class of neurons responded to the directions of the individual gratings. A second class of neurons, making up approximately 25% of MT neurons, responded maximally to the direction of motion predicted by the intersection of constraints solution. These findings suggest that MT neurons may solve the aperture problem with an IOC approach (for discussion, see Grzywacz & Yuille, 1991).

Role of Image Discontinuities

The above results provide one example of how the visual system might solve the aperture problem for superimposed gratings presented within a single receptive field or region of visual space. Two important aspects of the visual interpretation of object motion remain to be addressed. Firstly, when objects move in the physical world, the visual system must integrate motion signals across disconnected spatial locations. Secondly, real world visual scenes contain objects that have many different features. Such features can produce motion signals of differing degrees of ambiguity. For example, although the motion of a straight edge is ambiguous, the motion of an edge discontinuity, such as a corner or line ending, can be measured with greater certainty (because a discontinuity renders the component of motion parallel to an edge *visible*). Indeed, the evidence below suggests that such discontinuities can determine how image motion is interpreted.

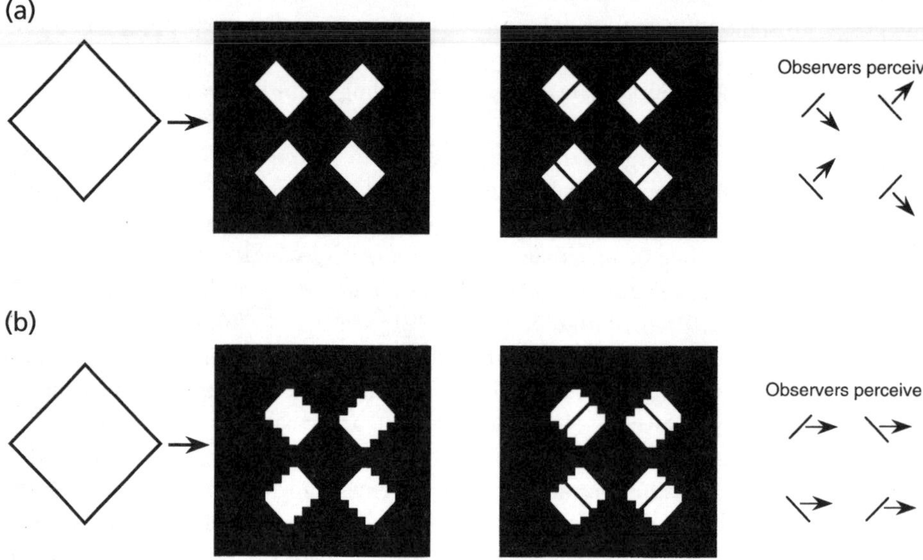

Figure 8.3. (a) A diamond translates rightward behind four rectangular windows. The four visible line segments appear to move in different directions. (b) However, if the shape of the window edges is changed so that positional noise is added to the visible line endings, the same four edges now appear to move coherently.

In one study of the role of image discontinuities in motion perception, subjects viewed simple diamond figures translating behind a set of disconnected apertures, as shown in Figure 8.3a. Each aperture displayed one edge of the diamond. When the diamond moved, its visible edges appeared to move independently of one another and, as a result, subjects could not determine the diamond's direction of motion (Lorenceau & Shiffrar, 1992). However, when the visible ends of these lines were rendered less visible, either through decreasing luminance, peripheral presentation, or the addition of positional noise, the diamond appeared to move as a coherent whole and subjects easily determined its direction of motion, as indicated in Figure 8.3b. Thus, the ends of the lines determined whether the line motion was integrated. Moreover, even when subjects had prior knowledge of the shape and rigidity of the diamond figure, this information was insufficient to promote the integration of motion information across the diamond's edges (Shiffrar & Pavel, 1991). This finding is inconsistent with the hypothesis that the visual system overcomes the aperture problem by assuming that line segments are rigidly connected (e.g., Ullman, 1979).

Corners, another type of image discontinuity, also play a critical role in the interpretation of object motion. For example, motion integration is enhanced when two edges form a corner but inhibited when the same two edges are repositioned so that they form a T-junction (Shiffrar, Lorenceau, & Pavel, 1995). Similarly, when an ambiguously translating edge is positioned so that it is collinear with two unambiguously translating corners, the visual system uses the corner motion to disambiguate the edge motion (Barchilon Ben-Av

& Shiffrar, 1995). Such "motion capture" does not occur when edge collinearity is broken. These findings suggest that the visual system can use structural cues to an object's shape to overcome ambiguities in the object's motion.

Motion Integration Over Time: The Correspondence Problem

In the previous section, we discussed how and why the visual system integrates motion information over space. Because physical motion involves simultaneous changes over space and time, no discussion of motion perception would be complete without a discussion of motion integration over time. The need to integrate motion information over time relates to the assumption made by many models of motion perception that the input to the visual system is a sequential series of snapshots or static retinal images. Given this input, the goal of motion perception then becomes the determination of how the features or objects in each images correspond, or can be tracked, across snapshots. Because it is not obvious how this tracking occurs, this domain of research is referred to as the correspondence problem.

The correspondence problem can be understood in terms of the perception of structure from motion, as indicated in Figure 8.4a. Consider a rotating cylinder that is defined by dots. The image of the 3-D cylinder is projected onto a flat, two-dimensional screen or retina. Even though the structure of the cylinder is defined only by the relative motion of the dots, observers readily interpret the flat projections of these dot displays as a three-dimensional cylinder (Ullman, 1979). If we assume that the visual system processes a series of static images of this display, then somehow the identity of the individual points must be tracked across images. That is, the visual system must be able to determine which dot at Time 1 corresponds to the same dot at Time 2.

Most models of motion perception propose that the visual system solve the correspondence problem by defaulting to a nearest neighbor or shortest path solution (Burt & Sperling, 1981; Ramachandran & Anstis, 1983; Ullman, 1979). This approach is based on the assumption that radical changes in object position or motion are unusual. As a result, if two points have the same or similar locations over time, then these points must correspond to the same object. You may have already noticed an example of the nearest neighbor solution if you have observed that the wagon wheels in TV Westerns sometimes appear to rotate backwards. This occurs because the film consists of a series of static images (see the Apparent Motion section). Because the spokes on the wagon wheels all appear to be identical, the visual system solves the correspondence problem by assuming that any spoke in one frame corresponds to the nearest spoke in the subsequent frame. If the wheel rolls quickly compared to the rate of the images in the film, the nearest spoke may be in the direction opposite to the actual motion of the wheel. As a result, the wheel appears to rotate backwards.

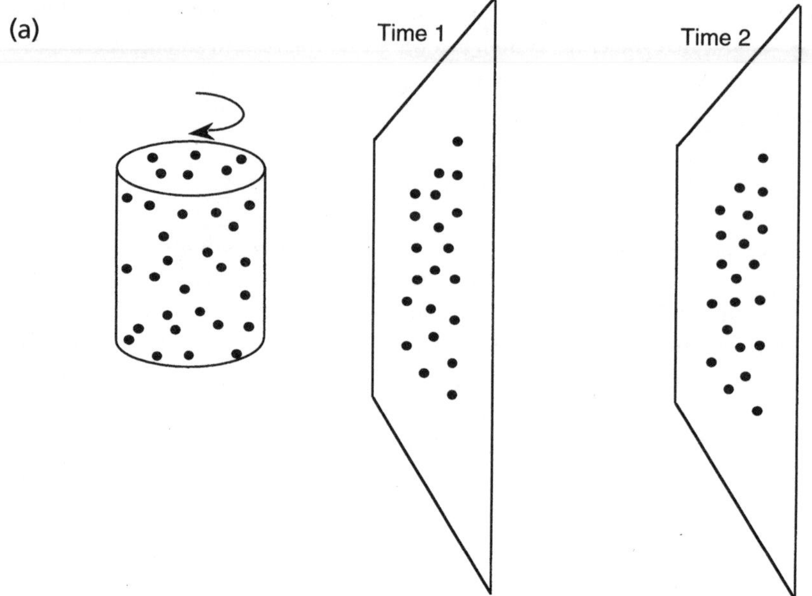

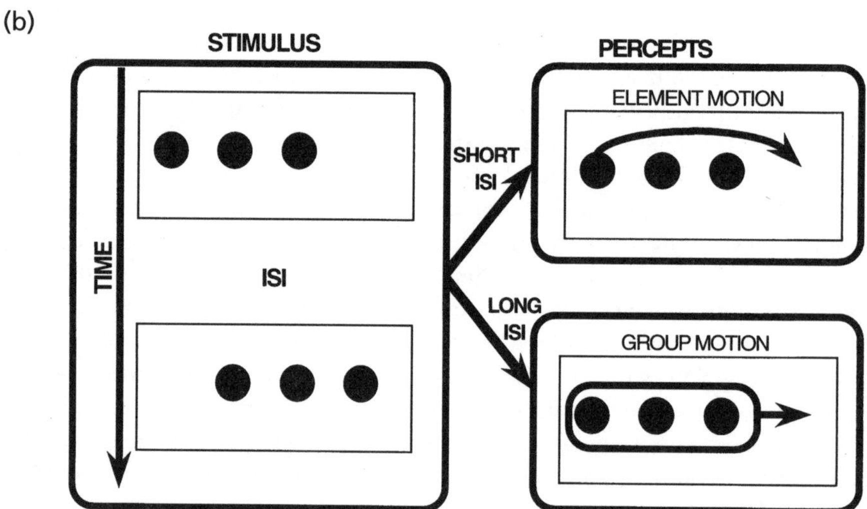

Figure 8.4. (a) The correspondence problem. The structure of a rotating cylinder can be perceptually defined from the relative motion of the cylinder's dots. However, this requires that the visual system can find a correspondence, or keep track of, individual dots over time. (b) The Ternus display. Element motion is perceived when the displays are rapidly presented (at short ISIs). Group motion is perceived when the displays are presented more slowly (at long ISIs).

Making Sense of Ambiguous Motion Information

In each of the previous sections concerning motion measurement, we have seen that the visual system is confronted with ambiguous information. In the following sections, we will examine how the visual system makes sense of such ambiguous information in the interpretation of object motion.

Apparent Motion

The phenomenon known as apparent motion represents an excellent example of the constructive nature of motion perception. Relatedly, apparent motion has played a critical role in the development of the perceptual sciences. During a 1910 train trip, Max Wertheimer developed some fundamentally important hypotheses about the perception of visual motion while watching some alternating lights on a railway signal (Ash, 1995). The resultant paper is traditionally cited as the founding moment of Gestalt psychology (Wertheimer, 1912). In this article, Wertheimer put forth the principle that perceptual processes are holistic because they differ significantly from the simple addition of low-level sensations. This principle was based on his observation that, although the railway signal consisted of stationary lights flashing in alternation, the lights gave rise to the perception of a single moving light. This perception of motion could not have been algebraically constructed from the stimulus array – it was something more.

If you have ever played with an old-fashioned flip book, you may have already noticed that sequentially presented static pictures can give rise to the perception of smooth motion. Whether we perceive apparent motion depends on how rapidly the images are presented as well as on the distance between figures within each image. For example, if the sequential presentation of a pair of dots is separated in time by approximately 30 msec or less, observers perceive two flashing dots rather than one moving dot. Good apparent motion requires that the amount of time between the presentation of the two images be approximately 50 to 250 msec (Braddick, 1980). If the delay between two briefly presented images is greater than 300 msec, the perception of motion tends to be replaced by the perception of slowly flashed individual pictures. These temporal windows should not be taken as fixed values because it has long been known that the temporal window for the perception of apparent motion is strongly influenced by the complexity of the display (DeSilva, 1926). Indeed, apparent motion can be seen with temporal gaps as long as 500 msec (Mather, 1988; Shiffrar & Freyd, 1990).

Short and Long Range

According to classic theories, the visual perception of apparent motion depends upon the activity of two different mechanisms (Anstis, 1980; Braddick, 1980). A short-range mechanism is thought to interpret objects separated by small differences in space and time. This short-range system may be related to very early levels of motion processing, possibly as early as directionally selective neurons in the primary visual cortex. A separate, long-range apparent motion system is thought to integrate information across larger spatio-temporal separations.

Studies of the Ternus (1926) display, shown in Figure 8.4b, have been used to illustrate the difference between short-range and long-range motion processes. The display contains only two frames. In the first frame, three small dots are positioned on the left side of the display. The second frame displays the same three dots with their horizontal position shifted rightward so that the two leftmost dots in this frame overlap with the two rightmost dots from the first frame. The two frames are separated by a blank known as the inter-stimulus interval or ISI. When the presentation rate of this sequence is rapid, so the ISI is less than 50 ms, subjects report the perception of two stationary dots and one dot that jumps from end to end. This perception, known as element motion, is thought to reflect activity of the short-range motion system. Conversely, if the display rate is slowed, then subjects perceive all three dots translating horizontally as a group. Long-range motion processes are thought to underlie this perception of group motion (Pantle & Picciano, 1976; Petersik, 1989).

The short- and long-range systems have also been reported to differ in their response to color and ocularity, as well as in their ability to generate motion aftereffects (Anstis, 1980; Braddick, 1980). Because the long-range mechanism is thought to reside in higher levels of the visual system, it is conceived of as a more interpretative mechanism that is sensitive to an observer's prior experience (Jones & Bruner, 1954; Rock, 1983), shadows (Shepard & Zare, 1983), occlusion (Anstis & Ramachandran, 1985), figural rigidity (Gerbino, 1984), size and slant (Mack, Klein, Hill & Palumbo, 1989), orientation (Foster, 1975; Hecht & Proffitt, 1991; McBeath & Shepard, 1989; Proffitt, Gilden, Kaiser & Whelan, 1988), surface characteristics (He & Nakayama, 1994), and kinematic geometry (Shepard, 1984). Thus, the long-range mechanism can be understood as a kind of problem-solving device which takes into account all of the available visual information and generates the most likely interpretation (Sigman & Rock, 1974).

Such evidence supports the existence of two distinct motion processes, but recent studies have challenged the nature of these two processes (Cavanagh, 1991; Cavanagh & Mather, 1989; Petersik, 1989, 1991). One concern is that apparent motion can be perceived over large spatial separations with stimuli that were thought to engage only the short-range system (Bischof & DiLollo, 1990). Long-range apparent motion can also be seen over short distances (Anstis, 1980). As a result of these and other violations of the traditional dichotomy between long- and short-range motion processes, some researchers have proposed a different understanding of motion mechanisms that is based on attentional tracking and image statistics (Cavanagh & Mather, 1989; Cavanagh, 1991; Lu & Sperling, 1995a). These models are summarized below.

First and Second Order

Traditional theories of short- and long-range apparent motion emphasize the importance of spatio-temporal differences in motion displays. Images can also differ in their statistical properties. First order statistics describe the frequency with which particular luminance values appear in an image. Two subregions of an image differ in their first order statistics if their mean luminances differ. For example, a simple, homogeneous luminance edge is a first order stimulus because the edge is defined by two areas each having a different luminance. Second order statistics, on the other hand, refer to differences in contrast or spatial-temporal structure. Thus, if two image regions have the same mean luminance but differ in the spatial or temporal distribution of their luminance values, then these regions can be differentiated on the basis of their second order statistics even though their first order properties are identical. For example, a black and white checkerboard may have the same first order statistics as a middle gray square of the same size but the two displays would have very different second order statistics.

From the point of view of the mammalian visual system, the difference between first and second order images is important because directionally selective neurons (see Area MT section) are responsive to first order images but not to second order images (Cavanagh & Mather, 1989). Nonetheless, the motion of second order images can be seen. Intriguingly, individual neurons in monkey area MT are selective for the direction of first order motion but not for second order motion (O'Keefe & Movshon, 1998). On the other hand, fMRI studies of the human visual cortex suggest that groups of MT neurons are activated by second order motion (Smith, Greenlee, Singh, Kraemer, & Hennig, 1998). Thus, the neurophysiological basis of the visual perception of second order motion remains a matter of debate.

Attentional Modulation

In addition to first and second order mechanisms, some researchers have proposed the existence of a third, attention-based motion mechanism (Cavanagh, 1992; Lu & Sperling, 1995a). Such active motion processes have been studied by asking subjects to attend to a subset of the features in a directionally ambiguous apparent motion display. A directionally ambiguous display is one in which, all things being equal, motion can be seen equally well in two or more different directions. Under conditions of attentional tracking, subjects report that these ambiguous displays yield an unambiguous impression of motion in a single direction (Cavanagh, 1992). Such behavioral results have led to the proposed existence of a motion mechanism within which the motion of attended features is heavily weighted (Lu & Sperling, 1995b).

Taken together, current research illustrates that apparent motion is a highly complex phenomenon that can be understood from a number of different perspectives. Temporal, spatial, and statistical image properties as well as the attentional state of the observer all contribute to the perception of apparent motion.

Motion Aftereffects

In 1834, Addams observed a waterfall in Scotland for several seconds. When he subsequently viewed a rock formation beside the waterfall, he noticed that the rocks appeared to move upwards in the direction opposite to the downward flow of the waterfall (Addams, 1834). Such motion aftereffects, which may have been first documented by Aristotle in 330 BC (Verstraten, 1996), illustrate that our current impression of visual motion depends upon our recent experiences. The strength of a motion aftereffect depends upon the spatial similarity and the temporal separation between the adapting motion display and the stationary, test display (Anstis, Verstraten, & Mather, 1998). The greater the similarity in space and time, the stronger the motion aftereffect. However, as Addams' original description suggests, motion aftereffects can be quite strong even when the adapting and test displays are as different as a waterfall and a rock formation. Motion aftereffects have also been shown to depend upon the perceived rather than the physical direction of the adapting motion (Culham & Cavanagh, 1994), the surrounding motion (Murakami & Shimojo, 1995), and the duration of the adapting stimulus (Hershenson, 1989). Given such complexity, it is perhaps not surprising that the physiological basis of motion aftereffects remains unclear (Anstis et al., 1998).

Compensating for Eye Movements

Motion aftereffects illustrate that we can perceive motion when none is physically present. Research on eye movements focuses on the reverse issue; namely, why does the world appear stationary when our eyes move (Gibson, 1994/1954)? Because our eyes are never fully at rest, images projected on our retinae are constantly in motion. Yet, we perceive the world as a stationary frame of reference. This ability may be related to analyses performed in extrastriate cortex, because bilateral damage to this area can lead to the perception of a moving world (Haarmeier, Thier, Repnow, & Petersen, 1997).

How do the neural processes underlying motion perception distinguish between the motion signals arising from eye movements and those arising from moving visual scenes? Helmholtz (1910) described two now classic mechanisms to disambiguate these signals. In both mechanisms, a signal is sent to the visual cortex which indicates that the eyes are moving. The difference between the two mechanisms concerns the proposed source of this signal. According to one approach, known as the outflow or corollary discharge theory, the signal is sent from the motor cortex. More specifically, whenever the motor system sends a signal to the muscles of the eyes, a copy of that signal is also sent to the visual system. In the second approach, the signal comes directly from eye muscle receptors. That is, this inflow theory suggests that the signals are sent by receptors measuring the forces exerted by the eye muscles to the visual cortex. In both cases, the eye movement signals are then compared with retinal motion signals so that the visual system can determine which motion signals are due to eye movements and which are due to image motion (e.g., von Holst, 1954; see "Connections with other Sensory Systems" for additional discussion).

Another means by which motion analyses compensate for motion signals generated by eye movements involves saccadic suppression. More specifically, whenever we want to study an object of interest, we must bring the image of that object to our fovea. This is accomplished through quick eye movements known as saccades. During these ballistic eye movements, visual sensitivity is significantly reduced (Bridgeman, van der Heijden, & Velichkovsky, 1994). This reduction in sensitivity during saccadic eye movements is known as saccadic suppression. For example, observers are oblivious to large changes in the location of objects in a visual scene if the displacement of those objects occurs during a saccadic eye movement (Bridgeman, Hendry, & Stark, 1975). Thus, by reducing visual signals during eye movements, the visual system can more easily determine object movement independent of the movement signals generated by the eyes themselves.

Furthermore, cognitive experience or probabilistic information about object movement plays an important role in our interpretation of eye movements (Kowler, 1989). For example, motion analyses may simply be based on the assumption that objects move relative to a stationary background (Gibson, 1979).

Event Perception

An event is generally defined as an occurrence that evolves over space and time (e.g., Johansson, von Hofsten, & Jansson, 1980; Proffitt & Kaiser, 1995; Shaw, Flascher, & Mace, 1996). Given the breadth of this definition, one could reasonably argue that it encompasses all of motion perception. However, for primarily historical reasons, event perception has been used to refer to the visual perception of optic flow, human movement, and objects relative to their surround. This convention is respected here. That is, the previous sections focused on relatively low-level aspects of motion perception examined in isolation. In this section, we switch to the discussion of higher-level aspects of motion perception. Namely, how do we perceive complex objects with multiple features moving through realistic environments?

Perception of Object Motion

Outside of the laboratory, visual scenes usually contain multiple objects moving relative to a variably textured background. If human observers are to function successfully within such environments, they must be able to separate each object from its background as well as from other objects. To solve this problem of separating objects from one another, Gestalt psychologists proposed that the visual system uses the law of common fate. This law proposes that image features that move with the same speed and direction probably belong to the same object and, as a result, their motion should be grouped together and analyzed as a whole perceptual unit (Wertheimer, 1923/1937). This similarity-based grouping principle underlies many of the current models of visual motion perception (e.g., Adelson & Movshon, 1982; Sejnowski & Nowlan, 1995).

Studies of motion capture have also been used to understand perceptual grouping. Motion capture refers to a biased motion analysis in which the perceived motion of an image feature is controlled or captured by the velocity of another feature (Ramachandran, 1985; Ramachandran & Cavanagh, 1987). Motion capture relies on numerous factors including spatial separation (Nawrot & Sekuler, 1990; Nakayama & Silverman, 1988) and collinearity (Barchilon Ben-Av & Shiffrar, 1995; Scott-Brown & Heeley, 1995). By considering many different sources of object information, including structural and surface cues, the visual system can perform object specific motion analyses.

Surfaces

In the physical world, objects are defined by their surfaces. Information about surface quality therefore plays a fundamental role in our perception of object motion (Braddick, 1994; Gibson, 1979; He & Nakayama, 1994; Kourtzi & Shiffrar, 2000). Although surfaces can be understood from a variety of different perspectives (Stroll, 1988), we limit our discussion to a subset of their most obvious physical characteristics.

The visual system uses the relative position of two or more surfaces to determine their motion. When objects appear to be moving together along the same perceived depth plane, their motion is interpreted as a coherent whole (DiVita & Rock, 1997). On the other hand, if one surface appears to move behind another surface, their motion is segregated (e.g., Trueswell & Hayhoe, 1993). When one surface moves in front of another surface, parts of the occluded surface become hidden (or deleted) and other parts come into view (or accreted). Such accretion and deletion plays a defining role in the perception of object motion (Gibson, Kaplan, Reynolds, & Wheeler, 1969; Shipley & Kellman, 1994).

The surfaces of an object can be opaque or transparent. A surface appears transparent when it has a luminance that falls in between the luminances of the adjacent image regions and has boundaries that are consistent with the occlusion of another surface (Metelli, 1974; Watanabe & Cavanagh, 1993). Because transparency is related to surface luminance and occlusion, the visual system is thought to use transparency to facilitate surface segmentation (Nakayama, Shimojo & Ramachandran, 1990). Consistent with this, transparency plays an important role in the interpretation of object motion. For example, if transparency cues indicate the presence of two independent surfaces, motion integration is less likely to occur (Stoner, Albright, & Ramachandran, 1990; but see Lindsey & Todd, 1996). Similarly, observers interpret two superimposed random-dot patterns translating in different directions as two transparent surfaces (Mulligan, 1992; van Doorn & Koenderink, 1983). However, motion segmentation only occurs when transparency is defined across relatively large image regions (Qian, Andersen, & Adelson, 1994).

Finally, surfaces cast shadows. These shadows are used, in turn, to interpret surface motion (Kersten, Mamassian, & Knill, 1997). All of these results indicate that motion processes are strongly biased towards the interpretation of objects and object parts. Thus, motion analyses can not be fully understood without taking into consideration the ultimate goal of such analyses – to help observers interact with their environment. The prediction of future events, discussed below, is a key component of this interaction.

Causality

All physical movement is caused by an ensemble of forces in action (for discussion, see Pailhous & Bonnard, 1993). The visual perception of object motion is strongly influenced by this causality. Research on the visual perception of causality was initiated by the classic studies of Albert Michotte (Michotte, 1946/1963). Michotte examined whether and how people interpret the causality of object motion by asking subjects to describe simple films. Several of his studies focused on the interpretations of collisions. For example, Michotte proposed that people directly perceive "launching" when one moving object contacts a second stationary object that is set in motion after a brief delay. More recent research indicates that observers can make fine discriminations between normal and physically impossible collisions (Kaiser & Proffitt, 1987). Furthermore, although Michotte argued that the perception of causality did not depend on experience, subsequent studies have suggested the opposite (Kaiser & Proffitt, 1984). An intriguing bias in the perception of causality is the tendency to attribute intentionality to moving objects, even when those objects are simple geometric figures (Heider & Simmel, 1944). For example, when people view two simple objects, such as a circle and a square, moving relative to one another, they frequently report that one object appears to "chase" the other object.

The importance of causality in the perception of moving objects can also be seen in the phenomenon of representational momentum. That is, our memory for the spatial location of an object is biased in the direction of the object's motion, even when the object is presented statically (Freyd, 1983). For example, when subjects view a picture of a man jumping off of a wall and are asked to remember the man's position, their memory for his position is systematically biased forward in the trajectory of his jump (Freyd & Finke, 1984). Thus, our memory for the location of a moving object depends upon the spatiotemporal characteristics of the movement that caused the object to occupy that particular location (Freyd, 1987). These and other findings (Kourtzi & Shiffrar, 1997, 1999, 2000; Martin et al., 1995) suggest that there is a tight connection between how an object moves and how it is represented in memory.

Wheels

To understand the perception of complex object motions, one must understand relative motion; that is, how motions are interpreted relative to each other and their environment. Such studies have often involved manipulations of wheel motion. When a single light is mounted on the rim of an otherwise invisible wheel, observers perceive the light to follow its actual path of a cycloid (Rubin, 1927; Duncker, 1929/1937). However, if a second light is attached to the hub of the wheel, the light on the rim now appears to move around the hub. Thus, the perception of the rim's motion depends upon whether it can be interpreted relative to another point.

These wheel displays have played a central role in the development of theories of motion perception (Gibson, 1979; Johansson, 1976; Wallach, 1976). An important issue of debate among these theorists concerns whether the motion of the lights relative to one another (relative or object-relative motion) or the motion of the lights relative to the observer (common or observer-relative motion) is extracted first. Subsequent research has suggested that both types of motion are extracted in parallel and minimized (Cutting & Proffitt, 1982). Moreover, each type of motion may be used by the visual system to interpret a different aspect of an event. For example, common motion may be used to determine where an object is moving while relative motion may be used to infer object structure (Proffitt & Cutting, 1980).

Perception of Human Motion

As social animals, humans behave largely in accordance with their interpretations and predictions of the actions of others. If the visual system has evolved so as to be maximally sensitive to those environmental factors upon which our survival depends (Shepard, 1984), then one would expect to find that human observers are particularly sensitive to the movements of humans and other animals. Twenty-five years of research supports this prediction.

Johansson (1973) initiated the systematic study of "biological motion" perception by demonstrating that observers could readily recognize simplified depictions of human locomotion. In a darkened environment, Johansson and his colleagues filmed the movements of individuals with point light sources attached to their major joints, as shown in Figure 8.5a. Observers of the films were rapidly able to identify the movements generated by the point-light-defined actors even though the displays were nearly devoid of form information. Importantly, observers rarely recognize the human form in static displays of these films (Johansson, 1973). Subsequent research has demonstrated that our perception of the human form in such displays is rapid (Johansson, 1976), orientation specific (Bertenthal & Pinto, 1994; Sumi, 1984), tolerates random contrast variations (Ahlström, Blake, & Ahlström, 1997), and extends to the perception of complex actions (Dittrich, 1993), social dispositions (MacArthur & Baron, 1983), gender (Kozlowski & Cutting, 1977, 1978), and sign language (Poizner, Bellugi & Lutes-Driscoll, 1981).

Several psychophysical experiments have suggested that the visual perception of human movement depends upon a spatially global mechanism (e.g., Ahlström et al., 1997; Cutting, Moore, & Morrison, 1988). One approach to this issue involves masked point-light-walker displays, as shown in Figures 8.5b and 8.5c. In this paradigm, observers view displays containing a point-light walker that is masked by the addition of superimposed moving point lights. This mask can be constructed from multiple point-light walkers that are positionally scrambled so that the spatial location of each point is randomized. The size, luminance, and velocity of the points remain unchanged. Thus, the motion of each point in the mask is identical to the motion of one of the points defining the walker. As a result, only the spatially global configuration of the points distinguishes the walker from the mask. The fact that subjects are able to detect the presence as well as the direction of an upright point-light walker "hidden" within such a scrambled walker mask implies that the mechanism underlying the perception of human movement operates over large spatial scales (Bertenthal & Pinto, 1994; Cutting et al., 1988; Pinto & Shiffrar, 1999).

The spatially global analysis of human movement is further supported by studies of the aperture problem. When viewing a walking stick figure through a multiple aperture display, observers readily perceive global human movement. Under identical conditions, however, observers fail to recognize moving non-biological objects and upside-down walkers (Shiffrar et al, 1997). This pattern of results suggests that the visual analysis of human locomotion can extend over a larger or more global spatial area than the visual analysis of other, non-biological motions (Pinto, Zhao, & Shiffrar, 1997; Shiffrar, 1994).

Apparent motion experiments suggest that the perception of human movement extends over long temporal intervals. In one series of experiments, subjects viewed photographs of

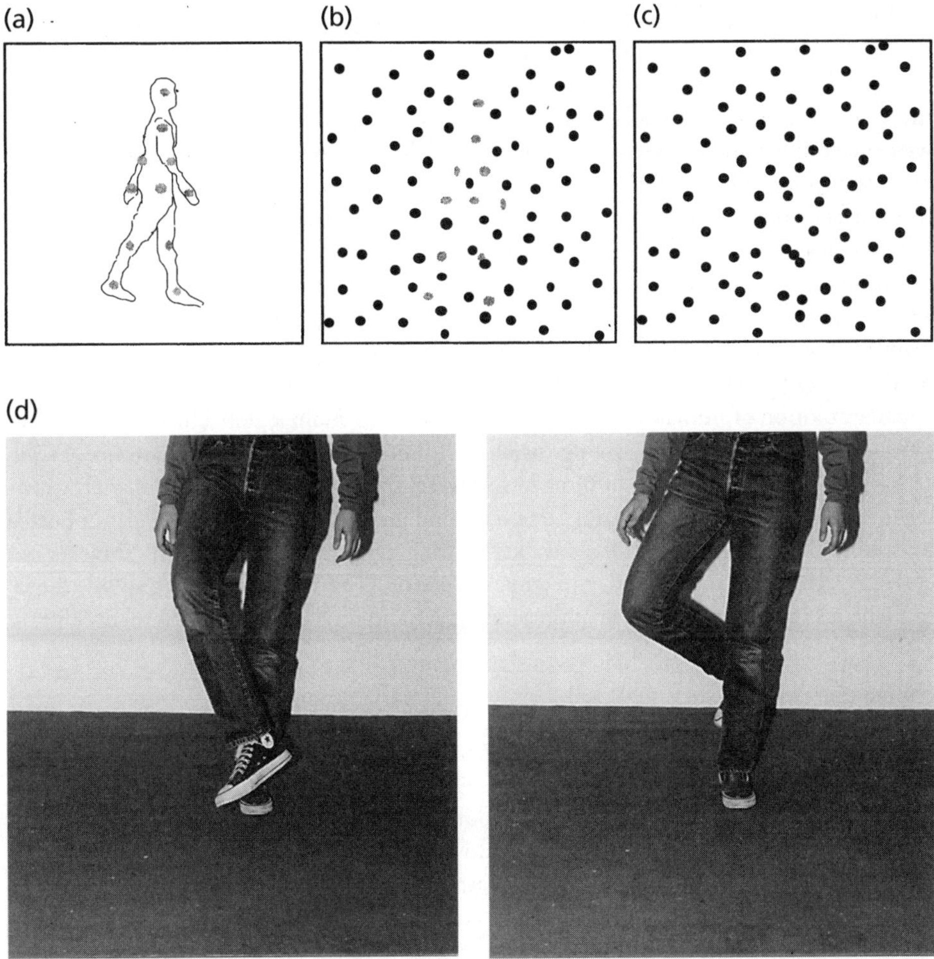

Figure 8.5. (a) A point-light walker. The outline of the walker is not presented during experiments. (b) The walker is placed in a mask of similarly moving points. Here the walker points are shown in gray and the mask points are black. (c) In experiments, the walker and mask points have the same color and luminance. As you can see, when presented statically, the walker is not visible. However, when display C is set in motion, observers can rapidly locate the walker. (d) A sample apparent motion stimulus from Shiffrar and Freyd (1990).

a human model in different positions created so that the biomechanically possible paths of motion conflicted with the shortest possible paths (Shiffrar & Freyd, 1990, 1993). A sample stimulus, shown in Figure 8.5d, consisted of two photographs in which the first displayed a woman with her right leg positioned in front of her left leg and the second showed her right leg bent around and behind her left leg. The shortest path connecting these two leg positions would involve the left leg breaking, and a biomechanically plausible path would entail the right leg rotating around the left leg.

When subjects viewed such stimuli, their perceived paths of motion changed with the stimulus onset asynchrony (SOA) or the amount time between the onset of one photograph and the onset of the next photograph. At short SOAs, subjects reported seeing the shortest, physically impossible motion path. However, with increasing SOAs, observers were increasingly likely to see apparent motion paths consistent with normal human movement (Shiffrar & Freyd, 1990). Conversely, when viewing photographs of inanimate control objects, subjects consistently perceived the same shortest path of apparent motion across increases in SOA. Importantly, when viewing photographs of a human model positioned so that the shortest movement path was a biomechanically plausible path, observers always reported seeing this shortest path (Shiffrar & Freyd, 1993). Thus, subjects do not simply report the perception of longer paths with longer presentation times. Moreover, observers can perceive apparent motion of non-biological objects in a manner similar to apparent motion of human bodies when these objects contain a global hierarchy of orientation and position cues resembling the entire human form (Heptulla-Chatterjee, Freyd, & Shiffrar, 1996). This pattern of results suggests that human movement is analyzed by motion processes that operate over large temporal intervals. This conclusion is supported by studies of a masked point-light walker in long-range apparent motion. Subjects can correctly determine the walker's direction of motion even when this task requires the simultaneous integration of information across space and time (Thornton, Pinto, & Shiffrar, 1998).

Perception of Self Motion

As we walk along any path, the entire retinal image projected on each of our eyes changes. We use such visual motion, known as optic flow, to determine where we are moving within a stationary environment (Gibson, 1950; Warren, 1995). When an observer moves straight ahead while keeping his or her eyes still, this optical flow field contains a radial focus of expansion that specifies the observer's direction of motion. When the eyes move during locomotion, the optic flow becomes more complex as additional motion signals are superimposed on the radial expansion. Nonetheless, observers can easily determine their heading while moving their eyes (Warren & Hannon, 1988). The use of optic flow in the determination of heading can also be generalized from straight to curved paths of locomotion (Warren, Mestre, Blackwell, & Morris, 1991). The manner in which visual motion analyses are actually used to determine heading is a matter of much debate (e.g., Cutting, Springer, Braren, & Johnson, 1992; Koenderink, 1986; Prazdny, 1983).

Studies of the perception of approaching objects, or time to contact, have been used to investigate the coordination between motion perception and action (Gibson, 1950, 1979). The amount of time before an observer collides with an object or an object passes or contacts an observer can be determined from optical information alone. That is, if an observer is correct in assuming that a directly approaching object has a constant velocity and a fixed size, then the time at which the object will collide with the observer can be determined from the angular extent of that object and its rate of change (Lee, 1976, 1980). This temporal variable, known as "tau," is readily calculable because, as a solid object directly approaches an observer, its angular extent increases geometrically. Behavioral evidence suggests that, under some conditions, people can accurately judge an object's time to contact (e.g., Todd, 1981). Moreover, infants readily associate visually expanding images with avoidance behavior (Yonas et al., 1977). Thus, the visual tau of a moving object can be used to control an observer's motor response. Observers may also use tau to control their actions when an approaching object accelerates or approaches at an angle (Bootsma & Oudejans, 1993; Kaiser & Mowafy, 1993; Lee et al., 1983).

The first temporal derivative of tau, known as "tau dot," is thought to control deceleration during braking behavior (Lee, 1976). Observers may use a "constant tau dot" strategy to optimize their rate of deceleration (Kim, Turvey, & Carello, 1993). However, this use of "tau dot" as the sole controlling variable in all braking situations has been challenged (Bardy & Warren, 1997). Instead, these researchers suggest that "tau dot" may be used in different ways in different braking tasks.

Connections With Other Sensory Systems

Visual perception is not a goal unto itself. Motion perception is simply an ability that enables animals to manipulate objects and navigate within their physical environment. It therefore makes little sense to assume that motion analyses are independent of other sensory processes. Instead, the sensory systems must work in concert to provide an animal with the most accurate understanding of its environment. In this section, we briefly describe some of the evidence suggesting that the analysis of visual motion occurs in collaboration with other sensory analyses.

Vestibular System

Bodily sway is important in the maintenance of posture. Optical flow analyses (as briefly described in "Perception of Self Motion") contribute to the control of standing posture (Stoffregen, 1985). Indeed, individuals have trouble correctly orienting their body when optical information is inadequate (Ross, 1974; Stoffregen & Riccio, 1988). People also naturally sway as they walk. Such balance control during locomotion is regulated by visual analyses of motion parallax and radial expansion (Bardy, Warren, & Kay, 1996). Even children under the age of two depend upon optic flow information to control their balance (Stoffregen, Schmückler, & Gibson, 1987).

Motor System

The visual perception of human movement may involve a functional linkage between the perception and production of motor activity (Viviani & Stucchi, 1992; Viviani, Baud-Bovy, & Redolfi, 1997). That is, the perception of human movement may be constrained by an observer's knowledge of or experience with his or her own movement limitations (Shiffrar, 1994; Shiffrar & Freyd, 1990, 1993). Given our extensive visual exposure to people in action, it is possible that this implicit knowledge may be derived solely from visual experience. On the other hand, physiological evidence increasingly suggests that motor experience may be crucial to this visual process. For example, "mirror" neurons in monkey premotor cortex respond both when a monkey performs a particular action and when that monkey observes another monkey or a human performing that same action (Rizzolatti, Fadiga, Gallese, & Fogassi, 1996). Recent imaging data clearly suggest that, in the human, the visual perception of human movement involves both visual and motor processes. That is, when subjects are asked to observe the actions of another human so that they can later imitate those actions, PET activity is found in those brain regions involved in motor planning (Decety et al., 1997). Thus, visual observation of another individual's movement can lead to activation within the motor system of the observer (Stevens, Fonlupt, Shiffrar, & Decety, 2000).

Optic flow can also initiate precise motor activity of the eyes, head, and entire body (Pailhous & Bonnard, 1992). Moreover, experimental manipulations of optic flow while an individual walks on a treadmill can result in systematic changes in the walker's stride length and cadence (Pailhous, Ferrandez, Flückiger, & Baumberger, 1990). Such locomotor changes occur even though the walker has no conscious awareness of them. Thus, there is a very tight linkage between the visual and motor systems.

Auditory System

Some sounds can influence the perception of ambiguous visual motion in a frontoparallel plane (Sekuler, Sekuler, & Lau, 1997). Sound perception can even induce motion perception when no motion is physically present (Shimojo, Miyauchi, & Hikosaka, 1997). These findings can be most easily understood in terms of human action. That is, humans, as all animals, must locate moving objects within their environment. When objects come in contact with each other, sounds are generated by their collision. Because objects can therefore be localized both by sound and visual motion, the visual and auditory systems interact.

Suggested Readings

Bruce, V., Green, P., & Georgeson, M. (1996). *Visual perception: Physiology, psychology, and ecology* (3rd ed.). East Sussex: Psychology Press.

Epstein, W., & Rogers, S. J. (Eds.) (1995). *Perception of space and motion.* Orlando, FL: Academic Press.

Gross, C. G. (1998). *Brain, vision, memory: Tales in the history of neuroscience.* Cambridge, MA: MIT Press.

Landy, M., & Movshon, J. A. (Eds.) (1991). *Computational models of visual processing.* Boston: MIT Press.

Wandell, B. (1995). *Foundations of vision.* Sunderland, MA: Sinauer Associates, Inc.

Zeki, S. (1993). *A vision of the brain.* Oxford: Blackwell Scientific Publications.

Additional Topics

Limits of Motion Sensitivity
Motion perception is limited by the contrast, luminance, spatial and temporal frequencies of an image. The range of conditions under which motion percepts can be successfully computed are thoroughly described in Epstein and Rogers (1995), Nakayama (1995), and Wandell (1995).

Historical Overviews of the Neurophysiological Bases of Motion Perception
Our knowledge of the physiological bases of motion perception depends on both case studies of patients and experimental studies. As can be seen in Gross (1998) and Zeki (1993), our understanding and interpretations of these data are constantly evolving.

References

Addams, R. (1834). An account of a peculiar optical phaenomenon seen after having looked at a moving body. *London and Edinburgh Philosophical Magazine and Journal of Science, 5*, 373–374.

Adelson, E. H., & Bergen, J. R. (1985). Spatiotemporal energy models for the perception of motion. *Journal of the Optical Society of America, A2*, 284–299.

Adelson, E. H. & Movshon, J. A. (1982). Phenomenal coherence of moving visual patterns. *Nature, 300*, 523–525.

Ahlström, V., Blake, R., & Ahlström, U. (1997). Perception of biological motion. *Perception, 26*, 1539–1548.

Alais, D., Wenderoth, P., & Burke, D. (1997). The size and number of plaid blobs mediate the misperception of type-II plaid direction. *Vision Research, 37*, 143–150.

Anstis, S. M. (1980). The perception of apparent movement. *Philosophical Transactions of the Royal Society of London, 290*, 153–168.

Anstis, S., & Ramachandran, V. (1985). Kinetic occlusion by apparent motion. *Perception, 14*, 145–149.

Anstis, S., Verstraten, F., & Mather, G. (1998). The motion aftereffect. *Trends in Cognitive Sciences, 2*, 111–117.

Ash, M. G. (1995). *Gestalt psychology in German culture, 1890–1967: Holism and the quest for objectivity.* Cambridge: Cambridge University Press.

Barchilon Ben-Av, M., & Shiffrar, M. (1995). Disambiguating velocity estimate across image space. *Vision Research, 35*, 2889–2895.

Bardy, B. G., & Warren, W. H. (1997). Visual control of braking in goal-directed action and sport. *Journal of Sports Sciences, 15*, 607–620.

Bardy, B. G., Warren, W. H., & Kay, B. A. (1996). Motion parallax is used to control sway during walking. *Experimental Brain Research, 111*, 271–282.

Beckers, G., & Zeki, S. (1995). The consequences of inactivating areas V1 and V5 on visual motion perception. *Brain, 118*, 49–60.

Bertenthal, B. I., & Pinto, J. (1994). Global processing of biological motions. *Psychological Science, 5*, 221–225.

Bischof, W. F., & DiLollo, V. (1990). Perception of directional sampled motion in relation to displacement and spatial frequency: Evidence for a unitary motion system. *Vision Research, 30*, 1341–1362.

Bonda, E., Petrides, M., Ostry, D., & Evans, A. (1996). Specific involvement of human parietal systems and the amygdala in the perception of biological motion. *Journal of Neuroscience, 16*, 3737–3744.

Bootsma, R. J., & Oudejans, R. R. D. (1993). Visual information about time-to-collision between two objects. *Journal of Experimental Psychology: Human Perception and Performance, 19*, 1041–1052.

Bowns, L. (1996). Evidence for a feature tracking explanation of why type II plaids move in the vector sum direction at short durations. *Vision Research, 36*, 3685–3694.

Braddick, O. J. (1980). Low-level and high-level process in apparent motion. *Philosophical Transactions of the Royal Society of London, 290*, 131–151.

Braddick, O. (1994). Moving on the surface. *Current Biology, 4*, 534–536.

Bradley, D. C., Maxwell, M., Andersen, R. A., Banks, M. S., & Shenoy, K. V. (1996). Mechanisms of heading perception in primate visual cortex. *Science, 273*, 1544–1547.

Bridgeman, B., Hendry, D., & Stark, L. (1975). Failure to detect displacement of the visual world during saccadic eye movements. *Vision Research, 15*, 719–722.

Bridgeman, B., van der Heijden, A. H. C., & Velichkovsky, B. M. (1994). A theory of visual stability across saccadic eye movements. *Behavioral and Brain Sciences, 17*, 247–258.

Britten, K. H., Shadlen, M., Newsome, W. T., & Movshon, J. A. (1992). The analysis of visual motion: A comparison of neuronal and psychophysical performance. *Journal of Neuroscience, 12*, 4745–4765.

Burt, P., & Sperling, G. (1981). Time, distance and feature trade-offs in visual apparent motion. *Psychological Review, 7*, 171–195.

Castet, E., Lorenceau, J., Shiffrar, M., & Bonnet, C. (1993). Perceived speed of moving lines depends on orientation, length, speed and luminance. *Vision Research, 33*, 1921–1936.

Cavanagh, P. (1991). Short-range vs long-range motion: Not a valid distinction. *Spatial Vision, 5*, 303–309.

Cavanagh, P. (1992). Attention based motion perception. *Science, 257*, 1563–1565.

Cavanagh, P., & Mather, G. (1989). Motion: The long and the short of it. *Spatial Vision, 4*, 103–129.

Culham, J. C., & Cavanagh, P. (1994). Motion capture of luminance stimuli by equiluminous color gratings and by attentive tracking. *Vision Research, 34*, 2701–2706.

Cutting, J. E., Moore, C., & Morrison, R. (1988). Masking the motions of human gait. *Perception & Psychophysics, 44*, 339–347.

Cutting, J. E., & Proffitt, D. R. (1982). The minimum principle and the perception of absolute, common, and relative motions. *Cognitive Psychology, 14*, 211–246.

Cutting, J. E., Springer, K., Braren, P. A., & Johnson, S. H. (1992). Wayfinding on foot from information in retinal, not optical, flow. *Journal of Experimental Psychology: General, 121*, 41–72.

Decety, J., Grezes, J., Costes, N., Perani, D., Jeannerod, M., Procyk, E., Grassi, F., & Fazio, F. (1997). Brain activity during observation of actions: Influence of action content and subject's strategy. *Brain, 120*, 1763–1777.

Derrington, A. M., & Lennie, P. (1984). Spatial and temporal contrast sensitivities of neurons in lateral geniculate nucleus of macaque. *Journal of Physiology, 357*, 219–240.

DeSilva, H. R. (1926). An experimental investigation of the determinants of apparent visual motion. *Journal of Experimental Psychology, 37*, 469–501.

Dittrich, W. H. (1993). Action categories and the perception of biological motion. *Perception, 22*, 15–22.

DiVita, J. C., & Rock, I. (1997). A belongingness principle of motion perception. *Journal of Experimental Psychology: Human Perception and Performance, 23*, 1343–1352.

Dubner, R., & Zeki, S. (1971). Response properties and receptive fields of cells in an anatomically defined region of the superior temporal sulcus in the monkey. *Brain Research, 35*, 528–532.

Duncker, K. (1929/1937). Induced motion. In W. D. Ellis (Ed.), *A source book of Gestalt psychology*. New York: Humanities Press.

Dursteller, M. R., & Wurtz, R. H. (1988). Pursuit and optokinetic deficits following lesions of cortical areas MT and MST. *Journal of Neurophysiology, 60*, 940–965.

Epstein, W., & Rogers, S. (1995). *Perception of space and motion*. London: Academic Press.

Foster, D. H. (1975). Visual apparent motion and some preferred paths in the rotation group SO(3). *Biological Cybernetics, 18*, 81–89.

Freyd, J. J. (1983). The mental representation of movement when static stimuli are viewed. *Perception & Psychophysics, 33*, 575–581.
Freyd, J. J. (1987). Dynamic mental representation. *Psychological Review, 94*, 427–438.
Freyd, J. J., & Finke, R. A. (1984). Representational momentum. *Journal of Experimental Psychology: Learning, Memory, and Cognition, 10*, 126–132.
Gerbino, W. (1984). Low-level and high-level processes in the perceptual organization of three-dimensional apparent motion. *Perception, 13*, 417–428.
Gibson, J. J. (1950). *The perception of the visual world.* Boston: Houghton Mifflin.
Gibson, J. J. (1979). *The ecological approach to visual perception.* Boston: Houghton Mifflin.
Gibson, J. J. (1994/1954). The visual perception of objective motion and subjective movement. *Psychological Review, 101*, 318–323.
Gibson, J. J., Kaplan, G. A., Reynolds, H. N., & Wheeler, K. (1969). The change from visible to invisible: A study of optical transitions. *Perception & Psychophysics, 5*, 113–116.
Graziano, M. S. A., Andersen, R. A., & Snowden, R. J. (1994). Tuning of MST neurons to spiral motions. *Journal of Neuroscience, 14*, 54–67.
Gross, C. G. (1998). *Brain, vision, memory: Tales in the history of neuroscience.* Cambridge, MA: MIT Press.
Grzywacz, N. M., & Yuille, A. L. (1991). Theories for the visual perception of local velocity and coherent motion. In M. S. Landy and J. A. Movshon (Eds.), *Computational models of visual processing* (pp. 231–252). Cambridge, MA: MIT Press.
Haarmeier, T., Thier, P., Repnow, M., & Petersen, D. (1997). False perception of motion in a patient who cannot compensate for eye movements. *Nature, 389*, 849–852.
Hawken, M., Parker, A., & Lund, J. (1988). Laminar organization and contrast sensitivity of direction and contrast sensitivity of direction-selective cells in the striate cortex of the Old World Monkey. *Journal of Neuroscience, 10*, 3541–3548.
He, Z. J., & Nakayama, K. (1994). Apparent motion determined by surface layout not by disparity or three-dimensional distance. *Nature, 367*, 173–175.
Hecht, H., & Proffitt, D. R. (1991). Apparent extended body motions in depth. *Journal of Experimental Psychology: Human Perception and Performance, 17*, 1090–1103.
Heider, F., & Simmel, M. (1944). An experimental study of apparent behaviour. *American Journal of Psychology, 57*, 243–259.
Helmholtz, H. von (1910). *Treatise on physiological optics* (Vol. III, J. P. C. Southall (Ed.)). New York: Dover.
Heptulla-Chatterjee, S., Freyd, J., & Shiffrar, M. (1996). Configural processing in the perception of apparent biological motion. *Journal of Experimental Psychology: Human Perception and Performance, 22*, 916–929.
Hershenson, M. (1989). Duration, time constant, and decay of the linear motion aftereffect as a function of inspection duration. *Perception & Psychophysics, 45*, 251–257.
Hildreth, E. (1984). *The measurement of visual motion.* Cambridge, MA: MIT Press.
Hubel, D., & Wiesel, T. (1968). Receptive fields and functional architecture of the monkey striate cortex. *Journal of Physiology, 195*, 215–243.
Johansson, G. (1973). Visual perception of biological motion and a model for its analysis. *Perception & Psychophysics, 14*, 201–211.
Johansson, G. (1976). Spatio-temporal differentiation and integration in visual motion perception. *Psychological Research, 38*, 379–393.
Johansson, G., von Hofsten, C., & Jansson, G. (1980). Event perception. *Annual Review of Psychology, 31*, 27–63.
Jones, E. E., & Bruner, J. S. (1954). Expectancy in apparent visual motion. *British Journal of Psychology, 45*, 157–165.
Kaiser, M. K., & Mowafy, L. (1993). Optical specification of time-to-passage: Observers' sensitivity to global tau. *Journal of Experimental Psychology: Human Perception and Performance, 19*, 194–202.
Kaiser, M. K., & Proffitt, D. R. (1984). The development of sensitivity to causally relevant dynamic

information. *Child Development, 55*, 1614–1624.
Kaiser, M. K., & Proffitt, D. R. (1987). Observers' sensitivity to dynamic anomalies in collisions. *Perception & Psychophysics, 42*, 275–280.
Kersten, D., Mamassian, P., & Knill, D. C. (1997). Moving cast shadows induce apparent motion in depth. *Perception, 26*, 171–192.
Kim, N.-G., Turvey, M. T., & Carello, C. (1993). Optical severity of upcoming contacts. *Journal of Experimental Psychology: Human Perception and Performance, 19*, 179–193.
Koenderink J. J. (1986). Optic flow. *Vision Research, 26*, 161–179.
Koffka, K. (1935). *Principles of Gestalt psychology*. New York: Harcourt, Brace.
Kourtzi, Z., & Shiffrar, M. (1997). One-shot view-invariance in a moving world. *Psychological Science, 8*, 461–466.
Kourtzi, Z., & Shiffrar, M. (1999). The representation of three-dimensional, rotating objects. *Acta Psychologica: A Special Issue on Object Perception & Memory, 102*, 265–292.
Kourtzi, Z., & Shiffrar, M. (2000). The visual representation of non-rigidly moving objects. *Journal of Experimental Psychology: Human Perception and Performance*, under review.
Kowler, E. (1989). Cognitive expectations, not habits, control anticipatory smooth oculomotor pursuit. *Vision Research, 29*, 1049–1058.
Kozlowski, L. T., & Cutting, J. E. (1977). Recognizing the sex of a walker from a dynamic point-light display. *Perception & Psychophysics, 21*, 575–580.
Kozlowski, L. T., & Cutting, J. E. (1978). Recognizing the sex of a walker from point-lights mounted on ankles: Some second thoughts. *Perception & Psychophysics, 23*, 459.
Lee, D. N. (1976). A theory of visual control of braking based on information about time-to-collision. *Perception, 5*, 437–459.
Lee, D. N. (1980). Visuo-motor coordination in space-time. In G. E. Stelmach & J. Requin (Eds.), *Tutorials in motor behavior* (pp. 281–293). Amsterdam: North-Holland.
Lee, D. N., Young, D. S., Reddish, P. E., Lough, S., & Clayton, T. M. H. (1983). Visual timing in hitting an accelerating ball. *Quarterly Journal of Experimental Psychology, 35*, 333–346.
Lindsey, D. T., & Todd, J. T. (1996). On the relative contributions of motion energy and transparency to the perception of moving plaids. *Vision Research, 36*, 207–222.
Livingstone, M., & Hubel, D. (1988). Segregation of form, color, movement, and depth: Anatomy, physiology, and perception. *Science, 240*, 740–749.
Lorenceau, J., & Shiffrar, M. (1992). The role of terminators in motion integration across contours. *Vision Research, 32*, 263–273.
Lu, Z.-L., & Sperling, G. (1995a). Attention-generated apparent motion. *Nature, 377*, 237–239.
Lu, Z.-L., & Sperling, G. (1995b). The functional architecture of human visual motion perception. *Vision Research, 35*, 2697–2722.
MacArthur, L. Z., & Baron, M. K. (1983). Toward an ecological theory of social perception. *Psychological Review, 90*, 215–238.
Mack, A., Klein, L., Hill, J., & Palumbo, D. (1989). Apparent motion: Evidence of the influence of shape, slant, and size on the correspondence process. *Perception & Psychophysics, 46*, 201–206.
Martin, A., Haxby, J.V., Lalonde, F. M., Wiggs, C. L., & Ungerleider, L. G. (1995). Discrete cortical regions associated with knowledge of color and knowledge of action. *Science, 270*, 102–105.
Mather, G. (1988). Temporal properties of apparent motion in subjective figures. *Perception, 17*, 729–736.
Maunsell, J. H. R., & Newsome, W. T. (1987). Visual processing in monkey extrastriate cortex. *Annual Review of Neuroscience, 10*, 363–401.
McBeath, M. K., & Shepard, R. N. (1989). Apparent motion between shapes differing in location and orientation: A window technique for estimating path curvature. *Perception & Psychophysics, 46*, 333–337.
Merigan, W. H., & Maunsell, J. H. R. (1993). How parallel are the primate visual pathways? *Annual Review of Neuroscience, 16*, 369–402.
Metelli, F. (1974). The perception of transparency. *Scientific American, 230*, 90–98.

Michotte, A. (1946/1963). *The perception of causality.* London: Methuen. (Originally published in French in 1946.)
Mingolla, E., Todd, J., & Norman, J. F. (1992). The perception of globally coherent motion. *Vision Research, 32,* 1015–1031.
Movshon, J. A., Adelson, E. H., Gizzi, M. S., & Newsome, W. T. (1985). The analysis of moving visual patterns. In C. Chagas, R. Gattas, & C. G. Gross (Eds.), *Pattern recognition mechanisms* (pp. 117–151). Rome: Vatican Press.
Movshon, J. A., & Newsome, W. T. (1996). Visual response properties of striate cortical neurons projecting to area MT in macaque monkeys. *Journal of Neuroscience, 16,* 7733–7741.
Mulligan, J. B. (1992). Nonlinear combination rules and the perception of visual motion transparency. *Vision Research, 33,* 2021–2030.
Murakami, I., & Shimojo, S. (1995). Modulation of motion aftereffect by surround motion and its dependence on stimulus size and eccentricity. *Vision Research, 35,* 1835–1844.
Nakayama, K. (1995). Biological image motion processing: A review. *Vision Research, 25,* 625–660.
Nakayama, K., Shimojo, S., & Ramachandran, V. (1990). Transparency: Relation to depth, subjective contours, and neon color spreading. *Perception, 19,* 497–513.
Nakayama, K., & Silverman, G. (1988). The aperture problem II: Spatial integration of velocity information along contours. *Vision Research, 28,* 747–753.
Nakayama, K., & Tyler, C. (1981). Psychophysical isolation of movement sensitivity by removal of familiar position cues. *Vision Research, 21,* 427–433.
Nawrot, M., & Sekuler, R. (1990). Assimilation and contrast in motion perception: Explorations in cooperativity. *Vision Research, 30,* 1439–1451.
Newsome, W. T., Britten, K. H., & Movshon, J. A. (1989). Neural correlates of a perceptual decision. *Nature, 341,* 52–54.
O'Craven, K. M., Rosen, B. R., Kwong, K.K., Treisman, A., & Savoy, R. L. (1997). Voluntary attention modulates fMRI activity in human MT-MST. *Neuron, 18,* 591–598.
O'Keefe, L. P., & Movshon, J. A. (1998). Processing of first- and second-order motion signals by neurons in area MT of the macaque monkey. *Visual Neuroscience, 15,* 305–317.
Oram, M., & Perrett, D. (1994). Responses of anterior superior temporal polysensory (STPa) neurons to "biological motion" stimuli. *Journal of Cognitive Neuroscience, 6,* 99–116.
Pailhous, J., & Bonnard, M. (1992). Locomotor automatism and visual feedback. In L. Proteau and D. Elliott (Eds.), *Vision and motor control.* London: Elsevier Science Publishers.
Pailhous, J., & Bonnard, M. (1993). L'espace locomoteur: Intégration sensorimotrice et cognitive. In *Le Corps en jeu* (pp. 33–38). Paris: Editions du CNRS, Collection Art du Spectacle.
Pailhous, J., Ferrandez, A. M., Flückiger, M., & Baumberger, B. (1990). Unintentional modulations of human gait by optical flow. *Behavioral and Brain Research, 38,* 275–281.
Pantle, A. J., & Picciano, L. (1976). A multistable movement display: Evidence for two separate motion systems in human vision. *Science, 193,* 500–502.
Perrett, D., Harries, M., Mistlin, A. J., & Chitty, A. J. (1990). Three stages in the classification of body movements by visual neurons. In H. B. Barlow, C. Blakemore, & M. Weston-Smith (Eds.), *Images and understanding* (pp. 94–107). Cambridge, UK: Cambridge University Press.
Petersik, J. T. (1989). The two process distinction in apparent motion. *Psychological Bulletin, 106,* 107–127.
Petersik, J. T. (1991). Comments on Cavanagh & Mather (1989): Coming up short (and long). *Spatial Vision, 5,* 291–301.
Pinto, J., & Shiffrar, M. (1999). Subconfigurations of the human form in the perception of biological motion displays. *Acta Psychologica: A Special Issue on Object Perception & Memory, 102,* 293–318.
Pinto, J., Zhao, Z., & Shiffrar, M. (May, 1997). What is biological motion? Part 2: Generalization to non-human animal forms. *Association for Research in Vision and Ophthalmology,* Ft. Lauderdale, FL.
Poizner, H., Bellugi, U., & Lutes-Driscoll, V. (1981). Perception of American Sign Language in dynamic point-light displays. *Journal of Experimental Psychology: Human Perception and Perform-*

ance, 7, 430–440.
Prazdny, K. (1983). On the information in optical flows. *Computer Vision, Graphics, and Image Processing, 22*, 239–259.
Proffitt, D. R., & Cutting, J. E. (1980). An invariant for wheel-generated motions and the logic of its determination. *Perception, 9*, 435–449.
Proffitt, D. R., Gilden, D. L., Kaiser, M. K., & Whelan, S. M. (1988). The effect of configural orientation on perceived trajectory in apparent motion. *Perception and Psychophysics, 43*, 465–474.
Proffitt, D. R., & Kaiser, M. K. (1995). Perceiving events. In W. Epstein and S. Rogers (Eds.), *Perception of space and motion*. London: Academic Press.
Qian, N., Andersen, R.A., & Adelson, E. H. (1994). Transparent motion perception as detection of unbalanced motion signals. I. Psychophysics. *Journal of Neurosciences, 14*, 7357–7366.
Ramachandran, V. S. (1985). Apparent motion of subjective surfaces. *Perception, 14*, 127–134.
Ramachandran, V. S., & Anstis, S. M. (1983). Perceptual organization in moving displays. *Nature, 304*, 529–531.
Ramachandran, V. S., & Cavanagh, P. (1987). Motion capture anisotropy. *Vision Research, 27*, 97–106.
Reichardt, W. (1969). Movement perception in insects. In W. Reichardt (Ed.), *Processing of optical data by organisms and by machines*. New York: Academic Press.
Rizzolatti, G., Fadiga, L., Gallese, V., & Fogassi, L. (1996). Premotor cortex and the recognition of motor actions. *Cognitive Brain Research, 3*, 131–141.
Rock, I. (1983). *The logic of perception*. Cambridge, MA.: Bradford Books/MIT Press.
Ross, H. E. (1974). *Behavior and perception in strange environments*. New York: Basic Books.
Rubin, E. (1927). Visuell wahrgenommene wirkliche Bewegungen. *Zeitschrift für Psychologie, 103*, 384–392.
Rubin, N., & Hochstein, S. (1993). Isolating the effect of one-dimensional motion signals on the perceived direction of two-dimensional objects. *Vision Research, 33*, 1385–1396.
Salzman, C. D., Britten, K. H., & Newsome, W. T. (1990). Cortical microstimulation influences perceptual judgments of motion direction. *Nature, 346*, 174–177.
Salzman, C. D., Murasugi, C. M., Britten, K. H., & Newsome, W. T. (1992). Microstimulation of visual area MT: Effects on direction discrimination performance. *Journal of Neuroscience, 12*, 2331–2355.
Scott-Brown, K. C., & Heeley, D. W. (1995). Topological arrangement affects the perceived speed of tilted lines in horizontal translation. *Investigative Ophthalmology and Visual Science, 36*, 261.
Sejnowski, T., & Nowlan, S. (1995). A model of visual motion processing in area MT of primates. In M. S. Gazzaniga (Ed.), *The cognitive neurosciences* (pp. 437–450). Cambridge, MA: MIT Press.
Sekuler, R., Sekuler, A. B., & Lau, R. (1997). Sound alters visual motion perception. *Nature, 385*, 308.
Shapley, R. (1995). Parallel neural pathways and visual function. In M. S. Gazzaniga (Ed.), *The cognitive neurosciences* (pp. 315–324). Cambridge: MIT Press.
Shapley, R., Kaplan, E., & Soodak, R. (1981). Spatial summation and contrast sensitivity of X and Y cells in the lateral geniculate nucleus of the macaque. *Nature, 292*, 543–545.
Shaw, R. E., Flascher, O. M., & Mace, W. M. (1996). Dimensions of event perception. In W. Prinz and B. Bridgeman (Eds.), *Handbook of perception and action: Volume 1* (pp. 345–395). London: Academic Press.
Shepard, R. N. (1984). Ecological constraints on internal representation: Resonant kinematics of perceiving, imagining, thinking, and dreaming. *Psychological Review, 91*, 417–447.
Shepard, R. N., & Zare, S. (1983). Path guided apparent motion. *Science, 220*, 632–634.
Shiffrar, M. (1994). When what meets where. *Current Directions in Psychological Science, 3*, 96–100.
Shiffrar, M., & Freyd, J. J. (1990). Apparent motion of the human body. *Psychological Science, 1*, 257–264.
Shiffrar, M., & Freyd, J. J. (1993). Timing and apparent motion path choice with human body photographs. *Psychological Science, 4*, 379–384.

Shiffrar, M., Lichtey, L., & Heptulla-Chatterjee, S. (1997). The perception of biological motion across apertures. *Perception & Psychophysics, 59,* 51–59.

Shiffrar, M., & Lorenceau, J. (1996). Improved motion linking across edges at decreased luminance contrast, edge width and duration. *Vision Research, 36,* 2061–2067.

Shiffrar, M., Lorenceau, J., & Pavel, M. (May, 1995). What is a corner? *Association for Research in Vision and Ophthalmology,* Ft. Lauderdale, FL.

Shiffrar, M., & Pavel, M. (1991). Percepts of rigid motion within and across apertures. *Journal of Experimental Psychology: Human Perception and Performance, 17,* 749–761.

Shimojo, S., Miyauchi, S., & Hikosaka, O. (1997). Visual motion sensation yielded by non-visually driven attention. *Vision Research, 37,* 1575–1580.

Shipley, T. F., & Kellman, P. J. (1994). Spatiotemporal boundary formation: Boundary, form, and motion perception from transformations of surface elements. *Journal of Experimental Psychology: General, 123,* 3–20.

Shipp, S., deJong, B. M., Zihl, J., Frackowiak, R. S. J., & Zeki, S. (1994). The brain activity related to residual activity in a patient with bilateral lesions of V5. *Brain, 117,* 1023–1038.

Siegel, R., & Anderson, R. A. (1988). Perception of three-dimensional structure from visual motion in monkey and humans. *Nature, 331,* 259–261.

Sigman, E., & Rock, I. (1974). Stroboscopic movement based on perceptual intelligence. *Perception, 3,* 9–28.

Silveira, L., & Perry, V. (1991). The topography of magnocellular projecting ganglion cells in the primate retina. *Neuroscience, 40,* 217–237.

Smith, A. T., Greenlee, M. W., Singh, K. D., Kraemer, F. M., & Hennig, J. (1998). The processing of first- and second-order motion in human visual cortex assessed by functional magnetic resonance imaging (fMRI). *Journal of Neuroscience, 18,* 3816– 3830.

Stevens, J., Fonlupt, P., Shiffrar, M., & Decety, J. (2000). New aspects of motion perception: Selective neural encoding for apparent human movements. *Neuroreport, 11,* 109–115.

Stoffregen, T. A. (1985). Flow structure versus retinal location in the optical control of stance. *Journal of Experimental Psychology: Human Perception and Performance, 11,* 554–565.

Stoffregen, T. A., & Riccio, G. (1988). An ecological theory of orientation and the vestibular system. *Psychological Review, 95,* 3–14.

Stoffregen, T. A., Schmückler, M. A., & Gibson, E. J. (1987). Use of central and peripheral optic flow in stance and locomotion in young walkers. *Perception, 16,* 121–133.

Stone, L. S., & Thompson, P. (1992). Human speed perception is contrast dependent. *Vision Research, 32,* 1535–1549.

Stoner, G. R., Albright, T. D., & Ramachandran, V. S. (1990). Transparency and coherence in human motion perception. *Nature, 334,* 153–155.

Stroll, A. (1988). *Surfaces.* Minneapolis: University of Minnesota Press.

Sumi, S. (1984). Upside-down presentation of the Johansson moving light-spot pattern. *Perception, 13,* 283–286.

Tanaka, K., Fukada, Y., & Saito, H. (1989). Underlying mechanisms of the response specificity of expansion/contraction and rotation cells in the dorsal part of the medial superior temporal area of the macaque monkey. *Journal of Neurophysiology, 62,* 642–656.

Ternus, J. (1926). Experimentelle Untersuchungen über phänomenale Identität. *Psychologische Forschung, 7,* 71–126.

Thornton, I., Pinto, J., & Shiffrar, M. (1998). The visual perception of human locomotion. *Cognitive Neuropsychology, 15,* 535–552.

Todd, J. T. (1981). Visual information about moving objects. *Journal of Experimental Psychology: Human Perception and Performance, 7,* 795–810.

Tootell, R. B. H., Reppas, J. B., Dale, A. M., Look, R. B., Sereno, M. I., Malach, R., Brady, T. J., & Rosen, B. R. (1995). Visual motion aftereffect in human cortical area MT revealed by functional magnetic resonance imaging. *Nature, 375,* 139–141.

Treue, S., & Maunsell, J. H. (1996). Attentional modulation of visual motion processing in cortical areas MT and MST. *Nature, 382,* 539.

Trueswell, J. & Hayhoe, M. (1993). Surface segmentation mechanisms and motion perception. *Vision Research, 33,* 313–328.

Ullman, S. (1979). *The interpretation of visual motion.* Cambridge, MA: MIT Press.

Vaina, L., Lemay, M., Bienfang, D., Choi, A., & Nakayama, K. (1990). Intact "biological motion" and "structure from motion" perception in a patient with impaired motion mechanisms: A case study. *Visual Neuroscience, 5,* 353–369.

van Doorn, A. J., & Koenderink, J. J. (1983). Detectability of velocity gradients in moving random-dot patterns. *Vision Research, 23,* 799–804.

van Santen, J. P. H., & Sperling, G. (1984). Temporal covariance model of human motion perception. *Journal of the Optical Society of America, A1,* 451–473.

Verstraten. F. A. (1996). On the ancient history of the direction of the motion aftereffect. *Perception, 25,* 1177–1187.

Viviani, P., Baud-Bovy, G., & Redolfi, M. (1997). Perceiving and tracking kinesthetic stimuli: Further evidence of motor-perceptual interactions. *Journal of Experimental Psychology: Human Perception and Performance, 23,* 1232–1252.

Viviani, P. & Stucchi, N. (1992). Biological movements look constant: Evidence of motor- perceptual interactions. *Journal of Experimental Psychology: Human Perception and Performance, 18,* 603–623.

von Holst, E. (1954). Relations between the central nervous system and the peripheral organs. *British Journal of Animal Behaviour, 2,* 89–94.

Wallach, H. (1935). Über visuell wahrgenommene Bewegungsrichtung. *Psychologische Forschung, 20,* 325–380.

Wallach, H. (1976). On perceived identity: I. The direction of motion of straight lines. In H. Wallach (Ed.), *On perception* (pp. 201–216). New York: Quadrangle, The New York Times Book Co.

Walsh, V., Ellison, A., Battelli, L., & Cowey, A. (1998). Task specific impairments and enhancements induced by magnetic stimulation of human visual area V5. *Proceedings of the Royal Society of London, Series B, 265,* 537–543.

Wandell, B. A. (1995). *Foundations of vision.* Sunderland, MA: Sinauer.

Warren, W. H. (1995). Self-motion: Visual perception and visual control. In W. Epstein and S. J. Rogers (Eds.), *Perception of space and motion.* Orlando: Academic Press.

Warren, W. H., & Hannon, D. J. (1988). Direction of self-motion is perceived from optical flow. *Nature, 336,* 162–163.

Warren, W. H., Mestre, D. R., Blackwell, A. W., & Morris, M. W. (1991). Perception of circular heading from optical flow. *Journal of Experimental Psychology: Human Perception and Performance, 17,* 28–43.

Watanabe, T. & Cavanagh, P. (1993). Transparent surfaces defined by implicit X junctions. *Vision Research, 33,* 2339–2346.

Watson, A. B., & Ahumada, A. J. (1985). Model of human visual-motion sensing. *Journal of the Optical Society of America, A2,* 322–341.

Wertheimer, M. (1912/1961). Experimental studies on the seeing of motion. In T. Shipley (Trans. and Ed.), *Classics in psychology* (pp. 1032–1088). New York: Philosophical Library.

Wertheimer, M. (1923/1937). Laws of organization in perceptual forms. In W. D. Ellis (Ed.), *A source-book in Gestalt psychology.* London: Routledge & Kegan Paul.

Wilson, H., Ferrera, V., & Yo, C. (1992). A psychophysically motivated model for two- dimensional motion perception. *Visual Neuroscience, 9,* 79–97.

Wurtz, R. H., Goldberg, M. E., & Robinson, D. L. (1982). Brain mechanisms of visual attention. *Scientific American, 244,* 124–135.

Yamasaki, D. S., & Wurtz, R. H. (1991). Recovery of function after lesions in the superior temporal sulcus in the monkey. *Journal of Neurophysiology, 66,* 651–673.

Yonas, A., Bechtold, A. G., Frankel, D., Gordon, F. R., McRoberts, G., Norcia, A., & Sternfels, S. (1977). Development of sensitivity to information for impending collisions. *Perception & Psychophysics, 21,* 97–104.

Zeki, S. (1993). *A vision of the brain.* Oxford: Blackwell Scientific Publications.
Zeki, S., Watson, J. D., Lueck C. J., Friston, K. J., Kennard, C., & Frackowiak R. S. (1991). A direct demonstration of functional specialization in human visual cortex. *Journal of Neuroscience, 11,* 641–649.
Zeki, S., Watson, J. D., & Frackowiak, R. S. (1993). Going beyond the information given: The relation of illusory visual motion to brain activity. *Proceedings of the Royal Society of London Series B, 252,* 215–222.
Zihl, J., von Cramon, D., & Mai, N. (1983). Selective disturbance of movement vision after bilateral brain disturbance. *Brain, 106,* 313–340.

Chapter Nine

Visual Attention

Marvin M. Chun and Jeremy M. Wolfe

What you see is determined by what you attend to. At any given time, the environment presents far more perceptual information than can be effectively processed. Visual attention allows people to select the information that is most relevant to ongoing behavior. The study of visual attention is relevant to any situation in which actions are based on visual information from the environment. For instance, driving safety critically depends on people's ability to detect and monitor stop signs, traffic lights, and other cars. Efficient and reliable attentional selection is critical because these various cues appear amidst a cluttered mosaic of other features, objects, and events. Complexity and information overload characterize almost every visual environment, including, but not limited to, such critical examples as airplane cockpits or nuclear power plant operation rooms.

To cope with this potential overload, the brain is equipped with a variety of attentional mechanisms. These serve two critical roles. First, attention can be used to select behaviorally relevant information and/or to ignore the irrelevant or interfering information. In other words, you are only aware of attended visual events. Second, attention can modulate or enhance this selected information according to the state and goals of the perceiver. With attention, the perceivers are more than passive receivers of information. They become active seekers and processors of information, able to interact intelligently with their environment.

The study of attention can be organized around any one of a variety of themes. In this chapter, we will concentrate on mechanisms and consequences of selection and attentional deployment across space and over time. Our review on spatial and temporal attention will consider theoretical, behavioral, and neurophysiological work. Our survey of the consequences of selection includes the effects of attention on perceptual performance, neurophysiological activity, memory, and visual awareness.

Selection

Given that perceptual systems cannot process all of the available information, how do such systems go about selecting a subset of the input? At the most basic level, a distinction can be made between active and passive selection. A sponge, thrown into a pool of water, is a passive selector. It cannot soak up all the water; it will soak up some water, and selection will be based on no principle other than proximity. The front end of a sensory system acts as a type of passive selector, admitting some stimuli and not others. Thus, the eye admits as "light" only a narrow segment of the electromagnetic spectrum. Further, essentially passive, selection continues beyond the receptors. For instance, high-resolution information about the retinal image is preserved only at the center of gaze. But even with these acts of passive selection, the visual system is still faced with far too much information (Broadbent, 1958). Our topic truly begins with the system's active efforts to select.

Active selection might occur early or late in processing. Four decades ago, this was presented as a dichotomous choice. Broadbent (1958) advocated filtering of irrelevant sensory information based on physical attributes such as location. A strong version of this *early-selection* theory posits that unattended, filtered information is not processed beyond its initial physical attributes. The alternative, *late-selection* view held that selection occurs only after categorization and semantic analysis of all input has occurred (Deutsch & Deutsch, 1963; Duncan, 1980). Intermediate views include *attenuation theory* which proposes that rejected information is attenuated rather than completely filtered or completely identified (Treisman, 1960). Pashler's (1998) review of the extensive literature to date suggests that unattended information is not completely filtered, but it is not processed to the same degree as attended information either.

Indeed, it is probably time to move away from this debate. Our review will reveal that attention is not a singular thing with a single locus, early or late. Rather, it is a multifaceted term referring to a number of different acts and loci of selection.

Spatial Attention: Visual Selection and Deployment Over Space

The Attentional Spotlight and Spatial Cueing

Active attentional selection occurs over space and time. Spatial selection studies typically have subjects focus attention on a subset of the spatial array, allowing for selective report of information at the focus of attention (Averbach & Coriell, 1961; Eriksen & Hoffman, 1973; Sperling, 1960). The spotlight has been a favorite metaphor for spatial attention because it captures some of the introspective phenomenology of attention – the feeling that attention can be deployed, like a beam of mental light, to reveal what was hidden in the world (one wonders if this feeling was the starting point for ancient extramission theories of vision in which vision was thought to require visual rays emitted from the eyes (Winer & Cottrell, 1996)).

Cueing experiments have been an important tool for understanding spatial attention as a spotlight. In a cueing paradigm, subjects are required to respond as quickly as possible to the onset of a light or other simple visual stimulus. This target stimulus is preceded by a "cue" whose function is to draw attention to the occurrence of a target in space (see Figure 9.1). Cues come in various forms, e.g., the brightening of an outline object (Posner & Cohen, 1984), the onset of some simple stimulus (Averbach & Coriell, 1961; Eriksen & Hoffman, 1973; Posner, Snyder, & Davidson, 1980), or a symbol, like an arrow, indicating where attention should be deployed (Jonides, 1981; Posner & Cohen, 1984). Although the mechanisms are debated, as a general rule, cues facilitate detection of and response to stimuli presented at the cued location (Cheal & Gregory, 1997; Luck et al., 1996; Shiu & Pashler, 1994; see Yeshurun & Carrasco, 1998, for an interesting exception in foveal texture segregation). Thus, Posner described attention as a "*spotlight* that enhances the efficiency of the detection of events within its beam" (Posner et al., 1980, p. 172).

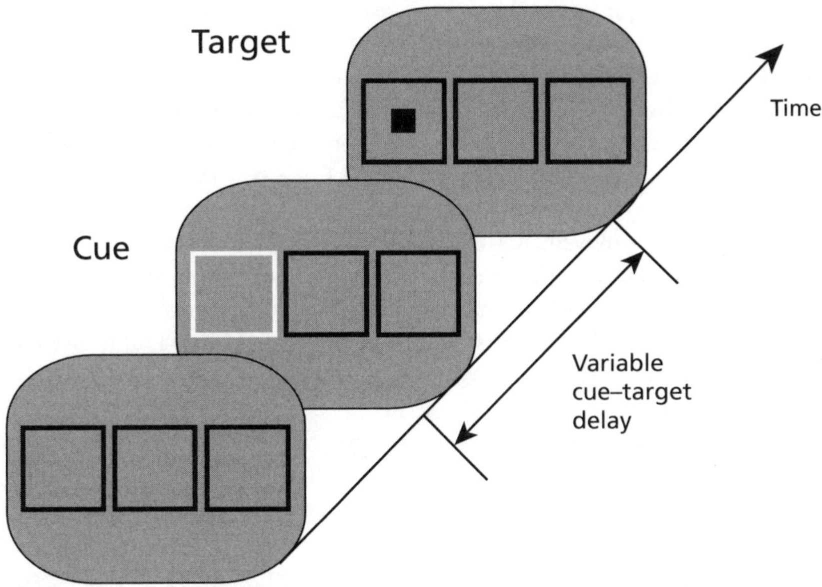

Figure 9.1. Posner cueing paradigm. Subjects fixate at central box at the beginning of trial. The outline of one peripheral box brightens briefly. At variable SOAs from the cue, a target appears in one of the boxes. Subjects press a button in response to target onset as quickly as possible. (Adapted from Posner & Cohen, 1984.)

Attentional Shifts, Splits, and Resolution

The spotlight metaphor raises several important questions (see Cave & Bichot, 1999, for more complete review and discussion).

Question 1: When attention is deployed from one location to another, do such attentional shifts occur in a digital, instantaneous fashion, magically appearing in a new location to be attended? Or does attention move from one location to another in an analog fashion, illuminating intermediate locations as it travels across visual space? It appears that the focus of attention can move instantaneously from one location to the other without a cost for the amount of distance traveled (Krose & Julesz, 1989; Kwak, Dagenbach, & Egeth, 1991; Remington & Pierce, 1984; Sagi & Julesz, 1985; Sperling & Weichselgartner, 1995). However, it is unclear whether attention has an effect on intermediate loci as it moves from point A to point B. The evidence remains inconclusive with Shulman, Remington, and McLean (1979) and Tsal (1983) arguing in the affirmative and Yantis (1988) and Eriksen and Murphy (1987) arguing in the negative.

Question 2: Can the spotlight of attention be split into multiple spots? That is, can attention be allocated to more than one object or one location at a time? One way to address this question is to have subjects attend to two spatially separate loci and measure attentional effects at intermediate loci. Eriksen and Yeh (1985) argued that attention could not be split into multiple beams. However, Castiello and Umilta (1992) argued that subjects can split focal attention and maintain two attentional foci across hemifields (though see McCormick, Klein, & Johnston, 1998, for an alternative explanation). Kramer and Hahn (1995) also showed that distractors appearing between two noncontiguous locations did not affect performance for targets. Recent new evidence further supports the view that attention can be split across two locations (Bichot, Cave, & Pashler, 1999).

Indeed, another way to explore whether there are multiple attentional spotlights is to ask subjects to track the movements of multiple objects. These experiments appear to show that subjects can allocate attention to something like four or five objects moving independently amongst other independently moving distractors (Pylyshyn & Storm, 1988; Yantis, 1992). This could mean that subjects can divide the spotlight into four to five independently targetable beams (Pylyshyn, 1989, but see Yantis, 1992, for an account based on perceptual grouping).

Question 3: Assuming that one has allocated one's full attention to a particular location, object or event, how focused is selection at that spot? The resolution of attention is studied by measuring the effects of distracting items on target processing. Distractors typically flank the target at various spatial distances. In a widely used paradigm known as the flanker task (also known as response interference task, flanker compatibility effect), the resolution of attention is revealed by examining the distance at which distractors start to impair target discrimination performance (Eriksen & Eriksen, 1974).

One general finding is that the acuity of attention is of coarser spatial resolution than visual acuity (reviewed in He, Cavanagh, & Intrilligator, 1997). Thus, items spaced more closely than the resolution of attention cannot be singled out (individuated) for further processing. This has been referred to as the *crowding effect* (Bouma, 1970; Eriksen & Eriksen, 1974; Levi, Klein, & Aitsebaomo, 1985; Miller, 1991; Townsend, Taylor, & Brown, 1971). An example of limited attentional resolution is shown in Figure 9.2. The resolution of attention limits the amount of visual detail that can be brought into awareness, and He, Cavanagh, and Intrilligator (1996) demonstrated that this limitation occurs in a stage beyond early visual processing in striate cortex.

Object-based Attention

As reviewed above, the spotlight metaphor is useful for understanding how attention is deployed across space. However, this metaphor has serious limitations. For example, attention can be allocated to regions of different size. Thus, the spotlight has a variable width of focus (*zoom lens model*), adjustable by subject's volition or by task demands (Eriksen & St. James, 1986; Eriksen & Yeh, 1985). Moving from metaphor to data, the speed of response to a stimulus is dependent on how narrowly attention is focused. The spatial distribution of attention follows a gradient with decreased effects of attention with increased eccentricity from its focus (Downing & Pinker, 1985; Eriksen & Yeh, 1985; Hoffman & Nelson, 1981; LaBerge, 1983; Shaw & Shaw, 1977). The spatial spread of attention around an attended object can also be measured with a probe technique (Cepeda, Cave, Bichot, & Kim, 1998; Kim & Cave, 1995).

Moreover, the focus of attention may be yoked to the overall load or difficulty of a task.

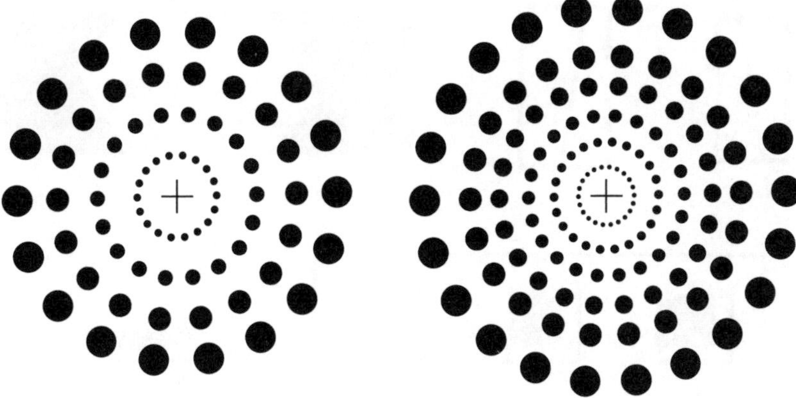

Figure 9.2. Attentional resolution. While fixating the cross in the center of the left-hand diagram, notice that it is fairly easy to attend to any of the items in the surrounding arrays. This is possible because each item is spaced at less than the critical density for individuation. The diagram on the right has a density that exceeds the resolution limit of attention, producing crowding effects. Fixating on the central cross, it is difficult to move attention from one item to another. (Reprinted from He, Cavanagh, & Intrilligator, 1997, with permission from Elsevier Science.)

In order for attention to remain focused on a target, the overall perceptual load of the task must be sufficiently high to ensure that no capacity remains to process other non-target events. In the absence of a sufficiently high load, attention spills over to non-target events (Kahneman & Chajczyk, 1983; Lavie, 1995; Lavie & Tsal, 1994). Lavie proposes that the early/late selection debate in attention can be resolved by considering the overall perceptual load of a task.

The spotlight metaphor runs into more serious difficulties when one considers that attention can be allocated to 3-D layouts (Atchley, Anderson, & Theeuwes, 1997; Downing & Pinker, 1985) and restricted to certain depth planes defining surfaces in space (Nakayama & Silverman, 1986). Thus, selection occurs after 3-D representations have been derived from the 2-D input (Marrara & Moore, 1998).

Along these lines, researchers have proposed that attention selects perceptual objects rather than simply "illuminating" locations in space (see Cave & Bichot, 1999, for a review). Such "object-based" attention can be considered independent of spatial selection (Duncan, 1984; Kahneman & Henik, 1981; Kanwisher & Driver, 1992). As an example, Neisser and Becklen (1975) presented two different movie sequences that overlapped each other in space. People were throwing a ball in one movie and playing a hand game in another. Subjects were asked to attend to only one of the two overlapping movies. Throughout viewing, subjects were able to follow actions in the attended movie and make responses to specific events in it, as instructed by the experimenter. Odd events in the unattended movie were rarely noticed. Because both scenes overlapped each other, this demonstrates a selective attention that cannot be space-based. Rather selection was based on objects and events. See Simons and Chabris (1999) for a modern version and extension of this study.

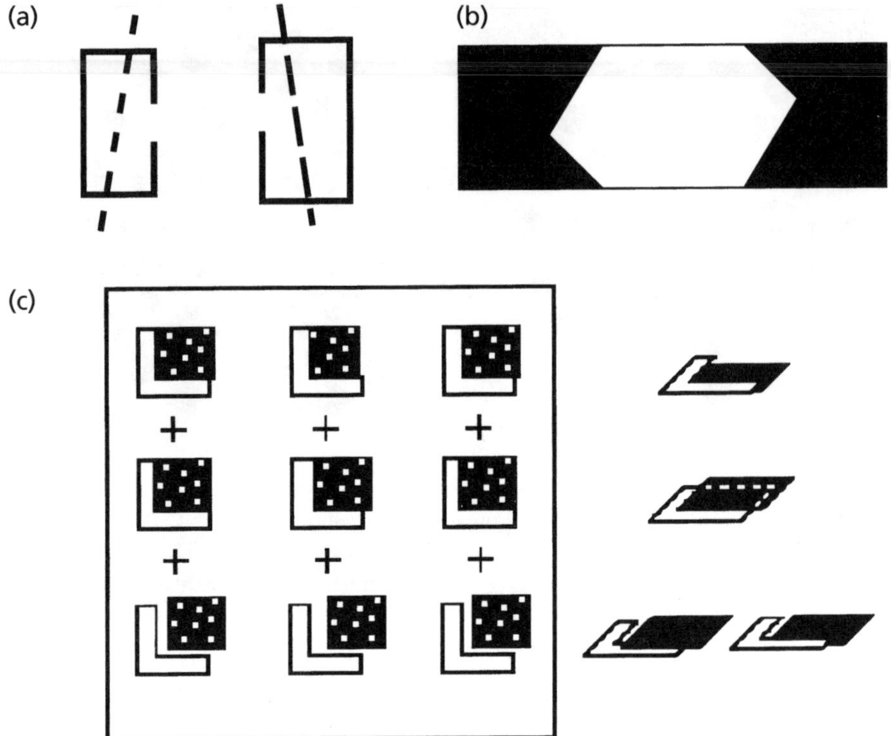

Figure 9.3. (a) Object-based attention. Each target is comprised of two overlapping objects, a box or a line. The box that could be large or small with a gap to the left or right. The line could be tilted right or left and comprised of either a dashed or a dotted line. Attending and reporting two attributes from a single object was easier than reporting two attributes, each from different objects. (Adapted from Duncan, 1984.) (b) Sample stimulus adapted from Baylis and Driver (1993). The task was to determine the relative vertical height of the apices formed at the angled outline of the center white figure. Depending on the subject's perceptual set, these apices can be considered to be part of one object (white figure) or two objects (black figures). Task performance was lower when the apices belonged to two objects, as manipulated by perceptual set. (c) In a search for a reversed L shape target, performance is much easier when the L shapes are perceived to be in front of the square than when they are perceived to appear behind the square (the apparent depth was manipulated using binocular disparity). Even though the retinal images were essentially identical in both conditions, setting the L shapes behind the squares causes the perceptual system to "complete" their shapes behind the occluder (look like squares behind occluding squares), making it difficult for observers to attend to the L-shape fragment alone. This demonstrates that attention operates over surfaces (objects) rather than raw visual features. (Adapted from He & Nakayama, 1992, © *Nature*, with permission.)

Figures 9.3a and 9.3b illustrate two other stimuli examples that argue against the spotlight metaphor. Subjects were asked to attend to one or two objects, occupying the same locations in space. Performance suffered when they had to attend to two objects rather than just one (Baylis & Driver, 1993; Duncan, 1984). Because the overlapping or abutting objects occupied the same location, the performance differences must be due to attentional allocation over object-based representations.

Object-based representations are "sophisticated" in the sense that they represent more than the raw visual input. For example, visual objects undergo substantial occlusion and fragmentation in real world raw images. Perceptual objects are created out of bits and pieces in the image by perceptual grouping and completion operations (Kanizsa, 1979; Kellman & Shipley, 1991; Nakayama, He, & Shimojo, 1995). It makes sense to direct attention to these object representations rather than the raw image features. Indeed, He and Nakayama (1992) have shown that attention cannot access raw image features, selecting the surfaces (objects) that the fragments represent instead (see Figure 9.3c; see also Rensink & Enns, 1995; Wolfe & Bennett, 1997). As a general rule, object-based deployment of attention is influenced by factors that determine perceptual grouping (Behrmann, Zemel, & Mozer, 1998; Driver & Baylis, 1989; Egly, Driver, & Rafal, 1994; Kramer & Jacobson, 1991; Moore, Yantis, & Vaughan, 1998; see also Berry & Klein, 1993, Kramer, Tham, & Yeh, 1991; see Cave & Bichot, 1999, for a review).

How is object-based selection achieved? A leading theory proposes that internal representations known as "object files" support our ability to attend to objects as they undergo occlusion and fragmentation or change over time (Kahneman & Treisman, 1984; Kahneman et al., 1992). Object files are episodic representations that "maintain the identity and continuity of an object perceived in a particular episode" (Kahneman & Treisman, 1984, p. 54). For instance, Kahneman et al. (1992) briefly presented two letters, each within a different outline box. Then the boxes moved to different locations, immediately after which another target letter appeared in one of the boxes. Subjects responded faster if the target was identical to the letter that had appeared earlier in the same box. This object-specific advantage was greater than when the target matched a letter that previously appeared in a different object. Phenomena like apparent motion can also be discussed in terms of object files. If the timing and spacing are correct, motion is perceived from two images flickering on and off in alternation (Anstis, 1980; Cavanagh & Mather, 1990). Object files provide the link to weave these two events into one, allowing the distinct states to be perceived as a single moving object (Chun & Cavanagh, 1997; Kanwisher & Driver, 1992).

To sum, converging evidence suggests that visual selection can operate over object-based representations. However, the broader literature indicates that location does play a critical role in visual attention (see Cave & Bichot, 1999), so understanding the spatial properties of attentional deployment and selection remains an important enterprise.

The Visual Search Paradigm

The preceding work was performed with very simple displays. However, the visual world rarely presents only one or two potential objects worthy of attention. A somewhat more realistic situation is found in the "visual search" paradigm. In visual search tasks, subjects look for a designated target item among a number of distracting items. This simple paradigm allows researchers to examine how visual stimuli are differentiated, what stimulus properties attract attention, how attention is deployed from one object to the next, how one keeps track of what was attended, and so on. Not surprisingly, the visual search paradigm has been used extensively.

Laboratory versions typically use highly artificial stimuli (colored line segments, letters, etc.). Still, these tasks approximate the visual search tasks that everyone does all the time (Wolfe, 1994b), whether it involves the efficient search for salient yellow dandelion flowers on a grassy lawn or the less efficient, frustrating search for a street sign when driving through an unfamiliar neighborhood at night. A sample lab task is shown in Figure 9.4. Fixating on the asterisk in the center, try to notice whether there are unique visual objects in the display. You should first notice the white "X" which appears to "pop out" of the array. This is an example of an easy, efficient search. Now try to locate the black letter "T". This exemplifies a more difficult, inefficient type of search.

In a typical lab study, subjects would perform many searches for such targets amongst a variable number of distractors. The total number of items in the display is known as the set size. The target is presented on some percentage of the trials, typically 50%. Subjects press one button if the target is present and another button if only distractors appear. Subjects are typically instructed to respond as quickly and accurately as possible. Both reaction time (RT) and accuracy are measured. In RT tasks, the display is usually present until a response is made. In accuracy tasks, the display is usually presented very briefly, followed by an interfering visual mask.

Critical insights into the mechanisms of search and attention can be obtained by examining the efficiency of search tasks. There are several ways to quantify search efficiency. The most common method is to vary the number of items in the display (set size) and RT as a function of set size. The slope of the RT X set size functions is a measure of search efficiency. A slope of zero msec/item indicates that the target item, when present, is detected without interference from the distractor items. Steeper slopes indicate less efficient search and a greater cost for each additional distractor. For search tasks in which acuity limitations are not an issue, slopes tend to range from 0 msec/item for the most efficient searches (e.g., a search for a red target among green distractors) to 20–30 msec item on target-present trials of inefficient searches (e.g., a search for a vowel among consonants) (see Figure 9.4b). Slopes for target-absent trials tend to be about twice those for target present (Chun & Wolfe, 1996; Wolfe, 1998c). Steeper slopes are found if the individual items take a long time to identify (e.g., imagine trying to find a cluster of 16 dots among clusters of 17 dots) or if eye movements are required to resolve items.

Accuracy measures are the second common method for quantifying search performance. Efficient searches produce high levels of accuracy independent of set size even when the display is presented very briefly. For less efficient tasks accuracy declines as set size increases unless exposure time is increased to compensate (Bergen & Julesz, 1983; Palmer, 1994).

Mechanisms Underlying Search Efficiency

What determines the efficiency of visual search? Is there a qualitative or merely a quantitative difference between efficient and inefficient search? Extensive reviews of specific search results can be found elsewhere (Wolfe, 1998b). For present purposes, a few basic principles will suffice, summarized in Table 9.1.

Treisman's Feature Integration Theory (Treisman, 1988; Treisman & Gelade, 1980;

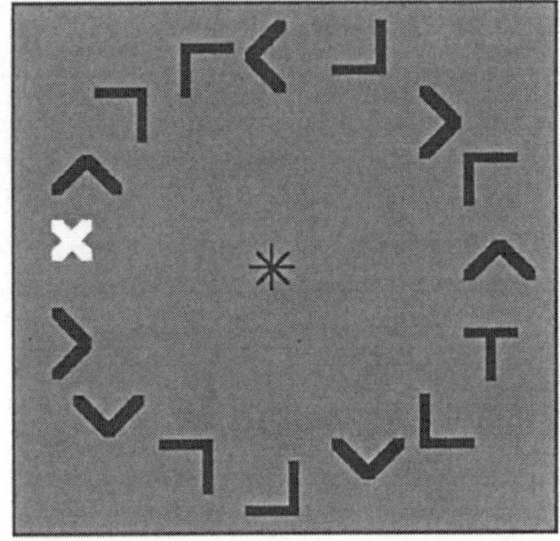

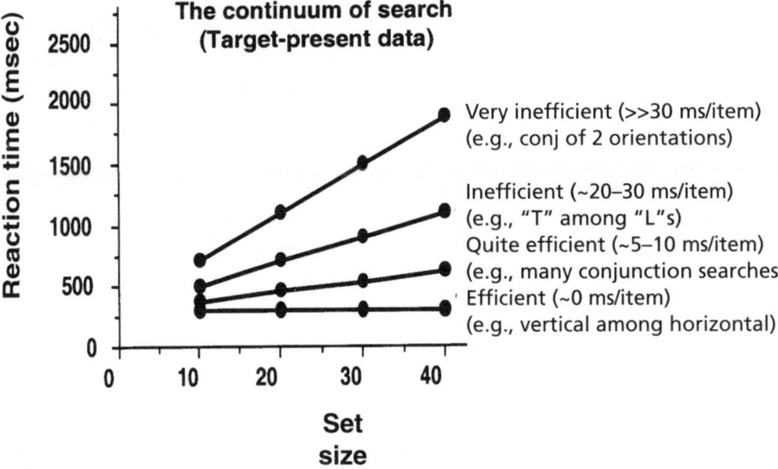

Figure 9.4. Visual search and hypothetical data. In the top figure, fixating on the asterisk, notice that the white X is much easier to detect than the black T. The bottom figure shows hypothetical data for visual search tasks of varying efficiency. (Adapted from Wolfe, 1998b, with permission.)

Treisman & Sato, 1990) was an early and influential account of differences in search efficiency. It held that efficient feature searches were performed by mechanisms capable of processing all items in parallel, and that all other searches relied on mechanisms that operated in a serial, item-by-item manner. In particular, attention was required to conjoin or bind multiple features into a single object. Hence, conjunction searches were serial (Treisman & Gelade, 1980), and withdrawing attention produced errors for binding features, known as "illusory conjunctions" (Treisman & Schmidt, 1982).

Although Feature Integration Theory was an elegant framework that stimulated much work in the field, the strict dichotomy between parallel and serial search tasks was not clearly supported in the data collected subsequently (see Wolfe, 1998c). Two broad classes of models have arisen to account for the data. One class abandons the serial/parallel

Table 9.1 Principles of search efficiency

Factors that decrease search efficiency	*Factors that increase search efficiency*
In general, as target-distractor differences get smaller, search becomes less efficient (e.g., Foster & Westland, 1992; Nagy & Sanchez, 1990).	Large target-distractor differences in features such as color, orientation, motion, size, curvature, some other form properties, and some 3-D properties (such as stereopsis, lighting, and linear perspective). See Wolfe (1998b) for a review.
Increasing distractor inhomogeneity. Consult Duncan and Humphreys (1989) for a detailed discussion of the role of similarity in visual search.	Increasing distractor homogeneity (Duncan, 1988).
Targets defined by conjunctions of two or more basic features (Treisman & Gelade, 1980; e.g., color X orientation: a red vertical line among green vertical and red horizontal distractors).	Conjunction targets can be found efficiently if the differences in target and distractor features are sufficiently salient (Wolfe, Cave, & Franzel, 1989).
Targets defined only by the spatial arrangement of basic features are, as a general rule, not found efficiently (Wolfe & Bennett, 1997). Thus, search for an "S" among mirror-reversed Ss will proceed at a rate of 20–30 msec per item on target present trials.	Difficult searches can become more efficient with extensive practice (Heathcote & Mewhort, 1993; Treisman, Vieira, & Hayes, 1992). However, such perceptual learning is specific to the training stimuli.

distinction altogether. These limited-capacity models argue that all items in a search are processed at once (e.g., Kinchla, 1974) or perhaps, in groups (e.g., Grossberg, Mingolla, & Ross, 1994; Pashler, 1987). Differences in search efficiency arise because different types of items make different demands on a limited processing resource. See Bundesen (1990, 1994), Logan (1996), Palmer (1995) for further discussion of models of this sort.

The second class of models preserves the distinction between serial and parallel processes. Following Neisser (1967), these models hold that the preattentive stages of vision are characterized by parallel processing of basic features and that there is a bottleneck after which processing is essentially serial. Selection of items for serial processing is under attentional control. Following Treisman, these models hold that the explicit knowledge of the relationship of features to each other (binding) requires serial processing. In these models, variation in the efficiency of search is determined by the ability of preattentive, parallel processes to *guide* attention toward candidate targets or away from likely distractors. (Hence "*Guided* Search," Cave & Wolfe, 1990; Wolfe, 1994a; Wolfe et al., 1989; Wolfe & Gancarz, 1996). Treisman's modified Feature Integration Theory has similar properties (e.g., Treisman & Sata, 1990; ; see also Hoffman, 1979; Tsotsos et al., 1995).

In a model like Guided Search, a simple feature search is efficient because preattentive processes can direct the first deployment of attention to the likely target item. Searches like a search for an S among mirror-Ss are inefficient because no preattentive information is available to distinguish one item from the next. Conjunction searches are of intermediate efficiency because preattentive feature guidance is available but it is not as strong as in a simple feature search.

Top-down and Bottom-up Control of Attention in Visual Search

In any visual task such as search, attention can be deployed to stimuli in one of two ways: endogenously or exogenously (Posner, 1980). In endogenous attention, attention is presumed to be under the overt control of the subject, (e.g., "I will attend to the left-side of the display"). This is also known as "top-down," goal-driven attention (Yantis, 1998). Endogenous attention is voluntary, effortful, and has a slow (sustained) time course. On the other hand, attention can be driven *exogenously*, by an external stimulus event that automatically draws attention to a particular location. This has been referred to as "bottom-up," stimulus-driven attention. The flashing lights of a highway patrol vehicle draw attention exogenously. Exogenous attention draws attention automatically and has a rapid, transient time course (Cheal & Lyon, 1991; Jonides, 1981; Nakayama & Mackeben, 1989; Posner et al., 1980; Weichselgartner & Sperling, 1987).

There are a wide variety of bottom-up, exogenous visual attributes that draw attention. For instance, in visual search, spatial cues and abrupt visual onsets (sudden luminance changes) draw attention. Hence, flat search slopes are obtained for abrupt-onset targets (Yantis & Jonides, 1984). Abrupt onsets may capture attention even when the cues were not informative of target location and even when subjects were instructed to ignore them (Jonides, 1981; Remington, Johnston, & Yantis, 1992).

Other salient visual features such as feature singletons (e.g., a red target amongst green distractors or a vertical target amongst horizontal items) can effectively draw attention but are under greater volitional control. That is, these features are easier to ignore than spatial cues or abrupt onsets (Jonides & Yantis, 1988). Specifically, the ability to ignore a singleton depends on the nature of the search task. When the task requires searching for a target defined by a singleton in one dimension (e.g., orientation), then singletons in other dimensions (e.g., color) automatically draw attention even when this is detrimental to performance (Pashler, 1988; Theeuwes, 1991, 1992). If, however, subjects are looking for a specific feature (e.g., vertical) then an irrelevant feature in another dimension does not capture attention.

In summary, bottom-up and top-down attentional control systems interact with each other. Hence, stimulus-driven attentional control depends on whether subjects are in singleton-detection mode (Bacon & Egeth, 1994) or have adopted the appropriate attentional control settings or perceptual set (Folk, Remington, & Johnston, 1992). More generally, nearly every visual search model proposes that the guidance of attention is determined by interactions between the bottom-up input and top-down perceptual set (Duncan & Humphreys, 1989; Grossberg et al., 1994; Muller, Humphreys, & Donnelly, 1994; Treisman & Sato, 1990; Wolfe, 1994a).

Inhibitory Mechanisms of Attention

Our review above discussed attentional selection, but how is selection achieved? Selection may be performed by excitation and enhancement of behaviorally relevant information, or by inhibition and suppression of irrelevant information. Of course both mechanisms may operate in concert, but the field is still debating how this occurs (Milliken & Tipper, 1998). Nevertheless, inhibitory mechanisms in selection can play a crucial role in reducing ambiguity (Luck et al., 1997b), they can protect central, capacity-limited mechanisms from interference (Dagenbach & Carr, 1994; Milliken & Tipper, 1998), and they can prioritize selection for new objects (Watson & Humphreys, 1997). Here, we review three extensively studied inhibitory phenomena: invalid cueing, negative priming, and inhibition of return.

Invalid Cueing

Inhibition effects can be measured as a decrement in performance relative to a neutral baseline. When a cue stimulus appearing before the target is informative, it will facilitate target performance compared to a baseline in which the prime is neutral. What if the prime is an invalid cue to the target? This should generate a negative expectation that slows down performance to the target. Inhibitory effects have been demonstrated using tasks such as letter matching (Posner & Snyder, 1975) and lexical decision (Neely, 1977); reviewed in Milliken & Tipper (1998). Of particular interest is the time course of inhibition. Neely varied the stimulus onset asynchrony (SOA) between prime and target. He found that inhibitory effects are only observed for targets appearing beyond 400 ms after the prime presentation.

Negative Priming

Evidence for item-specific inhibitory effects have been studied extensively using a paradigm known as *negative priming*, a term coined by Tipper (1985). In negative priming, subjects are slower at responding to targets (probes) that were distractors (referred to as primes) on the previous trials (usually the trial immediately before) (Dalrymple-Alford & Budayr, 1966; Neill, 1977; Tipper, 1985). This suggests that the representation of the ignored primes was actively suppressed, and that this inhibition was carried over to the following trial. Remarkably, pictures can prime words and vice versa, suggesting that negative priming operates at an abstract, semantic level (Tipper & Driver, 1988). Furthermore, single trial exposures to novel figures can produce negative priming, suggesting that implicit representations of unknown shapes can be formed and retained from ignored and unremembered events (DeSchepper & Treisman, 1996).

Inhibition of Return

The inhibition of return (IOR) paradigm is similar to that used in cued orienting (reviewed earlier; Posner et al., 1980). In Posner and Cohen's demonstration of this paradigm, the target was most likely to appear in the middle of three outline boxes arranged along the horizontal axis (See Figure 9.1). Peripheral cues occasionally appeared, either validly or invalidly cueing the onset of a target in the peripheral boxes. The SOA between cue and target was varied and the usual facilitatory effects of cueing were obtained for targets appearing within 300 ms of the cue in the same spatial location. Interestingly, when the SOA exceeded 300 ms, target detection performance was slowed, suggesting a transient bias *against* returning attention to visited locations. Inhibition of return makes ecological sense. For instance, in serial search tasks for a target amongst distractors, IOR would prevent an observer from continually rechecking the same location (Klein, 1988; Klein & McInnes, 1999). Note that other lines of evidence argue against IOR in search. Rather, covert attention may simply be deployed at random to relevant items without regard to the previous history of search (Horowitz & Wolfe, 1998). Further research is needed to resolve these two opposing views.

Temporal Attention: Visual Selection Over Time

Inhibition of return provides a good segue from spatial to temporal aspects of attention. The visual input changes from moment to moment. Perceivers need to extract behaviorally relevant information from this flux. How quickly can visual information be taken in? If there are limitations, what visual processes are affected? To address these questions, we must consider how attention is allocated in time as well as space.

A standard technique for studying temporal attention is to present rapidly presented sequences of visual items at rates of up to 20 items per second (rapid serial visual presentation, RSVP). This taxes processing and selection mechanisms to the limit, allowing researchers to assess the rate at which visual information can be extracted from a stream of changing input.

Single Target Search

Perhaps the most interesting property of temporal selection is that people are very good at it. For example, Sperling and his colleagues (1971) presented RSVP sequences of letter arrays. Each frame contained 9 or 16 letters each and were presented at rapid rates of 40 to 50 ms. The task was to detect a single target numeral embedded in one of the frames (also see Eriksen & Spencer, 1969; Lawrence, 1971). Accuracy performance in this sequential search task provides an estimate of the "scanning" rate, allowing Sperling to demonstrate that practiced observers can scan through up to 125 letters per second. This is higher than even the most liberal estimates of scanning rates from the spatial search literature (Horowitz and Wolfe, 1998). In another impressive demonstration of sequential search, Potter (1975) presented subjects with RSVP sequences of natural scene stimuli and asked them to search for target photos defined by verbal cues such as "wedding" or "picnic." Subjects performed well in such tasks at rates of up to eight pictures per second, suggesting that the "gist" of successive scenes could be extracted with only 125 msec per scene. Thus RSVP tasks show that it is possible to extract meaning from visual stimuli at rates much faster than the speed with which these meanings can be stored in any but the most fleeting of memories (Chun & Potter, 1995; Potter, 1993; see also Coltheart, 1999).

The Attentional Blink and Attentional Dwell Time

Although it is possible to report on the presence of a single target, presented in *one* brief moment in time, it does not follow that it is possible to report on a target in *every* brief moment in time. Intuition is clear on this point. While you can imagine monitoring a stream of letters for a target item at, say 15 Hz, you are unlikely to believe that you could echo all of the letters presented at that rate. This limitation can be assessed by presenting a second target (which we will refer to as T2) at various intervals after the first target (T1). This is known as the attentional blink paradigm described below.

Broadbent and Broadbent (1987) asked subjects to report two targets presented amongst an RSVP stream of distractors. The temporal lag between T1 and T2 was varied systematically across a range of intervals from 80 to 320 msec. Thus, the time course of interference could be examined as a function of time (see Figure 9.5a). This paradigm revealed a striking, robust impairment for detecting T2 if it appeared within half a second of T1 (see also Weichselgartner and Sperling (1987) and Figure 9.5b). This inability to report T2 for an extended time after T1 has come to be known as the attentional blink (AB) – a term coined by Raymond, Shapiro and Arnell (1992). Raymond et al. first proved that AB was an attentional effect rather than a sensory masking effect. This was illustrated by comparing dual-task performance with a control condition using identical stimulus sequences in which subjects were asked to ignore a differently colored target (T1) and just report a probe (T2). No impairment was obtained, suggesting that AB reflected the attentional demands of attending to and identifying T1. Raymond et al. also demonstrated that AB is dependent on the presence of a distractor or mask in the position immediately after T1 (called the +1 position). When this item was removed and replaced with a blank interval, AB disappeared. Although AB is not a masking effect itself, perceptual and/or conceptual interference with T1 is important (Chun & Potter, 1995; Grandison, Ghirardelli, & Egeth, 1997; Moore et al., 1996; Seiffert & Di Lollo, 1997). Interestingly, when T2 appears in the +1 position, it may be processed together with T1 (Chun & Potter, 1995; Raymond et al., 1992), allowing it to be reported at relatively high accuracy (known as Lag-1 sparing, see Figure 9.5b).

Thus, the AB reveals limitations in the rate at which visual stimuli can be processed, and it can be used to study fundamental questions of early/late selection and visual awareness (to be discussed in a later section). The reasoning behind the AB paradigm is simple. If a stage of processing is limited in capacity, then this will take a certain amount of time to complete (Duncan, 1980; Eriksen & Spencer, 1969; Hoffman, 1978; Pashler, 1984; Shiffrin & Gardner, 1972; Welford, 1952). This impairs or delays the system's ability to process a second stimulus presented during this busy interval, causing the attentional blink (Chun & Potter, 1995; Jolicoeur, 1999; Shapiro et al., 1994; Shapiro, Arnell et al., 1997).

Duncan, Ward, and Shapiro (1994; Ward et al., 1996) used AB to reveal the speed of attentional deployment, dubbed attentional "dwell time." Duncan et al. demonstrated that even distractor events to be ignored could produce significant AB. Duncan et al. considered this as evidence in favor of a long, 200–500 msec dwell time. On the other hand, visual search data can be interpreted as supporting serial search at a rate of one every 20–50 msec (Kwak et al., 1991). Even the AB literature supports two different dwell time estimates. Attention to T1 causes a blink of several hundred msec. At the same time, until T1 appears, the categorical status of items can be processed at RSVP rates of 8–12 Hz

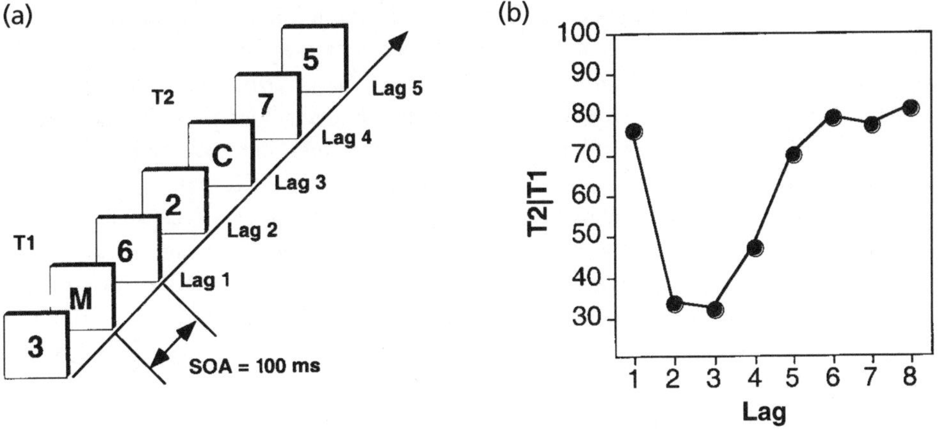

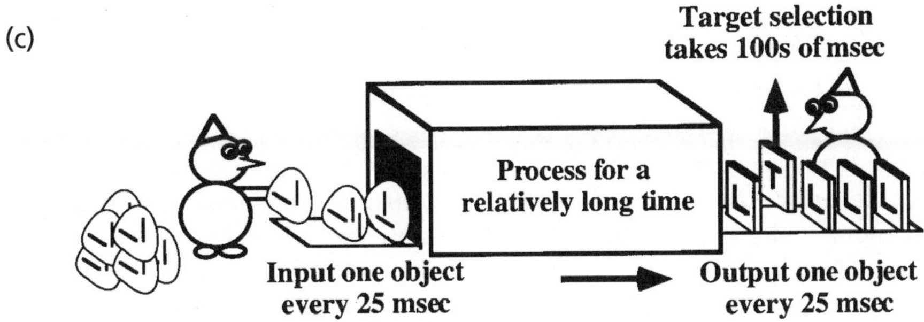

Figure 9.5. Temporal attention. (a) The RSVP paradigm. The task is to search for two letter targets presented amongst digits at a rate of 10 per second. (b) The attentional blink. Percent correct performance on reporting T2 given correct report of T1 is impaired at lags 2 to 5 (corresponding to SOAs of 200–500 ms). (Adapted from Chun & Potter, 1995.) (c) A conveyor belt model of multiple attentional dwell times.

(Broadbent & Broadbent, 1987; Chun & Potter, 1995; Lawrence, 1971; Potter, 1975, 1993; Shapiro, Driver, Ward, & Sorensen, 1997).

Perhaps these are estimates of two related but not identical aspects of attentional processing. Let us expand the standard metaphor of an attentional bottleneck into an attentional conveyor belt (see Figure 9.5c). Preattentively processed items are loaded onto the conveyer belt for further processing. One timing parameter describes how fast some mental demon can load items onto the conveyor belt. We can imagine the preattentive item moving along as if in some mental assembly line – its parts being bound into a recognizable whole. At the other end of the conveyor, another mental demon decides if the now-assembled item is worth keeping. If it is, that is, if it is a target, the demon must do something in order to save that item from oblivion, corresponding to Stage 2 of the Chun and Potter (1995) model. That "something" takes time, too. Suppose the loading demon puts an item on the conveyor every 20–50 msec, while the second demon can only properly handle one target item every 300 msec. This would give us both dwell times. In standard visual search, efficiency is governed by the loading demon. The discovery of a single target by the second demon ends the trial. In an AB task, the second demon grabs T1 and cannot go back to capture T2 until 300 msec or so have passed. The intervening items are no longer physically present when the second demon returns. If one of them was T2, then T2 is "blinked."

This account has a number of useful properties. Note that this is a "serial" conveyor belt but multiple items are being processed on it at the same time. This suggests a possible compromise solution to the serial/parallel arguments in visual search. Note, too, that we could call the first demon "early selection" and the second "late selection" and offer a compromise solution to that debate as well. Returning to the dwell time debate, visual search estimates for short dwell times may be based on loading demon operations (Treisman & Gelade, 1980; Wolfe et al., 1989), whereas Duncan et al.'s proposal for long dwell times may correctly refer to the second demon.

Repetition Blindness

In addition to the attentional blink, there are other factors that influence the subject's ability to report targets in RSVP. The AB is typically measured for two visual events that are different from each other, so what would happen if the two targets were identical? One might expect repetition shouldn't matter at all, or it may help performance through perceptual priming (Tulving & Schacter, 1990). The surprising finding is that performance is worse for repeated targets, a phenomenon known as *repetition blindness* (RB), first reported by Kanwisher (1987). As an example, some subjects expressed outrage at sentences like, "Unless they are hot enough, hotdogs don't taste very good," because they failed to perceive the second repetition of the word "hot" (Kanwisher & Potter, 1990). RB is the result of a failure to create separate object files for the second of two repeated items (Kanwisher, 1987). As noted in an earlier section, object files are used to represent perceptual events (Kahneman & Treisman, 1984). In RB, the visual system fails to treat the second repetition as a different object from the first. Thus no object file is created for the second event, and it is omitted from explicit report. Kanwisher's token individuation hypothesis is supported by a variety of studies (Bavelier, 1994; Chun, 1997; Chun & Cavanagh, 1997; Hochhaus & Johnston, 1996).

Neural Mechanisms of Attention

Thus far, this chapter has approached attention from a cognitive/experimental psychology standpoint. In this section, we examine how attentional behavior is implemented by the brain. A wide variety of methodologies exist to study the "attentive brain" (Parasuraman, 1998). Each technique has pros and cons, complementing each other as "converging operations" (Garner, Hake, & Eriksen, 1956). Here we survey a variety of neurophysiological methodologies and summarize critical findings as they relate to the cognitive descriptions of the attentional mechanisms described in the previous section.

Single-Cell Physiological Method

The single-cell recording method measures activity from individual neurons presumed to be participating in a perceptual or cognitive operation. An obvious advantage is that this methodology provides the highest spatial (individual neuron) and temporal (spike potentials) resolution of all the methods used to study attentional function in the brain. Current limitations include the invasiveness of cellular recording and the fact that only a few neurons can be examined at any given time. The latter feature makes it difficult to examine how multiple brain areas interact with each other to perform a particular task (c.f., note that researchers are developing methods to simultaneously record from multiple neurons and multiple cortical areas). Nevertheless, single-cell neurophysiology has led to several important insights.

What parts of the visual system show attentional modulation of activity (see Maunsell, 1995, for a review)? In some sense, this is the neuronal equivalent of the early/late selection debate, and neurophysiological evidence supports the view that attention operates at multiple stages in the visual system. An early selection account is supported by studies that demonstrate attentional modulation in V1 (Motter, 1993; see Posner & Gilbert, 1999, for a review). Modulatory activitity is even more prominent in extrastriate regions such as V4 (Haenny & Schiller, 1988; Luck et al., 1997a; Moran & Desimone, 1985; Motter, 1993, 1994; see Motter, 1998, for a review), as well as specialized cortical areas such as MT, where motion processing is enhanced by attention (Treue & Maunsell, 1996). Finally, attentional deployment is reflected in frontal eye field (FEF) neural activity that differs for targets and distractors (Schall and Hanes, 1993). Thus, like the behavioral data, the physiological data suggest that attentional effects occur at multiple loci.

A critical function of attention is to enhance behaviorally relevant information occupying a location in space while filtering out irrelevant information appearing at different spatial locations. What is the neural correlate of this spatial filter or attentional spotlight? In a now-classic study, Moran and Desimone (1985) identified one type of filtering process in V4 neuronal responses (see Figure 9.6). They presented two stimuli within the receptive field of a V4 neuron being recorded. One of the stimuli was "effective" for producing the cell's response, and the other "ineffective" stimulus wasn't. Monkeys were required to hold fixation on the same spot in all conditions, only their attentional focus varied. The main finding was that when monkeys attended to the location occupied by the ineffective stimulus, the cell failed to respond to the presence of the effective stimulus. In other words, attention modulated the cell's response such that the presence of a competing (effective) stimulus was filtered out. This can be characterized as an operation that resolves ambiguity or competition from neighboring items (Luck et al., 1997a, 1997b; Motter, 1993).

These results can be extended to spatial search paradigms. Chelazzi, Miller, Duncan, and Desimone (1993) employed a match-to-sample task in which monkeys were first shown a single target stimulus, then asked to make an eye movement to the same target item in a subsequent array which also contained a distractor item. Neural activity to the distractor stimulus was initially present, but subsequently suppressed at around 200 ms after the onset of the search array, illustrating a neural correlate of competitive selection.

As noted earlier, behavioral data show that attentional selection can be restricted to a set of items that contain a target attribute (e.g., search can be restricted to red items if subjects

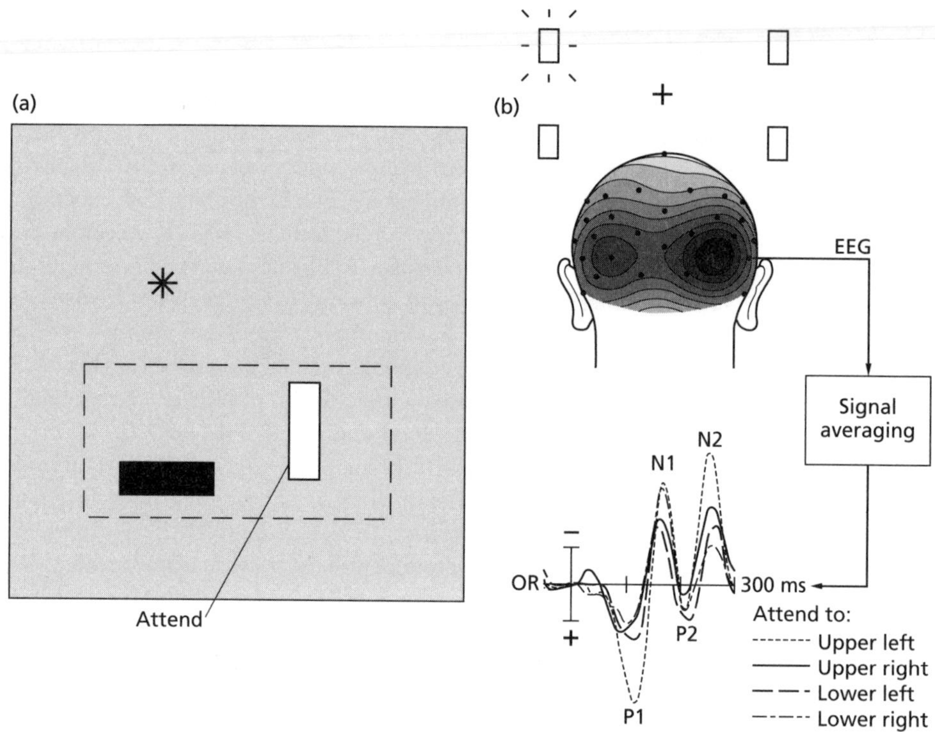

Figure 9.6. (a) Moran and Desimone's (1985) paradigm for studying selective attention in extrastriate cortical area V4. Monkeys fixate on the asterisk. The receptive field of the recorded neuron is indicated by the dotted frame, and this was plotted for the effective stimulus (red bar, shown here in black). When the animal attended to the location of an effective stimulus (red bar), the cell gave a good response. However, when the animal attended to the location of the ineffective stimulus (green bar, shown here in white) the cell gave almost no response, even though the effective stimulus was present in the receptive field. Thus, the cell's responses were determined by the attended stimulus. (Adapted from Moran & Desimone, 1985.) (b) ERP changes in a spatial-attention task. Subjects focused attention on one of the quadrants at a time. ERPs were recorded from 30 scalp sites (dots on the schematic head), and the bottom figure shows a larger P1 component in response to upper-left flashes while subjects attended to the upper-left quadrant. The scalp distribution of the P1 component for attended upper-left flashes (measured at 108 msec) is shown on the rear view of the head with darker areas representing greater positive voltages. (Mangun et al., 1993, © MIT Press, reproduced with permission.)

know that the target is red (Egeth et al., 1984; Wolfe et al., 1989). A neural correlate for such "Guided Search" has been identified by Motter (1994) for area V4 and by Bichot and Schall (1999) for the FEF. In Motter's study, monkeys were required to select an elongated bar target on the basis of color and then report its orientation. V4 neurons whose receptive fields included stimuli of the target color maintained their activity whereas V4 neurons whose receptive fields contained items of different colors had depressed activity.

Bichot and Schall (1999) demonstrated analogous effects of visual similarity in the FEF. The FEF plays an important role in visual selection and saccade generation (see Schall & Bichot, 1998, and Schall & Thompson, 1999, for reviews). A fundamental finding is that the activity of FEF neurons evolves to discriminate targets from distractors in search tasks, prior to initiating a saccade to the target (Schall & Hanes, 1993). Interestingly, the activity of FEF neurons was stronger to distractors that shared visual features to the target, suggesting a neural correlate of Guided Search. Bichot and Schall also discovered effects of perceptual history, as FEF activity was stronger to distractors that were targets on previous training sessions. This finding reveals a neurophysiological correlate of long-term priming, important for understanding how visual processing is modulated by perceptual experience.

Event-Related Potentials

The massed electrical activity of neurons can be measured through scalp electrodes. This non-invasive method can be used to assess neural activity in humans as well as animals. When these electrical events are correlated in time with sensory, cognitive, or motor processing, they are called "event-related potentials" (ERPs). ERP waveforms consist of a set of positive and negative voltage deflections, known as components. The sequence of ERP components that follows a stimulus event is thought to reflect the sequence of neural processes that is triggered by the onset of the stimulus. The amplitude and latency of each component is used to measure the magnitude and timing of a given process. In addition to being non-invasive, ERP measures provide high temporal precision. But, anatomical precision is limited for a number of reasons (see Luck, 1998). This can be overcome by combining ERP measures with other imaging techniques (Heinze et al., 1994), described in the next section.

The millisecond temporal resolution makes ERPs very useful for the study of attention. Consider the classic debate between early versus late selection (Broadbent, 1958; Deutsch & Deutsch, 1963). The locus-of-selection issue cannot be definitively resolved based on behavioral data because these reflect the sum of both early and late responses (Luck & Girelli, 1998). The temporal resolution of ERP, however, allows researchers to directly measure the impact of attentional processes at early stages of information processing. Evidence for early selection was first provided by Hillyard and colleagues in the auditory modality (Hillyard et al., 1973). Using a dichotic listening paradigm in which subjects attended to information from one ear versus the other, Hillyard et al. demonstrated that early sensory ERP components beginning within 100 ms post-stimulus were enhanced for attended stimuli. Importantly, these results generalize to visual selection in which subjects were required to attend to one of two spatial locations. Early components of the ERP waveform (P1 and N1) were typically larger for stimuli presented at attended locations versus unattended locations (reviewed in Mangun, Hillyard, & Luck, 1993). These effects also begin within 100 ms of stimulus onset, providing clear evidence for attentional modulation at early stages of visual information processing.

These early selection mechanisms also generalize to visual search tasks using multi-element displays (Luck, Fan, & Hillyard, 1993). A particularly interesting ERP component, the N2pc, reflects the focusing of attention onto a potential target item in order to suppress competing information from the surrounding distractor items (Luck & Hillyard, 1994). In fact, the N2pc may serve as a marker of where attention is focused and how it shifts across space. Recent evidence shows that this N2pc component rapidly shifts from one item to the next during visual search (Woodman & Luck, 1999). This finding lends provocative support to theories that propose attention moves in a serial manner between individual items rather than being evenly distributed across items in the visual field. The debate between serial and parallel models is a classic one that cannot be resolved by behavioral data or computational analyses (Wolfe, 1998c; Townsend & Ashby, 1983). However, the Woodman and Luck study indicates how neurophysiological data can provide novel insights towards resolving such classic questions.

ERP methodology has been successfully applied to understanding higher-level attentional processes also. Recall that in the attentional blink (AB) a target in RSVP can "blink" a subsequent target from awareness due to attentional limitations. Are such unreportable items semantically identified within the brain somewhere? Luck, Vogel, and Shapiro (1996; Vogel, Luck, & Shapiro, 1998) used ERP measures to examine this question. They looked at the N400 component which is sensitive to semantic mismatch. For example, consider the following sentence: "He went home for dinner and ate a worm." The last word "worm" does not fit the context of the sentence and will trigger an N400 (Kutas & Hillyard, 1980). Thus, the presence of N400 would indicate that a word has been processed up to its semantic meaning. If blinked items are suppressed early and not recognized, then little or no N400 should be observed for blinked targets. If AB is produced by capacity limitations after initial identification has occurred, then the N400 should be preserved even for blinked words which could not be reported. Luck et al. demonstrated that the N400 was preserved, providing direct evidence of semantic processing without awareness (or, at least, without awareness that lasts more than a few hundred milliseconds). Thus, electrophysiological techniques such as ERP can provide direct indices of perceptual and cognitive processing, not readily obtainable through behavioral measures alone.

Functional Imaging: PET and fMRI

Positron Emission Tomography (PET) and functional Magnetic Resonance Imaging (fMRI) methodologies allow non-invasive imaging of brain activity during performance of sensory, cognitive, and motor behavior. PET measures cerebral blood flow (rCBF) and fMRI measures deoxygenation signals in the brain (see Corbetta, 1998; Haxby, Courtney, & Clark, 1998). Both imaging techniques rely on the assumption that these metabolic measures are correlated with neuronal activity within the brain. Advantages of imaging techniques include their non-invasive nature and the ability to measure brain activity across the entire brain with relatively high spatial resolution compared to ERP. The temporal resolution is somewhat limited by the slowness of blood flow changes. Nevertheless, the spatial resolution and global imaging scale has allowed these two imaging techniques to provide critical insights into the neural networks that mediate attentional processing in the human brain.

One seminal contribution of functional imaging was to demonstrate that attention modulates the activity of extrastriate cortical areas specialized for feature dimensions such as color or motion. Importantly, this modulation depended on which feature was used as a template for selection (Corbetta et al., 1991). For instance, if attention was focused on the speed of the motion of the objects, increased rCBF activity was obtained in motion processing regions (presumed analogues of macaque areas MT/MST) (Corbetta et al., 1991; O'Craven et al., 1997). Attention to color activated a dorsal region in lateral occipital cortex and a region in the collateral sulcus between the fusiform and lingual gyri (Clark et al., 1997; Corbetta et al., 1991). Wojciulik, Kanwisher, & Driver (2000) showed that attentional modulation also occurs for more complex stimuli such as faces (face stimuli are selectively processed in an extrastriate area called the fusiform gyrus (Haxby et al., 1994; Kanwisher, McDermott, & Chun, 1997; Sergent, Ohta, & MacDonald, 1992)). In fact, attention modulates activity in specialized extrastriate areas, even when competing objects of different types (e.g., faces vs. houses) occupy the same location in space, providing evidence for object-based selection (O'Craven, Downing, & Kanwisher, 1999).

Attention also modulates visual processing in early visual areas such as V1 (Brefczynski & DeYoe, 1999; Gandhi, Heeger, & Boynton, 1999; Somers et al., 1999; Tootell et al., 1998). Most important, attentional modulation was demonstrated to occur in a retinotopic manner in visual cortex, revealing the physiological correlate of the spatial spotlight of attention. In other words, attending to specific locations enhanced cortical activity in a manner that corresponded closely with the cortical representations of the visual stimuli presented in isolation (see Figure 9.7). Note that attentional modulation effects were larger at extrastriate retinotopic areas in most of these studies, supporting psychophysical evidence that the resolution of attentional selection is limited at a processing stage beyond V1 (He et al., 1996).

In addition to revealing modulation effects, functional imaging has illuminated our understanding of mechanisms that drive attention to different spatial locations (Corbetta et al., 1993; Nobre et al., 1997). Corbetta et al. demonstrated that the superior parietal cortex may play an important role in shifting attention around locations in space. This would be particularly important for visual search tasks which require attention to move from one object to the other (according to some models). Consistent with this, significant superior parietal activation was obtained when subjects searched for conjunction targets defined by color and motion (Corbetta et al., 1995). Moreover, this activity was higher during search for conjunctions than for search for targets defined by individual color or motion features. This corroborates behavioral and theoretical work proposing that conjunction tasks require a serial spatial scanning mechanism (Treisman & Gelade, 1980; Wolfe et al., 1989; Yantis & Johnson, 1990).

Seeing: Attention, Memory, and Visual Awareness

The research reviewed so far described behavioral and neural mechanisms of attention, but how does this explain everyday visual experience? Namely, does attention play a central role in how we consciously perceive the world? Put more simply, can we see without attention? Does attention affect the appearance of things?

Answering this requires a definition of "seeing." One way to frame this problem is to

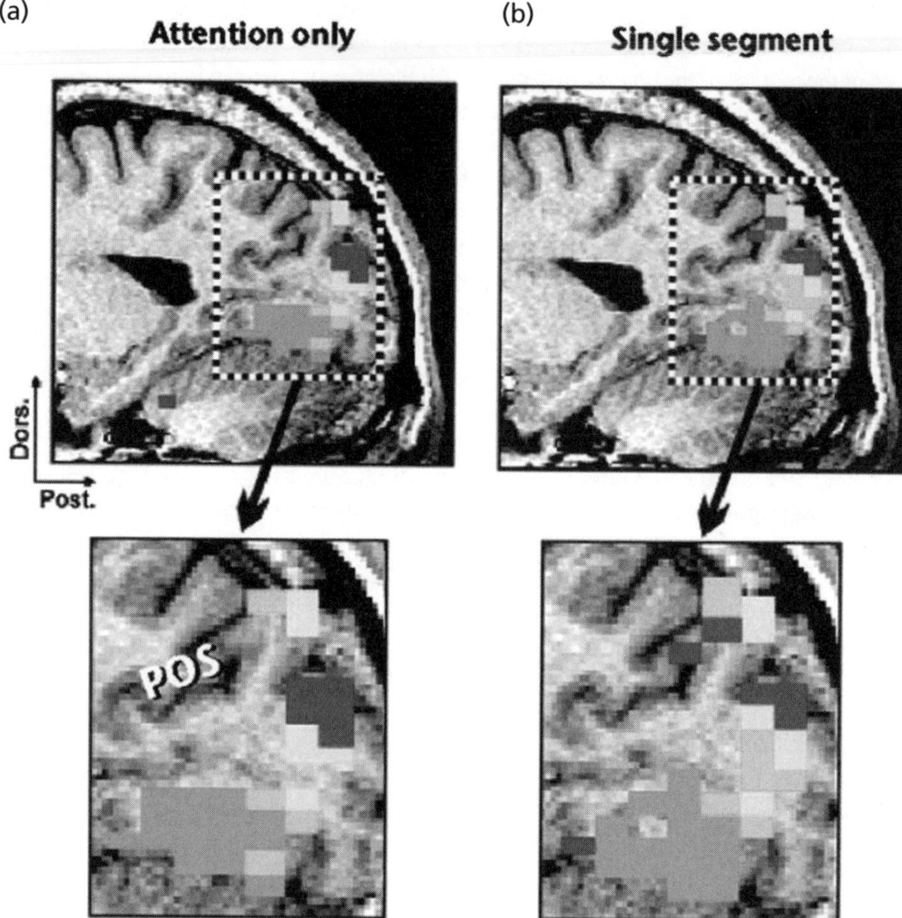

Figure 9.7. fMRI data that reveals retinotopic mapping of cortical activation produced by (a) shifts in spatial attention from the middle to the periphery (increasing polar angle) and (b) by the same visual targets presented in isolation (Brefczynski & DeYoe, 1999, © *Nature*, with permission). Note the close correspondence between the two patterns of cortical activation.

posit two levels of seeing (Kihlstrom, Barnhardt, & Tataryn, 1992; Mack & Rock, 1998). *Implicit seeing* occurs when visual stimuli have been identified, as measured by their impact on performance, but can't be explicitly reported by the subject. Masked priming paradigms provide a good example of implicit seeing. Masked prime stimuli that are too brief to reach awareness nevertheless facilitate performance for a subsequent target (Marcel, 1983). *Explicit seeing* occurs when subjects can explicitly report what visual event had occurred. This does not necessarily require perfect identification or description, but it should allow one visual event to be distinguished from another in a manner that can somehow be verbalized or articulated. Implicit and explicit seeing are not necessarily dichotomous and may represent different ends of a continuum of visual awareness.

This implicit/explicit seeing distinction appears tractable when the criterion is operationally defined as the overt reportability of a visual event. However, problems arise when we try to apply such terms to the phenomenal awareness of visual events, and the latter usage is more intrinsically interesting than the former. For instance, imagine you're sitting at a café looking out at a busy, colorful street scene. You clearly "perceive" the scene in a conscious manner. What do you "explicitly see" in such a situation? Recent work described below makes it clear that the phenomenal answer is *not* clear. Nevertheless, generalizations can be offered. Although objects outside the focus of attention (and awareness) can influence behavior, attention critically mediates the ability to experience, learn, and/or report something about visual events.

Attention and Explicit Seeing

Several researchers have argued that attention is needed for conscious perception (Nakayama & Joseph, 1998; Mack & Rock, 1998; Treisman & Kanwisher, 1998). Recall that subjects could only remember details from the attended movie in Neisser and Becklen's (1975) study (see "Object-based Attention" section). Also consider studies by Rock and Gutman (1981) and Goldstein and Fink (1981) who presented subjects with a series of drawings which consisted of two overlapping line shapes. Subjects were instructed to selectively attend to one of the two figures, inducing a state of *inattention* for the unattended figure. The question is whether the unattended forms are perceived. Subjects consistently failed to recognize the form of unattended items even when they were queried immediately after presentation. Rock and Gutman suggested that the form of unattended items was not perceived, hence "attention is necessary for form perception" (p. 275).

A similar conclusion can be drawn from a related finding known as *inattentional blindness* (Mack & Rock, 1998; Mack et al., 1992; Rock et al., 1992). This paradigm is simple and does not require the subject to actively ignore or inhibit the unattended event. In Rock et al.'s study, subjects performed several trials of a length judgment task for two lines bisecting each other in the form of a cross at the center of the computer screen. On one of the trials, an additional test figure was presented along with the cross figure, and subjects were queried of their awareness of this test stimulus. The remarkable finding is that a large proportion of subjects did not even notice the test figure, suggesting inattentional blindness. Mack and Rock (1998) concluded that attention is needed for conscious experience.

Much recent work in a new paradigm known as *change blindness* brings these lab results into the real world. People think that they simultaneously recognize multiple items. However, this appears to be an illusion. They are greatly impaired in their ability to notice changes in any but the currently attended object unless the change alters the "gist" or meaning of a scene (Simons & Levin, 1998). Awareness of the identity and attributes of visual objects can be probed by asking subjects to detect changes made across film cuts (Levin & Simons, 1997), between alternating images (Rensink, O'Regan, & Clark, 1997), or across eye movements (McConkie & Currie, 1996). Subjects perform miserably at detecting changes, even when this involves changing the identity of a real person in the real world asking for your directions to the local library (Simons & Levin, 1997)! Thus, although a great amount of detailed information is available in natural scenes, the amount of information that is consciously retained from one view to the next, or from one moment to the next, appears to be extremely low. Understanding these limitations is critical for understanding how visual information is integrated across views and eye movements (Henderson, 1992; Irwin, 1992).

The *attentional blink* paradigm described earlier is also pertinent to the issue of perceptual awareness. Recall that subjects typically fail to report a target appearing within about 500 ms following a correctly identified target. Joseph, Chun, and Nakayama (1997) demonstrated that even a "preattentive" task such as orientation pop-out target detection was impaired during AB. Thus, withdrawing attention makes it impossible to complete even the simplest and most efficient searches (see also Braun & Julesz, 1998; Braun & Sagi, 1990; Braun, 1998; Joseph, Chun, & Nakayama, 1998).

Perhaps many of these findings can be understood by noting that attention is necessary to prevent visual events from being overwritten by subsequent stimuli. Enns and Di Lollo (1997) demonstrated that under conditions when attention is not focused on an item, that item is subject to substitution or erasure by other, subsequent stimuli even when those other stimuli do not overlap the contours of the "erased" visual target. They termed this *attentional masking*. One could argue that change blindness is caused by the erasure of one scene by the next, and the same logic can be applied to unreportable targets appearing during the attentional blink (Chun & Potter, 1995; Giesbrecht & Di Lollo, 1998). Hence, attentional selection is required if the perceptual consequences of stimuli are to persist long enough to be reported.

Attention and Implicit Seeing

The studies reviewed above demonstrate that attention is very important for consciously perceiving and reporting on visual events. However, it is critical to remember that unattended stimuli do not simply disappear into oblivion, rather they may be implicitly registered (Treisman & Kanwisher, 1998). Using the overlapping line shapes similar to those in Rock and Gutman (1981), DeSchepper and Treisman (1996) have shown that the unattended shapes have an impact on performance in subsequent trials (negative priming, see "Inhibitory mechanisms of attention" section). In the inattentional blindness paradigm, Mack has shown that people are "less" blind to stimuli such as one's name or faces, suggesting that some meaning is extracted from those apparently unattended objects. Moore and Egeth (1997) employed an interesting variant of the inattentional blindness task to demonstrate that Gestalt grouping occurs without attention.

As reviewed earlier, unreportable items in the attentional blink are nevertheless identified (Luck et al., 1996; Shapiro et al., 1997b). Likewise, it is plausible that "unperceived" events in change blindness tasks are registered unconciously to influence scene interpretation (Simons, 2000). Similarly in the attentional blink phenomenon, unreportable visual targets that do not reach awareness are nevertheless identified (implicitly seen). In sum, attention limits what reaches conscious awareness and what can be reported through explicit seeing, but sophisticated implicit perception may proceed for unattended, unreportable visual stimuli.

Attention and Memory

Attention is also important for encoding information into visual working memory. Working memory for visual objects is limited in capacity, but interestingly the unit of capacity and selection is an integrated object rather than a collection of individual features comprising the object. Luck and Vogel (1997) showed that objects comprised of four conjoined features can be stored as well as the same number of objects comprised of one feature, even though the number of individual features is much larger for the integrated stimuli. Attentional encoding of these items into visual working memory makes all of their features available to awareness and report (Allport, 1971; Duncan, 1980; Luck & Vogel, 1997).

Not only does attention influence what you experience and remember, experience and memory influence what you attend to (see Chun and Nakayama, 2000, for a review). Memory traces of past perceptual interactions bias how attention should be allocated to the visual world (Chun & Jiang, 1998; Desimone & Duncan, 1995). For instance, there is a bias to orient towards novel items (Johnston et al., 1990). "Familiar" items can be examined more efficiently (Wang, Cavanagh, & Green, 1994). Furthermore, subjects attend more quickly to items which share the same color, spatial frequency, or location to targets attended to on preceding trials, a finding described as *priming of pop-out* (Maljkovic & Nakayama, 1994, 1996, 2000). In addition, the invariant context of a target experienced over time can guide attention and facilitate search (*contextual cueing*, Chun & Jiang, 1998, 1999).

Attention and the Phenomenology of Conscious Perception

Finally, one may ask whether attention affects the phenomenology of conscious visual experience (Prinzmetal et al., 1997, 1998). Most of the research reviewed in this chapter concerns *when* (how fast) a stimulus is perceived or *whether* it is perceived at all. This does not address the question of *how* a stimulus appears (Prinzmetal et al., 1998). Namely, how does attention affect the perceived brightness, color, location, or orientation of objects? Nineteenth-century researchers relied on introspection to suggest that attention may increase the intensity and clarity of images (James, 1890; Titchener, 1908). However, Prinzmetal and his colleagues (1997, 1998) used a matching procedure to demonstrate that attention did *not* affect the perceived intensity or clarity of a stimulus and had only a small, inconsistent effect on the veridicality of the perceived color or location of a stimulus. The main, consistent effect of reducing attention was to increase the variability in perceiving a wide variety of basic visual attributes.

Although attention does not change the experienced clarity and intensity of stimuli, it may determine *how* you perceive stimuli, especially ambiguous ones. Consider Rubin's ambiguous figure (Rubin, 1915/1958) which induces a percept that oscillates between two faces or a vase. Attention appears to determine which figure is perceived. In ambiguous motion displays, attention mediates the ability to track moving stimuli (Cavanagh, 1992). In binocular rivalry, presenting different images to each of the two eyes induces competing percepts which oscillate, and form-selective cortical areas in the brain are modulated according to what the subject "consciously" perceives (Leopald & Logothetis, 1996; Logothetis & Schall, 1989; Tong, Nakayama, Vaughan, & Kanwisher, 1998). Although the role of attention in binocular rivalry is unclear, it is intriguing that cortical areas important for attentional shifts are active as rivalrous percepts alternate (Lumer, Friston, & Rees, 1998). In several visual illusions, attentional cues can make a stationary line appear as if it were dynamically shooting out of a point in space (Hikosaka, Miyauchi, & Shimojo, 1993; see also Downing & Treisman, 1997, and Tse, Cavanagh, & Nakayama, 1998) or distort the form of simple figures (Suzuki & Cavanagh, 1997). Hence, attention can influence how you see and experience the perceptual world.

Closing Remarks

A large number of behavioral paradigms have elucidated many important mechanisms of attention. Attention is important for selecting and inhibiting visual information over space and over time. New paradigms continually emerge to illuminate how attention influences memory and perceptual awareness. Particularly exciting are the new technological developments such as fMRI that provide researchers with unprecedented tools for studying the neural basis of visual attention.

Our review of visual attention mirrors the state of the field, and if little else, one may come away with the sense that attention refers to a very diverse set of operations. Further integrative understanding should be a worthy goal of future research and theorizing. Such an understanding would specify how various attentional mechanisms interact with other perceptual, motor, and cognitive systems. However, we believe future research will be guided by the same, fundamental questions that have motivated the field up to now. How does attention facilitate our interactions with a rich visual world characterized by information overload? What ecological properties of the environment and what computational capacities of the brain constrain attentional selection? Finally, how does attentional selection and deployment influence the everyday qualia of seeing?

Suggested Readings

Coltheart, V. (Ed.) (1999). *Fleeting memories: Cognition of brief visual stimuli.* Cambridge, MA: MIT Press. [This edited volume contains chapters on visual cognition with a special focus on temporal attention in sentence, object, and scene processing. More information on the RSVP paradigm, the attentional blink, repetition blindness, inattentional amnesia, and scene processing can be found here.]

Dagenbach, D., & Carr, T. H. (Eds.) (1994). *Inhibitory processes in attention, memory, and language.* San Diego, CA: Academic Press. [This edited volume offers specialized chapters that discuss inhibitory processes in attention.]

Kramer, A. F., Coles, M. G. H., & Logan, G. D. (Eds.) (1996). *Converging operations in the study of visual selective attention.* Washington, DC: American Psychological Association. [This edited volume covers an extensive range of topics in selective attention. The chapters offer discussion of most of the major paradigms and issues in selective attention research.]

Pashler, H. (1998). *The psychology of attention.* Cambridge, MA: MIT Press. [An integrative and exhaustive survey of what the past few decades of attention research have taught us about attention.]

Pashler, H. (Ed.) (1998). *Attention.* East Sussex: Psychology Press Ltd. [Concise, edited volume of chapters on a variety of basic topics in attention. Useful, introductory surveys on the following topics can be found here: visual search, attention and eye movements, dual-task interference, inhibition, attentional control, neurophysiology and neuropsychology of selective attention, as well as computational modeling.]

Parasuraman, R. (Ed.) (1998). *The attentive brain.* Cambridge, MA: MIT Press. [This edited volume contains detailed discussion of methods (single cell electrophysiology, ERP, fMRI, PET, etc.), components of attention, and development and pathologies of attention. A particularly important volume for understanding the cognitive neuroscience of attention, as well as current issues and debates.]

Additional Topics

Attentional Networks

As evidenced in this chapter, there are different types of attention performing different functions. In addition, different aspects of attention appear to be mediated by different parts of the brain. These papers describe the function and anatomy of such attentional networks: Posner & Petersen (1990); Posner & Dehaene (1994).

Attention and Eye Movements

Perhaps one of the most important functions of attention is to guide eye movements (where visual acuity is the highest) towards objects and events that are relevant to behavior. Attention and eye movements are tightly coupled, and the chapter by Hoffman in Pashler (1998) reviews the relationship between the two.

Attention and Object Perception

The article by Treisman & Kanwisher (1998) reviews how attention influences the perception of objects. The authors also discuss the role of attention in perceptual awarenesss, and they review evidence for modularity of visual function in the brain.

Computational Modeling of Attentional Processes

Computational models are useful for describing and understanding complex functions such as attention. Considerable effort has been put into such quantitative models of attention. Bundesen (1994, see also Bundesen, 1990) and Mozer and Sitton's chapter in Pashler (1998) provide a useful review, while the articles by Grossberg, Mingolla, and Ross (1994), Logan (1996), and Wolfe (1994a, see also Cave & Wolfe, 1990; Chun & Wolfe, 1996; Wolfe & Gancarz, 1996) represent some of the most influential computational models in the field of attention.

Neuropsychology of Attention

Our understanding of attentional processing has been greatly informed by the neuropsychological investigations of attentional disorders caused by specific brain damage. These findings are reviewed in Humphreys' chapter (this volume). Further information on deficits such as neglect or Balint's syndrome can be found in Driver (1998) or Rafal (1995).

References

Allport, D. A. (1971). Parallel encoding within and between elementary stimulus dimensions. *Perception & Psychophysics, 10*, 104–108.

Anstis, S. M. (1980). The perception of apparent movement. *Philosophical Transactions of the Royal Society of London, B 290*, 153–168.

Atchley, P. F K. A., Andersen, G. J., & Theeuwes, J. (1997). Spatial cueing in a stereoscopic display: Evidence for a "depth-aware" attentional focus. *Psychonomic Bulletin & Review, 4*, 524–529.

Averbach, E., & Coriell, A. S. (1961). Short-term memory in vision. *Bell System Technical Journal, 40*, 309–328.

Bacon, W. F., & Egeth, H. E. (1994). Overriding stimulus-driven attentional capture. *Perception & Psychophysics, 55*, 485–496.

Bavelier, D. (1994). Repetition blindness between visually different items: The case of pictures and words. *Cognition, 51*, 199–236.

Baylis, G. C., & Driver, J. (1993). Visual attention and objects: Evidence for hierarchical coding of location. *Journal of Experimental Psychology: Human Perception & Performance, 19*, 451–470.

Behrmann, M., Zemel, R. S., & Mozer, M. C. (1998). Object-based attention and occlusion: Evidence from normal participants and a computational model. *Journal of Experimental Psychology: Human Perception and Performance, 24*, 1011–1036.

Bergen, J. R., & Julesz, B. (1983). Parallel versus serial processing in rapid pattern discrimination. *Nature, 303*(5919), 696–698.

Berry, G., & Klein, R. (1993). Does motion-induced grouping modulate the flanker compatibility effect? A failure to replicate Driver & Baylis. *Canadian Journal of Experimental Psychology, 47*, 714–729.

Bichot, N. P., Cave, K. R., & Pashler, H. (1999). Visual selection mediated by location: Feature-based selection of noncontiguous locations. *Perception & Psychophysics, 61*, 403–423.

Bichot, N. P., & Schall, J. D. (1999). Effects of similarity and history on neural mechanisms of visual selection. *Nature Neuroscience, 2*, 549–554.

Bouma, H. (1970). Interaction effects in parafoveal letter recognition. *Nature, 226*, 177–178.

Braun, J. (1998). Vision and attention: The role of training. *Nature, 393*(June 4), 424–425.

Braun, J., & Julesz, B. (1998). Withdrawing attention at little or no cost: Detection and discrimination tasks. *Perception & Psychophysics, 60*, 1–23.

Braun, J., & Sagi, D. (1990). Vision outside the focus of attention. *Perception & Psychophysics, 48*, 45–58.

Brefczynski, J. A., & DeYoe, E. A. (1999). A physiological correlate of the 'spotlight' of visual attention. *Nature Neuroscience*, 2, 370–374.

Broadbent, D. E. (1958). *Perception and communication*. London: Pergamon Press.

Broadbent, D. E., & Broadbent, M. H. (1987). From detection to identification: Response to multiple targets in rapid serial visual presentation. *Perception & Psychophysics, 42*, 105–113.

Bundesen, C. (1990). A theory of visual attention. *Psychological Review, 97*, 523–547.

Bundesen, C. (1994). Formal models of visual attention: A tutorial review. In A. Kramer, G. Logan, & M. G. H. Coles (Eds.), *Converging operations in the study of visual selective attention*. Washington DC: APA.

Castiello, U., & Umilta, C. (1992). Splitting focal attention. *Journal of Experimental Psychology: Human Perception & Performance, 18*, 837–848.

Cavanagh, P. (1992). Attention-based motion perception. *Science, 257*, 1563–1565.

Cavanagh, P., & Mather, G. (1990). Motion : The long and short of it. *Spatial Vision, 4*, 103–129.

Cave, K. R., & Bichot, N. P. (1999). Visuospatial attention: Beyond a spotlight model. *Psychonomic Bulletin & Review, 6*, 204–223.

Cave, K. R., & Wolfe, J. M. (1990). Modeling the role of parallel processing in visual search. *Cognitive Psychology, 22*, 225–271.

Cepeda, N. J., Cave, K. R., Bichot, N., & Kim, M.-S. (1998). Spatial selection via feature-driven

inhibition of distractor locations. *Perception and Psychophysics, 60* (5), 727–746.
Cheal, M., & Gregory, M. (1997). Evidence of limited capacity and noise reduction with single-element displays in the location-cuing paradigm. *Journal of Experimental Psychology: Human Perception & Performance, 23,* 51–71.
Cheal, M., & Lyon, D. R. (1991). Central and peripheral precuing of forced-choice discrimination. *Quarterly Journal of Experimental Psychology, A,* 859–880.
Chelazzi, L., Miller, E. K., Duncan, J., & Desimone, R. (1993). A neural basis for visual search in inferior temporal cortex. *Nature, 363,* 345–347.
Chun, M. M. (1997). Types and tokens in visual processing: A double dissociation between the attentional blink and repetition blindness. *Journal of Experimental Psychology: Human Perception and Performance, 23,* 738–755.
Chun, M. M., & Cavanagh, P. (1997). Seeing two as one: Linking apparent motion and repetition blindness. *Psychological Science, 8,* 74–79.
Chun, M. M., & Jiang, Y. (1998). Contextual cueing: Implicit learning and memory of visual context guides spatial attention. *Cognitive Psychology, 36,* 28–71.
Chun, M. M., & Jiang, Y. (1999). Top-down attentional guidance based on implicit learning of visual covariation. *Psychological Science, 10,* 360–365.
Chun, M. M., & Nakayama, K. (2000). On the functional role of implicit visual memory for the adaptive deployment of attention across scenes. *Visual Cognition, 7,* 65–81.
Chun, M. M., & Potter, M. C. (1995). A two-stage model for multiple target detection in rapid serial visual presentation. *Journal of Experimental Psychology: Human Perception and Performance, 21,* 109–127.
Chun, M. M., & Wolfe, J. M. (1996). Just say no: How are visual searches terminated when there is no target present? *Cognitive Psychology, 30,* 39–78.
Clark, V. P., Parasuraman, R., Keil, K., Kulanski, R., Fannon, S., Maisog, J. M., & Ungerleider, L. G. (1997). Selective attention to face identity and color studied with fMRI. *Human Brain Mapping, 5,* 293–297.
Coltheart, V. (Ed.) (1999). *Fleeting memories: Cognition of brief visual stimuli.* Cambridge, MA: MIT Press.
Corbetta, M. (1998). Functional anatomy of visual attention in the human brain: Studies with Positron Emission Tomography. In R. Parasuraman (Ed.), *The attentive brain* (pp. 95–122). Cambridge, MA: MIT Press.
Corbetta, M., Miezin, F. M., Dobmeyer, S., Shulman, G. L., & Petersen, S. E. (1991). Selective and divided attention during visual discrimination of shape, color, and speed: Functional anatomy by positron emission tomography. *Journal of Neuroscience, 11,* 2383–2492.
Corbetta, M., Miezin, F. M., Shulman, G. L., & Petersen, S. E. (1993). A PET study of visuospatial attention. *Journal of Neuroscience, 13,* 1202–1226.
Corbetta, M., Shulman, G. L., Miezin, F. M., & Petersen, S. E. (1995). Superior parietal cortex activation during spatial attention shifts and visual feature conjunction. *Science, 270,* 802–805.
Dagenbach, D., & Carr, T. H. (Eds.) (1994). *Inhibitory processes in attention, memory, and language.* San Diego, CA: Academic Press, Inc.
Dalrymple-Alford, E. C., & Budayr, B. (1966). Examination of some aspects of the Stroop color-word test. *Perceptual and Motor Skills, 23,* 1211–1214.
DeSchepper, B., & Treisman, A. (1996). Visual memory for novel shapes: Implicit coding without attention. *Journal of Experimental Psychology: Learning, Memory, & Cognition, 22,* 27–47.
Desimone, R., & Duncan, J. (1995). Neural mechanisms of selective visual attention. *Annual Review of Neuroscience, 18,* 193–222.
Deutsch, J. A., & Deutsch, D. (1963). Attention: Some theoretical considerations. *Psychological Review, 70,* 80–90.
Downing, C. J., & Pinker, S. (1985). The spatial structure of visual attention. In M. I. Posner & O. S. M. Marin (Eds.), *Attention and performance XI.* Hillsdale, NJ: Erlbaum.
Downing, P. E., & Treisman, A. M. (1997). The line-motion illusion: Attention or impletion? *Journal of Experimental Psychology: Human Perception & Performance, 23,* 768–779.

Driver, J. (1998). The neuropsychology of spatial attention. In H. Pashler (Ed.), *Attention* (pp. 297–340). London: University College London Press.

Driver, J., & Baylis, G. C. (1989). Movement and visual attention: The spotlight metaphor breaks down. *Journal of Experimental Psychology: Human Perception & Performance, 15*(3), 448–456.

Duncan, J. (1980). The locus of interference in the perception of simultaneous stimuli. *Psychological Review, 87*, 272–300.

Duncan, J. (1984). Selective attention and the organization of visual information. *Journal of Experimental Psychology: General, 113*, 501–517.

Duncan, J. (1988). Boundary conditions on parallel processing in human vision. *Perception, 17*, 358.

Duncan, J., & Humphreys, G. W. (1989). Visual search and stimulus similarity. *Psychological Review, 96*, 433–458.

Duncan, J., Ward, R., & Shapiro, K. L. (1994). Direct measurement of attentional dwell time in human vision. *Nature, 369*, 313–315.

Egeth, H. E., Virzi, R. A., & Garbart, H. (1984). Searching for conjunctively defined targets. *Journal of Experimental Psychology: Human Perception & Performance, 10*, 32–39.

Egly, R., Driver, J., & Rafal, R. D. (1994). Shifting visual attention between objects and locations: Evidence from normal and parietal lesion subjects. *Journal of Experimental Psychology: General, 123*, 161–177.

Enns, J. T., & Di Lollo, V. (1997). Object substitution: A new form of masking in unattended visual locations. *Psychological Science, 8*, 135–139.

Eriksen, B. A., & Eriksen, C. W. (1974). Effects of noise letters upon the identification of a target letter in a nonsearch task. *Perception & Psychophysics, 16*, 143–149.

Eriksen, C. W., & Hoffman, J. E. (1973). The extent of processing of noise elements during selective encoding from visual displays. *Perception & Psychophysics, 14*, 155–160.

Eriksen, C. W. & Murphy, T. D. (1987). Movement of attentional focus across the visual field: A critical look at the evidence. *Perception & Psychphysics, 42*(3), 299–305.

Eriksen, C. W., & Spencer, T. (1969). Rate of information processing in visual perception: Some results and methodological considerations. *Journal of Experimental Psychology Monograph, 79*, 1–16.

Eriksen, C. W., & St. James, J. D. (1986). Visual attention within and around the field of focal attention: A zoom lens model. *Perception & Psychophysics, 40*, 225–240.

Eriksen, C. W., & Yeh, Y.-y. (1985). Allocation of attention in the visual field. *Journal of Experimental Psychology: Human Perception & Performance, 11*, 583–597.

Folk, C. L., Remington, R. W., & Johnston, J. C. (1992). Involuntary covert orienting is contingent on attentional control settings. *Journal of Experimental Psychology: Human Perception & Performance, 18*, 1030–1044.

Foster, D. H., & Westland, S. (1992). Fine structure in the orientation threshold function for preattentive line-target detection. *Perception, 22*, (Supplement 2 (ECVP – Pisa)), 6.

Gandhi, S. P., Heeger, D. J., & Boynton, G. M. (1999). Spatial attention affects brain activity in human primary visual cortex. *Proceedings of the National Academy of Sciences of the United States of America, 96*, 3314–3319.

Garner, W. R., Hake, H. W., & Eriksen, C. W. (1956). Operationism and the concept of perception. *Psychological Review, 63*, 149–159.

Giesbrecht, B., & Di Lollo, V. (1998). Beyond the attentional blink: Visual masking by item substitution. *Journal of Experimental Psychology: Human Perception & Performance, 24* (5), 1454–1466.

Goldstein, E. B. and S. I. Fink (1981). Selective attention in vision: Recognition memory for superimposed line drawings. *Journal of Experimental Psychology: Human Perception & Performance, 7*, 954–967.

Grandison, T. D., Ghirardelli, T. G., & Egeth, H. E. (1997). Beyond similarity: Masking of the target is sufficient to cause the attentional blink. *Perception & Psychophysics, 59*, 266–274.

Grossberg, S., Mingolla, E., & Ross, W. D. (1994). A neural theory of attentive visual search:

Interactions of boundary, surface, spatial, and object representations. *Psychological Review, 101*(3), 470–489.
Haenny, P. E., & Schiller, P. H. (1988). State dependent activity in monkey visual cortex. I. Single cell activity in V1 and V4 on visual tasks. *Experimental Brain Research, 69*, 225–244.
Haxby, J. V., Courtney, S. M., & Clark, V. P. (1998). Functional magnetic resonance imaging and the study of attention. In R. Parasuraman (Ed.), *The attentive brain* (pp. 123–142). Cambridge, MA: MIT Press.
Haxby, J. V., Horwitz, B., Ungerleider, L. G., Maisog, J. M., Pietrini, P., & Grady, C. L. (1994). The functional organization of human extrastriate cortex: A PET-rCBF study of selective attention to faces and locations. *Journal of Neuroscience, 14*, 6336–6353.
He, S., Cavanagh, P., & Intrilligator, J. (1996). Attentional resolution and the locus of visual awareness. *Nature, 383*, 334–337.
He, S., Cavanagh, P., & Intrilligator, J. (1997). Attentional resolution. *Trends in Cognitive Science, 1*, 115–120.
He, Z. J., & Nakayama, K. (1992). Surfaces versus features in visual search. *Nature, 359*, 231–233.
Heathcote, A., & Mewhort, D. J. K. (1993). Representation and selection of relative position. *Journal of Experimental Psychology: Human Perception & Performance, 19*, 488–516.
Heinze, H. J., Mangun, G. R., Burchert, W., Hinrichs, H., Scholz, M., Munte, T. F., Gos, A., Johannes, S., & Hundeshagen, H. (1994). Combined spatial and temporal imaging of brain activity during visual selective attention in humans. *Nature, 372*, 543–546.
Henderson, J. M. (1992). Identifying objects across saccades: Effects of extrafoveal preview and flanker object context. *Journal of Experimental Psychology: Learning, Memory, & Cognition, 18*, 521–530.
Hikosaka, O., Miyauchi, S., & Shimojo, S. (1993). Focal visual attention produces illusory temporal order and motion sensation. *Vision Research, 33*, 1219–1240.
Hillyard, S. A., Hink, R. F., Schwent, V. L., & Picton, T. W. (1973). Electrical signs of selective attention in the human brain. *Science, 182*, 177–179.
Hochhaus, L., & Johnston, J. C. (1996). Perceptual repetition blindness effects. *Journal of Experimental Psychology: Human Perception & Performance, 22*, 355–366.
Hoffman, J. E. (1978). Search through a sequentially presented visual display. *Perception & Psychophysics, 23*, 1–11.
Hoffman, J. E. (1979). A two-stage model of visual search. *Perception & Psychophysics, 25*, 319–327.
Hoffman, J. E., & Nelson, B. (1981). Spatial selectivity in visual search. *Perception & Psychophysics, 30*, 283–290.
Horowitz, T. S., & Wolfe, J. M. (1998). Visual search has no memory. *Nature, 394*, 575–577.
Irwin, D. E. (1992). Perceiving an integrated visual world. In D. E. Meyer & S. Kornblum (Eds.), *Attention and performance XIV: Synergies in experimental psychology, artificial intelligence, and cognitive neuroscience* (pp. 121–142). Cambridge, MA: MIT Press.
James, W. (1890). *The principles of psychology*: Dover Publications, Inc.
Johnston, W. A., Hawley, K. J., Plew, S. H., Elliott, J. M., & DeWitt, M. J. (1990). Attention capture by novel stimuli. *Journal of Experimental Psychology: General, 119*, 397–411.
Jolicoeur, P. (1999). Concurrent response-selection demands modulate the attentional blink. *Journal of Experimental Psychology: Human Perception & Performance, 25* (4), 1097–1113.
Jonides, J. (1981). Voluntary versus automatic control over the mind's eye. In J. Long & A. Baddeley (Eds.), *Attention and performance IX* (pp. 187–203). Hillsdale, NJ: Lawrence Erlbaum Associates.
Jonides, J., & Yantis, S. (1988). Uniqueness of abrupt visual onset in capturing attention. *Perception & Psychophysics, 43*, 346–354.
Joseph, J. S., Chun, M. M., & Nakayama, K. (1997). Attentional requirements in a "preattentive" feature search task. *Nature, 387*, 805–808.
Joseph, J. S., Chun, M. M., & Nakayama, K. (1998). Vision and attention: The role of training – Reply. *Nature, 393*, 425.
Kahneman, D., & Chajczyk, D. (1983). Tests of the automaticity of reading: Dilution of Stroop

effects by color-irrelevant stimuli. *Journal of Experimental Psychology: Human Perception & Performance, 9*, 497–509.

Kahneman, D., & Henik, A. (1981). Perceptual organization and attention. In M. Kubovy & J. R. Pomerantz (Eds.), *Perceptual organization* (pp. 181–211). Hillsdale, NJ: Erlbaum.

Kahneman, D., & Treisman, A. (1984). Changing views of attention and automaticity. In R. Parasuraman & D. R. Davies (Eds.), *Varieties of attention* (pp. 29–61). Orlando, FL: Academic Press.

Kahneman, D., Treisman, A., & Gibbs, B. J. (1992). The reviewing of object files: Object-specific integration of information. *Cognitive Psychology, 24*, 175–219.

Kanizsa, G. (1979). *Organization in vision.* New York: Prager.

Kanwisher, N. (1987). Repetition blindness: Type recognition without token individuation. *Cognition, 27*, 117–143.

Kanwisher, N., & Driver, J. (1992). Objects, attributes, and visual attention: Which, what, and where. *Current Directions in Psychological Science, 1*, 26–31.

Kanwisher, N., McDermott, J., & Chun, M. M. (1997). The fusiform face area: A module in human extrastriate cortex specialized for face perception. *Journal of Neuroscience, 17*, 4302–4311.

Kanwisher, N., & Potter, M. C. (1990). Repetition blindness: Levels of processing. *Journal of Experimental Psychology: Human Perception & Performance, 16*, 30–47.

Kellman, P. J., & Shipley, T. F. (1991). A theory of visual interpolation in object perception. *Cognitive Psychology, 23*, 141–221.

Kihlstrom, J. F., Barnhardt, T. M., & Tataryn, D. J. (1992). Implicit perception. In T. S. P. Robert F. Bornstein (Ed.), *Perception without awareness: Cognitive, clinical, and social perspectives* (pp. 17–54). New York: Guilford Press.

Kim, M., & Cave, K. R. (1995). Spatial attention in visual search for features and feature conjunctions. *Psychological Science, 6*, 376–380.

Kinchla, R. A. (1974). Detecting targets in multi-element arrays: A confusability model. *Perception & Psychophysics, 15*, 149–158.

Klein, R. (1988). Inhibitory tagging system facilitates visual search. *Nature, 334*, 430–431.

Klein, R. M., & MacInnes, W. J. (1999). Inhibition of return is a foraging facilitator in visual search. *Psychological Science, 10*, 346–352.

Kramer, A. F., & Hahn, S. (1995). Splitting the beam: Distribution of attention over noncontiguous regions of the visual field. *Psychological Science, 6*, 381–386.

Kramer, A. F., & Jacobson, A. (1991). Perceptual organization and focused attention: The role of objects and proximity in visual processing. *Perception & Psychophysics, 50*, 267–284.

Kramer, A. F., Tham, M.-p., & Yeh, Y.-y. (1991). Movement and focused attention: A failure to replicate. *Perception & Psychophysics, 50*, 537–546.

Krose, B. J., & Julesz, B. (1989). The control and speed of shifts of attention. *Vision Research, 29*, 1607–1619.

Kutas, M., & Hillyard, S. A. (1980). Reading senseless sentences: Brain potentials reflect semantic incongruity. *Science, 207*, 203–205.

Kwak, H.-w., Dagenbach, D., & Egeth, H. (1991). Further evidence for a time-independent shift of the focus of attention. *Perception & Psychophysics, 49*, 473–480.

LaBerge, D. (1983). Spatial extent of attention to letters and words. *Journal of Experimental Psychology: Human Perception & Performance, 9*, 371–379.

Lavie, N. (1995). Perceptual load as a necessary condition for selective attention. *Journal of Experimental Psychology: Human Perception & Performance, 21*, 451–468.

Lavie, N., & Tsal, Y. (1994). Perceptual load as a major determinant of the locus of selection in visual attention. *Perception & Psychophysics, 56*, 183–197.

Lawrence, D. H. (1971). Two studies of visual search for word targets with controlled rates of presentation. *Perception & Psychophysics, 10*, 85–89.

Leopald, D. A., & Logothetis, N. K. (1996). Activity changes in early visual cortex reflect monkeys' percepts during binocular rivalry. *Nature, 379*, 549–553.

Levi, D. M., Klein, S. A., & Aitsebaomo, A. P. (1985). Vernier acuity, crowding and cortical magnification. *Vision Research, 25*, 963–977.

Levin, D. T., & Simons, D. J. (1997). Failure to detect changes to attended objects in motion pictures. *Psychonomic Bulletin & Review, 4*, 501–506.

Logan, G. D. (1996). The CODE theory of visual attention: An integration of space-based and object-based attention. *Psychological Review, 103*, 603–649.

Logothetis, N. K., & Schall, J. D. (1989). Neuronal correlates of subjective visual perception. *Science, 245*, 761–763.

Luck, S. (1998). Neurophysiology of selective attention. In H. Pashler (Ed.)., *Attention* (pp. 257–295). London: University College London Press.

Luck, S. J., Chelazzi, L., Hillyard, S. A., & Desimone, R. (1997a). Neural mechanisms of spatial selective attention in areas V1, V2, and V4 of macaque visual cortex. *Journal of Neurophysiology, 77*, 24–42.

Luck, S. J., Fan, S., & Hillyard, S. A. (1993). Attention-related modulation of sensory-evoked brain activity in a visual search task. *Journal of Cognitive Neuroscience, 5*, 188–195.

Luck, S. J., & Girelli, M. (1998). Electrophysiological approaches to the study of selective attention in the human brain. In R. Parasuraman (Ed.), *The attentive brain* (pp. 71–94). Cambridge, MA: MIT Press.

Luck, S. J., Girelli, M., McDermott, M. T., & Ford, M. A. (1997b). Bridging the gap between monkey neurophysiology and human perception: An ambiguity resolution theory of visual selective attention. *Cognitive Psychology, 33*, 64–87.

Luck, S. J., & Hillyard, S. A. (1994). Spatial filtering during visual search: Evidence from human electrophysiology. *Journal of Experimental Psychology: Human Perception & Performance, 20*, 1000–1014.

Luck, S. J., Hillyard, S. A., Mouloua, M., & Hawkins, H. L. (1996). Mechanisms of visual-spatial attention: Resource allocation or uncertainty reduction? *Journal of Experimental Psychology: Human Perception & Performance, 22*, 725–737.

Luck, S. J., & Vogel, E. K. (1997). The capacity of visual working memory for features and conjunctions. *Nature, 390*, 279–281.

Luck, S. J., Vogel, E. K., & Shapiro, K. L. (1996). Word meanings can be accessed but not reported during the attentional blink. *Nature, 383*, 616–618.

Lumer, E. D., Friston, K. J., & Rees, G. (1998). Neural correlates of perceptual rivalry in the human brain. *Science, 280*, 1930–1934.

Mack, A., & Rock, I. (1998). *Inattentional blindness*. Cambridge, MA: MIT Press.

Mack, A., Tang, B., Tuma, R., Kahn, S., & Rock, I. (1992). Perceptual organization and attention. *Cognitive Psychology, 24*, 475–501.

Maljkovic, V., & Nakayama, K. (1994). Priming of pop-out: I. Role of features. *Memory & Cognition, 22*(6), 657–672.

Maljkovic, V., & Nakayama, K. (1996). Priming of pop-out: II. The role of position. *Perception & Psychophysics, 58*(7), 977–991.

Maljkovic, V., & Nakayama, K. (2000). Priming of pop-out: III. A short-term implicit memory system beneficial for rapid target selection. *Visual Cognition, 7*, 571–595.

Mangun, G. R., Hillyard, S. A., & Luck, S. J. (1993). Electrocortical substrates of visual selective attention. In D. Meyer & S. Kornblum (Eds.), *Attention and performance XIV* (pp. 219–243). Cambridge, MA: MIT Press.

Marcel, A. J. (1983). Conscious and unconscious perception: Experiments on visual masking and word recognition. *Cognitive Psychology, 15*, 197–237.

Marrara, M. T., & Moore, C. M. (1998). Allocating visual attention in depth given surface information. *Investigative Ophthalmology & Visual Science, 39*, S631.

Maunsell, J. H. (1995). The brain's visual world: Representation of visual targets in cerebral cortex. *Science, 270*, 764–769.

McConkie, G. W., & Currie, C. B. (1996). Visual stability across saccades while viewing complex pictures. *Journal of Experimental Psychology: Human Perception & Performance, 22*(3), 563–581.

McCormick, P. A., Klein, R. M., & Johnston, S. (1998). Splitting versus sharing focal attention:

Comment on Castiello and Umilta (1992). *Journal of Experimental Psychology: Human Perception & Performance, 24*, 350–357.
Miller, J. (1991). The flanker compatibility effect as a function of visual angle, attentional focus, visual transients, and perceptual load: A search for boundary conditions. *Perception & Psychophysics, 49*, 270–288.
Milliken, B., & Tipper, S. P. (1998). Attention and inhibition. In H. Pashler (Ed.), *Attention* (pp. 191–221). East Sussex: Psychology Press Ltd.
Moore, C. M., & Egeth, H. (1997). Perception without attention: Evidence of grouping under conditions of inattention. *Journal of Experimental Psychology: Human Perception & Performance, 23*(2), 339–352.
Moore, C. M., Egeth, H., Berglan, L. R., & Luck, S. J. (1996). Are attentional dwell times inconsistent with serial visual search? *Psychonomic Bulletin & Review, 3*, 360–365.
Moore, C. M., Yantis, S., & Vaughan, B. (1998). Object-based visual selection: Evidence from perceptual completion. *Psychological Science, 9*, 104–110.
Moran, J., & Desimone, R. (1985). Selective attention gates visual processing in the extrastriate cortex. *Science, 229*, 782–784.
Motter, B. C. (1993). Focal attention produces spatially selective processing in visual cortical areas V1, V2, and V4 in the presence of competing stimuli. *Journal of Neurophysiology, 70*(3), 909–919.
Motter, B. C. (1994). Neural correlates of attentive selection for color or luminance in extrastriate area V4. *Journal of Neuroscience, 14*, 2178–2189.
Motter, B. C. (1998). Neurophysiology of visual attention. In R. Parasuraman (Ed.), *The attentive brain* (pp. 51–69). Cambridge, MA: MIT Press.
Mozer, M. C., & Sitton, M. (1998). Computational modeling of spatial attention. In H. Pashler (Ed.), *Attention* (pp. 341–393). East Sussex: Psychology Press Ltd.
Muller, H. J., Humphreys, G. W., & Donnelly, N. (1994). SEarch via Recursive Rejection (SERR): Visual search for single and dual form-conjunction targets. *Journal of Experimental Psychology: Human Perception & Performance, 20*, 235–258.
Nagy, A. L., & Sanchez, R. R. (1990). Critical color differences determined with a visual search task. *Journal of the Optical Society of America, 7*, 1209–1217.
Nakayama, K., He, Z. J., & Shimojo, S. (1995). Visual surface representation: A critical link between lower-level and higher-level vision. In S. M. Kosslyn and D. N. Osherson (Eds.), *An invitation to cognitive science: Visual cognition, Vol. 2* (pp. 1–70). Cambridge, MA: MIT Press.
Nakayama, K., & Joseph, J. S. (1998). Attention, pattern recognition, and pop-out in visual search. In R. Parasuraman (Ed.), *The attentive brain* (pp. 279–298). Cambridge, MA: MIT Press.
Nakayama, K., & Mackeben, M. (1989). Sustained and transient components of focal visual attention. *Vision Research, 29*, 1631–1647.
Nakayama, K., & Silverman, G. H. (1986). Serial and parallel processing of visual feature conjunctions. *Nature, 320*, 264–265.
Neely, J. H. (1977). Semantic priming and retrieval from lexical memory: Roles of inhibitionless spreading activation and limited-capacity attention. *Journal of Experimental Psychology: General, 106*, 226–254.
Neill, W. T. (1977). Inhibitory and facilitatory processes in selective attention. *Journal of Experimental Psychology: Human Perception & Performance, 3*, 444–450.
Neisser, U. (1967). *Cognitive psychology*. New York: Appleton-Century-Crofts.
Neisser, U., & Becklen, R. (1975). Selective looking: Attending to visually specified events. *Cognitive Psychology, 7*, 480–494.
Neumann, E., & DeSchepper, B. G. (1992). An inhibition-based fan effect: Evidence for an active suppression mechanism in selective attention. *Canadian Journal of Psychology, 46*, 1–40.
Nobre, A. C., Sebestyen, G. N., Gitelman, D. R., Mesulam, M. M., Frackowiak, R. S., & Frith, C. D. (1997). Functional localization of the system for visuospatial attention using positron emission tomography. *Brain, 120* (Pt 3), 515–533.
O'Craven, K. M., Downing, P. E., & Kanwisher, N. (1999). fMRI evidence for objects as the units

of attentional selection. *Nature, 401*, 584–587.
O'Craven, K. M., Rosen, B. R., Kwong, K. K., Treisman, A., & Savoy, R. L. (1997). Voluntary attention modulates fMRI activity in human MT-MST. *Neuron, 18*, 591–598.
Palmer, J. (1994). Set-size effects in visual search: The effect of attention is independent of the stimulus for simple tasks. *Vision Research, 34*, 1703–1721.
Palmer, J. (1995). Attention in visual search: Distinguishing four causes of a set size effect. *Current Directions in Psychological Science, 4*, 118–123.
Parasuraman, R. (Ed.) (1998). *The attentive brain.* Cambridge, MA: MIT Press.
Pashler, H. (1984). Processing stages in overlapping tasks: Evidence for a central bottleneck. *Journal of Experimental Psychology: Human Perception & Performance, 10*, 358–377.
Pashler, H. (1987). Detecting conjunctions of color and form: Reassessing the serial search hypothesis. *Perception & Psychophysics, 41*, 191–201.
Pashler, H. (1988). Cross-dimensional interaction and texture segregation. *Perception & Psychophysics, 43*, 307–318.
Pashler, H. (1998). *The psychology of attention.* Cambridge, MA: MIT Press.
Posner, M. I. (1980). Orienting of attention. *Quarterly Journal of Experimental Psychology, 32*, 3–25.
Posner, M. I., & Cohen, Y. (1984). Components of visual orienting. In H. Bouma & D. G. Bouwhuis (Eds.), *Attention and performance X* (pp. 55–66). Hillsdale, NJ: Erlbaum.
Posner, M. I., & Dehaene, S. (1994). Attentional networks. *Trends in Neurosciences, 17*, 75–79.
Posner, M. I., & Gilbert, C. D. (1999). Attention and primary visual cortex. *Proceedings of the National Academy of Sciences of the United States of America, 96*, 2585–2587.
Posner, M. I., & Petersen, S. (1990). The attention system of the human brain. *Annual Review of Neuroscience, 13*, 25–42.
Posner, M. I., Snyder, C. R., & Davidson, B. J. (1980). Attention and the detection of signals. *Journal of Experimental Psychology: General, 109*, 160–174.
Posner, M. I., & Snyder, C. R. R. (1975). Attention and cognitive control. In R. L. Solso (Ed.), *Information processing and cognition: The Loyola Symposium.* Hillsdale, NJ: Lawrence Erlbaum Associates Inc.
Potter, M. C. (1975). Meaning in visual search. *Science, 187*, 965–966.
Potter, M. C. (1993). Very short-term conceptual memory. *Memory & Cognition, 21*, 156–161.
Prinzmetal, W., Nwachuku, I., & Bodanski, L. (1997). The phenomenology of attention: 2. Brightness and contrast. *Consciousness & Cognition: An International Journal, 6*(2–3), 372–412.
Prinzmetal, W., Amiri, H., Allen, K., & Edwards, T. (1998). Phenomenology of attention: I. Color, location, orientation, and spatial frequency. *Journal of Experimental Psychology: Human Perception & Performance, 24*(1), 261–282.
Pylyshyn, Z. (1989). The role of location indexes in spatial perception: A sketch of the FINST spatial-index model. *Cognition, 32*, 65–97.
Pylyshyn, Z. W., & Storm, R. W. (1988). Tracking multiple independent targets : Evidence for a parallel tracking mechanism. *Spatial Vision, 3*, 179–197.
Rafal, R. (1995). Visual attention: Converging operations from neurology and psychology. In A. F. Kramer, M. G. H. Coles, & G. D. Logan (Eds.), *Converging operations in the study of visual selective attention* (pp. 193–223). Washington, DC: American Psychological Association.
Raymond, J. E., Shapiro, K. L., & Arnell, K. M. (1992). Temporary suppression of visual processing in an RSVP task: An attentional blink? *Journal of Experimental Psychology: Human Perception & Performance, 18*, 849–860.
Remington, R., & Pierce, L. (1984). Moving attention: Evidence for time-invariant shifts of visual selective attention. *Perception & Psychophysics, 35*, 393–399.
Remington, R. W., Johnston, J. C., & Yantis, S. (1992). Involuntary attentional capture by abrupt onsets. *Perception & Psychophysics, 51*, 279–290.
Rensink, R. A., & Enns, J. T. (1995). Preemption effects in visual search: Evidence for low-level grouping. *Psychological Review, 102*, 101–130.
Rensink, R. A., O'Regan, J. K., & Clark, J. J. (1997). To see or not to see: The need for attention to perceive changes in scenes. *Psychological Science, 8*, 368–373.

Rock, I., & Gutman, D. (1981). The effect of inattention on form perception. *Journal of Experimental Psychology: Human Perception & Performance, 7,* 275–285.
Rock, I., Linnett, C. M., Grant, P., & Mack, A. (1992). Perception without attention: Results of a new method. *Cognitive Psychology, 24,* 502–534.
Rubin, E. (1958). Figure and ground. In D. C. Beardslee & M. Wertheimer (Eds.), *Readings in perception.* New York: Van Nostrand.
Sagi, D., & Julesz, B. (1985). Fast noninertial shifts of attention. *Spatial Vision, 1,* 141–149.
Schall, J. D., & Bichot, N. P. (1998). Neural correlates of visual and motor decision processes. *Current Opinion in Neurobiology, 8*(2), 211–217.
Schall, J. D., & Hanes, D. P. (1993). Neural basis of saccade target selection in frontal eye field during visual search. *Nature, 366,* 467–469.
Schall, J. D., & Thompson, K. G. (1999). Neural selection and control of visually guided eye movements. *Annual Review of Neuroscience, 22,* 241–259.
Seiffert, A. E., & Di Lollo, V. (1997). Low-level masking in the attentional blink. *Journal of Experimental Psychology: Human Perception & Performance, 23,* 1061–1073.
Sergent, J., Ohta, S., & MacDonald, B. (1992). Functional neuroanatomy of face and object processing. A positron emission tomography study. *Brain, 115 Pt 1,* 15–36.
Shapiro, K. L., Arnell, K. M., & Raymond, J. E. (1997a). The attentional blink: A view on attention and glimpse on consciousness. *Trends in Cognitive Science, 1,* 291–296.
Shapiro, K., Driver, J., Ward, R., & Sorensen, R. E. (1997b). Priming from the attentional blink: A failure to extract visual tokens but not visual types. *Psychological Science, 8*(2), 95–100.
Shapiro, K. L., Raymond, J. E., & Arnell, K. M. (1994). Attention to visual pattern information produces the attentional blink in rapid serial visual presentation. *Journal of Experimental Psychology: Human Perception & Performance, 20,* 357–371.
Shaw, M. L., & Shaw, P. (1977). Optimal allocation of cognitive resources to spatial locations. *Journal of Experimental Psychology: Human Perception & Performance, 3,* 201–211.
Shiffrin, R. M., & Gardner, G. T. (1972). Visual processing capacity and attentional control. *Journal of Experimental Psychology, 93,* 72–82.
Shiu, L., & Pashler, H. (1994). Negligible effect of spatial precuing on identification of single digits. *Journal of Experimental Psychology: Human Perception & Performance, 20,* 1037–1054.
Shulman, G. L., Remington, R. W., & McLean, J. P. (1979). Moving attention through visual space. *Journal of Experimental Psychology: Human Perception and Performance, 5,* 522–526.
Simons, D. J. (2000). Current approaches to change blindness. *Visual Cognition: Special Issue on Change Detection and Visual Memory, 7,* 1–6.
Simons, D. J., & Chabris, C. F. (1999). Gorillas in our midst: Sustained inattentional blindness for dynamic events. *Perception, 28*(9), 1059–1074.
Simons, D., & Levin, D. (1997). Change blindness. *Trends in Cognitive Science, 1,* 261–267.
Simons, D. J., & Levin, D. (1997). Failure to detect changes to people during a real-world interaction. *Psychonomic Bulletin & Review, 37A,* 571–590.
Somers, D. C., Dale, A. M., Seiffert, A. E., & Tootell, R. B. (1999). Functional MRI reveals spatially specific attentional modulation in human primary visual cortex. *Proceedings of the National Academy of Sciences of the United States of America, 96,* 1663–1668.
Sperling, G. (1960). The information available in brief visual presentations. *Psychological Monographs: General and Applied, 74,* 1–29.
Sperling, G., Budiansky, J., Spivak, J. G., & Johnson, M. C. (1971). Extremely rapid visual search: The maximum rate of scanning letters for the presence of a numeral. *Science, 174,* 307–311.
Sperling, G., & Weichselgartner, E. (1995). Episodic theory of the dynamics of spatial attention. *Psychological Review, 102,* 503–532.
Suzuki, S., & Cavanagh, P. (1997). Focused attention distorts visual space: An attentional repulsion effect. *Journal of Experimental Psychology: Human Perception & Performance, 23,* 443–463.
Theeuwes, J. (1991). Cross-dimensional perceptual selectivity. *Perception & Psychophysics, 50,* 184–193.

Theeuwes, J. (1992). Perceptual selectivity for color and form. *Perception & Psychophysics, 51*, 599–606.

Tipper, S. P. (1985). The negative priming effect: Inhibitory priming by ignored objects. *Quarterly Journal of Experimental Psychology, 37A*, 571–590.

Tipper, S. P., & Driver, J. (1988). Negative priming between pictures and words in a selective attention task: Evidence for semantic processing of ignored stimuli. *Memory & Cognition, 16*, 64–70.

Titchener, E. B. (1908). *Lectures on the elementary psychology of feeling and attention.* New York: Macmillan.

Tong, F., Nakayama, K., Vaughan, J. T., & Kanwisher, N. (1998). Binocular rivalry and visual awareness in human extrastriate cortex. *Neuron, 21*, 753–759.

Tootell, R. B. H., Hadjikhani, N., Hall, E. K., Marrett, S., Vanduffel, W., Vaughan, J. T., & Dale, A. M. (1998). The retinotopy of visual spatial attention. *Neuron, 21*, 1409–1422.

Townsend, J. T., & Ashby, F. G. (1983). *The stochastic modeling of elementary psychological processes.* Cambridge: Cambridge University Press.

Townsend, J. T., Taylor, S. G., & Brown, D. R. (1971). Lateral masking for letters with unlimited viewing time. *Perception & Psychophysics, 10*, 375–378.

Treisman, A. (1960). Contextual cues in selective listening. *Quarterly Journal of Experimental Psychology, 12*, 242–248.

Treisman, A. (1988). Features and objects: The fourteenth Bartlett memorial lecture. *The Quarterly Journal of Experimental Psychology, 40A*(2), 201–237.

Treisman, A., & Gelade, G. (1980). A feature-integration theory of attention. *Cognitive Psychology, 12*, 97–136.

Treisman, A., & Schmidt, H. (1982). Illusory conjunctions in the perception of objects. *Cognitive Psychology, 14*, 107–141.

Treisman, A., & Kanwisher, N. G. (1998). Perceiving visually presented objects: Recognition, awareness, and modularity. *Current Opinion in Neurobiology, 8*, 218–226.

Treisman, A., & Sato, S. (1990). Conjunction search revisited. *Journal of Experimental Psychology: Human Perception & Performance, 16*, 459–478.

Treisman, A., Vieira, A., & Hayes, A. (1992). Automaticity and preattentive processing. Special Issue: Views and varieties of automaticity. *American Journal of Psychology, 105*, 341–362.

Treue, S., & Maunsell, J. H. (1996). Attentional modulation of visual motion processing in cortical areas MT and MST. *Nature, 382*, 539–541.

Tsal, Y. (1983). Movement of attention across the visual field. *Journal of Experimental Psychology: Human Perception & Performance, 9*, 523–530.

Tse, P., Cavanagh, P., & Nakayama, K. (1998). The role of parsing in high-level motion processing. In T. Watanabe (Ed.), *High-level motion processing: Computational, neurobiological, and psychophysical perspectives* (pp. 249–266). Cambridge: MIT Press.

Tsotsos, J. K., Culhane, S. N., Wai, W. Y. K., Lai, Y., Davis, N., & Nuflo, F. (1995). Modeling visual attention via selective tuning. *Artificial Intelligence, 78*, 507–545.

Tulving, E., & Schacter, D. L. (1990). Priming and human memory systems. *Science, 247*, 301–306.

Vecera, S. P., & Farah, M. J. (1994). Does visual attention select objects or locations? *Journal of Experimental Psychology: General, 123*, 146–160.

Vogel, E. K., Luck, S. J., & Shapiro, K. L. (1998). Electrophysiological evidence for a postperceptual locus of suppression during the attentional blink. *Journal of Experimental Psychology: Human Perception & Performance, 24* (6), 1656–1674.

Wang, Q., Cavanagh, P., & Green, M. (1994). Familiarity and pop-out in visual search. *Perception & Psychophysics, 56*, 495–500.

Ward, R., Duncan, J., & Shapiro, K. (1996). The slow time-course of visual attention. *Cognitive Psychology, 30*, 79–109.

Watson, D. G., & Humphreys, G. W. (1997). Visual marking: Prioritizing selection for new objects by top-down attentional inhibition of old objects. *Psychological Review, 104*, 90–122.

Weichselgartner, E., & Sperling, G. (1987). Dynamics of automatic and controlled visual attention. *Science, 238*, 778–780.

Welford, A. T. (1952). The "psychological refractory period" and the timing of high-speed performance: A review and theory. *British Journal of Psychology, 43*, 2–19.

Winer, G. A., & Cottrell, J. E. (1996). Does anything leave the eye when we see? Extramission beliefs of children and adults. *Current Directions in Psychological Science, 5*, 137–142.

Wojciulik, E., Kanwisher, N., & Driver, J. (2000). Covert visual attention modulates face-specific activity in the human fusiform gyrus: fMRI study. *Journal of Neurophysiology, 79*, 1574–1578.

Wolfe, J. M. (1994a). Guided Search 2.0: A revised model of guided search. *Psychonomic Bulletin & Review, 1*, 202–238.

Wolfe, J. M. (1994b). Visual search in continuous, naturalistic stimuli. *Vision Research, 34*, 1187–1195.

Wolfe, J. M. (1998a). Inattentional amnesia. In V. Coltheart (Ed.), *Fleeting memories*. Cambridge, MA: MIT Press.

Wolfe, J. M. (1998b). Visual search. In H. Pashler (Ed.), *Attention*. London: University College London Press.

Wolfe, J. M. (1998c). What can 1 million trials tell us about visual search? *Psychological Science, 9*, 33–39.

Wolfe, J. M., & Bennett, S. C. (1997). Preattentive object files: Shapeless bundles of basic features. *Vision Research, 37*, 25–43.

Wolfe, J. M., Cave, K. R., & Franzel, S. L. (1989). Guided search: An alternative to the feature integration model for visual search. *Journal of Experimental Psychology: Human Perception & Performance, 15*, 419–433.

Wolfe, J. M., & Gancarz, G. (1996). Guided Search 3.0: A model of visual search catches up with Jay Enoch 40 years later. In V. Lakshminarayana (Ed.), *Basic and clinical applications of vision science* (pp. 189–192). Dordrecht, Netherlands: Kluwer Academic.

Woodman, G. F., & Luck, S. J. (1999). Electrophysiological measurement of rapid shifts of attention during visual search. *Nature, 400*, 867–869.

Yantis, S. (1988). On analog movements of visual attention. *Perception & Psychophysics, 43*, 203–206.

Yantis, S. (1992). Multielement visual tracking: Attention and perceptual organization. *Cognitive Psychology, 24*, 295–340.

Yantis, S. (1998). Control of visual attention. In H. Pashler (Ed.), *Attention* (pp. 223–256). London: University College London Press.

Yantis, S., & Johnson, D. N. (1990). Mechanisms of attentional priority. *Journal of Experimental Psychology: Human Perception & Performance.*

Yantis, S., & Johnston, J. C. (1990). On the locus of visual selection: Evidence from focused attention tasks. *Journal of Experimental Psychology: Human Perception & Performance, 16*, 135–149.

Yantis, S., & Jonides, J. (1984). Abrupt visual onsets and selective attention: Evidence from visual search. *Journal of Experimental Psychology: Human Perception & Performance, 10*, 601–621.

Yeshurun, Y., & Carrasco, M. (1998). Attention improves or impairs visual performance by enhancing spatial resolution. *Nature, 396*, 72–75.

Chapter Ten

Separate Visual Systems for Action and Perception[1]

Melvyn A. Goodale and G. Keith Humphrey

What Is Vision For?

One of the most important functions of vision is the creation of an internal model or percept of the external world – a representation that allows us to think about objects and events and understand their relations. Most research in the psychology of sensation and perception has concentrated on this function of vision (for related discussion of this issue see Georgeson, 1997; Watt, 1991, 1992). There is another function of vision, however, which is concerned not with the perception of objects per se but with the control of actions directed at those objects. We will suggest that separate, but interacting, visual systems have evolved for the perception of objects on the one hand and the control of actions directed at those objects on the other. This "duplex" approach to high-level vision suggests that "reconstructive" approaches, perhaps best exemplified by Marr (1982), and "purposive-animate-behaviorist" approaches, such as that advocated by Gibson (1979), need not be mutually exclusive and may be actually complementary (for further discussion of this issue see Goodale & Humphrey, 1998).

For most people, there is nothing more to vision than visual experience. This everyday conception of vision was in fact the one put forward by Marr, who was perhaps the most influential visual theorist in recent years (see Marr, 1982, p. 3). There is plenty of evidence, however, that much of the work done by the visual system has nothing to do with sight or experiential perception. The pupillary light reflex, the synchronization of circadian rhythms with the local light-dark cycle, and the visual control of posture are but three examples of a range of visually modulated outputs where we have no direct experience of the controlling stimuli and where the underlying control mechanisms have little to do with our perception of the world. Yet most contemporary accounts of vision, while acknowledging the existence of these "extra-perceptual" visual phenomena, still assume that the main function of the visual system is the construction of some sort of internal model or percept of the external world (for a detailed discussion of this issue, see Goodale, 1983a, 1988, 1995, 1997). In such accounts, phenomena such as the pupillary light reflex are seen as simple servomechanisms which, although useful, are not part of the essential machinery for the construction of the visual percept. But, as we shall see, the visual control of far more complex behaviors, such as grasping or walking, are also in some sense extra-perceptual. Like the control of the pupillary reflex, the control of these behaviors depends on pathways in the brain that are quite independent from those mediating experiential perception.

Vision for Action

Vision evolved in animals not to enable them to "see" the world, but to guide their movements through it. Indeed, the visual system of most animals, rather than being a general-purpose network dedicated to reconstructing the rather limited world in which they live, consists instead of a set of relatively independent input-output lines, or visuomotor "modules," each of which is responsible for the visual control of a particular class of motor outputs.

A classic example of modularity in the vertebrate visual system is the so-called "bug detector," a specialized ganglion cell in the retina of the frog whose response characteristics are matched to "bug-like" stimuli – small, quick-moving, high-contrast targets (Lettvin, Maturana, McCulloch, & Pitts, 1959). These cells have been shown to project to structures in the midbrain of the frog that are specialized for the control of prey-catching (for review, see Ewert, 1987). One of the most compelling demonstrations of the modularity of this pathway comes from experiments with so-called "rewired" frogs.

Because the amphibian brain is capable of far more regeneration following damage than the mammalian brain, it is possible to "re-wire" some retinal projections, such as those going to the optic tectum in the midbrain, while leaving all the other retinal projections intact. Thus, the retinotectal projections in the frog can be induced to project to the optic tectum on the same side of the frog's brain instead of to the optic tectum on the opposite side, as is the case in the normal animal. In one such experiment, "re-wired" frogs showed "mirror-image" prey-catching movements – directing their sticky tongue to positions in space that were mirror-symmetrical to the location of prey objects (Ingle, 1973). These frogs also showed mirror-image predator avoidance and jumped towards rather than away from a looming visual stimulus, such as the experimenter's hand. These results suggest that the optic tectum plays a critical role in the visual control of these patterns of behavior in the frog. Remarkably, however, the same "rewired" frogs showed quite normal visually guided barrier avoidance as they locomoted from one place to another, even when the edge of the barrier was placed in the visual field where mirror-image feeding and predator avoidance could be elicited.

As it turns out, the reason the frogs showed normal visual control of barrier avoidance is quite straightforward; the retinal projections to the pretectum, a structure in the thalamus just in front of the optic tectum, were still intact and had not been redirected to the opposite side of the brain. A number of lesion studies have shown that this structure plays a critical role in the visual control of barrier avoidance (Ingle, 1980, 1982). In fact, frogs with a rewired pretectum show mirror-image barrier avoidance but normal prey-catching and visually-elicited escape (Ingle, personal communication). Thus, it would appear that there are at least two independent visuomotor systems in the frog: a tectal system, which mediates visually elicited prey-catching and predator-avoidance, and a pretectal system which mediates visually guided locomotion around barriers. In fact, more recent work suggests that the tectal system itself can be even further subdivided with the visual control of prey-catching and the visual control of escape behavior depending on separate circuits between the tectum and lower brainstem structures (Ingle, 1991). At last count, there may be upwards of five or more distinct visuomotor networks in the amphibian brain, each with its own set of retinal inputs and each controlling different arrays of motor outputs (Ewert, 1987; Ingle, 1991).

A good deal of work with rodents has also demonstrated the existence of independent visuomotor modules for many different behaviors from orienting head movements to barrier avoidance (e.g., Ellard & Goodale, 1986, 1988; Goodale, 1983b, 1996; Goodale & Carey, 1990). The behavior of rodents, however, is more flexible than the behavior of most amphibia, suggesting that the visuomotor networks are more complex than those in the frog.

In primates, of course, the complexity of their lives demands even more flexible organization of basic visuomotor circuitry than that seen in rodents. In monkeys (and thus presumably in humans as well), there is evidence that many of the phylogenetically ancient visuomotor circuits that were present in more primitive vertebrates are now modulated by more recently evolved control systems in the cerebral cortex (for review, see Milner & Goodale, 1995). Thus, the highly adaptive visuomotor behavior of humans and other higher primates is made possible by the evolution of other layers of control in a series of hierarchically organized networks. This idea of hierarchical control of behavior was proposed over a hundred years ago by John Hughlings Jackson (Jackson, 1875), an eminent nineteenth-century British neurologist who was heavily influenced by concepts of evolution.

Jackson tried to explain the effects of brain damage in his patients by suggesting that such damage, particularly in the cerebral cortex, removed the more highly evolved aspects of brain function. He argued that what one saw in the performance of many patients with cerebral insults was the expression of evolutionarily older mechanisms residing in more ancient brain structures. The emergence of more flexible visuomotor control has not been accomplished entirely by cortical modulation of older circuitry, however. The basic subcortical circuitry has itself changed to some extent and new visuomotor circuits have evolved. As a result of the emergence of this circuitry, modern primates can use vision to control an almost limitless range of motor outputs. Nevertheless, as we shall see later, for the most part, these visuomotor networks have remained separate from those mediating our visual perception of the world.

Vision for Perception

Flexible visuomotor control was only one of the demands put on the evolving visual system in primates and other animals. Survival also depended on being able to identify objects, to understand their significance and causal relations, to plan an appropriate course of action, and, in the case of social animals, to communicate with other members of the group. Vision began to play a role in all of this. But it was not enough to develop more visuomotor modules, however flexible they might be. What was needed was the development of *representational systems* that could model the world and serve as a platform for cognitive operations (Craik, 1943). The representational systems that use vision to generate such models or percepts of the world must carry out very different transformations on visual input from those carried out by the visuomotor modules described earlier. [The nature of these differences will be explored later.] Moreover, these representational systems, which generate our perception of the world, are not linked directly to specific motor outputs but are linked instead to cognitive systems involving memory, semantics, spatial reasoning, planning, and communication.

But even though such "higher-order" representational systems permit the formation of goals and the decision to engage in a specific act without reference to particular motor outputs, the actual execution of an action may nevertheless be mediated by dedicated visuomotor modules that are not dissimilar in principle from those found in frogs and toads. In summary, vision in humans and other primates (and presumably in other animals as well) has two distinct but interacting functions: (a) the perception of objects and their relations, which provides a foundation for the organism's cognitive life, and (b) the control of actions directed at (or with respect to) those objects, in which specific sets of motor outputs are programmed and guided "online".

Action and Perception Systems in the Primate Brain

It has been proposed that the two different requirements for vision outlined in the previous section – vision for perception and vision for action – are subserved by two different "streams of visual processing" (Goodale & Milner, 1992; Milner & Goodale, 1995). These distinct streams of visual processing were first identified by Ungerleider and Mishkin (1982) in the cerebral cortex of the macaque monkey. They described one stream, the so-called *ventral stream,* projecting from primary visual cortex to inferotemporal cortex, and another, the so-called *dorsal stream,* projecting from primary visual cortex to posterior parietal cortex. The major projections and cortical targets for these two streams are illustrated in Figure 10.1. Although one must always be cautious when drawing homologies between monkey and human neuroanatomy (Crick & Jones, 1993), it seems likely that the visual projections from the primary visual cortex to the temporal and parietal lobes in the human brain may involve a separation into ventral and dorsal streams similar to that seen in the macaque brain.

Ungerleider and Mishkin (1982) suggested initially, on the basis of a number of behavioral and electrophysiological studies in the monkey, that the ventral stream plays a critical role in object vision, enabling the monkey to identify an object while the dorsal stream is more involved in spatial vision, enabling the monkey to localize the object in space. Some have referred to this distinction in visual processing as one between "what" versus "where." Although the evidence for the Ungerleider and Mishkin proposal initially seemed quite compelling, recent findings from a broad range of studies in both humans and monkeys has led to a reinterpretation of the division of labor between the two streams. This reinterpretation, which was put forward by Goodale and Milner (1992; Milner & Goodale, 1995), rather than emphasizing differences in the visual information handled by the two streams (object vision versus spatial vision), focuses instead on the differences in the requirements of the *output systems* that each stream of processing serves. It should be noted that the Ungerleider and Mishkin proposal still influences the theoretical ideas of many cognitive neuroscientists (e.g., Kosslyn, 1994), although most investigators acknowledge that the posterior parietal cortex plays an important role in the visual control of action.

According to Goodale and Milner's (1992) new proposal, the ventral stream plays the major role in constructing the perceptual representation of the world and the objects within it, while the dorsal stream mediates the visual control of actions directed at those objects. In other words, processing within the ventral stream allows us to recognize an object, such as a banana in a bowl of fruit, while processing within the dorsal stream provides critical information about the location, orientation, size, and shape of that banana so that we can

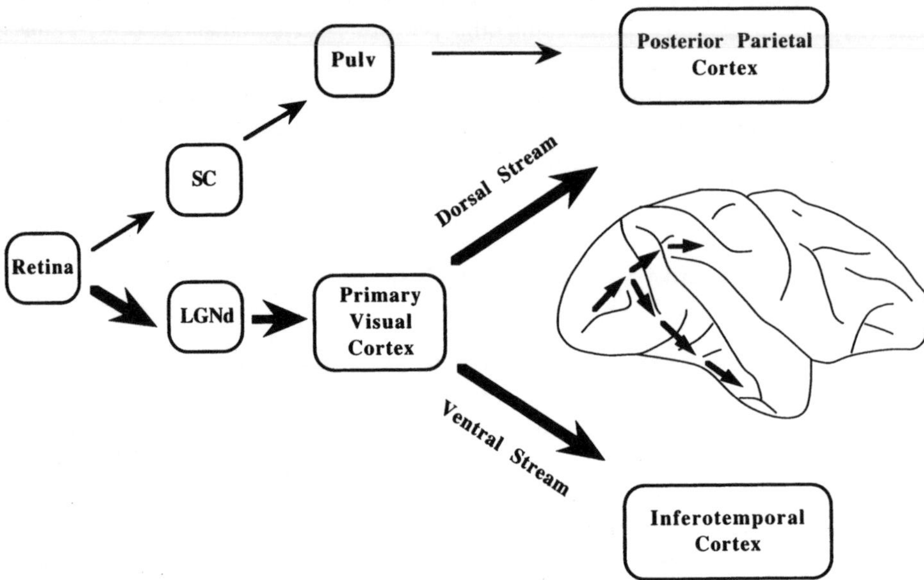

Figure 10.1. The major routes whereby retinal input reaches the dorsal and ventral streams. The diagram of the macaque brain (right hemisphere) on the right of the figure shows the approximate routes of the cortico-cortical projections from the primary visual cortex to the posterior parietal and the inferotemporal cortex, respectively. LGNd: lateral geniculate nucleus, pars dorsalis; Pulv: pulvinar; SC: superior colliculus.

reach out and pick it up. This is not a distinction between what and where. In this account, the structural and spatial attributes of the goal object are being processed by both streams, but for different purposes. In the case of the ventral stream, information about a broad range of object parameters is being transformed for perceptual purposes; in the case of the dorsal stream, some of these same object parameters are being transformed for the control of actions. This is not to say that the distribution of subcortical visual inputs does not differ between the two streams, but rather that the main difference lies in the nature of the transformations that each stream performs on those two sets of inputs.

Neuropsychological Evidence for Action and Perception Streams

Effects of Damage to the Human Dorsal Stream

Patients who have sustained damage to the superior portion of the posterior parietal cortex, the major terminus of the dorsal stream, are unable to use visual information to reach out and grasp objects in the hemifield contralateral to the lesion. Clinically, this deficit is called optic ataxia (Bálint, 1909). Such patients have no difficulty using other sensory information, such as proprioception, to control their reaching; nor do they usually have difficulty recognizing or describing objects that are presented in that part of the visual field. Thus, their deficit is neither "purely" visual nor "purely" motor; it is a visuomotor deficit. Moreover, this deficit cannot be explained as a disturbance in spatial vision. In fact, in one clear sense their "spatial vision" is quite intact, because they can often describe the relative location of objects in the visual field contralateral to their lesion, even though they cannot pick them up (Jeannerod, 1988).

Observations in several laboratories have shown that patients with lesions in the posterior parietal cortex can also show deficits in their ability to adjust the orientation of their hand when reaching toward an object (Perenin & Vighetto, 1988; Binkofski et al., 1998; Jeannerod, Decety, & Michel, 1994). At the same time, these same patients have no difficulty in verbally describing the orientation of the object (Perenin & Vighetto, 1988). Such patients can also have trouble adjusting their grasp to reflect the size of an object they are asked to pick up – although again their perceptual estimates of object size remain quite accurate (Jakobson, Archibald, Carey, & Goodale, 1991; Goodale, Murphy, Meenan, Racicot, & Nicolle, 1993).

To pick up an object successfully, however, it is not enough to orient the hand and scale the grip appropriately; the fingers and thumb must be placed at appropriate opposition points on the object's surface. To do this, the visuomotor system has to compute the outline shape or boundaries of the object. In a recent experiment (Goodale et al., 1994), a patient (RV) with bilateral lesions of the occipitoparietal region was asked to pick up a series of small, flat, non-symmetrical smoothly contoured objects using a precision grip, which required her to place her index finger and thumb in appropriate positions on either side of each object. If the fingers were incorrectly positioned, the objects would slip out of the subject's grasp. Presumably, the computation of the correct opposition points ("grasp points") can be achieved only if the overall shape or form of the object is taken into account. Despite the fact that the patient could readily distinguish these objects from one another, she often failed to place her fingers on the appropriate grasp points when she attempted to pick up the objects (Figure 10.2).

These observations are quite consistent with Goodale and Milner's (1992) proposal that the dorsal stream plays a critical role in the visuomotor transformations required for skilled actions, such as visually guided prehension – in which the control of an accurate grasp requires information about an object's location as well as its orientation, size, and shape. It should be emphasized that not all patients with damage to the posterior parietal region have difficulty shaping their hand to correspond to the structural features and orientation of the target object. Some have difficulty with hand postures, some with controlling the direction of their grasp, and some with foveating the target (e.g., Binkofski et al., 1998). Indeed, depending upon the size and locus of the lesion, a patient can demonstrate any combination of these visuomotor deficits (for review, see Milner & Goodale, 1995). Different sub-regions of the posterior parietal cortex, it appears, support transformations related to the visual control of specific motor outputs (for review, see Rizzolatti, Luppino, & Matelli, 1998).

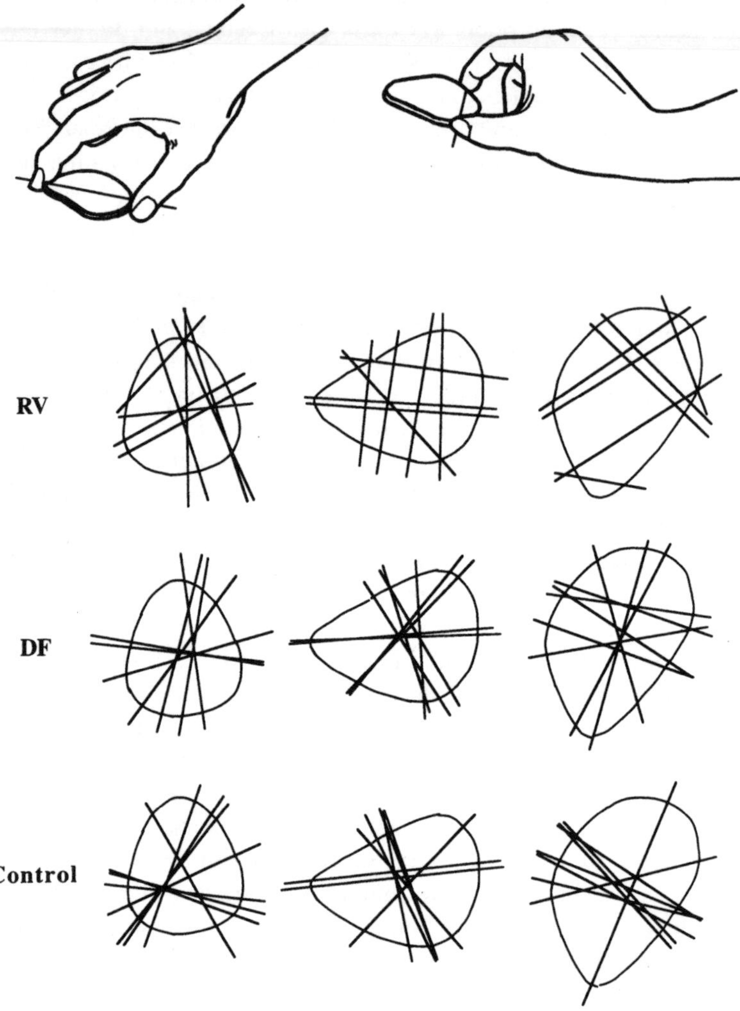

Figure 10.2. The top two drawings illustrate a "stable" grasp (left) that would allow one to pick up the object and an "unstable" grasp (right) that would likely result in the object slipping out of one's hand. The "grasp lines" (joining points where the index finger and the thumb first made contact with the shape) are also illustrated. The grasp lines selected by the optic ataxic patient (RV), the visual form agnosic patient (DF), and the control subject when picking up three of the 12 shapes used in the experiment by Goodale et al. (1994) are also shown. The four different orientations in which each shape was presented have been rotated so that they are aligned. No distinction is made between the points of contact for the thumb and finger in these plots. It can be seen that the optic ataxic patient made many more unstable grasps than did the agnosic patient or the control subject.

Effects of Damage to the Human Ventral Stream

Just as there are individuals with brain damage who are unable to pick up objects properly that they have no difficulty identifying, there are other individuals, with damage elsewhere in their brain, who show the opposite pattern of deficits and spared behavior. In other words, these individuals can grasp objects quite accurately despite their failure to recognize what it is they are picking up. One such patient is DF, a young woman who developed a profound visual form agnosia following near-asphyxiation by carbon monoxide. Not only is DF unable to recognize the faces of her relatives and friends or the visual shape of common objects, but she is also unable to discriminate between simple geometric forms such as a triangle and a circle. DF has no problem identifying people from their voices or identifying objects from how they feel. Her perceptual problems are exclusively visual. Moreover, her deficit seems largely restricted to the form of objects. She can use color and other surface features to identify objects (Humphrey, Goodale, Jakobson, & Servos, 1994; Humphrey, Symons, Herbert, & Goodale, 1996; Servos, Goodale, & Humphrey, 1993). What she seems unable to perceive are the contours of objects – no matter how the contours are defined (Milner et al.,1991). A selective deficit in form perception with spared color and other surface information is characteristic of the severe visual agnosia that sometimes follows an anoxic episode. Although MRI shows a pattern of diffuse brain damage in DF that is consistent with anoxia, most of the damage was evident in the ventrolateral region of the occipital lobe sparing primary visual cortex.

Not surprisingly, DF is unable to copy line drawings. Thus, her failure to identify the drawings in the left-hand side of Figure 10.3 is not due to a failure of the visual input to invoke the stored representations of the objects. Hers is a failure of perceptual organization, a deficit that Lissauer (1890) called "apperceptive agnosia." Although DF cannot copy line drawings, she can draw objects reasonably well from long-term memory (Servos et al., 1993). In fact, her visual imagery is remarkably intact, suggesting that it is possible to have a profound deficit in the perceptual processing of form without any deficit in the corresponding visual imagery (Servos & Goodale, 1995).

DF's deficit in form perception cannot be explained by appealing to disturbances in "low-level" sensory processing. She is able to detect luminance-defined targets out to at least 30°; her flicker detection and fusion rates are normal; and her spatial contrast sensitivity is normal above 10 cycles per degree and only moderately impaired at lower spatial frequencies (Milner et al., 1991). [Of course, even though she could detect the presence of the gratings used to measure her contrast sensitivity, she could not report their orientation. See also Humphrey, Goodale & Gurnsey, 1991.] But the most compelling reason to doubt that DF's perceptual deficit is due to a low-level disturbance in visual processing is the fact that in another domain, visuomotor control, she remains exquisitely sensitive to the form of objects.

Despite a profound inability to recognize the shape, size, and orientation of objects, DF shows strikingly accurate guidance of hand and finger movements directed at those very same objects. Thus, when DF was presented with a large slot which could be placed in one of a number of different orientations, she showed great difficulty in indicating the orientation of the slot either verbally or even manually by rotating a hand-held card (see Figure

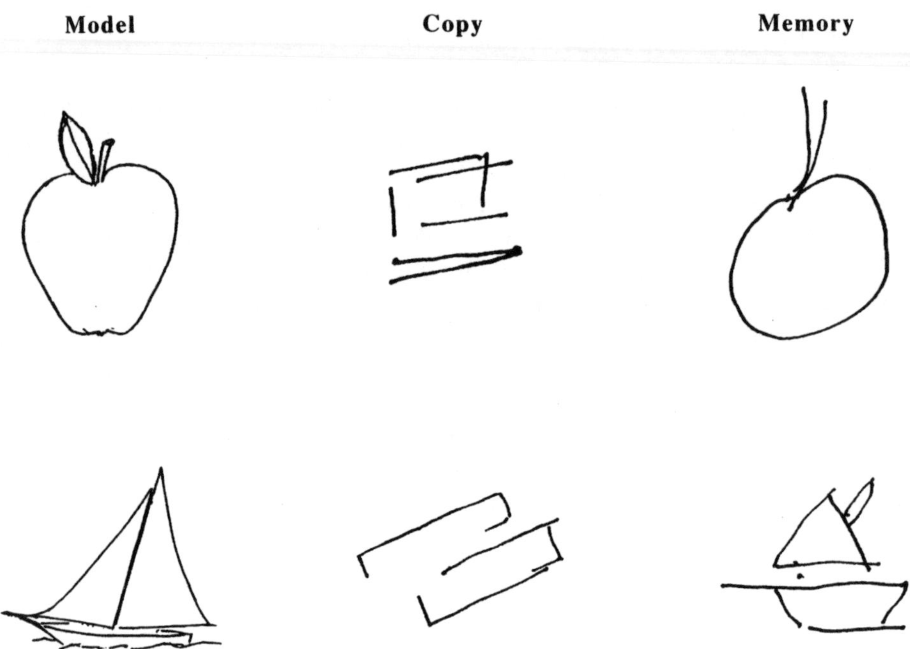

Figure 10.3. Samples of drawings made by DF. The left column shows examples of line drawings that were shown to DF, the right column shows some of DF's drawings of three objects from memory, and the middle column shows examples of DF's copies of the line drawings shown in the left column.

10.4, left). Nevertheless, when she was asked simply to reach out and insert the card, she performed as well as normal subjects, rotating her hand in the appropriate direction *as soon as she began the movement* (see Figure 10.4, right).

A similar dissociation was seen in DF's responses to the spatial dimensions of objects. When presented with a pair of rectangular blocks of the same or different dimensions, she was unable to distinguish between them. Even when she was asked to indicate the width of a single block by means of her index finger and thumb, her matches bore no relationship to the dimensions of the object and showed considerable trial-to-trial variability. In contrast, when she was asked simply to reach out and pick up the block, the aperture between her index finger and thumb changed systematically with the width of the object as the movement unfolded, just as in normal subjects (Goodale, Milner, Jakobson, & Carey, 1991). Finally, even though DF could not discriminate between target objects that differed in outline shape, she could nevertheless pick up such objects successfully, placing her index finger and thumb on stable grasp points (see Figure 10.2). In other words, DF matched the posture of her reaching hand to the orientation, size, and shape of the object she was about to pick up, even though she appeared to be unable to perceive those same object attributes.

These spared visuomotor skills are not limited to reaching and grasping movements; DF

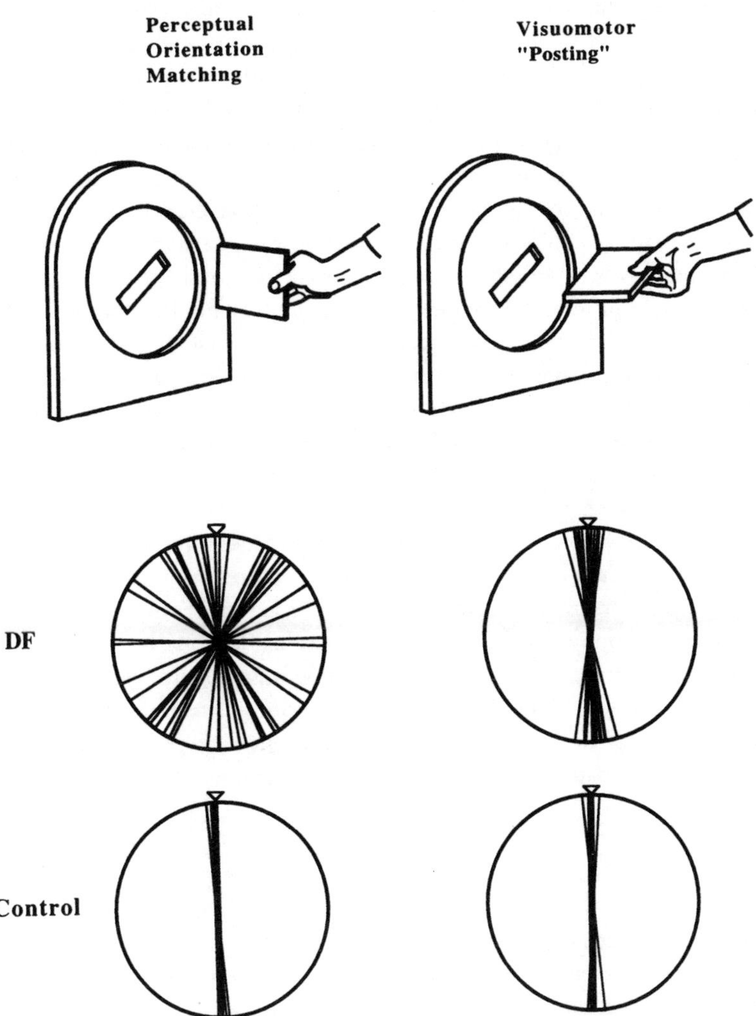

Figure 10.4. The top of the figure shows an illustration of the task in which DF and a control subject were asked to rotate a card to match the orientation of a slot (left), or to "post" the card into the slot (right). In the illustration of the matching task (top left), the orientation of the card is not well matched to the orientation of the slot. This is the sort of response that DF would often make. In contrast, when performing the posting task (top right) DF would orient the card appropriately to fit in the slot. Below are shown results of the study expressed as polar plots of the orientation of the hand-held card when DF and a control subject were each asked to rotate the card to match the orientation of the slot (left-hand column) or to "post" the card into the slot (right-hand column). The orientation of the card on the visuomotor task was measured at the instant before the card was placed in the slot. In both plots, the actual orientations of the slot have been normalized to vertical.

can also walk around quite well under visual control. In formal testing, we found that she is able to step over obstacles as well as control subjects even though her verbal descriptions of the heights of the obstacles were far from normal (Patla & Goodale, 1996).

These findings in DF provide additional support for Goodale and Milner's (1992) contention that there are separate neural pathways for transforming incoming visual information for action and perception. Presumably it is the latter and not the former that is compromised in DF. In other words, the brain damage that she suffered as a consequence of anoxia appears to have interrupted the normal flow of shape and contour information into her perceptual system without affecting the processing of shape and contour information by the visuomotor modules comprising her action system. If, as Goodale and Milner have suggested, the perception of objects and events is mediated by the ventral stream of visual projections to inferotemporal cortex, then DF should show evidence for damage relatively early in this pathway. An MRI of her brain taken a year after the accident showed that this was indeed the case. Even though DF showed the typical pattern of diffuse damage that follows anoxia, there was nevertheless a major focus of damage in the ventrolateral region of the occipital cortex, an area that is thought to be part of the human homologue of the ventral stream. Primary visual cortex, which provides input for both the dorsal and ventral streams, appeared to be largely intact. Thus, although input from primary visual cortex to the ventral stream may have been compromised in DF, input from this structure to the dorsal stream appeared to be essentially intact. In addition, the dorsal stream, unlike the ventral stream, also receives input from the superior colliculus via the pulvinar, a nucleus in the thalamus (see Figure 10.1). Input to the dorsal stream from both the superior colliculus (via the pulvinar) and the lateral geniculate nucleus (via primary visual cortex) could continue to mediate well-formed visuomotor responses in DF.

Blindsight

The dissociation between perception and action shown by DF is actually not the first such dissociation to be observed in neurological patients. An even more striking dissociation has been reported in patients who have sustained damage to primary visual cortex. These patients, unlike DF, claim to see nothing at all in the field contralateral to the lesion. Yet remarkably, even patients like these – patients who show a complete absence of visual experience in one half of their visual field – will demonstrate, under the right testing conditions, residual visual abilities in this "blind" field. The visual abilities of such "blindsight" patients can be quite astonishing (for review, see Weiskrantz, 1986, 1997). Perenin and Rossetti (1996), for example, described the behavior of a patient with a large occipital lesion that included all of primary visual cortex in the left hemisphere. Despite the absence of any awareness of visual stimuli in his right visual field, when the patient directed manual movements to objects presented in his blind field, the posture of his hand reflected the orientation and size of the object. How could such well-formed visually guided actions survive the removal of primary visual cortex? As we already mentioned, there is a pathway from the superior colliculus to the posterior parietal cortex (via the pulvinar) that could mediate the necessary transformations, even in the absence of input from primary visual cortex (see Figure 10.1). Of course, there are also inputs to visual areas in the cerebral cortex from the LGNd that bypass primary visual cortex, although they are extremely few in number. These projections might also mediate some of the spared visual abilities in blindsight patients.

In some ways, DF resembles patients with blindsight. She fails to perceive the form of objects, but can use the form information to direct many of her movements. Of course, unlike blindsight patients, she can still perceive the color and texture of objects and their motion. It would not be inaccurate to characterize her deficit as "form-specific blindsight."

Electrophysiological and Behavioral Evidence in the Monkey

The neuropsychological evidence reviewed above provides strong support for the proposed division of labor between the two streams suggested by Goodale and Milner (1992). It is important to remember, however, that the anatomical distinction between two streams of visual processing in the cerebral cortex has been most clearly demonstrated not in humans, but in monkeys. But even in monkeys, the functional distinction between perception and action appears to map rather well onto the ventral and dorsal streams respectively.

Ventral Stream Studies

It has been known for a long time that monkeys with lesions of inferotemporal cortex show profound deficits in object recognition. Nevertheless, a number of anecdotal accounts suggest that these animals are able to use visual information about the form of objects to guide their movements. Thus, Klüver and Bucy (1939) reported that monkeys with inferotemporal lesions are as capable as normal animals at picking up small food objects. Similarly, Pribram (1967) noted that his monkeys with inferotemporal lesions were remarkably adept at catching flying insects with their hand. More recent formal testing has revealed that these monkeys can orient their fingers in a precision grip to grasp morsels of food embedded in small slots placed at different orientations – even though their orientation discrimination abilities are profoundly impaired (Glickstein, Buchbinder, & May, 1998). In short, these animals behave much the same way as DF: They are unable to discriminate between objects on the basis of visual features that they can clearly use to direct their grasping movements.

There is a long history of electrophysiological work showing that cells in inferotemporal cortex are tuned to specific objects or object features (e.g., see Logothetis, 1998; Tanaka, 1996). Moreover, the responses of these cells are not affected by the animal's motor behavior, but are instead sensitive to the reinforcement history and significance of the visual stimuli that drive them. Indeed, sensitivity to particular objects can be created in ensembles of cells in inferotemporal cortex simply by training the animals to discriminate between different objects (Logothetis, Pauls, & Poggio, 1995). Finally, there is evidence for a specialization within separate regions of the ventral stream for the coding of certain categories of objects, such as faces and hands, which are of particular social significance to the monkey. (This review of work on the monkey ventral stream is far from complete. Interested readers are directed to Logothetis (1998), Logothetis and Sheinberg (1996), Perrett, Benson, Hietanen, Oram, and Dittrich (1995), Milner and Goodale (1995) and Tanaka (1996)).

Dorsal Stream Studies

A strikingly different picture is seen in the dorsal stream. Most visually sensitive cells in the posterior parietal cortex are modulated by the concurrent motor behavior of the animal (e.g., Hyvärinen & Poranen, 1974; Mountcastle, Lynch, Georgopoulos, Sakata, & Acuña, 1975). In reviewing the electrophysiological studies that have been carried out on the posterior parietal cortex, Andersen (1987) concluded that most neurons in these areas "exhibit both sensory-related and movement-related activity." The activity of some visually-driven cells in this region has been shown to be linked to saccadic eye movements; the activity of others to whether or not the animal is fixating a stimulus; and the activity of still other cells to whether or not the animal is engaged in visual pursuit or is making goal-directed reaching movements (e.g., Snyder, Batista, & Andersen, 1997). These different populations of cells are segregated in different regions of the posterior parietal cortex. Cells in still other regions of the posterior parietal cortex that fire when monkeys reach out to pick up objects are selective not for the spatially directed movement of the arm, but for the movements of the wrist, hand, and fingers that are made prior to and during the act of grasping the target (Hyvärinen & Poranen, 1974; Mountcastle et al., 1975). In a particularly interesting recent development, Sakata and his colleagues have shown that many of these so-called "manipulation" cells are visually selective and are tuned for objects of a particular shape and/or orientation (Sakata, Taira, Mine, & Murata, 1992; Taira, Mine, Georgopoulos, Murata, & Sakata, 1990; for review see Sakata & Taira, 1994; Sakata, Taira, Kusunoki, Murata, & Tanaka, 1997). These manipulation neurons thus appear to be tied to the properties of the goal object as well as to the distal movements that are required for grasping that object. Finally, it should be noted that lesions in the posterior parietal area in the monkey produce deficits in the visual control of saccades and/or reaching and grasping, similar in many respects to those seen in humans following damage to the homologous region (e.g., Haaxma & Kuypers, 1975; Ettlinger, 1990; Lynch & McLaren, 1989). In a recent study, small reversible pharmacological lesions were made in the region of the posterior parietal cortex where manipulation cells are located. When the circuitry in this region was inactivated, there was a selective interference with pre-shaping of the hand as the monkey reached out to grasp an object (Gallese, Murata, Kaseda, Niki, & Sakata, 1994). [This review of work on the monkey dorsal stream is clearly far from complete. Interested readers are directed to Andersen (1997), Rizzolatti et al. (1998), and Milner and Goodale (1995)].

The "Landmark" Test

In their original conception of the division of labor between the two streams, Ungerleider and Mishkin (1982) argued that "spatial vision" is mediated largely by the dorsal stream of visual processing. One of the important pieces of behavioral evidence for this claim was the observation that monkeys with posterior parietal lesions had little problem learning a conventional object discrimination, but had much more difficulty with a "landmark" task in which the animal is required to choose one of two covered foodwells on the basis of the proximity of a landmark object placed somewhere between the two (Pohl, 1973; Ungerleider & Brody, 1977). It has been commonly assumed that animals with inferotemporal lesions, while showing deficits on an object discrimination task, are unimpaired on the landmark task. Yet, even the early studies by Pohl and by Ungerleider and Brody found that animals with inferotemporal lesions were impaired relative to control animals on the landmark task, although not so severely as the monkeys with posterior parietal lesions. The monkeys with parietal damage have been shown to be particularly impaired on a version of the landmark task in which the task is made more difficult over successive training days by moving the landmark closer to the midpoint between the two foodwells. But then again, even normal monkeys have difficulty when the landmark is moved further and further away from the correct response site. Part of the problem seems to be that if the animal fails to look at the landmark, performance falls to chance (Sayner & Davis, 1972). In fact, looking at and touching the landmark before choosing a foodwell is a strategy that many normal monkeys adopt to solve the problem. Because monkeys, as we have already seen, often show deficits in the visual control of their saccadic eye movements and/or limb movements following posterior parietal lesions, such animals would be less likely to engage in this strategy and, as a consequence, might fail to choose the correct foodwell. This explanation for the poor performance of monkeys with parietal lesions is supported by the observation that such animals are also impaired on tasks in which the cue is separated from the foodwell but it is not the location of the cue but one of its object features (such as its color) that determines the correct foodwell choice (Bates & Ettlinger, 1960; Lawler & Cowey, 1987; Mendoza & Thomas, 1975). In summary, the impairment on landmark tasks following dorsal stream lesions is most likely due to disruption in the circuitry controlling particular visuomotor outputs such as shifts in gaze and goal-directed reaching, rather than a general disturbance in spatial vision. In fact, there is little other evidence to suggest that monkeys with posterior parietal lesions show deficits in spatial perception.

Neuroimaging Evidence in Humans

Recent neuroimaging studies have revealed an organization of visual areas in the human cerebral cortex that is remarkably similar to that seen in the macaque (reviewed in Tootell, Dale, Sereno, & Malach, 1996; Tootell, Hadjikhani, Mendola, Marrett, & Dale, 1998). Although clear differences in the topography of these areas emerges as one moves from monkey to human, the functional separation into a ventral occipitotemporal and a dorsal occipitoparietal pathway appears to be preserved. Thus, areas in the occipitotemporal region appear to be specialized for the processing of colour, texture, and form differences of objects (e.g., Kanwisher, Chun, McDermott & Ledden, 1996; Kiyosawa et al., 1996; Malach et al., 1995; Price, Moore, Humphreys, Frackowiak, & Friston, 1996; Puce, Allison, Asgari, Gore, & McCarthy, 1996; Vanni, Revonsuo, Saarinen, & Hari, 1996). In contrast, regions in the posterior parietal cortex have been found that are activated when subjects engage in visually guided movements such as saccades, reaching movements, and grasping (Matsumura et al., 1996).

As in the monkey, there is evidence for specialization within the occipitotemporal and occipitoparietal visual pathways. Thus, activation studies have identified regions in the occipitotemporal pathway for the processing of faces that are distinct from those involved in the processing of other objects (Kanwisher, McDermott, & Chun, 1997; McCarthy, Puce, Gore, & Allison, 1997; Sams, Hietanen, Hari, Ilmoniemi, & Lounasmaa, 1997; but see Gauthier, Anderson, Tarr, Skudlarski, & Gore, 1997). Similarly, there is evidence that different areas in and around the intraparietal sulcus are activated when subjects make saccadic eye movements as opposed to manual pointing movements towards visual targets (e.g., Kawashima et al., 1996). A region in the human brain that appears to correspond to that part of the monkey posterior parietal region where visually sensitive manipulation cells have been localized shows selective activation during visually guided grasping (Binkofski et al., 1998). Finally, a recent study of prism-adaptation shows that selective activation of the posterior parietal cortex occurs during the remapping of visual and proprioceptive representations of hand position (Clower et al., 1996).

Thus, as this brief review of the burgeoning neuroimaging literature indicates, many of the findings are consistent with the idea that there are two visual streams in the human cerebral cortex – just as there are in the monkey. In addition, the results of several studies suggest that areas in the posterior parietal cortex of the human brain are involved in the visual control of action, and that areas in the occipitotemporal region appear to play a role in object recognition.

The Control of Action Versus Perceptual Representation

The division of labor within the organization of the cerebral visual pathways in primates reflects the two important trends in the evolution of vision in higher vertebrates that were identified earlier. First, the emergence of a dorsal "action" stream reflects the need for more flexible programming and online control of visually guided motor outputs than was provided by the phylogenetically older subcortical visuomotor pathways. Second, the emergence of a ventral "perception" stream which can parse the visual array into discrete objects and events means that animals like ourselves can use perceptual representations of those objects and their relations for long-range planning, communication, and other cognitive activities. Indeed, the ventral stream projections to the inferotemporal cortex, which is intimately connected with structures in the medial temporal lobe and prefrontal cortex involved in long-term memory and other cognitive activities, is exquisitely poised to serve as interface between vision and cognition. In short, while the dorsal stream and its subcortical connections allows us visual control of our movements through the world, it is the ventral stream that gives us sight.

It seems clear that one important way in which the perception system differs from the visuomotor modules making up the action system is the way in which the visual world is represented in the brain. Of course, the notion of representation is one of the central ideas in perception and cognition, although the type(s) of representations used in visual perception and the very notion of representation itself have been the source of much debate. Nevertheless, the goal of visual perception is often taken to be the creation of a representation that is in some sense an internal model of the three-dimensional world. In this sense, a representation is a reconstruction of the world (for further critical discussion of this approach see Ballard & Brown, 1992; Churchland, Ramachandran, & Sejnowski, 1994; Cliff & Noble, 1997; Edelman, 1998 and accompanying commentaries; Tarr & Black, 1994 and accompanying commentaries; see also Goodale & Humphrey, 1998). This approach to vision is exemplified by Marr (1982) who concentrated on the representation of information about objects for the purposes of recognition. According to this approach, the major task of perception is to reconstruct a detailed and accurate model or replica of the three-dimensional world on the basis of the two-dimensional data present at the retinas. In the context of the arguments being made in this chapter, it is the construction of this kind of representation that is the major function of the perception system. In other words, the mechanisms in the ventral perception system construct representations that can serve as the substrate upon which a large range of cognitive operations can be mounted. Indeed, as we shall see below, the cognitive operations are themselves intimately involved in the construction of the representations upon which they operate.

Our perception of the world certainly appears remarkably rich and detailed. It is becoming increasingly apparent, however, that much of this perceptual representation is "virtual" and is derived from memory rather than visual input (e.g., McConkie & Currie, 1996; O'Regan, 1992; Rensink, O'Regan, & Clark, 1997). But although this representation allows us to think about the world and plan our actions, it offers a poor metric for the actions that we might wish to carry out (for review, see Goodale & Haffenden, 1998; Intraub, 1997). Further, the metrical information that is available is not computed with reference to the observer as much as it is to other objects in the visual array. Indeed, if perceptual representations were to attempt to deliver the real metrics of all objects in the visual array, the computational load would be astronomical. The solution that perception appears to have adopted is to use world-based coordinates – in which the real metric of that world need not be computed. Only the relative position, orientation, size, and motion of objects is of concern to perception. Such relative frames of reference are sometimes called allocentric. The use of relative or allocentric frames of reference means that we can, for example, watch the same scene unfold on television or on a movie screen without being confused by the enormous absolute change in the coordinate frame.

As soon as we direct a motor act towards an object, an entirely different set of constraints applies. No longer can we rely on the perception system's allocentric representations. To be accurate, an action must be finely tuned to the metrics of the real world. Moreover, different actions will engage different effectors. As a consequence, the computations for the visual control of actions must not only take into account the real metrics of the world, they must be specific to the particular motor output required. Directing a saccadic eye movement, for example, will demand different transformations of visual input to motor output from those required to direct a manual grasping movement. The former will involve coordinate systems centered on the retina and/or head, while the latter will involve shoulder and/or wrist centered coordinates. While it is theoretically possible that a highly sophisticated "general-purpose" representation could accommodate such transformations, such a possibility seems unlikely, unnecessary, and at odds with the empirical evidence we have already reviewed.

Dissociations Between Action and Perception in Normal Observers

As discussed above, the frames of reference for perception and action are very different. Perception depends almost entirely on allocentric frames of reference and relational metrics whereas the action system uses egocentric frames of reference and absolute metrics. For this reason, in normal observers, the visual information underlying the calibration and control of a skilled motor act directed at an object might not always match the perceptual judgments made about that object. In the following sections, we review some of the evidence that supports this idea.

Spatial Localization in Action and Perception

It has long been known that our perception of the position of a small dot is affected to a large degree by the position of the frame surrounding the dot. Thus, when the frame is moved unexpectedly to the left, we typically see the frame as stationary and the dot as moving to the right (Duncker, 1929/1938). Nevertheless, as a number of researchers have demonstrated, our visuomotor systems are not fooled by such manipulations, and when we are asked to point to the dot, our pointing movements are not influenced by changes in the position of the frame and we typically continue to point in the correct direction (e.g., Bridgeman, Lewis, Heit, & Nagle, 1979; Bridgeman, Kirch, & Sperling, 1981; Wong & Mack, 1981; for review, see Bridgeman, 1992; Goodale & Haffenden, 1998).

The Computation of Size in Action and Perception

Similar dissociations between perception and action have been demonstrated with object size. Although we can make subtle judgments about the relative sizes of objects, we rarely make judgments of their absolute size. Indeed, our perception of size is so inherently relative that we are subject to all sorts of pictorial illusions in which objects of the same size appear to be different because of the surrounding visual context. Take the Ebbinghaus Illusion, for example. In this familiar illusion, which is illustrated in Figure 10.5a, two target circles of equal size, each surrounded by a circular array of either smaller or larger circles, are presented side by side. Subjects typically report that the target circle surrounded by the array of smaller circles appears larger than the one surrounded by the array of larger circles, presumably because of the difference in the contrast in size between the target circles and the surrounding circles. In another version of the illusion, illustrated in Figure 10.5b, the target circles can be made to appear identical in size by increasing the actual size of the target circle surrounded by the larger circles.

Although our perceptual judgments are clearly affected by these manipulations of the stimulus array, there is good reason to believe that the calibration of size-dependent motor outputs, such as grip aperture during grasping, would not be. When we reach out to pick up an object, we must compute its real size if we are to pick it up efficiently. It is not

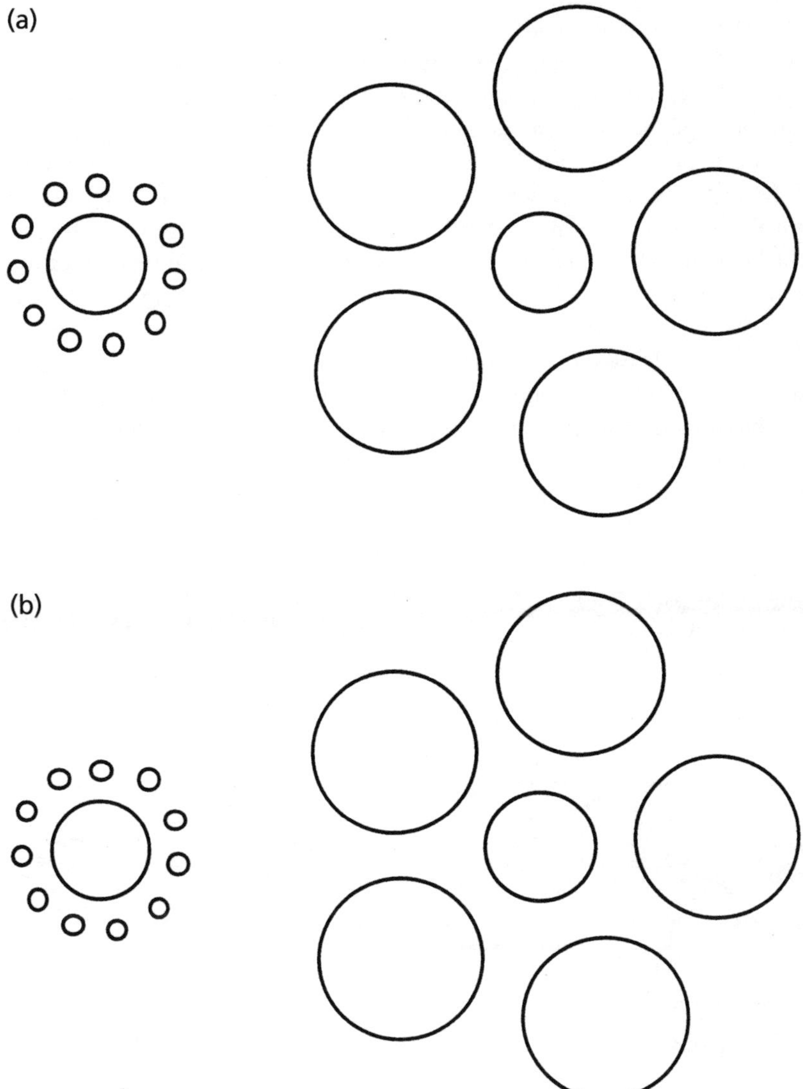

Figure 10.5. The "'Ebbinghaus" illusion. The standard version of the illusion, in which the target circles in the center of the two arrays appear to be different in size even though they are physically identical, is shown in (a). For most people, the circle in the annulus of smaller circles appears to be larger than the circle in the annulus of larger circles. (b) shows a version of the illusion in which the target circle in the array of larger circles has been made physically larger than the other target circle. The two target circles should now appear to be perceptually equivalent in size.

enough to know that it is larger or smaller than surrounding objects. One might expect, therefore, that grip scaling would be insensitive to size-contrast illusions. Such a result was recently found in two experiments that used a three-dimensional version of the Ebbinghaus illusion in which two thin "poker-chip" disks were arranged as pairs on a standard annular circle display (Aglioti, DeSouza, & Goodale, 1995; Haffenden & Goodale, 1998a; see Figure 10.6). Trials in which the two disks appeared perceptually identical but were physically different in size were randomly alternated with trials in which the disks appeared perceptually different but were physically identical. Even though subjects showed robust perceptual illusions – even in a matching task in which they opened their index finger and thumb to match the perceived diameter of one of the disks – their grip aperture was correlated with the real size of the disk when they reached out to pick it up (see Figure 10.6b).

The dissociation between perceptual judgments and the calibration of grasping is not limited to the Ebbinghaus Illusion. The relative insensitivity of reaching and grasping to pictorial illusions has also been demonstrated for the Müller-Lyer illusion (Gentilucci, Chieffi, Daprati, Saetti, & Toni, 1996), the horizontal-vertical illusion (Vishton & Cutting, 1995), and the Ponzo illusion (Brenner & Smeets, 1996). Most recently, Creem, Wraga, and Proffit (1998) demonstrated a similar dissociation between verbal judgments and locomotor accuracy using a large-scale Müller-Lyer illusion. Collectively, these studies of visual illusions demonstrate a separation in the mechanisms and visual representations underlying perception and action. Such a separation was described earlier in relation to the

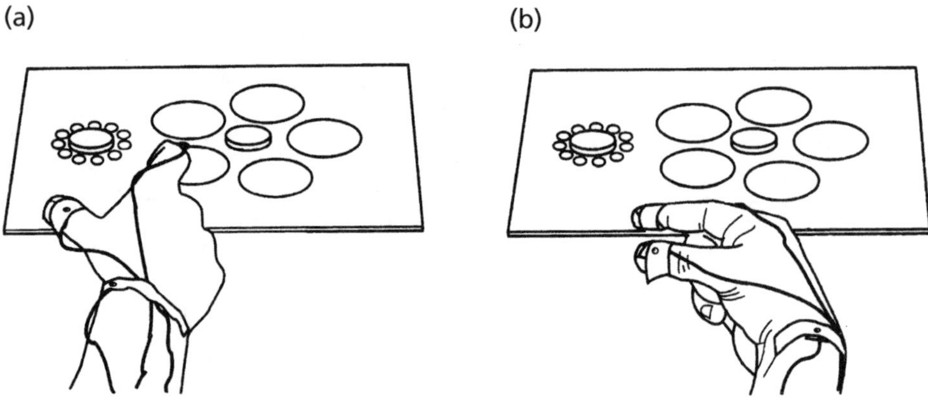

Figure 10.6. An illustration of the two tasks performed by each subject using a three-dimensional version of the Ebbinghaus illusion. Light-emitting diodes were attached to the finger, thumb, and wrist to allow for optoelectronic tracking. The grasping task is illustrated in (a). In this illustration the subject's hand is pictured in-flight on the way to the target disk. In the grasping task the grip aperture was correlated with the real size of the disk when they reached out to pick it up. (b) illustrates the manual estimation task. The heel of the subject's hand rested on the table and the subjects opened their thumb and index finger by an amount that matched the perceived size of the target disk. In the manual estimation task the subjects showed robust perceptual illusions, opening their index finger and thumb to match the perceived diameter of one of the disks.

brain-damaged patient DF. It seems that in the normal brain action systems also operate somewhat separately from perception systems.

It has been argued that pictorial illusions reveal something about how the perceptual system makes sense of the different elements in a particular scene (e.g., Gregory, 1998). These operations, in which the relations amongst a number of objects in the visual array are computed, are clearly central to perception. In contrast, the execution of a goal-directed act like manual prehension depends on metrical computations that are centered on only one object, the target itself. Moreover, the visual mechanisms within the action system that mediate the control of the grasping movements must compute the real distance of the object from the subject (presumably on the basis of reliable cues such as stereopsis, vergence, and retinal motion). As a consequence, computation of the retinal image size of the object coupled with an accurate estimate of distance will deliver the true size of the object for calibrating the grip – and such computations may be quite insensitive to the kinds of pictorial cues that drive our perception of familiar illusions.

In the absence of reliable distance information, such as that provided by binocular vision, grasping is no longer immune to the effects of pictorial illusions. Thus, when subjects viewed the 3-D Ebbinghaus display with only one eye, the calibration of their grasp was now affected by the illusion (Marotta, DeSouza, Haffenden, & Goodale, 1998). This result is consistent with a large body of data showing that binocular vision plays a critical role in the control of prehension (Jackson, Jones, Newport, & Pritchard, 1997; Servos, Goodale, & Jakobson, 1992; Servos & Goodale, 1994).

The paramount importance of binocular information to the programming and control of grasping is nicely illustrated in a recent study of grasping in DF and another individual (JW) with visual form agnosia (Marotta, Behrmann, & Goodale, 1997). Although both DF and JW showed relatively normal scaling of their grasp to objects placed at different distances from them with both eyes open, this "size constancy" in grip scaling disappeared when one eye was covered. Because they could not use pictorial cues to depth, such as linear perspective and familiar size, that remain available when binocular cues are removed, they had to scale their grasp using a retinal image of the target object that was uncalibrated for distance. As a consequence, they opened their hand wider for closer objects (presumably because the closer the object, the larger the retinal image). This result and a number of other findings both with normal subjects (Jackson et al., 1997; Servos et al., 1992; Servos & Goodale, 1994) and with patients (Dijkerman, Milner, & Carey, 1996) all point to the same conclusion: The visuomotor system "prefers" to use binocular vision when it can. Even when binocular information is not available, there is evidence that we turn not so much to pictorial cues but to the motion of the target image that occurs when we make head movements that sweep the visual scene across our retina (Marotta, Kruyer, & Goodale, 1998; Marotta, Perrot, Nicolle, Servos, & Goodale, 1995; Milner, Dijkerman, & Rogers, 1998). Such self-generated image motion (and the eye movements that keep the target on the retina when the head is moved) are, of course, mathematically equivalent to stereopsis and vergence.

Speed of Processing and Memory in Action and Perception

To be successful, our actions must often be rapidly initiated and executed. This premium on speed was probably even more evident in the world of our hunter-gatherer ancestors, who had to cope with predators and catch prey to survive. They had little time to ponder before acting. One would expect therefore, that the dorsal stream would be quicker at transforming visual inputs into action than the ventral stream would be in transforming visual inputs into perception. Electrophysiological research using monkeys has shown that this is indeed the case. Several studies have demonstrated that visual information is transmitted faster through the dorsal than through the ventral stream (Schroeder, Mehta, & Givre, 1998; Schmolesky, Wang, Hanes, Thompson, Leutgeb, Schall, & Leventhal, 1998; for review, see Nowak & Bullier, 1997). There is also evidence that actions made in response to a change in the location and size of a visual target are initiated well before such changes are perceived (Castiello & Jeannerod, 1991; Castiello, Paulignan, & Jeannerod, 1991; for review, see Goodale & Haffenden, 1998).

Another important difference between vision for action and vision for perception is the time scale over which each system operates. Because observers and goal objects rarely stay in the same location with respect to one another, that is, the egocentric coordinates of a goal object often change dramatically from one moment to the next, it would make sense to compute the required coordinates for action immediately before the movements are initiated and it would make little sense to store these coordinates (or the resulting motor programs) for more than a few milliseconds before executing the action. In the case of perception, conversely, it is the identity and meaning of the object that we are concerned with – not the precise size and position of the object with respect to the observer. We can, therefore, recognize objects we have seen minutes, hours, days – or even years before. In short, the time scale for visual perception is several orders of magnitude longer than the time scale for the visual control of action.

If visuomotor computations occur in "real time," then movements directed to remembered objects (objects that were present in the visual array, but are no longer there) might be expected to look rather different from movements directed to objects that remain visible. Indeed, Elliot and Madalena (1987) found that in a manual aiming task subjects exhibited greater errors in their movement amplitude after only a 2 s period of visual occlusion prior to movement initiation. A study by Gnadt, Bracewell, and Andersen (1991) showed that saccades to remembered targets and saccades to visual targets in both monkeys and humans have different spatial and temporal characteristics. Thus, the saccades made to remembered targets were slower than the saccades to visual targets and also showed markedly curved trajectories. The saccades to remembered targets were also much less accurate, showing an increase in both constant and variable end-point error. Gnadt et al. found that these distortions were evident after only a 100 ms delay and accumulated rapidly over the next 800 ms or so of delay with a much slower change after that.

More recently, Goodale, Jakobson, and Keillor (1994) demonstrated that grasping movements directed at a remembered goal object after a 2 s delay between seeing the object and movement initiation show different kinematics (spatiotemporal organization) from those made in real time. Reaching movements made to remembered objects were slower, showed a more curvilinear trajectory, and tended to undershoot the location at which the object had been presented. Furthermore, even though subjects continued to scale their grasp to the size of the remembered object, the hand did not open nearly as wide as it did when subjects grasped objects in "real time." These differences were evident after only 2 s of delay and showed little change after even a 30 s delay.

Although these studies involved different kinds of motor tasks, they all make the same general point: Actions directed to remembered objects are quite different from actions directed to seen objects – even when the action to the seen object is performed in visual "open loop," that is, when the lights are turned off as the movement begins. It appears as though the visuomotor program representing the actions is executed immediately and is not stored. Indeed, the program appears to decay almost immediately if it is not used (in less than 800 ms for saccades and in less than 2 s for manual aiming movements and grasping).

The programming of motor actions directed to remembered targets must rely, not on current visual information, but rather on a stored representation of the previously seen object and its spatial location – a representation that is presumably derived from earlier perceptual processing of the visual array. As was argued earlier, the perceptual system, which plays a major role in object recognition, is designed to represent objects and their spatial locations over quite long periods of time. For perceptual memory, a delay of 2 s is trivial.

If actions to remembered objects are based on perceptual memories, then one can make an interesting prediction about what a person like DF would do when asked to grasp an object that she saw 2 s earlier. Even though DF has no trouble grasping objects in real time, the introduction of even a short delay between object presentation and the initiation of the grasp should interfere enormously with her performance. In other words, she should no longer show any size-scaling in her grasp after a delay – because, unlike normal subjects, she would be unable to fall back on a visual memory of the object. This prediction was borne out in the study by Goodale et al. (1994) mentioned earlier. DF presumably could not invoke a visual memory of the object to scale her grasp following the delay because she never perceived the object in the first place!

Central Versus Peripheral Vision in Action and Perception

Although the visual fields of the two eyes together span about 200°, most of our perceptual experience is confined to the few degrees subtended by the foveal and parafoveal region. In short, we see what we are looking at. Yet as we move through the world, stepping over curbs, negotiating doorways, and grasping door handles, we often utilize visual information from the far periphery of vision. This differential use of the fovea and peripheral visual fields by perception and action systems may explain why in the monkey there is differential representation of these regions in the ventral and dorsal streams. The receptive fields of cells in the inferotemporal cortex almost always include the fovea and very little of the far peripheral visual fields whereas cells in the posterior parietal cortex have a very large representation of the peripheral visual fields (Baizer, Ungerleider, & Desimone, 1991). Indeed, in some areas of the dorsal stream, such as area PO (the parieto-occipital area), the portion of cortex devoted to the fovea is no larger than would be expected on the basis of the extent of the visual field it subtends; that is, there is no "cortical magnification" of central vision (Gattass, Sousa, & Covey, 1985).

If a similar retinotopic organization of cortical areas exists in the human brain, then one might expect that the visual control of motor behavior might be quite sensitive to differences in visual stimuli presented in the far peripheral visual field whereas perceptual judgments of the same stimuli might be relatively insensitive. In a recent experiment, Goodale and Murphy (1997) found exactly that. They found that subject's judgments of the dimensions of objects became much more variable as the objects were presented at more and more eccentric locations. In sharp contrast, when subjects were asked to pick up one of the objects, the relationship between the aperture of their grasp (before contact) and the width of the object was as well tuned in the far periphery (70°) as it was close to the fovea (5°). This dissociation between perceptual judgments and visuomotor control again emphasizes the specialization of different parts of the visual system for perception and action.

Interactions Between Action and Perception

Throughout this chapter, we have been advancing the idea that the ventral perception system and the dorsal action system are two independent and decidedly different visual systems within the primate brain. Nevertheless, the two evolved together and play complementary roles in the control of behavior. In some ways, the limitations of one system are the strengths of the other. Thus, although the ventral perception system delivers a rich and detailed representation of the world, the metrics of the world with respect to the organism are not well specified. In contrast, the dorsal action system delivers accurate metrical information in the required egocentric coordinates but these computations are spare and evanescent.

A useful analogy for understanding the different contributions of the dorsal and ventral stream to visually guided behavior can be found in robotic engineering. That analogy is *teleassistance* (Pook & Ballard, 1996). In teleassistance, a human operator identifies the goal and then uses a symbolic language to communicate with a semi-autonomous robot that actually performs the required motor act on the identified goal object. Teleassistance is much more flexible than completely autonomous robotic control, which is limited to the working environment for which it has been programmed and cannot cope easily with novel events. Teleassistance is also more efficient than teleoperation, in which a human operator simply controls the movement of a manipulandum at a distance. As Pook and Ballard (1996) have demonstrated, teleoperation (i.e., the human operator) cannot cope with sudden changes in scale or the delay between action and feedback from that action. In short, teleassistance combines the flexibility of teleoperation with the precision of autonomous routines.

The interaction between the ventral and dorsal streams is an excellent example of the principle of teleassistance, but in this case instantiated in biology. The perceptual-cognitive systems in the ventral stream, like the human operator in teleassistance, identify different objects in the scene – using a representational system that is rich and detailed but not metrically precise. When a particular goal object has been flagged, dedicated visuomotor networks in the dorsal stream (in conjunction with related circuits in premotor cortex, basal ganglia, and brainstem) are activated to perform the desired motor act. Thus, the networks in the dorsal stream, with their precise egocentric coding of the location, size, orientation, and shape of the goal object, are like the robotic component of teleassistance. Thus, both systems are required for purposive behavior – one system to select the goal object from the visual array, the other to carry out the required metrical computations for the goal-directed action. For example, suppose, while walking down the street, we recognize an old friend walking towards us, someone that we have not seen for a long time. As the friend draws near, we reach out and shake his outstretched hand. This is an experience we have all had – but it is also one that illustrates the different but complementary roles played by the two visual streams in mediating this familiar social act. It is our ventral stream, through its intimate connections with long-term memory, that enables us to recognize our friend – and his outstretched hand. But once our friend's hand has been selected as a "goal object" by the ventral stream, it is our dorsal stream that enables us to grasp his hand successfully.

What remains a central and outstanding issue is how the two streams communicate in the production of adaptive behavior. Certainly there is evidence that, on the neural level, the two systems are interconnected (see Milner & Goodale, 1995). To understand fully the integrated nature of our behavior, however, will require that we specify the nature of the interactions and information exchange that occur between the two systems. Research on interactions between the two streams is well under way (e.g., Bridgeman, Peery, & Anand, 1997; Creem & Proffit, 1998a, 1998b; Jeannerod, 1997; Haffenden & Goodale, 1998b; Harman, Humphrey, & Goodale, 1999) and holds the promise of explaining how "seeing" and "doing" work together.

Note

1. The preparation of this chapter was helped in part by grants from the Medical Research Council of Canada to MAG and the Natural Sciences and Engineering Research Council of Canada to GKH.

Suggested Readings

Bock, G. R., & Goode, J. A. (Eds.) (1998). *Sensory guidance of movement.* Novartis Foundation Symposium 218. New York: John Wiley & Sons.

Jeannerod, M. (1997). *The cognitive neuroscience of action.* Oxford: Blackwell Publishers Ltd.

Milner, A. D., & Goodale, M. A. (1995). *The visual brain in action.* Oxford: Oxford University Press.

Additional Topics

Spatial Neglect

Humans with lesions in the parietal cortex, particularly in the right hemisphere, often develop a syndrome called "spatial neglect," in which they ignore or fail to attend to visual stimuli presented to the side of space contralateral to the lesion. This observation has often been used to bolster the original suggestion by Ungerleider and Mishkin (1982) that the parietal lobe has a special role to play in "spatial vision." What is seldom appreciated, however, is that the critical region for neglect is located much more ventrally in the parietal cortex than the critical region visuomotor deficits such as optic ataxia. In fact, the circuitry in humans that corresponds to the dorsal stream in monkey may be confined largely to the more superior region of the posterior parietal cortex. For a detailed discussion of this topic see Driver and Mattingley (1998) and Milner (1997).

Evolution of Visual Systems

The evolution of visual systems in primates and other animals is a vast topic that we have only touched on briefly. For a fascinating discussion of current thinking on the evolution of the visual system, see Allman (1999).

Selective Attention

Selective attention plays a crucial role in perception and action. In fact, any comprehensive account of the functions of the two streams must deal with attention and the possibility that different attentional mechanisms might be at work in the dorsal and ventral pathways. See Allport (1987), Mack and Rock (1998), and Rizzolati, Riggio, and Sheliga (1994).

Mirror Neurons

Although we may not be conscious of the visual information that controls our actions, we are usually conscious of our actions. It may be that recently discovered "mirror neurons" play a role in the representation of our actions and in integrating them with our perception of the world. For review see Rizzolati and Arbib (1998).

References

Aglioti, S., DeSouza, J. F. X., & Goodale, M. A. (1995). Size-contrast illusions deceive the eye but not the hand. *Current Biology*, *5*, 679–685.

Allman, J. M. (1999). *Evolving brains.* New York: Scientific American Library.

Allport, D. A. (1987). Selection for action: Some behavioural and neurophysiological considerations of attention and action. In H. Heuer & A. F. Sanders (Eds.), *Perspectives on perception and action* (pp. 395–419). Hillsdale, NJ: Lawrence Erlbaum Associates.

Andersen, R. A. (1987). Inferior parietal lobule function in spatial perception and visuomotor integration. In V. B. Mountcastle, F. Plum, & S. R. Geiger (Eds.), *Handbook of physiology section 1: The nervous system, volume V: Higher functions of the brain, part 2* (pp. 483–518). Bethesda, MD: American Physiological Association.

Andersen, R. A. (1997). Multimodal integration for the representation of space in the posterior parietal cortex. *Philosophical Transactions of the Royal Society of London B*, *352*, 1421–1428.

Baizer, J. S., Ungerleider, L. G., & Desimone, R. (1991). Organization of visual input to the inferior temporal and posterior parietal cortex in macaques. *Journal of Neuroscience*, *11*, 168–190.

Bálint, R. (1909). Seelenlähmung des 'Schauens', optische Ataxie, räumliche Störung der Aufmerksamkeit. *Monatschrift für Psychiatrie und Neurologie, 25*, 51–81.

Ballard, D. H., & Brown, C. M (1992). Principles of animate vision. *CVGIP: Image Understanding, 56*, 3–21.

Bates, J. A. V., & Ettlinger, G. (1960). Posterior biparietal ablations in the monkey. *Archives of Neurology, 3*, 177–192.

Binkofski, F., Dohle, C., Posse, S., Stephan, K. M., Hefter, H., Seitz, R. J., & Freund, H.-J. (1998). Human anterior intraparietal area subserves prehension. *Neurology, 50*, 1253–1259.

Brenner, E., & Smeets, J. B. J. (1996). Size illusion influences how we lift but not how we grasp an object. *Experimental Brain Research, 111*, 473–476.

Bridgeman, B. (1992). Conscious vs unconscious processes: The case of vision. *Theory & Psychology, 2*, 73–88.

Bridgeman, B., Kirch, M., & Sperling, A. (1981). Segregation of cognitive and motor aspects of visual function using induced motion. *Perception & Psychophysics, 29*, 336–342.

Bridgeman, B., Lewis, S., Heit, G., & Nagle, M. (1979). Relation between cognitive and motor-oriented systems of visual position perception. *Journal of Experimental Psychology: Human Perception & Performance, 5*, 692–700.

Bridgeman, B., Peery, S., & Anand, S. (1997). Interaction of cognitive and sensorimotor maps of visual space. *Perception & Psychophysics, 59*, 456–469.

Castiello, U., & Jeannerod, M. (1991). Measuring time to awareness. *Neuroreport, 2*, 797–800.

Castiello, U., Paulignan, Y., & Jeannerod, M. (1991). Temporal dissociation of motor responses and subjective awareness. *Brain, 114*, 2639–2655.

Churchland, P. S., Ramachandran, V. S., & Sejnowski, T. J. (1994). A critique of pure vision. In C. Koch & J. L. Davis (Eds.), *Large-scale neuronal theories of the brain* (pp. 23–60). Cambridge, MA: MIT Press.

Cliff, D., & Noble, J. (1997). Knowledge-based vision and simple visual machines. *Philosophical Transactions of the Royal Society of London B, 352*, 1165–1175.

Clower, D. M., Hoffman, J. M., Votaw, J. R., Faber, T. L., Woods, R. P., & Alexander, G. E. (1996). Role of posterior parietal cortex in the calibration of visually guided reaching. *Nature, 383*, 618–621.

Craik, K. (1943). *The nature of explanation*. Cambridge: Cambridge University Press.

Creem, S. H., & Profitt, D. R. (1998a). Two memories for geographical slant: Separation and interdependence of action and awareness. *Psychonomic Bulletin & Review, 5*, 22–36.

Creem, S. H., & Proffitt, D. H. (1998b). Grasping meaningful objects: Interdependence of the two visual systems. *Abstracts of the Psychonomic Society, 3*, 35.

Creem, S. H., Wraga, M., & Profitt, D. R. (1998). Perception-action dissociations in a large-scale Müller-Lyer figure. *Investigative Ophthalmology & Visual Science* (Abstract Book), *39*, S1095.

Crick, F., & Jones, E. (1993). Backwardness of human neuroanatomy. *Nature, 361*, 109–110.

Dijkerman, H. C., Milner, A. D., & Carey, D. P. (1996). The perception and prehension of objects oriented in the depth plane. 1. Effects of visual form agnosia. *Experimental Brain Research, 112*, 442–451.

Driver, J., & Mattingley, J. B. (1998). Parietal neglect and visual awareness. *Nature Neuroscience, 1*, 17–22.

Duncker, K. (1929/1938). Induced motion. In W. D. Ellis (Ed.), *A source book of Gestalt psychology* (pp. 161–172). New York: Humanities Press.

Edelman, S. (1998). Representation is representation of similarities. *Behavioral and Brain Sciences, 21*, 449–498.

Ellard, C. G., & Goodale, M. A. (1986). The role of the predorsal bundle in head and body movements elicited by electrical stimulation of the superior colliculus in the Mongolian gerbil. *Experimental Brain Research, 64*, 421–433.

Ellard, C. G., & Goodale, M. A. (1988). A functional analysis of the collicular output pathways: A dissociation of deficits following lesions of the dorsal tegmental decussation and the ipsilateral collicular efferent bundle in the Mongolian gerbil. *Experimental Brain Research, 71*, 307–319.

Elliot, D., & Madalena, J. (1987). The influence of premovement visual information on manula aiming. *Quarterly Journal of Experimental Psychology, 39A*, 541–559.

Ettlinger, G. (1990). "Object vision" and "spatial vision": The neuropsychological evidence for the distinction. *Cortex, 26*, 319–341.

Ewert, J.-P. (1987). Neuroethology of releasing mechanisms: Prey-catching in toads. *Behavioral and Brain Sciences, 10*, 337–405.

Gallese, V., Murata, A., Kaseda, M., Niki, N., & Sakata, H. (1994). Deficit of hand preshaping after muscimol injection in monkey parietal cortex. *Neuroreport, 5*, 1525–1529.

Gattass, R., Sousa, A. P. B., & Covey, E. (1985). Cortical visual areas of the macaque: Possible substrates for pattern recognition mechanisms. In C. Chagas, R. Gattass, & C. G. Gross (Eds.), *Pattern recognition mechanisms* (pp. 1–20). Vatican City: Pontifical Academy of Sciences.

Gauthier, I., Anderson, A. W., Tarr, M. J., Skudlarski, P., & Gore, J. C. (1997). Levels of categorization in visual recognition studies using functional magnetic resonace imaging. *Current Biology*, 7, 645–651.

Gentilucci, M., Chieffi, S., Daprati, E., Saetti, M. C., & Toni, I. (1996). Visual illusion and action. *Neuropsychologia, 34*, 369–376.

Georgeson, M. (1997). Guest editorial: Vision and action: You ain't see nothin' yet . . . . *Perception*, 26, 1–6.

Gibson, J. J. (1979). *The ecological approach to visual perception*. Boston: Houghton Mifflin.

Glickstein, M., Buchbinder, S., & May, J. L. III. (1998). Visual control of the arm, the wrist and the fingers: Pathways through the brain. *Neuropsychologia, 36*, 981–1001.

Gnadt, J. W., Bracewell, R. M., & Andersen, R. A. (1991). Sensorimotor transformation during eye movements to remembered visual targets. *Vision Research, 31*, 693–715.

Goodale, M. A. (1983a). Vision as a sensorimotor system. In T. E. Robinson (Ed.), *Behavioral approaches to brain research* (pp. 41–61). New York: Oxford University Press.

Goodale, M. A. (1983b). Neural mechanisms of visual orientation in rodents: Targets versus places. In A. Hein & M. Jeannerod (Eds.), *Spatially oriented behavior* (pp. 35–61). Berlin: Springer-Verlag.

Goodale, M. A. (1988). Modularity in visuomotor control: From input to output. In Z. Pylyshyn (Ed.), *Computational processes in human vision: An interdisciplinary perspective* (pp. 262–285). Norwood, NJ: Ablex.

Goodale, M. A. (1993). Visual pathways supporting perception and action in the primate cerebral cortex. *Current Opinion in Neurobiology, 3*, 578–585.

Goodale, M. A. (1995). The cortical organization of visual perception and visuomotor control. In S. Kosslyn & D. Osherson (Eds.), *An invitation to cognitive science: Vol. 2. Visual cognition and action* (2nd ed., pp. 167–213). Cambridge, MA: MIT Press.

Goodale, M. A. (1996). Visuomotor modules in the vertebrate brain. *Canadian Journal of Physiology and Pharmacology, 74*, 390–400.

Goodale, M. A. (1997). Visual routes to perception and action in the cerebral cortex. In M. Jeannerod (Ed.), *Handbook of neuropsychology* (Vol. 11, pp. 91–109). Amsterdam: Elsevier.

Goodale, M. A., & Carey, D. P. (1990). The role of cerebral cortex in visuomotor control. In B. Kolb & R. C. Tees (Eds.), *The cerebral cortex of the rat* (pp. 309–340). Norwood NJ: Ablex.

Goodale, M. A., & Haffenden, A. (1998). Frames of reference for perception and action in the human visual system. *Neuroscience and Biobehavioral Reviews, 22*, 161–172.

Goodale, M. A., & Humphrey, G. K. (1998). The objects of action and perception. *Cognition, 67*, 181–207.

Goodale, M. A., Jakobson, L. S., & Keillor J. M. (1994). Differences in the visual control of pantomimed and natural grasping movements. *Neuropsychologia, 31*, 1159–1178.

Goodale, M. A., Meenan, J. P., Bülthoff, H. H., Nicolle, D. A., Murphy, K.S., & Racicot, C. I. (1994). Separate neural pathways for the visual analysis of object shape in perception and prehension. *Current Biology, 4*, 604–610.

Goodale, M. A., & Milner, A. D. (1992). Separate visual pathways for perception and action. *Trends in Neurosciences, 15*, 20–25.

Goodale, M. A., Milner, A. D., Jakobson, L. S., & Carey, D. P. (1991). A neurological dissociation between perceiving objects and grasping them. *Nature, 349,* 154–156.

Goodale, M. A., & Murphy, K. (1997). Action and perception in the visual periphery. In P. Thier & H.-O. Karnath (Eds.), *Parietal lobe contributions to orientation in 3D space* (pp. 447–461). Heidelberg: Springer-Verlag.

Goodale, M. A., Murphy, K., Meenan, J.-P., Racicot, C., & Nicolle, D. A. (1993). Spared object perception but poor object-calibrated grasping in a patient with optic ataxia. *Society for Neuroscience Abstracts, 19,* 775.

Gregory, R. L. (1998). *Eye and brain* (5th ed.). Oxford: Oxford University Press.

Haaxma, R., & Kuypers, H. G. J. M. (1975). Intrahemispheric cortical connexions and visual guidance of hand and finger movements in the rhesus monkey. *Brain, 98,* 239–260.

Haffenden, A., & Goodale, M. A. (1998a). The effect of pictorial illusion on prehension and perception. *Journal of Cognitive Neuroscience, 10.* 122–136.

Haffenden, A. M., & Goodale, M. A. (1998b). The influence of a learned color cue to size on visually guided prehension. *Investigative Ophthalmology & Visual Science* (Abstract Book), *39,* S558.

Harman, K. L., Humphrey, G. K., & Goodale, M. A. (1999). Active manual control of object views facilitates visual recognition. *Current Biology, 9,* 1315–1318.

Humphrey, G. K., Goodale, M. A., & Gurnsey, R. (1991). Orientation discrimination in a visual form agnosic: Evidence from the McCollough effect. *Psychological Science, 2,* 331–335.

Humphrey, G. K., Goodale, M. A., Jakobson, L. S., & Servos, P. (1994). The role of surface information in object recognition: Studies of a visual form agnosic and normal subjects. *Perception, 23,* 1457–1481.

Humphrey, G. K., Symons, L. A., Herbert, A. M., & Goodale, M. A. (1996). A neurological dissociation between shape from shading and shape from edges. *Behavioural Brain Research, 76,* 117–125.

Hyvärinen, J., & Poranen, A. (1974). Function of the parietal associative area 7 as revealed from cellular discharges in alert monkeys. *Brain, 97,* 673–692.

Ingle, D.J. (1973). Two visual systems in the frog. *Science, 181,* 1053–1055.

Ingle, D.J. (1980). Some effects of pretectum lesions in the frog's detection of stationary objects. *Behavioural Brain Research, 1,* 139–163.

Ingle, D. J. (1982). Organization of visuomotor behaviors in vertebrates. In D. J. Ingle, M. A. Goodale, & R. J. W. Mansfield (Eds.), *Analysis of visual behavior* (pp. 67–109). Cambridge MA: MIT Press.

Ingle, D. J. (1991). Functions of subcortical visual systems in vertebrates and the evolution of higher visual mechanisms. In R. L. Gregory & J. Cronly-Dillon (Eds.), *Vision and visual dysfunction: Vol. 2. Evolution of the eye and visual system* (pp. 152–164). London: Macmillan.

Intraub, H. (1997). The representation of visual scenes. *Trends in Cognitive Sciences, 1,* 217–222.

Jackson, J. H. (1875). *Clinical and physiological researches on the nervous system.* London: Churchill.

Jackson, S. R., Jones, C. A., Newport, R., & Pritchard, C. (1997). A kinematic analysis of goal-directed prehension movements executed under binocular, monocular, and memory-guided viewing conditions. *Visual Cognition, 4,* 113–142.

Jakobson, L. S., Archibald, Y. M., Carey, D. P., & Goodale, M. A. (1991). A kinematic analysis of reaching and grasping movements in a patient recovering from optic ataxia. *Neuropsychologia, 29,* 803–809.

Jeannerod, M. (1988). *The neural and behavioural organization of goal-directed movements.* Oxford: Oxford University Press.

Jeannerod, M. (1997). *The cognitive neuroscience of action.* Oxford: Blackwell Publishers Ltd.

Jeannerod, M., Decety, J., & Michel, F. (1994). Impairment of grasping movements following a bilateral posterior parietal lesion. *Neuropsychologia, 32,* 369–380.

Kanwisher, N., Chun, M. M., McDermott, J., & Ledden, P. J. (1996). Functional imaging of human visual recognition. *Cognitive Brain Research, 5,* 55–67.

Kanwisher, N., McDermott, J., & Chun, M. M. (1997). The fusiform face area: A module in human extrastriate cortex specialized for face perception. *The Journal of Neuroscience, 17,* 4302–4311.

Kawashima, R., Naitoh, E., Matsumura, M., Itoh, H., Ono, S., Satoh, K., Gotoh, R., Koyama, M., Inoue, K., Yoshioka, S., & Fukuda, H. (1996). Topographic representation in human intraparietal sulcus of reaching and saccade. *NeuroReport, 7,* 1253–1256.

Kiyosawa, M., Inoue, C., Kawasaki, T., Tokoro, T., Ishii, K., Ohyama, M., Senda, M., & Soma, Y. (1996). Functional neuroanatomy of visual object naming: A PET study. *Graefe's Archive of Clinical and Experimental Ophthalmology, 234,* 110–115.

Klüver, H., & Bucy, P. C. (1939). Preliminary analysis of functions of the temporal lobes of monkeys. *Archives of Neurological Psychiatry, 42,* 979–1000.

Kosslyn, S. M. (1994). *Image and brain: The resolution of the imagery debate.* Cambridge, MA: MIT Press.

Lawler, K. A., & Cowey, A. (1987). On the role of posterior parietal and prefrontal cortex in visuo-spatial perception and attention. *Experimental Brain Research, 65,* 695–698.

Lettvin, J. Y., Maturana, H. R., McCulloch, W. S., & Pitts, W. H. (1959). What the frog's eye tells the frog's brain. *Proceedings of the Institute of Radio Engineers, 47,* 1940–1951.

Lissauer, H. (1890). Ein Fall von Seelenblindheit nebst einem Beitrage zur Theorie derselben. *Archiv für Psychiatrie und Nervenkrankheiten, 21,* 222–270.

Logothetis, N. K., & Sheinberg, D. L. (1996). Visual object recognition. *Annual Review of Neuroscience, 19,* 577–621.

Logothetis, N. (1998). Object vision and visual awareness. *Current Opinion in Neurobiology, 8,* 536–544.

Logothetis, N. K., Pauls, J., & Poggio, T. (1995). Shape representation in the inferior temporal cortex of monkeys. *Current Biology, 5,* 552–563.

Lynch, J. C., & McLaren, J. W. (1989). Deficits of visual attention and saccadic eye movements after lesions of parieto-occipital cortex in monkeys. *Journal of Neurophysiology, 69,* 460–468.

Mack, A., & Rock, I. (1998). *Inattentional blindness.* Cambridge, MA: MIT Press.

Malach, R., Reppas, J. B., Benson, R. R., Kwong, K. K., Jiang, H., Kennedy, W. A., Ledden, P. J., Brady, T. J., Rosen, B. R., & Tootell, R. B. H. (1995). Object-related activity revealed by functional magnetic resonance imaging in human occipital cortex. *Proceedings of the National Academy of Sciences, USA, 92,* 8135–8139.

Marotta, J. J., Behrmann, M., & Goodale, M. A. (1997). The removal of binocular cues disrupts the calibration of grasping in patients with visual form agnosia. *Experimental Brain Research, 116,* 113–121.

Marotta, J. J., DeSouza, J. F., Haffenden, A. M., & Goodale, M. A. (1998). Does a monocularly presented size-contrast illusion influence grip aperture? *Neuropsychologia, 36,* 491–497.

Marotta, J. J., Kruyer, A., & Goodale, M. A. (1998). The role of head movements in the control of manual prehension. *Experimental Brain Research, 120,* 134–138.

Marotta, J. J., Perrot, T. S., Nicolle, D., & Goodale, M. A. (1995). The development of adaptive head movements following enucleation. *Eye, 9,* 333–336.

Marotta, J. J., Perrot, T. S., Nicolle, D., Servos, P., & Goodale, M. A. (1995). Adapting to monocular vision: Grasping with one eye. *Experimental Brain Research, 104,* 107–114.

Marr, D. (1982). *Vision.* San Francisco: Freeman.

Matsumura, M., Kawashima, R., Naito, E., Satoh, K., Takahashi, T., Yanagisawa, T., & Fukuda, H. (1996). Changes in rCBF during grasping in humans examined by PET. *NeuroReport, 7,* 749–752.

McCarthy, G., Puce, A., Gore, J. C., & Allison, T. (1997). Face specific processing in the human fusiform gyrus. *Journal of Cognitive Neuroscience, 9,* 605–610.

McConkie, G. W., & Currie, C. B. (1996). Visual stability across saccades while viewing complex pictures. *Journal of Experimental Psychology: Human Perception & Performance, 22,* 563–581.

Mendoza, J. E., & Thomas, R. K. (1975). Effects of posterior parietal and frontal neocortical lesions in squirrel monkeys. *Journal of Comparative and Physiological Psychology, 89,* 170–182.

Milner, A. D. (1997). Neglect, extinction, and the cortical streams of visual processing. In P. Thier

& H.-O. Karnath (Eds.), *Parietal lobe contributions to orientation in 3D space* (pp. 3–22). Heidelberg: Springer.

Milner, A. D., Dijkerman, H. C., & Rogers, B. J. (1998). Motion parallax can provide #D information for visually-guided action in a visual-form agnosic. *Society for Neuroscience Abstracts, 24*, 2097.

Milner, A. D. , & Goodale, M. A. (1993). Visual pathways to perception and action. In T. P. Hicks, S. Molotchnikoff, & T. Ono (Eds.), *The visually responsive neuron: From basic neurophysiology to behavior: Progress in brain research* (Vol. 95, pp. 317–338). Amsterdam: Elsevier .

Milner, A. D., & Goodale, M. A. (1995). *The visual brain in action*. Oxford: Oxford University Press.

Milner, A. D., Perrett, D. I., Johnston, R. S., Benson, P. J., Jordan, T. R., Heeley, D. W., Bettucci, D., Mortara, F., Mutani, R., Terazzi, E. & Davidson, D. L. W. (1991). Perception and action in visual form agnosia. *Brain, 114*, 405–428.

Mountcastle, V. B., Lynch, J. C., Georgopoulos, A., Sakata, H., & Acuña, C. (1975). Posterior parietal association cortex of the monkey: Command functions for operations within extrapersonal space. *Journal of Neurophysiology, 38*, 871–908.

Nowak, L. G., & Bullier, J. (1997). The timing of information transfer in the visual system. In K. S. Rockland, J. H. Kaas, & A. Peters (Eds.), *Cerebral cortex: Vol. 12. Extrastriate cortex in primates* (pp. 205–241). New York: Plenum Press.

O'Regan, J. K. (1992). Solving the "real" mysteries of visual perception: The world as an outside memory. *Canadian Journal of Psychology, 46*, 461–488.

Patla, A. E., & Goodale, M. A. (1996). Obstacle avoidance during locomotion is unaffected in a patient with visual form agnosia. *Neuroreport, 8*, 165–168.

Perenin, M. T., & Rossetti, Y. (1996). Grasping without form discrimination in a hemianopic field. *Neuroreport, 7*, 793–797.

Perenin, M.-T., & Vighetto, A. (1988). Optic ataxia: A specific disruption in visuomotor mechanisms. I. Different aspects of the deficit in reaching for objects. *Brain, 111*, 643–674.

Perrett, D., Benson, P. J., Hietanen, J. K., Oram, M. W., & Dittrich, W. H. (1995). When is a face not a face? In R. Gregory, J. Harris, P. Heard, & D. Rose (Eds.), *The artful eye* (pp. 95–124). Oxford: Oxford University Press.

Pohl, W. (1973). Dissociation of spatial discrimination deficits following frontal and parietal lesions in monkeys. *Journal of Comparative and Physiological Psychology, 82*, 227–239.

Pook, P. K., & Ballard, D. H. (1996). Deictic human/robot interaction. *Robotics and Autonomous Systems, 18*, 259–269.

Pribram, K. H. (1967). Memory and the organization of attention. In D. B. Lindsley & A. A. Lumsdaine (Eds.), *Brain function: Vol IV. UCLA Forum in Medical Sciences 6* (pp. 79–112). Berkeley: University of California Press.

Price, C. J., Moore, C. J., Humphreys, G. W., Frackowiak, R. S. J., & Friston, K. J. (1996). The neural regions subserving object recognition and naming. *Proceedings of the Royal Society of London (B), 263*, 1501–1507.

Puce, A., Allison, T., Asgari, M., Gore, J. C., & McCarthy, G. (1996). Differential sensitivity of human visual cortex to faces, letterstrings, and textures: A functional magnetic resonance imaging study. *The Journal of Neuroscience, 16*, 5205–5215.

Rensink, R. A., O'Regan, J. K., & Clark, J. J. (1997). To see or not to see: The need for attention to perceive changes in scenes. *Psychological Science, 8*, 368–373.

Rizzolatti, G. & Arbib, M. A. (1998). Language within our grasp. *Trends in Neurosciences, 21*, 188–194.

Rizzolatti, G., Luppino, G., & Matelli, M. (1998). The organization of the cortical motor system: New concepts. *Electroencephalography and Clinical Neurophysiology, 106*, 283–296.

Rizzolatti, G., Riggio, L., & Sheliga, B. M. (1994). Space and selective attention. In C. Umiltà & M. Moscovitch (Eds.), *Attention and performance XV: Conscious and nonconscious information processing* (pp. 231–265). Cambridge, MA: MIT Press.

Sakata, H., Taira, M., Mine, S., & Murata, A. (1992). Hand-movement-related neurons of the posterior parietal cortex of the monkey: Their role in visual guidance of hand movements. In R. Caminiti, P. B. Johnson, & Y. Burnod (Eds.), *Control of arm movement in space: Neurophysiological and computational approaches* (pp. 185–198). Berlin: Springer-Verlag.

Sakata, H., & Taira, M. (1994). Parietal control of hand action. *Current Opinion in Neurobiology, 4,* 847–856.

Sakata, H., Taira, M., Kusunoki, M., Murata, A., & Tanaka, Y. (1997). The TINS lecture: The parietal association cortex in depth perception and visual control of hand action. *Trends in Neurosciences, 20,* 350–357.

Sams, M., Hietanen, J. K., Hari, R., Ilmoniemi, R. J., & Lounasmaa, O. V. (1997). Face-specific responses from the human inferior occipito-temporal cortex. *Neuroscience, 77,* 49–55.

Sayner, R. B., & Davis, R. T. (1972). Significance of sign in an S-R separation problem. *Perceptual and Motor Skills, 34,* 671–676.

Schmolesky, M. T., Wang, Y., Hanes, D. P., Thompson, K. G., Leutgeb, S., Schall, J. D., & Leventhal, A. G. (1998). Signal timing across the macaque visual system. *Journal of Neurophysiology, 79,* 3272–3278.

Schroeder, C. E., Mehta, A. D., & Givre, S. J. (1998). A spatiotemporal profile of visual system activation revealed by current source density analysis in the awake macaque. *Cerebral Cortex, 8,* 575–592.

Servos, P., & Goodale, M. A. (1994). Binocular vision and the on-line control of human prehension. *Experimental Brain Research, 98,* 119–127.

Servos, P., & Goodale, M. A. (1995). Preserved visual imagery in visual form agnosia. *Neuropsychologia, 33,* 1383–1394.

Servos, P., Goodale, M. A., & Humphrey, G. K. (1993). The drawing of objects by a visual form agnosic: Contribution of surface properties and memorial representations. *Neuropsychologia, 31,* 251–259.

Servos, P., Goodale, M. A., & Jakobson, L. S. (1992). The role of binocular vision in prehension: A kinematic analysis. *Vision Research, 32,* 1513–1521.

Snyder, L. H., Batista, A. P., & Andersen, R. A. (1997). Coding of intention in the posterior parietal cortex. *Nature, 386,* 167–170.

Taira, M., Mine, S., Georgopoulos, A. P., Murata, A., & Sakata, H. (1990). Parietal cortex neurons of the monkey related to the visual guidance of hand movement. *Experimental Brain Research, 83,* 29–36.

Tanaka, K. (1996). Inferotemporal cortex and object vision. *Annual Review of Neuroscience, 19,* 109–139.

Tarr, M., & Black, M. (1994). A computational and evolutionary perspective on the role of representation in vision. *CVGIP: Image Understanding, 60,* 65–73.

Tootell, R. B. H., Dale, A. M., Sereno, M. I., & Malach, R. (1996). New images from human visual cortex. *Trends in Neurosciences, 19,* 481–489.

Tootell, R. B. H., Hadjikhani, N. K., Mendola, J. D., Marrett, S., & Dale, A. M. (1998). From retinotopy to recognition: fMRI in human visual cortex. *Trends in Cognitive Sciences, 2,* 174–183.

Ungerleider, L. G., & Brody, B. A. (1977). Extrapersonal spatial orientation:The role of posterior parietal, anterior frontal, and inferotemporal cortex. *Experimental Neurology, 56,* 265–280.

Ungerleider, L. G., & Mishkin, M. (1982). Two cortical visual systems. In D. J. Ingle, M. A. Goodale, & R. J. W. Mansfield (Eds.), *Analysis of visual behavior* (pp. 549–586). Cambridge MA: MIT Press.

Vanni, S., Revonsuo, A., Saarinin, J., & Hari, R. (1996). Visual awareness of objects correlates with activity of right occipital cortex. *Neuroreport, 8,* 183–186.

Vishton, P. M., & Cutting, J. E. (1995). Veridical size perception for action: Reaching vs. estimation. *Investigative Ophthalmology & Visual Science, 36* (Suppl.), 358.

Watt, R. J. (1991). *Understanding vision.* London: Academic Press.

Watt, R. J. (1992). Visual analysis and the representation of spatial relations. In G. W. Humphreys (Ed.), *Understanding vision* (pp. 19–38). Oxford: Basil Blackwell Ltd.

Weiskrantz, L. (1986). *Blindsight: A case study and its implications.* Oxford: Oxford University Press.
Weiskrantz, L. (1997). *Consciousness lost and found.* Oxford: Oxford University Press.
Wong, E., & Mack, A. (1981). Saccadic programming and perceived location. *Acta Psychologica, 48,* 123–131.

Chapter Eleven

Pictorial Perception and Art[1]

E. Bruce Goldstein

Pictorial Perception and Art

> Not a line is drawn without intention . . . as poetry admits not a letter that is insignificant, so painting admits not a grain of sand or a blade of grass insignificant, much less an insignificant blur or mark.
>
> (William Blake)

When artists talk of creating pictures they often describe the process as one of "making marks." These marks made by artists are not, however, just any marks. There is an intelligence behind them. They are made with the idea of creating a response, transmitting information, being seen as something more than mere marks.

How these marks are arranged in a picture and then are perceived by a viewer depends on many factors, not the least of which is the artist's intention in creating the picture. This intention can take many forms, including, but not limited to, the intention to tell a story (Hyman, 1979); to create a realistic representation of the environment (Martin, 1981); to create abstract compositions (Lane & Larsen, 1983); to create purely perceptual objects (Seitz, 1965); to capture an impression (Gombrich, 1960), or to self-referentially ask the question "what is art?" (Willats, 1997).

In this chapter, we will be concerned not with what makes a picture "art" (see Albright, 1989; Canaday, 1980), but with analyzing how we perceive the markings artists make on two-dimensional surfaces. Art becomes part of our discussion because art has provided a rich source of pictorial stimuli for study, and because we are interested in the implications of the perceptual motivations and hypotheses of artists and art theorists.

Pictorial Representation of Environmental Information

> The kind of vision we get from pictures is harder to understand than the kind we get from ambient light, not easier. . . . pictures . . . are deeply puzzling and endlessly interesting.
>
> (Gibson, 1978, p. 227)

Researchers and theorists have devoted a great deal of energy towards understanding the special properties of pictures (Cutting & Massironi, 1998; Gibson, 1971, 1978; Gombrich, 1960; Hagen, 1980a, 1980b; Hochberg, 1979, 1980, 1996; Nodine & Fisher, 1979). One of the major concerns of much of this research has been with the problem of representation: How can pictures *represent* the environment?

One approach to the problem of representation is to ask how information about the layout of the environment can be transferred onto the surface of a picture. One way to achieve this is through linear perspective, a geometrical system by which the layout of light and dark in the environment can be represented on the picture's surface.

Figure 11.1a shows the basic principle behind linear perspective. Lines extended to the object from the center of projection at the viewer's eye intersect a picture plane interposed between the eye and the object, and these intersections locate points on the picture plane that correspond to points on the object. The picture is therefore a projection of the object in which each point on the picture corresponds to a point on the object.

There are other methods of projection for representing objects or scenes on a flat surface (Dubery & Willats, 1972, 1983; Willats, 1997), but linear perspective has the distinction of creating a pictorial image that contains the same information for layout that a viewer receives directly from the scene itself. Note, however, that this information is a "freeze frame" of the environment, a point that has important perceptual implications.

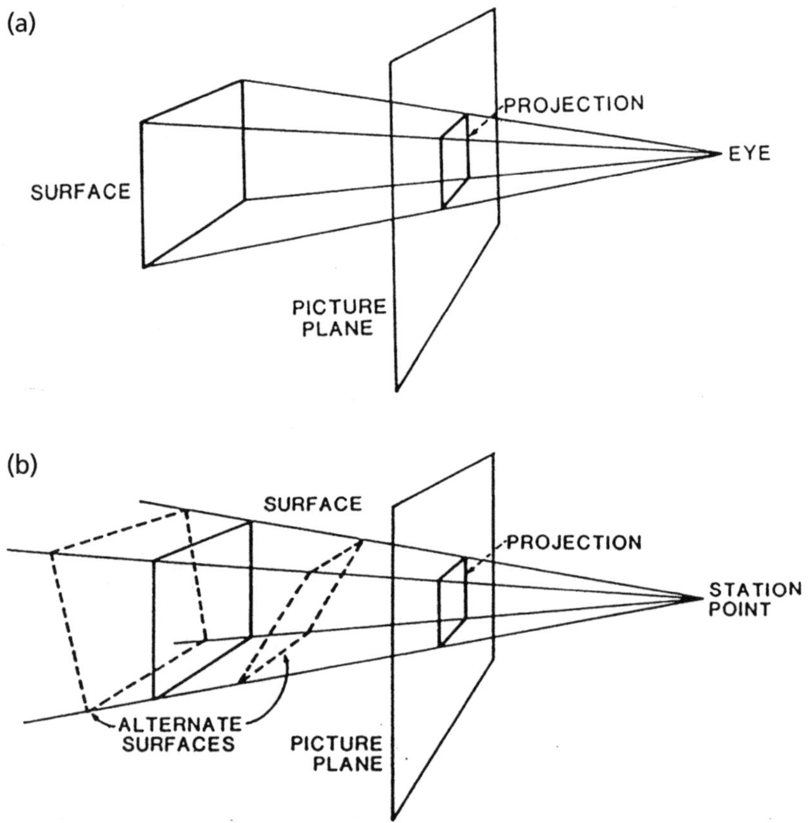

Figure 11.1. (a) The principle behind linear perspective. The intersection of lines extending from the center of projection (the eye) to the object define the projection of the object. (b) Projective ambiguity. The original object (solid line) *and* an infinite number of other objects (two shown by dashed lines) can create the same projection on the picture plane.

Having created this record of the environment, we might be tempted to announce that because the picture represents the environment with geometrical accuracy, we have solved the problem of representation. Our announcement would, however, be unjustified because when we start with the information in the picture and work backwards to reconstruct the environment, we find that there are an infinite number of three-dimensional objects that could have created the projection on the picture. This situation, shown in Figure 11.2b, is known as *projective ambiguity*.

This ambiguity is not, however, just a characteristic of pictures. It occurs when perceiving the three-dimensional environment as well, because the environment is represented on

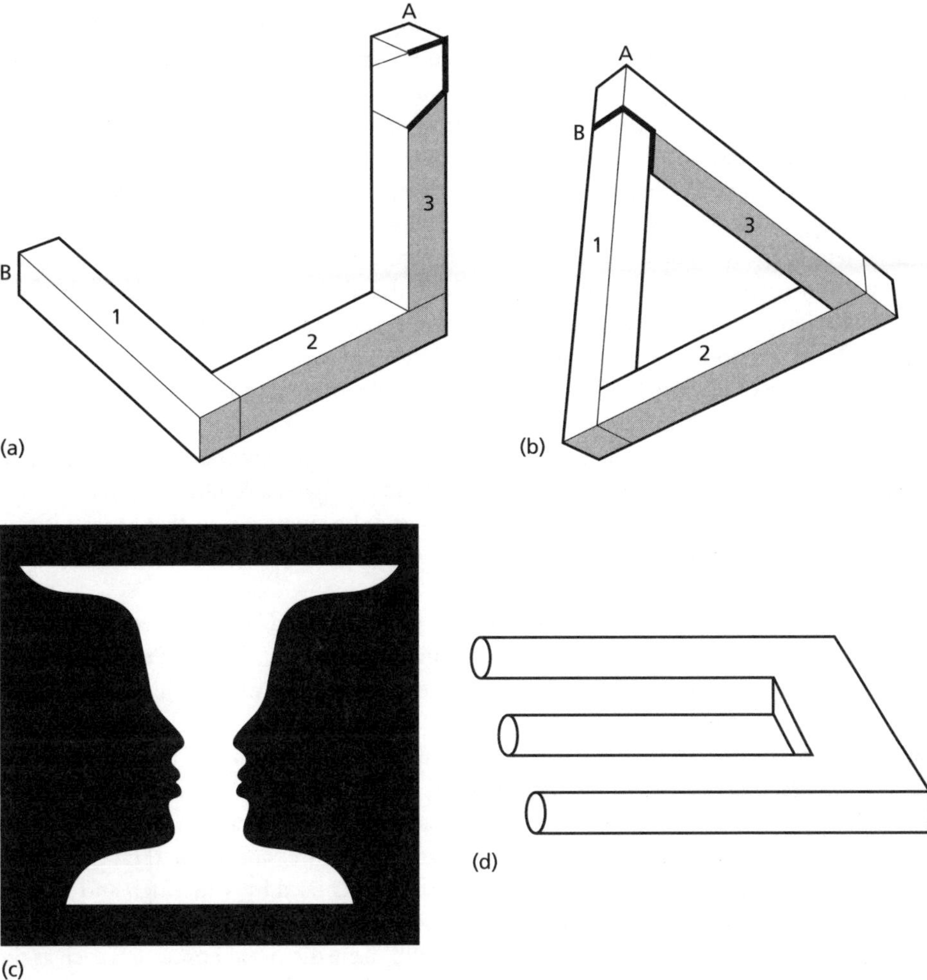

Figure 11.2. (a) A three-armed figure. (b) The same figure when viewed so that the end of leg B is aligned with the "cutout" on leg A. The numbers indicate the same sides in the two views. This figure is called the Penrose figure. (c) A reversible figure-ground display. (d) An impossible figure, which cannot exist in three dimensions.

the retina by the same perspective picture as the one on the artist's picture plane. Thus, when viewed through a peephole, from the correct station point, the distorted trapezoidal shape of the Ames room is perceived as a normal rectangular room. Similarly, when viewed from the correct viewpoint, the three-armed object in Figure 11.2a becomes the famous Penrose triangle in Figure 11.2b (Penrose & Penrose, 1958). [Note that Penrose and Penrose introduced the drawing of this figure and Gregory (1970) constructed the three-dimensional model which when viewed from the correct viewpoint becomes the Penrose triangle.]

The Penrose figure, which has been called "impossible," because it can't exist as a triangle in three dimensions, illustrates that the visual system often makes assumptions about what a projection represents. In the case of the Penrose triangle, the assumption is that because the projection of the ends at A and B are adjacent to one another, they are adjacent in three-dimensional space as well. (See Goldstein, 1998; Ittleson, 1996; Nakayama, He, & Shimojo, 1995; Perkins & Cooper, 1980 and Shepard, 1984 regarding perceptual assumptions.)

Although these misperceptions occur both when viewing the three-dimensional environment and in pictures created from the same viewpoint, an important difference between pictures and the three-dimensional environment is that the environment usually affords the potential of a changing viewpoint, whereas a picture does not. Thus, a slight movement of the head reveals that the three-dimensional version of the Penrose triangle is really a non-triangular three-armed figure. Similarly, liberating the viewer from the fixed peephole view of the Ames room reveals the room's true trapezoidal shape. No such liberation is, however, possible, when viewing still pictures of the same displays.

The fixed point of view that is achieved by pictorial representation also makes it possible to create displays such as reversible figure-ground figures (Figure 11.2c). These figures require precise alignment of matching positive and negative contours, which would be extremely unlikely to occur in the natural environment (Bayliss & Driver, 1995).

Other important differences between pictures and the environment that are significant both for the artist creating a picture and the viewer perceiving it are:

- Pictures can create impossible objects that cannot be realized as three-dimensional objects, no matter what the viewing angle (Figure 11.2d). Unlike the Penrose triangle, which is potentially a unique view of a three-dimensional object, this figure cannot exist in three-dimensional space.
- The information in pictures is different than the information in the environment, because pictures are pigmented markings on a surface, and not the objects themselves. These pigmented markings can be manipulated by artists in various ways: Line drawings eliminate information about light, shading, texture, and color (Hayes & Ross, 1995; Kennedy, 1974). Coarse brushstrokes, such as used by Van Gogh and Monet, add texture to the picture surface. Pointillistic dots, such as used by Seurat and Signac, add texture to the image. Rentschler et al. (1988) have discussed how artists such as the Impressionists and Neo-Impressionists have manipulated their depiction of the environment by selectively leaving out some information about a scene and emphasizing or adding other information.
- Pictures are flat but the depicted environment is usually three-dimensional. This obvious difference between pictures and the environment gives rise to the *dual reality of*

Table 11.1 Flatness cues

Flatness cue	*Description*	*How to eliminate*
Visibility of picture surface	Brushstrokes, surface texture of canvas is visible	Use fine brushstrokes, view picture from a distance
Visibility of picture border	Picture frame or edges of picture are visible	View picture through a peephole
Lack of movement parallax	When observer moves lateral to picture, there is no movement of near relative to far objects in the picture	View picture through a peephole so no movement relative to picture is possible
Identity of binocular fields	Left and right eyes receive essentially the same view of the objects in the picture, i.e., there is no binocular disparity	View picture through a peephole so it is viewed monocularly and images in left and right eyes can't be compared

pictures, the fact that "A picture is a surface that always specifies something other than what it is" (Gibson, 1978, p. 229). René Magritte comments on this dual reality with his painting of a pipe, which includes the caption, directly under the pipe, "Ceci n'est pas une pipe" (This is not a pipe). "What is it then?", the viewer might ask, and the answer is that it is a *representation* of a pipe.

- Pictures contain both depth information that helps create an impression of three dimensionality that mimics the space in the scene (Sedgwick, 1980 and Chapter 5, this volume) and flatness information such as the visibility of the picture's surface texture, which indicates that the picture's surface is flat (see Table 11.1). For example, the flatness cue of surface texture would be particularly strong in a Van Gogh, with its thickly applied paint. The simultaneous existence of information indicating both the depth of the depicted scene and the flatness of the picture surface is a manifestation of the dual reality of pictures.

It is clear that pictures are both similar to the environment and different from it. These similarities and differences play their role in determining how well artists and psychologists have succeeded in representing the environment in pictures. Our starting point for describing attempts to create these pictorial representations of the environment is the beginnings of linear perspective, which was first used by the ancient Romans, and then rediscovered and refined in the Italian Renaissance. It was during this rebirth of linear perspective in the Renaissance that artists attacked with a vengeance the problem of how to represent space and form in pictures (Edgerton, 1975; Kemp, 1989; Kubovy, 1986; White, 1967).

Perceptual Psychology in the Renaissance

> When the relationship between figure and ground in art changes, it reflects a change in man's definition of himself. With the Renaissance, for example, the figure was detached from the flat, anonymous surface it had dominated in the era of the religious icon, and placed in an illusionistic landscape space where it became, with the rest of the physical world, an object of objective examination.
>
> (Albright, 1989, p. 28)

The creation of illusionistic pictorial space by Renaissance artists has been called one of the great achievements of Western history (Edgerton, 1980). The widespread use of linear perspective that began in the Renaissance gave artists the ability to objectively depict the geometry of space, and to gain some control over it, two outcomes very much in concordance with the Renaissance quest to understand and control nature. The importance of Renaissance perspective from the vantage point of modern perceptual psychology is that it created pictures that were simultaneously high art and perceptual "experiments" that asked the question, "How well can pictures duplicate perception of a scene?"

Linear Perspective as a Way to Duplicate Reality

When, in about 1423, the Italian architect Filippo Brunelleschi created the first linear perspective depiction in the Renaissance, he used a special drawing apparatus that enabled him to transfer the geometry of the Baptistery in Florence onto his canvas (Kemp, 1989). In so doing, Brunelleschi created a realistic depiction of the Baptistery, which also duplicated the image that the Baptistery cast on his retinas.

This isomorphism between a depiction in linear perspective and the retinal image means that when a perspective picture is viewed from the correct station point (with the viewer's line of sight perpendicular to the picture and the viewer positioned at a distance so the visual angle of the picture matches the visual angle of the original scene as originally viewed by the artist), the picture will duplicate the image that the original scene cast on the artist's retina. But if a goal of perspective depiction is to create a perceptual surrogate of the original scene, that is, a perception that can be mistaken for the actual scene, then simply duplicating the scene's geometrical layout is not enough. One reason for this inadequacy of geometrical depiction is the flatness cues that indicate the existence of the picture's surface (Table 11.1). These flatness cues work against the goal of creating a perceptual surrogate of the scene, by making the viewer aware of the flat surface of the picture.

Flatness Cues

Brunelleschi minimized the flatness cues in his picture of the Baptistery by creating a viewing device in which viewers looked through a peephole at the picture's reflection in a mirror. The peephole viewing eliminated the flatness cues of visibility of the picture's border, the absence of motion parallax, and the absence of binocular disparity; and viewing the picture in a mirror may have minimized perception of the surface texture of the canvas. It is likely that this minimizing of flatness cues heightened the picture's illusory depth.

Later artists developed other ways of eliminating flatness cues. Fr. Andrea Pozzo created a painting on the interior of the dome of the church of St. Ignazio in Rome. The extreme height of the image made the surface of Pozzo's painting invisible, so when viewed from the correct position on the floor of the church (marked by a disc on the floor) the viewer perceives pictorial pillars and windows that add an illusory third story to the church's interior (Pirenne, 1970). Pirenne (1970) describes this perception as follows: ". . . From the position marked by the yellow marble disc, the arches supported by columns at both ends of the ceiling are seen to stand upright into space. They are seen in three dimensions. . . It is impossible to see that in fact they are painted on a cylindrical surface." (p. 84)

Leonardo Da Vinci, who was also aware of flatness cues, noted that the absence of binocular disparity can degrade the perception of depth in pictures (Kemp, 1989). Short of having viewers look at paintings through a peephole, or eliminating the depiction of depth from paintings, there is not much painters can do about this problem. However, Leonardo also realized that there is yet another problem with perspective, and one that the artist can control – the distortions that occur in wide-angle pictures.

Perspective Effects in Wide-Angle Pictures

Leonardo noted that linear perspective distorts the projections of objects in the periphery of wide-angle pictures. For example, the projection of a sphere located off to the side is an ellipse. Thus a perspective depiction of a sphere located at the left or right of a wide-angle picture is an ellipse, which will look unnatural when the picture is viewed from locations away from its center of projection (Figure 11.3a).

Painters have devised a number of solutions to this problem. Leonardo's solution was straightforward: He admonished painters not to paint pictures with a visual angle greater than 20–25 degrees. Another solution was to violate perspective by depicting peripherally located objects with the shapes we perceive when looking at them directly, as in Raphael's painting *School of Athens*, which depicts Voltaire standing far to the side of the room, holding a spherical globe, which is depicted as circular, in violation of perspective, but which appears perceptually correct. (See Figure 9.6 of Pirenne, 1970 or Figure 7.9 of Kubovy, 1986 for a reproduction of the painting and further discussion of this problem.)

The solution in which perspective is violated works, however, only for isolated objects, such as Voltaire's globe. One way some artists have dealt with depicting the space in wide-angle scenes is to use a curved picture plane. When the picture plane is curved, as is AB in Figure 11.3a, then projections of spheres in the periphery become circular. However, using a curved picture plane comes with a price, because the curvature of the picture plane creates a curvature of the projected space, which becomes obvious if the ground plane, such as a floor, is textured. This may explain the curvature of the floor in Van Gogh's *Bedroom at Arles* (Figure 11.3b) (also see Dubery & Willats, 1983, for a description of how the Dutch painters Vermeer and Saenredam dealt with this problem).

(a)

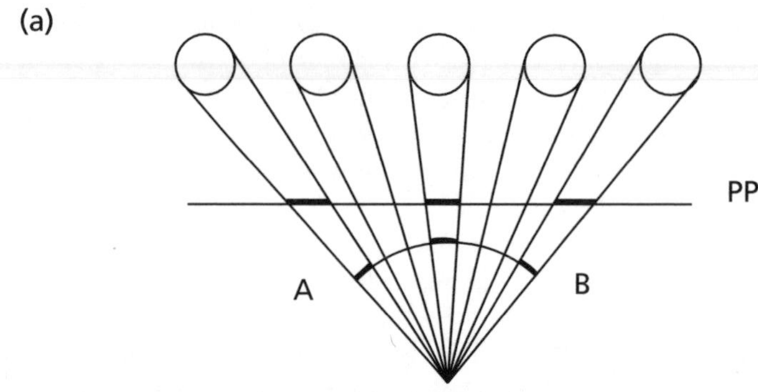

(b)

Figure 11.3. (a) The projections of spheres onto the picture plane (PP) become elliptical for the spheres off to the side. This is indicated in this top view by the darkened lines on the picture plane, which are longer for the spheres on the side than for the sphere in the middle. One way to make all of the spheres appear as circles on the picture plane is to use a curved picture plane (AB). Notice that the extents of each of the projections is the same for this picture plane. (b) Vincent Van Gogh's picture *The Bedroom* is a wide-angle picture that may have been composed using a curved picture plane, as indicated by the curvature of the floor (Vincent van Gogh, Dutch, 1853–1890, *The Bedroom*, oil on canvas, 1888, 73.6 × 92.3 cm, Helen Birch Bartlett Memorial Collection, 1926.417; photograph © 2000, The Art Institute of Chicago, All Rights Reserved).

Pictorial Perception in Art and the Laboratory

The achievement of the Renaissance was both the rediscovery of linear perspective as a tool for creating illusionistic space and the realization that simply recreating the scene's geometry did not guarantee perceptual duplication of the space. The history of art since the

Renaissance has been marked by a series of "movements" or "schools," many of which have also confronted the problem of depicting a three-dimensional scene on a flat surface. We will first consider two different artistic responses to this problem, and then some modern psychological research on pictorial representation.

Trompe l'oeil Art

Creating trompe l'oeil ("fool the eye") art has been a preoccupation of artists dating back to the discovery of perspective. The ultimate goal of the trompe l'oeil painter has been to create depictions that are perceived not as simply a realistic *picture* of an object or scene, but as *being* the actual object or scene itself. Examples of trompe l'oeil are architectural illusions such as Pozzo's ceiling, 15th-century wood inlays called *instarsia* (Tormey & Tormey, 1982), and paintings created by a group of American artists who were active in the late 19th century (Dars, 1979). Typical of these American trompe l'oeil paintings is William Harnett's *Old Models* (Figure 11.4), which is so striking in its realism that it is sometimes perceived as actual objects hanging on a wall.

The American trompe l'oeil painters achieved their illusory effects not by any new technique, but by combining extremely fine and realistic rendering with a judicious choice of subject matter. They depicted scenes such as objects hanging on a wall, or pictures of flat packages, that have little or no depth, thus eliminating the need to depict three-dimensional space. What the American trompe l'oeil artists demonstrated was that skillful painting technique can create a perceptual surrogate of nearly two-dimensional objects, on the two-dimensional surface of a picture. Their efforts tell us little about the more difficult problem of representing three-dimensional space on a two-dimensional surface.

Modifying Perspective to Achieve Perceptual Verisimilitude

As we have seen for the case of wide-angle pictures, the early practitioners of perspective realized that it was necessary to modify perspective in order to achieve perceptual verisimilitude. There are other situations as well in which a modification of perspective is necessary to create perceptually convincing depictions. One example of such a situation occurs in pictures of the sun or moon on the horizon. When the horizon sun or moon is viewed in the natural environment, it appears enlarged compared to its appearance when high in the sky. This enlarged perception, which is called the moon illusion, is substantial, with the horizon moon appearing enlarged about 50% (Hershenson, 1989). The enlarged perception of the horizon moon is considered illusory, because the angle subtended by the moon is the same whether it is high in the sky or near the horizon. (This follows geometrically from the fact that the moon remains at the same distance from the earth throughout the night.)

This constancy of the moon's visual angle would result in the full moon on the horizon being depicted by the same diameter circle as the full moon high in the sky, for a picture rendered in strict perspective. This becomes a problem, because the moon illusion occurs only weakly in pictures (Coren & Aks, 1990), presumably due to the presence of pictorial flatness cues and the lack of real depth in pictures. (See Hagen, Glick, & Morse, 1978 and

Figure 11.4. W. M. Harnett's *Old Models* 1892 is an example of trompe l'oeil painting. (The Hayden Collection, 1939; Courtesy, Museum of Fine Arts, Boston.)

Hagen, Jones, & Read, 1978 for research showing that the perception of depth in pictures is decreased by the presence of flatness information such as visibility of the picture plane.)

The painter's solution to the small moon illusion in perspective pictures is to violate perspective, enlarging the horizon moon's image beyond the dimensions specified by a strict perspective depiction. Tolansky (1964) cites examples of several painters who violated perspective, painting the horizon moon with an enlarged projective angle, in order to make its size look realistic, an example of how "artists have always accepted the primacy of perception over geometry" (Kubovy, 1986, p. 114).

Another example of accepting perception over geometry is Cézanne's depiction of bowls and bottles. Cézanne often painted the tops of bowls and bottles as more circular than the projective image, causing them to appear tilted forward. Cézanne may have done this by painting shapes as he saw them – that is, in terms of shape constancy, so circles-at-an-angle are painted as more circular than their elliptical projections, thereby achieving what Thouless (1931) called "regression towards the real object."

We do not, however, know the motivation behind the creation of Cézanne's "circularized" bowls. Was Cézanne painting shape constancy into his pictures, or was he motivated more by compositional considerations, perhaps tilting the bowls for conceptual reasons, such as wanting to bring elements of the picture towards the picture plane? Loran's (1947) report, that in setting up his still lives Cézanne tilted objects such as bowls and glasses forward by placing coins underneath them, is consistent with this hypothesis.

Whatever Cézanne's strategy for depiction, it is clear that he did not feel constrained to follow strict perspective. For example, many of the objects in Cézanne's pictures are depicted as if seen from multiple viewpoints, with some objects depicted as seen from one angle, and other objects depicted as seen from another angle. We can speculate that Cézanne's motive for doing this may have been to depict the defining views of many objects in one scene, thereby circumventing one of the properties of perspective – that parts of objects are hidden because they are depicted from a fixed viewpoint. (Also see Willats (1983, 1997) for a related analysis of a painting by Jean Gris.)

Illusionism and Space Perception

It is clear from our discussion above that artists have long been concerned with perceptual problems associated with pictorial depiction. It wasn't until the 20th century, however, that psychologists began applying the techniques of psychophysical measurement to some of the problems artists had been dealing with from a practical point of view for many hundreds of years.

One of the early experiments in pictorial depth perception is Smith and Smith's (1961) study in which subjects viewed a photomural through an eyepiece and threw a ball, in a space off to the side, at targets in the photograph. The balls were overthrown at short target distances (3 meters) and underthrown at longer distances (8 meters), but for all distances the maximum error was only about 10 percent. Not only were the subjects in this experiment fairly accurate in their throws, but they also seemed unaware of the fact that they were viewing a photograph, with no subject reporting that they had seen photographs rather than an actual room.

The accuracy of the motor response to pictorial depth in the Smith and Smith experiment is consistent with Smith and Gruber's (1958) finding of accurate estimation of depth in pictures. However, other studies have reported that estimates of pictorial depth tend to be compressed so that far distances from the observer are underestimated (Bengston, Stergios, Ward, & Jester, 1980; Kraft & Green, 1989; see Rogers, 1995 for a review) or distance in depth is underestimated compared to distance along the frontal plane (Goldstein, 1987), just as in natural scenes (Gilinski, 1951; Loomis, Da Silva, Fujita, & Fukusima, 1992; Toye, 1986; Wagner, 1985).

Unfortunately, few studies have directly compared space perception in pictures to space perception in the environment, and because "nonveridicality appears to be the case not just for pictorial perception but for the perception of real scenes, also" (Rogers, 1995), it is important that future research on pictorial space perception compare perception of pictures and natural scenes under equivalent viewing conditions.

Finally, Enright (1987) reports a particularly intriguing result of viewing pictures containing depth information: Monocular viewing of pictures that contain perspective depth information causes a vergence response, with the eyes diverging for far depicted distances and converging for near depicted distances. Perspective pictures can, therefore, cause an ocular motor response similar to that elicited by actual three-dimensional scenes. Enright suggests that this remarkable result may be responsible for a phenomenon called paradoxical monocular stereopsis, in which a photograph viewed with one eye can evoke a compelling illusion of depth (Ames, 1925; Koenderink, van Doorn, & Kappers, 1994; Schlosberg, 1941).

Changing the Station Point

> A theory of picture perception must also be a theory of the viewer's behavior in front of pictures.
>
> (Busey, Brady, & Cutting, 1990, p. 11).

A picture created in linear perspective must be viewed from the correct station point if the retinal image cast by the picture is to be the same as the retinal image cast by the original scene. In general this means that the picture must be viewed from the correct distance, so the picture's visual angle matches that of the original scene, and straight on, so the line of sight is perpendicular to the picture plane. (A deliberate exception is anamorphic art, which looks distorted when viewed from straight on, but becomes intelligible when viewed at an angle (see Leeman, Elffers & Schuyt, 1976).)

When viewing distance is varied, the geometry of the retinal image is changed so that the geometrical layout is magnified (for closer viewing) or minified (for farther viewing). If perception is controlled by the retinal image, then changing viewing distance should cause the perceived depth to be expanded for close viewing and compressed for far viewing. Corresponding perceptual changes do, in fact, occur with changes in viewing distance, with the extent depending on viewing conditions and the nature of the depicted scene (see Rogers, 1995, for a survey of this literature).

However, a different perceptual outcome occurs when pictures are viewed from an angle, because although the retinal image becomes distorted as the viewing angle becomes more oblique, viewers are usually unaware of such distortions (as when they walk past pictures in a museum) except at extreme viewing angles (as occurs when viewing a picture when standing off to the side and close to the wall) (Cutting, 1987; Pirenne, 1970). This seeming invulnerability of pictures-viewed-at-an-angle to distortion (at least at moderate angles) has been called the *robustness of perspective* (Kubovy, 1986).

This lack of perceived distortion has been explained by a compensation process that takes the viewer's deviation from straight-on viewing into account (Kubovy, 1986; Pirenne, 1970; Rogers, 1995; Rosinski & Farber, 1980; Wallach & Marshall, 1986). For example, Pirenne (1970) notes that an "unconscious intuitive process of compensation takes place which restores the correct view when the picture is looked at from the wrong position" (p. 99). Pirenne emphasizes that this compensation depends on the visibility of the picture surface. In cases in which the surface is not visible, as in Pozzo's ceiling, movement away from the correct station point creates easily perceived distortions.

However, the exact nature of this proposed compensation process has never been clearly specified, and it seems reasonable to consider alternative explanations for the lack of distortion. One explanation, proposed by Busey et al. (1990), is that the actual angles involved in normal viewing are not extreme. They propose that whatever geometrical distortion may occur at moderately oblique viewing angles (less than about 22°), it may not be noticed because the change in the geometry of the image is near the observer's threshold, so compensation is not necessary. According to this idea, the visual system ignores small transformations in the image because it never picks them up in the first place (Cutting, 1987).

Another reason for failure to notice distortions is because of the natural variability in the shapes of most environmental objects. There is no standard proportion for a face, for example, so there is some latitude as to which proportions are acceptable. As Gombrich (1960) notes regarding viewing at an angle: "If trees appear taller and narrower, and even persons somewhat slimmer, well there are such trees and such persons" (p. 144).

Although viewers may have only a limited awareness of distortions when viewing single pictures at an angle, awareness of this distortion becomes more obvious when the same picture is simultaneously viewed from two angles (see Pizlo & Scheessele, 1998). This awareness can be demonstrated by creating two identical copies of a picture by Xerography and positioning one on the left side of a page and the other on the right. By folding the page between the two images, it is possible to create a situation in which one image can be viewed at an angle while the other is viewed straight on. Comparison of the two pictures, when viewed simultaneously from different angles, reveals a large difference in the perception of the two views.

The phenomenology of this distortion aside, there is evidence that another aspect of pictures is affected little by even extreme changes in viewing angle. Goldstein (1987) has shown that an observer's judgment of the *spatial layout* of the scene depicted in a picture (as measured by the observer's arrangement of elements of the pictured scene on a three-dimensional plane in front of the picture) is relatively unaffected by changes in viewing angle. The mechanism responsible for this "layout constancy" is unclear; perhaps viewers are extracting some type of information that remains invariant with viewing angle.

The Meaning of the Picture Plane

René Magritte's painting *Les Promenades d' Euclide* (1955), shown in Figure 11.5, depicts the problem of the dual reality of pictures – on one hand markings on a flat surface, on the other hand representing something else, in this case a three-dimensional scene. The picture plane is the focus of Magritte's picture. If it is visible then we are looking at a flat painting of two cones on an easel standing in front of a window. If it is not visible, we are looking out of the window into a scene where the converging gray textures extend far into the distance on the right side and vertically into the cone of a tower roof on the left.

The visibility of the picture plane is a double-edged perceptual sword. When visible, it works against the achievement of illusionistic depth and towards perceiving objects more in terms of their visual angles, rather than their physical size in the environment. But while the picture plane is working against the achievement of illusionistic depth, it is helping achieve the robustness of perspective which minimizes the perceived distortion of pictures when they are viewed from incorrect station points.

Evidence that pictured objects are perceived more in terms of visual angle when the picture plane is visible is provided by Hagen et al.'s (1978) experiment in which subjects judged far objects as smaller, in accordance with their visual angle, when viewing them in a pictured scene, but more in terms of their physical size when viewing them in a natural scene, even though they both subtended the same visual angles. Evidence that the visibility of the picture plane helps prevent distortion is provided by the phenomenological descriptions of the severe distortions that occur when the picture plane is not visible, as when the scene on Pozzo's ceiling is viewed from an incorrect station point (Pirenne, 1970).

Another example of the effect of the picture plane is provided by Yang, Dixon, and Proffitt (1999), who found that overestimation of the length of the vertical stimulus in the vertical-horizontal illusion (Avery & Day, 1969; Prinzmetal & Gettleman, 1993) is reduced when subjects viewed the illusion stimuli on the screen of a small desktop monitor compared to when they viewed a natural scene containing large stimuli that subtended the same visual angle.

Why is the illusion reduced when the stimulus is viewed in the desktop monitor? The reduced illusion could be related to the flatness of the monitor's picture surface (as, for example, the moon illusion is reduced when viewed as a picture). But Yang et al. (1999) argue that the key variable is not the flatness of the picture plane per se, but the size of the image – small on the desktop monitor, large in the natural scene. Yang et al. claim that the visibility of the picture plane affects size perception indirectly, by signaling that the viewer looking at the desktop display is viewing a picture and so the image is small.

The most telling result of Yang's experiment is that the same difference between size estimation in the vertical-horizontal illusion in the outdoor scene and the desktop picture occurs when the scene and picture are viewed in a virtual reality (VR) condition created by viewing through a head-mounted device (HMD). Subjects viewed either VR depictions of an outdoor scene or VR depictions of a desktop display of the scene. Both of these VR depictions are pictures in that they are created by projections on a surface within the HMD, but in one case subjects interpret the pictures as the real scene and in the other, as a picture

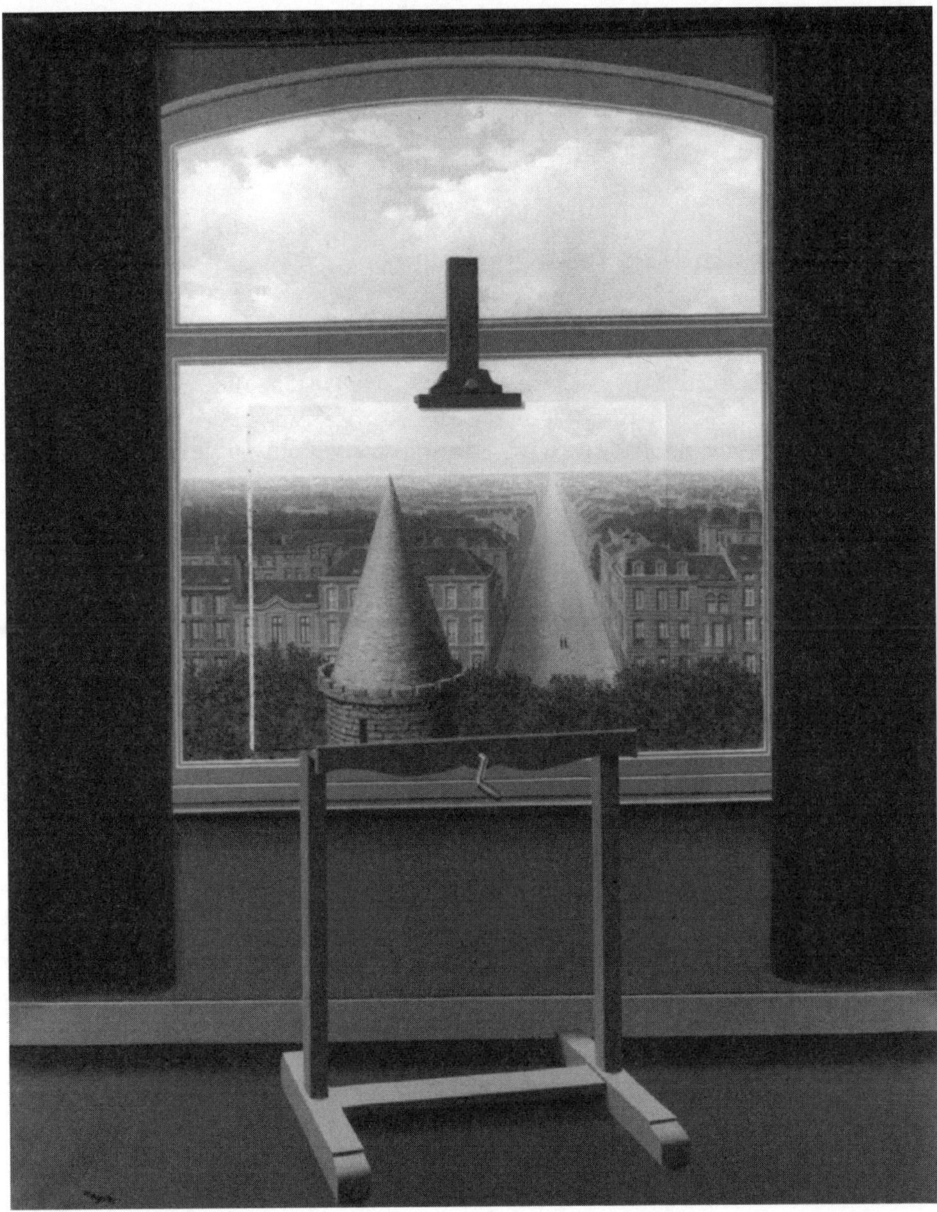

Figure 11.5. René Magritte. *Les Promenades d'Euclide*, 1955 (Minneapolis Institute of Arts).

in a desktop monitor. Thus, even though the pixels of the VR display are the same in both conditions, subjects related to one display as a picture and the other as a real scene, and it is this *interpretation* that they are seeing a small picture in one case and a large scene in the other that apparently influences their perception of size. The picture plane, therefore, becomes a cue that triggers a "picture understanding" perceptual response, whereas absence of the picture plane results in a "real world understanding" perceptual response.

The preceding examples of perceptual research illustrate some of the questions about pictures that have been posed by psychologists. We now consider some ideas about pictorial perception that have been proposed by artists and art theorists.

Composition

> Pictures are not randomly frozen slices . . . They are designed.
>
> (Rogers, 1995, p. 158)

> Drawing is a problem-solving exercise. What we observe on the page is the outcome of a great deal of mental work.
>
> (Freeman, 1987, p. 127)

The ideas expressed in the statements above are crucially important for understanding any psychology of art or pictorial perception, because they address the fact that pictures, whether they be children's drawings, family snapshots, or high art, are human creations, and as such are products of one human mind that are designed to be viewed and understood by another human mind.

Every picture is created by a process of composition, which we define as *any manipulation of the elements of a picture.* Generally, composition textbooks focus on how pictorial components are arranged in the picture. The importance of this arrangement, according to these texts, is that "good" composition has three perceptual effects: (a) it helps achieve perceptual clarity; (b) it directs the viewer's attention to various areas of the picture, and (c) it creates a feeling of harmony or balance.

Achieving Perceptual Clarity

> Pictorial communication is possible because pictures are *made* to be informative . . . paintings are easy to see. On the other hand, effective pictures are far from easy to produce.
>
> (Costall, 1985, p. 27)

Because they depict a frozen viewpoint, pictures are particularly vulnerable to ambiguity. For example, a cube depicted from a viewpoint that shows just one face may appear to be a square, or a person in the foreground of a photograph may appear to have a lamp, which is actually located in the background of the scene, growing out of his or her head. It is such pictorial "mistakes" that good composition seeks to avoid. Thus, Curtis (1947), in his composition text, cautions artists to avoid following or prolonging the line of the edge of one object, such as the trunk of a tree, directly into the edge of another object, such as the edge of a house. The result, which Willats (1997) calls *false attachment*, can be an unwanted perceptual joining of two objects that are actually separated from one another.

Another technique that has been employed to make pictures easier to "read" is the manipulation of contrast to ensure figure-ground segregation. Consider, for example, the Dürer print *Adam and Eve in the Garden of Eden* in Figure 11.6. At first glance this may appear to be a realistic (albeit somewhat fantastic) interpretation of Adam and Eve in the Garden of Eden. However, closer inspection indicates that Dürer has manipulated the illumination in this picture by darkening the background areas that surround human figures, thereby enhancing their visibility. (Notice, for example, the shading where Adam's arm crosses the tree.) Each aspect of the design of this picture has been carefully manipulated to make the picture easy to comprehend.

Directing Attention

> If you properly organize the picture, the viewers will never get lost. In fact, as long as the picture holds their attention . . . all areas of sight will constantly redirect their attention back to the chosen spot.
>
> (Henning, 1983, p. 126)

The above quote is representative of many statements in composition textbooks. Artists are taught that good composition can determine *where* a viewer looks, and the *order* in which the objects are viewed. Another goal of composition is to draw the viewer into the picture and to keep him or her from leaving it. The following statement by contemporary realist painter Jack Beal reflects one painter's approach to composition: ". . . I begin stressing diagonals as lines of entry and exit, as well as arrange empty chairs and other foreground objects as 'welcome mats,' and linear fractures and convolutions as a means of drawing the viewers into the image . . . ." (quoted in Shanes, 1993, p. 28). Beal relies on lines and objects to direct the viewer's attention, but lighting can have a powerful effect as well. This is particularly obvious in paintings by Caravaggio and Georges de la Tour, two Baroque artists who use chiaroscuro – lighting that makes forceful use of contrasting lights and darks – to direct the viewer's attention to areas that the artist considers most important (Hibbard, 1983).

The idea that composition can direct the viewer's attention is, however, only partially supported by empirical results. Measurements of the eye movements that occur while observers view pictures indicate that viewers fixate informative areas of pictures (Loftus & Mackworth, 1978; Mackworth & Morandi, 1967; Yarbus, 1967). It is, therefore, likely that artists can determine *where* a viewer will look in a picture by placement of high-information elements such as human figures. However, statements in composition texts notwithstanding, there is little empirical evidence to support the idea that compositional devices can control the *sequence* in which objects in a picture are scanned. In fact, there is a good deal of evidence that the sequence of scanning is more a function of the observer than the picture. Noton and Stark (1971) observed that sequences of fixations, which they call scanpaths, are variable across observers, so a particular picture might elicit 10 different scanpaths from 10 different observers (also see Buswell, 1935; Locher, Gray, & Nodine, 1996).

Figure 11.6. Albrecht Dürer. *Adam and Eve*, 1504 (Carnegie Museum of Art, Pittsburgh; bequest of Charles J. Rosenbloom).

To deal with empirical evidence for the individuality of eye movements, some art theorists have invoked "central processes." For example, Gaffron (1950), in describing a hypothesis called glance curve theory (also see Gordon, 1981; Gross & Bornstein, 1978), which contends that pictures are scanned from left to right, states that ". . . we are not dealing with a phenomenon dealing with voluntary or involuntary eye-movements. . . We are dealing with a phenomenon based upon the central process of visual perception" (p. 317). If this "central process" is related to attention, then Gaffron's statement seems unlikely to be true, because, although attention does not always have to exactly coincide with the locus of fixation (it is possible to steadily fixate in one place and attend to someplace else), there is evidence that we can't attend to one location and simultaneously move our eyes to another (Hoffman & Subramaniam, 1995). The close linkage between attention and eye movements that has been found in this study and others (Klein, Kingston, & Pontefract, 1992; Kowler, 1985) argues against the possibility that a trajectory of fixations moving in one direction could be accompanied by shifts of attention moving in another direction.

One of the reasons that art theoretical ideas about how the viewer's attention is distributed across a picture are so widely accepted by artists and theorists is that these principles are widely taught. Art students learn that certain compositional devices direct attention in a certain way, so they plan their paintings accordingly. It could be argued that because students of art are aware of the way paintings are *supposed to be scanned* they may therefore scan them (or think they are scanning them) in that way. The issue regarding whether pictorial composition can in fact control the sequence of scanning is still, however, open to investigation. The answer awaits a systematic investigation of the eye movement patterns in response to paintings that have been specifically composed according to principles designed to direct eye movements.

Creating Aesthetic Effect and Balance

> Balance is the primary design principle guiding the distribution of elements within a work.
>
> (Locher, Stappers & Overbeeke, 1998, p. 142)

Texts on composition generally agree that a goal of composition is to create balance. Ocvirk, Stinson, Wigg, Bone, and Cayton (1998), in a recent "Fundamentals of Art" textbook, define balance as *a sense of equilibrium achieved through implied weight, attention, or attraction, by manipulating the visual elements within an artwork* (p. 30) and as *the felt optimal equilibrium among all parts of the work* (p. 53). The key feature of these definitions, that balance is created by the action of individual elements of a picture, is contained in most conceptualizations of balance (also see Arnheim, 1974; Curtis, 1947; Locher et al., 1998). Balance is therefore a psychological state created by the arrangement of pictorial elements.

Authors differ on exactly how this translation from physical arrangement to psychological balance (or lack of it) occurs, but the explanation offered by Arnheim (1974) is representative. According to Arnheim, balance is determined by how the forces created by objects in a picture are distributed around a "center of balance" or fulcrum. The first step in analyzing a picture's balance is to determine the location of the fulcrum. The fulcrum is often at the center of the picture, but in asymmetrical pictures, in which most of the large objects are located off to the side, the fulcrum can be off to the side.

The next step is to determine the weights of various objects in a picture. Weights are determined both by qualities of the objects and their location in the picture. According to Arnheim (1974) some of the object qualities associated with "heavy" weight are high contrast, large size, jagged contours, and position on the picture plane. Objects in the top or right of the picture will be heavier than the same object on the bottom or left side. Because of this positional effect, larger objects are often placed lower on a picture or to the left, to compensate for the fact that those positions are associated with less weight.

Weights are converted into forces by the *rule of the steelyard*: force = weight times distance from the fulcrum. Thus, weights located farther from the fulcrum will exert more force than weights located near the fulcrum. Balance is achieved with "elements and qualities in a picture are organized around a balancing center so they appear anchored and stable" (Locher et al., 1998, p. 142).

Artists have generally accepted these ideas as a way to think about the process of ordering elements within a picture. This idea of arranging elements to create a balanced composition also has a certain face validity for non-artists. Most people have had the experience of arranging elements such as furniture in a room or pictures on a wall, with the goal of achieving a pleasing, or "balanced," result, and when doing this have noticed that some arrangements do seem more pleasing than others. Furthermore, when subjects in perceptual experiments are asked to arrange pictorial elements to create a balanced composition, or to locate the fulcrum of a composition, they are able to do so (McManis, Edmondson, & Rodger, 1985; Locher et al., 1996).

However, psychologists' attempts to test art theorists' ideas about balance have often failed to support the theorists' claims. The general strategy of much research on balance has been to start with paintings that are assumed to be balanced, by virtue of their status as "art" (i.e., they are in museum collections), and then to modify them by removing or moving elements of the painting or by creating a mirror image of the painting. The rationale for doing this is that if a balanced composition creates an equilibrium similar to balanced weights on two sides of a scale, then removal of a weight should destroy the equilibrium. Similarly, if there is a left-right asymmetry in the weights of pictured objects, then the mirror image, which is reversed from left to right, should appear unbalanced.

These predictions have been tested by presenting the original and modified pictures, usually in pairs, and asking observers to indicate which picture was the original or which picture they prefer. Results for mirror image reversals indicate no effect (original and modified pictures are preferred equally; Blount, Holmes, Rodger, Coltheart, & McManus, 1975; Freimuth & Wapner, 1979; Winner, Dion, Rosenblatt, & Gardner, 1987), or a small effect, such as Gordon and Gardner's (1974) observation that the original was preferred on 53% of the trials (also see Banich, Heller, & Levy, 1989; Levy, 1976; McLaughlin, Dean, & Stanley, 1983; Swartz &d Hewitt, 1970; Swartz & Swartz, 1971). Similarly, changing the picture content has only a small effect, as in McManus, Cheema, and Stoker's (1993) experiment in which original Mondrian paintings were preferred on 54% of the trials over the modified versions of paintings in which the proportions of the lines had been altered (also see Gordon & Gardner, 1974).

Perhaps most problematic for the idea that balance is created through an equilibrium between individual weights is McManus, Edmondson, and Rodger's (1985) finding that removing 10–30% from one end of "originals" that were judged to be balanced results in "chopped" pictures that are also judged to be balanced. McManus et al. concluded that balance is based on an integration of the picture as a whole, rather than on a simplistic balancing of individual weights (also see Locher et al., 1996, who reached a similar conclusion).

It is likely that, if weights are involved in determining balance, they are not part of a delicate balancing act, but are able to respond to changes by redistributing themselves into a new balanced configuration, much as an array of soap bubbles redistributes itself in response to the bursting of one of its members, to create a new pattern of equilibrium.

However, focusing on balance may be distracting research from other important variables that are worthy of study. Winner et al. (1987) speak to this point when they ask "why is it so often reported that a picture changes dramatically when it is reversed? . . . this effect cannot be explained in terms of balance: pictures do not look less balanced when shown in their mirror images" (p. 8). It is, therefore, perhaps more profitable to ask what perceptual changes actually do occur when pictures are reversed, and then to search for the mechanisms involved in these changes. One approach to this has been to hypothesize that reversal changes the relationship between the observer and the pictorial content, particularly in highly asymmetric pictures such as Janssen's *Reading Woman* (Figure 11.7). Gross and Bornstein (1978) observe that this painting clearly looks different upon reversal. Gaffron (1950) is more specific, claiming that when we view the original (Figure 11.7a) we look over the woman's right shoulder at her book, and towards the right side of the room. However, in the reversed picture (11.7b) we tend to look directly across the slippers, then more at the reading woman's lap. These phenomenal descriptions, while plausible, remain to be tested empirically (see Adair and Bartley, 1958).

Another left-right effect in pictures is one not of perception, but of creation. Portraits are more often oriented so the sitter's left cheek is visible (i.e., the sitter is facing leftward in the picture, from the perspective of the person viewing the picture). This effect is a robust one that extends over centuries of Western art, with proportions of left cheek visible pictures being about 60% (McManus & Humphrey, 1973; Gordon, 1981). Interestingly, the percentages are higher for portraits of women (68% face left versus 56% for portraits of males). This left-facing preference has generated speculation regarding possible mechanisms, most being unconvincing and/or unsupported by evidence. The most intriguing of the hypotheses, proposed by Coles (1974), is based on his finding that light is more likely to be depicted as coming from the left, so a sitter facing left will be turned towards the light and a sitter facing right will be turned away. This hypothesis further states that facing toward the left indicates "openness" and facing away indicates being "reserved." Gordon (1981) summarizes this theory by concluding that "the left face may signify openness for inspection and criticism, the right face will be enigmatic" (p. 239).

Yet another intriguing pattern in art is the placement of a portrait's eye on the picture plane. Tyler (1998a) found that one of the eyes of frontal or three-quarter portraits was frequently oriented so a line bisecting the picture passes through one of the eyes with an accuracy of ± 5%. This eye centering occurs for portraits throughout the history of Western art, ranging from the Mona Lisa to the statesmen on US Treasury Notes. An intriguing aspect of this result is that Tyler was unable to find any mention of a general principle of eye centering in the analytic literature of art. Because artists aren't taught to center eyes, the process must, according to Tyler (1998b), be subconscious, and may be related to the eye's role as a channel for the visual transmission of consciousness between people.

Figure 11.7. Pieter Janssen. *Reading Woman* (Bayerische Staatsgemäldesammlungen, Alte Pinakothek, Munich). (a) is the correct orientation. (b) is the mirror image.

Physiological Aspects of Art

> Hidden in the many billions of neuronal interactions, are the secrets of a consciousness that finds fulfillment, awe and beauty in the forms and configurations it makes.
> (Levy, 1988, p. 220)

> Through art, one can observe his/her reflection of reality in the brain.
> (Rentschler et al., 1988, p. 213)

Art, like any perceptual stimulus, has an underlying physiology. We will consider the physiological approach to art by describing the relationship between art and activity in various structures in the visual system.

Optics and Retinal Processing

The optical system and retina can influence the creation of artworks by degrading the artist's ability to see. For example, during the last decade of his life, Monet developed cataracts which blurred his vision. His late paintings therefore became increasingly blurred and shifted in color from blues and greens to yellows and browns. This color shift was probably due to the lack of short wavelength light transmitted by the cataracts (Trevor-Roper, 1970; Werner, 1998). Eventually, Monet had the cataract removed from his right eye, and because he had difficulty seeing clearly with both eyes open, he painted some pictures looking through either his left eye or his right eye. In one case he painted two paintings of the same view, one viewed with his left eye, the other viewed with his right eye. The difference between the two paintings is striking, with the one painted when viewing the scene through the lensless eye appearing far bluer (Werner, 1998). There is also evidence that defects such as "floaters" in the aqueous, color blindness, and retinal degenerations have affected the works of numerous artists (Forecast, 1986; Trevor-Roper, 1970).

Retinal circuitry influences perception by creating Mach bands, the heightening of the contrast at borders (Ratliff, 1965). Artists, most notably Georges Seurat and Paul Signac, have painted Mach bands into their pictures, thereby accentuating an effect naturally added by the retina, but which is often not obvious to the casual observer (Ratliff, 1992).

The most obvious addition of "visible physiology" to paintings has been the paintings that in the 1960s came to be known as "optical art." These paintings, by artists such as Bridget Riley and Victor Vasarely (Figure 11.8), exploit perceptual effects such as color and lightness contrast, in which juxtapositions of different colors enhance colors or cause shimmering; afterimages caused by high contrast areas of a painting which create images that seem to float over the surface of the painting in response to the observer's eye movements; and illusory movement effects, which create a shimmering effect. These effects share both high perceptual salience and connections to known physiological effects such as lateral neural interactions (Ratliff, 1965), visual pigment bleaching, and shifts in accommodation (McKay, 1957; Millodot, 1968; also see Zeki, Watson, & Frackowiak, 1993).

An earlier example of an optical effect, which predates the optical artists, is Ellsworth Kelly's painting *La Corbe I, 1950,* which includes striking illusory contours (Shapley, 1996).

This optical art, which reached its apogee with an exhibit at the Museum of Modern Art titled "The Responsive Eye" (Canaday, 1965; Seitz, 1965), was reviled by art critics as "pseudoscientism . . . having no lasting interest for most artists . . . " (Lippard, 1967) and as "empty and spiritless, though it may jangle the nerves and assault the eyeballs" (Rose, 1965). These aesthetic opinions notwithstanding, many of the optical art paintings provide impressive demonstrations of physiological effects made visible (Oster, 1965; Spillman, 1993; Wade, 1978).

Figure 11.8. Victor Vasarely. *Bora III*, 1964 (Collection Albright-Knox Art Gallery, Buffalo, NY; gift of Seymour H. Knox, Jr., 1966). The predominant optical effect in this painting is the horizontal subjective contours that are created by the alignment of the ends of the vertical bars. These subjective contours, in turn, create the perception of overlapping planes that can be seen when reading down the vertical centerline of the painting. These planes are not seen, however, when reading across the horizontal centerline of the painting.

Lateralization of Brain Function

It is well established that the brain is asymmetrically organized, with the left hemisphere being the site of language processing in most right handers, and the right hemisphere being important for both the recognition and expression of emotions, and the processing of spatial relationships (Springer & Deutsch, 1997).

The right hemisphere's role in the perception of spatial relations is reflected in Heller's (1991, 1994) description of an artist who, after sustaining damage to her right hemisphere, was unable to appreciate spatial relationships between the lines she was drawing, and, in fact, was initially not even aware of the severe distortions in her post-damage art work.[2]

There is also evidence that laterality of function affects the depiction of emotional material in pictures. Heller (1986, 1987, 1994) found that when children and adults draw pictures with emotional content, they place "happy" content to the right of center (which stimulates the left hemisphere, when the center of the picture is fixated), and sad content to the left of center (which stimulates the right hemisphere). Heller concludes that "the organization of space during the composition of a work of art may be influenced by the brain activity of the artist, which in turn is likely to depend, at least in part, on the artist's mood at the moment of creation" (p. 282). Interestingly, however, she found no such emotional bias in the organization of "famous paintings." She suggests that this may occur because serious artists (as opposed to the subjects who were asked to draw pictures for a psychological experiment) may be more interested in eliciting a complex blend of emotions in the viewer, rather than more straightforward positive or negative emotional experiences.

Asymmetric cortical processing may also be responsible for the finding that right-handed subjects prefer pictures with their major content displaced to the right, but left-handed subjects show no such preference (Banich et al., 1989; Levy, 1976; McLaughlin, Dean, &

Table 11.2 Three explanations for preference for right-biased pictorial content by right-hander

Reference	*Hemisphere activated*	*Result*
Levy (1976)	Right, because the stimulus is a picture	Attention to left so left appears heavier. Thus, more pictorial material is placed on the right to achieve balance
Beaumont (1985)	Right, because when the viewer directs eyes at important content on the right most of the picture falls in the left visual field (which activates the right hemisphere)	Pleasing effect since right hemisphere is more suited to spatial processing
Heller (1994)	Left, because attention is focused on information on the right	Pleasing, since the left hemisphere has a positive emotional valence

Stanley, 1983). The presumption here is that the preference in right-handed subjects is due to their consistent brain lateralization (with left usually being the hemisphere that controls language), whereas the lack of preference in the left-handed subjects may be due to the less consistent lateralization (with either the left or right hemisphere controlling language in different subjects).

While the right-side preference in right-handed subjects may be related to lateralization, the exact reason for this preference is not clear, with at least three different explanations having been proposed (see Table 11.2). We are left with empirical results that suggest an effect of brain lateralization on picture viewing, but the exact mechanisms involved remain in the realm of speculation (as does the mechanism behind the previously mentioned bias towards depicting the left cheek in portraits).

Modularity of Visual Processing

Even more speculative is the idea that the impact of art is related to its ability to selectively stimulate specific cortical pathways or nuclei. Zeki and Lamb (1994), in a paper titled *The Neurology of Kinetic Art*, put forth the idea that artists are exploring the organization of the visual brain. They illustrate this contention by focusing on kinetic artists such as Calder, who strive to emphasize motion over other visual qualities. Zeki and Lamb see Calder's mobiles as creating a perception that emphasizes movement, and they propose that this focus on motion strongly stimulates area V5 (also known as MT) of the extra striate cortex. As Zeki puts it, kinetic artists have worked to "tailor their art to the physiology of V5" (p. 632). In fact, Kourtzi and Kanwisher (2000) have used fMRI to show that static images that imply motion, such as athletes in action, stimulate more activity in area MT/MST than do images without implied motion. Thus, area MT, which is involved in the perceptual analysis of actual motion (Newsome and Pare, 1988), is also activated by still images depicting motion.

Cortical modules have also been implicated in the creation of some of the color effects associated with optical art. Livingstone (1988) suggests that the shimmering effect achieved by juxtapositions of different colors that have the same luminance may be due to strong activation of the parvocellular system, which is responsible for form perception, combined with weak activation of the magnocellular system, which cannot signal the borders between the colored objects because it is insensitive to color, and can't differentiate between the two equal luminance colored fields (see Chapter 3, this volume). The result is the perception of colors that "float," because the color is sensed but the border between them is indefinite.

Physiologically driven effects can also be created based on the simulation of multiple channels. For example, Latto (1995) suggests that artists may create artistic effects by simultaneously stimulating spatial frequency channels (see Goldstein, Chapter 1 and Frishman, Chapter 3, this volume) that serve high and low frequencies. As an example he cites Andy Warhol's *200 Soup Cans*, a display which simultaneously presents low frequency information, created by the alternating red and white stripes of the matrix of Campbell's soup cans, and high frequency information, contained in the lettering on the can labels. Of course, most pictures of natural scenes contain a large range of spatial frequencies, but artists have the luxury of manipulating their pictures to both emphasize certain frequencies and create juxtapositions of frequencies, thereby contributing to the perceptual and cognitive impact of works like Warhol's *Soup Cans*.

Conclusions

The application of perceptual and physiological principles to the analysis of pictures in general and art in particular is a two-way street. On one hand this analysis enhances our understanding of how pictures operate and, perhaps, how art creates its aesthetic effects. On the other hand, pictorial stimuli play a vital role in research dedicated to understanding perception in general. The richness of pictorial research is confirmed not only by the diversity of topics included in this chapter, but by other topics, such as color, contrast, and shadow, cross-cultural approaches to pictorial perception, and the various theoretical approaches to picture perception and art that had to be omitted from this chapter because of space limitations. Suggestions for readings relevant to these areas are included in the Additional Topics section below.

Notes

1. I thank Mary Peterson, Maggie Shiffrar, and Christopher Tyler for helpful comments on an earlier draft of the manuscript.
2. Another report of an effect of brain damage on artisitc creation describes Katherine Sherwood, a professor at the University of California, who was paralyzed on her right side by a massive stroke which damaged her left hemisphere. She taught herself to paint left-handed. Her post-stroke paintings, which are more abstract and have a freer more intuitive quality than her previous work, have garnered art awards and brisk sales, and two of Ms. Sherwood's paintings were recently exhibited in the Biennial Exhibition of the Whitney Museum of American Art in New York. Brain researchers conjecture that the newly found freedom of Ms. Sherwood's art may be due to the disabling of a site in the left hemisphere which is responsible for analysis, interpretation, and searching for deeper meanings. Freed of this left-hemisphere influence, processes in Ms. Sherwood's right hemisphere apparently took over the creative process. (Waldman, P. 'A tragedy transforms a right-handed artist into a lefty – and a star.' *Wall Street Journal*, May 12, 2000, page A1, A8.)

Suggested Readings

Arnheim, R. (1974). *Art and visual perception* (rev. ed.). Berkeley: University of California Press.
Goguen, J. A. (Ed.) (1999). *Art and the brain.* Thorverton, UK: Imprint Academic.
Gombrich, E. H. (1956). *Art and illusion.* Princeton, NJ: Princeton University Press.
Gombrich, E. H. (1982). *The image and the eye.* Ithaca, NY: Cornell University Press.
Gregory, R. L., & Gombrich, E. H. (Eds.) (1973). *Illusion in nature and art.* New York: Scribners.
Hagen, M. A. (Ed.) (1980). *The perception of pictures, Vols. 1* & 2. New York: Academic Press.
Hochberg, J. (1996). The perception of pictures and pictorial art. In M. F. Friedman & E. C.

Carterette (Eds.), *Cognitive ecology*. San Diego: Academic Press.
Ittleson, W. H. (1996). Visual perception of markings. *Psychonomic Bulletin & Review, 3*, 171–187.
Vitz, P. C., & Glimcher, A. B. (1984). *Modern art and modern science*. New York: Praeger.
Ziki, S. (2000). *Inner vision: an exploration of art and the brain*. Oxford, UK: Oxford University Press.

Additional Topics

Light and Color in Art

Light and color is a basic property of perception and a primary concern of many artists, notably the impressionists and modern abstract artists, among others (Baxandall, 1995; Gombrich, 1995; Jameson & Hurvich, 1975; Kemp, 1990; Lamb & Bourriau, 1995; Lee, 1987; Ratliff, 1971, 1992).

Developmental and Cross-Cultural Aspects of Picture Perception

Research on how children and people in cultures that have not traditionally viewed pictures provides insights on basic mechanisms of picture perception (Craton & Yonas, 1990; DeLoache, Pierroutsakos, Uttal, Risengren, & Gottlieb, 1998; Deregowski, 1989; Nye, Thomas, & Robinson, 1995).

Further Effects of Viewing Pictures at an Angle

Viewing pictures from an angle causes objects in the picture to appear to "rotate" to follow the observer (Goldstein, 1979, 1987).

Pictures as Stimuli in Psychological Research

This topic is less concerned with art, and more concerned with both the basic understanding of pictures, and how pictures have played a major role as stimuli in a large amount of research on perception and other psychological topics. It is not an exaggeration to say that without pictures, a large proportion of the psychological literature would not exist. When researchers refer to research on "real world scenes", that research often uses pictures, not three-dimensional scenes, as stimuli. A small selection of references from a few representative areas follows.

Figure-Ground Segregation: Bayliss and Driver (1995), Peterson (1994), Teuber (1974). *Illusions*: Coren and Girgus (1978). *Neurophysiology*: Perett, Hietanen, Oram, and Benson (1992), Rolls and Tovee (1995). *Neuropsychology*: Farah (1990), Humphreys and Riddoch (1987). *Event Perception*: Shiffrar and Freyd (1990), Simons and Levin (1997). *Object Perception*: Biederman (1981, 1987), Marr (1982). *Mental Imagery*: Kosslyn (1995). *Emotions*: Carroll and Russell (1996). *Personality Assessment*: Morgan and Murray (1935).

References

Adair, H., & Bartley, S. H. (1958). Nearness as a function of lateral orientation in pictures. *Perceptual and Motor Skills, 8*, 135–141.
Albright, T. (1989). *On art and artists*. San Francisco: Chronicle Books.
Ames, A. (1925). Depth in pictorial art. *Art Bulletin, 8*, 5–24.
Arnheim, R. (1974). *Art and visual perception*. Berkeley: University of California Press.
Avery, G. C., & Day, R. H. (1969). Basis of the horizontal-vertical illusion. *Journal of Experimental Psychology, 81*, 376–380.

Banich, M. T., Heller, W., & Levy, J. (1989). Aesthetic preference and picture asymmetries. *Cortex, 25*, 187–195.

Baxandall, M. (1995). *Shadows and enlightenment.* New Haven: Yale University Press.

Bayliss, G. C., & Driver, J. (1995). One-sided edge assignment in vision: 1. Figure-ground segmentation and attention to objects. *Current Directions in Psychological Science, 4*, 140–146.

Beaumont, J. G. (1985). Lateral organization and aesthetic preference: The importance of peripheral visual asymmetries. *Neuropsychologia, 23*, 103–113.

Bengston, J. K., Stergios, J. C., Ward, J. L., & Jester, R. E. (1980). Optic array determinants of apparent distance and size in pictures. *Journal of Experimental Psychology: Human Perception & Performance, 6*, 751–759.

Biederman, I. (1981). On the semantics of a glance at a scene. In M. Kubovy & J. Pomerantz (Eds.), *Perceptual organization.* Hillsdale, NJ: Erlbaum.

Biederman, I. (1987). Recognition-by-components: A theory of human image understanding. *Psychological Review, 94*, 115–147.

Blount, P., Holmes, J., Rodger, J., Coltheart, M., & McManus, C. (1975). On the ability to discriminate original from mirror-image reproductions of works of art. *Perception, 4*, 385–389.

Busey, T. A., Brady, N. P., & Cutting, J. E. (1990). Compensation is unnecessary for the perception of faces in slanted pictures. *Perception & Psychophysics, 48*, 1–11.

Buswell, G. T. (1935). *How people look at pictures.* Chicago: University of Chicago Press.

Canaday, J. (1965). Art that pulses, quivers, and fascinates. *The New York Times Magazine*, February 21.

Canaday, J. (1980). *What is art?* New York: Alfred Knopf.

Carroll, J. M., & Russell, J. A. (1996). Do facial expressions signal specific emotions? Judging emotion from the face in context. *Journal of Personality and Social Psychology, 70*, 205–218.

Coles, P.R. (1974). Profile orientation and social distance in portrait painting. *Perception, 3*, 303–308.

Coren, S., & Aks, D. J. (1990). Moon illusion in pictures: A multimechanism approach. *Journal of Experimental Psychology: Human Perception & Performance, 16*, 365–380.

Coren, S., & Girgus, J. S. (1978). *Seeing is deceiving: The psychology of visual illusions.* Hillsdale, NJ: Erlbaum.

Costall, A. (1985). In M. V. Cox (Ed.), *Visual order* (pp. 17–30). Cambridge: Cambridge University Press.

Craton, L. G., & Yonas, A. (1990). The role of motion in infants' perception of occlusion. In J. T. Enns (Ed.), *The development of attention: Research and theory* (pp. 21–46). London: Elsevier.

Curtis, E. P. (1947). *Composition and pictures.* Boston: American Photographic Publishing Co.

Cutting, J. E. (1987). Rigidity in cinema seen from the front row, side aisle. *Journal of Experimental Psychology: Human Perception & Performance, 13*, 323–334.

Cutting, J. E., & Massironi, M. (1998). Pictures and their special status in perceptual and cognitive inquiry. In J. Hochberg (Ed.), *Perception and cognition at century's end* (pp. 137–168). San Diego: Academic Press.

Dars, C. (1979). *Images of deception: The art of trompe l'oeil.* Oxford, UK: Phaidon.

DeLoache, J. S., Pierroutsakos, S. L., Uttal, D. H., Rosengren, K. S., & Gottlieb, A. (1998). Grasping the nature of pictures. *Psychological Science, 9*, 205–210.

Deregowski, J. (1989). Real space and represented space: Cross-cultural perspectives. *Behavioral and Brain Sciences, 12*, 51–119.

Dubery, F., & Willats, J. (1972). *Drawing systems.* New York: Van Nostrand Reinhold.

Dubery, F., & Willats, J. (1983). *Perspective and other drawing systems.* New York: Van Nostrand Reinhold.

Edgerton, S. Y. (1975). *The Renaissance rediscovery of linear perspective.* New York: Basic Books.

Edgerton, S. Y. (1980). The renaissance artist as quantifier. In M. A. Hagen (Ed.), *The perception of pictures* (Vol. 1, pp. 179–212). New York: Academic Press.

Enright, J. T. (1987). Art and the oculomotor system: Perspective illusions evoke vergence changes. *Perception, 16*, 731–746.

Farah, M. J. (1990). *Visual agnosia: Disorders of object recognition and what they tell us about normal vision.* Cambridge, MA: MIT Press.
Forecast (1986). *Art of the eye: An exhibition on vision.* Minneapolis, MN: Forecast.
Freeman, N. H. (1987). Current problems in the development of representational picture-production. *Archives de Psychologie, 55,* 127–152.
Freimuth, M., & Wapner, S. (1979). The influence of lateral organization on the evaluation of paintings. *British Journal of Psychology, 73,* 211-218.
Gaffron, M. (1950). Right and left in pictures. *Art Quarterly, 13,* 312–331.
Gibson, J. J. (1971). The information available in pictures. *Leonardo, 4,* 27–35.
Gibson, J. J. (1978). The ecological approach to the visual perception of pictures. *Leonardo, 11,* 227–235.
Gilinski, A. S. (1951). Perceived size and distance in visual space. *Psychological Review, 58,* 460-482.
Goldstein, E. B. (1979). Rotation of objects in pictures viewed at an angle: Evidence for different properties of two types of pictorial space. *Journal of Experimental Psychology: Human Perception & Performance, 5,* 78–87.
Goldstein, E. B. (1987). Spatial layout, orientation relative to the observer, and perceived projection in pictures viewed at an angle. *Journal of Experimental Psychology: Human Perception & Performance, 13,* 256–266.
Goldstein, E. B. (1998). When does visual processing become cognitive? *Contemporary Psychology, 43,* 127–129.
Gombrich, E. H. (1960). *Art and illusion.* Princeton, NJ: Princeton University Press.
Gombrich, E. H. (1982). *The image and the eye.* Ithaca, NY: Cornell University Press.
Gombrich, E. H. (1995). *Shadows: The depiction of cast shadows in Western art.* London: National Gallery Publications.
Gordon, I. (1981). Left and right in art. In D. O'Hare (Ed.), *Psychology and the arts* (pp. 211–241). New Jersey: Humanities Press.
Gordon, I. E., & Gardner, C. (1974). Responses to altered pictures. *British Journal of Psychology, 65,* 243–251.
Gregory, R. L. (1970). *The intelligent eye.* New York: McGraw-Hill.
Gross, C. G., & Bornstein, M. H. (1978). Left and right in science and art. *Leonardo, 11,* 29–38.
Hagen, M. A. (Ed.) (1980a). *The perception of pictures* (Vol. 1). New York: Academic Press.
Hagen, M. A. (Ed.) (1980b). *The perception of pictures* (Vol. 2). New York: Academic Press.
Hagen, M. A., Glick, R., & Morse, B. (1978). Role of two-dimensional surface characteristics in pictorial depth perception. *Perceptual and Motor Skills, 46,* 875–881.
Hagen, M. A., Jones, R. K., & Reed, E. S. (1978). On a neglected variable in theories of pictorial perception: Truncation of the visual field. *Perception & Psychophysics, 23,* 326–330.
Hayes, A., & Ross, J. (1995). Lines of sight. In R. L. Gregory, J. Harris, P. Heard, & D. Rose (Eds.), *The artful eye.* New York: Oxford University Press.
Heller, W. (1986). *Cerebral organization of emotional function in children.* Doctoral dissertation, University of Chicago.
Heller, W. (1987). Lateralization of emotional content in children's drawings. *Scientific Proceedings of the Annual Meeting of the American Academy of Child and Adolescent Psychiatry, 3,* 63.
Heller, W. (1991). New territory: Creativity and brain injury. *Creative Woman, 11,* 16–18.
Heller, W. (1994). Cognitive and emotional organization of the brain: Influences on the creation and perception of art. In D.W. Zaidel (Ed.), *Neuropsychology* (pp. 271–292). San Diego: Academic Press.
Henning, F. (1983). *The basis of successful art: Concept and composition.* Cincinatti: North Light Publishers.
Hershenson, M. (Ed.) (1989). *The moon illusion.* Hillsdale, NJ: Erlbaum.
Hibbard, H. (1983). *Caravaggio.* New York: Harper and Row.
Hochberg, J. (1979). Some of the things that paintings are. In C. F. Nodine & D. G. Fisher (Eds.), *Perception and pictorial representation* (pp. 17–41). New York: Praeger.
Hochberg, J. (1980). Pictorial functions and perceptual structures. In M. A. Hagen (Ed.), *The*

perception of pictures (Vol. 2). New York: Academic Press.

Hochberg, J. (1996). The perception of pictures and pictorial art. In M. F. Friedman & E. C. Carterette (Eds.), *Cognitive ecology* (pp. 151–203). San Diego: Academic Press.

Hoffman, J. E., & Subramaniam, B. (1995). The role of visual attention in saccadic eye movements. *Perception & Psychophysics, 57*, 787–795.

Humphreys, G. W., & Riddoch, M. J. (1987). *To see but not to see: A case of visual agnosia*. Hillsdale, NJ: Erlbaum.

Hyman, T. (1979). *Narrative paintings*. Bristol, UK: Arnolfini.

Ittleson, W. H. (1996). Visual perception of markings. *Psychonomic Bulletin & Review, 3*, 171–187.

Jameson, D., & Hurvich. L. M. (1975). From contrast to assimilation: In art and in the eye. *Leonardo, 8*, 125–131.

Kemp, M. (1989). *The science of art*. New Haven: Yale University Press.

Kennedy, J. M. (1974). *A psychology of picture perception*. San Francisco, CA: Jossey-Bass.

Klein, R. M., Kingston, A., & Pontefract, A. (1992). Orienting of visual attention. In K. Rayner (Ed.), *Eye movements and visual cognition* (pp. 46–65). New York: Springer-Verlag.

Koenderink, J. J., van Doorn, A. J., & Kappers, A. M. L. (1994). On so-called "paradoxical" monocular stereoscopy. *Perception, 23*, 583–594.

Kosslyn, S. M. (1995). Mental imagery. In S. M. Kosslyn & D. N. Osherson (Eds.), *Visual cognition* (Vol. 2, pp. 267–296). Cambridge, MA: MIT Press.

Kourtzi, Z., & Kanwisher, N. (2000). Activation in human MT/MST by static images with implied motion. *Journal of Cognitive Neuroscience*, in press.

Kowler, E. (1985). Smooth eye movements as indicators of selective attention. In M. I. Posner & O.S.M. Marin (Eds.), *Mechanisms of attention: Attention and performance XI* (pp. 333–350). Hillsdale, NJ: Erlbaum.

Kraft, R. N., & Green, J. S. (1989). Distance perception as a function of photographic area of view. *Perception & Psychophysics, 45*, 459–466.

Kubovy, M. (1986). *The psychology of perspective and Renaissance art*. Cambridge, UK: Cambridge University Press.

Lamb, T., & Bourriau, J. (Eds.) (1995). *Colour: Art and science*. Cambridge: Cambridge University Press.

Lane, J. R., & Larsen, S. C. (1983). *Abstract painting and sculpture in America, 1927–1944*. New York: Abrams.

Latto, R. (1995). The brain of the beholder. In R. Gregory, J. Harris, P. Heard, & D. Rose (Eds.), *The artful eye* (pp. 66–94). Oxford: Oxford University Press.

Lee, A. (1987). Seurat and science. *Art History, 10*, 203–225.

Leeman, F., Eiffers, J., & Schuyt, M. (1976). *Hidden images*. New York: Harry N. Abrams.

Levy, J. (1976). Lateral dominance and aesthetic preference. *Neuropsychologia, 14*, 431–445.

Levy, J. (1988). Cerebral asymmetry and aesthetic experience. In I. Rentschler et al. (Eds), *Beauty and the brain* (pp. 219–242). Basel: Birkhäuser Verlag.

Lippard, L. R. (1967). Perverse perspectives. *Art International, 11*, 28–33.

Livingstone, M. S. (1988). Art, illusion and the visual system. *Scientific American, 258*, 78–85.

Locher, P., Gray, S., & Nodine, C. (1996). The structural framework of pictorial balance. *Perception, 25*, 1419–1436.

Locher, P. J., Stappers, P. J., & Overbeeke, K. (1998). The role of balance as an organizing design principle underlying adults' compositional strategies for creating visual display. *Acta Psychologica, 99*, 141–161.

Loftus, G. R., & Mackworth, N. H. (1978). Cognitive determinants of fixation location during picture viewing. *Journal of Experimental Psychology: Human Perception & Performance, 4*, 565–572.

Loomis, J. M., Da Silva, J. A., Fujita, N., & Fukusima, S. S. (1992). Visual space perception and visually directed action. *Journal of Experimental Psychology: Human Perception & Performance, 18*, 906–920.

Loran, E. (1947). *Cézanne's composition*. Berkeley: University of California Press.

MacKay, D. M. (1957). Moving visual images produced by regular stationary patterns. *Nature, 180,* 849–850.
Mackworth, N. H., & Morandi, A. J. (1967). The gaze selects informative details within pictures. *Perception & Psychophysics, 2,* 547–551.
Marr, D. (1982). *Vision.* San Francisco: Freeman.
Martin, A. (1981). Modern realism is really real realism: Contemporary realism in context. In *Real, really real, super real: Directions in contemporary American realism.* San Antonio, TX: San Antonio Museum of Art.
McLaughlin, J. P., Dean, P., & Stanley, P. (1983). Aesthetic preference in dextrals and sinistrals. *Neuropsychologia, 21,* 147–153.
McManus, I., Edmondson, D., & Rodger, J. (1985). Balance in pictures. *British Journal of Psychology, 76,* 311–324.
McManus, I. C., Cheema, B. & Stoker, J. (1993). The aesthetics of composition: A study of Mondrian. *Empirical Studies of the Arts, 11,* 83–94.
McManus. I. C., & Humphrey, N. K. (1973). Turning the left cheek. *Nature, 243,* 271–272.
Millodot, M. (1968). Influence of accommodation on the viewing of an optical illusion. *Quarterly Journal of Experimental Psychology, 20,* 329–335.
Morgan, C. D., & Murray, H. A. (1935). A method for investigating fantasies: The Thematic Apperception Test. *Archives of Neurology and Psychiatry, 34,* 289–306.
Nakayama, K., He, Z. J., & Shimojo, S. (1995). Visual surface representation: A critical link between lower-level and higher-level vision. In S. M. Kosslyn & D. N. Osherson (Eds.), *Visual cognition* (Vol. 2, pp. 1–70). Cambridge, MA: MIT Press.
Newsome, W. T., & Pare, E. B. (1988). A selective impairment of motion perception following lesions of the middle temporal visual area (MT). *Journal of Neuroscience, 8,* 2201–2211.
Nodine, C. F., & Fisher, D. G. (Eds.) (1979). *Perception and pictorial representation.* New York: Praeger.
Nodine, C. F., Locher, P. J., & Krupinski, E. A. (1993). The role of formal art training on perception and aesthetic judgment of art compositions. *Leonardo, 26,* 219–227.
Noton, D., & Stark, L. (1971). Scanpaths in saccadic eye movements while viewing and recognizing patterns. *Vision Research, 11,* 929–942.
Nye, R., Thomas, G. V., & Robinson, E. (1995). Children's understanding about pictures. In C. Lange-Kuttner & G.V. Thomas (Eds.), *Drawing and looking* (pp. 123–134). New York: Harvester Wheatsheaf.
Ocvirk, O. G., Stinson, R. E., Wigg, P. R., Bone, R. O., & Cayton, D. L. (1998). *Art fundamentals: Theory and practice* (8th ed.). New York: McGraw-Hill
Oster, G. (1965). Optical art. *Applied Optics, 4,* 1359–1369.
Penrose, L. S., & Penrose, R. (1958). Impossible objects: A special type of illusion. *British Journal of Psychology, 49,* 31–33.
Perett, D. I., Hietanen, J. K., Oram, M. W., & Benson, P. J. (1992). Organization and function of cells responsive to faces in the temporal cortex. *Transactions of the Royal Society of London, B225,* 23–30.
Perkins, D. N., & Cooper, R. G. (1980). How the eye makes up what the light leaves out. In M. Hagen (Ed.), *The Perception of pictures* (Vol. II, pp. 95–129). New York: Academic Press.
Peterson, M. A. (1994). Object recognition processes can and do operate before figure-ground organization. *Current Directions in Psychological Science, 3,* 105–111.
Pirenne, M. H. (1970). *Optics, painting & photography.* Cambridge, UK: Cambridge University Press.
Pizlo, Z., & Scheessele, M. R. (1998). Perception of 3D scenes from pictures. *Proceedings of the SPIE, 3299,* 410–423.
Prinzmetal, W., & Gettleman, L. (1993). Vertical-horizontal illusion: One eye is better than two. *Perception & Psychophysics, 53,* 81–88.
Ratliff, F. (1965). *Mach bands: Quantitative studies on neural networks in the retina.* New York: Holden-Day.

Ratliff, F. (1971). Contour and contrast. *Proceedings of the American Philosophical Society, 115*, 150–163.

Ratliff, F. (1992). *Paul Signac and color in Neo Impressionism.* New York: Rockefeller University Press.

Rentschler, I., Caelli, T., & Maffei, L. (1988). Focusing in on art. In I. Rentschler et al. (Eds), *Beauty and the brain* (pp. 181–215). Basel: Birkhäuser Verlag.

Rogers, S. (1995). Perceiving pictorial space. In W. Epstein & S. Rogers (Eds.), *Perception of space and motion* (pp. 119–163). San Diego, CA: Academic Press.

Rolls, E. T., & Tovee, M. J. (1995). Sparseness of the neuronal representation of stimuli in the primate temporal visual cortex. *Journal of Neurophysiology, 73,* 713–726.

Rose, B. (1965). Beyond vertigo: Optical art at the Modern. *Art Forum, 3*, 31–33.

Rosinski, R. R., & Farber, J. (1980). Compensation for viewing point in the perception of pictured space. In W. A. Hagen (Ed.), *The perception of pictures* (Vol. 1, pp. 137–176). New York: Academic Press.

Schlosberg, H. (1941). Stereoscopic depth from single pictures. *American Journal of Psychology, 54*, 601–605.

Sedgwick, H. (1980). The geometry of spatial layout in pictorial representation. In M. A. Hagen (Ed.), *The perception of pictures* (Vol. 1, pp. 33–90). New York: Academic Press.

Seitz, W. C. (1965). *The responsive eye.* New York: Museum of Modern Art.

Shanes, E. (1993). *Jack Beal.* New York: Hudson Hills Press.

Shapley, R. (1996). Art and perception of nature: Illusory contours in the paintings of Ellsworth Kelly. *Perception, 25*, 1259–1261.

Shepard, R. N. (1984). Ecological constraints on internal representation: Resonant kinematics of perceiving, imagining, thinking, and dreaming. *Psychological Review, 91*, 417–447.

Shiffrar, M., & Freyd, J. J. (1990). Apparent motion of the human body. *Psychological Science, 1*, 257–264.

Simons, D. J., & Levin, D. T. (1997). Change blindness. *Trends in Cognitive Sciences, 1*, 261–267.

Smith, O. W., & Gruber, H. (1958). Perception of depth in photographs. *Perceptual and Motor Skills, 8*, 307–313.

Smith, P. C., & Smith, O. (1961). Ball throwing responses to photographically portrayed targets. *Journal of Experimental Psychology, 62*, 223–233.

Spillmann, L. (1993). The perception of movement and depth in Moiré patterns. *Perception, 22*, 287–308.

Springer, S. P., & Deutsch, G. (1997). *Left brain, right brain: Perspectives from cognitive neuroscience* (5th ed.). New York: W. H. Freeman.

Swartz, P., & Hewitt, D. (1970). Lateral organization in pictures and aesthetic preference. *Perceptual and Motor Skills, 30*, 991–1007.

Swartz, P., & Swartz, S. (1971). Lateral organization in pictures and aesthetic preference: II. A predictive study. *Perceptual and Motor Skills, 33*, 319–324.

Teuber, M. L. (1974, July). Sources of ambiguity in the prints of Maurits C. Escher. *Scientific American, 231*, 90–104.

Thouless, R. H. (1931). Phenomenal regression to the real object I. *British Journal of Psychology, 21*, 339–359.

Tolansky, S. (1964). *Optical illusions.* New York: Pergamon Press.

Tormey, A., & Tormey, J. F. (1982, July). Renaissance intarsia: The art of geometry. *Scientific American, 247*, 136–143.

Toye, R. (1986). The effect of viewing position on the perceived layout of space. *Perception & Psychophysics, 40*, 85–92.

Trevor-Roper, P. (1970). *The world through blunted sight.* Indianapolis. IN: Bobbs-Merrill.

Tyler, C. W. (1998a). Painters centre one eye in portraits. *Nature, 392*, 877–878.

Tyler, C. W. (1998b). The structure of interpersonal consciousness in art. *Consciousness research abstracts*, p. 174. Paper presented at Toward a Science of Consciousness: Tucson III.

Wade, N. J. (1978). Op art and visual perception. *Perception, 7*, 21–46.

Wagner, M. (1985). The metric of visual space. *Perception & Psychophysics, 38*, 483–495.
Wallach, H., & Marshall, F. J. (1986). Shape constancy in pictorial representation. *Perception & Psychophysics, 39*, 233–235.
Werner, J. S. (1998). Aging through the eyes of Monet. In. W. G. K. Backhaus, R. Kliegl, & J. S. Werner (Eds.), *Color vision*. Berlin: Walter de Gruyter.
White, J. (1967). *The birth and rebirth of pictorial space*. Boston: Boston Book and Art Shop.
Willats, J. (1983). Unusual pictures: An analysis of some abnormal pictorial structures in a painting by Juan Gris. *Leonardo, 16*, 188–192.
Willats, J. (1997). *Art and representation*. Princeton, NJ: Princeton University Press.
Winner, E., Dion, J., Rosenblatt, E., & Gardner, H. (1987). Do lateral or vertical reversals affect balance in paintings? *Visual Arts Research, 13*, 1–9.
Yang, T. L., Dixon, M. W., & Proffitt, D. R. (1999). Overestimation of heights is greater for real objects than for objects in pictures. *Perception, 28*, 445–467.
Yarbus, A. L. (1967). *Eye movements and vision*. New York: Plenum Press.
Zeki, S. (2000). *Inner vision: An exploration of art and the brain*. Oxford: Oxford University Press.
Zeki, S., & Lamb, M. (1994). The neurology of kinetic art. *Brain, 117*, 607–636.
Zeki, S., Watson, J. D. G., & Frackowiak, R. S. J. (1993). Going beyond the information given: The relation of illusory visual motion to brain activity. *Proceedings of the Royal Society of London, B., 252*, 215–222.

Chapter Twelve

Basic Auditory Processes

Brian C. J. Moore

The Importance and Function of Hearing

Hearing probably evolved primarily to alert organisms to events of significance in the environment. Unlike visual stimuli, auditory stimuli can be detected whatever their direction of incidence. Hearing can indicate the presence of predator or prey, and it can indicate the appropriate location to direct visual attention. In many species, and especially in humans, hearing has evolved further as a means of communication, speech communication being the prime example. Indeed, the ability to convey information using sounds as symbols for objects and actions is one of the characteristics that distinguishes humans from other animals. This chapter is mainly concerned with the physical description of sounds, the physiology of the auditory system, and with frequency selectivity in hearing. The latter plays a strong role in determining whether one sound will mask another, and it depends upon the analysis of sound in the peripheral auditory system. Chapter 13 is concerned with the perception of loudness, pitch, and timbre. Chapter 14 covers two main topics: sound localization; and the question of how the auditory system analyzes mixtures of sounds so as to achieve percepts of the individual sound sources that contributed to the mixture.

The Auditory Stimulus

Perceptual Dimensions of Sound and their Physical Correlates

Sound originates from the motion or vibration of an object. This motion is impressed upon the surrounding medium (usually air) as a pattern of changes in pressure. What actually happens is that the atmospheric particles, or molecules, are squeezed closer together than normal (called condensation), and then pulled farther apart than normal (called rarefaction). The sound wave moves outwards from the vibrating body, but the molecules do not advance with the wave: They vibrate around an average resting place. The vibrations occur along an axis that is aligned with the direction in which the sound is propagating. This form of wave is known as a "longitudinal wave." The sound wave generally weakens as it moves away from the source.

One of the simplest types of sound is the sine wave, also known as a sinusoid, which repeats regularly as a function of time. Its pressure variation as a function of time, $P(t)$, is described by the equation

$$P(t) = A \sin(2\pi f t),$$

where t is time, A is the peak amplitude (maximum deviation from the mean atmospheric pressure) and f is the frequency of the sound in Hz (number of cycles per second). The time taken for one complete cycle of the waveform is called the period, which is the reciprocal of the frequency. A sinusoid has a "pure" tone quality, like the sound produced by a tuning fork, and is also called a "pure tone" or "simple tone." Its subjective loudness is related to the peak amplitude, A; the greater the value of A, the greater the loudness, although the relationship is not linear, as is described in Chapter 13.

A sine wave is not the only kind of sound that repeats regularly. Many of the sounds encountered in everyday life, such as those produced by musical instruments, and certain speech sounds, also show such regularity, and hence are called periodic sounds. Although these sounds are generally more complex than sinusoids, they share a common subjective characteristic with sinusoids in that they have pitches. Pitch may be defined as that attribute of auditory sensation in terms of which sounds may be ordered on a musical scale. In other words, variations in pitch create a sense of melody. A sound that evokes a pitch is often called a "tone," especially when the pitch has a clear musical quality.

The pitch of a sound is related to its repetition rate and, hence, in the case of a sinusoid, to its frequency. It should be emphasized that pitch is a subjective attribute of a stimulus, and as such cannot be measured directly. However, for a sinusoid, the pitch is closely related to the frequency; the higher the frequency, the higher the pitch. For a more complex sound, the pitch is often investigated by asking the subject to adjust a sinusoid so that it has the same pitch as the complex sound. The frequency of the sinusoid is then taken as a measure of the pitch of the complex sound.

Fourier Analysis and Spectral Representations

Although all sounds can be specified in terms of variations in sound pressure occurring over time, it is often more convenient, and more meaningful, to specify them in a different way when the sounds are complex. This method is based on a theorem by Fourier, who proved that any complex waveform (with certain restrictions) can be analyzed, or broken down, into a series of sinusoids with specific frequencies, amplitudes, and phases. Such an analysis is called Fourier analysis, and each sinusoid is called a (Fourier) component of the complex sound. We may thus define a complex tone as a tone composed of a number of simple tones, or sinusoids.

The simplest type of complex tone to which Fourier analysis can be applied is one that is periodic. Such a tone is composed of a number of sinusoids, each of which has a frequency that is an integral multiple of the frequency of a common (not necessarily present) fundamental component. The fundamental component has a frequency equal to the repetition rate of the complex waveform as a whole. The frequency components of the complex tone are known as harmonics and are numbered, the fundamental being given harmonic number 1. Thus, for example, a note of A3 played on the piano has a fundamental component or first harmonic of frequency 220 Hz, a second harmonic of frequency 440 Hz, a third harmonic of frequency 660 Hz, etc. The nth harmonic has a frequency which is n times that of the fundamental.

One of the reasons for representing sounds in this way is that humans are able (if their attention is directed appropriately) to hear the lower harmonics of a periodic sound wave as individual pure tones, as will be described later in this chapter. Two simultaneous pure tones, whose frequencies are not too similar, are often heard as two separate tones each with its own pitch rather than as a single complex sound. Also, the subjective quality of a sound, its *timbre*, is partly determined by the way that energy is distributed over frequency, as will be described in Chapter 13.

The structure of a sound, in terms of its frequency components, is often represented by its magnitude spectrum, a plot of sound amplitude, energy, or power as a function of frequency. In these cases we would talk of the amplitude spectrum, energy spectrum, or power spectrum. Fourier's theorem in its original form can only be used to determine the spectrum of sounds with an infinite duration. However, a closely related mathematical device called the Fourier Transform can be used to determine the spectra of sounds with finite duration, as is always the case in practice. Examples of amplitude spectra are given in Figure 12.1. For periodic sounds of long duration, the energy falls at specific discrete frequencies and the spectrum is known as a line spectrum. The first three examples are of this type. The sinusoid, by definition, consists of a single frequency component. The square wave consists of the odd harmonics of the fundamental component (1 kHz in this example), and the amplitudes of the harmonics decrease with increasing harmonic number. The train of brief pulses, or clicks, contains all the harmonics of the fundamental at equal amplitude. However, since each pulse contains only a small amount of energy, and since there are many harmonics, each harmonic has a low amplitude.

For sounds that are not periodic, such as white noise (a hissing sound), the spectrum

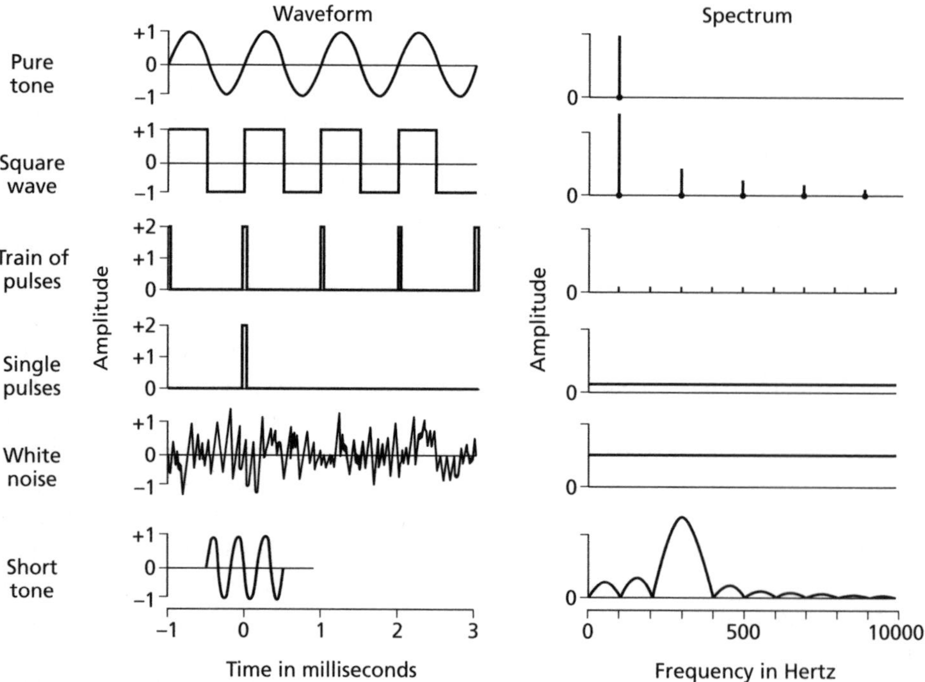

Figure 12.1. On the left are shown the waveforms of some common auditory stimuli, and on the right are the corresponding spectra. The periodic stimuli (pure tone, square wave, and train of pulses) have line spectra, while the non-periodic stimuli (single pulse, white noise, and short tone burst) have continuous spectra.

tends to be more complex. Non-periodic sounds can still have line spectra, for example a mixture of two non-harmonically related sinusoids. The term partial is used to describe any discrete sinusoidal component of a complex sound, whether it is a harmonic or not. More commonly, non-periodic sounds have continuous spectra; the energy is spread over certain frequency bands, rather than being concentrated at particular frequencies. The last three examples are of this type. The single pulse, or click, and the white noise both have flat amplitude spectra; the amplitude does not vary as a function of frequency (this is only true for very brief clicks). Although the pulse and the noise have spectra of the same shape, the amplitude of the spectrum of the pulse is lower, since it contains much less energy than the noise.

The final example shows a short burst of a sinusoid, often called a tone pulse or tone burst. In theory, the magnitude spectrum of a sinusoid is only a line if the sinusoid lasts an infinite time. For tone pulses of short duration, the magnitude spectrum contains energy over a range of frequencies around the nominal frequency of the sinusoid. This spread of energy increases as the duration of the tone pulse is shortened. Corresponding changes occur in our perception of such tone pulses; as a tone pulse is shortened in duration it sounds less tone-like and more click-like. If the tone pulse contains more than about 20 cycles (corresponding to a duration of 200 ms for a frequency of 100 Hz and 20 ms for a frequency of 1000 Hz), then the tonal sensation is dominant. If fewer than three cycles are present, the click-like sensation dominates.

The Measurement of Sound Level

Although the instruments used to measure the magnitudes of sounds, such as microphones, usually respond to changes in air pressure, sound magnitudes are often specified in terms of intensity, which is the sound energy transmitted per second (i.e., the power) through a unit area in a sound field. For a medium such as air there is a simple relationship between the pressure variation of a plane (flat-fronted) sound wave in a free field (i.e., in the absence of reflected sound) and the acoustic intensity; intensity is proportional to the square of the pressure variation.

The auditory system can deal with a huge range of sound intensities – about 10^{12}. This makes it inconvenient to deal with sound intensities directly. Instead a logarithmic scale expressing the ratio of two intensities is used. One intensity, I_0, is chosen as a reference and the other intensity, I_1, is expressed relative to this. One Bel corresponds to a ratio of intensities of 10:1. Thus the number of Bels corresponding to a given intensity ratio is obtained by taking the logarithm to the base 10 of the intensity ratio. For example, an intensity ratio of 100:1 corresponds to 2 Bels. The Bel is a rather large unit for everyday use, and to obtain units of convenient size the Bel is divided into 10 decibels (dB). Thus the number of decibels corresponding to a given ratio of acoustic intensity is:

$$\text{number of decibels} = 10\log_{10}(I_1/I_0)$$

When the magnitude of a sound is specified in decibels, it is customary to use the word "level" to refer to its magnitude. Notice that a given number of decibels represents an intensity or power ratio, not an absolute intensity. In order to specify the absolute intensity of a sound it is necessary to state that the intensity of the sound, I_1, is *n* dB above or below some reference intensity, I_0. The reference intensity most commonly used is 10^{-12} W/m^2, which is equivalent to a pressure of 2×10^{-5} N/m^2 or 20μPa (micropascal). A sound level specified using this reference level is referred to as a sound pressure level (SPL). Thus a sound at 60 dB SPL is 60 dB higher in level than the reference level of 0 dB, and has an intensity of 10^{-6} W/m^2. Notice that multiplying (or dividing) the ratio of intensities by 10 increases (or decreases) the number of decibels by 10. It is also convenient to remember that a twofold change in intensity corresponds to a change in level of 3 dB.

The reference sound level, 0 dB SPL, is a low sound level which was chosen to be close to the average human absolute threshold for a 1000-Hz sinusoid. The absolute threshold is the minimum detectable level of a sound in the absence of any other external sounds (see below for details). In fact the average human absolute threshold at 1000 Hz is about 6 dB SPL, when listening with one ear. Sometimes it is convenient to choose as a reference level the threshold of a subject for the sound being used. A sound level specified in this way is referred to as a sensation level (SL). Thus, for a given subject, a sound at 60 dB SL is 60 dB above the absolute threshold of that subject for that sound. The physical intensity corresponding to a given sensation level will, of course, differ from subject to subject and from sound to sound.

It is often convenient to use pressure as a unit rather than intensity, as the sound pressure generated by a transducer such as a loudspeaker or earphone is directly proportional to the voltage applied to the transducer, and this is easily measured. Thus, it is useful to adapt the decibel notation so that it expresses ratios of pressure as well as ratios of intensity. This may be done by recalling that intensity is proportional to the square of pressure. If one sound has an intensity of I_1 and a pressure P_1, and a second sound has an intensity I_2 and pressure P_2, then the difference in level between them is:

$$\text{number of decibels} = 10\log_{10}(I_1/I_2) = 10\log_{10}(P_1/P_2)^2 = 20\log_{10}(P_1/P_2).$$

Thus a tenfold increase in pressure corresponds to a 100-fold increase in intensity and is represented by +20 dB.

The Concept of Linearity

The auditory system is often conceived as being made up of successive stages, the output of a given stage providing the input to the next. Each of these stages can be considered as a device or system, with an input and an output. The analysis of the properties of a given stage is much simplified if that stage can be considered as linear. It turns out that some parts of the auditory system are linear or almost so (for example, the middle ear), while other parts (for example the inner ear) are distinctly nonlinear.

For a system to be linear, two conditions must be satisfied. (a) The output of the system in response to a number of independent inputs presented simultaneously should be equal to the sum of the outputs that would have been obtained if each input were presented alone. For example, if the response to input A is X, and the response to input B is Y, then the response to A and B together is simply X + Y. (b) If the input to the system is changed in magnitude by a factor *k*, then the output should also change in magnitude by a factor *k*, but be otherwise unaltered. For example, if the input is doubled, then the output is doubled, but without any change in the form of the output. These two conditions are known as superposition and homogeneity, respectively.

The output of a linear system never contains frequency components that were not present in the input signal. Thus, a sinusoidal input gives rise to a sinusoidal output of the same frequency (the amplitude and phase may, however, be changed). For other types of waveforms, the shape of the wave may be changed. For example, if the input to a linear system is a square wave, the output is not necessarily a square wave. This change in waveform occurs because the square wave contains many sinusoidal components, and the relative amplitudes and phases of the components may be altered by a linear system. This provides another reason for the popularity of sinusoids in auditory research; sinusoids are the only waveforms which are always "preserved" by a linear system.

Basic Structure and Function of the Auditory System

The Outer and Middle Ear and their Role in Determining Absolute Thresholds

Figure 12.2, panel (a) shows the structure of the peripheral part of the human auditory system. The outer ear is composed of the pinna (the part we actually see) and the auditory canal or meatus. The pinna significantly modifies the incoming sound, particularly at high frequencies, and this is important in our ability to localize sounds (see Chapter 14). Sound travels down the meatus and causes the eardrum, or tympanic membrane, to vibrate. These vibrations are transmitted through the middle ear by three small bones, called the malleus, incus, and stapes, collectively known as the ossicles. The stapes makes contact with the oval window, a membrane-covered opening in the bony wall of the cochlea, the spiral-shaped structure of the inner ear.

The major function of the middle ear is to ensure the efficient transfer of sound from the air to the fluids in the cochlea. If the sound were to impinge directly onto the oval window, most of it would simply be reflected back, rather than entering the cochlea. This happens because the resistance of the oval window to movement is very different to that of air. Technically, this is described as a difference in acoustical impedance. The middle ear acts as an impedance-matching device or transformer that improves sound transmission and reduces the amount of reflected sound. This is accomplished mainly by the difference in effective areas of the eardrum and the oval window, and to a small extent by the lever action of the ossicles. Transmission of sound through the middle ear is most efficient at middle frequencies (500–5000 Hz).

The ossicles have minute muscles attached to them which contract when we are exposed to intense sounds. This contraction, known as the middle ear reflex, is probably mediated by neural centers in the brain stem. The reflex reduces the transmission of sound through the middle ear, but only at low frequencies, and it may help to prevent damage to the delicate structures of the cochlea. However, the activation of the reflex is too slow to

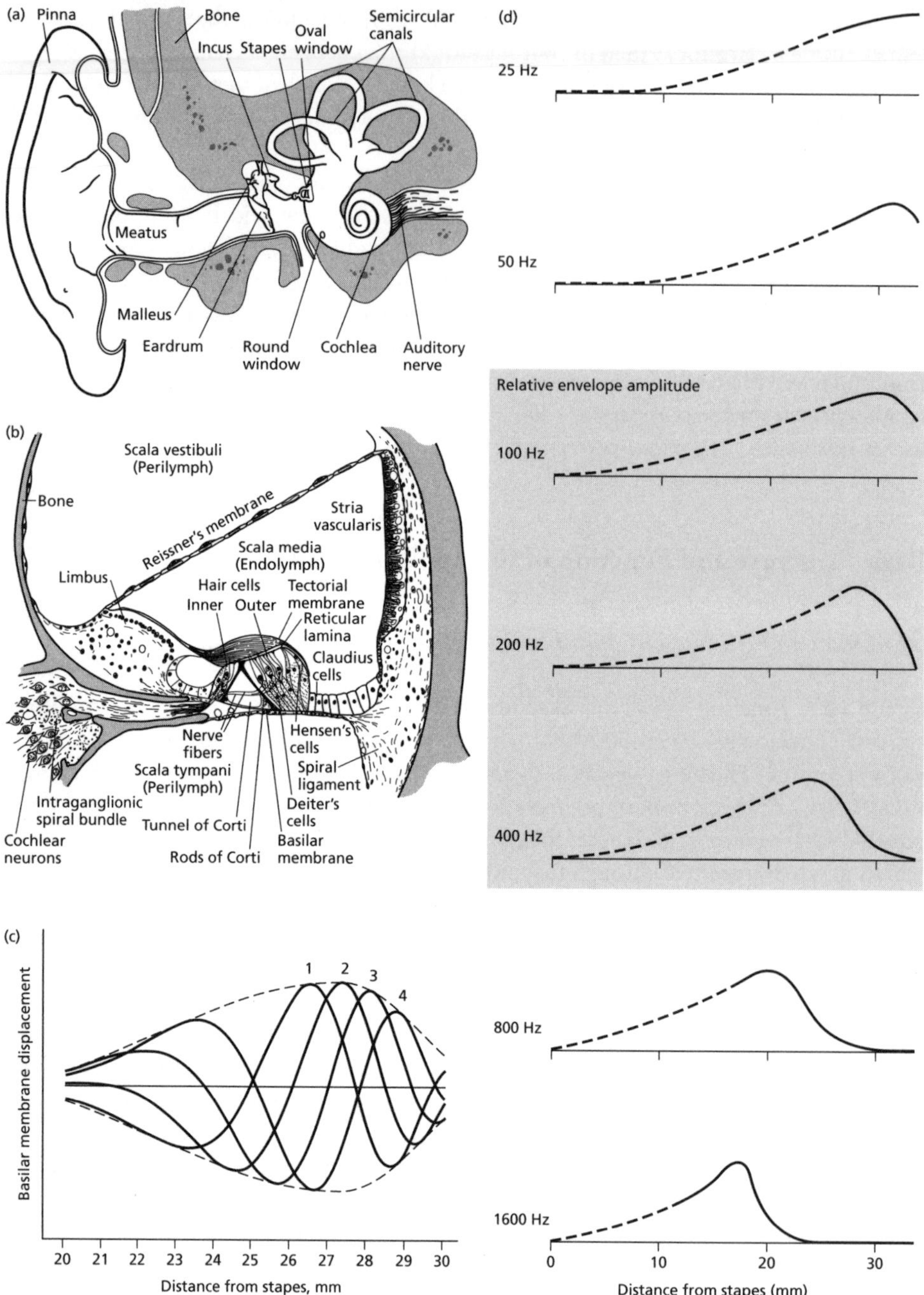

Figure 12.2. Panel (a) illustrates the structure of the peripheral auditory system showing the outer, middle and inner ear. Panel (b) shows a cross-section of the cochlea. Panel (c) shows schematically the waveform on the BM at four successive instants in time, in response to a low-frequency sinusoid. The pattern moves from left to right, building up gradually with distance, and decaying rapidly beyond the point of maximal displacement. The dashed line represents the envelope traced out by

provide any protection against impulsive sounds, such as gun shots or hammer blows. Two other functions have been suggested for the reflex. The first is the reduction of the audibility of self-generated sounds, particularly speech. It has been shown that the reflex is activated just before vocalization. The second is a reduction of the masking of middle and high frequencies by lower ones, a function which is particularly important at high sound levels; see later for details.

The absolute threshold for detecting sinusoids is largely determined by the sound transmission through the outer and middle ear; to a first approximation, the inner ear (see below) is equally sensitive to all frequencies, except perhaps at very low frequencies and very high frequencies (Moore, Glasberg, & Baer, 1997). Figure 12.3 shows estimates of the absolute threshold, measured in two ways. For the curve labeled MAP (Minimum Audible Pressure), the sound level is specified at a point close to the eardrum. For the curve labeled MAF (Minimum Audible Field), the measurement of sound level is made after the listener is removed from the sound field, at the point which had been occupied by the center of the listener's head. Note that the MAP estimates are for monaural listening and the MAF estimates are for binaural listening. On average, thresholds are about 2 dB lower when two ears are used as opposed to one. Both curves represent the average data from many young listeners with normal hearing. It should be noted, however, that individual people may have thresholds as much as 20 dB above or below the mean at a specific frequency and still be considered as "normal."

The MAP and MAF curves are somewhat differently shaped, because the head, the pinna, and the meatus have an influence on the sound field. The MAP curve shows only minor peaks and dips (5 dB) for frequencies between about 0.2 kHz and 13 kHz, whereas the MAF curves show a distinct dip around 3–4 kHz and a peak around 8–9 kHz. The difference derives mainly from a broad resonance produced by the meatus and pinna. The sound level at the eardrum is enhanced markedly for frequencies in the range 1.5–6 kHz, with a maximum enhancement at 3 kHz of about 15 dB.

The highest audible frequency varies considerably with age. Young children can often hear tones as high as 20 kHz, but for most adults threshold rises rapidly above about 15 kHz. The loss of sensitivity with increasing age (presbyacusis) is much greater at high frequencies than at low, and the variability between different people is also greater at high frequencies. There seems to be no well-defined low-frequency limit to hearing, although very intense low-frequency tones can sometimes be felt as vibration before they are heard. The low-frequency limit for the "true" hearing of pure tones probably lies about 20 Hz. This is close to the lowest frequency which evokes a pitch sensation.

←

the amplitude peaks in the waveform. Panel (d) shows envelopes of the patterns of vibration on the BM in response to sinusoids with various different frequencies. Solid lines indicate the results of actual measurements (von Békésy, 1960), while the dashed lines are von Békésy's extrapolations. Note that these patterns were obtained from damaged cochleas. The envelopes would have sharper peaks in a normal healthy cochlea.

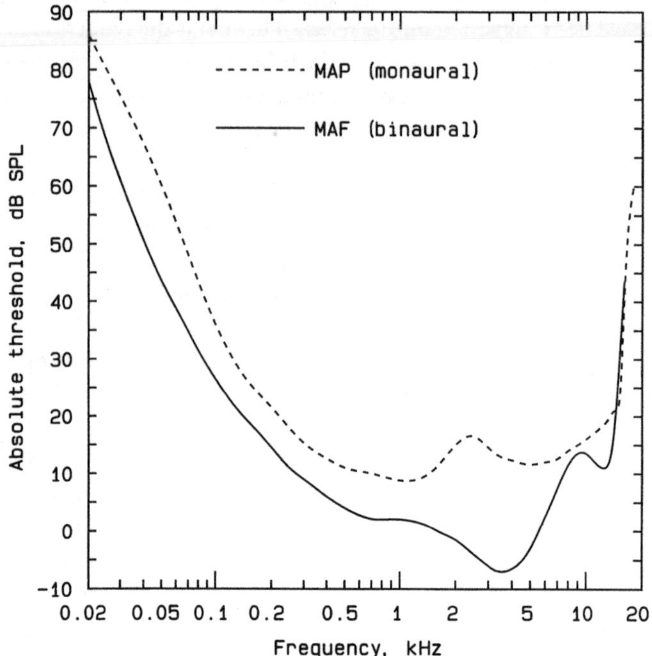

Figure 12.3. The minimum audible sound level as a function of frequency. The solid curve shows the Minimum Audible Field (MAF) for binaural listening published in a recent ISO standard (ISO 389-7, 1996). The dashed curve shows the Minimum Audible Pressure (MAP) for monaural listening.

The Inner Ear and the Basilar Membrane

The cochlea is filled with almost incompressible fluids, and it also has bony rigid walls. It is divided along its length by two membranes, Reissner's membrane and the basilar membrane (BM; see Figure 12.2, panel b). The start of the cochlea, where the oval window is situated, is known as the base; while the other end, the inner tip, is known as the apex. It is also common to talk about the basal end and the apical end. At the apex there is a small opening (the helicotrema) between the BM and the walls of the cochlea, which connects the two outer chambers of the cochlea, the scala vestibuli and the scala tympani. Inward movement of the oval window results in a corresponding outward movement in a membrane covering a second opening in the cochlea – the round window.

When the oval window is set in motion by an incoming sound, a pressure difference is applied across the BM, which causes the BM to move. The response of the BM to sinusoidal stimulation takes the form of a traveling wave which moves along the BM from the base towards the apex. The amplitude of the wave increases at first and then decreases rather abruptly. The basic form of the wave is illustrated in Figure 12.2, panel (c), which shows schematically the instantaneous displacement of the BM for four successive instants in time, in response to a low-frequency sinusoid. The four successive peaks in the wave are labelled 1, 2, 3, and 4. This figure also shows the line joining the amplitude peaks, which is called the envelope. The distance between peaks or zero-crossings in the wave decreases as the wave travels along, and the envelope shows a peak at a particular position on the BM.

The response of the BM to sounds of different frequencies is strongly affected by its mechanical properties, which vary considerably from base to apex. At the base it is relatively narrow and stiff, while at the apex it is wider and much less stiff. As a result, the position of the peak in the pattern of vibration differs according to the frequency of stimulation. High-frequency sounds produce a maximum displacement of the BM near the oval window, with little movement on the remainder of the membrane. Low-frequency sounds produce a pattern of vibration which extends all the way along the BM, but which reaches a maximum before the end of the membrane. This is illustrated in Figure 12.2, panel (d). The frequency that gives maximum response at a particular point on the BM is known as the Characteristic Frequency (CF) for that place. In response to steady sinusoidal stimulation each point on the BM vibrates in an approximately sinusoidal manner with a frequency equal to that of the input waveform, even though the amplitude of the response varies along the length of the BM.

Most of the pioneering work on patterns of vibration along the BM was done by von Békésy. His technique involved the use of a light microscope and stroboscopic illumination to measure the vibration amplitude at many points along the BM in human cadaver ears. However, there are a number of difficulties associated with the technique used by von Békésy. Firstly, the vibration amplitudes had to be at least of the order of one wavelength of visible light, which required very high sound levels – about 140 dB SPL. The vibration of the BM is now believed to be nonlinear, so that it is not valid to extrapolate from these high levels to more normal sound levels. Secondly, the frequency-analyzing mechanism is now known to be physiologically vulnerable, so that cadaver ears give markedly atypical responses.

Recent measurements of BM vibration, using different techniques in living animals, have shown that the BM is much more sharply tuned than found by von Békésy. The sharpness of tuning of the BM depends critically on the physiological condition of the animal; the better the condition, the sharper is the tuning (Khanna & Leonard, 1982; Leonard & Khanna, 1984; Robles, Ruggero, & Rich, 1986; Ruggero, 1992; Sellick, Patuzzi, & Johnstone, 1982). An example is given in Figure 12.4, panel (a), which shows the input sound level (in dB SPL) required to produce a constant velocity of motion at a particular point on the BM, as a function of stimulus frequency (data from Sellick et al. (1982)). This is sometimes called a "constant velocity tuning curve." At the start of the experiment, a very sharp tuning curve was obtained (open circles). After death (solid squares), the tuning became broader, and the sound level required to produce the criterion response increased markedly around the tip.

It seems likely that the sharp tuning and high sensitivity found in a healthy ear reflect an active process; that is, they do not result simply from the mechanical properties of the BM and surrounding fluid, but depend on biological structures actively influencing the mechanics (for a review, see Yates (1995)). The most likely structures to play this role are the outer hair cells, which will be described later.

(a)

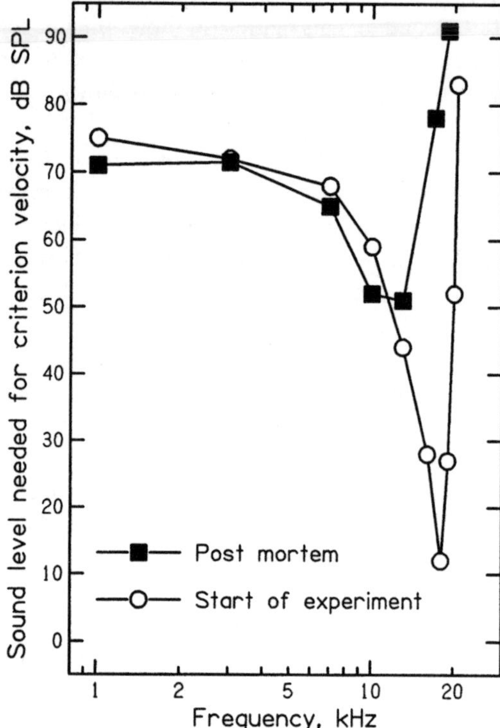
Sound level needed for criterion velocity, dB SPL
Post mortem
Start of experiment
Frequency, kHz
0
10
20
30
40
50
60
70
80
90
1
2
5
10
20

(b)

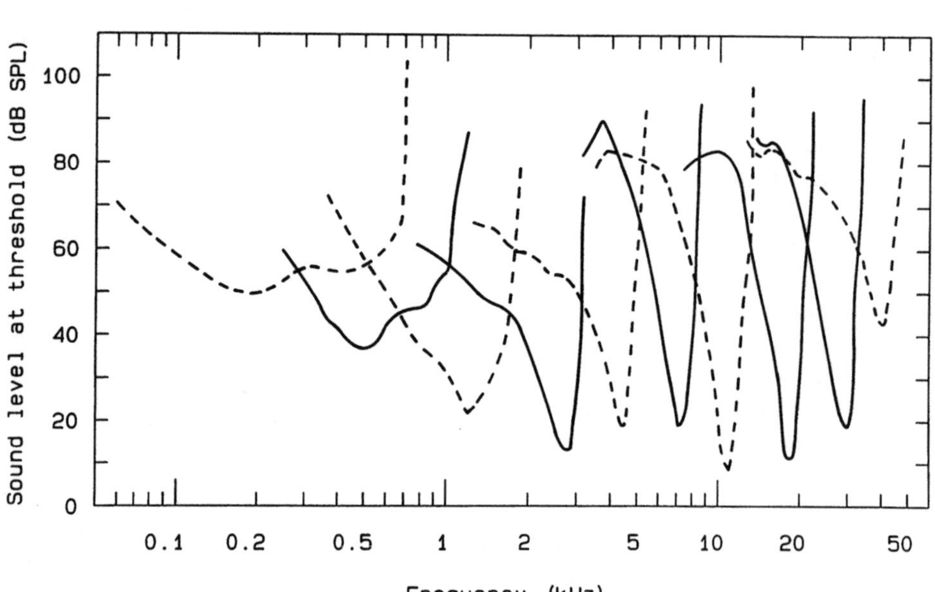
Sound level at threshold (dB SPL)
Frequency (kHz)
0
20
40
60
80
100
0.1
0.2
0.5
1
2
5
10
20
50

(c)

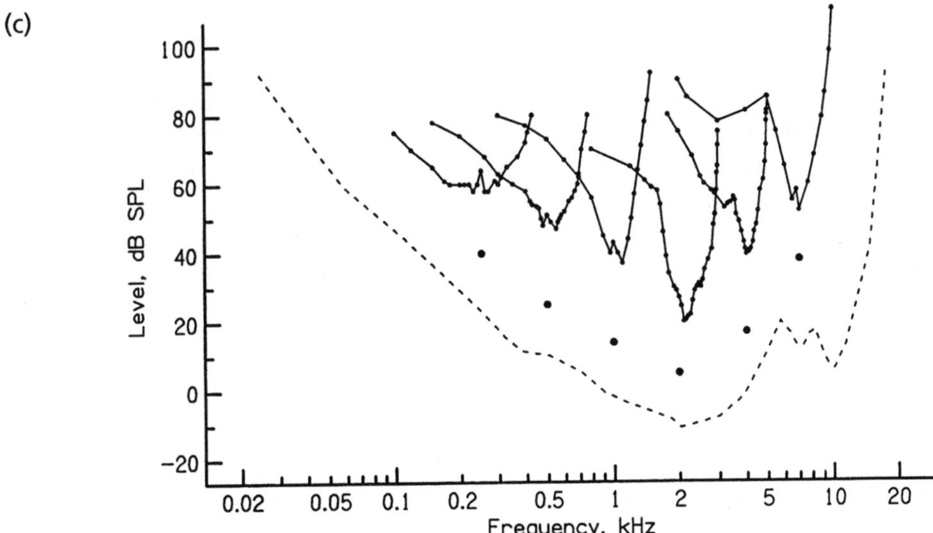

Figure 12.4. Panel (a) shows tuning curves measured at a single point on the BM. Each curve shows the input sound level required to produce a constant velocity on the BM, plotted as a function of stimulus frequency. The curve marked by open circles was obtained at the start of the experiment when the animal was in good physiological condition. Data from Sellick et al. (1982). Panel (b) shows a sample of tuning curves (also called frequency-threshold curves) obtained from single neurons in the auditory nerve of anesthetized cats. Each curve shows results for one neuron. The sound level required for threshold is plotted as a function of the stimulus frequency (logarithmic scale). Redrawn from Palmer (1987). Panel (c) shows psychophysical tuning curves (PTCs) determined using sinusoidal signals at 10 dB SL. For each curve, the solid circle below it indicates the frequency and level of the signal. The masker was a sinusoid which had a fixed starting phase relationship to the 50-ms signal. The masker level required for threshold is plotted as a function of masker frequency on a logarithmic scale. The dashed line shows the absolute threshold for the signal. Data from Vogten (1974).

Recent work has also shown that the BM vibration is nonlinear; the magnitude of the response does not grow directly in proportion with the magnitude of the input (Rhode, 1971; Rhode & Robles, 1974; Robles et al., 1986; Ruggero, 1992; Sellick et al., 1982). For a tone with frequency close to the CF of the place being studied, the response shows a *compressive* nonlinearity for mid-range sound levels (20–90 dB); a large range of input sound levels is compressed into a smaller range of responses on the BM. This helps to achieve the large range of sound levels over which the auditory system can operate, and it also influences many other aspects of perception; for a review, see Moore and Oxenham (1998). The response becomes more linear for very low sound levels and very high sound levels. This can be explained in the following way. At low and medium sound levels an active physiological mechanism amplifies the response on the BM. The amplification may be 50 dB or more. For very low input sound levels, below 20–30 dB, the amplification is roughly constant. As the sound level increases, the amplification progressively reduces. Thus the response grows more slowly than it would in a linear system. When the sound level is sufficiently high, around 90 dB SPL, the active mechanism is unable to contribute any amplification, and the response becomes linear. The nonlinearity mainly occurs when the stimulating frequency is close to the CF of the point on the BM that is being monitored. For stimuli with frequencies well away from the CF, the responses are more linear.

The response of the BM to complex sounds depends on the frequency separation of the components in the sounds. Consider first the case of two sinusoids, of different frequencies, presented simultaneously. If the frequency separation of the sinusoids is very large, then they produce two, effectively separate, patterns of vibration. Each produces a maximum at the place on the BM which would have been excited most had that tone been presented alone. The BM behaves like a Fourier analyzer, breaking down the complex sound into its sinusoidal components. When the two tones are close together in frequency, however, the Fourier analysis of the BM does not have sufficient resolution to separate them. The patterns of vibration on the BM interact, so that some points on the BM respond to both of the tones. At those points the displacement of the BM as a function of time is not sinusoidal, but is a complex waveform resulting from the interference of the two tones. When the two tones are sufficiently close in frequency, there is no longer a separate maximum in the pattern of vibration for each of the component tones; instead there is a single, broader, maximum. Thus, the BM has failed to resolve the individual frequency components. It is roughly true that two separate maxima occur when the peaks in the vibration patterns are separated by about 1.1 mm, out of a total length of the BM of about 35 mm. For medium to high frequencies, this corresponds to a frequency ratio between the two tones of about 1.16.

The Transduction Process and the Hair Cells

Between the BM and the tectorial membrane are hair cells, which form part of a structure called the organ of Corti (see Figure 12.2, panel b). The hair cells are divided into two groups by an arch known as the tunnel of Corti. Those on the side of the arch closest to the outside of the cochlea are known as outer hair cells, and they are arranged in three rows in the cat and up to five rows in humans. The hair cells on the other side of the arch form a single row, and are known as inner hair cells. There are about 25,000 outer hair cells, each with about 140 "hairs" (more correctly called stereocilia) protruding from it, while there are about 3,500 inner hair cells, each with about 40 hairs. The tectorial membrane, which has a gelatinous structure, lies above the hairs. It appears that the hairs of the outer hair cells actually make contact with the tectorial membrane, but this may not be true for the inner hair cells. The tectorial membrane appears to be effectively hinged at one side (the left in Figure 12.2(b)), so that when the BM moves up and down, a shearing motion is created between the BM and the tectorial membrane. As a result, fluid streams across the hairs at the tops of the hair cells and displaces them in a lateral direction. It is thought that this leads to excitation of the inner hair cells, which leads in turn to the generation of action potentials in the neurons of the auditory nerve.

The main role of the outer hair cells may be actively to influence the mechanics of the cochlea, so as to produce high sensitivity and sharp tuning. There is even evidence that the outer hair cells have a motor function, changing their length and shape in response to electrical stimulation (Ashmore, 1987). Drugs or other agents which selectively affect the operation of the outer hair cells result in a loss of sharp tuning and a reduction of sensitivity of the BM (Ruggero & Rich, 1991). Furthermore, it is likely that this action of the outer hair cells is partly under the control of higher centers of the auditory system. There are about 1,800 efferent nerve fibers which carry information from the auditory system to the cochlea, most of them originating in the superior olivary complex of the brain stem. Many of these efferent fibers make contact with the outer hair cells, and thus can affect their activity. It appears that even the earliest stages in the analysis of auditory signals are partly under the control of higher centers.

Neural Responses in the Auditory Nerve

Most neurons (nerve fibers) in the auditory nerve show background or spontaneous firing in the absence of sound stimulation. Liberman (1978) presented evidence that auditory nerve fibers could be classified into three groups on the basis of their spontaneous rates. About 61% of fibers have high spontaneous rates (18 to 250 spikes per second); 23% have medium rates (0.5 to 18 spikes per second); and 16% have low spontaneous rates (less than 0.5 spike per second). The spontaneous rates are correlated with the position and size of the synapses on the inner hair cells. High spontaneous rates are associated with large synapses, primarily located on the side of the inner hair cells facing the outer hair cells. Low spontaneous rates are associated with smaller synapses on the opposite side of the hair cells.

The threshold of a neuron is the lowest sound level at which a change in response of the neuron can be measured. Low thresholds tend to be associated with high spontaneous rates and vice versa. The most sensitive neurons may have thresholds close to 0 dB SPL, whereas the least sensitive neurons may have thresholds of 80 dB SPL or more.

The frequency selectivity of a single nerve fiber is often illustrated by a tuning curve, which shows the fiber's threshold as a function of frequency. This curve is also known as the frequency-threshold curve (FTC). The stimuli are usually tone bursts. The frequency at which the threshold of the fiber is lowest is called the characteristic frequency (CF). Some typical tuning curves are presented in Figure 12.4, panel (b). On the logarithmic frequency scale used, the tuning curves are generally steeper on the high-frequency side than on the low-frequency one. It is generally assumed that the frequency selectivity in single auditory nerve fibers occurs because those fibers are responding to vibration at one point on the BM. Experiments tracing single neurons whose tuning curves had been determined directly confirm this supposition (Liberman, 1982). Furthermore, CFs are distributed in an orderly manner in the auditory nerve. Fibers with high CFs are found in the periphery of the nerve bundle, and there is an orderly decrease in CF towards the center of the nerve bundle (Kiang, Watanabe, Thomas, & Clark, 1965). This kind of organization is known as tonotopic organization and it indicates that the place representation of frequency along the BM is preserved as a place representation in the auditory nerve. It appears that the sharpness of tuning of the BM is essentially the same as the sharpness of tuning of single neurons in the auditory nerve (Khanna & Leonard, 1982; Robles et al., 1986; Ruggero, Rich, Recio, Narayan, & Robles, 1997; Sellick et al., 1982); compare panels (a) and (b) of Figure 12.4.

The response of a single neuron usually increases progressively with increasing sound level, once the threshold of the neuron is exceeded. However, above a certain sound level the neuron no longer responds to increases in sound level with an increase in firing rate; the neuron is said to be saturated. The range of sound levels between threshold and the level at which saturation occurs is called the dynamic range. This range is correlated with the threshold and spontaneous rate of the neuron; high spontaneous rates and low thresholds are associated with small dynamic ranges. For most neurons the dynamic range is between 20 and 50 dB, but a few neurons do not show complete saturation; instead the firing rate continues to increase gradually with increasing sound level even at high sound levels. This has been called "sloping saturation" (Sachs & Abbas, 1974) and it occurs particularly for neurons with low spontaneous rates.

The tone-driven activity of a single fiber in response to one tone can be suppressed by the presence of a second tone. This was originally called two-tone inhibition (Sachs & Kiang, 1968), although the term "two-tone suppression" is now generally preferred, since the effect does not appear to involve neural inhibition. Typically the phenomenon is investigated by presenting a tone at, or close to, the CF of a neuron. A second tone is then presented, its frequency and intensity are varied, and the effects of this on the response of the neuron are noted. When the frequency and intensity of the second tone fall within the excitatory area bounded by the tuning curve, it usually produces an increase in firing rate. However, when it falls just outside that area, the response to the first tone is reduced or suppressed. The effect is usually greatest in two suppression regions at frequencies slightly above or below the area of the unit's excitatory response to a single tone. The suppression effects begin and cease very rapidly, within a few milliseconds of the onset and termination of the second tone (Arthur, Pfeiffer, & Suga, 1971). Thus it is unlikely that the suppression is established through any elaborate neural interconnections. In fact, there is good evidence that suppression occurs on the BM (Geisler & Nuttall, 1997; Rhode & Cooper, 1993; Rhode & Robles, 1974; Ruggero, Robles, & Rich, 1992). The *effects* of suppression may be similar to those of lateral inhibition in vision, even though the underlying mechanisms are different.

Information about sounds is also carried in the temporal patterning of the neural firings. In response to a pure tone the nerve firings tend to be phase locked or synchronized to the stimulating waveform. A given nerve fiber does not necessarily fire on every cycle of the stimulus but, when firings do occur, they occur at roughly the same phase of the waveform each time. Thus the time intervals between firings are (approximately) integral multiples of the period of the stimulating waveform. For example, a 500-Hz sinusoid has a period of 2 milliseconds (2 ms), so that the intervals between nerve firings might be 2 ms, or 4 ms, or 6 ms, or 8 ms, etc. In general, a neuron does not fire in a completely regular manner, so that there are not exactly 500, or 250, or 125 spikes/s. However, information about the period of the stimulating waveform is carried unambiguously in the temporal pattern of firing of a single neuron. Phase locking does not occur over the whole range of audible frequencies. The upper frequency limit lies at about 4-5 kHz, although it varies somewhat across species (Palmer & Russell, 1986; Rose, Brugge, Anderson, & Hind, 1968).

Neural Responses at Higher Levels in the Auditory System

The anatomy of the auditory system is exceedingly complex, and many of the neural pathways within and between the various nuclei in the auditory system have yet to be investigated in detail. Some of the more important neural centres or nuclei in the auditory pathway are illustrated in Figure 12.5. For a recent review see Palmer (1995). This section will briefly describe some properties of cortical neurons.

It is likely that the cortex is concerned with analyzing more complex aspects of stimuli than simple frequency or intensity. Many cortical neurons will not respond to steady pure tones at all, and the tuning properties of those that do respond to pure tones tend to differ from those found in primary auditory neurons. Some neurons show non-monotonic rate versus level functions, different neurons having different "best" sound levels (Pfingst & O'Conner, 1981). Abeles and Goldstein (1972) found three different types of tuning properties: narrow, broad, and multirange (responding to a number of preferred frequencies). They considered that this suggested a hierarchical organization, with several narrow range units converging on to one multirange unit. There has been some dispute about whether the tonotopic organization which is found at lower levels in the auditory system persists at the cortex. The general consensus is that the cortex is tonotopically organized, and there may be multiple "maps" (Palmer, 1995).

Evans (1968), using mostly unanesthetized cats, reported that 20% of cortical neurons respond only to complex stimuli such as clicks, bursts of noise, or "kissing" sounds. Of those neurons that would respond to tonal stimuli 10% would only do so if the tone frequency was changing. Whitfield and Evans (1965) reported that frequency-modulated tones were very effective stimuli for the majority of neurons responding to tones. Many neurons exhibited responses which were preferential to a specific direction of frequency change. These neurons have been called "frequency sweep detectors." Some neurons responded preferentially to particular rates of modulation or to particular rates of frequency sweep. Phillips, Mendelson, Cynader, and Douglas (1985) also reported cortical neurons with a preferred frequency-sweep direction, but the preferred sweep direction was always towards CF. For other neurons studied by Whitfield and Evans (1965), repetition rate and duration of tonal stimuli were critical parameters. Of all units studied, 17% responded only to the onset of a tonal stimulus, while 10% responded only to the termination and 2% responded to both onset and termination. Over 50% of neurons were preferentially or specifically sensitive to particular locations of the sound source. This general finding has been confirmed and extended by Brugge and Merzenich (1973) for restrained, unanesthetized monkeys.

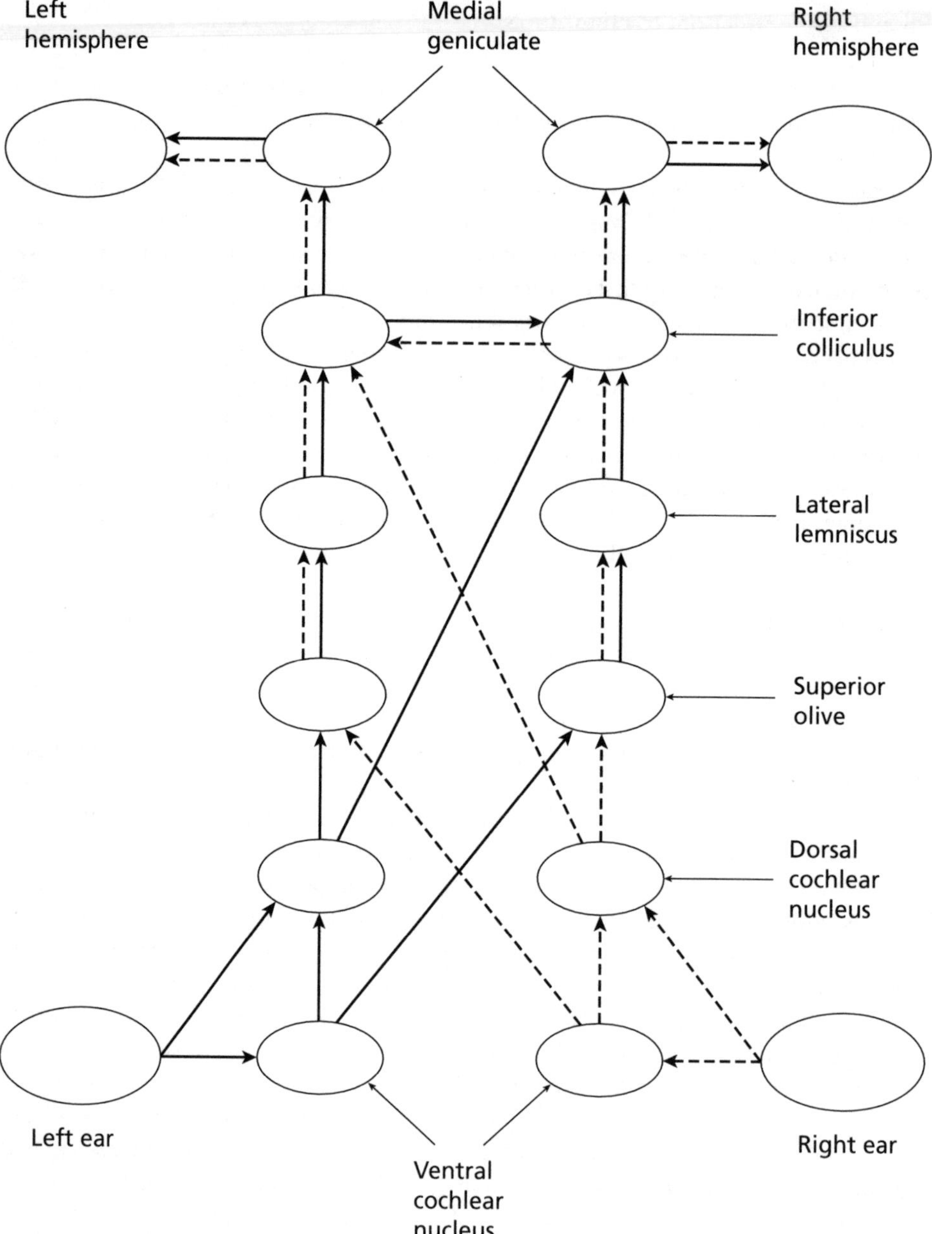

Figure 12.5. A schematic illustration of some of the more important neural centres or nuclei in the auditory pathway, showing ascending pathways. Descending pathways are not shown.

Frequency Selectivity and Masking

Frequency selectivity refers to the ability to resolve or separate the sinusoidal components in a complex sound. It is often demonstrated and measured by studying masking, which has been defined as "The process by which the threshold of audibility for one sound is raised by the presence of another (masking) sound" (American Standards Association, 1960). It has been known for many years that a signal is most easily masked by a sound having frequency components close to, or the same as, those of the signal (Wegel & Lane, 1924). This led to the idea that our ability to separate the components of a complex sound depends, at least in part, on the frequency-resolving power of the basilar membrane (BM). This idea will be elaborated later in this chapter.

The Concept of the Auditory Filter

Fletcher (1940), following Helmholtz (1863), suggested that the peripheral auditory system behaves as if it contains a bank of bandpass filters, with overlapping passbands. These filters are now called the "auditory filters." They are sometimes also called "critical bands." Fletcher thought that the BM provided the basis for the auditory filters. Each location on the BM responds to a limited range of frequencies, so each different point corresponds to a filter with a different center frequency. When trying to detect a signal in a noise background, the listener is assumed to make use of a filter with a center frequency close to that of the signal. This filter passes the signal but removes a great deal of the noise. Only the components in the noise which pass through the filter have any effect in masking the signal. It is usually assumed that the threshold for the signal is determined by the amount of noise passing through the auditory filter; specifically, threshold is assumed to correspond to a certain signal-to-noise ratio at the output of the filter. This set of assumptions has come to be known as the "power spectrum model" of masking (Patterson & Moore, 1986), because the stimuli are represented by their long-term power spectra; that is, the short-term fluctuations in the masker are ignored.

The question considered next is "What is the shape of the auditory filter?" In other words, how does its relative response change as a function of the input frequency? Most methods for estimating the shape of the auditory filter at a given center frequency are based on the assumptions of the power spectrum model of masking. The threshold of a signal whose frequency is fixed is measured in the presence of a masker whose spectral content is varied. It is assumed, as a first approximation, that the signal is detected using the single auditory filter which is centered on the frequency of the signal, and that threshold corresponds to a constant signal-to-masker ratio at the output of that filter. The methods described below both measure the shape of the filter using this technique.

Psychophysical Tuning Curves

One method of measuring the shape of the filter involves a procedure which is analogous in many ways to the determination of a neural tuning curve, and the resulting function is often called a psychophysical tuning curve (PTC). To determine a PTC, the signal is fixed in level, usually at a very low level, say, 10 dB SL. The masker can be either a sinusoid or a band of noise covering a small frequency range.

For each of several masker frequencies, the level of the masker needed just to mask the signal is determined. Because the signal is at a low level it is assumed that it produces activity primarily in one auditory filter. It is assumed further that at threshold the masker produces a constant output from that filter, in order to mask the fixed signal. Thus the PTC indicates the masker level required to produce a fixed output from the auditory filter as a function of frequency. Normally a filter characteristic is determined by plotting the output from the filter for an input varying in frequency and fixed in level. However, if the filter is linear the two methods give the same result. Thus, assuming linearity, the shape of the auditory filter can be obtained simply by inverting the PTC. Examples of some PTCs are given in Figure 12.4, panel (c).

PTCs are very similar in general form to neural tuning curves (see Figure 12.4, panel (b)). Remember that the neural tuning curves are obtained by determining the level of a tone required to produce a fixed output from a single neuron, as a function of the tone's frequency. The similarities in the procedures and the results encourage the belief that the basic frequency selectivity of the auditory system is established at the level of the auditory nerve, and that the shape of the human auditory filter (or PTC) corresponds to the shape of the neural tuning curve.

One problem in interpreting PTCs is that they inevitably involve activity over a group of neurons with slightly different CFs. Returning to the filter analogy, we have assumed in our analysis that, for a given signal frequency, only one auditory filter is involved. However, the listener may use the information from just one filter. When the masker frequency is above the signal frequency the listener might do better to use the information from a filter centered just below the signal frequency. If the filter has a relatively flat top, and sloping edges, this will considerably attenuate the masker at the filter output, while only slightly attenuating the signal. By using this off-center filter the listener can improve performance. This is known as "off-frequency listening," and there is now good evidence that humans do indeed listen "off-frequency" when it is advantageous to do so (Johnson-Davies & Patterson, 1979). The result of off-frequency listening is that the PTC has a sharper tip than would be obtained if only one auditory filter were involved (Johnson-Davies & Patterson, 1979; O'Loughlin & Moore, 1981).

The Notched-Noise Method

Patterson (1976) described a method of determining auditory filter shape which prevents off-frequency listening. The method is illustrated in Figure 12.6, panel (a). The signal (indicated by the bold vertical line) is fixed in frequency, and the masker is a noise with a

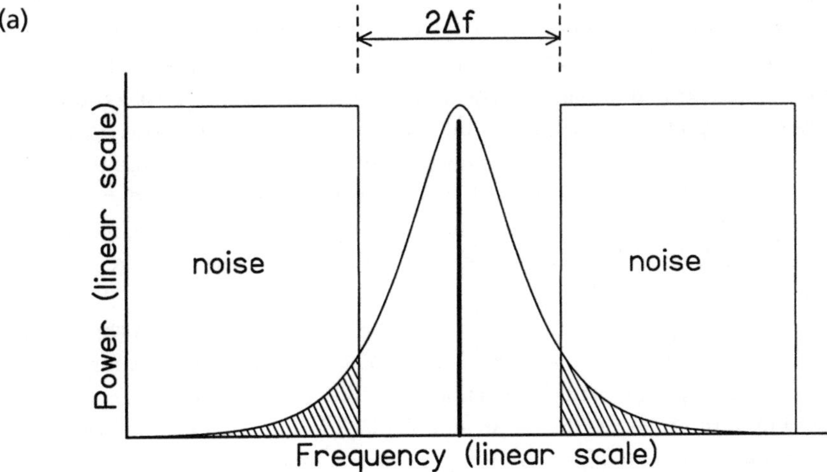

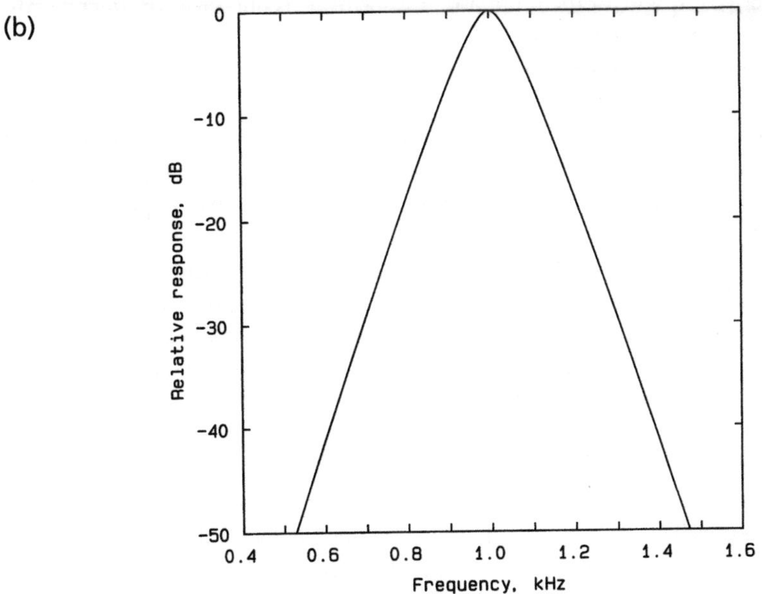

Figure 12.6. Panel (a) shows a schematic illustration of the technique used by Patterson (1976) to determine the shape of the auditory filter. The threshold of the sinusoidal signal is measured as a function of the width of a spectral notch in the noise masker. The amount of noise passing through the auditory filter centered at the signal frequency is proportional to the shaded areas. Panel (b) shows a typical auditory filter shape determined using Patterson's method. The filter is centered at 1 kHz. The relative response of the filter (in dB) is plotted as a function of frequency.

bandstop or notch centered at the signal frequency. The deviation of each edge of the noise from the center frequency is denoted by Δf. The width of the notch is varied, and the threshold of the signal is determined as a function of notch width. Because the notch is symmetrically placed around the signal frequency, the method cannot reveal asymmetries in the auditory filter, and the analysis assumes that the filter is symmetric on a linear frequency scale. This assumption appears not unreasonable, at least for the top part of the filter and at moderate sound levels, because PTCs are quite symmetric around the tips. For a signal symmetrically placed in a bandstop noise, the optimum signal-to-masker ratio at the output of the auditory filter is achieved with a filter centered at the signal frequency, as illustrated in Figure 12.6(a).

As the width of the spectral notch is increased, less and less noise passes through the auditory filter. Thus the threshold of the signal drops. The amount of noise passing through the auditory filter is proportional to the area under the filter in the frequency range covered by the noise. This is shown as the shaded areas in Figure 12.6(a). If we assume that threshold corresponds to a constant signal-to-masker ratio at the output of the filter, then the change in signal threshold with notch width tells us how the area under the filter varies with Δf. The area under a function between certain limits is obtained by integrating the value of the function over those limits. Hence by differentiating the function relating threshold to Δf, the relative response of the filter at that value of Δf is obtained. In other words, the relative response of the filter for a given deviation, Δf, from the center frequency is equal to the slope of the function relating signal threshold to notch width, at that value of Δf.

A typical auditory filter derived using this method is shown in Figure 12.6, panel (b). It has a rounded top and quite steep skirts. The sharpness of the filter is often specified as the bandwidth of the filter at which the response has fallen by a factor of two in power, that is, by 3 dB. The 3-dB bandwidths of the auditory filters derived using Patterson's method are typically between 10% and 15% of the center frequency. An alternative measure is the equivalent rectangular bandwidth (ERB), which is a little larger than the 3-dB bandwidth. The ERBs of the auditory filters derived using Patterson's method are typically between 11% and 17% of the center frequency. An equation describing the value of the ERB as a function of center frequency, F (in kHz), is (Glasberg & Moore, 1990):

$$\text{ERB} = 24.7(4.37F + 1)$$

Each ERB corresponds roughly to a fixed distance along the BM of about 0.89 mm. For example, for a center frequency of 1000 Hz, the ERB is about 132 Hz, so the ERB covers a frequency range from 935 Hz to 1066 Hz. The places on the BM with these CFs are separated by about 0.89 mm. The bandwidth of the auditory filter is sometimes referred to as the "critical bandwidth," although that term is also used to describe the bandwidth of a stimulus at which the perception of that stimulus starts to change in some way when the bandwidth is increased from a very small value (Moore, 1997a).

Patterson's method has been extended to include conditions where the spectral notch in the noise is placed asymmetrically about the signal frequency. This allows the measurement of any asymmetry in the auditory filter, but the analysis of the results is more difficult, and has to take off-frequency listening into account (Patterson & Nimmo-Smith,

1980). It is beyond the scope of this chapter to give details of the method of analysis; the interested reader is referred to Patterson and Moore (1985), Moore and Glasberg (1987) and Glasberg and Moore (1990). The results show that the auditory filter is reasonably symmetric at moderate sound levels, but becomes increasingly asymmetric at high levels, the low-frequency side becoming shallower than the high-frequency side. The filter shapes derived using the notched-noise method are quite similar to inverted PTCs (Glasberg, Moore, Patterson, & Nimmo-Smith, 1984).

Masking Patterns and Excitation Patterns

So far we have discussed masking experiments in which the frequency of the signal is held constant, while the masker is varied. These experiments are most appropriate for estimating the shape of the auditory filter at a given center frequency. However, many of the early experiments on masking did the opposite; the masker was held constant in both level and frequency and the signal threshold was measured as a function of the signal frequency.

The masking patterns obtained in these experiments show steep slopes on the low-frequency side, of between 55 and 240 dB/octave (an octave corresponds to a frequency ratio of 2:1). The slopes on the high-frequency side are less steep and depend on the level of the masker. A typical set of results is shown in Figure 12.7, panel (a). Notice that on the high-frequency side the curve is shallower at the highest level. For signal frequencies in the range from about 1300 to 2000 Hz, when the level of the masker is increased by 20 dB (from 65 to 85 dB SPL), the masked threshold increases by more than 20 dB; the amount of masking grows nonlinearly on the high-frequency side. This has been called the "upward spread of masking."

The masking patterns do not reflect the use of a single auditory filter. Rather, for each signal frequency the listener uses a filter centered close to the signal frequency. Thus the auditory filter is shifted as the signal frequency is altered. One way of interpreting the masking pattern is as a crude indicator of the excitation pattern of the masker. The excitation pattern is a representation of the effective amount of excitation produced by a stimulus as a function of CF, and is plotted as effective level (in dB) against CF. In the case of a masking sound, the excitation pattern can be thought of as representing the relative amount of vibration produced by the masker at different places along the BM. The signal is detected when the excitation it produces is some constant proportion of the excitation produced by the masker at places with CFs close to the signal frequency. Thus the threshold of the signal as a function of frequency is proportional to the masker excitation level. The masking pattern should be parallel to the excitation pattern of the masker, but shifted vertically by a small amount. In practice, the situation is not so straightforward, because the shape of the masking pattern is influenced by factors such as off-frequency listening.

Moore and Glasberg (1983) have described a way of deriving the shapes of excitation patterns using the concept of the auditory filter. They suggested that the excitation pattern of a given sound can be thought of as the output of the auditory filters plotted as a function of their center frequency. To calculate the excitation pattern of a given sound, it is necessary to calculate the output of each auditory filter in response to that sound, and to plot the output as a function of the filter center frequency. Panel (b) of Figure 12.7 shows

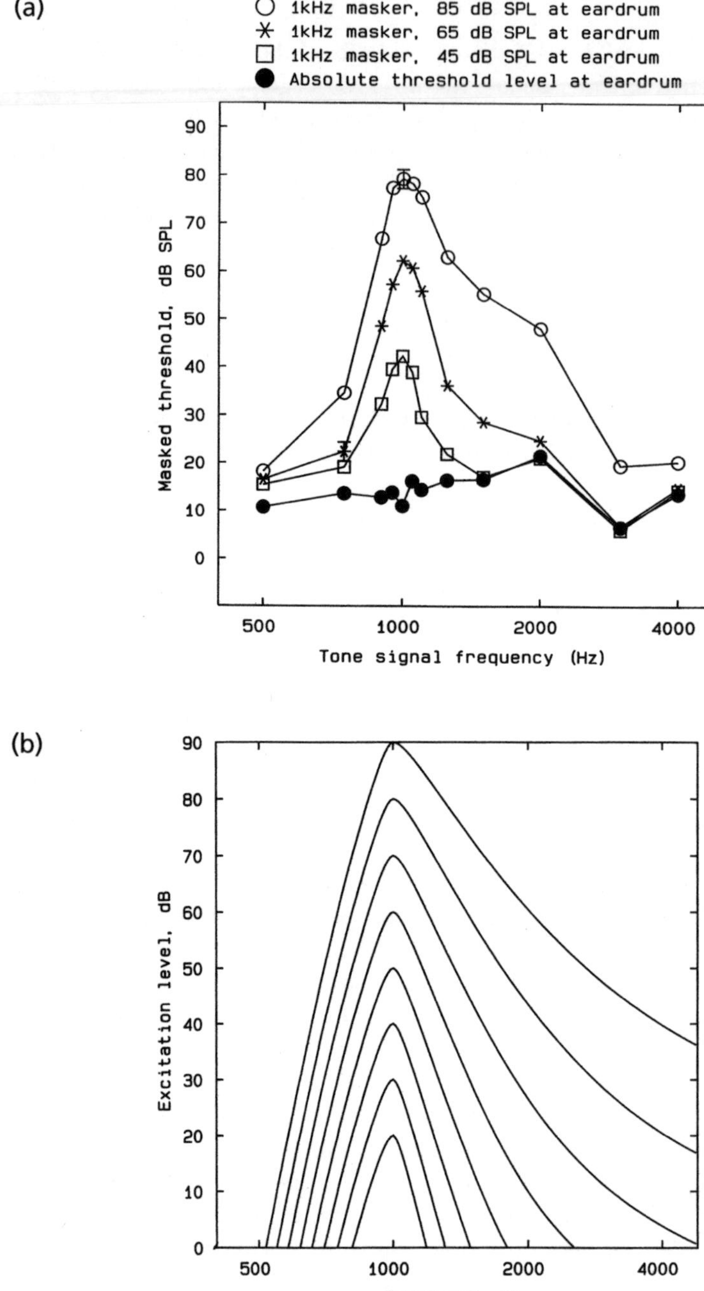

Figure 12.7. Panel (a) shows masking patterns for a narrow band of noise centered at 1000 Hz. Each curve shows masked threshold of a pure tone signal as a function of signal frequency. The overall noise level for each curve is indicated in the figure. Absolute thresholds for the signal (MAP values) are indicated by filled circles. Data from Moore et al. (1998). Panel (b) shows excitation patterns for 1-kHz sinusoids at various levels, calculated according to the method described by Moore and Glasberg (1983).

excitation patterns calculated in this way for sinusoids with various levels. The patterns are similar in form to the masking patterns shown in panel (a).

Hearing Out Partials in Complex Tones

When we listen to complex tones, such as those produced by musical instruments, we usually hear a single pitch (see Chapter 13), rather than hearing several pitches corresponding to the frequencies of individual partials. However, we can hear such pitches if our attention is directed appropriately. In other words, we can "hear out" the individual partials. Plomp (1964) and Plomp and Mimpen (1968) used complex tones with 12 sinusoidal components to investigate the limits of this ability. The listener was presented with two comparison tones, one of which was of the same frequency as a partial in the complex; the other lay halfway between that frequency and the frequency of the adjacent higher or lower partial. The listener had to judge which of these two tones was a component of the complex. Plomp used two types of complex: a harmonic complex containing harmonics 1 to 12, where the frequencies of the components were integer multiples of that of the fundamental; and a non-harmonic complex, where the frequencies of the components were mistuned from simple frequency ratios. He found that for both kinds of complex, partials could only be heard out if they were sufficiently far in frequency from neighboring partials. The data, and other more recent data (Moore & Ohgushi, 1993), are consistent with the hypothesis that a partial can be heard out (with 75% accuracy) when it is separated from neighboring partials by 1.25 times the ERB of the auditory filter (Moore, 1997a). For harmonic complex tones, only the first (lowest) five to eight harmonics can be heard out, as higher harmonics are separated by less than 1.25 ERBs.

It seems likely that the analysis of partials from a complex sound depends in part on factors other than the frequency analysis that takes place on the BM. Soderquist (1970) compared musicians and non-musicians in a task very similar to that of Plomp, and found that the musicians were markedly superior. This result could mean that musicians have smaller ERBs than non-musicians. However, Fine and Moore (1993) showed that ERBs, as estimated in a masking experiment, did not differ for musicians and non-musicians. It seems that some mechanism other than peripheral filtering is involved in hearing out partials from complex tones and that musicians, because of their greater experience, are able to make more efficient use of this mechanism.

The ability to hear out partials in complex tones is thought to play a role in the perception of the pitch of those tones. This is discussed in Chapter 13, which also describes the perception of loudness and of timbre.

Suggested Readings

Yates, G. K. (1995). Cochlear structure and function. In B. C. J. Moore (Ed.), *Hearing* (pp. 41–73). San Diego: Academic Press. [This provides a detailed overview of the physiology of the cochlea.]

Palmer, A. R. (1995). Neural signal processing. In B. C. J. Moore (Ed.), *Hearing* (pp. 75–121). San Diego: Academic Press. [This provides an overview of the coding of sounds at different levels in the auditory system.]

Moore, B. C. J. (1997). *An introduction to the psychology of hearing* (4th ed.). San Diego: Academic Press. [This provides a more comprehensive coverage of the psychoacoustic material presented in this chapter.]

Plomp, R. (1976). *Aspects of tone sensation.* London: Academic Press. [This book reviews many aspects of auditory perception that are affected by the frequency selectivity of the auditory system.]

Additional Topics

Perceptual Consequences of Compression on the Basilar Membrane

The compression on the basilar membrane, as revealed by the input-output function of the membrane, has effects on many different aspects of perception. For a review of some of these, see Moore and Oxenham (1998).

Effects of Cochlear Hearing Loss

Cochlear hearing loss is usually associated with damage to the hair cells within the cochlea. This produces many changes in the way that sounds are perceived. In particular it produces reduced frequency selectivity, which affects the ability to hear one sound in the presence of other sounds, and also influences the perception of pitch and timbre. For reviews of the perceptual consequences of cochlear hearing loss, see Moore (1995, 1998).

Simulations of the effects of cochlear hearing loss on absolute thresholds and on frequency selectivity are available on the CD "Audio demonstrations to accompany perceptual consequences of cochlear damage"; see Moore (1997b). The CD can be obtained by writing to Prof. B. C. J. Moore, Department of Experimental Psychology, University of Cambridge, Downing Street, Cambridge CB2 3EB, England. The cost of the disc is 12 pounds sterling or 20 US dollars. Payment (a check payable to B. C. J. Moore) should be enclosed with the order.

Across-channel Effects in Masking

Sometimes, the ability to detect a signal in the presence of a masking sound is enhanced by comparison of the outputs of different auditory filters. For example, listeners may detect a change in the shape of the spectrum of the sound produced by the addition of the signal to the masker. This is called *profile analysis*, and it occurs especially when the overall level of the masker-plus-signal varies randomly from one stimulus to the next. For a review, see Green (1988).

When a masking sound is amplitude modulated, the ability to detect a signal is often better when the modulation pattern is the same in all frequency bands than when the pattern of modulation differs across bands. This is called *co-modulation masking release (CMR)*. Again, the effect appears to depend on listeners comparing the outputs of different auditory filters. See Hall, Haggard, and Fernandes (1984).

In contrast, the ability to detect amplitude modulation of a target sound (for example a 1000-Hz sinusoid) can be impaired by the presence of an amplitude-modulated sound with a very different center frequency (for example a 4000-Hz sinusoid). This is called *modulation detection interference (MDI)*, and it indicates that the outputs of auditory filters remote in center frequency from the target can adversely affect discrimination of the target. See Yost, Sheft, and Opie (1989).

For general reviews of these across-channel effects in masking, see Hall, Grose, and Mendoza (1995) and Moore (1992).

References

Abeles, M., & Goldstein, M. H. (1972). Responses of single units in the primary auditory cortex of the cat to tones and to tone pairs. *Brain Research, 42*, 337–352.

American Standards Association (1960). *Acoustical terminology SI, 1–1960.* New York: American Standards Association.

Arthur, R. M., Pfeiffer, R. R., & Suga, N. (1971). Properties of "two-tone inhibition" in primary auditory neurones. *Journal of Physiology, 212*, 593–609.

Ashmore, J. F. (1987). A fast motile response in guinea pig outer hair cells: The cellular basis of the cochlear amplifier. *Journal of Physiology, 388*, 323–347.

Brugge, J. F., & Merzenich, M. M. (1973). Responses of neurones in auditory cortex of macaque monkey to monaural and binaural stimulation. *Journal of Neurophysiology, 36*, 1138–1158.

Evans, E. F. (1968). Cortical representation. In A. V. S. de Reuck & J. Knight (Eds.), *Hearing mechanisms in vertebrates.* London: Churchill.

Fine, P. A., & Moore, B. C. J. (1993). Frequency analysis and musical ability. *Music Perception, 11*, 39–53.

Fletcher, H. (1940). Auditory patterns. *Reviews of Modern Physics, 12*, 47–65.

Geisler, C. D., & Nuttall, A. L. (1997). Two-tone suppression of basilar-membrane vibrations in the base of the guinea pig cochlea using "low-side" suppressors. *Journal of the Acoustical Society of America, 102*, 430–440.

Glasberg, B. R., & Moore, B. C. J. (1990). Derivation of auditory filter shapes from notched-noise data. *Hearing Research, 47*, 103–138.

Glasberg, B. R., Moore, B. C. J., Patterson, R. D., & Nimmo-Smith, I. (1984). Dynamic range and asymmetry of the auditory filter. *Journal of the Acoustical Society of America, 76*, 419–427.

Green, D. M. (1988). *Profile analysis.* Oxford: Oxford University Press.

Hall, J. W., Grose, J. H., & Mendoza, L. (1995). Across-channel processes in masking. In B. C. J. Moore (Ed.), *Hearing* (pp. 243–266). San Diego: Academic Press.

Hall, J. W., Haggard, M. P., & Fernandes, M. A. (1984). Detection in noise by spectro-temporal pattern analysis. *Journal of the Acoustical Society of America, 76*, 50–56.

Helmholtz, H. L. F. (1863). *Die Lehre von den Tonempfindungen als physiologische Grundlage für die Theorie der Musik* (1st ed.). Braunschweig: F.Vieweg.

ISO 389–7 (1996). *Acoustics – Reference zero for the calibration of audiometric equipment. Part 7: Reference threshold of hearing under free-field listening conditions.* Geneva: International Organization for Standardization.

Johnson-Davies, D., & Patterson, R. D. (1979). Psychophysical tuning curves: Restricting the listening band to the signal region. *Journal of the Acoustical Society of America, 65*, 675–770.

Khanna, S. M., & Leonard, D. G. B. (1982). Basilar membrane tuning in the cat cochlea. *Science, 215*, 305–306.

Kiang, N. Y.-S., Watanabe, T., Thomas, E. C., & Clark, L. F. (1965). *Discharge patterns of single fibers in the cat's auditory nerve.* Cambridge, MA.: MIT Press.

Leonard, D. G. B., & Khanna, S. M. (1984). Histological evaluation of damage in cat cochleas used for measurement of basilar membrane mechanics. *Journal of the Acoustical Society of America, 75*, 515–527.

Liberman, M. C. (1978). Auditory-nerve response from cats raised in a low-noise chamber. *Journal of the Acoustical Society of America, 63*, 442–455.

Liberman, M. C. (1982). The cochlear frequency map for the cat: Labeling auditory-nerve fibers of known characteristic frequency. *Journal of the Acoustical Society of America, 72*, 1441–1449.

Moore, B. C. J. (1992). Across-channel processes in auditory masking. *Journal of the Acoustical Society of Japan (E), 13*, 25–37.

Moore, B. C. J. (1995). *Perceptual consequences of cochlear damage.* Oxford: Oxford University Press.

Moore, B. C. J. (1997a). *An introduction to the psychology of hearing* (4th ed.). San Diego: Academic Press.

Moore, B. C. J. (1997b). A compact disc containing simulations of hearing impairment. *British Journal of Audiology, 31*, 353–357.
Moore, B. C. J. (1998). *Cochlear hearing loss.* London: Whurr.
Moore, B. C. J., Alcántara, J. I., & Dau, T. (1998). Masking patterns for sinusoidal and narrowband noise maskers. *Journal of the Acoustical Society of America, 104*, 1023–1038.
Moore, B. C. J., & Glasberg, B. R. (1983). Suggested formulae for calculating auditory-filter bandwidths and excitation patterns. *Journal of the Acoustical Society of America, 74*, 750–753.
Moore, B. C. J., & Glasberg, B. R. (1987). Formulae describing frequency selectivity as a function of frequency and level and their use in calculating excitation patterns. *Hearing Research, 28*, 209–225.
Moore, B. C. J., Glasberg, B. R., & Baer, T. (1997). A model for the prediction of thresholds, loudness and partial loudness. *Journal of the Audio Engineering Society, 45*, 224–240.
Moore, B. C. J., & Ohgushi, K. (1993). Audibility of partials in inharmonic complex tones. *Journal of the Acoustical Society of America, 93*, 452–461.
Moore, B. C. J., & Oxenham, A. J. (1998). Psychoacoustic consequences of compression in the peripheral auditory system. *Psychological Review, 105*, 108–124.
O'Loughlin, B. J., & Moore, B. C. J. (1981). Improving psychoacoustical tuning curves. *Hearing Research, 5*, 343–346.
Palmer, A. R. (1987). Physiology of the cochlear nerve and cochlear nucleus. In M. P. Haggard and E. F. Evans (Eds.), *Hearing* (pp. 838-855). Edinburgh: Churchill Livingstone.
Palmer, A. R. (1995). Neural signal processing. In B. C. J. Moore (ed.), *Hearing* (pp. 75–121). San Diego: Academic Press.
Palmer, A. R., & Russell, I. J. (1986). Phase-locking in the cochlear nerve of the guinea-pig and its relation to the receptor potential of inner hair-cells. *Hearing Research, 24*, 1–15.
Patterson, R. D. (1976). Auditory filter shapes derived with noise stimuli. *Journal of the Acoustical Society of America, 59*, 640–654.
Patterson, R. D., & Moore, B. C. J. (1986). Auditory filters and excitation patterns as representations of frequency resolution. In B. C. J. Moore (Ed.), *Frequency selectivity in hearing* (pp. 123–177). London: Academic Press.
Patterson, R. D., & Nimmo-Smith, I. (1980). Off-frequency listening and auditory filter asymmetry. *Journal of the Acoustical Society of America, 67*, 229–245.
Pfingst, B. E.. & O'Conner, T. A. (1981). Characteristics of neurons in auditory cortex of monkeys performing a simple auditory task. *Journal of Neurophysiology, 45*, 16–34.
Phillips, D. P., Mendelson, J. R., Cynader, M. S., & Douglas, R. M. (1985). Responses of single neurones in the cat auditory cortex to time-varying stimuli: Frequency modulated tones of narrow excursion. *Experimental Brain Research, 58*, 443–454.
Plomp, R. (1964). The ear as a frequency analyzer. *Journal of the Acoustical Society of America, 36*, 1628-1636.
Plomp, R., & Mimpen, A. M. (1968). The ear as a frequency analyzer II. *Journal of the Acoustical Society of America, 43*, 764–767.
Rhode, W. S. (1971). Observations of the vibration of the basilar membrane in squirrel monkeys using the Mössbauer technique. *Journal of the Acoustical Society of America, 49*, 1218–1231.
Rhode, W. S., & Cooper, N. P. (1993). Two-tone suppression and distortion production on the basilar membrane in the hook region of the cat and guinea pig cochleae. *Hearing Research, 66*, 31–45.
Rhode, W. S., & Robles, L. (1974). Evidence from Mössbauer experiments for non-linear vibration in the cochlea. *Journal of the Acoustical Society of America, 55*, 588–596.
Robles, L., Ruggero, M. A., & Rich, N. C. (1986). Basilar membrane mechanics at the base of the chinchilla cochlea. I. Input-output functions, tuning curves, and response phases. *Journal of the Acoustical Society of America, 80*, 1364–1374.
Rose, J. E., Brugge, J. F., Anderson, D. J., & Hind, J. E. (1968). Patterns of activity in single auditory nerve fibres of the squirrel monkey. In A. V. S. de Reuck & J. Knight (Eds.), *Hearing mechanisms in vertebrates* (pp. 144–157). London: Churchill.

Ruggero, M. A. (1992). Responses to sound of the basilar membrane of the mammalian cochlea. *Current Opinion in Neurobiology, 2,* 449–456.

Ruggero, M. A., & Rich, N. C. (1991). Furosemide alters organ of Corti mechanics: Evidence for feedback of outer hair cells upon the basilar membrane. *Journal of Neuroscience, 11,* 1057–1067.

Ruggero, M. A., Rich, N. C., Recio, A., Narayan, S. S., & Robles, L. (1997). Basilar-membrane responses to tones at the base of the chinchilla cochlea. *Journal of the Acoustical Society of America, 101,* 2151–2163.

Ruggero, M. A., Robles, L., & Rich, N. C. (1992). Two-tone suppression in the basilar membrane of the cochlea: Mechanical basis of auditory-nerve rate suppression. *Journal of Neurophysiology, 68,* 1087–1099.

Sachs, M. B., & Abbas, P. J. (1974). Rate versus level functions for auditory-nerve fibers in cats: Tone-burst stimuli. *Journal of the Acoustical Society of America, 56,* 1835–1847.

Sachs, M. B., & Kiang, N. Y. S. (1968). Two-tone inhibition in auditory nerve fibers. *Journal of the Acoustical Society of America, 43,* 1120–1128.

Sellick, P. M., Patuzzi, R., & Johnstone, B. M. (1982). Measurement of basilar membrane motion in the guinea pig using the Mössbauer technique. *Journal of the Acoustical Society of America, 72,* 131–141.

Soderquist, D. R. (1970). Frequency analysis and the critical band. *Psychonomic Science, 21,* 117–119.

Vogten, L. L. M. (1974). Pure-tone masking: A new result from a new method. In E. Zwicker & E. Terhardt (Eds.), *Facts and models in hearing* (pp. 142–155). Berlin: Springer-Verlag.

von Békésy, G. (1947). The variations of phase along the basilar membrane with sinusoidal vibrations. *Journal of the Acoustical Society of America, 19,* 452–460.

von Békésy, G. (1960). *Experiments in hearing* (E. G. Wever, Trans.). New York: McGraw-Hill.

Wegel, R. L., & Lane, C. E. (1924). The auditory masking of one sound by another and its probable relation to the dynamics of the inner ear. *Physical Review, 23,* 266–285.

Whitfield, I. C., & Evans, E. F. (1965). Responses of auditory cortical neurones to stimuli of changing frequency. *Journal of Neurophysiology, 28,* 655–672.

Yates, G. K. (1995). Cochlear structure and function. In B. C. J. Moore (Ed.), *Hearing* (pp. 41–73). San Diego: Academic Press

Yost, W. A., Sheft, S., & Opie, J. (1989). Modulation interference in detection and discrimination of amplitude modulation. *Journal of the Acoustical Society of America, 86,* 2138–2147.

Chapter Thirteen

Loudness, Pitch and Timbre

Brian C. J. Moore

Loudness

Introduction

The human ear is remarkable both in terms of its absolute sensitivity and the range of sound intensities to which it can respond. The most intense sound we can hear without damaging our ears has a level about 120 dB above that of the faintest sound we can detect; this range is referred to as the dynamic range of the auditory system and it corresponds to a ratio of intensities of 1,000,000,000,000:1. One aim of this chapter is to discuss the possible ways in which such a range could be coded in the auditory system.

Loudness corresponds to the subjective impression of the magnitude of a sound. The formal definition of loudness is: that attribute of auditory sensation in terms of which sounds can be ordered on a scale extending from quiet to loud. Because loudness is subjective, it is very difficult to measure in a quantitative way. Estimates of loudness can be strongly affected by bias and context effects of various kinds (Gabriel, Kollmeier, & Mellert, 1997; Laming, 1997). For example, the impression of loudness of a sound with a moderate level (say, 60 dB SPL) can be affected by presenting a high-level sound (say, 100 dB SPL) before the moderate-level sound.

Loudness Level and Equal-Loudness Contours

It is often useful to be able to compare the loudness of sounds with that of a standard, reference sound. The most common reference sound is a 1000-Hz sinusoid. The *loudness level* of a sound is defined as the level of a 1000-Hz sinusoid that is equal in loudness to the sound. The unit of loudness level is the *phon*. Thus, the loudness level of any sound in phons is the level (in dB SPL) of the 1000-Hz sinusoid to which it sounds equal in loudness. For example, if a sound appears to be as loud as a 1000-Hz sinusoid with a level of 45 dB SPL, then the sound has a loudness level of 45 phons. To determine the loudness level of a given sound, the subject is asked to adjust the level of a 1000-Hz sinusoid until it appears to have the same loudness as that sound. The 1000-Hz sinusoid and the test sound are presented alternately rather than simultaneously.

In a variation of this procedure, the 1000-Hz sinusoid is fixed in level, and the test sound is adjusted to give a loudness match, again with alternating presentation. If this is repeated for various different frequencies of a sinusoidal test sound, an *equal-loudness contour* is generated (Fletcher & Munson, 1933). For example, if the 1000-Hz sinusoid is fixed in level at 40 dB SPL, then the 40-phon equal-loudness contour is generated. The exact shapes of equal-loudness contours vary markedly across studies (Gabriel et al., 1997), and there is currently no agreement as to the "correct" values. Some examples are shown in Figure 13.1, panel (a); the curves are actually predictions based on a model of loudness (Moore, Glasberg, & Baer, 1997), but they are similar in form to empirically obtained equal-loudness contours for young normally hearing people. The figure shows equal-loudness contours for binaural listening for loudness levels from 10 phons to 110 phons, and it also includes the absolute threshold (MAF) curve (see Chapter 12). The listening conditions were assumed to be similar to those for determining the MAF curve, namely that the sound came from a frontal direction in a free field (i.e., in a situation where there is no reflected sound from walls, floor or ceiling). The equal-loudness contours are of similar shape to the MAF curve, but tend to become flatter at high loudness levels.

Note that the subjective loudness of a sound is not directly proportional to its loudness level in phons. For example, a sound with a loudness level of 80 phons sounds much more than twice as loud as a sound with a loudness level of 40 phons.

The Scaling of Loudness

Several methods have been developed that attempt to measure "directly" the relationship between the physical magnitude of sound and perceived loudness (Stevens, 1957). In one, called *magnitude estimation*, sounds with various different levels are presented, and the subject is asked to assign a number to each one according to its perceived loudness. In a second method, called *magnitude production*, the subject is asked to adjust the level of a sound until it has a loudness corresponding to a specified number.

On the basis of results from these two methods, Stevens suggested that loudness, L, was a *power function* of physical intensity, I:

$$L = kI^{0.3}$$

where k is a constant depending on the subject and the units used. In other words, the loudness of a given sound is proportional to its intensity raised to the power 0.3. Note that this implies that loudness is *not* linearly related to intensity; rather, it is a *compressive* function of intensity. An approximation to this equation is that the loudness doubles when the intensity is increased by a factor of 10, or, equivalently, when the level is increased by 10 dB. In practice, this relationship only holds for sound levels above about 40 dB SPL. For lower levels than this, the loudness changes with intensity more rapidly than predicted by the power-law equation.

The unit of loudness is the *sone*. One sone is defined arbitrarily as the loudness of a 1000-Hz sinusoid at 40 dB SPL, presented binaurally from a frontal direction in a free-field. Figure 13.1, panel (b) shows the relationship between loudness in sones and the physical level of a 1000-Hz sinusoid, presented binaurally from a frontal direction in a free-field. Figure 13.1(b), like Figure 13.1(a), is based on predictions of a loudness model (Moore et al., 1997), but it is consistent with empirical data obtained using scaling methods (Hellman & Zwislocki, 1961). Because the loudness in sones is plotted on a logarithmic scale, and the decibel scale is itself logarithmic, the curve shown in Figure 13.1(b) approximates a straight line for levels above 40 dB SPL.

Neural Coding of Loudness

The mechanisms underlying the perception of loudness are not fully understood. Some possibilities are discussed more fully in the next section, on intensity discrimination. A com-

(a)

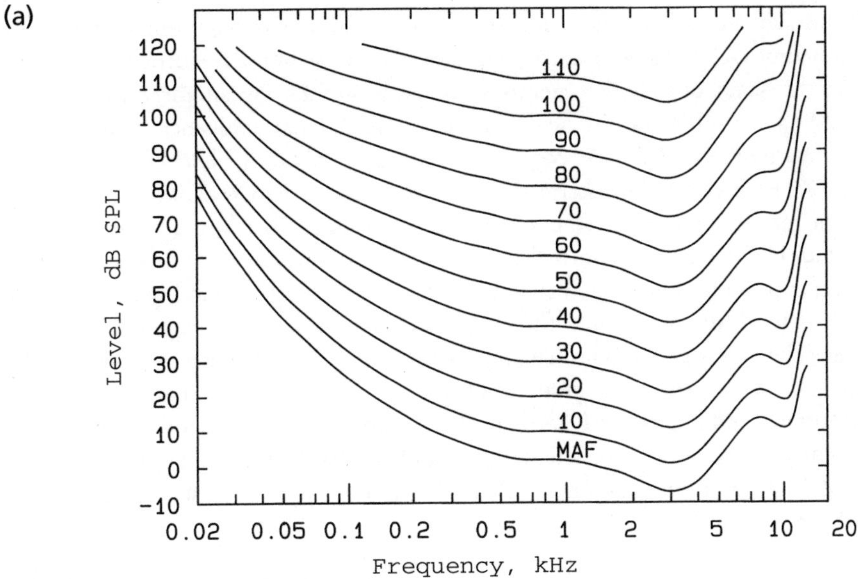

(b)

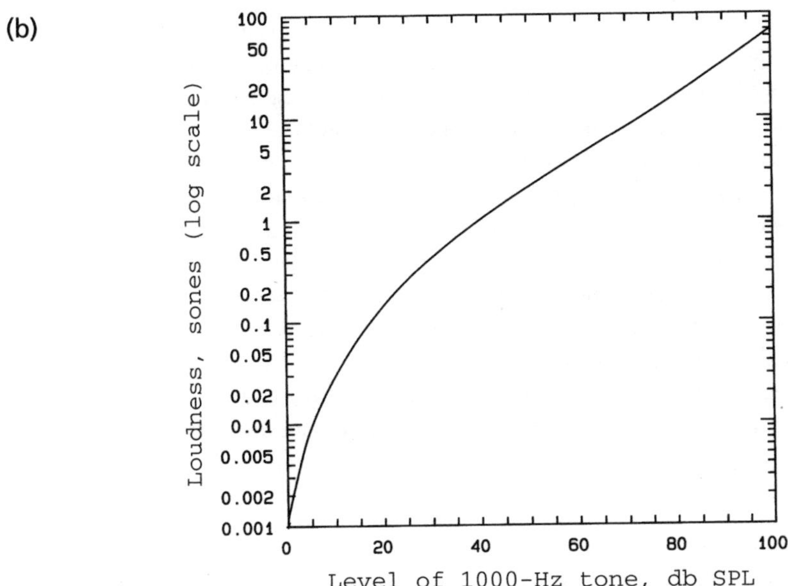

Figure 13.1. (a) Equal-loudness contours for various loudness levels. The lowest curve is the absolute threshold (MAF) curve. The curves are based on a loudness model (Moore et al., 1997a). (b) Loudness in sones (log scale), plotted as a function of the physical level of a 1000-Hz tone, presented binaurally from a frontal direction in free field. The curve is based on a loudness model (Moore et al., 1997a).

mon assumption is that loudness is somehow related to the total neural activity evoked by a sound. If this is the case, then the loudness of a sinusoidal tone is determined not only by activity in neurons with characteristic frequencies (CFs) close to the frequency of the tone, but also by the spread of activity to neurons with adjacent CFs. Put another way, loudness may depend upon a summation of neural activity across different frequency channels.

Models incorporating this basic concept have been proposed by Fletcher and Munson (1937), by Zwicker (1958; Zwicker & Scharf, 1965) and by Moore, Glasberg, and Baer (1997). The models attempt to calculate the average loudness that would be perceived by a large group of listeners with normal hearing under conditions where biases are minimized as far as possible. The models all have the basic form illustrated in Figure 13.2. The first stage is a fixed filter to account for the transmission of sound through the outer and middle ear. The next stage is the calculation of an *excitation pattern* for the sound under consideration; the concept of the excitation pattern was described in Chapter 12 (section Masking Patterns and Excitation Patterns). This pattern can be thought of as representing the distribution of excitation at different points along the basilar membrane (BM). In most of the models, the excitation pattern is calculated from psychoacoustical masking data, as described in Chapter 12.

The next stage is the transformation from excitation level (dB) to *specific loudness*, which is a kind of "loudness density." It represents the loudness that would be evoked by the excitation within a range small fixed distance along the BM if it were possible to present that excitation alone (without any excitation at adjacent regions on the BM). In the model of Moore et al. (1997), the distance is 0.89 mm, which corresponds to one ERB (see Chapter 12, section The Notched-Noise Method), so the specific loudness represents the loudness per ERB. The specific loudness cannot be measured either physically or subjectively. It is a theoretical construct used as an intermediate stage in the loudness models. The transformation from excitation level to specific loudness involves a compressive nonlinearity. Although the models are based on psychoacoustical data, this transformation can be thought of as representing the way that physical excitation is transformed into neural activity; the specific loudness is assumed to be related to the amount of neural activity at the corresponding CF. The *overall loudness* of a given sound, in sones, is assumed to be proportional to the total area under the specific loudness pattern. One might think of this area as approximately proportional to the total neural activity evoked by a sound.

Loudness models of this type have been rather successful in accounting for experimental data on the loudness of both simple sounds and complex sounds (Moore et al., 1997;

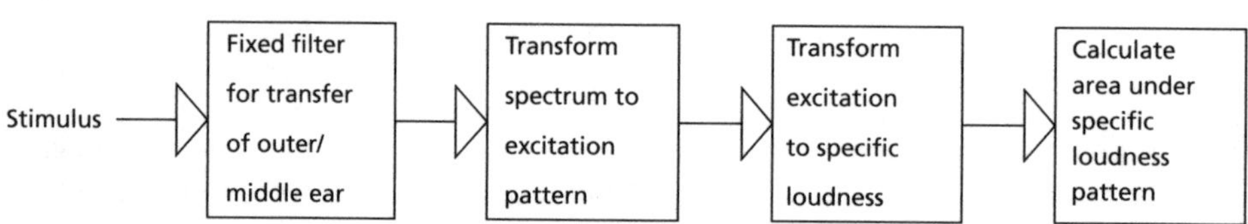

Figure 13.2. Block diagram of a typical loudness model.

Zwicker & Scharf, 1965). They have also been incorporated into "loudness meters" which can give an appropriate indication of the loudness of sounds even when they fluctuate over time (Fastl, 1993; Stone, Glasberg, & Moore, 1996; Zwicker & Fastl, 1990).

Intensity Discrimination

The smallest detectable change in intensity of a sound has been measured for many different types of stimuli by a variety of methods. The three main methods are:

1. Modulation detection. The stimulus is amplitude modulated (i.e., made to vary in amplitude) at a slow regular rate and the listener is required to detect the modulation. Usually, the modulation is sinusoidal.
2. Increment detection. A continuous background stimulus is presented, and the subject is required to detect a brief increment in the level of the background. Often the increment is presented at one of two possible times, indicated by lights, and the listener is required to indicate whether the increment occurred synchronously with the first light or the second light.
3. Intensity discrimination of gated or pulsed stimuli. Two (or more) separate pulses of sound are presented successively, one being more intense than the other(s), and the subject is required to indicate which pulse was the most intense.

In all of these tasks, the subjective impression of the listener is of a change in loudness. For example, in method 1 the modulation is heard as a fluctuation in loudness. In method 2 the increment is heard as a brief increase in loudness of the background, or sometimes as an extra sound superimposed on the background. In method 3, the most intense pulse appears louder than the other(s). Although there are some minor discrepancies in the experimental results for the different methods, the general trend is similar. For wideband noise, or for bandpass filtered noise, the smallest detectable intensity change, ΔI, is approximately a constant fraction of the intensity of the stimulus, I. In other words, $\Delta I/I$ is roughly constant. This is an example of Weber's Law, which states that the smallest detectable change in a stimulus is proportional to the magnitude of that stimulus. The value of $\Delta I/I$ is called the Weber fraction. Thresholds for detecting intensity changes are often specified as the change in level at threshold, ΔL, in decibels. The value of ΔL is given by

$$\Delta L = 10\log_{10}\{(I + \Delta I)/I\}$$

As $\Delta I/I$ is constant, ΔL is also constant, regardless of the absolute level, and for wideband noise has a value of about 0.5–1 dB. This holds from about 20 dB above threshold to 100 dB above threshold (Miller, 1947). The value of ΔL increases for sounds which are close to the absolute threshold.

For sinusoidal stimuli, the situation is somewhat different. If ΔI (in dB) is plotted against I (also in dB), a straight line is obtained with a slope of about 0.9; Weber's Law would give a slope of 1.0. Thus discrimination, as measured by the Weber fraction, improves at high levels. This has been termed the "near miss" to Weber's Law. The data of Riesz for modulation detection show a value of ΔL of 1.5 dB at 20 dB SL, 0.7 dB at 40 dB SL, and 0.3 dB at 80 dB SL (all at 1000 Hz). The Weber fraction may increase somewhat at very high sound levels (above 100 dB SPL) (Viemeister & Bacon, 1988).

In everyday life, a change in level of 1 dB would hardly be noticed, but a change in level of 3 dB (corresponding to a doubling or halving of intensity) would be fairly easily heard. This is worth bearing in mind when buying an amplifier for a stereo system. Upgrading from a 40 watt amplifier to a 50 watt amplifier would give only a barely noticeable (1 dB) change in maximum undistorted output. To produce a clearly audible change, the amplifier power would need to be increased to 80 watts (3 dB) and to produce a doubling of perceived loudness it would need to be increased to 400 watts (at which point the loudspeakers might blow up!).

We will consider now the implications of all of the above findings for the physiological coding of intensity in the auditory system. The three major phenomena which have to be explained are: (a) the auditory system is capable of detecting changes in level for a range of levels – the dynamic range – of at least 120 dB; (b) Weber's Law holds for the discrimination of bursts of noise; and (c) discrimination of the level of sinusoids improves (relative to Weber's Law) with increasing sound level up to about 100 dB SPL.

The Dynamic Range of the Auditory System

For many years the wide dynamic range of the auditory system was considered to be difficult to explain in terms of the properties of neurons in the auditory nerve. For example, following a survey of a large number of neurons, Palmer and Evans (1979) concluded that, in response to a sinusoidal stimulus, most neurons with CFs with frequencies close to the frequency of the sinusoid became saturated when its level was 60 dB SPL or higher. As most of the neurons had thresholds above 0 dB SPL, this means that most were saturated by a tone that was less than 60 dB above threshold. If intensity discrimination were based on changes in the firing rates of neurons with CFs close to the stimulus frequency, intensity discrimination would be expected to worsen at sound levels above 60 dB SPL, whereas in fact it does not.

This suggests that there is another mechanism for the coding of intensity changes at high intensities. One possibility lies in the way the excitation pattern of the stimulus spreads with increasing intensity (see Figure 12.6(b)). At high intensities, the majority of neurons at the center of the pattern would be saturated, but changes in intensity could still be signaled by changes in the firing rates of neurons at the edges of the pattern. The role of spread of excitation has been tested by measuring intensity discrimination in the presence of background noise chosen to mask the edges of the excitation pattern of the signal (Moore & Raab, 1974; Viemeister, 1972; Zwicker, 1956). Such noise typically impairs intensity discrimination at high levels, but has little effect at low levels. As a result, intensity discrimination roughly follows Weber's Law.

Although these experiments indicate that spread of excitation may play a role in intensity discrimination, they also show that reasonable performance is possible even when the edges of the excitation pattern are masked by noise. In other words, spread of excitation is not *essential* for maintaining the wide dynamic range of the auditory system. The small effect of masking the edges of the excitation pattern suggests that there is some further mechanism for intensity discrimination.

One possibility is that the timing of neural impulses provides a cue to the intensity of a tone in a noise background. When a tone is above threshold but is presented against a noise background, some neurons phase lock to the tone, while neurons with CFs far from that of the tone have a more random pattern of neural firing. When the tone is increased in intensity, more of the neurons become phase locked to it. Thus, a change in temporal regularity of the patterns of neural firing could signal the intensity change of the tone. Such a mechanism would, however, be limited to frequencies below about 4–5 kHz (see Chapter 12).

The possibility that phase locking plays a role in intensity discrimination has been tested using stimuli containing only frequencies above the range where phase locking occurs. Reasonably good performance is possible even when a background noise is used to mask the spread of excitation (Carlyon & Moore, 1984; Viemeister, 1983). This suggests that phase locking is not essential for intensity discrimination. However, Carlyon and Moore (1984) found that intensity discrimination did deteriorate at moderate sound levels when brief high-frequency tones were used as stimuli.

In recent years the "problem" of the wide dynamic range of the auditory system has been viewed in a rather different way. This new viewpoint has come from studies of the capacity of single neurons to carry information about intensity changes. This capacity depends both upon the shape of the rate versus level function, and upon the statistical properties of the neural responses, for example variability in the total number of spikes evoked by each stimulus presentation (Teich & Khanna, 1985). Such studies have indicated that information from only a small number of neurons is sufficient to account for intensity discrimination (Delgutte, 1987; Viemeister, 1988). The number required seems to be about 100. Indeed, if the information contained in the firing rates of all the 30,000 neurons in the auditory nerve were used optimally, then intensity discrimination would be much better than it actually is. Thus, rather than having to explain how intensity discrimination is possible over a wide range of sound levels, it has to be explained why intensity discrimination is not better than observed. It appears that, for most stimuli, intensity discrimination is not limited by the information carried in the auditory nerve, but by the use made of that information at more central levels of processing (Carlyon & Moore, 1984; Plack & Carlyon, 1995b).

Weber's Law

Weber's Law can be predicted by models which combine the firing rate information from a relatively small number of neurons (about 100) whose thresholds and dynamic ranges are appropriately staggered so as to cover the dynamic range of the auditory system (Delgutte, 1987; Viemeister, 1988). In models of this type it is generally assumed that the combination is done on a localized basis. In other words, information from neurons with similar CFs is combined, and there are many independent "channels" each responding to a limited range of CFs. Weber's Law is assumed to hold for each channel. Thus, information about the levels of components in complex sounds can be coded over a wide range of overall sound levels.

The Near Miss to Weber's Law

Assuming that Weber's Law reflects the "normal" mode of operation of a given frequency channel, an explanation is needed for the fact that the intensity discrimination of pure tones deviates from Weber's Law. There are probably at least two factors contributing to the improvement in intensity discrimination of pure tones with increasing level. The first was described by Zwicker (1956; 1970). He suggested that a change in intensity can be detected whenever the excitation pattern evoked by the stimulus changes somewhere by (approximately) 1 dB or more. The high-frequency side of the excitation pattern grows in a nonlinear way with increasing intensity; a 1-dB change in stimulus level gives rise to a greater than 1-dB change on the high-frequency side of the pattern (see Figure 12.7). This means that a 1-dB change in excitation on the high-frequency side will be produced by relatively smaller stimulus increments at high levels.

The second factor contributing to the near miss to Weber's Law has been described by Florentine and Buus (1981). They suggested that subjects do not make use of information only from a single channel. Rather, they combine information across the whole of the excitation pattern. As the level of a tone is increased, more channels become active, and the increase in the number of active channels allows improved performance. They presented a model based on this idea and showed that it was able to account for the near miss to Weber's Law and for the effects of masking noise on intensity discrimination.

Pitch Perception

Introduction

Pitch is an attribute of sound defined in terms of what is *heard*. It is defined formally as "that attribute of auditory sensation in terms of which sounds may be ordered on a musical scale" (American Standards Association, 1960). It is related to the physical repetition rate of the waveform of a sound; for a pure tone (a sinusoid) this corresponds to the frequency, and for a periodic complex tone to the *fundamental frequency* (see Chapter 12, section Fourier Analysis and Spectral Representations). Increasing the repetition rate gives a sensation of increasing pitch. Appropriate variations in repetition rate can give rise to a sense of melody. Variations in pitch are also associated with the intonation of voices, and they provide cues as to whether an utterance is a question or a statement and as to the emotion of the talker. Because pitch is a subjective attribute, it cannot be measured directly. Often, the pitch of a complex sound is assessed by adjusting the frequency of a sinusoid until the pitch of the sinusoid matches the pitch of the sound in question. The frequency of the sinusoid then gives a measure of the pitch of the sound. Sometimes a periodic complex sound, such as a pulse train, is used as a matching stimulus. In this case, the repetition rate of the pulse train gives a measure of pitch. Results are generally similar for the two methods, although it is easier to make a pitch match when the sounds to be matched do not differ very much in timbre (discussed later in this chapter).

Theories of Pitch Perception

For many years there have been two theories of pitch perception. One, the "place" theory, is based on the fact that different frequencies (or frequency components in a complex sound) excite different places along the basilar membrane, and hence neurons with different characteristic frequencies; the characteristic frequency of a given neuron is determined by the place along the BM of the inner hair cells which lead to excitation of that neuron. The place theory assumes that the pitch of a sound is related to the excitation pattern produced by that sound; for a pure tone the pitch is generally assumed to be determined by the position of maximum excitation.

An alternative theory, called the "temporal" theory, is based on the assumption that the pitch of a sound is related to the time pattern of the neural impulses evoked by that sound. These impulses tend to occur at a particular phase of the waveform on the basilar membrane, a phenomenon called phase locking (see Chapter 12). The intervals between successive neural impulses approximate integer multiples of the period of the waveform and these intervals are assumed to determine the perceived pitch. The temporal theory cannot be applicable at very high frequencies, since phase locking does not occur for frequencies above about 5 kHz. However, the tones produced by most musical instruments, the human voice, and most everyday sound sources have fundamental frequencies well below this range.

Many researchers believe that the perception of pitch involves both place mechanisms and temporal mechanisms. However, one mechanism may be dominant for a specific task or aspect of pitch perception, and the relative role of the two mechanisms almost certainly varies with center frequency. We next consider several aspects of the perception of the pitch of pure tones, assessing in each case the extent to which the results are consistent with one or the other mechanism.

The Perception of Pitch of Pure Tones

The Frequency Discrimination of Pure Tones

It is important to distinguish between frequency selectivity and frequency discrimination. The former refers to the ability to resolve the frequency components of a complex sound, as described in Chapter 12. If a complex tone with many harmonics is presented, a given harmonic can only be "heard out" from the complex tone if it is separated from neighboring harmonics by about 1.25 ERBs (Moore, 1997a; Moore & Ohgushi, 1993; Plomp, 1964; see Chapter 12, section Frequency Selectivity and Masking for a description of ERBs and for a description of the ability to hear out harmonics). For example, for a complex tone with a fundamental frequency of 150 Hz, the sixth harmonic (900 Hz) is separated from the neighboring harmonics (750 Hz and 1050 Hz) by about 1.25 ERBs and it would just be possible to "hear it out" as a separate tone. Frequency discrimination, on the other hand, refers to the ability to detect changes in frequency over time. Usually, the changes in frequency are heard as changes in pitch. The smallest detectable change in frequency is called the frequency difference limen (*DL*), and its value is usually much less than one ERB.

Place models of frequency discrimination (Henning, 1967; Siebert, 1970; Zwicker, 1970) predict that frequency discrimination should be related to frequency selectivity; both should depend on the sharpness of tuning on the basilar membrane. Zwicker (1970) has attempted to account for frequency discrimination in terms of changes in the excitation pattern evoked by the sound when the frequency is altered, inferring the shapes of the excitation patterns from masking patterns such as those shown in Figure 12.7(a) (see Chapter 12 for details). The model is illustrated in Figure 13.3. The figure shows two excitation patterns, corresponding to two tones with slightly different frequencies. A change in frequency results in a sideways shift of the excitation pattern. The change is assumed to be detectable whenever the excitation level at some point on the excitation pattern changes by more than a certain threshold value. Zwicker suggested that this value was about 1 dB.

The change in excitation level is greatest on the steeply sloping low-frequency side of the excitation pattern. Thus, in this model, the detection of a change in frequency is functionally equivalent to the detection of a change in level on the low-frequency side of the excitation pattern. The steepness of the low-frequency side is roughly constant when the frequency scale is expressed in units of the ERB of the auditory filter (see Chapter 12), rather than in terms of linear frequency. The slope is about 18 dB per ERB. To achieve a change in excitation level of 1 dB, the frequency has to be changed by one eighteenth of an ERB. Thus, Zwicker's model predicts that the frequency DL at any given frequency should be about one eighteenth (= 0.056) of the ERB at that frequency.

To test Zwicker's model, frequency *DL*s have been measured as a function of center frequency. There have been two common ways of measuring frequency discrimination. One measure involves the discrimination of two successive steady tones with slightly different frequencies. On each trial, the tones are presented in a random order and the listener is required to indicate whether the first or second tone is higher in frequency. The frequency difference between the two tones is adjusted until the listener achieves a criterion percentage correct, for example 75%. This measure will be called the *DLF* (difference limen for frequency). A second measure, called the *FMDL* (frequency modulation detection limen), uses tones which are frequency modulated. In such tones, the frequency moves up and down in a regular periodic manner about the mean (carrier) frequency. The number of times per second that the frequency goes up and down is called the modulation rate. Typically, the modulation rate is rather low (between 2 and 20 Hz), and the changes in frequency are heard as fluctuations in pitch – a kind of "warble." To determine a threshold for detecting frequency modulation, two tones are presented successively; one is modulated in frequency and the other has a steady frequency. The order of the tones on each trial is random. The listener is required to indicate whether the first or the second tone is modulated. The amount of modulation (also called the modulation depth) required to achieve a criterion response (e.g., 75% correct) is determined.

It turns out that the results obtained with these two methods are quite different, which suggests that different underlying mechanisms are involved. An example of results obtained with the two methods is given in Figure 13.4, panel (a) (data from Sek & Moore, 1995). For the FMDLs the modulation rate was 10 Hz. Expressed in Hz, both DLFs and

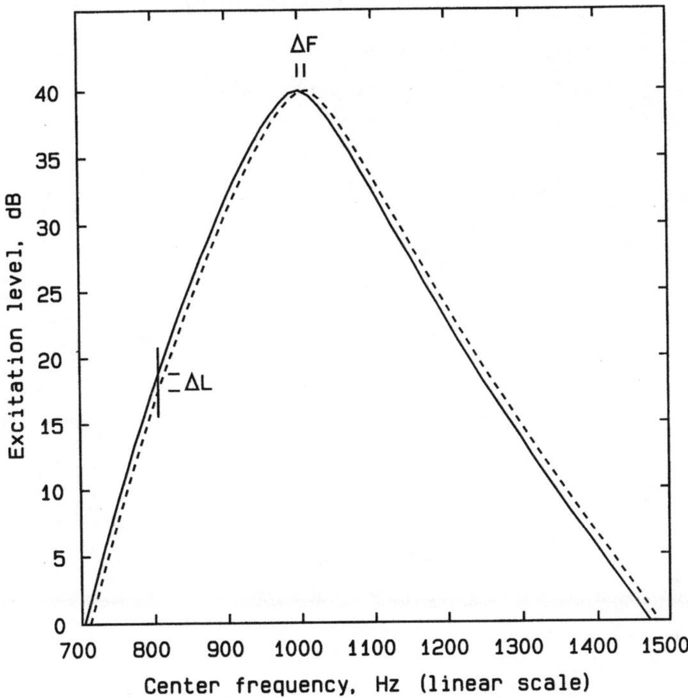

Figure 13.3. Schematic illustration of an excitation-pattern model for frequency discrimination. Excitation patterns are shown for two sinusoidal tones differing slightly in frequency; the two tones have frequencies of 1000 Hz and 1010 Hz. It is assumed that the difference in frequency, ΔF, can be detected if the excitation level changes anywhere by more than a criterion amount. The biggest change in excitation level is on the low-frequency side. The change is indicated by ΔL.

FMDLs are smallest at low frequencies, and increase monotonically with increasing frequency. Expressed as a proportion of center frequency, as in Figure 13.4, DLFs are smallest for middle frequencies, and are larger for very high and very low frequencies. FMDLs vary less with frequency than DLFs. Both DLFs and FMDLs tend to get somewhat smaller as the sound level increases; this is not shown in the figure, but see Wier, Jesteadt, and Green (1977) and Nelson, Stanton, and Freyman (1983).

To test Zwicker's model, the DLFs and FMDLs can be plotted as a proportion of the ERB at the same center frequency, as in panel (b) of Figure 13.4. According to his theory, the proportion should be independent of frequency. The proportion for FMDLs using a 10-Hz modulation rate, shown as the dashed line, is roughly constant, and its value is about 0.05, close to the value predicted by the model. However, DLFs vary more with frequency than predicted by the model (Moore, 1974; Moore & Glasberg, 1986, 1989; Sek & Moore, 1995). This is illustrated by the solid line in Figure 13.4(b), which shows the ratio DLF/ERB. The ratio varies markedly with center frequency. The DLFs for fre-

(a)

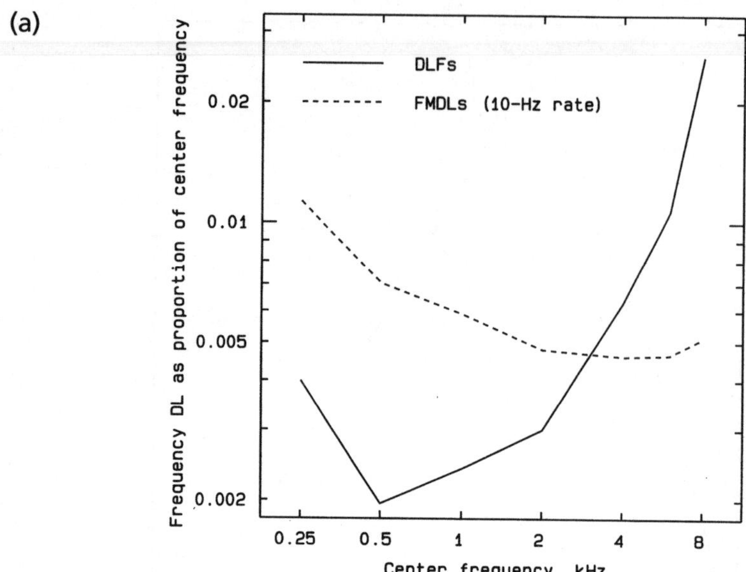

(b)

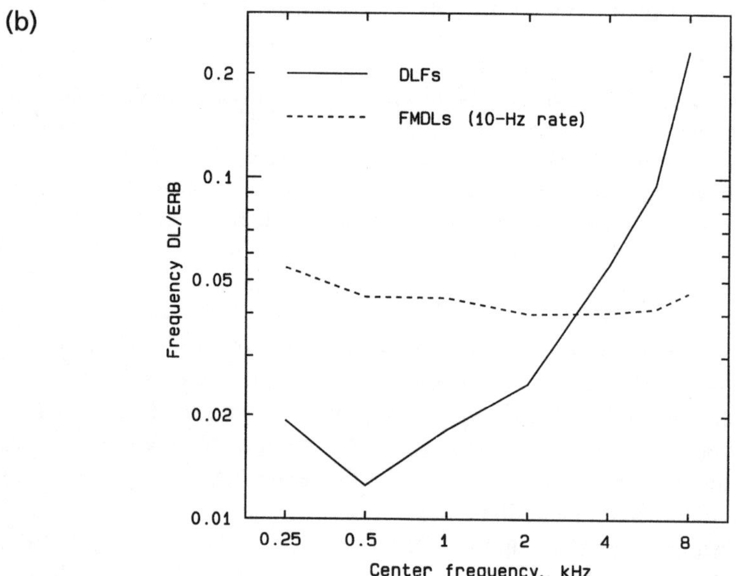

Figure 13.4. (a) Thresholds for detecting differences in frequency between steady pulsed tones (DLFs) and for detecting frequency modulation (FMDLs), plotted as a percentage of the center frequency and plotted against center frequency. The modulation rate for the FMDLs was 10 Hz. (b) The same data plotted relative to the ERB of the auditory filter at each center frequency. The data are taken from Sek and Moore (1995).

quencies of 2 kHz and below are smaller than predicted by Zwicker's model, while those for frequencies of 6 and 8 kHz are larger than predicted.

The results for the FMDLs are consistent with the place model, but the results for the DLFs are not. The reason for the deviation for DLFs is probably that DLFs at low frequencies depend on the use of temporal information from phase locking. Phase locking becomes less precise at frequencies above 1 kHz, and it is completely lost above 5 kHz. This can account for the marked increase in the DLFs at high frequencies (Goldstein & Srulovicz, 1977).

The ratio FMDL/ERB is not constant across center frequency when the modulation rate is very low (around 2 Hz), but increases with increasing frequency (Moore & Sek, 1995, 1996; Sek & Moore, 1995). For low center frequencies, FMDLs are smaller for a 2-Hz modulation rate than for a 10-Hz rate, while for high carrier frequencies (above 4 kHz) the reverse is true. For very low modulation rates, frequency modulation may be detected by virtue of the changes in phase locking to the carrier that occur over time. In other words, the frequency is determined over short intervals of time, using phase-locking information, and changes in the estimated frequency over time indicate the presence of frequency modulation. Moore and Sek (1996) suggested that the mechanism for decoding the phase-locking information was "sluggish"; it had to sample the sound for a certain time in order to estimate its frequency. Hence, it could not follow rapid changes in frequency and it played little role for high modulation rates.

In summary, measures of frequency discrimination are consistent with the idea that DLFs, and FMDLs for very low modulation rates, are determined by temporal information (phase locking) for frequencies up to about 4–5 kHz. The precision of phase locking decreases with increasing frequency above 1–2 kHz, and it is completely absent above about 5 kHz. This can explain why DLFs increase markedly at high frequencies. FMDLs for medium to high modulation rates may be determined by a place mechanism, that is, by the detection of changes in the excitation pattern. This mechanism may also account for DLFs and for FMDLs for low modulation rates, when the center frequency is above about 5 kHz.

The Perception of Musical Intervals

If temporal information plays a role in determining the pitch of pure tones, then we would expect changes in perception to occur for frequencies above 5 kHz, at which phase locking does not occur. Two aspects of perception do indeed change in the expected way, namely the perception of musical intervals, and the perception of melodies.

Two tones which are separated in frequency by an interval of one *octave* (i.e., one has twice the frequency of the other) sound similar. They are judged to have the same name on the musical scale (for example, C3 and C4). This has led several theorists to suggest that there are at least two dimensions to musical pitch. One aspect is related monotonically to frequency (for a pure tone) and is known as "tone height." The other is related to pitch class (i.e., the name of the note) and is called "tone chroma" (Bachem, 1950). For example, two sinusoids with frequencies of 220 and 440 Hz would have the same tone chroma (they would both be called A on the musical scale) but, as they are separated by an octave, they would have different tone heights.

If subjects are presented with a pure tone of a given frequency, f_1, and are asked to adjust the frequency, f_2 of a second tone so that it appears to be an octave higher in pitch, they generally adjust f_2 to be roughly twice f_1. However, when f_1 lies above 2.5 kHz, so that f_2 would lie above 5 kHz, octave matches become very erratic (Ward, 1954). It appears that the musical interval of an octave is only clearly perceived when both tones are below 5 kHz.

Other aspects of the perception of pitch also change above 5 kHz. A sequence of pure tones above 5 kHz does not produce a clear sense of melody (Attneave & Olson, 1971). It is possible to hear that the pitch changes when the frequency is changed, but the musical intervals are not heard clearly. Also, subjects with absolute pitch (the ability to assign names to notes without reference to other notes) are very poor at naming notes above 4–5 kHz (Ohgushi & Hatoh, 1991).

These results are consistent with the idea that the pitch of pure tones is determined by different mechanisms above and below 5 kHz, specifically, by a temporal mechanism at low frequencies and a place mechanism at high frequencies. It appears that the perceptual dimension of tone height persists over the whole audible frequency range, but tone chroma only occurs in the frequency range below 5 kHz. Musical intervals are only clearly perceived when the frequencies of the tones lie in the range where temporal information is available.

The Effect of Level on Pitch

The pitch of a pure tone is primarily determined by its frequency. However, sound level also plays a small role. On average, the pitch of tones below about 2 kHz decreases with increasing level, while the pitch of tones above about 4 kHz increases with increasing sound level. The early data of Stevens (1935) showed rather large effects of sound level on pitch, but more recent data generally show much smaller effects (Verschuure & van Meeteren, 1975). For tones between 1 and 2 kHz, changes in pitch with level are generally less than 1%. For tones of lower and higher frequencies, the changes can be larger (up to 5%). There are also considerable individual differences both in the size of the pitch shifts with level, and in the direction of the shifts (Terhardt, 1974a).

It has sometimes been argued that pitch shifts with level are inconsistent with the temporal theory of pitch; neural interspike intervals are hardly affected by changes in sound level over a wide range. However, changes in pitch with level could be explained by the place theory, if shifts in level were accompanied by shifts in the position of maximum excitation on the basilar membrane. On closer examination, both of these arguments turn out to be rather weak. Although the temporal theory assumes that pitch depends on the temporal pattern of nerve spikes, it also assumes that the temporal information has to be "decoded" at some level in the auditory system. In other words, the time intervals between neural spikes have to be measured. It is quite possible that the decoding mechanism is affected by the spike rate at its input and by the distribution of activity across neurons providing its input; these in turn depend on sound level.

The argument favoring the place mechanism is also weak. The peak in the pattern of excitation evoked by a tone shifts towards the base of the cochlea with increasing sound level (Ruggero, Rich, Recio, Narayan, & Robles, 1997). The base is tuned to higher frequencies, so a basalward shift should correspond to hearing an increase in pitch. An increase in sound level from 40 to 90 dB SPL can produce a basalward shift equivalent to that produced by a shift in frequency of one-half octave or more at a fixed sound level. Thus the place theory predicts that the pitch of pure tones should increase with increasing sound level, and the shift should correspond to half an octave or more if the level is changed from 40 to 90 dB SPL. In fact, for medium and low-frequency tones, the pitch tends to decrease with increasing sound level. For high-frequency tones, the shift is in the predicted direction, but the shift is always much less than half an octave. If pitch is determined by a place mechanism, then the auditory system must have some way of compensating for changes in excitation patterns with level.

At present there is no generally accepted explanation for the shifts in pitch with level. Given this, it seems that the existence of these pitch shifts cannot be used to draw any strong conclusions about theories of pitch. In any case, as already mentioned, the pitch shifts are rather small.

The Perception of the Pitch of Complex Tones

The Phenomenon of the Missing Fundamental

For complex tones the pitch does not, in general, correspond to the position of maximum excitation on the basilar membrane. Consider, as an example, a sound consisting of short impulses (clicks) occurring 200 times per second. This sound contains harmonics with frequencies at integer multiples of 200 Hz (200, 400, 600, 800 . . . Hz). The harmonic at 200 Hz is called the fundamental frequency. The sound has a low pitch, which is very close to the pitch of its fundamental component (200 Hz), and a sharp timbre (a "buzzy" tone quality). However, if the sound is filtered so as to remove the fundamental component, the pitch does not alter; the only result is a slight change in timbre. This is called the "phenomenon of the missing fundamental" (Ohm, 1843; Schouten, 1940). Indeed, all except a small group of mid-frequency harmonics can be eliminated, and the low pitch remains the same, although the timbre becomes markedly different.

Schouten (1940, 1970) called the low pitch associated with a group of high harmonics the *residue*. Several other names have been used to describe residue pitch, including *periodicity pitch*, *virtual pitch*, and *low pitch*. The term residue pitch will be used here. Schouten pointed out that it is possible to hear the change produced by removing the fundamental component and then reintroducing it. Indeed, when the fundamental component is present, it is possible to "hear it out" as a separate sound. The pitch of that component is almost the same as the pitch of the whole sound. Therefore, the presence or absence of the fundamental component does not markedly affect the pitch of the whole sound.

The perception of a residue pitch does not require activity at the point on the basilar membrane which would respond maximally to the fundamental component. Licklider (1956) showed that the low pitch of the residue could be heard when low-frequency noise was present that would mask any component at the fundamental frequency. Even when the fundamental component of a complex tone is present, the pitch of the tone is usually determined by harmonics other than the fundamental.

The phenomenon of the missing fundamental is not consistent with a simple place model of pitch based on the idea that pitch is determined by the position of the peak excitation on the basilar membrane. However, more elaborate place models have been proposed, and these are discussed below.

Theories of Pitch Perception for Complex Tones

To understand theories of pitch perception for complex tones, it is helpful to consider how complex tones are represented in the peripheral auditory system. A simulation of the response of the basilar membrane to a complex tone is illustrated in Figure 13.5. In this example, the complex tone is a regular series of brief pulses, whose spectrum contains many equal-amplitude harmonics. In the example, the number of pulses per second (also called the repetition rate) is 200, so the harmonics have frequencies that are integer multiples of 200 Hz. The lower harmonics are partly resolved on the basilar membrane, and give rise to distinct peaks in the pattern of activity along the basilar membrane. At a place tuned to the frequency of a low harmonic, the waveform on the basilar membrane is approximately a sinusoid at the harmonic frequency. For example, at the place with a characteristic frequency of 400 Hz the waveform is a 400-Hz sinusoid. At a place tuned between two low harmonics, for example the place tuned to 317 Hz, there is very little response. In contrast, the higher harmonics are not resolved, and do not give rise to distinct peaks on the basilar membrane. The waveforms at places on the basilar membrane responding to higher harmonics are complex, but they all have a repetition rate equal to the fundamental frequency of the sound.

There are two main (non-exclusive) ways in which the residue pitch of a complex sound might be extracted. Firstly, it might be derived from the frequencies of the lower harmonics that are resolved on the basilar membrane. The frequencies of the harmonics might be determined either by place mechanisms (e.g., from the positions of local maxima on the basilar membrane) or by temporal mechanisms (from the inter-spike intervals in neurons with CFs close to the frequencies of individual harmonics). For example, for the complex tone whose analysis is illustrated in Figure 13.5, the second harmonic, with a frequency of 400 Hz, would give rise to a local maximum at the place on the basilar membrane tuned to 400 Hz. The inter-spike intervals in neurons innervating that place would reflect the frequency of that harmonic; the intervals would cluster around integer multiples of 2.5 ms. Both of these forms of information may allow the auditory system to determine that there is a harmonic at 400 Hz.

The auditory system may contain a pattern recognizer which determines the residue pitch of the complex sound from the frequencies of the resolved components (Goldstein, 1973; Terhardt, 1974b). In essence the pattern recognizer tries to find the harmonic series giving the best match to the resolved frequency components; the fundamental frequency of this harmonic series determines the perceived pitch. Say, for example, that the initial analysis establishes frequencies of 800, 1000 and 1200 Hz to be present. The fundamental frequency whose harmonics would match these frequencies is 200 Hz. The perceived pitch corresponds to this inferred fundamental frequency of 200 Hz. Note that the inferred fundamental frequency is always the highest possible value that fits the frequencies determined in the initial analysis. For example, a fundamental frequency of 100 Hz would also

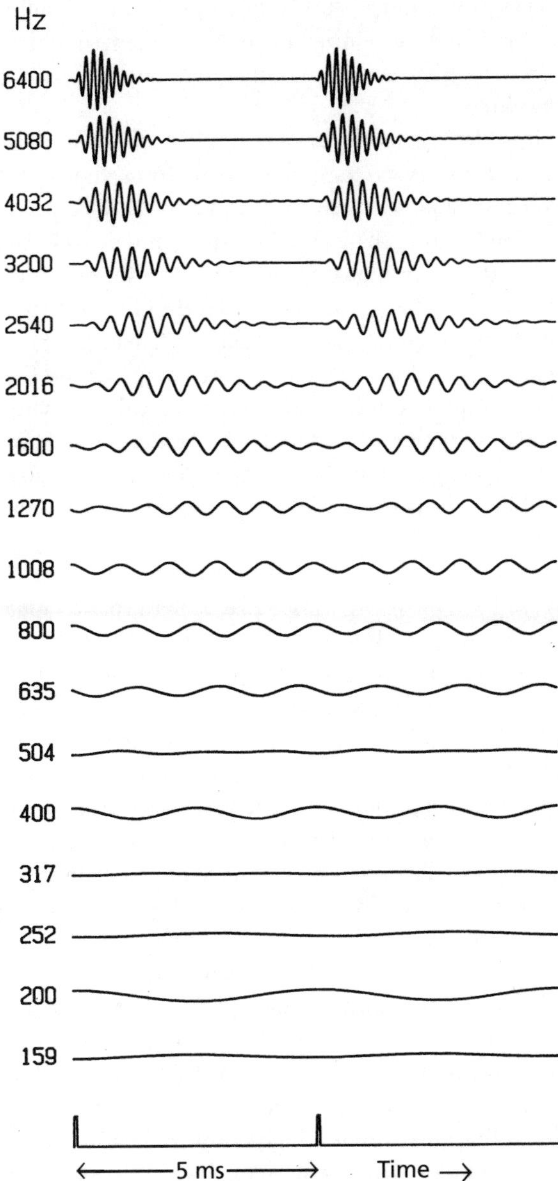

Figure 13.5. A simulation of the responses on the basilar membrane to periodic impulses of rate 200 pulses per second. The input waveform is shown at the bottom; impulses occur every 5 ms. Each number on the left represents the frequency which would maximally excite a given point on the basilar membrane. The waveform which would be observed at that point, as a function of time, is plotted opposite that number.

have harmonics at 800, 1000, and 1200 Hz, but a pitch corresponding to 100 Hz is *not* perceived. It is as if the pattern recognizer assumes that the harmonics are successive harmonics, such as the fourth, fifth, and sixth, rather than non-successive harmonics like the eighth, tenth, and twelfth.

Evidence supporting the idea that the residue pitch of a complex tone is derived by combining information from several harmonics comes from studies of the ability to detect changes in repetition rate (equivalent to the number of periods per second). When the repetition rate of a complex tone changes, all of the components change in frequency by the same *ratio*, and a change in residue pitch is heard. The ability to detect such changes is better than the ability to detect changes in a sinusoid at the fundamental frequency (Flanagan & Saslow, 1958) and it can be better than the ability to detect changes in the frequency of any of the individual sinusoidal components in the complex tone (Moore, Glasberg, & Shailer, 1984). This indicates that information from the different harmonics is combined or integrated in the determination of residue pitch. This can lead to very fine discrimination; changes in repetition rate of about 0.2% can be detected for fundamental frequencies in the range 100–400 Hz provided that low harmonics are present (e.g., the third, fourth, and fifth).

The pitch of a complex tone may also be extracted from the higher unresolved harmonics. As shown in Figure 13.5, the waveforms at places on the basilar membrane responding to higher harmonics are complex, but they all have a repetition rate equal to the fundamental frequency of the sound, namely 200 Hz. For the neurons with CFs corresponding to the higher harmonics, nerve impulses tend to be evoked by the biggest peaks in the waveform, that is, by the waveform peaks close to envelope maxima. Hence, the nerve impulses are separated by times corresponding to the period of the sound. For example, in Figure 13.5 the input has a repetition rate of 200 periods per second, so the period is 5 ms. The time intervals between nerve spikes would cluster around integer multiples of 5 ms, that is, 5, 10, 15, 20 . . . ms. The pitch may be determined from these time intervals. In this example, the time intervals are integer multiples of 5 ms, so the pitch corresponds to 200 Hz.

Experimental evidence suggests that pitch can be extracted *both* from the lower harmonics and from the higher harmonics. Usually, the lower, resolved harmonics give a clearer residue pitch, and are more important in determining residue pitch, than the upper unresolved harmonics (Moore, Glasberg, & Peters, 1985; Plomp, 1967; Ritsma, 1967). This idea is called the principle of "dominance"; when a complex tone contains many harmonics, including both low and high numbered harmonics, the pitch is mainly determined by a small group of lower harmonics. Also, the discrimination of changes in repetition rate of complex tones is better for tones containing only low harmonics than for tones containing only high harmonics (Carlyon, 1997; Carlyon & Shackleton, 1994; Hoekstra & Ritsma, 1977; Houtsma & Smurzynski, 1990; Moore et al., 1984; Plack & Carlyon, 1995a). However, a residue pitch can be heard when only high unresolvable harmonics are present (Moore, 1973; Ritsma, 1962, 1963). Although, this pitch is not as clear as when lower harmonics are present, it is clear enough to allow the recognition of musical intervals and of simple melodies (Houtsma & Smurzynski, 1990; Moore & Rosen, 1979).

Several researchers have proposed theories in which both place (spectral) and temporal mechanisms play a role; these are referred to as spectro-temporal theories. The theories assume that information from both low harmonics and high harmonics contributes to the determination of pitch. The initial place/spectral analysis in the cochlea is followed by an analysis of the time pattern of the neural spikes evoked at each characteristic frequency (Meddis & Hewitt, 1991; Meddis & O'Mard, 1997; Moore, 1982, 1989; Patterson, 1987b; Srulovicz & Goldstein, 1983). The temporal analysis is assumed to occur at a level of the auditory system higher than the auditory nerve, perhaps in the cochlear nucleus. The model proposed by Moore is illustrated in Figure 13.6. The sound is passed through an array of bandpass filters, each corresponding to a specific place on the basilar membrane. The time pattern of the neural impulses at each characteristic frequency (CF) is determined by the waveform at the corresponding point on the basilar membrane. The inter-spike intervals at each CF are determined. Then, a device compares the time intervals present at different CFs, and searches for common time intervals. The device may also integrate information over time. In general the time interval which is found most often corresponds to the period of the fundamental component. The perceived pitch corresponds to the reciprocal of this interval. For example, if the most prominent time interval is 5 ms, the perceived pitch corresponds to a frequency of 200 Hz.

As described above, complex tones with low, resolvable harmonics give rise to clear pitches. Changes in repetition rate for such tones are discriminated very well. Tones containing only high, unresolvable harmonics give less clear pitches, and changes in repetition rate are harder to detect. The differences between the two types of tones can be accounted for by spectro-temporal theories (Meddis & Hewitt, 1991; Meddis & O'Mard, 1997). They probably arise because the temporal information conveyed by the resolved harmonics is less ambiguous than the temporal information conveyed by the high harmonics (Moore, 1997a).

Consider two complex tones, one containing three low harmonics, say 800, 1000, and 1200 Hz, and the other containing three high harmonics, say 1800, 2000, and 2200 Hz. For the first tone, the components are largely resolved on the basilar membrane. The neurons with CFs close to 800 Hz respond as if the input were an 800-Hz sinusoid. The time intervals between successive nerve impulses are multiples of the period of that tone, that is, 1.25, 2.5, 3.75, 5.0 . . . ms. Similarly, in neurons with CFs close to 1000 Hz the intervals between successive nerve spikes are multiples of 1 ms, that is, 1, 2, 3, 4, 5 . . . , and in neurons with CFs close to 1200 Hz the intervals are 0.833, 1.67, 2.5, 3.33, 4.17, 5.0. . . . The only interval that is in common across CFs is 5 ms, and this unambiguously defines a pitch corresponding to 200 Hz (the missing fundamental).

Consider now the response to the second complex tone, with three high harmonics. These harmonics are not resolved. They give rise to maximum activity at a place on the basilar membrane with CF close to 2000 Hz. Neurons with CFs around 2000 Hz are driven by a complex waveform. The temporal structure of the response is correspondingly complex. Each peak in the fine structure of the waveform is capable of evoking a spike, so many different time intervals occur between successive spikes. The interval corresponding to the fundamental, 5 ms, is present, but other intervals, such as 4.0, 4.5, 5.5, and 6.0 ms, also occur (Evans, 1978; Javel, 1980). Hence, the pitch is somewhat ambiguous. Increasing the number of harmonics leads to activity across a greater range of places on the basilar membrane. The pattern of inter-spike intervals is slightly different for each place, and the only

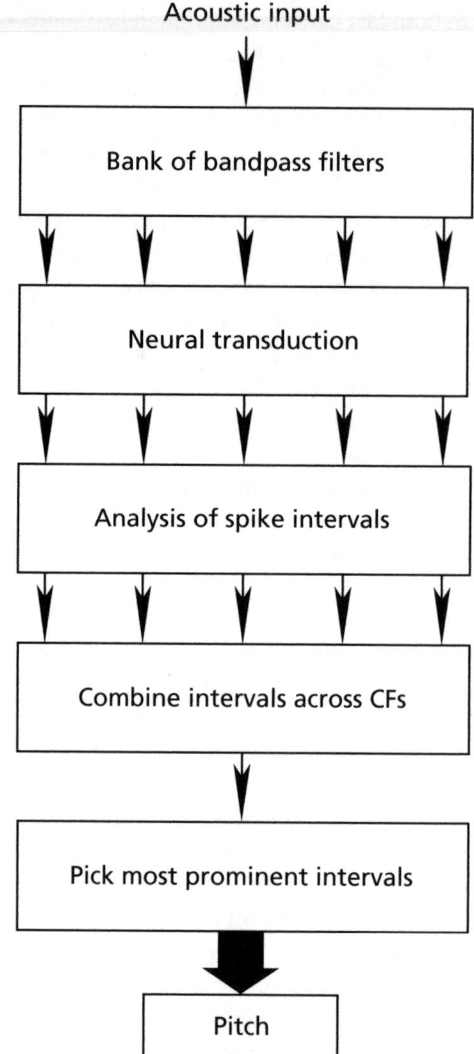

Figure 13.6. A schematic diagram of the spectro-temporal model of pitch perception for complex tones described in Moore (1997a).

interval that is in common across CFs is the one corresponding to the repetition period of the sound. Thus, the pitch becomes less ambiguous as the number of harmonics increases.

In summary, spectro-temporal theories can account for most existing data on the pitch perception of complex tones (Cariani & Delgutte, 1996a, 1996b; Meddis & O'Mard, 1997; Moore, 1997a). The theories assumes that both place analysis and temporal analysis are important, and that information about pitch can be extracted both from low harmonics and from high harmonics.

Timbre Perception

Time-Invariant Patterns and Timbre

If a single, steady sinusoid is presented, then the sound pattern can be described by just two numbers, specifying frequency and intensity. However, almost all of the sounds that we encounter in everyday life are considerably more complex than this, and contain a multitude of frequencies with particular levels and relative phases. The distribution of energy over frequency is one of the major determinants of the quality of a sound or its timbre. Timbre has been defined by the American Standards Association (ASA) (1960) as "that attribute of auditory sensation in terms of which a listener can judge that two sounds similarly presented and having the same loudness and pitch are dissimilar". Differences in timbre enable us to distinguish between the same note played on, say, the piano, the violin, or the flute.

Timbre as defined by the ASA depends upon more than just the frequency spectrum of the sound; fluctuations over time can play an important role (see the next section). For the purpose of this section we can adopt a more restricted definition suggested by Plomp (1970): "Timbre is that attribute of sensation in terms of which a listener can judge that two steady complex tones having the same loudness, pitch and duration are dissimilar." Timbre defined in this way depends mainly on the relative magnitudes of the partials of the tones.

Unlike pitch or loudness, which may be considered as unidimensional, timbre is multidimensional; there is no single scale along which the timbres of different sounds can be compared or ordered. Thus, a way is needed of describing the spectrum of a sound which takes into account this multidimensional aspect, and which can be related to the subjective timbre. A crude first approach is to look at the overall distribution of spectral energy. For example, complex tones with strong lower harmonics (below the 6th) sound mellow, whereas tones with strong harmonics beyond the 6th or 7th sound sharp and penetrating. However, a much more quantitative approach has been described by Plomp and his colleagues (Plomp, 1970, 1976; Plomp, Pols, & van de Geer, 1967; Pols, van der Kamp, & Plomp, 1969). They showed that the perceptual differences between different sounds, such as vowels, or steady tones produced by musical instruments, were closely related to the differences in the spectra of the sounds, when the spectra were specified as the levels in eighteen ⅓-octave frequency bands. A bandwidth of ⅓ octave is slightly greater than the ERB of the auditory filter over most of the audible frequency range. Thus, timbre is related to the relative level produced at the output of each auditory filter. Put another way, the timbre of a sound is related to the excitation pattern of that sound (see Chapter 12).

It is likely that the number of dimensions required to characterize timbre is limited by the number of ERBs required to cover the audible frequency range. This would give a maximum of about 37 dimensions. For a restricted class of sounds, however, a much smaller number of dimensions may be involved. It appears to be generally true, both for speech and non-speech sounds, that the timbres of steady tones are determined primarily by their magnitude spectra, although the relative phases of the components may also play a small role (Darwin & Gardner, 1986; Patterson, 1987a; Plomp & Steeneken, 1969).

Time-Varying Patterns and Auditory Object Identification

Differences in static timbre are not always sufficient to allow the absolute identification of an "auditory object," such as a musical instrument. One reason for this is that the magnitude and phase spectrum of the sound may be markedly altered by the transmission path and room reflections. In practice, the recognition of a particular timbre, and hence of an "auditory object," may depend upon several other factors. Schouten (1968) has suggested that these include: (a) whether the sound is periodic, having a tonal quality for repetition rates between about 20 and 20,000 per second, or irregular, and having a noise-like character; (b) whether the waveform envelope is constant, or fluctuates as a function of time, and in the latter case what the fluctuations are like; (c) whether any other aspect of the sound (e.g., spectrum or periodicity) is changing as a function of time; (d) what the preceding and following sounds are like.

The recognition of musical instruments, for example, depends quite strongly on onset transients and on the temporal structure of the sound envelope. The characteristic tone of a piano depends upon the fact that the notes have a rapid onset and a gradual decay. If a recording of a piano is reversed in time, the timbre is completely different. It now resembles that of a harmonium or accordion, in spite of the fact that the long-term magnitude spectrum is unchanged by time reversal. The perception of sounds with temporally-asymmetric envelopes has been studied by Patterson (1994a, 1994b). He used sinusoidal carriers that were amplitude modulated by a repeating exponential function. The envelope either increased abruptly and decayed gradually ("damped" sounds) or increased gradually and decayed abruptly ("ramped" sounds). The ramped sounds were time-reversed versions of the damped sounds and had the same long-term magnitude spectrum. The sounds were characterized by the repetition period of the envelope, which was 25 ms, and by the "half-life." For a damped sinusoid, the half-life is the time taken for the amplitude to decrease by a factor of two.

Patterson reported that the ramped and damped sounds had different qualities. For a half-life of 4 ms, the damped sound was perceived as a single source rather like a drum roll played on a hollow, resonant surface (like a drummer's wood block). The ramped sound was perceived as two sounds: a drum roll on a non-resonant surface (such as a leather table top) and a continuous tone corresponding to the carrier frequency. Ackeroyd and Patterson (1995) used sounds with similar envelopes, but the carrier was broadband noise rather than a sinusoid. They reported that the damped sound was heard as a drum struck by wire brushes. It did not have any hiss-like quality. In contrast, the ramped sound was heard as a noise, with a hiss-like quality, that was sharply cut off in time. These experiments clearly demonstrate the important role of temporal envelope in timbre perception.

Many instruments have noise-like qualities which strongly influence their subjective quality. A flute, for example, has a relatively simple harmonic structure, but synthetic tones with the same harmonic structure do not sound flute-like unless each note is preceded by a small "puff" of noise. In general, tones of standard musical instruments are poorly simulated by the summation of steady component frequencies, because such a synthesis cannot produce the dynamic variation with time characteristic of these instruments. Thus traditional electronic organs (pre-1965), which produced only tones with a fixed envelope shape, could produce a good simulation of the bagpipes, but could not be made to sound like a piano. Modern synthesizers shape the envelopes of the sounds they produce, and hence are capable of more accurate and convincing imitations of musical instruments. For a simulation to be completely convincing, it is sometimes necessary to give different time envelopes to different harmonics within a complex sound (Handel, 1995; Risset & Wessel, 1982).

Suggested Readings

For more detailed reviews of loudness perception and intensity discrimination, see:

Plack, C. J., & Carlyon, R. P. (1995). Loudness perception and intensity coding. In B. C. J. Moore (Ed.), *Handbook of perception and cognition: Vol. 6. Hearing* (pp. 123–160). Orlando, FL: Academic Press.

Scharf, B. (1978). Loudness. In E. C. Carterette & M. P. Friedman (Eds.), *Handbook of perception: Vol. IV. Hearing* (pp. 187–242). New York: Academic Press.

For more detailed reviews of pitch perception, see:

Houtsma, A. J. M. (1995). Pitch perception. In B. C. J. Moore (Ed.), *Hearing* (pp. 267–295). Orlando, FL: Academic Press.

Moore, B. C. J. (1993). Frequency analysis and pitch perception. In W. A. Yost, A. N. Popper, & R. R. Fay (Eds.), *Human psychophysics* (pp. 56–115). New York: Springer-Verlag.

For a review of timbre perception, see:

Handel, S. (1995). Timbre perception and auditory object identification. In B. C. J. Moore (Ed.), *Hearing* (pp. 425–461). San Diego: Academic Press.

Additional Topics

Perceptual Representation of the Pitch of Complex Tones

The perceptual representation of the pitch of complex tones is actually rather complex, and may depend both upon basic mechanisms of auditory analysis and upon musical experience in a particular culture. For reviews of the perceptual space associated with the pitches of complex tones see Krumhansl (1990) and Shepard (1964).

CD Demonstrating Auditory Effects

Auditory demonstrations illustrating several of the phenomena described in this chapter may be found on the compact disc (CD) "Auditory Demonstrations" produced by A. J. M. Houtsma, T. D. Rossing, and W. M. Wagenaars (1987). The disc can be obtained through the Acoustical Society of America, 500 Sunnyside Blvd., Woodbury, NY 11797–2999, USA. The cost is 20 dollars to members of the ASA and 26 dollars to non-members, payable in advance.

Loudness Recruitment

People with cochlear hearing loss often experience an abnormally rapid growth of loudness with increasing sound level. This effect, called loudness recruitment, is described in Moore (1998).

Simulations of the effects of loudness recruitment are available on the CD "Audio demonstrations to accompany perceptual consequences of cochlear damage"; see Moore (1997b).

The CD can be obtained by writing to Prof. B. C. J. Moore, Department of Experimental Psychology, University of Cambridge, Downing Street, Cambridge CB2 3EB, England. The cost of the disc is 12 pounds sterling or 20 US dollars. Payment (a check payable to B. C. J. Moore) should be enclosed with the order.

Loudness Adaptation

If a steady stimulus is presented for some time, its apparent magnitude often seems to decline, an effect called adaptation. While adaptation is very marked for some sensory modalities, for example the sense of smell, it is usually quite small for the sense of hearing. However, marked loudness adaptation can occur for high-frequency sounds. See Miskiewicz, Scharf, Hellman, and Meiselman (1993) and Scharf (1983).

Abnormal metabolic processes in the cochlea or auditory nerve sometimes result in a very rapid decrease in neural responses, although the response to the onset of a sound may be normal or near normal. The perceptual correlate of this is adaptation which is more extreme and more rapid than normal. This effect is usually greater when the abnormality occurs in the neurons than when it occurs in the cochlea, and "pathological adaptation" is often used as a sign of a problem in the auditory neural pathways, for example, a tumor growing on or close to the auditory nerve. See Jerger and Jerger (1975).

References

Ackeroyd, M. A., & Patterson, R. D. (1995). Discrimination of wideband noises modulated by a temporally asymmetric function. *Journal of the Acoustical Society of America, 98*, 2466–2474.

American Standards Association (1960). *Acoustical terminology SI, 1–1960.* New York: American Standards Association.

Attneave, F., & Olson, R. K. (1971). Pitch as a medium: A new approach to psychophysical scaling. *American Journal of Psychology, 84*, 147–166.

Bachem, A. (1950). Tone height and tone chroma as two different pitch qualities. *Acta Psychologica, 7*, 80–88.

Cariani, P. A., & Delgutte, B. (1996a). Neural correlates of the pitch of complex tones. I. Pitch and pitch salience. *Journal of Neurophysiology, 76*, 1698–1716.

Cariani, P. A., & Delgutte, B. (1996b). Neural correlates of the pitch of complex tones. II. Pitch shift, pitch ambiguity, phase invariance, pitch circularity, rate pitch and the dominance region for pitch. *Journal of Neurophysiology, 76*, 1717–1734.

Carlyon, R. P. (1997). The effects of two temporal cues on pitch judgements. *Journal of the Acoustical Society of America, 102*, 1097–1105.

Carlyon, R. P., & Moore, B. C. J. (1984). Intensity discrimination: A severe departure from Weber's Law. *Journal of the Acoustical Society of America, 76*, 1369–1376.

Carlyon, R. P., & Shackleton, T. M. (1994). Comparing the fundamental frequencies of resolved and unresolved harmonics: Evidence for two pitch mechanisms? *Journal of the Acoustical Society of America, 95*, 3541–3554.

Darwin, C. J., & Gardner, R. B. (1986). Mistuning a harmonic of a vowel: Grouping and phase effects on vowel quality. *Journal of the Acoustical Society of America, 79*, 838–845.

Delgutte, B. (1987). Peripheral auditory processing of speech information: Implications from a physiological study of intensity discrimination. In M. E. H. Schouten (Ed.), *The psychophysics of speech perception.* Dordrecht, Netherlands: Nijhoff.

Evans, E. F. (1978). Place and time coding of frequency in the peripheral auditory system: Some physiological pros and cons. *Audiology, 17*, 369–420.

Fastl, H. (1993). Loudness evaluation by subjects and by a loudness meter. In R. T. Verrillo (Ed.), *Sensory research – multimodal perspectives* (pp. 199–210). Hillsdale, NJ: Erlbaum.

Flanagan, J. L., & Saslow, M. G. (1958). Pitch discrimination for synthetic vowels. *Journal of the Acoustical Society of America, 30*, 435–442.

Fletcher, H., & Munson, W. A. (1933). Loudness, its definition, measurement and calculation. *Journal of the Acoustical Society of America, 5,* 82–108.

Fletcher, H., & Munson, W. A. (1937). Relation between loudness and masking. *Journal of the Acoustical Society of America, 9,* 1–10.

Florentine, M., & Buus, S. (1981). An excitation-pattern model for intensity discrimination. *Journal of the Acoustical Society of America, 70,* 1646–1654.

Gabriel, B., Kollmeier, B., & Mellert, V. (1997). Influence of individual listener, measurement room and choice of test-tone levels on the shape of equal-loudness level contours. *Acustica United with Acta Acustica, 83,* 670–683.

Goldstein, J. L. (1973). An optimum processor theory for the central formation of the pitch of complex tones. *Journal of the Acoustical Society of America, 54,* 1496–1516.

Goldstein, J. L., & Srulovicz, P. (1977). Auditory-nerve spike intervals as an adequate basis for aural frequency measurement. In E. F. Evans & J. P. Wilson (Eds.), *Psychophysics and physiology of hearing* (pp. 337–346). London: Academic Press.

Handel, S. (1995). Timbre perception and auditory object identification. In B. C. J. Moore (Ed.), *Hearing* (pp. 425–461). San Diego: Academic Press.

Hellman, R. P., & Zwislocki, J. J. (1961). Some factors affecting the estimation of loudness. *Journal of the Acoustical Society of America, 35,* 687–694.

Henning, G. B. (1967). A model for auditory discrimination and detection. *Journal of the Acoustical Society of America, 42,* 1325–1334.

Hoekstra, A., & Ritsma, R. J. (1977). Perceptive hearing loss and frequency selectivity. In E. F. Evans & J. P. Wilson (Eds.), *Psychophysics and physiology of hearing* (pp. 263–271). London: Academic Press.

Houtsma, A. J. M., & Smurzynski, J. (1990). Pitch identification and discrimination for complex tones with many harmonics. *Journal of the Acoustical Society of America, 87,* 304–310.

Javel, E. (1980). Coding of AM tones in the chinchilla auditory nerve: Implications for the pitch of complex tones. *Journal of the Acoustical Society of America, 68,* 133–146.

Jerger, J., & Jerger, S. (1975). A simplified tone decay test. *Archives of Otolaryngology, 102,* 403–407.

Krumhansl, C. L. (1990). *Cognitive foundations of musical pitch.* Oxford: Oxford University Press.

Laming, D. (1997). *The measurement of sensation.* Oxford: Oxford University Press.

Licklider, J. C. R. (1956). Auditory frequency analysis. In C. Cherry (Ed.), *Information theory* (pp. 253–268). New York: Academic Press.

Meddis, R., & Hewitt, M. (1991). Virtual pitch and phase sensitivity studied using a computer model of the auditory periphery: Pitch identification. *Journal of the Acoustical Society of America, 89,* 2866–2882.

Meddis, R., & O'Mard, L. (1997). A unitary model of pitch perception. *Journal of the Acoustical Society of America, 102,* 1811–1820.

Miller, G. A. (1947). Sensitivity to changes in the intensity of white noise and its relation to masking and loudness. *Journal of the Acoustical Society of America, 191,* 609–619.

Miskiewicz, A., Scharf, B., Hellman, R., & Meiselman, C. (1993). Loudness adaptation at high frequencies. *Journal of the Acoustical Society of America, 94,* 1281–1286.

Moore, B. C. J. (1973). Some experiments relating to the perception of complex tones. *Quarterly Journal of Experimental Psychology, 25,* 451–475.

Moore, B. C. J. (1974). Relation between the critical bandwidth and the frequency-difference limen. *Journal of the Acoustical Society of America, 55,* 359.

Moore, B. C. J. (1982). *An introduction to the psychology of hearing* (2nd ed.). London: Academic Press.

Moore, B. C. J. (1989). *An introduction to the psychology of hearing* (3rd ed.). London: Academic Press.

Moore, B. C. J. (1997a). *An introduction to the psychology of hearing* (4th ed.). San Diego: Academic Press.

Moore, B. C. J. (1997b). A compact disc containing simulations of hearing impairment. *British*

Journal of Audiology, 31, 353–357.

Moore, B. C. J. (1998). *Cochlear hearing loss*. London: Whurr.

Moore, B. C. J., & Glasberg, B. R. (1986). The role of frequency selectivity in the perception of loudness, pitch and time. In B. C. J. Moore (Ed.), *Frequency selectivity in hearing* (pp. 251–308). London: Academic Press.

Moore, B. C. J., & Glasberg, B. R. (1989). Mechanisms underlying the frequency discrimination of pulsed tones and the detection of frequency modulation. *Journal of the Acoustical Society of America, 86*, 1722-1732.

Moore, B. C. J., Glasberg, B. R., & Baer, T. (1997). A model for the prediction of thresholds, loudness and partial loudness. *Journal of the Audio Engineering Society, 45*, 224–240.

Moore, B. C. J., Glasberg, B. R., & Peters, R. W. (1985). Relative dominance of individual partials in determining the pitch of complex tones. *Journal of the Acoustical Society of America, 77*, 1853–1860.

Moore, B. C. J., Glasberg, B. R., & Shailer, M. J. (1984). Frequency and intensity difference limens for harmonics within complex tones. *Journal of the Acoustical Society of America, 75*, 550–561.

Moore, B. C. J., & Ohgushi, K. (1993). Audibility of partials in inharmonic complex tones. *Journal of the Acoustical Society of America, 93*, 452–461.

Moore, B. C. J., & Raab, D. H. (1974). Pure-tone intensity discrimination: Some experiments relating to the "near-miss" to Weber's Law. *Journal of the Acoustical Society of America, 55*, 1049–1054.

Moore, B. C. J., & Rosen, S. M. (1979). Tune recognition with reduced pitch and interval information. *Quarterly Journal of Experimental Psychology, 31*, 229–240.

Moore, B. C. J., & Sek, A. (1995). Effects of carrier frequency, modulation rate and modulation waveform on the detection of modulation and the discrimination of modulation type (AM vs FM). *Journal of the Acoustical Society of America, 97*, 2468–2478.

Moore, B. C. J., & Sek, A. (1996). Detection of frequency modulation at low modulation rates: Evidence for a mechanism based on phase locking. *Journal of the Acoustical Society of America, 100*, 2320–2331.

Nelson, D. A., Stanton, M. E., & Freyman, R. L. (1983). A general equation describing frequency discrimination as a function of frequency and sensation level. *Journal of the Acoustical Society of America, 73*, 2117–2123.

Ohgushi, K., & Hatoh, T. (1991). Perception of the musical pitch of high frequency tones. In Y. Cazals, L. Demany, & K. Horner (Eds.), *Ninth international symposium on hearing: Auditory physiology and perception* (pp. 207–212). Oxford: Pergamon.

Ohm, G. S. (1843). Über die Definition des Tones, nebst daran geknüpfter Theorie der Sirene und ähnlicher tonbildender Vorrichtungen. *Annalen der Physik und Chemie, 59*, 513–565.

Palmer, A. R., & Evans, E. F. (1979). On the peripheral coding of the level of individual frequency components of complex sounds at high sound levels. In O. Creutzfeldt, H. Scheich & C. Schreiner (Eds.), *Hearing mechanisms and speech* (pp. 19–26). Berlin: Springer-Verlag.

Patterson, R. D. (1987a). A pulse ribbon model of monaural phase perception. *Journal of the Acoustical Society of America, 82*, 1560–1586.

Patterson, R. D. (1987b). A pulse ribbon model of peripheral auditory processing. In W. A. Yost & C. S. Watson (Eds.), *Auditory processing of complex sounds*. Hillsdale, NJ: Erlbaum.

Patterson, R. D. (1994a). The sound of a sinusoid: Spectral models. *Journal of the Acoustical Society of America, 96*, 1409–1418.

Patterson, R. D. (1994b). The sound of a sinusoid: Time-interval models. *Journal of the Acoustical Society of America, 96*, 1419–1428.

Plack, C. J., & Carlyon, R. P. (1995a). Differences in frequency modulation detection and fundamental frequency discrimination between complex tones consisting of resolved and unresolved harmonics. *Journal of the Acoustical Society of America, 98*, 1355–1364.

Plack, C. J., & Carlyon, R. P. (1995b). Loudness perception and intensity coding. In B. C. J. Moore (Ed.), *Hearing* (pp. 123–160). Orlando, FL: Academic Press.

Plomp, R. (1964). The ear as a frequency analyzer. *Journal of the Acoustical Society of America, 36*,

1628–1636.

Plomp, R. (1967). Pitch of complex tones. *Journal of the Acoustical Society of America, 41*, 1526–1533.

Plomp, R. (1970). Timbre as a multidimensional attribute of complex tones. In R. Plomp & G. F. Smoorenburg (Eds.), *Frequency analysis and periodicity detection in hearing*. Leiden, Netherlands: Sijthoff.

Plomp, R. (1976). *Aspects of tone sensation*. London: Academic Press.

Plomp, R., Pols, L. C. W., & van de Geer, J. P. (1967). Dimensional analysis of vowel tones. *Journal of the Acoustical Society of America, 41*, 707–712.

Plomp, R., & Steeneken, H. J. M. (1969). Effect of phase on the timbre of complex tones. *Journal of the Acoustical Society of America, 46*, 409–421.

Pols, L. C. W., van der Kamp, L. J. T., & Plomp, R. (1969). Perceptual and physical space of vowel sounds. *Journal of the Acoustical Society of America, 46*, 458–467.

Risset, J. C., & Wessel, D. L. (1982). Exploration of timbre by analysis and synthesis. In D. Deutsch (ed.), *The psychology of music* (pp. 25–58). New York: Academic Press.

Ritsma, R. J. (1962). Existence region of the tonal residue. I. *Journal of the Acoustical Society of America, 34*, 1224–1229.

Ritsma, R. J. (1963). Existence region of the tonal residue. II. *Journal of the Acoustical Society of America, 35*, 1241–1245.

Ritsma, R. J. (1967). Frequencies dominant in the perception of the pitch of complex sounds. *Journal of the Acoustical Society of America, 42*, 191–198.

Ruggero, M. A., Rich, N. C., Recio, A., Narayan, S. S., & Robles, L. (1997). Basilar-membrane responses to tones at the base of the chinchilla cochlea. *Journal of the Acoustical Society of America, 101*, 2151–2163.

Scharf, B. (1983). Loudness adaptation. In J. V. Tobias & E. D. Schubert (Eds.), *Hearing research and theory* (Vol. 2, pp. 1–56). New York: Academic Press.

Schouten, J. F. (1940). The residue and the mechanism of hearing. *Proceedings of the Koninklijke Akademie van Wetenschappen, 43*, 991–999.

Schouten, J. F. (1968). The perception of timbre. *6th International Conference on Acoustics, 1*, GP-6–2.

Schouten, J. F. (1970). The residue revisited. In R. Plomp & G. F. Smoorenburg (Eds.), *Frequency analysis and periodicity detection in hearing* (pp. 41–54). Leiden, Netherlands: Sijthoff.

Sek, A., & Moore, B. C. J. (1995). Frequency discrimination as a function of frequency, measured in several ways. *Journal of the Acoustical Society of America, 97*, 2479–2486.

Shepard, R. N. (1964). Circularity in judgements of relative pitch. *Journal of the Acoustical Society of America, 36*, 2346–2353.

Siebert, W. M. (1970). Frequency discrimination in the auditory system: Place or periodicity mechanisms. *Proceedings of the IEEE, 58*, 723–730.

Srulovicz, P., & Goldstein, J. L. (1983). A central spectrum model: A synthesis of auditory-nerve timing and place cues in monaural communication of frequency spectrum. *Journal of the Acoustical Society of America, 73*, 1266–1276.

Stevens, S. S. (1935). The relation of pitch to intensity. *Journal of the Acoustical Society of America, 6*, 150–154.

Stevens, S. S. (1957). On the psychophysical law. *Psychological Review, 64*, 153–181.

Stone, M. A., Glasberg, B. R., & Moore, B. C. J. (1996). Dynamic aspects of loudness: A real-time loudness meter. *British Journal of Audiology, 30*, 124.

Teich, M. C., & Khanna, S. M. (1985). Pulse-number distribution for the neural spike train in the cat's auditory nerve. *Journal of the Acoustical Society of America, 77*, 1110–1128.

Terhardt, E. (1974a). Pitch of pure tones: Its relation to intensity. In E. Zwicker & E. Terhardt (Eds.), *Facts and models in hearing* (pp. 350–357). Berlin: Springer.

Terhardt, E. (1974b). Pitch, consonance, and harmony. *Journal of the Acoustical Society of America, 55*, 1061–1069.

Verschuure, J., & van Meeteren, A. A. (1975). The effect of intensity on pitch. *Acustica, 32*, 33–44.

Viemeister, N. F. (1972). Intensity discrimination of pulsed sinusoids: The effects of filtered noise.

Journal of the Acoustical Society of America, 51, 1265-1269.
Viemeister, N. F. (1983). Auditory intensity discrimination at high frequencies in the presence of noise. *Science, 221*, 1206–1208.
Viemeister, N. F. (1988). Psychophysical aspects of auditory intensity coding. In G. M. Edelman, W. E. Gall, & W. A. Cowan (Eds.), *Auditory function*. New York: Wiley.
Viemeister, N. F., & Bacon, S. P. (1988). Intensity discrimination, increment detection, and magnitude estimation for 1-kHz tones. *Journal of the Acoustical Society of America, 84*, 172–178.
Ward, W. D. (1954). Subjective musical pitch. *Journal of the Acoustical Society of America, 26*, 369–380.
Wier, C. C., Jesteadt, W., & Green, D. M. (1977). Frequency discrimination as a function of frequency and sensation level. *Journal of the Acoustical Society of America, 61*, 178–184.
Zwicker, E. (1956). Die elementären Grundlagen zur Bestimmung der Informationskapazität des Gehörs. *Acustica, 6*, 356–381.
Zwicker, E. (1958). Über psychologische und methodische Grundlagen der Lautheit. *Acustica, 8*, 237–258.
Zwicker, E. (1970). Masking and psychological excitation as consequences of the ear's frequency analysis. In R. Plomp & G. F. Smoorenburg (eds.), *Frequency analysis and periodicity detection in hearing* (pp. 376–394). Leiden, Netherlands: Sijthoff.
Zwicker, E., & Fastl, H. (1990). *Psychoacoustics – facts and models*. Berlin: Springer-Verlag.
Zwicker, E., & Scharf, B. (1965). A model of loudness summation. *Psychological Review, 72*, 3–26.

Chapter Fourteen

Auditory Localization and Scene Perception

William A. Yost

Introduction

Before you go any further, pause for a moment and concentrate on the various sounds that surround you. In every instance you probably perceive the sounds in terms of their sources: a car horn, the whirl of a fan, the closing of a door, the footsteps of a colleague, the hum of a computer terminal. Not only can you use the sounds produced by these objects for object identification, but you often determine several sound sources simultaneously. You are processing an auditory scene (Bregman, 1990) consisting of the perceptions of the various sound sources that constitute your acoustic environment. A moment of further reflection will suggest that the sounds from each source do not reach your auditory system as separate sounds. The sound entering your auditory system is a single acoustic event that is the mixture of all of the sounds from many sound sources. As such it must be that perceptual mechanisms determine the various sources that constitute this complex sound field. As described in Chapters 12 and 13, the peripheral auditory system provides a spectral-temporal code for the complex sound field consisting of the sounds of the many sound sources. That is, the auditory periphery is designed to code for the spectral and temporal properties of the sound field, not for sound sources per se. This chapter provides some of the data and theories about how the auditory system determines sound sources in a complex, multisource acoustic environment. That is, how is the auditory scene formed?

Figure 14.1 may help describe the problem confronted by the auditory system in forming an auditory scene. The figure shows the output of a computational model (Auditory Image Model, AIM, Patterson, Allerhand, & Giguere, 1995) of the function of the auditory periphery. The input to the model is a complex acoustic stimulus consisting of the sum of two spoken vowels (the /e/ in beat and the /a/ in bat), as if two people (two sound sources) simultaneously spoke these vowels. When listening to such simultaneously spoken vowels, it is usually easy to determine that two people are uttering these vowels (Summerfield & Assmann, 1989). The three-dimensional figure displays 100 ms (the x-axis) of the processed complex sound for each of 64 frequency-tuned auditory channels (the y-axis). Each tuned channel represents a simulation of the neural activity that exists within a small set of auditory nerve fibers tuned to a particular frequency. The model simulates the biomechanical action of the cochlea, inner haircell transduction of this biomechanical action into neural impulses, and auditory nerve fiber transmission of the neural impulses. Patterns seen across time represent the auditory peripheral code for the temporal structure of the complex sound. Patterns along the tuned channel dimension indicate the spectral code for the complex sound. This is the presumed neural pattern of information that flows from the auditory periphery to the central auditory nervous system. While the temporal and spectral properties of the complex sound field, consisting of the mixture of the two vowels, are well preserved in this neural code, it is not clear from such a representation that there are two vowels. That is, the auditory periphery is coding for the

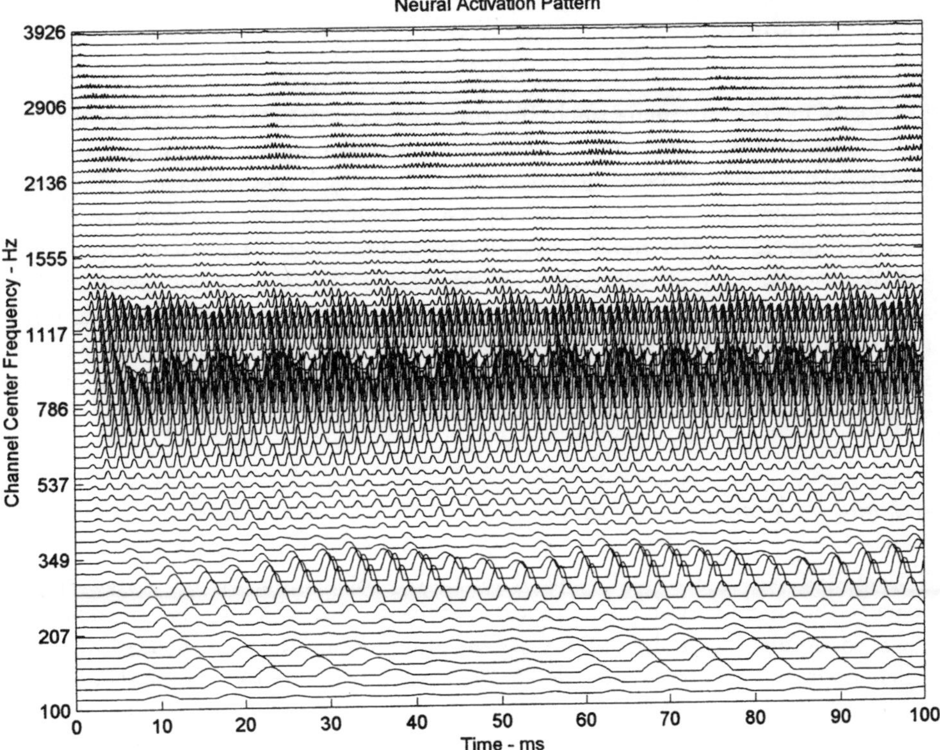

Figure 14.1. The neural activation pattern from the computational model (AIM, Patterson et al., 1995) of the auditory periphery to the input of the mixture of two vowels. 100 ms of the simulated neural activity from 64 frequency-tuned channels is shown. While the spectral-temporal properties of the mixture are well preserved by the auditory periphery, there is no direct code for sound sources (the two vowels) per se.

temporal-spectral properties of the complex sound field input and not for the sound sources themselves. However, within this peripheral representation are the codes for several important physical cues associated with each sound source that may aid higher neural centers in determining the auditory scene (Yost, 1991). This chapter reviews research on these cues and the type of perceptual organization that might mediate sound source determination. There are several ways in which the sound from one source may differ from that of another source. One sound source may differ from another in that it occurs at a different time (onset cues), or it has a different spectral content (spectral cues), or it is louder or softer (level-profile cues). These and other cues will be described in this chapter. We begin with a discussion of sound source localization, the ability to locate a sound source based entirely on the sound produced by the source.

Sound Localization

The spatial location of a source can be determined in three dimensions based on the sound it produces. Because sound, itself, has no spatial properties, sound localization is based on perceptual processing of the sound produced by vibrating objects. A different set of physical cues is presumably used by the auditory system for determining sound source location in each of the three spatial dimensions. The top part of Figure 14.2 describes these three spatial planes: azimuth or horizontal plane, which is the left-right direction; vertical plane which is the up-down direction; and distance or range plane, which is the near-far direction. The bottom part of Figure 14.2 indicates the cue(s) presumably used by the auditory system to locate a sound source in each dimension. These cues will be explained in more detail in the following sections.

Azimuth (Horizontal) Localization

If a sound source is placed to one side of a stationary listener, the sound will reach the ear closer to the sound first and with a greater level than that which reaches the other ear. Thus, sound arriving at the auditory system produces an interaural (between the ears) difference in onset of arrival and in level. These two interaural cues, *interaural time difference* and *interaural level difference*, provide information about the azimuthal location of a sound source: the greater the interaural differences become, the more toward one side of the listener the sound must be. In the bottom part of Figure 14.2 the pressure waveform reaches the right ear before it reaches the left ear and as a result the amplitude is greater at the right ear, thus signaling that the sound source is to the right of the listener.

Listeners are accurate in locating sound sources in the azimuthal plane. There are two general methods for estimating sound localization accuracy: location identification and the minimal audible angle. In location identification, a single sound source is presented somewhere in the sound field and the listener is asked to indicate its spatial position. Location error is often the mean square error between the listener's estimate of the sound source's location and the actual location. Such mean square error when expressed in terms of visual angle ranges between 5 and 10° for broad-band sound sources located directly in front of the listener and 10 and 25° when the source is toward the side of the listener (Makous & Middlebrooks, 1990). The errors are usually greater for narrow-band signals and depend on the frequency content of the sound, as will be discussed later. In addition, listeners have somewhat higher errors when judging the location of signals behind them compared to those in front (Wightman & Kistler, 1993).

In the minimal audible angle procedure two sound sources are presented in succession and listeners are to indicate if they can tell whether the left or right source delivered the sound first. The angular separation between the two sources is varied to obtain a threshold angle of separation (the minimal audible angle, MAA). The MAA is as small as 1° for sources directly in front and increases for sources off to one side (Mills, 1972). The MAA also varies with the spectral content and spectral complexity of the sound (Mills, 1972).

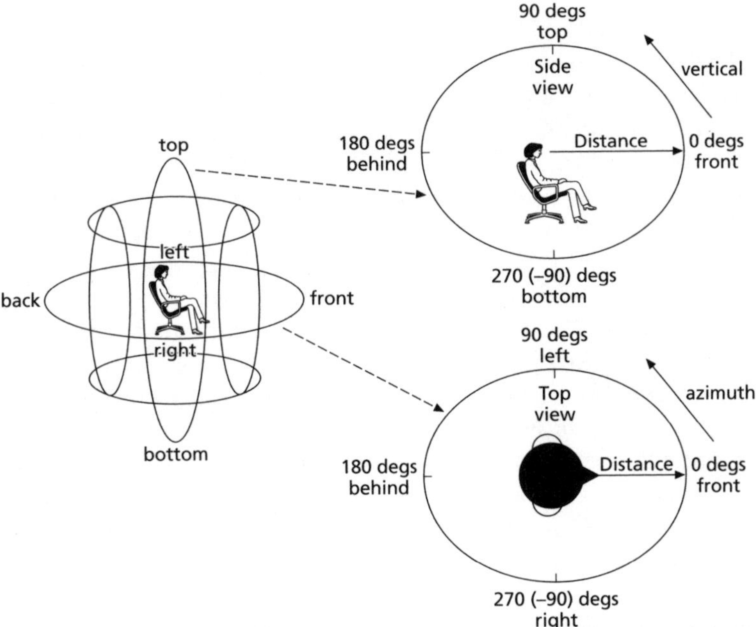

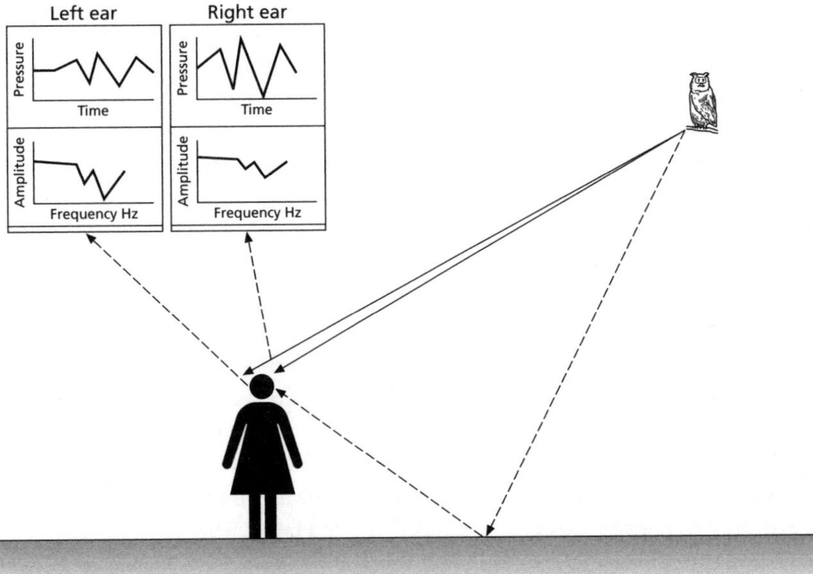

Figure 14.2. At the top is a schematic of the three spatial dimensions showing a top view of the azimuth plane and a side view of the vertical plane. On the bottom is a schematic of the information arriving at the two ears of a listener from a sound source (owl). The sound arrives at the right ear before it reaches the left ear and with a greater level. The amplitude spectra with a major spectral valley at each ear (HRTFs) represent the complex spectral pattern after the sound has passed over the body, head, and pinna. Reflections (dotted line from owl) off the ground are mixed with the sound from the source. All of these variables aid in sound localization.

Both location error and the MAA are small for tones with frequencies below 1000 Hz and above 2000 Hz. Thus, location accuracy is poorer in the spectral region between 1000 and 2000 Hz. The dependence of localization accuracy on sound frequency can be explained if we consider that the saliency of interaural time and level differences depends on frequency because of the way sound travels from a source to the ears of a listener. Interaural level differences are caused primarily by the head attenuating the sound arriving at the far ear (the head produces a "sound shadow"). The amount of attenuation is proportional to the frequency of the sound. High-frequency sounds having short wavelengths will be attenuated more than low-frequency sounds with longer wavelengths. Because the diameter of the average head is approximately 15 cm, significant attenuation occurs around 1600–1800 Hz. Thus, sounds with frequencies greater than 2000 Hz produce large interaural level differences. The large interaural level differences at high frequencies are more likely to provide a cue for localization than the smaller interaural level differences occurring at low frequencies.

Interaural time differences result because sound arrives at the far ear after it reaches the near ear. For instance, for a sound source off to the left, the first peak of the sound wave will reach the left ear before it reaches the right ear, producing an interaural onset time difference which is in the direction of the left ear. If the frequency of the sound is high, its period is short, and the time it takes sound to travel from one ear to the other may be relatively long compared to the period of this high-frequency sound. Thus, the later peaks in the high-frequency sound's waveform may not reach the two ears with the same time difference as that produced by the first peaks. While the first (onset) peaks produce one interaural time difference, the remaining peaks produce different interaural time differences. These later arriving peaks would indicate a different location of the sound source. Such confusions do not exist when the frequency of the tone is less than about 1200 Hz, because it takes about 700 to 800 microsecs for sound to travel from one ear to the other. That is, for frequencies below 1200 Hz the interaural time difference for all peaks in the waveform will be the same. Thus, all peaks will indicate the same location. The result is that only sounds below about 1200 Hz produce an unambiguous interaural time difference which can be used as a cue for sound localization.

Stevens and Newman (1936, following earlier work by Lord Rayleigh, 1907) suggested that in the spectral region below 1000 Hz, the interaural time difference cue was used for sound localization and for the region above 2000 Hz interaural level difference was the primary cue. In the 1000- to 2000-Hz region neither interaural difference provides a good cue and, thus, sound localization accuracy is poor. This is known as the *Duplex Theory of Sound Localization*. The theory does a good job of describing sound localization of narrow-band signals in free-field listening conditions (Yost & Hafter, 1987).

Vertical Localization

Interaural time and level differences may not always be usable for sound localization. With the head in a fixed position, it is possible for sounds from sources at different spatial locations to produce identical interaural time and level differences. For instance, a sound source directly in front of a listener and one directly behind the listener will both produce zero interaural time and level differences. If interaural differences are the basis for sound localization, then the two sound sources would be perceived at the same place (referred to as front-back or back-front confusions). In fact, all sound sources that lie along the vertical plane that is at zero azimuth produce zero interaural differences. This plane (see Figure 14.2), called the *mid-sagittal plane*, runs from directly in front of the listener to directly overhead to directly behind to directly below the listener. The mid-sagittal plane is one "*cone of confusion*" in which all spatial locations on a cone of confusion produce the same interaural differences (Mills, 1972).

There are usually more localization errors when sound sources lie on a cone of confusion. In the real world a small head movement will break up a cone of confusion and the listener can use interaural differences to locate sound sources, at least when the sound sources differ in azimuthal location. That is, suppose there is a sound source directly in front and one directly behind a listener. Each sound source will produce no interaural differences and thus their locations can be confused. If the listener moves his or her head slightly to one side, then the two sources produce different interaural differences and each set of interaural differences can be used to localize each sound source. Sound localization errors are greater if listeners cannot or do not move their head.

Even though listeners have more difficulty locating sound sources on cones of confusion without head movements, they can still locate them with some accuracy even though they cannot be using interaural differences for localization. Most of the research into how this is accomplished is based on work in the mid-sagittal plane, and this research is the basis for the conjectures about the cues used for vertical localization. That is, the ability to localize sound sources in the vertical direction is not based on interaural differences, but on a different set of cues.

The cues used for vertical sound localization are based on complex spectral information reaching the ears after the sound has traveled from the source across the body and head to the ear canals. In the real world an acoustic signal passes over the torso, head, and pinna of the listener before entering the ear canal. Each of these structures provides an obstacle to the path of the sound. These structures reduce the amplitude of the sound and delay its passage. However, the amount of the attenuation and delay is determined by the interaction between the sound's wavelength (wavelength is reciprocally related to frequency) and the size of the obstacle. That is, for a complex signal there is a spectral pattern of attenuation and phase shifts imparted to the signal before it reaches the ear canal. These spectral changes transform the spectral information of the sound from the source and as such these complex spectral transformations produced by the head and torso are called *Head Related Transfer Functions (HRTF)* (Wightman & Kistler, 1993).

HRTFs are determined by first measuring the spectrum of the sound at the source and then measuring the spectrum in a listener's ear canal with very small microphones. With proper digital signal processing, the difference in the spectra will reveal the HRTF for each ear. Thus, each point in space is represented by a pair of HRTFs, one for each ear. The differences in the amplitude spectra of the HRTFs between each ear reveal the frequency-dependent interaural level differences for that point in space, and the differences in the phase spectra reveal the frequency-dependent interaural phase shifts. Each point in space produces a different pair of HRTFs, such that for any one listener the spectral structure of the HRTFs could be used to indicate a location in space. Thus, the spectral structure of the HRTF is the presumable cue for vertical localization.

The amplitude spectra of HRTFs are usually relatively flat out to about 3000–4000 Hz, and then major spectral peaks and valleys occur at higher frequencies. The spectral location of these peaks and valleys differ for sounds from sources located at different vertical positions. Thus, the spectral location of these peaks and valleys may provide a cue for vertical sound localization. In the bottom part of Figure 14.2 the amplitude spectrum of the sound at the ears (i.e., the amplitude spectrum after the HRTF has been applied) has a spectral valley whose spectral location might indicate the vertical location of the owl. Both the spectral structure of the stimulus that arrives at any one ear and the interaural spectral differences are the *spectral cues* used for vertical localization.

Human listeners are not as accurate in vertical localization as they are in azimuthal localization. The mean square errors tend to be 1.125 to 1.25 times greater for vertical localization compared with azimuthal localization (Middlebrooks, 1992; Wightman & Kistler, 1993, 1997). Errors for vertical localization are lower for sounds with high frequencies than for sounds that contain only low frequencies. The fact that vertical localization accuracy is best for high-frequency sounds where the HRTFs show the most spectral fluctuations is one line of evidence for the use of spectral cues for vertical localization.

It is possible that the spectrum of the sound from the originating source will have a spectral structure that is the same as that provided by a particular HRTF. That is, the spectrum of the sound from a sound source located at one position might have a spectral peak that would, if it were caused by the HRTF, indicate the sound source is at a different location. Thus, there is the possibility that listeners could mislocalize such a stimulus, as the spectral information provided by the stimulus itself might indicate one location and that provided by the HRTF another location (Wightman & Kistler, 1993). There is some evidence that this can occur, but usually the spectral structure of HRTFs is so unique that such mislocalizations are unlikely to occur in the real world. It is also possible that an interaural comparison of the spectra from the two ears could help determine the correct vertical location of a sound source. In any event, there is considerable evidence that vertical localization is based on spectral information provided by HRTFs.

Distance Localization

Far less is known about locating the distance of a sound source than is known about azimuthal and vertical localization. Stationary listeners are poor at judging the distance of a stationary sound source (Loomis, Klatsky, Philbeck, & Golledge, 1998). One obvious cue for distance judgments is loudness (Gardner, 1969; Loomis, et al., 1998; Mershon, 1997). Near sound sources are louder than far sound sources because a sound's level decreases as a function of distance (the inverse square law). Thus, if a listener has independent information about the source's overall intensity (e.g., the sound source is familiar), then the absolute distance of the source can be calculated from the relative loudness of the sound. Even when loudness cannot be used as a distance cue, listeners can judge a sound source's distance. Another possible cue for distance judgments is the reflections that come from reflective surfaces. The early reflections from near surfaces (such as the ground) can be used to aid a listener in determining the distance of a sound source. That is, a sound source near a listener will have a higher proportion of the total sound arriving at the listener coming from the reflection than that from a far away sound source. In the bottom part of Figure 14.2 a reflected path (dotted line) for the sound from the ground is shown to indicate that reflected sound might provide a useful cue for judging the distance of a sound source.

Thus, interaural differences of time and level are the primary cues for localization in the azimuth plane, spectral differences provide cues for sound sources located in the vertical planes, and loudness and early reflections can aid in judging the distance of a sound source.

The Precedence Effect – Localization in the Presence of Reflections

The sounds that arrive at the auditory system from most sound sources in the real world are accompanied by reflections from surfaces. Reflections might influence sound localization, in that the source of the sound might be perceived as coming from the location of a reflection rather than from the source. However, in most listening environments reflections are not perceived as separate acoustic events (i.e., as echoes) and they do not greatly influence the ability to locate the originating sound source in the horizontal or vertical direction (as mentioned previously reflections may assist in distance location). Because reflections take a longer path to the listener than that from the sound source, the sound from the source reaches the auditory system before that of any reflection. The fact that reflections are not heard separately and have only a small influence on localization is called the *precedence effect* (also called *the law of the first wavefront),* as if the sound from the source takes precedence over later arriving reflections (Blauert, 1997; Litovsky, Colburn, Yost, & Guzman, forthcoming). The sound from the source plus its reflections is perceived as different from the sound of the source alone. However, the reflections are not perceived as separate from the source (*fusion* of the source and reflected sounds), and the perceived azimuth and vertical location of the sound source is dominated by the location of the source (*localization dominance*). Precedence usually occurs (i.e., both fusion and localization dominance occur) when the level of the reflection is equal to or less intense than that of the source, when the reflection is delayed by 3–10 ms relative to the source, when the reflection arrives from a different spatial location than the source, and when the reflection is temporally and spectrally similar to the source (Blauert, 1997).

Headphone Delivered Stimuli: Lateralization

In the free field it is often difficult to control the many variables that influence sound localization. For instance, interaural level and time differences covary for real-world sounds and the characteristics of the HRTF cannot be independently varied. By presenting sounds over headphones these many variables can be manipulated. If an acoustic signal is presented over headphones, listeners often report that a sound image is "inside" their head at a location between the ears. In these conditions the sound is not externalized as it would be if the sound had originated from a real-world sound source. Rather the sound is internalized or *lateralized* (Yost & Hafter, 1987). The lateralized image is located toward the ear that receives the sound first and/or receives the more intense sound. The greater the interaural time or level difference, the further toward one side (one ear) the sound image is perceived (Yost, 1981). Thus, changes in lateral location mirror those for the azimuthal location of real-world sound sources; interaural level or time differences that favor one side (ear) are perceived toward that side (ear).

The ability to just detect a change in an interaural time or level difference can be used to define the acuity of the auditory system to these important binaural variables. Thresholds for discriminating a change in interaural time difference for a 200-Hz tone are about 45 microsecs. The difference thresholds fall to about 10 microsecs at 1000 Hz, and rise again as frequency increases until interaural time difference thresholds cannot be measured for tones with frequencies above about 1500 Hz (Yost, 1974). Above about 1500 Hz, changes in interaural time are not perceptible. These results from lateralization experiments are consistent with the Duplex Theory of Localization, which states that sound sources with low frequencies are localized based on interaural time differences.

The difference threshold for determining a just noticeable change in interaural level difference is between 0.5 and 1 dB at all frequencies, except around 1000 Hz where it is slightly higher (Yost & Dye, 1988). In the real world a low-frequency sound below about 1000 Hz will produce interaural level differences that are less than 1 dB. Again these lateralization data support the Duplex Theory of Localization, in that the small size of the interaural level difference produced by low-frequency sounds from real-world sound sources would not be detectable.

If complex high-frequency sounds are produced with low rates of overall amplitude modulation (e.g., amplitude modulated high-frequency carrier tones; high-pass filtered pulse trains; and narrow bandwidth, high center-frequency noises), then they can be lateralized on the basis of interaural time differences. For instance, a 300-Hz amplitude modulated, 3600-Hz carrier tone has an interaural time difference threshold of about 70 microsecs (slightly larger than the threshold for a 300-Hz pure tone), whereas an interaural time difference threshold cannot be measured for an unmodulated 3600-Hz tone (Henning, 1974). The modulated sound has spectral energy only in the region of 3600 Hz and thus, according to the Duplex Theory of Localization, should not be lateralized based on interaural time differences. However, the sound can be lateralized based on the 300-Hz (low) rate of amplitude modulation (Henning, 1974). These and other data suggest a modification to the Duplex Theory of Localization (Yost & Hafter, 1987). The revised theory states that interaural time is a potential cue for azimuthal localization for sound sources that have sounds with low-spectral frequencies or slow rates of amplitude modulation, and interaural level is a potential cue for azimuthal localization of sound sources with high frequencies.

Recall that stimuli presented over headphones with an interaural time or level difference are lateralized inside the head and thus are not perceived the same as sounds coming from real- world sound sources. When a complex sound is presented over headphones with just an interaural difference, the complexities of the HRTF have not been provided. If the spectrum of a sound presented over headphones had the spectral complexity provided by an appropriate HRTF, then the headphone delivered sound arriving in the ear canal would be the same as that from a real sound source. A sound can be filtered with a filter that reflects the spectral complexities of a particular HRTF. Each point in space will have a different pair (one for each ear) of HRTFs. If these HRTFs were used to design filters, then

HRTF-filtered stimuli should be localized just like real-world sound sources (Wightman & Kistler, 1989a, 1989b), because the HRTF-filtered stimuli delivered over headphones would produce the same acoustical signal in the ear canal as that which would have arrived from the real sound source that produced the HRTFs.

Experiments comparing localization accuracy for real sound sources as compared with HRTF-filtered sounds delivered over headphones show a strong correlation between the two localization tasks (Wightman & Kistler, 1989b). These experiments suggest that HRTF-filtered stimuli delivered over headphones are localized almost the same as sound coming from real-world sound sources. Although such virtual sound sources can be perceived as if they were real sound sources (Hartmann & Wittenburg, 1996), this virtual auditory experience is not always exactly like listening to real sound sources. For instance, the virtual sound sources are often not externalized to the same extent as their real-world counterparts. Also, listeners make more back-front (and front-back) errors (cone of confusion errors) with virtual sound sources than with real sound sources (Wightman & Kistler, 1993).

Several aspects of normal listening to real-world sound sources are still not present when HRTF-filtered stimuli are presented over headphones; for example, head movements are not incorporated properly into the listening condition. That is, if an HRFT-filtered stimulus were presented as if it came from behind a listener, the listener could not turn to face the stimulus, because no matter what position the head is in, the virtual sound delivered over headphones will always be perceived as coming from behind. As even very small head movements help listeners localize sound sources (e.g., when cone of confusion errors occur), head movements appear to be important for sound localization. If a head-movement sensor were coupled to an HRTF-filter system, such that the proper HRTF filter is used for each position of the head and for a particular source location, listeners could face a virtual sound source as they could for a real-world sound source. The use of a head-position monitor (Wenzel, 1995) or other ways of providing appropriate head movements (Hartmann & Wittenburg, 1996) improves externalization of the virtual sound source and decreases cone-of-confusion errors. A completely accurate virtual auditory sound system may also have to include proper integration of visual, proprioceptive, and vestibular cues (Wightman & Kistler, 1993).

Thus, sounds presented over headphones often do not produce the same spatial perceptions as sounds coming from sound sources located in the real world. While delivering sounds over headphones allows one to carefully study the cues used for sound localization, understanding the differences between lateralization and localization is also crucial for forming theories of sound localization.

Neural Processing of Information About Auditory Space

Much of the research seeking physiological correlates of sound localization has investigated binaural coincidence neural network as suggested by Jeffress (1948). Jeffress theorized that interaural time differences could be determined by cross-correlating the signals arriving at the two ears. The lag in the cross-correlation function for the first peak in the cross-correlation function indicates the interaural time difference. This lag serves as the indicator of

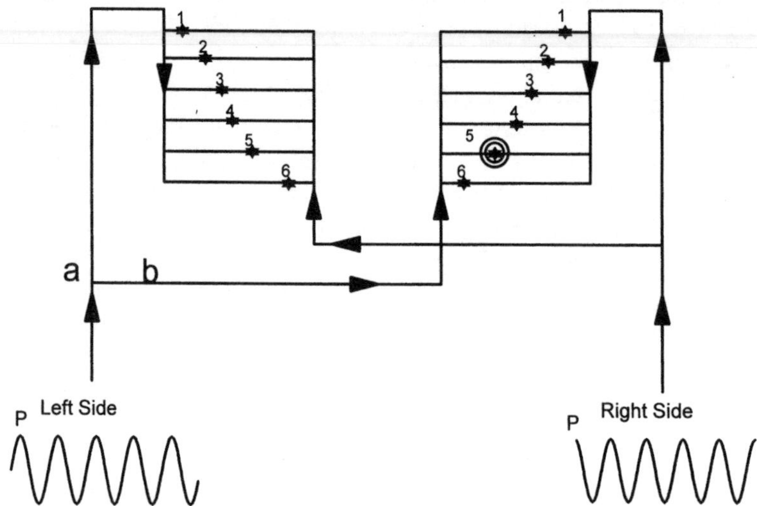

Figure 14.3. A Jeffress coincidence network that could produce a neural spatial map based on interaural time differences. Each cell (star) in the network fires maximally when the inputs from the two sides arrive simultaneously. In the example, a sound coming from the right leads that from the left and will therefore arrive at cell 5 on the right (the circled cell) simultaneously with that coming from the left.

spatial location, in that cross-correlation peaks that occur at large lags indicate spatial locations toward one side. Jeffress further suggested that a coincidence network as is shown in Figure 14.3 could serve as a neural network that would perform a type of cross-correlation. Such a coincidence network of binaural cells produces a maximal output at a particular place in the network based on the interaural time difference, and that place in the network provides an indication of the spatial location of the sound source. Such a coincidence network could provide a spatial map for processing the location of sound sources based on interaural time differences.

Various implementations of coincidence networks have proved successful in accounting for lateralization data based on interaural time differences (Colburn & Durlach, 1978). Additional modifications to these networks have also been suggested to enable the networks to account for lateralization data based on interaural level differences. For instance, early work (Jeffress, 1948) argued that an interaural level difference could be turned into an interaural time difference based on the relationship between the time course of neural conduction and stimulus level. An intense sound travels faster in the nervous system than a weak sound, so the more intense sound reaching the near ear would arrive at a neural center before the weak sound from the far ear, producing an time difference between the two signals. That is, an interaural level difference could be traded into an interaural time difference. Later work (Yost & Hafter, 1987), however, demonstrated that it was unlikely that interaural level differences could be traded for interaural time differences in this matter. Additional mechanisms have been proposed for incorporating interaural level differences into a coincidence network (Stern & Trahiotis, 1997). As such, coincidence networks have provided excellent models for azimuthal localization.

The site of any such binaural or spatial hearing processor must be relatively high in the nervous system. Sound enters each ear and is transduced by each cochlea such that the auditory nerve provides a spectral-temporal code of the incoming signal. The spectral-temporal code provided by the auditory nerve is further processed by the next stage of neural processing, the cochlear nucleus. The neural outputs of the two cochlear nuclei feed into the two olivary complexes. The olivary complex is the first brainstem site where there are strong bilateral (binaural) connections. The medial superior olive (MSO) appears appropriate for processing interaural time differences, and the lateral superior olive (LSO) appears suited for processing interaural level differences (Kuwada & Yin, 1983). In some species (especially birds like the barn owl) structures similar to the MSO appear to have a neural network that resembles a Jeffress coincidence network (Knudsen & Konishi, 1978). Recently investigators (Young, Rice, & Tong, 1996) have suggested that the cochlear nucleus might be the site for processing the spectral differences associated with the HRTF that are crucial for vertical localization. Fibers from the cochlear nucleus and the olivary complex flow into the inferior colliculus (IC), where there is a rich array of neurons that are sensitive to the cues responsible for sound localization. Additional research, especially ablation studies (Casseday & Covey, 1987), also suggest that cortical neurons play a crucial role in sound localization. That is, sound localization in animals is often not significantly impaired until auditory cortex or part of auditory cortex is ablated.

In the MSO, LSO, IC, and auditory cortex, binaurally driven neurons often have an interaural time or level difference to which the cell is most sensitive. The interaural difference to which the cell is most sensitive is called the *characteristic delay or level difference* and suggests that these cells are tuned to that interaural difference (Kuwada & Yin, 1987). These cells are thought to provide input into maps of auditory space. Although such spatial maps have been measured in the auditory cortex of mammals, they are often very large (Brugge. Reale, & Hind, 1997). That is, stimuli located over a wide range of spatial locations can elicit a response from a single cell in such a spatial map. This lack of spatial resolution for cortically measured auditory spatial maps presents a challenge for how such maps might aid sound localization. Spatial maps measured in the barn owl (Knudsen & Konishi, 1978) show a much closer correspondence to the spatial abilities of the barn owl, and so the barn owl has been an excellent animal model for the study of auditory spatial processing.

Auditory Scene Perception

Even when two different sound sources are at the exact same location, we often perceive each sound source. Thus, there must be cues in addition to those that support sound localization that aid in sound source determination. As will be discussed in the following sections several acoustic cues may be used by the auditory system in segregating sound sources in a complex acoustic environment. Perceptual processes use the cues available in the complex sound field to aid the auditory system in determining sound sources. Table

Table 14.1 Seven classes of stimulus cues that might aid in sound source determination

Stimulus cue	*Effect*
Spatial separation	The spatial separation of sound sources and the ability to localize sound source
Spectral separation	Spectral differences that exist among sounds
Temporal separation	Temporal separation of sounds from different sound sources
Intensity/Spectral profile	Level differences among the sounds from different sources
Harmonicity	Sounds with harmonic structure often have a complex pitch associated with the fundamental frequency of the harmonic structure and this complex pitch may aid in sound source determination
Common onsets/offsets	A sound could be segregated from sounds from other sound sources based on its asynchronous onset or offset
Common patterns of modulation	Most vibrating sources impart a slow temporal modulation to the level and frequency of the sound produced by the source. The unique patterns of modulation may aid in segregating one sound source from another

14.1 indicates seven classes of cues that are likely candidates for those used by auditory system for sound source determination (Yost & Sheft, 1993). Sound source determination refers to the use of these cues for describing how a single source is perceived as well as how the various sound sources in an auditory scene may be segregated. Although in many situations listeners might be able to identify the sources, sound source determination does not assume that the ability to label a source is a necessary and sufficient condition for the auditory system to recognize that a sound source exists (Yost, 1991; Yost & Sheft, 1993). Some of the research investigating the seven classes of cues shown in Table 14.1 is described below.

Spatial Separation: The Cocktail Party Effect and The Masking-Level Difference

It is often the case that being able to locate one sound source in a background of many sources makes attending to that source easier. Cherry (1953) proposed that our ability to locate sound sources aids the auditory system in its ability to determine sources in multisource acoustic environments. He labeled this ability the *cocktail party effect,* alluding to the ability to attend to a few people at a noisy cocktail party of many people and other sound sources. Although very few studies have directly investigated the ability to attend to sound sources in complex, real-world acoustic environments, there is evidence that spatially separated sound sources aid in resolving differences among them (Yost, 1997).

Many studies have investigated the ability to detect a signal in a background of masking noise, when the signal is presented with one interaural difference and the masking noise is presented with a different interaural difference, as if the signal and masker were spatially separated on the basis of the interaural differences. The threshold for detecting a signal presented with one interaural difference in a masker which has a different interaural difference is lower than when the signal and masker have the same interaural difference. This improvement in detection is called the *masking-level difference (MLD)* (Green & Yost, 1975). The MLD occurs when the signal would be lateralized at one location and the masker at a different location. Thus, the spatial separation of the signal and masker aids in signal detection as suggested by Cherry.

The MLD is obtained by first determining the threshold level of the signal in the presence of the masker when both are presented to the same ear. Then the signal and masker are presented to both ears such that the signal has one interaural difference and the masker another interaural difference. When the signal (S) and maskers (N for noise masker) are dichotic (dichotic means presented with an interaural difference) and the interaural differences differ between the masker and signal, the threshold for detecting the signal is lower than when the signal and masker are presented to one ear (NmSm, "m" for monaural) or the same to both ears (NoSo, "o" for no difference between the ears, which is called diotic). The masked threshold for detecting signals is always the same for the NoSo and NmSm conditions. When the signal is a low-frequency tone presented with an interaural phase shift of 180° (a 180° shift is a π phase shift) and the masker is a broad-band noise presented the same to both ears, the MLD for this NoS_π condition is approximately 15 dB. That is, the signal threshold in the NoS_π condition is 15 dB lower than in either the NoSo or NmSm conditions. Masked thresholds for NoS_π conditions are about the largest MLD that can be measured for a wide-band noise masker. Many other interaural configurations and stimulus conditions for the masker and signal have been used to study the MLD. The largest MLDs occur for signals with energy below about 1500 Hz. In general, the greater the spatial separation between the signal and the masker, the greater the MLD.

Several models (Colburn & Durlach, 1978) have been proposed to account for the MLD. One class of models is based on the concept of cross-correlation as described previously for the Jeffress coincidence network (Colburn & Durlach, 1978). These models rely on the interaural time and level differences that exist for the signal and maskers in MLD conditions. For instance, an S_π signal has a large interaural time difference as compared to a No masker (which has no interaural differences), and thus the MLD should be large for the NoS_π condition, which it is. Cross-correlation models provide quantitative predictions of the relationship between the interaural differences and the MLD (Colburn, 1977). Another class of models assumes that the powers of the signal and masker at one ear are subtracted from those occurring at the other ear after the stimuli are equalized in one of several ways (Durlach, 1972). The subtraction (cancellation) is modeled as a noisy process resulting in imperfect cancellation. The resulting signal-to-noise ratio after the equalization-cancellation process is used to determine the MLD. For instance, in the NoS_π condition the noise would be nearly canceled because it is the same at both ears, while the signal would be added because subtraction of signals 180° out of phase with each other is the same as addition. Thus, the output of the equalization-cancellation process produces a large signal-to-noise ratio for the NoS_π condition, predicting the large MLD. Both classes of model do an excellent job of accounting for many MLD data, and under several circumstances the two types of model may be functionally related (Colburn & Durlach, 1978).

Although the MLD and cocktail party effects suggest that spatial separation is a means to segregate sound sources in a complex acoustic world, spatial separation is not necessary and sufficient for sound source segregation. Consider listening to a symphony orchestra recorded with one microphone and played back over a single loudspeaker. One can perceive many of the instruments in the orchestra although no spatial cues are provided. Thus, spatial separation is simply one possible cue for sound source determination.

Spectral and Temporal Separation

Sounds from sources that occur at different times or in different frequency regions can be separated as a basis for sound source determination. However, when the sounds appear in close temporal and spectral proximity, it is less obvious how sound source segregation might be accomplished. Consider a simple case of two tones that alternate in frequency over time. That is, a tone of one frequency (f1) is pulsed on and off along with a tone of a slightly different frequency (f2) such that when f1 is on, f2 is off, and vice versa. Under several stimulus conditions, listeners do not perceive a sequence of pitches going from f1 to f2 and back again, that is, a single sound source whose pitch is alternating. Rather they perceive two sounds as if there were two sound sources, one a source of f1 pulses and one of f2 pulses. It as if there were two perceptual streams of source f1 and source f2 running side by side. This is an example of a study conducted by Bregman (1990). Bregman and his colleagues have studied such stimulus conditions extensively and have called these conditions and the perceptions *auditory streaming or auditory stream segregation.* It is usually argued that a form of perceptual continuity organizes the sound into the two streams because a sound that alternates over time but at the same frequency is likely to be from a single source. The two tones, f1 and f2, are perceived as coming from two different sound sources, causing the perceptual segregation of the two tones into two streams. Many different acoustic variables have been investigated in their ability to support auditory stream segregation. For instance, having sounds alternate between the two ears can be used to investigate spatial separation as a basis for streaming. That is, a sound presented to the left ear simulates a source located on the left and a sound presented to the right ear simulates a sound source on the right. Listeners can be tested as to whether or not alternating sounds between the ears leads to the perception that the sounds at each ear belong to different streams as if they were from different sound sources. Although such a dichotic experiment can produce stream segregation, the effects are much weaker than those produced when different frequencies are used as the basis for forming different streams (Bregman, 1990). Although many variables support stream segregation, spectral manipulations usually produce the strongest effects (Bregman, 1990).

Other percepts that can be interpreted in terms of sound source segregation occur when sounds are presented in close temporal proximity. Consider the condition in which one sound is presented continuously while a second sound is pulsed on and off and added to the continuous sound. For instance, a pulsed tone is added to a continuous noise background. At the appropriate signal-to-noise ratio the pulsed tone is perceived as a low-level continuous tone. The level of the pulsing tone can be adjusted until the listener perceives it to be steady, and the tonal level required for such a threshold is often called a *pulsation threshold* (Houtgast, 1972). Warren and his colleagues (Warren, Obusek, & Ackroff, 1972) have studied these conditions in detail and refer to such continuity effects as *auditory induction*. If two tones are presented, one continuous and one pulsing, and the level of the pulsing tone is varied to find a pulsation threshold, then the pulsation threshold varies as a function of the frequency separation between the two tones much in the same way that masked thresholds differ (see Chapter 12). That is, the closer in frequency the two tones become, the higher the pulsation threshold becomes (the more intense the pulsing tone must be in order for it to be perceived as continuous). Thus, such pulsation threshold contours reflect frequency resolution and are partially determined by aspects of the critical band. Explanations of auditory induction often suggest that the pulsing tone would likely be perceived as coming from a different source than the continuous tone because each tone occupies a different frequency region. At low levels of the pulsing tone, the continuous tone "fills in" the time between the pulsing tone to support sound source segregation.

Intensity/Spectral Profile

In a mixture of several sound sources the louder one sound source becomes, the more likely it is to be perceived as a separate sound source. It is the level of the loud sound relative to that of the background that supports sound source segregation. How might the auditory system judge the relative level differences of complex sounds? Consider the following experiment involving a complex of 11 tones presented simultaneously. For one complex, 10 of the tones have the same level, but the 11th tone, the target tone, (whose frequency is in the spectral middle of the 11 frequencies) is slightly more intense. For the other complex all 11 tones have the same level. Now imagine that a listener is to discriminate between the two complexes to determine which one contains the incremented target tone. On each stimulus presentation the overall level of the complex is randomly varied over a very large range of levels. One strategy for making such a discrimination would be to attend to the frequency of the tone whose level was incremented. However, because the random variation applies to both complexes it would take a very large increment in the target tone for discrimination to occur. That is, on one trial the target complex might have a level of 60 dB and on another trial it might be 50 dB. The 10-dB difference could be due to the random variation in overall level or to the fact that for one of these stimuli the target tone had an increment added to its level. The only way to determine which situation occurred is for the added target level increment to be large compared to the overall range of randomized level changes. About the same level increment in the target tone would be required if the decision strategy were to determine which entire complex was more intense. An increment in one tone of the complex will increase the overall level of that complex. However, because of the random overall level randomization, the target increment would have to be almost as large as the range of the random level change if overall level were the cue for discrimination.

When listeners are asked to make such discriminations between these two types of complexes, they require only a very modest increase in the level of the target tone to discriminate one complex from the other (Green, 1988). Such modest increments suggest that the listener is comparing the level of the target tone to that of the other tones in the complex. The complex with the target tone has a spectral level profile with an increment in it, while the other complex has a flat level profile. If a comparison is made within a complex across frequencies, then it is possible that a small target increment can be detected, because the increment in the target level relative to that of the other tones is the same no matter what the overall level of the complex. Figure 14.4 displays the stimulus conditions and some results from such an *intensity profile* experiment (Green, 1988). For this experiment tones in the complexes were arranged on a log scale so that there was a constant ratio among successive frequencies. The frequency range for the tonal components was the same for all complexes. The tone with the middle frequency was the target tone whose level was incremented above that of the other equal-level tones. An independent variable was the number of tones in the complex. For each condition the level of the target tone was adjusted until the listener was at threshold in being able to discriminate the complex with the incremented target tone from the complex with the flat level profile. The overall level of the complexes was randomly varied over a 40-dB range. The spectral profiles of the various target complexes are depicted along the bottom of Figure 14.4. The data show the relative level of the target tone required for threshold discrimination as a function of the number of tones in the complex. Included in the figure are data for judging an increment of a single tone (the asterisk). As can be seen, performance is best for 11 tones in the complex, and performance is about the same as it was for a single tone. The data are explained by noting that with just a few components the increment of the target tone does not "stand out" from the background of the other tones as well as it does for complexes with more tonal components. That is, for few tonal components, the spectral intensity contrast is difficult to determine due to the large spectral region over which such a contrast must be made. As the number of components increases, the high density of components makes the spectral contrast between the level of the target tone and that of the background easier to discern. With a great many tonal components, they become close enough together in frequency that they begin to interact directly with the target. That is, there is considerable direct masking of the target component by nearby non-target tonal components. So the increase in threshold for the 21- and 43-component complexes is explained by masking (Green, 1988).

Work on profile analysis indicates the ability of the auditory system to make cross-spectral comparisons. This work suggests that listeners place attentional weight on the tonal components near the target (Berg, 1990). The ability to compare levels across a wide frequency range is crucial for sound source determination. That is, in a multisource real-world acoustic environment, the sound from one source will have a spectral profile that is different from that of another source. To segregate the spectral information into the constituent sources, the auditory system must be able to make comparisons across the audio spectrum. Green (Green, 1988) and his colleagues have used profile experiments to describe many conditions that support such cross-spectral level processing.

Watson (Watson, 1976) and his colleagues have used a different type of tonal complex to study auditory processing of complex sounds. This work involves complexes of tones of different frequencies where the tones appear in sequence (rather than simultaneously as in level-profile experiments). Such a tonal complex is a complex waveform where the frequency content of the sound changes over time like that of most complex real-world sound sources, such as speech. In fact the parameters of the tonal patterns are often chosen to mimic aspects of speech waveforms. For instance, the frequency range over which the tone

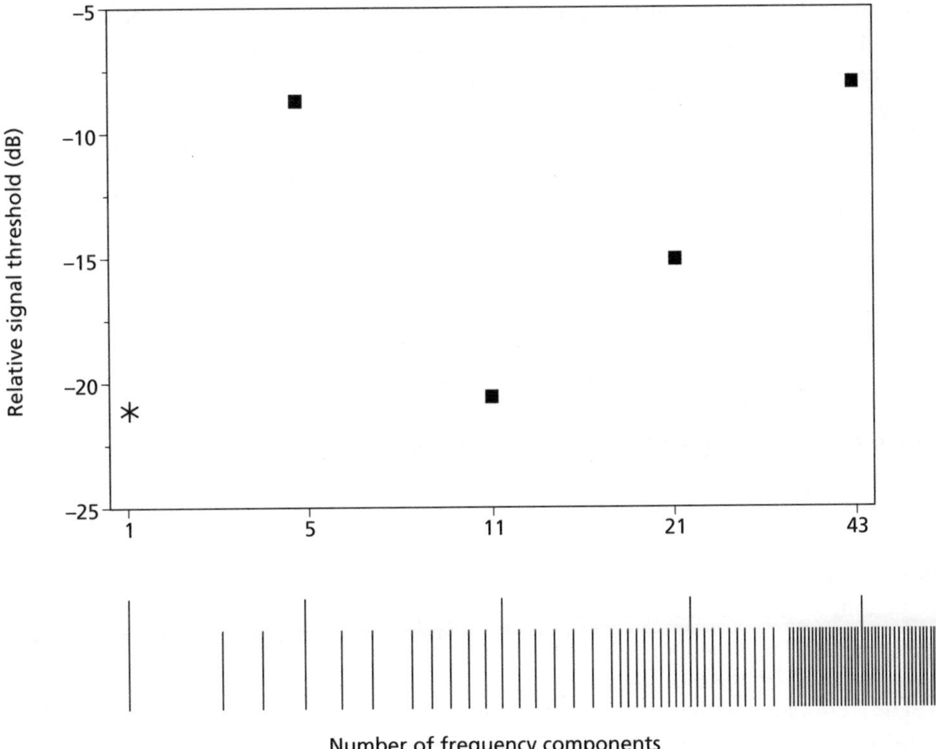

Figure 14.4. A level-profile experiment in which tonal patterns of 1 to 43 tones (spectral schematics are shown along the bottom) are presented and listeners are to decide if one pattern has an increment added to its middle tonal component. The overall level of the patterns is randomly varied over a 40-dB range. The relative level of the increment required for threshold discrimination is plotted as a function of the number of tonal components in the pattern such that best performance is obtained when only one component is present (asterisk) or when 11 tones are in the pattern (adapted from Green, 1988 in Yost, 1994).

is varied covers the bandwidth of speech. The duration of each successive tone in the sequence is often about 40 ms, which is the common duration of a phoneme. Ten such tones in sequence make a 400-ms complex that approximates word-length utterances. The general goal of these tonal-pattern experiments is to determine listeners' acuity for detecting changes in auditory patterns. That is, how much change in a sound source needs to be introduced so that listeners can discriminate one sound from another. In a typical experiment, listeners are presented two tonal patterns that are either the same or one of the patterns has the frequency of one of its tonal components changed. The frequency shift required to just notice the frequency difference is determined as a function of which of the 10 tones had its frequency shifted. That is, is a frequency shift required for discrimination of the first tone in the pattern different from that for a tone that occurs later in the pattern?

Watson and his collaborators (Watson & Kelly, 1981) are often interested in how such discriminations are affected by the fact that real-world sounds vary for moment to moment. Thus, listeners are often asked to make these frequency discriminations when a new 10-tone pattern is randomly presented on each trial. That is, the 10 tones presented on a trial are chosen at random over a specified range of frequencies. For a particular experiment a particular tone in each pattern (say the third tone in the sequence) will have its frequency increased. Thus on a particular trial, 10 tones are sampled at random. Then, this 10-tone pattern is presented during both observation intervals or one of the tones in the pattern (in the example the third tone) will be presented with a different frequency during the second observation interval. The frequency shift required for threshold discrimination in this same-different procedure is measured as a function of the temporal position of the tone whose frequency was varied. When the tonal patterns are randomized from trial to trial in this manner, very large frequency increments are required for threshold and frequency changes for tones at the beginning of the pattern are much more difficult to discriminate than tones toward the end of the pattern. As the variation in the patterns from trial to trial is reduced (e.g., by not sampling a different pattern on each trial but only every 10th trial), performance improves and the differences in threshold from tone to tone are also reduced. When the same 10-tone tonal pattern is presented on every trial, performance is almost as good as that achieved for discriminating a change in the frequency of a single tone presented in isolation of the 10-tone pattern. When there is no trial-to-trial variation in the 10-tone patterns there is very little difference in the discrimination thresholds across the 10 tones.

The additional interference of frequency processing caused by varying the 10-tone patterns from trial to trial is an example of *informational masking* (Neff & Jesteadt, 1996). Informational masking is contrasted with *energy masking*, which is masking caused by the direct interaction among the acoustic stimuli. Informational masking is masking that occurs in addition to energy masking caused by the context in which the stimuli are presented.

Many similar experiments have demonstrated the types of stimulus variables required to notice a change in a complex sound. This work has also documented the fact that variation in complex sounds, especially without a context for the variation, makes it difficult to discern differences in complex sounds. Thus, the details of the complex spectral pattern or profile are crucial for determining how such complexes are perceived and segregated.

Harmonicity

Many sources in the real world vibrate so that the sound consists of a fundamental frequency of vibration and its many higher harmonics. Stimuli with this harmonic structure often have a characteristic pitch (see Chapter 13), which is often at the frequency of the fundamental. This complex pitch can be used as a basis for sound source determination and segregation. That is, a difference in pitch can be used to segregate one sound source from another, or a distinctive pitch can be used to label a particular sound source. For instance, stream segregation can be achieved on the basis of the pitch of one complex stimulus alternating with the different complex pitch of a second complex stimulus (Bregman, 1990).

The pitch of complex tones results from processes that operate on the entire spectrum of the sound. As such these processes are cross-spectral in nature. Studies of complex pitch have provided valuable insights into the types of processes that might mediate cross-spectral processing, which is a crucial element in auditory scene perception. If one tone in a harmonic series of several simultaneously presented tones is mistuned (its frequency is shifted) by 4–8%, the frequency-shifted tone is perceived separately from the harmonic sequence (Hartmann, McAdams, & Smith, 1990; Moore, Peters, & Glasberg, 1985). That is, a sound with the timbre and complex pitch associated with a harmonic series and a pure tone are both perceived as if there were two sound sources. This type of experiment demonstrates the degree to which spectral components must remain in harmonic relationship in order to support the generation of a single complex pitch and the perception of a single sound source.

Common Onsets/Offsets

In most multisource complex acoustic environments, sounds from different sources start and stop at different times. Thus, all of the spectral components of the sound from one source will come on and go off together at a different time than those associated with another sound source. This common onset and offset is often a powerful cue for segregating sound sources. For instance, if two harmonic complexes are played simultaneously, the complex pitches associated with each harmonic complex may not be perceived. That is, the individual tonal components of each harmonic complex may interact when they are combined, making it difficult to sort out the two original complex pitches. However if the onset of one harmonic complex is delayed a couple of hundred milliseconds relative to that of the other complex, the two complex pitches can often be perceived, even though there is considerable temporal overlap of the two sounds (Darwin & Ciocca, 1992). The asynchronous onsets (and often offsets) support the segregation of the pitches of two or more sounds. There are many examples of temporal asynchrony supporting sound source segregation (Yost & Sheft, 1993).

The way in which a sound comes on (its *attack*) or goes off (its *decay*) often provides a distinctive timbre that distinguishes the quality of the sound even more than the steady state portion of the sound. The distinctive timbre of many musical instruments is provided by the spectral characteristics of the attack and decay. The art of musical instrument synthesis is to accurately simulate the characteristics of the attack and decay as well as the instrument's harmonic structure.

Common Patterns of Modulation

The sounds emanating from most sources have a unique temporal change in their amplitude (amplitude modulation) or frequency (frequency modulation). Thus, the spectral components of the sound may change in time in a matter that is unique to that source. For instance, the vocal cords do not open and close in precise rhythm. The periodicity (vibrato) with which they open and close varies, as does the amplitude (jitter). The vibrato and jitter for each speaker is different and hence could be the basis for distinguishing between two talkers uttering the same words at the same time and pitch.

Although it appears that frequency modulation per se is not a basis for sound source segregation (Carylon, 1991; Gardner & Darwin, 1986), amplitude modulation can be. Hall and Grose (1990) have shown that a cross-spectral comparison of sounds with a common pattern of amplitude modulation can help separate a tonal signal from a modulated noise background. Figure 14.5 depicts the stimulus conditions and an example of some typical results (Hall, Haggard, & Fernandes, 1984). A narrow band of noise serves as a masker for a tonal signal centered in the spectral bandwidth of the noise. A narrow-band noise has a pattern of amplitude modulation that varies in rate in proportion to the bandwidth. While the pattern of amplitude modulation is not regular, the average rate at which the overall amplitude fluctuates is faster as the bandwidth of the noise increases. The threshold for

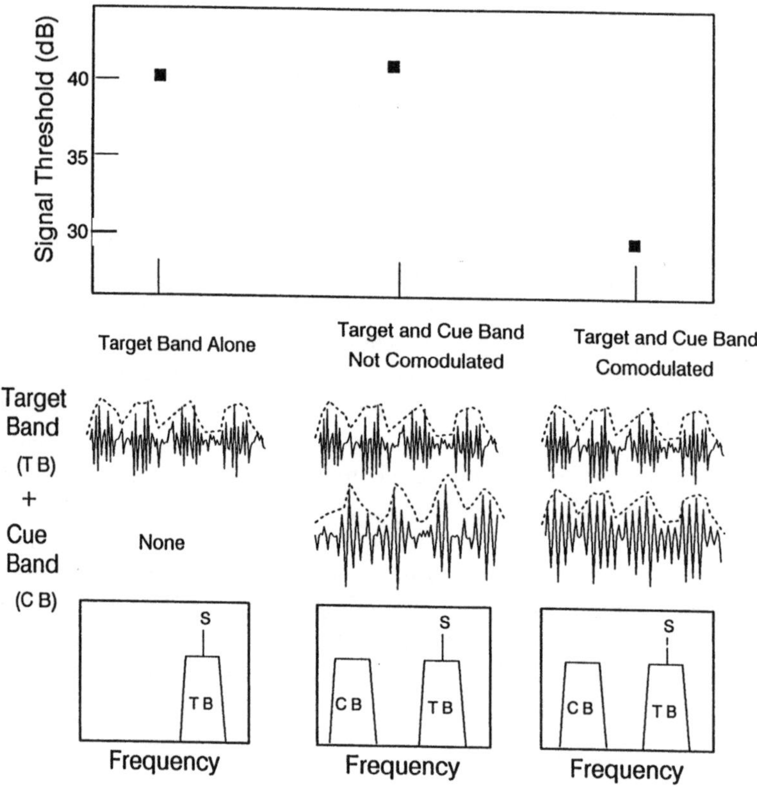

Figure 14.5. Examples of CMR stimuli and data. In the target band condition where thresholds for detecting a tonal signal are high, a narrow band (target) serves as the masker. When a cue band that is spectrally separated from the target band and is comodulated (dotted line on top of waveforms indicates the modulation pattern) with the target, masked thresholds decline. If the cue band is not comodulated, there is little reduction in masked threshold. (Adapted from Hall et al., 1984 in Yost, 1994.)

detecting a tonal signal in the narrow-band noise (the target band) can be lowered if another narrow-band noise, that is spectrally separate from the target band (the cue band), has the same pattern of amplitude modulation as the target band (the target and cues band are comodulated). If the cue band has a different pattern of modulation (is not comodulated), then there is no lowering of the signal threshold. The improvement in signal detection due to the comodulated cue and target bands is called *comodulation masking release (CMR)*. One explanation of CMR is that the comodulated bands form a single sound source, and, as such, it is easier to segregate the tonal signal from this coherent background (Hall & Grose, 1990). When the cue and target band are not comodulated, they each would be perceived as being from different sources, and it is not as easy to segregate the tonal signal from several sound sources. Thus, comodulation supports sound source determination.

Another line of inquiry also indicates how a common pattern of amplitude modulation can affect auditory processing. Yost and his collaborators (Yost & Sheft, 1989) asked listeners to detect a change in the depth of amplitude modulation of a tonal carrier. An example of one of their experiments is shown in Figure 14.6 (Yost, 1992). In the probe-alone condition, listeners are asked to determine which stimulus has a greater depth of amplitude modulation. Listeners require about a 3% change in depth of modulation to perform this discrimination. If a tone (masker tone) of a very different frequency from that of the probe carrier is added simultaneously to the modulated probe tone, then there is very little change in the ability of listeners to discriminate a change in the depth of probe amplitude modulation. Because there is a large spectral difference between the probe and masker stimuli, it is not surprising that a spectrally remote masker provides very little interference. However, if this masker is now amplitude modulated with the same pattern of modulation used for the probe carrier, listeners have difficulty determining a change in the depth of amplitude modulation for the probe. If the masker and probe are each amplitude modulated but with a different modulation pattern, then it is not as difficult to discriminate a change in the depth of amplitude modulation of the probe. The increase in threshold for detecting a change in the depth of probe amplitude modulation when the masker and probe are comodulated is called *modulation detection or discrimination interference (MDI)*. An explanation for MDI is that when the probe and masker are comodulated they form a single sound source; and because modulation was the cue used to perceptually fuse the probe and masker as a single sound source it is difficult to process the modulation of the probe (Yost & Sheft, 1994).

Moore and colleagues (Moore & Alcantara, 1996) have shown that providing a common form of modulation does help in segregating one sound source from another. They asked listeners to identify synthetic vowel sounds mixed together (as described in Figure 14.1). It is easier for listeners to identify an individual target vowel in the mixture of several vowels when the target vowel is amplitude modulated at a slow rate. However, amplitude modulation per se might not have aided the listeners in vowel identification. Listeners could have more easily discerned the other vowels in the mixture during periods when the amplitude of the target vowel was low. That is, the level of the target vowel is modulated and when the level is low, the listener can better detect the other vowels. This example points out a difficulty often encountered when attempts are made to decide which aspect of a complex stimulus supports sound source determination. Many times several aspects of the stimulus covary when a particular cue is used to study sound source determination. It can be difficult to determine which cue is actually being used as a basis for sound source segregation.

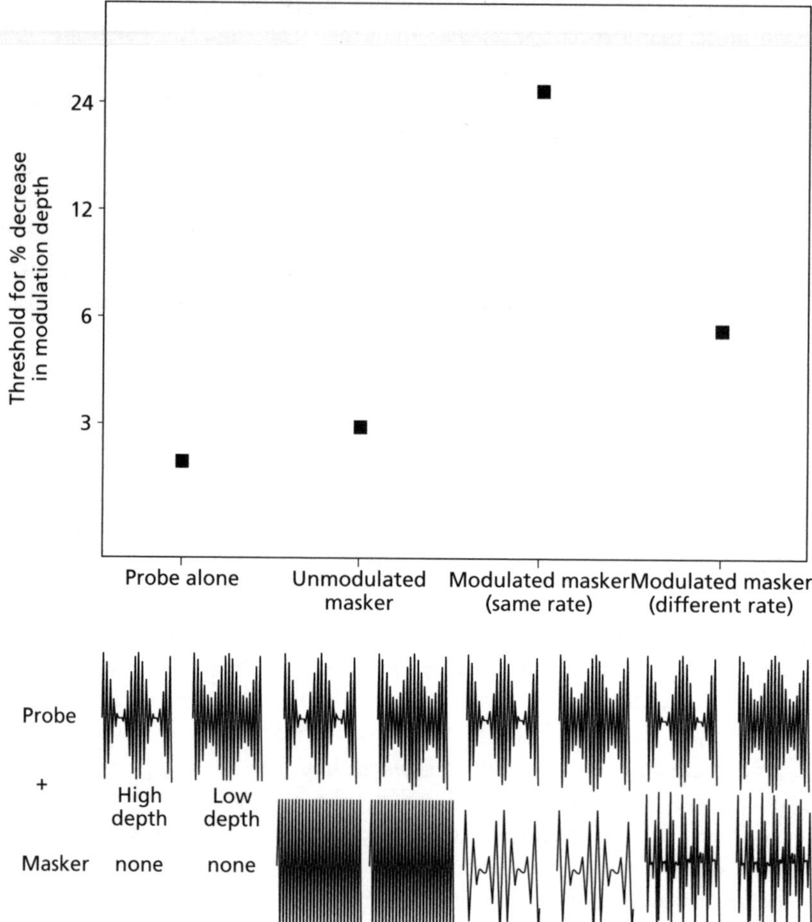

Figure 14.6. Examples of MDI stimuli and data. In the probe-alone condition the thresholds for detecting a change in modulation depth of a tonal carrier are low. When an unmodulated masker carrier of a different frequency is added to the probe, there is little change in modulation depth threshold. When the masker carrier is modulated with the same pattern as the probe carrier, there is a large increase in modulation depth threshold. There is much less change in modulation depth threshold when the masker carrier is modulated but with a different pattern than that used to modulate the probe carrier. (Adapted from Yost, 1992 in Yost, 1994.)

Explanations for Sound Source Determination

Being able to parse the sound from a multisource acoustic environment into its constituent sound sources appears to require an ability to process sound across a wide range of frequencies and over time. Far less is known about auditory analysis across the spectrum and time than about auditory processing in narrow regions of the spectrum and at short moments of time. Studies of the critical band (see Chapter 12) are examples of how the auditory system detects a signal of one frequency from a background of sound containing many frequencies. The critical band suggests that in detecting a tonal signal in a noise background, the auditory system monitors those frequency channels tuned to the frequency of the tonal signal and ignores all other channels. Sound source determination suggests that the auditory system must operate in a wide-band mode to process information from all of the channels, and thus cannot ignore any channel. Profile analysis experiments clearly show that the auditory system can make cross-spectral comparisons with high acuity. Modulation detection interference experiments indicate that there are situations in which the auditory system operates only in a wide-band mode and cannot use a narrow-band or critical band mode. The MDI results showed that there is no interference of processing amplitude modulation of the probe when a nonmodulated masker is presented, presumably because the auditory system can monitor the frequency channel containing the probe and ignore that containing the masker. However, when the masker is modulated the auditory system can no longer ignore the frequency channel containing the masker. The results of MDI experiments suggest that information from both channels is combined such that the system cannot attend to any one channel. Experiments on auditory streaming lead to similar conclusions about processing over time. That is, there are cases in which the auditory system integrates over long sections of time (on the order of seconds) in order to accomplish the task of sound source determination.

There have been two types of attempts to build models or theories of sound source determination. Several investigators (Assmann & Summerfield, 1990; Beauvois & Meddis, 1991; Meddis & Hewitt, 1992) have built computational models to account for aspects of sound source determination, especially auditory stream segregation. The front end to these models is similar to that described in Figure 14.1. Then processes compare the spectral-temporal code across the spectrum and time to arrive at an output that can account for a particular data set. Often such models include some aspect of prior knowledge about the stimulus context to guide the decision process.

Bregman (1990) has proposed a perceptually guided framework, in the spirit of Gestalt principles, to formulate a way to organize aspects of auditory scene analysis. He differentiates between *primitive* operations of integration and segregation and *schema-based* operations. By primitive he means simple, innate, bottom-up processing. Schema-based operations are hypotheses-driven processes that often depend on prior knowledge. Primitive operations like the Gestalt principle of grouping are used to describe the continuity effects that occur for pulsation threshold and auditory induction. He describes a principle of *exclusive allocation* which states that a stimulus attribute cannot be assigned to two sources at the same time. Thus, when all of the spectral components of a sound go off together, it is likely that only one sound source existed. Often the ability to determine the sources of sound in a complex sound field requires practice or some additional information about the stimulus context. Such situations would be schema-based. For instance, in the work of Watson and colleagues using 10-tone patterns, listeners are able to discriminate a change in the frequency of one tone in the pattern, if the tones are repeated over and over for several trials without changing. Thus, the fact that practice improves listeners' acuity would be a schema-based operation. That is, much of information masking may be schema-based.

Although determining the sound sources in our complex world often appears to be an automatic, effortless process, it is not clear the extent to which such processing requires high levels of attention, experience, and cognition. Clearly the ability to label the sound sources we perceive requires aspects of such top-down processing. It is less clear if just the ability to determine that a sound source exists without being able to label it requires such processing. Current research has identified some of the physical cues that may be used for sound source determination. A great deal more research is needed to know how these cues are used.

Basic Data

Table 14.2 Various measures of localization and lateralization accuracy for pure-tone stimuli. Nm = not measurable, none = not measured

	Frequency (Hz)						
Conditions	*250*	*500*	*1000*	*1500*	*2000*	*5000*	*7000*
Lateralization:							
Interaural time-difference thresholds, ITD(microsecs, μs), Yost, 1974 and Yost & Hafter, 1987	45 μs	22 μs	10 μs	70 μs	Nm	Nm	Nm
Interaural level-difference thresholds, ILD (dB), Yost & Dye, 1988 and Yost & Hafter, 1987	0.7 dB	0.6 dB	1.1 dB	0.7 dB	0.4 dB	0.5 dB	none
Localization:							
Minimal audible angle (MAA at 0° azimuth) (degrees), Mills, 1972	1.2°	1°	1.5°	3°	3.2°	1.7°	1.8°
Minimal audible angle (MAA at 60° azimuth) (degrees), Mills, 1972	3.75°	3.5°	3.7°	14°	16°	8°	12°
Localization error (% error), Stevens & Newman, 1936	11%	12%	13%	16%	Nm	15%	13%

Table 14.3 The stimulus configurations for the maskers (N) and signals (S) used in many MLD conditions. The typical size of the MLD (in dB) relative to the NmSm condition is shown. The size of the MLD depends on many stimulus variables. The size of the MLDs shown in this table represents those that might be obtained when the masker is a moderately intense continuous noise and the signal a 500-Hz tone on for 500 ms

Binaural condition	*Description*	*MLD*
NmSm (monotic)	Masker (N) at only one ear (m) Signal (S) at only one ear (m)	Referent
NoSo (diotic)	Masker (N) the same at both ears (o) Signal (S) the same at both ears (o)	0 dB
NπSm	Masker (N) out-of-phase between ears (π) Signal (S) at only one (m)	2 dB
NuSo	Masker (N) uncorrelated between ears (u) Signal (S) the same at both ears (o)	6 dB
NuSπ	Masker (N) uncorrelated between ears (u) Signal (S) out-of-phase between ears (π)	6 dB
NoSm	Masker (N) the same at both ears (o) Signal (S) at only one ear (m)	10 dB
NπSo	Masker (N) out-of-phase between ears (π) Signal (S) the same at both ears (o)	12 dB
NoSπ	Masker (N) the same at both ears (o) Signal (S) out-of-phase between ears (π)	15 dB

Suggested Readings

Sound Localization

Blauert, J. (1997). *Spatial hearing* (3rd ed.). Cambridge, MA: MIT Press.

Gilkey, R. H., & Anderson, T. (1997). *Binaural and spatial hearing in real and virtual environments.* Hillsdale, NJ: Lawrence Erlbaum.

Yost, W. A., & Gourevitch, G. (1987). *Directional hearing.* New York: Springer-Verlag.

Auditory Scene Perception

Bregman, A. S. (1990). *Auditory scene analysis.* Cambridge, MA: MIT Press.

Hartmann, W. (1988). Pitch perception and the organization and integration of auditory entities. In G. W. Edelman, W. E. Gall, & W. M. Cowan (Eds.), *Auditory function: Neurobiological bases of hearing.* New York: John Wiley and Sons.

Yost, W. A., & Sheft, S. (1993). Auditory perception. In W. A. Yost, R. R. Fay, & A. Popper (Eds.), *Psychoacoustics.* New York: Springer-Verlag.

Additional Topics

Monaural Localization

There is evidence that listeners can monaurally localize sound sources, especially in the vertical plane (Butler, 1986, 1997; Butler & Humanski, 1992). That is, binaural processing may not be required to localize sound sources, especially in the vertical direction.

Additional HRTF Studies

Investigation of the HRTF cues used for localization (Wightman & Kistler, 1992) and how one adapts to changes in the spatial information provided by HRTFs can be studied by altering the characteristics of the HRTF filters (Shinn-Cunningham, Durlach, & Held, 1998) or by physically changing the properties of the pinna (Hoffman, Van Riswick, & Van Opstal, 1998).

Auditory Motion Perception

Studies of moving sound sources have been conducted using both real moving sound sources (Perrott & Musicant, 1977) and simulations (Grantham, 1986). Localization by moving people and stationary sound sources has also been investigated (Loomis et al., 1998). These and other experiments involving dynamically changing interaural time or level differences (Grantham, 1986 and Grantham & Wightman, 1978) suggest that the binaural system is "sluggish" in responding to changes in interaural time and level.

Bat and Dolphin Echo Processing

Bats and dolphins emit high-frequency sounds that reflect off objects in their environment (often very small objects such as insects). These mammals use the return echoes to locate insects and other objects. This form of "active" echo-localization has provided valuable insights into the possible neural mechanisms for sound localization (Popper & Fay, 1995; Simmons, 1987).

Dichotic Pitches

When the same noise is presented to both ears, but with an interaural time (phase) difference in a small spectral region, listeners perceive a pitch associated with that spectral region. This dichotic pitch (Huggins Pitch, after Huggins who first demonstrated its existence, Huggins & Cramer, 1958) can only be perceived when the noises are delivered to both ears, and dichotic pitches are an interesting example of sound source segregation based on interaural differences (Culling, Summerfield, & Marshall, 1998).

Source Segregation with Speech and Music

Studying sound source segregation when listeners can label the sounds is often easier than when identification is not possible. As a consequence, musical notes or melodies and speech utterances have been widely used in studies of sound source segregation (Deutsch, 1998). The sounds of different musical instruments playing the same note at the same loudness and with the same duration differ along the dimension of timbre. Different speech phonemes can be characterized as differing in timbre. Thus, the study of timbre and sound source determination often involves studies of speech or music perception (see Yost & Sheft, 1993).

Adaptation and Auditory Enhancement

Several forms of auditory afterimages have been studied as a form of auditory enhancement

(Summerfield & Assmann, 1989; Viemeister & Bacon, 1982; Wilson, 1970; Zwicker, 1964). These enhancement phenomena are often explained in terms of long-term adaptation. Enhancement and long-term adaptation may help in sound source determination.

Modulation Channels

There is both psychoacoustical (Dau, 1997) and physiological (Kim & Chang, 1976; Langner, 1992; Rees & Palmer, 1989; Schreiner & Langer, 1988) evidence that there are channels tuned to modulation period, especially to amplitude modulation period.

References

Assmann, P.F., & Summerfield, Q. (1990). Modeling the perception of concurrent vowels: Vowels with different fundamental frequencies. *Journal of the Acoustical Society of America, 88*, 680–697.

Beauvois, M. W., & Meddis, R. (1991). A computer model of auditory stream segregation. *Quarterly Journal of Experimental Psychology, 43A*, 517–541.

Berg, B. G. (1990). Observer efficiency and weights in a multiple observation task. *Journal of the Acoustical Society of America, 88*, 148–158.

Blauert, J. (1997). *Spatial hearing.* Cambridge, MA: MIT Press.

Bregman, A. S. (1990). *Auditory scene analysis.* Cambridge, MA: MIT Press.

Brugge, J. F., Reale, R. A., & Hind, J.E. (1997). Auditory cortex and spatial hearing. In R. H. Gilkey & T. R. Anderson (Eds.), *Binaural and spatial hearing in real and virtual environments.* Hillsdale, NJ: Lawrence Erlbaum Assoc.

Butler, R. A. (1986). The bandwidth effect on monaural and binaural localization. *Hearing Research, 21*, 67–73.

Butler, R. A. (1997). Spatial referents of stimulus frequencies, their role in sound localization. In R. H. Gilkey & T. R. Anderson (Eds.), *Binaural and spatial hearing in real and virtual environments.* Hillsdale, NJ: Lawrence Erlbaum Assoc.

Butler, R. A., & Humanski, R. A. (1992). Localization of sounds in the vertical plane with and without high-frequency spectral cues. *Perception & Psychophysics, 51*, 182–186.

Casseday, J. H., & Covey, E. (1987). Central auditory pathways in directional hearing. In W. A. Yost & G. Gourevitch (Eds.), *Directional hearing.* New York: Springer-Verlag.

Cherry, E. C. (1953). Some experiments on the recognition of speech, with one and two ears. *Journal of the Acoustical Society of America, 25*, 975–979.

Colburn, H. S. (1977). Theory of binaural interaction based on auditory-nerve data II. Detection of tones in noise. *Journal of the Acoustical Society of America, 61*, 525–533.

Colburn, H. S., & Durlach N. I. (1978). Binaural models. In E. C. Carterette & M. P. Friedman (Eds.), *Handbook of perception: Vol. IV. Hearing.* New York: Academic Press.

Cramer, E. M., & Huggins, W. H. (1958). Creation of pitch through binaural interaction. *Journal of the Acoustical Society of America, 30*, 413–417.

Culling, J. F., Summerfield, Q. A., & Marshall, D. H. (1998). Dichotic pitches as illusions of binaural unmasking I: Huggins Pitch and the "binaural edge pitch." *Journal of the Acoustical Society of America, 103*, 3527–3539.

Darwin, C. J., & Ciocca, V. (1992). Grouping in pitch perception, Effects of onset asynchrony and ear of presentation of a mistuned component. *Journal of the Acoustical Society of America, 91*, 3381–3391.

Dau, T. (1997). Modeling auditory processing of amplitude modulation. II Spectral and temporal interactions. *Journal of the Acoustical Society of America, 102*, 2906–2919.

Deutsch, D. (1998). The tritone paradox: A link between music and speech. *Current Directions in Psychological Science, 6*, 174–180.

Durlach, N. I. (1972). Binaural signal detection, equalization-cancellation theory. In J. V. Tobias (Ed.), *Foundations of modern auditory theory* (Vol. II). New York: Academic Press.

Gardner, M. B. (1969). Distance estimation of 0° or apparent 0°-oriented speech signals in anechoic space. *Journal of the Acoustical Society of America, 45*, 47–53.

Gardner, R. B., & Darwin, C. J. (1986). Grouping vowel harmonics by frequency modulation, Absence of effects on phonemic categorization. *Perception & Psychophysics, 40*, 183–187.

Grantham, D. W. (1986). Detection and discrimination of simulated motion of auditory targets in the horizontal plane. *Journal of the Acoustical Society of America, 79*, 1939–1949.

Grantham, D. W. (1997). Auditory motion perception, snapshot revisited. In R. H. Gilkey & T. R. Anderson (Eds.), *Binaural and spatial hearing in real and virtual environments.* Hillsdale, NJ: Lawrence Erlbaum Assoc.

Grantham, D. W., & Wightman, F. L. (1978). Detectability of varying interaural temporal differences. *Journal of the Acoustical Society of America, 63*, 511–523.

Green, D. M. (1988). *Profile analysis.* New York: Oxford University Press.

Green, D. M., & Yost, W. A. (1975). Binaural analysis. In W. D. Keidel & W. D. Neff (Eds.), *Handbook of sensory physiology* (Vol. V). Berlin/Heidelberg: Springer-Verlag.

Hall, J. W., & Grose, J. H. (1990). Comodulation masking release and auditory grouping. *Journal of the Acoustical Society of America, 88*, 119-125.

Hall III, J. W., Haggard, M., & Fernandes, M. A. (1984). Detection in noise by spectro-temporal pattern analysis. *Journal of the Acoustical Society of America, 76* (1), 50–61.

Hartmann, W. M., McAdams, S., & Smith, B. K. (1990). Hearing a mistuned harmonic in an otherwise periodic complex tone. *Journal of the Acoustical Society of America, 88*, 1712–1724.

Henning, G. B. (1974). Detectability of interaural delay in high-frequency complex waveforms. *Journal of the Acoustical Society of America, 55*, 84–90.

Hoffman, P. M., Van Riswick, J. G. A., & Van Opstal, A. J. (1998). Relearning sound localization with new ears. *Nature Neuroscience, 1*, 417–421.

Houtgast, T. (1972). Psychophysical evidence for lateral inhibition in hearing. *Journal of the Acoustical Society of America, 51*, 1885.

Jeffress, L. A. (1948). A place mechanism of sound localization. *Journal of Comparative Physiology and Psychology, 41*, 35–39.

Kim, D. O., & Chang, S. O. (1990). Responses of DCN-PVCN neurons and auditory nerve fibers in unanesthetized decerebrate cats to AM and pure tones. Analysis with autocorrelation/power spectrum. *Hearing Research, 45*, 95–113.

Knudsen, E. I., & Konishi, M. (1978). A neural map of auditory space in the owl. *Science, 200*, 795-797.

Kuwada, S., & Yin, T. C. T (1983). Physiological studies of directional hearing. In W. A. Yost & G. Gourevitch (Eds.), *Directional hearing.* New York: Springer-Verlag.

Langner, B. (1992). Periodicity coding in the auditory nervous system. *Hearing Research, 60*, 115–142.

Litovsky, R., Colburn, S., Yost, W. A., & Guzman, S. (forthcoming). The precedence effect: A review. *Journal of the Acoustical Society of America*, in press.

Loomis, J. A., Klatzky, R. L., Philbeck, J. W., & Golledge, R. G. (1998). Assessing auditory distance using perceptually directed action. *Perception & Psychophysics, 60*, 966–980.

Makous, J. C., & Middlebrooks J. C. (1990). Two-dimensional sound localization by human observers. *Journal of the Acoustical Society of America, 87*, 2188–2200.

Meddis, R., & Hewitt, M. J. (1992). Modeling the identification of concurrent vowels with different fundamental frequencies. *Journal of the Acoustical Society of America, 91*, 233–245.

Mershon, D. H. (1997). Phenomenal geometry and the measurement of perceived auditory distance. In R. H. Gilkey & T. R. Anderson (Eds.), *Binaural and spatial hearing in real and virtual environments.* Hillsdale, NJ: Lawrence Erlbaum Assoc.

Middlebrooks, J. C. (1992). Narrow-band sound localization related to external ear acoustics. *Journal of the Acoustical Society of America, 92*, 2607–2624.

Mills, A. W. (1972). Auditory localization. In J. V. Tobias (Ed.), *Foundations of modern auditory theory* (Vol. 2). New York: Academic Press.

Moore, B. C. J., & Alcantara, J. I. (1996). Vowel identification based on amplitude modulation.

Journal of the Acoustical Society of America, 99, 2332–2343.

Moore, B. C. J., Peters, R. W., & Glasberg, B. R. (1985). Thresholds for the detection of inharmonicity in complex tones. *Journal of the Acoustical Society of America, 77*, 1861–1867.

Neff, D. L., & Jeasteadt, W. (1996). Intensity discrimination in the presence of random-frequency, multicomponent maskers and broadband noise. *Journal of the Acoustical Society of America, 100*, 2289–2298.

Patterson, R. D., Allerhand, M., & Giguere, C. (1995). Time-domain modeling of peripheral auditory processing. A modular architecture and a software platform. *Journal of the Acoustical Society of America, 98*, 1890–1895.

Perrott, D. R., & Musicant, A. D. (1977). Minimum auditory moment angle. Binaural localization of moving sound sources. *Journal of the Acoustical Society of America, 62*, 1463–1466.

Popper, A. N., & Fay, R. R (1995). *Hearing in bats*. New York: Springer-Verlag.

Rayleigh, Lord (1907). On our perception of sound direction. *Philosophical Magazine, 13*, 214–232.

Rees, A., & Palmer, A .R. (1989). Neuronal responses to amplitude-modulated and pure-tone stimuli in the guinea pig inferior colliculus, and their modification by broadband noise. *Journal of the Acoustical Society of America, 85*,1978–1994.

Schreiner, C. E., & Langer, G. (1988). Periodicity coding in the inferior colliculus of the cat. II. Topographical organization. *Journal of Neurophysiology, 60*,1823–1840.

Shinn-Cunningham, B. L., Durlach, N. I., & Held, R. M. (1998). Adapting to supernormal auditory localization cues I: Bias and resolution. *Journal of the Acoustical Society of America, 103*, 3656–3666.

Simmons, J. A. (1987). Directional hearing and sound localization in echolocating animals. In W. A. Yost & G. Gourevitch (Eds.), *Directional hearing*. New York: Springer-Verlag.

Stern, R. M., & Trahiotis, T. (1997). Models of binaural perception. In R. H. Gilkey & T. R. Anderson (Eds.), *Binaural and spatial hearing in real and virtual environments*. Hillsdale, NJ: Lawrence Erlbaum Assoc.

Stevens, S. S., & Newman, E. B. (1936). The localization of actual sound sources. *American Journal of Psychology, 48*, 297–306.

Summerfield, Q., & Assmann, P. F. (1989). Auditory enhancement and the perception of concurrent vowels. *Perception & Psychophysics, 45*, 529–536.

Viemeister, N. F., & Bacon, S. P. (1982). Forward masking by enhanced components in harmonic complexes. *Journal of the Acoustical Society of America, 71*, 1502–1507.

Warren, R. M., Obusek, C. J., & Ackroff, J. M. (1972). Auditory induction. Perceptual synthesis of absent sounds. *Science, 176*, 1149–1151.

Watson, C. S. (1976). Auditory pattern discrimination. In S. K. Hirsh, D. H. Eldredge, I. J. Hirsh, & S. Silverman (Eds.), *Hearing and Davis*. St. Louis: Washington University Press.

Watson, C. S., & Kelly, W. J. (1981). The role of stimulus uncertainty in the discrimination of auditory patterns. In D. J. Getty & J. Howard (Eds,), *Auditory and visual pattern recognition*. New York: Lawrence Erlbaum Press.

Wenzel, E. M. (1995). The relative contribution of interaural time and magnitude cues to dynamic sound localization. *Proceedings of IEEE Workshop on Applications of Signal Processing to Audio and Acoustics*, New Paltz, NY.

Wightman, F. L., & Kistler, D. J. (1989a). Headphone simulation of free-field listening, I. Stimulus synthesis. *Journal of the Acoustical Society of America, 85*, 858–867.

Wightman, F. L., & Kistler, D. J. (1989b). Headphone simulation of free-field listening, II. Psychophysical validation. *Journal of the Acoustical Society of America, 85*, 868–878.

Wightman, F. L., & Kistler, D. J. (1992). The dominant role of low-frequency interaural time differences in sound localization. *Journal of the Acoustical Society of America, 91*, 1648–1661.

Wightman, F. L., & Kistler, D. J. (1993). Localization. In W. A. Yost, R. R. Fay, & A. N. Popper (Eds.), *Human psychoacoustics*. New York: Springer-Verlag.

Wightman, F. L., & Kistler, D. (1997). Factors affecting the relative saliance of sound localization cues. In R. H. Gilkey & T. R. Anderson (Eds.), *Binaural and spatial hearing in real and virtual environments.* Hillsdale, NJ: Lawrence Erlbaum Assoc.

Wilson, J. P. (1970). An auditory afterimage. In R. Plomp & G. Smoorenburg (Eds.), *Frequency analysis and periodicity detection in hearing.* Leiden, Netherlands: AW Sijthoff.

Yost, W. A. (1974). Discrimination of interaural phase-differences. *Journal of the Acoustical Society of America, 55,* 1294–1304.

Yost, W. A. (1981). Lateral position of sinusoids presented with interaural intensive and temporal differences. *Journal of the Acoustical Society of America, 70,* 397–409.

Yost, W. A. (1991). Auditory image perception and analysis. The basis for hearing. *Hearing Research, 56,* 8–18.

Yost, W. A. (1992). Auditory perception and sound source determination. *Current Directions in Psychological Science, 1,* 12–15.

Yost, W. A. (1994). *Fundamentals of hearing. An introduction* (3rd ed.). San Diego, CA: Academic Press.

Yost, W. A. (1997). The cocktail party effect, 40 years later. In R. H. Gilkey & T. R. Anderson (Eds.), *Binaural and spatial hearing in real and virtual environments.* Hillsdale, NJ: Lawrence Erlbaum Assoc.

Yost, W. A., & Dye, R. H. (1988). Discrimination of interaural differences of level as a function of frequency. *Journal of the Acoustical Society of America, 83,* 1846–1851.

Yost, W. A., & Gourevitch G. (Eds.) (1987). *Directional hearing.* New York: Springer-Verlag.

Yost, W. A., & Hafter, E. (1987). Lateralization of simple stimuli. In W. A. Yost & G. Gourevitch (Eds.), *Directional hearing.* New York: Springer-Verlag.

Yost, W. A., & Sheft, S. (1989). Across-critical-band processing of amplitude-modulated tones. *Journal of the Acoustical Society of America, 85,* 848–857.

Yost, W. A., & Sheft, S. (1993). Auditory perception. In W. A. Yost, R. R. Fay, & A. N. Popper (Eds.), *Human psychoacoustics.* New York: Springer-Verlag.

Yost, W. A., & Sheft, S. (1994). Modulation detection interference, across-spectral processing and sound source determination. *Hearing Research, 79* (1/2), 48–59.

Young, E. D., Rice, J. J., & Tong, S. C. (1996). Effects of pinna position on the head related transfer function in cats. *Journal of the Acoustical Society of America, 99,* 3064–3076.

Zwicker, E. (1964). Negative after images in hearing. *Journal of the Acoustical Society of America, 36,* 2413–2415.

Chapter Fifteen

Perception of Music

W. Jay Dowling

Music consists of sound organized in time, intended for, or perceived as, aesthetic experience (Rodriguez, 1995). The perceptual dimensions of musical sound include pitch, loudness, duration, and timbre or tone color. When we study the perception of music we study the listener's processing of those perceptual attributes in the global context of musical structure. This investigation can start with the perception of isolated sounds (as, for example, in determining the threshold of hearing), but what is important is how meaningful patterns of sound are perceived in a musical context. The perception of music involves auditory mechanisms and general cognitive constraints that characterize people the world over, shaped by cultural patterns which, through perceptual learning, govern expectancies and experience for individuals in various cultures.

When we begin to think about the perception of music we realize immediately that we are dealing with perception in a culturally defined domain. The case is parallel to that of speech perception. All the human cultures in the world have both language and music, and in both domains there is not only considerable variation from culture to culture, but also definite constraints on that variation imposed by the capacities of the human auditory system and of human information processing. With music, as with speech and language, we have neither a biological determinism casting all the musics of the world into a common mold or "universal language," nor a total cultural relativism with an unlimited range of possibilities. What we have is a cultural pluralism of the kind outlined by Isaiah Berlin (1998; Hampshire, 1989) in which there are many ways of structuring a cultural domain, all constrained by human information processing capacities. Music perception is the study of those constraints and of how music is perceived and understood in various cultures. Because most students of music perception have come from a European musical tradition, most of what we know at present concerns that tradition. However, future research will deal more and more with non-European cultures and with twentieth-century developments in the European tradition.

A major theme growing out of this concern with the cultural framework of music perception is that we find individual differences in the perception of the very same stimulus, based upon listeners' differing experiences. What listeners hear is shaped by their expectancies, in turn shaped by the lifelong experience of the individual.

Human Information Processing and Music

The broadest set of constraints on music perception are imposed by the limitations of psychophysics: a range of hearing roughly between 20 and 20,000 Hz, and 10 and 120 dB SPL. To these limits we can add that of temporal resolution. We are able to resolve separate events in sequences presented at rates of up to 10–12 per second, and we have difficulty linking events into a coherent pattern when they proceed much slower than one every 2 seconds (Warren, 1993). Thus we have a window in frequency, intensity, and time in which musical events occur. Those events are extended in time (and space) with properties of pitch, loudness, and timbre. The domain of timbre or tone color – what makes "ah" different from "eeh," "mah" different from "tah," and a trumpet different from a flute (playing the same pitch) – is much less constrained than those of loudness and pitch. Computer synthesis of sounds expands that domain in ways previously unimagined, for example, by making possible the creation of novel timbre contrasts tailored to the perceptions of a particular composer or listener (Wessel, 1979).

Adaptive pressures on our auditory system worked to create a system designed to understand a nonmusical natural world, and many of the constraints built into it concern what Bregman (1990, 1993) has called "auditory scene analysis" (see Chapter 14, this volume). Music presents us with a particularly interesting family of auditory scenes. The first part of this chapter concentrates on the perception of musical pitch, and later considers time and rhythm.

Pitch

Beyond the basic psychophysical constraints on pitch mentioned above, several constraints are imposed by more complex aspects of the auditory system, as well as by limitations of human cognition (Dowling & Harwood, 1986). The first of these is that the various musics of the world use discrete levels of pitch (see Table 15.1). Songs in virtually all cultures, as well as the spontaneous songs of children, make use of vowel sounds sustained on steady, discrete pitches. Helmholtz (1877/1954) thought that this was to provide the cognitive system with anchor points to measure melodic motion, and he may have been right. Second, the discrete pitch levels used in music should be discriminable from each other. This constraint is easy to meet, because in the midrange of musical pitches (100–2000 Hz) the size of the just noticeable difference (JND) is very small compared with the smallest micro-intervals in the world's music.

A third constraint is that tones an octave apart are treated as functionally equivalent. For

Table 15.1 Constraints on the structure of musical pitch arising from the human auditory system and cognitive processing

Constraint	*Definition*	*Example or comment*
Discrete pitch levels	Pitches in music are sustained for long durations relative to the transitions between them	Children in their first spontaneous songs hold vowels steady on pitches, unlike in speech
Discriminable pitch levels	Pitches should not be easily confused when they occur in succession	Even the micro-tonal intervals in various cultures are well above JND
Octave equivalence	Tones an octave apart share musical function and belong to the same pitch class	Even nonmusicians are precise in tuning successive notes to an octave
5 to 7 tones per octave	Musical scales out of which melodies are made have 5 to 7 pitch classes	This agrees with what we expect from the limitation on humans' ability to use categories with consistency

example, the tonic pitch "do" is a resting point where a melody can begin or end, and this is true no matter what octave the "do" falls in. Similarly, the pitch above the tonic, "re," is less stable, in the sense that it would sound odd to end a melody on re. (Try singing *Twinkle, Twinkle*, and stop on the next-to-last note.) In virtually all cultures men and women sing together at octave intervals. In cultures that name pitches (like do, re, mi, etc.), pitches an octave apart have similar names. And because the second harmonic of a complex tone coincides with the frequency of a tone an octave higher, the two are acoustically consonant with each other (Plomp & Levelt, 1965). Fourth, there is a limit to the number of pitches within the octave: five to seven in most cultures. The same pattern of pitches recurs in each octave, and the set of functionally equivalent pitches at octave intervals from each other is called a "pitch class"; for example, all the Cs on the piano. The seven pitch classes in the European major scale are labeled do, re, mi, fa, sol, la, si. The quality of do-ness, re-ness, etc., shared by members of a pitch class is called "chroma." The major scale is called "diatonic" because it contains two sizes of pitch intervals. The small intervals are 1 semitone and occur between mi and fa, and si and do. All the other intervals are 2 semitones. A semitone represents a frequency ratio of 1.05946/1 – the twelfth root of 2. There are 12 semitones in an octave. If we go up in pitch by 12 semitones, multiplying the frequency by 1.05946 for each semitone, we will arrive at a frequency twice the one we started with: one octave higher. A scale with seven pitch classes is about what we would expect in terms of limitations on the number of categories humans can use consistently (Miller, 1956). The scale serves as a cognitive schema or framework in terms of which the pitches of music are perceived.

In any brief section of a tonal piece of music seven pitch classes are usually in play. In European music, however, even simple songs include contrasts of key introduced by modulation – shifting the tonal center – to a new key (for example, Schubert's song in Figure 15.1e). Lerdahl (1988b) provides a theoretical framework characterizing the relationships among pitch classes in different keys: neighboring keys that overlap with the original key, and more distant keys that share fewer pitches with the starting key.

We could ask whether music could make extensive use of more than seven pitch classes, and of course it can, as in Schönberg's 12-tone system of serial composition where all 12 semitones in the octave occur equally often. This is accomplished by organizing the 12 pitches into a "row" – a carefully structured permutation of the 12 pitches. A row is like a signature "theme." It is transformed into variants by transposition to other pitch levels, inversion (reversing ups and downs of pitch reversed), retrograde (backwards), and retrograde inversion (upside-down-backwards). Putting more pitch categories in play inevitably increases cognitive complexity. This complexity sometimes causes difficulties even for expert musicians in recognizing structural patterns in 12-tone music (Francès, 1958/1988, Experiment 6). However, Krumhansl, Sandell, and Sergeant (1987) found that listeners (largely familiar with serial works) performed well above chance in such tasks as identifying the transformations of a 12-tone row in a musical context. One task was to rate how good a continuation of the start of a row a test tone would be. Because one of the rules for constructing a row is to avoid repeating pitches, the "right answer" is to give high ratings to pitches that have not yet occurred. Krumhansl et al.'s listeners were able to do that both with simplified materials and in a complex musical context.

Certain 12-tone pieces succeed in engaging and even thrilling relatively naive listeners. We might suppose that it is through dimensions other than the serial organization of

Figure 15.1. Melodies serving as examples of tonal relationships. The brackets indicate the critical notes or intervals. (a) *Greensleeves*. (b) *Over There*. (c) *There's a Place for Us*. (d) *Bali Hai*. (e) *The Trout*. (f) *Three Blind Mice*. (g) A melody shifted from the tonic to the dominant without altering its intervals.

pitches that the listener understands the music (cf. Lerdahl, 1988a). For example, Clarke and Krumhansl (1990) found that listeners parsed a serial piece (Stockhausen's *Klavierstück IX*) into sections using cues similar to those they used with Mozart's *Fantasie in C Minor*. Twentieth-century 12-tone composers often used dimensions of musical organization other than pitch in relatively traditional ways, making contrasts of tone color, pitch height, tempo, rhythm, and loudness. Certain of their masterpieces are immediately accessible in this way: Schönberg's *Pierrot Lunaire* and *Five Pieces for Orchestra*; Berg's *Violin Concerto* and *Wozzeck*, for example. And such pieces grow in accessibility as warmed-over usages of their techniques filter into popular movie and television scores, as Brown (1981) has noted.

It is difficult to foresee the effect of raising a child with only 12-tone music, but we should note that even children raised with the traditional tonality system hear the simplest materials as infants. Nursery tunes stay within a single key. Adult folk tunes generally use seven or fewer pitch classes. Slightly more complex, Schubert's songs typically move between two related keys, thereby using eight pitch classes (Dowling & Harwood, 1986).

These are the main constraints on pitch, though others sometimes operate (Balzano, 1980; Dowling & Harwood, 1986). In several theoretically sophisticated cultures (Chinese, Indian, European) the pitch system is rationalized in terms of a basic, modular interval (such as the semitone) out of which all the other intervals are constructed. Further, there is the property of "coherence" of scale-step sizes in scales (like the diatonic) with different sized intervals. Coherence requires that no interval of one scale step be larger than any interval of two scale steps, no two-step interval larger than any three-step interval, etc. Finally, the variety of available intervals might be maximized. For example, a "whole-tone scale" is made of six pitch classes using two-semitone intervals (C, D, E, F#, G#, A#). Then the only possible larger intervals (C-E, C-F#, D-F#, etc.) have even numbers of semitones; there would be no minor third (3 semitones) or perfect fifth (7 semitones). That reduces variety. The diatonic major scale, in contrast, contains intervals of odd numbers of semitones as well as even, though the even are more prevalent.

Some theorists (including Schönberg, 1978) have claimed that the integer ratios of the harmonic series (present in vowels and musical tones) provide a guiding principle for the auditory system. It is true that the 2/1 frequency ratio of the octave, and less so the 3/2 ratio of the fifth, influence the structure of pitch relations in music in many cultures. And small integer ratios are important in determining the consonance of simultaneous complex tones (but not sine waves – Plomp & Levelt, 1965). However, there is no reason to suppose that European scales (or those of any other culture) are built out of ratios beyond 2/1, 3/2, and perhaps 5/4 and 4/3. We could build a C major scale out of 4/5/6 ratios of the three principal three-note chords ("triads") in the key: C-E-G, G-B-D, and F-A-C. (This is called "just" intonation.) Note that that scheme accounts for all seven pitch classes. But the next more complicated ratio, 7/1, is not represented anywhere in that set of pitches. The ratio 7/1 in fact lands in the crack between two semitones, about 9.3 semitones above the starting point (between A and B♭, reckoning from C). Thus if integer ratios are important, it is only the very simplest ones that play a role in scale construction. (For further discussion of the relationship between integer ratios and scales, see Burns, 1999; Carterette & Kendall, 1999; Dowling & Harwood, 1986; and Shepard, 1999.)

Time

In addition to the constraints on pitch, there are constraints on the organization of time. Virtually all the music of the world relies on some system of regular divisions of time, or beats. (These beats may or may not be organized into higher-order units such as the measures of European music.) In addition to the beats there is an additional level of temporal organization involving more complex rhythmic patterns that are overlaid on the beats. For example, at the start of the song *Some Enchanted Evening* the syllables "some," "chant," "eve," and "ning" occur on beats, while the timings of "en" and "ed" are placed in accordance with some more complicated rhythmic scheme. This division of time into a beat structure and more complex rhythmic overlays is present in the spontaneous songs of 2- and 3-year-olds (Dowling, 1999).

Musical Pitch

The example of pitch perception illustrates how the study of music perception complements and extends what we know from psychophysics. The problems addressed by psychophysics are detection, discrimination, and scaling. Music is limited by the range of detectable frequencies. In terms of discrimination, psychophysics assures us that the pitch intervals in music, even micro-intervals, are well above discrimination thresholds. Psychophysics should also provide a scale of pitch, assigning subjective pitch relationships to relationships among frequencies.

The Psychophysical Scale

Stevens, Volkmann, and Newmann (1937) proposed a "mel" scale for pitch based on listeners' judgments of "twice as high" and "half as high," etc. However, as Ward (1954) points out, the variability of those judgments is enormous compared with the precision of even musically untrained listeners' judgments of the octave. Ward had listeners adjust two alternating notes to an octave interval. Listeners were very precise. Ward proposes the octave as the foundation of a psychophysical scale for pitch. The correspondence of the subjective octave and the 2/1 frequency ratio means that the psychophysical function should be essentially logarithmic; that is, for every increase of one subjective octave there should be an approximate doubling of frequency. (I say "approximate" because Ward's data show that listeners adjust a subjective octave to a ratio slightly greater than 2/1, growing even larger in the upper register; for a discussion, see Dowling, 1978, and Carterette & Kendall, 1999).

One implication of the logarithmic pitch scale is that melodies should retain their shapes when moved along it, as long as the ratios among the frequencies are preserved. Attneave and Olson (1971) demonstrated this using the NBC chime pattern. They ascertained that the chimes had always been played over the air at exactly the same pitch level (G–E–C in the midrange). Listeners would never have heard instances of a transposed pattern (except perhaps in the ephemeral Gillette commercial jingle "Look Sharp, Be Sharp"). Listeners recreated the pattern at different pitch levels using adjustable oscillators, and even untrained listeners produced precise logarithmic transpositions. Melodic patterns remain invariant across transpositions of pitch.

Shepard (1982) suggests that a psychophysical scale of pitch should capture this invariance. This leads him to a pitch scale that is helical in shape, because the screw-like motion of translation along a helix preserves patterns represented along it. The helical pattern furthermore captures multidimensional aspects of pitch implied by octave equivalence by separating the dimensions of "tone height" and "chroma." Tone height is the property of pitch represented on the logarithmic scale described above, measuring the distance in octaves between two pitches, and corresponds to distance along the piano keyboard. Chroma refers to the quality shared by pitches exactly an octave apart; for example, the quality shared by all the members of a pitch class – all the Cs on the piano, or all the D#s. Figure 15.2a shows Shepard's helical scale for pitch. The vertical dimension represents tone height. Going around the helix pitch rises, passing through a succession of chromas. The vertical lines in the figure connect members of a pitch class.

One of Shepard's most compelling demonstrations of the appropriateness of the helical representation of pitch is his auditory barber pole. Shepard (1964) presented the listener with a pattern of tones arranged at octave intervals (solid lines in Figure 15.2b). The upper and lower components are attenuated in intensity and shade off into inaudibility at the extremes. Then all the tones shift upward by the same logarithmic interval – say a whole step of 2 semitones from C to D (an increase of 12.25% – dashed lines). The pitch rises. Then we continue: D to E, E to F#, F# to G#, G# to A# (= B♭), B♭ to C – all 1.1225 ratios – with tones fading in at the bottom while they disappear at the top. We end with the very same stimulus we started with, after six steps upward! (Note that the sixth power of 1.1225 is 2.) We could continue this upward motion perpetually, just as with a barber pole. The perception is of a continually rising pitch in terms of chromas, even though in terms of tone height it isn't going anywhere at all. This is the auditory analog of Escher's endless staircase in which the soldiers march around and around, stepping up with each step, and never get any higher.

This demonstration shows that subjective pitch has at least two aspects: chroma and tone height. You can create a similar demonstration of the independence of chroma and tone height by playing the four highest Cs on a piano; then drop almost an octave and play four Ds; then drop again to four Es, etc. – you will have chroma rising while tone height descends. (Be careful, this may cause vertigo.) Similarly, you can demonstrate the importance of tone height in the absence of chroma by striking five or six adjacent notes at the bottom of the piano keyboard, and then in the middle, and then at the top end. Tone height changes even though there is no clear chroma, or pitch class.

Shepard's helical psychophysical function captures succinctly the relationships of chroma, tone height, and frequency. Figure 15.3 shows the helical psychophysical function in relation to culturally determined levels of analysis of musical pitch, outlined in Table 15.2.

(a)

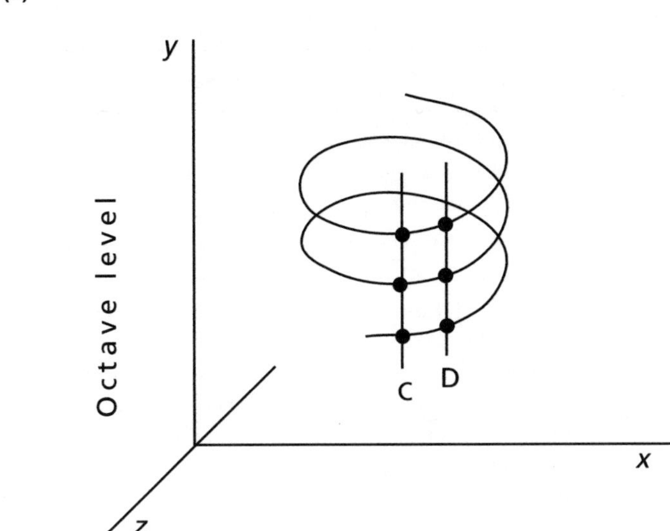

(b)

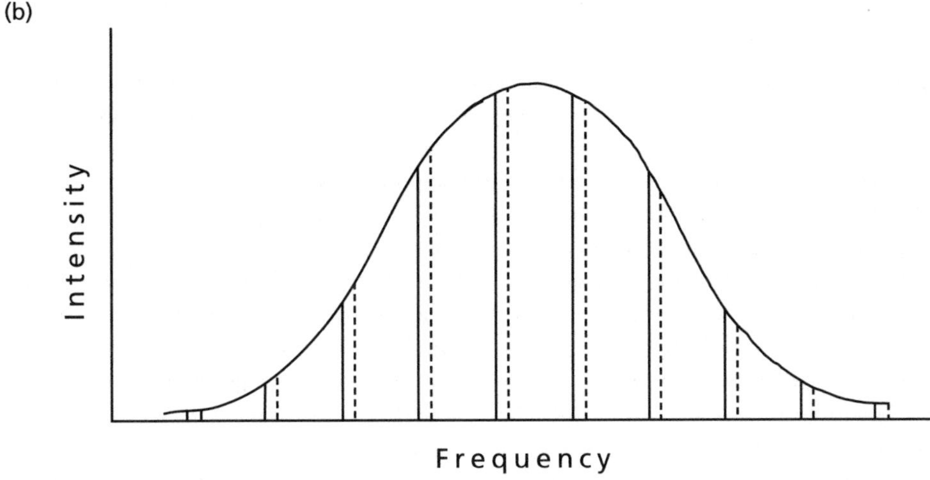

Figure 15.2. (a) Shepard's helical representation of pitch. The helix cycles through several octaves. Tone height is represented on the vertical axis, and chroma or pitch class around the helix. Note that all the members of the same pitch class fall on a vertical line. (b) Shepard's tones having tone chroma or the quality of a pitch class. Intensities are governed by a bell-shaped curve, and components are 1 octave apart. When the pitch is raised by a step, the initial components (solid lines) all move up to those represented by dashed lines. New components are phased in at the bottom of the spectrum as old components are phased out at the top. (From Dowling & Harwood, 2000; with permission.)

Table 15.2 Levels of analysis of pitch material used in music

Level	*Definition*	*Example*
Psychophysical scale	Function describing how the auditory system assigns perceived pitches to frequencies	This is an undifferentiated continuum, as in a fire siren
Tonal material	Set of pitches that potentially could be used in a culture	In European music, the chromatic scale of all the notes on the piano
Tuning system	Set of pitches forming the basis of a set of modal scales	All the white notes on the piano
Modal scale	Set of pitches that could be used in a melody, including their patterns of hierarchical relationships	A scale in a particular mode (e.g., major) and anchored to a particular key (e.g., C major)

Levels of Analysis

The continuous psychophysical scale represented at the top of Figure 15.3 is inherent in the auditory system, and perhaps shaped by early experience with harmonic complex tones. The patterns depicted on the other levels in Figure 15.3 arise out of the culture. I believe that the three levels of cultural differentiation described below operate for all cultures that are sufficiently advanced technologically to have elaborate accounts of musical practice (especially tuning) – certainly the Chinese, Japanese, Indonesian, Indian, Persian, European, and numerous African cultures (Dowling & Harwood, 1986). These levels progressively divide the infinity of pitches available in the continuum of the psychophysical scale into sets of categories used in the music of a culture. The set of pitches in the "tonal material" represents all the possible pitches for music. The "tuning system" selects those pitches that can be used in a set of related scales. And the "modal scale" selects those pitches (and their relationships) that can be used in a piece (or section of a piece). If a level is lacking in a culture, it is usually tonal material. It is sometimes difficult to establish that there are more pitches available in a culture than those present in a particular piece of music. Evidence pertaining to the psychological reality of these levels of abstraction will be presented below. (See also Dowling & Harwood, 1986, and Carterette & Kendall, 1999.)

As we move to the second level in Figure 15.3, the first cultural constraint on the psychophysical function is to select, out of the infinity of pitches, a set of pitches for music. This set is called the tonal material. In European music the tonal material consists of the set of semitone intervals represented on the piano keyboard. Chinese and Indian music use much the same set of 12 semitones, to which Indian music adds micro-intervals used for melodic ornamentation. Other cultures divide the pitch continuum in other ways. In Indonesia, for example, the tonal material is only generally specified by the culture, precise specification being left to the tuning of a particular set of instruments.

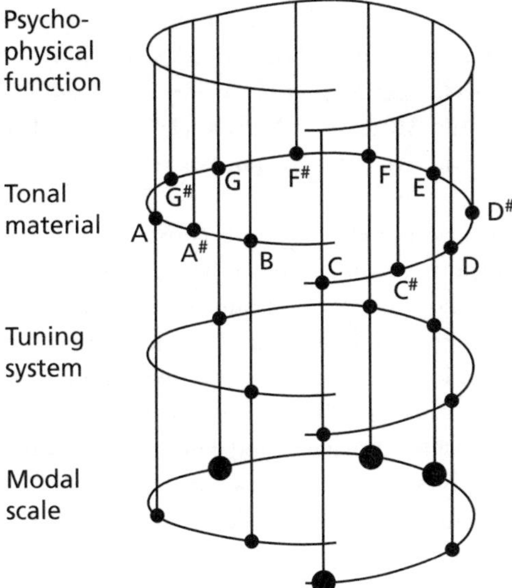

Figure 15.3. Differentiation of the continuous psychophysical scale (top) into culturally defined sets of categories (here exemplified by European categories): tonal material, tuning system, and modal scale. (From Dowling & Harwood, 2000; with permission.)

Out of the tonal material comes a more limited pitch set used as the basis for a set of modal scales – in European music, for a set of keys: a tuning system. For example, in European music we could select the tuning pattern of just the white notes on the piano as a basis for a set of scales. Chinese and Celtic music select pentatonic sets of pitches similar to the black notes on the piano (for example, in the song *Oh Bury Me Not on the Lone Prairie*). North Indian music selects a tuning system (*that* – Sanskrit for "framework") out of 35 possibilities defined by the choice of upper or lower variants of the seven scale pitches (Jairazbhoy, 1971).

The final step in specifying the set of pitches available for a melody is that of imposing a tonal hierarchy on the tuning system to define a modal scale. For example, selecting C as the tonic in the white note tuning system defines a modal scale in the key of C major. Selecting A as the tonic defines the A minor scale. It sometimes happens, as in the European minor mode and the Indian rag, that certain pitches are altered in context from those of the tuning system. It is largely at the level of the modal scale, or rag (India), or maqam (Persia), or patet (Indonesia), that culturally conditioned expectancies operate. It is typical in nonwestern musical cultures for a "mode" to have numerous musical and extra-musical connotations governing its performance, including characteristic melodic patterns and cadences, as well as social expectations involving appropriate occasions and time of day. Extramusical associations (including social contexts, emotions, and moods) are involved with the European major and minor modes as well (Carterette & Kendall, 1999). For example, we would not use a slow march in a minor mode for a wedding.

"Mode" and "key" are used somewhat interchangeably in the foregoing paragraph. "Mode" refers to a set of intervals with a functional hierarchy of scale degrees imposed upon it (tonic, dominant, etc.), but not anchored to a specific pitch height. A "key" is a mode that is anchored to a specific pitch, as in "C major" or "D minor." Thus we can say that the NBC chimes used in the Attneave and Olson (1971) study had always been presented in the key of C major, and that listeners transposed the pattern to other keys while preserving the major mode.

The number of pitch classes within each octave is constrained by cognitive limitations on the use of categories along a single dimension. However, the number of different tuning systems and modal scales is not subject to the same severe constraints, and at those two levels we find the greatest variation among cultures: from the major-minor system with close to a single tuning system in European music, to two tuning systems each having a variety of modes in Indonesian music, to the multiplicity of South Indian music, with 72 theoretically possible tuning systems of which a large number are in use.

In the above discussion of pitch we can see how the properties of the auditory system that determine the form of the psychophysical scale are overlaid with cultural constraints that govern the use of pitches in musical contexts. One consequence of the effect of these overlays on acculturation and perceptual learning is that the perception of musical pitches is almost never the pure and context-free auditory perception studied in isolation by psychophysics.

For example, musical context strongly affects the perception of individual pitches. The pattern of relations among the pitches in a modal scale affects the precision with which they are perceived. There are tonal tendencies that "pull" less stable pitches toward neighboring stable pitches. The leading tone, the seventh degree of the scale (si), pulls upward to the tonic; the pitch just above the tonic (re) tends to pull downward. Francès (1958/1988, Experiment 2) demonstrated that these tendencies arising out of the tonal hierarchy affect perception. Francès studied musically sophisticated listeners' ability to notice the mistuning of pitches presented in the midst of complex piano pieces. For some of the presentations he altered the tuning of the piano by lowering ("flatting") the frequencies of an E♭ and an A♭ in the middle of the keyboard. The pieces were in C minor and E major, keys in which the altered pitches have different functions and different tonal tendencies. In C minor the E♭ and A♭ are the lowered third and sixth degrees of the scale, and have generally downward tendencies in musical context; while in E major they function as the seventh (D#=E♭) and third (G#=A♭) degrees of the scale and have upward tendencies. Francès found that listeners noticed the flatting of the pitches much more often when that went against their inherent tonal tendencies; that is, the flatting was more obvious in E major, where the pitches tended upward, than in C minor, where they tended downward. A particular pitch, defined in terms of pitch class (chroma) and pitch height (octave level), is perceived differently depending on the tonal tendency that pitch has in the modal scale. These tendencies, attractions and repulsions that are immediately felt in connection with musical elements in context, may well exert a powerful emotional effect (Bharucha, 1999; Sloboda, 1998). For the acculturated listener something as basic as the precision of pitch perception depends on musical context. The pitch of a particular note on the piano is not a static given in perception, but rather a dynamic property that depends on a context flowing in time.

Cultural Relativism vs. Pluralism

We can return now to Berlin's (1998) contrast of cultural relativism vs. cultural pluralism. There are numerous ways in which pitch in music has been organized in various cultures. The traditional European pattern is only one of a myriad of possibilities. At each step differentiating the pitches of music out of the continuum of the psychophysical function, different cultures make different choices. However, those choices are not entirely arbitrary. The initial configuration of the psychophysical scale, capturing as it does the underlying features of octave equivalence and overall pitch height, expresses properties universally present in the human auditory system.

In ethics the issue of cultural pluralism vs. relativism has its normative side; there we may want to rule out the possibility that "anything goes." In music perception the pluralism described here is simply an empirical generalization to which we would definitely not want to give normative status. It is simply true that all the musical cultures of the world that use a range of greater than one octave use octave equivalence. For the few cultures that rarely go beyond one octave, the evidence for the use of some principle other than logarithmic intervals is extremely weak (Dowling, 1988). This does not mean that interesting and exciting music could not be put together on the basis of more than seven pitch classes to the octave, as in the 12-tone works of Schönberg and Berg, discussed above, or in Harry Partch's microtonal intervals, or that we might not dispense with the octave altogether as in the Bohlen-Pierce scale (Pierce, 1999).

Pitch Organization in Practice

The four levels outlined in Table 15.2 represent an abstraction based on musical practice and on listeners' behavior in making similarity judgments. In practice the sung or played melody is primary, and the modal scale, tuning system, and tonal material are inferred from that. One rarely hears modal scales presented in anything close to their entirety – perhaps only in fairly technical solos in jazz or "classical" music. And one almost never hears a chromatic scale (the tonal material) of any length in isolation. We know that the modal scale and its intervals are represented cognitively because when someone in a culture makes up a new song they use the scale of a set of previous well-known melodies. The scale serves as a schema or framework guiding the creation of new songs. Listeners can tell when a novel song is "out of tune" – not conforming to the scale steps. But that scale representation is implicit for people with no music lessons, unless they have learned some song that encodes it explicitly such as *Do, Re, Mi* or *Ut Queant Laxis* (the medieval *Do, Re, Mi*).

The primacy of the set of songs can be seen in the way music students in college ear-training classes remember musical intervals. When posed the task of singing a particular interval they recall a phrase from an already well-known song (see Figure 15.1b–d). A descending major sixth can be found at the start of the World War I song *Over There*; an ascending minor seventh in *Somewhere* from *West Side Story*; an ascending major seventh in *Bali Hai* from *South Pacific* (skipping the second note), an ascending major sixth in the NBC chimes. Everyone can produce an in-tune ascending major sixth (Attneave & Olson,

1971); only the music student needs (eventually) to know what it's called. Even though the fact that they sing the intervals of familiar songs in tune, nonmusicians sometimes even claim explicitly to hear the pitches of the do-re-mi scale as equally spaced when they are not (Shepard, 1999). Both musicians and nonmusicians access their implicit representation of the unequally spaced scale via well-known melodies.

Elements of the underlying tonal material are made explicit in melodies in a similar way to elements of the scale and tuning system. For example, the song *Greensleeves* (Figure 15.1a) alternates between a raised and lowered sixth degree in the minor, and uses a raised seventh. A typical Schubert song such as *The Trout* (Figure 15.1e) introduces a raised fourth in modulating to the key of the dominant at the end of the second phrase. Thus the information required for the abstraction of the tonal material is available in the explicit surface representations of familiar melodies.

Expectancies and Their Role in Music Perception

Acculturation and the Development of Expectancies

Clearly, given the range of cultural variation in the use of pitch in music, listeners must learn from experience the particular patterns of tonal material, tuning systems, and scales in use in their culture. This acculturation begins with the learning of nursery songs and other simple folk songs. European nursery songs generally use only seven or fewer pitch classes of the major or minor scale, avoiding altered pitches and changes of key (Dowling, 1999). Acculturation involves perceptual learning during which the listener extracts the pattern invariants of the musical system(s) of the culture. Acculturated listeners' automatic perceptual habits lead them to hear music in a way appropriate to that particular culture. The expectancies of an acculturated listener will be tuned to a particular set of invariants. Those expectancies can serve as a basis for aesthetic dimensions of listening. It is also clear that there will be wide individual differences in music perception, both across and within cultures, as the result of differing patterns of experience.

Returning briefly to the cultural-pluralism theme: Musical materials vary in the degree to which they push the limits of the system of invariants described here. In the European tradition we could imagine a continuum of complexity going from simple nursery songs using just five or seven pitch classes at one end, to music such as Schönberg's using twelve pitch classes at the other. Through perceptual learning listeners accommodate themselves to various positions along the continuum.

There is some confusion in the current literature concerning how much we know concerning individual differences in music perception, and how much we can learn using traditional methods of experimental psychology exemplified by the studies of Francès (1958/1988), Ward (1954), Shepard (1964), and Attneave and Olson (1971) described above. Cook (1994) and Smith (1997) claim that cognitive psychologists have neglected musically untrained listeners, and that what we do know shows that untrained listeners do not implicitly grasp the abstract levels of Table 15.2. Neither claim is true. We have already encountered a prime example demonstrating the implicit grasp of the pattern of pitch intervals in the modal scale by untrained listeners in Attneave and Olson's (1971) NBC chimes study. Below I review other examples of individual differences based on musical experience.

Expectancy and Attention

Expectancies developed in lifelong perceptual learning with music function in a variety of ways. Expectancies guide perceptual processing to important aspects of complicated patterns, and they facilitate the processing of expected elements when they occur. Further, expectancies are important to the aesthetic impact of a piece of music in setting up subtle surprises that make music interesting and exciting (Meyer, 1956). The pattern of expectancies mirrors the musical structure. As Jones says, people

> generate subjective space-time paths of their own in response to certain features of the external stimulus pattern. These mental "paths" function as psychological expectancies. And it is through extrapolation of these mental spatio-temporal patterns that a person comes to anticipate "where" in space [pitch] and "when" in time future events may occur. Expectancies, at least initially, are typically ideal or simplified paths. They are continuous, rhythmically generated paths that allow us to guide our attention to approximately correct neighborhoods. But what is most important is that organisms possess subjective generators that resemble those outlined in the representation of world patterns. (Jones, 1981, p. 571)

We can see the facilitation due to expectancies in a study by Bharucha (1987). Bharucha had listeners judge whether a target chord was out of tune or not. Out-of-tune chords had one pitch mistuned by a quarter of a semitone, a sufficiently obvious alteration for nonmusicians to notice. The target chord was preceded by a priming context chord either from the same key or from a distant key (in which the target would have been very unlikely to occur). Listeners were quicker to respond (800 msec vs. 1,000 msec) and made far fewer errors (5% vs. 30%) when the target was primed with a near-key chord that invoked the appropriate expectancies. Though musicians were quicker and made fewer errors than nonmusicians, expectancies facilitated performance equally for both groups. Furthermore, facilitation operated not only when the target shared no tones with the priming chord, but also when it shared no harmonics with the harmonics of the tones of the priming chord. That is, no explanation could be found in the physical stimuli. Bharucha (1987) also presented Indian listeners with contexts consisting of characteristic melodic phrases in the rag *Bhairav*, followed by either an expected or an unexpected target. As before, listeners had to judge target intonation. The same pattern of facilitation occurred; listeners were faster and more accurate in judging the expected target.

We can think of the facilitation due to expectancies as being mediated by implicit representations of musical structure – schemas. These representations are explicitly accessible to well-trained musicians, and in fact explicit access is a major goal of musical training. However, it is clear that an implicit appreciation of pattern invariants operates even in untrained listeners. In music listening as in Bharucha's experiment, a priming cue triggers the activation of an appropriate schema. That schema then guides the perceptual systems in picking out relevant events in the music and facilitates their processing. Everyone has had experience of noticing something out of place in a familiar scene, even though we weren't exactly looking for that particular detail. Our expectancies, derived from familiarity, led to our noticing a relevant detail. This kind of facilitation is critical in an information-rich domain such as music where there is always more detail available in the stimulus pattern than we could possibly attend to at once.

We should maintain a distinction between the function of expectancies guiding the automatic processing of information in a scene, without our concentrating on it, and that of guiding our focused attention – selecting the things we will consciously perceive. Expectancies guide both processes, but the activation of an implicit schema doesn't mean that we will necessarily focus conscious attention on the things it picks out. Several parallel schemas, concerning different aspects of the scene, can be activated at once.

Consider the example of a conductor rehearsing an orchestra. The conductor's focal attention may be devoted to the overall shape of the phrase at hand, and how that fits the broader shape of the piece. However, if the bassoonist plays a wrong note, the conductor notices it immediately and perhaps frowns at the bassoonist. Does this mean that the conductor was (luckily or unluckily) focusing attention on the bassoon at the very moment the wrong note occurred? No. Through a long process of perceptual learning – familiarization with the piece both in global shape and minute detail – the conductor has developed schemas that are activated during performance. Those schemas tacitly monitor the performance as long as nothing unexpected happens. But when the bassoonist plays a wrong note, or when the clarinetist plays a solo in an especially beautiful way, the schema registers something new, and focal attention is drawn to that detail. The conductor is able, just like everyone else, to focus conscious attention on one thing at a time (or perhaps a cluster of closely related things). The difference lies in the ability to track implicitly a number of different sequences of events at the same time.

In considering the perceptual organization of music, we might ask how complex events become parsed into meaningful components. That is, how do we comprehend the auditory scene before us? In line with Bregman's (1990, 1993; see Chapter 14) suggestions, we might suppose that clusters of events, though separated in time, are assigned in initial auditory processing to distinct sources of sound. Here we observe the operation of Gestalt principles of perceptual grouping: Streams of notes that are proximate in pitch and of similar loudness and timbre will be grouped together (see Figure 15.4a). Streams of notes that are distant in pitch (Figure 15.4b) or different in loudness or timbre (Figure 15.4c) will be segregated.

In patterns like that of Figure 15.4b we can easily focus our attention on the upper or the lower melody, even though the notes of one melody are interleaved in time with the notes of the other. This effect is more compelling as the notes go faster (up to about 12 notes/sec) and as the pitches of the melodies move farther apart (van Noorden, 1975). In the Baroque period in European music (1600–1750) pieces for solo violin or flute or cello, with no accompaniment, were popular, and composers such as Bach used this effect to provide the soloist with a means of producing polyphony – more than one melodic line at a time.

The segregation of the two streams in Figure 15.4b depends on temporal organization as well as pitch. When the listener is trying to judge the order of a pair of target tones, distractor tones at neighboring pitches interfere with the task. That is, if the listener is

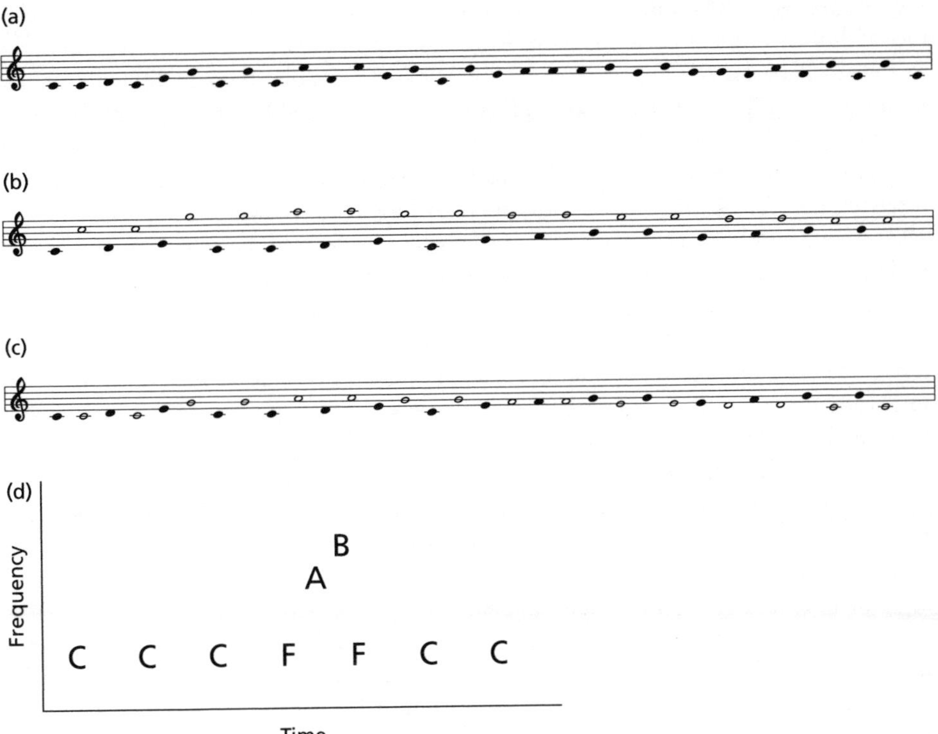

Figure 15.4. (a) Two temporally interleaved melodies (*Twinkle, Twinkle* and *Frère Jacques*) in the same pitch range with the same loudness and timbre. (b) The same melodies played in different pitch ranges. (c) The same melodies played in different timbres (represented by open and filled notes). (d) Target pattern for which distractors are "captured" by a neighboring pattern (Bregman & Rudnicky, 1975).

trying to judge the order of tones A and B in Figure 15.4d (AB vs. BA), adding the tones at F interferes. Bregman and Rudnicky (1975) showed that adding additional distractors C before and after the F distractors made the task easier again. The series of C distractors "captures" the F distractors. Initially, FABF was grouped into a coherent pattern, making AB harder to discern. But with the addition of the Cs, the pattern is grouped into CCCF, AB, and FCCC.

Timing can be an important determinant of stream segregation in cases where potential distractors are captured by another stream. Jones, Kidd, and Wetzel (1981) found that in patterns such as that of Figure 15.4d, if the stream CCCF/FCCC has a different tempo from the stream AB, performance is much better than when they all go at the same rate. Temporal differentiation aids focusing attention on the target. The capacity of expectancies to guide attention even extends to facilitating perceptual grouping in ways other than grouping on the basis of physical characteristics such as similarity of pitch, location, or timbre. This is what Bregman (1990) calls "schema-based segregation." The pattern in

Figure 15.4a is initially unintelligible to the listener. It really consists of two familiar melodies with their notes interleaved. Now, if we raise the pitches of alternate notes, soon the melodies will become distinct (Figure 15.4b). We could also play them in different timbres (denoted by filled and open symbols in Figure 15.4c). The auditory system uses the physical grouping to focus on one or the other melody. However, if we present listeners with the mixed, undifferentiated pattern of Figure 15.4a, now that they know what melodies to listen for, they can discern the two melodies (Dowling, 1973; Dowling, Lung, & Herrbold, 1987). Expectancies direct attention to the points in pitch and time where relevant target-melody notes are going to occur, and those notes can be checked against memory to verify that it really is the target. The listener who knows that *Twinkle, Twinkle* is hidden in a particular pattern, and who is familiar with *Twinkle, Twinkle*, can hear the melody if it is there. The listener who lacks either of those components cannot do that. This study has implications for the effect of past experience on present perceptions: The listener who is familiar with a particular piece will be able to hear different things in it from a person hearing it for the first time. In fact, once you hear the hidden melody it is difficult to ignore. This case is analogous to that of hidden-figures drawings in children's books, such as the "find six lions in the picture" type of drawing. Since you know more or less what a lion looks like, you will be able to pick them out when you search. But once you have identified them, they will be hard to ignore.

It is clear from listeners' success in discerning the melodies in Figure 15.4a, once they have been alerted to which melodies to listen for, that processes other than low-level parsing of the auditory input are responsible for stimulus selection and grouping. As Jones and Yee (1993) suggest, attention can be guided by expectancies involving the timing of target events.

Expectancies can operate on either a global or a local level. In the preceding study expectancies were clearly operating on a local level to direct attention to specific notes of the target melody. But those local expectancies were probably under the control of more global expectancies concerned with the contour – the ups and downs – of the melody. As Deutsch (1972) showed, a melody becomes all but unrecognizable when its notes are scattered randomly into several octaves; that is, when its set of pitch classes is preserved, but not the pitch heights of the notes. However, if the octave-scrambled melody preserves the contour of the original melody, then listeners are able to use that information, and succeed in recognizing the target (Dowling & Hollombe, 1977).

The Organization of Pitch and Time

Expectancies in music, though they apply to every perceptual aspect, are organized in elaborate structural ways in pitch and time. We now consider those patterns of organization in detail.

Pitch

As tuning systems and modal scales arise out of the tonal material in a culture, not only is a subset of pitches selected for use, but a tonal hierarchy is imposed on them. This hierarchy assigns a relative importance to each of the pitches in a scale, designating some as potential resting places for melodic motion, and others as less stable transitional points. A stable pitch in a tonal context is one on which a melody could pause with a sense of closure. The tonal hierarchy influences both expectancies and perceptual processing. The hierarchy imposes not only relative degrees of stability, but also governs the tendencies of the less stable tones toward stable ones (which Bharucha, 1996, calls "anchors"). In the European major mode stability is greatest for the tonic (do). Next is the dominant or fifth degree of the scale (sol), and then the third degree (mi). These are members of the tonic chord with which a piece might end, and all are potential beginnings and endings of melodies. (*Twinkle, Twinkle* begins on do, *Mary Had a Little Lamb* on mi, and *Happy Birthday* on sol; all three end on do.) The other pitches of the diatonic scale are lower in stability than the tonic triad pitches. Least stable are the nondiatonic pitches from the tonal material lying outside the scale. Their appearance in music often signals a shift to another key.

Direct evidence for the psychological reality of the tonal hierarchy comes from an extensive series of studies by Krumhansl (1990). In a typical study Krumhansl played listeners a tonic chord followed by a target tone. The listeners were asked to rate how well the target tone fit the context. Typical results are shown in Figure 15.5a (Krumhansl & Kessler, 1982).

Members of the tonic triad (C-E-G) received the highest ratings, followed by other members of the diatonic scale, with nondiatonic chromatic tones rated lowest. A qualitatively similar pattern emerges for the minor mode. In a similar study, Krumhansl and Shepard (1979) found that musicians produced ratings like those in Figure 15.5, while nonmusicians were more influenced by the pitch height of the target (in terms of pitch distance from the context) rather than its place in the tonal hierarchy.

The cross-cultural generality of this approach is illustrated by a study by Castellano, Bharucha, and Krumhansl (1984) who had Indian and Western listeners judge test tones following contexts drawn from Indian rags. They found that Western listeners were able to pick up the surface hierarchy very rapidly from the frequency of occurrence of pitches in the contexts. However, the responses of Indian listeners also showed a sensitivity to the underlying *that* tuning systems.

In a converging study, Krumhansl (1979) had listeners rate pairs of target tones, judging how well the second tone followed the first, given the tonal context that was provided. She used the ratings to estimate distances representing how closely the tones in a pair were related in the listener's mental representation of the tonal hierarchy. If a pair of tones received a low rating, that meant that they must be fairly distant from each other; pairs with high ratings must be relatively close. Krumhansl used multidimensional scaling to fit these distances into a three-dimensional representation, shown in Figure 15.5b. As you can see the members of the tonic chord (C-E-G) are clustered together at the bottom of the cone, followed by a layer with the other diatonic pitches (D-F-A-B). Farthest away from the center, in the top circle, are the nondiatonic pitches (C#, D#, F#, G#, and A#).

(a)

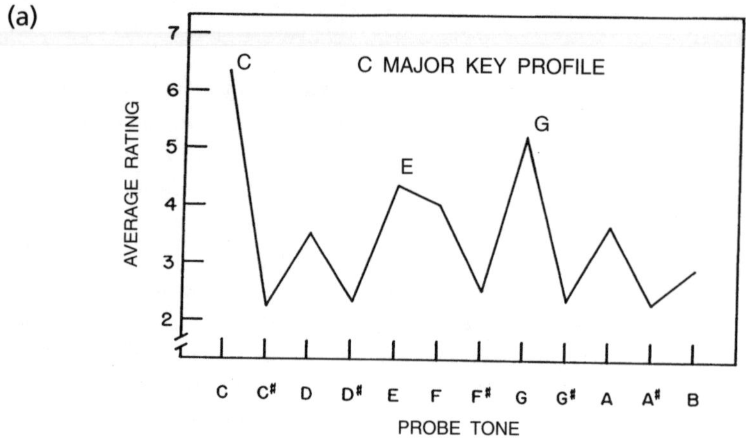

(b)

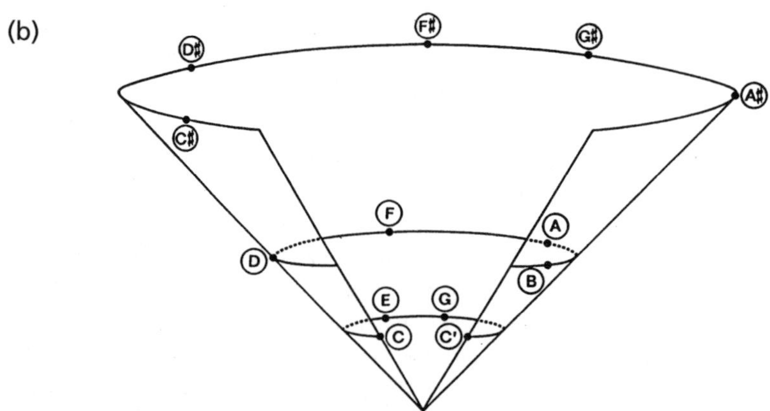

Figure 15.5. (a) Krumhansl's profile of judgments of suitability of probe tones to a key. Pitches of the tonic triad receive higher ratings than those of the diatonic scale, which in turn receive higher ratings than nonscalar pitches. (Adapted from Krumhansl & Kessler, 1982a; copyright © 1982 by the American Psychological Association. Reprinted with permission.) (b) Krumhansl's three-dimensional multidimensional scaling solution in which distances represent the affinity of the pitches for the key, illustrating the relationship between pitch classes within an key and those outside it. (Adapted from Krumhansl, 1979; with permission.)

The arrangement of the out-of-key pitches in relation to the in-key pitches in Figure 15.5b suggests another psychophysical dimension of pitch in addition to chroma and pitch height: that of key distance. You can easily demonstrate for yourself the independence of key distance from the first two dimensions. Put the right pedal down and play a cluster of adjacent white notes at the bottom of the piano, say from the lowest B to the next B up. Lift and depress the pedal again, and play a cluster of mostly black notes, still with the Bs on the top and bottom. It will sound different, but the difference is neither in chroma (the pitch classes are indistinguishable) nor in pitch height (we haven't moved along the keyboard). The difference lies in the selection of pitches from the periphery of Figure 15.5b versus the interior: key distance. Shepard (1982, 1999) has devised various ways of incorporating this information into the helix of Figure 15.2a, using a double helix or even a torus. Shepard's more elaborate model has similar implications to those of Lerdahl's (1988b) model of key relationships mentioned above. And those models' predictions are largely borne out in listeners' judgments of single tones and chords in a tonal context involving key changes (Kwak, 1994).

A general characteristic of perceptual frameworks such as the tonal hierarchy is that pairs of stimuli differing in stability within the framework will be judged differently depending on the order in which they are presented. If we take stability as an indication of conformity to the schema, then a stable tone followed by an unstable one should be judged less closely related than an unstable followed by a stable (Kahneman & Miller, 1986). This is exactly what Krumhansl (1979) found. Bartlett and Dowling (1988) found a converging result having listeners rate the similarity of pairs of melodies that were strongly tonal (conforming to the framework) or containing an out-of-key pitch (which sounds like a wrong note). Listeners rated nontonal-tonal pairs more similar than tonal-nontonal. The degree to which these perceptual reactions are implicit and not under conscious control was demonstrated when Bartlett and Dowling had listeners judge whether the two melodies in the pair had the same contour (pattern of ups and downs), presumably a judgment depending on a feature of the melodies independent of tonal strength. However, both musicians and nonmusicians in the contour-judgment task were heavily influenced by the tonal relationships. Tonal-nontonal pairs were judged to have the same contour less often than nontonal-tonal pairs, even when listeners were not supposed to be judging tonality. Further, nonmusicians' ratings of tonal strength are closely parallel to those of musicians (Cross, Howell, & West, 1983), and nonmusicians readily detect out-of-key pitches (Dewar, Cuddy, & Mewhort, 1977).

Memory tasks can be used to discover how listeners initially hear and encode the pitches of melodies. An encoding specificity effect is one in which context during the encoding of a target pattern is shown to affect the way in which that pattern is later remembered. One such study illustrates the importance of the tonal hierarchy. Dowling (1986) presented listeners with brief melodies introduced and concluded by chordal contexts that strongly established a key. The context set the melody up as either centered around the tonic (for example, do, re, mi, re, do, sol, do), or around the fifth degree or dominant (where the same melodic pattern of pitch intervals would be sol, la, si, la, sol, re, sol – see Figure 15.1g). (This translation along the scale works if we avoid the fourth and seventh degrees (fa and si) in the tonic-centered version.) Listeners had to detect when a note had been changed in the test melody. All test items were in different keys from the initial versions, so listeners were judging whether the test melody had been accurately transposed. The critical variable was whether the relationship of the melody to the chordal context was preserved at test. For half the melodies it was, and a melody originally based on do was tested with a context that kept it on do. For the other half the context shifted, and do melodies were moved to sol and vice versa.

Nonmusicians were unaffected by the context shift, and performed moderately well. Listeners with some musical training (an average of 5 years of music lessons in their youth) performed very well when the context was preserved, but at chance when the context was shifted. This suggests that these listeners were encoding the pitches in the initial melody in terms of their do-re-mi values in the tonal hierarchy. When those values were preserved at test, their performance was good. But when the context shifted and the tonal values of the notes changed, they were unable to retrieve the information encoded in a different way. (Professional musicians achieved high performance in both conditions, and in fact often commented on the fact that the task required them to ignore the context.) A simpler type of encoding specificity effect is that tonal melodies are easier to remember than nontonal ones, and that is true for both musicians and nonmusicians (Dowling, 1991).

Another line of converging evidence for the importance of the tonal framework in perception comes from experiments using the very rapid temporally interleaved melodies described above (Figure 15.4a). When listeners are given the task of judging the pitches of particular target tones in such patterns, both musicians and nonmusicians assimilate quarter steps (that lie outside the tonal material, Figure 15.3) to neighboring semitones (Dowling, 1992). That is, when the target pitch was a note on the piano keyboard, listeners were accurate in judging its pitch, but when the target fell in the "cracks" between keyboard notes, listeners were inaccurate and judged that a keyboard note had been presented.

The organization of pitch in music is based on a framework that specifies the standard pitches to be expected in a given context. In the midst of a piece nonstandard pitches that depart from the framework occur, generating excitement and interest. This tension between the expected and the unexpected that the framework sets up is found also in relation to the organization of time.

Time

Music is necessarily extended in time. There is even a piece, Cage's *4:33*, that consists only of time, with the dimensions of pitch, loudness, timbre, and location suppressed; to play it, the soloist simply sits at the piano for 4 minutes and 33 seconds.

Expectancies involving the timing of target events can serve to guide attention to important features of a target (Jones & Yee, 1993). For example, Dewitt and Samuel (1990) found that alterations in the pitch of a target are easier to detect when that target is part of a highly predictable, steady temporal sequence, rather than an irregular sequence. And Bharucha and Pryor (1986) found that listeners were better able to detect brief disruptive pauses hidden in tone sequences when those sequences exemplified a regular meter, than when they were less regular variants.

As the foregoing results suggest, time in music is organized in terms of a regular metrical structure of beats. A level of more elaborate rhythmic events is overlaid on that metric structure. We can observe this pattern in a song such as *Three Blind Mice* (Figure 15.1f). If you clap along with the metrical beat, you find that for the first two phrases there is one syllable per beat. In phrases three and four, the word "they" occurs off the beat, involving a more complicated rhythm than that of the regular beats. And you find still more complications in phrases five, six, and seven.

Povel and Essens (1985) demonstrated the importance of the metrical structure in a study in which they had listeners tap along with a rhythmic pattern (upper lines in Figure 15.6) that was either a good match to the underlying meter represented at 125 Hz (Figure

15.6a) or not as good a match (Figure 15.6b). Povel and Essens had found that when the beat (lower line) and the rhythmic pattern (upper line) were desynchronized (that is, when the time delay of the beats was not an integer multiple of the smallest time delay of the rhythmic elements) listeners found the task virtually impossible. But even with beat timings and rhythmic-element timings synchronized (as in Figure 15.6), the sequences were much harder to learn when the relationship between the rhythmic sequence and the beat was complicated (Figure 15.6b) than when it was not (Figure 15.6a).

The importance of the metrical framework to the perception of temporal relationships is well established. Clarke (1999) points out the seeming paradox that while regularly patterned time delays expressing simple integer ratios are easy for listeners to process, it is nevertheless the case that exact, simple integer ratios in event timing are quite rare in actual music, even in rhythmically simple music, due to variations in timing by the performer. Clarke suggests that the solution lies in distinguishing between the structural properties of rhythm (described by the metrical scheme) and the timings of actual notes, which are responsive to expressive properties of the music. A musical performance in which all of the timings of notes are regularized to integer ratios sounds dull and lifeless. Performers vary from the norm in timings to add interest and excitement. Clarke suggests that the listener copes with the variation by means of categorical perception. A quarter note will be heard as a quarter note even if it is delayed or hurried. Listeners will be able both to retrieve the metrical structure and to appreciate the subtle deviations from it in an actual performance.

In terms of universal constraints on the structure of music, it seems very likely that the presence of a metrical beat structure constitutes just such a constraint. For example, Drake (1998) notes that even at the age of 2 months infants are able to notice irregularities in a regular beat sequence.

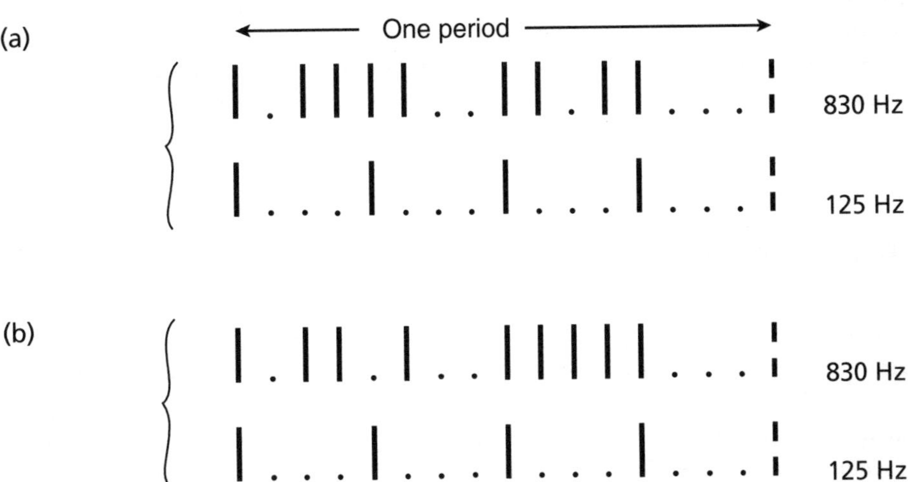

Figure 15.6. (a) Rhythmic pattern in which the upper track (830 Hz) is organized compatibly with the beat in the lower track (125 Hz). (b) Pattern in which the upper track is less compatible with the beat (from Povel & Essens, 1985; with permission).

Melodic Contour

When the basic elements of pitch and time are combined in a melody, a dynamic shape emerges: the melodic contour. This contour has both pitch and rhythmic aspects. Both pitch and rhythm are integrated into a unified pattern. When we ask whether the pitch or the rhythmic pattern is more fundamental to our recognition of a melody, we get a complicated answer. For novel patterns the rhythm clearly dominates. Monahan and Carterette (1985; Monahan, Kendall, & Carterette, 1987) found rhythm more important to listeners' similarity judgments of brief unfamiliar melodies. For familiar melodies the pitch pattern appears to be more important. Though we can often recognize a familiar tune from the rhythmic pattern alone (as William James, 1890, noted), Hebert and Peretz (1997) found that listeners identified familiar nursery tunes much more easily when their pitch patterns were presented isochronously (with same-length notes) than when their rhythms were presented on a repeating pitch. These results with novel and familiar melodies may be the result of differing ranges of available alternatives in the pitch and rhythm domains (Garner, 1974). A case could be made that there is more freedom for variation in pitch than in rhythm for nursery tunes (though Hebert and Peretz try to counter this argument), and in novel tonal melodies restricted to seven pitch classes there may well be a wider range of possibilities in rhythm.

Melodic contour is an easily accessible feature for musically inexperienced and experienced listeners alike. Inexperienced listeners are usually as good as or better than experienced listeners in recognizing the pitch contours of distorted melodies (Dowling & Fujitani, 1971). And in memory tasks novel melodies with the same contour are often confused with each other (Dowling, 1978; Dowling, Kwak, & Andrews, 1995).

Varying melodic material while preserving contour is a standard structural principle not only in European music but in most of the musics of the world. Think of the first movement of Beethoven's *Fifth Symphony* as an extreme example. After the first two presentations (in which the pitch interval between the two notes changes), the kernel theme is presented nine times in quick succession with almost as many interval sizes between the pitches as possible. Not only classical composers, but preschoolers when they sing spontaneously generate variations of melodic contour patterns (Dowling, 1999).

Perception and Memory

In the 1960s it was common practice to draw modular flow diagrams for the mind (or brain). In such diagrams one or more modules were designated as some form of memory – short-term, long-term, immediate, etc. Sensory information was interpreted by perceptual systems, and then if a task or mental set required, related that information to information in memory (Dowling, 1993). Implicit in this approach was the notion that cognitive psychologists were primarily interested in declarative information in memory – information subject to verbal report. In fact, even today "cognitive" connotes access to conscious control for some theorists. And because it constituted a separate module, memory could be studied separately from perception.

For the past several years, Robert Crowder (1993) has been campaigning against the notion of a separate memory module. In Crowder's view, memory is just the residue of perceptual processing, remaining in the same modules that did the processing initially. Memory retrieval is not necessarily a separate operation, but occurs when new stimuli enter the system.

One implication of Crowder's approach is that remembering something activates much the same set of modules as perceiving it. Imagining a sound – say a trumpet playing an A of 440 Hz – should activate some of the same neural pathways that hearing that sound would activate. Crowder (1989) found that the processing of a trumpet sound can be primed by the sound of a trumpet. That is, if you have to judge whether the pitch of a trumpet tone is the same as a pitch you've just heard, you will be faster making that judgment if you've just heard the pitch played on a trumpet, than if you heard it on a flute. Crowder reasoned that if the listener is given a neutral, sine-wave pitch cue, and then imagines the trumpet sound, that should also speed processing by comparison with imagining a flute sound. And that turned out to be the case. Listeners were quicker to respond to trumpet sounds after imagining a trumpet, and quicker to respond to flute sounds after imagining a flute, etc. (Crowder, 1989; for complications, see Pitt & Crowder, 1992). This makes a very strong case that remembering a trumpet sound, which would seem to be necessary to imagining it, is being carried out by brain processes that are closely associated with those involved in perceiving it. Perception and memory are convenient headings for considering various sorts of phenomena and functional behaviors. But it seems less and less likely that they are carried out by separate modules.

Summary

This chapter has described music perception as involving a combination of the built-in structure of the human auditory system and an overlay of culturally determined patterns that the listener develops in a lifetime of hearing and producing music. The listener's perceptual learning builds frameworks in terms of which newly encountered music is perceived and understood. Musical scales in pitch and metrical patterns in time are examples of patterns of such frameworks that hold for numerous individual pieces, and that govern expectancies and facilitate perceptual processing. These frameworks embody the listener's implicit knowledge of the music of the culture. Depending on the prior experience of each listener we should expect individual differences in perception and understanding of a particular piece. This implicit knowledge is invoked automatically in the process of perceiving musical sound. It is not some separate body of knowledge that is "looked up" after the sounds are perceived, as Crowder's (1989) experiment shows.

Suggested Readings

Helmholtz, H. von (1954). *On the sensations of tone* (A. J. Ellis, Trans.). New York: Dover. (Original work published 1877) [A seminal work that lays out the major issues in the field and provides thoughtful discussions, at least in terms of the organization of pitch. An appendix by Ellis on nineteenth-century European organ tunings shows how recent our standardization on an A of 440 Hz is.]

Meyer, L. (1956). *Emotion and meaning in music.* Chicago: University of Chicago Press. [The principal modern statement from a musicological perspective.]

Dowling, W. J., & Harwood, D. L. (1986). *Music cognition.* Orlando, FL: Academic Press. [An overview of major trends in research applying cognitive psychology to music.]

McAdams, S., & Bigand, E. (Eds.) (1993). *Thinking in sound: The cognitive psychology of human audition.* Oxford: Oxford University Press. [A collection of stimulating and thoughtful chapters by well-selected cognitive psychologists.]

Deutsch, D. (Ed.) (1999). *The psychology of music* (2nd ed.). San Diego: Academic Press. [Up-to-date and thorough chapters on selected topics.]

Additional Topics

Consonance and Dissonance

Plomp and Levelt (1965) settled several issues concerning consonance and dissonance, indicating the sources of acoustic dissonance and showing why small integer ratios of fundamental frequencies of complex tones lead to consonance. Kameoka and Kuriyagawa (1969a, 1969b) extended this approach to chords of more than two tones.

Beats, Rhythm, and Expressive Timing

There is more to the story of the temporal organization of music and its relationship to time keeping in human cognition than was discussed in this chapter. Essens (1995) and Large and his co-authors (1995, 1999) provide useful continuations. The other aspect of timing that was only mentioned in the chapter is that of expressive timing in performance. Repp's two recent articles (1999a, 1999b) provide a window on an extensive literature.

Words and Music

People often ask whether the music helps you remember the words to a song, and vice versa. See Crowder, Serafine, & Repp (1990) and Rubin (1995).

Emotion and Meaning

Why does music have powerful emotional effects, and how does it do it? We don't know the answers yet, but the articles by Sloboda (1991) and Panksepp (1995) go in that direction.

References

Attneave, F., & Olson, R. K. (1971). Pitch as medium: A new approach to psychophysical scaling. *American Journal of Psychology, 84,* 147–166.

Balzano, G. J. (1980). The group-theoretic description of 12-fold and microtonal pitch systems. *Computer Music Journal, 4*(4), 66–84.

Bartlett, J. C., & Dowling, W. J. (1988). Scale structure and similarity of melodies. *Music Perception, 5,* 285–314.

Berlin, I. (1998). My intellectual path. *New York Review of Books,* May 14.

Bharucha, J. J. (1987). Music cognition and perceptual facilitation: A connectionist framework. *Music Perception, 5,* 1–30.

Bharucha, J. J. (1996). Melodic anchoring. *Music Perception, 13*, 383–400.

Bharucha, J. J. (1999). Neural nets, temporal composites, and tonality. In D. Deutsch (Ed.), *The psychology of music* (2nd ed., pp. 413–440). San Diego: Academic Press.

Bharucha, J. J., & Pryor, J. H. (1986). Disrupting the isochrony underlying rhythm: An asymmetry in discrimination. *Perception & Psychophysics, 40*, 137–141.

Bregman, A. S. (1990). *Auditory scene analysis: The perceptual organization of sound.* Cambridge, MA: MIT Press.

Bregman, A. S. (1993). Auditory scene analysis: Hearing in complex environments. In S. McAdams & E. Bigand (Eds.), *Thinking in sound: The cognitive psychology of human audition* (pp. 10–36). Oxford: Oxford University Press.

Bregman, A. S., & Rudnicky, A. (1975). Auditory segregation: Stream or streams? *Journal of Experimental Psychology: Human Perception & Performance, 1*, 263–267.

Brown, R. W. (1981). Music and language. In *Documentary Report of the Ann Arbor Symposium: Applications of Psychology to the Teaching and Learning of Music* (pp. 233–265). Reston, VA: Music Educators National Conference.

Burns, E. M. (1999). Intervals, scales, and tuning. In D. Deutsch (Ed.), *The psychology of music* (2nd ed., pp. 215–264). San Diego: Academic Press.

Carterette, E. C., & Kendall, R. A. (1999). Comparative music perception and cognition. In D. Deutsch (Ed.), *The psychology of music* (2nd ed., pp. 725–791). San Diego: Academic Press.

Castellano, M. A., Bharucha, J. J., & Krumhansl, C. L. (1984). Tonal hierarchies in the music of North India. *Journal of Experimental Psychology: General, 113*, 394–412.

Clarke, E. F. (1999). Rhythm and timing in music. In D. Deutsch (Ed.), *The psychology of music* (2nd ed., pp. 473–500). San Diego: Academic Press.

Clarke, E. F., & Krumhansl, C. L. (1990). Perceiving musical time. *Music Perception, 7*, 213–252.

Cook, N. (1994). Perception: A perspective from music theory. In R. Aiello & J. Sloboda (Eds.), *Musical perceptions* (pp. 64–95). New York: Oxford University Press.

Cross, I., Howell, P., & West, R. (1983). Preference for scale structure in melodic sequences. *Journal of Experimental Psychology: Human Perception & Performance, 9*, 444–460.

Crowder, R. G. (1989). Imagery for musical timbre. *Journal of Experimental Psychology: Human Perception & Performance, 15*, 472–478.

Crowder, R. G. (1993). Auditory memory. In S. McAdams & E. Bigand (Eds.), *Thinking in sound: The cognitive psychology of human audition* (pp. 113–145). Oxford: Oxford University Press.

Crowder, R. G., Serafine, M. L., & Repp, B. (1990). Physical interaction and association by contiguity in memory for the words and melodies of songs. *Memory & Cognition, 18*, 469–476.

Deutsch, D. (1972). Octave generalization and tune recognition. *Perception & Psychophysics, 11*, 411–412.

Dewar, K. M., Cuddy, L. L., & Mewhort, D. J. K. (1977). Recognition memory for single tones with and without context. *Journal of Experimental Psychology: Human Learning & Memory, 3*, 60–67.

Dewitt, L. A., & Samuel, A. G. (1990). The role of knowledge-based expectations in music perception: Evidence from musical restoration. *Journal of Experimental Psychology: General, 119*, 123–144.

Dowling, W. J. (1973). The perception of interleaved melodies. *Cognitive Psychology, 5*, 322–337.

Dowling, W. J. (1978). Scale and contour: Two components of a theory of memory for melodies. *Psychological Review, 85*, 341–354.

Dowling, W. J. (1986). Context effects on melody recognition: Scale-step versus interval representations. *Music Perception, 3*, 281–296.

Dowling, W. J. (1988). The cognitive framework for musical scales in various cultures. *Journal of the Acoustical Society of America, 84*, S204 (Abstract).

Dowling, W. J. (1991). Tonal strength and melody recognition after long and short delays. *Perception & Psychophysics, 50*, 305–313.

Dowling, W. J. (1992). Perceptual grouping, attention and expectancy in listening to music. In J. Sundberg (Ed.), Gluing tones: Grouping in music composition, performance and listening. *Publications of the Royal Swedish Academy of Music*, no. 72, pp. 77–98.

Dowling, W. J. (1993). Procedural and declarative knowledge in music cognition and education. In T. J. Tighe & W. J. Dowling (Eds.), *Psychology and music: The understanding of melody and rhythm* (pp. 5–18). Hillsdale, NJ: Erlbaum.
Dowling, W. J. (1999). The development of music perception and cognition. In D. Deutsch (Ed.), *The psychology of music* (2nd ed., pp. 603–625). San Diego: Academic Press.
Dowling, W. J., & Fujitani, D. S. (1971). Contour, interval, and pitch recognition in memory for melodies. *Journal of the Acoustical Society of America, 49*, 524–531.
Dowling, W. J., & Harwood, D. L. (1986). *Music cognition*. Orlando, FL: Academic Press.
Dowling, W. J., & Hollombe, A. W. (1977). The perception of melodies distorted by splitting into several octaves: Effects of increasing proximity and melodic contour. *Perception & Psychophysics, 21*, 60–64.
Dowling, W. J., Kwak, S.-Y., & Andrews, M. W. (1995). The time course of recognition of novel melodies. *Perception & Psychophysics, 57*, 197–210.
Dowling, W. J., Lung, K. M.-T., & Herrbold, S. (1987). Aiming attention in pitch and time in the perception of interleaved melodies. *Perception & Psychophysics, 41*, 642–656.
Drake, C. (1998). Psychological processes involved in the temporal organization of complex auditory sequences: Universal and acquired processes. *Music Perception, 16*, 11–26.
Essens, P. (1995). Structuring temporal sequences: Comparison of models and factors of complexity. *Perception & Psychophysics, 57*, 519–532.
Francès, R. (1988). *The perception of music* (W. J. Dowling, Trans.). Hillsdale, NJ: Erlbaum. (Original work published 1958)
Garner, W. R. (1974). *The processing of information and structure*. Hillsdale, NJ: Erlbaum.
Hampshire, S. (1989). *Innocence and experience*. Cambridge, MA: Harvard University Press.
Hebert, S., & Peretz, I. (1997). Recognition of music in long-term memory: Are melodic and temporal patterns equal partners? *Memory & Cognition, 25*, 519–533.
Helmholtz, H. von (1954). *On the sensations of tone* (A. J. Ellis, Trans.). New York: Dover. (Original work published 1877)
Jairazbhoy, N. A. (1971). *The rags of North Indian music*. London: Faber & Faber.
James, W. (1890). *The principles of psychology*. New York: Holt.
Jones, M. R. (1981). Only time can tell: On the topology of mental space and time. *Critical Inquiry, 7*, 557–576.
Jones, M. R., Kidd, G., & Wetzel, R. (1981). Evidence for rhythmic attention. *Journal of Experimental Psychology: Human Perception & Performance, 7*, 1059–1073.
Jones, M. R., & Yee, W. (1993). Attending to auditory events: The role of temporal organization. In S. McAdams & E. Bigand (Eds.), *Thinking in sound: The cognitive psychology of human audition* (pp. 69-112). Oxford: Oxford University Press.
Kahneman, D., & Miller, D. T. (1986). Norm theory: Comparing reality to its alternatives. *Psychological Review, 92*, 136–153.
Kameoka, A., & Kuriyagawa, M. (1969a). Consonance theory part I: Consonance of dyads. *Journal of the Acoustical Society of America, 45*, 1451–1459.
Kameoka, A., & Kuriyagawa, M. (1969b). Consonance theory part II: Consonance of complex tones and its calculation method. *Journal of the Acoustical Society of America, 45*, 1460–1471.
Krumhansl, C. L. (1979). The psychological representation of musical pitch in a tonal context. *Cognitive Psychology, 11*, 346–374.
Krumhansl, C. L. (1990). *Cognitive foundations of musical pitch*. New York: Oxford University Press.
Krumhansl, C. L., Sandell, G. J., & Sergeant, D. C. (1987). The perception of tone hierarchies and mirror forms in twelve-tone serial music. *Music Perception, 5*, 31–78.
Krumhansl, C. L., & Kessler, E. J. (1982). Acquisition of the hierarchy of tonal functions in music. *Memory & Cognition, 10*, 243–251.
Krumhansl, C. L., & Kessler, E. J. (1982a). Tracing the dynamic changes in perceived tonal organization in a spatial representation of musical keys. *Psychological Review, 89*, 334–368.
Krumhansl, C. L., & Shepard, R. N. (1979). Quantification of the hierarchy of tonal functions

within a diatonic context. *Journal of Experimental Psychology: Human Perception & Performance, 5*, 579–594.
Kwak, S. Y. (1994). *Mental representations of nonmusicians and musicians for pitches, chords, and musical keys*. Unpublished doctoral dissertation, University of Texas at Dallas.
Large, E. W., & Jones, M. R. (1999). The dynamics of attending: How we track time-varying events. *Psychological Review,106*, 119–159.
Large, E. W., & Kolen, J. F. (1995). Resonance and the perception of musical meter. *Connection Science, 6*, 177–208.
Lerdahl, F. (1988a). Cognitive constraints on compositional systems. In J. A. Sloboda (Ed.), *Generative processes in music* (pp. 231-259). Oxford: Oxford University Press.
Lerdahl, F. (1988b). Tonal pitch space. *Music Perception, 5*, 315–350.
McAdams, S., & Bigand, E. (Eds.) (1993). *Thinking in sound: The cognitive psychology of human audition*. Oxford: Oxford University Press.
Meyer, L. (1956). *Emotion and meaning in music*. Chicago: University of Chicago Press.
Miller, G. A. (1956). The magical number seven, plus or minus two: Some limits on our capacity for processing information. *Psychological Review, 63*, 81–97.
Monahan, C. B., & Carterette, E. C. (1985). Pitch and duration of musical space. *Music Perception, 3*, 1–32.
Monahan, C. B., Kendall, R. A., & Carterette, E. C. (1987). The effect of melodic and temporal contour on recognition memory for pitch change. *Perception & Psychophysics, 41*, 576–600.
Panksepp, J. (1995). The emotional sources of "chills" induced by music. *Music Perception, 13*, 171–207.
Pierce, J. R. (1999). Consonance and scales. In P. R. Cook (Ed.), *Music, cognition, and computerized sound* (pp. 167–185). Cambridge, MA: MIT Press.
Pitt, M. A., & Crowder, R. G. (1992). The role of spectral and dynamic cues in imagery for musical timbre. *Journal of Experimental Psychology: Human Perception & Performance, 18*, 728–738.
Plomp, R., & Levelt, W. J. M. (1965). Tonal consonance and critical bandwidth. *Journal of the Acoustical Society of America, 38*, 548–560.
Povel, D. J., & Essens, P. (1985). Perception of temporal patterns. *Music Perception, 2*, 411-440.
Repp, B. H. (1999a). Detecting deviations from metronomic timing in music: Effects of perceptual structure on the mental timekeeper. *Perception & Psychophysics, 61*, 529–548.
Repp, B. H. (1999b). A microcosm of musical expression, III: Contributions of timing and dynamics to the aesthetic impression of pianists' performances of the initial measures of Chopin's *Etude in E Major*. *Journal of the Acoustical Society of America, 106*, 469–478.
Rodriguez, R. X. (1995). *The mystery of two worlds*. Polykarp Kusch Lecture, University of Texas at Dallas.
Rubin, D. C. (1995). *Memory in oral traditions: The cognitive psychology of epic, ballads, and counting-out rhymes*. New York: Oxford University Press.
Schönberg, A. (1978). *Theory of harmony*. Berkeley: University of California Press.
Shepard, R. N. (1964). Circularity in judgments of relative pitch. *Journal of the Acoustical Society of America, 36*, 2345–2353.
Shepard, R. N. (1982). Musical pitch. In D. Deutsch (Ed.), *The psychology of music* (1st ed., pp. 343–390). Orlando, FL: Academic Press.
Shepard, R. N. (1999). Tonal structure and scales. In P. R. Cook (Ed.), *Music, cognition, and computerized sound* (pp. 187-194). Cambridge, MA: MIT Press.
Sloboda, J. (1991). Music structure and emotional response: Some empirical findings. *Psychology of Music, 19*, 110–120.
Sloboda, J. (1998). Does music mean anything? *Musicae Scientiae, 2*, 21–31.
Smith, J. D. (1997). The place of musical novices in music science. *Music Perception, 14*, 227–262.
Stevens, S. S., Volkmann, S. J., & Newman, E. B. (1937). A scale for the measurement of the psychological magnitude of pitch. *Journal of the Acoustical Society of America, 8*, 185–190.
van Noorden, L. P. A. A. (1975). *Temporal coherence in the perception of tone sequences*. Eindhoven, Netherlands: Institute for Perceptual Research.

Ward, W. D. (1954). Subjective musical pitch. *Journal of the Acoustical Society of America, 26*, 369–380.

Warren, R. M. (1993). Perception of acoustic sequences: Global integration versus temporal resolution. In S. McAdams & E. Bigand (Eds.), *Thinking in sound: The cognitive psychology of human audition* (pp. 37–68). Oxford: Oxford University Press.

Wessel, D. (1979). Timbre space as a musical control structure. *Computer Music Journal, 3*(2), 45–52.

Chapter Sixteen

Speech Perception and Spoken Word Recognition: Research and Theory

Miranda Cleary and David B. Pisoni

Introduction

The study of speech perception investigates how we are able to identify in the human voice the meaningful patterns that define spoken language. Research in this area has tended to focus on how humans perceive minimal linguistic contrasts known as "phonemes" – how we distinguish "pat" from "bat" or "bit" from "bet" for example. Although speech perception has traditionally been the study of phoneme perception,[1] an account is also needed for how we identify spoken words and comprehend sentences in *connected fluent* speech. Defining "speech perception" very narrowly in terms of phoneme perception or nonsense syllable identification was a useful and reasonable simplification in the early days of the field, but the drawbacks of conceptualizing the problem purely in these terms have become increasingly apparent in recent years.

Speech Perception in the Context of the Other Senses

Speech perception stands to audition much as face perception stands to vision, in that it is a differentially developed response to a particular type of physical signal within a more general sensory modality. Because speech perception involves how we categorize vocalizations characteristic of our own species, the key issues cannot be addressed through the use of animal models; the relevant data come, almost exclusively, from external observations of human behavior. The relevance of how other species perceive human speech signals is doubtful (see Trout, 1998), although to the extent that such research helps provide a psychophysical account of the early processing activity that takes place at the auditory periphery, it can have some limited value (see Kluender, 1994 for review).

Speech is only one type of auditory signal of interest to humans. Perceiving speech is an ability arguably lying intermediate between the fundamentally pragmatic skill of perceiving meaningful environmental sounds (where the sound-meaning correspondence is relatively static across members of the species), and the somewhat more mysterious perceptual capacity we have to store, process, and appreciate musical input (of rather more ambiguous semantic content). Several acoustic characteristics, however, differentiate spoken language from other auditory signals. It therefore makes sense to review these fundamentals before proceeding to a discussion of the key theoretical issues.

The Acoustic Speech Signal

In speech production, the lungs act as a sophisticated pair of bellows with the moving larynx, jaw, tongue, lips, and soft palate serving to constrain the air-stream in characteristic ways. Figure 16.1b shows a speech waveform, plotting overall amplitude as a function of time. A magnified portion of the waveform is shown in Figure 16.1a. The articulators (many of which are shown in Figure 16.2) impose continually shifting filtering functions atop temporally quasi-periodic or aperiodic sound sources, causing the acoustic energy to be attenuated at certain frequencies and amplified at others. It is possible to analyze the resulting complex signal as the summation of a large number of simple sinusoidal frequency components. A two-dimensional plot showing the relative amplitude of these various frequency components over some small window of time is called an amplitude spectrum. A single spectrum from Point X in Figure 16.1b is shown in Figure 16.1f, with frequency plotted on the horizontal axis. A third dimension can be added to this 2-D representation by computing *many* spectra consecutively over time to form a spectrogram. A spectrogram provides a visual three-dimensional representation of energy (indicated by darkness of shading) at a range of frequencies (Y-axis) as a function of time (X-axis). Wide-band spectrograms (Figure 16.1c) are used when temporal fidelity is important for measurement, with actual amplitudes at adjacent frequencies averaged by the analysis. Narrow-band spectrograms, on the other hand, provide high resolution frequency resolution averaged over larger time domains (Figure 16.1d).

Laryngeal Source Characteristics

The complex acoustic patterns in speech arise from the anatomy and physiology of the human vocal tract and the physics of sound (Denes & Pinson, 1993; Flanagan, 1972; Rossing, 1990). The most basic characteristic of a human voice is its fundamental frequency, symbolized as "f0", which closely corresponds to the perceived pitch of a speaker's voice (perception of a "deep" versus "high" voice, for example). Determined by the rate at which the vocal folds within the larynx flap open and shut, f0 is the lowest harmonic component of the complex quasi-periodic sound made when air presses through these folds. In a wide-band spectrogram, each of the semi-regularly spaced vertical striations corresponds to one opening and closing cycle of the vocal folds. Narrow-band spectrograms, on the other hand, illustrate f0 via the spacing of the horizontally running harmonics.

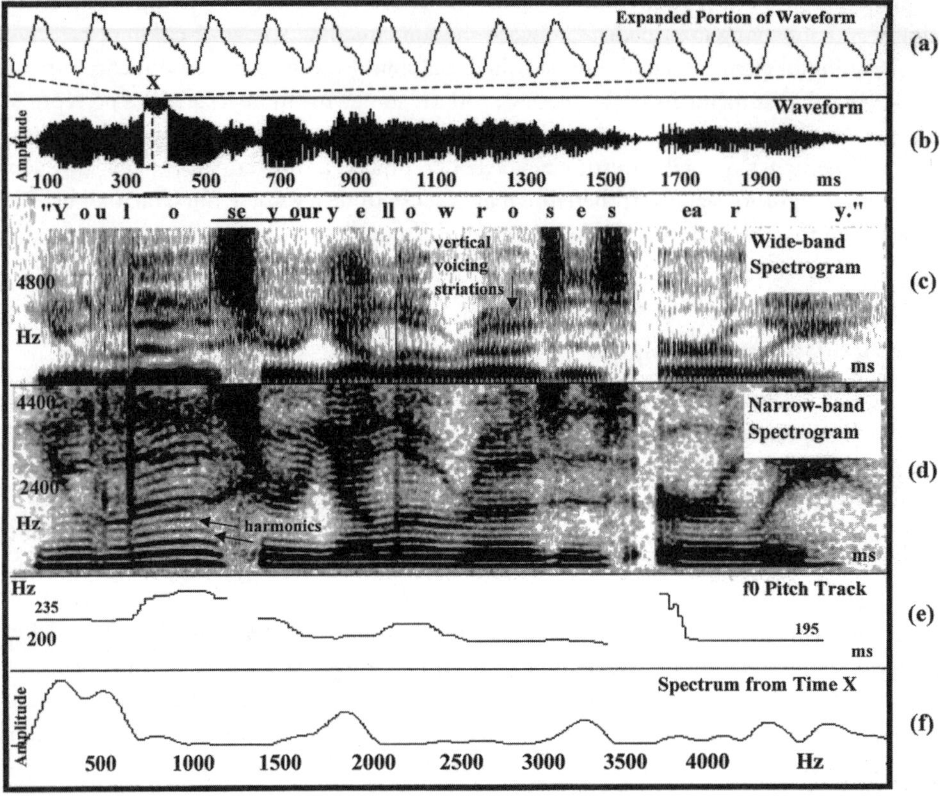

Figure 16.1. Acoustic characteristics of the utterance "You lose your yellow roses early," spoken by an adult female speaker. (a) Expanded detail of the selected section of full waveform as shown in (b). (c) A wide-band spectrogram of the entire utterance. (d) A narrow-band spectrogram of the same sentence. (e) An f0 pitch track of the utterance. (f) A single spectrum from point X in the waveform. Note that despite the apparent lack of clear-cut word boundaries (e.g., pauses/silent intervals) in this utterance, a native listener will have no trouble comprehending the sentence. One (among many) instances of coarticulation can be seen in the underlined sounds in "lose" and "your." A comparison of the "z" in "lose" with the two "z" sounds in "roses" makes clear the influence of the preceding "oo" vowel and the following "y" sound on the acoustic representation of the "z" in "lose." That is, there is evidence of formant structure in the 2500 Hz range that would not be observed if the "z" sound was produced in isolation.

Widely spaced harmonics indicate high pitch, whereas closely spaced harmonics indicate lower pitch. During fluent speech, the vocal cords are vibrating about 70% of the time (Fry, 1979). The rate of vibration can be influenced by many factors, but the mass and flexibility of the folds largely constrain this value so as to produce the average fundamental frequencies associated with the speech of men (about 125 Hz), women (~200+ Hz), and children (~300+ Hz).

Talker-controlled adjustments in f0 play a major role in perception of intonation, pho-

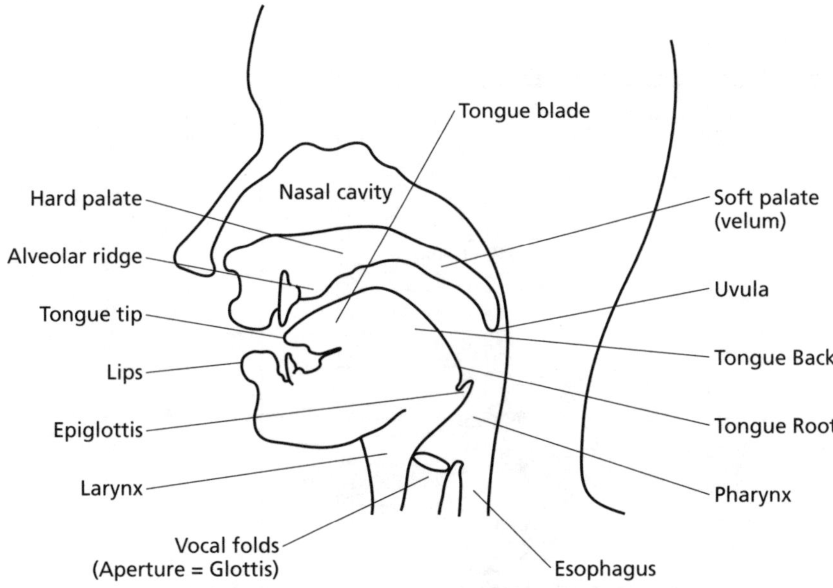

Figure 16.2. A sagittal view of the human vocal tract showing the main speech articulators as labeled.

nemic tone, and word stress. The "pitch-track" in Figure 16.1e, for example, shows the f0 of this female voice dropping from 235 Hz to 195 Hz in a declarative intonation pattern (with some local f0 maxima intervening). Variations on a general declination pattern are used for different purposes; for instance, in English, a prominent end-of-utterance pitch-rise can indicate a question. Relative f0 levels (or "tones") are used by a number of so-called "tone languages" (such as Mandarin Chinese), such that words may be distinguished in meaning only by the pitch or pitch contour of the vowel. In a language such as English, the perception of word or syllable stress results from a combination of adjusted pitch (local maxima or minima), amplitude (usually louder), and duration (longer). Stress, like tone, is defined, not in absolute terms, but relative to its surrounding speech context.

The timing of the onset of vocal cord vibration can also serve to distinguish one spoken word from another. The delay between a noise burst caused by sharply releasing a set of closed articulators (such as the lips) to the first vocal fold vibration following, such as occurs in producing a syllable like "pah," is called "voice onset time" (VOT) (see Figure 16.3), and is used in many languages to contrast consonant sounds that are otherwise alike in how they are produced before vowels. A VOT difference distinguishes, for example, early "voiced" (short VOT) sounds like [b] and late-voiced (long VOT) "voiceless" sounds like [p]. There are also "pre-voiced" sounds in the world's languages for which vocal cord activity starts at, or before, the release of closure. Thai, for example, uses a pre-voiced bilabial stop.

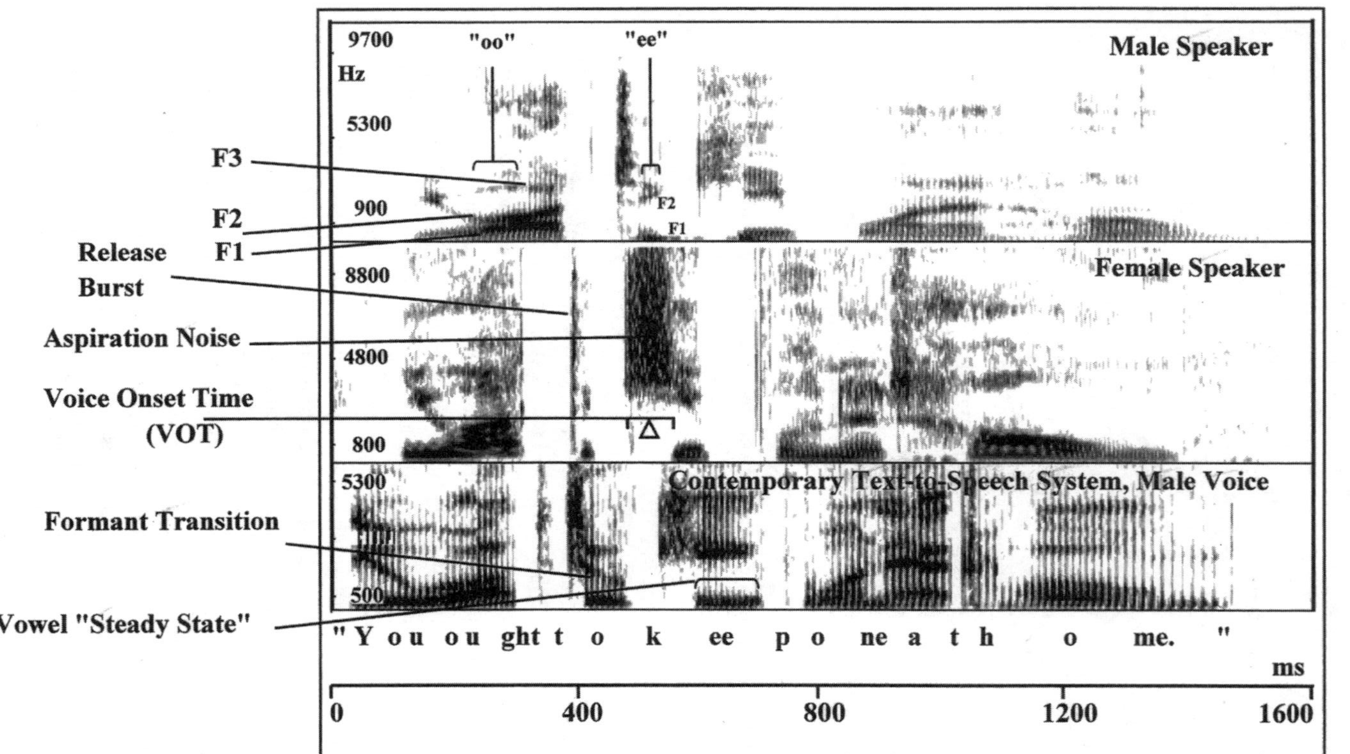

Figure 16.3. Wide-band spectrograms of the utterance "You ought to keep one at home," spoken by male talker, a female talker, and one machine text-to-speech system, all with American English pronunciation. Some commonly used "acoustic cues" are identified as labeled. The delta symbol indicates the VOT duration for the word-initial [k] in "keep." The VOT duration is measured from the velar release just prior to the aspiration noise until the first voicing striation following. Note that as these are wide-band spectrograms, although the formants are quite clear, the harmonics are not distinguishable. Each formant is typically composed of several relatively intense harmonics, visually "smeared together" by the wide-band analysis technique, as can be more clearly observed by comparing (c) with (d) in Figure 16.1. Note also the low F2 in the vowel "oo" in "you" as compared to the high F2 of "ee" in "keep".

Coarticulation and the Phoneme

In fluent speech no tidy one-to-one mapping necessarily exists between the acoustic signal and our percepts. Even word boundaries are often not well defined physically. (See Figure 16.1, caption.) While a certain sound X may be heard as preceding sound Y, the acoustic characteristics of X do not necessarily leave off where the acoustics of sound Y begin. For example in Figure 16.1 ("You lose your yellow roses early"), the final sound in "lose" clearly shows the influence of the "y" sound in "your" that immediately follows (see caption). This "spreading" influence of certain articulations, known technically as "coarticulation," can extend many milliseconds beyond the perceived temporal center of a particular speech sound. Coarticulation can be partially understood as a necessary result of the articulators moving into position for an upcoming sound even while the current sound is still being produced. Both anticipatory and perseverative types of coarticulation exist. As the combinatorial possibilities of one sound following another are enormous, this means that a particular percept exists in a one-to-many relation with its acoustic expressions in the physical signal.

The prevalence of coarticulation means that discrete perceptual units like consonants and vowels are linguistic abstractions that do not exist in the raw acoustic signal. Most models of speech perception and spoken word recognition, however, assume the extraction of some intermediate representational unit such as the phoneme. In response to the problem that coarticulation poses to characterization of individual phonemes, several other alternative units of perceptual analysis have been proposed over the years, including the syllable, context-sensitive units such as the diphone[2] or triphone[3], or even entire word forms. The issue of what unit of analysis is "most fundamental" is often hotly debated. Because speech perception is a temporally unfolding process, however, involving hierarchically related neural representations of the input being constructed "on-line," the "unit" upon which a particular experimental response is based most likely depends on the precise nature of the information processing task assigned to the human perceiver.

Even so, for many years, the predominant focus of study has been on phoneme-level units of perception (Liberman, Cooper, Shankweiler, & Studdert-Kennedy, 1967; Nearey, 1990). While these efforts have not yielded necessary and sufficient invariant predictors for the perception of phonemic categories, they have provided valuable information about the acoustic correlates of larger classes of sounds (e.g., vowels vs. consonants).

Articulatory and Acoustic Correlates of Vowel Perception

In wide-band spectrograms of carefully articulated speech, vowels are visually quite prominent, usually marked clearly by a sequence of vertical voicing striations and characterized by dark bands of horizontally-running formants (Figure 16.3). Formants are concentrated regions of acoustic energy created through the enhanced intensity of certain harmonics of the fundamental frequency and the attenuation of other f0 harmonics due to the natural resonance characteristics of the vocal tract. The lowest frequency formant is typically referred to as "F1," the next highest formant as "F2," and so on. These resonances were first investigated by Chiba and Kajiyama (1941), Fant (1960), and Stevens (Stevens & House, 1955), by modeling the human vocal tract during vowel production as a pair of simple tube resonators, one representing the front oral cavity and one representing the back pharynx cavity. In a spectrogram, steeply sloping formants indicate rapid changes in the resonant frequencies due to articulator movement and are typically referred to as "formant transitions." Non-sloping, horizontal formants of relatively long duration indicate a stable articulatory configuration and are sometimes referred to as "steady-state" portions of the vowel.

The relative positioning of the two or three lowest frequency formants over time helps to perceptually distinguish the different vowel sounds. Low-frequency first formants tend to be caused by the raising or arching of the tongue up towards the roof of the mouth. The further back the location of this tongue-raising within the oral cavity, the lower the F2 frequency. Relative duration is also used to distinguish some vowels. Often, the brief vowels found in rapid speech or unstressed syllables are said to "lose their spectral quality" because their formant values do not change rapidly enough to reach the frequency values typical of longer instances, and are thus less characteristic, or "undershot" (Fant, 1960). Although this might be seen as problematic for perceptually discriminating different vowels, it has been shown that some information about vowel identity is present in the rapid formant transitions that initiate and conclude a vowel sound flanked by consonants (Strange, Jenkins, & Johnson, 1983).

Every speaker uses some range of possible formant frequencies to produce recognizable vowels. The bounds of this acoustic space are defined by the physiology of the speaker's vocal tract and translate into a "vowel space" whose edges are defined by the most extreme values of the first two or three formants in the speaker's vowel set (Gerstman, 1968; Hillenbrand, Getty, Clark, & Wheeler, 1995; Peterson & Barney, 1952). Perceptually, the vowels produced in these extreme regions correspond to the so-called "point vowels" – the [u] as in "who'd," the [i] as in "heed" and the [ɑ] as in "hod" or "haughty" (Figure 16.4). Languages differ on how many regions within this perceptual-acoustic space they use to represent different vowels, and in where these regions lie in the space.

Articulatory and Acoustic Correlates of Consonant Perception

Most of the acoustic cues that differentiate consonants lie in the interval of about 1500 to 6000 Hz, and although the intensity of these cues is weak in absolute terms compared to those of vowels, the human auditory system's increased sensitivity in this range partially compensates for this fact.

Consonants in English can be roughly sorted along three major articulatory dimensions: (a) manner of articulation (very generally, how the articulators move), (b) place of articulation (where the most constriction occurs in the vocal tract), and (c) voicing (whether and when the vocal cords are vibrating during articulation).

Fricatives utilize a narrow but incomplete closure of the articulators and are distinguished phonetically by intervals of aperiodic noise at particular frequencies. The fricatives [s], [ʃ], [z], [ʒ][4] have noise energy concentrated at the higher frequencies (higher for [s] and [z] than for [ʃ] and [ʒ]) and are of relatively long duration, while [f], [θ], [v], [ð][5] have

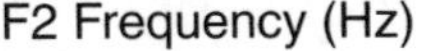

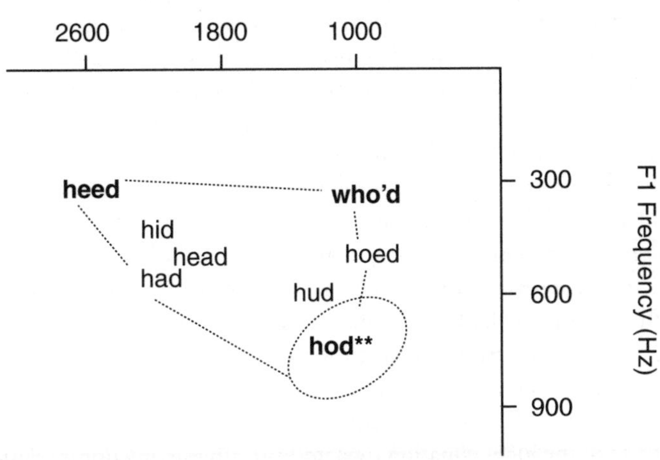

Figure 16.4. An average vowel space for a male speaker of American English. The "point-vowels" [i], [u], and [ɑ] are shown in bold.

shorter duration, and consist of weaker energy spread over a wider frequency range.

Stops involve making a complete vocal tract closure which is then abruptly released, allowing air to escape (as in [b], [d], and [g], for example). Thus, abrupt stretches of silence often indicate the presence of stop consonants in spectrograms. The release of a stop closure is obligatorily marked by a very brief high-frequency noise burst, the intensity and frequency of which tend to vary predictably for the different stop consonants. This release burst may be followed by additional "aspiration" noise generated at the larynx.

The nasal stops [n], [m], and [ŋ][6] are produced with the bulk of the air traveling from the lungs up into the nasal cavity via a "side-branch" route channeled off by lowering the velum, a flap of tissue at the extreme back of the mouth. Because the nasal cavity is relatively soft and large, the bandwidth of the nasal formants is wider than that of orally produced (non-nasal) formants. The shape of the tract during nasal production also results in antiformants, frequency ranges where the lack of intensity is due to active interference and canceling-out of some frequencies by others. Nasals show voicing striations and weak higher formant structure, with low and relatively intense F1s.

Finally, the American English "liquids" [l] and [ɹ] involve only partial constriction, permitting strong "vowel-like" formant structure.[7] The "glides" [j] and [w][8] closely resemble the liquids, but have their own characteristic formant patterns.

Each of these "manner" classes (fricative vs. stop vs. nasal, etc.) contains sounds distinguished from each other only by place of stricture in the vocal tract. Although clearly invariant acoustic cues to place of articulation have proved elusive, perception of place contrasts has been a long-standing area of research and debate. The bilabial (closure at the lips), alveolar (closure at the alveolar ridge), and velar (closure at the velum) stops of English all have a similar effect on the F1 frequency values transitioning into a following vowel but differ in their effect on F2 and F3 transitions. Early work by Delattre, Liberman, and Cooper (1955) suggested that consonants produced at each constriction location possessed invariant "loci" or frequencies from which these higher formant transitions would emerge (after a silent closure interval in the case of stops) and interpolate toward the frequencies characteristic of the following sound, for example, of a vowel. Unfortunately, this notion of a "locus equation" did not work well for velar consonants in different vowel contexts. A similar problem was encountered trying to use a static "template" defined by an amplitude spectrum calculated across the release burst and the formant transitions directly following (Stevens & Blumstein, 1981). In subsequent years, the search for invariant acoustic information for place of articulation turned to somewhat more complex measures of the rate and direction of spectral change over time (e.g., Kewley-Port, 1983; Kewley-Port, Pisoni, & Studdert-Kennedy, 1983). More recently, Sussman and colleagues have tried to revive a modified version of the locus equation by demonstrating strong linear relationships in CV syllables between the frequency at which the F2 transition begins and the value of F2 once it reaches the temporal midpoint of the vowel that follows (Sussman & Shore, 1996). This correlation appears to be an informative though not infallible predictor of consonant place (see Brancazio & Fowler, 1998 for counter-arguments and discussion).

The type of findings surveyed above provide useful heuristics for predicting the phoneme category associated with a particular acoustic signal, but they do not constitute invariant acoustic "markers" unique to particular phonemes. Phonemes are linguistic abstractions, not physical entities. Nevertheless, as mentioned in the introduction, speech perception was equated for many years with what we would term "phoneme perception." As an outgrowth of this approach, there have been a handful of largely phoneme-based perceptual phenomena that have been quite extensively studied. Although for completeness' sake we will review a selection of these below, it can be argued that these particular perceptual effects have, in a sense, been exhausted in their usefulness, and may be distracting from more pressing fundamental problems of fluent speech perception and spoken language processing. It is doubtful that a comprehensive theory of speech perception can be built from a selective smorgasbord of relatively low-level perceptual effects without a unified theoretical framework that binds together these different levels of analysis (see Lively, Pisoni & Goldinger, 1994 for review).

Findings From the Traditional Domain of Inquiry: Phoneme Perception

Categorical Perception

Categorical perception refers to the phenomenon of perceiving items from a large and varied stimulus set in terms of only a small number of discrete categories. Typically, in speech perception research, categorical perception is studied using a large set of synthetic stimuli varying continuously along a manipulated acoustic parameter. In a seminal paper, Liberman, Harris, Hoffman, and Griffith (1957) reported that listeners "categorically" perceived continuously varied F2 transitions in synthesized consonant-vowel syllables. A syllable best labeled as "bah" was reported for steeply rising F2 transitions, "dah" for short gradually falling F2 transitions, and "gah" for longer, steeply falling F2 transitions. Sharp "cutoff points" were found along the manipulated F2 dimension, with a single unequivocal label favored within each interval. From performance on an identification task that required the listener to label members of the stimulus set as either "bah," "dah," or "gah," it was possible to predict how well acoustically similar stimulus pairs taken from along the continuum could be discriminated (Figure 16.5a). Discrimination ability varied sharply along the continuum, with good discrimination between pairs on either side of a category label, and relatively poor discrimination for within-category pairs.

Other consonantal characteristics, such as voice-onset time, have also been manipulated to produce "categorical" responses (Liberman, 1970). Although discrimination of sustained "steady-state" vowels does not show the same general pattern (Fry, Abramson, Eimas, & Liberman, 1962), reducing the duration of the vowel (Pisoni, 1973) or placing vowels in dynamic context (Stevens, 1968; Sachs, 1969) generates discrimination functions that better resemble the data from the consonant studies. Based on comparisons drawn between the fine discriminatory abilities humans have for tones (or, in vision, for color), and the apparent phonetic insensitivity within perceptual categories that define native speech sounds, a claim from this early work on categorical perception was that different perceptual mechanisms processed speech versus non-speech auditory stimuli (e.g., Eimas, 1963).

Later evidence suggested, however, that within-category discrimination was not as poor as the strong version of categorical perception claimed, and that categorical perception effects appeared to be enhanced by the response format of the discrimination task used in the earlier studies (Fujisaki & Kawashima, 1968; Pisoni & Lazarus, 1974; Pisoni & Tash, 1974). Peripheral auditory processing limitations on the temporal resolution of acoustic detail were found to partially account for categorical perception of VOT differences, and it was discovered that non-speech stimuli with roughly similar temporal characteristics could also be discriminated categorically (Miller, Wier, Pastore, Kelly, & Dooling, 1976; Pisoni, 1977). Additionally, various researchers reported that non-human species such as the chinchilla (Kuhl & Miller, 1975), macaque (Kuhl & Padden, 1983), and Japanese quail (Kluender, Diehl, & Kileen, 1987) could be trained to categorically discriminate the type of stimuli used in categorical perception studies, although they could not be shown to be able to identify these signals in the same manner that human listeners do. The necessity of

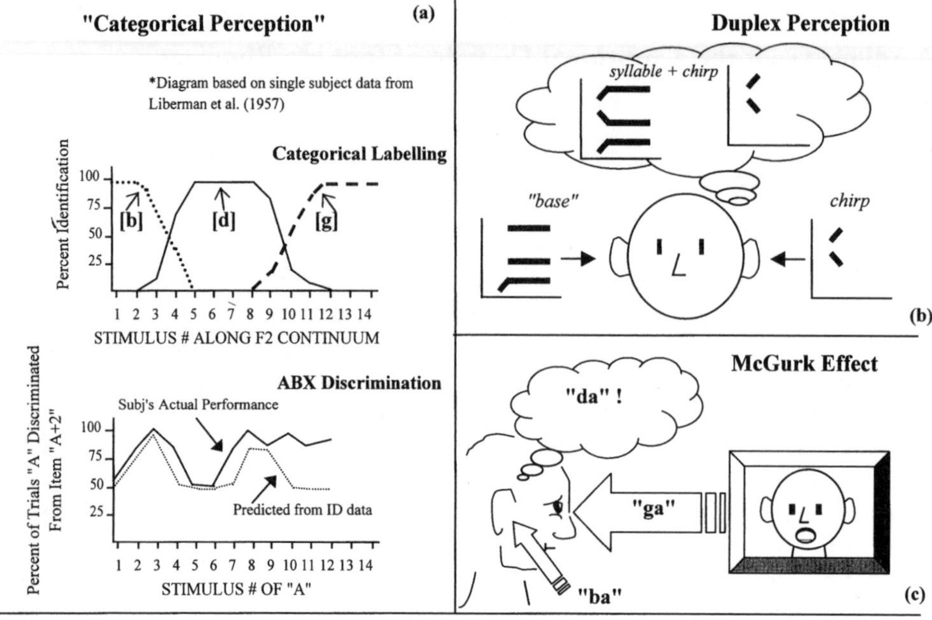

Figure 16.5. (a) Sample identification and discrimination functions relevant to the discussion of categorical perception of voiced English stop consonants. The top graph shows how each stimulus along the manipulated continuum of F2 transition rate was labeled by the subject. The bottom graph shows what occurred when the subject was asked to listen to pairs of different stimuli ("A", "B") and then decide whether a third stimulus "X" was identical to the first or to the second item in the pair. In this data, the presented pairs were always two steps apart on the manipulated continuum, and for each plotted "A" stimulus shown on the x-axis, the comparison "B" stimulus was two steps to the right. A minimum at stimulus number "5" for example, means that when the comparison pair was composed of Stimulus 5 and Stimulus 7, the third stimulus (which could have been either Stimulus 5 or Stimulus 7) was matched at chance levels to the comparison stimuli. (Illustration based on Liberman et al., 1957, © American Psychological Association, with permission.) (b) Typical stimuli and the resulting percepts in a duplex perception experiment. Although the stimuli used in these experiments may vary, this example shows a "base" constructed from the steady-state portions of the syllable, plus the F1 formant transition. The "chirp" consists of the F2 and F3 formant transitions. Note the "reconstruction" of the full syllable shown on the upper left-hand side. (c) Visual and auditory inputs that result in the "fused" McGurk percept. The effect has partially been explained in terms of the visual prominence of labial closures (as in "ba") when they occur. Because in the McGurk paradigm the visual input is inconsistent with the usually obvious labial closure, the perceiver is influenced to hear the relatively fragile high-frequency auditory cue to place of articulation as evidence of a closure further back in the vocal tract.

postulating an innate mechanism unique to the human brain specifically for making speech (as opposed to non-speech) distinctions using this particular paradigm has therefore been rejected, although the more fundamental issue of whether this form of "categorical" perception should ever have been proposed as the litmus test for the existence of specialized speech mechanisms in the first place continues to be debated.

Research in categorical perception nevertheless fueled considerable interest in how "categorical-like" discrimination of speech sounds in humans might develop. (For reviews see Aslin, Jusczyk, & Pisoni, 1998; Werker, 1992.) Pioneering work by Eimas, Siqueland, Jusczyk, and Vigorito (1971) used a habituation-based high-amplitude sucking procedure to show that infants as young as one month of age demonstrated categorical-type responses to voiced vs. voiceless stimuli. Subsequent research suggested that infants under six months of age responded in a "categorical" fashion along many of the acoustic dimensions used by the world's languages to distinguish different phonemes, regardless of whether these particular contrasts were used in the language native to the child. After the first half year of life, however, infants appeared to show lessened sensitivity to some sound contrasts foreign to the child's linguistic environment, particularly when these contrasts conflicted with the phonemic distinctions of their native language (Werker & Tees, 1984). As in the animal studies mentioned above, whether or not infants were explicitly *identifying* phonetic categories in the tasks employed remained at issue, but unlike the non-human species, human infants did not require hundreds of training trials to show discrimination (Eimas, 1985). More recent research has shown that the "lessened sensitivity" shown by older infants and adults is not strictly irreversible or absolute, and that an accurate theory of early sensitivity to speech contrasts requires more complicated assumptions than first thought. The most important insight to be taken from this research, however, is that the experiences of even very young infants constitute the groundwork for adult speech perception.

A natural extension has been the exploration of categorical perception in the context of perceiving and learning a second language. For example, it has been shown that listeners often demonstrate an apparent inability to perceptually discriminate speech stimuli that resemble items of a single phonemic category in their native language but which represent different phonemic categories in the nonnative language (e.g., Lisker & Abramson, 1967; Goto, 1971). The difficulty that native Japanese speakers encounter trying to perceive the distinction in English between [ɹ] and [l], a contrast not utilized in Japanese, is one case that has attracted considerable attention (Miyawaki et al., 1975). Although initial reports indicated that very little "re-acquisition" of this particular contrast was possible, high-variability training that incorporates a wide variety of phonetic contexts and different speakers has demonstrated reliable improvements in this discrimination by adult Japanese monolinguals (Logan, Lively, & Pisoni, 1991; Bradlow, Pisoni, Akahane-Yamada, & Tohkura, 1997). Reacquisition success appears to also depend crucially on the particular contrast involved and its relation to an individual's native sound inventory (Best, 1994; Best, McRoberts, & Sithole, 1988). These results have served to warn against relying too heavily on generalizations made from the study of phoneme perception under highly limited contexts as this has led to underestimating the plasticity of the adult perceptual system.

Duplex Perception

Another laboratory phenomenon frequently cited as evidence for specialized speech perception mechanisms is duplex perception (for review, see Repp, 1982). Given a synthetic

CV syllable, if the brief frequency transitions into the higher vowel formants are presented in isolation to one ear, and a complex "base" consisting of the complete first formant plus the remaining steady-state portions of the higher formants is presented to the other, listeners report not one, but *two* percepts – a "fused" speech syllable in the ear that was played the "base" with the missing upper formant transitions, and a non-speech "chirp" in the ear into which the lone transitions were played (Figure 16.5b) (Rand, 1974).

It has been argued by Liberman and his colleagues that a speech-specific route of perception leads to the fused syllable percept, while a separate "general auditory" process results in the non-speech percept. Other researchers have reported, however, that these "duplex" percepts can be elicited by using components analogously isolated from complex non-speech stimuli – the sound of a slamming door, or a musical chord, for example (Fowler & Rosenblum, 1990; Pastore, Schmuckler, Rosenblum, & Szczesiul, 1983). These non-speech results clearly call into question the idea that a specialized speech perception mechanism is necessarily responsible for the duplex perception results. It remains possible, however, that the duplex percept arises from a special system designed to attribute causal sources to familiar sounds (Ballas, 1993; Gaver, 1993), or general perceptual organization and auditory grouping mechanisms (e.g., Remez, Rubin, Berns, Pardo, & Lang, 1994).

Perception of the duplex syllable component suggests automatic integration of acoustic information from different sources into a single speech percept having a perceived common source. Stored information reflecting a statistical correlation between the past occurrences of similar spectral components may favor this type of processing for familiar complex sounds. As we next discuss, a similar kind of learning appears to underlie yet another type of integration in speech perception, that is, integration of inputs across different modalities.

Visual Contributions to Phoneme Perception and the McGurk Effect

It has been known since the early days of telephone communications research that certain sounds are more susceptible to being misheard than others (Fletcher, 1929). Often the resulting confusions ([v] for [b], for example) tend to share acoustic attributes along dimensions such as voicing and nasality, but differ along dimensions such as place of articulation (Miller & Nicely, 1955). Some of this ambiguity is removed in natural settings by the fact that a speaker's face is often available to the perceiver. Access to a speaker's face has been shown to significantly improve intelligibility under less than ideal conditions, such as low signal-to-noise ratios (Sumby & Pollack, 1954). However, it is not only under auditorily degraded conditions that visual information has a functional impact. A now-classic paper published by McGurk and MacDonald (1976) reported that auditory recordings of "ba" dubbed to filmed articulations of a person saying "ga" often led to reports of "da" – a "fused" utterance with an intermediate place of articulation (at the alveolar ridge) that was never actually presented (see Figure 16.5c).[9] This "fusion effect" is not lost by an awareness of the manipulation or by repeated exposure. The McGurk effect is an illusion based on an unnatural co-occurrence of inputs, but it helps to demonstrate that speech perception is susceptible to the influence of visual information even when the auditory signal is not degraded. This finding has led to interest in just how much information the visual channel can provide during speech perception (Massaro, 1998). "Viseme" has been the term coined to refer to an abstract linguistic unit of visual analysis analogous to the phoneme (Fisher, 1968). An example of a viseme is the set of speech sounds that all involve a visually apparent closure of the lips (i.e., [p], [b], and [m]). In general, the equivalence classes for visemes are somewhat larger than those for phonemes. Confusability statistics have been generated for different visemes and the idea of "viseme-defined" lexicons has been explored (Auer & Bernstein, 1997).

Coarticulatory Context Effects

We have just seen how a single acoustic signal may be perceived differently given different visual contexts. Similar phenomena have been shown to occur naturally in the auditory channel alone. Single spectrographically salient acoustic cues are often perceived differently depending on other sounds in their immediate context. These data are usually described as coarticulatory context effects (Repp, 1982). A synthetic release burst centered at 1600 Hz, for example, is perceived as [p] before vowels with low F1s such as [i], but as a [k] before the vowel [ɑ] (Liberman, Delattre & Cooper, 1952). Frication noise with spectral intensities ambiguous between an alveolar and a palatal will be perceived as an [s] (an alveolar sound) if preceding a rounded vowel such as in "Sue," but more often as a [ʃ] before the vowel [ɑ] as in "shot" (Mann & Repp, 1980). Such "context-conditioned" effects are common and have been used to argue for a syllable-based rather than phoneme-based "unit" of speech perception.

Lexical Influences on Phoneme Perception

In naturalistic circumstances, we distinguish between phonemes in the larger context of spoken words. A number of studies have shown that a listener's lexical knowledge can subtly influence the interpretation of acoustic cues to phoneme identity. A common illustration of this is the finding that the VOT criterion for what constitutes the voiced vs. voiceless contrast for stimuli with ambiguous VOTs is affected by the lexical status of the sound pattern formed by interpreting the acoustic information as one phoneme versus the other (Ganong, 1980). For example, if two VOT continua of voiced-to-voiceless synthetic stimuli are constructed, one ranging from the word "beef" to the non-word "peef," and the other from the non-word "beace" to the real word "peace," the "cut-off" VOT value for labeling a stimulus as beginning with a "b" vs. a "p" will not be the same for the two continua. That is, listeners will tend to more often label a stimulus having a single "ambiguous" VOT value as a word over a non-word, or as a high-frequency word over a low-frequency word, given the option (Connine, Titone, & Wang, 1993).

Lexical knowledge can even cause a "filling-in effect" to occur when part of a familiar or contextually predicable word is artificially obliterated with a patch of noise. Listeners often report hearing the missing segment in addition to the noise. This phenomenon is called the "phoneme restoration effect" (Bagley, 1900/1901; Cole & Rudnicky, 1983; Warren, 1970). Mispronunciations within familiar words often go undetected for apparently similar reasons. It has also been found that although utterances filtered to remove high-frequency information are usually difficult to understand "in the clear," they are, almost paradoxically, *more* intelligible when played through noise – presumably because "restoration mechanisms" are recruited to process this degraded form of input (Miller, 1956).

Some theorists believe that a discussion of lexical effects on perceiving phonemic contrasts does not properly belong in a discussion of speech perception, arguing that lexical influences are merely "biases" that operate "post-perceptually" only in circumstances where the auditory signal is degraded. Although we do not believe this to be a tenable position, clearly a major issue in speech perception is how and when different types of "top-down" knowledge and information in long-term memory come in contact with incoming "bottom-up" data (Luce & Pisoni, 1998; Massaro & Oden, 1995; McQueen, 1991; Pitt 1995; Pitt & Samuel, 1993). Thanks in part to this recruitment of both "top-down" and "bottom-up" information, our perceptual systems are remarkably robust to the wide variability that can exist in the raw acoustic speech signal, and it is to this topic that we now turn.

From Phoneme Perception to Perceiving Fluent Speech

Trading Relations

While the immediately previous sections focused on the finding that a single acoustic feature can map onto multiple percepts depending on surrounding context, as we have already mentioned it is also the case that a single percept can be cued by multiple forms of acoustic information. Most speech sound contrasts are supported redundantly by several different sets of "speech cues" in the acoustic signal. Some of these cues manifest themselves in a "trading relation," in that the stronger presence of one cue can (or must) potentially compensate for the weaker presence or non-expression of another. For example, there are several aspects of the speech signal that can contribute to the perception of voicing in stops, including the duration of voice onset time and the first formant onset frequency following release. If one shortens the VOT of a particular synthetic stimulus, the onset frequency of the F1 transition must also be increased in order to generate the same percept as previously obtained – as would naturally occur in a faster rate of speech. In natural speech speakers make use of this limited flexibility in producing variable acoustic "cues" from which listeners (having learned these constellations of articulatory compensations) are still able to perceive the intended linguistic contrasts.

The Intelligibility of Speech Under Transformation

Because phonemically contrastive information is widely and variably distributed temporally across the incoming speech signal, and because "top-down" information can be recruited, the speech signal can be characterized as informationally redundant and consequently quite resistant to degradation. Just how robust is the speech signal? Consider that in a telephone conversation, not only does one not have the option of looking at the talker's face, but the typical telephone receiver only reproduces frequencies between 350 and 3500 Hz. Nevertheless, this filtered speech is usually quite intelligible. In more extreme examples, researchers looking at the intelligibility of speech under gross distortion have shown that listeners can still recognize many words in a non-anomalous sentence even if, for example, the signal is interrupted by silence at rates faster than 10 times a second (Miller & Licklider, 1950), or is transformed to pitch-preserving time-compressed speech (Foulke, 1971). Other studies have shown that speech waveforms that have been "clipped and squared off" at their intensity peaks, or speech that has had each of its formant centers replaced with only a simple frequency-varying sinusoidal tone with all other intensities removed (Remez, Rubin, Pisoni, & Carrell, 1981), can also be linguistically intelligible. Another rarely cited extreme manipulation conducted by Blesser (1969, 1972) took the spectral information in the speech signal between 200 and 3000 Hz and rotated it around an axis at 1600 Hz. This spectral transformation seriously distorted place cues but managed to maintain perceived pitch and intonation. Despite this highly unnatural degraded format, listeners were able to partially comprehend sentences after several training sessions, leading Blesser to conclude that "learning to comprehend sentences or holding a conversation through the spectral transformation does not require the pre-requisite ability of perceiving isolated phonemes or syllables. Speech perception under normal conversing is not simply the result of processing a sequence of speech segments" (Blesser, 1969, p. 5). Findings in a similar vein have been reported more recently by Shannon, Zeng, Kamath, Wygonski, et al. (1995).

Normalization Issues and Indexical Information

The fact that the speech signal is so redundantly specified to the experienced listener suggests that it might be possible to perform some type of stimulus reduction such that only non-redundant information would play a role in the recognition process. The variety of distortion types that can be successfully dealt with, however, makes this a daunting proposition. Nevertheless, implicit in nearly all work in speech perception is the assumption that hearers "normalize" the acoustic speech signal in order to recognize an abstract idealized symbolic linguistic message (Pisoni, 1997). That is to say, signal variability not directly associated with the abstract linguistic message, such as information about speech rate or talker identity or speaking mode, is somehow culled from the signal, providing a "standardized" representation of an idealized canonical linguistic form. This "normalized" signal is thought to be the true object of speech perception, according to this abstractionist/symbolic view. Through normalization, it is argued, the perceptual equivalence of utterances spoken at different rates, or by individuals with different-sized vocal tracts is possible.

Some researchers have conceptualized perceptual normalization as an "on-line adjustment" made by a listener to deal with different speakers and speaking styles. It has been suggested that once this "calibration" takes place, it continues to apply to all input perceived as coming from the same source. One proposed mechanism is that the bounds of a speaker's vowel space are extracted from early portions of the signal and then used to "scale" the utterance into a normalized form (Gerstman, 1968; Ladefoged & Broadbent 1957).

Normalized information used to make "linguistic" discriminations has traditionally been conceived of as having an independent existence apart from non-linguistic, "indexical" information also contained in the signal. The term "indexical" refers to those aspects of the speech signal that provide information regarding the speaker's identity and condition. (The speaker is John, the speaker is sad, etc.) Traditionally, this type of information was thought to be "channeled-off" to some other processing mechanism during a normalization stage of speech perception, and not thought to have much of a short- or long-term impact on perceiving phonemic contrasts or recognizing spoken words (e.g., Halle, 1985). In recent years, however, evidence has begun to accumulate suggesting that indexical information in speech is not discarded during or after normalization. Theories of speech perception grounded in general theories of cognition and human information processing now recognize that indexical properties of the signal interact with memory and attention processes and contribute to how linguistic messages are perceived (Johnson & Mullennix, 1997).

Short-term as well as long-term influences of indexical properties on speech perception have been demonstrated. Nygaard, Sommers, and Pisoni (1994) and Nygaard and Pisoni (1998), among others, have shown that familiarization with a talker's voice facilitates the accuracy of identification (intelligibility) of novel utterances by that same talker. Memory studies reported in Goldinger (1996) demonstrate that recognition of studied words as "old" or "new" items at test is facilitated if the same voice is used in the test phase as in study (with as much as a week between study and test). In this last example, the facilitative voice information appears to be stored in an "implicit" form of memory, able to impact performance on a variety of speech-related tasks, even if no explicit memory for indexical information can be reported by listeners (see Goldinger, 1998).

A number of experiments have shown decrements in word and phoneme identification when stimuli are spoken by different talkers from trial to trial (see Mullennix, 1997, for a review). Lippman (1997) has suggested that experiencing several seconds of continuous speech from a talker is necessary for a listener to perform word identification at optimal levels. These interference effects caused by shifts in indexical information are not easily avoided; Mullennix and Pisoni (1990) reported, for example, that listeners cannot simply choose to completely ignore one type of information (phoneme identifying characteristics vs. voice identifying characteristics), even when explicitly instructed to do so.

In short, there is now a large and growing body of evidence suggesting that speech perception involves extracting both indexical information and a "symbolic" linguistic message from the speech signal, and that perception is necessarily influenced by representations of both kinds of information in memory. These sources of information are likely to be extracted at different rates from the signal, but these extraction processes are not independent of each other as once thought.

Findings generated using indexically poor "laboratory speech" may be difficult to generalize to speech perception under more realistic conditions. "Lab-speech" has traditionally involved items spoken (or synthesized) in isolation, consisting typically of nonsense syllables, and sometimes monosyllabic and spondaic single words. It is typically spoken slowly, using very careful articulation, and often read rather than spontaneously spoken. Often stimuli are created using only a single talker or speech synthesis system. These simplifications were practical and necessary in the past; however, a less conservative and more naturalistic corpus will permit the development of more comprehensive theories of speech perception (see also Stevens, 1996). The next section outlines why this issue of "lab speech" is of importance to speech perception and spoken language processing.

The Impact of Speaking Styles on Perception

One of the most interesting current issues in speech perception concerns the nature of the communication process and how this is reflected in the production provided to a hearer's perceptual system. Speaker and hearer typically share knowledge about what is "old" and "new" information in a conversation (Haviland & Clark, 1974). With this knowledge, it has been argued, " . . . the (ideal) speaker makes a running estimate of the listener's need for explicit signal information on a moment to moment basis. He then adapts the production of the utterance elements (words, syllables, or phonemes) to those needs" (Lindblom, 1996, p. 1687; Lindblom, 1990).

Do these different speaking modes impact perception? Almost certainly. Hearers regularly benefit from speakers' automatic tendency to raise their voices in the presence of competing background noise (Lane & Tranel, 1971). Speakers also tend to place greater stress on rare words or when introducing a new topic (Berry, 1953; Fowler & Housum, 1987). More recently, Wright (1997) has shown that speakers modify their speech as a function of the estimated confusability of the word spoken. Specifically, words that sound similar to many high-frequency words are articulated using vowels that define a larger, more expanded vowel space than equally familiar words which have very few similar-sounding words. Note however, that there is also the countering influence of speaker effort: Lindblom (1996, p. 1688) argues that " . . . phonetic form . . . is determined by the speaker's assumptions about the informational needs of the listener and by his own tacit propensity to make articulatory simplifications." When a speaker and listener do not share the same experiences and expectations regarding the content of the signal, speech communication can be expected to suffer.

It is therefore misleading to conceive of the "interactive" aspect of naturalistic speech perception as "beginning strictly after peripheral auditory processing finishes." Rather, the raw acoustic signal itself is produced as a function of another speech user's knowledge about speech and language. In this sense, a "cognitive" influence on speech production has helped to determine perceptual outcome long before the signal has reached the listener's brain.

Although we have first presented what we view as some of the most promising approaches in current speech perception research, these ideas have not developed in a vacuum. Next we briefly review theoretical approaches to speech perception that have contributed to shaping the ideas already presented.

General Theoretical Approaches to the Study of Speech Perception

Motor Theory of Speech Perception

The lack of invariance in the acoustic signal caused speculation for many years that perceptual data might somehow align better with facts of articulation (Liberman, Cooper, Harris, & MacNeilage, 1963). For example, Liberman et al. pointed out that the acoustic cues for a [d] in a syllable onset differ depending on the vowel that follows, yet an articulatory description of [d] as "an alveolar constriction" is comparable in each environment. They proposed that speech is decoded into an abstract phoneme-based representation via a listener's own knowledge of the effects of coarticulation on his/her own productions. This "motor theory" of speech perception argued that listeners make use of their own internalized articulator motor patterns, encapsulated in a "specialized speech module," to interpret heard speech (Liberman, 1970; Liberman & Mattingly, 1989).

It was soon found, however, that low-level articulatory motor activity maps no less variably to perception than does the acoustic signal. Both within and across individual speakers, articulatory variability is very high even when the perceptual result is relatively stable (e.g., Harris, 1977; Johnson, Ladefoged & Lindau, 1993; MacNeilage, 1970). Motor theory was subsequently revised, such that the proposed motor correspondence no longer referred to externally measurable articulatory motions, but rather to the recovery of abstract sets of motor commands, or "intended phonetic gestures." With this change, however, motor theory's main hypothesis became extremely difficult, if not impossible to test. Researchers, however, continue to explore the idea that the role of the perceiver as also a producer should contribute a potentially valuable information source in a model of speech perception.

The Direct Realist Approach

The "direct realist" approach to speech perception is based on the legacy of Gibsonian ideas of "direct perception," particularly in the areas of vision and haptic sensation (Gibson, 1966). With reference to speech, direct realism is largely associated with the work of Fowler and colleagues (Fowler, 1986, 1996). The main point being made in the direct realist approach is that in delving only deeper into the intricacies of acoustic variation, the ecological function of speech perception is in danger of being ignored. What animals directly perceive is information about events in their environment, not the intermediate structure conveyed to some intervening medium such as the air. Explanation, it is argued, can be couched in terms of the "public aspect" of perception. Proponents of this view suggest that "there is no need to look inside the perceiver to explain how the percept acquires its motor character" (Fowler & Rosenblum, 1990, p. 743). In other words, there is no need for positing the intermediate mental representations of a levels-of-processing model.

The "motor character" of the percept is referred to above, because ostensibly, the objects of perception in direct realism are still abstract gestures. The abstract gestures described by direct realist approaches span more than a single modality, however, thereby providing the potential basis for a type of parity relation between perception and production. A basic premise of direct realism is that speech is directly perceived like any other meaningful sound in a creature's environment, in terms of a hypothesis about its source (Gaver, 1993), using perceptual mechanisms that are not necessarily unique to humans.

Although a direct realist perspective provides a valuable reminder of the need to step back and consider speech perception in relation to its larger environment, designing methods for testing its basic claims is difficult. (For discussion see Fowler, 1996; Lindblom, 1996; Ohala, 1996; Studdert-Kennedy, 1986.)

Integration of Multiple Information Sources

The "fuzzy logical model of perception" (FLMP) proposed by Massaro (Massaro, 1987, 1989, 1998; Oden & Massaro, 1978) attempts to model both auditory and visual influences on speech perception under very specific response constraints. Massaro's theory of speech perception is probably best characterized as a parameter-tailored version of a more general Bayesian model for general categorization of stimuli into mutually exclusive categories. The motivation for this model is to see if perception of bimodal speech can or cannot be explained in terms of a simple mixture or weighting of the two channels of information, auditory and visual. FLMP assumes that the information conveyed in the two sensory input channels is independently evaluated before integration. Inputs are specified in terms of continuously valued feature values – "partial truth values" which reflect the probability of a feature's presence (i.e., x is partially voiced). This is the "fuzzy logic" aspect of FLMP. Following evaluation, the two sources of information are integrated and then compared to (modality-independent feature-based) best "example" prototypes in long-term memory. The best match constitutes the most probable perceptual report.

This model has been formalized so generally (in terms of basic axioms of formal probability) that some have commented (e.g., Crowder, 1989; Cutting, Bruno, Brady & Moore, 1992) that FLMP in a sense works "too well." Indeed, by adjusting the probability and prior probability parameters on a case by case basis, FLMP can be tightly fit to a variety of existing response data from forced-choice discrimination and goodness-ratings tasks involving stimulus items ranging along a single continuum between two perceptual categories.

Massaro has used signal detection theory and FLMP to try to disentangle "pure" perceptual sensitivity for phonemic contrasts from different kinds of response "biases." Lexical influences are often mentioned by Massaro as being among these "biases" (Massaro, 1994). Future versions of FLMP will hopefully begin to examine these important "biases" in more detail, allowing generalizability beyond simple closed-set response choices involving a minimal number of contrasts using only synthetic speech.

Bridging the Gap Between Speech Perception and Spoken Word Recognition

General Points Regarding Spoken Word Recognition

The study of speech sound perception has traditionally minimized, or simply ignored, the possible influences of lexical and other linguistic knowledge. On the other hand, spoken word recognition models often assume, as their input, the very output that models of speech perception have a difficult time accounting for, that is, sequences of idealized, symbolic phonemes, neatly segmented at word boundaries. Clearly, some future integration of these approaches is to be aimed at.

In the following sections we review – in highly abbreviated form – a selection of current spoken word recognition models.

Cohort Theory

The Cohort model (Marslen-Wilson & Welsh, 1978; Marslen-Wilson, 1987) was among the first to make detailed predictions about the time course of the recognition process in the context of acoustic-phonetic similarities between known words. Early versions of cohort theory conceived of the recognition process as the temporally unfolding "weeding-out" of a competitive cohort of possible word candidates as each new bit of acoustic input becomes available. Recognition occurred, according to the model, when only a single word candidate remained in the cohort. (See Figure 16.6a.)

The Cohort model has been studied extensively using the gating paradigm introduced by Grosjean (1980). The gating paradigm asks listeners to identify a word given successively longer segments of the signal (usually measured from its onset). Performance on this task provides some insight into the time course of word recognition and factors influencing the selection of lexical candidates (see also Salasoo & Pisoni, 1985).

The original Cohort model assumed that candidates were fatally eliminated from consideration immediately upon receiving inconsistent acoustic-phonetic information. This assumption has since been relaxed to permit instances of successful identification given degraded or distorted input. Elimination of candidates is also possible via "top-down" contextual information. Data showing that humans identify high-frequency words more quickly and accurately than low-frequency words can be accounted for by having stored representations of familiar words advantageously possess elevated resting activation levels. While these activation levels can be gradually suppressed in the face of counter-evidence, higher-frequency words will tend to remain in the active cohort longer than low-frequency candidates.

Cohort theory fails, however, to incorporate any influence of cohort *size* during the time course of recognition. It also assumes knowledge of where one word starts and another begins. The way in which this model deals with spoken non-words presented for lexical decision is also not ideal. It predicts that *non-words* will be identified as such immediately after

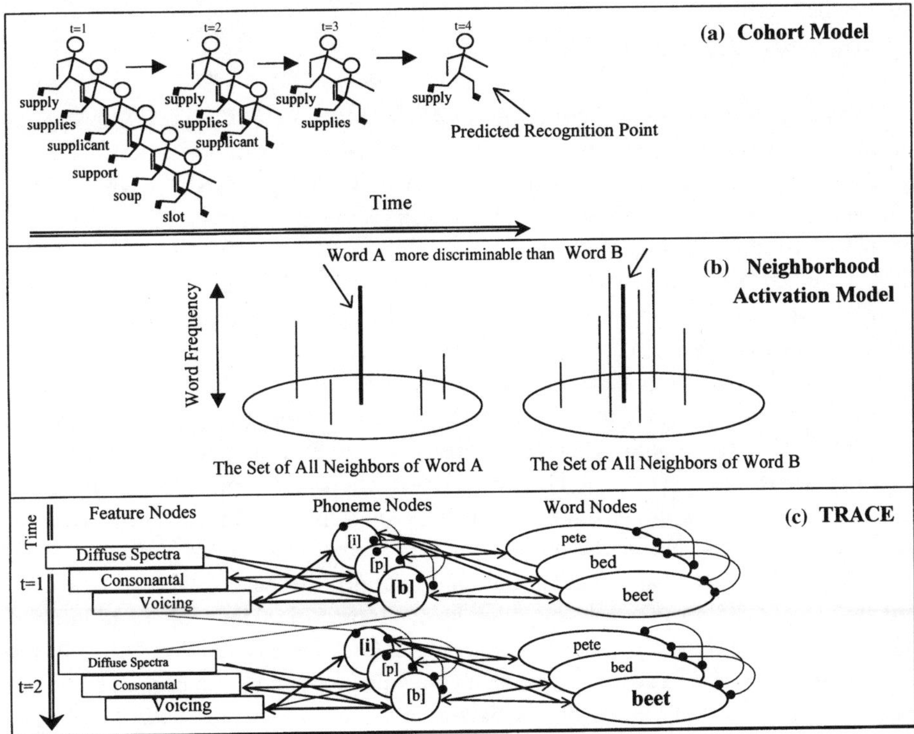

Figure 16.6. The basic structure of the three models of spoken word recognition discussed in this chapter, simplified for illustrative purposes. An illustration of how the Cohort model might predict the time-course of recognition for the word "supply" is shown in (a). Note how members of the cohort gradually drop out. The relative discriminability of two words of comparable frequency is shown in (b) as predicted by the NAM model. Word A as shown has only a few relatively low-frequency neighbors. Word B is similar-sounding to many other high-frequency words and thus is less likely to be correctly identified than Word A. A greatly simplified representation of the TRACE model is shown in (c). Connections ending in arrowheads indicate excitatory connections. Round-knobbed connections indicate inhibitory links. The example is intended to illustrate how the relative activations within each layer might change within the transition from the initial consonant to the medial vowel in the word "beet." Larger typeface symbolizes greater activation of a particular node. Connections with negligible weights are not shown.

they structurally "diverge" from all known words; the data, however, suggest that information occurring after the divergence point can influence non-word decision speed (Taft & Hambly, 1986). Also problematic for cohort theory are findings that real words are often *not* recognized immediately upon the theoretical point at which all other candidates are supposedly eliminated; in many situations some delay is experienced (Bard, Shillcock, & Altmann,1988; Grosjean & Gee, 1987). These results have encouraged exploration of other, more flexible ways of defining "cohort" candidate sets during word recognition.

The Neighborhood Activation Model

The basis of the Neighborhood Activation Model (NAM) (Luce & Pisoni, 1998) is a large body of evidence suggesting that words are recognized relationally in the context of knowledge about other similar-sounding words (Treisman, 1978). The term "neighborhood" simply refers to the set of words that are phonetically similar to a given word according to a particular criterion (see Figure 16.6b).

NAM predicts that all other factors being equal, lower probabilities of correct identification will be associated with words that have any of the following factors "working against them": (a) low frequency, (b) many neighbors, (c) many high-frequency neighbors, (d) many acoustically fragile/confusable constituent phonemes, or (e) many neighbors with acoustically fragile/confusable constituent phonemes. Phonemic transcriptions, corpora-based frequency statistics, and behavioral auditory confusion data provide the parameters for NAM's specialized version of R. D. Luce's (1959) "choice rule." NAM has been used to make a number of successful qualitative predictions about speed and accuracy measures for lexical decision and naming tasks as a function of the above factors (Luce & Pisoni, 1998).

In practice, this model has usually operationally defined the "neighborhood" of a given word as the set of all known words that differ by one substitution, deletion, or addition of a phoneme from the transcription of the target word (Greenberg & Jenkins, 1964). NAM generally assumes access to a segmented, phoneme-based representation of speech and has been criticized for lacking much of a dynamic temporal component. Luce, Goldinger, Auer, and Vitevitch (in press) have suggested, however, that NAM might be revised to reflect a probability computation unfolding continuously in time as input is received.

The TRACE Model

Connectionist approaches to spoken word recognition involve computing activation values in parallel across different layers of computational units called "nodes." Each layer of nodes is assumed to represent a different level of abstract linguistic structure. Nodes may have their activation levels influenced by relationships defined with other nodes in terms of weighted connection strengths. The network's behavior is determined by deploying an activation function and an update rule on its architecture. Connectionist models have the attraction of both formal specification and potentially physical implementation. They are often extensively pre-designed to accomplish a certain task (as is the case with TRACE, discussed below), but it is worth keeping in mind that a more interesting case is the self-organizing net that adapts itself via a learning process often (but not necessarily) provided by the designer (see Grossberg, Boardman, & Cohen, 1997).

TRACE (McClelland & Elman, 1986) is an interactive activation model of speech perception that uses three layers of nodes, one layer representing an acoustic feature level of analysis, a second layer, a phoneme level, and the last layer, word categories (see Figure 16.6c). Nodes within each layer represent particular acoustic features, phonemes, or lexical items. Nodes that are mutually consistent (e.g., the node for the "voicing feature," the node representing the voiced phoneme [b], and the node for the lexical item "beet") are bidirectionally connected by excitatory connections. There are also bidirectional within-layer inhibitory connections, such that a highly activated unit will tend to send negative activation to its "competitor" within-level category nodes. Observing the most active nodes within each level across the time-steps provides a simulation of the time course of recognition.

The TRACE model has been implemented using a "mock speech" input consisting of values provided for seven acoustic feature dimensions at every time-step of 25 ms.[10] Some of the coarticulation present in natural speech is retained in this representation. Additional coarticulatory influences are modeled by having each phoneme node linked to the feature nodes associated with the previous and following time-step.

TRACE can simulate many of the classic effects in the literature, and is able to recover from and "fill in" noisy input. One of TRACE's inelegances, however, is a reduplication of the entire network at each time-step. Newer neural network designs suggest ways to avoid this, and also ways of dealing with the temporal structure of the speech signal via involvement of memory resources (e.g., Grossberg et al., 1997 on ARTPHONE).

Among TRACE's weaknesses are its limited lexicon of only several hundred words and its failure to use information that can constrain the likelihood that all time slices represent plausible beginnings of words. These characteristics motivated the development of Shortlist (Norris, 1994), another connectionist model of spoken word recognition. This alternative model uses prosodic characteristics such as stress to find word beginnings. It also minimizes the impact of "top-down" lexical influences on phoneme identification under favorable listening conditions by *not* allowing alternative lexical candidates that are only partially consistent with available information to sway subsequent "lower-level" phoneme classifications via top-down excitatory connections to their mutually consistent phoneme nodes.

The models thus far presented were designed with the primary goal of accurately characterizing certain well-documented phenomena of human spoken language processing behavior. Practicality of physical implementation was not necessarily at the forefront of their concerns. The progress made towards addressing the problems of spoken language recognition from this alternative perspective has, however, yielded some useful insights about what components cannot be left out of even a minimal working speech recognition system.

Contributions from Continuous Automatic Speech Recognition

At this point, readers familiar with current commercial speech-to-text software applications may be wondering if any of the systems used in continuous automatic speech recognition by machines constitute models of human speech perception. Many automatic speech recognition (ASR) systems operate on series of spectra, smoothed to bring out formant information and reduce random noise. These are then compared to stored sets of canonical smoothed spectra, combinations of which are matched to phoneme or word representations. These matches do not go on *in vacuo*, as it were – probabilistically encoded information about what phonemes typically occur together, and how probable various word combinations are in the language, also get figured in. This "language module" or "long-term linguistic knowledge storage component" of ASR systems has turned out to be *crucial* to successful performance (Jelinek, 1997).

For ASR, within-speaker coarticulation has turned out to be the more tractable problem, but one that has been handled, not by assuming that words can be extracted phoneme by phoneme from the signal, but rather that stored knowledge about words, language, and the world can be brought to bear on the process. Variability arising from environmental conditions and cross-speaker differences (e.g., regional dialect, age), has posed a much more difficult problem, partly countered by extensive training sessions, storage of different "talker" templates, and noise-canceling microphones.

Klatt's (1979, 1986, 1989) "lexical access from spectra" model (LAFS) is a well-known ASR-derived model of human spoken word recognition based on an early speech recognition system called Harpy (Lowerre & Reddy, 1980). LAFS assumes that word recognition is a process of matching an incoming series of short-term spectra to the stored contents of a very large branching tree-structure network of temporally ordered spectra. The spectra used by this model approximate the neurally transformed signals generated by the peripheral auditory system. LAFS's method for constructing the "precompiled" decoding network is not very satisfactory, however, in that it assumes that a tree of phoneme-based representations of a speaker's vocabulary is modified to reflect all possible acoustic realizations of contextual coarticulation, thus creating a much larger tree containing spectra sequences corresponding to several thousand different diphones.

LAFS is clearly a model of a "mature" recognition system - how new words would be acquired was never addressed in detail. In fact, none of the models reviewed above provides an understanding of how the perceptual categories each model assumes arise during development.

Development of Spoken Word Recognition

Several proposals have been recently made to account for how children begin to perceptually segment words and potential words from a continuous speech stream. One theory is that sensitivity to stress patterns is key. Jusczyk, Cutler, and Redanz (1993) have shown that by nine months, American infants show evidence of developing a preference for words with a strong-weak stress pattern – the most common pattern for content words in their native language (Cutler & Carter, 1987). The learning of language-specific phonotactic distributions, that is, where particular sounds tend to occur within utterances, may also aid in segmentation (Brent & Cartwright, 1996). Evidence suggesting that infants can acquire prenatal experience with native language prosody indicates that the groundwork for dealing with the word segmentation problem may be established even before birth (DeCasper & Spence, 1986).

Although a large literature exists concerning infant and adult speech perception (albeit based on rather different operational definitions of what constitutes speech perception), the dearth of practical experimental methods has resulted in relatively little data from young children beyond infancy. It has been argued that young school-age children show the phoneme perception skills of an adult, but clearly, young children's word recognition skills are much more limited than those of adults, even while their capacity for learning the sound forms of new words is at its height. A handful of studies have begun to examine how speech perception changes as a function of a growing lexicon (Charles-Luce & Luce, 1990, 1995; Dollaghan, 1994; Gerken, Murphy, & Aslin, 1995; Walley & Metsala, 1990). Research in this area is helping to clarify how low-level auditory representations of speech interface with long-term lexical knowledge.

Some of these ideas have recently been fleshed out by Jusczyk (1993, 1997) into a theory of word recognition and phonetic structure acquisition (WRAPSA). WRASPA accounts for developmental changes in discrimination sensitivity in terms of experience-dependent changes in "weighting-schemes" applied to the acoustic-phonetic input. WRAPSA adopts an account of these weighting shifts, analogous to proposals in the general categorization literature of cognitive psychology, that "shrinking or stretching" of certain perceptual dimensions relative to their corresponding physical dimensions occurs as a result of experience (Nosofsky, 1987).

What is stored in long-term memory when a speech event is experienced? For many years, the assumption that storage space in the brain was "at a premium" favored the notion of abstract phonetic representations. "Memory space" could be used more efficiently, it was suggested, by storing a prototype (perhaps formed by averaging each new instance with the existing prototype), instead of individual experiences ("exemplars") (Posner, 1969). Research published over the past 20 years suggests, however, that massive reductions in information storage are not necessarily required or even desirable (Hintzman, 1986; Nosofsky, 1988). Listeners show evidence of storing more in their brains than simply a symbolic representation of speech, and appear to advantageously use the redundancy and variability inherent in the speech signal. Exemplar-based computational models provide ways of accounting for such findings (Estes, 1994). The WRAPSA model discussed above argues for an exemplar-based learning and storage process, as have recent models of adult vowel identification (Johnson, 1997) and results from word recognition (Goldinger, 1998).

Current Trends and Some Future Directions

While we have covered a wide variety of topics, there are several core issues touched on in this chapter that we feel are fundamental to future progress of the field. Briefly, in review: Firstly, we urge that serious attempts be made to address issues of stimulus variability now. If tackling these issues is postponed further, the problem will be compounded when issues of perceiving typical "lab speech" versus naturalistic speech are to be resolved. Variability in the speech signal may in fact represent a clever training recipe for insuring the communicative robustness of speech, rather than an inconvenient complication (as it has sometimes been treated in the past 50 years of speech science research).

Second, the organization of long-term memory representations of speech-relevant data is extremely relevant to the perception of fluent speech and must be dealt with explicitly. An account of speech perception needs to be situated in a position where it can be plausibly integrated with other aspects of cognitive functioning and development. One such example is research looking at the effects of age-related changes in short-term memory, long-term memory, and attention, on speech perception and spoken word recognition (e.g., Sommers, 1996, 1997).

More work is needed regarding audiovisual aspects of speech perception. That people can and do make use of visual information in perceiving spoken language has been firmly established. However, we still know little about when and how this information is used, and whether differences may exist between language populations (e.g. Sekiyama, 1997) or individuals.

Lastly, speech perception does not necessarily involve matching to, or storing only abstract idealized canonical units. The capacity to store data relevant to speech has been seriously underestimated in the past, and this assumption has constrained the design of speech perception and spoken word recognition models. In order to account for a number of the findings reviewed in this chapter, new types of process models must be developed. This effort will require continued cooperation from the research areas of sensory, cognitive, and developmental psychology, speech and hearing sciences, linguistics, and speech technology/engineering.

Notes

1 A "phoneme" is an abstract linguistic entity referring to the smallest unit of sound that can distinguish one meaningful word from another in a particular language. What constitutes a phoneme differs from language to language. Phoneme symbols are convenient shorthand for particular combinations of acoustic feature attributes – the attributes judged to be most critical to identification being simplified to an abstract binary labeling of either present (+) or absent (−). Specific combinations of these features are categorized as instances of a particular phoneme. The term "phone" is sometimes used to refer to one possible acoustic instantiation of a phoneme.
2 Defined by from the approximate center of one phone [see Note 1] to the midpoint of the following phone.
3 Defined from the midpoint of the preceding phone, through the target phone, to the midpoint of the following phone.
4 [s] as in "*s*ip," [ʃ] as in "*sh*ip," [z] as in "*z*ip," and [ʒ] as in "a*z*ure"
5 [f] as in "*f*in," [θ] as in "*th*in," [v] as in "*v*an," and [ð] as in "*th*en"
6 [ŋ] as in "si*ng*," "wro*ng*" and "ra*ng*"
7 [l] as in "*l*ight," [ɹ] as in "*r*ight"
8 [j] as in "yawn," [w] as in "want"
9 An auditory "ga" dubbed to a visual "ba" led, however, to reports of a "combination" of both sounds (e.g., "gabga," "baga").
10 Elman & McClelland (1986) reported a separate version of the TRACE model (TRACE I) which utilizes input values derived from actual spectra in order to identify phonemes.

Suggested Readings

Borden, G. J., Harris, K. S., & Raphael, L. J. (1994). *Speech science primer: Physiology, acoustics, and perception of speech* (3rd ed.). Baltimore, MA: Williams & Wilkins.

Denes, P. D., & Pinson, E. N. (1993). *The speech chain: The physics and biology of spoken language* (2nd ed.). New York: W. H. Freeman.

Johnson, K., & Mullennix, J. W. (1997). *Talker variability in speech processing.*. San Diego, CA: Academic Press.

Johnson, K. (1997). *Acoustic and auditory phonetics.* Cambridge: Blackwell.

Kent, R. D. (1997). *The speech sciences.* San Diego: Singular Pub. Group.

Lively, S. E., Pisoni, D. B., & Goldinger, S. D. (1994). Spoken word recognition: Research and theory. In M. Gernsbacher (Ed.), *Handbook of psycholinguistics.* New York: Academic Press.

Luce, P. A., & Pisoni, D. B. (1998). Recognizing spoken words: The Neighborhood Activation Model. *Ear and Hearing, 19,* 1–39.

Pisoni, D. B. (1993). Long-term memory in speech perception: Some new findings on variability, speaking rate and perceptual learning. *Speech Communication, 13 Special Issue,* 109–125.

Stevens, K. N. (1998). *Acoustic phonetics.* Cambridge, MA: MIT Press.

Additional Topics

Cross-linguistic Issues in Speech Perception

Examining diverse languages and drawing cross-language comparisons are vital when making general claims about human speech perception skills. Research is ongoing concerning the role of learning and experience in perceiving nonnative contrasts. The case of bilingual and multilingual speakers also poses an interesting challenge to current theories of speech perception. See Strange (1995).

Speech Perception and Development

The structure of the adult perceptual system may prove easier to understand if we can learn more about how this structure is derived. Recent research has demonstrated that infants show remarkable evidence of encoding subtle characteristics of spoken language at a very early age, paving the way for a rapid proliferation of word learning. See Goodman and Nusbaum (1994), Jusczyk (1997), and Locke (1993).

Neuropsychology and Speech

New methods of brain imaging are providing provocative new evidence about the distribution of speech processing functions in the human cortex. Current research documents distinctive patterns of cortical activity in individuals as they engage in linguistic processing, as well as interesting case studies of language-related pathologies. See Caplan (1994) and Zurif and Swinney (1994).

Speech Perception and Hearing Impairment

Studying speech perception under situations where audition is unavailable or compromised can provide valuable information concerning the role of peripheral processing constraints and the extent of visual contributions to speech perception. Data from adult and pediatric users of cochlear implants, prosthetic devices that directly stimulate the basilar membrane with an electrically coded representation of the speech signal via a surgically implanted electrode array, are providing compelling new evidence regarding the acquisition of speech perception skills. See Bernstein, Demorest, and Tucker (2000), Jesteadt (1997), Mendel and Danhauer (1997), and Tyler (1993).

Speech Recognition and Synthesis

Understanding the methods developed for automatic speech recognition by machines, and the strategies and limitations they embody, can provide an appreciation of the complexity of the task being performed by the human speech perceiver. Issues of how humans perceive and remember artificially synthesized speech are also becoming increasingly relevant to daily life as these technologies begin to be widely used in the user interfaces of commercial products. See Lippman (1997), Rabiner and Juang (1993), Syrdal, Bennett, and Greenspan (1995), and van Saten, Sproat, Olive, and Hirshberg (1997).

Speech and Animal Communication
"Language" may be "uniquely human" but communication clearly is not. Consideration of other species' native communication systems may be able to provide insight into the characteristics necessary for a robust and efficient communicative signal. See Hauser (1996).

Useful Resources Regarding Data Collection
This chapter has made reference to several well-known paradigms such as "word identification" and "gating," for example. Although the use of converging operations in investigating a particular claim is valuable, the details of the various different methodologies are sometimes difficult to grasp. See Grosjean and Frauenfelder (1997) and Sawusch (1996).

References

Aslin, R. N., Jusczyk, P. W., & Pisoni, D. B. (1998). Speech and auditory processing during infancy: Constraints on and precursors to language. In W. Damon (Ed.), *Handbook of child psychology (5th ed.), Vol. 2. Cognition, perception, & language.* New York: John Wiley & Sons.

Auer, E. T. & Bernstein, L. E. (1997). Speech reading and the structure of the lexicon: Computationally modeling the effects of reduced phonetic distinctiveness on lexical uniqueness. *Journal of the Acoustical Society of America, 102*, 3704–3710.

Bagley, W. C. (1900/1901). The apperception of the spoken sentence: A study in the psychology of language. *American Journal of Psychology, 12*, 80–130.

Ballas, J. A. (1993). Common factors in the identification of an assortment of brief everyday sounds. *Journal of Experimental Psychology: Human Perception & Performance, 19*, 250–267.

Bard, E. G., Shillcock, R. C., & Altmann, G. E. (1988). The recognition of words after their acoustic offsets in spontaneous speech: Evidence of subsequent context. *Perception & Psychophysics, 44*, 395–408.

Bernstein, L., Demorest, M. E., & Tucker, P. E. (2000). Speech perception without hearing. *Perception & Psychophysics, 62*, 233–252.

Berry, J. (1953). Some statistical aspects of conversational speech. In W. Jackson (Ed.), *Communication theory*. London: Butterworth.

Best, C. T. (1994). The emergence of native-language phonological influences in infants: A perceptual assimilation model. In J. C. Goodman & H. C. Nusbaum (Eds.), *The development of speech perception: The transition from speech sounds to spoken words.* Cambridge, MA: MIT Press.

Best, C. T., McRoberts, G. W., & Sithole, N .N. (1988). Examination of perceptual reorganization for non-native speech contrasts: Zulu click perception by English-speaking adults and infants. *Journal of Experimental Psychology: Human Perception & Performance, 14*, 345–360.

Blesser, B. (1969). The inadequacy of a spectral description in relationship to speech perception. Presentation to Acoustical Society Meeting, November, San Diego, CA.

Blesser, B. (1972). Speech perception under conditions of spectral transformation: I. Phonetic characteristics. *Journal of Speech and Hearing Research, 15*, 5–41.

Bradlow, A. R., Pisoni, D. B., Akahane-Yamada, R., & Tohkura, Y. (1997). Training Japanese listeners to identify English /r/ and /l/: IV. Effects of perceptual learning on speech production. *Journal of the Acoustical Society of America, 101*, 2299–2310.

Brancazio, L., & Fowler, C. A. (1998). On the relevance of locus equations for production and perception stop consonants. *Perception & Psychophysics, 60*, 24–50.

Brent, M. R., & Cartwright, T. A. (1996). Distributional regularity and phonotactic constraints are useful for segmentation. *Cognition, 61*, 93–125.

Caplan, D. (1994). Language and the brain. In M. A. Gersbacher (Ed.), *Handbook of psycholinguistics.* San Diego: Academic Press.

Charles-Luce, J., & Luce, P. A. (1995). An examination of similarity neighbourhoods in young children's receptive vocabularies. *Journal of Child Language, 22*, 727–735.

Charles-Luce, J., & Luce, P. A. (1990). Similarity neighbourhoods of words in young children's lexicons. *Journal of Child Language, 17,* 205–215.

Chiba, T., & Kajiyama, M. (1941). *The vowel: Its nature and structure.* Tokyo: Kaiseikan.

Cole, R. A., & Rudnicky, A. I. (1983). What's new in speech perception? The research and ideas of William Chandler Bagley, 1874–1946. *Psychological Review, 90,* 94–101.

Connine, C. M., Titone, D., & Wang, J. (1993). Auditory word recognition: Extrinsic and intrinsic effects of word frequency. *Journal of Experimental Psychology: Learning, Memory, & Cognition, 19,* 81–94.

Crowder, R. G. (1989). Categorical perception of speech: A largely dead horse, surpassingly well kicked. *Behavioral and Brain Sciences, 12,* 760.

Cutler, A., & Carter, D. M. (1987). The predominance of strong initial syllables in the English vocabulary. *Computer Speech and Language, 2,* 133–142.

Cutting, J. E., Bruno, N., Brady, N. P., & Moore, C. (1992). Selectivity, scope, and simplicity of models: A lesson from fitting judgements of perceived depth. *Journal of Experimental Psychology: General, 121,* 364–381.

DeCasper, A. J., & Spence, M. J. (1986). Prenatal maternal speech influences newborns' perception of speech sounds. *Infant Behavior and Development, 9,* 133–150.

Delattre, P., Liberman, A., & Cooper, F. S. (1955). Acoustic loci and transitional cues for consonants. *Journal of the Acoustical Society of America, 27,* 769–773.

Denes, P. B., & Pinson, E. N. (1993). *The speech chain: The physics and biology of spoken language.* New York: W. H. Freeman.

Dollaghan, C. A. (1994). Children's phonological neighbourhoods: Half empty or half full? *Journal of Child Language, 21,* 257–271.

Eimas, P. D. (1963). The relation between identification and discrimination along speech and non-speech continua. *Language and Speech, 6,* 206–217.

Eimas, P. D. (1985). The perception of speech in early infancy. *Scientific American, January,* 46–52.

Eimas, P. D., Siqueland, E. R., Jusczyk, P. W., & Vigorito, J. (1971). Speech perception in infants. *Science, 171,* 303–306.

Elman, J. L., & McClelland, J. L. (1986). Exploiting lawful variability in the speech waveform. In J. S. Perkell & D. H. Klatt (Eds.), *Invariance and variability in speech processes.* Hillsdale, NJ: Erlbaum.

Estes, W. K. (1994). *Classification and cognition.* New York: Oxford University Press.

Fant, G. (1960). *Acoustic theory of speech production, with calculations based on X-ray studies of Russian articulations.* s'Gravenhage, Netherlands: Mouton.

Fisher, C. G. (1968). Confusions among visually perceived consonants. *Journal of Speech and Hearing Research, 11,* 796–804.

Flanagan, J. L. (1972). *Speech analysis, synthesis & perception* (2nd ed.). New York: Springer-Verlag.

Fletcher, H. (1929). *Speech and hearing.* New York: Van Nostrand.

Foulke, E. (1971). The perception of time compressed speech. In D. L. Horton & J. J. Jenkins (Eds.), *The perception of language.* Columbus, Ohio: Charles E. Merrrill Publishing.

Fowler, C. A. (1986). An event approach to the study of speech perception from a direct realist perspective. *Journal of Phonetics, 14,* 3–28.

Fowler, C. A. (1996). Listeners do hear sounds, not tongues. *Journal of the Acoustical Society of America, 99,* 1730–1741.

Fowler, C. A., & Housum, J. (1987). Talker's signaling of "new" and "old" words in speech and listeners' perception and use of the distinction. *Journal of Memory and Language, 26,* 489–504.

Fowler, C. A., & Rosenblum, L. D. (1990). Duplex perception: A comparison of monosyllables and slamming doors. *Journal of Experimental Psychology: Perception & Performance, 16,* 742–754.

Fry, D. B. (1979). *The Physics of speech.* Cambridge UK: Cambridge University Press.

Fry, D. B., Abramson, A. S., Eimas, P. D., & Liberman, A. M. (1962). The identification and discrimination of synthetic vowels. *Language and Speech, 5,* 171–189.

Fujisaki, H., & Kawashima, T. (1968). The influence of various factors on the identification and discrimination of synthetic speech sounds. *Reports of the 6th International Congress on Acoustics.* Tokyo.

Ganong, W. F. (1980). Phonetic categorization in auditory word perception. *Journal of Experimental Psychology: Human Perception & Performance, 6*, 110–125.
Gaver, W. W. (1993). What in the world do we hear?: An ecological approach to auditory event perception. *Ecological Psychology, 5*, 1–29.
Gerken, L., Murphy, W. D., & Aslin, R. N. (1995). Three- and four-year-olds' perceptual confusions for spoken words. *Perception & Psychophysics, 57*, 475–486.
Gerstman, L. J. (1968). Classification of self-normalized vowels. *IEEE Transactions on Audio and Electroacoustics, AU-16, 1*, 78–80.
Gibson, J. J. (1966). *The senses considered as perceptual systems.* Boston, MA: Houghton Mifflin.
Goldinger, S. D. (1996). Words and voices: Episodic traces in spoken word identification and recognition memory. *Journal of Experimental Psychology: Learning, Memory, & Cognition, 22*, 1166–1183.
Goldinger, S. D. (1998). Echoes of echoes? An episodic theory of lexical access. *Psychological Review, 105*, 251-279.
Goodman, J. C., & Nusbaum, H. C. (1994). *The development of speech perception: The transition from speech sounds to spoken words.* Cambridge, MA: MIT Press.
Goto, H. (1971). Auditory perception by normal Japanese adults of the sounds 'l' and 'r'. *Neuropsychologia, 9*, 317–323.
Greenberg, J. H., & Jenkins, J. J. (1964). Studies in the psychological correlates of the sound system of American English. *Word, 20*, 157–177.
Grosjean, F. (1980). Spoken word recognition and the gating paradigm. *Perception & Psychophysics, 28*, 267-283.
Grosjean, F., & Frauenfelder, U. H. (Eds.) (1997). *A guide to spoken word recognition paradigms.* Hove, UK: Psychology Press.
Grosjean, F., & Gee, J. P. (1987). Prosodic structure and spoken word recognition. *Cognition, 25*, 135–155.
Grossberg, S., Boardman, I., & Cohen, M. (1997). Neural dynamics of variable-rate speech categorization. *Journal of Experimental Psychology: Human Perception & Performance, 23*, 481–503.
Halle, M. (1985). Speculations about the representation of words in memory. In V. A. Fromkin (Ed.), *Phonetic linguistics.* New York: Academic Press.
Harris, K. S. (1977). The study of articulatory organization: Some negative progress. *Haskins Laboratories Status Report on Speech Research, 50, Apr-Jun*, 13–20.
Hauser, M. D. (1996). *The evolution of communication.* Cambridge, MA: MIT Press.
Haviland, S. E., & Clark, H. H. (1974). What's new? Acquiring new information as a process in comprehension. *Journal of Verbal Learning and Verbal Behavior, 13*, 512–521.
Hillenbrand, J., Getty, L. A., Clark, M. J., & Wheeler, K. (1995). Acoustic characteristics of American English vowels. *Journal of the Acoustical Society of America, 97*, 3099–3111.
Hintzman, D. (1986). Schema abstraction in a multiple-trace model. *Psychological Review, 93*, 411-428.
Jelinek, F. (1997). *Statistical methods for speech recognition.* Cambridge, MA: MIT Press.
Jesteadt, W. (1997). *Modeling sensorineural hearing loss.* Mahwah, NJ: Lawrence Erlbaum.
Johnson, K. (1997). Speech perception without speaker normalization: An exemplar model. In K. Johnson & J. W. Mullennix (Eds.), *Talker variability in speech processing.* San Diego: Academic Press.
Johnson, K., Ladefoged, P., & Lindau, M. (1993). Individual differences in vowel production. *Journal of the Acoustical Society of America, 94*, 701–714.
Jusczyk, P. W. (1993). From general to language-specific capacities: The WRAPSA model of how speech perception develops. *Journal of Phonetics, 21*, 3–28.
Jusczyk, P. W. (1997). *The discovery of spoken language.* Cambridge, MA: MIT Press.
Jusczyk, P. W., Cutler, A., & Redenz, N. J. (1993). Infants' preference for the predominant stress patterns of English words. *Child Development, 64*, 675–687.
Kewley-Port, D. (1983). Time-varying features as correlates of place of articulation in stop consonants. *Journal of the Acoustical Society of America, 73*, 322–335.

Kewley-Port, D., Pisoni, D. B., & Studdert-Kennedy, M. (1983). Perception of static and dynamic acoustic cues to place of articulation in initial stop consonants. *Journal of the Acoustical Society of America, 73,* 1779–1793.

Klatt, D. H. (1979). Speech perception: A model of acoustic-phonetic analysis and lexical access. *Journal of Phonetics, 7,* 279–312.

Klatt, D. H. (1986). The problem of variability in speech recognition and in models of speech perception. In J. Perkell & D. H. Klatt (Eds.), *Invariance and variability in speech processes.* Hillsdale, NJ: Erlbaum.

Klatt, D. H. (1989). Review of selected models of speech perception. In W. D. Marslen-Wilson (Ed.), *Lexical representation and process.* Cambridge, MA: MIT Press.

Kluender, K. R. (1994). Speech perception as a tractable problem. In M. A. Gernsbacher (Ed.), *The handbook of psycholinguistics.* San Diego, CA: Academic Press.

Kluender, K. R., Diehl, R. L., & Kileen, P. R. (1987). Japanese quail can learn phonetic categories. *Science, 237,* 1195–1197.

Kuhl, P. K., & Miller, J. D. (1975). Speech perception by the chinchilla: Voiced-voiceless distinction in alveolar plosive consonants. *Science, 190,* 69–72.

Kuhl, P. K., & Padden, D. M. (1983). Enhanced discriminability at the phonetic boundaries for the place feature in macaques. *Journal of the Acoustical Society of America, 73,* 1003–1010.

Ladefoged, P., & Broadbent, D. E. (1957). Information conveyed by vowels. *Journal of the Acoustical Society of America, 29,* 98–104.

Lane, H., & Tranel, B. (1971). The Lombard sign and the role of hearing in speech. *Journal of Speech and Hearing Research, 14,* 677–709.

Liberman, A. M. (1970). Some characteristics of perception in the speech mode. In D. A. Hamburg (Ed.), *Perception and its disorders, Proceedings of ARNMD.* Baltimore: Williams and Wilkins.

Liberman, A. M., Cooper, F. S., Harris, K. S., & MacNeilage, P. F. (1963). A motor theory of speech perception. In *Proceedings of the Speech Communication Seminar, Stockholm 1962.* Stockholm: Royal Institute of Technology, D3.

Liberman, A. L., Cooper, F. S., Shankweiler, D. P., & Studdert-Kennedy, M. (1967). Perception of the speech code. *Psychological Review, 74,* 431–461.

Liberman, A. M., Delattre, P. C.,& Cooper, F. S. (1952). The role of selected stimulus variables in the perception of unvoiced stop consonants. *American Journal of Psychology, 65,* 497–516.

Liberman, A. M., Harris, K. S., Hoffman, H. S., & Griffith, B. C. (1957). The discrimination of speech sounds within and across phoneme boundaries. *Journal of Experimental Psychology, 54,* 358–368.

Liberman, A. M., & Mattingly, I. G. (1989). A specialization for speech perception. *Science, 243,* 489–494.

Lindblom, B. (1990). Explaining phonetic variation: A sketch of the H&H theory. In W. J. Hardcastle & A. Marchal (Eds.), *Speech production and speech modelling.* Dordrecht: Kluwer Academic.

Lindblom, B. (1996). Role of articulation in speech perception: Clues from production. *Journal of the Acoustical Society of America, 99,* 1683–1692.

Lippman, R. P. (1997). Speech recognition by machines and humans. *Speech Communication, 22,* 1–15.

Lisker, L., & Abramson, A. D. (1967). The voicing dimension: Some experiments in comparative phonetics. *Proceedings of the 6th International Congress of Phonetic Sciences.* Prague: Academia.

Locke, J. L. (1993). *The child's path to spoken language.* Cambridge, MA: Harvard University Press.

Logan, J. S., Lively, S. E., & Pisoni, D. B. (1991). Training Japanese listeners to identify English /r/ and /l/: A first report. *Journal of the Acoustical Society of America, 89,* 874–886.

Lowerre, B. T., & Reddy, D. R. (1980). The harpy speech understanding system. In W. A. Lea (Ed.), *Trends in speech recognition.* Englewood-Cliffs: Prentice Hall.

Luce, P. A., & Pisoni, D. B. (1998). Recognizing spoken words: The Neighborhood Activation Model. *Ear and Hearing, 19,* 1–39.

Luce, P. A., Goldinger, S. D., Auer, E. T., & Vitevitch, M. S. (in press). Phonetic priming, neighborhood activation, and PARSYN. *Perception & Psychophysics.*

Luce, R. D. (1959). *Individual choice behavior.* New York: Wiley.

MacNeilage, P. F. (1970). Motor control of serial ordering of speech. *Psychological Review, 77,* 182–196.

Mann, V. A., & Repp, B. H. (1980). Influence of vocalic context on perception of the [<sh>]-[s] distinction. *Perception & Psychophysics, 28,* 213–228.

Marslen-Wilson, W. G. (1987). Functional parallelism in spoken word recognition. *Cognition, 25,* 71–102.

Marslen-Wilson, W. G., & Welsh, A. (1978). Processing interactions and lexical access during word-recognition in continuous speech. *Cognitive Psychology, 10,* 29–63.

Massaro, D. W. (1987). *Speech perception by ear and eye. A paradigm for psychological inquiry.* Hillsdale NJ: Erlbaum.

Massaro, D. W. (1989). Testing between the TRACE model and the fuzzy logical model of speech perception. *Cognitive Psychology, 21,* 398–421.

Massaro, D. W. (1994). Psychological aspects of speech perception: Implications for research and theory. In M. A. Gernsbacher (Ed.), *Handbook of psycholinguistics.* San Diego: Academic Press.

Massaro, D. W. (1998). *Perceiving talking faces: From speech perception to a behavioral principle.* Cambridge, MA: MIT Press.

Massaro, D. W., & Oden, G. C. (1995). Independence of lexical context and phonological information in speech perception. *Journal of Experimental Psychology: Learning, Memory, & Cognition, 21,* 1053-1064.

McClelland, J. L., & Elman, J. L. (1986). The TRACE model of speech perception. *Cognitive Psychology, 18,* 1–86.

McGurk, H., & MacDonald, J. (1976). Hearing lips and seeing voices. *Nature, 264,* 746–748.

McQueen, J. M. (1991). The effect of the lexicon on phonetic categorization: Stimulus quality in word-final ambiguity. *Journal of Experimental Psychology: Human Perception & Performance, 17,* 433–443.

Mendel, L. L., & Danhauer, J. L. (1997). *Audiologic evaluation and management and speech perception assessment.* San Diego, CA: Singular.

Miller, G. A. (1956). The perception of speech. In M. Halle (Ed.), *For Roman Jakobson: Essays on the occasion of his sixtieth birthday, 11 October 1956.* The Hague: Mouton.

Miller, G. A., & Licklider, J. C. R. (1950). The intelligibility of interrupted speech. *Journal of the Acoustical Society of America, 22,* 167–173.

Miller, G. A., & Nicely, P. E. (1955). An analysis of perceptual confusions among some English consonants. *Journal of the Acoustical Society of America, 27,* 338–352.

Miller, J. D., Wier, C. C., Pastore, R., Kelly, W. J., & Dooling, R. J. (1976). Discrimination and labeling of noise-buzz sequences with varying noise-lead times: An example of categorical perception. *Journal of the Acoustical Society of America, 60,* 410–417.

Miyawaki, K., Strange, W., Verbrugge, R., Liberman, A. M., Jenkins, J. J., & Fujimura, O. (1975). An effect of linguistic experience: The discrimination of [r] and [l] by native speakers of Japanese and English. *Perception & Psychophysics, 18,* 331–340.

Mullennix, J. W. (1997). On the nature of perceptual adjustments to voice. In K. Johnson & J. W. Mullennix (Eds.), *Talker variability in speech processing.* San Diego: Academic Press.

Mullennix, J. W., & Pisoni, D. B. (1990). Stimulus variability and processing dependencies in speech perception. *Perception & Psychophysics, 47,* 379–390.

Nearey, T. M. (1990). The segment as a unit of speech perception. *Journal of Phonetics, 18,* 347–373.

Norris, D. (1994). Shortlist: A connectionist model of continuous recognition. *Cognition, 52,* 189–234.

Nosofsky, R. M. (1987). Attention and learning processes in the identification and categorization of integral stimuli. *Journal of Experimental Psychology: Learning, Memory, & Cognition, 13,* 87–108.

Nosofsky, R. M. (1988). Exemplar-based accounts of relations between classification, recognition, and typicality. *Journal of Experimental Psychology: Learning, Memory & Cognition, 14,* 700–708.

Nygaard, L C., & Pisoni, D. B. (1998). Talker-specific learning in speech perception. *Perception & Psychophysics, 60,* 355–376.

Nygaard, L. C., Sommers, M. S., & Pisoni, D. B. (1994). Speech perception as a talker-contingent process. *Psychological Science, 5*, 42–46.
Oden, G. C., & Massaro, D. W. (1978). Integration of featural information in speech perception. *Psychological Review, 85*, 172–191.
Ohala, J. J. (1996). Speech perception is hearing sounds, not tongues. *Journal of the Acoustical Society of America, 99*, 1718–1725.
Pastore, R. E., Schmuckler, M. A., Rosenblum, L., & Szczesiul, R. (1983). Duplex perception with musical stimuli. *Perception & Psychophysics, 33*, 469–474.
Peterson, G. E., & Barney, H. L. (1952). Control methods used in a study of the vowels. *Journal of the Acoustical Society of America, 24*, 175–184.
Pisoni, D. B. (1973). Auditory and phonetic memory codes in the discrimination of consonants and vowels. *Perception & Psychophysics, 13*, 253–260.
Pisoni, D. B. (1977). Identification and discrimination of the relative onset of two-component tones: Implications for the perception of voicing in stops. *Journal of the Acoustical Society of America, 61*, 1352–1361.
Pisoni, D. B. (1997). Some thoughts on "normalization" in speech perception. In K. Johnson & J. W. Mullennix (Eds.), *Talker variability in speech processing.* San Diego: Academic Press.
Pisoni, D. B., & Lazarus, J. H. (1974). Categorical and non-categorical modes of speech perception along the voicing continuum. *Journal of the Acoustical Society of America, 55*, 328–333.
Pisoni, D. B., & Tash, T. (1974). Reaction times to comparisons within and across phonetic categories. *Perception & Psychophysics, 15*, 285–290.
Pitt, M. A. (1995). The locus of the lexical shift in phoneme identification. *Journal of Experimental Psychology: Learning, Memory, & Cognition, 21*, 1037–1052.
Pitt, M. A., & Samuel, A. G. (1993). An empirical and meta-analytic evaluation of the phoneme identification task. *Journal of Experimental Psychology: Human Perception and Performance, 19*, 699–725.
Posner, M. I. (1969). Abstraction and the process of recognition. In J. T. Spence & G. H. Bower (Eds.), *The psychology of learning and motivation.* New York: Academic Press.
Rabiner, L. R., & Juang, B-H. (1993). *Fundamentals of speech recognition.* Englewood Cliffs, NJ: PTR Prentice Hall.
Rand, T. C. (1974). Dichotic release from masking for speech. *Journal of the Acoustical Society of America, 55*, 678–680.
Remez, R. E., Rubin, P. E., Pisoni, D. B., & Carrell, T. (1981). Speech perception without traditional speech cues. *Science, 212*, 947–950.
Remez, R. E., Rubin, P. E., Berns, S. M., Pardo, J. S., & Lang, J. M. (1994). On the perceptual organization of speech. *Psychological Review, 101*, 129-156.
Repp, B. H. (1982). Phonetic trading relations and context effects: New experimental evidence for a speech mode of perception. *Psychological Bulletin, 92*, 81–110.
Rossing, T. D. (1990). *The science of sound*, 2nd ed. Reading, MA: Addison-Wesley.
Sachs, R. M. (1969). Vowel identification and discrimination in isolation vs. word context. *Quarterly progress report No. 93.* Cambridge, MA: Research Laboratory of Electronics, MIT.
Salasoo, A., & Pisoni, D. B. (1985). Interaction of knowledge sources in spoken word identification. *Journal of Memory and Language, 24*, 210–231.
Sawusch, J. R. (1996). Instrumentation and methodology for the study of speech perception. In N. J. Lass (Ed.), *Principles of experimental phonetics* (pp. 525–550). St. Louis: Mosby.
Sekiyama, K. (1997). Cultural and linguistic factors in audiovisual speech processing: The McGurk Effect in Chinese subjects. *Perception & Psychophysics, 59*, 73–80.
Shannon, R. V., Zeng, F. G., Kamath, V., Wygonski, J., et al. (1995). Speech recognition with primarily temporal cues. *Science, 270*, 303–304.
Sommers, M. S. (1996). The structural organization of the mental lexicon and its contribution to age-related declines in spoken-word recognition. *Psychology and Aging, 11*, 333–341.
Sommers, M. S. (1997). Stimulus variability and spoken word recognition. II. The effects of age and hearing impairment. *Journal of the Acoustical Society of America, 101*, 2278–2288.

Stevens, K. N. (1968). On the relations between speech movements and speech perception. *Zeitschrift für Phonetik, Sprachwissenschaft und Kommunikationsforschung, 21*, 102–106.

Stevens, K. N. (1996). Understanding variability in speech: A requisite for advances in speech synthesis and recognition. *2aSC3 in Session 2aSC – Speech communication: Speech communication for the next decade: New directions of research, technological development, and evolving applications.* Acoustical Society of America and Acoustical Society of Japan, Third Joint Meeting, December 1996, Honolulu, Hawaii.

Stevens, K. N., & Blumstein, S. (1981). The search for invariant acoustic correlates of phonetic features. In P. D. Eimas & J. L. Miller (Eds.), *Perspectives on the study of speech.* Hillsdale, NJ: Lawrence Erlbaum.

Stevens, K. N., & House, A. S. (1955). Development of a quantitative description of vowel articulation. *Journal of the Acoustical Society of America, 27*, 484–493.

Strange, W. (1995). *Speech perception and linguistic experience: Issues in cross-language speech research.* Timonium, MD: York Press.

Strange, W., Jenkins, J. J., & Johnson, T. L. (1983). Dynamic specification of coarticulated vowels. *Journal of the Acoustical Society of America, 74*, 695–705.

Studdert-Kennedy, M. (1986). Two cheers for direct realism. *Journal of Phonetics, 14*, 99–104.

Sumby, W. H., & Pollack, I. (1954). Visual contribution to speech intelligibility in noise. *Journal of the Acoustical Society of America, 26*, 212–215.

Sussman, H. M., & Shore, J. (1996). Locus equations as phonetic descriptors of consonantal place of articulation. *Perception & Psychophysics, 58*, 936–946.

Syrdal, A., Bennett, R., & Greenspan, S. (1995). *Applied speech technology.* Boca Raton, FL: CRC Press.

Taft, M., & Hambly, G. (1986). Exploring the Cohort Model of spoken word recognition. *Cognition, 22*, 259–282.

Treisman, M. (1978). Space or lexicon? The word frequency effect and the error response frequency effect. *Journal of Verbal Learning and Verbal Behavior, 17*, 37–59.

Trout, J. D. (1998). The biological basis of speech: What to infer from talking to the animals. Manuscript submitted for publication.

Tyler, R. S. (1993). *Cochlear implants: Audiological foundations.* San Diego, CA: Singular.

van Saten, J. P. H., Sproat, R. W., Olive, J. P., & Hirshberg, J. (1997). *Progress in speech synthesis.* New York: Springer-Verlag.

Walley, A. C., & Metsala, J. L. (1990). The growth of lexical constraints on spoken word recognition. *Perception & Psychophysics, 47*, 267–280.

Warren, R. (1970). Perceptual restoration of missing speech sounds. *Science, 167*, 392–393.

Werker, J. F. (1992). Cross-language speech perception: Developmental change does not involve loss. In J. Goodman & H. C. Nusbaum (Eds.), *Speech perception and spoken word recognition.* Cambridge, MA: MIT Press.

Werker, J. F., & Tees, R. C. (1984). Cross-language speech perception: Evidence for perceptual reorganization during the first year of life. *Infant Behaviour and Development, 7*, 49–63.

Wright, R. (1997). Lexical competition and reduction in speech: A preliminary report. *In Research on spoken language processing progess report no. 21* (pp. 471–485). Bloomington, IN: Speech Research Laboratory, Indiana University.

Zurif, E., & Swinney, D. (1994). The neuropsychology of language. In M. A. Gersbacher (Ed.), *Handbook of psycholinguistics.* San Diego: Academic Press.

Chapter Seventeen

Cutaneous Perception

Janet M. Weisenberger

Introduction – Why Study the Sense of Touch?

A cursory scan of textbooks on the topic of human perception shows far greater emphasis on vision (and perhaps audition) than on the so-called "minor" senses, underscoring the notion held by many researchers that touch serves merely as an inferior form of vision, providing information about objects in space in a poor imitation of visual ability (Lederman & Pawluk, 1993). However, the body of research on the sense of touch indicates that it can convey certain object aspects more accurately than other senses, in particular object properties such as surface texture, compliance, and thermal conductivity. In addition, the sense of touch is unique among the human senses in that it is the only system that simultaneously interacts with objects in passive perception and active manipulation.

The cutaneous senses are inherently multimodal in nature. The receptors under the skin surface are responsible for conveying sensations of light and deep pressure, vibration, temperature, and pain. Further, some of the same receptors also work in concert with motor movement to provide information about joint angle, limb position, and direction and extent of limb movement. The ability to sense the position of the body and limbs in space is referred to as *proprioception*, and the sensing of body and limb movement is called *kinesthesia*. However, these two terms are often used interchangeably. Although a detailed discussion of proprioceptive or kinesthetic perception is beyond the scope of this chapter, this form of feedback is a critical component in what is referred to as *haptics,* or *active touch*. Haptic perception refers to the combination of cues provided by tactile and kinesthetic receptors during active manipulation of objects in the environment. When stimuli are presented to a stationary observer, the cues arising from tactile receptors are referred to as *passive touch*.

The receptors for these diverse sensory abilities respond to several different forms of energy. *Mechanoreceptors* are sensitive to stimuli involving mechanical pressure, or deformation of the skin surface; *thermoreceptors* respond to thermal stimulation of the skin; and *nociceptors* mediate pain sensations arising from potentially damaging application of mechanical, thermal, chemical, or electrical stimulation of the skin. The underlying anatomical and physiological framework of the cutaneous senses is described in the following section, followed by a description of the basic psychophysical capabilities for each form of sensation. This is in turn followed by a discussion of some higher-level perceptual abilities. Finally, applied aspects and future research directions of cutaneous perception are outlined.

Anatomy and Physiology of the Somatosensory System

The skin surface constitutes the largest sensory organ of the body, with a surface area of some 1.7 m^2 in the adult. The skin actually consists of numerous layers of tissue, or *strata,* which can be divided into two main sections, the *epidermis,* or outer layer, and the *dermis,* or inner layer. On the body surface are three kinds of skin: *hairy skin,* characterized by the presence of hair; *glabrous skin,* a hairless surface found on the palm of the hand and sole of the foot; and *mucocutaneous skin,* found at the entrance to various body cavities at the junction with mucous membrane. Although these skin types differ in the density and distribution of sensory receptors that they contain, there are some general features that characterize most areas, as described below. It is important to note that the small size, complex innervation, and diffuseness of some of the receptor types make it very difficult to identify their actual functions. Rather, researchers have often been able to identify the characteristics of the primary afferent fibers that respond to a particular form of stimulation, and from these characteristics to postulate the probable depth and location of the receptor that activates those afferents. Thus, some of the receptors described in this chapter are more accurately referred to as putative receptors.

More recent research has attempted to identify functional roles for primary afferents via microneurography, a technique in which activity is recorded by percutaneous micro-electrodes from primary afferent fibers in awake human subjects, who can report sensations based on stimuli delivered to the skin at the same time as afferent activity is measured. This technique permits somewhat greater confidence in assigning roles to particular cutaneous end organs.

Mechanoreceptors

There are a number of structures that are believed to serve as receptors for transducing tactile stimulation. For sensations of touch, pressure, and vibration, four different structures have been investigated as putative mechanoreceptors. These include the Pacinian corpuscle, Meissner corpuscle, Merkel disk, and Ruffini cylinder, all shown in Figure 17.1.

The primary afferent responses measured for mechanical indentation of the skin are of two types: (a) slowly adapting (SA), indicating a response at stimulus onset that continues for the duration of the stimulation; and (b) rapidly adapting (RA), indicating a vigorous onset response, and perhaps an offset response, but no sustained response to a prolonged stimulus. Each of these two types of afferent response can be further subdivided, based on the size of the receptive field (skin surface area) that excites a particular afferent fiber. Thus, afferent responses fall into four categories: SA types I and II, and RA types I and II.

The relationship between afferent response and end organ is best understood for the Pacinian corpuscle. It is a relatively large receptor, which in the adult has numerous layers, or lamellae, that produce an onion-like appearance. Pacinian corpuscles are located deep in the dermis, as well as in joints. Each Pacinian corpuscle is innervated by a single afferent, and thus it is straightforward to assume that transduction for a fiber is mediated by the

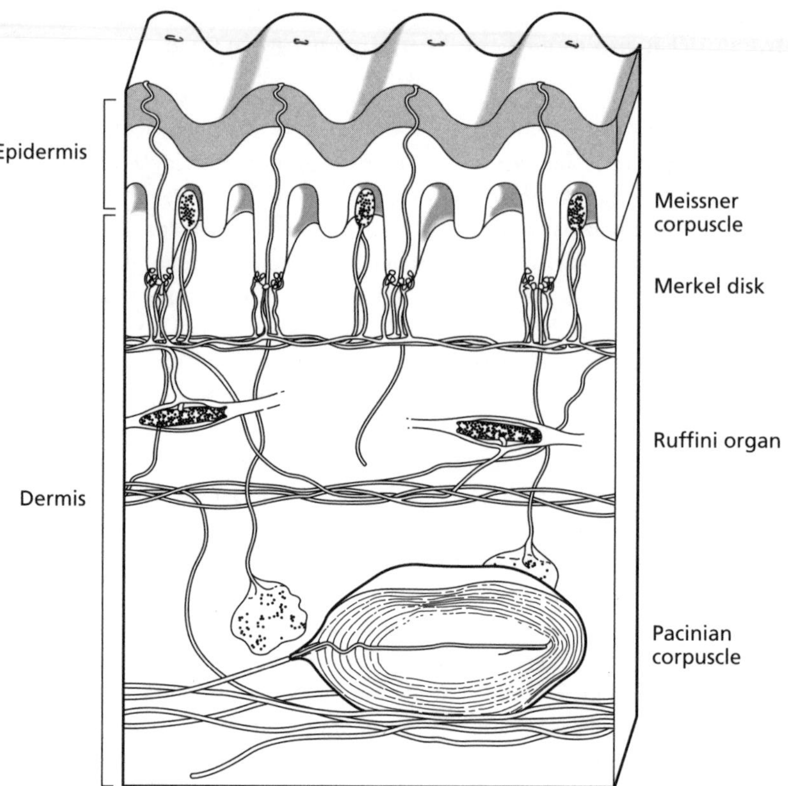

Figure 17.1. Schematic representation of the primary cutaneous mechanoreceptors and their approximate locations beneath the skin surface. (Adapted with permission from Darian-Smith (1982) from the *Annual Review of Psychology*, Volume 33, © 1982, by Annual Reviews www.AnnualReviews.org.)

Pacinian corpuscle at the fiber's termination. Based on this relationship, it has been determined that the Pacinian corpuscle is rapidly-adapting and has a large receptive field. Thus, the RA type II fiber is typically called a Pacinian, or PC fiber.

The distribution and placement of Meissner corpuscles, located at the junction of dermis and epidermis in the dermal papillae, suggests that they serve as the other RA (type I) mechanoreceptor. Meissner corpuscles are surrounded by an elastic capsule that is attached to the epidermis above and to the dermis below, and are innervated by 2–6 afferent fibers. Receptive field size for the Meissner corpuscle is small, particularly in comparison to the large field of the Pacinian corpuscle.

Likely candidates for the two SA fiber types are the Merkel disk for the small receptive-field SA I fibers, and the Ruffini cylinder for the larger receptive-field SA II fibers. The Merkel disk is a small terminal located on certain basal epidermal cells. The Ruffini cylinder is a spindle-shaped, capsule-like structure found in the upper layers of the dermis, as well as in joint areas; in many cases the Ruffini structure is considered too loosely organized to reflect true encapsulation, which compounds the difficulty in identifying it as a mechanoreceptor. A further problem with assignment of a mechanoreceptive role to the Ruffini cylinder is the fact that much of the anatomical and physiological work describing the somatosensory system is performed in species of monkeys (such as macaques) who do not exhibit an SA type II response (e.g., Phillips & Johnson, 1981).

Thermoreceptors

The situation for thermal receptors is even less certain than that for the mechanoreceptors. A variety of receptor structures at different levels of the skin show a response to thermal stimulation. However, many of these also respond to mechanical stimulation. For example, the response of the Pacinian corpuscle is quite affected by changes in skin temperature (Bolanowski, Gescheider, Verrillo, & Checkosky, 1988), but the primary function of the Pacinian corpuscle is thought to be mechanoreceptive rather than thermoreceptive. Some researchers have suggested a thermoreceptive role for the Krause end bulb, but others have been less willing to speculate about the identity of individual thermoreceptors. The main source of information about the thermoreceptive system has been the response profiles of individual primary afferent fibers, which appear to change their firing rates in response to either temperature increases or temperature decreases from some neutral point, but not both. Thus, one can speak of "cold" fibers and "warm" fibers.

Nociceptors

For sensations of pain, there appear to be several classes of receptors that respond to excessive heat, excessive cold, extreme mechanical deformation, chemical irritation, high-level electrical current, or all of these. The fibers delivering information about noxious stimulation appear to terminate in free nerve endings scattered throughout the epidermis and dermis. A common feature of many pain receptors, or nociceptors, is their high thresholds for stimulation; however, some so-called "wide dynamic range" receptors have also been identified, which respond weakly to low stimulation levels, but vigorously to high levels. In the case of pressure-induced pain, the threshold for a nociceptor may be as much as 1,000 times the displacement needed to detect pressure for a low-threshold mechanoreceptor. Similarly, thermal nociceptors may have thresholds of 45 °C or higher for heat, or 15 °C or lower for cold (Price, 1988). Overall, it appears that the stimulus for nociceptors must be intense enough to cause actual or potential damage to skin tissues.

Central Pathways

All of the receptor types discussed above pass information via primary afferent fibers from the periphery to more central structures via the spinal cord (with the exception of receptors located on the face and head, which project upward through the cranial nerves). Cell bodies for these afferents are located in the dorsal root ganglia. Within the spinal cord, larger diameter fibers (Aα or Aδ), carrying primarily mechanoreceptive information, project upward in the lemniscal bundle, whereas smaller diameter fibers, carrying thermoreceptive and nociceptive information, form the spinothalamic bundle. Lemniscal fibers ascend to the medulla, where they cross to the contralateral side before continuing upward to the ventral posterolateral nucleus of the thalamus, and from there to somatosensory cortex, located in the parietal lobe of the brain on the postcentral gyrus. Spinothalamic fibers actually cross contralaterally in the spinal cord, and ascend to the ventrobasal portions of the thalamus, from which they project to somatosensory cortex. These pathways are shown schematically in Figure 17.2a, adapted from Geldard (1972), with the left panel representing the lemniscal pathway (associated with touch) and the right panel representing the spinothalamic pathway (associated with temperature and pain).

Representation of different areas of the body in somatosensory cortex is *somatotopic*, that is, different parts of cortex are devoted to input from different body sites, and adjacent body structures are likely to activate adjacent areas of cortex. The cortex itself is organized into two general areas, SI and SII, both of which contain multiple complete representations of all body areas. SI has four such representations, in areas 3b, 3a, 1, and 2; 3b contains the simplest receptive fields and receives the bulk of inputs from the thalamus. From 3b, cortico-cortical projectsions carry information to 3a, 1, and 2. An example of a cortical map in monkey is shown in Figure 17.2b, indicating a dual body representation in two subregions of SI.

More central projections of somatosensory cortex are characterized by a high degree of specialization exhibited by some cortical cells. In area 2, the most posterior portion of SI, there appear to be cells that respond only to stimuli in a particular orientation, or to stimulus movement in a particular direction (Hyvarinen & Poranen, 1978), in a manner analogous to that observed in visual cortex. Other evidence suggests that there may be cells that respond preferentially to particular hand positions (Iwamura & Tanaka, 1978). Chapman and her colleagues (Chapman, Tremblay, & Ageranioti-Belanger, 1996) have investigated changes in somatosensory cortical firing rates when subjects are engaged in attention-directed or attention-divided tasks under haptic and passive touch conditions. Their findings suggest substantial interactions between tactile and kinesthetic inputs in tactile sensing and manipulation tasks, with changes in the locus of cortical activity with the addition of an active movement component to the task.

Even in the mature adult, the somatosensory cortex displays a remarkable plasticity. Studies with both animal and human subjects have shown that changes in the pattern of peripheral stimulation result in alterations of the cortical map for the stimulated area. Work by Merzenich and his colleagues (e.g., Allard, Clark, Jenkins, & Merzenich, 1991) showed that temporarily sewing together the index and middle finger on one hand of monkeys led to a "blurring" of the receptive fields that served the two digits in the contralateral cortex, such that stimulation of either digit evoked a broad response across an area that had earlier been sharply divided between the digits. Similar studies of long-term deafferentation in monkeys (Pons et al., 1991); of human amputees (Yang et al., 1994); and of patients undergoing surgery for separation of webbed fingers, or syndactyly (Mogilner et al., 1993) have suggested similar reorganization of cortical receptive fields (see also a review of this topic by Merzenich & Jenkins, 1993). Further, long-term stimulation/training of particular body sites can result in alterations of the cortical receptive fields. Craig

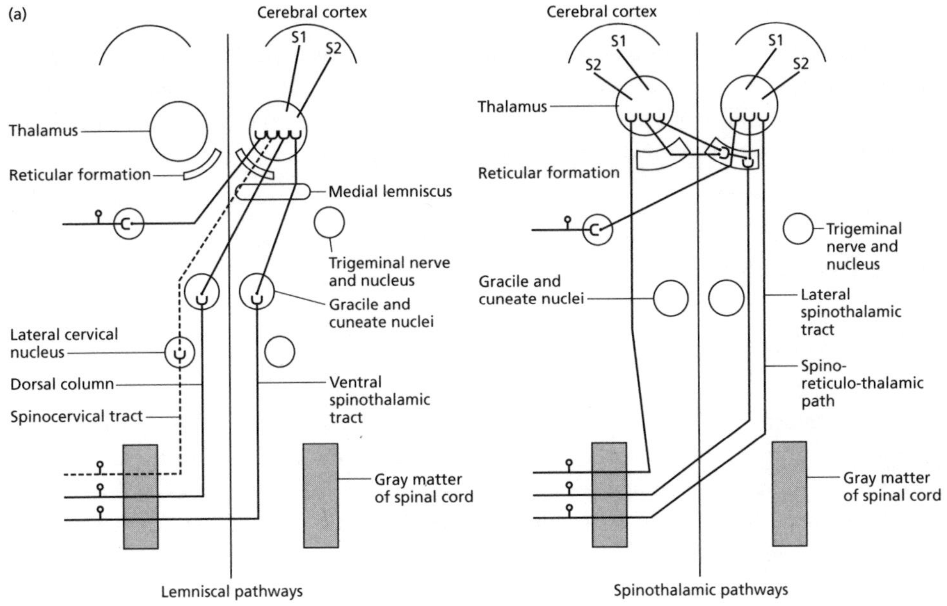

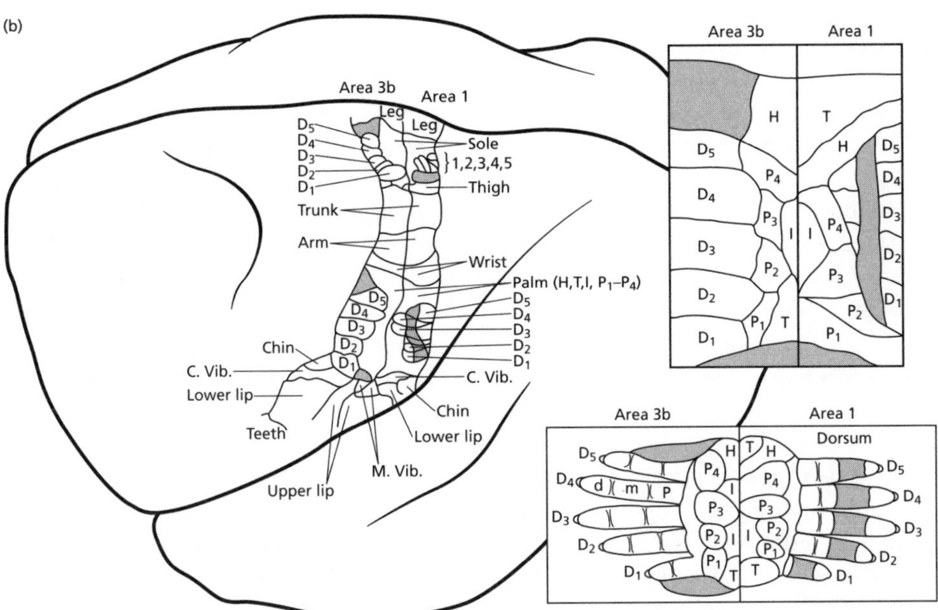

Figure 17.2. (a) Highly schematic renderings of the central pathways for the medial lemniscal system, serving touch sensations (left panel), and the spinothalamic system, serving temperature and pain sensations (right panel). (Adapted from Geldard (1972), with permission.) (b) Representation of receptive fields in the primary somatosensory cortex of spider monkey, areas 3b and 1, with inset panels detailing the representation of the hand and finger areas. (Adapted from Pons et al. (1991).)

(1993) reported changes in psychophysical abilities such as point localization in subjects receiving long-term bursts of vibration to three sites on the forearm. Overall, these studies suggest that the ability of somatosensory cortex to reorganize following injury or training continues well into adulthood.

Basic Psychophysics

Stimulus Specification

For measurements of the sense of touch, or pressure, a number of techniques have been developed for presenting stimuli to the skin surface. Traditional implements such as two-point aesthesiometers (a compass-like device designed to measure spatial sensitivity) and von Frey hairs (filaments designed to measure absolute pressure sensitivity) were simple in design and promoted ease in administration of tests; however, such apparatuses did not control certain crucial variables affecting cutaneous perception, such as skin indentation, contact force, contact duration, and temporal simultaneity of contact. Recent work has benefited from a more systematic approach, with considerable care to control for these variables. In addition, recent studies have often combined psychophysical/perceptual observations with physiological recording from afferent fibers, thus providing important links between mechanoreceptor activity and perceptual response.

Presentation of thermal stimulation is also bound by certain important considerations. For example, stimulus presentation using a thermal source that actually contacts the skin surface produces contact-temperature interactions in sensitivity (Stevens, 1991); for this reason some investigators prefer to use radiant thermal sources, which can heat or cool the skin surface without actual contact. The type of thermal source (e.g., infrared, microwave, etc.) can also affect measures of sensitivity, depending on whether multiple skin layers are affected simultaneously or sequentially. The device of choice for many studies of thermal perception has been a Peltier thermocouple, which can change its temperature rapidly, and thus can be useful in studies investigating the perception of temperature change.

For experimental measurements of pain, the situation is even more complex. As Rollman (1991) points out, it is difficult even to define pain; he asks "Is pain a sensation, a perception, an emotion, or a thought?" (p. 91). Human responsiveness to noxious stimuli also varies substantially depending on whether the pain is experienced in conjunction with a physical problem (i.e., clinical pain), or is delivered by an experimenter in a laboratory setting (experimental pain). There are numerous sources of stimulation that have the potential to cause tissue damage, and many of these have been utilized in experimental studies of pain, including intense pressure, chemical irritants, electrical stimulation, etc. It is likely, however, that each of these produces subtle differences in the pain sensation experienced by subjects, and thus it is somewhat difficult to compare results from studies using different stimulation modes.

Thresholds

Touch

One important tactile ability is the differentiation of spatially distributed stimuli. Earlier work of Weinstein (1968) established punctate detection thresholds for different areas of the body, and provided experimental verification for differences in sensitivity to tactile stimulation at different body sites. He found that certain body areas, in particular the fingertips and facial regions, show exquisite sensitivity, with detection thresholds for skin indentation of a few microns. Studies employing vibratory stimulation, where repeated skin indentation keeps the rapidly-adapting receptor populations (Pacinian and Meissner corpuscles) engaged for the duration of the stimulus, have reported much lower thresholds for detection. On the fingertips, vibratory thresholds for stimuli in the 250 Hz range can be as low as 0.2 mm (Gescheider, Capraro, Frisina, Hamer, & Verrillo, 1978). Again, there are differences in vibratory sensitivity across body regions, with the trunk and leg regions showing poorer thresholds. Variations in detection threshold for different body sites are shown in Figure 17.3a (see Sherrick & Cholewiak, 1986, for a more complete discussion).

Vibratory thresholds are critically dependent on vibration frequency. Verrillo and his colleagues (e.g., Verrillo, 1963, 1966) established thresholds for the thenar eminence (area of the palm just below the thumb) for frequencies between 25 and 600 Hz, as shown in Figure 17.3b. This figure shows the characteristic U-shaped function for frequencies above about 40 Hz, such that threshold reaches its minimum point at approximately 250 Hz, and then increases as frequency is further increased. For frequencies below 40 Hz, there is no particular change as frequency is varied. Possible mechanoreceptive mechanisms underlying these threshold characteristics are discussed below.

Note also in Figure 17.3b that threshold for the higher frequencies also appears to vary as a function of contactor size, such that larger contactors produce the lowest thresholds. Thus, tactile sensitivity shows *spatial summation*, the ability to sum energy from different locations to minimize the total energy required for detection. Vibratory detection has also been shown to exhibit *temporal summation*, the ability to sum energy over extended stimulus durations, in a manner similar to the visual and auditory modalities. For the tactile system, temporal summation persists for up to a second (Verrillo, 1965), but appears to occur only for higher vibration frequencies (Gescheider, 1976).

Frequency discrimination is rather poor for vibrotactile stimuli (Goff, 1967; Rothenberg, Verrillo, Zahorian, Brachman, & Bolanowski, 1977). These studies generally report Weber fractions ($\Delta f/f$) in the vicinity of 30 percent, with discrimination being worse for high frequencies than for lower frequencies. However, some studies indicate that temporal resolution of vibratory stimuli is actually rather good. Gap detection, for example, can show thresholds as low as 5 ms for highly damped stimuli (Gescheider, 1974; Sherrick, 1982), whereas temporal modulation transfer functions employing amplitude-modulated sinusoids suggest a time constant of 3–4 ms for vibratory sensitivity (Weisenberger, 1986). Temporal order thresholds, as reported by Hirsh and Sherrick (1961), are similar across the visual, auditory, and tactile modalities at about 20 ms (but see McFarland, Cacace, & Setzen, 1998, for a discussion of temporal order judgments for different stimulus dimensions). For more than two stimuli, this threshold increases rapidly (Sherrick, 1982).

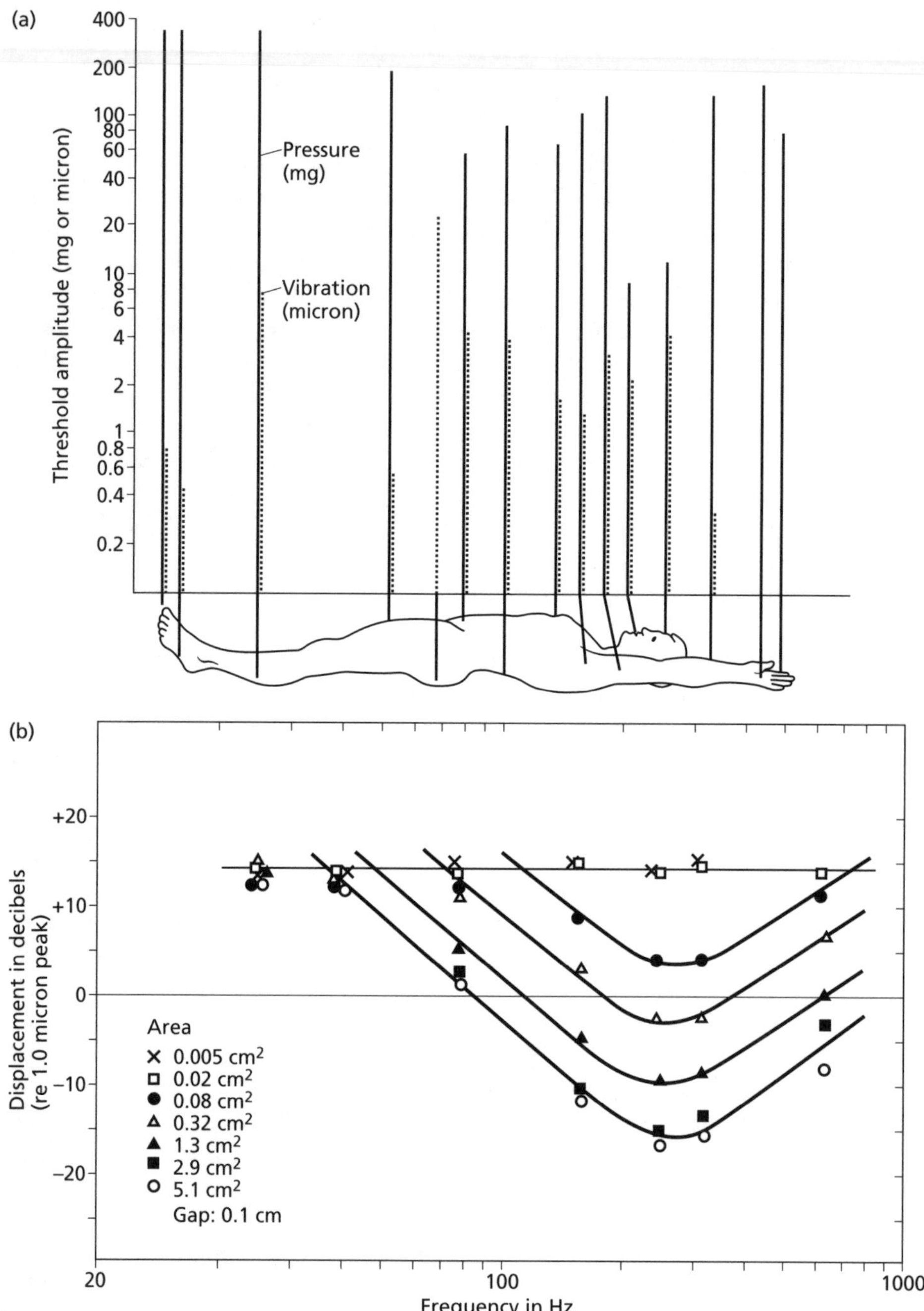

Figure 17.3. (a) Threshold values (in microns) for detection of pressure (solid lines) and vibration (dotted lines) for different body locations. (Adapted from Sherrick and Cholewiak (1986), with permission from Academic Press.) (b) Threshold values (in decibels re 1 μ) for detection of vibration as a function of frequency, for different contactor sizes. (Adapted from Verrillo (1966), with permission from the American Institute of Physics.)

Spatial discrimination ability for touch, like detection threshold, varies according to body location. The earlier work of Weinstein (1968) was revisited by Stevens and Choo (1996), who measured spatial sensitivity at 13 body sites, and found the highest acuity in the fingertips and face areas. Johnson and colleagues (e.g., Van Boven & Johnson, 1994; Johnson & Phillips, 1981) measured spatial acuity on the fingertips of humans and monkeys using square-wave grating stimuli, which, if applied carefully, do not fall prey to the temporal simultaneity issue that clouds results for the two-point threshold. They found that under optimal conditions, a groove width of 0.5 mm was sufficient for discrimination of grating orientation.

The presentation of multiple tactile stimuli can produce cross-stimulus interactions, which can occur over both space and time. These interactions can be integrative, as is seen in spatial and temporal summation, or inhibitory, as in spatial and temporal masking effects. The integration of inputs may not be different neurally, but the task demands may be. Sherrick (1964) conducted the first systematic investigation of spatial and temporal masking effects for vibratory stimuli, looking at thresholds for vibratory detection on one fingertip while a second stimulus was presented on the same or another fingertip, either simultaneously or in close temporal proximity. Sherrick found that the amount of masking decreased as the location of the masker was moved farther from the target. He also observed temporal masking effects that extended over several hundred ms, with a greater amount of masking for forward maskers (maskers that precede the target in time) than for backward maskers (maskers that follow the target in time).

Taken as a whole, measurements of temporal summation, temporal enhancement, and temporal masking reflect the tendency of the tactile system to integrate stimuli over time. The size of the temporal window over which integration occurs is not definitively known; rather, it appears to be at least somewhat task-dependent and may range from several hundred ms up to 1s or more. Similarly, it is clear that the tactile system can integrate information over space, and that integration is a fundamental characteristic of tactile processing.

Temperature

The measurement of thermal sensations is particularly complicated by the fact that the skin is already at some temperature even before a thermal stimulus is applied. Thus, the question of thermal detection is actually a question of detecting a change in skin temperature from some initial point. However, the issue is even more complicated, because the initial neutral "point" is actually a range of temperatures within which complete adaptation to the stimulus can be achieved, known as *physiological zero*. This attribute further implies that the detection of a thermal stimulus will depend on the rate at which the stimulus changes the ambient skin temperature; thus, it is possible that some methods of thermal stimulation (e.g., microwave) might evoke a different sensation from others, because of differential rates and depths of skin temperature change.

Nonetheless, even older data, obtained using radiant heat sources, show the perception of a warm stimulus to be highly acute, with a change of only 0.003 °C necessary for detection (Hardy & Oppel, 1937). Similar acuity is observed for the detection of a cooling stimulus. Also, like pressure sensitivity, thermal sensitivity shows attributes of spatial and temporal summation, such that increasing the area or the duration of the stimulus results in lower thresholds.

Just as for pressure and vibration, differential sensitivity has been found across body sites. Stevens, Marks, and Simonson (1974) reported that the most sensitive areas to warm stimulation were the forehead and cheek, whereas the least sensitive were the calf and thigh. However, unlike sensations of pressure, spatial acuity for thermal stimulation is quite poor. When two areas of thermal stimulation are in close proximity, they tend to fuse into a single merged percept. Further, Cain (1973) noted that subjects even confused a stimulus presented on the front of the body with one presented on the back, an interesting finding in view of the earlier research that systematically mapped small-diameter, discrete "cold" and "warm" spots at different body locations (Blix, 1884, cited in Stevens, 1991). It is likely that these thermal spots reflect a more complex touch-temperature interaction.

Thermotactile interactions have been noted under a variety of circumstances. For example, warming or cooling of the skin can have a substantial effect on tactile acuity (Stevens, Green, & Krimsley, 1977), and on vibratory perception of high-frequency stimuli (Bolanowski et al., 1988); in fact, as described below, the finding that the Pacinian corpuscle shows a marked alteration in its responsiveness at different temperatures was very useful in differentiating the vibration response of different mechanoreceptor systems.

Changes in the thermal properties of an object can also affect other perceived characteristics, as in the well-known observation that cold objects tend to feel heavier than warm ones. In addition, simultaneously presented stimuli with different thermal properties can interact; the most long-standing example of this is the sensation of "synthetic heat," in which alternating cold and warm stimuli in close proximity are perceived as being intensely hot (Alrutz, 1898). This paradoxical effect has to date not been satisfactorily explained. It is generally assumed that somehow the simultaneous firing of warm and cold afferent fibers signals to the brain the potential for tissue damage, and thus evokes the sensation of stinging heat.

Pain

Of all the cutaneous attributes, pain is the most difficult to describe in basic psychophysical terms, for the reasons cited above. Still further complications arise in the measurement of persistent pain that continues even after the healing of a wound, as in the painful sensations localized to so-called "phantom limbs." However, although the basic pain experience typically has both sensory and affective components (and may, in the case of long-term pain, have cognitive components as well), researchers have employed methodology that permits the separation of these components.

Although pain experiences can be highly differentiable qualitatively (note, for example, terms applied to painful sensations, such as burning, stinging, stabbing, aching), Rollman (1991) suggests that for evaluation purposes, pain can be categorized in terms of its duration, into transient, acute, or chronic pain. A transient pain, as its name implies, is extremely brief, such as the prick of a needle, and typically evokes little or no emotional response. Pain associated with a more sustained injury that induces the release of prostaglandins begins to have an emotional aspect, that is, a sense of unpleasantness and a desire to withdraw from the painful stimulus. If such pain persists over a term greater than

6 months, it becomes classified as chronic pain, which has strong affective components, and can lead to more wide-ranging emotional reactions (e.g., depression). It is likely, then, that these different kinds of pain will produce very different responses in pain measurement. Some researchers (e.g., Rollman, 1979) have attempted to use the analysis techniques of signal detection theory to separate the sensory and nonsensory aspects of pain, and have met with some success.

Psychophysical scaling approaches have also been employed to evoke descriptions of the effects of duration, intensity, and location on the pain percept. Again, it is possible to evaluate the sensory and nonsensory aspects to some degree, through the use of instruments such as the McGill Pain Questionnaire, or MPQ (Melzack, 1975), in which words typically used to describe painful sensations are grouped into subcategories (e.g., hot/burning/scalding/searing, or fearful/frightened/terrifying), and subjects are asked to select a word from each category if it can appropriately describe the pain. Responses are scored with a ranking scale (the Pain Ranking Index) that provides an overall index of the painful experience. Further, the MPQ is useful in differentiating types of pain, and factor analysis techniques suggest that it is based on three underlying factors, which are loosely related to sensory, emotional, and cognitive aspects.

Why does it matter whether different aspects of pain can be can be distinguished? For one thing, it seems that different pharmacological interventions may selectively alleviate different components of pain. Low doses of morphine appear to reduce the affective but not the sensory aspects of pain, whereas higher doses reduce both components (Price, Von Der Gruen, Miller, Rafii, & Price, 1985). Similar results have been reported for acupuncture therapy. This type of information is important for the alleviation and clinical management of pain. Further studies have found that in cases of pain associated with life-threatening conditions, such as some cancers, the affective components of the pain are likely to take precedence (Price, Harkins, & Baker, 1987). Laboratory-induced pain, on the other hand, appears in many studies to have a stronger sensory component.

Issues such as those just described reflect the dual goals of pain research: first, to understand the nature of the pain experience; and second, to find effective procedures for the alleviation of clinical pain. Considerable research has been performed on the analgesic effects produced by pharmacologic agents, including endogenous opiates (enkephalins, dynorphans, and beta-endorphins). These latter substances appear to be activated by stimulation elsewhere on the body, which may explain the effectiveness of such treatments as "audio analgesia," in which sound produces a reduction in pain. Some research suggests that these analgesic effects are mediated by a descending inhibition projecting to the raphe nucleus in the medulla and down to the dorsal horn of the spinal cord (Young, 1989); this possibility is discussed further below.

Just as for touch and temperature responsiveness, multiple painful stimuli can interact. If in close proximity and similar in quality, multiple painful stimulation can show summation effects (Algom, Raphaeli, & Cohen-Raz, 1986), but if widely separated on the body, one painful stimulus can reduce the painful sensation evoked by another (Rollman, 1991).

Complex Perceptual Tasks

In everyday life, the sense of touch is routinely used to identify, or at least extract the material properties of, objects and surfaces. The information available from tactile and thermal stimulation allows judgments of weight, stiffness, elasticity, material (e.g., metal, plastic, etc.), and roughness. This information is often rendered imperfectly by other sensory systems, such as vision, and thus touch supplements visual information about size, shape, color, etc. in object identification. Equally important is the role of tactile feedback in the manipulation of objects, where touch and thermal information permit fine-tuning of the motor response in precision grip and movement. Finally, because vision and touch can provide some degree of *redundant* information about objects (size, shape, roughness, location), the tactile sense has been evaluated for its potential as a substitute for vision in cases where visual information is not available, such as blindness. All of these possible roles for tactile feedback have led researchers to investigate tactile capabilities in tasks requiring fine spatial and temporal resolution. Several examples from this literature are discussed in the following sections.

Tactile Pattern Perception

A number of studies have examined human perceptual response to complex tactile patterns; these studies have employed a large variety of stimuli, including raised lines and letters, Braille symbols, and vibratory patterns. Although the majority of experiments have focused on presentation to the fingertip, other sites have also been studied, including back, abdomen, and thigh.

Raised Patterns and Braille

Perception of embossed letters was examined by Loomis (1980), who manipulated pattern size to assess spatial acuity. His results suggested that the skin acts as a lowpass filter, and that tactile perception of raised letters can be accurately modeled as analogous to the visual perception of blurred stimuli. Although normal tactile sensing tasks would not necessarily involve the perception of raised letters, they have certain advantages as a stimulus for evaluating tactile acuity, in that they are relatively spatially complex, require no training of the subjects, and can yield data that can be compared across laboratories and tasks (Johnson & Hsiao, 1992). Other studies of raised letter recognition have shown that subjects differ considerably in their ability to identify them (e.g., Loomis, 1981).

Considerable attention has been given to the analysis of patterns of confusions, or identification errors, observed in different studies. It is often assumed that the same "features" that comprise visually presented letters of the alphabet will also govern perception of tactually presented letters. However, although there are similarities, the confusions generated with tactually and visually presented letters are not identical. A confusion matrix for raised letters was reported by Vega-Bermudez, Johnson, and Hsaio (1991) showing certain characteristics that are typical for tactile presentation. First, there is a large range of identifiability of different letters, with relatively simple, low spatial frequency letters, such as I or T, proving easily identifiable and only infrequently confused with other letters, whereas other letters, such as N or G, produce much lower levels of performance and frequent confusions. Further, substantial asymmetries in confusions are observed; the letter C is misidentified as G much more often than G is misidentified as C. Possible explanations for these confusion asymmetries based on physiological responses in peripheral afferents are discussed below.

The confusion matrices obtained for letters presented on vibratory arrays for the fingertip (Craig, 1979; Weisenberger, Hasser, & Holtman, 1998) show similar trends, suggesting that the features extracted from vibratory patterns are not substantially different from those for nonvibrating patterns. However, the mechanoreceptor population that mediates detection might be different for the two types of presentation.

The patterns that comprise Braille are a specific case of raised patterns. Braille symbols, originally introduced by Louis Braille in 1829, have proven to be much more easily identified than raised letters, most likely because of their less complex spatial structure. The Braille code rather fortuitously employs dots separated by a little more than 2 mm, with a dot height of 0.5 mm, and thus the patterns of Braille do not tax the spatial resolution ability of the fingertip. Trained Braille readers typically read at rates around 100 words per minute (Nolan & Kederis, 1969); many Braille readers employ both hands in the task, indicating good transfer of perceptual training across hands (Foulke, 1991).

The Braille reading task, like the identification of raised letters, is also of interest because the scanning behavior introduces a temporal component into the basic spatial acuity task. Data for raised letters suggest that, over a moderate range (20–80 mm/s), scanning velocity does not impact perception (e.g., Vega-Bermudez et al., 1991). Performance across scanning velocities is also stable for vibratory patterns, for moderate speeds (Craig, 1980). However, in Braille reading, the fingertip moves across patterns in rapid sequence, which can lead to cross-pattern interactions. These interactions will be subject to temporal integrative processes (as described above) that can be either facilitative or inhibitory, depending on the task. For skilled Braille readers, this integration permits the reader to construct "higher-order" patterns that make syllables or words, thus speeding the act of reading (Foulke, 1991).

Vibratory Patterns

Researchers using vibratory displays have been able to map out the parameters of spatial and temporal interaction of complex patterns. Work by Craig and his colleagues (1976, 1980, 1995, 1996) has shown that pattern perception on the fingertip is subject to both forward and backward masking effects. Unlike the case for vibratory detection, vibratory pattern identification exhibits more backward masking (masker following target) than forward masking (masker preceding target); however, the deleterious effects of a forward masker persist over a longer period of time (Craig & Evans, 1995). Further, these studies show that the masking effect itself often reflects an integration of target and masker patterns; if the masker is itself an identifiable pattern, subjects may choose it as a response, an effect known as response competition (Craig & Evans, 1995).

Masking effects can also be observed when the masker is in close *spatial* proximity to the target (Craig & Evans, 1995; Weisenberger & Craig, 1982). These effects can follow a rather complicated time course, and are also subject to response competition effects. Subjects also appear to have some difficulty in monitoring multiple locations on the skin simultaneously, if both locations are on the same hand (Craig & Evans, 1995). When the patterns are presented to different hands, no decrement in dividing attention is observed. As in other sensory modalities, cueing can facilitate the direction of attention and improve performance over non-cued conditions (Whang, Burton, & Shulman, 1991). Misleading cueing, unsurprisingly, disrupts performance.

The question of attention is of particular interest for the tactile sense, given the great extent of the receptor surface. Specifically, one can ask: How many locations can be monitored simultaneously? Is it more difficult to divide attention over very widely spaced locations? Does cortical hemispheric specialization impact the ability to divide attention successfully across hands? These questions have not yet been conclusively answered.

Texture Perception

One task at which the tactile system excels is the perception of surface texture. Anecdotal reports indicate that in commercial ventures that require fine texture discrimination, such as the selection of fabric or the detection of irregularities in a surface finish, touch may be far superior to vision as an information channel.

Johnson and Hsiao (1992) point out that the perception of texture depends on repetitive spatial or temporal structure, which can be random, as in sandpaper, or more regular, as in fabric. The primary perceptual judgment of texture is of surface roughness, but there may be other perceptual aspects (Hollins, Faldowski, Rao, & Young, 1993).

Lederman and colleagues have studied roughness perception extensively using magnitude estimation techniques (1974, 1981; Lederman & Taylor, 1972). Their work showed that although movement is necessary for roughness judgments, it does not matter whether the movement is active (i.e., the perceiver moves the fingers across the surface) or passive (the surface is moved under a stationary finger). Further, the velocity of movement, at least in the range of 10–250 mm/s, does not affect the perception of roughness. However, increasing contact force tends to elevate roughness judgments. Much of their work involved judgments of raised gratings, with gap widths between 0.4 and 1.6 mm. In general, Lederman's results indicate that the perception of roughness is a curvilinear function of gap width, increasing with increases in gap width up to 1 mm, and decreasing thereafter. Sathian, Goodwin, John, and Darian-Smith (1989) and Connor, Hsaio, Phillips, and Johnson (1990) observed a similar curvilinear relationship.

Several investigators have evaluated the ability to perceive texture using primarily temporal cues, as occurs when an object such as a pencil or stylus is dragged across a surface. In this case the contact with the surface is a point source, and the information delivered to the mechanoreceptors in the fingertips is primarily vibratory in nature. This form of texture sensing was described as early as 1925 by Katz, and is of interest precisely because the stimulus cue is temporal only, rather than spatio-temporal. Even without spatial information, roughness perception appears to be possible. Extensions of this form of texture perception include work of Weisenberger and Krier (1997) and Weisenberger, Krier, and Rinker (1998) with virtual displays. They found that subjects could discriminate surprisingly fine spatial periods, on the order of 1 mm, even though these surfaces contained no sharp edges. Craig and Rollman (1999) note that texture discrimination may be perceptually different from judging surface roughness, and may also involve different neural codes, as discussed below.

Object Identification

Klatzky, Lederman, and Metzger (1985) describe haptic touch as an "expert system" for the identification of object shape. Indeed, this is a primary function of the cutaneous system in everyday life. Lederman and Klatzky (1987) identify stereotyped *exploratory procedures* (EPs), hand movements used by the perceiver to gain information about different kinds of object properties. For example, an EP that applies pressure to an object most appropriately conveys object hardness, whereas an EP employing lateral motion may convey aspects of object texture, and a contour-following EP will provide exact shape information.

As for pattern perception, there is also no consensus regarding the existence of distinctive perceptual features of objects. Garbin and Bernstein (1984) reported that although subjects noted distinctive features on objects, such as ridges, they tended to classify objects on the basis of metric attributes, such as size. Increases in the complexity of an object, as might be expected, increase the time necessary for object identification, while simultaneously decreasing accuracy (Ballesteros, Manga, & Reales, 1997).

The Role of Kinesthetic Feedback in Cutaneous Sensing

How important is the "active" aspect of haptic touch? It might be assumed that the additional information from kinesthetic feedback provided when the hand is actively moved across an object surface would prove valuable. Gibson (1966), in fact, argued for the preeminence of the haptic mode of touch, in his equivalence of perception and action. However, a number of researchers have found that, for tasks dependent on motion between stimulus and perceiver, it makes no difference how the movement is achieved; comparable perceptual experiences are obtained when the hand moves across a surfaces as well as when the surface is moved under a stationary hand. Lederman (1981), as noted, reported such a result for judgments of texture roughness. Similarly, Vega-Bermudez et al. (1991) found no difference in the identifiability of raised letters when active or passive movement was permitted, and Weisenberger and Hasser (1998) reported equivalent performance under haptic and passive scanning of vibratory patterns when other aspects of the stimulus were accounted for.

Nonetheless, there exist circumstances under which kinesthetic information can benefit tactile perception. Weisenberger et al. (1998) studied the effects of reducing the tactile "field of view" by systematically reducing the number of activated elements on a 30-element vibratory array. As the display size decreased from 25 to 9 to 4 elements, no decrease in performance was observed as long as haptic scanning of the stimulus patterns was permitted, even though the display size was smaller than the stimulus pattern. They argued that kinesthetic feedback could partially compensate for the loss of direct spatial information. However, when the display size was reduced to a single element, effectively eliminating all tactile spatial information, performance dropped substantially (though still remaining above chance). This result indicates that kinesthesis cannot completely replace spatially distributed information, at least for this task. Nonetheless, it can partially compensate for the loss of such information.

Theoretical Frameworks and Neural Mechanisms of Touch, Temperature, and Pain

The most exciting recent theoretical formulations in cutaneous perception have involved attempts to link physiology and psychophysics for various stimuli, providing potential neural codes and mechanoreceptive substrates for different perceptual attributes. The peripheral coding of many stimulus aspects is relatively well understood, and current work now focuses on the more central physiology of touch, where higher-order aspects of perception, such as attention and context effects, can be examined.

Touch

Current consensus among researchers holds that the four mechanoreceptors described in the section on Anatomy and Physiology of the Somatosensory System all play a role in the

Table 17.1 Sensory receptors

	Afferent fibers	*Receptive field size*	*Preferred vibratory range*	*Functions*
Mechanoreceptors				
Pacinian corpuscle	RA (PC)	Large	40–500 Hz	Vibration, texture from manipulation of tools
Meissner corpuscle	RA	Small	10–40 Hz	Slip, texture, features of fine surfaces
Merkel disk	SA I	Small	0.1–10 Hz	Spatial detail, texture, edges
Ruffini cylinder	SA II	Large	0.1–10 Hz	Static force, skin stretch
Thermoreceptors				
Free nerve endings	Aβ, Aδ	Large	–	Warm, cold
Nociceptors				
Free nerve endings	Aδ, C	Large	–	Pain

perception of pressure and vibration. With respect to vibratory stimuli, Bolanowski et al. (1988; see also Greenspan & Bolanowski, 1996) proposed a four-channel model that can explain the threshold data shown in Figure 17.4. In this model, vibratory detection for frequencies above about 40 Hz is mediated by the PC channel, served by the Pacinian corpuscle. Between 10 and 40 Hz, the NP (non-Pacinian) I channel mediates detection, and below 40 Hz, the NP III channel mediates detection. (See Table 17.1.)

Bolanowski et al. provided supporting evidence for this model from both physiological and psychophysical studies. Neural response curves for the Pacinian corpuscle obtained by Talbot, Darian-Smith, Kornhuber, and Mountcastle (1968) show the characteristic U-shaped response as a function of frequency that also describes psychophysical sensitivity. Manipulation of spatial summation (shown by the PC channel but not by the NP I channel); adaptation of specific channels by prolonged exposure to either a 200-Hz vibration fatiguing the PC channel or a 20-Hz vibration fatiguing the NP I and NP III channels; or manipulation of stimulus and skin temperature, elevating PC thresholds, all helped to isolate specific channels. Physiological investigations offer supporting data suggesting that the NP I system is most likely the Meissner corpuscle/RA afferent combination, and the NP III system is mostly likely the Merkel disk/SA I afferent combination. The physiological substrate of the NP II channel has not been conclusively identified.

The work of Johnson and his colleagues (see Johnson and Hsiao, 1992 for a review), has provided us with substantial insights into the peripheral codes for form and texture. Their

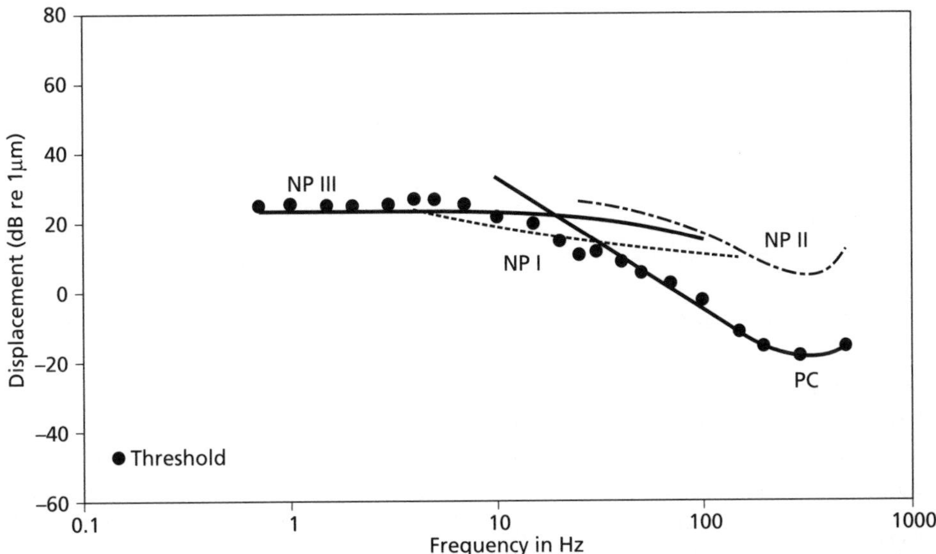

Figure 17.4. Representation of the four-channel model of vibrotaction of Bolanowski, Gescheider, Verrillo, and Checkosky (1988). (Reproduced with permission of the American Institute of Physics.) Threshold for detection of vibration is plotted across frequencies, with indications of the mechanoreceptive channel serving different frequency ranges. PC = Pacinian corpuscle; NP I = Non-Pacinian channel I (Meissner corpuscle); NP II = Non-Pacinian channel II (Ruffini cylinder?); NP III = Non-Pacinian channel III (Merkel disk).

work is characterized by an elegant combination of psychophysical and physiological experimentation, using the same stimuli, and where possible, the same subjects. These studies have shown that the peripheral neural coding of fine spatial detail, such as that necessary for grating discrimination, Braille reading, and raised letter identification, is most accurately represented in the firing patterns of SA I afferents (Vega-Bermudez et al., 1991; Johnson & Phillips, 1981). Figure 17.5a, from Vega-Bermudez et al. (1991), provides a compelling representation of this finding, showing summed responses over space (spatial event plots) for monkey SA I fibers in contact with raised letters. One particularly interesting feature of this representation is the greater fidelity in spatial detail of the left side of the letters than the right side, which Vega-Bermudez et al. link to the patterns of psychophysical confusion obtained from human subjects for the same stimuli. Figure 17.5b shows spatial event plots for the SA I, RA, and PC afferent types in response to raised dot patterns. These results provide additional support for the argument that the SA I afferents show the necessary spatial resolution to mediate fine spatial perception, and that the other afferent types, at least when responses are plotted in this manner, do not.

Johnson and Hsiao (1992) argue that although these physiological data provide a "causal link" to the perceptual results, they do not provide a quantitative theoretical framework that completely explains this link and permits further analysis. They point to Loomis's (1990) model of character recognition and legibility as a step in this direction.

One aspect of the SA I response that is not evident in the plots of Figure 17.5a and b, but that might play a crucial role in the spatial fidelity of the SA I system, is illustrated in Figure 17.5c, from Phillips and Johnson (1981). This figure shows SA I firing rates to portions of an irregular grating pressed against the fingertip. For this stimulus, the SA I afferents show a finely differentiated spatial response. In addition, the SA I fibers appear to show edge enhancement effects, with sharp increases in firing rate at the edges of the grating bars. This edge enhancement, together with the already acute spatial response, is not observed for RA or PC afferents.

Peripheral neural codes for texture are less well understood. Connor et al. (1990) suggest that roughness perception is in most cases coded by SA I fibers; however, a simple rate code does not appear to provide an adequate explanation for roughness estimates. A more complex code, involving higher-order neurons with excitatory and inhibitory subregions, can be used to model roughness perception for surfaces that evoke significant SA I activity. However, in cases where the SA I response is poor, such as surfaces with a microstructure too fine for SA I resolution, or the case where textural cues are transmitted via a rigid stylus, it is likely that RA and PC afferents play a role in mediating perception (see Hollins, Bensmaia, & Risner, 1998 for a model proposing this). RA fiber responses do account for some frictional percepts, such as slip when grasping an object (Johansson & Westling, 1987; Srinivasan, Whitehouse, & LaMotte, 1990), and the high density of RA innervation in the fingertip implicates this channel as a potential conveyor of information about fine microstructure. Finally, the vibrational sensitivity of the PC afferents makes this system a prime candidate for mediating texture perception via a stylus.

Johnson and Hsiao (1992) propose several working hypotheses for the neural coding of form and texture. First, they argue that the SA I system is responsible for most tasks requiring fine spatial acuity. The RA system provides a good representation of local movements, as in slip, and signals aspects of surface form and texture when the stimulus microstructure

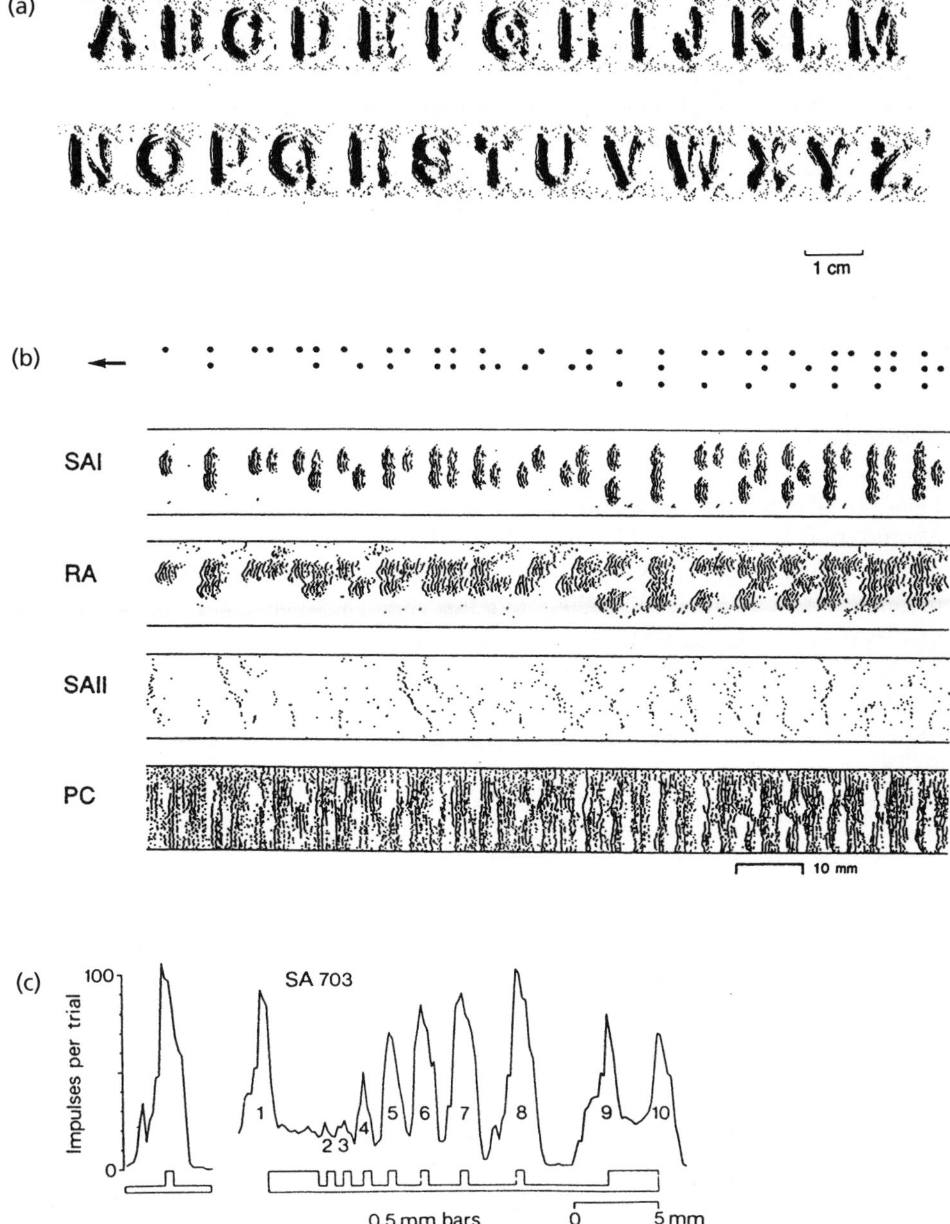

Figure 17.5. (a) Spatial event plots of SA I mechanoreceptive fibers in response to raised letters presented to the fingertip. (b) Spatial event plots for SA I, RA, SA II, and PC afferents to raised Braille dots. (a & b adapted with permission from Johnson and Hsiao (1992) from the *Annual Review of Neuroscience*, Volume 15, © 1992, by Annual Reviews www.AnnualReviews.org.) (c) Firing rates for SA I afferents in response to raised gratings. (Adapted with permission from Phillips and Johnson (1981).)

is too fine for SA resolution. The PC system is sensitive to high-frequency vibrations and as a population may be able to signal roughness perception from vibrations transmitted via rigid probes in tool manipulation tasks.

Current work in the physiological substrates for touch has focused on central mediation of peripheral inputs. It is clear that central structures play a role in focusing attention on different aspects of peripheral stimulation, and in the temporal integration/masking observed with events occurring in close temporal proximity (e.g., Chapman, Tremblay, & Ageranioti-Belanger, 1996; Tremblay, Ageranioti-Belanger, & Chapman,1996). Further, sensory-motor interactions and tactile-kinesthetic interactions must be mediated by higher-order centers. Future investigations should elucidate the role of cortical mechanisms in more complex tactile perceptual tasks.

Temperature

Fiber populations that signal warmth or cold, but not both, have been identified and recorded from by Sumino and Dubner (1981). However, as mentioned above, no specific terminals, such as the encapsulated mechanoreceptive structures, have been identified as thermoreceptors. Further, rate coding, to a first approximation, appears to describe the psychophysical data, depending on the state of prior adaptation of the skin. Lederman and Pawluk (1993) note that the division of thermal sensing into dual channels may improve perceptual acuity; in addition, the considerable spatial summation evidenced by thermal fibers reduces the spatial acuity of thermal sensation, but enhances detectability, which may be adaptive for survival. Less is known about the cortical mediation of thermal sensitivity.

Pain

The most comprehensive theory of pain sensitivity was proposed by Melzack and Wall (1965), and is known as *gate control theory*. Although subsequent physiological findings have required the alteration of the theory, its basic premise of inhibitory interaction of larger and smaller diameter fibers at both peripheral and central levels remains sound.

Melzack and Wall's (1988; Wall & Melzack, 1994) revision of gate control theory is shown in Figure 17.6. Briefly, the spinal cord receives input from both large-diameter (Aβ) and smaller-diameter (Aδ and C) fibers, which in turn innervate transmission (T) cells, projecting up to more central structures. In this version of the theory, the small diameter fibers can exert multiple excitatory effects, either directly onto the T-cells, or via interneurons in the spinal cord. Similarly, the large diameter fibers, which are myelinated and respond to lower input levels, can also exert multiple effects on the T-cells. However, in the model the interneurons activated by the large fibers have inhibitory effects on the T-cells, while direct large-fiber inputs to the T-cells are excitatory.

An additional important aspect of this theory is the operation of centrally mediated inhibition. Physiological evidence for such a system has been reported in recent years, in cases of stimulation analgesia, in which electrical stimulation of central fibers produces a

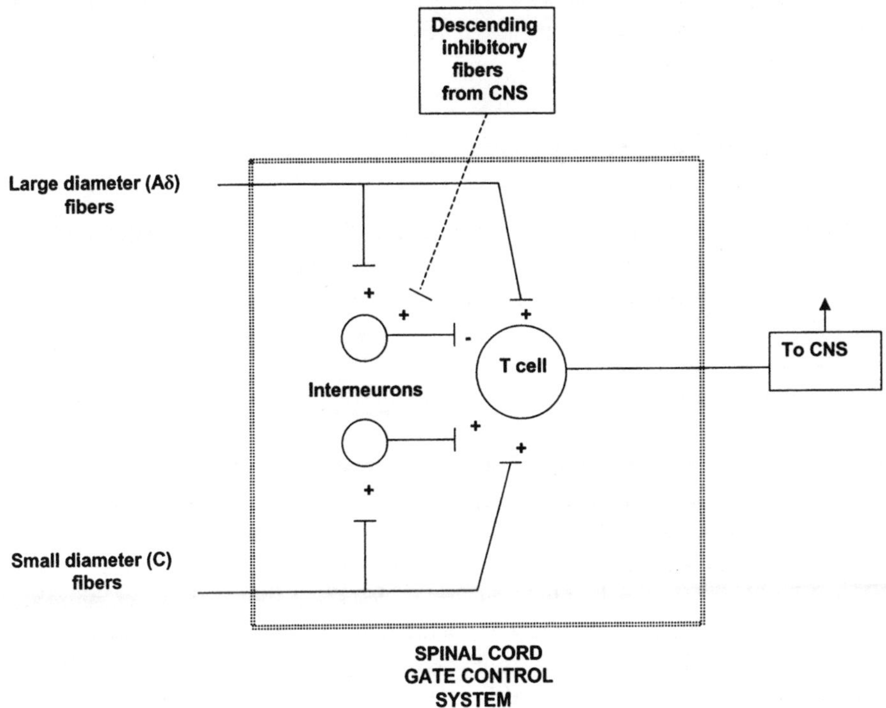

Figure 17.6. Schematic representation of Melzack and Wall's revised gate theory of pain. (Adapted from Rollman (1991).)

long-lasting analgesic effect (Young, 1989). This effect appears to be controlled by a descending circuit from frontal cortex to the raphe nucleus of the medulla, and from there to the dorsal horn of the spinal cord. Although this descending system seems to be involved as well in the suppression of pain by endogenous opiates, there is another pain suppression mechanism that is not opiate-mediated but instead controls the suppressive effects of stress-induced analgesia (Coderre & Rollman, 1984). The analgesia produced by acupuncture and TENS (transcutaneous electrical nerve stimulation), which involve peripheral rather than central stimulation, also has been found to have both opiate-mediated and non-opiate-mediated aspects (Sjolund & Eriksson, 1979).

The gate control theory of pain, in its general form, is consistent with stimulation-induced analgesic effects. Inputs from high-threshold nociceptors would excite T-cells in the spinal cord and cause transmission to higher centers that is interpreted as painful. Subsequent activation of lower-threshold fibers via electrical or mechanical means would exert inhibitory effects on the T-cells via interneurons, and would thus reduce the painful sensation. Such a mechanism explains the everyday observation that the sensation of pain is often reduced by simply rubbing the affected area.

However, as previously mentioned, pain is a much more complex perception in many cases, involving not only sensory, but cognitive and emotional factors. A more comprehensive theoretical account of human pain response must also take these factors into account.

Applications of Cutaneous Perception

Thus far we have focused on basic findings about the nature of the cutaneous senses. However, applied aspects of research on touch have followed very exciting directions in recent years. Several applications are described below.

Touch in Sensory Substitution and Supplementation

The relatively acute spatial and temporal responsiveness of the tactile system has led researchers to investigate the potential utility of touch as a transmission channel for information normally provided via the visual or auditory systems. It may be possible to use the sense of touch to substitute for the impaired sensory channel. One obvious application is the use of Braille for reading by blind persons, as described above. However, more ambitious applications have included the vibrotactile fingertip display of the Optacon, originally developed as a reading aid that would permit access to regular printed text, thus not requiring specially printed material. Although subsequent developments in text-recognition and text-to-speech algorithms have made talking readers a more common choice, many blind individuals were trained to become successful readers with the Optacon. Optacon-like devices have more recently been investigated as a means of conveying tangible graphical information, an area not yet well served by text-to-speech devices.

Similarly, considerable effort has been invested in developing and evaluating tactile devices to convey acoustic information to hearing-impaired persons. The history of such efforts extends back to the work of Gault (1926). Recent efforts have shown some success (see reviews by Reed, Durlach, & Braida, 1982; Weisenberger, 1992). However, the most compelling demonstration of tactile capabilities for speech reception does not involve an external device. Rather, direct sensing via the fingertips of the articulatory movements of a talker provides the tactile input of *Tadoma*, a method of speech reception used by some deaf-blind persons. In Tadoma, the receiver places the thumb and fingertips on the face and neck of the talker, and gains running feedback conveying laryngeal vibration, upper and lower jaw tension and movement, airflow, lip extension, and nasal resonance. Highly trained Tadoma users can understand speech at rates only slightly slower than normal speech (Reed et al., 1985). This level of success in speech comprehension via tactile input alone has led Tadoma to be designated as an "existence proof" of the feasibility of tactile speech transmission. Other tactile devices do not reach this goal at present, although some devices do provide substantial benefits to visual input from speechreading (e.g., Brooks, Frost, Mason, & Gibson, 1986; Weisenberger, Broadstone, & Saunders, 1989).

Force Feedback in Motor Performance

Consider the practical problem of manipulating a tool, such as a computer mouse, to contact a specific point, such as an icon on the screen or an item on a pull-down menu. A certain degree of skill is required to reach the desired point rapidly, without overshoot. Recent research has investigated the potential assistive role of force feedback in such tasks. The simplified task commonly used for experimental evaluation is referred to as the Fitts-Law task, in which the subject must move a tool from point A to point B as rapidly as possible. Eberhardt, Neverov, West, and Saunders (1997) evaluated the use of force feedback in this task, by setting up a situation where the tool initially moves freely toward the icon to be contacted, but when it is in close proximity, the tool is "pulled" onto the icon, and greater effort is needed to move the tool away from the icon. The use of such force areas improved response times in the Fitts-Law task substantially. Findings such as these have led to the development of the force-feedback computer mouse (Immersion Corporation). Force feedback can also play a role in more complex tasks. Repperger, Phillips, and Chelette (1995) showed that accuracy in a target-tracking task in a cockpit simulation was enhanced when "force tunnels" added to the navigation stick provided information about the best tracking path. It is easy to imagine a whole realm of tasks whose execution could be benefited by the provision of force feedback cues.

Virtual Displays

The explosion of interest in "virtual reality" has focused largely on the development of sophisticated computer graphics to provide realistic simulation of a three-dimensional visual world. Somewhat less attention has been paid to developing realistic auditory displays for externalized sound (Durlach & Mavor, 1994). However, true simulation of the real world will require that the user be able to touch and manipulate the objects in a virtual environment, and receive appropriate feedback when doing so.

Haptic interfaces to provide this capability are still in their infancy, partly because of the preponderance of interest in visual aspects of virtual environments, but partly because the technological issues to be overcome in constructing such interfaces are formidable. Despite these challenges, several haptic interfaces have been developed in recent years. A few examples are described below.

Several groups have incorporated force feedback into a joystick. These devices permit the user to move about in two dimensions, with forces exerted in the X-Y domain. Although such devices are typically envisioned as assisting human-computer interaction in game-type tasks, they can also be used to represent surface features and textures, and to assist in tasks like computer-assisted design (e.g., Weisenberger et al., 1998).

Haptic interfaces become more complex when additional degrees of freedom of movement must be specified. In the simplest case, the user senses virtual objects with the fingertip via a thimble, or with a stylus. In both of these, the exerted force is provided at a single point, thus improving computational and mechanical tractability. Glove devices and hand exoskeletons that provide multiple forces simultaneously to different fingers face an even greater challenge in implementation. Still more challenging are efforts to combine force, vibratory, and thermal actuators in glove devices, in an attempt to provide most of the cutaneous cues normally available to the human perceiver (e.g., Caldwell, Kocak, & Andersen, 1995).

To what uses could such devices be directed? Some potential applications that have been investigated include virtual medicine and surgery, and telerobotics. Virtual medical applications might involve the use of simulated medical procedures for training and evaluation of surgeons, particularly for cases in which animal or cadaver models are inadequate. Additional possibilities include laparoscopic procedures, where surgeons often complain about the lack of "feel" provided by the instrumentation. *Telerobotics* refers to the control of a robot at a remote site; here, movement of a robot's "hands" by a human controller to perform some task in a hostile environment could be substantially benefited by tactile feedback about the objects contacted by the robot hand. Without such feedback, the situation is analogous to, but even worse than, object manipulation while wearing thick gloves. Without tactile feedback, manipulation is clumsy and inaccurate.

These are just a few examples of the potential uses of haptic interfaces in virtual environments. The spectrum of such applications runs through entertainment, education, and training, and new possibilities are constantly being proposed and explored. The future of virtual environments is truly multisensory.

The Present and Future of Cutaneous Research

Although recent studies have advanced our knowledge of cutaneous capabilities, our understanding of this complex of sensory functions remains incomplete. Future work that explores further the linkage between psychophysical and perceptual aspects, on the one hand, and physiological and neural substrates, on the other, should provide substantial new insights into the operation of somatosensory abilities. Elucidating the role of kinesthetic feedback in tactile perception will require inventive new research paradigms, but will fundamentally advance somatosensory science. Investigations of intersensory integration and information transmission should lead to a more comprehensive picture of multimodal perception. The influence of cognitive and affective factors, already known to be of great importance in the perception and alleviation of pain, will require further specification. Finally, the availability of new technology in the design of tactile actuators and haptic interfaces will allow researchers to broaden the scope of their investigations, and ask questions that have heretofore not been experimentally accessible. There are still many unanswered questions in cutaneous perception. Filling the gaps in our knowledge provides an exciting challenge for researchers in this field.

Suggested Readings

Craig, J. C., & Rollman G. B. (1999). Somesthesis. *Annual Review of Psychology, 50*, 305–331. [Craig and Rollman provide a comprehensive review of recent research in the areas of touch, temperature, and pain.]

Kruger, L. (Ed.) (1996). *Pain and touch.* San Diego: Academic Press. [Kruger's update for the second edition of the *Handbook of perception and cognition* series contains a number of excellent tutorial chapters, including ones on the physiology and psychophysics of tactile perception (Greenspan & Bolanowski, Chapter 2); somatosensory cortex (Burton & Sinclair, Chapter 3); afferent mechanisms of pain (Lynn & Perl, Chapter 5); and measurement of pain sensation (Gracely & Naliboff, Chapter 6).]

Wall, P. O., & Melzack, R. (1994). *Textbook of pain* (3rd ed.). Edinburgh: Churchill Livingstone. [Wall and Melzack have compiled an encyclopedic reference on all aspects of pain, including physiology, measurement, and control of pain sensations.]

Sherrick, C. E., & Cholewiak, R. W. (1986). Cutaneous sensitivity. In K. Boff, L. Kaufman, & J. L. Thomas (Eds.), *Handbook of perception and human performance* (pp. 12-1–12-58). New York: Academic Press. [Sherrick and Cholewiak's chapter remains one of the most complete accounts of the physiology and psychophysics of touch.]

Johnson, K. O., & Hsiao, S. S. (1992). Neural mechanisms of tactual form and texture perception. *Annual Review in Neuroscience, 15,* 227–250. [Johnson and Hsiao provide an in-depth review of peripheral neural mechanisms underlying the sensing of object shape and texture.]

Burdea, G. C. (1996). *Force and touch feedback for virtual reality.* New York: John Wiley & Sons. [This book provides an overview of the issues involved in using haptic and tactile interfaces in virtual environment applications.]

Additional Topics

Plasticity in Somatosensory Cortex

One of the most exciting topics in cutaneous research is the high degree of plasticity observed in the organization of receptive fields in somatosensory cortex. Findings from controlled laboratory studies have suggested that our traditional notions of fixed cortical organization are not an accurate description of cortical processing. For further information see Merzenich and Jenkins (1993).

Phantom Limb Sensations and Causalgia

The concept of "phantom limb" sensations, the report from amputees that they continue to experience sensations of touch and pain (causalgia) from the amputated site, is another fascinating aspect of cortical mediation of cutaneous and pain inputs. For additional information on this topic, see Melzack (1990) and Ramachandran and Blakeslee (1998).

Sensory-Motor Interactions in Active Touch

A substantial body of research has studied how movement and touch interact in our manipulation of objects in the environment. Although this chapter refers briefly to the combination of tactile and kinesthetic inputs in the perception of objects, the motor aspects of this activity are not addressed. An excellent source of recent work on this topic is found in Wing, Haggard, and Flanagan (1996). Various chapters address physiology, psychophysics, kinematics, and cortical mediation of active touch.

Attention and Cognition in Unisensory and Multisensory Tasks

Recent research into cognitive mediation of sensory inputs from one or more sensory modalities has focused on the role of attention in processing these inputs. Such studies have immediate real-world relevance, in that our normal experience of the world involves simultaneous inputs from multiple sensory sources. For additional information on this topic, see Hsiao, Johnson, Twombly and DiCarlo (1996).

References

Algom, D., Raphaeli, N., & Cohen-Raz, L. (1986). Integration of noxious stimulation across separate somatosensory communications systems: A functional theory of pain. *Journal of Experimental Psychology: Human Perception & Performance, 12*, 92–102.

Allard, T., Clark, S. A., Jenkins, W. M., & Merzenich, M. M. (1991). Reorganization of somatosensory area 3b representations in adult owl monkeys after digital syndactyly. *Journal of Neurophysiology, 66* (3), 1048–1058.

Alrutz, S. (1898). On the temperature senses: II. The sensation "hot". *Mind, 7* (2), 140–144.

Ballesteros, S., Manga, D., & Reales, J. M. (1997). Haptic discrimination of bilateral symmetry in 2-dimensional and 3-dimensional unfamiliar displays. *Perception & Psychophysics, 59*, 37-50.

Blix, M. (1884). Experimentale Beiträge zur Lösung der Frage über die spezifische Energie der Hautnerven. *Zeitschrift für Biologie, 20*, 141–156.

Bolanowski, S. J., Jr., Gescheider, G. A., Verrillo, R. T., & Checkosky, C. M. (1988). Four channels mediate the mechanical aspects of touch. *Journal of the Acoustical Society of America, 84*, 1680–1694.

Brooks, P. L., Frost, B. J., Mason, J. L., & Gibson, D. M. (1986). Continuing evaluation of the Queens University Tactile Vocoder II: Identification of open-set sentences and tracking narrative. *Journal of Rehabilitation Research and Development, 23*, 129–138.

Cain, W. S. (1973). Spatial discrimination of cutaneous warm. *American Journal of Psychology, 86*, 169–181.

Caldwell, D., Kocak, O., & Andersen, U. (1995). Multi-armed dextrous manipulator operation using glove/exoskeleton control and sensory feedback. *Proceedings of IROS'95*, (Pittsburgh, PA), 567–572.

Chapman, E. C., Tremblay, F., & Ageranioti-Belanger, S.A. (1996). Role of a primary somatosensory cortex in active and passive touch. In A. M. Wing, P. Haggard, & J. Flanagan (Eds.), *Hand and brain* (pp. 329–347). New York: Academic Press.

Coderre, T. J., & Rollman, G. B. (1984). Stress analgesia: Effects of PCPA, yohimbine, and maloxone. *Pharmacology, Biochemistry and Behavior, 21*, 681–686.

Connor, C. E., Hsiao, S. S., Phillips, J. R., & Johnson, K. O. (1990). Tactile roughness: Neural codes that account for psychophysical magnitude estimates. *Journal of Neuroscience, 10*, 3823–3836.

Craig, J. C. (1976). Vibrotactile letter recognition: The effects of a masking stimulus. *Perception & Psychophysics, 20*, 317–326.

Craig, J. C. (1979). A confusion matrix for tactually presented letters. *Perception & Psychophysics, 26*, 409–411.

Craig, J. C. (1980). Modes of vibrotactile pattern generation. *Journal of Experimental Psychology: Human Perception & Performance, 6*, 151–166.

Craig, J. C. (1993). Anomalous sensations following prolonged tactile stimulation. *Neuropsychologia, 31* (3), 277–291.

Craig, J. C. (1995). Vibrotactile masking: The role of response competition. *Perception & Psychophysics, 57*, 1190–2000.

Craig, J. C. (1996). Interference identifying tactile patterns: Response competition and temporal integration. *Somatosensory & Motor Research, 13* (3–4), 199–213.

Craig, J. C., & Evans, P. M. (1995). Tactile selective attention and temporal masking. *Perception & Psychophysics, 57*, 511–518.

Craig, J. C., & Rollman, G. B. (1999). Somesthesis. *Annual Review of Psychology, 50*, 305–331.

Darian-Smith, I. (1982). Touch in primates. *Annual Review of Psychology, 33*, 155–194.

Durlach, N. I., & Mavor, A. S. (Eds.) (1994). *Virtual reality: Scientific and technological challenges.* Washington, DC: National Academy Press.

Eberhardt, S., Neverov, M., West, T., & Sanders, C. (1997). Force reflection for WIMPs: A button acquisition experiment. *Proceedings of the ASME Dynamic Systems and Control Division, DSC-61,* 23–27.

Foulke, E. (1991). Braille. In M. A. Heller & W. Schiff (Eds.), *The psychology of touch* (pp. 219–33). Hillsdale, NJ: Lawrence Erlbaum Associates.

Garbin, C. P., & Bernstein, I. H. (1984). Visual and haptic perception of three-dimensional solid forms. *Perception & Psychophysics, 36,* 104–110.

Gault, R. H. (1926). Touch as a substitute for hearing in the interpretation and control of speech. *Archives of Otolaryngology, 3,* 121–135.

Geldard, F. A. (1972). *The human senses.* New York; John Wiley & Sons, Inc.

Gescheider, G. A. (1974). Temporal relations in cutaneous stimulation. In F. A. Geldard (Ed.), *Cutaneous communication systems and devices* (pp. 33–37). Austin, TX: Psychonomic Society.

Gescheider, G. A. (1976). Evidence in support of the duplex theory of mechanoreception. *Sensory Processes, 1,* 68–76.

Gescheider, G. A., Capraro, A. J., Frisina, R. D., Hamer, R. D., & Verrillo, R. T. (1978). The effects of a surround on vibrotactile thresholds. *Sensory Processes, 2* (2), 99–115.

Gibson, J. J. (1966). *The senses considered as perceptual systems.* Boston: Houghton-Mifflin.

Goff, G. D. (1967). Differential discrimination of frequency of cutaneous mechanical vibration. *Journal of Psychology, 71,* 655–658.

Greenspan, J. D., & Bolanowski, S. J. (1996). In L. Kruger (Ed.), *Pain and touch* (*Handbook of perception and cognition,* 2nd ed.). San Diego: Academic Press.

Hardy, J. D., & Oppel, T. W. (1937). Studies in temperature sensation III. The sensitivity of the body to heat and the spatial summation of the end organ responses. *Journal of Clinical Investigation, 16,* 533–540.

Hirsh, I. J., & Sherrick, C. E. (1961). Perceived order in different sense modalities. *Journal of Experimental Psychology, 62,* 423–432.

Hollins, M., Bensmaia, S., & Risner, M. (1998). The duplex theory of tactile texture perception. *Proceedings of the International Society for Psychophysics, Fourth Annual Meeting* (pp. 115–120).

Hollins, M., Faldowski, R., Rao, S., & Young, F. (1993). Perceptual dimensions of tactile surface texture: A multidimensional scaling analysis. *Perception & Psychophysics, 6,* 697–705.

Hsiao, S. S., Johnson, K. O., Twombly, A., & DiCarlo, J. (1996). Form processing and attention effects in the somatosensory system. In O. Franzen, R. Johanson, & L. Terenius (Eds.), *Somesthesis and the neurobiology of the somatosensory cortex* (pp. 229–248). Boston: Birkhauser Verlag.

Hyvarinen, J., & Poranen, A. (1978). Movement-sensitive or direction- or orientation-selective cutaneous receptive fields in the hand area of the postcentral gyrus in monkeys. *Journal of Physiology, 283,* 523–537.

Iwamura, Y., &Tanaka, M. (1978). Postcentral neurons in hand region of area 2: Their possible role in the form discrimination of tactile objects. *Brain Research, 150,* 662–666.

Johansson, R. S., & Westling, G. (1987). Signals in tactile afferents from the fingers eliciting adaptive motor responses during precision grip. *Experimental Brain Research, 66,* 141–154.

Johnson, K. O., & Hsiao, S. S. (1992). Neural mechanisms of tactual form and texture perception. *Annual Review in Neuroscience, 15,* 227–250.

Johnson, K. O., & Phillips, F. R. (1981). Tactile spatial resolution: I. Two-point discrimination, gap detection, grating resolution, and letter recognition. *Journal of Neurophysiology, 46,* 1177–1191.

Katz, D. (1925). *Der Aufbau der Tastwelt.* Leipzig, Germany: Barth. (For an English translation, see L. E. Krueger (Ed.) (1989). *The world of touch.* Hillsdale, NJ: Lawrence Erlbaum Associates.)

Klatzky, R. L., Lederman, S. J., & Metzger, V. A. (1985). Identifying objects by touch: An expert system. *Perception & Psychophysics, 37,* 299–302.

Lederman, S. J. (1974). Tactile roughness of grooved surfaces: The touching process and effects of macro- and microsurface structure. *Perception & Psychophysics, 16,* 385–395.

Lederman, S. J. (1981). The perception of surface roughness by active and passive touch. *Bulletin of the Psychonomic Society, 18,* 253–255.

Lederman, S. J., & Klatzky, R. L. (1987). Hand movements: A window into haptic object recognition. *Cognitive Psychology, 19,* 342–368.

Lederman, S. J., & Pawluk, D. T. (1993). Lessons from the study of biological touch for robot tactile sensing. In H. Nichols (Ed.), *Advanced tactile sensing for robotics* (pp. 1–44). London: World Press.

Lederman, S. J., & Taylor, M. M. (1972). Fingertip force, surface geometry, and the perception of roughness by active force. *Perception & Psychophysics, 12,* 401–408.

Loomis, J. M. (1980). Interaction of display mode and character size in vibrotactile letter recognition. *Bulletin of the Psychonomic Society, 16,* 385–387.

Loomis, J. M. (1981). On the tangibility of letters and Braille. *Perception & Psychophysics, 29,* 37–46.

McFarland, D. J., Cacace, A. T., & Setzen, G. (1998). Temporal-order discrimination for selected auditory and visual stimulus dimensions. *Journal of Speech, Language, and Hearing Research, 41,* 300–314.

Melzack, R. (1975). The McGill pain questionnaire: Major properties and scoring methods. *Pain, 1,* 277–300.

Melzack, R. (1990). Phantom limbs and the concept of a neuromatrix. *Trends in Neuroscience, 13,* 88–92.

Melzack, R., & Wall, P. D. (1965). Pain mechanisms: A new theory. *Science, 150,* 971–979.

Melzack, R., & Wall, P. D. (1988). *The challenge of pain.* London: Penguin.

Merzenich, M. M., & Jenkins, W. M. (1993). Reorganization of cortical representations of hand following alterations of skin inputs induced by nerve injury, skin island transfers, and experience. *Journal of Hand Therapy, 6* (2), 89–104.

Mogilner, A., Grossman, J. A., Ribary, U., Joliot, M., Volkmann, J., Rapaport, D., Beasley, R. W., & Llinas, R. R. (1993). Somatosensory cortical plasticity in adult humans revealed by magnetoencephalography. *Proceedings of the National Academy of Sciences of the United States of America, 90* (8), 3593–3597.

Nolan, C. Y., & Kederis, C. J. (1969). Perceptual factors in Braille word recognition. *American Foundation for Blind Research Services, 20.*

Phillips, J. R., & Johnson, K. O. (1981). Tactile spatial resolution III: A continuum-mechanics model of skin predicting mechanoreceptor responses to bars, edges, and gratings. *Journal of Neurophysiology, 59,* 607–622.

Pons, T. P., Garraghty, P. E., Ommaya, A. K., Kaas, J. H., Taub, E., & Mishkin, M. (1991). Massive cortical reorganization after sensory deafferentation in adult macaques. *Science, 252* (5014), 1857–1860.

Price, D. D. (1988). *Psychological and neural mechanisms of pain.* New York: Raven Press.

Price, D. D., Harkins, S. W., & Baker, C. (1987). Sensory affective relationships among different types of clinical and experimental pain. *Pain, 28,* 297-308.

Price, D. D., Von Der Gruen, A., Miller, J., Rafii, A., & Price, C. (1985). A psychophysical analysis of morphine analgesia. *Pain, 22,* 261–270.

Ramachandran, V., & Blakeslee, S. (1998). *Phantoms in the brain.* New York: William Morrow & Co.

Reed, C. M., Durlach, N. I., & Braida, L. D. (1982). Research on tactile communication of speech: A review. *ASHA Monographs, 20.* Rockville, MD: American Speech-Language-Hearing Association.

Reed, C. M., Rabinowitz, W. M., Durlach, N. I., Braida, L. D., Conway-Fithian, S., & Schultz, M. C. (1985). Research on the Tadoma method of speech communication. *Journal of the Acoustical Society of America, 62,* 1003–1012.

Repperger, D. W., Phillips, C. A., & Chelette, T. L. (1995). A study on spatially induced virtual force with an information theoretic investigation of human performance. *IEEE Transactions on Systems, Man, And Cybernetics, 25* (100), 1392–1403.

Rollman, G. B. (1979). Signal detection theory pain measures: Empirical validation studies and adaptation level effects. *Pain, 6*, 9–21.

Rollman, G. B. (1991). Pain responsiveness. In M.A. Heller & W. Schiff (Eds.), The *psychology of touch* (pp. 91–114). Hillsdale, NJ: Lawrence Erlbaum Associates.

Rothenberg, M., Verrillo, R. T., Zahorian, S. A., Brachman, M. L., & Bolanowski, Jr. S. J. (1977). Vibrotactile frequency for encoding a speech parameter. *Journal of the Acoustical Society of America, 62*, 1003–1012.

Sathian, K., Goodwin, A. W., John, K. T., & Darian-Smith, I. (1989). Perceived roughness of a grating: Correlation with responses of mechanoreceptive afferents innervating the monkey's fingerpad. *Journal of Neuroscience, 9*, 1273–1279.

Sherrick, C. E. (1964). Effects of double simultaneous stimulation of the skin. *American Journal of Psychology, 77*, 42–53.

Sherrick, C. E. (1982). Cutaneous communication. In W. D. Neff (Ed.), *Contributions to sensory physiology* (pp. 1–43). New York: Academic Press.

Sherrick, C. E., & Cholewiak, R. W. (1986). Cutaneous sensitivity. In K. Boff, L. Kaufman, & J. L. Thomas (Eds.), *Handbook of perception and human performance* (Vol. 1, pp. 12-1–12-58). New York: Academic Press.

Sjolund, B. H., & Eriksson, M. B. E. (1979). Endorphins and analgesia stimulation. In J. J. Bonica, J. C. Liebesking, & D. Albe-Fessard (Eds.), *Advances in pain research and therapy* (pp. 587–599). New York: Raven Press.

Srinivasan, M. A., Whitehouse, J. M., & LaMotte, R. H. (1990). Tactile detection of slip: Surface microgeometry and peripheral neural codes. *Journal of Neurophysiology, 63*, 1312–1332.

Stevens, J. C. (1991). Thermal sensibility. In M. A. Heller & W. Schiff (Eds.), *The psychology of touch* (pp. 61–90). Hillsdale, NJ: Lawrence Erlbaum Associates.

Stevens, J. C., & Choo, K. K. (1996). Spatial acuity of the body surface over the life span. *Somatosensory & Motor Research, 13* (2), 153–166.

Stevens, J. C., Green, B. G., & Krimsley, A. S. (1977). Punctate pressure sensitivity: Effects of skin temperature. *Sensory Processes, 1*, 238–243.

Stevens, J. C., Marks, L. E., & Simonson, D. C. (1974). Regional sensitivity and spatial summation in the warmth sense. *Physiology and Behavior, 13*, 825–836.

Sumino, R., & Dubner, R. (1981). Response characteristics of specific thermoreceptive afferents innervating monkey facial skin and their relationship to human thermal sensitivity. *Brain Research Reviews, 3* (2), 105–122.

Talbot, W. H., Darian-Smith, I., Kornhuber, H. H., & Mountcastle, V. B. (1968). The sense of flutter-vibration: Comparison of the human capacity with response patterns of mechanoreceptive afferents from the monkey hand. *Journal of Neurophysiology, 31*, 301–334.

Tremblay, F., Ageranioti-Belanger, S. A., & Chapman, C. E. (1996). Cortical mechanisms underlying tactile discrimination in the monkey. 1. Role of primary somatosensory cortex in passive texture discrimination. *Journal of Neurophysiology, 76*, 3382–3403.

Van Boven, R. W., & Johnson, K. O. (1994). A psychophysical study of the mechanisms of sensory recovery following nerve injury in humans. *Brain, 117*, 149–167.

Vega-Bermudez, F., Johnson, K. O., & Hsiao, S. S. (1991). Human tactile pattern recognition: Active versus passive touch, velocity effects, and patterns of confusion. *Journal of Neurophysiology, 65*, 531–546.

Verrillo, R. T. (1963). Effect of contactor area on the vibrotactile threshold. *Journal of the Acoustical Society of America, 35*, 1962–1966.

Verrillo, R. T. (1965). Temporal summation in vibrotactile sensitivity. *Journal of the Acoustical Society of America, 37*, 843–846.

Verrillo, R. T. (1966). Effect of spatial parameters on the vibrotactile threshold. *Journal of the Acoustical Society of America, 35*, 1962–1966.

Wall, P. O., & Melzack, R. (1994). *Textbook of pain* (3rd ed.). Edinburgh: Churchill Livingstone.

Weinstein, S. (1968). Intensive and extensive aspects of tactile sensitivity as a function of body part, sex and laterality. In D. R. Kenshalo (Ed.), *The skin senses* (pp. 195–222). Springfield, IL: Thomas.

Weisenberger, J. M. (1986). Sensitivity to amplitude-modulated vibrotactile signals. *Journal of the Acoustical Society of America, 80,* 1707–1715.

Weisenberger, J. M. (1992). Communication of the acoustic environment via tactile stimuli. In I.R. Summers (Ed.), *Tactile aids for the hearing impaired* (pp. 83–109). London: Whurr Publishers.

Weisenberger, J. M., Broadstone, S. M., & Saunders, F. A. (1989). Evaluation of two multichannel tactile aids for the hearing-impaired. *Journal of the Acoustical Society of America, 86,* 1764–1775.

Weisenberger, J. M., & Craig, J. C. (1982). A tactile metacontrast effect. *Perception & Psychophysics, 31,* 530–536.

Weisenberger, J. M., & Hasser, C. J. (1998). Role of active and passive movement in vibrotactile pattern perception. *Perception & Psychophysics,* submitted.

Weisenberger, J. M., Hasser, C. J., & Holtman, K. M. (1998). Changing the tactile "field of view": Effects on pattern perception with haptic displays. *Presence: Teloperators and virtual environments,* submitted.

Weisenberger, J. M., & Krier, M. J. (1997). Haptic perception of simulated surface textures via vibratory and force feedback displays. *ASME Dynamic Systems and Control, DSC 53,* 83–91.

Weisenberger, J. M., Krier, M. J., & Rinker, M. A. (1998). Resolution of virtual grating orientation with 2-DOF and 3-DOF force feedback systems. *ASME Dynamic Systems and Control, DSC-64,* 295–301.

Whang, K. C., Burton, H., & Shulman, G. L. (1991). Selective attention in vibrotactile tasks: Detecting the presence of amplitude change. *Perception & Psychophysics, 50,* 157–165.

Wing, A. M., Haggard, P., & Flanagan, J. (Eds.) (1996). *Hand and brain.* San Diego: Academic Press.

Yang, T. T., Gallen, C. C., Ramachandran, V. S., Cobb, S., Schwartz, B. J., & Bloom, F. E. (1994). Noninvasive detection of cerebral plasticity in adult human somatosensory cortex. *Neuroreport, 5* (6), 701–704.

Young, R. F. (1989). Brain stimulation. In P. D. Wall & R. Melzack (Eds.), *Textbook of pain* (pp. 925–931). Edinburgh: Churchill Livingstone.

Chapter Eighteen

Olfaction

Beverly J. Cowart and Nancy E. Rawson

Introduction

Smell, like taste, is a concrete sense in which receptors respond to what are literally pieces of the thing perceived. When one tastes, however, the stimulus is known in that it is also seen, felt, and placed into the mouth, whereas smells often seem to come from nowhere – and to disappear into nothingness. It is, perhaps, the contrast in our olfactory experience between the compelling perception of a physical thing and its ambiguous source, often undetected by any other sense, that lends smell its peculiar mystery and contributes to the strong emotional responses it can evoke in humans, and to the significance frequently attached to it: the smell of life, the smell of death, the "odour of the soul" (Howes, 1988). Societal attitudes towards smells have varied greatly (Howes, 1988) and no doubt influenced the scientific study and understanding of this sense. For many years, in modern Western societies, smells were simply not spoken of in polite company (McKenzie, 1923). There has, however, been increasing popular interest in – indeed, almost an obsession with – smell (e.g., global fragrance consumption is now valued at over 2.8 billion dollars (Rossiter, 1996)), and a concomitant increase in research in this area. Although much remains to be learned, we are beginning to understand some of the unique characteristics of this intriguing sensory system.

The Nature of the Stimulus

The olfactory system is remarkable in the absolute number of different types of stimuli it can detect, its sensitivity, and its discriminatory ability. The number of chemical substances known to be odorous reaches the tens of thousands, and a trained perfumer can discriminate among thousands of different odorants. The variety in both structural and perceptual characteristics represented by these odorous chemicals attests to the impressive ability of the olfactory system to perceive and describe our environment.

The key chemical features that render a chemical "odorous" include its volatility and its solubility in the mucus overlying the olfactory receptor cells. Chemicals meeting these criteria typically are nonionic compounds with a molecular weight of less than 300 (Rossiter, 1996). Available evidence indicates that numerous chemical and molecular features (e.g., molecular weight, molecular mass and shape, polarity, resonance structure, types of bonds and sidegroups) can all influence the odorous characteristics of a chemical. However, no systematic description of how these characteristics relate to particular odor qualities has been developed. Odor qualities have been classified in a variety of ways, but schemes based on perceptual qualities reflect neither chemical nor physiological referents. In other words,

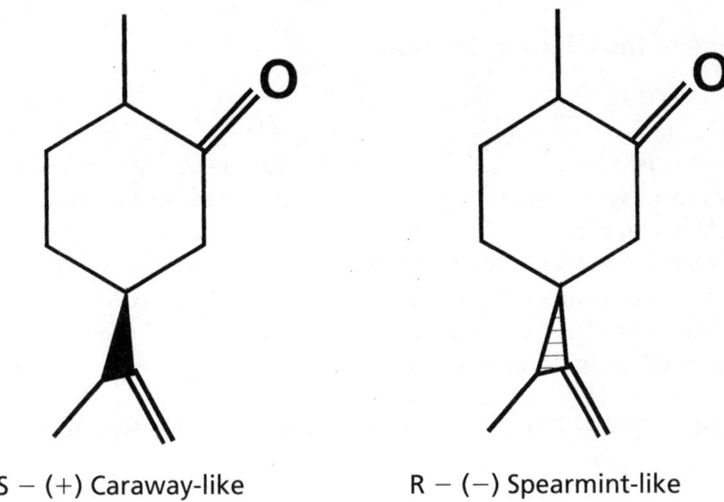

Figure 18.1. The two enantiomers of carvone, (+) and (−) are structurally similar but the (+) form has the odor of caraway, while the (−) form smells like spearmint.

chemicals that bear little resemblance structurally can smell the same, and chemicals that are nearly identical structurally can elicit very different perceptual qualities (Figure 18.1).

Odorants may be classified according to common chemical features, such as aldehydes or alcohols, and according to such characteristics as chain length, number and polarity of side groups, etc. (Rossiter, 1996). These basic chemical traits play an important part in determining how volatile a stimulus is, and thus how easily it will traverse into the nasal cavity, and how soluble it is in the mucus, and thus how easily it will penetrate to access the receptor on the cell membrane. These features, as well as the three-dimensional structure of the molecule, determine what receptor protein, or docking site on the olfactory neuron, a chemical is able to interact with, and thus what pattern of olfactory neuron activity it will elicit. A particular odorant may interact with more than one type of receptor protein with different affinities or activities (Malnic, Hirono, Sato, & Buck, 1999), and may activate one cell and inhibit another (Bacigalupo, Morales, Labarca, Ugarte, & Madrid, 1997). Current evidence suggests that it is the resulting overall pattern of activity across the olfactory epithelium, which lines the upper portions of the nasal cavity, that is detected by the central nervous system and determines the perceptual quality of a given odorant. As no structure-based classification scheme has yet been devised that is consistently capable of predicting odor quality across more than a limited number of possibilities, new approaches have been suggested. One proposed model takes into account the physical attributes that result from a chemical structure interacting with its environment, such as the resonance or vibration resulting from charge interactions (Turin, 1996). Until more is known about the molecular basis for odor perception, however, a truly accurate scheme for classifying structural qualities that can reliably predict perceptual impact remains a challenge to the field.

Anatomy of the Olfactory System

The human nose is responsible for a wide variety of tasks – warming the air we breath and filtering particles from it, detoxifying potentially harmful chemicals, and sensing airborne chemicals that tell us a great deal about the world around us. The tissue responsible for much of this sensory ability is the olfactory epithelium. Located within the upper portions of the nasal cavity and the olfactory cleft (Figure 18.2), the epithelium has a surface area of $\approx$ 3–5 cm^2 and contains 6–12 million receptor neurons (Silver & Walker, 1997). Volatile chemicals are inhaled into the nasal cavity, and this air plume is broken up by convolutions in the tissue called turbinates that contain olfactory and respiratory epithelium (Lanza & Clerico, 1995). Volatile chemicals also enter the nasal cavity from the mouth and during swallowing via the nasopharynx, or what is referred to as the retronasal pathway ("behind

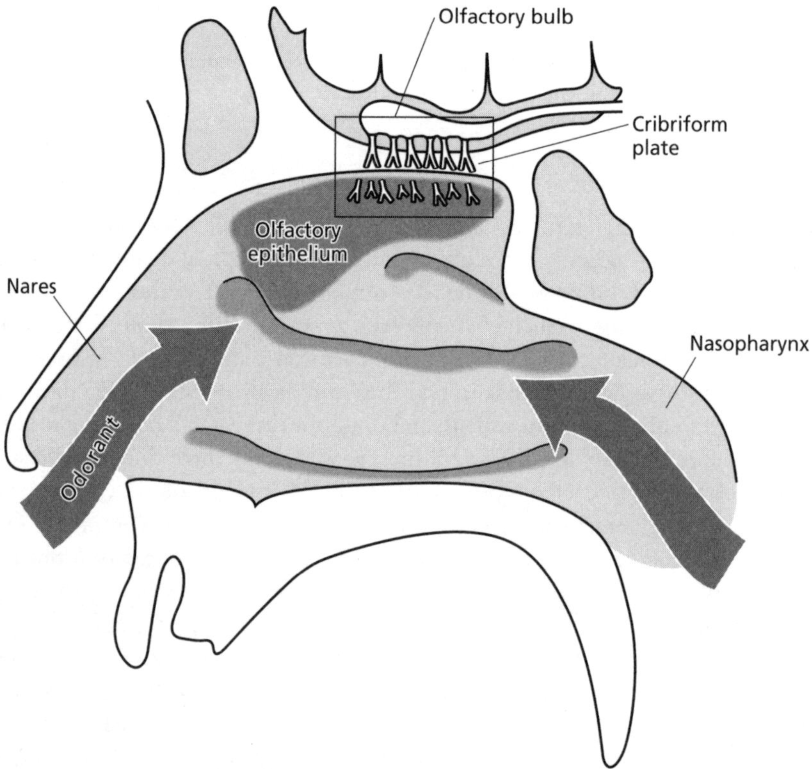

Figure 18.2. Diagram of human nasal cavity. Volatile chemicals enter via the nares (orthonasal) or nasopharynx (retronasal) to interact with ciliated sensory receptor cells. Sensory epithelium is present within the olfactory cleft (boxed region), as well as along the superior and high middle turbinates (shaded area), although the extent varies among individuals. Boxed region shows olfactory receptor cell axons passing through the cribriform plate to synapse within the olfactory bulb, which relays signals along the olfactory nerve to the olfactory cortex.

the nose" vs. "orthonasal," or through the front of the nose). This retronasal pathway plays a particularly important role in the sensory enjoyment of food, as olfactory components of food flavors are released and access the olfactory epithelium during consumption (see Retronasal Olfaction, below).

Olfactory receptor neurons within the epithelium project cilia into the mucus lining the nasal cavity, and it is within these cilia that the initial steps in olfaction occur (Figure 18.3). One to two liters of mucus are secreted daily by the Bowman's glands and goblet cells within the nasal epithelium of an average adult (see Getchell & Mellert, 1991, for review). This mucus is crucial for protecting the delicate cilia where olfactory detection takes place, and also influences what chemicals can be perceived. Because the mucus plays an important role in olfactory reception, medications or conditions that affect its ion or protein composition or viscosity can alter the ability to perceive volatile chemicals. Among the proteins within the mucus are odorant binding proteins (see Pelosi, 1994 for review). These proteins form families that are thought to interact with odorous chemicals of different chemical classes, and may aid in carrying the odorant through the mucus to the receptors and/or in carrying it away via mucus being swept through the nasal cavity into the back of the throat by the motile cilia of the respiratory epithelial cells (at a rate of 6–8 mm/min (Saketkhoo, Januszkiewicz, & Sackner, 1978)).

The olfactory receptor neurons (ORNs) are unusual in that even though they are primary neurons directly connected to the central nervous system, they have a limited life span (approximately one month), and are replaced from a population of continually dividing globose basal cells (Caggiano, Kauer, & Hunter, 1994). The basal cells give rise to immature neurons, which differentiate into mature olfactory receptor neurons. This

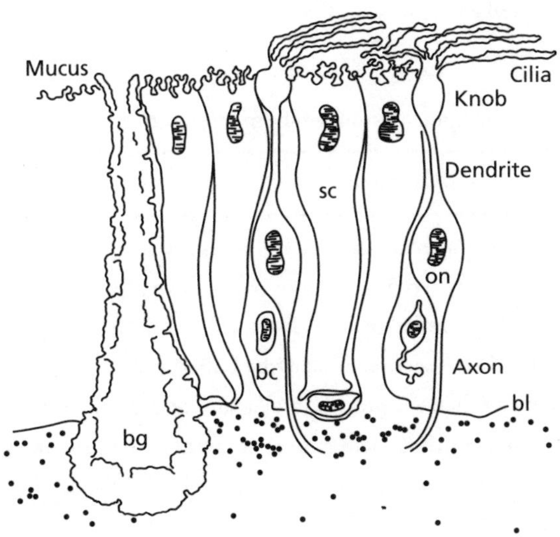

Figure 18.3. Diagram of the olfactory epithelium. bg: Bowman's gland; bc: basal cell; sc: sustentacular (supporting) cell; on: olfactory receptor neuron; bl: basal lamina. (Drawing courtesy of P. O. Rawson.)

regeneration within the olfactory system is almost unique within the adult mammalian brain. Also present in the epithelium are sustentacular or supporting cells, which contain a variety of detoxification enzymes such as cytochrome P450 (Lazard, 1990) and phenol sulfotransferase (Miyawaki, Homma, Tamura, Matsui, & Mikoshiba, 1996), and probably play an important role in degrading and detoxifying inhaled chemicals (xenobiotic metabolism), although there is little direct evidence for their function.

Olfactory neurons extend their axons through the cribriform plate to synapse in glomeruli in the olfactory bulbs – the first relay station in the brain (see Figure 18.2). There are ≈7,800 glomeruli in the bulbs of young adults, with the number declining to around 2,100 in old age (Meisami, Mikhail, Baim, & Bhatnagar, 1998). The glomeruli are circular structures where the axons of the olfactory neurons synapse with the dendrites of mitral cells, which project their axons to higher-order processing centers in the olfactory cortex. In addition, interneurons, such as periglomerular cells that surround the glomeruli and tufted cells found within the outer plexiform layer of the olfactory bulb, connect with the axons of the olfactory neurons and may modulate incoming signals. Mitral cells and some interneurons express receptors for a variety of neuroactive peptides such as estrogen, insulin, neuropeptide Y and dopamine (Coronas, Srivastava, Liang, Jourdan, & Moyse, 1997; Duchamp-Viret, Coronas, Delaleu, Moyse, & Duchamp, 1997; and see Halasz & Shepherd, 1983, for review), and these substances may play an important role in influencing the sensitivity of the system to meet the needs of the organism. Table 18.1 outlines the early development of structures in the primary olfactory system.

Functional magnetic resonance imaging studies are helping to reveal the central structures that are activated by the processes of sniffing and smelling odors (Sobel et al., 1998). The primary olfactory cortex is thought to lie in the pyriform cortex of the temporal lobe, and this region is activated when an odorant is sniffed, but not when no odorant is present. However, these studies also found activation of regions of the orbito-frontal cortex, not previously viewed as part of the primary olfactory cortex (Sobel et al., 1998). The olfactory

Table 18.1 Development of the human primary olfactory system[a]

Gestational age (wks)	*Anatomical observations*
9	Initial stages of olfactory epithelial development
11	Olfactory receptor neurons morphologically identifiable
12	Some neuronal markers expressed by ORNs
13	Laminar structure of olfactory bulb appears
16	Neurofilament protein in olfactory cells, not in axons
17	Axo-dendritic synapses begin to form in olfactory bulb
28	Olfactory marker protein expressed by ORNs; dendrodritic synapses form in olfactory bulb
32	Olfactory marker protein expressed in olfactory nerve layer

[a] From Chuah & Zheng (1992)

system is also closely linked to areas of the brain involved with emotion (amygdala), and learning and memory (hippocampus), and it is perhaps because of this that odor-associated memories may be particularly emotionally evocative (Herz & Cupchik, 1995).

Detection of Odorous Chemicals

Advances in molecular biology have led to substantial progress in our understanding of the molecular basis of olfaction. Within the last 10 years we have developed some understanding of the receptor proteins responsible for detecting odorous molecules, and of the molecular machinery inside the cell responsible for converting the chemical stimulation into an electrical signal that is carried to the olfactory bulbs. By understanding these cellular components, we hope one day to understand how odor qualities are determined and defined.

Olfactory Receptors

The first step in odorant detection occurs upon interaction of an odorant with a receptor protein located within the cilia of the olfactory neuron (Figures 18.3, 18.4). These proteins resemble other types of receptor proteins linked to G-proteins that stimulate the activity of enzymes (adenylate cyclase or phospholipase C) to produce the messenger molecules cyclic adenosine monophosphate (cAMP) or inositol trisphosphate ($InsP_3$), respectively. In fact, it was known that olfactory reception was mediated by the activity of G-proteins before the nature of the receptors was known. This feature was exploited to lead to the discovery of the olfactory receptor genes, as they exhibited DNA sequences that are similar across all such G-protein linked receptors, which include the adrenergic receptors (Buck & Axel, 1991). Messenger RNA, which represents that part of the genetic code that is translated into protein, or "expressed," was extracted from olfactory tissue and found to contain a large number of such sequences exhibiting regions within their sequence that were nearly identical ("homologous") and other regions that were highly variable. These sequences could be grouped into families on the basis of their homologies, and in rodents, there are predicted to be as many as 1,000 different proteins, comprising about 10 main families (Buck, 1992). In humans, many of the olfactory receptor genes have been identified by screening genomic DNA for patterns of sequences similar to those identified in other species (Ben-Arie et al., 1993). These studies have identified a very large number of potential olfactory receptor genes – occupying over 1% of the human genome spread across 19 of our 23 chromosomes (Roquier et al., 1998)! However, studies identifying those sequences that are actually used to generate functional receptor proteins indicate that many, perhaps as many as 40–60%, contain DNA sequences that prevent them from being expressed as proteins (termed "pseudogenes") (Crowe, Perry, & Connerton, 1996). In addition, a great degree of polymorphism (variability) exists between individuals in the olfactory receptor genes that can be expressed (Trask et al., 1998). It is not yet clear whether these genetic variations affect the odorant affinity or specificity of the receptors, but it is likely that these differences affect the perceived qualities of odors, as well as influencing the ability to discriminate among odors. Genetic differences in receptor expression probably account for the occurrence of at least some "specific anosmias," in which olfactory function is normal with the exception of a single odorant or small group of closely related odorants that cannot be detected or are poorly detected (see Specific Anosmia, below). Thus, it is likely that the olfactory world of each individual is slightly different and colored by the population of receptor proteins that individual is using.

Functional and molecular studies suggest that each receptor is capable of interacting with a structurally defined group of odorants, although few receptor proteins have been linked with their preferred ligands. The most definitive case is for the diacetyl receptor of the nematode *c. elegans* (Sengupta, Chou, & Bargmann, 1996). In more complex animals, receptor proteins are thought to be able to interact with broad classes of odorous stimuli with varying degrees of affinity, such that a given odor will activate a particular set of receptor neurons. Recently, a molecular technique was used to induce the nasal epithelium of mice to produce an overabundance of a particular rat olfactory receptor protein, by linking the gene for this protein to a virus that infects the epithelium. Mice exhibiting increased levels of this receptor protein showed an increased electrical response to the eight-carbon aldehyde octanal (Zhao et al., 1998). The response to closely related aldehydes containing 7, 9 or 10 carbons was slightly enhanced compared to controls, and responses to approximately 65 other chemicals that were tested were not affected by the genetic manipulation. These data suggest that the genetic sequence with which the mice were infected coded for a receptor protein with a very narrow range of chemical sensitivity, whose preferred ligand was octanal. More recently, the homologue of this receptor was cloned from mice and functionally expressed in a mammalian cell line (Krautwurst, Yau, & Reed, 1998). Remarkably, although its sequence differed by only one amino acid, the odorant specificity was shifted to heptanal rather than octanal. Although this receptor may represent an unusual case, these findings contrast with the widely held view of broadly tuned receptors described above, and suggest that olfactory receptors are quite narrow in their selectivity. If generally true, this further suggests that cells responding to chemicals that vary widely in structure are expressing multiple receptor types, rather than one receptor per cell as suggested by much of the molecular biological data (see also Coding of Odor Qualities, below). The resolution of this controversy awaits further research, which is likely to come rapidly with the rapid advances in molecular tools enabling functional characterization of large numbers of cloned receptors.

Recent data indicate that the receptor proteins are also involved in mediating guidance of the receptor cell axon to the appropriate location within the olfactory bulb (Wang, Nemes, Mendelsohn, & Axel, 1998). This feature may explain the remarkable ability of the olfactory system to maintain functional stability in the face of ongoing receptor cell replacement (but see Clinical Problems, below).

Signal Transduction

Most of what we know about how odorant stimulation is conveyed to the brain is based on studies in a variety of invertebrate and non-human vertebrate systems. This discussion will present the current models of olfactory transduction developed on the basis of those studies, and will then describe recent research that has tested these models in human ORNs. Importantly, while a great degree of similarity across species has been observed, significant species differences have also been found, a fact that should be kept in mind in interpreting the body of olfactory research currently available.

The information that an odor has bound to its receptor is converted into an electrical signal by a signal transduction cascade initiated by activation of G-proteins linked to the receptor protein (Figure 18.4). These G-proteins include adenylate cyclase, which generates cAMP from adenosine triphosphate (ATP), and phospholipase C, which breaks down membrane phospholipids to form diacylglycerol and $InsP_3$. The second messengers cAMP or $InsP_3$ diffuse through the cytoplasm to open ion channels within the membrane. In mammals, cAMP opens a nonselective cation channel that has been cloned and sequenced, the cyclic nucleotide-gated channel (cNc; Dhallan, Yau, Schrader, & Reed, 1990). Activation of a similar but, as yet, unidentified channel by $InsP_3$ has been demonstrated in response to excitatory odorants in lobster, but the existence of such a channel in mammals remains controversial. Convincing, but not conclusive evidence exists for the presence of an IP_3-gated ion current in at least some mammalian ORNs that is involved in mediating transduction of certain types of odors (see Restrepo, Teeter, & Schild, 1996; Schild & Restrepo, 1998, for reviews).

Opening of these cation channels allows sodium, calcium, and other cations to enter the cell, resulting in a change in membrane potential (see Breer, Raming & Krieger, 1994, for review). In cells where this is an excitatory response, depolarization ensues, leading to an action potential. Hyperpolarizing, inhibitory responses are also seen in invertebrate ORNs, and odorants may either increase or decrease basal firing rates in catfish (Kang & Caprio, 1995) and rat ORNs (Duchamp-Viret, Chaput, & Duchamp, 1999). Olfactory neurons

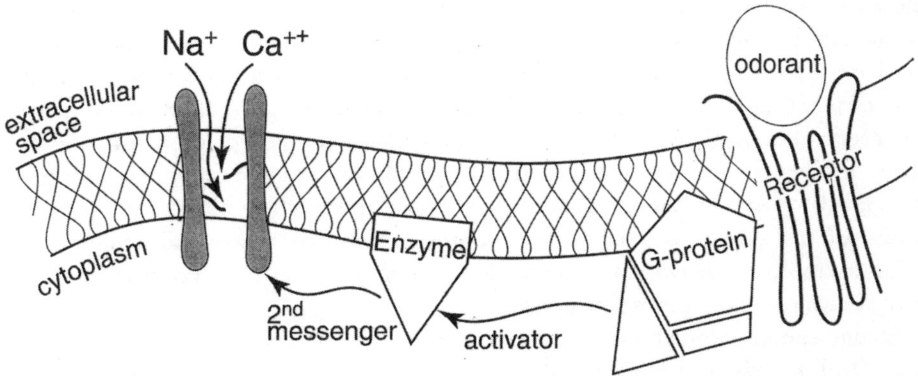

Figure 18.4. Odorants interact with olfactory receptor proteins which span the membrane of the cilia on the tip of the olfactory receptor cell. These proteins are coupled to G-proteins that when activated, release a component which activates an enzyme, adenylate cyclase (AC) which produces the 2nd messenger, cAMP. The cAMP then opens cation channels allowing positive ions into the cell. Phospholipase C (PLC) may also mediate transduction for some odorants, or may activate other processes within the cell (see text).

are unusual in the high concentration of chloride they contain (Restrepo et al., 1996). This enables an outward chloride current to contribute to the depolarization of the cell, which may play a particularly important role under conditions where extracellular ionic conditions are altered, such as in amphibians encountering varying salinities in a river approaching the ocean (Kleene, 1993; Kurahashi & Yau, 1993).

Studies of human ORNs reveal that odorants can induce increases in intracellular calcium that are mediated by at least two transduction pathways that can be distinguished pharmacologically (Rawson et al., 1997; Restrepo et al., 1993). These studies employ imaging techniques to characterize odorant responses in living ORNs freshly isolated from biopsies from the olfactory epithelium of live human volunteers (Lowry & Pribitkin, 1995). Exposure to odorants shown to elicit increases in cAMP but not $InsP_3$ in preparations of isolated rat olfactory cilia trigger increases in intracellular calcium in about 25% of human ORNs tested. This calcium response can be blocked with 1-*cis*-diltiazem, a chemical that selectively blocks the cyclic nucleotide-gated channel (Figure 18.4). In contrast, this chemical has no effect on cells that respond to odorants that trigger increases in $InsP_3$ without affecting cAMP levels in isolated rat olfactory cilia (Rawson et al., 1997). Thus two pathways mediating calcium influx must exist in human ORNs, although the molecular basis for these pathways remains uncertain.

The influx of cations into the cell results in depolarization of the cell and an action potential, which is carried along the axon of the olfactory neuron directly to the olfactory bulb. This electrical signal triggers release of a neurotransmitter, most likely glutamate (Berkowicz, Trombley, & Shepherd, 1994), which activates mitral and tufted cells within the olfactory bulb to carry the information further into the brain. Electrophysiological studies indicate that there is always a certain amount of baseline electrical activity in olfactory neurons (i.e., in the absence of stimulation), due to intrinsic instability in the ion channels (Lowe & Gold, 1995). This baseline "noise" serves to increase the sensitivity of the system, possibly at the expense of specificity – in other words, by being easily opened, the channels are more likely to be shifted into the "open state" by a very low concentration of stimulus, but are also more likely to open in response to a stimulus that is not the best fit for that receptor. This characteristic also provides an additional option for the encoding of odor quality information – via either increases or decreases in electrical activity. It is possible that conditions related to mucus composition, blood composition or pressure, medications, or other environmental or health factors could under some conditions increase or decrease this inherent noise to create a sensation of odor where none exists. Olfactory hallucinations, also called "phantosmia," occur in a variety of diseases and conditions (see Clinical Problems, below), and may be due to dysfunction at the level of the receptor, perireceptor or central processing events.

In some species, odorants can either activate or inhibit different receptor cells (Bacigalupo et al., 1997). This dual modality may serve to increase the coding and discriminatory capabilities of the system by improving the signal to noise ratio. It is not yet known whether odorants can inhibit human ORNs; however, we have found that some cells respond to odorant stimuli with a decrease rather than an increase in intracellular calcium (Rawson et al., 1997). This type of response is unusual in that it is not seen in rat ORNs (Restrepo, Okada, & Teeter, 1993; Tareilus, Noe, & Breer, 1995). The mechanism for this decrease in calcium is not explained by any model of olfaction yet proposed, and suggests that odor characteristics may be coded somewhat differently in the human olfactory system than in other animals.

Coding of Odor Qualities

Earlier efforts to understand odor quality coding focused on characterizing the electrical response properties of the receptors using single-unit or multi-unit (electro-olfactogram) approaches (e.g., Maue & Dionne, 1987; Sicard, 1984; Sicard & Holley, 1984). Recent advances in molecular and functional methods have enabled a more comprehensive approach to this issue.

In situ hybridization analyses, which localize the messenger RNA for specific genes, show that different families of receptor genes are expressed in different zones across the olfactory epithelium (Strotmann et al., 1994), and cells expressing a given receptor project their axons to the same glomeruli within the olfactory bulb (Ressler, Sullivan, & Buck, 1994). These zones of receptor expression coincide, to some degree, with zones of odorant sensitivity determined using electrophysiological techniques (Scott, Davis, Shannon, & Kaplan, 1996). The integration of structural and functional studies such as these leads to the view that odor qualities are coded on the basis of activity patterns of sets of olfactory receptor neurons, each of which expresses a single receptor sensitive to a particular group of odors.

One of the more intriguing conundrums is that in many species individual olfactory receptor neurons can sometimes respond to many odorants that differ considerably in structure and quality (Ivanova & Caprio, 1993; Sato, Hirono, Tonoike, & Takebayashi, 1994). In a recent study of rat single-unit recordings, Duchamp-Viret et al. (1999) found that the odorant selectivity of individual cells was quite broad, with over 30% responding to six different pure stimuli that bore neither structural nor perceptual similarity (see Figure 18.5). In this study, odorant concentrations were carefully controlled using an olfactometer, and stimuli were applied in a physiological manner (vapor phase). These authors also found that the same cell could be excited by one stimulus and inhibited by another. The most parsimonious explanation for these data is that an individual cell may express multiple types of receptors.

In contrast, molecular biological studies of the genes coding for odorant receptor proteins suggest that an individual cell is likely to express only one receptor protein (Chess, Simon, Cedar, & Axel, 1994; Kang & Caprio, 1995). If the receptors are nonselective, as indicated by the molecular biological studies, it is hard to understand how so many different odor qualities can be perceived – that is, where is the quality coding taking place? On the other hand, if the receptors are quite specific, cells that respond to many odors must have many types of receptors. This would enable each receptor to be connected to different transduction machinery and potentially elicit a different pattern of electrical activity that could be incorporated into the coding scheme. Studies with frog olfactory neurons (Kashiwayanagi, Shimano, & Kurihara, 1996), and in our laboratory with single rat olfactory neurons, suggest that both situations are likely to occur, with some cells having multiple receptor types and others only one or a few (Rawson, Ulrich, Jackson, Eberwine, &

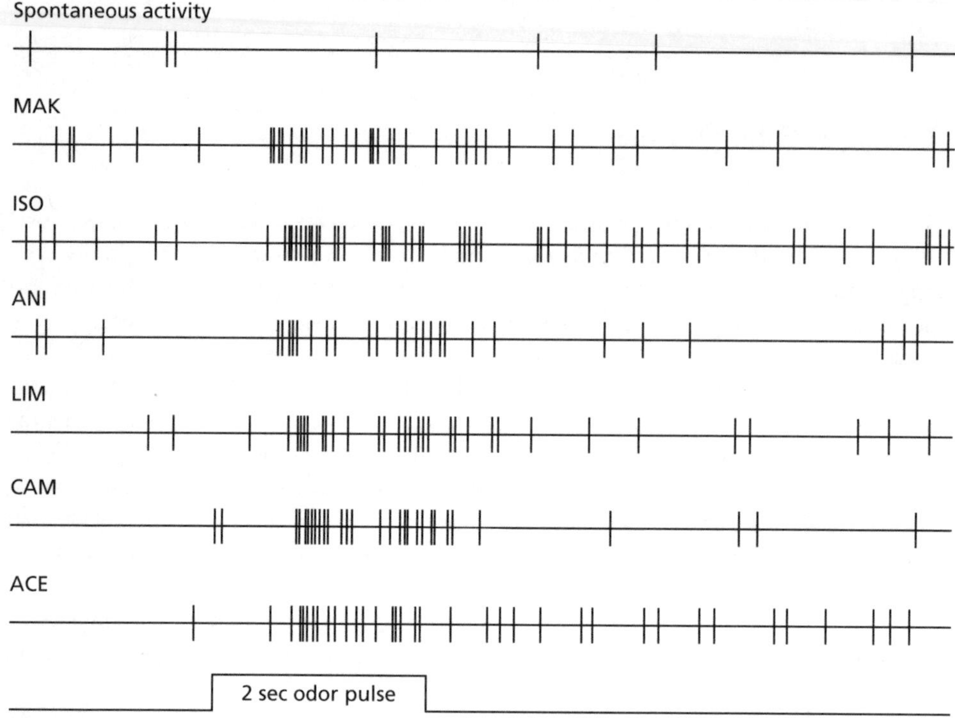

Figure 18.5. Data shown represent recordings from an individual cell stimulated with odors delivered at the same concentration, taking into account the saturated vapor pressure. This cell responded to 5 of the 16 odors used, even at concentrations as low as 2.5×10^{-8} mol/liter. These odors represent diverse chemical classes and perceptual qualities. Eighty-eight percent of the 540 cells tested responded to two or more odorants, demonstrating that these mammalian ORNs are broadly tuned. MAK = methylamyl ketone; ISO = isoamyl acetate; ANI = anisole; LIM = limonene; CAM = camphor; ACE = acetophenone. (Reproduced with permission from Duchamp-Viret et al., 1999, copyright © 1999 American Association for the Advancement of Science.)

Restrepo, in press). This would be consistent with electrophysiological recordings from individual ORNs from mice demonstrating that some cells respond to only a few, closely related odorants (e.g., only the 5 and 6 carbon straight-chain alcohols), while others respond to broader classes of odorants (e.g., 4–9 carbon straight and branched-chain alcohols) (Sato et al., 1994). Such a scenario would vastly increase the number of combinations available for coding the quality attributes of volatile stimuli. Recent data from two laboratories in which both function and gene expression were characterized in individual mouse olfactory neurons have shown that individual cells are activated by a small number of odorants, and different cells respond to distinct but occasionally overlapping sets of odorants (Malnic et al., 1999; Touhara et al., 1999). These data provide further support for the notion that odor qualities are coded on the basis of the combinations of receptor cells that are activated by a given odorant. However, until we know definitively how many functional receptors individual ORNs express, we cannot say whether the ligand specificity of a given receptor will reflect that of a cell. Until then, the physiological data suggest that the receptor cells possess a repertoire of mechanisms with which to respond to odorants and therefore may actively participate in the quality coding process.

Unexpectedly, human olfactory cells appear to be more selective than other vertebrate species. For instance, when tested with two odorant mixtures, 30% of rat olfactory neurons responded to both with a characteristic change in intracellular calcium, but none of the hundreds of cells from young adult humans that we have tested with these same mixtures responded to both (Rawson et al., 1997). This raises the possibility that odor coding occurs somewhat differently in humans than in rodents, with a greater emphasis on recognition of the individual receptor cell activated and less integration or pattern recognition needed at the level of the olfactory bulb. This would tend to produce a system designed more for quality recognition and less for sensitivity – a situation that is reflected in human psychophysical performance.

Results from studies examining patterns of neural activity within the olfactory bulbs in response to odorant stimuli are consistent with the notion that specific glomeruli represent activation of specific receptor subtypes (Johnson, Woo, & Leon, 1998). Some odorants seem to activate a very discrete set of glomeruli, while others activate a larger number of more distributed regions (Rubin & Katz, 1999), but these regions are consistent across animals and concentration-dependent (i.e., more glomeruli activated at higher concentrations). These findings are consistent with recent evidence demonstrating that in some cases, cells expressing a particular receptor can project axons to more than one glomeruli (Royal & Key, 1999). In addition, data suggest that cross-talk can occur between glomeruli, and that the signal sent via the mitral cells to their respective connections in the entorhinal cortex is already processed and synthesized to a large extent. In other words, there does not appear to be an odor map in the cortex similar to that found in the visual system. Rather, odor-elicited activity in higher brain centers seems to be influenced by familiarity, hedonics (i.e., pleasantness), intensity, and perhaps even the associated memories and images triggered by the odorant to a greater extent than is activity elicited by visual stimuli (Fulbright et al., 1998).

The picture we now have of odor quality coding begins in the periphery, where a subset of receptors differing in their range of chemical sensitivity is activated by a given odorant or group of odorants containing some, as yet undetermined common feature, or "odotype" (Mori & Yoshihara, 1995). The resulting electrical signals are carried along axons converging to a given glomerulus within the olfactory bulb. It is possible that each glomerulus represents an "odor primary," but evidence for this is lacking, and the molecular and physiological data described do not seem to support such a concept. Cross-talk within transduction pathways in the receptor neuron (Anholt & Rivers, 1990), between receptor neurons and between glomeruli may occur to tune and modulate the incoming signal, which is passed to the olfactory cortex for comparison with previously stored information and conversion into what we perceive as an odor sensation.

Basic Olfactory Perception

Measurement Issues

Two general issues, relating to stimulus control and stimulus selection, complicate the interpretation of studies of human odor perception. Odor stimuli travel in turbulent plumes, arriving at the olfactory epithelium in discrete bursts that can vary considerably in concentration (Moore & Atema, 1991; Murlis & Jones, 1981). In addition to the intrinsic signal fluctuations within odor plumes, the organism's sampling behavior (e.g., sniffing) can further alter local stimulus patterns (Moore, 1994). Moreover, olfactory stimuli may remain in the receptor environment for some period of time prior to clearance via desorption back into air during exhalation, mucociliary transport away from the receptor organs, circulatory uptake or, possibly, xenobiotic metabolism (Dahl & Hadley, 1997; Hornung & Mozell, 1977). Thus, varying degrees of stimulus accumulation will occur during odor exposure, depending on both the physicochemical properties of the odorant (affecting its diffusion rates through air, mucus, and blood) and characteristics of the organism at the time of stimulation (e.g., breathing pattern, blood and mucus flow rates). All of these complexities render fine measurement and control of the effective stimulus impossible in human studies of olfactory perception, and at least some of the apparent "noisiness" of the olfactory system in such studies in fact reflects this problem of inherent stimulus fluctuation (Cain, 1977).

The stimulus selection issue, which is relevant to biochemical and neurophysiological as well as psychophysical studies, arises from the previously mentioned absence of an accurate odorant classification scheme, based on some physiologically significant, physical metric (such as wavelength for color vision) or set of "primary" qualities (as in taste), to define relationships among stimuli. As a result, the specific stimuli used in research studies vary widely and unsystematically, often making broad statements and across-study comparisons questionable.

Thresholds and Sensitivity

The olfactory neurons serve as distance receptors for ambient chemical stimuli and respond to extremely low concentrations of most odorants. There are, however, considerable differences among compounds in their potency as olfactory stimuli, with threshold concentrations varying over many orders of magnitude. This is illustrated in Table 18.2, which lists average threshold values for several common odorous compounds that were drawn from a careful literature survey by Amoore and Hautala (1983). Attempts to model absolute olfactory sensitivity, in order to predict thresholds for specific compounds, have not been successful, but it seems clear that parameters of stimulus solubility affecting dispersion through the mucus play a key role in determining stimulus efficacy (Cain, 1988).

There are also considerable individual differences in olfactory sensitivity, even in the absence of olfactory dysfunction or specific anosmia (see Olfactory Anomalies/Dysfunc-

Table 18.2 Selected odor detection thresholds[a]

Compound	*Odor threshold in air (ppm; v/v)*
Butane	2700
Ethyl alcohol	84
Acetone	13
Acetic acid	0.84
Isoamyl acetate	0.025
Hydrogen sulfide	0.0081
Ethyl mercaptan	0.00076
Triethylamine	0.00044

[a] From Amoore & Hautala (1983)

tion, below). The range of individual thresholds observed in brief tests varies across compounds (e.g., Punter, 1983), but is frequently found to be several hundred to one or greater (see Rabin & Cain, 1986). Much of this variation appears to reflect *intra*-individual fluctuations in measured thresholds. Whereas average group thresholds for a given compound, obtained under similar conditions, are fairly stable, individual thresholds may be highly unreliable (Punter, 1983). With repeated testing, there is both an increase in individual reliability and a decrease in the range of individual differences (Cain & Gent, 1991; Rabin & Cain, 1986; Stevens, Cain, & Burke, 1988; Stevens & Dadarwala, 1993); nonetheless, stable individual differences remain, and these tend to extend across odorants, presumably reflecting a general olfactory sensitivity factor (Cain & Gent, 1991; Rabin & Cain, 1986).

Odor Intensity

As in other sensory continua (Stevens, 1975), odor intensity grows as a power function of stimulus magnitude, and the rate of growth can be characterized by the slope of the straight-line function relating the two in log-log coordinates. Just as thresholds vary across odor compounds, so does the relative steepness of the psychophysical function; in general, however, olfactory sensation is characterized by a great deal of compression, with slopes almost always reported to be under 0.80, and often under 0.20 (Berglund, Berglund, Ekman, & Engen, 1971; Cain, 1969). That is, rather large increases in stimulus concentration are required to produce appreciable increases in perceived intensity; for example, a 32-fold increase in the concentration of an odor compound whose psychophysical function has a slope of 0.20 would be necessary to double its rated intensity. In contrast, in most other sensory continua, the slopes of psychophysical functions tend to approach, and occasionally exceed, 1.0 (Stevens, 1975).

Significant correlations between odorant thresholds and the steepness of their psychophysical functions have been reported, but account for less than about 25% of the variance

(Laffort, Patte, & Etcheto, 1974). Thus, there can be substantial discrepancies between the threshold and suprathreshold efficacies of odor stimuli. A particularly striking example of this is seen with the optical isomers of carvone (see Figure 18.1). Whereas threshold sensitivity to (–)-carvone (which smells like spearmint) is significantly greater than to (+)-carvone (which has a caraway-like smell) (Cowart, 1990; Hormann & Cowart, 1993; Leitereg, Guadagni, Harris, Mon, & Teranishi, 1971a, 1971b), at equivalent suprathreshold concentrations of these isomeric forms, (+)-carvone elicits the more intense odor sensation (Cowart, 1990; Hormann & Cowart, 1993; Pike, Enns, & Hornung, 1988).

A complicating factor in the characterization of odor intensity perception is that, at moderate to high concentrations, virtually all olfactory stimuli also stimulate free nerve endings of the ethmoid branch of the trigeminal nerve, embedded in the nasal mucosa. In humans, there is converging psychophysical and electrophysiological evidence only for phenylethyl alcohol, vanillin, and hydrogen sulfide being essentially pure olfactory stimuli at high concentrations (Doty et al., 1978; Kobal, 1982; Kobal & Hummel, 1998; Kobal, Van Toller, & Hummel, 1989; Wysocki, Cowart, & Radil, in press) (although the substantial data indicating that some individuals fail to detect any sensation from concentrated androstenone strongly suggest it is too; see Specific Anosmia, below). Thus, the perceived intensities of volatile compounds typically reflect a combination of olfactory and trigeminal stimulation at some concentrations (Cain, 1974). Determination of the point at which different compounds begin to elicit a nasal-trigeminal response has been difficult, but a promising technique takes advantage of an interesting distinction between the olfactory and nasal-trigeminal systems in their ability to encode spatial information (Wysocki et al., in press; Wysocki, Dalton, Brody, & Lawley, 1997; Wysocki, Green, & Malia, 1992). Specifically, humans cannot identify to which side of the nose a pure olfactory stimulus is presented, but can do so readily when the stimulus elicits a trigeminal response (e.g., von Skramlik, 1925; Kobal et al., 1989). Assessment of the threshold for localization or "lateralization" of an inhaled stimulus therefore provides an estimate of the concentration at which trigeminal stimulation begins to contribute to perceived "odor" magnitude (and quality).

Recognition Memory and Identification

Memory for odors is long-lived, but it may be hard-earned. That is, once an odor has been encoded into memory, it tends to persist there: Long-term odor recognition memory shows relatively little decay over extended periods of time, under a variety of conditions (Engen & Ross, 1973; Lawless, 1978; Rabin & Cain, 1984). On the other hand, effective encoding appears to be difficult to achieve: Short-term recognition memory for odors is, in fact, very poor unless the target odors can be correctly identified on initial presentation (Rabin & Cain, 1984).

Lyman and McDaniel (1986) suggest that the significance of identifiability in odor recognition memory lies in its providing the opportunity for dual encoding in both a verbal-linguistic and a presumably non-verbal, olfactory imagery system, with veridical identifications allowing for more precise elaborative processing (c.f., Pavio, 1986). Notably, unlike verbal labels, the generation of visual images does not seem to enhance odor recognition as it has been shown to enhance recognition of concrete verbal stimuli (Lyman & McDaniel, 1986).

However, coming up with accurate verbal labels for odors is extremely difficult, even when the odors are recognized as being highly familiar (what has been called the "tip-of-the-nose state" (Lawless & Engen, 1977)). On average, subjects are able to name correctly fewer than half (35–45%) of any given set of commonly encountered smells (Cain, 1982; Cain, 1979; Cain & Potts, 1996; Desor & Beauchamp, 1974). Desor and Beauchamp (1974) were the first to demonstrate that, despite this initially poor performance, subjects can quickly approach perfect identification of large sets of odors if prompted with their names and given subsequent corrective feedback. That seems to be possible, however, only when the prompts are accurate names for familiar odors (Cain, 1982; Cain, 1979; Desor & Beauchamp, 1974). In other words, it is not the case that new or arbitrary names for odors are easy to learn (Davis, 1975, 1977). Rather, the connection between olfactory percepts and verbal labels seems to be one that requires extensive experience to forge and that is not easily accessed in the absence of recent and/or frequent use.

Mixtures

In the real world, single odorous compounds are almost never encountered in isolation. Not only are most common smells that we perceive to be unitary, such as coffee, banana, or chocolate, actually elicited by complex mixtures of compounds, but they are always experienced against an ambient background of at least low levels of a variety of other odorous molecules. Thus, mixture perception is central to olfactory experience. The systematic psychophysical study of odor mixtures is, however, still in its infancy.

At the level of detection threshold, combinations of odor stimuli appear to have an approximately additive effect, irrespective of their chemical structure or perceptual quality (Laska & Hudson, 1991; Patterson, Stevens, Cain, & Cometto-Muñiz, 1993). As a result, the complexity of natural odors allows for the detection of the mixture even though the concentrations of constituent compounds are well below their individual detection thresholds (e.g., Teleky-Vámossy & Petró-Turza, 1986). This also suggests that, consistent with physiological studies in animals, the repertoire of responses exhibited by receptor neurons allows for integration at the level of the receptor as well as within the bulb and higher brain regions. Moreover, the detection of odor mixtures appears to be more stable than that of individual compounds; that is, intra- and inter-individual variability tends to decline with increasing stimulus complexity (Laska & Hudson, 1991; Patterson et al., 1993).

On the other hand, the perceived intensities of suprathreshold mixtures of odorants are characterized by hypoadditivity: The intensity of a mixture is almost always less than the sum of intensities of its unmixed components, and frequently falls below the rated intensity of its strongest component (e.g., Bell, Laing, & Panhuber, 1987; Cain, 1975; Laing & Willcox, 1987). Suppression is often evident when two odor compounds are presented separately but simultaneously to each nostril, as well as when an actual physical mixture is sniffed, although the degree of suppression tends to be less under the former circumstances (Cain, 1975; Laing & Willcox, 1987). This observation, together with other lines of psychophysical and electrophysiological evidence (Bell et al., 1987; Derby, Ache, & Kennel,

1985; Kurahashi, Lowe, & Gold, 1994; Lawless, 1987; Leveteau & MacLeod, 1969; Schiet & Frijters, 1988), indicates that both peripheral and central mechanisms can contribute to mixture suppression in olfaction.

Although the suppression of overall intensity is ubiquitously observed in odor mixtures, the degree to which specific components of simple (2–3 odor) mixtures are suppressed varies. Not surprisingly, weaker smelling components are generally suppressed to a greater extent than are stronger smelling ones (Cain, 1975), but exceptions have been reported (Laing & Willcox 1987). A study by Laing, Eddy, and Best (1994) suggests that the relative speed with which different odorants are processed (this can vary by hundreds of milliseconds, and is itself partially concentration dependent) is the key factor in determining which will show the greatest suppression, with "faster" odorants suppressing "slower" ones.

Laing et al. (1994) also suggest that limitations in temporal processing may ultimately limit the ability to perceive components in mixtures; that is, to the extent temporal differences are obscured, as they will be in complex mixtures, so is the ability to distinguish olfactory mixture components. In fact, people do not seem to be able to distinguish the individual components in mixtures that include more than four compounds (Laing & Francis, 1989). Instead, more chemically complex odor stimuli (3+ compounds) may be perceived to be *less* complex than binary mixtures (Moskowitz & Barbe, 1977), as odors blend to form new, homogenous percepts. Thus, a combination of two compounds, such as amyl acetate (banana-like) and eugenol (clove-like), will be perceived as a mixture of odors, whereas the 800+-compound mixture that comprises the aroma of coffee (Deibler, Acree, & Lavin, 1998) will be perceived simply as "coffee."

Olfactory Adaptation

Self-adaptation: Short- and Long-term

Most people have had the experience of gradually "losing" the scent of a flower after repeated sniffing, or becoming unaware of cooking odors after having been in the kitchen for a while. This waning of response with repeated or continuous stimulation is typically referred to as *adaptation*, whether the underlying process is of peripheral or central origin (that is, a distinction is generally not made between peripheral *adaptation* and central *habituation*).

In fact, both peripheral and central (including high-level cognitive) processes probably play a role in most instances of olfactory adaptation. For example, olfactory adaptation is observed even when the adapting and test stimuli are presented unilaterally to opposite nostrils, and thus stimulate different sets of peripheral receptors; however, the degree of adaptation is not as profound as when the same sets are stimulated (Cain, 1977). This finding implicates both peripheral and more central neural structures in the adaptation process. In addition, purely cognitive factors, such as perceived health risk from odor exposure, have been shown to impact significantly on adaptation to suprathreshold odor stimuli, with the direction of influence depending on the type of information provided about the nature of the stimulus (Dalton, 1996).

The majority of research in the area of olfactory adaptation has focused on the effects of limited (≤20 minutes) exposures to an adapting stimulus on perceived intensity and/or detection threshold. Under these conditions, the perceived intensity of the stimulus declines rapidly, in an exponential fashion, with a steady-state often being reached within a minute or less (e.g. Cain, 1974; Dalton & Wysocki, 1996) (although odor mixtures may be more resistant to adaptation than are the odors of single compounds (Schiet & Cain, 1990)). Absolute sensitivity (as assessed by threshold) also declines rapidly, although the rate of decline may be more linear (Pryor, Steinmetz, & Stone, 1970). With removal of the adapting stimulus, complete recovery of function at both threshold and suprathreshold levels is also quite rapid, and may be achieved in less time than was required for adaptation to reach asymptotic levels (Pryor et al., 1970; Steinmetz, Pryor, & Stone, 1970).

In addition to these types of short-term exposures, individuals may be exposed to particular odors for extended periods of time in the home or workplace. Available data suggest that such long-term exposures can produce much more long-lasting olfactory adaptation than is seen following brief exposures. For example, Gagnon, Mergler, and Lapare (1994) found that threshold sensitivity to methyl isobutyl ketone had not fully recovered more than one and a half hours after a 7-hour exposure to low-levels of this odorant. The results of a naturalistic study by Dalton and Wysocki (1996) are even more striking. In this case, an odor compound was continuously released in subjects' bedrooms for two weeks; thus, although exposed to the odor for hours every day, subjects were typically away from it for hours as well. Nonetheless, a gradual decline in threshold sensitivity was observed, and the return to pre-exposure sensitivity required two weeks.

Cross-adaptation

At the suprathreshold level, adaptation to any odorant is associated with a slight reduction in the perceived intensity of subsequent probes with another odorant (Köster, 1971). This, however, probably reflects a context effect and/or mixture suppression (given the potential for slow clearance of odor molecules from the receptor environment; see Measurement Issues, above). More profound, stimulus-specific cross-adaptation also occurs, although it is difficult to predict and often asymmetric (that is, responses to odor 1 are more affected by prior adaptation to odor 2 than vice versa) (Köster, 1971; Pierce, Jr., Wysocki, Aronov, Webb, & Boden, 1996; Pierce, Jr., Zeng, Aronov, Preti, & Wysocki, 1995; Todrank, Wysocki, & Beauchamp, 1991). Odors that are perceptually similar, especially if they share multiple qualitative characteristics, typically cross-adapt (Pierce, Jr. et al., 1996). However, even odors that seem to be perceptually indiscriminable may show asymmetric cross-adaptation (Todrank et al., 1991), and perceptual similarity does not appear to be necessary for cross-adaptation. Cross-adaptation has also been observed between compounds with similar chemical structures but quite distinctive qualitative characteristics (Pierce, Jr. et al., 1995), as well as between those that seem to be both perceptually and structurally dissimilar (Pierce, Jr. et al., 1996). Thus, studies of olfactory cross-adaptation have not pointed to any simple organizing principles for encoding in the olfactory system.

Retronasal Olfaction

What most people think of as *smelling* involves drawing odorous compounds from the external environment through the nostrils by inhalation or sniffing, or what is sometimes referred to as *orthonasal* olfaction. In fact, we also smell when odorants in the mouth (or lungs) reach the olfactory epithelium through the posterior nares of the nasopharynx during respiratory exhalation or after swallowing. The smell sensations evoked via this retronasal stimulation constitute a substantial portion of what is colloquially called *taste*, but is actually a complex mixture of the gustatory, textural, temperature, and olfactory properties of foods that is perhaps most accurately captured in the term *flavor* (Rozin, 1982).

Rozin (1982) has argued that olfaction is really a dual sense, with retronasal and orthonasal olfaction being perceptually independent and giving rise to qualitatively different perceptions of the same stimuli. This contention has some intuitive appeal; many people can, for example, think of foods (such as strong cheeses) whose smells they find unpleasant when sniffed but whose flavors, including those same olfactory components experienced retronasally, they enjoy. Subsequent tests of Rozin's hypothesis have not, however, been supportive (Chifala & Polzella, 1995; Pierce & Halpern, 1996). That is, there is no empirical evidence for substantial qualitative differences in orthonasal and retronasal olfactory perception.

On the other hand, there certainly are differences in the patterns of stimulus input and flow properties of retronasal versus orthonasal stimulation, which are likely to affect sensitivity to stimuli presented via these two routes (Burdach & Doty, 1987; Pierce & Halpern, 1996; Voirol & Daget, 1986). Although a significant relationship between orthonasal and retronasal olfactory acuity has been reported, correlations between these modes of presentation were substantially lower than test-retest correlations within each mode, suggesting there may be some dissociation in sensitivity to stimuli presented by way of one or the other pathway (Burdach, Köster, & Kroeze, 1985). This has also been observed in a clinical sample of patients complaining of diminished smell and/or flavor perception (n=40), 27.5% of whom showed markedly better orthonasal than retronasal responsiveness to olfactory stimuli (Cowart, Halpern, & Varga, 1999). The bases for this discrepancy remain to be elucidated. As Pierce and Halpern (1996) have noted, there is still a great need for studies examining retronasal olfaction, and the factors affecting it, as a primary subject of interest rather than simply as a poor cousin to orthonasal olfaction.

Olfactory Anomalies/Dysfunction

Specific Anosmia

Specific anosmia refers to a deficit in olfactory sensitivity to a specific compound or limited class of compounds, with intact general olfactory abilities. A large number of specific anosmias have been described (see Amoore, 1977); however, these often reflect relative rather than absolute insensitivities (which the use of the term "anosmia" implies). In addition, for some compounds, the underlying distribution of sensitivities may be essentially Gaussian, with what is referred to as a specific anosmia representing one extreme of that distribution, whereas for others, there appear to be true bi- (or multi-) modal distributions of sensitivities.

Guillot (1948, cited in Amoore, 1977) was apparently the first to suggest that each specific anosmia reflects the absence of, or an alteration in, the receptor site for a "primary" odor, and that these deficits could, therefore, be used to classify odors and understand odor quality coding. Amoore (e.g., 1967, 1977) was the principal advocate of this idea, which influenced views of odor coding for many years. Perhaps in part because of the mixed bag of perceptual anomalies comprising the so-called specific anosmias, however, that endeavor has not been entirely successful. Nonetheless, the study of some specific anosmias, most notably that to 5α-androst-16-en-3-one (androstenone), has yielded insights into the overlapping roles of genetic and non-genetic factors in human olfactory perception.

Androstenone is a volatile steroid, described variously by humans who can smell it as urinous, sweaty, musky, or sandalwood-like. A strikingly large proportion of adults (40–50%) are, however, unable to detect it even at vapor saturation (Amoore, Pelosi, & Forrester, 1977; Wysocki & Beauchamp, 1984). In a study of 17 identical and 21 fraternal twin pairs, Wysocki and Beauchamp (1984) found 100% concordance among identical twins in their sensitivity to androstenone, but only 62% concordance among fraternal twins. This suggested that olfactory sensitivity to androstenone might be inherited as a dominant Mendelian trait. A subsequent study of 67 families, however, found a more complex pattern of familial relationships in androstenone anosmia than would be predicted by that simple genetic model, as well as a sex difference in the incidence of anosmia (proportionally higher in males than in females), raising the possibility of one or more X-linked genes regulating androstenone sensitivity (Wysocki & Beauchamp, 1991).

Further complicating factors in the expression of specific anosmia to androstenone have also been identified. For example, there is now evidence that the incidence of androstenone insensitivity increases, especially among males, from early childhood through adolescence; that is, some individuals apparently lose an initial sensitivity to this compound by the time they reach young adulthood (Dorries, Schmidt, Beauchamp, & Wysocki, 1989; Gilbert & Wysocki, 1987; Schmidt & Beauchamp, 1988). Even more surprising, given a trait with an apparently large genetic component, is the finding that androstenone sensitivity can be induced in some (but not all) previously anosmic adults with systematic exposure to the compound (Wysocki, Dorries, & Beauchamp, 1989). In a parallel study of inbred mice, selected for their relative insensitivity to either androstenone or isovaleric acid, odorant-specific increases in peripheral olfactory sensitivity to these chemicals (as measured by the magnitude of the stimulus-induced voltage response across the olfactory epithelium) were observed in each type of insensitive breed with repeated exposure to the relevant odorant (Wang, Wysocki, & Gold, 1993), suggesting that in the continuous turnover of olfactory receptor neurons, their full differentiation, and the determination of their odorant specificity, may be partially controlled by olfactory stimulation. Finally, a study by Stevens and O'Connell (1995) suggests this stimulation need not be by the specific compound to which sensitivity is induced, but may be by a chemically distinct *but perceptually similar* compound.

Thus, studies of specific anosmia have strengthened the idea that we each live in a distinct olfactory world. Like cross-adaptation studies, however, they have pointed to a remarkable complexity in olfactory coding, and raised as many questions as they have answered.

Clinical Problems

Although olfactory dysfunction is not as obvious to the observer as is dysfunction in vision or audition, nor does it have the broad lifestyle implications, it can impact substantially on quality of life, impede performance in some occupations (e.g., food preparation, perfumery), lead to nutritional difficulties (Mattes & Cowart, 1994; Mattes et al., 1990; Mattes-Kulig & Henkin, 1985), and render individuals more vulnerable to the hazards of fire, chemical toxins in the environment, and spoiled food. Moreover, it is becoming increasingly clear that this type of dysfunction is not rare, but affects a substantial portion of the population at some point in their lives. At the very least, many if not most individuals experience measurable loss in olfactory sensitivity with aging (see Aging, below). In addition, a number of common medical conditions are associated with long-term, permanent or recurrent chemosensory dysfunction. For example, it has been shown that clinically significant diminutions in olfactory sensitivity are present in over 23% of patients suffering from allergic rhinitis (Cowart, Flynn-Roden, McGeady, & Lowry, 1993). Because nasal allergies are estimated to afflict 10–15% of the general population (Fadal, 1987; Seebolm, 1978), 2.5–3.5% of the population could be expected to suffer from smell loss as a result of this etiologic factor alone.

Several aspects of the anatomy of the olfactory system contribute to its vulnerability to damage (see also Anatomy of the Olfactory System, above). First, olfactory receptors are localized in a relatively small patch of tissue high in the nasal cavity, and any number of factors producing changes in nasal patency or air flow patterns could potentially limit the access of stimulus molecules to those receptors. In addition, the olfactory nerve is located in a somewhat vulnerable position in that the axons must pass through the cribriform plate of the ethmoid bone prior to dissemination on the surface of the olfactory bulb. They are, therefore, potentially subject to tearing or severing as a result of shearing forces produced when the brain is displaced forward or backward with blows to the head (Costanzo & Zasler, 1991). Finally, as has been noted, the olfactory neurons *are* the receptor cells and, as neurons, are uniquely exposed to the external environment and subject to a constant barrage of chemical stimuli, some of which are potentially toxic, as well as being susceptible to direct injury from microbes. Although there is ongoing regeneration of these elements, this process is a complex one, requiring reinnervation of the olfactory bulb.

Given these considerations, it is not surprising that the three major causes of olfactory problems seen in clinical settings are ongoing nasal/sinus disease (NSD), head trauma, and upper respiratory viral infections (URI) (Cowart, Young, Feldman, & Lowry, 1997). Of these, only NSD-related loss is currently amenable to treatment, as it does not typically involve sensori-neural damage (Douek, Bannister, & Dodson, 1975; Jafek, Eller, Esses, & Moran, 1989; Jafek et al., 1990; Yamagishi, Hasegawa, & Nakano, 1988). However, dysfunctions secondary to nerve damage may show gradual spontaneous recovery due to the regenerative capacity of the olfactory system (see Anatomy of the Olfactory System, above).

This appears to be more common in URI-related disorders than in those secondary to head trauma (Costanzo & Becker, 1986; Cowart, Varga, Young, & Lowry, 1998; Duncan & Seiden, 1995).

In addition to simple losses in sensitivity, olfactory dysfunctions may manifest either as the constant or recurring experience of a smell sensation in the absence of an odorous stimulus (phantosmia) or as distortions in the perceived qualities of odorous stimuli (dysosmia or parosmia). As suggested in Signal Transduction (above), olfactory phantoms may arise from problems at the perireceptor as well as at the neural level, and they are almost as likely to be reported by patients with NSD-related olfactory symptoms as by those whose dysfunctions develop following URI or head trauma (Cowart et al., 1997). On the other hand, distortions in odor quality independent of a phantom seem to be associated with sensori-neural damage, and are virtually never reported by NSD patients. The precise conditions that give rise to disruptions in olfactory quality perception are not known. However, this type of symptom typically develops following a period during which there is simply a loss of sensitivity, and patients who experience dysosmia are more likely than those who do not to report subsequent improvement in olfactory function, suggesting that, in many cases, the distortions are associated with regenerative changes in the olfactory epithelium and/or bulb (Cowart et al., 1997).

Despite its potentially positive prognostic significance, dysosmia is an extremely disconcerting experience for patients. It is like being aware a symphony is being performed, but hearing only cacophonous noise. This is a symphony that never ends, however; it is continuously played out in the smells of those who are closest and the flavors of foods that were once most desired – all now tainted by a sour note for some sufferers or distorted beyond recognition for others. Moreover, the recovery process may, for unknown reasons, be quite extended, requiring up to two years (or possibly more) for return to normal or "near-normal" function (Cowart et al., 1998). Thus, a better basic understanding of olfactory regeneration, and how it might be facilitated, would be of great clinical benefit.

Aging

Age-related decline in average olfactory sensitivity, even in the healthy elderly, has been extensively documented (e.g., Doty, Shaman, & Dann, 1984; Gilbert & Wysocki, 1987; Ship, 1993). This form of loss apparently occurs gradually, is not typically complete and often seems to go unnoticed by individuals experiencing it (Cowart, 1989; Nordin, Monsch, & Murphy, 1995; Stevens & Cain, 1985). Nonetheless, it may be of sufficient magnitude to render them vulnerable to chemical hazards such as gas leaks (Chalke & Dewhurst, 1957; Stevens, Cain, & Weinstein, 1987; Wysocki & Gilbert, 1989) and to impact on food flavor perception (Cain, Reid, & Stevens, 1990; Murphy, 1985; Schiffman, 1977, 1979; Stevens & Cain, 1986).

There is some debate about the uniformity of age-related olfactory loss, both across compounds and across individuals. Based on their own and others' studies of sensitivity to a variety of odorants, Cain and Stevens (1989) argued that, although there is some variation in the degree of loss reported for specific compounds, the range is relatively small and age-related change in olfaction is best characterized as non-specific. As these authors note, however, the vast majority of studies of aging in olfaction have simply contrasted the performance of an elderly group (mean age 70+ years) with that of a group of young adults (mean age < 30 years). This design does not allow estimation of either the onset or rate of decline in sensitivity to specific odors. In one of the few studies that examined responses to several different odors across the adult life span, substantial compound-specific variation in these parameters was observed (Wysocki & Gilbert, 1989).

At the individual level, extreme differences among elderly subjects in their ability to detect odors, exceeding the variability observed among young subjects, have frequently been noted, with many performing as well as the average young person (Cain & Stevens, 1989; Stevens & Dadarwala, 1993). A study by Stevens and Dadarwala (1993) suggests that the apparent overlap between the young and elderly in olfactory threshold sensitivity is an artifact of the poor reliability of this measure (see Threshold Sensitivity, above), and that with repeated testing to obtain a better estimate of individual function, the thresholds of all elderly subjects fall above the highest produced by young subjects. Given the relatively small group sizes (n=20) in this study, however, it seems premature to conclude that a substantial decline in olfactory sensitivity is an inevitable feature of aging.

Conclusion

Olfaction has traditionally been considered a "minor" sense, and it is, in some respects, a rather primitive sensory system, lacking specialized receptor organs and providing a direct and seemingly unfiltered connection between environmental stimuli and the brain. Nonetheless, both psychophysical studies and everyday experience indicate this is a quite sensitive system that is also capable of exceedingly fine quality discriminations. Neurophysiological and molecular biological studies now point to the existence of complex mechanisms within the olfactory receptor neurons that allow for substantial peripheral coding. These include a large number of receptor subtypes with varying degrees of specificity, at least two transduction pathways (which may interact), and probable inhibitory as well as excitatory responses to odor stimuli. In addition, there may be cross-talk among receptor neurons, as well as among glomeruli representing specific receptor subtypes at the level of the olfactory bulb. Thus, we are beginning to understand the fine tuning and modulation of signals that occur within this "primitive" system, and that underlie the richness of our olfactory experience.

Suggested Readings

Amoore, J. E. (1967). Molecular shape and odour: Pattern analysis of PAPA. *Nature, 216*, 1084–1087.

Amoore, J. E. (1977). Specific anosmia and the concept of primary odors. *Chemical Senses and Flavour, 2*, 267–281. [A classic paper that set the stage for how odor quality coding was viewed for over two decades.]

Getchell, T. V., Doty, R. L., Bartoshuk, L. M., & Snow, J. B., Jr. (Eds.) (1991). *Smell and taste in health and disease*. New York: Raven Press. [A comprehensive collection of papers that focus on clinical issues in smell (and taste), but also provide coverage of many neurobiological, psychophysical and nutritional/dietary issues relating to the chemical senses.]

Getchell, T. V., Margolis, F. L., & Getchell, M. L. (1984). Perireceptor and receptor events in vertebrate olfaction. *Progress in Neurobiology, 23*, 317–345. [A review that is unique in its coverage of the perireceptor events that are critical to understanding olfactory function.]

Rossiter, K. J. (1996). Structure-odor relationships. *Chemical Reviews, 96*, 3201–3240. [An excellent review of the science underlying fragrance development and current approaches to studying structure-activity relationships; includes examples of synthetic pathways and chemical features common to specific odor qualities.]

Additional Topics

Cellular Adaptation/Desensitization

The role of phosphorylation and calcium in termination of the receptor cell response to odorant stimulation: Breer and Boekhoff (1992); Kramer and Siegelbaum (1992).

Growth Factors Involved in Maintenance/Development of the Olfactory Receptor Cells

Studies using human tissue and cultured olfactory cells to understand the neurotrophic factors that enable the olfactory neurons to regenerate: Balboni, Zonefrat, Repice, Barni, and Vannelli (1991); Murrell et al. (1996).

Development of the Human Olfactory System

The developmental biology of the olfactory system and its role in development of central reproductive pathways: Chuah and Zheng (1992), Schwanzel-Fukuda et al. (1994).

Significance of Olfaction in Infant Behavior

Increasing evidence points to the salience of olfactory cues to the human infant, and their possible role in infant-mother bonding, as well as feeding behavior: Mennella and Beauchamp (1996); Porter, Makin, Davis, and Christensen (1991); Varendi, Christensson, Porter, and Winberg (1998); Varendi, Porter, and Winberg (1994).

Cephalic Phase Reflexes

A variety of physiological reflexes are triggered by orosensory stimulation ("cephalic phase reflexes"); these reflexes include salivary flow, release of gastric acid and even insulin and other pancreatic hormones that prepare the organism for the incoming nutrients: Feldman and Richardson (1986); Teff (1996).

Odor-Evoked Memory and Emotion

The possibly unique status of odors in influencing mood and evoking emotional memories: Ehrlichman and Bastone (1992); Herz and Engen (1996).

Nasal Trigeminal Chemosensitivity

Virtually all volatile molecules that stimulate the olfactory system also, at least at some concentrations, stimulate free nerve endings of the nasal trigeminal system, eliciting sensations of irritation, coolness, warmth and possibly other qualities that contribute to our experience of "smell": Cain and

Murphy (1980); Dalton, Wysocki, Brody, and Lawley (1997); Wysocki, Cowart and Radil (in press).

References

Amoore, J. E. (1967). Specific anosmia: A clue to the olfactory code. *Nature (London)*, *214*, 1095–1098.

Amoore, J. E. (1977). Specific anosmia and the concept of primary odors. *Chemical Senses and Flavour*, *2*, 267–281.

Amoore, J. E., & Hautala, E. (1983). Odor as an aid to chemical safety: Odor thresholds compared with threshold limit values and volatilities for 214 industrial chemicals in air and water dilution. *Journal of Applied Toxicology*, *3*, 272–290.

Amoore, J. E., Pelosi, P., & Forrester, L. J. (1977). Specific anosmia to 5α-androst-16-en-3-one and ω-pentadecalactone: The urinous and musky primary odors. *Chemical Senses and Flavour*, *2*, 401–425.

Anholt, R. R. H., & Rivers, A. M. (1990). Olfactory transduction: Cross-talk between second-messenger systems. *Biochemistry*, *29*, 4049–4054.

Bacigalupo, J., Morales, B., Labarca, P., Ugarte, G., & Madrid, R. (1997). Inhibitory responses to odorants in vertebrate olfactory neurons. In R. Latorre & J.C. Saez (Eds.), *From ion channels to cell-to-cell conversations* (pp. 269–285). New York: Plenum Press.

Balboni G. C., Zonefrat, R., Repice, F., Barni, T., & Vannelli, G. B. (1991). Immunohistochemical detection of EGF and NGF receptors in human olfactory epithelium. *Bollettino-Societa Italiana Biologia Sperimentale*, *671*, 901–906.

Bell, G. A., Laing, D. G., & Panhuber, H. (1987). Odour mixture suppression: Evidence for a peripheral mechanism in human and rat. *Brain Research*, *426*, 8–18.

Ben-Arie, N., Lancet, D., Taylor, C., Ken, M., Walker, N., Ledbetter, D. H., Carrozzo, R., Patel, K., Sheer, D., Lehrach, H., & Morth, M. A. (1993). Olfactory receptor gene cluster on human chromosome 17: Possible duplication of an ancestral receptor repertoire. *Human Molecular Genetics*, *3*, 229–235.

Berglund, B., Berglund, U., Ekman, G., & Engen, T. (1971). Individual psychophysical functions for 28 odorants. *Perception & Psychophysics*, *9*, 379–384.

Berkowicz, D. A., Trombley, P. Q., & Shepherd, G. M. (1994). Evidence for glutamate as the olfactory receptor cell neurotransmitter. *Journal of Neurophysiology*, *71*, 2557–2561.

Breer, H., & Boekhoff, I. (1992). Termination of second messenger signaling in olfaction. *Proceedings of the National Academy of Sciences*, *89*, 471–474.

Breer, H., Raming, K., & Krieger, J. (1994). Signal recognition and transduction in olfactory neurons. *Biochemical and Biophysical Acta*, *1224*, 277–287.

Buck, L., & Axel, R. (1991). A novel multigene family may encode odorant receptors: A molecular basis for odor recognition. *Cell*, *65*, 175–187.

Buck, L. B. (1992). The olfactory multigene family. *Current Opinion in Neurobiology*, *2*, 282–288.

Burdach, K. J., & Doty, R. L. (1987). The effects of mouth movements, swallowing, and spitting on retronasal odor perception. *Physiology & Behavior*, *41*, 353–356.

Burdach, K. J., Köster, E. P., & Kroeze, J. H. (1985). Interindividual differences in acuity for odor and aroma. *Perceptual and Motor Skills*, *60*, 723–730.

Caggiano, M., Kauer, J. S., & Hunter, D. D. (1994). Globose basal cells are neuronal progenitors in the olfactory epithelium: A lineage analysis using a replication-incompetent retrovirus. *Neuron*, *13*, 339–352.

Cain, W. S. (1969). Odor intensity: Differences in the exponent of the psychophysical function. *Perception & Psychophysics*, *6*, 349–354.

Cain, W. S. (1974). Contribution of the trigeminal nerve to perceived odor magnitude. *Annals New York Academy of Sciences*, *237*, 28–34.

Cain, W. S. (1975). Odor intensity: Mixtures and masking. *Chemical Senses and Flavour, 1*, 339–352.

Cain, W. S. (1977). Differential sensitivity for smell: "Noise" at the nose. *Science, 195*, 796–798.

Cain, W. S. (1979). To know with the nose: Keys to odor identification. *Science, 203*, 467–470.

Cain, W. S. (1982). Odor identification by males and females: Predictions vs performance. *Chemical Senses, 7*, 129–142.

Cain, W.S. (1988). Olfaction. In R. C. Atkinson, R. J. Herrnstein, G. Lindzey, & R. D. Luce (Eds.), *Stevens' handbook of experimental psychology: Vol. 1. Perception and motivation* (pp. 409–459). New York: Wiley.

Cain, W. S., & Gent, J. F. (1991). Olfactory sensitivity: Reliability, generality, and association with aging. *Journal of Experimental Psychology, 17*, 382–391.

Cain, W. S., & Murphy, C. L. (1980). Interaction between chemoreceptive modalities of odour and irritation. *Nature, 284*, 255–257.

Cain, W. S., & Potts, B. C. (1996). Switch and bait: Probing the discriminative basis of odor identification via recognition memory. *Chemical Senses, 21*, 35–44.

Cain, W. S., & Stevens, J. C. (1989). Uniformity of olfactory loss in aging. *Annals New York Academy of Sciences, 561*, 29–38.

Cain, W. S., Reid, F., & Stevens, J. C. (1990). Missing ingredients: Aging and the discrimination of flavor. *Journal of Nutrition for the Elderly, 9*, 3–15.

Cain, W. S., Schiet, F. T., Olsson, M. J., & de Wijk, R. A. (1995). Comparison of models of odor interaction. *Chemical Senses, 20*, 625–637.

Chalke, H. D., & Dewhurst, J. R. (1957). Accidental coal-gas poisoning: Loss of sense of smell as a possible contributory factor with old people. *British Medical Journal, 2*, 915–917.

Chess, A., Simon, I., Cedar, H., & Axel, R. (1994). Allelic inactivation regulates olfactory receptor gene expression. *Cell, 78*, 823–834.

Chifala, W. M., & Polzella, D. J. (1995). Smell and taste classification of the same stimuli. *The Journal of General Psychology, 122*, 287–294.

Chuah, M. I., & Zheng, D. R. (1992). The human primary olfactory pathway: Fine structural and cytochemical aspects during development and in adults. *Microscopy Research and Technique, 23*, 76–85.

Cometto-Muñiz, J. E., Cain, W. S., & Hudnell, H. K. (1997). Agonistic sensory effects of airborne chemical in mixtures: Odor, nasal pungency, and eye irritation. *Perception & Psychophysics, 59*, 665–674.

Coronas, V., Srivastava, L. K., Liang, J.-J., Jourdan, F., & Moyse, E. (1997). Identification and localization of dopamine receptor subtypes in rat olfactory mucosa and bulb: A combined *in situ* hybridization and ligand binding radioautographic approach. *Journal of Chemical Neuroanatomy, 12*, 243–257.

Costanzo, R. M., & Becker, D. P. (1986). Smell and taste disorders in head injury and neurosurgery patients. In H. L. Meiselman & R. S. Rivlin (Eds.), *Clinical measurement of taste and smell* (pp. 565–578). New York: Macmillan Publishing Co.

Costanzo, R. M., & Zasler, N. D. (1991). Head trauma. In T. V. Getchell, R. L. Doty, L. M. Bartoshuk, & J. B. Snow, Jr. (Eds.), *Smell and taste in health and disease* (pp. 711–730). New York: Raven Press.

Cowart, B. J. (1989). Relationships between taste and smell across the adult life span. *Annals New York Academy of Sciences, 561*, 39-55.

Cowart, B. J. (1990). Olfactory responses to enantiomers [Abstract]. *Chemical Senses, 15*, 562–563.

Cowart, B. J., Flynn-Rodden, K., McGeady, S. J., & Lowry, L. D. (1993). Hyposmia in allergic rhinitis. *Journal of Allergy and Clinical Immunology, 91*, 747–751.

Cowart, B. J., Halpern, B.P., & Varga, E. K. (1999). A clinical test of retronasal olfactory function [Abstract]. *Chemical Senses*, 24, 608.

Cowart, B. J., Varga, E. K., Young, I. M., & Lowry, L. D. (1998). The natural history of smell dysfunctions secondary to upper respiratory infection (URI) [Abstract]. *Chemical Senses, 23*, 608.

Cowart, B. J., Young, I. M., Feldman, R. S., & Lowry, L. D. (1997). Clinical disorders of smell and taste. *Occupational Medicine: State of the Art Reviews, 12*, 465–483.

Crowe, M. L., Perry, B. N., & Connerton, I. F. (1996). Olfactory receptor-encoding genes and pseudogenes are expressed in humans. *Gene, 169*, 247–249.

Dahl, A. R., & Hadley, W. M. (1997). Nasal cavity enzymes involved in xenobiotic metabolism: Effects on the toxicity of inhalants. *Toxicology, 21*, 345–358.

Dalton, P. (1996). Odor perception and beliefs about risk. *Chemical Senses, 21*, 447–458.

Dalton, P., & Wysocki, C. J. (1996). The nature and duration of adaptation following long-term odor exposure. *Perception & Psychophysics, 58*, 781–792.

Dalton, P., Wysọcki, C. J., Brody, M. J., & Lawley, H.J. (1997). The influence of cognitive bias on the perceived odor, irritation and health symptoms from chemical exposure. *International Archives of Occupational and Environmental Health, 69*, 407–417.

Davis, R. G. (1975). Acquisition of verbal associations to olfactory stimuli of varying familiarity and to abstract visual stimuli. *Journal of Experimental Psychology: Human Learning & Memory*, 104, 134–142.

Davis, R. G. (1977). Acquisition and retention of verbal associations to olfactory and abstract visual stimuli of varying similarity. *Journal of Experimental Psychology: Human Learning & Memory, 3*, 37–51.

Deibler, K. D., Acree, T. E., & Lavin, E. H. (1998). Aroma analysis of coffee brew by gas chromatography-olfactometry. In E. T. Contis, C.-T. Ho, C. J. Mussinan, T. H. Parliament, F. Shahidi, & A. M. Spanier (Eds.), *Food Flavors: Formation, analysis and packaging influences* (pp. 69–78). Amsterdam: Elsevier Science.

Derby, C. D., Ache, B. W., & Kennel, E. W. (1985). Mixture suppression in olfaction: Electrophysiological evaluation of the contribution of peripheral and central neural components. *Chemical Senses, 10*, 301–316.

Desor, J. A., & Beauchamp, G. K. (1974). The human capacity to transmit olfactory information. *Perception & Psychophysics, 16*, 551–556.

Dhallan, R. S., Yau, K.-W., Schrader, K. A., & Reed, R. R. (1990). Primary structure and functional expression of a cyclic nucleotide-activated channel from olfactory neurons. *Nature, 347*, 184–187.

Dorries, K., Schmidt, H. J., Beauchamp, G. K., & Wysocki, C. J. (1989). Changes in sensitivity to the odor of androstenone during adolescence. *Developmental Psychobiology, 22*, 423–435.

Doty, R. L., Brugger, W. E., Jurs, P. C., Orndorff, M. A., Snyder, P. J., & Lowry, L. D. (1978). Intranasal trigeminal stimulation from odorous volatiles: Psychometric responses from anosmic and normal humans. *Physiology & Behavior, 20*, 175–185.

Doty, R. L., Shaman, P., & Dann, M. (1984). Development of the University of Pennsylvania smell identification test: A standardized microencapsulated test of olfactory function. *Physiology & Behavior, 32*, 489–502.

Douek, E., Bannister, L. H., & Dodson, H. C. (1975). Recent advances in the pathology of olfaction. *Proceedings of the Royal Society of Medicine, 68*, 467–470.

Duchamp-Viret, P., Coronas, V., Delaleu, J. C., Moyse, E., & Duchamp, A. (1997). Dopaminergic modulation of mitral cell activity in the frog olfactory bulb: A combined radioligand binding-electrophysiological study. *Neuroscience, 79*, 203–216.

Duchamp-Viret, P., Chaput, M. A., & Duchamp, A. (1999). Odor response properties of rat olfactory receptor neurons. *Science, 284*, 2171–2174.

Duncan, H. J., & Seiden, A. M. (1995). Long-term follow-up of olfactory loss secondary to head trauma and upper respiratory tract infection. *Archives of Otolaryngology,Head and Neck Surgery, 121*, 1183–1187.

Engen, T., & Ross, B. M. (1973). Long-term memory of odors with and without verbal descriptors. *Journal of Experimental Psychology, 100*, 221–227.

Ehrlichman, H., & Bastone, L. (1992). Olfaction and emotion. In M. J. Serby & K. L. Chobor (Eds.), *Science of olfaction* (pp. 410–438). NY: Springer-Verlag.

Fadal, R. G. (1987). The medical management of rhinitis. In G. M. English (Ed.), *Otolaryngology* (Vol. 2, pp. 1–25). Philadelphia: JB Lippincott.

Feldman, M., & C. T. Richardson (1986). Role of thought, sight, smell, and taste of food in the cephalic phase of gastric acid secretion in humans. *Gastroenterology, 90,* 428–433.
Fulbright, R. K., Skudlarski, P., Lacadie, C. M., Warrenburg, S., Bowers, A. A., Gore, J. C., & Wexler, B. E. (1998). Functional MR imaging of regional brain responses to pleasant and unpleasant odors. *American Journal of Neuroradiology, 19,* 1721–1726 .
Gagnon, P., Mergler, D., & Lapare, S. (1994). Olfactory adaptation, threshold shift and recovery at low levels of exposure to methyl isobutyl ketone (MIBK). *Neurotoxicology, 15,* 637–642.
Getchell, M. L, & Mellert, T. K. (1991). Olfactory mucus secretion. In T. V. Getchell, R. L. Doty, L. M. Bartoshuk, & J. B. Snow Jr. (Eds.), *Smell and taste in health and disease* (pp. 83–95). New York: Raven Press.
Gilbert, A. N., & Wysocki, C. J. (1987). The smell survey results. *National Geographic Magazine, 172,* 514–525.
Halasz, N., & Shepherd, G. M. (1983). Neurochemistry of the vertebrate olfactory bulb. *Neuroscience, 10,* 579–619.
Herz, R., & Cupchik, G. C. (1995). The emotional distinctiveness of odor-evoked memories. *Chemical Senses, 20,* 517–528.
Herz, R. S., & Engen, T. (1996). Odor memory: Review and analysis. *Psychonomic Bulletin & Review, 3,* 300–313.
Hormann, C. A., & Cowart, B. J. (1993). Olfactory discrimination of carvone enantiomers [Abstract]. *Chemical Senses, 18,* 573.
Hornung, D. E., & Mozell, M. M. (1977). Odorant removal from the frog olfactory mucosa. *Brain Research, 128,* 158–163.
Howes, D. (1988). On the odour of the soul: Spatial representation and olfactory classification in eastern Indonesia and western Melanesia. *Bijdragen tot de Taal-, Land- en Volkenkunde, 144,* 84–113.
Ivanova, T., & Caprio, J. (1993). Odorant receptor activated by amino acids in sensory neurons of the channel catfish *Ictalurus punctatus. Journal of General Physiology, 102,* 1085–1105.
Jafek, B. W., Eller, P. M., Esses, B. A., & Moran, D. T. (1989). Post-traumatic anosmia: Ultrastructural correlates. *Archives of Neurology, 46,* 300–304.
Jafek, B. W., Hartman, D., Eller, P. M., Johnson, E. W., Strahan, R. C., & Moran, D. T. (1990). Postviral olfactory dysfunction. *American Journal of Rhinology, 4,* 91–100.
Johnson, B. A., Woo, C. C., & Leon, M. M. (1998). Spatial coding of odorant features in the glomerular layer of the rat olfactory bulb. *The Journal of Comparative Neurology, 393,* 457–471.
Kang, J., & Caprio, J. (1995). *In vivo* responses of single olfactory receptor neurons in the channel catfish, *ictalurus punctatus. Journal of Neurophysiology, 73,* 172–177.
Kashiwayanagi, M., Shimano, K., & Kurihara, K. (1996). Existence of multiple receptors in single neurons: Responses of single bullfrog olfactory neurons to many cAMP-dependent and independent odorants. *Brain Research, 738,* 222–228.
Kleene, S. J. (1993). Origin of the chloride current in olfactory transduction. *Neuron, 11,* 123–132.
Kobal, G. (1982). A new method for determination of the olfactory and the trigeminal nerve's dysfunction: Olfactory (OEP) and chemical somatosensory (CSEP) evoked potentials. In A. Rothenberger (Ed.), *Event-related potentials in children* (pp. 455–461). Amsterdam: Elsevier Biomedical Press.
Kobal, G., & Hummel, T. (1998). Olfactory and intranasal trigeminal event-related potentials in anosmic patients. *Laryngoscope, 108,* 1033–1035.
Kobal, G., Van Toller, S., & Hummel, T. (1989). Is there directional smelling? *Experientia, 45,* 130–132.
Köster, E. P. (1971). *Adaptation and cross-adaptation in olfaction: An experimental study with olfactory stimuli at low levels of intensity.* University of Utrecht.
Kramer, R. H., & Siegelbaum, S. A. (1992). Intracellular Ca^{2+} regulates the sensitivity of cyclic nucleotide-gated channels in olfactory receptor neurons. *Neuron, 9,* 897–906.
Krautwurst, D., Yau, K.-W., & Reed, R. R. (1998). Identification of ligands for olfactory receptors by functional expression of a receptor library. *Cell, 95,* 917–926.

Kurahashi, T., & Yau, K.-W. (1993). Co-existence of cationic and chloride components in odorant-induced current of vertebrate olfactory receptor cells. *Nature, 363*, 71–74.
Kurahashi, T., Lowe, G., & Gold, G. H. (1994). Suppression of odorant responses by odorants in olfactory receptor cells. *Science, 265*, 118–120.
Laffort, P., Patte, F., & Etcheto, M. (1974). Olfactory coding on the basis of physiochemical properties. *Annals New York Academy of Sciences, 237*, 193–208.
Laing, D. G., & Francis, G. W. (1989). The capacity of humans to identify odors in mixtures. *Physiology & Behavior, 46*, 809–814.
Laing, D. G., & Willcox, M. E. (1987). An investigation of the mechanisms of odor suppression using physical and dichorhinic mixtures. *Behavioural Brain Research, 26*, 79–87.
Laing, D. G., Eddy, A., & Best, D. J. (1994). Perceptual characteristics of binary, trinary, and quaternary odor mixtures consisting of unpleasant constituents. *Physiology & Behavior, 56*, 81–93.
Lanza, D. C. & Clerico, D. M. (1995). Anatomy of the human nasal passages. In R.L. Doty (Ed.), *Handbook of olfaction and gustation* (pp. 53–73). New York: Marcel Dekker, Inc.
Laska, M., & Hudson, R. (1991). A comparison of the detection threshold of odour mixtures and their components. *Chemical Senses, 16*, 651–662.
Lawless, H., & Engen, T. (1977). Associations to odors: Interference, mnemonics, and verbal labeling. *Journal of Experimental Psychology: Human Learning & Memory, 3*, 52–59.
Lawless, H. T. (1987). An olfactory analogy to release from mixture suppression in taste. *Bulletin of the Psychonomic Society, 25*, 266–268.
Lazard, D. (1990). Identification and biochemical analysis of novel olfactory-specific cytochrome P-450IIA and UDP-glucuronosyl transferase. *Biochemistry, 29*(32), 7433–7440.
Leitereg, T. J., Guadagni, D. G., Harris, J., Mon, T. R., & Teranishi, R. (1971a). Chemical and sensory data supporting the difference between the odors of the enantiomeric carvones. *Journal of Agriculture and Food Chemistry*, 19, 785–787.
Leitereg, T. J., Guadagni, D. G., Harris, J., Mon, T. R., & Teranishi, R. (1971b). Evidence for the difference between the odours of the optical isomers (+) and (-) carvone. *Nature, 230*, 455–456.
Leveteau, J., & MacLeod, P. (1969). Reciprocal inhibition at glomerular level during bilateral olfactory stimulation. In C. Pfaffmann (Ed.), *Olfaction and taste III* (pp. 212–215). New York: Rockefeller University Press.
Livermore, A., & Laing, D.G. (1998). The influence of odor type on the discrimination and identification of odorants in multicomponent odor mixtures. *Physiology & Behavior, 65*, 311–320.
Lowe, G., & Gold, G. H. (1995). Olfactory transduction is intrinsically noisy. *Proceedings of the National Academy of Sciences, 92*, 7864–7868.
Lowry, L. D., & Pribitkin, E. A. (1995). Collection of human olfactory tissue. In A. I. Spielman & J. G. Brand (Eds.), *Experimental cell biology of taste and olfaction* (pp. 47–48). Boca Raton: CRC Press.
Lyman, B. J., & McDaniel, M. A. (1986). Effects of encoding strategy on long-term memory for odours. *The Quarterly Journal of Experimental Psychology, 38A*, 753–765.
Malnic, B., Hirono, J., Sato, T., & Buck, L. B. (1999). Combinatorial receptor codes for odors. *Cell, 96*, 713–723.
Mattes, R. D., & Cowart, B. J. (1994). Dietary assessment of patients with chemosensory disorders. *Journal of the American Dietetic Association, 94*, 50–56.
Mattes, R. D., Cowart, B. J., Schiavo, M. A., Arnold, C., Garrison, B., Kare, M. R., & Lowry, L. D. (1990). Dietary evaluation of patients with smell and/or taste disorders. *American Journal of Clinical Nutrition, 51*, 233–240.
Mattes-Kulig, D. A., & Henkin, R. I. (1985). Energy and nutrient consumption of patients with dysgeusia. *Journal of the American Dietetic Association, 85*, 822–826.
Maue, R. A., & Dionne, V. E. (1987). Patch-clamp studies of isolated mouse olfactory receptor neurons. *Journal of General Physiology, 90*, 95–125.
McKenzie, D. (1923). *Aromatic and the soul: A study of smells.* London: William Heinemann.
Meisami, E., Mikhail, L., Baim, D., & Bhatnagar, K. (1998). Human olfactory bulb: Aging of

glomeruli and mitral cells and a search for the accessory olfactory bulb. *Annals New York Academy of Sciences, 855*, 708–715.

Mennella, J. A., & Beauchamp, G. K. (1996). The human infants' response to vanilla flavors in mother's milk and formula. *Infant Behavior and Development, 19*, 13–19.

Miyawaki, A., Homma, H., Tamura, H., Matsui, M., & Mikoshiba, K. (1996). Zonal distribution of sulfotransferase for phenol in olfactory sustentacular cells. *EMBO Journal, 15*, 2050–2055.

Moore, P. A. (1994). A model of the role of adaptation and disadaptation in olfactory receptor neurons: Implications for the coding of temporal and intensity patterns in odor signals. *Chemical Senses, 19*, 71–86.

Moore, P. A., & Atema, J. (1991). Spatial information in the three-dimensional fine structure of an aquatic odor plume. *Biological Bulletin, 181*, 408–418.

Mori, K., & Yoshihara, Y. (1995). Molecular recognition and olfactory processing in the mammalian olfactory system. *Progress in Neurobiology, 45*, 585–619.

Moskowitz, H. R., & Barbe, C. D. (1977). Profiling of odor components and their mixtures. *Sensory Processes, 1*, 212–226.

Murlis, J., & Jones, C. D. (1981). Fine-scale structure of odour plumes in relation to insect orientation to distant pheromone and other attractant sources. *Physiological Entomology, 6*, 71–86.

Murphy, C. (1985). Cognitive and chemosensory influences on age-related changes in the ability to identify blended foods. *Journal of Gerontology, 40*, 47–52.

Murrell, W. G., Bushell, R., Livesey, J., McGrath, J., MacDonald, K. P. A., Bates, P. R., & Mackay-Sim, A. (1996). Neurogenesis in adult human. *NeuroReport, 7*, 1189–1194.

Nordin, S., Monsch, A. U., & Murphy, C. (1995). Unawareness of smell loss in normal aging and Alzheimer's disease: Discrepancy between self-reported and diagnosed smell sensitivity. *Journal of Gerontology: Psychological Sciences, 50B*, 187–192.

Patterson, M. Q., Stevens, J. C., Cain, W. S., & Cometto-Muñiz, J. E. (1993). Detection thresholds for an olfactory mixture and its three constituent compounds. *Chemical Senses, 18*, 723–734.

Pavio, A. (1986). *Mental representation: A dual coding approach*. New York: Oxford University Press.

Pelosi, P. (1994). Odorant-binding proteins. *Critical Reviews in Biochemistry and Molecular Biology, 29*, 199–228.

Pierce, J., & Halpern, B. P. (1996). Orthonasal and retronasal odorant identification based upon vapor phase input from common substances. *Chemical Senses, 21*, 529–543.

Pierce, J. D., Jr., Wysocki, C. J., Aronov, E. V., Webb, J. B., & Boden, R. M. (1996). The role of perceptual and structural similarity in cross-adaptation. *Chemical Senses, 21*, 223–237.

Pierce, J. D., Jr., Zeng, X.-N., Aronov, E. V., Preti, G., & Wysocki, C. J. (1995). Cross-adaptation of sweaty-smelling 3-methyl-2-hexenoic acid by a structurally-similar, pleasant-smelling odorant. *Chemical Senses, 20*, 401–411.

Pike, L. M., Enns, M. P., & Hornung, D. E. (1988). Quality and intensity differences of carvone enantiomers when tested separately and in mixtures. *Chemical Senses, 13*, 307–309.

Porter, R. J., Makin, J. W., Davis, L. B., & Christensen, K. M. (1991). An assessment of the salient olfactory environment of formula-fed infants. *Physiology & Behavior, 50*, 907–911.

Pryor, G. T., Steinmetz, G., & Stone, H. (1970). Changes in absolute detection threshold and in subjective intensity of suprathreshold stimuli during olfactory adaptation and recovery. *Perception & Psychophysics, 8*, 331–335.

Punter, P. H. (1983). Measurement of human olfactory thresholds for several groups of structurally related compounds. *Chemical Senses, 7*, 215–235.

Rabin, M. D., & Cain, W. S. (1984). Odor recognition: Familiarity, identifiability, and encoding consistency. *Journal of Experimental Psychology: Learning, Memory, & Cognition, 10*, 316–325.

Rabin, M. D., & Cain, W. S. (1986). Determinants of measured olfactory sensitivity. *Perception & Psychophysics, 39*, 281–286.

Rawson, N. E., Ulrich, P., Jackson, J., Eberwine, J., & Restrepo, D. (in press). Single olfactory receptor neurons may express more than on receptor mRNA. *Journal of Neurochemistry*.

Rawson, N. E., Gomez, G., Cowart, B., Brand, J. G., Lowry, L. D., Pribitkin, E. A., & Restrepo, D. (1997). Selectivity and response characteristics of human olfactory neurons. *Journal of Neuro-*

physiology, 22, 1606–1613.
Ressler, K., Sullivan, S., & Buck, L. (1994). Information coding in the olfactory system: Evidence for a stereotyped and highly organized epitope map in the olfactory bulb. *Cell, 79*, 1245–1255.
Restrepo, D., Okada, Y., & Teeter, J. H. (1993). Odorant-regulated Ca^{2+} gradients in rat olfactory neurons. *Journal of General Physiology, 102*, 907–924.
Restrepo, D., Okada, Y., Teeter, J. H., Lowry, L. D., Cowart, B., & Brand, J. G. (1993). Human olfactory neurons respond to odor stimuli with an increase in cytoplasmic Ca^{++}. *Biophysical Journal, 64*, 1961–1966.
Restrepo, D., Teeter, J. H., & Schild, D. (1996). Second messenger signaling in olfactory transduction. *Journal of Neurobiology, 30*, 37–48.
Rossiter, K. J. (1996). Structure-odor relationships. *Chemical Reviews, 96*, 3201–3240.
Rouquier, S., Taviaux, S., Trask, B. J., Brand-Arpon, V., van den Engh, G., Demaille, J., & Giorgi, D. (1998). Distribution of olfactory receptor genes in the human genome. *Nature Genetics, 18*, 243–250.
Royal, S. J., & Key, B. (1999). Development of P2 olfactory glomeruli in P2-internal ribosome entry site-tau-lacZ transgenic mice. *Journal of Neuroscience, 19*, 9856–9864.
Rozin, P. (1982). "Taste-smell confusions" and the duality of the olfactory sense. *Perception & Psychophysics, 31*, 397–401.
Rubin, B. D., & Katz, L. C. (1999). Optical imaging of odorant representations in the mammalian olfactory bulb. *Neuron, 23*, 489–511.
Saketkhoo, K., Januszkiewicz, A., & Sackner, M. A. (1978). Effects of drinking hot water, cold water, and chicken soup on nasal mucus velocity and nasal airflow resistance. *Chest, 74*, 408–410.
Sato, T., Hirono, J., Tonoike, M., & Takebayashi, M. (1994). Tuning specificities to aliphatic odorants in mouse olfactory receptor neurons and their local distribution. *Journal of Neurophysiology, 72*, 2980–2989.
Schiet, F. T., & Cain, W. S. (1990). Odor intensity of mixed and unmixed stimuli under environmentally realistic conditions. *Perception, 19*, 123–132.
Schiet, F. T., & Frijters, J. E. R. (1988). An investigation of the equiratio-mixture model in olfactory psychophysics: A case study. *Perception & Psychophysics, 44*, 304–308.
Schiffman, S. S. (1977). Food recognition by the elderly. *Journal of Gerontology, 32*, 586–592.
Schiffman, S. S. (1979). Changes in taste and smell with age: Psychophysical aspects. In J.M. Ordy & K. Brizzee (Eds.), *Sensory systems and communication in the elderly: Vol. 10. Aging* (pp. 227–246). New York: Raven Press.
Schild, D., & Restrepo, D. (1998). Transduction mechanisms in vertebrate olfactory receptor cells. *Physiological Reviews, 78*, 429–466.
Schmidt, H. J., & Beauchamp, G. K. (1988). Adult-like preferences and aversions in three-year-old children. *Child Development, 59*, 1136–1143.
Schwanzel-Fukuda, M., Reinhard, G. R., Abraham, S., Crossin, K. L., Edelman, G. M., & Pfaff, D. W. (1994). Antibody to neural cell adhesion molecule can disrupt the migration of luteinizing hormone-releasing hormone neurons into the mouse brain. *Journal of Comparative Neurology, 342*, 174–185.
Scott, J., Davis, L., Shannon, D., & Kaplan, C. (1996). Relation of chemical structure to spatial distribution of sensory responses in rat olfactory epithelium. *Journal of Neurophysiology, 75*, 2036–2049.
Seebolm, P. M. (1978). Allergic and nonallergic rhinitis. In E. Middleton, C. Reed, & E. Ellis (Eds.), *Allergy principles and practice* (Vol. 2, pp. 868–876). St. Louis: CV Mosby.
Sengupta, P., Chou, J. H., & Bargmann, C. I. (1996). odr-10 encodes a seven transmembrane domain olfactory receptor required for responses to the odorant Diacetyl. *Cell, 84*, 899–909.
Ship, J. A. (1993). Gustatory and olfactory considerations: Examination and treatment in general practice. *Journal of the American Dental Association, 124*, 55–62.
Sicard, G. (1984). Electrophysiological recordings from olfactory receptor cells in adult mice. *Brain Research, 397*, 405–408.
Sicard, G., & Holley, A. (1984). Receptor cell responses to odorants: Similarities and differences

among odorants. *Brain Research, 292*, 283–296.

Silver, W. L., & Walker, J. C. (1997). Odors. In J. J. Lagowski (Ed.), *MacMillan encyclopedia of chemistry* (pp. 1067–1071). New York: Macmillan Reference.

Sobel, N., Prabhakaran, V., Desmond, J. E., Glover, G. H., Goode, R. L., Sullivan, E. V., & Gabrirell, D. E. (1998). Sniffing and smelling: Separate subsystems in the human olfactory cortex. *Nature, 392*, 282–286.

Steinmetz, G., Pryor, G. T., & Stone, H. (1970). Olfactory adaptation and recovery in man as measured by two psychophysical techniques. *Perception & Psychophysics, 8*, 327–330.

Stevens, D. A., & O'Connell, R. J. (1995). Enhanced sensitivity to androstenone following regular exposure to pemenone. *Chemical Senses, 20*, 413–419.

Stevens, J. C., & Cain, W. S. (1985). Age-related deficiency in the perceived strength of six odorants. *Chemical Senses, 10*, 517–529.

Stevens, J. C., & Cain, W. S. (1986). Smelling via the mouth: Effect of aging. *Perception & Psychophysics, 40*, 142–146.

Stevens, J. C., & Dadarwala, A. D. (1993). Variability of olfactory threshold and its role in assessment of aging. *Perception & Psychophysics, 54*, 296–302.

Stevens, J. C., Cain, W.S., & Burke, R. J. (1988). Variability of olfactory thresholds. *Chemical Senses, 13*, 643–653.

Stevens, J. C., Cain, W. S., & Weinstein, D. E. (1987). Aging impairs the ability to detect gas odor. *Fire Technology, 23*, 198–204.

Stevens, S. S. (1975). *Psychophysics: Introduction to its perceptual, neural and social prospects.* New York: Wiley.

Strotmann, J., Wanner, I., Helfrich, T., Beck, A., Neinken, C., Kubick, S., & Breer, H. (1994). Olfactory neurones expressing distinct odorant receptor subtypes are spatially segregated in the nasal neuroepithelium. *Cell and Tissue Research, 276*, 429–438.

Tareilus, E., Noe, J., & Breer, H. (1995). Calcium signaling in olfactory neurons. *Biochemical and Biophysical Acta, 1269*, 129–138.

Teff, K. L. (1996). Physiological effects of flavour perception. *Trends in Food Science and Technology, 7*, 448–452.

Teleky-Vámossy, Gy., & Petró-Turza, M. (1986). Evaluation of odour intensity versus concentration of natural garlic oil and some of its individual aroma compounds. *Die Nahrung, 30*, 775–782.

Todrank, J., Wysocki, C. J., & Beauchamp, G. K. (1991). The effects of adaptation on the perception of similar and dissimilar odors. *Chemical Senses, 16*, 467-482.

Touhara, K., Sengoku, S., Inaki, K., Tsuboi, A., Hirono, J., Sato, T., Sakano, H., & Haga, T. (1999). Functional identification and reconstitution of an odorant receptor in single olfactory neurons. *Proceedings of the National Academy of Sciences, 96*, 4040–4045.

Trask, B. J., Friedman, C., Martin-Gallardo, A., Rowen, L., Akinbami, C., Blankenship, J., Collins, C., Giorgi, D., Iadonato, S., Johnson, F., Kuo, W. L., Massa, H., Morrish, T., Naylor, S., Nguyen, O. T. H., Rouquier, S., Smith, T., Wong, D. J., Youngblom, J., & van den Engh, G. (1998). Members of the olfactory receptor gene family are contained in large blocks of DNA duplicated polymorphically near the ends of human chromosomes. *Human Molecular Genetics*, 7, 13–26.

Turin, A. (1996). Spectroscopic mechanism for primary olfactory reception. *Chemical Senses, 21*(6), 773–791.

Varendi, H., Christensson, K., Porter, R. H., & Winberg, J. (1998). Soothing effect of amniotic fluid smell in newborn infants. *Early Human Development, 51*, 47–55.

Varendi, H., Porter, R. H., & Winberg, J. (1994). Does the newborn baby find the nipple by smell? *Lancet, 344*, 989–990.

Voirol, E., & Daget, N. (1986). Comparative study of nasal and retronasal olfactory perception. *Lebensmittel-Wissenschaft und Technologie, 319*, 316–319.

von Skramlik, E. (1925). Über die Lokalisation der Empfindungen bei den niederen Sinnen. *Zeitschrift für Sinnesphysiologie, 56*, 69–140.

Wang, F., Nemes, A., Mendelsohn, M., & Axel, R. (1998). Odorant receptors govern the formation of a precise topographic map. *Cell, 93*,47–60.

Wang, H-W., Wysocki, C. J., & Gold, G. H. (1993). Induction of olfactory receptor sensitivity in mice. *Science, 260*, 998–1000.

Wysocki, C. J., & Beauchamp, G. K. (1984). Ability to smell androstenone is genetically determined. *Proceedings of the National Academy of Sciences, 81*, 4899-4902.

Wysocki, C. J., & Beauchamp, G. K. (1991). Individual differences in human olfaction. In C. J. Wysocki & M. R. Kare (Eds.), *Chemical senses: Vol. 3. Genetics of perception and communication* (pp. 353–373). New York: Marcel-Dekker.

Wysocki, C. J., & Gilbert, A. N. (1989). National Geographic smell survey: Effects of age are heterogenous. *Annals New York Academy of Sciences, 561*, 12–28.

Wysocki, C. J., Cowart, B. J., & Radil, T. (in press). Nasal-trigeminal chemosensitivity across the adult life-span. *Perception & Psychophysics.*

Wysocki, C. J., Dalton, P., Brody, M. J., & Lawley, H. J. (1997). Acetone odor and irritation thresholds obtained from acetone-exposed factory workers and from control (occupationally unexposed) subjects. *American Industrial Hygiene Association Journal, 58*, 704–712.

Wysocki, C. J., Dorries, K. M., & Beauchamp, G. K. (1989). Ability to perceive androstenone can be acquired by ostensibly anosmic people. *Proceedings of the National Academy of Sciences, 86*, 7976–7978.

Wysocki, C. J., Green, B. G., & Malia, T. P. (1992). Monorhinal stimulation as a method for differentiating between thresholds for irritation and odor [Abstract]. *Chemical Senses, 17*, 722–723.

Yamagishi, M., Hasegawa, S., & Nakano, Y. (1988). Examination and classification of human olfactory mucosa in patients with clinical olfactory disturbances. *Archives of Otorhinolaryngology, 245*, 316–320.

Zhao, H., Ivic, L., Otaki, J. M., Hashimoto, M., Mikoshiba, K., & Firestein, S. (1998). Functional expression of a mammalian odorant receptor. *Science, 279*, 237–242.

Chapter Nineteen

Taste

Harry T. Lawless

Overview and Anatomy

The sense of taste functions as a gatekeeper to the alimentary tract. Its most important functional property is to determine our reactions to items placed in the mouth. Taste sensations carry information about the palatability of potential foods and play a major role in appetitive behaviors. Its importance is clear if you think about what the experience of eating might be like without taste. Reduced to a collection of odiferous and tactile sensations, even the greatest vintage of wine would fail to impress us. This chapter will focus on the functional aspects of the sense of taste such as taste quality, adaptation, temporal response characteristics, mixture effects, and genetic factors. Basic information is also provided on the anatomy and physiology of taste. A brief overview of general chemical sensitivity to irritants in the oral cavity is included as these sensations are regarded as part of the taste sense by current workers in the chemical senses.

Taste as Part of the Chemical Senses

The sense of taste comprises one part of the chemical sensitivity on and in the human body. Many other systems are responsive to chemicals such as various mucous membranes (eyes, nasal passages, anus), the external skin, and even within the body there are specialized chemoreceptors such as the carotid body responsible for sensing levels of carbon dioxide in the blood (Marshall, 1994). Taste can be defined as those sensory systems responding to chemical stimuli placed in the oral cavity. Smell can likewise be thought of as those sensory systems responding to chemical stimuli entering the airways of the nasal passages. Flavor is the overall impression from nasal and oral chemical sensations. The anatomical divisions of the flavor senses are shown in Figure 19.1. In the oral cavity, taste can be divided into gustation proper and the general chemical sensitivity of the mouth. Gustation may be defined as those sensations mediated by structures that contain taste buds, and that are not sensed on areas without taste buds. Sensations such as sweetness, saltiness, sourness and bitterness are mediated by these structures and are classified as gustatory. These sensations are to be distinguished from chemically induced tactile or irritative sensations that are felt in areas that do not contain taste buds. Examples include astringency or drying from tannins in foods, the cooling effects of menthol, and the warmth or irritation from hot pepper felt throughout the oral cavity.

Taste is usually differentiated from smell on two grounds – taste is oral and smell is nasal, and the sense of taste responds to stimuli that are dissolved in an aqueous carrier like saliva while olfaction responds to chemicals in the vapor phase. Taste is further complicated by the fact that nongustatory stimuli such as temperature and tactile stimuli modu-

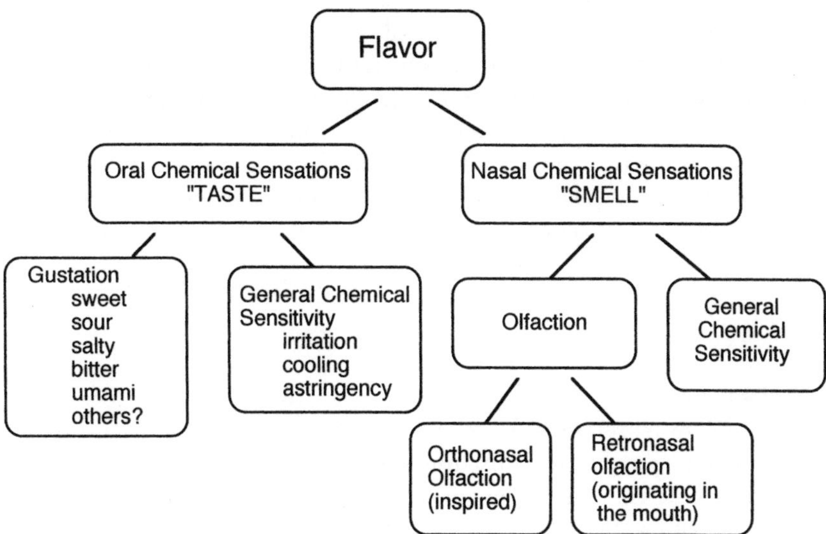

Figure 19.1. Anatomical classification of the flavor senses. Based upon whether the stimulus-receptor interaction occurs in the oral or nasal cavities, the chemical senses are divided into taste and smell. Taste can be divided into general chemical sensitivity, mediated largely by the trigeminal nerves, and the more specialized functions of the taste buds that signal gustatory sensations such as sweet, sour, salty, bitter, and umami.

late the responses of taste nerves (Halpern, 1997). Although we can make some anatomical distinctions separating gustation from other oral senses, their interaction in sensations from everyday eating is common in natural settings. Generally, when we think about the ecological function of taste it is one of the important systems that modulates food choice via flavor perception. Flavor is thus a combination of taste and olfactory sensations, and includes the generalized chemical sense carried by other nerves besides the classical gustatory and olfactory pathways.

Another important chemoreceptive pathway within the taste senses is the trigeminal nerve innervations of the mouth. The fifth cranial nerves transmit information about heat, cold, dental pain, touch, and pressure in the oral cavity. They are also responsive to chemical stimuli that contribute to our perceptions of flavors. Examples include the burn of pepper, the irritation from cinnamon, mustard, horseradish, and other spices and condiments (Lawless, 1984). Even the prototypical stimulus for salty taste, sodium chloride, will stimulate the oral irritation sense when concentration levels are high (Green & Gelhard, 1989). So the sense of taste is one component of the flavor senses, but is also a system with several anatomical divisions.

Study of the sense of taste has faced several methodological challenges. Simply placing a chemical in the mouth or on the tongue does not stimulate the taste sense the way that activating a switch can begin visual or auditory stimulation. Stimulus removal is likewise not as easy as switching off a light or a tone. When a solid chemical is placed on the tongue, it first must dissolve in order to stimulate the gustatory apparatus. If a liquid solution is used complications also occur. The solution will mix with existing saliva thus changing the effective stimulus concentration. Next, it will often evoke a salivary reflex further changing the content, potency, and duration of the stimulus. Finally, the chemical stimulus itself may penetrate the receptor cell membrane, so that stimulus removal becomes a matter of intracellular deactivation or disposal. It should be apparent to researchers in other sense modalities that many of the paradigms applied to the understanding of visual and auditory phenomena are poorly suited or even unworkable for studying the sense of taste.

The Gustatory Sense Organs

Specialized sense organs on the tongue and soft palate contain the receptors for our sense of taste. The following summary is derived from Beidler (1978), Pritchard (1991), and Brand (1997). Taste receptor cells are clustered in a layered ball called a taste bud. Different numbers of cells are cited as contained in the average mammalian taste bud, with Mistretta (1991) citing 40 to 60 and Brand (1997) citing 75 to 150. A schematic drawing of a typical mammalian taste bud is shown in Figure 19.2a. These cells are modified epithelial cells (skin-like cells) rather than neurons and have a life span of about a week. New cells differentiate from the surrounding epithelium, migrate into the taste bud and make synaptic contact with sensory nerves. A pore at the top of the taste bud makes contact with the fluid environment in the mouth and taste molecules are believed to bind to hair-like cilia that project from the top of the taste cells, near the opening of the pore. Some of the taste cells in each bud make contact with the primary taste nerves over a synaptic connection. Packets of neurotransmitter molecules are released into this gap to stimulate the primary afferent nerves.

The taste buds are contained in specialized structures called papillae consisting of bumps and grooves on the tongue. The tongue is not a smooth uniform surface. The upper surface is covered with small cone-shaped filiform papillae. These serve a tactile function but do not contain taste buds. Interspersed among the filiform papillae, especially on the front and edges of the tongue, are slightly larger mushroom-shaped fungiform papillae, often more reddish in color. These small button-shaped structures contain from two to four taste buds each, on the average, although many contain no taste buds at all (Arvidson, 1979). There are over a hundred on each side of the anterior tongue, suggesting an average of several hundred taste buds in the normal adult fungiform papillae (Miller & Bartoshuk, 1991) accounting for about 18% of the lingual total. Numbers of taste buds in different areas of the tongue and mouth are shown in Table 19.1. Along the sides of the tongue there are several parallel grooves called the foliate papillae, located about two-thirds of the way back from the tip to the root. Each groove may contain over a hundred taste buds, with about 2,400 total buds in the foliate papillae of the human tongue, about 34% of the lingual total. Other specialized structures include the large circular bumps arranged in an inverted-V on the back of the tongue, the circumvallate papillae. They contain several hundred taste buds each in the outer grooves or moat-like fissures that surround them. The vallate papillae in total possess about two to three times as many taste buds as the fungiform papillae (Miller & Bartoshuk, 1991). Extra-lingual taste buds are located on the

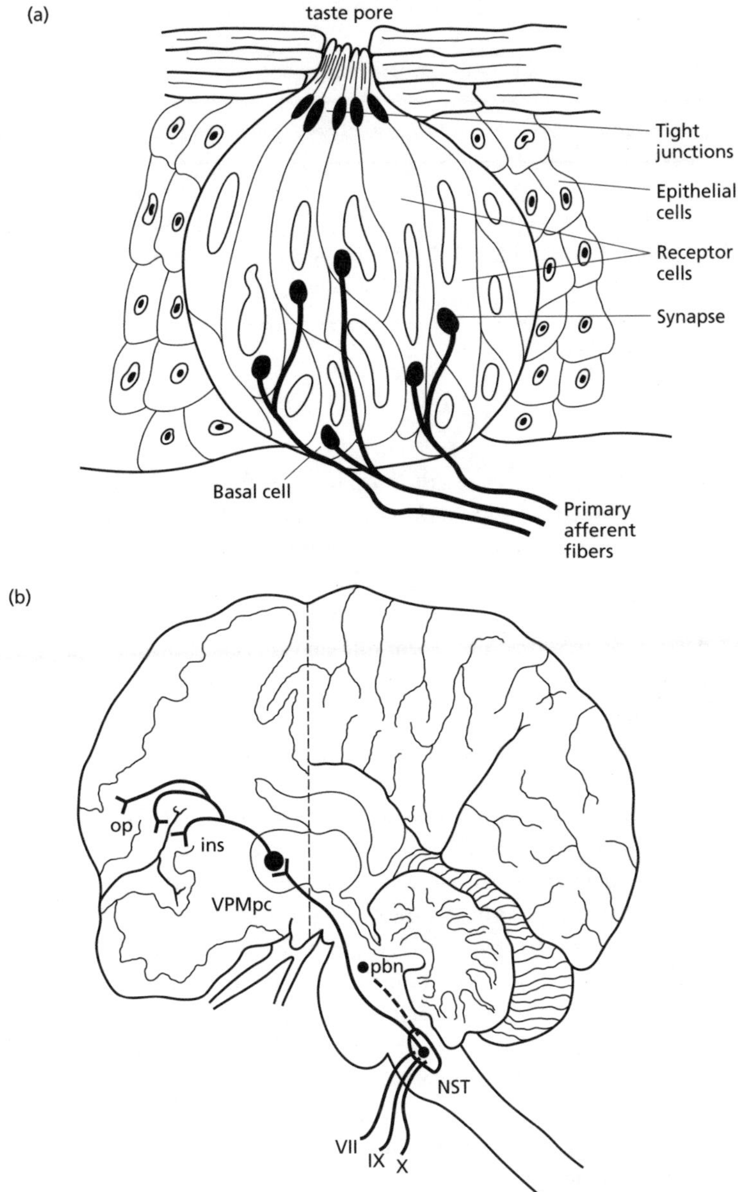

Figure 19.2. (a) Schematic drawing of mammalian taste bud (after Mistretta, 1991 and Brand, 1997). (b) Projections of the mammalian taste system (after Pritchard, 1991 and Smith & Vogt, 1997). VII, IX, X – input to the nucleus of the solitary tract (NST) from gustatory afferent fibers of the seventh, ninth, and tenth cranial nerves. The NST projects to the parvicellular portion of the venteroposteromedial nucleus of the thalamus (VMPpc). Thalamocortical fibers terminate in the anterior opercular cortex (op) and the agranular insular cortex (ins). Note that the drawing has a midline cut to the right of the vertical dashed line and a saggital cut to the left of the dashed line to show the lateral progress of the thalamocortical fibers. The parabrachial relay of the pons (PBN) appears not to be present in primates.

Table 19.1 Papillae and taste buds in different oral regions

Papillae	*Numbers*	*Taste buds per papilla*	*Range*	*Total taste buds*
Vallate	9.2±1.8	240±125	12–800	2,150
Foliate	5.4±1.45 per side	117±72	13–441	2,540
Fungiform	About 100 per side	3.4±1.8 tongue tip 2.6±1.6 midregion	0–32	800

Source: Miller & Bartoshuk (1991)

soft palate just behind the line where the hard or bony part of the palate stops, an important but often overlooked area for sensing taste. The root of the tongue, epiglottis and upper part of the esophagus also contain taste receptors. Frequency counts of taste buds show wide individual differences and that people with higher taste sensitivity tend to possess more fungiform papillae and more taste buds (Bartoshuk, Duffy, & Miller, 1994). Miller and Bartoshuk presented data from human cadavers showing a range over 18-fold in the total number of taste buds, from 398 to 6,974 (mean 2,755 ± 2,099).

Four different pairs of nerves innervate the tongue to make contact with these structures. This may explain in part why the sense of taste is fairly robust. It would be difficult to knock out all taste areas through trauma or disease and the sense of taste remains functional until very late in life, in contrast to smell (Weiffenbach, 1991). The fungiform papillae and possibly the anterior foliate are innervated by the chorda tympani branches of the facial nerves (cranial nerves VII) which as their name suggests, cross the eardrums. This circuitous route has actually permitted recording of human taste nerve impulses during surgery on the middle ear (Diamant, Oakley, Strom, & Zotterman, 1965). The glossopharyngeal nerves (cranial nerve IX) send branches to the foliate and vallate papillae and the vagus nerve (cranial X) to the far posterior areas of the tongue root and upper esophagus. The superior petrosal nerve, also a branch of cranial VII, innervates the palatal taste area (Miller & Spangler, 1982; Pritchard, 1991). Afferent taste nerves from cranial nerves VII, IX, and X terminate in the nucleus of the solitary tract (NST) in the medulla. The NST has rostro-caudal organization that corresponds to the anterior-posterior innervation of the oral cavity (terminations from VII rostral and terminations from X caudal, with some overlapping fields). Although the NST is the obligatory relay for taste signals, cells therein also respond to tactile and thermal stimuli, as do many fibers in the primary afferent taste nerves. This mix of chemosensory and somatosensory function persists in the higher projections of the CNS.

In primates, the medullary fibers project to the parvicellular portion of the ventero-posteromedial nucleus of the thalamus (VPMpc in Figure 19.2b) and the thalamus relays to the gustatory neocortex within the agranular insular cortex (ins) (Pritchard, 1991). Taste projects ipsilaterally in primates although the pattern in humans is unclear. In other mammals such as cats and rodents, there is an additional relay from the NST into the parabrachial nucleus of the pons (PBN). The existence of the pontine taste relay in humans is controversial (Pritchard, 1991) and in Old World monkeys, there is clear evidence of a direct projection from the NST to the thalamus. Pritchard speculates that the PBN in primates may receive input from the caudal NST and subserve visceral and alimentary functions. In other species, the parabrachial nuclei send parallel projections to limbic structures involved in appetitive behavior including the lateral hypothalamus, the amygdala, and the bed nucleus of the stria terminalis. Evidence from epileptic patients with gustatory auras, patients with skull damage, and labeling experiments in animal models all point to two neighboring areas of the neocortex as the gustatory cortical centers, the parietal operculum (op) and the posterior insular cortex (Pritchard, 1991). A secondary gustatory cortex is located in areas 12 and 13 of the posterior orbitofrontal cortex. Responses from cells in this region are to highly complex multimodal stimuli, and gustatory responses of monkeys in this area are modulated by satiety. Pritchard suggests that it may subserve perceptual or pattern recognition functions influencing food selection and intake.

Transduction

Several cellular mechanisms for the transduction of chemical into neural signals have been proposed for taste. These different mechanisms arise from application of compounds from the classical taste categories (or from stimulation with glutamate). Different physiological mechanisms are consistent with the view of taste as being comprised of four or five separate chemosensory submodalities tuned to specific taste primaries. What events are necessary in order to create an afferent signal in the primary taste nerves? To do this, receptor cells must spill neurotransmitter across the synapse. Release of neurotransmitter is dependent upon increases in intracellular calcium, either from calcium influx or release from intracellular stores. Changes in intracellular calcium are either caused by or are congruent with depolarization of the receptor cell. Cellular biologists studying taste have looked at the potential mechanisms for modulating cell polarization and calcium levels as the link between the stimulus and signal transduction.

Three general classes of mechanisms have been proposed (reviewed by Brand, 1997). The simplest is the passage of an ionic stimulus (such as sodium ions) through an existing ion channel in the cell membrane. The second consists of a second messenger system, in which the stimulus binds to a receptor that then activates a protein subunit that further stimulates an enzymatic cascade within the cell. The enzymes are capable of modulating intracellular calcium or modulating cell membrane polarization through the phosphorylation of ion channels. A third mechanism is a stimulus-gated ion channel complex, where the stimulus binds to a receptor which controls the activity in a linked ion channel, thus modulating ion flux across the cell membrane. Figure 19.3 shows how these kinds of mechanisms could work for different taste stimuli.

Since only sodium, lithium and to a lesser extent, potassium ions are salty, the mechanism for salty taste transduction must be one that is stimulated by these ions. Salt taste transduction is probably transduced by a membrane-bound ion channel similar to those found in other epithelial cells and kidney (Heck, Mierson, & DeSimone, 1984; Brand, 1997). Salt taste is blocked in some animals by the application of the diuretic drug, amiloride (Brand, Teeter, & Silver, 1985) although the effect in humans is less clear. The specificity

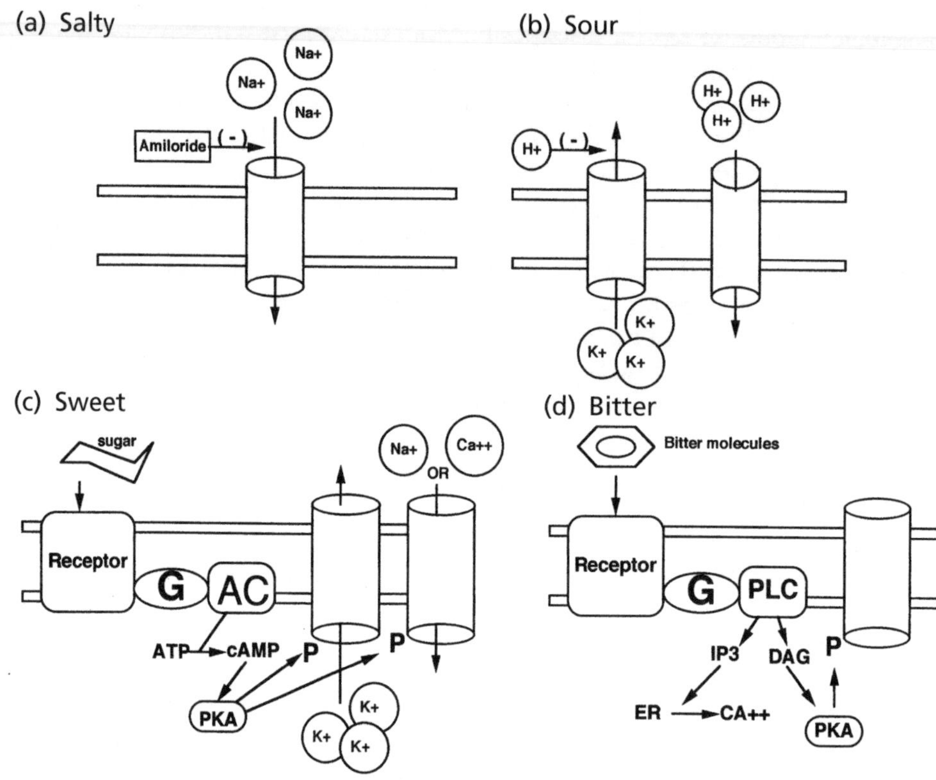

Figure 19.3. Proposed mechanisms of gustatory transduction (from Brand, 1997 and Spielman et al., 1992). (a) Sodium ions may enter the taste cell through a channel in the membrane which is sensitive to the diuretic blocking agent, amiloride. (b) Protons from acid stimuli may function to block outward flowing potassium ion channels or may enter the cell directly. (c) Carbohydrate sweet stimuli may interact with receptors coupled to G-proteins. Dissociation of the G-protein subunits leads to activation of adenylate cyclase enzyme and production of cyclic AMP (cAMP). cAMP activates a protein kinase that phosphorylates ion channels, activating or inhibiting them. (d) Bitter molecules interact with a receptor coupled to G-proteins and phospholipase C enzyme (PLC). PLC stimulates production of the second messengers inositol 3-phosphate (IP3) and diacyl glycerol (DAG). IP3 may affect release of intracellular calcium stores (ER) and DAG can activate a protein kinase A (PKA) capable of phosphorylating ion channels. In all cases, increases in intracellular calcium associated with cell depolarization are seen as a necessary step in stimulating neurotransmitter release.

of the ion channel that transduces saltiness creates a difficult problem for developers of potential salt substitutes, leading to the search for potential salt enhancers. Such taste enhancing agents could work by increasing the gain or efficiency of the sodium ion channels.

Sour taste is also likely linked to modulation of ion channels. The efficacy of sour stimuli appears most closely linked to the titratable acidity of a stimulus (rather than its pH), leading to the notion that the sour receptor mechanism must function as a proton counter of sorts. One cellular mechanism that is sensitive to protons is blockage of an outward-flowing potassium channel as found in some amphibians (Brand, 1997). Other possibilities include direct influx through an ion channel or modulation of a stimulus-gated ion channel capable of admitting calcium (Brand, 1997).

In contrast to these ionic mechanisms, there is growing evidence that transduction of sweet and bitter tastes involves second messenger systems, with receptors linked to G-protein complexes. G-proteins are expressed in a number of receptor systems, and the one that has so far been isolated to taste, gustducin, shows a strong homology with the G-proteins of the visual system, the transducins (McLaughlin, McKinnon, & Margolskee, 1992). Mice that are bred with a depletion of the gustducin gene ("knock-out" mice) show impairments in sweet and bitter reactivity, but not in sour or salty (Wong, Gannon, & Margolskee, 1996). The link between a receptor, G-protein, and the enzyme cascade is thought to work as follows (Brand, 1997; Streim et al., 1989): Cyclic AMP (adenosine monophosphate) is produced in response to stimulation with carbohydrates. Cyclic AMP production is controlled by the dissociation of a subunit of a G-protein. This dissociation is thought to arise from stimulation of a membrane-bound protein receptor that affects the association of three G-protein subunits. Cyclic AMP is capable of stimulating production of a protein kinase that controls the phosphorylation of ion channels. The resulting phosphorylation leads to cellular depolarization and ultimately an increase in inward calcium flow. Having several biochemical steps may act to amplify the chemical signal at each step. For non-sugar sweeteners another important second messenger is inositol-3-phosphate (IP3) which is also known to modulate intracellular calcium stores in chemosensory receptor cells.

Bitter taste transduction is likely to be more complicated, given the large diversity in bitter molecules and the genetic diversity in both humans and other mammals in their sensitivity to different bitter compounds. Multiple mechanisms are likely (Spielman et al., 1996). Taste cells and membrane preparations isolated from circumvallate regions of various mammals have been used to study bitter taste transduction. One important mechanism appears to be blockage of outward potassium flow by substances such as the potent bitter compound denatonium (Brand, 1997). Denatonium also appears to result in a release of intracellular calcium stores, possibly mediated through a second messenger system. IP3 and diacyl glycerol (DAG) have both been implicated as second messengers in bitter taste transduction. DAG controls a protein kinase and IP3 could affect the release of calcium from intracellular stores. Another possibility is that the activation of gustducin stimulates a phosphodiesterase enzyme. This would somewhat paradoxically cause a decrease in cyclic nucleotides like cAPM. If cAMP is gating an inhibitory channel, reduction could stimulate membrane depolarizing events (Brand, 1997).

The glutamate mechanism is not well understood in mammals, but should be able to explain the synergistic interaction of glutamate and ribosides in stimulating taste (Brand, 1997). The possibility of a stimulus gated ion channel has been raised by the reconstitution of a glutamate-stimulated ion channel in mouse circumvallate membrane preparations (Teeter et al., 1992). Developments of biochemical tools to study intracellular mechanisms, advances in microscopy, the identification of transduction proteins, and techniques for studying genetic expression have created a recent explosion in our understanding of how taste receptor cells function.

General Sensitivity and Potency of Gustatory Stimuli

Stimulus Specification

A wide variety of chemical compounds are sensed by the gustatory apparatus and an even wider group by the general oral irritation sense. Furthermore, most chemicals have multiple sensory effects and the identification of a single chemical compound as being representative of a taste quality is potentially misleading. Acids, for example, primarily thought of as prototypical stimuli for sour taste, have astringent and tactile properties (Rubico & McDaniel, 1992; Lawless, Horne, & Giasi, 1996). Even sodium chloride, long used as the prototypical salty stimulus, is sweet when low in concentration and irritative when high (Bartoshuk, Murphy, & Cleveland, 1978; Green & Gelhard, 1989). Salts other than sodium chloride are not purely salty, and many are more bitter than salty (Murphy, Cardello, & Brand, 1981). Rather than ask what prototypical stimuli are representative of single taste qualities, it may be more informative to ask what kinds of different chemicals have primarily one or another taste property. The issue of whether the sense of taste can be conceptualized as consisting of four or more distinct qualities is discussed below.

Although there are no purely monogustatory chemicals, some stimuli are associated primarily with one taste quality. Sweetness is characteristic of the carbohydrate sugars and may have evolved to provide an appetitive sensing apparatus for a concentrated source of edible energy. However, many other molecules are sweet and some are more potent than sugars. These include the so-called artificial sweeteners such as saccharin and aspartame as well as some protein molecules like Monellin and Thaumatin (van der Heijden, 1993). Sodium and lithium chlorides are primarily salty in taste. Other halides and multivalent salts have complex tastes, often including a bitter component. Acids are primarily sour. This includes both organic acids like acetic and citric acids, and inorganic acids like hydrochloric and sulfuric (used when suitably dilute). Bitter compounds are perhaps the most diverse and difficult to characterize chemically. They include moderately large organic compounds such as the citrus compound naringin, the large organic acids found in hop oils, small molecules like urea, and even some sugars. Van der Heijden (1993) tabulated no fewer than 19 distinct chemical families of bitter substances.

Salivary Modulation, Stimulus Interface, the Peri-receptor Environment

One factor that is shared in common among tastants is that all must enter a solution if they are to be perceived, either dissolved in water or into the salivary medium that bathes the receptors. The interplay of dissolved molecules with their surrounding water molecules may be an important factor in determining taste quality, potency, and access to the receptors (Birch & Kemp, 1989; Kemp, Birch, Portmann, & Mathlouthi, 1990). Ionic molecules are known to loosely attract a shell of hydration from the water molecules around them. Hydrophobic molecules such as bitter tastants impose structure on the water molecules surrounding them, causing a kind of organization that has energetic (entropic) consequences. The chemistry of solute-tastant interactions has received surprisingly little attention.

Saliva plays an important part in taste function, both as a carrier of sapid molecules to the receptors and because it contains substances capable of modulating taste response. Saliva contains sodium and other cations, bicarbonate capable of buffering acids, and a range of proteins and mucopolysaccharides that give it its slippery and coating properties (Bradley, 1991). There are recent suggestions that salivary glutamate may be capable of altering food flavor perception (Yamaguchi & Kobori, 1994). Whether saliva is actually necessary for taste response is a matter of historical controversy. Over short time spans saliva is not required for taste perception. Rinsing the tongue with deionized water does not inhibit the taste response, but actually sharpens it (McBurney, 1966).

Potency and Structure Activity Relationships

The potency or stimulatory efficiency of a compound may be expressed as that concentration that yields a given level of response, or an isointense response across different compounds. Response to taste has been characterized primarily through threshold estimation and scaling work. Either may be used to specify an isointense point for the characterization of stimulus-response efficiency. In the case of thresholds, the isointensity point is that which is just perceivable. Above threshold, some common benchmarks have been used such as a 10% (wt/vol) sucrose equivalency in sweetener research. After finding the concentrations that yield a given level of scaled response for two stimuli, their concentrations may be compared to create a measure of relative potency.

Threshold studies have been difficult in the sense of taste, due to the need to remove saliva as well as residual molecules from previous stimuli within a series of stimulus presentations. Thus the concept of an absolute threshold may in fact be unattainable in taste research, as it would require water rinses of infinite purity and complete removal of

Table 19.2 Taste detection thresholds in water for common test substances

Substance	*Threshold (moles/liter)*
Sucrose	0.019 (5)*
Saccharin	0.000043 (3)
NaCl	0.008 (5)
Acetic acid	0.0031 (3)
Hydrochloric acid	0.00013 (3)**
Citric	0.0017 (5)
Quinine	0.0000032 (5)
Urea	0.012 (1)

* Numbers in parentheses are numbers of studies averaged to obtain the listed value.

** Recognition thresholds, detection thresholds unavailable.

Source: Fazzalari (1978)

residual stimulus molecules. Taste thresholds are probabilistic estimates of the concentration range within which sensations will appear (Marin, Barnard, Darlington, & Acree, 1991). Thresholds depend upon methodological details and show practice effects. They are prone to wide individual differences of factors of a hundred or thousand fold in concentration. Thresholds for common test substances are shown in Table 19.2. Carbohydrate sugars become tastable in the range of about 0.001 M, as does sodium chloride. Acids have different thresholds depending upon their pK values, that is, among organic acids, their tendency to dissociate. Bitter compounds as a class are among the most potent, with thresholds for common substances such as quinine and caffeine in the range of 0.000001 M. However, there are important exceptions within each class, as discussed below.

Suprathreshold intensity responses have been assessed by methods such as category scales and magnitude estimation. The notion that magnitude estimation provided a ratio scale for sensation intensity and characteristic power function exponents for particular tastants was an influential paradigm in the 1960s and 1970s (e.g., Moskowitz, 1971). The validity of magnitude estimation as a ratio scaling procedure was later challenged (Anderson, 1974; Birnbaum, 1982). Other procedures include the labeled magnitude scale (Green, Shaffer, & Gilmore, 1993; Green et al., 1996), a line-marking technique with verbal anchors (weak, moderate, strong, etc.) in a quasi-logarithmic spacing that yields data similar to magnitude estimation. Not only has magnitude estimation been challenged, but its concomitant result, the power function, has been called into question. Much psychophysical data from taste fits a function associated with the Law of Mass Action, and the associated enzyme kinetic equations of Michaelis, Menten, and Hill (Curtis, Stevens, & Lawless, 1984; Lawless, 1978; McBride, 1987). This type of relationship was used by Beidler and co-workers to model stimulus binding phenomena and describe taste cell responses (Beidler, 1954, 1978). The equation may be cast as

$$R = (R_{max}\, C) / (k + C)$$

where R is response, R_{max} is the maximal response, C is the concentration, and k is the concentration at which response is half-maximal. In enzyme kinetics, k is a quantity proportional to the dissociation constant of the enzyme-substrate complex and can be used as an index of binding energy or stimulus efficacy. The equation is attractive as a description of taste response because it is based on molecular events in stimulus binding. As taste responses may involve the binding of a molecule to a receptor, it is perhaps not surprising that there is a parallel between taste response and an enzyme-substrate binding relationship. The faster the binding, the more receptor sites that should be filled at any one time, and the greater the response of the sensory nerves. In a plot of log concentration versus response, the function forms an S-shaped curve, with an initial flat portion, a steep rise and then another flat zone representing saturation of response at high levels. This seems intuitively appealing as inflection points should logically occur as threshold is surpassed and as the system saturates in terms of filled receptor sites or the maximal response rate of gustatory nerves.

Research on sweeteners has been the most productive with regard to understanding the critical molecular parameters that affect taste potency. Shallenberger and Acree (1967) proposed that a complementary hydrogen bond pair between a sweet molecule and a receptor could explain why many molecules were sweet and others were not. The second insight was that a third binding site involving a lipophilic or hydrophobic interaction could explain why some molecules such as aspartame were much more potent than the carbohydrate sugars (Kier, 1972; van der Heijden, 1993). Recently, even more efficacious or "hyperpotent" molecules have been identified, such as the sucrononic acid that is several hundred thousand times more potent than sucrose (Tinti & Nofre, 1991). Study of such molecules has led to the proposition that yet additional binding sites are available in the taste receptor-ligand arrangement (Tinti & Nofre, 1991). Thus a search for molecules of potential commercial importance has also yielded insights into the nature and requirements of the receptor interaction for taste. Note that potency is used as an indication that the threshold (or concentrations derived from another isointensity point of reference through scaling) is some proportion lower than the threshold for sucrose, so that potency is inverse to threshold concentration. This avoids the common mistake of using of nonsensical phrases like "compound X is 200 times as sweet as sucrose," to describe stimulus activity. Sweetness is a subjective experience, not a ratio of concentrations.

Modulating Affects: Area and Locus

To state a physical concentration value for a taste substance at threshold or to provide a single number that characterizes the psychophysical function is misleading unless the conditions under which those observations were made are considered. There are methodological factors and practical questions of carriers for the taste molecules, which can affect response (Stahl, 1973). A number of physical and anatomical variables can affect taste responses, including the size of the area stimulated, the locus of stimulation within the mouth, the flow rate of a stimulus and its temperature. Taste responses increase with flow rate and are most robust when the test stimulus is between room temperature and body temperature (McBurney, Collings, & Glanz, 1973; Meiselman, Bose, & Nykvist, 1972).

A common but mistaken diagram of the tongue sometimes shows areas labeled with basic tastes, with sweet at the front and bitter at the back, etc. This oversimplification is the result of poor translation of work on discrimination thresholds and is not an accurate picture of spatial sensitivity to taste. Such a "tongue map" does not recognize the area for taste on the soft palate at the posterior of the roof of the mouth (Nilsson, 1977). The inaccurate map leaves the impression that *only* sweetness is perceived on the front of the tongue, bitterness on the back, etc. This is false. Any one of the classical taste qualities can be perceived on any part of the tongue or soft palate. Collings (1974) examined recognition thresholds and suprathreshold intensity functions in different oral areas and found some results different from the common tongue map notions (Figure 19.4). Thresholds for quinine were lowest on the front of the tongue and the palate and not on the circumvallate areas on the back of the tongue, as expected. However, the psychophysical scaling functions on the circumvallate areas (responses above threshold) grew more steeply with concentration than the other areas. This may in part explain why people feel that the backs of their tongues are more responsive to bitterness.

The size of the area stimulated on the tongue has an effect on threshold and suprathreshold intensity. McBurney (1969) found a hyperbolic relationship for taste thresholds of the

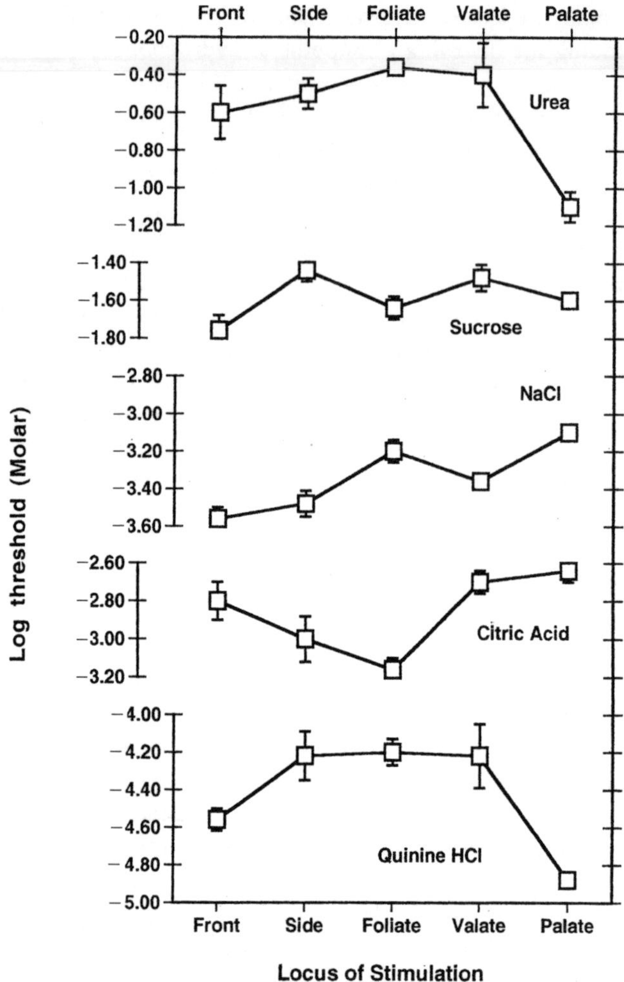

Figure 19.4. Taste recognition thresholds in different areas of the tongue and mouth. Note that as thresholds decline, sensitivity is increased. (From Collings (1974), with permission.)

form $C = k / (A^n)$, where C is the threshold concentration, A is the area and n is an exponent characteristic of a given chemical stimulus. Smith (1971) used a flow chamber to restrict the exposed area on the front of the tongue. He showed increasing intensity with increasing area with approximately the same characteristic area exponent across different taste compounds. Across small areas on the tongue there is considerable spatial summation. However, a different picture of inhibitory interactions emerges when more widely dispersed gustatory areas are stimulated. When the chorda tympani is anesthetized, taste intensity of quinine is enhanced in posterior regions subserved by the glossopharyngeal nerve (Lehman, Bartoshuk, Catalanotto, Kveton, & Lolicht, 1995; Yanigasawa, Bartoshuk, Catalanotto, Karrer, & Kveton, 1998). This suggests a central inhibitory interaction between anterior and posterior oral taste zones. Contralateral inhibition has also been observed between the two sides of the tongue for sweet and bitter substances (Kroeze & Bartoshuk, 1985; Lawless, 1978). An inhibitory interaction between the back and front of the tongue, coupled with Collings's observation of steeper bitter functions on the circumvallate papillae, may further explain the introspection that bitterness appears to be localized posteriorly.

Genetic Factors and PTC/PROP Bitterness Differences

For bitter compounds, there are wide individual differences in taste sensitivity. The best example is the genetically inherited insensitivity to compounds containing the functional group $-N-C=S$ typified by certain aromatic thiourea compounds. This taste "blindness" was primarily studied using the compound phenylthiourea, originally called phenylthiocarbamide or PTC (Blakeslee, 1932; Fox, 1932). Due to the potential toxicity of PTC as well as its tendency to give off an odor, more recent studies have used the compound 6-n-propylthiouracil (PROP) which is highly correlated with PTC response (Lawless, 1980). The minimum detectable concentrations (thresholds) of these compounds, PTC and PROP, follow a bimodal distribution, with about one-third of Caucasian persons unable to detect the substance until it is a hundred or a thousand-fold higher than the mean concentration detected by the majority. Threshold tests as well as ratings for bitterness above threshold (Lawless, 1980) both allow differentiation into "taster" (sensitive) and "nontaster" (insensitive) groups. Nontasters are most likely homozygous recessive individuals for a single gene, demonstrating a simple Mendelian pattern of inheritance. Other bitter substances such as quinine show wide variation, but none so dramatic as PTC and related compounds. The mechanism for PTC tasting appears to be a different bitter receptor process from that of other bitter compounds (Lawless, 1979b). The possibility of multiple mechanisms contributing to a single taste category like bitterness is contrary to the notion of four simple taste primaries. Recent studies have proposed a third classification of hypersensitive groups of "supertasters." Counts of papillae and taste buds are correlated with taster status (Miller & Bartoshuk, 1991), providing evidence of an anatomical determinant of these differences among individuals. Persons who are insensitive to PTC will not show some mixture suppression effects (discussed in the section on Mixture Effects, Inhibition and Synergy, below). Because they perceive no bitterness, there is no inhibition (Lawless, 1979a). Thus, depending upon what we *don't* sense in a product, the balance of flavors in a product may shift.

Relationships of various bitter substances to the PTC/PROP effect and the potential overlap of bitter taste mechanisms have been studied in three ways. One approach has been to classify taster and nontaster groups, and then see if they show differences in response to another test compound. For example, PTC tasters show higher response to the bitterness of caffeine and saccharin at some concentrations (Bartoshuk, 1979; Hall, Bartoshuk, Cain, & Stevens, 1975). This would imply that caffeine, for example, could stimulate the PTC/PROP receptor mechanism, as well as others. The approach thus uses genetic classification as a means to study bitter receptor mechanisms via psychophysical methods. In general, these taster-nontaster differences are small effects at low concentrations. The significance of taster-nontaster differences in everyday food flavor perception is unclear, and some differences have been difficult to reproduce (Mattes & Labov, 1989; Schifferstein & Frijters, 1991). One problem is whether general taste sensitivity factors (influences of aging, disease, medications, nutrition, general health, etc.) can be contributing to the observed group differences. Common controls for overall taste responsiveness in comparisons of PTC taster groups are cross-referencing to salt sensitivity or cross-modality matching to the loudness of tones, but it not clear that these approaches adequately eliminate an overall responsiveness factor from the picture.

A second approach to studying the potential overlap in mechanisms across compounds is cross-adaptation, discussed further below. In a cross-adaptation paradigm, the receptors are exposed to one compound and then a second test compound is presented. If the second compound has reduced taste intensity relative to its response following water adaptation (an important baseline condition) then some overlap in peripheral mechanisms of stimulation, possibly even common receptors, is expected. For bitter compounds, there is good differentiation of PTC responses from quinine responses, that is, little or no cross-adaptation (Lawless, 1979b; McBurney, Smith, & Shick, 1972). The third approach to examination of overlap in mechanisms is to examine response correlations. For example, do people who have high thresholds for one compound tend to have high thresholds for another? Using this approach, the multiplicity of bitterness mechanisms and independence of PTC sensitivity from sensitivity to other compounds has been supported (Yokomukai, Cowart, & Beauchamp, 1993). Strong individual differences were noted for quinine and urea sensitivity, but no correlation was observed in thresholds for PTC, caffeine, sucrose octa-acetate (SOA), or $MgSO_4$. Above threshold, responsiveness was correlated among quinine, caffeine and SOA. Correlation results are consistent with the picture from cross-adaptation studies. There are at least two mechanisms for bitter tasting, one related to PTC and one to quinine, while a third mechanism typified by urea and bitter salts is also possible. No relationship of PTC status to isohumulone sensitivity is found, suggesting that the compounds that give beer its bitter taste should belong in the quinine category (Mela, 1990). Different aging patterns for urea and quinine sensitivity have been used as further evidence of different physiological reception/transduction mechanisms (Cowart, Yokomukai, & Beauchamp, 1993).

Taste Qualities

Four or More Taste Categories?

Various perceptual qualities have been proposed as taste descriptions throughout history (Bartoshuk, 1978) but the consistent theme is that four qualities suffice for most purposes. These are the classical taste qualities of sweet, salty, sour, and bitter. Other proposed tastes include metallic, astringent, and umami. Umami is an oral sensation stimulated by monosodium glutamate. Astringency is a chemically induced complex of tactile sensations. The metallic taste is little understood although it is occasionally used to describe the side tastes of sweeteners such as acesulfam-K and is a descriptor used in certain pathological recurrent phantom taste disorders (Lawless & Zwillinberg, 1983) and burning mouth syndromes

(Grushka & Sessle, 1991). There are ongoing controversies about whether the classical four taste qualities are sufficient to describe all taste sensations (O'Mahony & Ishii, 1986). However, they can be used to characterize most taste experiences as is common in industrial sensory testing.

McBurney and Gent (1979) reviewed several arguments for the existence of four categorical taste qualities. They conceptualized the qualities as interacting submodalities, much like the modalities of temperature, touch, pressure, and pain within the skin senses. Introspection reveals that the four or five qualities are distinct experiences. The study of taste psychophysics and the understanding of functional processes like adaptation and mixture interactions have been advanced under paradigms in which taste responses are described using the classical four qualities. For example, cross-adaptation experiments using prototypical stimuli representing the four tastes have provided evidence that the physiological mechanisms underlying the four qualities are independent channels, although with the possibility that sweetness and bitterness have multiple channels within each category (discussed below). Equally important is the observation that taste mixtures can be readily described by four or five terms alone or in combination (Bartoshuk, 1975). This implies that no new or emergent qualities arise when prototypical substances are mixed. While there is a certain circularity in the use of four taste words as responses in experiments to substantiate this conceptualization, the system seems to work. However, others argue that taste qualities perceptually fuse in mixtures (McBurney, 1986), or that new singular qualities arise (Erickson, Priolo, Warwick, & Schiffman, 1990).

The notion of primary or basic tastes is not without its contestants, who view the evidence for basic tastes as circular, not in keeping with experimental observations and even biased (Halpern, 1997). One alternative view states that the four taste qualities are merely reference points on a continuum of taste experience (Schiffman & Erickson, 1980). Four response categories are insufficient to capture the groupings people make of diverse taste stimuli (Ishii & O'Mahony, 1987). However, that experiment included several substances commonly thought of as savory or umami in flavor. Furthermore, the use of duplicate words to describe some categories does not negate the within-category similarity nor the between-category distinctiveness. For example, some people claim they can distinguish intensive sweeteners such as aspartame from carbohydrate sweeteners like sugars. However, such discrimination, if possible, does not mean that sweetness as a category is not a useful concept, only that there is some perceptual variation within the category of those things termed sweet. Discrimination experiments have shown that acids can not be discriminated once intensities have been equated (Breslin & Beauchamp, 1995a). As Delwiche (1996) noted in a recent review of this controversy, there is no better alternative at this time to a four or five category system of describing taste experience.

The Umami Controversy

The umami sensation, roughly translated from Japanese as "delicious taste," is attributed to the taste of monosodium glutamate (MSG) and ribosides such as salts of 5' inosine monophosphate (IMP) and 5' guanine monophosphate (GMP) (Karamura & Kare, 1987). In my experience, glutamate salts and the ribosides produce a mouth-filling sensation that seems partly tactile in nature. The sensation is distinguishable from that of saltiness, as direct comparison with equally intense NaCl solutions clearly demonstrates. The sensation is perhaps best rendered in English by the term "brothy" due to its resemblance to the taste of protein-rich soup stocks. "Savory" or "meaty" are alternatives, as MSG-related sensations form part of the savory class of flavors (Nagodawithana, 1995). Whether the sensation is merely a complex of more basic taste sensations or is justified as a separate category of experience in its own right is a matter of some controversy. The taste properties of glutamate and aspartate salts form the building blocks of flavor principles in some ethnic (notably Asian) cuisines, so perhaps it is not surprising that Japanese, for example, have no difficulty in using this taste term (O'Mahony & Ishii, 1986). Occidental subjects, on the other hand, seem to be able to fractionate the taste of MSG into the traditional four categories (Bartoshuk et al., 1974). From an ecological perspective, it would be surprising if omnivorous humans lack a receptor process to signal the presence of a category of important nutrients (amino acids) while other species have been shown to possess receptors for glutamate (Scott & Plata-Salaman, 1991).

Cross-Adaptation and Modalities Within Modalities

One early source of evidence for the notion that there were at least four independent sensory channels within the sense of taste came from psychophysical experiments on cross-adaptation. Adaptation is a decrease in the responsiveness of the taste system under conditions of constant stimulation. One approach to assessing the overlap vs. independence of mechanisms giving rise to different taste qualities is cross-adaptation. In this paradigm, the usual approach is to adapt the tongue to one of the prototypical substances (i.e., a chemical that is mostly sweet, or salty, etc.) and see if a second substance is also decreased in its response. It is expected that substances within the same taste quality category will cross-adapt one another assuming they share common reception and transduction mechanisms and that chemicals of differing taste qualities (and different underlying mechanisms) will be unaffected. This is the predominant pattern of results, with some qualifications. The first problem arises in that most chemicals are not monogustatory from the point of view of possessing only one of the classical taste qualities. So many salts are bitter as well as salty. This leads to a situation in which adaptation to sodium chloride will not fully cross-adapt other salts, because of their non-salty side tastes. However, adaptation to sodium chloride effectively reduces the saltiness of other salts (Smith & McBurney, 1969). Similarly, adaptation to sucrose reduces the sweetness of most sweet substances (McBurney, 1972). So the perceptual task must involve a profiling of the individual taste qualities in order to see this result. Simple estimation of the overall taste intensity will not show the pattern.

Conversely, looking at other prototypical classic tastants (salt, acid, quinine) reveals a pattern of little or no cross-adaptation between the modalities, implying independent physiological mechanisms at the periphery (McBurney & Bartoshuk, 1973). Note that this paradigm requires several tests to establish the importance of a finding of no cross-adaptation. This is essentially a null effect, and failures to reject the null are rarely conclusive. To lend credence to this finding, two other effects must be demonstrated (Lawless & Stevens, 1983). First, the adapting efficiency of the first stimulus must be demonstrated by self-adaptation. Second, the susceptibility of the second substance to self-adaptation under the experimental conditions must also be demonstrated. When both of these findings are obtained, that is, that the first stimulus is an effective adapter and the second is a potential adaptee, then the result of no cross-adaptation becomes meaningful.

However, the pattern of independent taste qualities and full cross-adaptation within a category was challenged when further work was done on a greater number of taste stimuli and fully reciprocal patterns were examined. Lawless and Stevens (1983) and Schiffman, Cahn, and Lindley (1981) found patterns of asymmetric cross-adaptation among sucrose and intensive sweeteners. As noted above, McBurney et al. (1972) and Lawless (1979b) had found asymmetric cross-adaptation among PTC and other bitter substances. These studies provide psychophysical evidence that there might be multiple receptors and/or multiple mechanisms for transduction of sweet and bitter taste. This is consistent with the evidence for multiple intracellular transduction mechanisms for sweet and bitter, as discussed earlier (Brand, 1997; Spielman, Huque, Whitney, & Brand, 1992).

Neural Coding: Ensembles or Labeled Lines?

In parallel to the question of taste quality categories vs. a continuum, physiological theorists have developed two opposing views of how taste quality is encoded in the afferent pathways. The debate has grown around several key experimental observations. The first was the observation that the primary afferent neurons in the chorda tympani of the rat were somewhat broadly tuned in the sense that they responded to multiple chemical stimuli such as salts and acids that cut across the traditional introspective categories of four basic tastes (Frank, 1973; Pfaffman, 1941). This led early workers such as Pfaffman and Erickson (1963) to propose that taste quality was encoded as an across-fiber pattern. The across-fiber similarities among compounds were able to predict generalization in an avoidance paradigm as well as human psychophysical data on taste similarity (Schiffman & Erickson, 1971).

However, even from the beginning of recordings from taste neurons, researchers had attempted to classify neurons into response groups (Frank, Beiber, & Smith, 1988). Frank (1973) noted that afferent fibers tend to have a best response to one of the four commonly used tastants. This supported an older notion of Zotterman's that taste quality information might be carried in terms of the activity of a fiber that is characterized by its best stimulus. This has come to be known as the labeled line theory. Current thought (reviewed by Smith & Vogt, 1997) has it that even though there may be neuron types, the activity in one neuron type alone is insufficient to allow for taste discrimination. They proposed that it is the relative activity across broadly tuned neuron types that allows for taste qualities to be discerned in an analogy similar to the color coding in the peripheral visual system in which three broadly tuned cone pigments give rise to four focal colors. Recent work with primates suggests the existence of four distinct classes, sucrose-best, NaCl-best, HCl-best, and quinine-best fibers (Sato et al., 1975, 1994). By calling them "best" there is the acknowledgement that the cell may respond to many chemicals, but that sucrose is particularly efficient. This classification is consistent with a mechanism for taste quality experience based encoding in a set of labeled lines of specific fiber types. The presence of a given taste quality from the classical quartet would be signaled by a high level of activity in the labeled line associated with that quality of taste. In support of the notion of distinct and functional fiber groupings, Jacobs, Mark, and Scott (1988) found sodium deprivation to decrease the sensitivity of sodium-best neurons in the rat medulla, but not other fiber types.

It is possible to find correlations between across-fiber patterns and taste similarities when the patterns contain such fiber groups (Smith, Van Buskirk, Travers, & Beiber, 1983). So either theory can fit the correlational evidence. Smith et al. used multidimensional scaling of neural responses to generate a spatial model of taste similarities. The model showed a good grouping of sweet molecules when sucrose-best fibers in the hamster brain stem were included in the data set. Deletion of these fibers from the input data (a sort of statistical ablation experiment) caused the sweet compounds to lose their group identity and disperse throughout the space. This is consistent with requiring the information present in sucrose-best fibers to perceive the similarities among sweet compounds and their distinctiveness from other taste qualities. A similar result was found for acid-best fibers but not for salt-specific neurons.

At this time the resolution of this debate is not clear and may be clouded by species differences. However, most work with primates appears to support the existence of specific fiber groups. Furthermore the specificity of transduction mechanisms and drug effects on specific fiber categories (Scott & Giza, 1990) are consistent with a specificity theory. It is also possible that general taste qualities are determined by groups while variations within or between groups may render some sense of nuance or quality variation within the category (Scott & Plata-Salaman, 1991). Not all sweet molecules have exactly the same taste as shown in cross-adaptation studies (Lawless & Stevens, 1983).

Taste Perception

Mixture Effects, Inhibition and Synergy

The sense of taste has two important functional properties: mixture interactions and adaptation. Mixtures of different tastes show partially inhibitory or masking interactions. Thus a solution of quinine and sucrose is less sweet than an equal concentration of sucrose tasted alone (i.e., when the sucrose in the two solutions is in equimolar concentration). Similarly the mixture is less bitter than equimolar quinine tasted alone. The general pattern is that all four classical taste qualities show this inhibitory pattern, commonly called mixture suppression (Bartoshuk, 1975). In many foods these interactions are important in determining the overall appeal of the flavors and how they are balanced. For example, in fruit beverages and wines, the sourness of acids can be partially masked by sweetness from sugar. The sugar thus serves a dual role – adding its own pleasant taste while decreasing the intensity of what could be an objectionable level of sourness (Lawless, 1977). Some of these mixture inhibition effects, like the inhibition of bitterness by sweetness, appear to reside in the central nervous system (Lawless, 1979a) while others, such as the inhibition of bitterness by salt, are more likely due to peripheral mechanisms at the receptor level (Breslin & Beauchamp, 1995b; Kroeze & Bartoshuk, 1985).

There are a few exceptions to the pattern of inhibition where hyperadditive relationships, sometimes called enhancement or synergism occur. Claims of hyperadditive effects imply that there is a higher taste intensity in the mixture than would be predicted on the basis of simple addition of component effects. However, how this addition is actually performed and how the mixture outcome is to be modeled or predicted is a matter of some controversy (Ayya & Lawless, 1992; Frank, Mize, & Carter, 1989). The most well-known claim of synergy is the interaction of MSG with the ribosides responsible for umami taste mentioned above. These are clearly hyperadditive by any definition. Addition of even small subthreshold amounts in mixtures will produce strong taste sensations (Yamaguchi, 1967). Binding enhancement at taste receptors could provide the physiological substrate for this effect (Cagan, 1981).

A second area of enhancement is seen with sweetness from salt in low concentrations added to sugar. NaCl has an intrinsic sweet taste that is normally masked by the saltiness at higher levels (Murphy, Cain, & Bartoshuk, 1977). So the small increase in sweetness noted with addition of NaCl is due to this intrinsic sweet taste of dilute NaCl. This may explain the beneficial effects of small amounts of salt in foods, or effects like the improvement in the taste of melons with light salting. Synergy or hyperadditivity is observed for some sweetener mixtures, although the methods of comparison are themselves the point of some debate (Frank et al., 1989; Lawless, 1998). Nonetheless the search for synergistic mixtures of sweeteners is an ongoing topic, due to potential cost savings in the multi-billion dollar food ingredient business.

Taste Adaptation and Water Tastes

Adaptation can be defined as a decrease in responsiveness under conditions of constant stimulation. It is a property of most sensory systems as they act to alert an organism to changes; the status quo is rarely of interest. We become largely unaware of the ambient level of stimulation, especially in the chemical, tactile, and thermal senses. After putting on your socks, you don't think much anymore about how they feel. Likewise placing your foot in a hot bath can be alarming at first, but the skin senses adapt. Our eyes adjust to ambient levels of light, as we notice upon entering a dark movie theater. Adaptation is easily demonstrated in taste if a constant stimulus can be maintained on a controlled area of the tongue. This was often done in laboratory experiments where a solution would be flowed over the extended tongue or through a chamber around the tongue (Kroeze, 1979; McBurney, 1966). Under these conditions, most taste sensations will disappear in a minute or two. We are generally unaware of the sodium in our saliva, but rinsing the tongue with deionized water and re-presenting that concentration of NaCl will produce a sensation above threshold. However, when the stimulus is not so neatly controlled, as in eating, drinking, or in pulsatile stimulation, the tendency for taste to adapt is less robust and may disappear entirely (Halpern et al., 1986; Meiselman & Halpern, 1973).

One other important discovery accompanied the early flow experiments on taste adaptation. These investigators noticed that concentrations below the adapting level – of which pure water was the extreme example – would take on other taste qualities. Thus water after salt adaptation tastes sour or bitter to most people. Water tastes sweet after quinine or acid

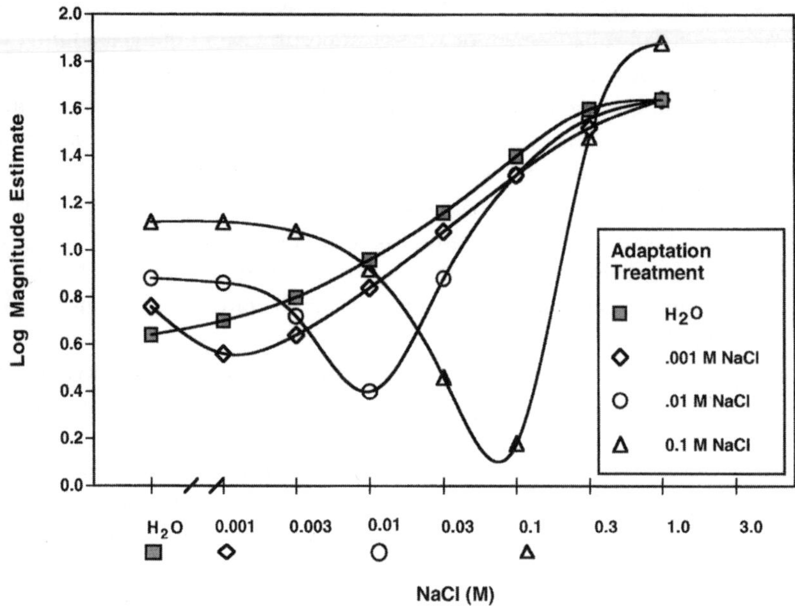

Figure 19.5. Taste and water taste of NaCl following different adapting concentrations. Symbols below the concentration axis show the concentrations of the adapting solutions. Below the adapting concentration the modal response is sour or bitter, reaching a maximum with water. Note that the functions appear to steepen above the adapting point, reminiscent of a recruitment phenomenon and suggesting sharper intensity discrimination around the adapting point. (From McBurney, copyright © 1966 by the American Psychological Association. Reprinted with permission.)

and tastes bitter after sucrose (McBurney & Shick, 1971). Figure 19.5 shows the response to concentrations of NaCl after different adaptation conditions. Above the adapting concentration, there is a salty taste. At the adapting concentration, there is little or no taste. Below the adapting concentration the taste is characterized as a sour-bitter taste. The sour-bitter taste is strongest when water itself is presented after salt adaptation. Water can take on any one of the four qualities, depending upon what has preceded it. Both the diluent and taste molecules themselves can elicit sensory responses.

Release From Inhibition Effects

How are mixture interactions changed when one of the components is subject to adaptation? This has been studied extensively in two component mixtures of sweet and salty tastes (Kroeze, 1979) and sweet and bitter tastes (Lawless, 1979a). In mixtures of sucrose and quinine, both the sweetness of sucrose and the bitterness of quinine are partially suppressed when present in a mixture. After adaptation to sucrose, the bitterness of a quinine/

sucrose mixture rebounds to the level it would be perceived at in an equimolar unmixed quinine solution. Likewise the sweetness rebounds after the bitterness is reduced by adaptation to quinine. This rebound is called release from suppression (Figure 19.6). Release effects are quite common in everyday eating. They can be observed during a meal with wines, as wines are primarily sugar/acid (sweet/sour) taste mixtures. A wine will seem too sour after eating a very sweet dessert. Similarly, tasting a wine after eating a salad dressed with vinegar makes the wine seem too sweet and lacking in acid. These are simply the adapting effects of strong taste stimuli upon the components of the wine, decreasing some tastes and enhancing others through release from inhibition effects. Try eating chocolate after orange juice or drinking orange juice after chocolate. Each has a disruptive effect on the flavor balance of the other, due to release from suppression.

Breslin and Beauchamp (1997) noted a similar effect in complex taste mixtures containing salt and a bitter tastant. As noted above, evidence for bitterness suppression by sodium favors a peripheral mechanism probably at the level of gustatory receptors (Breslin & Beauchamp, 1995b; Kroeze & Bartoshuk, 1985). Salt-bitter suppression is occurring at a level in the incoming sensory channel that precedes the mechanism of sweet suppression by bitterness. Breslin and Beauchamp recognized that any reduction in bitterness due to a peripheral mechanism like salt addition should also enhance the level of sweetness in a three-way mixture of salt, sweet, and bitter. The apparent flavor enhancement by salt in mixtures with bitter tastes is analogous to a release from suppression effect. By inhibiting the inhibitor, a third taste quality can be increased in intensity.

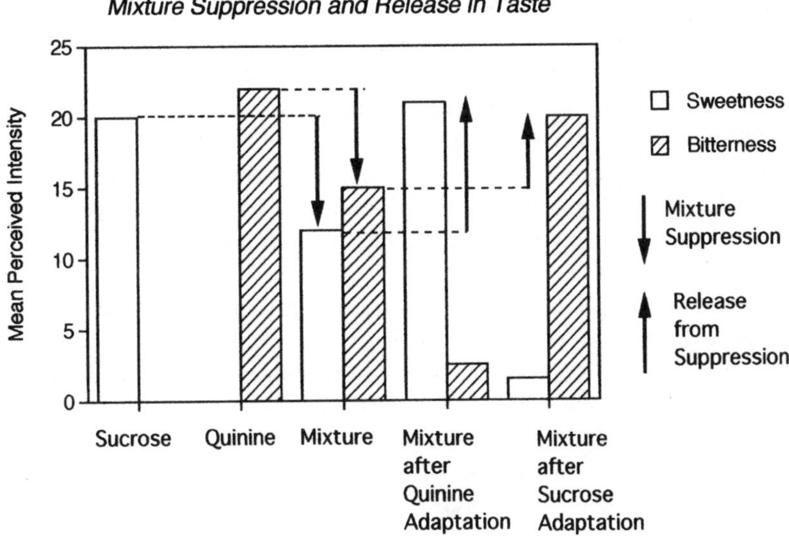

Figure 19.6. Mixture suppression and release effects in taste. Open bars indicate the sweetness of 0.32 M sucrose and hatched bars the bitterness of 0.0001 M quinine sulfate. In a mixture, both sensations are suppressed. After adaptation to one component, the other returns to its unmixed level, an effect termed "release from suppression." (From Lawless (1982).)

Temporal Factors: Reaction Times, Persistence After Stimulus Removal, Quality Over Time

The phenomenon of taste adaptation alerts us to the fact that taste responses are dynamic and temporally labile. Furthermore, taste receptors do not track stimulus onset and offset very closely. The system may continue to respond long after stimulus flow has ceased and response declines under conditions of constant stimulation. In one respect, this makes the sense of taste much more difficult to study than visual or auditory phenomena where stimulus control is easily achieved and sensory response is locked in close temporal contiguity to stimulus onset and cessation. On the other hand, these very temporal phenomena are worthy of study, part and parcel of defining the operating characteristics of the gustatory sense. In a system with built-in problems in effective stimulus onset and removal, it becomes critical to define the time of stimulus arrival if one is going to measure temporal phenomena. In using flow systems for gustatory psychophysics, this requires some "plumbing" with sensors near the tongue to indicate stimulus arrival. This can be achieved by using conductivity detectors near the tongue and using chemical stimuli with some ionic character capable of effecting a conductivity change compared with a deionized water pretreatment.

Given this kind of setup, some general observations about taste can be drawn. Compared with the visual and auditory senses, the gustatory sense is slow to react. Simple reaction times (detection) to moderate intensity stimuli are well over 1,000 msec for many substances (Halpern, 1991). Yet such generalizations ignore several salient stimulus variables that affect gustatory reaction time. Stimulus duration, concentration, and the response task can all affect gustatory reaction times. Simple reaction times for detection are fastest, followed by quality identification times, followed by magnitude estimation response times (Halpern, 1991). When tracking taste intensity using an analogue response device like a joystick the onset of response is similar to the simple detection reaction time, ranging between 500 and 1,000 msec under optimal conditions. However, these lower limits of response may not correspond very well to ecologically relevant situations of eating and drinking. Halpern (1997) points out that various studies of sipping and decisions to ingest vs. expectorate produce minimum durations of 1 to 2 seconds and up to 4 to 5 seconds of stimulation in some cases.

The converse of adaptation is taste persistence. Some taste sensations persist for a time, following expectoration or swallowing, especially noticeable with bitter substances and trigeminal irritants like hot pepper. In sensory evaluation of food flavors, a useful method is the continuous tracking of perceived intensity (Lee & Pangborn, 1986), an example of time-intensity scaling (TI) (Lawless & Heymann, 1997). The TI methods allow differentiation of subtle differences in the time course of the sensory experience that might not be evident from a single judgment of sensory intensity. Various parameters can be extracted from the individual curves such as time to maximum, total duration, area under the curve, and so on. Such time parameters are of great practical interest in flavor research. For example, it is widely believed that the more an intensive sweetener resembles sucrose in its TI profile, the more acceptable it will be to consumers.

Continuous tracking of perceived intensity has also found its way into the psychophysi-

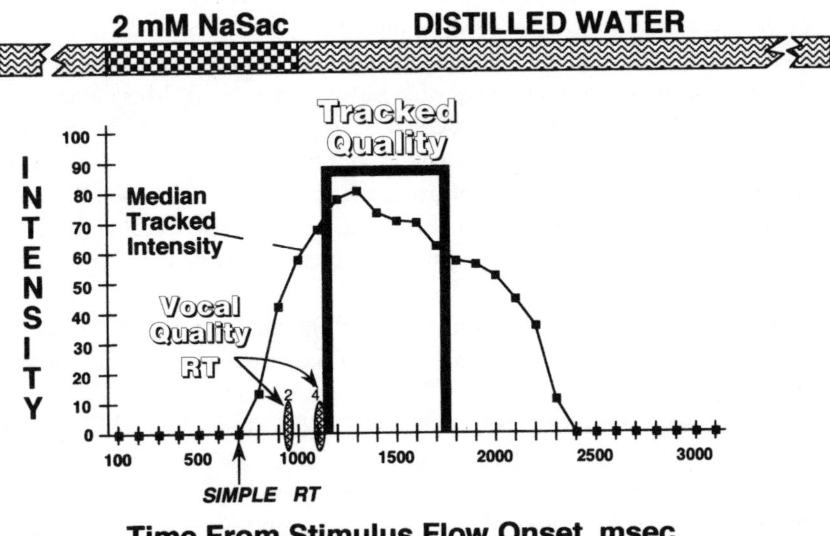

Figure 19.7. A comparison of tracked taste intensity, tracked taste quality, and vocal quality reaction times to 2 or 4 alternative experiments. The rectangle shows the time of mean onset, duration and offset of tracked quality response via a typewriter keyboard. Note the later onset and faster offset relative to the tracked intensity curve. Vertical ellipses marked "2" and "4" are vocal response times to taste quality from two studies with two or four stimulus alternatives. Responses are to 2 mM sodium saccharin flowed over the anterior dorsal tongue surface. (Reprinted from Halpern (1991, p. 91) by courtesy of Marcel Dekker, Inc.)

cal laboratory (Halpern, 1991; Kelling & Halpern, 1986, 1988; Zwillinger et al., 1991) with some curious results. When tastes are tracked for intensity, a typical curve is shown in Figure 19.7. The rectangle in this plot represents the response to tracked quality of 2 mM sodium saccharin. Note that the quality response starts later and ends sooner than the intensity record. This leads to the speculation that intensity perception is possible without knowing exactly what is being tasted, or that there is some general or a qualitative impression that accompanies some part of our taste experience.

Interactions With the Other Flavor Senses

Taste Perception and Olfactory Stimulation; Retronasal Smell Referred to Taste

Arguably, the largest contribution to the diversity of flavors comes from the volatile or airborne molecules sensed by the olfactory receptors. Whether sniffed through the external nares in the direction of normal inspiration or arising from odors present in the mouth, the vast diversity of what we come to know as food flavors is mediated by smell. Due to the tendency to localize aromatics from foods in the mouth, many people do not realize that the olfactory sense is responsible for sensing flavors other than the simple tastes described above. Much of what we normally speak of as taste is really smell (Murphy et al., 1977; Murphy & Cain, 1980). The lemon character of a lemon, for example, is derived not from lemon taste (which is only sour, sweet, and bitter) but from the terpene aroma compounds that arise in the mouth and pass up into the nasal cavity from the rear direction (retronasally), opposite to that from sniffing. This highlights the dual role of olfaction as both an external sensory system and an internal sensory system, attuned to volatile flavors present in the oral cavity (Rozin, 1982).

A simple demonstration can convince anyone of the importance of the orally derived smells, sometimes referred to as "retronasal" smell. Take a sip of a simple fruit beverage or juice while holding the nose pinched shut. Take care to note the sensations present in the mouth (the true sweet and sour tastes). Next swallow the sample and while keeping the mouth shut, release the nostrils and exhale (you must release the nose pinch, obviously, to exhale). In about a second or so, the fruit flavor will appear. Pinching the nose shut effectively blocks the retronasal passage of flavor volatiles up to the olfactory receptors (Murphy & Cain, 1980). When that route is facilitated by swallowing and exhaling, the contribution of smell becomes clear. The tendency of people to label retronasal smells as "tastes" probably contributes to the claims of sweetness enhancement by volatile flavors such as vanilla and maltol. This is a simple mislocation and mislabeling of the sensation.

Trigeminal Chemical Sensitivity; Oral Irritancy

In addition to the taste and smell systems for chemical sensation, there is a more generalized chemical sensitivity in the nose, mouth, the eyes, and over the whole body, a system recently termed "chemesthesis" in an analogy to somesthesis (Green & Lawless, 1991). An old Hungarian saying has it that the good paprika burns twice. Many common flavor experiences arise from stimulation of the trigeminal nerves in the mouth or nose – the fizzy tingle from carbon dioxide in soda, the burn from hot peppers, pungency from black pepper and from spices such as ginger and cumin, the nasal pungency of mustard and horseradish, the bite from raw onions and garlic, not to mention their lachrymatory effects.

The importance of chemesthesis is evident from both anatomical and economic considerations. One study found three times as many trigeminal fibers in the fungiform papillae of the rat as facial (taste) nerve fibers innervating taste buds (Farbman & Hellekant, 1978). Consideration of the trigeminal innervation of the fungiform papilla would suggest that it is more accurately classified as an organ for the perception of chili pepper than a gustatory sensor. Trigeminal fibers also ascend around the taste bud forming a chalice-like structure (Whitehead, Beeman, & Kinsella, 1985) perhaps using the specialized structure of the taste bud to enhance access to the external environment. This speculation is consistent with the observation of high responsiveness to pepper chemicals in areas such as the top of the tongue that are rich in fungiform papillae (Lawless & Stevens, 1988).

A great deal of the literature on human oral sensitivity to chemical irritants is devoted to controlled studies using the chili pepper compound, capsaicin, and to a lesser extent, the black pepper irritant, piperine (reviewed by Green & Lawless, 1991). The potency of capsaicin is noteworthy, with thresholds below 1 ppm. This is about 100 times as potent as piperine and other irritants. In pure form, capsaicin causes a warm or burning type of irritation with little or no apparent taste or smell (Lawless, 1984). The most obvious sensory characteristic of stimulation with the pepper compounds is their long-lasting nature. Stimulation with capsaicin, piperine, or ginger oleoresin at concentrations above threshold may last 10 minutes or longer (Lawless, 1984).

The temporal properties of capsaicin are complex. When stimulation is followed by a short rest period, a type of desensitization or numbing of the oral tissues sets in (Green, 1989). Application of capsaicin to the skin or oral epithelium has profound desensitizing effects (Jansco, 1960; Lawless & Gillette, 1985; Szolscanyi, 1977). This also occurs with systemic administration of capsaicin – animals injected with capsaicin become inured to chemical irritants (Burks, Buck, & Miller, 1985; Szolcsanyi, 1977). Desensitization effects are seen in repeated presentations in psychophysical studies and chronic desensitization occurs in people who consume chili peppers or spices derived from red pepper on a regular basis (Lawless, Rozin, & Shenker, 1985). Desensitization is believed to result from the depletion of substance P, a neurotransmitter in the somatic pain system. Substance P has also been linked to the functioning of endorphins (Andersen, Lund, & Puil, 1978). In contrast, when the rest period is omitted and stimulation proceeds in rapid sequences, the irritation continues to build to higher levels (Green, 1989; Stevens & Lawless, 1987). In addition to their numbing and sensitizing effects, irritant stimulation in the oral or nasal cavity evokes strong defensive reflexes in the body, including sweating, tearing, and salivary flow. There is a good parallel between the peak perceived intensity from scaling and the mean evoked salivary flow (Lawless, 1984), a useful correlation of "subjective" and objective measures of bodily response.

An unresolved question in the realm of chemical irritation is the degree to which different sensory qualities are evoked (Green & Lawless, 1991). This is difficult to study due to a lack of vocabulary to describe, at least in English, the experiences from pepper burn, CO_2, mustard, and so on. Experience with spices suggests that there are a variety of irritative flavor experiences and not all irritations are the same. Yet these differences could arise on the basis of intensity differences or from taste and odor properties, rather than from irritation per se. Studies of synergistic interaction in mixtures and potentiation with different irritants presented in rapid sequences are suggestive of the possibility of multiple receptor mechanisms for oral chemical irritation (Lawless & Stevens, 1989, 1990). So the anatomical substrate for different qualities (i.e., some non-overlapping receptor mechanisms) is present. Direct measurement of qualitative differences was attempted in a descriptive study by Cliff and Heymann (1992) using a variety of irritant flavor materials. They found evidence for differences in lag time (short vs. long onset) and burning vs. tingling sensations among the irritants tested.

In spite of its commercial importance, relatively little has been published on the perception of CO_2 in solution. Using the method of magnitude estimation, Yau and McDaniel (1990) examined the power function exponent for carbonation and found an unusually high value of about 2.4. The high exponent is consistent with good sensitivity to changes in carbonation level in the levels occurring in common beverages. Yau and McDaniel

(1991) also looked at the interaction of carbonation with different solution temperatures. A small increase in tactile intensity was noted at very low temperatures (3 to 10 °C), possible an example of Weber's illusion. Weber noted that a cold coin seemed heavier than a warm one. The general effect that cold things seem heavier suggests some overlap in nerve fibers subserving of cold and tactile sensory processes.

An area of some overlap between chemical and somatosensory function is the phenomenon of astringency. Tannins in foods are chemical stimuli, but they have tactile effects (ASTM, 1989; Bate Smith, 1954). Astringency is a group of chemically induced oral tactile sensations defined by Lee and Lawless (1991) as "A complex sensation combining three distinct aspects: drying of the mouth, roughing of oral tissues, and puckery or drawing sensations felt in the cheeks and muscles of the face." Multivariate analysis of scaling data supports the notion that these sub-qualities are independent sensory cues and separate from gustatory sensations such as sourness (Lawless & Corrigan, 1994).

These tactile effects of chemical stimuli may differ in important ways from true tastes and smells. For example, repeated stimulation with astringent substances tends to cause a buildup of tactile effects rather than a decrement as one might see in taste adaptation or capsaicin desensitization (Guinard, Pangborn, & Lewis, 1986). The mechanisms giving rise to astringency are poorly understood, but one longstanding theory has it that tannins bind to salivary proteins and mucopolysaccharides (slippery constituents of saliva), causing them to aggregate or precipitate, thus robbing saliva of its ability to coat and lubricate oral tissues (Clifford, 1986; McManus, Davis, Lilley, & Halsam, 1981). We feel this as rough and dry sensations on oral tissues, even when there is fluid in the mouth. Note that "roughness" and "dryness" are difficult to perceive unless a person moves the tongue against other oral tissues (as we do when eating). An active perceiver is required for astringency perception. Acids commonly thought of as prototypical sour stimuli are potent inducers of astringency (Rubico & McDaniel, 1992; Thomas & Lawless, 1995). This serves to remind us that any chemical placed in the oral cavity is likely to have multiple sensory effects, even if they are conceptualized as pure in taste.

Suggested Readings

Green, B. G., & Lawless, H. T. (1991). The psychophysics of somatosensory chemoreception in the nose and mouth. In T. V. Getchell, L. M. Bartoshuk, R. L. Doty, & J. B. Snow (Eds.). *Smell and taste in health and disease* (pp. 235–253). New York: Raven Press. [Provides an overview of the trigeminal and irritative chemical senses in the oral cavity.]

Halpern, B. P. (1997). Psychophysics of taste. In G. K. Beauchamp & L. M. Bartoshuk (Eds.), *Tasting and smelling* (pp. 77–123). San Diego: Academic Press. [Provides a good overview of several key issues, including issues of taste quality description, the importance of temporal properties of taste stimuli and laboratory vs. natural observations of taste phenomena.]

Lawless, H. T. (1996). Flavor. In E. C. Carterette & M. P. Friedman (Eds.), *Handbook of perception and cognition, vol. 16, cognitive ecology* (pp. 325–380). San Diego: Academic Press. [The sense of taste and smell within the larger context of flavor perception is discussed.]

Additional Topics

Development of Gustation and Olfaction

Like other neural systems, the chemical senses are not fixed at birth but undergo changes during maturation, show plasticity and effects of exposure to specific stimuli. Some loss of chemosensory function is found as people age. Developmental aspects of gustation and olfaction are discussed in Menella and Beauchamp (1997). This chapter includes a thorough discussion of the transmission of flavors in mother's milk. See also Chapter 21 in this volume by Werner and Bernstein. The effects of aging on chemical sense function are reviewed by Weiffenbach (1991).

Clinical Aspects of Taste and Smell Disfunction

Loss of chemosensory function as a result of disease, medication or therapy can change the quality of life and possibly have detrimental effects on nutritional intake. The development of clinical taste and smell research centers over the last two decades have enhanced our understanding of how taste and smell sensitivity can be impaired and the prospects for recovery. Clinical disorders of taste and smell are discussed by Cowart, Young, Feldman, and Lowry (1997). Further information on clinical problems can be found in the volumes edited by Getchell, Doty, Bartoshuk, and Snow (1991), Meiselman and Rivlin (1986), and Chapter 18 of this volume.

The Chemical Senses and Nutrition

Long considered the "gatekeepers of the alimentary tract," the senses of taste and smell are known to influence food choice and therefore nutritional status. However, this is a two-way street, and nutritional status can also influence chemosensory function. The interplay of the chemical senses and nutrition is reviewed by Friedman and Mattes (1991).

References

Andersen, R. K., Lund, J. P., & Puil, E. (1978). Enkephalin and substance P effects related to trigeminal pain. *Canadian Journal of Physiology and Pharmacology, 56*, 216–222.

Anderson, N. (1974). Algebraic models in perception. In E. C. Carterette & M. P. Friedman (Eds.), *Handbook of perception. II. Psychophysical judgment and measurement* (pp. 215–298). New York: Academic Press.

Arvidson, K. (1979). Location and variation in number of taste buds in human fungiform papillae. *Scandinavian Journal of Dental Research, 87*, 435–442.

ASTM (1989). Standard definitions of terms relating to sensory evaluation of materials and products. In *Annual book of ASTM standards* (p. 2). Philadelphia: American Society for Testing and Materials.

Ayya, N., & Lawless, H. T. (1992). Qualitative and quantitative evaluation of high-intensity sweeteners and sweetener mixtures. *Chemical Senses, 17*, 245–259.

Bartoshuk, L. M. (1975). Taste mixtures: Is mixture suppression related to compression? *Physiology and Behavior, 14*, 643–649.

Bartoshuk, L. M. (1978). History of taste research. In E. C. Carterette & M. P. Friedman (Eds.), *Handbook of perception. IVA, tasting and smelling* (pp. 2–18). New York: Academic Press.

Bartoshuk, L. M. (1979). Bitter taste of saccharin related to the genetic ability to taste the bitter substance 6-N-Propylthiouracil. *Science, 205*, 934–935.

Bartoshuk, L. M., Duffy, V. B., & Miller, I. J. (1994). PTC/PROP tasting: Anatomy, psychophysics and sex effects. *Physiology and Behavior, 56*, 1165–1171.

Bartoshuk, L. M., Murphy, C. L., & Cleveland, C. T. (1978). Sweet taste of dilute NaCl. *Physiology*

and Behavior, 21, 609–613.
Bartoshuk, L. M., Cain, W. S., Cleveland, C. T., Grossman, L. S., Marks, L. E., Stevens, J. C., & Stolwijk, J. A. (1974). Saltiness of monosodium glutamate and sodium intake. *Journal of the American Medical Association, 230*, 670.
Bate Smith, E. C. (1954). Astringency in foods. *Food Processing and Packaging, 23*, 124–127.
Beidler, L. M. (1954). A theory of taste stimulation. *Journal of General Physiology, 38*, 133–139.
Beidler, L. M. (1978). Biophysics and chemistry of taste. In E. C. Carterette & M. P. Friedman (Eds.), *Handbook of perception. IVA, tasting and smelling* (pp. 21–49). New York: Academic Press.
Birch, G. G., & Kemp, S. E. (1989). Apparent specific volumes and tastes of amino acids. *Chemical Senses, 14*, 249–285.
Birnbaum, M. H. (1982). Problems with so called "direct" scaling. In J. T. Kuznicki, A. F. Rutkiewic, & R. A. Johnson (Eds.), *Problems and approaches to measuring hedonics (ASTM STP 773)* (pp. 34–48). Philadelphia: American Society for Testing and Materials.
Blakeslee, A. F. (1932). Genetics of sensory thresholds: Taste for phenylthiocarbamide. *Proceedings of the National Academy of Sciences USA, 18*, 120–130.
Bradley, R. M. (1991). Salivary secretion. In T. V. Getchell, L. M. Bartoshuk, R. L. Doty, & J. B. Snow (Eds.), *Smell and taste in health and disease* (pp. 127–144). New York: Raven Press.
Brand, J. G. (1997). Biophysics of taste. In G. K. Beauchamp & L. M. Bartoshuk (Eds.), *Smelling and tasting* (pp. 1–24). San Diego: Academic Press.
Brand, J. G., Teeter, J. H., & Silver, W. (1985). Inhibition by amiloride of chorda tympani responses evoked by monovalent salts. *Brain Research, 334*, 207–214.
Breslin, P. A. S., & Beauchamp, G. K. (1995a). Weak acids are indiscriminable from one another and from HCl. *Chemical Senses, 20*, 670–671.
Breslin, P. A. S., & Beauchamp, G. K. (1995b). Suppression of bitterness by sodium: Variation among bitter taste stimuli. *Chemical Senses, 20*, 609–623.
Breslin, P. A. S., & Beauchamp, G. K. (1997). Salt enhances flavour by suppressing bitterness. *Nature, 387*, 563.
Burks, T. F., Buck, S. H., & Miller, M. S. (1985). Mechanisms of depletion of substance P by capsaicin. *Federation Proceedings, 44*, 2531–2534.
Cagan, R. H. (1981). Recognition of taste stimuli at the initial binding interaction. In R. H. Cagan & M. R. Kare (Eds.), *Biochemistry of taste and olfaction* (pp. 175–204). New York: Academic Press.
Cliff, M., & Heymann, H. (1992). Descriptive analysis of oral pungency. *Journal of Sensory Studies, 7*, 279–290.
Clifford, M. N. (1986). Phenol-protein interactions and their possible significance for astringency. In G. G. Birch & M. G. Lindley (Eds.), *Interactions of food components* (pp. 143–163). London: Elsevier.
Collings, V. B. (1974). Human taste response as a function of locus on the tongue and soft palate. *Perception & Psychophysics, 16*, 169–174.
Cowart, B. J., Yokomukai, Y. & Beauchamp, G. K. (1993). Development of bitter taste perception in humans. In G. K. Beauchamp (Ed.), *Kirin International Symposium on Bitter Taste, Physiology and Behavior, 56*, 1237–1241.
Cowart, B. J., Young, I. M., Feldman, R. S., & Lowry, L.D. (1997). Clinical disorders of smell and taste. In G. K. Beauchamp & L. M. Bartoshuk (Eds.), *Tasting and smelling* (pp. 175–198). San Diego: Academic Press.
Curtis, D. W., Stevens, D. A., & Lawless, H. T. (1984). Perceived intensity of the taste of sugar mixtures and acid mixtures. *Chemical Senses, 9*, 107–120.
Delwiche, J. (1996). Are there "basic" tastes? *Trends in Food Science & Technology, 7*, 411–415.
Diamant, H., Oakley, B., Strom, L., & Zotterman, Y. (1965). A comparison of neural and psychophysical responses to taste stimuli in man. *Acta Physiologica Scandinavica, 64*, 67–74.
Erickson, R. P. (1963). Sensory neural patterns in gustation. In Zotterman, Y. (Ed.), *Olfaction and taste* (pp. 205–213). New York: Pergamon.
Erickson, R. P., Priolo, C. V., Warwick, Z. R., & Schiffman, S. S. (1990). Synthesis of tastes other

than the primaries: Implications for neural coding and theories and the concept of "suppression." *Chemical Senses, 15*, 495–504.
Farbman, A. I., & Hellekant, G. (1978). Quantitative analyses of fiber population in rat chorda tympani nerves and fungiform papillae. *American Journal of Anatomy, 153*, 509–521.
Fazzalari, F. A. (Ed.) (1978). *Compilation of odor and taste threshold values data*, DS 48A. Philadelphia: American Society for Testing and Materials.
Fox, A. L. (1932). The relationship between chemical constitution and taste. *Proceedings of the National Academy of Sciences USA, 18*, 115–120.
Frank, M. E. (1973). An analysis of hamster afferent taste nerve response functions. *Journal of General Physiology, 61*, 588–618.
Frank, M. E., Beiber, S. L., & Smith, D. V. (1988). The organization of taste sensibilities in hamster chorda tympani nerve fibers. *Journal of General Physiology, 91*, 861–896.
Frank, R. A., Mize, S. J., & Carter, R. (1989). An assessment of binary mixture interactions for nine sweeteners. *Chemical Senses, 14*, 621–632.
Friedman, M. I., & Mattes, R. D. (1991). Chemical senses and nutrition. In T. V. Getchell, R. L. Doty, L. M. Bartoshuk, & J. B. Snow (Eds.), *Smell and taste in health and disease* (pp. 391–404). New York: Raven Press.
Getchell, T. V., Doty, R. L., Bartoshuk, L. M., & Snow, J. B. (1991). *Smell and taste in health and disease.* New York: Raven Press.
Green, B. G. (1989). Capsaicin sensitization and desensitization on the tongue produced by brief exposures to a low concentration. *Neuroscience Letters, 107*, 173–178.
Green, B. G., & Gelhard, B. (1989). Salt as an oral irritant. *Chemical Senses, 14*, 259–271.
Green, B. G., & Lawless, H. T. (1991). The psychophysics of somatosensory chemoreception in the nose and mouth. In T. V. Getchell, R. L. Doty, L. M. Bartoshuk, & J. B. Snow (Eds.), *Smell and taste in health and disease* (pp. 235–253). New York: Raven Press.
Green, B. G., Shaffer, G. S., & Gilmore, M. M. (1993). Derivation and evaluation of a semantic scale of oral sensation magnitude with apparent ratio properties. *Chemical Senses, 18*, 683–702.
Green, B. G., Dalton, P., Cowart, B., Shaffer, G., Rankin, K., & Higgins, J. (1996). Evaluating the "labeled" magnitude scale for measuring sensations of taste and smell. *Chemical Senses, 21*, 323–334.
Grushka, M., & Sessle, B. J. (1991). Burning mouth syndrome. In T. V. Getchell, R. L. Doty, L. M. Bartoshuk, & J. B. Snow (Eds.), *Smell and taste in health and disease* (pp. 665–682). New York: Raven Press.
Guinard, J.-X., Pangborn, R. M., & Lewis, M. J. (1986). The time course of astringency in wine upon repeated ingestion. *American Journal of Enology and Viticulture, 37*, 184–189.
Hall, M. L., Bartoshuk, L. M., Cain, W. S., & Stevens, J. C. (1975). PTC taste blindness and the taste of caffeine. *Nature, 253*, 442–443.
Halpern, B. P. (1991). More than meets the tongue: Temporal characteristics of taste intensity and quality. In H. T. Lawless & B. P. Klein (Eds.), *Sensory science theory and applications in foods* (pp. 37–105). New York: Marcel Dekker.
Halpern, B. P. (1997). Psychophysics of taste. In G. K. Beauchamp & L. M. Bartoshuk (Eds.), *Tasting and smelling* (pp. 77–123). San Diego: Academic Press.
Halpern, B. P., Kelling, S. T., & Meiselman, H. L. (1986). An analysis of the role of stimulus removal in taste adaptation by means of simulated drinking. *Physiology and Behavior, 36*, 925–928.
Heck, G. L., Mierson, S., & DeSimone, J. A. (1984). Salt taste transduction occurs through an amiloride-sensitive sodium transport pathway. *Science, 233*, 403–405.
Ishii, R., & O'Mahony, M. (1987). Taste sorting and naming: Can taste concepts be misrepresented by traditional psychophysical labelling systems? *Chemical Senses, 12*, 37–51.
Jacobs, K., Mark, G. P., & Scott, T. R. (1988). Taste responses in the nucleus tractus solitarius of sodium-deprived rats. *Journal of Physiology, 406*, 393–410.
Jansco, N. (1960). Role of the nerve terminals in the mechanism of inflammatory reactions. *Bulletin of Millard Fillmore Hospital*, Buffalo, 7, 53–77.
Kawamura, Y., & Kare, M. R. (Eds.) (1987). *Umami: A basic taste.* New York: Marcel Dekker.

Kelling, S. T., & Halpern, B. P. (1986). Physical characteristics of open flow and closed flow taste delivery apparatus. *Chemical Senses, 13*, 559–586.
Kelling, S. T., & Halpern, B. P. (1988). Taste judgments and gustatory stimulus duration: Taste quality, taste intensity and reaction time. *Chemical Senses, 11*, 89–104.
Kemp, S. E., Birch, G. G., Portmann, M. O., & Mathlouthi, M. (1990). Intrinsic viscosities and apparent specific volumes of amino acids and sugars. *Journal of the Science of Food and Agriculture, 51*, 97–107.
Kier, L. B. (1972). A molecular theory of sweet taste. *Journal of Pharmaceutical Sciences, 61*, 1394–1397.
Kroeze, J. H. A. (1979). Masking and adaptation of sugar sweetness intensity. *Physiology and Behavior, 22*, 347–351.
Kroeze, J. H. A., & Bartoshuk, L.M. (1985). Bitterness suppression as revealed by split-tongue taste stimulation in humans. *Physiology and Behavior, 35*, 779–783.
Lawless, H. (1977). The pleasantness of mixtures in taste and olfaction. *Sensory Processes, 1*, 227–237.
Lawless, H. T. (1978). *Evidence for neural inhibition in bittersweet mixtures.* Dissertation, Brown University, Department of Psychology.
Lawless, H. T. (1979a). Evidence for neural inhibition in bittersweet taste mixtures. *Journal of Comparative and Physiological Psychology, 93*, 538–547.
Lawless, H. T. (1979b). The taste of creatine and creatinine. *Chemical Senses, 4*, 249–252.
Lawless, H. T. (1980). A comparison of different methods for assessing sensitivity to the taste of phenylthiocarbamide PTC. *Chemical Senses, 5*, 247–256.
Lawless, H. T. (1982). Adapting efficiency of salt-sucrose mixtures. *Perception & Psychophysics, 32*, 419–422.
Lawless, H. T. (1984). Oral chemical irritation: Psychophysical properties. *Chemical Senses, 9*, 143–155.
Lawless, H. T. (1998). Theoretical note: Tests of synergy in sweetener mixtures. *Chemical Senses, 23*, 447–451.
Lawless, H. T., & Corrigan, C. J. (1994). Semantics of astringency. In K. Kurihara (Ed.), *Olfaction and taste XI. Proceedings of the 11th International Symposium on Olfaction and Taste and 27th Meeting, Japanese Association for Smell and Taste Sciences* (pp. 288–292). Tokyo: Springer-Verlag.
Lawless, H. T., & Gillette, M. (1985). Sensory responses to oral chemical heat. In D. D. Bills & C. J. Mussinan (Eds.), *Characterization and measurement of flavor compounds* (pp. 27–42). Washington, DC: American Chemical Society.
Lawless, H. T., & Heymann, H. (1997). *Sensory evaluation of food, principles and practices.* New York: Chapman & Hall.
Lawless, H. T., Horne, J., & Giasi, P. (1996). Astringency of acids is related to pH. *Chemical Senses, 21*, 397–403.
Lawless, H. T., Rozin, P., & Shenker, J. (1985). Effects of oral capsaicin on gustatory, olfactory and irritant sensations and flavor identification in humans who regularly or rarely consume chili pepper. *Chemical Senses, 10*, 579–589.
Lawless, H. T., & Stevens, D. A. (1983). Cross-adaptation of sucrose and intensive sweeteners. *Chemical Senses, 7*, 309–315.
Lawless, H. T., & Stevens, D. A. (1988). Responses by humans to oral chemical irritants as a function of locus of stimulation. *Perception & Psychophysics, 43*, 72–78.
Lawless, H. T., & Stevens, D. A. (1989). Mixtures of oral chemical irritants. In D. G. Laing, W. S. Cain, R. L. McBride & B. W. Ache (Eds.), *Perception of complex smells and tastes* (pp. 297–309). Sydney: Academic Press Australia.
Lawless, H. T., & Stevens, D. A. (1990). Differences between and interactions of oral irritants: Neurophysiological and perceptual implications. In B. G. Green & J. R. Mason (Eds.), *Chemical irritation in the nose and mouth* (pp. 197–216). New York: Marcel Dekker.
Lawless, H. T., & Zwillenberg, D. (1983). Clinical methods for testing taste and olfaction. *Transactions of the Pennsylvania Academy of Ophthalmology and Otolaryngology*, Fall, 190–196.

Lee, C. B., & Lawless, H. T. (1991). Time-course of astringent sensations. *Chemical Senses, 16*, 225–238.

Lee, W. E., & Pangborn, R. M. (1986). Time-intensity: The temporal aspects of sensory perception. *Food Technology, 40*(11), 71–77, 82.

Lehman, C. D., Bartoshuk, L.M., Catalanotto, F. C., Kveton, J. F., & Lolicht, R. A. (1995). Effect of anesthesia of the chorda tympani nerve on taste perception in humans. *Physiology and Behavior, 57*, 943–951.

Marin, A. B., Barnard, J., Darlington, R. B., & Acree, T. E. (1991. Sensory thresholds: Estimation from dose-response curves. *Journal of Sensory Studies, 6*(4), 205–225.

Marshall, J. M. (1994). Peripheral chemoreceptors and cardiovascular regulation. *Physiological Review, 74*, 543–594.

Mattes, R., & Labov, J. (1989). Bitter taste responses to phenylthiocarbamide are not related to dietary goitrogen intake in human beings. *Journal of the American Dietetic Association, 89*(5), 692–694.

McBride, R. L. (1987). Taste psychophysics and the Beidler equation. *Chemical Senses, 12*, 323–332.

McBurney, D. H. (1966). Magnitude estimation of the taste of sodium chloride after adaptation to sodium chloride. *Journal of Experimental Psychology, 72*, 869–873.

McBurney, D. H. (1969). A note on the relation between area and concentration in taste. *Perception & Psychophysics, 6*, 250.

McBurney, D. H. (1972). Gustatory cross adaptation between sweet tasting compounds. *Perception & Psychophysics, 11*, 225–227.

McBurney, D. H. (1986). Taste, smell and flavor terminology: Taking the confusion out of fusion. In H. L. Meiselman & R. S. Rivlin (Eds.), *Clinical measurement of taste and smell* (pp. 117–125). New York: Raven Press.

McBurney, D. H., & Bartoshuk, L. M. (1973). Interactions between stimuli with different taste qualities. *Physiology and Behavior, 10*, 1101–1106.

McBurney, D. H., Collings, V. B., & Glanz, L. M. (1973). Temperature dependence of human taste responses. *Physiology and Behavior, 11*, 89–94.

McBurney, D. H, & Gent, J. F. (1979). On the nature of taste qualities. *Psychological Bulletin, 86*, 151–167.

McBurney, D. H., & Shick, T. R. (1971). Taste and water taste of 26 compounds for man. *Perception & Psychophysics, 11*, 228–232.

McBurney, D. H., Smith, D. V., & Shick, T. R. (1972). Gustatory cross-adaptation, sourness and bitterness. *Perception & Psychophysics, 11*, 228–232.

McLaughlin, S. K., McKinnon, P. J., & Margolskee, R. F. (1992). Gustducin is a taste-cell-specific G protein subunit closely related to the a-transducins. *Nature, 357*, 563–569.

McManus, J. P., Davis, K. G., Lilley, T. H., & Halsam, E. (1981). Polyphenol interactions. *Journal of the Chemical Society, Chemical Communications*, 309–311.

Meiselman, H. L., Bose, H. E., & Nykvist, W. E. (1972). Effect of flow rate on taste intensity responses in humans. *Physiology and Behavior, 9*, 35–38.

Meiselman, H. L., & Halpern, B. P. (1973). Enhancement of taste intensity through pulsatile stimulation. *Physiology and Behavior, 11*, 713–716.

Meiselman, H. L., & Rivlin, R. S. (1986). *Clinical measurement of taste and smell.* New York: Macmillan.

Mela, D. J. (1990). Gustatory perception of isohumulones: Influence of sex and thiourea taster status. *Chemical Senses, 15*, 485–490.

Menella, J. A., & Beauchamp, G. K. (1997). The ontogeny of human flavor perception. In G. K. Beauchamp & L. M. Bartoshuk (Eds.), *Tasting and smelling* (pp. 199–221). San Diego: Academic Press.

Miller, I. J., & Bartoshuk, L. M. (1991). Taste perception, taste bud distribution and spatial relationships. In T. V. Getchell, R. L. Doty, L. M. Bartoshuk, & J. B. Snow (Eds.), *Smell and taste in health and disease* (pp. 205–233). New York: Raven Press.

Miller, I. J., & Spangler, K. M. (1982). Taste bud distribution and innervation on the palate of the rat. *Chemical Senses, 7,* 99–108.
Mistretta, C. M. (1991). Developmental neurobiology of the taste system. In T. V. Getchell, R. L. Doty, L. M. Bartoshuk, & J. B. Snow (eds.), *Smell and taste in health and disease* (pp. 35–64). New York: Raven Press.
Moskowitz, H. R. (1971). The sweetness and pleasantness of sugars. *American Journal of Psychology, 84,* 387–405.
Murphy, C., & Cain, W. S. (1980). Taste and olfaction: Independence vs. interaction. *Physiology and Behavior, 24,* 601–605.
Murphy, C., Cain, W. S., & Bartoshuk, L. M. (1977). Mutual action of taste and olfaction. *Sensory Processes, 1,* 204–211.
Murphy, C. L., Cardello, A. V., & Brand, J. G. (1981). Tastes of fifteen halide salts following water and NaCl: Anion and cation effects. *Physiology and Behavior, 26,* 1083–1095.
Murray, N. J., Williamson, M. P., Lilley, T. H., & Haslam, E. (1994). Study of the interaction between salivary proline-rich proteins and a polyphenol by 1H-NMR spectroscopy. *European Journal of Biochemistry, 219,* 923–935.
Nagodawithana, T. W. (1995. *Savory flavors.* Milwaukee, WI: Esteekay Associates.
Nilsson, B. (1977). Taste acuity of the human palate. *Acta Odontologica Scandinavica, 53,* 51–62.
O'Mahony, M., & Ishii, R. (1986). Umami taste concept: Implications for the dogma of four basic tastes. In Y. Kawamura & M. R. Kare (Eds.), *Umami: A basic taste* (pp. 75–93). New York: Marcel Dekker.
Pfaffman, C. (1941). Gustatory afferent impulses. *Journal of Cellular and Comparative Physiology, 17,* 243–258.
Pritchard, T. C. (1991). The primate gustatory system. In T. V. Getchell, R. L. Doty, L. M. Bartoshuk, & J. B. Snow (Eds.), *Smell and taste in health and disease* (pp. 109–125). New York: Raven Press.
Rozin, P. (1982). "Taste-smell confusions" and the duality of the olfactory sense. *Perception & Psychophysics, 31,* 397–401.
Rubico, S. M., & McDaniel, M. R. (1992). Sensory evaluation of acids by free-choice profiling. *Chemical Senses, 17,* 273–289.
Sato, M., Ogawa, H., & Yamashita, S. (1975). Response properties of macaque monkey chorda tympani fibers. *Journal of General Physiology, 66,* 781–810.
Sato, M., Ogawa, H., & Yamashita, S. (1994). Gustatory responsiveness of chorda tympani fibers in the cynomolgus monkey. *Chemical Senses, 19,* 381–400.
Schifferstein, H. N. J., & Frijters, J. E. R. (1991). The perception of the taste of KCl, NaCl and quinine HCl is not related to PROP sensitivity. *Chemical Senses, 16*(4), 303–317.
Schiffman, S. S., Cahn, H., & Lindley, M. G. (1981). Multiple receptor sites mediate sweetness: Evidence from cross-adaptation. *Pharmacology, Biochemistry and Behavior, 15,* 377–388.
Schiffman, S. S., & Erickson, R. P. (1971). A psychophysical model for gustatory quality. *Physiology and Behavior, 7,* 617–633.
Schiffman, S. S., & Erickson, R. P. (1980). The issue of primary tastes vs. a taste continuum. *Neuroscience and Biobehavioral Reviews, 4,* 109–117.
Scott, T. R., & Giza, B. K. (1990). Coding channels in the taste system of the rat. *Science, 249,* 1585–1587.
Scott, T. R., & Plata-Salaman, C. R. (1991). Coding of taste quality. In T. V. Getchell, R. L. Doty, L. M. Bartoshuk, & J. B. Snow (Eds.), *Smell and taste in health and disease* (pp. 345–368). New York: Raven Press.
Shallenberger, R. S., & Acree, T. E. (1967). Molecular theory of sweet taste. *Nature, 216,* 480–482.
Smith, D. V. (1971). Taste intensity as a function of area and concentration: Differentiation between compounds. *Journal of Experimental Psychology, 87,* 163–171.
Smith, D. V., & McBurney, D. H. (1969). Gustatory cross-adaptation: Does a single mechanism code the salty taste? *Journal of Experimental Psychology, 80,* 101–105.
Smith, D. V., Van Buskirk, R. L., Travers, J. B., & Beiber, S. L. (1983). Coding of taste stimuli by hamster brain stem neurons. *Journal of Neurophysiology, 50,* 541–558.

Smith, D. V., & Vogt, M. B. (1997). The neural code and integrative processes of taste. In G. K. Beauchamp & L. M. Bartoshuk (Eds.), *Tasting and smelling* (pp. 25–76). San Diego: Academic Press.

Spielman, A. I., Huque, T., Whitney, G., Brand, J. G. (1992). The diversity of bitter taste signal transduction mechanisms. In D. P. Corey & S. D. Roper, *Sensory transduction* (pp. 307–324). New York: Rockefeller University Press.

Stahl, W. H. (Ed.) (1973). *Compilation of odor and taste threshold values data.* Philadelphia: American Society for Testing and Materials.

Stevens, D. A., & Lawless, H. T. (1987). Enhancement of responses to sequential presentation of oral chemical irritants. *Physiology and Behavior, 39,* 63–65.

Streim, B. J., Yamamoto, T., Naim, M., Lancet, D., Jackinovich, W., & Zehavi, U. (1989). Sweet tastants stimulate adenylate cyclase coupled to GTP-binding protein in rat tongue membranes. *Biochemical Journal, 260,* 121–126.

Szolscanyi, J. (1977). A pharmacological approach to elucidation of the role of different nerve fibers and receptor endings in mediation of pain. *Journal of Physiology (Paris), 73,* 251–259.

Teeter, J. H., Kumazawa, T., Brand, J. G., Kalinowski, D. L., Honda, E., & Smutzer, G. (1992). Amino acid receptor channels in taste cells. In D. P. Corey & S. D. Roper (Eds.), *Sensory transduction* (pp. 291–306). New York: Rockefeller University Press.

Thomas, C. J. C., & Lawless, H. T. (1995). Astringent subqualities in acids. *Chemical Senses, 20,* 593–600.

Tinti, J.-M., & Nofre, C. (1991). Why does a sweetener taste sweet? A new model. In D. E. Walters, F. T. Orthoefer, & G. E. Dubois (Eds.), *Sweeteners, discover, molecular design and chemoreception* (pp. 206–213). Washington: ACS Books.

van der Heijden, A. (1993). Sweet and bitter tastes. In T. E. Acree & R. Teranishi (Eds.), *Flavor science: Sensible principles and techniques* (pp. 76–115). Washington, DC: ACS Books.

Weiffenbach, J. M. (1991. Chemical senses in aging. In T. V. Getchell, R. L. Doty, L. M. Bartoshuk and J. B. Snow (eds.), *Smell and taste in health and disease* (pp. 369–378). New York: Raven Press.

Whitehead, M. C., Beeman, C. S., & Kinsella, B. A. (1985). Distribution of taste and general sensory nerve endings in fungiform papillae of the hamster. *American Journal of Anatomy, 173,* 185–201.

Wong, G. T., Gannon, K. S., & Margolskee, R. F. (1996). Transduction of bitter and sweet tastes by gustducin. *Nature, 381,* 796–800.

Yamaguchi, S. (1967). The synergistic taste effect of monosodium glutamate and disodium 5' inosinate. *Journal of Food Science, 32,* 473–475.

Yamaguchi, S., & Kobori, I. (1994). Humans and appreciation of umami taste. In K. Kurihara (Ed.). *Olfaction and taste XI. Proceedings of the 11th International Symposium on Olfaction and Taste and 27th Meeting, Japanese Association for Smell and Taste Sciences* (pp. 353–356). Tokyo: Springer-Verlag.

Yanigasawa, K., Bartoshuk, L. M., Catalanotto, F. A., Karrer, T. A., & Kveton, J. F. (1998). Anesthesia of the chorda tympani nerve and taste phantoms. *Physiology and Behavior, 63,* 329–335.

Yau, N. J. N., & McDaniel, M. R. (1990). The power function of carbonation. *Journal of Sensory Studies, 5,* 117–128.

Yau, N. J. N., & McDaniel, M. R. (1991). The effect of temperature on carbonation perception. *Chemical Senses, 16,* 337–348.

Yokomukai, Y., Cowart, B. J. & Beauchamp, G. K. (1993). Individual differences in sensitivity to bitter-tasting substances. *Chemical Senses, 18,* 669–681.

Zwillinger, S. A., Kelling, S. T., & Halpern, B. P. (1991). Time-quality tracking of monosodium glutamate, sodium saccharin and a citric acid-saccharin mixture. *Physiology and Behavior, 49,* 855–862.

Chapter Twenty

Perceptual Development: Vision

Jane Gwiazda and Eileen E. Birch

Introduction

A recurring question posed by parents to pediatricians and vision researchers is, "What can my baby see?" With the vast amount of research on infant visual development accumulated over the past 25 years, we can now provide them with a reasonably complete account of what their infant can see at different ages, as described in this chapter. This summary shows that a remarkable amount of visual development occurs over the first year of life, but all visual functions do not mature at the same rate.

Although the developmental course of many visual functions is known, we still know little about the development of more global aspects of perception, such as object recognition and image segmentation. Further research, including consolidation and modeling of existing data, will be necessary to explain how the infant is able to integrate all of the low-level information into a coherent view of the world.

Methods for Measuring Infant Perception

Behavioral Techniques

Preferential Looking

Unbelievable as it may be to a new generation of vision researchers, many of the techniques in standard use today, both in the laboratory and the clinic, did not exist when they were infants. Preferential looking (PL) is one of the oldest and among the most widely used today. The technique is based on the observation that infants prefer some stimuli over others (e.g., stripes over plain gray). In the original preferential looking paradigm of Fantz (1961), an infant was given a choice between two stimuli varying along some dimension. The infant indicated its ability to differentiate between the two stimuli by looking more at one than the other. An observer, who was naïve as to the relative location of the stimuli, recorded the amount of time that the infant looked at one stimulus over another. Data obtained from this technique, based on time spent looking at a particular pattern, do not lend themselves to plots of individual psychometric functions.

Subsequently, Teller and colleagues (Teller, Morse et al., 1974) introduced adult psychophysics into the field of infant testing. The preferential looking technique was modified to include a two-alternative forced-choice paradigm for the observer's decision as to which of two stimuli the infant was fixating. Many trials were run per infant, such that individual psychometric functions could be plotted. Early studies using this procedure delineated the development of grating acuity, which is the spatial frequency of a high contrast grating that can just be resolved.

In order to measure grating acuity using preferential looking, a grating pattern is paired with an adjacent gray pattern matched in overall luminance. The side of presentation of the grating changes randomly from trial to trial, while the infant sits and gazes at the two patterns. An observer, unaware of what is being presented, watches the infant's head and eye movements and decides whether the infant prefers to look to the left or right. After a series of gratings covering a range of spatial frequencies is presented, the highest spatial frequency at which the infant looks on some criterion percentage of trials, often 75%, is taken as the acuity threshold. Usually at least 50 trials are required to get a threshold estimate. In addition to being used to measure grating acuity, the forced-choice preferential looking procedure (FPL) has been used to investigate the development of many of the visual functions discussed in this chapter.

A number of features of laboratory-based methods of assessing acuity make them impractical for use in a clinical setting. Paramount is the time it takes to run a sufficient number of trials for determination of a threshold. For a quick assessment of acuity that is often needed to make a clinical judgment, Teller Acuity Cards (TAC) were developed (McDonald, Dobson et al., 1985). The TAC procedure is similar to the standard PL procedure described above, but only one card is used for each spatial frequency, so the total test time is reduced to three to five minutes per eye. Although precise acuity thresholds cannot be obtained with so few trials, estimates from this quick procedure can be used in conjunction with other clinical tests to aid in making diagnoses and monitoring treatment.

Habituation

This technique is based on the observation that an infant's fixation of a particular stimulus tends to decrease over many trials, but recovers when a novel stimulus is presented. The decrease in looking time over trials is referred to as habituation, and the increase in looking time with the presentation of a novel stimulus is called dishabituation. If an infant cannot discriminate between the new and the old stimulus, then looking time to the new one will continue to drop with repeated trials. Habituation has proven to be a popular method, especially for studies of higher-order perception. One drawback of this method is that conclusions must be based on group averages due to the variability in individual infant's responses.

Monitoring Eye Movements

Infant eye movements can be used to assess basic visual functions such as acuity and contrast sensitivity. Optokinetic nystagmus (OKN) is the series of smooth eye movements elicited by a succession of objects passing across the visual field. The direction of OKN matches the direction of the stimulus. Early studies made use of subjective reports on the part of adult observers as to whether an infant exhibited OKN to a variety of stimuli, such as different size spheres or grating patterns. More recent OKN techniques have incorporated a two-alternative forced-choice paradigm. For example, eye movement voting (EMV) is a technique in which an observer, naïve with respect to stimulus conditions, votes on the direction of stimulus movement on each trial using information provided by a record of the subject's eye movements (Hainline, Abramov et al., 1987).

Electrophysiological Techniques

Electroretinograms

Electroretinograms (ERGs) are massed electrical signals generated by the retina in response to visual stimulation. Typically, ERGs are recorded using a bipolar corneal electrode, with a ground electrode located on the forehead. Signals are led from the electrodes to a differential preamplifier to boost signal amplitude and then averaged and digitally filtered by computer. ERGs are typically elicited by flashes of light or flickering light presented in a full-field (Ganzfeld) dome. Specialized ERG testing can also be conducted by using focal flashes of light to the macula (Sandberg, Jacobson et al., 1979), multifocal (Bearse & Sutter, 1996) or patterned stimuli (Arden & Wooding, 1985). The full-field ERG provides an objective measure of health and maturity of retinal elements, including the rod and cone photoreceptors and the inner retina; it is dominated by the mid-peripheral and peripheral retinal regions and is insensitive to immaturity or dysfunction in the macula.

A standard full-field ERG protocol for assessing rod- and cone-mediated function has been adopted by the International Society for Clinical Electrophysiology and Vision (ISCEV, 1995). This protocol consists of a rod response, a maximal response, oscillatory potentials, a cone response, and a flicker response. In addition, specialized protocols are available for isolating rod and cone function. Recently, protocols have been established for directly assessing the integrity and maturation of activation and deactivation stages of phototransduction using the a-wave of the ERG (Hood & Birch, 1993, 1994; Pepperberg et al., 1997). These protocols utilize quantitative models based on a comprehensive knowledge of the phototransduction cascade in isolated photoreceptors (Lamb & Pugh, 1992) to provide sensitivity, maximum response, and recovery of sensitivity of the photoreceptors. Developmental changes in photoreceptor sensitivity are likely to reflect lower quantal catch in infants and/or reduced gain of phototransduction. Developmental changes in the maximum amplitude are likely to reflect immaturities in the circulating current of the outer segment membrane. These include the number of mitochondria in the photoreceptors, the electrical resistance/leakage of the photoreceptor layer, permeability of the outer limiting membrane, and/or the density of light sensitive channels distributed along the outer segment membrane.

Visual Evoked Potentials

Visual evoked potentials (VEPs) are massed electrical signals generated by the occipital cortex in response to visual stimulation. VEPs differ from the electroencephalogram (EEG) in that the EEG derives from ongoing activity of many cortical areas while the VEP is primarily a specific occipital lobe response triggered by a visual stimulus. Thus, VEPs can used to assess the integrity or maturational state of the visual pathway in infants and preverbal children.

VEPs are recorded by placing one or more active electrodes over the occipital lobes and reference and ground electrodes elsewhere on the scalp. Signals are led from the electrodes to a bandpass differential preamplifier to boost amplitude and signal-to-noise ratio and then typically are averaged and digitally filtered by computer. There are two common types of visual stimuli used to elicit VEPs, light flashes and pattern contrast reversal. When light flashes or contrast reversals are presented infrequently (≤ 1/sec), the entire VEP waveform can be seen; this is called a *transient* response. When light flashes or contrast reversals are repeated frequently at regular intervals (≥ 10/sec), a simple periodic waveform can be recorded; this is called a *steady-state* response.

Flash VEPs. The transient luminance flash VEP is a complex waveform with multiple negative and positive voltage peaks. Recently, recommendations for standardized reporting of flash VEP responses have been made by the International Society for Clinical Electrophysiology and Vision (ISCEV, 1995). ISCEV proposed that peaks be designated as positive and negative in numerical sequence (P1, P2, . . . , and N1, N2 . . .). The most commonly reported amplitude is the N2-P2 peak-to-peak amplitude. Several source localization and intracortical recording studies suggest that the transient luminance flash VEP primarily reflects the activity of striate and extra-striate cortex (Ducati, Fava et al., 1988; Kraut, Arezzo et al., 1985; van der Marel, Dagnelie et al., 1984; Wilson, Babb et al., 1983). There are also some wavelets in the VEP which appear to be subcortical in origin; these wavelets are not major components of the flash VEPs of healthy infants but may be more prominent in pediatric patients for whom the cortical components of the VEP are missing (Ducati et al., 1988; Kraut et al., 1985; Schanel-Klitsch et al., 1987). Thus, the presence of a flash VEP response cannot be taken as unequivocal evidence for cortical function unless it can be established that the recorded response is not composed of subcortical wavelets.

Pattern Reversal VEPs. The transient pattern reversal VEP typically contains a small negative peak followed by a large positive peak and a second negative peak. ISCEV proposed that these components be termed N75, P100, and N135 to indicate their polarity and their approximate latency (in msec) in normal adults (ISCEV, 1995). The most commonly reported amplitude is the N75-P100 peak-to-peak amplitude. The steady-state pattern reversal VEP has a relatively simple, almost sinusoidal waveform; amplitude and phase of the response typically are reported. The majority of the pattern reversal VEP response is generated by the cortical projection of the macular area (central 6 to 8 degrees of the visual field. The pattern reversal VEP primarily reflects primarily the activity of striate cortex (Dagnalie, De Vries et al., 1986; Spekreijse, Dagnelie et al., 1985). There have been no reports of pattern reversal VEPs being recorded in newborns who lack functional striate and extra-striate cortex. Thus, the presence of a pattern reversal VEP response may be a good indicator of the integrity of cortical function.

Both transient and steady state pattern VEPs can provide a method for estimating visual acuity by examining the relationship between amplitude and pattern element size (Marg, Freeman et al., 1976; Sokol, 1978). Traditionally, responses to 4 to 6 pattern element sizes are recorded and linear regression of amplitude on pattern element size is used to extrapolate the pattern element size which corresponds to 0.0 μ V amplitude as the visual acuity estimate. More recently, a new "swept" approach to VEP assessment of infant acuity has been developed (Norcia, Sutter et al., 1985). The "swept" protocol presents 10–20 pattern reversal stimuli ranging from coarse to fine during a 10-second test period and uses Fourier analytic techniques to extract the response to each of the brief stimuli. The technique has significant advantages over more traditional methods. Test time is greatly reduced, the infant's behavioral state is less likely to change during the brief test session, and many more pattern element sizes can be included in the test protocol so that acuity estimates are more precise.

Development of Basic Visual Functions

Electrophysiological Responses to Light and Pattern

ERGs. Full-field ERGs to ISCEV standard maximum intensity bright flashes of white light have been recorded from preterm infants as early as 36 weeks PMA (post-menstrual age, used to correct for preterm birth) (Birch, Birch et al., 1990, 1992). The response shows considerable immaturity at 36 weeks PMA, both in terms of amplitude (1.1 log μV lower than adult values) and implicit time (23 msec slower than adult values). It rapidly matures, so that by 4 months post-term (57 weeks PMA), the amplitude is within 0.4 log μV of adult values and implicit time is within 12 msec of adult values. Cone responses recorded with an adapting background also mature early; by 4 months post-term amplitude is within 0.2 log μV of adult values. Cone responses to 30 Hz flicker are within 0.3 log μV of adult values by 4 months of age. The rod response to dim blue flashes of light matures later (Figure 20.1). At 36 weeks PMA amplitude is 1.7 log μV lower than adult values and, even at 4 months post-term, amplitude is 0.6 log mV lower than adult values. Using stimulus-response functions over a range of stimulus intensities to determine rod and cone thresholds, rod thresholds drop an average of 2.0 log units over the 5-month period between 36 weeks PMA and 4 months post-term age (Birch et al. 1992). This change reflects maturation of both sensitivity (log k) and the maximum response (log Vmax).

Analysis of the leading edge of the rod a-wave of infants shows that both sensitivity and the maximum saturated photoreceptor response increase over the first 4 months of life, but that sensitivity approaches adult-like values sooner than the maximum saturated photoreceptor response (Nusinowitz, Birch et al., 1998). To date, no focal or multifocal ERGs have been reported for the infant age range.

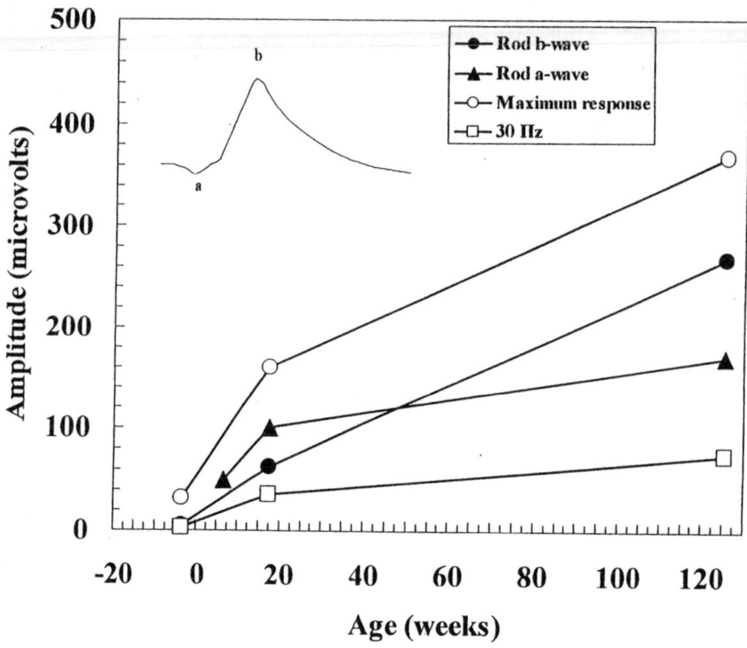

Figure 20.1. ERG waveform and changes in rod and cone parameters of the ERG as a function of age. Rod responses mature later than cone responses.

VEPs. Flash VEPs have been recorded from preterm infants as early as 24 weeks PMA. Typically, a single long latency (about 300 msec) negative peak is seen in the response, possibly N3 (Taylor, Menzies et al., 1987). The youngest infants reported to show a positive flash VEP peak (P2) were 32 weeks PMA (Ellingson, 1958, 1960). When present, the latency of the positive component decreases from about 220 msec at 34 weeks PMA to 190 msec at term, and to 120 msec by 52 weeks PMA (Ellingson, 1958, 1960). The P2 peak is present in the VEPs of healthy infants by 46 weeks PMA and its amplitude exceeds N3 amplitude by 48 weeks PMA (Ellingson, 1958, 1960; Ellingson, Lathrup et al, 1973). Changes in the waveform with age may reflect changes in alertness of the infants with age rather than visual development per se. There is a rapid increase in the amplitudes of most of the flash VEP peaks during early childhood, with the largest amplitudes present at about 6 years of age; amplitudes of the various peaks reach adult levels by about 16 years of age (Dustman, Schenckenberg et al., 1977). The maturational changes in amplitude, however, are only age trends as there are large individual differences in amplitudes within any given age group (Calloway & Halliday, 1973).

Transient pattern-reversal VEPs have been recorded from preterm infants as early as 30 weeks PMA (Grose, Harding et al., 1989; Harding, Grose et al., 1989). At this age, the pattern-reversal VEP to a coarse checkerboard has a simple waveform, consisting of a single positive peak with a latency of approximately 330 msec. Latency decreases to 240 msec by 40 weeks PMA and to 125 msec by 53 weeks PMA. Beyond 44 weeks PMA, the VEP waveform changes from a simple one to a more complex waveform with multiple peaks, and latency grows progressively shorter (Moskowitz & Sokol, 1983). Latency is dependent on pattern element size, with latency to large element patterns decreasing rapidly over the first months of life and latency for small element patterns decreasing more gradually (Moskowitz & Sokol, 1983; Porciatti, Vizzoni et al., 1982; Sokol, Moskowitz et al., 1987).

Steady-state pattern VEPs have been recorded from preterm infants as early as 35 weeks PMA when large pattern element sizes and relatively slow pattern alternation rates are used (Birch et al., 1990, 1992). As infants mature and their acuity increases, responses can be recorded to progressively smaller pattern element sizes and progressively faster pattern alternation rates (Porciatti, 1984; Birch et al., 1992).

Grating Acuity

Preferential Looking

The development of grating acuity using variations of preferential looking shows good agreement across laboratories, with estimates falling within an octave of each other, as shown in Figure 20.2 (Atkinson, Braddick et al., 1982; Birch & Hale, 1988; Gwiazda, Brill et al., 1980; Salamao, Berezovsky et al., 1997). Binocular acuity is approximately 1 cy/deg in the first month, increasing to around 9 to 12 cy/deg by one year, and achieving adult levels (30 cy/deg or 20/20 Snellen) at 3 to 4 years of age. A handy mnemonic is that age in months is approximately equal to acuity in cycles per degree.

Optokinetic Nystagmus

Optokinetic nystagmus (OKN) has been used to assess visual acuity much less frequently than preferential looking. OKN resolution of newborns is reported to be approximately 20 minutes, improving to 5 minutes by 6 months (Fantz, Ordy et al., 1962; Gorman, Cogan et al., 1957). In a recent study OKN was used to assess the monocular visual resolution of a large group of infants and toddlers (Lewis, Maurer et al., 1990). Results indicated that OKN bar resolution improved from 40 min at 2 months to at least 6 min (the smallest stimulus value) at 36 months, with a plateau in the second year. However, given the low estimates of visual resolution obtained with some OKN procedures and the relative ease of use of many current preferential looking procedures, OKN has not gained wide acceptance in either the laboratory or clinic.

VEP Acuity Development

Two classic studies of the maturation of VEP acuity during infancy were conducted during the mid-70s by Marg et al. (1976) and by Sokol (1978). From an initial acuity of approximately 20 minutes (20/400) soon after birth, visual acuity rapidly matures to near adult levels of 1 minute (20/20), as shown in Figure 20.2. These early studies of VEP acuity

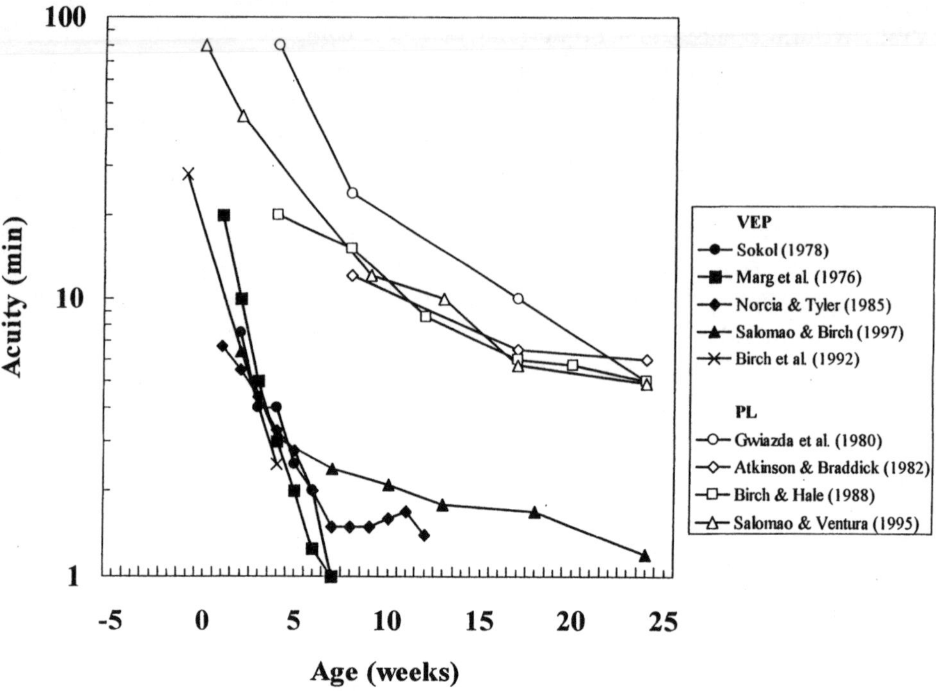

Figure 20.2. Acuity estimates as a function of age obtained using preferential looking and VEP techniques. VEP acuity is better than PL acuity during infancy.

maturation generally have been confirmed in subsequent swept VEP studies. However, it is now known that the precise time course of VEP visual acuity maturation depends on the spatial and temporal parameters used and that subtle improvements in VEP acuity continue well beyond the first year of life, reaching adult-level acuity at 18 to 24 months.

Comparison of VEP and PL Acuity

As shown in Figure 20.2, VEP acuity is better than PL acuity during infancy. Variables which clearly contribute to the difference include: (a) stimulus properties (pattern reversal versus static, differences in mean luminance and contrast); (b) methods of threshold estimation (extrapolation to zero amplitude versus determination of the 75% correct response point of the psychometric function); (c) area of the visual field tapped by the protocol (central 6 to 8 degrees versus full-field); and (d) task requirements (fixation of the display versus localization and fixation). Although, in general, both tests have been shown to be valid in older children through comparison with acuity data obtained from eye charts, there are also reported instances where each of the tests fails. Normal pattern VEPs have been reported in blind children and absence of a PL response has been reported in children with oculomotor abnormalities but normal acuity. Clearly, the VEP and PL acuity protocols are complementary techniques that do not measure solely the capacity of the infant to resolve pattern stimuli.

Contrast Sensitivity

Two general trends emerge from behavioral studies of infant contrast sensitivity: (a) contrast sensitivity, especially at higher spatial frequencies, improves with age; and (b) the peak of the contrast sensitivity function (CSF) shifts to higher spatial frequencies with increasing age (Atkinson, Braddick et al., 1977; Banks & Salapatek, 1976; Gwiazda, Bauer et al., 1997; Peterzell, Werner et al., 1995). As shown in Figure 20.3, sensitivity at the peak approaches 1.0 at 8 months, lower than adult levels of 2.5 log contrast. The peak of the infant CSF toward the end of the first year is 1.5 cy/deg, an octave lower than the peak in older children. The increase in sensitivity and the shift in the peak occur concurrently in behavioral studies.

Unlike CSFs measured with behavioral techniques, contrast sensitivity measured with the sweep VEP shows an early increase in sensitivity, followed by a later shift in the peak frequency (Norcia, Sutter et al., 1985). In the first 10 weeks, contrast sensitivity for low spatial frequencies increases rapidly, asymptoting between 10 and 40 weeks of age at a log contrast of 2.3, about half of the adult level. Sensitivity to higher frequencies is also immature at 40 weeks.

At the end of the first year contrast sensitivity measured with both behavioral and electrophysiological techniques is lower than adult sensitivity. In fact, sensitivity has not reached adult levels even by 8 years of age, as shown in Figure 20.3. Reduced stereoacuity and vernier acuity have also been reported in school-aged children compared to adults (Gwiazda, Bauer et al., 1989). The reductions found in children might be due to nonvisual factors, such as attention and motivation. Another possibility is that neural development could underlie the continued improvement during childhood.

It is not sufficient to specify only the spatial properties of a stimulus. When measuring contrast sensitivity, the temporal properties of the stimulus, and the interaction of spatial and temporal properties, also must be considered. However, due to the practical problem of obtaining multiple data points from infant subjects, most studies of the development of the CSF have varied only spatial frequency, while holding temporal properties constant, usually with sustained presentation of gratings or use of one temporal frequency. Swanson and Birch (1990) investigated the interaction of spatial and temporal properties in the development of contrast sensitivity. They reported that the temporal tuning function changed from lowpass (attenuating all frequencies above a certain frequency) at 4 months to bandpass (attenuating all frequencies above one frequency and below a lower one) at 8 months.

Vernier Acuity

Vernier acuity during infancy has been of great interest because it represents a hyperacuity, which is the capacity to make spatial discriminations finer than the spacing of photoreceptors. As such, vernier acuity may provide an opportunity to directly evaluate

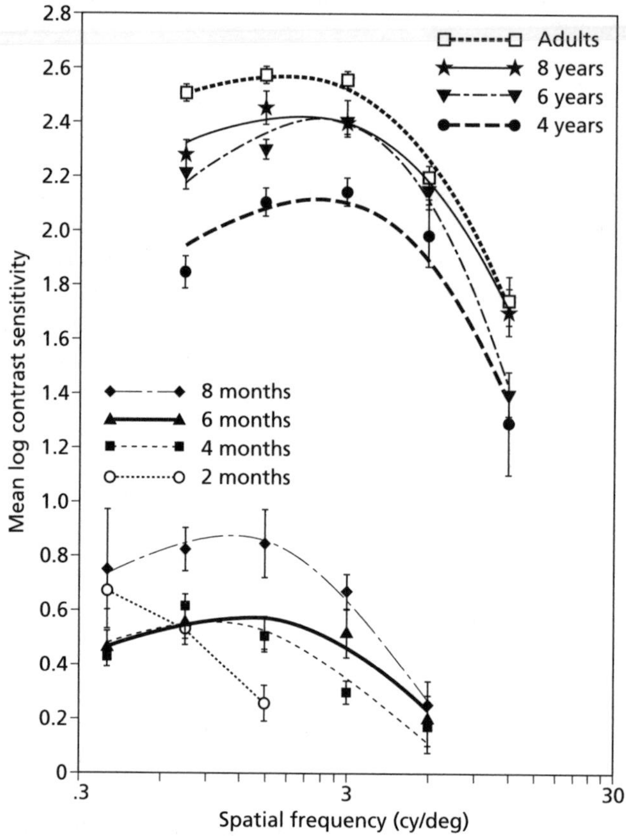

Figure 20.3. Mean CSFs for infants, children, and adults, measured using behavioral techniques. Error bars represent standard errors. (Reprinted with permission from Gwiazda et al. (1997), copyright © The American Academy of Optometry 1997.)

cortical maturation. There have been several attempts to measure the maturation of vernier acuity during infancy. Initial attempts used static multiple vernier offsets of square-wave gratings and a preferential looking response (for a description, see Shimojo, Birch et al., 1984). In general, these studies found very poor vernier acuity throughout infancy; indeed, the measured vernier acuities were so coarse that they often were poorer than grating thresholds. Although these results may accurately represent the visual capabilities of infants, it is also possible that the stimuli failed to capture the interest of the infant observers sufficiently to mediate optimum discrimination performance. The vernier thresholds, in fact, were so poor that the data were consistent with a scenario in which the infants failed to demonstrate a fixation preference unless the vernier offset was so large that the grating was converted to a "checkerboard-like" appearance.

In order to provide a more salient visual stimulus for mediating fixation preference, two research laboratories independently devised moving vernier offset stimuli (Manny & Klein, 1984, 1985; Shimojo et al., 1984; Shimojo & Held, 1987). Here the grating patterns contained an offset which jumped back and forth in conjunction with an auditory cue. These stimuli turned out to be quite interesting to infants, who consistently displayed a fixation preference for a grating containing moving vernier offsets over a static grating. Before 4 months of age, infants' vernier acuity appears to be poorer than their grating acuity in some studies. At about 4 to 5 months of age, infants perform this discrimination task at a finer level than they perform a grating acuity task; that is, they demonstrate hyperacuity (Figure 20.4). Rapid development of vernier acuity, relative to grating acuity, continues through at least 8 months of age. However, development does not appear to be complete during infancy; two reports show continued improvement in vernier acuity until about 10 years of age (Carkeet, Levi et al. 1997; Gwiazda et al. 1989).

The moving vernier offsets used to gather these psychophysical responses confound the interpretation of the data. The infant may be responding to vernier offsets per se or may be responding to local motion cues which occur simultaneously. Thus, this paradigm does not provide unique access to vernier discrimination. More recently, a promising VEP technique has been developed (Manny, 1988; Norcia, Manny et al., 1988) which separates the vernier response from the motion response. This technique uses a moving vernier offset grating stimulus and capitalizes on the novel finding that the breaking of co-linearity yields a larger response amplitude that the transition back to co-linearity. What this means is that the vernier VEP response occurs at half the temporal frequency of the motion response, as it occurs only for one direction of motion. Thus, by looking at frequency-specific components of the VEP response, the vernier and motion responses are separable. In adults, the VEP vernier response has reasonable amplitude, high signal-to-noise ratio and, most

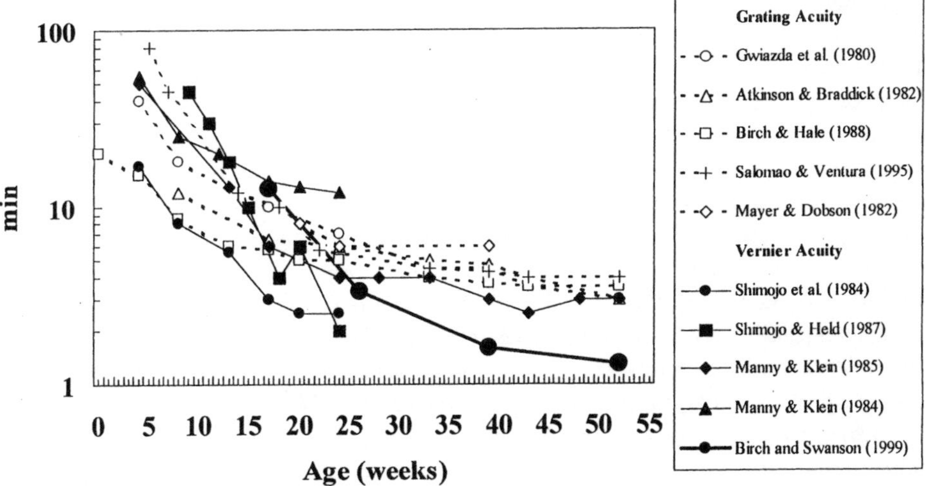

Figure 20.4. Vernier acuity versus grating acuity as a function of age. Vernier acuity becomes a hyperacuity at 4 to 5 months of age.

importantly, the vernier threshold is comparable to psychophysical vernier acuity and exhibits an eccentricity dependence similar to psychophysical vernier acuity. Unfortunately, so far this promising technique has failed in infants. Although initial reports suggested that a vernier offset VEP could be recorded in infants, studies of spatio-temporal variables which should have affected vernier thresholds in predictable ways have failed to provide confirmatory data that a vernier-specific response is being measured in infants (Manny, 1988). Whether this failure represents an immaturity of visual responses or whether the source geometry of the occipital cortex of infants precludes recording responses that are easily obtainable from adults is unknown.

Thus, there remain many questions to be answered about the development of vernier acuity. None of the research paradigms to date has provided an unambiguous description of the time course for maturation and none has yet clearly defined the critical immaturities in the infant visual system which restrict performance during development.

Color Vision

Human trichromacy is based on the activity of three univariant cone photoreceptor classes, the short-wavelength S-cone, the middle wavelength M-cone, and the long-wavelength L-cone, and the neural pathways that encode their output. The maturation of the three photoreceptor classes has been a major focus of color vision research in infants, addressing both spectral sensitivity and chromatic discrimination. Neonatal foveal photoreceptors are known to be both shorter and wider than adults (Hendrickson, 1994; Hendrickson & Drucker, 1992; Youdelis & Hendrickson, 1986). These differences clearly affect both spectral sensitivity and efficiency in absorbing quanta.

Early studies of infant color vision were confounded by the failure to equate stimuli for brightness because the infant's photopic spectral sensitivity function was unknown; it is impossible to know whether the infants were responding to brightness or chromatic differences in these paradigms. In the 1970s, several research groups developed paradigms to overcome confounding by brightness cues and, since that time, a great deal has been learned about the spectral sensitivity of infants (Bornstein, 1975; Peeples & Teller, 1975). The spectral sensitivity of rods and S-cones has been measured as early as 4 weeks postnatal (Volbrecht & Werner, 1987) and the photopic spectral sensitivity function has been assessed at 8 weeks postnatal (Bebier, Volbrecht et al., 1995; Dobson, 1976; Moskowitz-Cook, 1979; Peeples & Teller, 1978). These data leave little doubt that rods, S-cones, and L-cones are functional in early infancy. That M-cones are also functional in early infancy is supported by the finding that 8-week-old infants can make Rayleigh discriminations, although it is possible that rods rather than M-cones mediated these discriminations (Hamer, Alexander et al., 1982). Stronger evidence of M-cone function early in infancy comes from recent studies using receptor-isolating stimuli to measure field sensitivities and action spectra (Bebier, Knoblaugh et al., 1998; Knoblauch, Bieber et al., 1998). Several studies have failed to find evidence of red-green color discrimination prior to 5–8 weeks of age using chromatic VEPs, OKN responses to moving isoluminant red-green gratings, or Rayleigh stimuli (Allen, Banks et al., 1993; Crognale, Switkes et al., 1996; Morrone, Burr et al., 1993). The possible causes for these failures are still under active investigation.

Infants as young as 2 months clearly are able to demonstrate responses which meet the classic definition of color vision as the ability to make chromatic discriminations, but what about the perception of chromatic differences? Teller recently has suggested an approach to investigating color perception in infants. The rationale is based on the hypothesis that, as has been shown in adults, color perception is mediated primarily by the P-cell pathway; the M-cell pathway may also respond to chromatic differences but does not mediate perceived color. She proposes that studies which "rule out" M-cell mediation of infants' chromatic discriminations would help to establish that infants not only make chromatic discriminations but also perceive chromatic differences.

Orientation Selectivity

Understanding how orientation selectivity develops in infants is critical for assessing the maturity of specific areas in primary visual cortex. One approach to studying the development of orientation selectivity has been to record VEPs specific to orientation changes in the stimulus. Orientation reversal VEPs were reported in infants starting at 6 weeks of age, but newborns failed to show evidence of responses to changes in stimulus orientation (Braddick, Atkinson et al., 1986). A follow-up study using different spatial and temporal frequencies showed that the orientation-selective response could be recorded in 3-week-old infants using low temporal frequency stimulation (3 reversals/second) . Evidence from behavioral studies using preferential looking provides support for gradual improvement in orientation selectivity from 2 to 8 months (Held, Yoshida et al., 1989; Yoshida, Gwiazda et al., 1990).

Some of the earliest studies of infant visual development were motivated by the demonstration of plasticity in the developing visual system of animals. Exposure of kittens to stripes of only one orientation resulted in a failure to develop cells responsive to edges of other orientations (Blakemore & Cooper, 1970). Researchers sought to explore human parallels, one of which is the oblique effect, reduced acuity for oblique compared to horizontal and vertical edges. Unlike in animals, testing young human infants revealed the presence of an oblique effect early in life, suggesting that the underlying substrate develops independently of biased environments (Leehey, Moskowitz-Cook et al., 1975; Gwiazda, Brill et al., 1978).

Visual Fields

The effective visual field expands gradually during infancy. Young infants orient only toward peripheral stimuli near the midline, but with increasing age they are more likely to produce an orienting response toward targets at increasing eccentricities. Early in life they orient better toward objects in the temporal than in the nasal field (Lewis & Maurer, 1992).

Kinetic perimetry, in which stimuli are moved slowly from the periphery into the visual field while the infant fixates a central spot, has the advantage of being simple to produce and administer. The downside is that variability with this technique is large.

Static perimetry has the advantage of not having a central fixation target when the peripheral targets are presented, and the peripheral target is present until the infant makes an eye movement. However, large numbers of trials are required for this method, more than can be obtained from individual infants. Hybrid procedures combining the advantages of each are now becoming popular.

The age at which the extent of the field becomes adult-like depends on the method used. In a recent study Dobson, Brown et al. (1998) compared different methods on children aged 3 months to 3 years. They found that with kinetic perimetry, children had large fields that approached adult levels around 1½ years of age, while with static and hybrid perimetry children had smaller fields that only became adult-like at 2½ years.

Development of Binocular and Oculomotor Processes

Stereopsis

Prior to 1980, there was little information in the literature about the normal maturation of stereopsis. Since that time, a variety of psychophysical, electrophysiological, and eye movement protocols have been used to assess both local and global stereopsis during infancy and early childhood. Both line stereograms and random dot stereograms have been employed in the various protocols. Virtually all studies report an abrupt onset of stereopsis at 3 to 4 months of age, as shown in Figure 20.5 (for review, see Birch, 1993). The agreement on the age of onset for stereopsis among psychophysical, electrophysiological, and eye movement protocols is unique among infant visual development studies. Moreover, this concordance regarding the onset of stereopsis argues against interpretation of discrepancies regarding other aspects of visual function (e.g., acuity) simply in terms of differences in sensitivity among techniques.

The onset of stereopsis does not appear to depend solely on the maturation of eye alignment nor on the maturation of visual acuity (Birch, Gwiazda et al., 1982; Birch, 1993). That the infant is not only able to detect and discriminate horizontal binocular disparity but also appreciates a depth percept is supported by the finding that very large disparities, which exceed the range that supports depth perception in adults, do not support preferential looking in infants and may actually elicit an avoidance response (Birch, Gwiazda et al., 1982; Fox, Aslin et al., 1980). In addition, infants show appropriate reaching responses to horizontally disparate stimuli (Granrud, 1986). In the few studies which also measured the maturation of stereoacuity, rapid stereoacuity development follows the abrupt onset, and 40 to 80 sec of arc stereoacuity was achieved by 8 to 12 months of age (Birch et al., 1982; Birch & Salomao, 1998; Birch, Stager et al., 1986).

Recently, a new random dot stereo card test has been developed for rapid assessment of stereoacuity in infants (Birch & Salomao, 1998). This test consists of a series of "flashcards" which contain pairs of disparate and non-disparate random dot vectographs. The infant is shown progressively smaller disparities in the series of cards in a preferential looking paradigm in order to determine stereothreshold. Initial results suggest that this rapid protocol provides similar results, both in terms of the onset of stereopsis and the development of

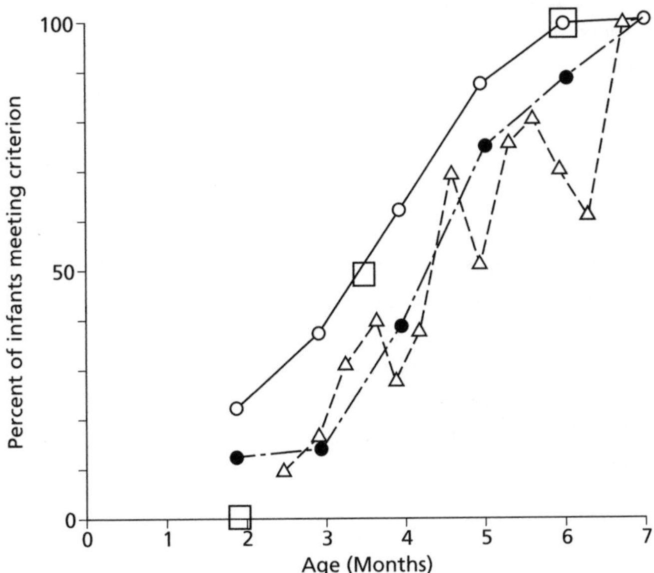

Figure 20.5. Stereoacuity using different techniques as a function of age. Rapid development of stereoacuity follows the abrupt onset at 3 to 4 months of age. The large open squares represent VEP data; the other symbols are behavioral data. (From a composite by Teller (1982), *Current eye research*, pp. 199–210, © Swets & Zeitlinger. Used with permission.)

stereoacuity, to more lengthy test protocols which utilize more complex stimulus equipment.

Stereo processing has been proposed to consist of two ranges of disparities with different properties, coarse and fine. Different perceptual phenomena are associated with the two ranges and separate physiological substrates have been proposed. The processing of coarse and fine disparity ranges in infants has been explored using an adaptation of a VEP paradigm initially applied to adults (Norcia & Tyler, 1985). The disparity versus VEP amplitude function of adults is non-monotonic, with two amplitude peaks. A dip in amplitude occurs at approximately 20 min arc, and a step change in the phase of the response occurs between the coarse and fine disparity ranges defined by this amplitude minimum. Extrapolation of a linear fit of the descending portion of the log disparity versus amplitude function to 0 μV provides an estimate of stereoacuity which agrees within reasonable limits with psychophysical stereoacuity thresholds for the same stimulus. The disparity versus VEP amplitude function shows the same coarse and fine disparity clusters in children aged 6 months and older (Birch & Petrig, 1996).

While stereoacuity approaches adult levels (40 sec arc) by 8 to 12 months of age, maturation of stereoacuity appears to continue through at least 36 months as determined by operant testing protocols using random dot stimuli (Birch & Hale, 1989). Until recently, there were no simple tests of random dot stereoacuity for the preschool age range. During the past two years, two new tests have been commercially produced and normative and clinical data are available which demonstrate their high success rate and sensitivity to disorders of binocular vision (Birch, Williams et al., 1997; Ciner, Schanel-Klitsch et al., 1996).

Fusion and Rivalry

As the onset of stereopsis does not occur until 3 to 4 months of age, the question of how the younger infant's prestereoptic visual system processes the two monocular images naturally arises. One alternative might be that the infant alternately sees the right eye and then the left eye image, similar to rivalry. A second alternative is that the images from the two eyes are simply superimposed. To date, the evidence from psychophysical studies of infants supports the superimposition theory (Shimo, Bauer et al., 1986; Held, 1993). Infants less than 3 months of age prefer dichoptic square-wave gratings that are oriented orthogonally to dichoptic square-wave gratings with matched orientation. The similarity of this preference to the preference for plaids over stripes supports the superposition hypothesis. Moreover, at about the same age as the onset of stereopsis, the infant switches preference from the dichoptic orthogonal square-wave gratings to the dichoptic square-wave gratings with matched orientation (Gwiazda et al., 1989). This abrupt switch is consistent with the replacement of superimposition with binocular rivalry. To date, this is the only well-explored experimental paradigm which has attempted to determine the binocular function of the pre-stereoptic infant. On the other hand, a recently developed VEP protocol which appears to provide a valid index of rivalry in adults has failed to show evidence of rivalry in infants aged 5 to 12 months (Brown, Candy et al., 1998). However, it is not clear as yet whether this failure represents a true discrepancy or whether this VEP protocol simply does not provide a valid measure of rivalry in infants due to non-binocular factors such as differences in the source geometry of the VEP.

If the hypothesis of superimposition is supported by other data, it will be unique in the field of visual development in that the infant shows a qualitative difference in visual processing compared with the adult rather than the more typical quantitative differences of gradual improvement toward adult performance. Although the initial psychophysical data support the superimposition hypothesis for the prestereoptic infant, another interpretation of the data has been offered. Binocular rivalry can have a very long latency in adults when stimulus contrast is low and, prior to the onset of rivalry, the dichoptic stimuli appear superimposed. Tyler has suggested that it is possible that the low contrast sensitivity of the prestereoptic infant, rather than a qualitative difference in binocular processing, prevents appreciation of rivalry before 3 to 4 months of age.

Another electrophysiological paradigm that has been developed to assess binocular status is the motion VEP protocol (Norcia, Hamer et al., 1995). The infant monocularly views gratings which jitter back and forth nasalward and temporalward. Young infants under 4 months of age display nasal-temporal asymmetries in the VEP motion response while older infants respond equally well to both nasalward and temporalward motion (Salamao et al., 1997). The exact time course depends on the spatial-temporal parameters of the stimulus (Norcia & Hamer, 1990). Given the similarity of the general time course of development of a symmetric response to that of the development of stereopsis, along with the clinical data showing persistent asymmetries in stereoblind patients with a history of infantile strabismus, it has been suggested that this monocular testing protocol may provide a valid index of binocular status (Jamplosky, Norcia et al., 1994; Norcia et al., 1995).

Convergence and Accommodation

Early studies of accommodation reported that neonates had a focus of about 20 cm (5 diopters) that did not change in response to targets at different viewing distances (Haynes, White et al. 1965). More recent work has demonstrated that even infants under 1 month of age can accommodate in the appropriate direction to targets at various viewing distances, but that they "over-accommodate" for targets beyond 75 cm (>1.3 diopters) (Hainline, Riddell et al. 1992). This failure in neonates to relax accommodation for distant targets has been termed "spurious myopia" (Hainline et al., 1992). The failure to observe appropriate accommodative response in young infants may be due to their lack of interest and/or motivation in looking at distant targets rather than a true immaturity of the accommodative response (Hainline et al. 1992). This suggestion gains at least some weak support from the finding that looking time for a variety of stimuli negatively correlates with stimulus distance in neonates (McKenzie & Day, 1972).

Even the youngest infants appear to have appropriate convergence in response to targets presented at 25 to 200 cm, although younger infants do exhibit greater variability in vergence responses (Hainline & Riddell, 1995). The finding of accurate, although more variable, vergence responses in prestereoptic infants suggests that vergence movements in the youngest infants may be driven by a qualitatively different form of binocular information than the binocular disparity-driven vergence of adults. For example, in the superposition model discussed above (Shimojo, Bauer et al., 1986; Held, 1993), vergence movements in the prestereoptic infant may be driven by maximizing the correlation of the images on the two retinas. Alternatively, recent evidence suggests that disparity sensitivity is present in the striate cortex of neonatal humans and monkeys. Together with other data, this finding is consistent with the hypothesis that disparity processing in the striate cortex mediates vergence but higher cortical function is necessary for stereopsis (Cumming & Parker, 1997).

The finding that convergence is accurate at the same age at which accommodation is inaccurate argues strongly against the hypothesis that poor accommodation is simply due to inattention on the part of the youngest infants. The causes of the relative lag in the maturation of accommodation relative to convergence have not been established. However, the poor acuity and contrast sensitivity of neonates are logical candidates because these factors would reduce sensitivity to the blur which drives the accommodative response.

Development of Object and Pattern Perception

Size and Shape Constancy

Size constancy, the perception of objects' real size despite changes in retinal image size, has been reported to be present at birth (Granrud, 1987; Slater, Mattock et al., 1991). Granrud

(1987) compared rates of habituation for two kinds of sequences of objects in which retinal sizes varied identically. In one sequence real object size also varied, while in the other it remained the same. Slower habituation was found when the real object size varied, suggesting that this was noticed by the infants.

Research on newborns also provides evidence for shape constancy, in this case the perception of constant shape despite detectable variations in slant. In a study using preferential looking, newborns' preferences for an outline of a square were found to change with changes in slant (Slater & Morison, 1985). An outline of a square that changed orientation was paired with an outline of a trapezium that remained in the frontal plane relative to the infant. When the orientation of the square was shifted away from the frontal plane by larger and still larger amounts, it was preferred on fewer and fewer trials.

Perception of Faces

As summarized in this chapter, young infants show consistent preferences for patterned over plain stimuli, three-dimensional over two-dimensional stimuli, moving over static stimuli, and high contrast over low contrast stimuli. As all of these preferred stimulus attributes are found in the human face, it is not surprising that infants attend to faces. Within two days of birth infants show reliable preferences for their mother's face compared to a female stranger (Bushnell, Sai et al., 1989). Newborns also produce more sucking responses to seeing a video version of their mother's face than that of a stranger (Walton, Bower et al., 1992). Parental preference aside, infants, even newborns, prefer to look at attractive faces over unattractive ones (Langlois, Roggman et al., 1987). This result is found across gender, age, and race.

Newborn infants also imitate adult facial gestures, such as mouth opening, lip pursing, and tongue protrusion (Meltzoff & Moore, 1977). More recently, the same investigators have shown that 6-week-old infants can imitate facial gestures of adults, even after a one-day delay (Meltzoff & Moore, 1994). On one day an adult made either a mouth opening or tongue protrusion gesture, witnessed by the infant. On the next day the adult made no gesture, but the infants imitated the gesture which they had observed on the previous day.

These results on face perception can be interpreted either in terms of an innate mechanism that recognizes and responds to the human face or in terms of rapid learning about faces in the hours after birth.

Texture

The ability of the brain to extract figures out of a visual scene is called segmentation. An aspect of visual segmentation that has been studied extensively in adults is segmentation of textures, consisting of elementary features called textons (Julesz, 1981) or primitives (Triesman & Gelade, 1980). Examples include color, brightness, and orientation. If the features described by Julesz and Triesman are fundamental perceptual units of vision, then we might expect to see evidence that they are involved in perception early in development. Although limited data are available, there is some evidence that 3-month-old infants are sensitive to textons (Rovee-Collier, Hankins & Bhatt, 1992).

Development of Motion Perception

The observation of parents and others that newborn infants attend to moving stimuli suggests that sensitivity to motion is well developed at birth. Young infants, however, may be sensitive to temporal modulation and not to direction and speed. Sensitivity to the latter two components is required for full use of motion information, at least in the first stages of motion analysis.

The development of sensitivity to direction, usually discrimination between opposite directions, has been assessed by both electrophysiological and behavioral methods. Longitudinally tested infants first showed a statistically significant direction reversal component in the VEP at approximately 2½ months of age to stimulus velocities of 5 deg/sec and at 3 months of age to velocities of 20 deg/sec (Wattam-Bell, 1991).

The majority of behavioral studies on motion processing in infants have used FPL to measure thresholds for discrimination between moving and stationary patterns, rather than tasks requiring discrimination of direction. Studies of directional sensitivity show that development is characterized by a decrease in lower velocity thresholds and a simultaneous increase in upper velocity thresholds between 6 and 20 weeks of age (Aslin & Shea, 1990; Wattam-Bell, 1993). Habituation experiments have shown that sensitivity to direction emerges at about 6–8 weeks of age.

These results, taken together, show that directional sensitivity is poor in the first weeks of life. The suggestion has been made that this may be due to the absence of motion detectors sensitive to large spatial displacements at short time intervals. However, since newborns show OKN responses and are able to track slowly moving stimuli, the presence of sensitivity to direction soon after birth cannot be ruled out. In the first experiment described above, the use of test velocities below 5 deg/sec might have produced directional responses at an earlier age. More experimentation is needed on infants between 0 and 3 months of age.

Low-level motion mechanisms, as discussed above, form the first stage of motion analysis and emerge by 3 months of age. More global processes are involved in using motion information for perception and these emerge soon after 3 months. It has been shown that by 3 to 4 months of age, infants can use motion cues for image segmentation. For example, 3-month-olds can detect motion-defined contours and are sensitive to the shape of objects defined by them (Kaufmann-Hayoz, Kaufmann et al., 1986). Four-month-olds can group the spatially separated parts of a partially occluded object sharing a common motion (Kellmann & Spelke, 1983) and can also extract structure from motion (Arterberry & Yonas, 1988).

Clinical Topics

Amblyopia and Visual Impairment

Although the first FPL and VEP studies of the maturation of visual acuity in normal infants were published only 20 years ago, rapid advances in protocols and international standardization have led to the acceptance of these measures in clinical research and for clinical evaluation of infants and young children. Psychophysical and electrophysiological protocols have been used to measure visual acuity in infants and children with known or suspected visual impairment due to retinal or cortical abnormalities and due to amblyogenic conditions. In general, such studies have addressed either the natural history of visual acuity development in pediatric visual disorders or the response of various treatment regimens. Indeed, with the recent availability of rapid protocols for both preferential-looking acuity (Teller Acuity Cards) (McDonald et al., 1985) and VEP acuity (sweep VEP) (Norcia & Tyler, 1985) these acuity tests are becoming more prevalent in routine clinical evaluation of pediatric patients.

Amblyopia is a visual acuity deficit due to abnormal visual experience during the early months of life, including visual deprivation (e.g., a congenital cataract), strabismus (misaligned visual axes), and anisometropia (blurred vision in one eye due to unequal refractive error). Studies of FPL acuity development in strabismic amblyopia quickly revealed the insensitivity of grating acuity tests to this condition (Mayer & Fulton, 1985). The spatial distortions which result from strabismic amblyopia have a much more devastating effect on recognition acuity tests with letter targets which have complex spatial details than on grating detection which is only mildly disrupted by spatial distortions. On the other hand, FPL and VEP acuity tests have been useful in both clinical research and clinical management of infants with congenital cataracts or unequal refractive error. Perhaps the most impressive success story from this avenue of research is the use of infant acuity tests to monitor the success of occlusion therapy for deprivation amblyopia due to congenital unilateral cataracts. Compared with the typical visual acuity outcome of 20/200 or poorer that was routine in the 1970s, a shift to earlier surgery and monitoring of acuity development by PL or VEP methods in the 1980s and 1990s has led to visual acuity outcomes of 20/50 or better being routinely achieved (Beller, Hoyt et al., 1981; Birch et al., 1986; Birch, Stager et al., 1998; Birch & Stager, 1988; Catalano, Simon et al., 1987; Maurer & Lewis, 1993; Salamao et al., 1997).

In cases of infantile esotropia (crossed eyes), infant stereopsis tests have been used to examine the question of whether the eyes are misaligned because the infant congenitally lacks normal binocular vision or whether the infant loses the capacity for stereopsis because of prolonged misalignment of the visual axes during the critical period of development. Using a test paradigm which compensates for misalignment of the visual axes, the same proportion of 4- to 6-month-old esotropic infants were able to demonstrate the sensory capacity for stereopsis as normal (Birch & Stager, 1984). This finding of innate capacity for stereopsis in infants with esotropia has led to a new approach to clinical treatment trials for infantile esotropia with a focus on early intervention during the critical period for the maturation of stereopsis.

VEP motion responses to jittering gratings have also been used to investigate binocular function in infantile and late-onset esotropia. Like normal infants aged 2 to 4 months, infantile esotropes show a nasal-temporal asymmetry in the VEP response to motion (Norcia, Garcia et al., 1991). Unlike normal infants, whose responses mature toward symmetry, infantile esotropes retain the asymmetry on long-term follow-up (Norcia et al., 1995). In late onset esotropia, many children show symmetric VEP motion responses, suggesting that only infantile disruption of binocular function disturbs the normal maturation of this response (Brosnaha, Norcia et al., 1998). Recent evidence suggests that symmetry/asymmetry of the VEP motion response in patients with esotropia may be an index of whether fusion or suppression is present (Fawcett & Birch, 1998). This provides a new approach to the investigation of cause and effect questions about the wide variety of binocular sensory abnormalities that accompany infantile esotropia. Initial data suggest that young infantile esotropes have symmetric VEP motion responses and develop asymmetry only after prolonged misalignment of the visual axes (Birch, Fawcett et al., 1999). These data are indicative of normal maturation of the capacity for fusion followed by a disruption of normal binocular capacity by abnormal binocular experience.

Infant visual acuity tests have also been used to study retinal and cortical abnormalities. A multicenter trial of cryotherapy treatment for retinopathy of prematurity, a disorder of retinal vascular development which affects many infants born at 1,000 g or less, included preferential-looking acuity as the primary sensory outcome measure (CRYO-ROP, 1990). A clear relationship between the retinal structural outcome and the acuity outcome was found in this study and in other studies of ROP (Birch & Spencer, 1991; CRYO-ROP, 1992). The degree to which the retina was damaged due to retinopathy (e.g., normal posterior pole, macular dragging, partial retinal detachment, total retinal detachment) was strongly associated with the acuity outcome. In addition, acuity test outcomes during infancy are predictive of final acuity outcomes several years later (Birch & Spencer, 1991). The predictive value of visual acuity tests conducted during infancy for long-term acuity outcomes has also been demonstrated in cases of delayed visual maturation (Fielder, Russell-Eggitt et al., 1985) and cortical visual impairment (Birch & Bane, 1991).

Refractive Errors

Evidence is accumulating from both human and animal studies that environmental factors play a role in the development of refractive errors. In contrast to previously held views that refractive errors were solely a consequence of genetically programmed patterns of eye growth, it has now been established that the growth of the eye also is guided by visual feedback. An active, vision-dependent mechanism of emmetropization coordinates eye growth to reduce neonatal refractive errors and achieve emmetropia, the absence of refractive error.

Young infants have a wide range of refractive errors, with only a small percent close to emmetropia. Longitudinal refraction studies have shown that in the first years of life both hyperopic and myopic refractive errors are reduced, with the majority of children achieving emmetropia by 5–6 years of age, as shown in Figure 20.6 (Cook & Glasscock, 1951; Gwiazda, 1993). The fact that most infants are either hyperopic or myopic at birth but become emmetropic in the early months raises an interesting question: Are the infants

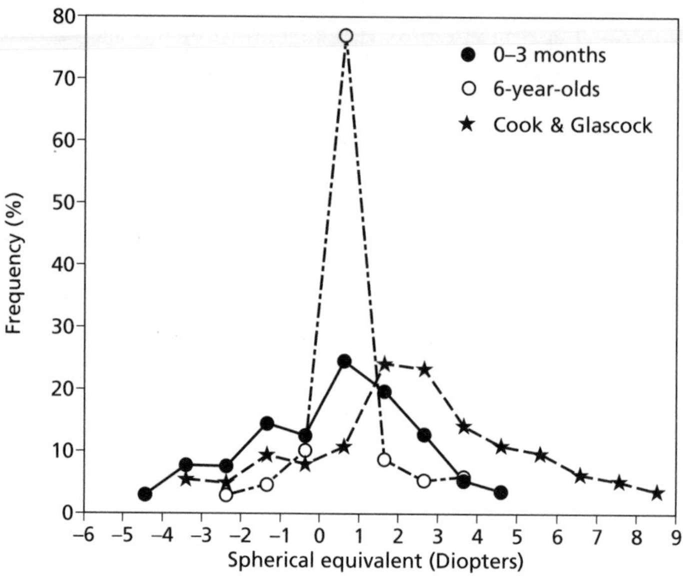

Figure 20.6. Distribution of refractive errors in infancy (●) and at 6 years (○) obtained without cycloplegia, and in infancy obtained with cycloplegia (*). Six-year-olds are predominately emmetropic, unlike infants, who exhibit a wide range of refractive errors. (Reprinted from Gwiazda et al. (1993), copyright © 1993, with permission from Elsevier Science.)

with significant refractive errors the same children who once again become myopic or hyperopic at school-age? For at least one group of children the answer appears to be "Yes." In a longitudinal study of refraction spanning more than 20 years, Gwiazda et al. (1993) reported that manifest refractions in infancy were predictive of refraction at school-age, after a period of emmetropization.

The duration of the daily light period affects eye growth in chicks (Stone, Lin et al., 1995). An intriguing finding related to this is a strong association between childhood myopia and night-time exposure to light (Quinn, Shinn et al., 1999). Children who slept with room lights on in their first two years (by parental report) were found to have 5 times the prevalence of myopia as those who slept in the dark. Those who slept with nightlights had 3 times the prevalence of myopia as those who slept without lights. The strength of the association between myopia and ambient lighting at night led to the recommendation that children sleep without lights in the bedroom. Two subsequent studies, however, failed to confirm the original finding, instead showing that the use of ambient light at night is associated with myopia in parents, not children (Gwiazda, Ong, Held, & Thorn, 2000; Zadnik et al., 2000).

Recent studies provide evidence that the eyes of animals show compensatory growth to focusing errors imposed by externally applied lenses (Wildsoet, 1997). These findings have direct clinical implications. They suggest that the naturally occurring emmetropization process could be inhibited in young children by intervening too early with spectacles.

Furthermore, they also predict that correction of myopia with negative lenses could lead to increased progression. However, limited data from human studies that bear on these predictions do not appear to show these dire effects (Ong, Grice et al., 1999). It is therefore premature to alarm children and their parents with the specter of higher refractive errors caused by the very lenses prescribed to help them see clearly.

Moreover, hyperopic children treated with corrective lenses that reduced their effective hyperopia to +1.0D in the least hyperopic meridian showed the same amount of emmetropization as a group of untreated hyperopes (Atkinson, Braddick et al., 1996). In addition, the children who wore corrective lenses were much less likely to have strabismus or amblyopia than the untreated hyperopes. Overall, then, the lenses were quite beneficial: They did not appear to disrupt emmetropization and did appear to help protect against strabismus and amblyopia.

Astigmatism and Meridional Amblyopia

Although it is now established that the prevalence of astigmatism in infants and young children is higher than in the adult population, percentages vary according to many factors, including the method of refraction, the criterion for significant astigmatism, and the children's ethnicity. The early cylindrical error is greatly reduced or eliminated during the first two years of life, but little is known about the functional significance of the infantile astigmatism, especially its role, if any, in emmetropization and the development of refractive errors. It is known that corneal and lens flattening in infancy, during the time when axial elongation is occurring, moves the refractive state of the eye toward emmetropia.

It is possible that early astigmatic blur might disrupt the emmetropization process, but at present only limited data from chicks and monkeys lend support for this possibility. A recent study of emmetropization in hyperopic children (Ehrlich, Braddick et al., 1997) reported that changes in the cylinder power and mean spherical equivalent over the period from 9 to 20 months were independent of each other, suggesting independent mechanisms for axial elongation and corneal change. The possibility was raised that a passive process is responsible for corneal change and an active process for axial growth.

What happens in the preschool years to the refractive errors and acuity of those children who show significant astigmatism at a year of age? Abrahamsson, Fabian et al. (1990) tracked changes in refractive error, with emphasis on astigmatism, in a group of 310 children with at least 1.0 diopter of astigmatism at a year of age. Over the next 3 years the astigmatism decreased in 90% of the children. The remaining 10% of children with constant or increasing astigmatism were found to be at greater risk for developing amblyopia than those with reduced astigmatism.

Some of the amblyopia found in astigmats might be meridional amblyopia, which is characterized by reduced acuity for certain orientations even with best optical correction and which is presumed to be a form of neural dysfunction. There is a strong likelihood that this meridional amblyopia is produced by blurred visual input early in life. Although young infants do not show evidence of this form of amblyopia (Gwiazda, Mohindra et al., 1985), older children and adults do (Cobb & MacDonald, 1978; Mitchell, Freeman et al., 1973). Furthermore, meridional amblyopia may be present even when the astigmatism is gone.

Astigmatism present from 6–24 months of age has been found to be correlated with meridional amblyopia measured in a group of non-astigmatic school-age children with known refraction histories (Gwiazda, Bauer et al., 1986). Some of these subjects also showed slight reductions in Snellen acuity, another presumed consequence of the early astigmatism.

Effect of Diet on Visual Development

Just as it is clear that there are critical periods during which abnormal visual experience may result in permanent adverse changes in the way that the visual system matures, recently it has become clear that some dietary deficiencies during infancy may have long-term adverse effects on visual function. Studies have addressed the role of dietary taurine, vitamin A and E, and other nutrients. Recently, there has been a focus on the differences in long-chain polyunsaturated fatty acid levels in human milk versus infant formula. Over 60% of the structural material in the brain is lipids, including cholesterol and phosphoglycerides of neural membranes which are rich in docosahexaenoic acid (DHA). As a component of the central nervous system with a common embryonic origin, the retina contains similarly high levels of DHA as structural lipids, particularly in the metabolically active photoreceptor outer segments. Changes in the relative proportions of different brain and retinal phospholipids, especially large changes in DHA levels, during late fetal development and infancy may be reflected in cellular and neural maturation.

To date, the main focus for evaluation of differences in neural function among infant populations with or without a dietary long-chain polyunsaturated fatty acid supply during development largely has been on visual maturation and, specifically, on ERG measures of retinal function, VEP acuity, and PL acuity. A focus on visual function as an index of the functional status of the retina and brain makes sense from the point of view that quantitative, reliable, valid techniques are available for the infant age range.

There have been a large number of non-randomized studies comparing the visual development of human-milk fed infants with that of infants fed commercial formulas; currently, all US commercial formulas lack DHA. There have also been several randomized clinical trials in which the visual development of infants assigned to formulas which do or do not contain DHA are compared (for reviews, see Bendich & Brock, 1997). Overall, the evidence suggests that infants are at risk for DHA deficiency due to their limited ability to metabolize these fatty acids during the first weeks or months of life, particularly preterm infants who are also deprived of the last trimester of maternal-to-fetal transfer of DHA. Infants who lack an adequate dietary supply of DHA consistently show poorer retinal function during the first weeks of life, poorer acuity during the first year of life, and poorer stereoacuity at 3 years of age. In addition, there is accumulating evidence that infants fed commercial formula which lacks long-chain polyunsaturated fatty acids have lower DHA levels in red blood cell membranes (Hoffman, Birch et al., 1993) and in cerebral cortex (Gibson, Neumann et al., 1996). Thus, an adequate supply of long-chain polyunsaturated fatty acids provided by the early diet may be of vital importance to the developing brain and eye in the human infant.

Suggested Readings

Hamer, R. D., & Mayer, D. L. (1994). The development of spatial vision. *Principles and Practices of Ophthalmology: Basic Sciences*, 578–608.
Mohn, G., Van, H.V., & Duin, J. (1990). Development of spatial vision. In D. M. Regan (Ed.), *Vision and visual dysfunction* (pp. 179–211). London: Macmillan Press.
Simons, K. (1993). *Early visual development, normal and abnormal.* New York: Oxford University Press.
Teller, D. Y. (1997). First glances: The vision of infants. *Investigative Ophthalmology & Visual Science, 38*, 2183–2199.

Additional Topics

Perceptual Organization/Object Perception
Recent investigations have demonstrated that infants perceive a more coherent world than Piaget suggested. Infants may begin life with an innate conception of the underlying unity and coherence of objects. See Kellman, Spelke, and Short (1986), Slater, Morrison, Somers, Mattock, Brown, and Taylor (1990), and Spelke, Gutheil, and Van de Walle (1995).

Pictorial Depth Cues
Infants begin to use these cues, such as shading, interposition, and familiar size, between 5 and 7 months of age; later than they use retinal disparity. See Granrud and Yonas (1984) and Granrud, Yonas, and Opland (1985).

Animal Models
Increased understanding of immaturities in the human visual system that limit visual capacities at different ages requires studying animal models. See Movshon and Kiorpes (1988) and Chino, Smith, Hatta, and Cheng (1997).

References

Abrahamsson, M., Fabian, G. et al. (1990). A longitudinal study of a population based sample of astigmatic children. *Acta Ophthalmologica, 68*, 428–434.
Allen, D., Banks, M. S. et al. (1993). Does chromatic sensitivity develop more slowly than luminance sensitivity? *Vision Research, 33*(17), 2553–2562.
Arden, G. B., & Wooding, S. L. (1985). Pattern ERG in amblyopia. *Investigative Ophthalmology & Visual Science, 26*(1), 88–96.
Arterberry, M. E., & Yonas, A. (1988). Infants' sensitivity to kinetic information for three-dimensional object shape. *Perception & Psychophysics, 44*, 1–6.
Aslin, R. N., & Shea, S. L. (1990). Velocity thresholds in human infants implications for the perception of motion. *Developmental Psychology, 26*, 589–598.
Atkinson, J., Braddick, O. et al. (1977). Contrast sensitivity of the human infant for moving and static patterns. *Vision Research, 17*, 1045–1047.
Atkinson, J., Braddick, O. et al. (1982). Preferential looking for monocular and binocular acuity testing of infants. *British Journal of Ophthalmology, 66*, 264–268.
Atkinson, J., Braddick, O. et al. (1996). Two infant vision screening programmes: Prediction and

prevention of strabismus and amblyopia from photo-and-videorefractive screening. *Eye, 10,* 189–198.

Banks, M. S., & Salapatek, P. (1976). Contrast sensitivity function of the infant visual system. *Vision Research, 16,* 867–869.

Bearse, M. A., Jr., & Sutter, E. E. (1996). Imaging localized retinal dysfunction with the multifocal electroretinogram. *Journal of the Optical Society of America A-Optics & Image Science, 13*(3), 634–640.

Bebier, M., Volbrecht, V. et al. (1995). Spectral efficiency measured by heterochromatic flicker photometry is similar in human infants and adults. *Vision Research, 35,* 1385–1392.

Bebier, M., Knoblauch, K. et al. (1998). M- and L-cones in early infancy: II. Action spectra at 8 weeks of age. *Vision Research, 38,* 1765–1773.

Beller, R., Hoyt, C. S. et al. (1981). Good visual function after neonatal surgery for congenital monocular cataracts. *American Journal of Ophthalmology, 91*(5), 559–565.

Bendich, A., & Brock, P. E. (1997). Rationale for the introduction of long chain polyunsaturated fatty acids and for concomitant increase in the level of vitamin E in infant formulas. *International Journal for Vitamin & Nutrition Research, 67*(4), 213–231.

Birch, D. G., Birch, E. E. et al. (1992). Retinal development in very-low-birth-weight infants fed diets differing in omega-3 fatty acids. *Investigative Ophthalmology & Visual Science, 33*(8), 2365–2376.

Birch, E. (1993). Stereopsis and its developmental relationship to visual acuity. In K. Simons (Ed.), *Early visual development: Normal and abnormal* (pp. 224–236). New York: Oxford University Press.

Birch, E., Birch, D. et al. (1990). Retinal and cortical function of very low birth weight infants at 36 and 57 weeks postconception. *Clinical Vision Research, 5,* 363–373.

Birch, E., Fawcett, S. et al. (1999). Codevelopment of VEP motion response symmetry and binocular vision in normal infants and infantile esotropes. *Vision Science and Its Applications,* OSA Technical Digest (Optical Society of America Washington, DC), 70–73.

Birch, E., & Hale, L. (1989). Operant assessment of stereoacuity. *Clinical Vision Sciences, 4,* 295–300.

Birch, E. E. & Hale, L. A. (1988). Criteria for monocular acuity deficit in infancy and early childhood. *Investigative Ophthalmology & Visual Science, 29,* 636–643.

Birch, E., & Petrig, G. (1996). FPL and VEP measures of fusion, stereopsis and stereoacuity in normal infants. *Vision Research, 36*(9), 1321–1327.

Birch, E., Stager, D. et al. (1998). Effects of unequal competition are minimized by very early treatment of congenital unilateral cataract. *Investigative Ophthalmology & Visual Science, 39,* 1560–1566.

Birch, E., Williams, C. et al. (1997). Random dot stereoactivity of preschool children. *Journal of Pediatric Ophthalmology & Strabismus, 34,* 217–222.

Birch, E. E., & Bane, M. C. (1991). Forced-choice preferential looking acuity of children with cortical visual impairment. *Developmental Medicine & Child Neurology, 33*(8), 722–729.

Birch, E. E., Gwiazda, J. et al. (1982). Stereoacuity development for crossed and uncrossed disparities in human infants. *Vision Research, 22,* 507–513.

Birch, E. E., & Salomao, S. (1998). Infant random dot stereoacuity cards. *Journal of Pediatric Ophthalmology & Strabismus, 35*(2), 86–90.

Birch, E. E., & Spencer, R. (1991). Monocular grating acuity of healthy preterm infants. *Clinical Vision Sciences, 6,* 331–334.

Birch, E. E., & Stager, D. R. (1984). Monocular acuity and stereopsis in infantile esotropia. *Investigative Ophthalmology & Visual Science (Supplement), 25,* 217.

Birch, E. E., & Stager, D. R. (1988). Prevalence of good visual acuity following surgery for congenital unilateral cataract. *Archives of Ophthalmology, 106*(1), 40–43.

Birch, E. E., Stager, D. R. et al. (1986). Grating acuity development after early surgery for congenital unilateral cataract. *Archives of Ophthalmology, 104*(12), 1783–1787.

Blakemore, C., & Cooper, G. (1970). Development of the brain depends on the visual environment. *Nature, 228*, 477–478.

Bornstein, M. H. (1975). Qualities of color vision in infancy. *Journal of Experimental Child Psychology, 19*, 401–419.

Braddick, O., Atkinson, J. et al. (1986). Orientation-specific cortical responses develop in early infancy. *Nature, 320*, 617–619.

Brosnahan, D., Norcia, A. M. et al. (1998). OKN, perceptual and VEP direction biases in strabismus. *Vision Research, 38*(18), 2833–2840.

Brown , R., Candy, T. et al. (1998). Late maturation of rivalry and binocular suppression in infants. *Investigative Ophthalmology & Visual Science, 39*, 5023S.

Bushnell, I., Sai, F. et al. (1989). Neonatal recognition of the mother's face. *British Journal of Developmental Psychology, 7*, 3–15.

Calloway, E., & Halliday, R. (1973). Evoked potential variability: Effects of age, amplitude, and methods of measurement. *Electroencephalography & Clinical Neurophysiology, 34*, 125–131.

Carkeet, A., Levi, D. M. et al. (1997). Development of Vernier acuity in childhood. *Optometry & Vision Science, 74*(9), 741–50.

Catalano, R. A., Simon, J. W. et al. (1987). Preferential looking as a guide for amblyopia therapy in monocular infantile cataracts. *Journal of Pediatric Ophthalmology & Strabismus, 24*(2), 56–63.

Chino, Y., Smith, E., Hatta, S., and Cheng, H. (1997). Postnatal development of binocular disparity sensitivity in neurons of the primate visual cortex. *Journal of Neuroscience, 17*, 296–307.

Ciner, E. B., Schanel-Klitsch, E. et al. (1996). Stereoacuity development: 6 months to 5 years. A new tool for testing and screening. *Optometry & Vision Science, 73*(1), 43–48.

Cobb, S. R., & MacDonald, C. F. (1978). Resolution acuity in astigmats: Evidence for a critical period in the human visual system. *British Journal of Physiological Optics, 32*, 38–49.

Cook, R., & Glasscock, R. (1951). Refractive and ocular findings in the new born. *American Journal of Ophthalmology, 34*, 1407–1413.

Crognale, M., Switkes, E. et al. (1996). Temporal response characteristics of the spatiochromatic visual evoked. *Journal of the Optical Society of America, 14*, 2595–2607.

CRYO-ROP (1990). Multicenter trial of cryotherapy for retinopathy of prematurity – one year outcome: Structure and function. *Archives of Ophthalmology, 108*, 1408–1416.

CRYO-ROP (1992). The correlation of visual function with posterior retinal structure in severe retinopathy of prematurity. *Archives of Ophthalmology, 110*, 625–631.

Cumming, B. G., & Parker, A. J. (1997). Responses of primary visual cortical neurons to binocular disparity without depth perception [see comments]. *Nature, 389*(6648), 280–283.

Dagnalie, G., De Vries, M. et al. (1986). Pattern reversal stimuli: Motion or contrast? *Documenta Ophthalmologica, 31*, 343–349.

Dobson, V. (1976). Spectral sensitivity of the 2-month infant as measured by the visually evoked cortical potential. *Vision Research, 16*(4), 367–374.

Dobson, V., Brown, A. et al. (1998). Visual field in children 3.5–30 months of age tested with a double-arc LED perimeter. *Vision Research, 38*, 2743–2760.

Ducati, A., Fava, E. et al. (1988). Neuronal generators of the visual evoked potentials: Intracerebral recording in awake humans. *Electroencephalography & Clinical Neurophysiology, 71*(2), 89–99.

Dustman, R., Schenckenberg, T. et al. (1977). The cerebral evoked potential: Life span changes and twin studies. In J. Desmedt (Ed.), *Visual evoked potentials in man* (pp. 363–377). Oxford: Clarendon.

Ehrlich, D., Braddick, O. et al. (1997). Infant emmetropization: Longitudinal changes in refraction components from nine to twenty months of age. *Optometry & Vision Science,74*(10), 822–843.

Ellingson, R. (1958). Electroencephalograms of normal fullterm infants immediately after birth with observations on arousal and visual evoked responses. *Electroencephalography & Clinical Neurophysiology, 10*, 31–37.

Ellingson, R. (1960). Cortical electrical responses to visual stimulation in the human infant. *Electroencephalography & Clinical Neurophysiology, 12*, 663–669.

Ellingson, R., Lathrup, G. et al. (1973). Variability of visual evoked potentials in newborn infants and adults. *Electroencephalography & Clinical Neurophysiology, 34*, 113–124.

Fantz, R. L. (1961). A method for studying depth perception in infants 6 months of age. *Psychological Record, 11*, 27–32.

Fantz, R. L., Ordy, J. M. et al. (1962). Maturation of pattern vision in infants during the first six months. *Journal of Comparative and Physiological Psychology, 55*, 907–917.

Fawcett, S., & Birch, E. (1998). Asymmetric motion VEPs infer binocular suppression not stereopsis in infantile esotropia. *Investigative Ophthalmology & Visual Science, 39*, 15S.

Fielder, A. R., Russell-Eggitt, I. R. et al. (1985). Delayed visual maturation. *Transactions of the Ophthalmological Societies of the United Kingdom, 104*(Pt 6), 653–661.

Fox, R., Aslin, R. N. et al. (1980). Stereopsis in human infants. *Science, 207*(4428), 323–324.

Gibson, R. A., Neumann, M. A. et al. (1996). Effect of dietary docosahexaenoic acid on brain composition and neural function in term infants. *Lipids, 31 Suppl*, S177–181.

Gorman, J., Cogan, D. et al. (1957). An apparatus for grading the visual acuity on the basis of optokinetic nystagmus. *Pediatrics, 19*, 1088–1092.

Granrud, C. E. (1986). Binocular vision and spatial perception in 4- and 5-month-old infants. *Journal of Experimental Psychology: Human Perception & Performance, 12*(1), 36–49.

Granrud, C., & Yonas, A. (1984). Infants' perception of pictorially specified interposition. *Journal of Experimental Child Psychology, 37*, 500–511.

Granrud, C., Yonas, A., & Opland, E. (1985). Infants' sensitivity to the depth cue of shading. *Perception & Psychophysics, 37*, 415–419.

Grose, J., Harding, G. et al. (1989). The maturation of pattern reversal VEP and flash ERG in preterm infants. *Clinical Vision Sciences, 4*, 239–246.

Gwiazda, J., Bauer, J. et al. (1989). Binocular function in human infants: Correlation of stereoptic and fusion-rivalry discriminations. *Journal of Pediatric Ophthalmology & Strabismus, 26*, 128–132.

Gwiazda, J., Bauer, J. et al. (1986). Meridional amblyopia *does* result from astigmatism in early childhood. *Clinical Vision Sciences, 1*(2), 145–152.

Gwiazda, J., Bauer, J. et al. (1997). Development of spatial contrast sensitivity from infancy to adulthood: Psychophysical data. *Optometry & Vision Science, 74*, 785–789.

Gwiazda, J., Brill, S. et al. (1978). Infant visual acuity and its meridional variation. *Vision Research, 18*, 1557–1564.

Gwiazda, J., Brill, S. et al. (1980). Preferential looking acuity in infants from two to fifty-eight weeks of age. *American Journal of Optometry & Physiological Optics, 57*, 428–432.

Gwiazda, J., Mohindra, I. et al. (1985). Infant astigmatism and meridional amblyopia. *Vision Research, 25*(9), 1269–1276.

Gwiazda, J., Ong, E., Held, R., & Thorn, F. (2000). Myopia and ambient night-time lighting. *Nature, 404*, 144.

Gwiazda, J., Thorn, F. et al. (1993). Emmetropization and the progression of manifest refraction in children followed from infancy to puberty. *Clinical Vision Sciences, 8*, 337–344.

Hainline, L., Riddell, P. et al. (1992). Development of accommodation and convergence in infancy. *Behavioural Brain Research, 49*, 33–50.

Hainline, L., & Riddell, P. M. (1995). Binocular alignment and vergence in early infancy. *Vision Research, 35*(23–24), 3229–3236.

Hamer, R. D., Alexander, K. et al. (1982). Raleigh discriminations in young human infants. *Vision Research, 22*, 575–587.

Harding, G. F., Grose, J. et al. (1989). The pattern reversal VEP in short-gestation infants. *Electroencephalography & Clinical Neurophysiology, 74*(1), 76–80.

Haynes, H., White, B. L. et al. (1965). Vision accommodation in human infants. *Science, 148*, 528–530.

Held, R. (1993). The stages in the development of binocular vision and eye alignment. In K. Simons (Ed.), *Early visual development: Normal and abnormal* (pp. 250–257). New York, Oxford University Press.

Held, R., Yoshida, H. et al. (1989). Development of orientation selectivity measured by a masking procedure. *Investigative Ophthalmology & Visual Science Supplement, 30*, 312.

Hendrickson, A. (1994). Primate foveal development: A microcosm of current questions in neuro-

biology. *Investigative Ophthalmology & Visual Science, 35*, 3129–3133.
Hendrickson, A., & Drucker, D. (1992). The development of parafoveal and midperipheral retina. *Behavior Brain Research, 49*, 21–31.
Hoffman, D. R., Birch, E. E. et al. (1993). Effects of supplementation with omega 3 long chain polyunsaturated fatty acids on retinal and cortical development in premature infants. *American Journal of Clinical Nutrition, 57*(5 Suppl), 807S–812S.
Hood, D. C., & Birch, D. G. (1993). Light adaptation of human rod receptors: The leading edge of the human a-wave and models of rod receptor activity. *Vision Research, 33*(12), 1605–1618.
Hood, D. C., & Birch, D. G. (1994). Rod phototransduction in retinitis pigmentosa: Estimation and interpretation of parameters derived from the rod a-wave. *Investigative Ophthalmology & Visual Science, 35*(7), 2948–2961.
ISCEV (1995). Standard for clinical electroretinography. *Documenta Ophthalmologica, 89*, 199–210.
Jamplosky, A., Norcia, A. et al. (1994). Preoperative alternate occlusion decreases motion processing abnormalities in infantile esotropia. *Journal of Pediatric Ophthalmology & Strabismus, 31*, 6–17.
Julesz, B. (1981). Textons, the elements of texture perception, and their interaction. *Nature, 290*, 91–97.
Kaufmann-Hayoz, R., Kaufmann, F. et al. (1986). Kinetic contours in infants' visual perception. *Child Development, 57*, 292–299.
Kellmann, P., & Spelke, E. (1983). Perception of partly occluded object in infancy. *Cognitive Psychology, 15*, 483–524.
Kellman, P., Spelke, E., & Short, K. (1986). Infant perception of object unity from translatory motion in depth and vertical translation. *Child Development, 57*, 72–86.
Knoblauch, K., Bieber, M. L. et al. (1998). M- and L-cones in early infancy: I. VEP responses to receptor-isolating stimuli at 4- and 8-weeks of age. *Vision Research, 38*(12), 1753–1764.
Kraut, M., Arezzo, J. et al. (1985). Intracortical generators of the flash VEP in monkeys. *Electroencephalography & Clinical Neurophysiology, 62*, 300–312.
Lamb, T. D., & E. N. Pugh, Jr. (1992). A quantitative account of the activation steps involved in phototransduction in amphibian photoreceptors. *Journal of Physiology, 449*, 719–758.
Langlois, J., Roggman, L. et al. (1987). Infant preferences for attractive faces: Rudiments of a stereotype. *Developmental Psychology, 23*, 363–369.
Leehey, S. C., Moskowitz-Cook, A. et al. (1975). Orientational anisotropy in infant vision. *Science, 190*, 900–902.
Lewis, T., Maurer, D. et al. (1990). The development of visual resolution in infants and toddlers tested monocularly with optokinetic nystagmus. *Clinical Vision Sciences, 5*, 231–241.
Lewis, T., & Maurer, D. (1992). The development of the temporal and nasal visual fields during infancy. *Vision Research, 32*, 903–911.
Manny, R., & Klein, S. (1984). The development of vernier acuity in infants. *Current Eye Research, 3*, 453–462.
Manny, R. E. (1988). The visually evoked potential in response to vernier offsets in infants. *Human Neurobiology, 6*(4), 273–279.
Manny, R. E., & Klein, S. A. (1985). A three alternative tracking paradigm to measure vernier acuity of older infants. *Vision Research, 25*(9), 1245–1252.
Marg, E., Freeman, D. et al. (1976). Visual acuity development in human infants: Evoked potential measurements. *Investigative Ophthalmology & Visual Science, 15*, 150–154.
Maurer, D., & Lewis, T. (1993). Visual outcomes in infantile cataract. In K. Simons (Ed.), *Early visual development* (pp. 454–484). New York: Oxford University Press.
Mayer, D. L., & Fulton, A. B. (1985). Preferential looking grating acuities of infants at risk of amblyopia. *Transactions of the Ophthalmological Societies of the United Kingdom, 104*(Pt 8), 903–911.
McDonald, M. A., Dobson, V. et al. (1985). The acuity card procedure: A rapid test of infant acuity. *Investigative Ophthalmology & Visual Science, 26*(8), 1158–1162.
McKenzie, B., & Day, R. (1972). Distance as a determinant of visual fixation in early infancy.

Science, 178, 1108–1110.

Meltzoff, A., & Moore, M. (1977). Imitation of facial and manual gestures by human neonates. *Science, 198*, 75–78.

Meltzoff, A., & Moore, M. (1994). Imitation, memory, and the representation of persons. *Infant Behavior and Development, 17*, 83–99.

Mitchell, D. E., Freeman, R. D. et al. (1973). Meridional amblyopia: Evidence for the modification of the human visual system by early visual experience. *Vision Research, 13*, 535–557.

Morrone, M. C., Burr, D. C. et al. (1993). Development of infant contrast sensitivity to chromatic stimuli. *Vision Research, 33*(17), 2535–2552.

Moskowitz, A., & Sokol, S. (1983). Developmental changes in the human visual system as reflected by the latency of the pattern reversal VEP. *Electroencephalography & Clinical Neurophysiology, 56*, 1–15.

Moskowitz-Cook, A. (1979). The development of photopic spectral sensitivity in human infants. *Vision Research, 19*(10), 1133–1142.

Movshon, A. & Kiorpes, L. (1988) Analysis of the development of spatial contrast sensitivity in monkey and human infants. *Journal of the Optical Society of America, 5*, 2166–2172.

Norcia, A., Garcia, H. et al. (1991). Anomalous motion VEPs in infants and in infantile esotropia. *Investigative Ophthalmology & Visual Science, 32*, 436–439.

Norcia, A., & Hamer, R. (1990). Temporal tuning of the motion VEP in infants. *Investigative Ophthalmology & Visual Science, 31*, 10S.

Norcia, A., Manny, R. et al. (1988). Vernier acuity measured using the sweep VEP. *Optical Society of America Technical Digest Series, 3*, 151–154.

Norcia, A. M., Hamer, R. D. et al. (1995). Plasticity of human motion processing mechanisms following surgery for infantile esotropia. *Vision Research*, 35(23–24), 3279–3296.

Norcia, A. M., Sutter, E. E. et al. (1985). Electrophysiological evidence for the existence of coarse and fine disparity mechanisms in human. *Vision Research, 25*(11), 1603–1611.

Norcia, A. M., & Tyler, C. W. (1985). Spatial frequency sweep VEP: Visual acuity during the first year of life. *Vision Research, 25*(10), 1399–1408.

Nusinowitz, S., Birch, D. G. et al. (1998). Rod photoresponses in 6-week and 4-month-old human infants. *Vision Research, 38*(5), 627–635.

Ong, E., Grice, K. et al. (1999). Effects of spectacle intervention on the progression of myopia in children. *Optometry and Vision Science, 76*, 363–369.

Peeples, D. R., & Teller, D. Y. (1975). Color vision and brightness discrimination in two month-old human infants. *Science, 189*, 1102–1103.

Peeples, D. R., & Teller, D. Y. (1978). White-adapted photopic spectral sensitivity in human infants. *Vision Research, 18*(1), 49–53.

Pepperberg, D. R., Birch, D. G. et al. (1997). Photoresponses of human rods in vivo derived from paired-flash electroretinograms. *Visual Neuroscience, 14*(1), 73–82.

Peterzell, D., Werner, J. et al. (1995). Individual differences in contrast sensitivity functions: Longitudinal study of 4-, 6-, and 8-month-old human infants. *Vision Research, 35*(7), 961–979.

Porciatti, V. (1984). Temporal and spatial properties of the pattern-reversal VEPs in infants below 2 months of age. *Human Neurobiology, 3*(2), 97–102.

Porciatti, V., Vizzoni, L. et al. (1982). Neurological age determined by evoked potentials. *Pediatric ophthalmology* (pp. 345–348). New York: John Wiley & Sons.

Quinn, G. E., Shinn, C. H. et al. (1999). Myopia and ambient lighting at night. *Nature, 399*, 113–114.

Rovee-Collier, C., Hankins, E., & Bhatt, R. (1992). Textons, visual pop-out effects, and object recognition in infancy. *Journal of Experimental Psychology: General, 121*, 435–445.

Salamao, S., Berezovsky, A. et al. (1997). Motion VEP in infantile esotropia before and after surgery. *Vision Science and Its Applications, 1*, 112–113.

Sandberg, M. A., Jacobson, S. G. et al. (1979). Foveal cone electroretinograms in retinitis pigmentosa and juvenile macular degeneration. *American Journal of Ophthalmology, 88*(4), 702–707.

Schanel-Klitsch, E., Siegfried, J. et al. (1987). Developmental differences in visual evoked potential slow waves and high frequency wavelets across the lifespan: Effects of luminance variation of flash and background. In C. Barber and T. Blum (Eds.), *Evoked potentials III*. Boston: Butterworth.

Shimojo, S., Bauer, J. A. et al. (1986). Pre-stereoptic binocular vision in infants. *Vision Research, 26*, 501–510.

Shimojo, S., Birch, E. E. et al. (1984). Development of vernier acuity in infants. *Vision Research, 24*(7), 721–728.

Shimojo, S., & Held, R. (1987). Vernier acuity is less than grating acuity in 2 and 3-month olds. *Vision Research, 27*, 77–86.

Slater, A., Mattock, A. et al. (1991). Form perception at birth: Cohen and Younger. *Journal of Experimental Child Psychology, 51*, 395–406.

Slater, A., & Morison, V. (1985). Shape constancy and slant perception at birth. *Perception, 14*, 337–344.

Slater, A., Morison, V., Somers, M., Mattock, A., Brown, E., and Taylor, D. (1990). Newborn and older infants' perception of partly occluded objects. *Infant Behavior and Development, 13*, 33–49.

Sokol, S. (1978). Measurement of infant visual acuity from pattern reversal evoked potentials. *Vision Research, 18*(1), 33–39.

Sokol, S., Moskowitz, A. et al. (1987). Electrophysiological evidence for the oblique effect in human infants. *Investigative Ophthalmology & Visual Science, 28*, 731–735.

Spekreijse, H., Dagnelie, G. et al. (1985). Flicker and movement constituents of the pattern reversal response. *Vision Research, 25*(9), 1297–1304.

Spelke, E. S., Gutheil, G., & Van de Walle, G. (1995). The development of object perception. In S. M. Kosslyn & D. N. Osherson (Eds.), *Visual cognition* (pp. 297–330). Cambridge, MA: MIT Press.

Stone, R. A., Lin, T. et al. (1995). Photoperiod, early post-natal eye growth, and visual deprivation. *Vision Research, 35*(9), 1195–1202.

Swanson, W., & Birch, E. (1990). Infant spatiotemporal vision: Dependence of spatial contrast sensitivity on temporal frequency. *Vision Research, 30*(7), 1033–1048.

Taylor, M. J., Menzies, R. et al. (1987). VEPs in normal full-term and premature neonates: Longitudinal versus cross-sectional data. *Electroencephalography & Clinical Neurophysiology, 68*(1), 20–27.

Teller, D. Y., Morse, R. et al. (1974). Visual acuity for vertical and diagonal gratings in human infants. *Vision Research, 14*, 1433–1439.

Treisman, A., & Gelade, G. (1980). A feature integration theory of attention. *Cognitive Psychology, 12*, 97–136.

Tyler, C. (1993). On the development of threshold nonlinearity, peripheral acuity, binocularity, and complex stereoscopic processing. In K. Simons (Ed.), *Early visual development: Normal and abnormal* (pp. 258–284). New York: Oxford University Press.

van der Marel, E., Dagnelie, G. et al. (1984). Subdurally recorded pattern and luminance Eps in the alert Rhesus monkey. *Electroencephalography & Clinical Neurophysiology, 57*, 354–368.

Volbrecht, V. J., & Werner, J. S. (1987). Isolation of short-wavelength-sensitive cone photoreceptors in 4–6-week-old human infants. *Vision Research, 27*(3), 469–478.

Walton, G. E., Bower, N. J. A. et al. (1992). Recognition of familiar faces by newborns. *Infant Behavior and Development, 15*, 265–269.

Wattam-Bell, J. (1991). Development of motion-specific cortical responses in infancy. *Vision Research, 31*, 287–297.

Wattam-Bell, J. (1993). One-month-old infants fail in a motion discretion discrimination task. *Investigative Ophthalmology & Visual Science, 34S*, 1356.

Wildsoet, C. (1997). Active emmetropization – evidence for its existence and ramifications for clinical practice. *American Journal of Ophthalmology & Physiological Optics*, 1–12.

Wilson, C. L., Babb, T. L. et al. (1983). Visual receptive fields and response properties of neurons in human temporal lobe and visual pathways. *Brain, 106*(Pt 2), 473–502.

Yoshida, H., Gwiazda, J. et al. (1990). Orientation selectivity is present in the first month and subsequently sharpens. *Investigative Ophthalmology & Visual Science Supplement, 31*, 8.

Youdelis, C., & Hendrickson, A. (1986). A qualitative and quantitative analysis of the human fovea during development. *Vision Research, 26*, 847–855.
Zadnik, K., Jones, L., Irvin, B., Kleinstein, R., Manny, R., Shin, J., & Mutti, D. (2000). Myopia and ambient night-time lighting. *Nature*, *404*, 143–144.

Chapter Twenty-One

Development of the Auditory, Gustatory, Olfactory, and Somatosensory Systems[1]

Lynne A. Werner and Ilene L. Bernstein

Introduction

The purpose of this review is to highlight the major events in the development of audition, somesthesis, taste and olfaction. The senses in birds and mammals develop in a specified order: cutaneous, chemical, vestibular, auditory, visual (Gottlieb, 1971). That the senses considered here occur early in this sequence suggests that they are important in early development. With this idea in mind, the following review includes a consideration of the importance of these sensory systems to development in general.

Audition

Methods for Assessing Function in Infants and Children

Psychophysiological Methods

Heart rate is the only psychophysiological method that has been used extensively in the study of auditory development. Specifically, heart rate deceleration in response to sound has been taken as evidence that an infant hears a sound (Morrongiello & Clifton, 1984) or a change in a sound (Kinney & Kagan, 1976). Because heart rate deceleration to sound declines in amplitude and frequency with repeated stimulation, the spontaneous response is limited as a means for exploring the auditory capacity of infants and children.

Behavioral Methods

CONDITIONED HEAD-TURN PROCEDURES. Infants make many spontaneous behavioral responses to sound (Watrous, McConnel, Sitton, & Fleet, 1975), but threshold estimates based on such responses are very high and inconsistent with other observations of infants' auditory capacities (Gerber & Mencher, 1979). After about 6 months, infants often make spontaneous short-latency head turns toward sound sources. The development of procedures to assess hearing by bringing the infant's head turn under stimulus control, rather than depending entirely on the spontaneous response, represented a significant advance (Liden & Kankkonen, 1961; Moore, Thompson, & Thompson, 1975; Suzuki & Ogiba, 1961). Infants can be taught to make a head turn toward a single sound source when a sound is presented. The head turn is reinforced by the presentation of an interesting visual display, such as a mechanical toy or a video segment. Once the response is learned, sound intensity can be varied to estimate the infant's detection threshold. Infants will learn to turn toward the visual reinforcer when sounds are presented under earphones. The procedure has been modified to test discrimination: One sound is presented repeatedly as a background; the infant learns to respond when the sound changes in a defined way (Eilers & Minifie, 1975). A variant has been developed by Trehub and Schneider and their colleagues (Schneider & Trehub, 1985; Trehub, Schneider, & Endman, 1980) in which the infant makes a head turn to the left or right, toward the one of two speakers producing a sound, to receive visual reinforcement. This method can only be used to test detection.

OBSERVER-BASED PROCEDURES. The observer-based method (Werner, 1995) is another operant procedure in which a head turn is not specifically required as a response. It depends on an observer's ability to tell that a sound has occurred or changed, on the basis of the infant's response, such as a change in motor activity or a directional eye movement. The advantage of this method is that it allows testing of infants younger than 6 months.

HABITUATION PROCEDURES. Other methods have been widely used in behavioral studies of infant audition to demonstrate that infants can make a discrimination, though not how sensitive infants are to a particular stimulus change. These methods rely on habituation. The logic is that if a response that has habituated to one stimulus is reinstated when the stimulus is changed in some way, then the infant must have noticed the change. Most methods combine habituation with operant techniques. One example is the High Amplitude Sucking technique, in which infants are reinforced by the presentation of a sound for sucking on a pacifier. Another is the visual fixation technique, in which infants are reinforced for looking at a patterned visual stimulus by the presentation of a sound. Other operant conditioning procedures based on sucking and visual fixation rely on the infant's preference for one sound over another to demonstrate discrimination. If the infant responds more in the presence of one signal than the other, the conclusion is that the infant preferred the sound presented during that signal and that the infant could discriminate between the two sounds (DeCasper & Spence, 1986; Jusczyk, Bertoncini, Bijeljac-Babic, Kennedy, & Mehler, 1990; Jusczyk, Friederici, Wessels, Svenkerud, & Jusczyk, 1993).

Procedures for Testing Older Children. Schneider, Trehub, Morrongiello, and Thorpe (1989) have extended their variant of the conditioned-head-turn procedure to children older than 1.5–2 years by having children push buttons on the left or right to indicate where a sound is coming from. The testing of children between 2 and 4 years of age is considered very difficult, and to date, no acceptable laboratory procedure has been developed for assessing many aspects of audition for that age group. Once children are about 4 years old, they can perform in the psychophysical procedures that are used for adults, such as two- or three-alternative, forced-choice procedures. Clever displays are used to indicate the listening intervals and changes in the display provide feedback for the child (Wightman, Allen, Dolan, Kistler, & Jamieson, 1989).

Physiological Methods

Otoacoustic Emissions. Otoacoustic emissions (OAEs), sounds produced by the inner ear, provide a relatively direct measure of inner ear function (Kemp, 1978). OAEs can be quickly recorded in the ear canal of individuals with normal hearing and do not require that the subject be still for very long. Several varieties of OAEs are commonly used in the study of development. Transient (T)OAEs are usually recorded in response to a click; the spectrum of TOAEs is broadband. Distortion product (DP)OAEs are generated by presenting two tones to the ear simultaneously. DPOAEs provide information about cochlear function at specific frequencies.

Evoked Potentials. Scalp-recorded evoked potentials can be used to assess the status of the auditory nervous system. The auditory brainstem response (ABR) is the most widely used both clinically and in the laboratory. Wave I of the ABR arises from the auditory nerve; Wave V arises from the brainstem. The difference between the latencies of these two waves, the I–V interval, is taken as a measure of neural processing independent of the periphery. Middle latency and late responses have also been recorded in infants and children, but only the ABR is widely used in the study of development, because while recording all these potentials requires a quiet, typically sleeping infant, subject, only the ABR appears to be unaffected by state of arousal (Kraus & McGee, 1992).

Overview of Morphological and Physiological Development

Morphological Development

In humans, the structures of the ear are readily identifiable by 4–5 wk conceptional age (CA). By 18–20 wk CA, the inner ear has formed its full 2½ turns, both inner and outer hair cells are well differentiated, and the fluid spaces within the organ of Corti are formed, at least in the base of the cochlea. It is at this point in the structural development of the ear that responses to intense sounds are first observed. The primary ascending circuits of the auditory nervous system are also laid down prior to the 18th week of gestation, and descending projections to the ear and within the brain are identifiable well before the onset of sound-evoked cochlear responses (Cant, 1998; Fritzch & Nichols, 1993; Payne, Pearson, & Cornwell, 1988; Pujol, Lavigne-Rebillard, & Lenoir, 1998).

Although the basic structural properties of the auditory system are established in the absence of experience with sound, the initial responses to sound arise before the structural properties of the auditory system are completely mature. The pinna, ear canal and middle ear cavity continue to grow into childhood. Cochlear mechanical and receptor maturation continues, particularly at the apex (Rübsamen & Lippe, 1998). The basilar membrane decreases in thickness throughout the cochlea. Outer hair cell innervation and support cells continue to mature, in humans for about 10 weeks after the cochlea has matured sufficiently to demonstrate sound-evoked activity (Lavigne-Rebillard & Pujol, 1988).

The important neural structural developments that occur after the onset of response to sound are increases in neuron and nucleus size, redistribution of synapses, and the refinement of axonal and dendritic processes (Cant, 1998; Konigsmark & Murphy, 1972; Larsen, 1984; Schweitzer, 1991). Callosal connections, connections between cortical areas (Feng & Brugge, 1983; Payne, 1992), and the circuitry underlying the representation of auditory space in the superior colliculus (Withington-Wray, Binns, & Keating, 1990a) also continue to mature. Finally, the myelination of the auditory pathways and increases in the vascular support of the auditory nervous system are important developmental events, in humans beginning at 22–23 weeks CA, but continuing through 3–4 years of age at the cortical level (Moore, Perazzo, & Braun, 1995).

Physiological Development

Cochlear Intensity Processing. High sound intensity is required to elicit the earliest cochlear responses. For example, threshold of the cochlear microphonic (CM), a receptor potential, exceeds 110 dB SPL (Woolf & Ryan, 1988). Both sensitivity and dynamic range, however, improve rapidly (e.g., Uziel, Romand, & Marot, 1981). The sources of early improvements in sensitivity to sound are not completely understood, but include maturation of the middle ear (Woolf & Ryan, 1988), increases in the endocochlear potential – the cochlear resting potential that controls the gain of the cochlear amplifier (Rybak, Whitworth, & Scott, 1992) – and changes in the mass and stiffness of the basilar membrane (Mills, Norton, & Rubel, 1994). The gain of the cochlear amplifier increases, as indicated by DPOAEs, reaching a maximum before CM thresholds and the endocochlear potential mature (Mills et al., 1994; Mills & Rubel, 1996). The improvement in cochlear amplification reflects, in part, maturation of the outer hair cell system. Changes in the passive mechanical response of the basilar membrane, however, are largely responsible for the fact that the base of the cochlea responds to progressively higher frequencies over the course of development (Mills & Rubel, 1996).

Studies of human cochlear sensitivity during development are only beginning to be conducted (Abdala, 1998). At term birth, thresholds for eliciting TOAEs are within 10–15 dB of those of adults (Stevens, Webb, Smith, & Buffin, 1990). The ABR can first be recorded from premature infants at about 28 weeks conceptional age. The delay between the apparent onset of cochlear function and the appearance of the ABR is usually explained by an early lack of myelination in brainstem pathways. Click-evoked ABR threshold decreases from about 40 dB re: adult threshold at 27 weeks CA to about 10 dB re: adult threshold at 38 weeks CA (Lary, Briassoulis, de Vries, Dubowitz, & Dubowitz, 1985). Sininger, Abdala, and Cone-Wesson (1997) found that term neonates had tone-burst-evoked ABR thresholds that were quite close to those of adults at 500 Hz, about 10 dB higher than those of adults at 1500 Hz, and 20–25 dB higher than those of adults at 4000 and 8000 Hz, when sound pressure level was measured in the ear canal. In term neonates, the threshold differences are largely due to middle ear and brainstem, rather than inner ear, immaturity (Okabe, Tanaka, Hamada, Miura, & Funai, 1988; Keefe, Bulem, Arehart, & Burns, 1993).

Cochlear Frequency Resolution. Early in development frequency resolution, the precision with which frequency is represented by the activity pattern along the basilar membrane improves. Each auditory nerve fiber initially responds to a broad range of frequencies. The finely tuned frequency response evident in mature auditory nerve fibers emerges in parallel with improvement in thresholds, as expected given its dependence on many of the same mechanisms responsible for good absolute sensitivity. OAE studies indicate that cochlear frequency resolution is mature by term birth in humans (Abdala & Sininger, 1996; Bargones & Burns, 1988), but results from premature infants suggest some immaturity at 31–36 weeks CA (Abdala, 1998).

Cochlear Temporal Coding. Phase-locking, the tendency of neurons to fire at a fixed phase of a periodic sound, is the basis for the temporal code for frequency, as well as for representations of the time-varying aspects of sound. Phase-locking in the auditory nerve improves progressively with age, but the time course of phase-locking development is prolonged relative to that of other aspects of the cochlear response (Kettner, Feng, & Brugge, 1985). An evoked potential believed to reflect phase-locking to low-frequency tones at the level of the auditory nerve is the frequency following response (FFR). The FFR has been recorded in 1-month-old term human infants; it appears to be adult-like at that age (Levi, Folsom, & Dobie, 1995).

Responses of the Central Auditory Nervous System. Immature sound-evoked neural responses generally can be recorded as soon as cochlear responses are observed. Subsequent maturation of the neural response has two sources. First, the input to the auditory nervous system from the ear is immature. Cochlear immaturity is reflected directly in neural responses, and indirectly in neural processes that involve integration of peripheral information, such as localization. Second, the maturation of some neural response properties, such as maximum response rate, depend on maturation of the neural auditory pathway (Sanes & Walsh, 1998; Sanes, 1993; Kettner et al., 1985). In humans, for example, it is clear from studies of OAEs that cochlear frequency resolution is mature by term birth (Abdala & Sininger, 1996), but ABR measures indicate that frequency resolution at the level of the brain stem is immature at high frequencies until some time between 3 and 6 months postnatal age (Folsom & Wynne, 1987).

Development of Sensitivity

Initial Differential Responses

Behavioral responses to sound are generally observed soon after the onset of cochlear responses. For example, in mouse pups behavioral responses to sound appear a day or two after cochlear responses can first be recorded (Ehret, 1976). In humans, the first cochlear responses can probably be recorded at about 22 weeks CA, and heart rate and motor responses to sound have been reported at 28 weeks CA (Birnholz & Benacerraf, 1983).

It is frequently stated that young animals respond preferentially to species-typical sounds (Gottlieb, 1991; Gray & Jahrsdoerfer, 1986). In humans, one would expect a preferential response to speech, and in those cases where this expectation has been tested, it is generally confirmed. Hutt, Hutt, Lenard, von Bernuth, and Muntjewerff (1968), for example, showed that infants moved more in response to a voice saying "Hi baby" than to a tone. However, to date, no study has determined the basis of that preference.

Psychophysical Studies

Intensity Processing. The development of the audibility curve, absolute threshold as a function of frequency, has been described in a few species (Werner & Gray, 1998). The course of human postnatal threshold development is consistent with the general pattern. In nonhumans, early threshold development is characterized by very high thresholds and no response to very low or very high frequencies. The initial stage of human threshold development has not been well studied, because much of it occurs prenatally (Lecanuet, Granier-Deferre, & Busnel, 1988). At term birth the human audibility curve is still fairly flat and elevated by about 30–40 dB relative to that of adults (Weir, 1979; Werner & Gillenwater, 1990; Figure 21.1). Because adults have relatively high thresholds at low frequencies, newborns' thresholds are closer to those of adults at low than at high frequencies. However, between 3 and 6 months, high-frequency (> 4000 Hz) thresholds improve by about 20 dB, while low-frequency thresholds change by only a few dB (Olsho, Koch,

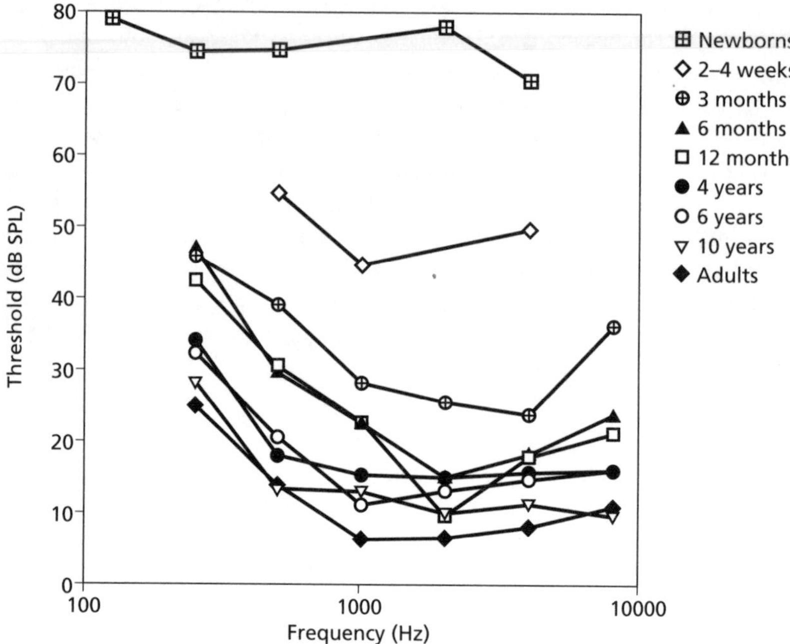

Figure 21.1. Audibility curves based on pure-tone thresholds measured under earphones at different ages in human development, based on averages of available data. Newborns: Weir (1979); 2–4-week-olds: Werner & Gillenwater (1990); 3-month-olds: Olsho et al. (1988); 6-month-olds: Moore, Wilson, & Thompson (1977), Nozza & Wilson (1984), Olsho et al. (1988); 12-month-olds: Moore & Wilson (1977), Nozza & Wilson (1984), Olsho et al. (1988); 4-year-olds: Maxon & Hochberg (1982); 6-year-olds: Elliott & Katz (1980), Maxon & Hochberg (1982); 10-year-olds: Elliott & Katz (1980), Maxon & Hochberg (1982); Adults: ANSI-S3.6-1989 – TDH39 (1989), Olsho et al. (1988), Watson et al. (1972).

Carter, Halpin, & Spetner, 1988). High-frequency thresholds are adult-like by 2 or 3 years of age, but low-frequency thresholds continue to improve until about 10 years of age (Trehub, Schneider, Morrongiello, & Thorpe, 1988).

Unlike absolute sensitivity, other aspects of intensity processing are mature by school age (Figure 21.2). For example, the just noticeable difference (jnd) for intensity in infants appears to be on the order of 2–6 dB under conditions in which adults discriminate changes on the order of 1–2 dB (Bull, Eilers, & Oller, 1984; Sinnott & Aslin, 1985). The jnd for intensity at 4 years of age has been estimated as 2–3 dB in one report (Maxon & Hochberg, 1982) and as 7 dB in another (Jensen & Neff, 1993). There is general agreement that the jnd for intensity becomes mature by about 6 years. Detection in noise develops along a similar time course (Schneider et al., 1989). Although the development of loudness perception has been little studied, it is apparently adult-like by 5–6 years (Bond & Stevens, 1969; Collins & Gescheider, 1989; Kawell, Kopun, & Stelmachowicz, 1988).

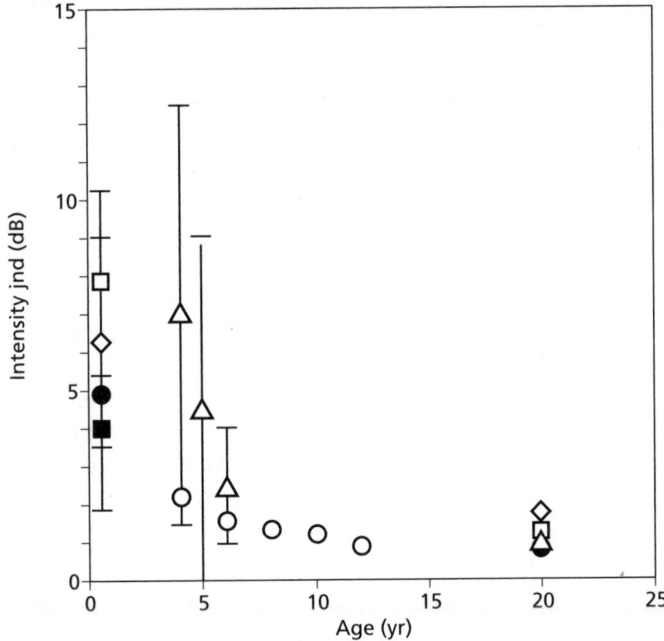

Figure 21.2. Intensity jnd as a function of age from five studies. Error bars represent ±1 standard deviation; in some cases the error bars are smaller than the symbol. Open symbols represent pure-tone data; filled symbols represent broadband stimulus data. *Filled square,* Bull et al. (1984); *open triangle,* Jensen & Neff (1993); *filled circle and open circle,* Kopyar (1997); *open circle,* Maxon & Hochberg (1982); *open diamond,* Sinnott & Aslin (1985).

The mechanisms underlying the development of intensity processing are relatively well understood. Maturation of the external and middle ear plays a role throughout the course of absolute threshold development, and may be the only factor involved after 5 or 6 years of age (Keefe et al., 1993; Okabe et al., 1988). Cochlear maturation appears to be complete by term birth (Abdala, 1996). Neural maturation at the level of the brainstem is important early in development, as thresholds are correlated with the I–V interval of the ABR prior to 6 months of age (Werner, Folsom, & Mancl, 1994). Neural maturation in other auditory centers (Schneider & Trehub, 1992) and the development of listening strategies (Bargones & Werner, 1994; Greenberg, Bray, & Beasley, 1970) may be involved in the development of intensity processing to 5–6 years of age. Inattentiveness makes only a small (2–3 dB) contribution to immature detection thresholds throughout infancy and childhood (Bargones, Werner, & Marean, 1995; Green, 1995).

Frequency Processing. The results of Spetner and Olsho (1990) suggest that frequency resolution is immature early in infancy, primarily at high frequencies, consistent with physiological studies of frequency resolution in early infancy (Abdala & Folsom, 1995; Folsom & Wynne, 1987) and suggesting a neural origin of the immaturity. Several studies agree that by 6 months of age frequency resolution is mature, as indicated by critical bandwidth (Schneider, Morrongiello, & Trehub, 1990) and psychophysical tuning curve widths (Olsho, 1985; Spetner & Olsho, 1990). Although initial studies of frequency resolution in older children suggested immaturities among preschool children (Allen, Wightman, Kistler, & Dolan, 1989; Irwin, Stillman, & Schade, 1986), Hall and Grose (1991) demonstrated that frequency resolution is mature at 4 years of age when an appropriate test procedure is used, consistent with the infant studies.

The development of frequency discrimination follows a longer time course (Figure 21.3). The high-frequency jnd appears to mature before 3 years of age, but the low-frequency jnd may not reach adult values until 8–10 years (Maxon & Hochberg, 1982; Olsho, Koch, & Halpin, 1987; Sinnott & Aslin, 1985). The early changes in frequency discrimination at high frequencies may well be related to maturation of high-frequency resolution. The persistent immaturity in low-frequency discrimination suggests that children are able to use the place-based code before they are able to use the time-based code for frequency (Moore, 1973). However, by 7 months infants appear to hear the pitch of a harmonic complex with missing fundamental as adults do (Clarkson & Clifton, 1985) and their perception of the complex is similarly affected by stimulus manipulations (Clarkson & Clifton, 1995; Clarkson & Rogers, 1995). The status of complex pitch perception in younger infants has not been examined.

TEMPORAL PROCESSING. The developmental course of temporal processing is less well established than that of other auditory capacities. Duration discrimination and detection of a temporal gap in a sound improve from infancy to about 6 years of age (Elfenbein, Small, & Davis, 1993; Irwin, Ball, Kay, Stillman, & Rosser, 1985; Jensen & Neff, 1993; Morrongiello, 1985; Trehub, Schneider, & Henderson, 1995; Werner, Marean, Halpin, Spetner, & Gillenwater, 1992; Wightman et al., 1989), but measures based on the detection of amplitude modulation or on forward masking suggest that temporal resolution may be mature by 6 months of age (Hall & Grose, 1994; Levi & Werner, 1995, 1996; Werner, 1996).

LOCALIZATION. Because the head and external ears grow, the cues that are used to localize sounds change continually during that period of growth (Clifton, Gwiazda, Bauer, Clarkson, & Held, 1988). Sound localization has been quantified during development using the minimum audible angle (MAA), threshold for discriminating a difference in location between two sound sources. The MAA for location in the horizontal plane, or azimuth, is based on interaural comparisons. It improves progressively from 3 months to about 5 years of age (Clifton, 1992; Figure 21.4). The MAA for location in elevation is based on direction-dependent changes in spectrum imposed on incoming sound by the external ear. Morrongiello and Rocca (1987) reported that the MAA for elevation also improves during infancy, but reaches adult values earlier, at about 18 months of age. Infants' MAA in azimuth improves over an age period during which their ability to discriminate interaural differences does not improve (Ashmead, Davis, Whalem & Odom, 1991). It has been suggested that much of the development of sound localization depends not on the ability to calculate interaural differences, but in the construction of a "map" of auditory space (Werner & Gray, 1998). The neonate may hear changes in interaural differences when a

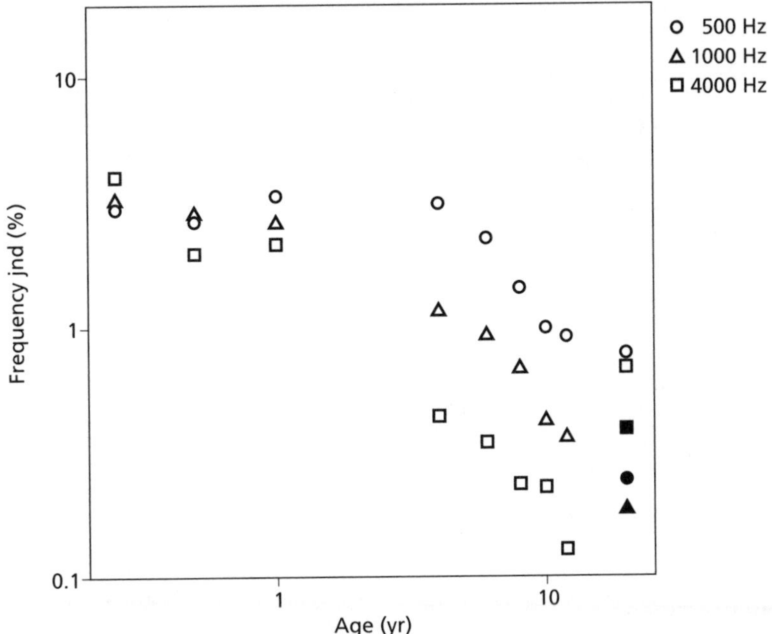

Figure 21.3. Frequency jnd as a function of age from three studies. Data for infants from Olsho et al. (1987); data for children from Maxon & Hochberg (1982); data for adults (far right hand points) are from Olsho et al. (1987), *open symbols*, and from Weir et al. (1977), *closed symbols*. The "age" axis is logarithmic only for clarity.

sound moves, but not be able to match locations in space to the interaural differences heard.

Role in Early Development

Newborns appear to prefer to listen to their own mother's voice over the voice of another woman (DeCasper & Fifer, 1980). They prefer to hear speech to which they have been exposed prenatally (DeCasper & Spence, 1986). They may even prefer to listen to the language spoken by their mother, rather than other languages, even when the speaker is not their mother (Nazzi, Bertoncini, & Mehler, 1998). It is quite likely that these preferences are based upon prenatal experience with sound: Under many conditions, infants prefer familiar sounds (Spence, 1996). However, newborns also prefer the highly inflected speech that adults typically direct to infants over the speech that adults typically direct to adults (Cooper & Aslin, 1994), even though they would not have heard it prenatally. Thus, infant-directed speech may be more attractive to infants because of its acoustic properties.

Enhanced attention to speech may well be important in the development of speech perception (Kemler Nelson, Hirsh-Pasek, Jusczyk, & Cassidy, 1989). Whether or not

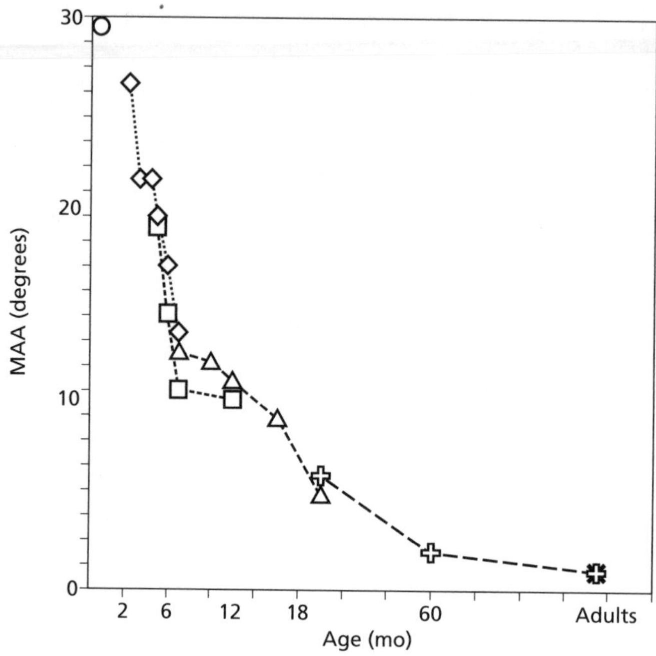

Figure 21.4. Minimum audible angle (MAA) in the horizontal plane as a function of age from several studies. *Squares*, Ashmead et al. (1988); *crosses*, Litovsky (1991); *diamonds*, Morrongiello (1988); *triangles*, Morrongiello et al. (1990); *circle*, Morrongiello et al. (1994); *asterisk*, Mills (1972).

enhanced attention to speech promotes the development of speech perception, however, it most certainly promotes social interactions between infant and caregiver. Infants clearly look at a talking human and show evidence of attention and interest. In fact, infants appeared distressed when they see their mother looking at them without speaking (Weinberg & Tronick, 1996). In general, vocalization is an important component of infants' social interactions (Bornstein et al., 1992).

Atypical interactions with hearing parents have frequently been reported for deaf infants and children (Greenberg, 1980; Koester, 1995; Schlesinger & Meadow, 1972). However, recent studies suggest that modalities other than hearing are capable of supporting normal social interactions and communication development. Both parents and infants can substitute visual and tactile signals for auditory signals in their interactions (Koester, Karkowski, & Traci, 1998; Smith-Gray & Koester, 1995). In fact, infant-directed sign has many of the same characteristics as infant-directed speech (Erting, Prezioso, & O'Grandy Hines, 1990; Masataka, 1992), and both hearing and deaf infants are more attentive and responsive to infant-directed than to adult-directed sign (Masataka, 1996, 1998). It appears, however, that hearing parents may be less successful than deaf parents in adapting their behaviors to accommodate deaf infants' dependence on visual and tactile input (Koester et al., 1998; Smith-Gray & Koester, 1995).

Effects of Early Experience

Despite the fact that nearly all aspects of auditory system morphology are established in the absence of experience with sound, the presence of the cochlea appears to be important to the maintenance of neurons and connections in the central auditory nervous system. Cochlear ablation prior to the onset of cochlear responses to sound results in reduction in neuronal size and number, and disruption of projections in the brainstem following hearing onset (Pasic, Moore, & Rubel, 1994; Russell & Moore, 1995). Physiological studies suggest that experience with sound is important to the maintenance and refinement of the neural connections established prior to the onset of cochlear response (Poon, Chen, & Hwang, 1990; Sanes & Constantine-Paton, 1985). Furthermore, if either auditory or visual input is disrupted, a precise map of auditory space fails to emerge in the superior colliculus of mammals (King, Hutchings, Moore, & Blakemore, 1988; Withington-Wray, Binns, & Keating, 1990b). Knudsen and his colleagues have detailed the critical period for such effects in the barn owl (Knudsen, 1985; Mogdans & Knudsen, 1993).

Speech Perception

Important changes in the perception of speech occur during infancy, such that the ability to discriminate among native speech sounds comes to differ from the ability to discriminate nonnative speech sounds. In a series of studies Werker and her colleagues showed that while 6-month-old infants living in homes where English was spoken exclusively could reliably distinguish between Hindi or Nthlakampx speech contrasts that do not occur in English, 12-month-old infants could not (Werker, 1994; Werker & Tees, 1984). Kuhl, Williams, Lacerda, Stevens, and Lindblom (1992) have shown that native vowel categories are also defined in the course of development, but by 6 months. Best (1993) subsequently showed that this pattern of development does not occur for all nonnative speech sounds. Best's results suggest that the effect of experience with native speech is to define the acoustic limits of the speech categories employed in the native language, which may or may not interfere with the perception of nonnative speech sounds. For example, Best found that a native speaker of English has trouble distinguishing between two variations of /k/ produced in Zulu; both variations are acceptable "k" in English. But the same listener has no trouble distinguishing between two Zulu "click" consonants that are unlike any speech sound used in English.

Sound Localization

It is generally argued that the development of processes like sound localization should depend upon experience with sound, because the system must adjust to small differences between the ears or slight asymmetries of the head. There are some indications that abnormal experience with sound in humans affects the accuracy of binaural processing. Wilmington, Gray, and Jahrsdorfer (1994) provide a particularly comprehensive account of the effects of early interaural disruption on binaural hearing following surgical correction of a congenital malformation of the external ear. Nearly all aspects of binaural hearing were abnormal in these patients prior to surgery, suggesting that the system had not been able to compensate for the imbalance between the ears. However, following surgery, several measures of binaural hearing approached normal values, including interaural difference discrimination. At the same time, these individuals were quite poor at localizing sound sources in space, suggesting that abnormal experience with interaural differences had prevented the formation of a map of auditory space.

Somesthesis

The term somesthesis encompasses a multitude of senses: touch, pain, temperature, kinesthesia, and proprioception. The review that follows concentrates on the development of tactile sensitivity and the neural pathways subserving it.

Methods for Assessing Function in Infants and Children

Behavioral Responses

Infant tactile sensitivity has been assessed primarily by observing reflex responses to tactile stimulation, providing a view of infant somatosensory processing that is limited in several ways. First, the occurrence of the reflex depends on the maturity of the entire sensorimotor pathway. Second, reflex responses often habituate, so few responses may be observed. Third, the reflexes typically used to study infants are normally only observed during infancy, precluding comparison to older individuals. If a reflex occurs, then it is clear that the periphery, at least, is functioning. It does not indicate whether other parts of the pathway are functioning. Standard psychophysical procedures have been used to assess the tactile sensitivity of children older than 4 or 5 years.

Evoked Potentials

Somatosensory evoked potentials (SEPs) have been widely used to assess the integrity of the nervous system in premature and high-risk infants (Gilmore, 1988). SEPs are generally elicited by electrical stimulation of the median nerve (MN), although a few studies have examined the response elicited by stimulation of the posterior tibial nerve (PTN). The components of the SEP have been well described in adults, including responses arising in the peripheral nerve, spinal cord, brainstem, thalamus, primary cortex and other cortical areas. Response latency is the most common SEP measure recorded. N1, with a latency of 19–20 ms in adults, is believed to represent the initial primary cortical response and is most frequently described. However, electrical stimulation generates a rather nonspecific response from the system, and it is never clear which pathways are generating the response. In addition, response latency is obviously affected by the length of the pathway, which in the case of peripheral nerves increases substantially during development. The use of latency divided by height as a more meaningful SEP measure has been advocated (Desmedt,

Brunko, & Debecker, 1976), but it is frequently not used in papers concerning SEP development.

Overview of Morphological and Physiological Development

Morphological Development

RECEPTORS. Developing nerve trunks are seen in human fetal skin as early as 6 wk CA, and fine nerve branches extending toward the epidermis are evident by 8–10 wk (Hogg, 1941; Holbrook, Bothwell, Schatteman, & Underwood, 1988). Adult-like nerve patterns, though of reduced density, were established in the dermis and epidermis of the limbs at 12 wk CA, throughout the body surface by 35 wk CA (Humphrey, 1964; Valman & Pearson, 1980). Cauna (1965) reported that Pacinian corpuscles make their appearance during the 4th month of gestation, and that Merkel's disks and Meissner's corpuscles are numerous in the skin of late term fetuses. However, Cauna also noted that Pacinian and Meissner's corpuscles changed in size, shape, and attachment to the epidermis throughout life. The density of these specialized endings also appeared to decrease with age. Thus, while the skin is innervated very early in development, accessory structures and nerve fiber density continue to mature into the third trimester and beyond.

SPINAL AND CRANIAL NERVES. At the periphery, basic circuitry is established early, but the efficiency of transmission continues to improve into childhood. Synapses have been reported in the marginal layer of the human dorsal horn at 6–7 wk CA (Okado, 1981; Wozniak, O'Rahilly, & Olszewska, 1980). However, the peripheral endings of trigeminal ganglion cells only reach their targets after central projections make contacts in the brainstem (Mirnics & Koerber, 1995a, 1995b; McKinnis, 1936), and peripheral myelinated nerve fiber diameter continues to increase until approximately 5 years postnatal age (Gutrecht & Dyck, 1969). Thus, development of peripheral nerves begins very early but its course is prolonged.

CENTRAL SOMATOSENSORY NERVOUS SYSTEM. The development of the central somatosensory nervous system has been less studied in humans, but predictions can be made on the basis of studies of other mammals (Belford & Killackey, 1979; Catalano, Robertson, & Killackey, 1996; Schlagger & O'Leary, 1994; Wise, Fleshman, & Jones, 1979). Central circuitry is probably established by about 11–12 weeks CA. Over the next 4–5 weeks, the somatotopic representation of the entire body is completed, and primary somatosensory cortex is functionally connected to the periphery around 19 weeks CA. During the second half of the human gestational period, however, the axonal and dendritic configurations and synaptic density and distribution at all levels of the system undergo considerable development (De Biasi, Amadeo, Arcelli, Frassoni, & Spreafico, 1997; Scheibel, Davies, & Scheibel, 1976). Myelination of the human somatosensory system continues throughout gestation and for about 2 years after birth (Yakovlev & Lecours, 1967). Both rostral-to-caudal and peripheral-to-central developmental gradients are evident in somatosensory development (Belford & Killackey, 1979; Killackey, Jacquin, & Rhoades, 1990; Mirnics & Koerber, 1995b).

Physiological Development

Structural and other comparisons to nonhuman species (Code & Juliano, 1992; Wu & Gonzalez, 1997) suggest that a cortical response to tactile stimulation could be observed at 17–19 weeks CA in human fetuses. Cortical responses to peripheral electrical stimulation can be recorded earlier than responses to tactile stimulation (Rubel, 1971), suggesting that peripheral immaturity may be a limiting factor in early responses to tactile stimulation.

In the mature somatosensory system, four different channels, differing in frequency response range and adaptation rate, are believed to carry vibrotactile information from the skin to the brain (Bolanowski, 1996). The development of these channels has been examined in single-unit studies of kittens. These studies show that slowly adapting fibers mature before rapidly adapting fibers and that low-frequency response thresholds are adult-like before high-frequency (Ferrington & Rowe, 1980). The development of Pacinian-afferent threshold and frequency response is particularly prolonged (Ferrington, Hora, & Rowe, 1984). Responses of neurons in the nuclei to which these fibers project mirror the immaturities observed in the peripheral response at the same age (Connor, Ferrington, & Rowe, 1984; Ferrington & Rowe, 1981, 1982). It is not clear whether the early receptive fields of somatosensory neurons are larger than those seen in adults or not (Armstrong-James, 1975; Eckholm, 1967; Fitzgerald, 1985; Juliano, Code, Tommerdahl, & Eslin, 1993; Rhoades, Killackey, Chiaia, & Jacquin, 1990; Rubel, 1971). The studies that have examined this question have produced discrepant results, but used different species, ages, and methodologies.

Maturation of the physiological response of the somatosensory system occurs in the second half of human gestation, and to date, little is known with regard to physiological thresholds or receptive field properties during human development. MN-SEPs have been recorded in infants as young as 25 weeks CA, but N1, with a latency of as long as 60 ms, is not evident in the response until about 29 wk CA (Bongers-Schokking, Colon, Hoogland, de Groot, & Van den Brande, 1991; Hrbek, Karlberg, & Olsson, 1973; Karniski, Wyble, Lease, & Blair, 1992; Klimach & Cooke, 1988; Majnemer, Rosenblatt, Willis, & Lavallee 1990). Peripheral nerve, dorsal horn and brainstem components are also observed in both MN-SEP and PTN-SEP at this age (Bongers-Schokking,Colon, Hoogland, Van den Brande, & de Groot, 1990; Gilmore, Brock, Hermansen, & Baumann, 1987). Response threshold decreases progressively between 34 weeks CA and about 5 years of age and is constant to at least 52 years (Eyre, Miller, & Ramesh, 1991). Adjusting response latencies for the length of the pathway by dividing latency by height (Desmedt et al., 1976) results in response latencies that decline progressively with age into childhood or adolescence. The latencies of peripheral nerve responses reach adult values at about 5–6 years of age and spinal responses reach adult values at about 7–10 years, while brainstem and cortical response latencies continue to decline until adolescence (Kimura, 1989; Tomita, Nishimura, & Tanaka, 1986). Myelination of the somatosensory pathway and increases in fiber diameter are typically offered as explanations for this developmental pattern (Gilmore, 1988). Improvements in synaptic transmission efficiency are also likely contributors, as indicated in several anatomical studies (Eggermont, 1988).

Development of Sensitivity

Initial Responses

Tactile reflexes mediated by the spinal reflex arc are first observed by the 8th week of gestation (Prechtl, 1989; Rayburn, 1989). Other tactile reflexes, such as rooting and grasping, typically appear around 24–28 wk CA (Hill, 1998). Cardiac and motor responses to "vibroacoustic" stimulation delivered through the maternal abdomen have been observed consistently in fetuses of 28–29 wk gestation age (Birnholz & Benacerraf, 1983; Kisilevsky, Muir, & Lowe, 1992). However, the artificial larynx used to generate the stimulus in these studies has a frequency response that extends from about 50 Hz to over 1000 Hz, so it is not clear whether fetuses are responding to stimulation of the skin or the ears.

Psychophysical Studies

Many fetal reflex responses to tactile stimulation are immature. For example, placing responses to footpad stimulation are observed in newborn rats and kittens, but these responses do not achieve adult form for 1–2 months (Clarke & Williams, 1994; Villablanca & Olmstead, 1979). Several studies have examined the development of tactile limb withdrawal reflexes in humans using von Frey hairs applied to the foot as the stimulus. Threshold for the response appears to increase from 0.5 g at 27 weeks CA to 1–2 g among full-term infants (Andrews & Fitzgerald, 1994; Fitzgerald, Shaw, & MacIntosh, 1988; Jacklin, Snow, & Maccoby, 1981; Figure 21.5). Those values are much smaller than the 40 g touch threshold on the sole of the foot reported for adults (Weinstein, 1968). The receptive field of the response seems to decrease in size with age (Andrews & Fitzgerald, 1994). A similar developmental pattern has been observed in rat pups where it has been noted that response latency and amplitude decrease progressively with age (Issler & Stephens, 1983; Vecchierini-Blineau & Guihneuc, 1982). Development of the limb withdrawal reflex is typically explained in terms of the development of descending inhibitory inputs to the spinal cord (Fitzgerald & Koltzenburg, 1986). However, in adults, the flexion withdrawal reflex occurs in response to noxious stimulation, and the fact that the response occurs in premature and full-term infants to low-intensity mechanical stimulation, suggests that different sensory receptors may mediate the reflex early in development.

Studies of touch in older children are consistent with a trend of decreasing sensitivity with age, at least in some cutaneous submodalities. For example, Schiff and Dytell (1972) found that two-point thresholds increased between 7.5 and 19.5 years of age. Verrillo (1977) also demonstrated that vibrotactile thresholds on the thenar eminence of 10-year-old children were lower than those of young adults from 40–160 Hz and above 320 Hz, but about the same as those of adults at 25 Hz and in the vicinity of 250 Hz. Subsequent studies have confirmed that school-age children have lower vibrotactile thresholds than adults, at frequencies between 40 and 250 Hz (Frisina & Gescheider, 1977; Fucci, Petrosino, Harris, & Randolph-Tyler, 1987; Halonen, Ylitalo, Holonen, & Lang, 1986; Figure 21.5). The results of these studies also suggest that the greatest age-related change occurs in Pacinian channels. The data of Fucci et al. (1987) also suggest that the perceived magnitude

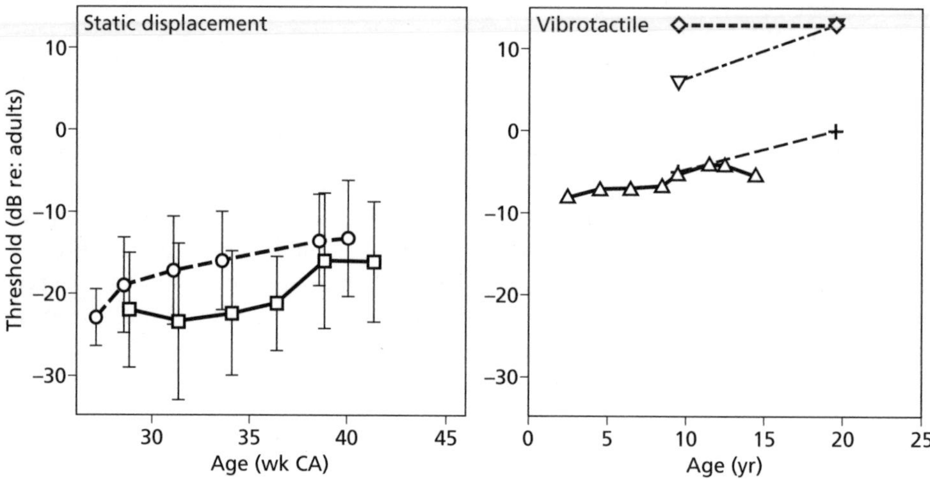

Figure 21.5. Thresholds for two different types of tactile stimulation as a function of age. Left panel shows thresholds for static displacement with a von Frey hair applied to the sole of the foot of preterm and term infants from two studies: *squares*, Andrews & Fitzgerald (1994); *circles*, Fitzgerald et al. (1988). Error bars represent ± 1 sem. Thresholds are expressed in dB re: adult thresholds reported by Weinstein (1968). Right panel shows thresholds for vibrotactile stimulation of the thenar eminance from two studies: *up triangles*, Halonen et al. (1986) – 100 Hz; *diamonds*, Verrillo (1979) – 25 Hz; *down triangles*, Verrillo (1979) – 40 Hz; *crosses*, Verrillo (1979) – 80 Hz. Thresholds are expressed re: thresholds for 20-year-olds at 80 Hz reported by Verrillo (1979).

of a vibrotactile stimulus to the tongue increases more rapidly with increasing intensity among younger subjects. Age-related changes in receptors (Cauna, 1965) are typically offered as explanations for these changes in sensitivity.

Although absolute sensitivity to tactile stimulation decreases with age, the ability to use tactile information, for example to identify objects or to make judgments of size, improves with age. Infants appear to be able to recognize a familiar object on the basis of touch alone (Gottfried & Rose, 1980). However, Schiff and Dytell (1972) showed that the ability to discriminate among patterns and to identify objects improved between 7.5 and 19 years of age, in the same subjects whose tactile sensitivity was reported to grow poorer with age. Similarly, Pick, Klein, and Pick (1966) demonstrated that tactile discrimination of arbitrary line figures improved into late childhood. In monkeys Carlson (1984) found that while younger monkeys were more efficient at learning texture discrimination than were older monkeys, older monkeys were more efficient at learning size discrimination. In other words, younger monkeys had better sensitivity, but older monkeys were better at tasks that required integration of tactile information.

Role in Early Development

Sensitivity to tactile stimulation is clearly important to early postnatal survival: Many feeding behaviors depend on tactile stimulation. For example, Larson and Stein (1984) showed that rat pups with impaired tactile input had no trouble locating their mothers, but could not attach to the nipple. Along the same lines, rooting and sucking are elicited specifically by tactile stimulation in human infants.

Tactile stimulation is an important determinant of infant behavioral state. Touch has been shown to be an effective means of soothing a distressed infant (Korner & Thoman, 1972). Blass and Ciaramitaro (1994a) reported that orotactile stimulation (a pacifier) led to reductions in crying, heart rate, and motor activity as well as increased eye opening and hand-mouth coordination among newborns. Tactile stimulation also apparently supports normal development of perceptual processes. Rose, Schmidt, Riese, and Bridger (1980) showed that premature infants who were systematically massaged and stroked in the weeks following their birth exhibited greater cardiac and behavioral response to suprathreshold tactile stimulation than did premature infants who did not receive this intervention. Moreover, infants who received the touch intervention also demonstrated greater auditory responsiveness (Dorros, Brody, & Rose, 1980) and enhanced visual recognition memory 6 months later (Rose, 1980).

Touch also plays an important role in the development of social interactions. When adults are asked to play with an infant in face-to-face interaction, they typically touch the infant. While infants normally look away from an adult who maintains a neutral, silent face, if the adult actively touches the infant in this condition, the infant continues to look at the adult's face (Stack & Muir, 1992). In fact, 3-month-olds' attention to visual and auditory stimulation tends to wane more quickly in the absence of tactile stimulation (Gusella, Muir, & Tronick, 1988). Brossard and Decarie (1968) have also shown that tactile stimulation is an especially effective reinforcer of infant smiling.

Effects of Early Experience

The mechanisms underlying the development of somatotopy have been a topic of considerable interest for the past 15 years, since it was first reported that peripheral deafferentation prevented the development of the orderly representation of the periphery in somatosensory cortex (Woolsey, 1990). Interest has been concentrated on the development of the neural representation of facial vibrissae, or whiskers. Peripheral lesion (vibrissa cauterization or nerve section) during a critical period in development leads to extensive loss of ganglion volume and cell number (e.g., Jacquin, Mooney, & Rhoades, 1986; Savy, Margules, Farkas-Bargeton, & Verley, 1981) and the development of abnormal peripheral innervation (Rhoades et al., 1987), as well as failure of the formation of organized neural representations at all levels (Killackey & Belford, 1980; Ma & Woolsey, 1984; Woolsey, Anderson, Wann, & Stanfield, 1979). Many neurons are unresponsive to tactile stimulation following such procedures, and responsive neurons have abnormally large receptive fields. Eliminating afferent input from some whiskers, but not others, during a critical period in development also leads to a reduction in the neural area representing the missing whisker and expansion of the area representing the remaining whiskers (Jacquin, McCasland, Henderson, Rhoades, & Woolsey, 1993; Killackey, Chiaia, Bennett-Clarke, Eck, & Rhoades, 1994). The response characteristics of neurons in the somatosensory pathway can also be altered by preventing young animals from moving their whiskers while leaving the afferent pathway intact (Nicolelis, De Oliveira, Lin, & Chapin, 1996) or by artificially connecting two nearby body parts (e.g., ear and shoulder) so that stimulation of one results in simultaneous stimulation of the other (Benedetti, 1995).

The behavioral consequences of deafferentation have not been studied extensively, but the results of the existing studies are consistent with the anatomical and physiological observations. For example, Carvell and Simons (1996) reported that rats that had their whiskers clipped daily from birth to 45 days of age were largely unable to perform difficult tactile discriminations after their whiskers were allowed to regrow. Moreover, the way rats moved their whiskers across the stimulus surface was abnormal.

Taste

Methods for Assessing Function in Infants and Children

There is a general consensus regarding the categorization of taste quality. Most investigators agree on the identity of four basic tastes, sweet, bitter, sour, and salty. As a consequence, taste stimuli used in most studies include representatives of these categories leading to considerable methodological consistency.

In infants, indicators of gustatory function involve differential responding to tastants, usually with responding to water used as a baseline. The earliest approaches involved consummatory responding or obtaining intake measures (Peterson & Rainey, 1910). Such approaches have numerous problems, including a reluctance to allow infants to ingest tastants that may be harmful. When consumption is compared to water, the failure to differentially consume may not imply a failure to detect the taste, but merely a failure to prefer or avoid it relative to water. Further, some have suggested that water is not neutral for infants, but rather that they dislike it. Finally some have questioned whether infants are even capable of inhibiting ingestion of aversive tastes, based on incidents such as the inadvertent poisoning of a group of newborns fed a formula which had been made with salt instead of sugar.

Significant methodological advances over intake measures have been made. These include the direct measurement of nonnutritive sucking patterns and tongue movements in response to the delivery of minute amounts of taste solutions (Crook, 1987; Nowlis & Kesson, 1976). This approach circumvents the problem of reluctance to offer infants highly concentrated or potentially unwholesome substances in quantity and also avoids the confound of postingestional effects of tastants consumed in larger amounts. Another approach has been to use the infant's reflexive gustofacial responses to tastants, most recently by videotaping infants' faces during the delivery of very small amounts of tastant solution. Distinctive patterns of facial reactions have been described in response to the presentation of different solutions (Peterson & Rainey, 1910; Steiner, 1977). In addition to the elicitation of facial reactions, gustatory stimulation of newborns has measurable effects on autonomic activity, such as heart rate, providing another index of detection (Crook & Lipsitt, 1976).

It may be noted that methods for assessing gustatory function in infants rely to some extent on hedonic reactions to tastes and are therefore of limited value in the assessment of hedonically neutral but detectable stimuli. In addition, although these methods can provide unequivocal evidence for the detection and discrimination of tastants, they are unsuitable for finer distinctions such as the determination of thresholds.

The assessment of gustatory function of children has typically relied on the standard psychophysical methods utilized with adults, often with minimal adaptation to the cognitive limitations or response biases of young children (Cowart, 1981). Because the appropriateness of the methods used has been questioned, the occasional reports of lower gustatory sensitivity in young children have been hard to interpret. On the other hand, because children over the age of four years can generally be expected to understand instructions, assessments at this age and beyond tend not to be limited to responses based on reflexive hedonic reactions, and measures of gustatory sensitivity can be attempted.

Overview of Morphological and Physiological Development

Morphological evidence reveals the presence of taste buds as early as the 7th or 8th week of gestation in human fetuses, and these buds are structurally mature by around the 13th week of gestation (Bradley & Mistretta, 1975). Postnatally, the density of papillae and taste buds on the tongue appears to change with age. There have been reports that the number of foliate and circumvallate papillae is highest in childhood whereas the number of taste buds per papillae peaks in young adulthood (Cowart, 1981). Functionally, the gustatory system of fetal sheep, whose gustatory development appears to parallel that of the human fetus, has been shown to respond to chemical stimulation of the tongue early in gestation (Mistretta & Bradley, 1977). Electrophysiologically, responses to salt appear to develop more slowly than those to other basic tastes (Hill & Mistretta, 1990).

Development of Sensitivity

Initial Differential Responses. The evidence is suggestive of gustatory function in the fetus although methodological limitations have precluded clear experimental documentation. There appears to be significant fetal swallowing activity (Ross & Nijland, 1997). Amniotic fluid contains a wide variety of chemicals which would be effective gustatory stimuli (glucose, fructose, citric acid, urea, salts) and the chemical composition of the amniotic fluid changes frequently, further contributing to its effectiveness in providing gustatory stimulation. Reports exist (Cowart, 1981; Lecanuet, 1996) that fetal swallowing can be increased by the injection of saccharin into the amniotic fluid and swallowing can be inhibited by the addition of a bitter chemical. This suggests not only a very early responsiveness of the taste system, but some ability to discriminate between tastants.

Preterm and term infants, within hours of birth, have been tested for gustofacial responding to prototypes of the four basic tastants (Peterson & Rainey, 1910 cited by Cowart, 1981; Rosenstein & Oster, 1988; Steiner, 1977). Consistent responses of short latency were elicited by sweet, sour, and bitter stimuli and these responses differed for the different tastes. Facial expressions were similar to those made by adults exposed to those stimuli and they were judged as clearly indicative of an innate preference for sweet and an aversion to bitter and sour tastes. Consistent rejection of bitter tastes is seen with quinine but not urea solutions. Because there is evidence that these two bitter tastants may involve different receptor mechanisms (Kinnamon & Cummings, 1992), this suggests that the receptor system for the bitter taste of quinine matures sooner than that for urea. Responses of neonates to salt were judged as ambiguous. These studies employed fairly concentrated solutions and no attempt was made to assess sensitivity. Crook (1978) measured burst-pause patterns of nonnutritive sucking and found that this pattern was altered by sucrose and salt, as compared to water. Sucrose lengthened the bursts while salt shortened them.

PSYCHOPHYSICAL STUDIES. The data on taste development in children using psychophysical methods have been somewhat spotty. Most studies of threshold determination have not tested all four basic tastes and findings are frequently inconsistent. Thresholds have been reported to be higher in children than in young adults but it is not clear whether this was due to sensory factors or to attentional or motivational differences (Richter & Campbell, 1940; reviewed by Cowart, 1981). Age effects are generally weak. More consistent is the evidence of gender differences, with girls generally being more sensitive than boys.

The situation is improved considerably by a recent study (James, Laing, & Oram, 1997) which provides a careful comparison of the ability of 8–9-year-old children and adults to detect taste stimuli. All four basic tastants were included and gender, as well as age, differences were assessed. The results showed 8–9-year-old girls did not differ significantly from adult men and women in their detection thresholds for any of the four tastes, nor did the men and women differ from each other. In contrast, the 8–9-year-old boys had significantly higher thresholds for all tastants than women; significantly higher thresholds for sucrose, sodium chloride, and citric acid than men; and significantly higher thresholds for sucrose and sodium chloride than girls of their age. Thresholds tended to be from 2 to 7 fold higher in the boys than in the other groups. These differences do not appear to stem from the boys' difficulty in performing the detection task but instead tend to support immature gustatory sensitivity in boys, but not girls, of this age.

Role in Early Development

In children and adults gustatory signals play a critical role in food selection. Such cues provide information regarding the nutritiousness of foods and drinks, with sweetness generally signaling caloric value and saltiness signaling the presence of sodium. Furthermore, unpleasant tastes such as sour and bitter can signal spoilage and toxicity. The ability to detect such important features of ingestants before swallowing them is of clear survival value. However, the initial diet of the human infant in the months after birth is not varied, nor does the infant do much selecting. Instead the infant is either breast or bottle fed and taste would appear to play a relatively minor role in these situations. Yet the evidence reviewed here clearly indicates that the gustatory system of the newborn functions well before the time of weaning. This raises the question of whether taste plays a role in early development aside from its usual role in food selection.

Recent studies have found that tasting sugar solutions or milk enables infants to cope more successfully with pain or stress. For example, Blass and his colleagues found that sucrose delivered to the mouth of infants in volumes as low as 100 to 200 ml elevated pain thresholds and quieted distressed infants (Blass & Hoffmeyer, 1991). These effects are believed to be mediated by endogenous opioids released in response to sweet tastes. Evidence for opioid mediation includes the observation that, in rats, these effects are blocked by the administration of the specific opioid antagonists naloxone and naltrexone (Blass & Fitzgerald, 1988) and that, in human infants born to women who were maintained on methadone during pregnancy, sucrose was not effective in quieting them (Blass & Ciaramitaro, 1994b).

Effects of Early Experience

There is little or no evidence for an important facilitative or maintenance role for early taste experience in gustatory development in humans. Although there is good evidence for varied gustatory experience prenatally and a functioning gustatory system postnatally, deprivation or distortion of this experience has not been attempted. In addition, animal models provide little indication that gustatory experience, per se, plays a crucial role in development of the gustatory pathway. Those animal studies which find significant, lasting effects of neonatal manipulations on adult function have introduced fairly extreme treatments (e.g. destruction of taste buds; severe sodium deprivation), the effects of which were unlikely to have been limited to gustatory stimulation alone (Hill & Prezekop, 1988; Lasiter, 1991). The gustatory system may be buffered against gross distortion or deprivation of stimulation. Unlike other sensory systems, in gustatory development evidence for a significant role for stimulation during critical periods is lacking.

Olfaction

Methods for Assessing Function in Infants and Children

Unlike the taste system, there are no agreed upon primary olfactory qualities, and hence there is startling variety in the chemicals that have been used to assess olfaction. Reasons for the choice of particular chemicals is not often explained. Sometimes they are volatiles of known safety and strong odor to adults. Sometimes they are chemicals of ecological validity for infants (e.g. breast odors; amniotic fluid) and in these cases the stimuli are not defined chemically.

Early efforts to assess olfactory competence of neonates based on spontaneous responses produced generally inconsistent results. More recent psychophysical methods incorporate simultaneous measurement of different physiological responses during odor presentation with videotaping of behavioral responses to the odor, including head orientation and facial expression. The studies aim to assess whether or not the infant can detect an odor and whether two odors can be discriminated from each other. For the latter question a habituation paradigm has proven useful, even with infants as young as 2–3 days of age. Hedonic reactions to odors have been assessed using a head-turn response with odors presented to the left and right of the infant's head.

Measures of olfactory sensitivity have been obtained from children using detection and recognition thresholds. Additionally, discrimination and recognition abilities using odors well above threshold have been assessed. Perhaps most interesting have been the hedonic assessments which have been attempted to address the question of when strong hedonic responses, particularly strong negative responses to "disgusting" odors, emerge. These studies have used verbal and nonverbal indices of pleasantness or unpleasantness for odors commonly viewed by adults as extremely unpleasant (e.g. sweat; feces) or pleasant (e.g. lavender; vanilla).

Overview of Morphological and Physiological Development

The primary olfactory bulbs can be identified as early as the 8th to 10th week of gestation and the receptor cells begin to appear between the 9th and 11th week. Olfactory marker protein, a possible correlate of olfactory receptor function, has been demonstrated in the olfactory bulb of human fetuses between the 28th and the 35th week of gestation (Schaal, 1988). The external nares are obstructed by epithelial nasal plugs until the 4th to 6th month of gestation, after which the nasal passages are clear and amniotic fluid flows through them. Despite suggestions to the contrary, it is generally agreed that the fluid medium of the uterine cavity is capable of effectively delivering olfactant molecules to the olfactory receptors, and that such stimulus delivery may yield even greater sensitivity than delivery of those molecules in air. Together these findings suggest an early time course for development of the olfactory system, and once the nasal plugs disappear, the amniotic fluid provides a rich source of chemicals capable of stimulating the system.

Development of Sensitivity

Initial Differential Responses

There is evidence for olfactory function in preterm neonates as young as 6–7 months CA. For example, 8 of 11 premature newborns, between 7 and 8 months CA, displayed arousal reactions to the presentation of a mint odor (Sarnat, 1978). However, it is not clear whether these responses were mediated principally by olfactory, vomeronasal or trigeminal systems.

A number of studies have demonstrated that healthy, term infants can detect and discriminate among a range of olfactory stimuli, although thresholds vary both with the nature of the odorant and across different infants. In an early, controlled study (Engen, Lipsitt, & Kaye, 1963) newborns were exposed to a variety of odors during sleep. General activity, leg withdrawal, respiration, and heart rate were measured. Infants were reported to be sensitive to a variety of odors. Other studies confirm sensitivity to odors in newborns and suggest that sensitivity increases over the first few days after birth (Schaal, 1988).

Psychophysical Studies

There is a relative scarcity of developmental studies of olfactory function in childhood and adolescence. Those that exist tend to point to good sensitivity to odors and a well-developed ability to discriminate among odors in young children 5 years and beyond. Studies also report lower thresholds for odor detection in children and adolescents than in adults, with females outperforming males in most studies. On the other hand, odor identification (e.g., the ability to identify an odor by name or picture) tends to improve with age, up to adulthood (Schaal, 1988).

Despite clear evidence of olfactory function at birth there is some controversy regarding the emergence of hedonic responses to odors. A number of studies have failed to find expected patterns of odor preference in children under 5 years of age. For example, almost all 3–4-year-olds in one study (Stein, Ottenberg, & Roulet, 1958) rated odors of synthetic sweat and feces to be as pleasant as that of synthetic banana. In recent studies in which observable behaviors are scored or sorting tasks are used which are geared to the capabilities and interests of 3-year-olds, hedonic reactions to odorants conform fairly closely to those of adults (Schmidt & Beauchamp, 1988). Thus, when methodologies are utilized which are appropriate to age, children as young as 3 years of age show clearly defined hedonic responses to odors.

Role in Early Development

The apparent olfactory competence of newborns and the distinct possibility of olfactory function *in utero* provide a potential mechanism for olfactory mediation of early maternal attachment. This possibility has been examined in a variety of studies in humans and animals. In rats, studies have found that the odor of amniotic fluid (which the postpartum rat dam distributes over her ventrum) promotes the newborn pup's first nipple attachment (Teicher & Blass, 1977). The introduction of an exogenous odorant, citral, into the uterine cavity alters the behavior of the newborn pup, making it more likely to attach to nipples with citral odor (Pederson & Blass, 1982). Thus, prenatal exposure to natural amniotic fluid or odors introduced into the amniotic fluid, can influence postnatal rat behavior. An important role in attachment for odor cues also has been demonstrated in the squirrel monkey. Eight-week-old infant squirrel monkeys show behavioral preference for their own mother relative to an unfamiliar lactating mother, but they no longer do so when maternal odor cues are removed (Kaplan, 1977).

Studies in humans have shown that breast-fed infants will preferentially orient towards the odor of their mothers' breast relative to an unscented stimulus or the odor of an unfamiliar lactating female (Macfarlane, 1975). Reliable preference emerges over the early neonatal period and clearly indicates that human neonates can discriminate subtle distinctions among olfactory stimuli when these stimuli are in low concentration but of considerable social significance. The degree to which this odor preference is based on positive associations, familiarity, or some other mechanism remains to be determined.

Effects of Early Experience

A substantial body of research, mostly in rodents, supports the notion that early olfactory experience has significant effects on brain and behavior. Unilateral deprivation of olfactory stimulation, by surgical sealing of the external nares, has dramatic effects on development of the olfactory bulbs. When mice or rats have their nares occluded within the first 10 days of life they display a 25% decrease in the size of the ipsilateral olfactory bulb (Benson, Ryugo, & Hinds, 1984; Meisami, 1976). Deprivation effects are seen without receptor degeneration. The contralateral bulb appears unaffected, neither reduced nor augmented by the treatment. Thus, olfactory stimulation appears necessary for normal olfactory bulb development and deprivation of stimulation has clear anatomical and neurochemical effects which are lateralized to the side of the head in which occlusion occurred.

Conclusions

The development of the senses described in this chapter can be grossly summarized: Function starts early in the prenatal period and is well-established at term birth in humans, but development continues well into childhood or beyond. The function of these sensory systems at birth is generally affected by early experience, and these effects are critical to orienting the neonate toward the important sources of stimulation in the postnatal environment. Finally, a general theme in sensory development seems to be that the capacity to process the features of a stimulus develop early, but perceptual processes that involve synthesis or integration of sensory information continue to improve until adolescence or adulthood.

Basic Data

Hearing Development

Some psychophysical quantities

Age/Measure	*1 month*	*3 months*	*6 months*	*6 years*	*Adult*
Pure-tone threshold, 500 Hz (dB SPL)[a]	56	39	29	18	14
Pure-tone threshold, 4000 Hz (dB SPL)[a]	38	24	13	12	11
Frequency jnd, 500 Hz (%)[b]	na	3	3.5	2.8	0.8
Frequency jnd, 4000 Hz (%)[b]	na	4.2	2	0.7	0.6
Duration jnd (ms)[c]	na	na	20	15	10
ABR Wave I latency (ms)[d]	1.7	1.6	1.6	1.5	1.5
ABR Wave V latency (ms)[d]	6.8	6.3	6.1	5.6	5.6

[a] Based on results of Olsho et al. (1988), Trehub et al. (1988), Maxon & Hochberg (1982), Elliott & Katz (1980)
[b] Based on results of Olsho et al. (1987), Maxon & Hachberg (1982)
[c] Based on results of Morrongiello & Trehub (1987)
[d] Based on results of Gorga et al. (1989)

Age at onset of hearing for various species

Species	*Age/Gestational period*
Cat	62 days/64 days
Rat	30 days/22 days
Guinea pig	48 days/69 days
Gerbil	37 days/25 days
Humans	20 weeks/40 weeks

Somatosensory Development

Age/Measure	*1 month*	*3 years*	*10 years*	*Adult*
Vibrotactile threshold, 100 Hz (dB re: 1 μm)[a]	na	−8	−5	0
MN-SEP N1 latency/body height (ms/cm)[b]	0.34	0.18	0.15	0.12

[a] Based on results of Halonen et al. (1986) and Verrillo (1977)

[b] Based on results of Tomita et al. (1986)

Note

1. The preparation of this chapter was supported by NIDCD grant number R01 DC00369 to L. A. Werner and DC00248 to I. L. Bernstein.

Suggested Readings

Hearing Development

Rubel, E. W., Fay, R. R. & Popper, A. N. (Eds) (1998). *Development of the auditory system.* New York: Springer Verlag. [A comprehensive and up-to-date edited volume covering all aspects of auditory development.]

Werner, L. A., & Marean, G. C. (1996). *Human auditory development.* Boulder, CO: Westview Press. [Concentrates on the development of hearing in humans, using data from nonhumans to try to explicate the mechanisms of development.]

Tactile Development

Purves, D., Riddle, D. R., White, L. E., & Gutierrez-Ospina, G. (1994). Neural activity and the development of the somatic sensory system. *Current Opinions in Neurobiology, 4,* 120–123. [This volume of *Current Opinions in Neurobiology* includes several outstanding papers dealing with current issues in the development of the somatosensory system. The Purves et al. paper is a particularly enthusiastic example.]

Taste and Olfactory Development

Doty, R. L. (Ed.) (1995) *Handbook of olfaction and gustation.* New York: Marcel Dekker, Inc. [Although it addresses olfaction and gustation in general, this volume has several interesting chapters which focus on development. Of particular interest would be the ones by Porter and Schaal, by Mistretta and Hill, and by Ganchrow.]

Additional Topics

Event Related Potentials (ERPs)

ERPs have engendered recent interest in the area of auditory development. ERPs occur not simply in response to sound, but to a change in sound or to an unexpected sound. See Kraus, McGee, Micco, Sharma, Carrell, and Nicol (1993) and Shibasaki and Miyazaki (1992).

Tonotopic Organization is not Stable during Development.

While the most mature part of the cochlea at the onset of sound evoked responses was the base, where high frequencies are coded in the adult, the initial responses to sound tended to be restricted to mid-to-low frequencies. Rubel and colleagues hypothesized that the base of the cochlea actually responds best to mid-to-low frequencies when it begins to respond, and subsequent studies have generally confirmed this hypothesis. See Rübsamen and Lippe (1998) and Mills and Rubel (1996).

The Binaural Masking Level Difference

The improvement in masked threshold under dichotic listening conditions, has been shown to be smaller among 6- and 12-month-olds than among adults, but adult-like by 5 years of age. See Hall and Grose (1990) and Nozza, Wagner, and Crandell (1988).

Sensitivity to Noxious Stimulation

See Falcon, Guendellman, Stolberg, Frenk, and Urca (1996) and Johnston, Stevens, Yang, and Horton (1996).

References

Abdala, C. (1996). Distortion product otoacoustic emission (2f1–f2) amplitude as a function of f2/f1 frequency ratio and primary tone level separation in human adults and neonates. *Journal of the Acoustical Society of America, 100*, 3726–3740.

Abdala, C. (1998). A developmental study of distortion product otoacoustic emission (2f1–f2) suppression in humans. *Hearing Research, 121*, 125–138.

Abdala, C., & Folsom, R. C. (1995). The development of frequency resolution in humans as revealed by the auditory brain-stem response recorded with notched-noise masking. *Journal of the Acoustical Society of America, 98*, 921–930.

Abdala, C., & Sininger, Y. S. (1996). The development of cochlear frequency resolution in the human auditory system. *Ear and Hearing, 17*, 374–385.

Allen, P., Wightman, F., Kistler, D., & Dolan, T. (1989). Frequency resolution in children. *Journal of Speech and Hearing Research, 32*, 317–322.

American National Standards Institute (1989). *American national standard specifications for audiometers.* ANSI-S3.6–1989.

Andrews, K., & Fitzgerald, M. (1994). The cutaneous withdrawal reflex in human neonates:

Sensitization, receptive fields, and the effects of contralateral stimulation. *Pain, 56,* 95–101.

Armstrong-James, M. (1975). The functional status and columnar organization of single cells responding to cutaneous stimulation in neonatal rat somatosensory cortex SI. *Journal of Physiology (London), 246,* 501–538.

Ashmead, D., Davis, D., Whalen, T., & Odom, R. (1991). Sound localization and sensitivity to interaural time differences in human infants. *Child Development, 62,* 1211–1226.

Ashstead, D. H., Clifton, R. K., & Perris, E. E. (1987). Precision of auditory localization in human infants. *Developmental Psychology, 24* (5), 641–647.

Bargones, J. Y., & Burns, E. M. (1988). Suppression tuning curves for spontaneous otoacoustic emissions in infants and adults. *Journal of the Acoustical Society of America, 83,* 1809–1816.

Bargones, J. Y., & Werner, L. A. (1994). Adults listen selectively; infants do not. *Psychological Science, 5,* 170–174.

Bargones, J. Y., Werner, L. A., & Marean, G. C. (1995). Infant psychometric functions for detection: Mechanisms of immature sensitivity. *Journal of the Acoustical Society of America, 98,* 99–111.

Belford, G. R., & Killackey, H. P. (1979). The development of vibrissae representation in subcortical trigeminal centers of the neonatal rat. *Journal of Comparative Neurology, 188,* 63–74.

Benedetti, F. (1995). Differential formation of topographic maps on the cerebral cortex and superior colliculus of the mouse by temporally correlated tactile-tactile and tactile-visual inputs. *European Journal of Neuroscience, 7,* 1942–1951.

Benson, T. E., Ryugo, D. K., & Hinds, J. W. (1984). Effects of sensory deprivation on the developing mouse olfactory system: A light and electron microscopic, morphometric analysis. *Journal of Neuroscience, 4,* 638–653.

Best, C. T. (1993). Emergence of language-specific constraints in perception of non-native speech: A window on early phonological development. In B. de Boysson-Bardies, S. de Schonen, P. Jusczyk, P. McNeilage, & J. Morton (Eds.), *Developmental neurocognition: Speech and face processing in the first year of life* (pp. 289–304). Boston: Kluwer Academic Publishers.

Birnholz, J. C., & Benacerraf, B. R. (1983). The development of human fetal hearing. *Science, 222,* 516–518.

Blass, E. M., & Ciaramitaro, V. (1994a). A new look at some old mechanisms in human newborns: Taste and tactile determinants of state, affect, and action. *Monographs of the Society for Research in Child Development, 59,* 1–81.

Blass, E. M., & Ciaramitaro, V. (1994b). Oral determinants of state, affect, and action in newborn humans. *Monographs of the Society for Research in Child Development, 59,* 1–96.

Blass, E. M., & Fitzgerald, E. (1988). Milk-induced analgesia and comforting in 10-day-old rats: Opioid mediation. *Pharmacology, Biochemistry and Behavior, 29,* 9–13.

Blass, E. M., & Hoffmeyer, L. N. (1991). Sucrose as an analgesic in newborn humans. *Pediatrics, 87,* 215–218.

Bolanowski, S. J. (1996). Information processing channels in the sense of touch. In G. Franzén, R. Johansson, & L. Terenius (Eds.), *Somesthesis and the neurobiology of the somatosensory cortex* (pp. 49–58). Basel: Birkhäuser Verlag.

Bond, B., & Stevens, S. S. (1969). Cross-modality matching of brightness to loudness by 5-year-olds. *Perception and Psychophysics, 6,* 337–339.

Bongers-Schokking, C. J., Colon, E. J., Hoogland, R. A., de Groot, C. J., & Van den Brande, J. L. (1991). Somatosensory evoked potentials in neonates with primary congenital hypothyroidism during the first week of therapy. *Pediatric Research, 30,* 34–39.

Bongers-Schokking, J. J., Colon, E. J., Hoogland, R. A., Van den Brande, J. L., & de Groot, C. J. (1990). Somatosensory evoked potentials in term and preterm infants in relation to postconceptional age and birth weight. *Neuropediatrics, 21,* 32–36.

Bornstein, M. H., Tamis-LeMonda, C. S., Tal, J., Ludemann, P., Toda, S., Rahn, C. W., Pecheux, M. G., Azuma, H., & Vardi, D. (1992). Maternal responsiveness to infants in three societies: The United States, France, and Japan. *Child Development, 63,* 808–821.

Bradley, R. M., & Mistretta, C. M. (1975). Fetal sensory receptors. *Physiological Reviews, 55,* 352–

382.
Brossard, L. M., & Decarie, T. G. (1968). Comparative reinforcing effect of eight stimulations on the smiling response of infants. *Journal of Child Psychology and Psychiatry, 9,* 51–59.
Bull, D., Eilers, R. E., & Oller, D. K. (1984). Infants' discrimination of intensity variation in multisyllabic stimuli. *Journal of the Acoustical Society of America, 76,* 13–17.
Cant, N. B. (1998). Structural development of the mammalian central auditory pathways. In E. W. Rubel, R. R. Fay, & A. N. Popper (Eds.), *Development of the auditory system* (pp. 315–414). New York: Springer Verlag.
Carlson, M. (1984). Development of tactile discrimination capacity in Macaca mulatta. I. Normal infants. *Brain Research, 318,* 69–82.
Carvell, G. E., & Simons, D. J. (1996). Abnormal tactile experience early in life disrupts active touch. *Journal of Neuroscience, 16,* 2750–2757.
Catalano, S. M., Robertson, R. T., & Killackey, H. P. (1996). Individual axon morphology and thalamocortical topography in developing rat somatosensory cortex. *Journal of Comparative Neurology, 367,* 36–53.
Cauna, N. (1965). The effects of aging on the receptor organs of the human dermis. In W. Montagna (Eds.), *Advances in biology of skin: Vol. 6. Aging.* New York: Pergamon Press.
Clarke, K. A., & Williams, E. (1994). Development of locomotion in the rat – spatiotemporal footfall patterns. *Physiology and Behavior, 55,* 151–155.
Clarkson, M. G., & Clifton, R. K. (1985). Infant pitch perception: Evidence for responding to pitch categories and the missing fundamental. *Journal of the Acoustical Society of America, 77,* 1521–1528.
Clarkson, M. G., & Clifton, R. K. (1995). Infants' pitch perception: Inharmonic tonal complexes. *Journal of the Acoustical Society of America, 98,* 1372–1379.
Clarkson, M. G., & Rogers, E. C. (1995). Infants require low-frequency energy to hear the pitch of the missing fundamental. *Journal of the Acoustical Society of America, 98,* 148–154.
Clifton, R. K. (1992). The development of spatial hearing in human infants. In L. A. Werner & E. W. Rubel (Eds.), *Developmental psychoacoustics* (pp. 135–157). Washington, DC: American Psychological Association.
Clifton, R. K., Gwiazda, J., Bauer, J., Clarkson, M., & Held, R. (1988). Growth in head size during infancy: Implications for sound localization. *Developmental Psychology, 24,* 477–483.
Code, R. A., & Juliano, S. L. (1992). Development of cat somatosensory cortex: Structural and metabolic considerations. *Cerebral Cortex,* 2, 231–243.
Collins, A. A., & Gescheider, G. A. (1989). The measurement of loudness in individual children and adults by absolute magnitude estimation and cross-modality matching. *Journal of the Acoustical Society of America, 85,* 2012–2021.
Connor, K. M., Ferrington, D. G., & Rowe, M. J. (1984). Tactile sensory coding during development: Signaling capacities of neurons in kitten dorsal column nuclei. *Journal of Neurophysiology, 52,* 86–98.
Cooper, R. P., & Aslin, R. N. (1994). Developmental differences in infant attention to the spectral properties of infant-directed speech. *Child Development, 65,* 1663–1677.
Cowart, B. J. (1981). Development of taste perception in humans: Sensitivity and preference throughout the life span. *Psychological Bulletin, 90,* 43–73.
Crook, C. (1978). Taste perception in the newborn infant. *Infant Behavior and Development, 1,* 52–69.
Crook, C. (1987). Taste and olfaction. In P. Salapatek & L. Cohen (Eds.), *Handbook of infant perception* (pp. 237–264). Orlando: Academic Press.
Crook, C. & Lipsitt, L. P. (1976). Neonatal nutritive sucking: Effects of taste stimulation upon sucking and heart rate. *Child Development, 47,* 518–522.
De Biasi, S., Amadeo, A., Arcelli, P., Frassoni, C., & Spreafico, R. (1997). Postnatal development of GABA-immunoreactive terminals in the reticular and ventrobasal nuclei of the rat thalamus: A light and electron microscopic study. *Neuroscience, 76,* 503–515.
DeCasper, A. J., & Fifer, W. P. (1980). Of human bonding: Newborns prefer their mothers' voices.

Science, 208, 1174–1176.

DeCasper, A. J., & Spence, M. J. (1986). Prenatal maternal speech influences newborns' perception of speech sounds. *Infant Behavior and Development, 9*, 133–150.

Desmedt, J. E., Brunko, E., & Debecker, J. (1976). Maturation of the somatosensory evoked potentials in normal infants and children, with special reference to the early N1 component. *Electroencephalography & Clinical Neurophysiology, 40*, 43–58.

Dorros, K. G., Brody, N., & Rose, S. A. (1980). A comparison of auditory behavior in the premature and fullterm infant: The effects of intervention. In H. D. Kimmel, E. H. v. Olst, & J. F. Orlebeke (Eds.), *The orienting reflex in humans*. New York: Erlbaum.

Eckholm, J. (1967). Postnatal changes in cutaneous reflexes and in the discharge pattern of cutaneous and articular sense organs. *Acta Physiologica Scandinavica, 297*, 1–130.

Eggermont, J. J. (1988). On the rate of maturation of sensory evoked potentials. *Electroencephalography & Clinical Neurophysiology, 70*, 293–305.

Ehret, G. (1976). Development of absolute auditory thresholds in the house mouse (mus musculus). *Journal of the American Audiological Society, 1*, 179–184.

Eilers, R. E., & Minifie, F. D. (1975). Fricative discrimination in early infancy. *Journal of Speech and Hearing Research, 18*, 158–167.

Elfenbein, J. L., Small, A. M., & Davis, M. (1993). Developmental patterns of duration discrimination. *Journal of Speech and Hearing Research, 36*, 842–849.

Elliott, L. L., & Katz, D. R. (1980). Children's pure-tone detection. *Journal of the Acoustical Society of America, 67*, 343–344.

Engen, T., Lipsitt, L. P., & Kaye, H. (1963). Olfactory responses and adaptation in the human neonate. *Journal of Comparative Physiological Psychology, 59*, 312–316.

Erting, C. J., Prezioso, C., & O'Grandy Hynes, M. (1990). The interactional context of deaf mother-infant communication. In V. Voltera & C. J. Erting (Eds.), *From gesture to language in hearing and deaf children* (pp. 97–106). Berlin: Springer.

Eyre, J. A., Miller, S., & Ramesh, V. (1991). Constancy of central conduction delays during development in man: Investigation of motor and somatosensory pathways. *Journal of Physiology (London), 434*, 441–452.

Falcon, M., Guendellman, D., Stolberg, A., Frenk, H., & Urca, G. (1996). Development of thermal nociception in rats. *Pain, 67*, 203–208.

Feng, J. Z., & Brugge, J. F. (1983). Postnatal development of auditory callosal connections in the kitten. *Journal of Comparative Neurology, 214*, 416–426.

Ferrington, D. G., Hora, M. O., & Rowe, M. J. (1984). Functional maturation of tactile sensory fibers in the kitten. *Journal of Neurophysiology, 52*, 74–85.

Ferrington, D. G., & Rowe, M. J. (1980). Functional capacities of tactile afferent fibres in neonatal kittens. *Journal of Physiology (London), 307*, 335–353.

Ferrington, D. G., & Rowe, M. J. (1981). Specificity of tactile connections in neonatal cuneate nucleus. *Brain Research, 227*, 429–433.

Ferrington, D. G., & Rowe, M. J. (1982). Specificity of connections and tactile coding capacities in cuneate nucleus of the neonatal kitten. *Journal of Neurophysiology, 47*, 622–640.

Fitzgerald, M. (1985). The post-natal development of cutaneous afferent fibre input and receptive field organization in the rat dorsal horn. *Journal of Physiology (London), 364*, 1–18.

Fitzgerald, M., & Koltzenburg, M. (1986). The functional development of descending inhibitory pathways in the dorsolateral funiculus of the newborn rat spinal cord. *Brain Research, 389*, 261–270.

Fitzgerald, M., Shaw, A., & MacIntosh, N. (1988). Postnatal development of the cutaneous flexor reflex: Comparative study of preterm infants and newborn rat pups. *Developmental Medicine and Child Neurology, 30*, 520–526.

Folsom, R. C., & Wynne, M. K. (1987). Auditory brain stem responses from human adults and infants: Wave V tuning curves. *Journal of the Acoustical Society of America, 81*, 412–417.

Frisina, R. D., & Gescheider, G. A. (1977). Comparison of child and adult vibrotactile thresholds as a function of frequency and duration. *Perception and Psychophysics, 22*, 100–103.

Fritzch, B., & Nichols, D. H. (1993). DiI reveals a prenatal arrival of efferents in the differentiating otocyst of mice. *Hearing Research, 65*, 51–60.

Fucci, D., Petrosino, L., Harris, D., & Randolph-Tyler, E. (1987). Effects of aging on responses to suprathreshold lingual vibrotactile stimulation. *Perceptual and Motor Skills, 64*, 683–694.

Gerber, S. E., & Mencher, G. T. (1979). Arousal responses of neonates to wide band and narrow band noise. Paper presented to the annual meeting of the American Speech-Language-Hearing Association, Atlanta, GA, November.

Gilmore, R. (1988). Use of somatosensory evoked potentials in infants and children. *Neurologic Clinics, 6*, 839–859.

Gilmore, R., Brock, J., Hermansen, M. C., & Baumann, R. (1987). Development of lumbar spinal cord and cortical evoked potentials after tibial nerve stimulation in the pre-term newborns: Effects of gestational age and other factors. *Electroencephalography & Clinical Neurophysiology, 68*, 28–39.

Gorga, M. P., Kaminski, J. R., Beauchaine, K. L., Jesteadt, W., & Neely, S. T. (1989). Auditory brainstem responses from children three months to three years of age: Normal patterns of response II. *Journal of Speech and Hearing Research, 32*, 281–288.

Gottfried, A. W., & Rose, S. A. (1980). Tactile recognition memory in infants. *Child Development*, 51, 69–74.

Gottlieb, G. (1971). Ontogenesis of sensory function in birds and mammals. In E. Tobach, L. R. Aronson, & E. F. Shaw (Eds.), *The biopsychology of development* (pp. 67–128). New York: Academic Press.

Gottlieb, G. (1991). Experiential canalization of behavioral development: Results. *Developmental Psychology, 27*, 35–39.

Gray, L., & Jahrsdoerfer, R. (1986). Naturalistic psychophysics: Thresholds of ducklings (*Anas platyrhynchos*) and chicks (*Gallus gallus*) to tones that resemble mallard calls. *Journal of Comparative Psychology, 100*, 91–94.

Green, D. M. (1995). Maximum likelihood procedures and the inattentive listener. *Journal of the Acoustical Society of America, 97*, 3749–3760.

Greenberg, G. Z., Bray, N. W., & Beasley, D. S. (1970). Children's frequency-selective detection of signals in noise. *Perception and Psychophysics, 8*, 173–175.

Greenberg, M. T. (1980). Hearing families with deaf children: Stress and functioning as related to communication method. *American Annals of the Deaf, 125*, 1063–1071.

Gusella, J. L., Muir, D., & Tronick, E. Z. (1988). The effect of manipulating maternal behavior during an interaction on three- and six-month-olds' affect and attention. *Child Development, 59*, 1111–1124.

Gutrecht, J. A., & Dyck, P. J. (1969). Quantitative teased-fiber and histologic studies of human sural nerve during postnatal development. *Journal of Comparative Neurology, 138*, 117–130.

Hall, J. W., III, & Grose, J. H. (1990). The masking level difference in children. *Journal of the American Academy of Audiology, 1*, 81–88.

Hall, J. W., III, & Grose, J. H. (1991). Notched-noise measures of frequency selectivity in adults and children using fixed-masker-level and fixed-signal-level presentation. *Journal of Speech and Hearing Research*, 34, 651–660.

Hall, J. W., I., & Grose, J. H. (1994). Development of temporal resolution in children as measured by the temporal modulation transfer function. *Journal of the Acoustical Society of America, 96*, 150–154.

Halonen, P., Ylitalo, V., Halonen, J. P., & Lang, H. (1986). Quantitative vibratory perception thresholds of healthy and epileptic children. *Developmental Medicine and Child Neurology, 28*, 772–778.

Hill, A. (1998). Development of tone and reflexes in the fetus and newborn. In R. A. Polin & W. W. Fox (Eds.), *Fetal and neonatal physiology* (pp. 2166–2174). Philadelphia: W.B. Saunders.

Hill, D. L., & Mistretta, C.M. (1990). Developmental neurobiology of salt taste sensation. *Trends in Neuroscience, 13*,188–195.

Hill, D. L., & Prezekop, P. R. (1988). Influence of dietary sodium on functional taste receptor development: A sensitive period. *Science, 241*, 1826–1828.

Hogg, I. D. (1941). Sensory nerves and associated structures in the skin of human fetuses of 8 to 14 weeks of menstrual age correlate with functional capability. *Journal of Comparative Neurology, 75*, 371.

Holbrook, K. A., Bothwell, M. A., Schatteman, G., & Underwood, R. (1988). Nerve growth factor receptor labelling defines developing nerve networks and stains follicle connective tissue cells in human embryonic and fetal skin. *Journal of Investigative Dermatology, 90*, 570.

Hrbek, A., Karlberg, P., & Olsson, T. (1973). Development of visual and somatosensory evoked responses in pre-term newborn infants. *Electroencephalography & Clinical Neurophysiology, 34*, 225–232.

Humphrey, T. (1964). Some correlations between the appearance of human fetal reflexes and the development of the nervous system. *Progress in Brain Research, 4*, 93–135.

Hutt, S. J., Hutt, C., Lenard, H. G., von Bernuth, H., & Muntjewerff, W. J. (1968). Auditory responsivity in the human neonate. *Nature, 218*, 888–890.

Irwin, R. J., Ball, A. K. R., Kay, N., Stillman, J. A., & Rosser, J. (1985). The development of auditory temporal acuity in children. *Child Development, 56*, 614–620.

Irwin, R. J., Stillman, J. A., & Schade, A. (1986). The width of the auditory filter in children. *Journal of Experimental Child Psychology, 41*, 429–442.

Issler, H., & Stephens, J. A. (1983). The maturation of cutaneous reflexes studied in the upper limb in man. *Journal of Physiology (London), 335*, 643–654.

Jacklin, C. N., Snow, M. E., & Maccoby, E. E. (1981). Tactile sensitivity and muscle strength in newborn boys and girls. *Infant Behavior and Development, 4*, 261–268.

Jacquin, M. F., McCasland, J. S., Henderson, T. A., Rhoades, R. W., & Woolsey, T. A. (1993). 2-DG uptake patterns related to single vibrissae during exploratory behaviors in the hamster trigeminal system. *Journal of Comparative Neurology, 332*, 38–58.

Jacquin, M. F., Mooney, R. D., & Rhoades, R. W. (1986). Morphology, response properties, and collateral projections of trigeminothalamic neurons in brainstem subnucleus interpolaris of rat. *Experimental Brain Research, 61*, 457–468.

James, C. E., Laing, D. G., & Oram, N. A. (1997). A comparison of the ability of 8–9-year-old children and adults to detect taste stimuli. *Physiological Behavior, 62*, 193–197.

Jensen, J. K., & Neff, D. L. (1993). Development of basic auditory discrimination in preschool children. *Psychological Science, 4*, 104–107.

Johnston, C. C., Stevens, B., Yang, F., & Horton, L. (1996). Developmental changes in response to heelstick in preterm infants: A prospective cohort study. *Developmental Medicine and Child Neurology, 38*, 438–445.

Juliano, S. L., Code, R. A., Tommerdahl, M., & Eslin, D. E. (1993). Development of metabolic activity patterns in the somatosensory cortex of cats. *Journal of Neurophysiology, 70*, 2117–2127.

Jusczyk, P. W., Bertoncini, J., Bijeljac-Babic, R., Kennedy, L. J., & Mehler, J. (1990). The role of attention in speech perception by young infants. *Cognitive Development, 5*, 265–286.

Jusczyk, P. W., Friederici, A. D., Wessels, J. M. I., Svenkerud, V. Y., & Jusczyk, A. M. (1993). Infants' sensitivity to the sound patterns of native language words. *Journal of Memory and Language, 32*, 402–420.

Kaplan, J. N. (1977) Perceptual properties of attachment in surrogate-reared and mother-reared squirrel monkeys. In S. Chevalier-Skolnikiff & F.E. Poirier (Eds.), *Primate bio-social development* (pp. 225-234). New York: Garland.

Karniski, W., Wyble, L., Lease, L., & Blair, R. C. (1992). The late somatosensory evoked potential in premature and term infants. II. Topography and latency development. *Electroencephalograpy & Clinical Neurophysiology, 84*, 44–54.

Kawell, M. E., Kopun, J. G., & Stelmachowicz, P. G. (1988). Loudness discomfort levels in children. *Ear and Hearing, 9*, 133–136.

Keefe, D. H., Bulen, J. C., Arehart, K. H., & Burns, E. M. (1993). Ear-canal impedance and reflection coefficient in human infants and adults. *Journal of the Acoustical Society of America, 94*,

2617–2638.

Kemler Nelson, D. G., Hirsh-Pasek, K., Jusczyk, P. W., & Cassidy, K. W. (1989). How the prosodic cues in motherese might assist language learning. *Journal of Child Language, 16*, 55–68.

Kemp, D. T. (1978). Stimulated acoustic emissions from within the human auditory system. *Journal of the Acoustical Society of America, 64*, 1386–1391.

Kettner, R. E., Feng, J.-Z., & Brugge, J. F. (1985). Postnatal development of the phase-locked response to low frequency tones of the auditory nerve fibers in the cat. *Journal of Neuroscience, 5*, 275–283.

Killackey, H. P., & Belford, G. R. (1980). Central correlates of peripheral pattern alterations in the trigeminal system of the rat. *Brain Research, 183*, 205–210.

Killackey, H. P., Chiaia, N. L., Bennett-Clarke, C. A., Eck, M., & Rhoades, R. W. (1994). Peripheral influences on the size and organization of somatotopic representations in the fetal rat cortex. *Journal of Neuroscience, 14*, 1496–1506.

Killackey, H. P., Jacquin, M. F., & Rhoades, R. W. (1990). Development of somatosensory system structures. In J. R. Coleman (Ed.), *Development of sensory systems in mammals* (pp. 403–430). New York: John Wiley & Sons.

Kimura, K. (1989). Development of the somatosensory evoked potential (SEP): Particularly to peak latencies of early SEP components. *No To Shinkei, 41*, 503–511.

King, A. J., Hutchings, M. E., Moore, D. R., & Blakemore, C. (1988). Developmental plasticity in the visual and auditory representations in the mammalian superior colliculus. *Nature, 332*, 73–76.

Kinnamon, S. C. & Cummings, T. A. (1992). Chemosensory transduction mechanisms in taste. *Annual Review of Physiology, 54*, 715–731.

Kinney, D. K., & Kagan, J. (1976). Infant attention to auditory discrepancy. *Child Development, 47*, 155–164.

Kisilevsky, B. S., Muir, D. W., & Low, J. A. (1992). Maturation of human fetal responses to vibroacoustic stimulation. *Child Development, 63*, 1497–1508.

Klimach, V. J., & Cooke, R. W. (1988). Maturation of the neonatal somatosensory evoked response in preterm infants. *Developmental Medicine and Child Neurology, 30*, 208–214.

Knudsen, E. I. (1985). Experience alters the spatial tuning of auditory units in the optic tectum during a sensitive period in the barn owl. *Journal of Neuroscience, 5*, 3094–3109.

Knudsen, E. I., Knudsen, P. F., & Esterly, S. D. (1982). Early auditory experience modifies sound localization in barn owls. *Nature, 295*, 238–240.

Koester, L. S. (1995). Face-to-face interactions between hearing mothers and their deaf or hearing infants. *Infant Behavior and Development, 18*, 145–154.

Koester, L. S., Karkowski, A. M., & Traci, M. A. (1998). How do deaf and hearing mothers regain eye contact when their infants look away? *American Annals of the Deaf, 143*, 5–13.

Konigsmark, B. W., & Murphy, E. A. (1972). Volume of the ventral cochlear nucleus in man: Its relationship to neuronal population and age. *Journal of Neuropathological Experimental Neurology, 31*, 304–316.

Kopyar, B.A. (1997). *Intensity discrimination abilities of infants and adults: Implications for underlying processes.* Unpublished doctoral dissertation, University of Washington.

Korner, A. F., & Thoman, E. B. (1972). The relative efficacy of contact and vestibular-proprioceptive stimulation in soothing neonates. *Child Development, 43*, 443–453.

Kraus, N., & McGee, T. (1992). Electrophysiology of the human auditory system. In A. N. Popper & R. R. Fay (Eds.), *The mammalian auditory pathway: Neurophysiology* (pp. 335–404). New York: Springer-Verlag.

Kraus, N., McGee, T., Micco, A., Sharma, A., Carrell, T., & Nicol, T. (1993). Mismatch negativity in school-age children to speech stimuli that are just perceptibly different. *Electroencephalography & Clinical Neurophysiology, 88*, 123–130.

Kuhl, P. K., Williams, K. A., Lacerda, F., Stevens, K. N., & Lindblom, B. (1992). Linguistic experience alters phonetic perception in infants by 6 months of age. *Science, 255*, 606–608.

Larsen, S. A. (1984). Postnatal maturation of the cat cochlear nuclear complex. *Oto-Laryngologica,*

417.

Larson, M. A., & Stein, B. E. (1984). The use of tactile and olfactory cues in neonatal orientation and localization of the nipple. *Developmental Psychobiology, 17*, 423–436.

Lary, S., Briassoulis, G., de Vries, L., Dubowitz, L. M. S., & Dubowitz, V. (1985). Hearing threshold in preterm and term infants by auditory brainstem response. *Journal of Pediatrics, 107*, 593–599.

Lasiter, P. S. (1991). Effects of early postnatal receptor damage on dendritic development in gustatory recipient zones of the rostral nucleus of the solitary tract. *Developments in Brain Research, 61*, 197–206.

Lavigne-Rebillard, M., & Pujol, R. (1988). Hair cell innervation in the fetal human cochlea. *Acta Oto-Laryngologica (Stockh), 105*, 398–402.

Lecanuet, J.-P., Granier-Deferre, C., & Busnel, M.-C. (1988). Fetal cardiac and motor responses to octave-band noises as a function of central frequency, intensity and heart rate variability. *Early Human Development, 18*, 81–93.

Lecanuet, J. P. (1996). Fetal sensory competencies. *European Journal of Obstetrics and Gynecology, 68*, 1–23.

Levi, E. C., Folsom, R. C., & Dobie, R. A. (1995). Coherence analysis of envelope-following responses (EFRs) and frequency-following responses (FFRs) in infants and adults. *Hearing Research, 89*, 21–27.

Levi, E. C., & Werner, L. A. (1995). Modulation detection of sinusoidally amplitude-modulated (SAM) noise in 3- and 6-month-old infants: Preliminary data. *Abstracts of the Association for Research in Oto-Laryngology, 18*, 56.

Levi, E. C., & Werner, L. A. (1996). Amplitude modulation detection in infancy: Update on 3-month-olds. *Abstracts of the Association for Research in Oto-Laryngology, 19*, 142.

Liden, G., & Kankkonen, A. (1961). Visual reinforcement audiometry. *Acta Oto-Laryngologica (Stockh), 67*, 281–292.

Litovsky, R. (1991). *Developmental changes in sound localization precision under conditions of the precedence effect*. Unpublished doctoral dissertation, University of Massachusetts.

Ma, P. K. M., & Woolsey, T. A. (1984). Cytoarchitectonic correlates of the vibrissae in the medullary trigeminal complex of the mouse. *Brain Research, 306*, 374–379.

Macfarlane, A. J. (1975). Olfaction in the development of social preferences in the human neonate. *Ciba Foundation Symposium, 33*, 103–117.

Majnemer, A., Rosenblatt, B., Willis, D., & Lavallee, J. (1990). The effect of gestational age at birth on somatosensory-evoked potentials performed at term. *Journal of Child Neurology, 5*, 329–335.

Masataka, N. (1992). Motherese in a signed language. *Infant Behavior and Development, 15*, 453–460.

Masataka, N. (1996). Perception of motherese in a signed language by 6-month-old deaf infants. *Developmental Psychology, 32*, 874–879.

Masataka, N. (1998). Perception of motherese in Japanese sign language by 6-month-old hearing infants. *Developmental Psychology, 34*, 241–246.

Maxon, A. B., & Hochberg, I. (1982). Development of psychoacoustic behavior: Sensitivity and discrimination. *Ear and Hearing, 3*, 301–308.

McKinnis, M. E. (1936). The number of ganglion cells in dorsal root ganglia of the second and third cervical nerves in human fetuses of various ages. *Anatomical Record, 65*, 255–259.

Meisami, R. (1976). Effects of olfactory deprivation on postnatal growth of the rat olfactory bulb utilizing a new method for production of neonatal unilateral anosmia. *Brain Research, 107*, 437–444.

Mills, A. W. (1972). Auditory localization. In J. V. Tobias (Ed.), *Foundations of modern auditory theory* (pp. 303–348). New York: Academic Press.

Mills, D., Norton, S., & Rubel, E. (1994). Development of active and passive mechanics in the mammalian cochlea. *Auditory Neuroscience, 1*, 77–99.

Mills, D. M., & Rubel, E. W. (1996). Development of the cochlear amplifier. *Journal of the Acoustical Society of America, 100*, 1–15.

Mirnics, K., & Koerber, H. R. (1995a). Prenatal development of rat primary afferent fibers: I. Peripheral projections. *Journal of Comparative Neurology, 355*, 589–600.

Mirnics, K., & Koerber, H. R. (1995b). Prenatal development of rat primary afferent fibers: II. Central projections. *Journal of Comparative Neurology, 355*, 601–614.

Mistretta, C. M., & Bradley, R. M. (1977). Taste in utero: Theoretical considerations. In J. M. Weiffenbach (Ed.), *Taste and development: The genesis of sweet preference (DHEW Publication No. NIH 77–1068)*. Washington, DC: US Government Printing Office.

Mogdans, J., & Knudsen, E. I. (1993). Early monaural occlusion alters the neural map of interaural level differences in the inferior colliculus of the barn owl. *Brain Research, 619*, 29–38.

Moore, B. C. J. (1973). Frequency difference limens for short-duration tones. *Journal of the Acoustical Society of America, 54*, 610–619.

Moore, J. K., Perazzo, L. M., & Braun, A. (1995). Time course of axonal myelination in human brainstem auditory pathway. *Hearing Research, 87*, 21–31.

Moore, J. M., Thompson, G., & Thompson, M. (1975). Auditory localization of infants as a function of reinforcement conditions. *Journal of Speech and Hearing Disorders, 40*, 29–34.

Moore, J. M., Wilson, W. R., & Thompson, G. (1977). Visual reinforcement of head-turn responses in infants under 12 months of age. *Journal of Speech and Hearing Disorders, 42*, 328–334.

Morrongiello, B. A. (1985). Age-related changes in duration discrimination. *Abstracts of the Society for Research in Child Development, 5*, 248.

Morrongiello, B. A. (1988). Infants' localization of sounds in the horizontal plane: Estimates of minimum audible angle. *Developmental Psychology, 24*, 8–13.

Morrongiello, B. A., & Clifton, R. K. (1984). Effects of sound frequency on behavioral and cardiac orienting in newborn and five-month-old infants. *Journal of Experimental Child Psychology, 38*, 429–446.

Morrongiello, B. A., Fenwick, K., & Chance, G. (1990). Sound localization acuity in very young infants: An observer-based testing procedure. *Developmental Psychology, 26*, 75–84.

Morrongiello, B. A., Fenwick, K. D., Hillier, L., & Chance, G. (1994). Sound localization in newborn human infants. *Developmental Psychobiology, 27* (8), 519–538.

Morrongiello, B. A., & Rocca, P. T. (1987). Infants' localization of sounds in the median vertical plane: Estimates of minimal audible angle. *Journal of Experimental Child Psychology, 43*, 181–193.

Morrongiello, B. A., & Trehub, S. E. (1987). Age related changes in auditory temporal perception. *Journal of Experimental Child Psychology, 44*, 413–426.

Nazzi, T., Bertoncini, J., & Mehler, J. (1998). Language discrimination by newborns: Toward an understanding of the role of rhythm. *Journal of Experimental Psychology: Human Perception & Performance, 24*, 756–766.

Nicolelis, M. A., De Oliveira, L. M., Lin, R. C., & Chapin, J. K. (1996). Active tactile exploration influences the functional maturation of the somatosensory system. *Journal of Neurophysiology, 75*, 2192–2196.

Nowlis, G. H., & Kessen, W. (1976). Human newborns differentiate differing concentrations of sucrose and glucose. *Science, 191*, 865–866.

Nozza, R. J., Wagner, E. F., & Crandell, M. A. (1988). Binaural release from masking for a speech sound in infants, preschoolers, and adults. *Journal of Speech and Hearing Research, 31*, 212–218.

Nozza, R. J., & Wilson, W. R. (1984). Masked and unmasked pure-tone thresholds of infants and adults: Development of auditory frequency selectivity and sensitivity. *Journal of Speech and Hearing Research, 27*, 613–622.

Okabe, K. S., Tanaka, S., Hamada, H., Miura, T., & Funai, H. (1988). Acoustic impedance measured on normal ears of children. *Journal of the Acoustical Society of Japan, 9*, 287–294.

Okado, N. (1981). Onset of synapse formation in the human spinal cord. *Journal of Comparative Neurology, 201*, 211–219.

Olsho, L. W. (1985). Infant auditory perception: Tonal masking. *Infant Behavior and Development, 7*, 27-35.

Olsho, L. W., Koch, E. G., Carter, E. A., Halpin, C. F., & Spetner, N. B. (1988). Pure-tone sensitivity of human infants. *Journal of the Acoustical Society of America, 84,* 1316–1324.

Olsho, L. W., Koch, E. G., & Halpin, C. F. (1987). Level and age effects in infant frequency discrimination. *Journal of the Acoustical Society of America, 82,* 454–464.

Pasic, T. R., Moore, D. R., & Rubel, E. W. (1994). Effect of altered neuronal activity on cell size in the medial nucleus of the trapezoid body and ventral cochlear nucleus of the gerbil. *Journal of Comparative Neurology, 348,* 111–120.

Payne, B., Pearson, H., & Cornwell, P. (1988). Development of visual and auditory cortical connections in the cat. In A. Peters & E. G. Jones (Eds.), *Cerebral cortex: Vol. 7. Development and maturation of cerebral cortex* (pp. 309–389). New York: Plenum Press.

Payne, B. R. (1992). Development of the auditory cortex. In R. Romand (Ed.), *Development of auditory and vestibular systems 2* (pp. 357–389). Amsterdam: Elsevier Science Publishers.

Pederson, P.E., & Blass, E.M. (1982). Prenatal and postnatal determinants of the first suckling episode in albino rats. *Developmental Psychobiology, 15,* 349–355.

Peterson, F., & Rainey, L. H. (1910). The beginnings of mind in the newborn. *Bulletin of the Lying-in Hospital, City of New York, 7,* 99–122.

Pick, H. L., Jr., Klein, R. E., & Pick, A. D. (1966). Visual and tactual identification of form orientation. *Journal of Experimental Child Psychology, 4,* 391–397.

Poon, P. W. F., Chen, X., & Hwang, J. C. (1990). Altered sensitivities of auditory neurons in the rat midbrain following early postnatal exposure to patterned sounds. *Brain Research, 524,* 327–330.

Prechtl, H. F. (1989). Fetal behaviour. *European Journal of Obstetrics and Gynecological Reproductive Biology, 32,* 32.

Pujol, R., Lavigne-Rebillard, M., & Lenoir, M. (1998). Development of sensory and neural structures in the mammalian cochlea. In E. W. Rubel, R. R. Fay, & A. N. Popper (Eds.), *Development of the auditory system* (pp. 146–192). New York: Springer Verlag.

Rayburn, W. F. (1989). Antepartum fetal monitoring: Fetal movement. In A. Hill & J. J. Volpe (Eds.), *Fetal neurology* (pp. 17–36). New York: Raven Press.

Rhoades, R. W., Chiaia, N. L., Mooney, R. D., Klein, B. G., Renehan, W. E., & Jacquin, M. F. (1987). Reorganization of the peripheral projections of the trigeminal ganglion following neonatal transection of the infraorbital nerve. *Somatosensory Research, 5,* 35–62.

Rhoades, R. W., Killackey, H. P., Chiaia, N. L., & Jacquin, M. F. (1990). Physiological development and plasticity of somatosensory neurons. In J. R. Coleman (Ed.), *Development of sensory systems in mammals* (pp. 431–459). New York: John Wiley & Sons.

Richter, C. P. & Campbell, H. K. (1940). Sucrose taste thresholds of rats and humans. *American Journal of Physiology, 128,* 291–297.

Rose, S. A. (1980). Enhancing visual recognition memory in preterm infants. *Developmental Psychology, 16,* 85–92.

Rose, S. A., Schmidt, K., Riese, M. L., & Bridger, W. H. (1980). Effects of prematurity and early intervention on responsivity to tactual stimuli: A comparison of preterm and full-term infants. *Child Development, 51,* 416–425.

Rosenstein, D., & Oster, H. (1988). Differential facial responses to four basic tastes in newborns. *Child Development, 59,* 1555–1568.

Ross, M. G., & Nijland, M. J. (1997). Fetal swallowing: Relation to amniotic fluid regulation. *Clinical Obstetrics and Gynecology, 40,* 352–365.

Rubel, E. W. (1971). A comparison of somatotopic organization in sensory neocortex of newborn kittens and adult cats. *Journal of Comparative Neurology, 143,* 447–480.

Rübsamen, R., & Lippe, W. (1998). The development of cochlear function. In E. W. Rubel, R. R. Fay, & A. N. Popper (Eds.), *Development of the auditory system* (pp. 193–270). New York: Springer Verlag.

Russell, F. A., & Moore, D. R. (1995). Afferent reorganization within the superior olivary complex of the gerbil: Development and induction by neonatal, unilateral cochlear removal. *Journal of Comparative Neurology, 352,* 607–625.

Rybak, L. P., Whitworth, C., & Scott, V. (1992). Development of the endocochlear potential and

compound action potential in the rat. *Hearing Research, 59*, 189–194.
Sanes, D. H. (1993). The development of synaptic function and integration in the central auditory system. *Journal of Neuroscience, 13*, 2627–2637.
Sanes, D. H., & Constantine-Paton, M. (1985). The sharpening of frequency tuning curves requires patterned activity during development in the mouse, *Mus musculus*. *Journal of Neuroscience, 5*, 1152–1166.
Sanes, D. H., & Walsh, E. J. (1998). The development of central auditory function. In E. W. Rubel, R. R. Fay, & A. N. Popper (Eds.), *Development of the auditory system* (pp. 271–314). New York: Springer Verlag.
Sarnat, H. B. (1978). Olfactory reflexes in the newborn infant. *Journal of Pediatrics, 92*, 624–626.
Savy, C. S., Margules, S., Farkas-Bargeton, C., & Verley, R. (1981). A morphometric study of mouse trigeminal ganglion after unilateral destruction of vibrissae follicles at birth. *Brain Research, 217*, 265–277.
Schaal, B. (1988). Olfaction in infants and children: Developmental and functional perspectives. *Chemical Senses, 13*, 145–190.
Scheibel, M. E., Davies, T. L., & Scheibel, A. B. (1976). Ontogenetic development of somatosensory thalamus. I. Morphogenesis. *Experimental Neurology, 51*, 392–406.
Schiff, W., & Dytell, R. S. (1972). Deaf and hearing children's performance on a tactual perception battery. *Perception and Motor Skills, 35*, 683–706.
Schlaggar, B. L., & O'Leary, D. D. (1994). Early development of the somatotopic map and barrel patterning in rat somatosensory cortex. *Journal of Comparative Neurology, 346*, 80–96.
Schlesinger, H. S., & Meadow, K. P. (1972). Development of maturity in deaf children. *Exceptional Child, 38*, 461–467.
Schmidt, H. J., & Beauchamp, G. K. (1988). Adult-like odor preferences and aversions in 3-year-old children. *Child Development, 59*, 1136–1143.
Schneider, B. A., Morrongiello, B. A., & Trehub, S. E. (1990). The size of the critical band in infants, children, and adults. *Journal of Experimental Psychology [Human Perception], 16*, 642–652.
Schneider, B. A., & Trehub, S. E. (1985). Behavioral assessment of basic auditory abilities. In S. E. Trehub & B. Schneider (Eds.), *Auditory development in infancy* (pp. 101–113). New York: Plenum Press.
Schneider, B. A., & Trehub, S. E. (1992). Sources of developmental change in auditory sensitivity. In L. A. Werner & E. W. Rubel (Eds.), *Developmental psychoacoustics* (pp. 3–46). Washington, DC: American Psychological Association.
Schneider, R. A., Trehub, S. E., Morrongiello, B. A., & Thorpe, L. A. (1989). Developmental changes in masked thresholds. *Journal of the Acoustical Society of America, 86*, 1733–1742.
Schweitzer, L. (1991). Morphometric analysis of developing neuronal geometry in the dorsal cochlear nucleus of the hamster. *Developments in Brain Research, 59*, 39–47.
Shibasaki, H., & Miyazaki, M. (1992). Event-related potential studies in infants and children. *Journal of Clinical Neurophysiology, 9*, 408–418.
Sininger, Y. S., Abdala, C., & Cone-Wesson, B. (1997). Auditory threshold sensitivity of the human neonate as measured by the auditory brainstem response. *Hearing Research, 104*, 27–38.
Sinnott, J. M., & Aslin, R. N. (1985). Frequency and intensity discrimination in human infants and adults. *Journal of the Acoustical Society of America, 78*, 1986–1992.
Smith-Gray, S., & Koester, L. S. (1995). Defining and observing social signals in deaf and hearing infants. *American Annals of the Deaf, 140*, 422–427.
Spence, M. J. (1996). Young infants' long-term auditory memory: Evidence for changes in preference as a function of delay. *Developmental Psychobiology, 29*, 685–695.
Spetner, N. B., & Olsho, L. W. (1990). Auditory frequency resolution in human infancy. *Child Development, 61*, 632–652.
Stack, D. M., & Muir, D. W. (1992). Adult tactile stimulation during face-to-face interactions modulates five-month-olds' affect and attention. *Child Development, 63*, 1509–1525.
Stein, M., Ottenberg, P., & Roulet, N. (1958). A study of the development of olfactory preferences.

AMA Archives of Neurology and Pyschiatry, 80, 264–266.

Steiner, J. E. (1977). Facial expressions of the neonate infant indicating the hedonics of food-related chemical stimuli. In J. M. Weiffenbach (Eds.), *Taste and development: The genesis of sweet preference (DHEW Publication No. NIH 77–1068).* Washington, DC: US Government Printing Office.

Stevens, J. C., Webb, H. D., Smith, M. F., & Buffin, J. T. (1990). The effect of stimulus level on click evoked oto-acoustic emissions and brainstem responses in neonates under intensive care. *British Journal of Audiology, 24,* 293–300.

Suzuki, T., & Ogiba, Y. (1961). Conditioned orientation reflex audiometry. *Archives of Oto-Laryngology - Head and Neck Surgery, 74,* 84–90.

Teicher, M.H. & Blass, E.M. (1977) First suckling response of the newborn: The roles of olfaction and amniotic fluid. *Science, 198,* 635–636.

Tomita, Y., Nishimura, S., & Tanaka, T. (1986). Short latency SEPs in infants and children: Developmental changes and maturational index of SEPs. *Electroencephalography & Clinical Neurophysiology, 65,* 335–343.

Trehub, S. E., Schneider, B. A., & Endman, M. (1980). Developmental changes in infants' sensitivity to octave-band noises. *Journal of Experimental Child Psychology, 29,* 282–293.

Trehub, S. E., Schneider, B. A., & Henderson, J. (1995). Gap detection in infants, children, and adults. *Journal of the Acoustical Society of America, 98,* 2532–2541.

Trehub, S. E., Schneider, B. A., Morrongiello, B. A., & Thorpe, L. A. (1988). Auditory sensitivity in school-age children. *Journal of Experimental Child Psychology, 46,* 273–285.

Uziel, A., Romand, R., & Marot, M. (1981). Development of cochlear potentials in rats. *Audiology, 20,* 89–100.

Valman, H. B., & Pearson, J. F. (1980). What the fetus feels. *British Medical Journal, 280,* 233–234.

Vecchierini-Blineau, M. F., & Guihneuc, P. (1982). Lower limb cutaneous polysynaptic reflexes in the child, according to age and state of waking or sleeping. *Journal of Neurology Neurosurgery and Psychiatry, 45,* 531–538.

Verrillo, R. T. (1977). Comparison of child and adult vibrotactile thresholds. *Bulletin of the Psychonomic Society, 9,* 197–200.

Verrillo, R. T. (1979). Change in vibrotactile thresholds as a function of age. *Sensory Processes, 3,* 49–59.

Villablanca, J. R., & Olmstead, C. E. (1979). Neurological development of kittens. *Developmental Psychobiology, 12,* 101–127.

Watrous, B. S., McConnell, F., Sitton, A. B., & Fleet, W. F. (1975). Auditory responses of infants. *Journal of Speech and Hearing Disorders, 40,* 357–366.

Watson, C. S., Franks, J. R., & Hood, D. C. (1972). Detection of tones in the absence of external masking noise. I. Effects of signal intensity and signal frequency. *Journal of the Acoustical Society of America, 52,* 633–643.

Weinberg, M. K., & Tronick, E. Z. (1996). Infant affective reactions to the resumption of maternal interaction after the still-face. *Child Development, 67,* 905–914.

Weinstein, S. (1968). Intensive and extensive aspects of tactile sensitivity as a function of body part, sex, and laterality. In D. R. Kenshalo (Ed.), *The skin senses* (pp. 195–222). Springfield, IL: Charles C. Thomas.

Weir, C. (1979). Auditory frequency sensitivity of human newborns: Some data with improved acoustic and behavioral controls. *Perception and Psychophysics, 26,* 287–294.

Weir, C. C., Jesteadt, W., & Green, D. M. (1977). Frequency discrimination as a function of frequency and sensation level. *Journal of the Acoustical Society of America, 61,* 178–184.

Werker, J. F. (1994). Cross-language speech perception: Developmental change does not involve loss. In J. C. Goodman & H. C. Nusbaum (Eds.), *The development of speech perception* (pp. 93–120). Cambridge, MA: MIT Press.

Werker, J. F., & Tees, R. C. (1984). Cross-language speech perception: Evidence for perceptual reorganization during the first year of life. *Infant Behavior and Development, 7,* 49–63.

Werner, L. A. (1995). Observer-based approaches to human infant psychoacoustics. In G. M. Klump, R. J. Dooling, R. R. Fay, & W. C. Stebbins (Eds.), *Methods in comparative psychoacoustics* (pp. 135–146). Boston: Birkhauser Verlag.

Werner, L. A. (1996). The development of auditory behavior (or what the anatomists and physiologists have to explain). *Ear and Hearing, 17*, 438–446.

Werner, L. A., Folsom, R. C., & Mancl, L. R. (1994). The relationship between auditory brainstem response latency and behavioral thresholds in normal hearing infants and adults. *Hearing Research, 77*, 88–98.

Werner, L. A., & Gillenwater, J. M. (1990). Pure-tone sensitivity of 2- to 5-week-old infants. *Infant Behavior and Development, 13*, 355–375.

Werner, L. A., & Gray, L. (1998). Behavioral studies of hearing development. In E. W. Rubel, R. R. Fay, & A. N. Popper (Eds.), *Development of the auditory system* (pp. 12–79). New York: Springer Verlag.

Werner, L. A., Marean, G. C., Halpin, C. F., Spetner, N. B., & Gillenwater, J. M. (1992). Infant auditory temporal acuity: Gap detection. *Child Development, 63*, 260–272.

Wightman, F., Allen, P., Dolan, T., Kistler, D., & Jamieson, D. (1989). Temporal resolution in children. *Child Development, 60*, 611–624.

Wilmington, D., Gray, L., & Jahrsdorfer, R. (1994). Binaural processing after corrected congenital unilateral conductive hearing loss. *Hearing Research, 74*, 99–114.

Wise, S. P., Fleshman, J. W., Jr., & Jones, E. G. (1979). Maturation of pyramidal cell form in relation to developing afferent and efferent connections of rat somatic sensory cortex. *Neuroscience, 4*, 1275–1297.

Withington-Wray, D. J., Binns, K. E., & Keating, M. J. (1990a). The developmental emergence of a map of auditory space in the superior colliculus of the guinea pig. *Developments in Brain Research, 51*, 225–236.

Withington-Wray, D. J., Binns, K. E., & Keating, M. J. (1990b). A four-day period of bimodality auditory and visual experience is sufficient to permit normal emergence of the map of auditory space in the guinea pig superior colliculus. *Neuroscience Letters, 116*, 280–286.

Woolf, N. K., & Ryan, A. F. (1988). Contributions of the middle ear to the development of function in the cochlea. *Hearing Research, 35*, 131–142.

Woolsey, T. (1990). Peripheral alterations and plasticity of somatosensory neurons. In J. R. Coleman (Ed.), *Development of sensory systems in mammals* (pp. 461–516). New York: John Wiley & Sons.

Woolsey, T. A., Anderson, J. R., Wann, J. R., & Stanfield, B. B. (1979). Effects of early vibrissae damage on neurons in the ventrobasal (VB) thalamus of the mouse. *Journal of Comparative Neurology, 184*, 363–380.

Wozniak, W., O'Rahilly, R., & Olszewska, B. (1980). The fine structure of the spinal cord in human embryos and early fetuses. *Journal für Hirnforschung, 21*, 101–124.

Wu, C. C., & Gonzalez, M. F. (1997). Functional development of the vibrissae somatosensory system of the rat: (14C) 2-deoxyglucose metabolic mapping study. *Journal of Comparative Neurology, 384*, 323–336.

Yakovlev, P. I., & Lecours, A.-R. (1967). The myelogenetic cycles of regional maturation of the brain. In A. Minkowski (Ed.), *Regional development of the brain in early life* (pp. 3–70). Oxford: Blackwell.

Chapter Twenty-Two

Brain Mechanisms for Synthesizing Information From Different Sensory Modalities[1]

Barry E. Stein, Mark T. Wallace, and Terrence R. Stanford

Perceptual and Behavioral Evidence for Interactions Among the Senses

Sensory Systems Function in Parallel

Decoding and interpreting incoming sensory information are among the brain's most important tasks. These are ongoing processes that make it possible for us not only to know the world in which we live, but to plan and initiate behaviors that are appropriate for a particular circumstance. Because survival depends on the speed and accuracy of such processes, it is not surprising to find that encoding, decoding, and evaluating sensory information have been powerful driving forces in evolution. Consequently, extant organisms have an impressive array of specialized sensory systems.

Having multiple sensory systems provides significant benefits; it allows an organism to monitor simultaneously a host of environmental cues, and also provides a means of substituting one sensory system for another when necessary (e.g., hearing and/or touch can substitute for vision in the dark). The ability to monitor and process multiple sensory cues in "parallel" not only increases the likelihood that a given stimulus will be detected, but, because the information carried along each sensory channel reflects a different feature of that stimulus, it increases the chances that the stimulus will be properly identified. Stimuli that may be difficult to distinguish by means of a single sensory modality (e.g., how they look) can become quite distinct via information from another modality (how they sound or feel). Indeed, we deal so successfully with sensory cues that we have come to have great faith in the ability of our sensory systems to distinguish among important stimuli and provide us with impressions that are accurate reflections of the physical world. So, it is sometimes amusing and occasionally distressing to discover that these perceptual judgments are relative rather than absolute, and that they can be radically different in different contexts. For example, manipulating context by altering perspective and contrast in painting, photography, and cinematography can give apparent depth to a flat surface, make small objects appear large, or large objects appear small, or make objects appear far away when they are really very near, or the reverse. Yet, despite our extensive experience and sophistication with these effects, visual illusions continue to delight us. Apparently, understanding the concept of an illusion does not mitigate the surprise induced by experiencing it.

The relative nature of a sensory judgment is also evident when dealing with combinations of cues from different modalities. There is, in fact, a rather rich literature filled with examples in which the presence of a cue from one modality can substantially alter perceptual judgments of cues in other modalities. For example, the presence of a visual cue can substantially change a subject's perception of proprioceptive and auditory cues, and proprioceptive cues can alter the subject's perception of where an auditory cue is located (Held, 1955; Pick, Warren, & Hay, 1969; Shelton & Searle, 1980; Thurlow & Rosenthal, 1976; Warren, Welch, & McCarthy, 1981; Welch & Warren, 1980). These cross-modality perceptual effects can be quite potent. Thus, when watching some of the new films on Imax or in a planetarium (e.g., illustrating flight through mountainous terrain or through a starry night) the viewer is apt to experience many of the same vestibular and gastrointestinal sensations that make clear air turbulence and amusement park rides so delightful.

Still, our readiness to acknowledge that judgments of one sensory cue can be altered by another sensory cue comes most easily when the effects are restricted to the same modality, as when the appearance of a visual cue is altered by the visual background against which it is judged, or when the pitch or intensity of a sound seems different when linked to other sounds. The possibility that seemingly "irrelevant" cues, such as those derived from modalities other than the one being evaluated, can substantially alter its perception is less obvious. Although cross-modality influences on perception and behavior are as common as their within-modality counterparts, the fact that a brief sound can strongly alter one's judgment of light intensity (Stein, London, Wilkinson, & Price, 1996) is generally met with greater surprise than the observation that one looks slimmer wearing vertical rather than horizontal stripes.

Sensory Systems Also Function in an Interdependent Fashion

The commonly held impression that sensory systems are unlikely to have an ongoing dialogue with one another may be due, in part, to the fact that the senses have evolved unique subjective impressions, or qualia, for which there are no cross-modality equivalents. Tickle and itch are specific to the somatosensory system, hue to the visual system, and pitch to the auditory system. Therefore, it seems logical that to maintain the modality-specificity of these qualia, the brain must avoid cross-talk between the senses – an issue that harkens back to Johannes Muller's concept that each modality has "specific nerve energies" associated with it, and that these energies provide the basis for their subjective impressions. A modern parallel might be found in the concept of "labeled lines" of information in the central nervous system. However, the different senses not only affect one another quite regularly, but frequently do so with unexpected consequences.

The influences of different sensory modalities on one another are quite obvious in a host of cross-modality illusions, and the reader is referred to Welch and Warren (1986) and Stein and Meredith (1993) for more in-depth discussions. However, consideration of a few cross-modality illusions here is helpful to underscore their potency. The so-called "McGurk Effect" (McGurk & MacDonald, 1976) is an excellent example, and one that is very popular among speech professionals because it shows how strongly a discordant visual signal (i.e., lip movements) can influence the perception of speech. If one hears the word "bows," but sees the mouth form the word "goes," the perception is "doze" or "those," percepts that match neither of the two inputs, but rather reflect their synthesis (see Figure 16.5c, p. 510). Similarly, "ga" and "ba" are usually combined to form the percept "da."

While cross-modality influences like the McGurk Effect change (or abolish) the perceived meaning of the signal, others can cause a misperception of its location. For example, a dynamic (e.g., moving) visual cue can cause an observer to believe that an accompanying auditory cue originating from a different location actually comes from the same location as the visual stimulus. For obvious reasons illusions of this type are categorized as examples of the "ventriloquism effect" (Howard & Templeton, 1966). They are also far more common than one might first imagine, and explain why, when watching a movie, speech seems to be emanating from the actors, even as they are moving from one end of the screen to the other, rather than from speakers that are far away and fixed in space. In similar fashion, tactile and/or vestibular cues can lead us to mislocalize visual and auditory cues (Biguer, Donaldson, Hein, & Jeannerod, 1988; Clark & Graybiel, 1966; Graybiel & Niven, 1951; Lackner, 1974a,1974b; Roll, Velay, & Roll, 1991; Wade & Day, 1968).

Cross-modality illusions are simply an extension of the "normal" perceptions produced by combining sensory cues from different modalities that occur close together in space and time. They depend on a critical degree of distortion in the spatial and/or temporal relationships among sensory cues that normally originate from a common event. A larger distortion would lead to an unambiguous perception that these cues originate from separate events, and a smaller distortion would be lost within the "noise" of normal cross-modality coherence. A key factor in the discussions of multisensory integration is that these distortions are not generally provided by cues derived from the same event.

The normal close temporal and spatial linkage between sensory stimuli from different modalities originating from the same event generally produce signals that the brain uses synergistically. This is why being able to see a speaker's face makes it far easier to understand his words, particularly in a noisy room (Sumby & Pollack, 1954). The adaptive significance of multisensory integration is also obvious in enhancing the detection of a stimulus and the speed with which a reaction to it can be organized. Thus, a number of studies have shown that our ability to detect a stimulus is better and our reaction times are shorter when the cues are spatially and temporally concordant multisensory stimuli as opposed to their individual sensory components (e.g., see Andreassi & Greco, 1975; Bernstein, Clark, & Edelstein, 1969; Gielen, Schmidt, & van den Heuvel, 1983; Goldring et al., 1996; Hershenson, 1962; Hughes, Reuter-Lorenz, Nozawa, & Fendrich, 1994; Morrell, 1968a, 1968b, 1972; Posner, Nissen, & Klein, 1976).

The synergistic interaction of concordant cross-modality cues also has been demonstrated in experiments examining the attentive and orientation responses of cats (Stein, Meredith, Huneycutt, & McDade, 1989). The animals show a striking enhancement in their detection of, and orientation to, a dim visual stimulus when it is paired with a neutral auditory stimulus (the animals are either naive with respect to the auditory stimulus or have learned not to respond to it). Similarly, in humans and nonhuman primates, where eye movements often are used as an index of attentive and orientation reactions, the latency of ballistic (i.e., saccadic) eye movements to a visual or auditory cue is significantly reduced when these cues are combined in a concordant manner (Frens, Van Opstal, & Van der Willigen, 1995; Hughes et al., 1994; Lee, Chung, Kim, & Park, 1991; Perrott, Saberi, Brown, & Strybel, 1990; Zahn, Abel, & Dell'Osso, 1978). On the other hand, when visual and auditory cues are significantly discordant, their combination can have the opposite effect and depress responses (Stein et al., 1989).

Oddly enough, there are individuals called "synesthetes" who are sometimes unable to separate sensory impressions from one another. For them, a stimulus in one modality can elicit an entire complex of subjective impressions in another modality. A humorous example of such a synesthetic experience, described by Ackerman (1990), is that of a woman who tasted baked beans whenever she heard the word "Francis."

The literal meaning of "synesthesia" is "joining of the senses", and it has been said to reflect ". . . an involuntary joining in which the real information of one sense is accompanied by a perception in another sense" (Cytowic, 1989, also see Marks, 1975, 1978). Although at present there is no adequate neural explanation for this "syndrome," modern functional imaging studies have shown that it is associated with a complex of changes in cortical activity that is quite different than that observed in nonsynesthetic individuals (Paulesu et al., 1995).

On the basis of some published observations, one might suppose that the synesthetic experience is less an oddity than a reflection of arrested sensory development. Some researchers have indicated that even among normal neonates, the various sensory impressions are not well differentiated and form what has been called a "primitive unity" (see Bower, 1977; Gibson, 1966; Marks, 1978; Ryan, 1940; Turkewitz & Mellon, 1989; von Hornbostel, 1938). In this scenario, a single, modality-specific stimulus can produce ". . . sensations (that) spill from one sensory system into another" (Maurer & Maurer, 1988, p. 164). This is by no means a generally held view. Some investigators believe quite the opposite, and hold that the senses are well differentiated from one another at birth and that the ability to associate among them is learned during postnatal development (e.g., Piaget, 1952; von Helmholtz, 1884/1968).

As is often true when dealing with conflicting theories seeking to explain complex phenomena without the benefit of a comprehensive database, it is difficult to conclude that one is correct and the other is incorrect. Thus, while the idea of a gradual acquisition of associations during postnatal life seems the more conservative of the two views (and indeed, fits with some of the more recent data from experiments with single neurons, see below), there are a number of observations that conflict with the idea that all intersensory capabilities are acquired gradually via learned associations during early life. One of the most interesting of these comes from studies conducted by Meltzoff and colleagues (e.g., Meltzoff & Moore, 1977, 1983a, 1983b). These investigators reported that newborn human babies could mimic facial expressions very soon after birth; too soon, in fact, to have had the opportunity to develop associations between what they were seeing and what they were doing. For some researchers, these observations are consistent with the idea that human infants are synesthetic, because they appear able to match a visual image with tactile and/or proprioceptive sensations (e.g., Maurer & Maurer, 1988), a process referred to by Meltzoff as "active intermodal mapping."

There are also observations from animal studies that are consistent with the idea that the brain is sensitive to at least some intersensory influences at or before birth. For example, when patterned visual input is provided before it normally occurs (by surgically separating the eyelids in mammals before they normally open, or making it possible for bird embryos to see outside their shells (see Gottlieb, Tomlinson, & Radell, 1989; Lickliter, 1990;

Turkewitz & Mellon, 1989)), there is a striking impact on the animals' ability to use cues from other sensory modalities. Such a result is not surprising in light of anatomical evidence, which suggests that in many species inputs from different sensory modalities are extensively intermingled early in development. Some rodents and at least one species of carnivore are now known to have "exuberant" sensory inputs from "inappropriate" (e.g., visual) modalities converging onto the same target structures as the "appropriate" inputs (e.g., auditory or somatosensory). The former are at a competitive disadvantage with the latter and are retracted during early development unless extraordinary surgical means are taken to eliminate the more competitive, and thus the normally surviving, inputs (Asanuma, Ohkawa, Stanfield, & Cowan, 1988; Frost, 1984; Innocenti & Clarke, 1984; Sur, Garraghty, & Roe, 1988).

Neurophysiological Evidence for Interactions Among the Senses

From the foregoing discussion it should be evident that there is an interesting organizational duality in the brain. Some regions, such as those along the primary projection pathways, are dedicated for modality-specific function. By and large, these regions segregate information on a sense-by-sense basis, so they are likely to be responsible for the qualia that are closely linked to modality-specific experiences (e.g., hue in vision, tickle in somatosensation, etc.). In contrast, other areas are specialized for pooling information regardless of modality. Presumably, these latter areas play a significant role in cross-modality phenomena, with some regions contributing more to overt behavior and others contributing more to perceptual or emotive experiences.

Inputs From Different Senses Converge on Individual Neurons at Many Levels in the Neuraxis

Despite the long history of documenting the potent influences of cross-modality cues on both perception and behavior, and the various suppositions about the brain regions that might be involved, it is only within the past few years that we have begun to identify the neural structures and mechanisms through which these different sensory inputs interact. Although these neuroanatomical/neurophysiological studies have not yet "explained" cross-modal perception, they have been quite successful in furthering our understanding of the impact of cross-modality processing on some overt behaviors, determining the distribution of multisensory neurons in various areas of the brain, and providing intriguing insights into some of the principles by which multisensory neurons integrate cross-modality information.

Many sites in the nervous system have been identified as receiving inputs from different sensory modalities, and many neurons in these sites have been shown to receive converging afferents from multiple modalities (i.e., these neurons are "multisensory"). In some systems (e.g., vestibular), convergence of inputs from different sensory modalities takes place even at the level of first and second order neurons (Highstein & Baker, 1985). However, the overwhelming majority of this convergence takes place in the brain. A brief list of brain structures in which such multisensory convergence is commonplace includes: reticular formation, superior colliculus, pretectum, posterior thalamus, basal ganglia, and areas of association cortex. Indeed, outside of the primary sensory projection pathways, convergence among sensory modalities is quite common at each level of brain organization (see Stein & Meredith, 1993 for a review).

The Superior Colliculus as a Model to Study Multisensory Processes

One of the best models with which to study sensory convergence and multisensory integration is a midbrain structure, the superior colliculus (SC). The choice of this structure is based on the high incidence of visual-, auditory- and somatosensory-responsive multisensory neurons in its deep layers, and its well-documented involvement in overt attentive and orientation behaviors (Casagrande, Harting, Hall, & Diamond, 1972; Schneider, 1969; Sprague & Meikle, 1965; Stein & Meredith, 1993). Perhaps more than any other brain structure, the SC functions at the interface of sensory and motor processing. It receives inputs from multiple sensory modalities and issues motor commands to produce coordinated movements of the eyes, ears, head, and body toward stimuli in each of these modalities. Consistent with its sensorimotor role, the discharge of an individual SC neuron shows a strong selectivity for the location of a sensory stimulus and/or the metrics (i.e., amplitude and direction) of a movement toward that stimulus. Neurons with sensory-related activity have distinct receptive fields and respond only to stimuli within a restricted region of space. Such neurons may be unimodal, responding only to visual, auditory, or somatosensory stimuli. Alternatively, these neurons can be multisensory, responding to stimuli from two (or even three) sensory modalities. Analogously, neurons with motor-related activity have movement fields, and these neurons discharge in association with orienting movements within a particular range of amplitude and direction.

The Topographic Organization of the Superior Colliculus

In the SC, the representations of sensory space and movement metrics are topographic; that is, SC neurons are arranged in an orderly fashion according to the position of their receptive and/or movement fields to form sensory and motor "maps." In such an organization, sensory stimulus location or movement metrics are represented by the location of activity within the map. Understanding the relationships of the visual, auditory, and somatosensory maps to each other and to the motor maps is important for understanding how multisensory stimuli are translated into motor output. Of particular concern are the relationships among the sensory representations, for they have profound implications for the synthesis of cross-modal sensory cues and the motor behaviors they elicit.

Receptive Field Correspondence in Multisensory Neurons

The notion that inputs from different sensory modalities have access to the same motor maps dictates the need for mechanisms to establish and maintain a correspondence among the receptive fields of the different modalities. Whether a particular location in space is the source of a visual, auditory, or somatosensory stimulus, or some combination thereof, an orienting movement to that location requires activating the same region of a motor map. If sensory activity is a prelude to motor activity in the corresponding region of the SC, then the site of sensory SC activity should be the same regardless of whether the initiating stimulus is visual, auditory, or somatosensory. The register among the receptive fields of different modalities ensures consistent spatial selectivity and, presumably, consistent behavioral outcomes (e.g. movement vectors) across modalities. The presence of this cross-

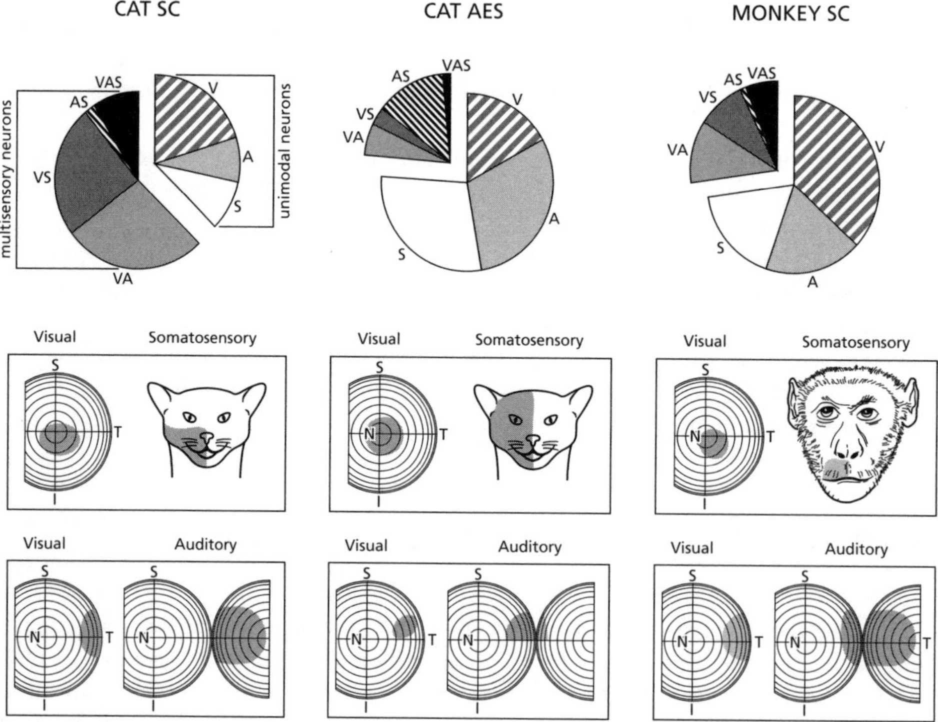

Figure 22.1. Top: Shown are the relative proportions of the various multisensory neurons obtained in cat (SC and AES) (AES = anterior ectosylvian sulcus, see p. 725) and monkey (SC). V – visual, A – auditory, S – somatosensory. Bottom: These multisensory neurons are all characterized by an alignment among their different modality-specific receptive fields (shading), and six characteristic examples are illustrated. In the representation of auditory space (lower left), the caudal half of contralateral space is depicted by a semicircle that is folded forward (the caudal half of ipsilateral space is not shown). S – superior, I – inferior, T – temporal, N – nasal. (Adapted from Wallace et al. (1992) and Wallace & Stein (1996), the latter © 1996 Elsevier Science, with permission.)

modality alignment of receptive fields is particularly evident in multisensory neurons (Figure 22.1), whose role is to integrate cross-modal information, a role which will be described in detail below.

Maintaining Receptive Field Alignment

While it appears simple conceptually, establishing and maintaining receptive field alignment across modalities is not a trivial problem from the standpoint of neural computation. Each sensory system uses distinctly different referents: visual axes are centered on the retina, the acoustic axes are aligned with respect to the head (i.e., the position of the external ears), and the location of a tactile stimulus is referred to the body surface. Given that these reference frames can move independently of one another, there is no unique relationship between a coordinate in one reference frame and that in another. As described below, this places substantial constraints on the neural mechanisms that establish and maintain receptive field alignment in instances in which the eyes, head, ears, and body move with respect to one another.

The receptive field properties of SC multisensory neurons have been examined most often when the eyes, head, and body are aligned so that the axes of visual, auditory, and tactile "space" are in approximate co-registration. With only rare exceptions, these experiments have demonstrated that there is excellent alignment among the modality-specific receptive fields of multisensory neurons. A few examples from different species and brain structures are presented in Figure 22.1. Note that in each case there is an overlap, or spatial register, among the receptive fields. This is easiest to see in the case of a visual-auditory neuron, for which both receptive fields are in extrapersonal space. However, visual-somatosensory and auditory-somatosensory receptive fields show a similar organization. Thus, when the visual or auditory receptive field is in central (i.e., frontal) space, the corresponding somatosensory receptive field is on the face; when the visual or auditory receptive field is more peripheral, the corresponding somatosensory receptive field is further back on the body. Similar observations have now been made in alert animals (e.g., see Frens & van Opstal, 1998; Wallace, Meredith, & Stein, 1998).

But what happens when one set of sensory organs is moved relative to the others? Given that the eyes, ears, head, and body can move independently of one another (to a degree that is species-specific), modality-specific signals cannot be encoded in their original reference frames (e.g., eye-centered, head-centered, body-centered) if receptive field register is to be maintained in the behaving animal. For example, eye movements deviate the eyes in the orbit, and each eye movement changes the relationship between the visual axis and those of the auditory and somatosensory domains. The same result is produced by head, ear, and/or limb movements.

Is receptive field alignment disrupted by relative movement of modality-specific reference frames? Studies in awake animals indicate that compensatory mechanisms attempt to maintain receptive field register. Evidence that many SC auditory and somatosensory RFs are remapped as a function of eye position to maintain alignment with the visual RFs has been obtained in both monkeys and cats (Groh & Sparks, 1996; Hartline, Pandey Vimal, King, Kurylo, & Northmore, 1995; Jay & Sparks, 1987a, 1987b; Peck, Baro, & Warder,

1995). These results suggest that multisensory representations are of a higher order, that is, the product of neural computations that transform signals from different modalities into a common coordinate frame. One possibility, as discussed by Sparks and colleagues (e.g., Sparks & Nelson, 1987), is that SC sensory maps are the end-product of coordinate transformations designed to represent modality-specific information in a common "motor" frame of reference. In such a scheme, the locus of sensory-contingent activity is more closely allied with the movement vector required to orient to the stimulus than to the spatial location of the stimulus itself. The result of this would be a modality-independent code in which stimulus location with respect to the current gaze position is the major determinant of the spatial distribution of activity across the multisensory population.

In the SC, different modalities of sensory information may be represented in a coordinate frame that makes for an easy interface with the motor map that produces gaze shifts. Because the visual reference frame is tied to the direction of gaze, it makes sense that the auditory and somatosensory receptive fields shift to maintain alignment with the visual representation. Reinforcing these findings are data from another area involved in movement, the ventral premotor cortex of monkey (Graziano, Yap, & Gross, 1994). Rather than being active in association with shifts in gaze, ventral premotor cortex is active in association with reaching movements. Accordingly, because it is the tactile sensory surface that is bound to the position of the arm, Graziano and colleagues found that the visual receptive fields of visual-tactile neurons are remapped with changes in arm position, so that visual information, like tactile information, is represented in a body-part-centered frame of reference.

Principles of Cross-Modality ("Multisensory") Integration in the Superior Colliculus

The synthesis of multisensory information accomplished by SC neurons is critically dependent upon the relationships between the different sensory stimuli, as well as their individual physical characteristics. Several of the more important factors in dictating an integrated multisensory response are detailed below.

Space

Because cues that are derived from the same event are likely to originate from the same location in space, they also are likely to activate the same multisensory neurons (because of the receptive field overlap described above). These neurons integrate the different sensory inputs, yielding a multisensory response "product" far different from either of the responses to the individual stimuli. Typically, this is manifested as a discharge train with more impulses than that evoked by either of the single-modality stimuli and often exceeding the sum of the unimodal responses (Figure 22.2) (Meredith & Stein, 1986; Wallace, Wilkinson, & Stein, 1996).

If the auditory stimulus is presented outside its receptive field (and is thereby spatially

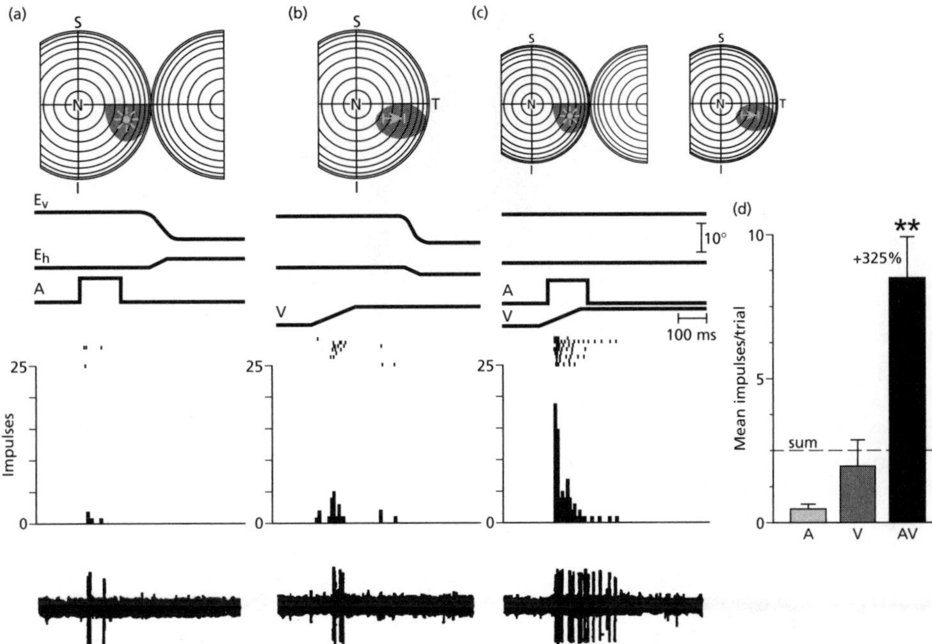

Figure 22.2. Multisensory enhancement in a visual-auditory SC neuron of an awake cat. (a) Shown at the top are the auditory receptive field and the location of the stimulus (icon of speaker). E_v and E_h represent vertical and horizontal components of eye position during a single trial, and the electronic trace labeled "A" illustrates the timing of the auditory stimulus. Raster and peristimulus time histogram show this neuron's response to six presentations of the auditory stimulus alone, and a single response is shown in the oscillograph below. (b) The visual receptive field (shading) and visual stimulus (bar moving as depicted by the arrow) are shown at the top, and the responses to the visual stimulus alone are shown below. (c) Pairing the auditory and visual stimuli produced a marked response enhancement that exceeded the sum of the unimodal responses. The magnitude of the response enhancement is shown in the summary bar graph (d). ** $p < 0.01$. (From Wallace et al. (1998), with permission.)

discordant with the visual stimulus), no such response enhancement is produced. In fact, under such circumstances there is a good probability that the opposite effect – response depression – will occur (Figure 22.3). In this case, even a robust visual response can be abolished by the spatially disparate auditory stimulus (Kadunce, Vaughan, Wallace, Benedek, & Stein, 1997; Meredith & Stein, 1996; Wallace et al., 1996). Multisensory depression can be evoked in many of the same neurons that exhibit multisensory enhancement. There is a parallel phenomenon in behavioral experiments in which spatially coincident visual and auditory stimuli enhance attentive and orientation responses, and spatially disparate visual and auditory stimuli degrade them. This is discussed below in the section entitled SC-Mediated Multisensory Behaviors.

An explanation for the opposing effects that can be evoked with the same stimuli in the

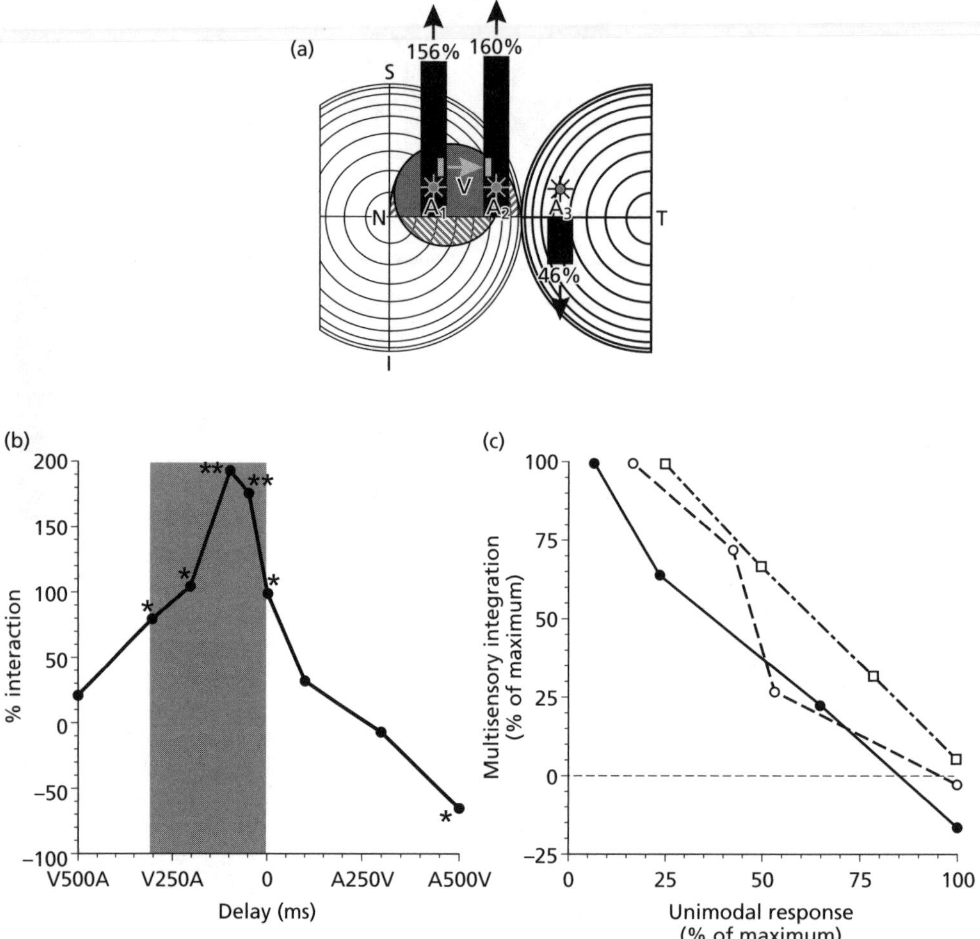

Figure 22.3. Multisensory integration is affected by spatial and temporal factors, as well as by the effectiveness of the modality-specific stimuli. (a) When the two stimuli are presented within their respective receptive fields, their combination results in response enhancement. For this visual-auditory SC neuron in the cat, the auditory receptive field is shown as upward hatch lines, the visual receptive field as downward hatch lines, and the region of overlap as gray shading. The visual stimulus is a bar of light moving as indicated by the arrow (V). The auditory stimulus, depicted by the speaker icon, was presented at three different locations (A_1, A_2 and A_3) in each of three different test series. When the visual and auditory stimuli were within their receptive fields, response enhancement (A_1 = 156% and A_2 = 160%) resulted, but when the auditory stimulus was outside of its receptive field (A_3), response depression was obtained. (b) In this visual-auditory neuron, multisensory interactions were greatest when the visual stimulus preceded the auditory by 100 ms (V100A) and became progressively smaller as the temporal disparity between the stimuli increased or decreased. Nonetheless, significant interactions were generated within a temporal window of 300 ms (gray shading). * $p < 0.05$; ** $p < 0.01$. (c) In the three multisensory neurons depicted, the largest multisensory interactions were generated when the modality-specific stimuli were at minimal levels of effectiveness. As these stimuli became more effective, the magnitude of the multisensory interactions declined. While other SC neurons also exhibited this effect of "inverse effectiveness," they were far less linear in their response profiles.

same neurons is based on the spatial relationships of the two stimuli to one another and to their respective receptive fields. Response enhancement is the result of the synergistic interaction of two excitatory inputs that occurs when stimuli appear within their respective receptive fields. But, because some receptive fields have an inhibitory, or suppressive, region at their borders, response depression can be explained by the antagonism between the inhibitory input from the stimulus outside the receptive field and the excitatory input produced by the within-field stimulus (Kadunce et al., 1997).

Effectiveness

In addition to the spatial relationships between the stimuli, the effectiveness, or strength, of the individual stimuli in eliciting a response plays an important role in determining the multisensory product produced by their combination. This relationship makes intuitive sense, because highly effective stimuli typically result in a large neuronal response (and, likely, a consequent behavioral response) and gain little from the additional information provided by the second modality. However, when the stimuli are weakly effective on their own, the benefit of multisensory integration is most obvious. For here, the stimulus combination results in a largely enhanced response, often far exceeding that predicted by summing the two unimodal responses (i.e., superadditive; see Figure 22.3). Not surprisingly, and highlighting the parallels here between the physiology of single neurons and behavior, such a stimulus combination will also have a high probability of evoking an SC-mediated behavior (see below). This principle, known as "inverse effectiveness," is illustrated in Figure 22.3.

Time

Producing an integrated multisensory response, and the magnitude of that response, depends not only on the location and effectiveness of the stimuli, but on their relative timing as well (Figure. 22.3). Not surprisingly, when there is too great an interval between two stimuli, they are treated as independent events, even if they are derived from the same location in space. Yet, the "window" of time during which multisensory interactions can occur is surprisingly long, often exceeding hundreds of milliseconds (Meredith, Nemitz, & Stein, 1987; Wallace & Stein, 1997). This is perhaps most important because it permits stimuli from two sensory modalities to interact despite very different input latencies. For example, the latency range for auditory and somatosensory responses in multisensory SC neurons is approximately 10–25 msec, while the latency range for visual responses spans 40–120 msec. Therefore, if a visual-auditory or a visual-somatosensory neuron depended on an exact latency match in order to integrate cross-modal information, the vast majority of events that take place near the animal (and which produce near-simultaneous sensory cues) would result in signals arriving at the SC at different times and produce very little, if any, cross-modal integration. This is clearly not the case, in large part because each sensory input has a long-lasting effect on a multisensory neuron.

Nonetheless, within the wide temporal window there generally exists an optimum difference in the time between the onsets of the two stimuli that will result in the largest multisensory interaction. Most SC neurons appear to be "tuned" so that their best multisensory response occurs at one stimulus onset asynchrony (SOA – the difference between the onset of the two stimuli), and progressively smaller interactions are generated at greater or lesser SOAs (Figure 22.3). Some neurons even exhibit response depression at SOAs transitional between those that evoke two unique responses and those that elicit a single integrated response. This finding suggests that such neurons are tuned to events that take place at different distances from the animal and thus respond best to stimuli that have SOAs that are consistent with these distances.

Preservation of Receptive Field Properties

It is interesting to note that the marked changes induced by multisensory enhancement generally do not alter a neuron's fundamental receptive field properties. For example, if a visual-auditory neuron responds best to a certain direction of visual movement, and/or a certain velocity, and/or proves to be binocular when examined with a unimodal visual cue, it will maintain these properties in the presence of an auditory stimulus even when that auditory stimulus enhances the neuron's responses dramatically. Whether this also holds true during response depression is not yet known.

Receptive Field Alignment is Critical for Normal Multisensory Integration

It is apparent from the discussion above that the alignment of the different receptive fields in multisensory neurons is important for the enhancement of responses to stimuli derived from the same event and the depression of responses to stimuli derived from competing events. However, early in life, receptive field alignment in multisensory SC neurons is not readily apparent. Neonatal SC neurons typically have very large receptive fields; many can be activated by stimuli anywhere in sensory space and it is only after a substantial postnatal developmental period that the different receptive fields of multisensory neurons achieve their adult-like precision and cross-modality register (Wallace & Stein, 1997; see also King & Carlile, 1993; Knudsen & Brainard, 1991; Withington-Wray, Binns, & Keating, 1990; Withington-Wray, Binns, Dhanjal, Brickley, & Keating, 1990). Presumably, the same Hebbian mechanisms that operate to strengthen synchronous inputs in any modality-specific system are also likely to strengthen synchronous cross-modality inputs derived from the same event, thereby leading to cross-modality receptive field alignment.

SC-Mediated Multisensory Behaviors

The most direct effects of the SC on overt behavior are mediated via its crossed descending output pathway, the predorsal bundle. It is through this pathway that SC neurons gain access to regions of the brainstem and spinal cord that influence movements of the eyes, ears, mouth, and head (see Stein & Meredith, 1991). The overwhelming majority of SC neurons projecting into this pathway are responsive to sensory stimuli, with most of these being multisensory (Meredith, Wallace, & Stein, 1992; Wallace, Meredith, & Stein, 1993).

This observation prompted a number of behavioral experiments to test a pair of seemingly straightforward predictions: that the multisensory stimulus configurations that produce enhanced responses in SC neurons will be more salient and will increase SC-mediated attentive and orientation behaviors; and that those multisensory stimulus combinations that reduce SC neuronal responses will be less salient, and will degrade SC-mediated behaviors. These predictions proved to be correct.

Cats were trained using food reward in a perimetry device (see Figure 22.4) to look directly ahead of them and then orient toward, and immediately approach, a briefly illuminated visual target (a light-emitting diode, or LED). Some of the animals were also trained to approach a sound – a very brief, low-intensity broad-band noise burst delivered from a speaker. Still other animals either had no experience with the auditory stimulus, or were trained to ignore it (it was never paired with reinforcement). When the visual and auditory stimuli were presented at the same time and in the same location during testing, the correct responses of animals in the first group were increased far more than was expected based on statistical predictions. Correct responding also was significantly enhanced in all other animals regardless of their training history. But, if the auditory stimulus was presented in a location disparate (e.g., 60° medial) to the visual stimulus, it decreased the probability of correct responses, and did so not only in animals that learned to ignore the auditory stimulus during their training sessions, but also in animals that were never exposed to the auditory stimulus during training (Stein et al., 1989).

The results of these behavioral experiments closely parallel those obtained in physiological studies. As it turns out, the key to the multisensory integration seen both physiologically in the activity of individual SC neurons, and behaviorally in changes in attentive and orientation performance, depends on the development and maintenance of a critical connection between the neocortex and the SC.

Role of Cortex in Mediating Multisensory Integration in the Superior Colliculus

Physiological Studies

Because the SC receives sensory inputs from a large number of ascending and descending (corticotectal) visual, auditory and somatosensory structures (Edwards, Ginsburgh, Henke, & Stein, 1979; Huerta & Harting, 1984; Stein & Meredith, 1991), its neurons could, theoretically, become multisensory by virtue of a host of different afferent convergence patterns. Oddly enough, they appear to receive few, if any, inputs from multisensory neurons in other structures (Wallace et al., 1993; Jiang, McHaffie & Stein, unpublished observations), but become multisensory as a result of the convergence of unimodal inputs. Therefore, it seemed reasonable to expect that any neuron that receives convergent sensory input from two or more modalities will be capable of the kind of multisensory integration

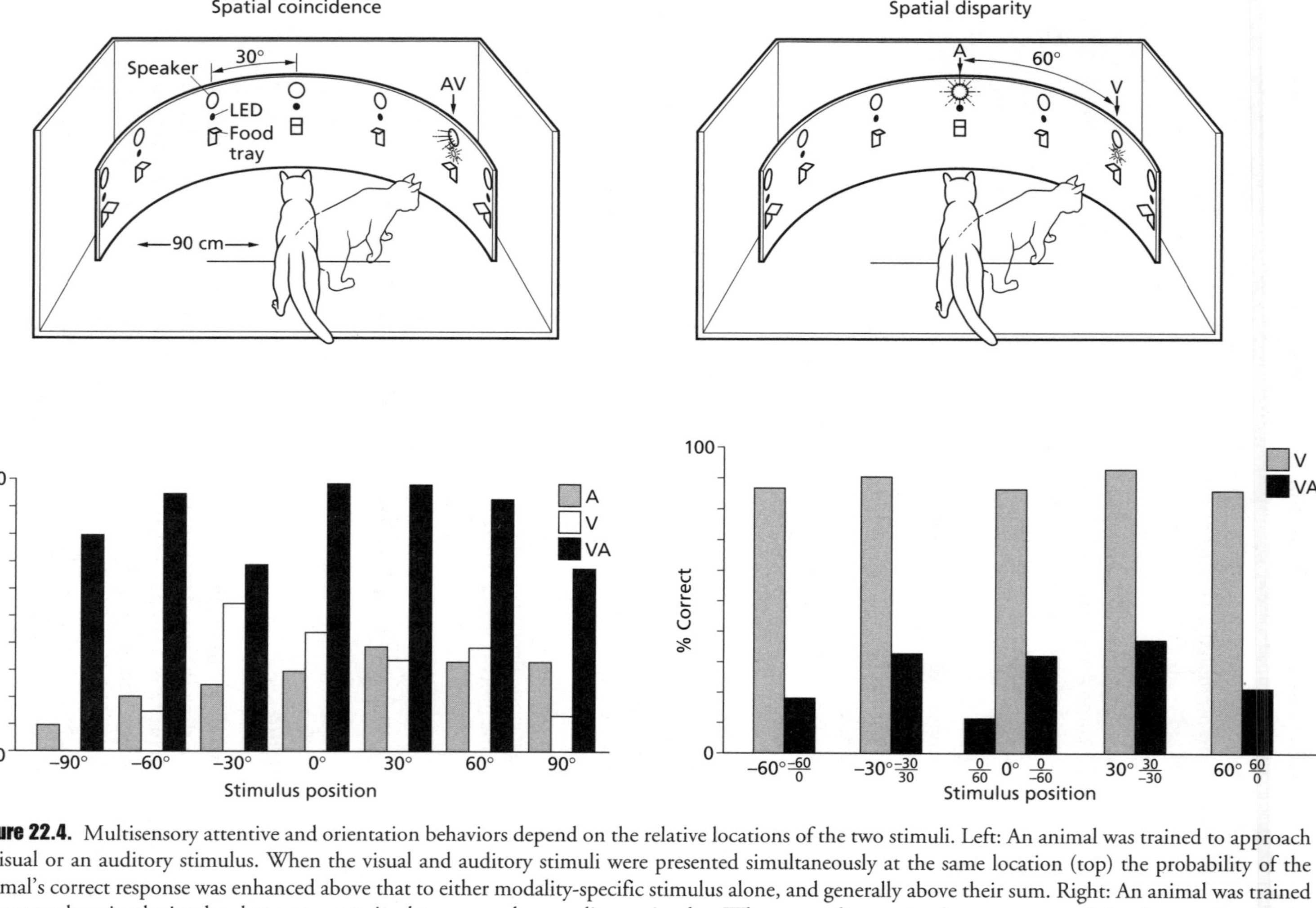

Figure 22.4. Multisensory attentive and orientation behaviors depend on the relative locations of the two stimuli. Left: An animal was trained to approach a visual or an auditory stimulus. When the visual and auditory stimuli were presented simultaneously at the same location (top) the probability of the animal's correct response was enhanced above that to either modality-specific stimulus alone, and generally above their sum. Right: An animal was trained to approach a visual stimulus, but was not trained to approach an auditory stimulus. When an auditory stimulus was presented simultaneously with the visual (but 60% disparate), the probability of a correct response to the visual stimulus was markedly depressed. (Adapted from Stein et al. (1989), with permission from MIT Press.)

discussed above. This proved not to be the case, and as discussed below, not all converging sensory inputs proved to be capable of supporting this process.

In the cat, inputs derived from one region of neocortex, the anterior ectosylvian sulcus (AES), turned out to make a very special contribution to multisensory integration in the SC. Traditionally, the AES has been described as an area of sensory "association cortex." It does not receive its primary inputs from the major thalamic sensory relay nuclei, and it has multiple subregions representing different sensory modalities: a somatosensory area, SIV (Clemo & Stein, 1982); a visual area, AEV (Mucke, Norita, Benedek, & Creutzfeldt, 1982; Olson & Graybiel, 1987); and an auditory area, Field AES (Clarey & Irvine, 1986). It also has many multisensory neurons distributed throughout these subregions (Clemo, Meredith, Wallace, & Stein, 1991; Jiang, Lepore, Ptito, & Guillemot, 1994a, 1994b; Wallace, Meredith, & Stein, 1992). This region of cortex is a rich source of input to the SC, providing one of the largest descending corticotectal projections (Stein, Spencer, & Edwards, 1983; Wallace et al., 1993). Although, as noted above, only unimodal AES neurons send their axons to the SC, they do so in convergence patterns that match the multisensory nature of the SC neuron they contact. For example, AES inputs onto visual-auditory SC neurons will arise from its visual (i.e., AEV) and auditory (i.e., FAES) subdivisions, but not from its somatosensory subdivision (i.e., SIV). However, of primary importance in the present context is the observation that the influences of the AES are essential for normal multisensory integration in SC neurons. For when the AES is temporarily deactivated, most SC neurons continue to respond to the individual sensory cues (because their various other sources of sensory information are unimpaired), but they can no longer integrate these inputs to produce an enhanced response (Figure 22.5). By using its target neurons in the SC in this way, the AES not only controls these cross-modality associative functions, but takes advantage of a circuitry that mediates attentive and orientation behaviors to multiple sensory stimuli. In the few multisensory neurons in which multisensory integration could not be demonstrated, AES inputs were found to be absent (Wallace & Stein, 1994).

Behavioral Studies

Based on these physiological observations, one would predict that the ability to use different sensory cues synergistically to guide SC-mediated behaviors would also depend on the integrity of the AES. Confirmation of this prediction was obtained in behavioral studies with cats that used the same paradigm and perimetry device described above. The animals were trained and then tested for multisensory orientation behaviors with AES intact or temporarily deactivated by infusion with an anesthetic agent, lidocaine. When the AES was deactivated there was no observable effect on orientation to unimodal cues, whereas the behavioral enhancements resulting from spatially-coincident multisensory stimulus combinations were abolished. Furthermore, the ability of spatially-disparate cues to decrease the probability of correct responses was also degraded (Wilkinson, Meredith, & Stein, 1996) (Figure 22.6). These effects were specific to AES deactivation and were not observed during the deactivation of other visual or auditory cortical regions. The behavioral data, in conjunction with data from the electrophysiological studies described above, strongly

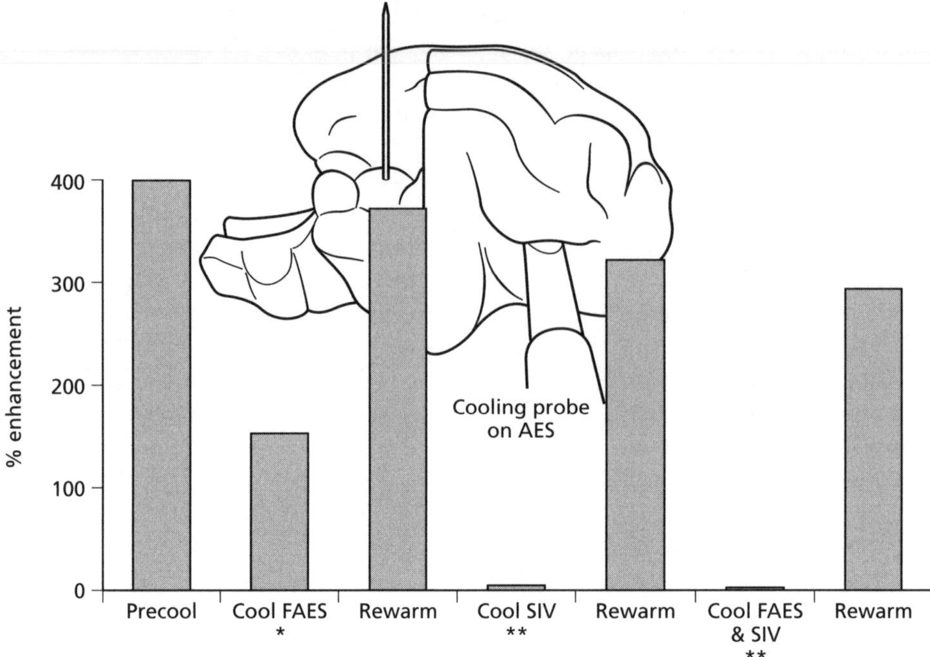

Figure 22.5. Deactivation of AES cortex abolishes multisensory integration in cat SC neurons. In this example a significant multisensory response enhancement was induced in an SC neuron by pairing auditory and somatosensory stimuli. Deactivating (cooling) the auditory (FAES) and somatosensory (SIV) subdivisions of the AES abolished the enhanced response, but did not substantially alter responses to the modality-specific stimuli (not shown). Rewarming the AES reinstituted the SC neuron's response enhancement. * $p < 0.05$, ** $p < 0.01$. (Adapted from Wallace & Stein (1994).)

suggest that an intimate relationship must be maintained between the AES and SC in order to support these multisensory attentive and orientation functions.

Development of Multisensory Integration

Animals are not born with the neural processes through which multisensory integration is effected in the SC, and young animals exhibit little of the behavioral facility with multisensory cues that characterizes the adult cat. In fact, during the first few days after birth, the SC functions essentially as a unimodal structure (see Stein, Labos, & Kruger, 1973). During this period the animal's eyelids and ear canals are closed and, not surprisingly, SC neurons do not respond to visual or auditory stimuli. However, some neurons do respond to somatosensory cues and the animal's responsiveness to tactile stimuli is particularly evident in its use of these cues to initiate suckling behaviors (Larson & Stein, 1984). As

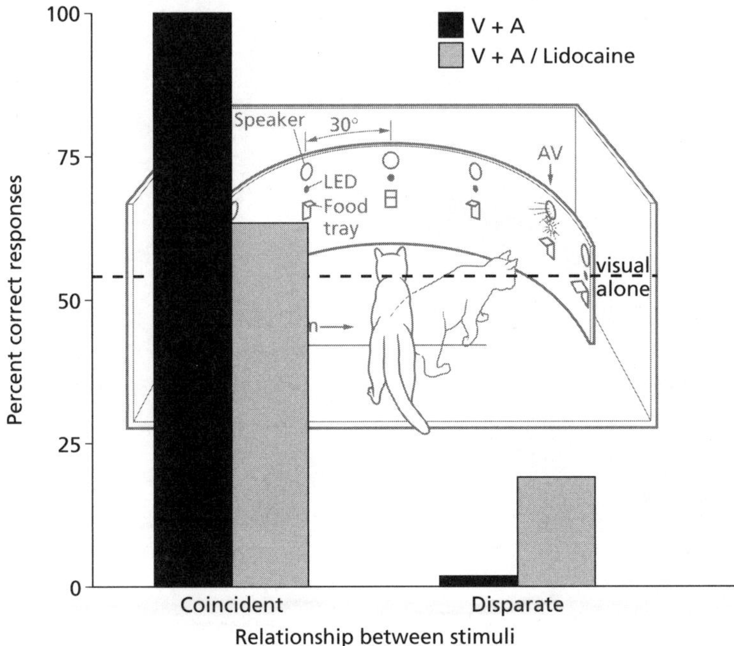

Figure 22.6. Deactivating AES cortex severely disrupts multisensory orientation behavior. Both the enhanced responses to a spatially coincident multisensory combination and the depressed responses to a spatially disparate combination are compromised during transient AES deactivation (lidocaine injections via indwelling cannulae). (Adapted from Wilkinson et al. (1996).)

postnatal development progresses, the incidence of sensory-responsive SC neurons increases. By about the fifth day after birth the first SC neurons become responsive to auditory cues (Stein et al., 1973), and at about 3 postnatal weeks neurons in the multisensory layers begin to respond to visual inputs (Wallace & Stein, 1997). However, these early neurons are very different from their adult counterparts.

The earliest multisensory neurons have very large receptive fields, and they are unable to synthesize their different sensory inputs to increase or decrease their responses (Figure 22.7). This immaturity is not specific to the cat, but is apparent in multisensory SC neurons of the newborn rhesus monkey as well. In many respects, the rhesus monkey is far more mature than the kitten at birth, having already developed a complement of multisensory neurons. Yet, just as in the young cat, these neonatal multisensory neurons have receptive fields that are much larger than they are in adults and they are incapable of synthesizing multisensory cues to significantly enhance or degrade their responses (see Wallace, McHaffie, & Stein, 1995).

By the end of the first postnatal month the cat's multisensory capabilities have matured substantially. Some multisensory SC neurons have developed spatially restricted receptive

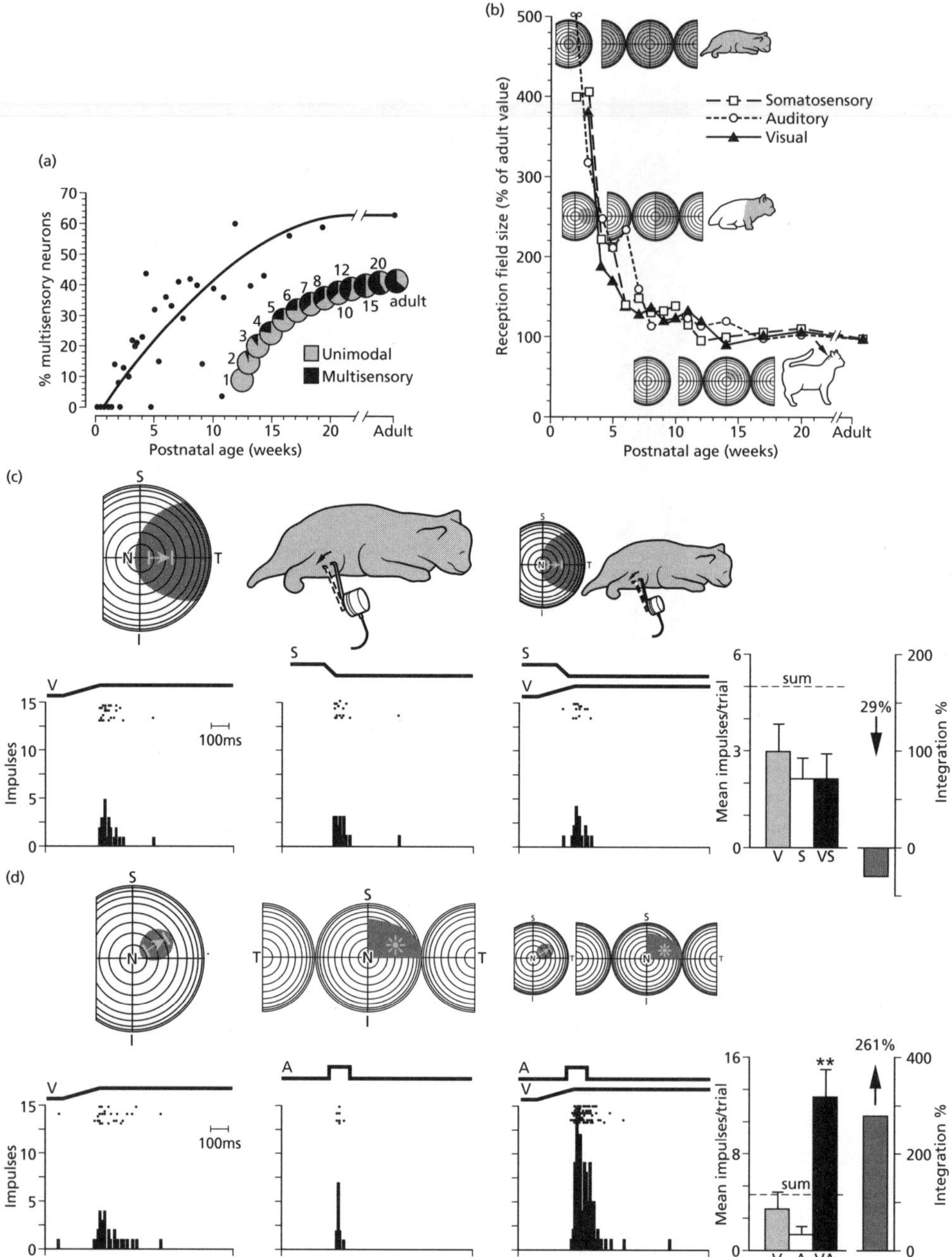

Figure 22.7. The development of cat SC multisensory neurons, multisensory receptive fields, and multisensory integration. (a) Multisensory SC neurons appear gradually over the first several postnatal months. (b) Visual, auditory and somatosensory receptive fields also contract during this period and develop an increasingly obvious spatial register (insets). (c) Early multisensory neurons, which typically have large receptive fields, lack the capacity for multisensory integration (as shown in this example from a 20 dpn animal). (d) shortly thereafter, in neurons in which receptive fields have consolidated (as in this example from a 30 dpn animal), multisensory integration appears. ** $p < 0.01$. (Adapted from Wallace & Stein (1997), with permission.)

fields and are able to integrate cross-modality cues very much like the adult. Such neurons exhibit significant response enhancement when these cues are spatially coincident, and either no enhancement or response depression when these same cues are spatially disparate (Figure 22.7). During the next two months there is a progressive increase in the incidence of these seemingly mature multisensory neurons.

Unexpectedly, when the first SC neurons exhibit the capacity to engage in multisensory integration, they do so in a manner that appears very much like that observed in the adult. The magnitude of the enhanced (or depressed) product is the same as in the adult, and interactions closely follow the established principles of multisensory integration (e.g., receptive field overlap, spatial coincidence among stimuli yields response enhancement, spatial disparity yields no interaction or a depressed response, inverse effectiveness, etc.). The only characteristic that appears to be different is that early multisensory neurons have a much more limited temporal window during which integration can take place. Generally, these neurons require near simultaneous presentation of the different sensory stimuli in order to exhibit an integrated product. Given the critical nature of AES-SC connections for multisensory integration in adult animals, it seems quite probable that the abrupt onset of multisensory integration in these neurons reflects a rapid transition to the state in which there is an active influence of AES over SC neurons. That a corticotectal influence can develop in a seemingly abrupt fashion is not without precedent, as corticotectal influences from visual cortex show a similar developmental profile (see Stein & Gallagher, 1981).

Fundamental Commonalities in Multisensory Integration

The topographic organization of the sensory representations and the spatial register of the different receptive fields of multisensory neurons are characteristic not only of cat and monkey, but are seen also in hamster (Chalupa & Rhoades, 1977; Finlay, Schneps, Wilson, & Schneider, 1978; Stein & Dixon, 1979; Tiao & Blakemore, 1976), mouse (Benedetti, 1991; Drager & Hubel, 1975), rat (McHaffie, Kao, & Stein, 1989), and guinea pig (King & Palmer, 1985). In addition, these organizational principles have been described in the nonmammalian homologue of the SC, the optic tectum, in a number of species, including birds, reptiles, amphibians, and fish (Bullock, 1984; Hartline, Kass, & Loop, 1978; Knudsen, 1982; Stein & Gaither, 1981; see also Stein & Meredith, 1993). The striking phyletic constancy in the manner in which the different sensory modalities are represented in the midbrain suggests that this multisensory organizational scheme antedates the evolution and radiation of mammals.

The presence of receptive field register in multisensory neurons also characterizes neurons in a variety of neocortical areas (e.g., Bruce, Desimone, & Gross, 1981; Duhamel, Colby, & Goldberg, 1991; Fogassi et al., 1996; Graziano, Hu, & Gross, 1997; Ramachandran, Wallace, Clemo, & Stein, 1993; Rizzolatti, Scandolara, Matelli, & Gentilucci, 1981a, 1981b; Stein, Meredith, & Wallace, 1993; Wallace et al., 1992), where such neurons are likely to be involved in functional roles very different from those in the SC. However, unlike the midbrain, a global topography for each sensory modality is not apparent in all cortical regions, even though individual multisensory neurons exhibit a striking register.

For example, in cat AES, only SIV has been found to have a demonstrable sensory map. The corresponding visual (AEV) and auditory (FAES) regions are far less systematically arranged. Despite this, multisensory AES neurons, regardless of where they are found, have overlapping receptive fields. Furthermore, these multisensory neurons exhibit a number of the integrative properties that are characteristic of SC neurons. These include the spatial principle, inverse effectiveness, and response enhancements that exceed the sum of the unimodal responses (Wallace et al., 1992). These commonalities are consistent with the idea that some of the fundamental principles of multisensory integration are general and supersede structure, function, and species.

This should not be taken to indicate that there are no significant differences in unimodal or multisensory neurons that are associated with different species or structures. There is little doubt that high frequency sounds are more effective in rodent than in primate, that sound is of primary importance in some species (e.g., bats) whereas vision is primary in others (e.g., monkey) and somesthesis in still others (e.g., blind mole). These differences are reflected in the proportion and response characteristics of neurons devoted to processing modality-specific information and are essential adaptations that reflect an animal's ecological specialization. They are also very likely to be reflected in the convergence patterns and responses of multisensory neurons. Specialization is almost certainly the case for different structures as well. For example, multisensory depression appears to be less frequent and less pronounced in cortex than in SC (see Stein & Wallace, 1996). In this context it is interesting to note that the influence of an auditory cue on perceptual judgments of visual intensity (presumably a cortical function) does not require that the auditory and visual cues originate from the same spatial location, an effect very different from that governing SC-mediated attentive and orientation functions (Stein et al., 1996).

Nevertheless, it is likely that specialized characteristics are imposed on a core of common properties, such as those shared by the midbrain and cortex. A common foundation of properties that characterize multisensory integration at different levels of the neuraxis ensures that cues are enhanced (or degraded) simultaneously in areas of the brain involved in different response components of an integrated behavior. The preservation and elaboration of these properties in animals at different phyletic levels attest to the utility of such a scheme in both very primitive and more advanced species.

Note

1. The research described here was supported by NIH grants EY06562 and NS22543. We thank Nancy London for editorial assistance.

Suggested Readings

Baron-Cohen, S., & Harrison, J. E. (1997). *Synesthesia.* Cambridge, MA: Blackwell.

Lewkowicz, D. J., & Lickliter, R. (1994). *The development of intersensory perception: Comparative perspectives.* Hillsdale, NJ: Erlbaum.

Sparks, D.L., & Groh, J.M. (1994). The superior colliculus: A window for viewing issues in integrative neuroscience. In M. Gazzaniga (Ed.), *The cognitive neurosciences* (pp. 565–584). Cambridge, MA: MIT Press.

Stein, B. E., & Meredith, M. A. (1993). *The merging of the senses.* Cambridge, MA: MIT Press.

Stein, B. E., Meredith, M. A., & Wallace, M. T. (1994). Neural mechanisms mediating attention and orientation to multisensory cues. In M. Gazzaniga (Ed.), *The cognitive neurosciences* (pp. 683–702). Cambridge, MA: MIT Press.

Additional Topics

Cross-modal Plasticity

Of substantial interest is whether, and the degree to which, the different sensory modalities can compensate for each other after abnormal experience, disuse, or damage. See Rauschecker (1995) and Neville (1990).

Map Development

Although the formation of topographic maps for the different sensory modalities has been well documented, the issue of how overlapping sensory representations come about in cross-modal structures is of substantial interest. See Knudsen and Brainard (1995) and Schnupp, King, Smith, and Thompson (1995).

Attention

Attentive mechanisms influence much of what we do and the speed with which we do it. Although much of the literature on sensory attention examines intramodal processes, they apply equally well to questions of whether attending to a cue in one modality affects the ability to attend and react to a cue from another modality. See Hillyard, Mangun, Woldorff, and Luck (1995). Sparks and Groh (1994) is a review of the unique role of the superior colliculus in the transformation of sensory information into appropriate motor commands.

References

Ackerman, D. (1990). *A natural history of the senses.* New York: Vintage Books/Random House.

Andreassi, J. L., & Greco, J. R. (1975). Effects of bisensory stimulation on reaction time and the evoked cortical potential. *Physiology and Psychology, 3*,189–194.

Asanuma, C., Ohkawa, R., Stanfield, B. B., & Cowan, W. M. (1988). Observations on the development of certain ascending inputs to the thalamus in rats. I. Postnatal development. *Developments in Brain Research, 41*, 159–170.

Benedetti, F. (1991). The postnatal emergence of a functional somatosensory representation in the superior colliculus of the mouse. *Developments in Brain Research, 60*, 51–57.

Bernstein, I. H., Clark, M. H., & Edelstein, B. A. (1969). Effects of an auditory signal on visual reaction time. *Journal of Experimental Psychology, 80*, 567–569.

Biguer, B., Donaldson, I. M. L., Hein, A., & Jeannerod, M. (1988). Neck muscle vibration modifies the representation of visual motion and direction in man. *Brain, 111*, 1405–1424.

Bower, T. G. R. (1977). *A primer of infant development.* San Francisco: WH Freeman.

Bruce, C., Desimone, R., & Gross, C. G. (1981). Visual properties of neurons in a polysensory area in superior temporal sulcus of the macaque. *Journal of Neurophysiology, 46*, 369–384.

Bullock, T. H. (1984). Physiology of the tectum mesencephali in elasmobranchs. In H. Vanegas (Ed.), *Comparative neurology of the optic tectum* (pp 47–68). New York: Plenum Press.

Casagrande, V. A., Harting. J. K., Hall, W. C., & Diamond, I. T. (1972). Superior colliculus of the tree shrew: A structural and functional subdivision into superficial and deep layers. *Science, 177*, 444–447.

Chalupa, L. M., & Rhoades, R. W. (1977). Responses of visual, somatosensory, and auditory neurones in the golden hamster's superior colliculus. *Journal of Physiology (London), 207*, 595–626.

Clarey, J. C., & Irvine, D. R. F. (1986). Auditory response properties of neurons in the anterior ectosylvian sulcus of the cat. *Brain Research, 386*, 12–19.

Clark, B., & Graybiel, A. (1966). Contributing factors in the perception of the oculogravic illusion. *American Journal of Psychology, 79*, 377–388.

Clemo, H. R., Meredith, M. A., Wallace, M. T., & Stein, B. E. (1991). Is the cortex of cat anterior ectosylvian sulcus a polysensory area? *Society of Neuroscience Abstracts, 17*, 1585.

Clemo, H. R., & Stein, B. E. (1982). Somatosensory cortex: A "new" somatotopic representation. *Brain Research, 235*, 162–168.

Cytowic, R. E. (1989). *Synesthesia: A union of the senses*. New York: Springer-Verlag.

Drager, U. C., & Hubel, D. H. (1975). Responses to visual stimulation and relationship between visual, auditory and somatosensory inputs in mouse superior colliculus. *Journal of Neurophysiology, 38*, 690–713.

Duhamel, J.-R., Colby, C. L., & Goldberg, M. E. (1991). Congruent representations of visual and somatosensory space in single neurons of monkey ventral intraparietal cortex (Area VIP). In J. Paillard (Ed.), *Brain and space* (pp. 223–236). New York: Oxford University Press.

Edwards, S. B., Ginsburgh, C. L., Henkel, C. K., & Stein, B. E. (1979). Sources of subcortical projections to the superior colliculus in the cat. *Journal of Comparative Neurology, 184*, 309–330.

Finlay, B. L., Schneps, S. E., Wilson, K. G., & Schneider, G. E. (1978). Topography of visual and somatosensory projections to the superior colliculus of the golden hamster. *Brain Research, 142*, 223–235.

Fogassi, L., Gallese, V., Fadiga, L., Luppino, G., Matelli, M., & Rizzolatti, G. (1996). Coding of peripersonal space in inferior premotor cortex (area F4). *Journal of Neurophysiology, 76*, 141–157.

Frens, M. A., & Van Opstal, A. J. (1998). Visual-auditory interactions modulate saccade-related activity in monkey superior colliculus. *Brain Research Bulletin, 46*, 211–224.

Frens, M. A., Van Opstal, A. J., & Van der Willigen, R. F. (1995). Spatial and temporal factors determine audio-visual interactions in human saccadic eye movements. *Perception & Psychophysics, 57*, 802–816.

Frost, D. O. (1984). Axonal growth and target selection during development: Retinal projections to the ventrobasal complex and other "nonvisual" structures in neonatal Syrian hamsters. *Journal of Comparative Neurology, 230*, 576–592.

Gibson, J. J. (1966). *The senses considered as perceptual systems*. Boston: Houghton Mifflin.

Gielen, S. C. A. M., Schmidt, R. A., & van den Heuvel, P. J. M. (1983). On the nature of intersensory facilitation of reaction time. *Perception & Psychophysics, 34*, 161–168.

Goldring, J. E., Dorris, M. C., Corneil, B. D., Ballantyne, P. A., & Munoz, D. P. (1996). Combined eye-head gaze shifts to visual and auditory targets in humans. *Experimental Brain Research, 111*, 68–78.

Gottlieb, G., Tomlinson, W. R., & Radell, P. L. (1989). Developmental intersensory interference: Premature visual experience suppresses auditory learning in ducklings. *Infant Behavior and Development, 12*, 1–12.

Graybiel, A., & Niven, J. I. (1951). The effect of a change in direction of resultant force on sound localization: The audiogravic illusion. *Journal of Experimental Psychology, 42*, 227–230.

Graziano, M. S., Hu, X. T., & Gross, C. G. (1997). Visuospatial properties of ventral premotor cortex. *Journal of Neurophysiology, 77*, 2268–2292.

Graziano, M. S., Yap, G. S., & Gross, C. G. (1994). Coding of visual space by premotor neurons. *Science, 266*, 1054–1057.

Groh, J. M., & Sparks, D. L. (1996). Saccades to somatosensory targets. III. Eye-position-dependent somatosensory activity in primate superior colliculus. *Journal of Neurophysiology, 75*, 439–453.

Hartline, P. H., Kass, L., & Loop, M. S. (1978). Merging of modalities in the optic tectum: Infrared and visual integration in rattlesnakes. *Science, 199,* 1225–1229.

Hartline, P. H., Pandey Vimal, R. L., King, A. J., Kurylo, D. D., & Northmore, D. P. M. (1995). Effects of eye position on auditory localization and neural representation of space in superior colliculus of cats. *Experimental Brain Research, 104,* 402–408.

Held, R. (1955). Shifts in binaural localization after prolonged exposures to atypical combinations of stimuli. *American Journal of Psychology, 68,* 526–548.

Helmholtz, H. von (1968). The origin of the correct interpretation of our sensory impressions. In R. M. Warren & R. P. Warren (Eds.), *Helmholtz on perception: Its physiology and development* (pp 247–266). New York: Wiley.

Hershenson, M. (1962). Reaction time as a measure of intersensory facilitation. *Journal of Experimental Psychology, 63,* 289–293.

Highstein, S. M., & Baker, R. (1985). Action of the efferent vestibular system on primary afferents in the toadfish, *Opsanus tau. Journal of Neurophysiology, 54,* 370–384.

Hillyard, S. A., Mangun, G. R., Woldorff, M. G., & Luck, S. J. (1995). Neural mechanisms mediating selective attention. In M. Gazzaniga (Ed.), *The cognitive neurosciences* (pp. 665–681). Cambridge, MA: MIT Press.

Howard, I. P., & Templeton, W. B. (1966). *Human spatial orientation.* London: Wiley.

Huerta, M. F., & Harting, J. K. (1984). The mammalian superior colliculus: Studies of its morphology and connections. In H. Vanegas (Ed.), *Comparative neurology of the optic tectum* (pp. 687–773). New York: Plenum Press.

Hughes, H. C., Reuter-Lorenz, P. A., Nozawa, G., & Fendrich, R. (1994). Visual-auditory interactions in sensorimotor processing: Saccades versus manual responses. *Journal of Experimental Psychology: Human Perception & Performance, 20,* 131–153.

Innocenti, G. M., & Clarke, S. (1984). Bilateral transitory projection to visual areas from auditory cortex in kittens. *Developments in Brain Research, 14,* 143–148.

Jay, M. F., & Sparks, D. L. (1987a). Sensorimotor integration in the primate superior colliculus. I. Motor convergence. *Journal of Neurophysiology, 57,* 22–34.

Jay, M. F., & Sparks, D. L. (1987b). Sensorimotor integration in the primate superior colliculus. II. Coordinates of auditory signals. *Journal of Neurophysiology, 57,* 35–55.

Jiang, H., Lepore, F., Ptito, M. & Guillemot, J. P. (1994a). Sensory modality distribution in the anterior ectosylvian cortex (AEC) of cats. *Experimental Brain Research, 97,* 404–414.

Jiang, H., Lepore, F., Ptito, M. & Guillemot, J. P. (1994b). Sensory interactions in the anterior ectosylvian cortex of cats. *Experimental Brain Res*earch, *101,* 385–396.

Kadunce, D. C., Vaughan, J. W., Wallace, M. T., Benedek, G., & Stein, B. E. (1997). Mechanisms of within-modality and cross-modality suppression in the superior colliculus. *Journal of Neurophysiology, 78,* 2834–2847.

King, A. J., & Carlile, S. (1993). Changes induced in the representation of auditory space in the superior colliculus by rearing ferrets with binocular lid suture. *Experimental Brain Research, 94,* 444–455.

King, A. J., & Palmer, A. R. (1985). Integration of visual and auditory information in bimodal neurones in the guinea-pig superior colliculus. *Experimental Brain Research, 60,* 492–500.

Knudsen, E. I. (1982). Auditory and visual maps of space in the optic tectum of the owl. *Journal of Neuroscience, 2,* 1177–1194.

Knudsen, E. I., & Brainard, M. S. (1991). Visual instruction of the neural map of auditory space in the developing optic tectum. *Science, 253,* 85–87.

Lackner, J. R. (1974a). Changes in auditory localization during body tilt. *Acta Oto-Laryngologica (Stockh), 77,* 19–28.

Lackner, J. R. (1974b). Influence of visual rearrangement and visual motion on sound localization. *Neuropsychologia, 12,* 291–293.

Larson, M., & Stein, B. E. (1984). The use of tactile and olfactory cues in neonatal orientation and localization of the nipple. *Developmental Psychobiology, 17,* 423–436.

Lee, C., Chung, S., Kim, J., & Park, J. (1991). Auditory facilitation of visually guided saccades. *Society of Neuroscience Abstracts, 17,* 862.

Lickliter, R. (1990). Premature visual stimulation accelerates intersensory functioning in bobwhite quail neonates. *Developmental Psychobiology, 23*, 15–27.

Marks, L. E. (1975). On colored-hearing synesthesia: Cross-modal translations of sensory dimensions. *Psychological Bulletin, 82*, 303–331.

Marks, L. E. (1978). *The unity of the senses: Interrelations among the modalities.* New York: Academic Press.

Massaro, D. W., & Stork, D. G. (1998). Speech recognition and sensory integration. *American Science, 86*, 236–244.

Maurer, D., & Maurer, C. (1988). *The world of the newborn.* New York: Basic Books.

McGurk, H., & MacDonald, J. (1976). Hearing lips and seeing voices. *Nature, 264*, 746–748.

McHaffie, J. G., Kao, C.-Q., & Stein, B. E. (1989). Nociceptive neurons in rat superior colliculus: Response properties, topography and functional implications. *Journal of Neurophysiology, 62*, 510–525.

Meltzoff, A. N., & Moore, M. K. (1977). Imitation of facial and manual gestures by human neonates. *Science, 198*, 75–78.

Meltzoff, A. N., & Moore, M. K. (1983a). The origins of imitation in infancy: Paradigm, phenomena, and theories. In L. P. Lipsitt (Ed.), *Advances in infancy research* (Vol. 2, pp. 265–301). Norwood, NJ: Ablex.

Meltzoff, A. N., & Moore, M. K. (1983b). Newborn infants imitate adult facial gestures. *Child Development, 54*, 702–709.

Meredith, M. A., Nemitz, J. W., & Stein, B. E. (1987). Determinants of multisensory integration in superior colliculus neurons. I. Temporal factors. *Journal of Neuroscience, 10*, 3215–3229.

Meredith, M. A., & Stein, B. E. (1986). Visual, auditory and somatosensory convergence on cells in superior colliculus results in multisensory integration. *Journal of Neurophysiology, 56*, 640–662.

Meredith, M. A., & Stein, B. E. (1996). Spatial determinants of multisensory integration in cat superior colliculus. *Journal of Neurophysiology, 75*, 1843–1857.

Meredith, M. A., Wallace, M. T., & Stein, B. E. (1992). Visual, auditory and somatosensory convergence in output neurons of the cat superior colliculus: Multisensory properties of the tecto-reticulo-spinal projection. *Experimental Brain Research, 88*, 181–186.

Morrell, L. K. (1968a). Cross-modality effects upon choice reaction time. *Psychonomic Science, 11*, 129–130.

Morrell, L. K. (1968b). Temporal characteristics of sensory interaction in choice reaction times. *Journal of Experimental Psychology, 77*, 14–18.

Morrell, L. K. (1972). Visual system's view of acoustic space. *Nature, 238*, 44–46.

Mucke, L., Norita, M., Benedek, G., & Creutzfeldt, O. (1982). Physiologic and anatomic investigation of a visual cortical area situated in the ventral bank of the anterior ectosylvian sulcus of the cat. *Experimental Brain Research, 46*, 1–11.

Neville, H. J. (1990). Intermodal competition and compensation in development. Evidence from studies of the visual system in congenitally deaf adults. *Annals of the New York Academy of Science, 608*, 71–87.

Olson, C. R., & Graybiel, A. M. (1987). Ectosylvian visual area of the cat: Location, retinotopic organization, and connections. *Journal of Comparative Neurology, 261*, 277–294.

Paulesu, E., Harrison, J., Baron-Cohen, S., Watson, J. D., Goldstein, L., Heather, J., Frackowiak, R. S., & Frith, C. D. (1995). The physiology of coloured hearing. A PET activation study of colour-word synaesthesia. *Brain, 118*, 661–676.

Peck, C. K., Baro, J. A., & Warder, S. M. (1995). Effects of eye position on saccadic eye movements and on the neural responses to auditory and visual stimuli in cat superior colliculus. *Experimental Brain Research, 103*, 227–242.

Perrott, D. R., Saberi, K., Brown, K., & Strybel, T. Z (1990). Auditory psychomotor coordination and visual search performance. *Perception & Psychophysics, 48*, 214–226.

Piaget, J. (1952). *The origins of intelligence in children.* New York: International Universities Press.

Pick, H. L., Jr., Warren, D. H., & Hay, J. C. (1969). Sensory conflict in judgements of spatial direction. *Perception & Psychophysics, 6*, 203–205.

Posner, M. I., Nissen, M. J., & Klein, R. M. (1976). Visual dominance: An information-processing account of its origins and significance. *Psychological Reviews, 83,* 157–171.

Ramachandran, R., Wallace, M. T., Clemo, H. R., & Stein, B. E. (1993). Multisensory convergence and integration in rat cortex. *Society of Neuroscience Abstracts, 19,* 1447.

Rauschecker, J. P. (1995). Compensatory plasticity and sensory substitution in the cerebral cortex. *Trends in Neuroscience, 18,* 36–43.

Rizzolatti, G., Scandolara, C., Matelli, M., & Gentilucci, M. (1981a). Afferent properties of periarcuate neurons in macaque monkeys. I. Somatosensory responses. *Behavioral Brain Research, 2,* 125–146.

Rizzolatti, G., Scandolara, C., Matelli, M., & Gentilucci, M. (1981b). Afferent properties of periarcuate neurons in macaque monkeys. II. Visual responses. *Behavioral Brain Research, 2,* 147–163.

Roll, R., Velay, J. L., Roll, J. P. (1991). Eye and neck proprioceptive messages contribute to the spatial coding of retinal input in visually oriented activities. *Experimental Brain Research, 85,* 423–431.

Ryan, T. A. (1940). Interrelations of the sensory systems in perception. *Psychological Bulletin, 37,* 659–698.

Schneider, G. E. (1969). Two visual systems: Brain mechanisms for localization and discrimination are dissociated by tectal and cortical lesions. *Science, 163,* 895–902.

Schnupp, J. W. H., King, A. J., Smith, A. L., & Thompson, I. D. (1995). NMDA-receptor antagonists disrupt the formation of the auditory space map in the mammalian superior colliculus. *Journal of Neuroscience, 15,* 1516–1531.

Shelton, B. R., & Searle, C. L. (1980). The influence of vision on the absolute identification of sound-source position. *Perception & Psychophyics, 28,* 589–596.

Sparks, D. L., & Groh, J. M. (1994). The superior colliculus: A window for viewing issues in integrative neuroscience. In M. Gazzaniga (Ed.), *The cognitive neurosciences* (pp. 565–584). Cambridge, MA: MIT Press..

Sparks, D. L., & Nelson, J. S. (1987). Sensory and motor maps in the mammalian superior colliculus. *Trends in Neuroscience, 10,* 312–317.

Sprague, J. M., & Meikle, T. H., Jr. (1965). The role of the superior colliculus in visually guided behavior. *Experimental Neurology, 11,* 115–146.

Stein, B. E., & Dixon, J. P. (1979). Properties of superior colliculus neurons in the golden hamster. *Journal of Comparative Neurology, 183,* 269–284.

Stein, B. E., & Gaither, N. (1981). Sensory representation in reptilian optic tectum: Some comparisons with mammals. *Journal of Comparative Neurology, 202,* 69–87.

Stein, B. E., & Gallagher, H. (1981). Maturation of cortical control over superior colliculus cells in cat. *Brain Research, 223,* 429–435.

Stein, B. E., Labos, E., & Kruger, L. (1973). Sequence of changes in properties of neurons of superior colliculus of the kitten during maturation. *Journal of Neurophysiology, 36,* 667–679.

Stein, B. E., London, N., Wilkinson, L. K., & Price, D. D. (1996). Enhancement of perceived visual intensity by auditory stimuli: A psychophysical analysis. *Journal of Cognitive Neuroscience, 8,* 497–506.

Stein, B. E., & Meredith, M. A. (1991). Functional organization of the superior colliculus. In A. G. Leventhal (Ed.), *The neural basis of visual function* (pp. 85–110). Hampshire, UK: Macmillan.

Stein, B. E., & Meredith, M. A. (1993). *The merging of the senses.* Cambridge, MA: MIT Press.

Stein, B. E., Meredith, M. A., Huneycutt, W. S., McDade, L. (1989). Behavioral indices of multisensory integration: Orientation to visual cues is affected by auditory stimuli. *Journal of Cognitive Neuroscience, 1,* 12–24.

Stein, B. E., Meredith, M. A., & Wallace, M. T. (1993). The visually responsive neuron and beyond: Multisensory integration in cat and monkey. *Progress in Brain Research, 95,* 79–90.

Stein, B. E., Spencer, R. F., & Edwards, S. B. (1983). Corticotectal and corticothalamic efferent projections of SIV somatosensory cortex in cat. *Journal of Neurophysiology, 50,* 896–909.

Stein, B. E., & Wallace, M. T. (1996). Comparisons of cross-modality integration in midbrain and cortex. *Progress in Brain Research, 112*, 289–299.

Sumby, W. H., & Pollack, I. (1954). Visual contribution to speech intelligibility in noise. *Journal of the Acoustical Society of America, 26*, 212–215.

Sur, M., Garraghty, P. E., & Roe, A. W. (1988). Experimentally induced visual projections into auditory thalamus and cortex. *Science, 242*, 1437–1441.

Thurlow, W. R., & Rosenthal, T. M. (1976). Further study of existence regions for the "ventriloquism effect." *Journal of the American Audiological Society, 1*, 280–286.

Tiao, Y.-C., & Blakemore, C. (1976). Functional organization in the superior colliculus of the golden hamster. *Journal of Comparative Neurology, 168*, 483–504.

Turkewitz, G., & Mellon, R. C. (1989). Dynamic organization of intersensory function. *Canadian Journal of Psychology, 43*, 286–307.

von Hornbostel, E. M. (1938). The unity of the senses. In W. D. Ellis (Ed.), *A sourcebook of Gestalt psychology* (pp 211–216). New York: Harcourt Brace.

Wade, N. J., & Day, R. H. (1968). Apparent head position as a basis for a visual aftereffect of prolonged head tilt. *Perception & Psychophysics, 3*, 324–326.

Wallace, M. T., McHaffie, J. G., & Stein, B. E. (1995). Sensory response properties in the superior colliculus (SC) of the newborn rhesus monkey. *Society of Neuroscience Abstracts, 21*, 655.

Wallace, M. T., Meredith, M. A., & Stein, B. E. (1992). Integration of multiple sensory modalities in cat cortex. *Experimental Brain Research, 91*, 484–488.

Wallace, M. T., Meredith, M. A., & Stein, B. E. (1993). Converging influences from visual, auditory and somatosensory cortices onto output neurons of the superior colliculus. *Journal of Neurophysiology, 69*, 1797–1809.

Wallace, M. T., Meredith, M. A., & Stein, B. E. (1998). Multisensory integration in the superior colliculus of the alert cat. *Journal of Neurophysiology, 80*, 1006–1010.

Wallace, M. T., & Stein, B. E. (1994). Cross-modal synthesis in the midbrain depends on input from association cortex. *Journal of Neurophysiology, 71*, 429–432.

Wallace, M. T., & Stein, B. E. (1996). Sensory organization of the superior colliculus in cat and monkey. *Progress in Brain Research, 112*, 301–311.

Wallace, M. T., & Stein, B. E. (1997). Development of multisensory neurons and multisensory integration in cat superior colliculus. *Journal of Neuroscience, 17*, 2429–2444.

Wallace, M. T., Wilkinson, L. K., & Stein, B. E. (1996). Representation and integration of multiple sensory inputs in primate superior colliculus. *Journal of Neurophysiology, 76*, 1246–1266.

Warren, D. H., Welch, R. B., & McCarth, T. J. (1981). The role of visual-auditory "compellingness" in the ventriloquism effect: Implications for transitivity among the spatial senses. *Perception & Psychophyics, 30*, 557–564.

Welch, R. B., & Warren, D. H. (1980). Immediate perceptual response to intersensory discrepancy. *Psychological Bulletin, 88*, 638–667.

Welch, R. B., & Warren, D. H. (1986). Intersensory interactions. In K. R. Boff, L. Kaufman, & J. P. Thomas (Eds.), *Handbook of perception and human performance, Volume I: Sensory processes and perception* (pp.1–36). New York: Wiley.

Wilkinson, L. K., Meredith, M. A., & Stein, B. E. (1996). The role of anterior ectosylvian cortex in cross-modality orientation and approach behavior. *Experimental Brain Research, 112*, 1–10 .

Withington-Wray, D. J., Binns, K. E., & Keating, M. J. (1990). The maturation of the superior collicular map of auditory space in the guinea pig is disrupted by developmental visual deprivation. *European Journal of Neuroscience, 2*, 682–692.

Withington-Wray, D. J., Binns, K. E., Dhanjal, S. S., Brickley, S. G., & Keating, M. J. (1990). The maturation of the collicular map of auditory space in the guinea pig is disrupted by developmental auditory deprivation. *European Journal of Neuroscience, 2*, 693–703.

Zahn, J. R., Abel, L. A., & Dell'Osso, L. F. (1978). Audio-ocular response characteristics. *Sensory Process, 2*, 32–37.

Chapter Twenty-Three

Modularity in Perception, its Relation to Cognition and Knowledge

Ken Nakayama

> Nature has contrived to have it both ways, to get the best out of fast dumb mechanisms and slow contemplative ones, by simply refusing to choose between them.
>
> (Fodor, 1983, p. 4)

Although, as lay people, we take it for granted that perception offers us sure knowledge of the world, perception is deficient in some rather fundamental ways. It doesn't reveal *all* that we know about the world. Unaided, it says very little, for example, about the microscopic structure of matter. Perception can also be mistaken at the scale of the everyday, showing a host of well-known errors, so-called illusions. Yet, these obvious limitations do not shake our confidence in perceptual experience. Seeing is believing and we take perception as a reliable source to bolster our most deeply held beliefs.

Yet, this seemingly natural acceptance of perception as corresponding to "reality" has not gone unchallenged. Descartes (1649) began his foundational approach to philosophy with the posture of radical doubt, raising the possibility that the material world might not exist at all, that our sensory experience could be the conceivable handiwork of a malevolent demon, cleverly constructing what we sense for some evil purpose to fool us. In a more scientific vein, a different though related question continues to be of importance. Does perception inform us directly or is perception a construction, mediated not necessarily by Descartes' demon, but by our own and possibly flawed mental apparatus? Berkeley's *New Theory of Vision* (1709) addressed the critical issue of perceived size and distance and argued that the various cues to vision, accommodation, convergence, etc., required learned associations with motor and tactile feedback to get the correct impression of distance. For Berkeley, the process of vision from such cues was analogous to that of deriving meaning from language. As we learn the meaning of words from their association with objects and events in childhood, so do we learn the distances of objects from their association with our motor activity and various associated kinesthetic sensations.

Seventy years earlier, Descartes and followers argued for a different answer, assuming that by some form of innate calculation, distance could be immediately derived. For three-dimensional vision, Descartes suggested that we can know distance (as does the blind man in Figure 23.1a) using some form of geometrical reasoning. Assuming that we can sense the length of our eye muscles (Figure 23.1b), the calculation of distance is a straightforward problem in trigonometry.

Berkeley's and Descartes' ideas have survived very well in this modern age. Berkeley's thinking suggests the continuity of perception with thought in general, citing the analogy of perception to language, whereas Descartes' views suggests that perception is pre-

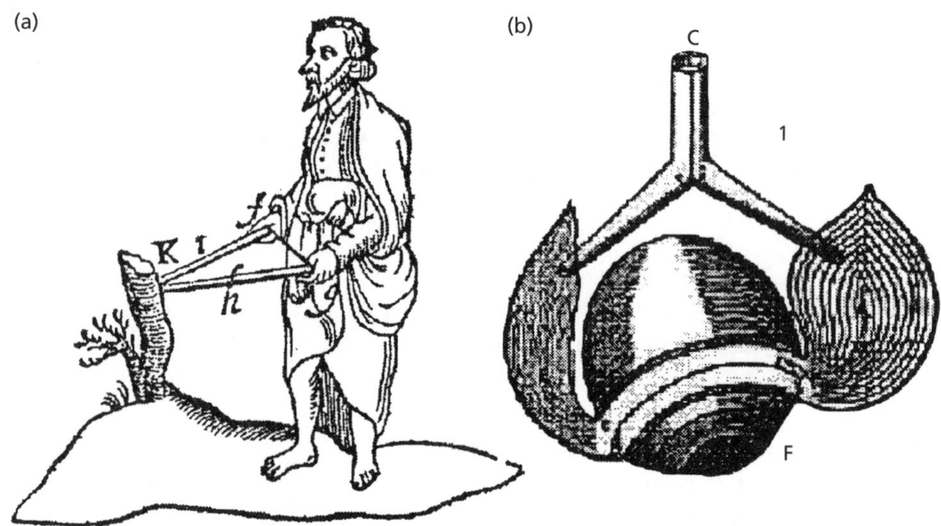

Figure 23.1 (a) Blind man obtaining information from the distance of a point in the environment using trigonometry, utilizing the known angle between the sticks which are hand-held (from Descartes, 1649). (b) Eye muscles as described by Descartes (Treatise on man).

ordained, more machine-like, and very different from thought. As we will see, current ideas about perception tilt more in favor of Descartes and this in turn leads to the following question. If perception is more machine-like and distinctively different from thought in general, what happens when the results obtained from perception contradict knowledge of the world obtained from other sources mediated by thinking?

In this chapter I argue that errors from perceptual mechanisms are almost inevitable and are very likely. On the other hand, consequential, that is, life-threatening or even inconveniencing errors of perception are rare in real life. This might be regarded as surprising because perceptual experience can make such a strong impression on us and the long history of research in perception contains a catalog of errors and illusions. To address this seeming paradox, we take a wide tour. In brief, we argue that perception can be regarded as modular in Fodor's (1983) sense. Then we identify some unusual situations where modularity can lead to consequential error. The singular nature of these situations implies that perception's modularity leads to no particular problem under normal circumstances. Perception's distinctly close coupling to the real world and its selectivity renders any error as inconsequential. We conclude this chapter on a cautiously ambitious note, suggesting that the characteristics of perception's modularity are such that a greater understanding of perception offers particular benefits for the study of cognition and psychology more generally.

Modular Systems

To begin this discussion, I suggest we reflect on the seminal essay by Jerry Fodor (1983), *Modularity of the mind.* Although many disagree with the specific assertions made (see later), this short book, more than any other, has articulated the agenda for contemporary cognitive science. In *Modularity*, Fodor suggests that we resurrect faculty psychology, that we create a modern version of Gall and Spurzheim's phrenology. Fodor's point was that we need to think of the mind as a distinct set of units or modules, each of which is complete in itself, fully devoted to a specific function. Fodor was emboldened and inspired by the Chomskian revolution which assumed innate structures for the processing of speech and language. Using language as his main example, Fodor suggested that speech processing uses dedicated hardware that is specific to the language task, that this hardware is not shared by other cognitive systems. Furthermore, it is activated in an automatic and obligatory manner. Thus for speech in a native speaker's language, utterances are automatically processed as speech, with each word individuated. Because speech processing is obligatory, native speakers always process the sounds of their language as speech; they cannot hear their own language as the continuous stream of sound experienced by the foreigner.

According to Fodor, such modular systems as exemplified by human language are likely to have very specific characteristics. Modular systems are (a) domain specific, (b) encapsulated, (c) obligatory, (d) have shallow outputs, (e) are rapid, (f) are generally inaccessible to consciousness except at their outputs, (g) have a characteristic ontogenetic course, (h) have dedicated neural hardware, and finally, as a consequence, (i) have characteristic patterns of breakdown.

Color and Classical Stereopsis as Modules

Foundational studies on the visual system began many years before Fodor's *Modularity* and still provide its best examples. Consider color vision which can be seen to be in easy accord with Fodor's modular system's concept. It is (a) domain specific as it processes only visual stimuli, in particular wavelength as it has been broken down into three broad bands by the receptors. It is (b) encapsulated in that it is impervious to thinking or to other high-level cognitive processes. It is (c) obligatory insofar as we cannot turn off color vision at will. When we view a scene at photopic levels, we *always* see it in color. We don't have the option of seeing the world as shades of gray, as in a black and white movie. It has very (d) shallow outputs in the sense that it does not supply information as to its own inner workings or the results of intermediate processes. We have no conscious knowledge of the tristimulus values, the excitations of each cone type. This is consistent with the view that the workings of the color system (e) are generally inaccessible to consciousness except at their outputs. Furthermore, the chromatic system has a (f) characteristic ontogenetic course, particularly evident at the earliest stages. Specific pigment molecules are confined to different classes of receptor (Baylor, 1987) and the anatomy of the visual system appears to contain (g) dedicated neural hardware devoted to color. Color vision shows very (h) characteristic patterns of breakdown. Each photoreceptor loss is associated with subtle color deficiencies which form distinct classes (protanopia, deuteranopia, tritanopia). Profound and often total loss of color vision can accompany circumscribed lesions in extrastriate visual cortex in the case of cerebral achromotopsia (Cowey & Heywood, 1995). This cortical deficiency reinforces the "shallow output" nature of the process because *primary* visual cortex with its rich supply of color selective cells is intact in these patients. Yet, color vision is absent. As such, there must be a higher cortical area (beyond the striate cortex) which must comprise the critical output portion of the color module upon which the conscious perception of color depends.

So closely does color vision conform to Fodor's modularity that it is probably its best documented example. Yet binocular depth perception might qualify as a plausible second. With classical stereopsis as in Wheatstone's original demonstration, tiny differences in image distances between the two can lead, when fused, to the vivid perception of three dimensions (Wheatstone, 1838). This became particularly evident with the invention of the random dot stereogram (Julesz, 1960). With Julesz's stimulus, the perception of depth is ineffable, not further analyzable through introspection. We are completely unaware of the differences in disparity in this figure and simply see a square hovering in front of a background. Further support for a specialized binocular system comes from neurophysiology with the discovery of disparity-specific neurons tuned to various degrees of binocular image alignment between the two eyes (Barlow, Blakemore, & Pettigrew, 1967). In addition, there is a characteristic breakdown of binocular depth perception with damage to this early visual cortical system as evidenced by the case of strabismus, where eye misalignment prevents the normal development of binocular neurons in the visual cortex.

Although these examples from low-level vision are evident examples of modularity they do not come as much surprise to those who have spent their careers in the field of visual perception. At either an implicit or explicit level, vision was thought to be special, not explainable by more general laws of psychology, like, say, conditioning. Thus the Gestalt psychologist rejected the associationist foundation of vision, suggesting that perception was autonomous with its own laws. The single unit revolution of visual neurophysiology beginning back in the 1950s only strengthened this view, showing unforeseen structure and regularities within the visual system. Neurons in the retina of the frog were detectors of bugs and looming objects (Barlow, 1953; Lettvin et al., 1959). Neurons in the cat visual system were arranged in a hierarchy such that LGN cells coded local aspects of an image with concentric receptive fields and this was elaborated with cortical processing, showing several stages of integration where cells here were sensitive to oriented lines, to motion, to binocular disparity (Hubel & Wiesel, 1962).

Building upon these success stories in early vision, a larger challenge of the modularity thesis is to see whether more cognitive visual processes would be similarly constituted. Would higher-level visual processing, obviously requiring experience and learning, be understood as modular systems as well? Here of course the objects of study would be much less known and the establishment of modularity would be more difficult to accomplish. Yet recalling Fodor's speculation that such systems would be modular at least to "an interesting extent," it is clear that very recent research has been very supportive of the modularity, extending it in new directions.

Face Recognition as a Module

Face recognition emerges as a very strong candidate for modularity with probable genetic constraints. Higher primates and especially humans are inherently social animals and there is no question that faces have been both important and ubiquitous throughout recent phylogeny and over the course of an individual's development. As such, it is plausible that a specialized face processor emerges during development with help from mechanisms which have been bequeathed by evolution (Johnson & Morton, 1991). This important idea has been underappreciated partly because faces can be recognized by a variety of routes, not exclusively connected to a specialized face processor itself. For example, we can recognize faces from the presence of a defining feature such as a peculiar-shaped mustache or, say, a birthmark. Yet, it is becoming more evident that there is something more characteristic about face processing that enables us to recognize familiar persons under very different guises, after they have shaved off their beards or had changes in hairstyle or cosmetics. For such familiar faces, it is clear that we can recognize faces with great certainty and under a wide variety of conditions (see Tong & Nakayama, 1999) but often we as "perceivers" or "knowers" cannot analyze our knowledge about faces with any more insight from introspection than we did for stereopsis or color. We are certain of a friend's identity even if the face is stripped of all features that can be verbally described. The process remains ineffable and immediate and we don't have conscious insight as to what underlies our knowledge. This is consistent with the notion of face recognition as mediated at least in part by a Fodorian module with shallow outputs.

Some of the most striking evidence that face recognition is a module comes from clinical cases, particularly those sets of findings which constitute a double dissociation. Prosopagnosia, the absence of face recognition (Meadows, 1974), can occur in observers whose ability to do object recognition is largely intact. Such patients often have lesions in the ventral occipital regions, just where more recent evoked potential and fMRI studies show activation to the presentation of faces (Allison, Ginter, McCarthy, & Nobre, 1994; Kanwisher, McDermott, & Chun, 1997). Second is the converse phenomenon, a situation where a patient has an almost total loss of ordinary object perception but is normal or even above normal in the identification of faces (Moscovitch, Winocur, & Behrmann, 1997). Their patient CK is particularly informative because his remaining abilities reveal a putative face module in isolation, uncontaminated by other recognition systems available in persons with an intact visual brain. For example, when CK was shown the unusual paintings of Giuseppe Archimboldo (Kriegskorte, 1990) where faces are composites of vegetables (Figure 23.2), he was easily able to identify them as faces, presumably because his face module was intact. Yet because of the shallow output of this putative face module and his lack of any other recognition abilities, he could see the face only but *not* its vegetarian constituents. A very recent case study of prosopagnosia due to very early damage (infantile encephalitis) in this same cortical area (Farah, Rabinowitz, Quinn, & Liu, 1999) suggests that the dedicated neural hardware responsible for face recognition is likely to be constrained by genetic factors.

Modules Without Genetic Specification? The Case of Written Language

All of these cases (color, stereo depth, and face recognition) subserve functions that would have been beneficial over the course of evolution. As such, they do not challenge Fodor's strong claim that modules are to some extent innately specified. Each of course requires some degree of environmental input and the higher one goes in the visual system, the more obvious is the likely dependence. Thus, for faces, it seems self-evident that one needs to be exposed to a specific face to recognize it. Yet, the existence of and the importance of learning does not indicate that genetic factors are not at play. Each of these functions is likely to have a long evolutionary history with genetic specification aided by additional learning. So, all of these examples fulfill more or less all of the specifications listed by Fodor for modular systems, including the important property of having a characteristic ontogenetic course.

There remains the possibility, however, that Fodor may have been unnecessarily specific in indicating the requirement for strong genetic control. It has been suggested that modules having many of the characteristics of Fodor modules may indeed exist but that they are more likely to be the result of a developmental process, that modularity *increases* as a consequence of experience (Karmiloff-Smith, 1992).

The characteristics of our visual recognition of written language argues this point. Writing is an instructive case because the adoption of written language is a very recent development on the scale of human evolutionary time. Skills in writing and reading cannot have played a role in human evolution because mass literacy emerged only within the past century and is still incomplete. Yet, despite its recency, the processing of written language shows many of the characteristics of a Fodorian module. For example, the reading of the written word is automatic and mandatory. Like speech, it is not a matter of choice as to whether we will process written words as having meaning. This has been amply confirmed

Figure 23.2. A face by Giuseppe Archimboldo (Kriegskorte, 1990) composed of vegetables. Patient CK (Moscovitch et al., 1997) sees such paintings as faces but is not aware of the vegetables.

by the well-known Stroop effect where the meaning of a presented word can interfere with ongoing tasks despite the greatest efforts to ignore the words or their meaning (MacLeod, 1991).

Neuropsychological studies on the recognition of written words reveal some unusually specific patterns of breakdown with brain damage. For example, Caramazza and Hillis (1990) show that left parietal lesions can selectively impair word recognition in surprisingly characteristic ways. In these patients the first (left) portion of a word can be identified but not the right. Yet, it is not simply a portion of the visual representation of the word that is selectively degraded. The damage is more subtle and reveals that the representation of words is more abstractly represented. Thus if the words are presented vertically or left right reversed, the deficit is still confined to the second half of the word. The findings indicate that specific brain lesions can lead to very characteristic breakdowns in the processing, occasionally revealing the characteristics of underlying modules.

In some forms of acquired dyslexias, patients cannot read the letters of words or word-like non-words (Coltheart et al., 1993). Yet they can read whole words and understand their meaning. This indicates the existence of a "whole word" module which makes available the identity of the word but not its constituents, strikingly similar to the case of face recognition (Moscovitch et al., 1997) where patient CK sees the faces but not the constituent vegetables. Further studies of word recognition under conditions of backward masking also reveal the "shallowness" of the outputs of a putative word recognition module. Words with upper, lower, or mixed case letters are correctly recognized, yet subjects are unaware of such changes and variations of case.

Given these examples of modular processing in the absence of obvious genetic constraints, Fodor's modularity idea has been strongly criticized (see Elman et al., 1997; Karmiloff-Smith, 1992). Yet, even the severest critics leave much of Fodor's speculative framework intact, differing mainly on the single issue of nurture vs. nature. These commentators take great pains to dismiss the likelihood that these modular systems are inborn, relying on learning mechanisms as could be realized in connectionist networks. Yet, they concede, and in fact embrace, much of Fodor's program, arguing that if modules can be built during development and if they are highly over-learned, they will exhibit many characteristics that Fodor reserved for inborn systems (Karmiloff-Smith, 1992).

This example of written language suggests that Fodor's postulation of innateness for modular systems might be overly rigid, missing possible systems that are modular to "an interesting extent," particularly if we seek explanations as to the underlying characteristics of higher visual processes. It suggests that there might be many more modules, somewhat unsuspected, and not as easily identifiable as, say, for reading, but that have many of the properties outlined by Fodor and followers. It also suggests that it is the outcome of module formation that is important, that the mechanism of formation of a module is less important than its operation.

From the examples we have given so far, it is clear that modular systems exist and they clearly have some decisive advantages in their ability to deal with domain-specific material in a very rapid and effective manner. This array of "fast dumb mechanisms" (Fodor, 1983) is at odds with Berkeley's now dated view of perception as a general associative process. We should note, however, that there is plenty of room for association too in modular processing (Hebb, 1949; Linsker, 1990) but it seems that it is carried out over a restricted range of inputs, "within" a domain. Thus for visual surface perception, it has been argued that the associations are not domain general but restricted to local visual surface information within vision (Nakayama, He, & Shimojo, 1995).

Yet in reflecting about behavior and mind as a whole, it seems unlikely that modular systems by themselves can provide a full explanation as to the function of the mind and brain. Much of our mental life seems too varied and rich to be subserved only by such arrays of specialized sub-systems. Furthermore, our behavior seems wielded to serve more general goals; it is not simply the result of smaller piecemeal activities, acting independently. For this reason, it is important to think about what else may be necessary for the mind and brain to act as a whole.

Central Systems

Fodor's speculative psychology in *Modularity* has been prophetic. The study of modular systems is today's most dominant research agenda. So popular has the idea of modularity become that its scope has grown enormously. It is suggested that there are modules for a wide range of functions, rivaling Gall's original phrenology with jealousy organs and cheating detection organs posited by advocates of evolutionary psychology (Cosmides & Tooby, 1986), and theory of mind modules posited to account for aspects of development and autism (Baron-Cohen, 1997). These are recent additions, taking their place alongside color vision, face recognition, etc.

In contrast to these recent developments, Fodor took a surprisingly different stance on the applicability of modular systems to cognition in general. Fodor made much effort to indicate that modular systems are *not* the whole story about the mind. He argued that the mind must also contain in its essentials central systems which have the opposite characteristics of modules; they need to be widely distributed, flexible, slow, accessible to consciousness, etc. These aspects of Fodor's (1983) essay have been largely forgotten, amidst the rapid progress in identifying modules. Yet his point bears closer examination because he makes an extreme, yet lucid argument about the relation of perceptual modules to cognition more generally.

To distill the essence of this boundlessness and flexibility of central systems, Fodor claimed they are (a) isotropic and (b) Quinean. By isotropic, he means that the sources of belief for central systems can come from *anywhere*; they are *not* domain specific. Any information in any domain can influence the outcome, can contribute to the knowledge possessed by central systems. As such, information in central systems is not encapsulated.

By Quinean, Fodor refers to the fact that no specific sorts of sensory information (experience) are decisive in affirming or contradicting a belief. This derives from Quine's (1953) attack on the foundations of logical positivism and its assertion that there is some special identifiable sense data that can validate or invalidate a scientific theory.

> The totality of our so-called knowledge or beliefs, from the most casual matters of geography and history to the profoundest laws of atomic physics or even of pure mathematics and logic, is a man-made fabric which impinges on experience only along the edges. Or, to change the

> figure, total science is like a field of force whose boundary conditions are experience. A conflict with experience at the periphery occasions readjustments in the interior of the field. . . . the total field is so underdetermined by its boundary conditions, experience, that there is much latitude of choice as to what statements to reevaluate in the light of any single contrary experience. *No particular experiences* are linked with any particular statements in the interior of the field, except indirectly through considerations of equilibrium affecting the field as a whole. (Quine, 1965, p. 42, italics added)

This describes science or at least its quest for empirical knowledge. By analogy, Fodor considers science to be the mind writ large, or at least the central systems of the mind. Thus in distinction to modular systems which have enduring or at least lawful characteristics, central systems are essentially holistic, capricious and unknowable.

Seeming to take unusual delight in a gloomy prognosis regarding the understanding of central systems, Fodor asserts that modular systems are the *only* valid topic of inquiry. The extent to which the mind is modular is the extent to which we will understand it. Central systems are just too capricious, contingent on countless random factors and must forever lie outside the bounds of science. Cognitive science is stuck with the study of modular systems and when that task is complete, the enterprise will have reached its limit. By implication, any statements about central systems are off limits, at least as scientific discourse.

The argument here is implicit and indirect. Rather than examining the properties of the mind's central systems (which by his definition are essentially unknowable), he uses science itself and its history as a metaphor for the growth of knowledge in the mind. Thus "knowledge" at any given era in science is prey to remote and possibly tiny causes. There are no laws of scientific discovery and there are no privileged domains of relevant experience. In the field of astronomy, the Copernican outlook denied that the earth stood still, and asserted that it moves around the sun. As such, it became evident that the palpable perceptual experience indicating that the earth is stationary, with the sun making its daily path across the sky, was suspect. This indicated that our perceptual apparatus is too insensitive to rule on the motion of the earth, challenging perception's privileged position regarding the fixation of belief.

Prior to Newton it would seem that our understanding of celestial and terrestrial motion were separate, comprising discrete encapsulated domains of knowledge. After Newton this division disappeared and all motion was subject to the same universal laws, illustrating Fodor's notion of isotropy. In all of these cases new beliefs were acquired over a long uneven history. Supporting data came from unexpected and seemingly unrelated fields; that is, planetary motion was informed by the properties of terrestrial motion and vice versa. Furthermore, whole frameworks of thought, Quine's "web of belief," were influenced by metaphysical presuppositions (Burtt, 1924). As such, the path delineating the growth of knowledge could not be foreordained or perhaps not understood even *post hoc* (Feyerabend, 1975). So too with the mind, at least that part which corresponds to its central systems. The mind's beliefs are historically conditioned, subject to our individual histories and to the exigencies of the moment. There can be no science pertaining to this aspect of mind and its acquired knowledge.

A Possible Science of Central Systems

Fodor's views about the futility of studying central systems does not seem to have led to the wholesale abandonment of his implied "off limits" areas of psychology. For example, the field of developmental psychology continues to exist, despite Fodor's disinterest and his tacit dismissal of development. Nor has the field of reasoning and decision making, likely to be mediated by central systems, been deserted. Yet, one can discern developments in these fields that are not unrelated to Fodor's main thesis. Topics related to Fodor's central systems have been co-opted by ideas related to modularity. In developmental psychology, there has been a recent emphasis on innate structures, the notion that children are born with built-in primitive knowledge mechanisms to encode and interpret the world and from this base, development unfolds (Carey & Spelke, 1994; Hermer & Spelke, 1996). Second, in the field of thinking and reasoning, there has been the view that reason itself is not as central, logical, and abstract as normative theories of logic would suggest, that it too is domain specific. It is argued that abstract reasoning is a fiction and that we use heuristics, more akin to perception than logic, when faced with the uncertainties of decision making in daily life (Kahneman & Tversky, 1984). These developments indicate an "invasion" of Fodor's territory of central systems by what begins to look suspiciously like modular processing.

Overall we seem to be in a historic period where the study of modules is ascendant, and where other fields of inquiry are less regarded. Curiously, the rapid progress and concomitant optimism about modules has not prompted much effort in thinking of how such piecemeal mechanisms could be functionally coordinated. In other words, there hasn't been a comparably high-profile research program showing the necessity for or characteristics of inter-module organization. The situation is perhaps like the "discovery" of reflexes in the spinal cord a century earlier. Sherrington (1906) indicated that there are reflexes (although he was wary enough to call them useful fictions). He wondered how all of these myriad processes could be wielded together to the smooth seamless behavior observed. A similar problem appears now. How can a finite number of modules, especially ones that are mandatory (many of Sherrington's reflexes were not mandatory), be woven into something that resembles what we consider to correspond to our behavior and mental life?

Some writers have considered this problem at length. Gazzaniga (1985) suggests a kind of autonomous competition between modules such that the orderliness and seamlessness of behavior that we "experience" is actually an illusion, that it is actually rather disconnected, wielded together *post hoc* by our story-telling verbal left hemisphere. This is particularly graphic when actions initiated in the silent and autonomous right hemisphere require a cover story to be told by the left hemisphere, sometimes with bizarre reasons, especially by patients with split brains. In his view, modules appear to rule but there is some kind of *post hoc* mediation function served by language. No doubt, there are many obvious rationalizations afforded by such cases of brain damage (see later). Dramatic as these important findings are, one should be cautious in interpreting such examples from very abnormal brains as illuminating the norm for behavior under ordinary circumstances. Researchers interested in both animal (Tinbergen, 1951) and human behavior (Miller, Galanter, & Pribram, 1960) have postulated broad hierarchical theories to account for the purposive flow of behavior which are not incompatible with rather fixed modules or subunits of behavior. In each case, the animal or person has higher-order goals which activate various subgoals which in turn activate smaller bits of behavioral routines. Thus, for the ethologist Tinbergen (1951), when an animal has a predisposition to nest build, it engages in behaviors appropriate to it, not engaging in competing or distracting behaviors, courtship, exploration, etc.

Baars (1988) in his *A cognitive theory of consciousness* agrees and observes that the integration and modification of various modules is exactly what consciousness helps to facilitate. This rests on his argument that modules by themselves are too inflexible to deal with behavior and that they have to be knit and modified by his virtual central system (which also require consciousness) to coordinate actions which are in line with the organism's goals. Baars suggests that not only is there a need for integration to coordinate modules smoothly when they do not perform appropriately to serve the higher-order goals of the animal but that they are also needed to tune, or in more challenging situations, to rewire modules so that they perform up to the standard required. The latter case is similar to the concept of accommodation outlined many years earlier by Piaget (1950). Thus central systems could both coordinate the operations of modules and help to fashion new ones.

Prolonged Clash of Modular and Central Systems: Perception of the Vertical

Given what we know about modular and central systems, it would seem that we cannot rely on perceptual modules unconditionally. For if perception or at least a significant part of perception is mediated by relatively inflexible domain-specific modules, there is the likely chance of error. It is almost inevitable that at some time central and modular systems will arrive at very different conceptions of reality. With perception, we are informed by a system that is geared for the long haul of evolutionary or life history and is generally appropriate for the majority of situations. Perception is more suited to embody the "wisdom of the ages," providing rapid response, not requiring reasoning which is too time consuming and perhaps even more error prone. Yet such a modular system could give us wrong information.

Take the most often quoted example, the Muller-Lyer illusion, which is inevitably mentioned when discussing the modularity of perception. We are told that the two lines are of the same length and if need be, we can measure them with a ruler. The illusion persists, even after it is explained to us, arguing for inflexible perceptual mechanisms that constantly err despite "corrections." Few if any of these discrepancies cause distress in daily life. Such illusions are carefully contrived by researchers to establish some unexpected properties of our visual system but they do not occur with any regularity in nature and even if they did, it is not clear that we would notice them.

Some illusions do occur in normal life, however, and are more noticeable. These are the illusions of self-movement and the perception of one's bodily orientation in space. The illusions are the likely consequence of modular systems doing their job with characteristic inflexibility. Linear vection is a good example. We are familiar with the compelling yet illusory experience of our own movement, sensing that our stationary train is moving when it is only the movement of another train in the station. Such motion must start very slowly so that associated vestibular cues ordinarily accompanied by such movements would be too small to be sensed. Usually there are no untoward consequences because the perceptual illusion is short lived.

Some illusions of bodily position in space are not so fleeting. Consider illusions related to the classic rod and frame experiments (Witken, 1954) and studied more recently by Matin and colleagues (Matin & Li, 1992). The most dramatic example of such an illusion can be seen when stationed in a house that has been pitched so that normally vertical walls are inclined (see Figure 23.3). Our "modular" perceptual system uses visual cues in the environment to determine our own reference to upright in the environment and this continues even if we know that the house is pitched. The adherence to the wrong and in his case the local visual coordinate frame (the house) is so strong that our companions can appear as either shorter or taller than ourselves depending how they stand in relation to us and the internal room. This is the phenomenon of the alteration of perceived eye height (Matin & Li, 1992). We also notice that a freely rolling ball appears to move uphill, as does spilt water, appearing to defy gravity. Several of these examples have become well-known tourist attractions. The Mystery Spot in California's Santa Cruz Mountains is a particularly good example (Murphy, 1986). Here and in more controlled laboratory situations, it is evident that we have a visually based module (with shallow outputs) which tells us about the direction of the upright. These "mandatory" mechanisms cannot be shut down and continue to give us false information even though we are aware of the circumstances giving rise to the illusion. Under these circumstances, the perceptual module is so strong and ubiquitous that it cannot be ignored. Observers, including the proprietors of such establishments, not familiar with these phenomena of visual perception, explain the rather disparate array of phenomena as due to a "mysterious physical force" yet to be explained by physicists. For example, my tour guide in the Santa Cruz mountains assured us that the place was visited by America's top rocket scientists, Werner von Braun and Albert Einstein, and that neither could explain it.

A Possible Lesson From Virtual Reality

In general, it is clear that perceptual errors occur in everyday life and one question is why we aren't more disturbed by them and more often. A goal of this chapter is to suggest that the answer must lie in the extreme richness of perception, its potential to get the most detailed information about a local scene so as to render anomalous information as spurious in relation to the wealth of consistent information available. We are not passive observers but can be informed by active interrogation of our environment, by the mobile movement of visual attention, the rotations of our eyes and, most important, the movement of our head to sample our vast environment from an infinity of vantage points (Gibson, 1966). So rich is our visual perception and so closely coupled is it with the outside world, that fully simulating it in all its range and detail is not possible Such is argued by Dennett (1991) who notes that few have ever been fooled or ever will be fooled by virtual reality (VR) displays, no matter how advanced they become. Dennett argues that for any VR simulation of a real-life situation, there would always be instances of sensory motor exploration that would reveal VR's illusory character, that the real world is usually such an

(a) Physical situation

(b) Perceived situation

Figure 23.3. (a) Real tilted room that is part of a tilted house. (b) Cues from the room are very strong (as opposed to the sense of the gravitational vertical) and the observer perceives up in relation to the room, not gravity. (Adapted from Palmer, 1999.)

infinitely rich source of information that it could never be fully simulated. Added to these considerations is the difficulty in also providing simulated input to our vestibular apparatus, which provides almost unerring information as to changes in our orientation and positions in space. This does not take away the appeal of virtual reality displays, however, because we do not seek information regarding those aspects that would break the spell. We can attend to the game in a video arcade and the simulative experience provided is adequate for the occasion. Such interactive displays have been found to be very useful for the training and testing of commercial airline pilots. Yet, echoing Dennett, there is always the opportunity for the observer to see full well that this environment is indeed artificial. Furthermore, if the vestibular system inputs are inappropriate to the motion experienced, motion sickness is a frequent by-product (Reason, 1974).

Yet there exists at least one counter-example and possibly there are more, where a simulated environment is more than usually successful in creating an environment that is "perceptually" indistinguishable from reality. The example I have in mind is not the latest from high technology but is a more modest effort. It comes from the simulation of a very slowly moving ship moving in a harbor at nightfall. Here the participant is allowed to steer a very large ship, the size of an oil tanker, in a harbor, in a simulation at the Institute of Perception in Soesterberg, the Netherlands. Although the display is rather impoverished, simply a dim landscape portrayed panoramically in silhouette on distant walls, the simulated experience is fully convincing, exceeding higher-technology VR displays. The participant has the uncanny experience of being on a ship, steering it through the harbor. Linear vection, the sense of oneself and the boat moving through the harbor, is maintained, as are very slow rotational components of vection as the ship changes course slightly under one's command. From the point of view of perception, the simulation is completely convincing; there is no perceptual distinction between simulation and reality.

The reasons for success with this relatively modest simulation as opposed to obvious hi-tech failures elsewhere are of interest, particularly as they might be classified under reasons of omission: (a) there were no cues that the spatial information depicted was not that of a real as opposed to a simulated scene, and (b) there were no vestibular cues to contradict the perception of self-motion. Instead of attempting to provide the most detail as is so often done in the case of the most technically advanced virtual reality displays, the approach taken here was essentially the opposite, to provide only the minimum optical information to obtain the sense of vection in a stationary environment and to arrange it so that there is no conflict between visual and vestibular cues. Because the simulation was that of nightfall, we as observers were forced to rely on the information available from our visual system under low illumination where it is well known that sensitivity to high spatial and high temporal frequency information is markedly attenuated (van Nes, Koenderink, Nas, & Bouman, 1967). Because the simulation was that of a very large ship, it could only make the smallest changes of direction and course consistent with its tonnage and associated linear and angular momentum. This meant that all appropriate motions of the ship were in the very low temporal frequency range, just where our vestibular system is the least sensitive. This ensured that contradictory vestibular stimulation accompanying any possible course of action would be below or at near threshold levels and not readily perceptible.

All of this adds up to an interesting minimalist slogan, an apt handbook subtitle for any would-be Cartesian demon: *Supply only the minimal information and no more.* Of course, it is not terribly practical in the domain of virtual reality because the range of perceptual situations where there is such an opportunity for such deception is too limited. Yet, more generally, it is likely that this slogan would serve *any* liar or deceiver. One of the important rules of lying is to embellish only in areas where one is certain one's listener is ignorant and otherwise not to volunteer any additional information.

Given the fact that virtual reality's purpose is to deceive, its successes and failures might illuminate the question of knowledge and perception more generally. By understanding the reasons for virtual reality's success in limited situations we gain a different perspective on how perception might work in normal and abnormal circumstances. Our main thesis is that in ordinary perception (as opposed to contrived VR simulations), the potential of perception to "check up" on reality with fast dumb mechanisms is virtually endless. The special virtue of perception is not its infinite wisdom, but its access to near infinite data. By way of exception, this point is further supported by a special psychopathological case where perceptual errors are consequential, where they go unchecked and where psychopathology can be the unhappy result. We describe this next.

Cognition Trumped by Perception in Psychopathology?

Psychopathology is instructive because it offers some vivid examples of what might be taken as deception. Consider hallucinations, altered perceptual states which often accompany mental disorders. How do they stack up in terms of verisimilitude? Do they seem more or less "real" than a virtual reality display? Is a hallucination incorporated into our awareness as something "out there" or is it regarded as something separate, perhaps internal, reflecting some property of our mind or brain? We can identify some "technical" problems that need to be overcome before a hallucination might be considered as real. Much of it has to do with the rendering of the scene at what we might call mid-level vision (Nakayama et al., 1995; Nakayama, 1999), whether the hallucination can be appropriately interwoven into the scene. Obvious are two problems related to occlusion. First, does the hallucinated phantom occlude the background so that those surfaces behind the phantom are now invisible? Second, suppose the phantom steps behind an opaque object. Will its body be partially occluded as if it were a real person or real object? A similar set of questions could be asked of scene lighting. For example, does the hallucinated phantom cast a shadow on neighboring regions which is in accord with the position of the lighting sources in the scene? Are the shading and highlights on the phantom's face appropriate for the composition of the lighting in the scene? These are the classic problems of what is called scene rendering in the computer graphics world, that is, how to make a real object fit into the scene as if it was lit and arranged at different depths in relation to other objects. They apply equally well to the handiwork of any would-be Cartesian demon and no less to a hallucination.

Yet these considerations might be regarded as somewhat off the point for they are based on the assumption that hallucinations are centrally based, that altered perception is the consequence of a dysfunctional mental apparatus which actually constructs or interprets so that perception is different. This is a strongly top-down notion, one that is in accord with psycho-dynamic and cognitive explanations of mental disorders. But we have been pursuing a different question, asking how an altered perceptual experience, say through some kind of abnormality in Fodor's perceptual modules, might lead to mischievous and deleterious effects further along. Maher (1974, 1992) has been developing this point for a number of years; the basic idea being that some mental disorders might be traced to anomalous perceptual disorders. This is the reverse of the usual logic employed in psycho-dynamic or cognitive interpretations of psychopathology. Instead of attributing misperception and delusion to hidden urges or conflicts or to disordered thinking, Maher (1992) is suggesting an opposite causal route, hypothesizing that a primary event in the etiology of at least some forms of psychopathology could be an altered perceptual state and that psychopathology is its reasonable conclusion. He implies that a more or less normal mind, given the same circumstances, would find itself in a similar state. This could occur because perception has priority in the fixation of belief and that otherwise unopposed, perception trumps cognition. Recall that the distorted sense of the upright in a pitched house leads immediately to the false belief that there are mysterious forces afoot, contradicting our longstanding physical knowledge of the world. So too, says Maher, in the generation of psychopathological states. So compelling are some anomalous perceptual experiences that beliefs otherwise labeled as pathological are the plausible consequences.

To be fully convincing, abnormal perception should be such that it cannot be easily contradicted by other sorts of experience. As such, more undifferentiated perceptual experiences having less detail are perhaps more suitable. This is the lesson learned from the ship simulation at nightfall where visual detail is missing, yet given the circumstances, it is not considered as anomalous. Private perceptual experiences, less able to be disconfirmed by others, are most likely to be effective. Such is indeed the case in Maher's argument; he cites subjective perceptual feeling states as the prime examples, where persons have abnormally increased or decreased feelings of familiarity with a scene or person. Others might sense a feeling of foreboding about a scene, etc. Thus, Maher suggests that a schizophrenic patient might know that a particular person is familiar but there would be such a feeling state associated with that person that is so anomalous that unusual thoughts might be the unhappy results, so unusual as to lead to some kind of psychiatric diagnosis.

This line of thinking has received much greater attention of late, defining a new subspecialty combining cognitive neuropsychology and psychiatry (Stone & Young, 1997), and also providing novel explanations for otherwise puzzling and bizarre symptoms. For example, consider the now well-publicized but rare Capgras syndrome, where patients have a very specific delusion. They are sure that a very close relative has been replaced by an imposter. Because such patients were often diagnosed as mentally ill, psychodynamic explanations were initially proffered, thus the patient's beliefs were attributed to ambivalent feelings for a spouse or close family member, etc. This sort of explanation, however, became less plausible as the number of such cases increased and even more telling was the fact that Capgras patients were found to have damage in right ventral occipital temporal cortical regions, close to regions having to do with face recognition. As such, a more satisfying explanation was required, one that accounted for the specific delusion in relation to putative face recognition machinery.

Ellis and Young's (1990) new psychiatric theory is based on recent findings suggesting a dual nature of face perception, the idea that face recognition mechanisms have two distinct and separable outputs. For example, prosopagnosics who lack the ability to recognize faces overtly still are able to make differential emotional responses to faces that are different as measured by various physiological measures (DeHaan, Young, & Newcomb,1987; Tranel & Damasio, 1985). This suggests that there are at least two ways in which face recognition can occur: first is an overt route leading to identification, calling forth explicit memories about the person; second is a covert route, an unconscious identification process activating implicit knowledge of the individual, including vaguer yet powerful emotional states. Ellis and Young (1990) draw upon this dual theory to explain the Capgras syndrome. In this syndrome, opposite to what is found in prosopagnosia, they assume that overt face recognition is normal, but covert is not. When confronting strange faces, Capgras patients would not be different than normals. Recognition would be lacking when seeing such faces and also lacking would be any feelings of familiarity. When confronted with very close associates and loved ones, however, there would be a large discrepancy; patients would recognize the faces of others and have all sorts of memory associations, but there would be no feeling of familiarity. Such a strong discrepancy is then hypothesized to call for a set of cognitive readjustments, "beliefs." The patient resolves the matter with what would otherwise seem like an unlikely conclusion, that these people are imposters!

The specificity of the clinical phenomenon in relation to face perception is supported by recent observations by Hirstein and Ramachandran (1997). Persons who are regarded as imposters when seen face-to-face are less likely to be regarded as such when speaking to them over the telephone. In sum, the Capgras syndrome is in accord with Maher's original hypothesis, that the origin of some types of psychopathology is disordered perception and not the other way around.

Other syndromes as strange and dramatic as the Capgras syndrome have been documented and suggest a similar explanation. Ramachandran (1995) has called attention to a class of parietal cortical damaged patients who are not normally regarded as psychopathological because of obvious brain damage, but who also demonstrate that false perception can lead to even more preposterous false beliefs. Parietal patients can have striking perceptual anomalies; particularly well documented are disorders of body image. For example, right hemispheric parietal patients can insist that the left half of their body is alien, that it belongs to someone else. More pertinent for our topic, parietal patients can be paralyzed say on the contralesional side and because of some peculiarity of such damage, they lack the awareness that they are paralyzed (Ramachandran, 1995). Called anosognosia in the clinical literature, such patients insist that their paralyzed limbs are normal even after aggressive questioning by a physician. Thus patients will repeatedly insist that they can use their paralyzed limbs and so strong is their belief that they do not make any effort to fabricate credible explanations as to why the outcome of using their so-called paralyzed arm is so unsuccessful. Such patients will offer obviously incorrect accounts of why the outcome of a neurologist's challenge is to be explained. Patients, for example, will claim that others have three hands, that they are touching their nose at the same time their arm is immobile, etc. If we regard the body image as including the perceived ability to move as a given state of affairs revealed by perception, then the abandonment of common sense and logical thinking becomes comprehensible. If the body image is the consequence of a perceptual module and its outputs are simply given, no questioning is possible. So compelling is perception here that all logic and knowledge pales in its wake.

Conclusions: Fast Dumb Mechanisms in World Rich in Information

At the beginning of this chapter we asked how potentially contradictory information, from perception and from other higher-level sources, might be reconciled. In the last several sections we have described very rare and unusual situations where errors in perception are consequential, where the organism's ability to select coherent true information from other sources is either unavailable or unexpected and where false beliefs are a possible outcome. In the tilted mystery house, the perception of the upright is dominated by vision, not gravity, and this leads to persistent error. In turn, this can lead to the belief that there are mysterious physical forces. In the ship simulation, there are no other perceptual clues and if persons were temporarily blindfolded and taken to this spot, they could be fooled. In some forms of psychopathology, there are strong feelings, of familiarity or of body competence, which are so strong as to trigger very bizarre thoughts or to violate logical thinking.

Yet, these are very peculiar circumstances where other sources of contradictory information are not available, and where mistaken perception, unchecked by normal perception, can lead to mistaken thoughts. It should be obvious, however, that everyday life is very different. The richness and redundancy of information supplied by the ambient visual array is almost limitless for ordinary terrestrial environments (Gibson, 1966). As such, any small amount of inconsistent misinformation is tiny in comparison to the wealth of coherent information available. Also critical is the fact that perception is highly selective. The organism can determine what is perceived. Much of this is simply physical. Moving to different places affords very different visual vantage points. Shifts of gaze are also critical. We can't see an object in much detail if our eyes are not fixated on it. Most important and becoming deservedly appreciated of late is the role of visual attention. Studied extensively in the past but not in its fullest form, visual attention is now seen as a prerequisite for vision. Thus if we don't attend to an object in a scene, we simply do not see it. This is the phenomenon of inattentional blindness which has become well documented in the past few years (Joseph, Chun, & Nakayama, 1997; Mack & Rock, 1998; Rensink, O'Regan, & O'Regan, 1997; Simons & Levin, 1998). Thus misinformation, along with all other information not of interest to the organism, can be safely ignored. As such, perceptual modules, dumb as they are, are not a significant source of error. This suggests that our worried question, the issue of reconciling perception and cognition, is not a troublesome one. Perception, by being so closely coupled to the environment, is, in aggregate, correct and even when it is wrong, it rarely matters.

Postscript: Broader Lessons From the Study of Perception's Modularity?

Having considered perception as an assemblage of modules which work surprisingly well to keep us informed about our environment, I speculate as to whether this understanding might help to understand other mental functions. If we agree with Fodor's thesis, it would seem that there are no obvious riches in attempting to use perception's modularity for understanding broader questions of cognition. The very modularity of perception, particularly its encapsulation, protects it from central systems, allowing perception to be studied with such evident success (witness the treasures in this book). Detailed and satisfying answers are forthcoming but the accumulated knowledge may generalize less and less. Perhaps this is the price to be paid in the study of perceptual modules. This would support Fodor's gloomy prognosis, dashing hopes for a greater and more extended cognitive science.

It is very likely, however, that Fodor's pessimism is too pervasive, resting so heavily on a strict division of the mind into distinct categories, modular and central systems. Although this division has been clarifying, idealizing two extremes, we have already mentioned the existence of transitional cases. For example, studies of visual word recognition indicate the existence of modular systems which are not genetically specified. Yet, these show strong formal similarities with so-called inborn systems. We also mentioned putative modules for higher-level psychological functions. In recent developments in the "theory of mind," it is suggested that a "theory of mind module" develops from more primitive modules, those having to do with eye gaze detection, the detection of animacy, shared attention, etc. (Baron-Cohen, 1997). Although less firmly established, they indicate the fruitfulness of dividing up what would otherwise be too large a terrain. These examples suggest that a variety of mental processes could be described at least in part as modular, that there may be no clear dividing line between modular and non-modular.

I suggest we abandon Fodor's strong views yet retain his property list characterizing modular systems. From this we inherit a useful, open-ended set of distinctions. For a given psychological process, we can determine the degree to which it satisfies various modular criteria. Then by looking over a variety of processes we may see illustrative patterns. So far, we have suggested that genetic specificity is not essential in defining a module, citing the perception of written language. Other properties might also be diminished or absent. As just one example, consider the degree to which a module's operation is obligatory or mandatory. For the bulk of this chapter, we considered perceptual modules as obligatory. Yet, there is the likelihood that all modules are not always obligatory. Earlier stages in the perception of writing and in the learning of a second language in adulthood are transitional examples. Proficiency for the beginner would be limited and as a consequence, the operations of a putative module would become mandatory only at a later time. The opposite might also be the case. Modularity might decrease or be overshadowed over time. Perceptual modules ensure that we see the world as it is. As such, when we look at a scene, we can't help but see it as three-dimensional. There is no choice. Yet, if we were to learn to draw, this would be a great handicap, witness children's drawings. It takes training to see 3-D scenes as 2-D and to render the shapes of objects on a flat surface. This suggests that as expertise develops, the mandatory seeing of 3-D might be superseded by seeing in 2-D.

What determines whether one system will become modular or will be overshadowed by another? Clearly experience and practice must be of importance. But structural considerations are also likely to be relevant. One obvious constraint is the brain itself. The existence of modules seems inevitable if we realize that a given neuron in the brain can connect on average with only 10,000 other neurons at most. Given the 100,000,000,000 neurons in the brain, we can see that some form of nesting of neural connections is required, that neurons can connect widely only by being parts of larger assemblies that can connect to other assemblies over longer distances. This suggests that modules can emerge most easily over regions of high interconnectivity, say over cortical columns or adjacent sets of columns.

As such, it seems reasonable to suppose that modules formed by long-distance connections in the brain would be much harder to establish. Consider an audio-visual speech recognition mechanism that is suggested by the advantages of lip reading and the McGurk effect. The latter is demonstrated by the altered hearing of speech with changes in facial motion (McGurk & MacDonald, 1976). Because brain regions specialized for the processing of faces and speech sounds are not adjacent, such a presumed mechanism presents an interesting challenge. Is acoustic visual speech processing a module? Little is known on the topic but Green, Kuhl, Meltzoff, and Stevens (1991) suggest that such a process is at least domain specific. The McGurk effect is as strong for voices and faces of differing sexes as it is for conditions where the sex of the voice and face is the same. If it is a module, by what anatomical route is the coordination of such a module accomplished, and is there a characteristic way that other multi-modal modules in general can emerge?

By answering these questions and others motivated by questions of modularity, I suggest that we can obtain much more systematic knowledge, not only about perception, but for a wider range of topics where the presumption of modularity might also be informed by a closer examination of perception's modularity. Perception has long been held up as an example for understanding other mental processes. Its methodologies have been appropriated (Green & Swets, 1966) and broader theoretical concepts (Marr, 1982) have gained wide currency in cognitive sciences. Yet, in all of these endeavors, it has been easy to ignore the specific findings of perception, to regard them as too detailed and technical and not relevant for the understanding of higher-order processes. Yet closer attention to the field of perception might offer more than has been previously appreciated. Perception may furnish the best and most extensive set of examples regarding the nature of, the development of, and the interaction of modules. As such, the degree to which other systems can be understood as modular or partially modular may be informed by progress here. In short, the specific contents derived from the study of perception, not just its methods, may be more useful than has been generally apparent.

References

Allison, T., Ginter, H., McCarthy, G., & Nobre, A. (1994). Face recognition in human extrastriate cortex. *Journal of Neurophysiology, 71*, 821–825.

Baars, B. J. (1988). *A cognitive theory of consciousness.* New York: Cambridge University Press.

Barlow, H. B. (1953). Summation and inhibition in the frog's retina. *Journal of Physiology, 119*, 69–88.

Barlow, H. B., Blakemore, C., & Pettigrew, J. D. (1967). The neural mechanism of binocular depth discrimination. *Journal of Physiology, 193*, 327–342.

Baron-Cohen, S. (1997). *Mindblindness: An essay on autism and theory of mind.* Cambridge, MA: Bradford Books.

Baylor, D. A. (1987). Photoreceptor signals and vision: Proctor Lecture. *Investigative Ophthalmology & Visual Science, 28*, 34–49.

Berkeley, G. (1709). *An essay towards a new theory of vision.* Dublin: Aaron Rhames.

Burtt, E. A. (1924). *The metaphysical foundations of modern physical science.* New York: Harcourt, Brace.

Caramazza, A., & Hillis, A. E. (1990). Spatial representation of words in the brain implied by studies of a unilateral neglect patient. *Nature, 346*, 267–269.

Carey, S., & Spelke, E. (1994). Domain-specific knowledge and conceptual change. In L. Hirschfeld, R. Gelman, & A. Susan (Eds.), *Domain specificity in cognition and culture* (pp. 169–200). New York: Cambridge University Press.

Coltheart, M., Curtis, B., Atkins, P., & Haller, M. (1993). Models of reading aloud: Dual route and parallel distributed approaches. *Psychological Review, 100*, 589–608.

Cosmides, L., & Tooby, J. (1986). From evolution to behavior: Evolutionary psychology as the missing link. In J. Dupre (Ed.), *The latest on the best: Essays on evolution and optimality* (pp. 1–56). Cambridge: MIT Press.

Cowey, A., & Heywood, C. (1995). There's more to colour than meets the eye. *Behavioral Brain Research, 71*, 89–100.

DeHaan, E. H., Young, A., & Newcomb, F. (1987). Face recognition without awareness. *Cognitive Neuropsychology*, 4, 385–415.

Dennett, D. C (1991). *Consciousness explained.* Boston: Little Brown.

Descartes, R. (1649). *A discourse of a method for well-guiding of reason and the discovery of truth in the sciences.* London: Tho. Newcomb.

Ellis, H. D., & Young, A. W. (1990). Accounting for delusional misidentifications. *British Journal of Psychiatry, 157*, 239–248.

Elman, J. L., Bates, L. A., Johnson, M. H., Karmiloff-Smith, A., Parisi, D., & Plunkett, K. (1997). *Rethinking innateness: A connectionist perspective on development.* Cambridge: MIT Press.

Farah, M. J., Rabinowitz, C., Quinn, G. E., & Liu, G. T. (2000). Early commitment of neural substrates for face recognition. *Cognitive Neuropsychology, 1/2/3*, 117–124.

Feyerabend, P. (1975). *Against method.* London: Verso.

Fodor, J. A. (1983). *Modularity of mind: An essay on faculty psychology.* Cambridge, MA: MIT Press.

Gazzaniga, M. S. (1985). *The social brain: Discovering the networks of the mind.* New York: Basic Books.

Gibson, J. J. (1966). *The senses considered as perceptual systems.* Boston: Houghton-Mifflin.

Green, K. P., Kuhl, P. K., Meltzoff, A. N., & Stevens, E. B. (1991). Integrating speech information across talkers, gender, and sensory modality: Female faces and male voices in the McGurk effect. *Perception & Psychophysics, 50*, 524–536.

Green, D. M., & Swets, J. A. (1966). *Signal detection theory and psychophysics.* New York: John Wiley.

Hebb, D. O. (1949). *The organization of behavior, a neuropsychological theory.* John Wiley & Sons.

Hermer, L., & Spelke, E. (1996). Modularity and development: The case of spatial reorientation. *Cognition, 61,* 195–232.

Hirstein, W., & Ramachandran, V. S. (1997). Capgras Syndrome: A novel probe for understanding the neural representation of the identity and familiarity of persons. *Proceedings of the Royal Society: Biological Sciences, B264,* 437–444.

Hubel, D. H., & Wiesel, T. N. (1962). Receptive fields, binocular interaction and functional architecture in the cat's visual cortex. *Journal of Physiology, London, 160,* 106–154.

Johnson, M. H., & Morton, J. (1991). *Biology and cognitive development: The case of face recognition.* Oxford: Blackwell.

Joseph, J. S., Chun, M. M., & Nakayama, K. (1997). Attentional requirements in a "preattentive" feature search task. *Nature, 387,* 805–807.

Julesz, B. (1960). Binocular depth perception of computer generated patterns. *Bell Systems Technical Journal, 29,* 1125–1162.

Kahneman, D., & Tversky, A. (1984). Choices, values and frames. *American Psychologist, 39* (4), April, 341–350.

Kanwisher, N., McDermott, J., & Chun, M. (1997). The fusiform face area: A module in human extrastriate cortex specialized for face perception. *Journal of Neuroscience, 17,* 4302–4311.

Karmiloff-Smith, A. (1992). *Beyond modularity: A developmental perspective on cognitive science.* Cambridge, MA: MIT Press.

Kriegeskorte, W. (1990). *Giuseppe Archimboldo.* Köln: Benedikt Taschenbuch Verlag.

Lettvin, J. Y., Maturana, H. R., Pitts, W. H., & McCulloch, W. S. (1961). Two remarks on the visual system of the frog. In W. A. Rosenblith (Eds.), *Sensory communication.* New York: MIT Press and John Wiley & Sons.

Linsker, R. (1990). Perceptual neural organization: Some approaches based on network models and information theory. *Annual Review of Neuroscience, 13,* 257–281.

Mack, A., & Rock, I. (1998). *Inattentional blindness.* Cambridge, MA: MIT Press.

MacLeod, C. M. (1991). Half a century of research on the Stroop effect: An integrative review. *Psychological Bulletin, 192,* 163–203.

Maher, B. A. (1974). Delusional thinking and perceptual disorder. *Journal of Individual Psychology, 30,* 98–113.

Maher, B. A. (1992). Delusions: Contemporary etiological hypotheses. *Psychiatric Annals, 22,* 260–268.

Marr, D. (1982). *Vision: A computational investigation into the human representation and processing of visual information.* San Francisco: W. H. Freeman.

Matin, L., & Li, W. (1992). Visually perceived eye level: Changes induced by a pitched-from-vertical 2-line visual field. *Journal of Experimental Psychology: Human Perception & Performance, 18,* 257–289.

McGurk, H., & MacDonald, J. (1976). Hearing lips and seeing voices. *Nature, 264,* 746–748.

Meadows, J. C. (1974). The anatomical basis of prosopagnosia. *Journal of Neurology, Neurosurgery and Psychiatry, 37,* 489–501.

Miller, G. A., Galanter, E., & Pribram, K. H. (1960). *Plans and the structure of behavior.* New York: Adams-Bannister-Cox.

Moscovitch, M., Winocur, G., & Behrmann, M. (1997). What is special about face recognition? Nineteen experiments on a person with visual object agnosia and dyslexia but normal face recognition. *Journal of Cognitive Neuroscience, 9,* 555–564.

Murphy, P. (1986). The mystery spot. *Exploratorium Quarterly,* Spring issue, 23–27.

Nakayama, K. (1999). Mid-level vision. In R. A. Wilson & F. C. Keil (Eds.), *The MIT encyclopedia of the cognitive sciences* (pp. 545–546). Cambridge, MA: MIT Press.

Nakayama, K., He, Z. J., & Shimojo, S. (1995). Visual surface representation: A critical link between lower-level and higher-level vision. In S. M. Kosslyn & D. N. Osherson (Eds.), *Visual cognition* (pp. 1–70). Cambridge, MA: MIT Press.

Palmer, S. (1999). *Vison science: From photons to phenomenology.* Cambridge, MA: MIT Press.

Piaget, J. (1950). *The psychology of intelligence.* London: Routledge & Kegan Paul.

Quine, W. V. O. (1953). Two dogmas of empiricism. In *From a logical point of view.* Cambridge, MA: Harvard University Press.

Ramachandran, V. S. (1995). Anosognosia in parietal lobe syndrome. *Consciousness and Cognition, 4,* 22–51.

Reason, J. (1974). *Man in motion: The psychology of travel.* London: Weidenfeld and Nicolson.

Rensink, R. A., O'Regan, J. K., & O'Regan, J. J. C. (1997). To see or not to see: The need for attention to perceive changes in scenes. *Psychological Science, 8,* 368–373.

Sherrington, C. S. (1906). *The integrative action of the nervous system.* New Haven: Yale University Press.

Simons, D., & Levin, D. (1998). Failure to detect changes to people during a real-world interaction. *Psychonomic Bulletin and Review, 5,* 644–649.

Stone, T., & Young, A. W. (1997). Delusions and brain injury: The philosophy and psychology of belief. *Mind and Language, 12,* 327–364.

Tinbergen, N. (1951). *The study of instinct.* Oxford: Oxford Clarendon Press.

Tong, F., & Nakayama, K. (1999). Robust representations for faces: Evidence from visual search. *Journal of Experimental Psychology: Human Perception & Performance, 25,*1016–1035.

Tranel, D., & Damasio, A. R. (1985). Knowledge without awareness. An autonomic index of facial recognition by prosopagnosics. *Science, 228,* 1453–1454.

van Nes, F. L., Koenderink, J. J., Nas, H., & Bouman, M. A. (1967). Spatiotemporal modulation transfer in the human eye. *Journal of the Ophthalmic Society of America, 57,* 1082–1088.

Wheatstone, C. (1838). On some remarkable, and hitherto unobserved, phenomena of binocular vision. *Philosophical Transactions of the Royal Society of London, B128,* 371.

Witkin, H. A. (1954). *Personality through perception, an experimental and clinical study* (Harper's psychological series). New York: Harper.

Index